Indiana, 1816–1850: The Pioneer Era

THE HISTORY OF INDIANA

VOL. II

INDIANA, 1816–1850: THE PIONEER ERA

Donald F. Carmony

INDIANA HISTORICAL BUREAU &
INDIANA HISTORICAL SOCIETY
Indianapolis 1998

The paper in this publication meets the minimum requirements of American National Standard for Information Sciences—Permanence of Paper for Printed Library Materials, ANSI Z39.48-1984 ∞

Library of Congress Cataloging-in-Publication Data

Carmony, Donald F. (Donald Francis)
    Indiana, 1816-1850 : the pioneer era / Donald F. Carmony
       p.   cm. — (The history of Indiana : vol. 2)
    Includes bibliographical references and index.
    ISBN 0-87195-124-X. — ISBN 0-87195-125-8 (pbk.)
    1. Indiana—History.   I. Title.   II. Series.
F526.C295   1998   97-36392
977.2—dc21   CIP

This book is dedicated to my parents, Bert and Golda (Wicker) Carmony, whose love, support, and sacrifice made it possible for me to become a historian, and to Edith B. (Hagelskamp) Carmony, a student in one of the first classes I taught at Indiana Central College and my wife of fifty-seven years (1934–91), without whose love, support, and very outstanding contributions to my life this book never could have been written.

CONTENTS

Preface   ix

Acknowledgments   xii

Chapter 1   Statehood on Borrowed Money, 1816–1822   1

Chapter 2   The Economy, 1816–1850   45

Chapter 3   Political Parties Founded, 1822–1831   80

Chapter 4   Banking and Internal Improvements, 1831–1837   146

Chapter 5   Depression and Debt, 1837–1843   202

Chapter 6   Repudiation, 1843–1850   278

Chapter 7   Education, 1816–1850   363

Chapter 8   Jacksonian Constitution of 1851   403

Chapter 9   Jeffersonian Democracy Reinterpreted, 1816–1829   452

Chapter 10   Jacksonian Democracy Reinterpreted, 1829–1841   514

Chapter 11   Western Expansion Amid Sectional Strife, 1841–1850   573

Notes   633

Bibliography   861

Index   879

(2)   Despite a considerable diversity of views and backgrounds the pioneers had a strong attachment to English common law and English traditions of representative government.

(3)   Separation of church and state, essential because of the variety of religious views and practices, was emphasized in the Constitution of 1816, but interpreted in differing ways and at times violated.

(4)   Indiana's location, well west of the crest of the Appalachian Mountains, increased its detachment from most of the other states, located mainly between this barrier and the Atlantic Ocean, and enhanced the isolation and self-sufficiency of pioneer life.

(5)   The state's location within a region of much fertile land, with a climate suitable for agriculture, attracted settlers.

(6)   Most of the pioneers had experience in pioneering or at least they came from families with such experience.

(7)   Indiana's interior location, however, made it extremely costly to receive imports and send exports to markets in other states and countries.

(8)   In an unsuccessful attempt to decrease the costs of imports and exports, the Hoosier state borrowed millions of dollars for building canals, railroads, and roads which soon caused bankruptcy and a repudiation of most of the bonded debt for same.

(9)   The state's location in the vast interior of the country partly in the upper reaches of the St. Lawrence and Mississippi drainage basins, with the Appalachian barrier between it and most other states, made the pioneers, regardless of party preference, overwhelmingly ardent for preservation of the Union and willing to make considerable compromises for its preservation.

(10) Because the federal government, which owned the public domain and sold land to settlers on rather modest terms, was generous in tolerating squatters on unsold land, the state settled at a rather rapid rate.

(11) The role of the United States in establishing trading posts with the Indians provided an important source of wealth to some pioneers who engaged in the Indian trade.

(12) Among the pioneers very strong hostility existed to the presence of Negroes. This resulted in a prohibition in the Constitution of 1851 against further immigration of Negroes into the state, and an attempt to remove many of those already in the state.

(13) During the 1830s and 1840s the movement for a statewide system of common schools, supported by public revenue, and open to all youth without charge, stimulated the General Assembly to enact such legislation in the 1850s.

The chapters which follow indicate and explain how I believe these and other factors and circumstances influenced Indiana to develop as it did, 1816-1850. As the notes and citations illustrate, I make frequent and numerous citations to both primary and secondary sources. Readers, however, are encouraged to form their own opinions. The evidence offered is often subject to differing interpretations.

In writing this volume I have had in mind the so-called general reader more than scholars. Citizens generally should be encouraged to learn more about the history of their communities, states, and countries. Many scholars are themselves general readers, save for books in their specialized areas. In the pioneer era a considerable number of Hoosiers were illiterate, but many of them were very intelligent. Some of them as legislators helped enact the laws that governed the state, and some of them helped draft the Constitutions of 1816 and 1851.

ACKNOWLEDGMENTS

It is impossible to mention all of the individuals to whom I became indebted during the research for and the writing of this book. To none am I more indebted than Lorna Lutes Sylvester. A native of Brown County, where frontier life lingered much longer than in most Indiana counties, she was one of the best students I ever had in my classes in Indiana history. Her parents were both natives of Southern Indiana, her father taught school for forty-three years, and she also taught school for a number of years. For thirty-three years she has served me and others as the indispensable associate editor of the *Indiana Magazine of History*. Concerning this book, she has given much help about sources, reviewed preliminary copy, and done miscellaneous research for me.

I am also very much indebted to Shirley McCord, for many years an editor for the Indiana Historical Bureau and, more recently, for the Indiana Historical Society. She has reviewed and carefully checked the text and citations on a chapter by chapter basis, at times making helpful comments about additional sources and items which needed more or less emphasis—all reflecting her abundant knowledge and thoughtful understanding of Indiana history.

Several individuals made significant contributions to this volume. Paula Corpuz, an experienced and very capable editor for the Indiana Historical Society, assisted Shirley McCord in the careful manner in which the completed manuscript was reviewed and made ready for publication. Hubert H. Hawkins, while director of both the Indiana Historical Bureau and the Indiana Historical Society, generously provided me with photocopied material and made helpful comments about miscellaneous items. Frances Krauskopf, who served with me for a brief period as assistant editor of the *Indiana Magazine of History*, did much research and considerable checking of notes concerning citations for previous writing relevant to this volume. During the 1960s Pamela J. Bennett contributed to my research and writing while serving with me as an assistant editor of the *Indiana Magazine of History*.

I am also indebted to countless other individuals. Many students asked questions which at times caused me to do further research and modify my views about particular items. Librarians and archivists, especially those at Indiana University, the Indiana Division of the Indiana State Library, and the Indiana Historical Society, were extremely helpful in my search for sources relevant to Indiana in the pioneer era.

It is appropriate that this book be published cooperatively by the Indiana Historical Bureau and the Indiana Historical Society. As the bibliography abundantly illustrates, citations to their publications are common throughout this volume. I thank

Pamela J. Bennett, Director of the Indiana Historical Bureau; Peter T. Harstad, Executive Director of the Indiana Historical Society; and Thomas A. Mason, Director of Publications for the Indiana Historical Society, for the manner in which my draft manuscript was transformed into this book.

Donald F. Carmony,
Emeritus Professor History
Indiana University

PREFACE

I was born on a farm in Shelby County, Indiana, in 1910, near where my great, great, paternal grandfather and family had settled in the 1820s. They arrived soon after various Indian tribes had ceded much of central Indiana to the United States. For a year or so after my paternal grandmother died, my parents lived with grandfather in the double log cabin where my father was born. A frame lean-to along its back provided two additional rooms, making four rooms for three adults and three small children. The dug well was between the cabins and the log barn, with its frame addition, and the outhouse was nearby on the other side of the cabins.

My elementary education was completed in seven years in four one-room, red brick schoolhouses, which offered grades one through eight, taught by my father. I was one of nineteen who graduated from Manilla High School, across the line in Rush County, in 1925. Because I had never missed a day since entering the first grade, the county superintendent gave me a medallion.

During the teens and twenties I did a variety of chores and labor on the family farm before mechanization and electricity revolutionized farming and farm life. Despite long hours and much hard work, I enjoyed these years, which in some respects resembled the pioneer life, about which I write in this book, more than life of the 1990s.

In the fall of 1925 I entered Indiana Central College, now the University of Indianapolis, expecting to major in mathematics and probably combine farming and teaching at the high school level as my career. Soon my interest in history exceeded that in mathematics, and I completed majors in both subjects, graduating cum laude in June, 1929. During the summer I was invited to teach history at Indiana Central College on a part-time basis, while pursuing the doctorate in history from Indiana University. I soon became full-time, and continued on its faculty for a decade.

As a graduate student at Indiana University during the thirties, I became much interested in Indiana history under the capable and charming teaching of Logan Esarey. From 1939 until "retirement" in 1980, I was a member of the faculty in history at Indiana University, teaching at the Fort Wayne, South Bend, and Indianapolis Extension Centers, but principally on the Bloomington campus. I began teaching Indiana history while on the faculty of Indiana Central College, but the transfer to Indiana University gave me much more time for its study and teaching. I received the Ph.D. in history from Indiana University in 1941. The pioneer era has long been my area of principal interest. From 1954 until 1975 I edited the *Indiana Magazine of History*.

From service on several state commissions and committees, including that as chair of the Indiana Sesquicentennial Commission, 1959-1967, I gained valuable insights about politics, politicians, and government. This experience increased my understanding of and appreciation for the role that politicians exercise in local, state, and national government.

In writing *Indiana, 1816-1850: The Pioneer Era*, my primary purpose was to describe how and why Indiana developed as it did during its formative years and also to describe its role as a member of the United States. Too often, state history has been presented mainly as history of the United States, with a miscellany of items and episodes about the state described. To achieve my purpose, I emphasized research in primary sources, greatly decreasing reliance on secondary sources.

A variety of factors and circumstances help explain why and how Indiana developed as it did, 1816-1850. Among them, are these:

(1)   The state's population came overwhelmingly from western Europe or was of western European extraction, and largely from England, Germany, Ireland, and Scotland.

CHAPTER 1

STATEHOOD ON BORROWED MONEY, 1816–1822

JONATHAN JENNINGS was the central figure in Indiana's transition from a territory to a state. Already a popular political leader, he had served as Indiana's territorial delegate to Congress since 1809 by repeated choice of the voters. In this capacity he aided passage of the Enabling Act by which Congress authorized Indiana to frame a constitution and organize a state government. As a delegate to and president of the Corydon Constitutional Convention in June, 1816, he helped draft the state's first constitution. At the initial state election in August Jennings was elected governor by a comfortable majority, and he won reelection three years later by an increased margin. Shortly before completing his second term in 1822, Jennings was elected to Congress, then resigned as chief executive and served in the House of Representatives until 1831. More than any other individual, Jennings was the architect of statehood for Indiana, despite the fact that he was only about thirty-two years of age when Congress admitted Indiana to the Union.[1]

The Constitution of 1816 established a modest but an effective framework for state and local government.[2] Imbued with liberal Jeffersonian Republican principles, it provided a republican or representative government which was somewhat democratic for its time. Its preamble and bill of rights guaranteed important individual rights and freedoms, affirmed the separation of church and state, and declared that the people were the source of power and authority for all free governments. Suffrage was granted white male citizens of the United States who were at least twenty-one years of age and had resided within the state a minimum of one year. Hence, neither blacks, Indians, nor women could vote. Persons enlisted in the army of the United States or its allies were not allowed to vote. Slavery and involuntary servitude were emphatically prohibited. High goals were set concerning education and libraries under public auspices, as well as for reformation of the penal code and care of the poor. In accordance with the Jeffersonian Republican philosophy that the people have the right to change their government, it mandated the General Assembly to hold a referendum every twelfth year to afford the sovereign electorate an opportunity to decide whether a convention should be called to amend or revise the constitution.[3]

Despite the constitutional emphasis regarding separation of powers and checks and balances, the General Assembly was much the strongest department of state government. The legislative power of the General Assembly, only partly indicated by the constitution, was enormous and varied. It enacted laws concerning revenues and expenditures, the criminal code, elaboration of the judiciary, county and township government, the status of towns, transportation facilities, care of the poor, education, and miscellaneous items.[4] The General Assembly met annually, with no limit on the duration of sessions. Unless called into special session, it convened on the first Monday in December. Legislation and resolutions could be advanced and approved in each house by a mere majority vote so long as a quorum of at least two thirds of the members was present.

The assembly also had a substantial role in the selection of public officials. By majority vote on joint ballot the two houses elected the secretary, treasurer, and auditor of state. In like manner it chose president judges of the circuit courts, while executive nominations for the three judges of the Supreme Court were subject to confirmation by the Senate. Less often exercised was the judicial power of the General Assembly, which authorized it to remove the governor and all civil officers of the state if found guilty of treason, bribery, or other high crimes and misdemeanors. The House of Representatives had the exclusive power of impeachment in these cases, whereas trial and possible conviction rested with the Senate. In exercising this removal power, a majority of the membership of each house was needed to concur with actions taken.

The General Assembly, more than either the executive or judicial department, was subject to close and frequent review by the electorate. Annually on the first Monday of August, all the representatives and approximately one third of the senators were elected. Representatives and senators could serve as many annual and triennial terms as they could win from their constituents. No property or religious qualification was required, but legislators must have paid either a state or county tax and be citizens of the United States. Representatives had to be at least twenty-one years of age, and a resident of the area served for not less than one year; senators at least twenty-five years of age, a resident of the state for two years, and a resident of the area served for not less than one year. During their elected terms, legislators were ineligible for any office filled by the assembly, while a collector of tax revenue or holder of public money could not sit in the legislature until all money due had been paid into the treasury. Persons occupying an office under the authority of the president of the United States or any state office, militia offices excepted, were ineligible to a legislative seat unless the office held was vacated prior to such election. The prohibition against legislators accepting offices created by the state and federal constitutions was waived for members of the first state legislative session.

The General Assembly was subject to constitutional mandate concerning its size and apportionment. The constitution fixed the initial number of representatives at twenty-nine and that of senators at ten. At five-year intervals the assembly was required to make a new apportionment. Reapportionments were to be made "among the several counties, according to the number of" voters in each as determined by an enumeration taken pursuant to legislative provision. Until the aggregate of voters reached 22,000, membership of the House of Representatives could vary between twenty-five and thirty-six, after which it must not be less than thirty-six or more than one hundred. The number of senators was never to be less than one third or more than one half that for representatives.[5]

The Constitution of 1816 vested the "Supreme Executive power" of the state in the governor, but this official had far less power than his territorial counterpart had enjoyed. The governor was commander in chief of the state's military forces, save when they were called into federal service, and he appointed certain high militia officials. He could remit fines and forfeitures and grant reprieves and pardons, except for persons convicted of impeachment charges. He named members of the Supreme Court, subject to Senate approval, and made recess appointments to various executive and judicial positions. The governor could call special sessions of the assembly and submit information and recommendations for its consideration. He had a suspensive veto over legislation and resolutions, but his negative could be overridden by concurrence of a majority of the membership in each house. The governor was authorized to require information in writing from other executive officials, and he was charged to "take care that the laws be faithfully executed." Elected by the voters for three years, he could not serve "longer than six years in any term of nine years." A governor had to be at least thirty years of age, have been a citizen of the United States for ten years, and a resident of the state for five years (or of the territory for two), but there was neither a religious test, property qualification, nor tax prerequisite. While serving as governor, it was not possible to hold any federal or another state office.

A lieutenant governor, secretary of state, treasurer, and auditor comprised the other officials of the executive department mandated by the constitution. The lieutenant governor had to possess the same qualifications as the chief executive. He was elected in like manner, with identical provisions regarding tenure. Although not a member of the Senate, he was its presiding officer or president, could vote when this body sat in committee of the whole, and cast the deciding vote when the Senate was evenly divided regarding matters under consideration. In addition to these modest part-time duties, he became governor if this office became vacant through death, removal, or absence from the state. As already observed, the secretary, treasurer, and auditor were elected by joint ballot of the General Assembly. The secretary served four years, the treasurer and auditor three. These officials were eligible for reelection without limitation, no constitutional criteria were prescribed concerning their qualifications, and their duties were left largely for statutory determination.[6]

The judicial department had much strength and considerable independence. The judicial power of the state was vested, both as regards matters of law and equity, in a Supreme Court, circuit courts, and justices of the peace, plus such inferior courts as the legislature might establish. The Supreme Court consisted of three judges, any two of whom made a quorum. Nominated by the governor for seven-year terms, subject to confirmation by the Senate, they were eligible for indefinite reappointment. The Supreme Court had appellate jurisdiction only, but the assembly could give it original jurisdiction in capital or chancery cases if a president judge of a circuit court was considered an interested or prejudiced party. Members of the Supreme Court appointed their own clerk. No residence, legal training, or other qualifications were prescribed for the Supreme judges or their clerk.

Immediately below the highest court were the all important circuit courts, one for every county. In each county voters elected two associate judges for this court, and the General Assembly chose a president judge who rode circuit from county to county as the third judge for the counties within his district as established by the assembly. All three judges served terms of seven years, with eligibility for continued reelection. The circuit courts had a large role concerning common law, chancery, and criminal jurisdiction. The voters of each county elected a clerk for this court, but no one could seek this position unless he obtained a certificate from one or more members of the Supreme Court, or one or more of the president judges, certifying his qualifications. No qualifications were specified for associate or president judges.

The lowest courts mandated by the constitution were the justices of the peace courts. A "competent number" of justices were to be elected by the voters in each township for five-year terms, with no limit on tenure, their duties and powers to be determined by legislation.[7]

County, township, and town government was left largely to legislative discretion. In addition to the clerk and two associate judges for the circuit court, the constitution required that the voters of each county elect a sheriff, coroner, and recorder. The sheriff and coroner were given two-year terms with the sheriff limited to a maximum of four years in any period of six and the coroner eligible for continued reelection. The recorder and the clerk were chosen for seven years without restriction about tenure. The clerk might concurrently hold the office of recorder. No person could be "appointed as a County officer" unless he had been a citizen and resident of the county, or area from which it was created, for a minimum of one year. No particular township or town officials were mandated, but the constitution stated that "All town, and township officers shall be appointed in such manner as shall be directed by law."[8]

The Constitution of 1816 provided for continuity in the transition to statehood. Territorial legislation, unless inconsistent with the new constitution, remained in effect until it was repealed, modified, or expired. Civil and military officials under the territorial government continued in office until superseded by persons named pursuant to the constitution. All contracts, actions, rights, suits, claims, and prosecutions, respecting both individuals and corporate bodies, persisted as if no change in government had taken place. Fines, penalties, and forfeitures owing the territory or a county became due the state or relevant county. Actions and proceedings in the territorial courts were to continue as if the constitution had not been adopted. The General Assembly, however, was empowered to transfer actions and proceedings pending in the territorial General Court to the new state Supreme Court and those pending in the territorial circuit courts to the new state circuit courts. Every individual "appointed to any office of trust or profit" under state authority was required to take an oath or affirmation for performance of his duties in support of both the federal and state constitutions.[9]

With only about five weeks between the adjournment of the constitutional convention on June 29, 1816, and the initial state election on August 5, office seekers had limited time for campaigning. Most likely, however, considerable discussion had occurred among delegates about who would be candidates before the people in August as well as who might be named by the General Assembly subsequent to its meeting. According to writs of election, sent to county sheriffs by Jonathan Jennings as president of the convention, voters of the territory elected a governor, lieutenant governor, and one congressman. Voters of each county elected a sheriff and coroner, and those of legislative districts elected representatives and senators to the General Assembly.[10] These officials were needed as a basis for *commencing* state government.

The major contest at the August election was that for governor. Thomas Posey, Indiana's last territorial governor, who had privately viewed statehood as premature, announced his candidacy to the four delegates from Gibson County shortly before the convention adjourned. Jennings had doubtless informed various delegates that he would seek the governorship. By early July both men had been announced as candidates.[11]

Using columns of the Vincennes *Western Sun*, whose editor was unfriendly to Jennings, anonymous writers attacked him and supported Posey. "A Farmer of Knox County" contended that Jennings had failed to press the federal government for payments due rangers and militiamen for service in the War of 1812; helped Canadians, who aided the Americans in this war, secure *choice lands* in Indiana; and had urged statehood against the wishes of citizens in Knox and adjacent counties. "Farmer" advocated the election of the "venerable & respectable" Posey, whose experienced judgment was "unimpaired by age," and who had held important offices with credit to himself and the country. "A Citizen of Gibson County" voiced similar complaints concerning the rangers, militiamen, and Canadians. He asked whether Jennings had attended a congressional caucus to nominate candidates for president and vice president. Both writers tried to convey the idea that Jennings had helped obtain a recent salary increase for members of Congress.[12]

These critics, however, were not representative of voters generally. Jennings privately reported in mid-July that the change in the form of government "is generally well received" and had created but little noise. After the August balloting the *Western Sun* acknowledged that Jennings had won "with a handsome majority" of the vote. The speaker of the House of Representatives reported that Jennings had received 5,211 votes to 3,934 for Posey. Jennings probably won his majority mainly in the eastern half of the state, while Posey probably got most of the votes in the western portion.[13]

In the race for lieutenant governor, Christopher Harrison of Washington County was an easy victor. The returns, as reported by the speaker of the House of Representatives, registered 6,570 votes for him against 847 for John Vawter of Jennings County, his nearest rival. At the election in August the voters also elected William Hendricks as the state's first congressman.[14]

Pursuant to the apportionment set by the constitutional convention, voters from the fifteen counties elected ten senators and twenty-nine representatives. Sixteen of the legislators had been delegates to the constitutional convention, while a number of them had served in the territorial assembly.[15] When the General Assembly convened on November 4, Isaac Blackford of Knox County was named speaker of the House of Representatives and John Paul of Jefferson County president pro tem of the Senate.[16]

Three days after the General Assembly convened Jennings and Harrison were sworn in as governor and lieutenant governor. In a brief inaugural Jennings suggested that "the shackles of the colonial should be forgotten," and he admonished legislators not to lose "the simplicity of our republican institutions . . . in dangerous expedients and political design." Jennings called attention to the plan of education set forth in the constitution and stated that the dissemination of useful knowledge was essential to sustain morals and restrain vice.[17]

Between its convening on November 4 and adjournment the ensuing January 3, the General Assembly on joint ballot elected three state officials, two United States senators, three president judges of the circuit courts, and three presidential electors. Two days after the assembly convened, Robert A. New was elected secretary of state by a two to one margin over a competitor. On November 16 Daniel C. Lane was chosen treasurer, apparently without opposition, and William H. Lilly was named auditor over a rival by a slim margin.[18] Not until December 20, however, did the assembly name president judges for the three judicial districts into which the circuit courts were grouped. Benjamin Parke was designated for the first or western district, David Raymond for the second or middle district, and John Test for the third or eastern district.[19] Next day the Senate received a message from Governor

Jennings nominating John Johnson, James Scott, and Jesse L. Holman "as suitable persons" for judges of the Supreme Court. These nominations were quickly confirmed without a formal vote.[20] Meantime, the General Assembly had elected James Noble and Waller Taylor to the United States Senate, and it had chosen Indiana's three electors for the presidential election of 1816.[21]

When Indiana became a state is a question that has no simple answer. As already noted, legislative and executive officials of state government began functioning during November, 1816, while the president judges of the circuit courts and members of the state Supreme Court were not even named until December.[22] Congressman Hendricks was given his seat December 2, the day Congress convened, even though the formal act admitting Indiana was not approved until December 11. Although on hand when Congress began, Senators Noble and Taylor were not seated until the day after formal admission.[23] But a congressional law for the extension and execution of federal legislation over Indiana was not approved until March 3, 1817, the closing day of Madison's administration. This measure created a federal district court for Indiana. A few days later the Senate approved the nomination of Benjamin Parke as judge for the new district, along with Thomas H. Blake as prosecutor and John Vawter as its marshal.[24] Thus, the substance of statehood was achieved on a piecemeal basis, but December 11, 1816, is as appropriate a date as any to symbolize Indiana's becoming the nineteenth state of the Union.

The transition to county government, the key unit of local government, was likewise achieved piecemeal. While the constitution empowered voters of each county to elect a sheriff, coroner, clerk of the circuit court, and two associate justices of this court, it made no provision for a county governing board. The clerk could serve as both recorder and clerk. A county official had to have lived in his county for one year, or in the area from which it was carved if a new county. In creating new counties, the existing ones could not be reduced to less than four hundred square miles in area.[25] The initial state legislature set the first Monday in February, 1817, for the election of a clerk of the circuit court, two associate justices of this court, a recorder, and three commissioners as the county governing board for each county. The clerk of the circuit court was made the clerk of this board to record its proceedings, and the sheriff or his deputy was to attend its sessions and execute its orders. The commissioners were instructed to divide their county into a suitable number of townships, provide for the election of justices of the peace by local voters, and name constables for the various townships. When the legislature created new counties, the governor appointed a sheriff and a coroner for them, and the sheriff had the responsibility for holding an election at which voters chose the officials subject to their selection.[26] In related legislation the commissioners were empowered to elect a treasurer annually for their county. Moreover, in the early years of statehood the governor named county surveyors, and the judges of the county circuit court named a prosecutor for their county.[27] Hence, as state government commenced, county government was considerably decentralized with legislative and administrative functions diffused.

The first legislative session enacted a general law for the incorporation of towns. After explaining that granting towns separate charters would swell the volume of published laws and entail "considerable expense," this act provided that if two thirds of the voters of a town expressed a desire for incorporation they could elect five trustees to adopt by-laws and ordinances for its government not inconsistent with the constitution and state laws. Thus incorporated towns, in contrast to townships, were given substantial autonomy and a status separate from their counties. Towns which had obtained charters from the territorial legislature were invited to incorporate in accordance with this general law, but, if so, anything in their former charter not consistent with it became void. In addition, the assembly reserved the right to change the terms of incorporation.[28]

The transition to statehood augmented fiscal burdens for citizens of the infant commonwealth over what they had been for the territorial era. As the accompanying tables show, during the Jennings-Boon administrations, 1816-1822, *ordinary expenditures* for state government averaged $23,396.40 annually.[29] Legislative costs, averaging $8,162.00, were considerably more than double

Ordinary Expenditures, 1816–1822

Fiscal Year	Legislative	Judiciary	Executive	Contingent	Territorial Debt	Constitutional Convention
1816–17	$ 7,325.12	$ 2,100.00	$ 2,000.00	$ 222.37	$5,331.63	$3,076.21
1817–18	9,753.45	5,207.15	2,078.00	108.11	66.66	0.00
1818–19	4,411.88	3,977.78	2,542.00	318.87	0.00	0.00
1819–20	7,918.33	4,923.66	2,220.00	773.89	0.00	0.00
1820–21	9,180.45	5,501.72	2,300.00	501.86	0.00	0.00
1821–22	10,382.80	3,664.00	1,595.80	529.80	27.61	0.00
Total	48,972.03	25,374.31	12,735.80	2,454.90	5,425.90	3,076.21
Average	8,162.00	4,229.05	2,122.63	409.15	904.31	512.70

Ordinary Expenditures, 1816–1822

Fiscal Year	Debt to State Bank	State Bank	State Prison	Wolves Killed	Militia	Misc. Costs	Taxes Paid Collectors	Total
1816–17	$ 0.00	$ 0.00	$ 0.00	$ 0.00	$ 0.00	$ 0.00	$ 382.59	$ 20,437.92
1817–18	0.00	1,084.00	0.00	823.00	126.80	0.00	1,324.60	20,571.77
1818–19	0.00	0.00	0.00	346.00	105.36	91.00	665.95	12,458.84
1819–20	0.00	3,105.00	0.00	496.00	336.17	0.00	1,402.31	21,175.36
1820–21	0.00	1,800.00	0.00	90.00	262.29	99.00	1,063.94	20,799.26
1821–22	25,164.33	0.00	1,000.00	12.00	231.97	249.56	2,077.40	44,935.27
Total	25,164.33	5,989.00	1,000.00	1,767.00	1,062.59	439.56	6,916.79	140,378.42
Average	4,194.05	998.16	166.66	294.50	177.09	73.26	1,152.79	23,396.40

those for the judicial and executive departments combined. Pay to legislators, and the officers who served them, ranked first among legislative items. Costs for printing and distributing the session journals were the major part of it, and laws ranked second among legislative costs. Lawmakers were given $2 per day, plus this sum for every twenty-five miles traveled to and from the sessions. Since the annual meetings usually lasted less than fifty days, legislators normally received roughly $100 per session. From this modest amount some members paid for the care of horses which carried them to and from the capital as well as for their own board and lodging. The lieutenant governor, while serving as president of the Senate, and the speaker of the House got the same per diem and travel allowance as did members.[30] Judicial costs were nearly double that for the executive department. The highest paid official, the governor, was given $1,000 annually; Supreme judges and president judges of the circuit courts, $800; and the treasurer, auditor, and secretary of state $400 each. A lieutenant governor becoming governor received the pay provided for this office.[31]

Among other costs, principal and interest paid the State Bank totaled $5,989.00, consuming over one fifth of all expenditures. The territorial debt and cost of the Corydon Constitutional Convention — items inherited from the territorial era — totaled $8,502.11 for an average of $1,417.01. Payments for contingent items, wolves killed, and militia costs were modest. Items considered as miscellaneous revenue included $99 of revenue lost from the depreciation of bank paper received at the treasury; $140 paid a committee on education; and $9.56 paid county censors, apparently for enumerating eligible voters in preparation for the legislative apportionment of 1821. Though not embraced in the annual reports of the treasurer, an average of $1,152.79 of the revenue from taxes was paid the collectors of state revenue.[32] For practical purposes during 1816-1821, no state tax money was spent for schools, libraries, benevolent institutions, roads, or poor relief. This situation reflects the sparse and limited population, meager economic resources, the primitive aspect of early pioneer society, and especially the heavy reliance on individual efforts and local government for these services.

Despite the extremely modest ordinary expenditures, they exceeded the revenue from taxation. As shown in the accompanying table the ordinary revenue averaged $22,447.96, but the tax money paid into the treasury averaged only $12,808.92, which was only moderately above half of the average cost of state government in its infant years. Moreover, the aggregate of costs received exceeded the total of revenue collected by an average of $948.42 yearly. Of the $50,800 obtained by borrowing, $30,800 was secured from the First State Bank, making it the First State Creditor! As the bank sank into insolvency and disgrace after the Panic of 1819, the state issued $20,000 in paper money called treasury notes during 1820-1822. Items considered as miscellaneous revenue embrace $26.56 obtained from sale of depreciated bank paper, plus $91 secured from a suit against citizens of Harrison County.[33]

Meanwhile, when the legislature convened in November, 1816, Governor Jennings presented a gloomy view of fiscal prospects. He advised: "It is not to be expected that the annual revenue of the state, especially for the present year [1816-1817], will be equal to the annual expenditure without resorting to taxes too heavy for the existing circumstances of the country." The governor recommended a loan in preference to an issue of treasury notes; and he asserted that though a state debt "may be found unavoidable for a time" it could "with facility be reimbursed hereafter without additional taxes" as the taxable land increased and income was gained from federal grants. The legislature levied a tax on land at $1, 87½ cents, and 50 cents respectively per 100 acres of first, second, and third rate tracts. The next legislative session raised the levy on third rate land to 62½ cents per 100 acres.[34] But, as noted in the table regarding ordinary revenue, in these first two years of statehood $25,000 had been borrowed from the First State Bank, with an additional $4,000 obtained from it during fiscal 1819-1820.

By late 1820 the state's fiscal status was much embarrassed, made worse by the depression which began the previous year. When the General Assembly met in November, Governor Jennings told members that tax revenue had averaged more than $4,000 yearly less than expenditures since statehood. He advised

Ordinary Revenue, 1816–1822

Fiscal Year	Taxes Received	Taxes Paid Collectors	Borrowing	Miscellaneous	Total
1816–17	$ 4,251.09½	$ 382.59	$20,000.00	$ 0.00	$ 24,633.68
1817–18	14,717.82	1,324.60	5,000.00	0.00	21,042.42
1818–19	7,399.51	665.95	0.00	0.00	8,065.46
1819–20	15,581.23	1,402.31	4,000.00	0.00	20,983.54
1820–21	11,821.59	1,063.94	11,800.00	117.56	24,803.09
1821–22	23,082.29	2,077.40	10,000.00	0.00	35,159.69
Total	76,853.53	6,916.79	50,800.00	117.56	134,687.88
Average	12,808.92	1,152.79	8,466.66	19.59	22,447.96

that either "additional taxes" or a loan was essential to maintain public credit. The Ways and Means Committee of the House concluded that "under existing circumstances it would be improper to provide for taxation for the discharge of the public debt," and it supported "a resort to loans as heretofore or an issue of treasury notes."[35] The legislature authorized a loan to pay the interest owed the First State Bank; approved the issuance of $10,000 of noninterest bearing treasury notes; and raised the levy on land to $1.50, $1.25, and $1 respectively on each 100 acres of taxable first, second, and third rate land.[36] This increased levy on land, however, yielded only modest revenue for fiscal 1820-1821 during which tax revenue fell below that for the preceding fiscal year.

The state's financial situation worsened during 1821. Shortly before the assembly convened in November, "C," perhaps a well informed state official, stressed that the treasury had had a deficit of about $5,000 annually from statehood; and had accumulated a debt of about $40,000 which should be paid immediately. "C" noted that the increased number of legislators, resulting from their reapportionment at the previous session, would further augment costs, and he argued that salaries could not be reduced while some should be raised. After observing that taxes had been increased nearly 50 percent at the previous session, "C" declared that if taxes were raised again by this percentage the public debt could be liquidated within five years. He also proposed that treasury notes be doubled to $20,000. Governor Jennings concurred with much that "C" had said. He urged that current revenue, apart from borrowing, be made to equal current costs; and he agreed that treasury notes should be doubled. But Jennings, commenting somewhat as he had to the legislature five years earlier, observed that the yearly increments of land becoming taxable, starting in December, 1822, "should be regarded, as a certain means of extinguishing the public debt."[37] By the time the assembly adjourned early in 1822, it had approved an additional $10,000 of treasury notes; levied a poll tax of 50 cents on most adult males; and lowered the levy on second and third rate land to $1 and 75 cents respectively per 100 acres. The levy on first rate land remained at $1.50 per 100 acres. The *Indiana Gazette*, published at the capital, commended this legislation. Its editor estimated that tax revenue would increase one fourth, and he explained that the poll tax had been "laid for the purpose of embracing the *New Purchase* . . . ." If future lawmakers would continue the existing taxes, "without bowing at the shrine of popularity, to lessen the revenue," the Corydon editor hoped that the expanding acreage of land and growing number of polls would make possible the extinguishment of the state debt within a few years.[38] During fiscal 1821-1822 tax revenue greatly increased, totaling almost double that for the preceding year. As the Jennings-Boon era ended in December, 1822, the light at the end of the state's fiscal tunnel burned brightly.

Modest as expenditures were, critics considered them too high. An organ at the capital observed that the printing of the ayes and nays for the House journal at a recent session "must have cost the state about five hundred dollars" which seemed intended as preparation "for some future election." In the early twenties a legislator called the office of attorney general "new and expensive" and "altogether useless, unless it be to harrass our people and eat out their substance." The salary of this official was $200, plus fees.[39] A township meeting in Switzerland County resolved to support only legislative candidates pledged to reduce fees and salaries and repeal the poll tax. This meeting wanted to "see a Spartan economy introduced into our councils and the days of republican plainness revived." "Simonides" complained of too many officials "and the paying of taxes, which comes yearly and grows higher every year."[40] In these early years it seems likely that not many citizens contributed more than one dollar yearly to the state treasury.[41] But in the primitive and undeveloped economy of frontier Indiana, even small sums were hard for citizens to secure, especially amid the depression of the late teens and early twenties.

Although the General Assembly levied state taxes, the local officials who assessed and collected county taxes did likewise for the state. An act of 1817 required county commissioners to name a lister (or assessor) for each township to list taxable land as first, second, or third rate. The rosters of tracts so listed were reported to the commissioners who were empowered to make corrections and review appeals. The county clerk gave the sheriff a copy of the assessment roll as approved by the commissioners. The sheriff collected the tax due the state, which he was to deposit in the state treasury by December 1. If individuals failed to pay by the time designated, the sheriff was to sell personal property and then land if necessary to obtain the amount owed. If the sheriff was delinquent in depositing the revenue, the state auditor was to bring suit against him for the sum owed plus a penalty for his delinquency. A law, effective for 1818, provided that commissioners name only one lister for the entire county, but it was soon changed to allow the option of naming a lister for each township.[42] During the teens and early twenties state officials at times commented about the inequality in the listing or assessing of land according to first, second, or third class. Considerable difficulty was experienced in obtaining revenue from collectors when due, and the magnitude of this problem was one of the important reasons for establishing the office of attorney general in 1822, with authority to bring suits against delinquent collectors.[43]

Closely intertwined with Indiana's troubled fiscal affairs was the development of banking. Various circumstances created an unfavorable context for successful banking. Among them were the extremely limited economic and population base; the debtor nature of early pioneer economy; the substantial use of barter and thus the modest use of money in exchanging goods and services; the tendency of settlers to be unduly optimistic, hence less cautious than desirable, in making financial commitments; the negligible experience with and understanding of banking on the part of politicians and citizens alike; and the devastating impact of the depression of the late teens and early twenties. Indiana banking rested on a shaky foundation even in the prosperous years preceding the Panic of 1819.[44]

The Constitution of 1816 favored privileged or monopolistic banking. It stated: "There shall not be established or incorporated, in this state, any Bank or Banking company or monied institution, for the purpose of issuing bills of credit, or bills payable to order or bearer"; however, the General Assembly could establish "a State Bank, and branches, not exceeding one branch for any three Counties," at places selected by directors of the state bank. Before a state bank could be established, individuals must subscribe and pay at least $30,000 in specie. Express recognition was given territorial charters, approved in 1814, incorporating the Farmers and Mechanics Bank of Madison and the Bank of Vincennes. Although unchartered banking had existed in the territorial period, the framers of the constitution apparently sought to prohibit such banking. Nothing was said about the recently chartered Second Bank of the United States, but if strictly observed the new constitution would prohibit its branches in Indiana.[45]

The chartered bank at Vincennes, and apparently the one at Madison, commenced banking before Indiana became a state. Their charters, valid to 1835, authorized up to $500,000 in capital stock with one fourth of it reserved for purchase by the territory or state. Both charters restricted the rate for loans and discounts to 6 percent, and declared their stock liable to taxation by the territory or state. Neither charter made payment of specie for notes issued an explicit requirement for continued banking.[46]

The initial legislative session under state government offered to adopt the Vincennes bank as the parent unit of a state bank and branches. If adopted its capital would be trebled to $1,500,000, with one fourth reserved for purchase by the state. Whether purchased or not the General Assembly would elect three directors of the state bank, as an addition to the twelve selected by private stockholders pursuant to its charter. The adoption act was silent about redemption of the bank's notes in specie, but explicit that the bank would be required to loan the state up to $50,000 "in specie or in bank notes on chartered banks current and at par throughout the state," bearing interest at 6 percent, for not to exceed five years. The directors of the Bank of Vincennes quickly accepted this offer, and in March, 1817, the governor proclaimed it the state bank.[47] Although the Farmers and Mechanics Bank of Madison was invited to become a branch of the state bank, its directors chose to remain a separate institution under its 1814 charter.

Various scholars have said incorrectly that the legislature attempted to establish fourteen branches for the First State Bank. The adoption act named individuals to take subscriptions to augment the stock of the bank in fourteen counties, all save Knox in which the parent bank was located, but it explicitly restricted the state bank directors from establishing more than one branch for any three counties. The only branches established were the three soon commenced at Brookville, Corydon, and Vevay.[48]

The First State Bank was closely associated with political and economic leaders of the infant commonwealth. Among persons connected with it in some official capacity were James Noble, United States senator; Nathaniel Ewing, receiver for the Vincennes Land Office; Daniel C. Lane, state treasurer; Thomas Posey, son of the last territorial governor; William Eads, Brookville merchant; Noah Noble, later governor and a brother of James Noble; Jordan Vigus, Corydon merchant; John D. Hay, Vincennes merchant; Armstrong Brandon, editor of the Corydon *Indiana Gazette*; Ratliff Boon, who succeeded Jonathan Jennings as governor; and John F. Dufour, of the Swiss community at Vevay. In 1819, perhaps influenced by the growing criticism and troubles of the bank, Governor Jennings resigned as a director of the Corydon branch.[49]

The First State Bank quickly became a depository for federal money. Apparently in the hopes of obtaining this privilege, the president of the Bank of Vincennes informed the secretary of the federal treasury that as of February 20, 1817, it had authorized resumption of specie payment for its notes. During May the First State Bank, as successor to the Bank of Vincennes, began receiving federal deposits.[50] But the president of the Second Bank of the United States, which preferred to handle federal money through its branches, objected that the risk regarding these deposits was too much for it to be responsible. Secretary of the Treasury William H. Crawford, however, considered deposits in some banks other than branches of the Bank of the United States essential to the national interest as well as to that of numerous individuals and the banking system. Indicating concern about the $20,000,000 due the treasury from persons who had bought land on credit, he later asserted that the government would have had more to lose by ending such deposits than by assuming the risk for their continuation.[51] In the spring of 1819 the First State Bank was among the banks, not branches of the federal bank, approved for further deposits with the risk assumed by the federal treasury.

From April, 1819, through June, 1820, the Vincennes bank obtained nearly $295,325.77 in deposits, while becoming delinquent for nonpayment of drafts against it totaling $140,000, with $218,262.90 of federal deposits on hand as this period ended. Consequently, by about the end of 1820 it apparently lost the privilege of securing deposits, and its notes ceased to be accepted for purchases from federal land offices.[52]

The First State Bank was tottering toward collapse even before it lost the deposits. At its birth Indiana's earliest newspaper editor, Elihu Stout, called the bank "a political machine" for which there was insufficient "active capital in the State to afford stamina for its intended branches." After it began circulating its paper twenty-one citizens of Posey County told the legislature that they wanted a bank which bound "the shearholders [sic] property" for its true performance. They asked for a medium that would circulate throughout the state in lieu of the existing one which would scarcely pass from one town to another.[53] In May, 1819, "A Citizen" branded the state bank as "the engine thro which" the Vincennes Steam Mill Company foisted an enormous issue of its money on the public. He wanted this paper terminated, or else those who issued it be required to redeem it "in money really current, not nominally so." At the legislative session of 1819-1820, the first after the onset of the Depression of 1819, members of the House considered such items as making stockholders liable for bank notes issued; forfeiting charters of banks failing to redeem their paper in specie; requiring payment of interest at 6 percent on notes, not redeemed upon request, until redeemed; and investigating the abuses and evils attributed to banking. These items, however, were not adopted.[54] Several months after the legislature adjourned, Elihu Stout's paper asserted that there was "an overgrown band of Bank-Mongers in our land," whose influence extended in "our state councils . . . ." Indicating regret that the legislators had not investigated the state bank and branches, Stout maintained that an investigation would be in the interest of good banks; while if fraud and injustice were practiced, it should be corrected. In reporting toasts offered at Fourth of July observances Stout printed this one: "'*The Banking System*—The swindler's God; the honest man's Devil.—3 cheers.'"[55]

During the last half of 1820 the precarious status of the bank became increasingly apparent. The loss of federal deposits and refusal of land offices to take its notes was followed by an unusually large turnover of legislators at the election in August, apparently caused in part by augmented opposition to the bank. During September, by authority granted by the act creating the state bank, Governor Jennings asked its president and directors for information concerning "the respective situation of each of the branches." Want of such information, he explained, had caused "some inconvenience" at the previous legislative session. In addressing the General Assembly on November 28, the governor asserted: "Although most of our banks, from want of foresight, have acted imprudently in issuing paper too freely; yet, from the best information, they have generally been engaged in recalling it from circulation for more than a year past." He recommended that the assembly give careful thought to setting a time when banks would be required to resume specie payment on their notes. Jennings viewed forced resumption of specie payment by banks as a way to "remove that uncertainty which is entertained in relation to their ultimate solvency . . . ." The following day the governor gave legislators a statement from the cashier of the Bank of Vincennes, the State Bank, which included statements from its three branches. According to the cashier of the Bank of Vincennes, it, the parent bank, had credits and debits aggregating $545,559.67. Its debits included $128,469 of "paid in" capital; $13,102 of its bank notes issued and in circulation; $167,158 of such notes issued on its branches; and $215,357.51 on deposit from the federal government. On the credit side the parent bank held $199,259.91 of discounted notes; the sum of $29,000 for loans to the state treasury; $33,168.92 in specie; and $239,234.59 of deposits in the three branches. The statements from the Corydon, Vevay, and Brookville branches indicated that their credits and debits totaled $273,404.58; and they also were anything but solvent operations. The report by the president of the Vevay branch asserted that an unnamed officer had conducted its business "for his own benefit and that of his immediate friends" rather than that of the branch. A Brookville editor, presumably acquainted with the data the bank's cashier had given

Jennings, wryly commented: "The report is not as gratifying as we expected it to be."[56] The General Assembly considered a variety of items concerning banks, but only modest legislation resulted. No date was set for resumption of specie payment, but those not paying specie on demand were mandated to pay interest on same at 6 percent until redeemed. An editor at the capital shrewdly quipped: "On this [bank] hobby a number of the members rode to the legislature, and now they must appear to do something at least to satisfy the expectations of their constituents at home." At this session the legislative pot was hardly in a position to call the state bank kettle black inasmuch as it authorized the issuance of $10,000 in treasury notes and the borrowing of $1,800 from the insolvent bank in part to pay interest on previous loans from the bank.[57]

Shortly after the legislature adjourned early in 1821, twelve stockholders called a meeting of the stockholders to consider "the propriety of surrendering" its charter. Before this meeting occurred the Vincennes Steam Mill Company, much indebted to the bank, was destroyed by fire.[58] At the March meeting a committee was named to investigate the situation of the bank, and David Brown was elected its president. After seeking forbearance on behalf of the bank from Treasury Secretary Crawford, Brown ruefully told the secretary: "It was an unfortunate day which brought me to preside over an already, ruined institution."[59] Nonetheless, before a meeting of the stockholders on June 13, the directors approved a 10 percent dividend on paid in stock. On June 13 Brown stated that the bank was insolvent, and he blamed much of its trouble on its close association with the Steam Mill Company. Resolutions adopted by the stockholders seem to have contemplated gradual closing of its business, but their actual intent is uncertain.[60] An editor at Vincennes, where the stockholders met, told his readers that the meeting reminded him "of an old-fashioned *Carolina Gander Pulling*. The poor old Mother Bank," he said, "was tied up by the legs, and every one present, friend and foe, appeared anxious to have a jerk at her neck." But when the gander appeared nearly dead, someone "tenderly *greased* it a little . . . so that it outlived the frolic, and probably will survive until another *pulling match*." The editor was uncertain "*who greased the gander*," but termed him "a great goose for doing so, unless he expected a share in the next crop." An editor at Corydon, who had likewise been probank, bluntly declared, "That the bank has been prostrated, by means which deserve no better name than swindling," as indicated by the resolutions adopted. Their manifest intent, this capital editor asserted, was "to wrest the stock of the Company, the only security for creditors, from the grasp of the United States; and at the same time to pay their own debt to the bank, in the easiest manner possible." At a public meeting at Princeton, Gibson County, on June 9, Senator Richard Daniel offered this toast: "The state Bank of Indiana—more corruption than money."[61]

Concern that the bonded debt owed the bank had been transferred to the federal government prompted Governor Jennings to advance the start of the legislative session of 1821-1822 about two weeks. This possibility had been noted in the press for more than a month. On October 25 a paper at the capital commented that if this were true: "The whole revenue of the present year, which is collected in the depreciated paper of the State Bank and Branches, & intended to pay the debt to the bank, must remain an useless mass in the treasury." The federal treasury, however, generously returned the bonds to the state, enabling the use of the bank's depreciated paper toward their liquidation.[62] Perhaps spurred by the bank's action regarding the debt, the legislators ended acceptance of the bank's paper for payment of taxes and other obligations to the state; and mandated the executive to appoint an agent to bring a quo warranto suit against the institution in the Knox County circuit court. If the suit resulted in forfeiture of the charter the governor would name three commissioners to settle its affairs.[63] Before the outcome of this suit was known, control of the bank apparently largely passed to directors at or near Brookville. The new directors reportedly paid some stockholders a 40 percent dividend, and gave Nathaniel Ewing $3,500 for his former services as its president.[64] In June, 1822, the Knox County circuit court declared the charter forfeited, and directed the seizure of all bank property for the benefit of creditors.[65] Bank officials appealed this decision, and in November, 1823, the state Supreme Court upheld termination of the charter but ruled that the property of the bank remained with the stockholders. In a scathing indictment of how the bank had been conducted, the high court concluded that it had "embezzled" $250,000 of federal deposits; had debts above that permitted by its charter; had issued more paper than it could redeem; had established more branches than its capital and specie justified; had paid large dividends while refusing to meet demands against it; and had taken steps to dissolve without paying large debts owed.[66] The conclusion of an anonymous author, perhaps Samuel Merrill, offers an epitaph for the First State Bank: "There were few Bank failures more discreditable than that of the . . . State Bank of Indiana, with branches at Corydon, Vevay and Brookville. A large amount of the paper became entirely worthless in the hands of the holders, and the General Government never obtained but a small portion of about $200,000 of its deposits for lands sold."[67]

The Farmers and Mechanics Bank of Madison, which declined becoming a branch of the state bank, had a more honorable record than the latter. It resumed specie payment in 1817, by which time it had a branch at Lawrenceburg.[68] How consistently it maintained specie payment is uncertain, but at various times from at least 1818 to 1826 its notes were accepted at specified land offices.[69] About the time the First State Bank lost the receipt of federal deposits, the Madison bank obtained them and received at least $140,000 of deposits during 1820 and 1821. In recommending the bank for federal deposits, Congressman William Hendricks and Senator James Noble asserted that "its solvency and good management [is] as well ascertained as that of any bank in the western country." Its officers and stockholders included "men of wealth and integrity," they said, adding that federal funds would be "perfectly safe" in this bank.[70] Although Logan Esarey says the bank closed in 1824-1825, after meeting all its obligations in an honorable manner, this seems to be a premature burial since its notes were received at some land offices at times during 1825 and 1826. In any event, it recommenced banking in 1832, during which year Congress authorized a compromise settlement with it.[71] Its charter expired on January 1, 1835, but the legislature gave it three years to terminate its business. The anonymous author who gave a scathing indictment of the demise of the First State Bank also observed: "The paper of the Farmers and Mechanics Bank, at Madison, was ultimately redeemed, after passing, at depreciated rates, for several years."[72]

Not all of the major questions which arose in the teens and early twenties concerned state finances and banking. Before Jonathan Jennings completed his initial term as governor, his right to retain the office was questioned because of his service in 1818 as a commissioner to treat with the Indians by appointment of President James Madison.[73] Editor Elihu Stout, his persistent critic, allowed anonymous critics to use his paper to heap abuse upon the youthful governor. "A Farmer," charging that Jennings and his advocates had abused and vilified their political opponents, especially territorial Governor William Henry Harrison, asserted that in Congress the latter was "caressed . . . as a statesman and a warrior," while Jennings was "known and viewed as a drunken sot."[74]

When this sharp thrust appeared against Jennings, he was at St. Mary's, Ohio, seeking land from the Indians as one of three federal commissioners. While in Ohio the governor wrote Lieutenant Governor Christopher Harrison: "Understanding that some official business is necessary to be transacted . . . it may be necessary for you to attend at the seat of government to discharge such duties as involve on the executive of Indiana."[75] According to Harrison, upon receipt of this communication he obtained the state seal from Secretary of State Robert A. New, but needing to be away from Corydon for a brief period left it with New upon the assurance that it would be surrendered only to him. Upon Harrison's return, however, New explained that Jennings "came into his office and took the seal from off the press or table." Harrison contended that Jennings "had abandoned the office of governor," and asked for the seal, but Jennings responded that he would keep it, and "be answerable for his own conduct." "Who has the constitutional right and authority to administer the government," Harrison averred, "and from whom will the general assembly receive communications as chief magistrate at the commencement of their approaching session, are questions fairly laid before the public without [further] comment."[76]

The contest between Jennings and Harrison gave Editor Stout an opportunity to try to secure the ouster of the incumbent governor. Referring to Jennings' "late breach of the constitution, and consequent relinquishment of the gubernatorial chair," Stout commended "acting gov. Harrison" for his intelligence, uprightness, and firmness of spirit, which as a contrast to Jennings' "double dealing" would insure the support and confidence of the people in his administration. Harrison would have been "liable to impeachment," Stout asserted, had he "tacitly permitted" Jennings to act unchallenged.[77]

But the Constitution of 1816 was subject to differing interpretation regarding this item. It prohibited the holding of "any office" under the federal or state government while serving as chief executive, nor could a state official have "more than one lucrative office at the same time" except as authorized by the constitution. During a governor's "absence from the State, the Lieutenant Governor" was to "exercise all the powers and authority appertaining to the office of Governor, until" the executive's return.[78] If serving temporarily as a federal Indian commissioner meant holding a federal office or another lucrative one, Jennings had violated the constitution.

When the General Assembly met on December 7, 1818, the impasse between Jennings and Harrison was on its doorstep. On this day the House named a committee to ask Harrison "to communicate . . . the resignation of Jonathan Jennings as Governor . . . and by what way the state seal has been taken out of his possession[.]" Next day, however, the House abolished this committee and sought Senate concurrence for a joint committee to call upon both claimants to learn "the true situation of the office of the Executive" and report its findings.[79] Unable to gain Senate concurrence, on the third day the House agreed, by a vote of 15 to 12 to a joint committee to invite communications from Jennings. That afternoon, Jennings submitted his annual address, affording at least tacit recognition of him as governor.[80]

Nonetheless, the House continued to investigate the dispute. Even before the address from Jennings it appointed a committee to consider "the existing differences" regarding the executive department, and another to inform "the Lieutenant Governor" that it would receive any communication he might wish to offer about the situation. The day after Jennings addressed the assembly, the Senate proposed a joint committee "to wait on the Lieutenant and late acting Governor" to receive any communication he wished to give. The House concurred with this proposal but Harrison responded, "That as Lieutenant Governor he had no communication to make . . . , but as Lieutenant and acting Governor, if recognized as such, he had."[81] The joint committee apparently closed its probe at this point.

The House investigating committee, however, chaired by Samuel Milroy, asked Jennings for "any documents" he might provide concerning "this unfortunate subject." The governor explained that from a conviction of its propriety he and others had "successfully" negotiated with the Indians in obtaining "a large and fertile tract of country" which the people of the state desired. Although not explicit whether he had received a federal commission, the executive stated that had he "any public documents, calculated to advance the public interest" it would be a pleasure to provide them. Milroy's committee took sworn testimony from James Dill, William Prince, and John Conner, all present at the treaty negotiations, who said they had neither seen nor heard anything which proved that Jennings had had an official commission. Secretary of State Robert A. New and Auditor William H. Lilly professed lack of information about such a document.[82] Milroy's committee concluded that Jennings had accepted a federal commission, but asserted that it was not prepared to say what its effect might be. Next day, by a vote of 15 to 13, the House terminated its investigation.[83] Thus, despite substantial opposition in the House, largely from western counties, Jennings was sustained by the General Assembly. His personal popularity and the importance of the cession obtained—known as the New Purchase —seemingly outweighed concern about any constitutional question involved in his service as commissioner. But with the close of the House investigation Harrison resigned as lieutenant governor with the pithy comment: "As the officers of the Executive Department of Government and the General Assembly have refused to recognize and acknowledge that authority, which, according to my understanding, is constitutionally attached to the office, the name itself in my estimation is not worth retaining."[84]

The gubernatorial election of 1819 gave voters an indirect referendum between Harrison and Jennings. Early in 1819 "Man in the Moon" observed that Indiana's governor could apparently "bend" the laws and constitution "with impunity to suit himself." Jennings was charged with having concurrently received pay as Indian commissioner and governor, but a pro-Jennings editor asserted that the auditor's books would show that Harrison had received compensation as governor during the absence of the former.[85] By April various papers viewed Judge Jesse L. Holman of the Supreme Court and Jennings as candidates, but some doubted whether the judge was an aspirant and pictured him as having been urged to run by opponents of the governor.[86] A correspondent advised John Tipton that "The allegations against Governor Jennings, for Serving his Country as a commissioner in the purchase of the Indian Lands, will have a very different affect from what his enemies intended—[.]" In the Whitewater Valley "A Voter" emphasized that some "new" and "weighty matter" must be brought against Jennings "before we shall consent to abandon our old friend" who "has protected and cherished our infancy, and assisted in laying the foundation of our future greatness." In May Jennings confirmed his candidacy, merely stating: "ALLOW me to announce to the citizens of Indiana, that I consider myself a candidate for the office of Governor at the next general election."[87]

Stout's *Western Sun* gave much space to items against the reelection of Jennings. Among the litany of abuses against the incumbent governor, by anonymous critics, were those that he had: come to Indiana as a Federalist and so far as known was still one; continued to serve as a director of the branch bank at Corydon, thus conflicting with his duty to oversee the conduct of the First State Bank; violated the state constitution by serving as a federal commissioner to treat with the Indians; been "*indisposed*" for a "number of days" while serving as such, as the federal government supplied excellent liquors; and in 1811, when the Indians were daily committing savage murders, had "done all in his power to oppose and frustrate the Indian war."[88] On July 3 the *Western*

Sun happily announced former Lieutenant Governor Christopher Harrison as a candidate in opposition to Jennings. In this issue "A Subscriber," responding to those who called Harrison's candidacy too late, emphasized that it was "never too late to get clear of a man, who has violated the Constitution in three years oftener than an honest man would in a century"; or "to substitute a moral, upright man, for one who is notoriously the reverse." Harrison, "A Subscriber" said, had yielded to his friends to become a candidate after Holman declined doing so.[89] Harrison's friends presented him as: a moral and upright man who would not violate either the laws or constitution of the state, a firm and longtime Republican, a person of intelligence and experience, and as one who neither owned any bank stock nor had any involvement with banks. On the eve of the election, "A Voter" stirred various criticisms against Jennings, and jabbed that if the people "want a notorious drunkard," hardly qualified for any office, "then it is proper to vote for Jonathan Jennings."[90]

At the election on August 2, Jennings apparently trounced Harrison by roughly a three to one margin. Unofficial returns for twenty-one of thirty-one counties show 9,038 votes for the governor to 2,900 for his rival, with Jennings obtaining majorities in six of the eight western counties for which votes are available.[91] The executive doubtless won his decisive triumph in part because of the popularity he had achieved since his election as a territorial delegate a decade earlier. His role in obtaining the vast New Purchase area from the Indians in 1818 most likely enlarged his total, while most voters were apparently not unduly perturbed by the attacks on his character.

Significant interest was manifested in the contest for lieutenant governor, an office vacant since December, 1818, when Harrison had resigned. For a time three state senators—Ratliff Boon, John DePauw, and Dennis Pennington—were viewed as leading aspirants for this office. Marston G. Clark, an early settler who had fought in Indian campaigns, also became a candidate.[92] Late in May Boon and DePauw resigned their Senate seats helping establish the precedent that a candidate should not retain one office while seeking another.[93] During July Clark and Pennington withdrew from the competition,[94] and according to unofficial and incomplete returns Boon defeated DePauw by about a two to one margin.[95] This substantial triumph for Boon, from Warrick County in the western half of the state, indicates that voters from the more populous eastern counties were willing to support a popular candidate from the western area. Boon's strength in the eastern counties and that of Jennings in the western counties suggests that the east-west sectionalism of the later territorial era was fading.

Since the General Assembly chose the treasurer, auditor, and secretary of state, elections for these officials were held at appropriate intervals. When this body convened in December, 1819, House and Senate committees reported favorably concerning the manner in which Treasurer Daniel C. Lane and Auditor William H. Lilly had performed their duties. In a joint session the legislature reelected them for three-year terms.[96] Because the secretary served four years, his election came up at the ensuing session. Jennings told the General Assembly that he had personal acquaintance "of gross neglect and direct carelessness" on the part of incumbent Robert A. New. Although a joint committee of the legislature took exception to the secretary's not keeping records on a current basis, it reported that his records and books were in good condition. New then won reelection to a four-year term, despite considerable opposition.[97] The new terms for these three officials, and especially for that of Governor Jennings, provided substantial continuity to the executive department from statehood into the early twenties.

While the governor and most state officials held three-year terms, members of the General Assembly were subject to more frequent scrutiny by the sovereign voters. Annually on the first Monday in August the voters elected all of the representatives and about one third of the senators, with the latter serving terms of three years. But with a rapidly growing and shifting population frequent apportionments were essential if anything approaching equitable distribution of legislative seats was to be maintained. The Constitution of 1816 mandated an enumeration "of all the white male inhabitants above the age of twenty-one years" at five-year intervals beginning in 1820. Subsequent to these enumerations representatives were to be "apportioned among the several counties" and senators "among the several Counties or districts" according to the number of voters. The aggregate of senators was never to "be less than one third, nor more than one half of the number of Representatives." This wording suggests that county lines were to be respected in forming both representative and senatorial districts.[98] If this was not the intent of its framers, it is strange that the initial legislative apportionment which they made respected county lines in spite of considerable inequality in the total of voters from district to district.

The distribution of legislative seats pursuant to the constitution rested on an enumeration made the preceding year which reported 12,112 voters. Inasmuch as the constitutional apportionment of 1816 provided twenty-nine representatives and ten senators, if all representatives had been given an equal number of voters each would have served 418 members of the electorate. Had senatorial representation been likewise distributed, each senator would have served 1,211 voters. Since two new counties had been created after the enumeration—raising the number from thirteen to fifteen—county lines had been significantly modified. Six of the fifteen counties received one representative each, four two, and five three. Seven counties obtained their own senator, one senatorial district was formed by joining two counties, and the two remaining districts each embraced three counties. Considerable disparity in the number of voters from district to district is indicated since five counties with three representatives each acquired its senator, but so did Dearborn and Gibson which had only two representatives. Moreover, Washington, Jackson, and Orange constituted a senatorial district, as did Perry, Posey, and Warrick, but the former counties combined had four representatives while the latter trio had but three.[99] Legislative districts which gained two or more members of the assembly elected them on an at large basis.[100] The apportionment of 1816 showed complete respect for county lines. As noted above, each county got at least one representative, and counties were never divided in establishing senatorial districts. Since political parties had not yet developed, it seems that local and personal rivalries had considerable to do with which counties

got more than one representative, and which counties were combined to form senatorial districts. The fourteen counties of Southern Indiana gained overwhelming dominance of the House of
Representatives, obtaining twenty-six of twenty-nine of them.
Wayne County, in the eastern part of Central Indiana, was given
the three remaining representatives. The eight eastern counties of
Southern Indiana, with seventeen representatives, had a majority
of the members of the House. As yet there was no organized
county in the western portion of Central Indiana, or in Northern
Indiana. In proportion to the number of eligible voters, it appears
that the representative ratio for this apportionment favored
Wayne County and the western counties of Southern Indiana.[101]

Because the number of counties more than doubled while Jennings and Boon were governor, the question of how and when
their voters were to be represented in the General Assembly was of
major importance.[102] Though the constitution mandated a reapportionment every fifth year, save for one exception, it was silent
whether general or limited apportionments could be made at
other times. The assembly dealt with this question in a practical
manner. Various acts at the legislative session of 1816-1817 creating new counties stated that voters in them should continue to
vote in legislative districts as provided in the constitution. At the
ensuing session the legislature affirmed this principle and specified
that persons were "entitled to vote in the same districts (and no
other) for senators and representatives, as though no change had
taken place in the bounds of the counties since the adoption of the
constitution, until a new apportionment shall be made by law."[103]

Pursuant to the injunction of the constitution, early in 1820 the
General Assembly provided for a county by county enumeration
of voters preparatory to the initial legislative reapportionment.[104]
A Brookville editor expressed concern that the commissioners of
Franklin and other counties had been tardy in naming an individual to make the enumeration. He advised that if necessary commissioners should hold an extra meeting, name the enumerator,
and ask the next assembly to legalize their action. Otherwise, the
eastern counties would "lose that weight in the Legislature they
have hitherto enjoyed, and to which they are justly entitled." The

enumeration was made for Franklin and most other counties, however, the secretary of state later advised legislators that "but few of the returns, can be said to be strictly official." The aggregate of voters in 1820 cannot be determined from the official enumeration, but in terms of the population as of the federal census of 1820 the total was probably roughly 28,000.[105]

The reapportionment of 1821 increased the aggregate of legislators by slightly more than half. The number of representatives rose from twenty-nine to forty-three, of senators from ten to sixteen. The guideline apparently called for one representative per 700 voters, and one senator per 1,800 voters.[106] But because the total of counties included had jumped from fifteen to thirty-seven, more combining of them was necessary than had been required in 1816. Again, save for Warrick—split for both representative and senatorial districts—county lines were respected. While in 1816 every county got at least one representative, in several instances the new distribution joined two or more counties. Counties with plural representation were located mainly in the eastern half of the state. Only three counties gained their own senator, none secured more than one. Most senatorial districts included two or three counties, and one included five counties. The unequal distribution among counties is illustrated by the fact that Wayne and Dearborn obtained three representatives each, whereas the latter got a senator of its own and the former shared one with Randolph. For eight counties with two representatives each, only Washington and Franklin got their own senator, while Knox, with two representatives, was put in a senatorial district which included Daviess and Martin.

For the apportionment of 1821, the disparity among counties was in contrast to the equitable manner in which representation was spread among geographical areas. Of the forty-three representatives, thirty-five were given counties of Southern Indiana, eight to those in Central Indiana, and none to Northern Indiana in which a separate county had not yet been organized. The eastern counties of the state received twenty-seven representatives against sixteen for the western ones. The eastern counties of Southern Indiana obtained twenty-one representatives, or slightly less than half the total. Thus, representatives from southeastern Indiana still had the dominant voice in the General Assembly, but already political power had commenced advancing across the state both northward and westward. Despite this slippage of power, approved by an assembly in which representatives from the southeast were a majority, membership in the House of Representatives seems to have been extended to other sections of the state in a generous manner.[107]

Constitutional provisions about suffrage and elections strengthened popular control over state government. Suffrage was extended to "every white male" citizen of the United States in the county of his residence, subject to a year's residence in Indiana, except for those "enlisted in the army of the united States or their allies." Voting was to be "by ballot," unless changed to the *viva voce* or oral method at the 1821-1822 session of the legislature. Since these items were never changed in the pioneer era, both blacks and women were not allowed to vote.[108] Although ballot voting had existed briefly in the territorial period, oral voting had been restored on the eve of statehood.[109] At the constitutional convention the committee regarding suffrage and elections reported a section calling for oral voting, but the Committee of the Whole decided that votes be "'given by ballot.'" An effort to strike out this section failed by a tally of 26 to 17. Then the section was amended so that ballot voting would prevail for "'four years and afterwards be regulated by the legislature; and when thereafter established'" remain unalterable unless changed by another convention. This amendment prevailed by a razor thin vote of 22 to 21, after which it was agreed that if the mode of voting was not changed at the fifth legislative session, the General Assembly could not thereafter do so.[110] The legislative session of 1820-1821 asked voters to indicate their preference between the two modes at the election in August, 1821. The Vincennes *Western Sun* viewed this referendum as one of "the utmost importance," meriting mature and careful consideration. The Vincennes *Centinel*, friendly to Governor Jennings, said there was "much difference of opinion" about this question, but it called voting by ballot "the safest, purest, and most correct and reasonable mode which can possibly be devised."[111] The August referendum yielded scanty and indecisive data, but Knox County, whose county seat was Vincennes, cast 387 ballots for ballot voting and 250 for a return to oral voting.[112]

At the legislative session of 1821-1822 the General Assembly declined to restore oral voting. On two important votes the House favored the return of oral voting by a tally of 23 to 19, but on two such votes the Senate stood by ballot voting by the narrow margin of 8 to 7.[113] Fifteen representatives protested the House support for oral voting. They claimed that a majority of the vote on the referendum in 1821 had been for ballot voting, asserted that oral voting would subject debtors and tenants to the influence of those on whom they were dependent, and cause "personal controversies amongst neighbors . . . calculated to deter peaceable citizens from attending the polls." The preamble to the Senate resolution in favor of ballot voting contended that oral voting would make it "impossible for the votes of each county to be taken at the county seat in one day," defeating the "beneficial consequences" of having elections "at one place" giving candidates the "power to refute the falsehoods and misrepresentations . . . too frequently circulated for the accomplishment of improper purposes."[114] Hence, ballot voting persisted throughout the pioneer era.

A law passed early in 1817 established the basic pattern for the conduct of elections which prevailed under the Constitution of 1816. At their initial meeting each year, according to this law, the county commissioners named a "respectable elector" inspector of elections for every township. Each inspector named two voters to serve with him as judges for elections, and the three of them chose "two suitable persons" as clerks. The county commissioners provided inspectors with ballot boxes and blank forms for use in making poll books and recording votes. At 9 A.M. on election day inspectors proclaimed "aloud" that the polls were open. They remained open until 4 P.M., after which if fifteen minutes elapsed without a voter appearing, the polls could be closed. Voting, however, must cease at 6 P.M. When a prospective voter arrived the inspector called out his name, took sworn testimony of his eligibility if his vote was questioned, after which the three judges decided whether he could or could not vote. Each voter handed his ballot to the inspector, who placed it in the ballot box in the presence of the other judges. One judge repeated the voter's name and both clerks kept separate and consecutively numbered lists of those who voted. When the counting of the vote began, the inspector took ballots from the box one by one, and read "aloud" the persons voted for. A judge received each ballot, again read the vote, and the remaining judge strung the ballots "on a thread of twine" as they were given him. Both clerks kept separate lists of the vote for all the candidates in columns prepared for this record. The judges gave certificates of the vote for each candidate to the county clerk, plus one of the numbered lists of those who had voted, and one of the lists of the vote for the candidates. The county clerk, in the presence of judges from the townships, compared the returns and gave certificates of election to local candidates having the highest number of votes. In the event of a tie vote, the clerk and judges determined the winner by lot. The clerk sent certificates stating the vote for governor and lieutenant governor to the speaker of the Indiana House of Representatives. Those for sheriff, coroner, and congressmen were sent to the secretary of state who reviewed them and certified the winners to the governor who gave them certificates of election.[115] Pursuant to the Constitution of 1816, the General Assembly was the final judge of the qualifications and elections of its members; and contested elections for governor and lieutenant governor were to be settled by a joint committee of the assembly. The ultimate decision about the qualifications and elections of congressmen rested with the federal House of Representatives.[116]

Heavy penalties were provided for improper voting and inappropriately influencing voters. Every ballot cast was to state "in writing or print" those supported and their offices. No ballot was to be "lost for want of form" if the judges could determine its intent to their satisfaction. A person who voted more than once or submitted two or more ballots deceitfully "folded together" was subject to a fine of up to $50 and disbarment from voting or holding office for two years. The state constitution mandated that a candidate for governor, lieutenant governor, or the legislature be disqualified for his elected term if found guilty of giving or offering "any bribe, treat, or reward to procure his election." The election law of 1817 made persons seeking to influence voters by threats, violence, or force; by offering a fee, meat, drink, or otherwise; or by public treating on election day subject to a fine of $500 and prohibition from voting and holding office for two years.[117] Before the state election in 1819 a paper at Madison called an election day "The Sabbath of Liberty," and it urged that "men of talents, virtue and patriotism" be elected to preserve the privileges and freedoms so happily enjoyed. But the "Sabbath of Liberty," like other Sabbaths, was often violated. Editors and others objected to the use of flattery, promises, threats, treats, slanders, lies, whiskey, and otherwise to affect voters.[118] Soon after the election in August, 1822, an editor at the capital reported that it had been accompanied by "less riotting and drunkinness" than previously. Though uncertain whether this resulted from candidates having "less confidence in whiskey" or because voters were rising "above the degradation of selling their votes for a dram," this editor strongly urged that the law be changed and voters be required to vote in their townships. Under existing law, he said, "the great body of the people collect at the county seats, and chiefly those who are fondest of Drinking and Riotting."[119] Restricting voters to their townships of residence probably would have reduced the abuses complained of, but voting at the county seats gave them an opportunity to obtain information about candidates at a time when newspapers were scarce and their readers were limited in number.

The desire of the pioneers to perpetuate representative government was matched by their eagerness to expand and develop the economy. As a debtor society, living on the northwestern frontier of the United States, with much emphasis on self-sufficiency, they urgently needed an excess of exports over imports to gain capital to pay debts and augment the economy. Roads were needed to link the scattered and spreading settlements, largely located on or near the borders with Ohio, Kentucky, and Illinois in a U shape around the southern half of the state. The Ohio River and its main tributaries offered a natural outlet for trade with southern markets and beyond via the Mississippi outlet, but upriver traffic was slow and extremely costly. Trade with the Atlantic Seaboard was limited and very expensive, thanks to the Appalachian Mountain barrier and the lack of any through natural waterway for its conveyance. Despite the urgent need for increased and improved transportation facilities, because of the meager population and economic base but little could be accomplished toward this goal during the Jennings-Boon era. It is well to keep in view that the ordinary expenditures of state government averaged about $23,396.40 annually in these years, and the population was only 147,178 in 1820 and roughly a little over half this number when statehood was achieved.[120]

Difficult and hazardous conditions of travel prevailed in the teens and early twenties. The navigation of rivers was impaired by fallen trees, rocks, rapids, shoals, ice, sandbars, strong currents, islands, floods, and other obstructions. Roads varied from deep mud to dust, depending upon the weather, with stumps, ruts, mudholes, hilly terrain, fallen trees, rocks, and swamps as common obstacles. Crossing unbridged streams was frequently dangerous and at times impossible. Whether travel was by water or by land exposure to rain, heat, cold, snow, mosquitoes, and wind was often experienced as the seasons came and went. Finding suitable drinking water along the way was at times a matter of concern. Goods and persons were transported principally by flatboats, keelboats, and canoes, if by water; and by wagons, carts, sleds, and horseback, if on land. Individuals did much travel afoot.[121]

Contemporary accounts vividly illustrate the difficulties and hazards of frontier travel and transportation. In 1817 it took Thomas Dean and party about eleven days to pole, oar, push, and perhaps sail, their schooner from the mouth of the Wabash upstream to Vincennes—a distance of perhaps roughly eighty to one hundred miles. Below New Harmony "great exertion" was required and an hour and forty minutes consumed in navigating a chute of approximately two miles through "a swift current" full of logs and trees. At the Grand Rapids near Vincennes, because of the swift water and slippery rock bottom, the members "had to get out and wade to find the channel, and shove the boat up." During the fall of 1822 an English traveler found roads in southern Indiana "almost impassable, even on horseback." With difficulty one day he made only "eighteen to twenty miles between sun-rise and sun-set," walking and leading his horse much of the way. Oliver H. Smith, who traveled the state in the teens and early twenties as a lawyer, later explained that attorneys paid "the highest prices . . . for the very best traveling horses," which "were trained to the cross-pole mud roads, and to swimming" the rivers.[122]

The early settlers found a sprawling network of trails which had been used by Indians and animals for an unknown period of time. Perhaps roughly four fifths of Indiana was forested when statehood began thus this network principally wound through timbered areas.[123] The overhanging branches of trees often spread across the trails, and travelers might proceed for miles without the rays of the sun occasionally penetrating through the dense forest canopy. Removing fallen timber and other obstacles from these paths, plus adding stone or logs in some of the soft places, was a necessary first step in pioneer road building. But in reality new roads were *cut* or *opened* rather than built, and the stumps of larger trees often were left in the roadway.[124]

The responsibility for opening and maintaining public roads rested almost entirely with local officials and citizens. The initial state legislative session gave county commissioners the power to open, relocate, or vacate roads. The commissioners were annually to name an adequate number of freeholders within each township as road supervisors. Males, "eighteen years of age and under fifty," were obligated to donate, in person or by a hired substitute, up to six days of labor yearly. The supervisors notified workers when and where labor was to be done, and whether it would be for six days or less. If an individual provided "a pair of horses or oxen and driver, with a plough, cart, or waggon" each, such day counted as three days of individual labor. The commissioners at their option could levy a road tax on land at not to exceed one fourth the state levy on land. Owners so taxed, however, could offer road labor, either in person or via a substitute, in lieu of paying the tax. Supervisors were to erect signposts at points where roads forked with "the most remarkable places on each road" mentioned and the way to them indicated.[125]

The General Assembly soon increased the obligation of landowners for opening and clearing roads. An act of 1819 made able bodied males, "between the ages of eighteen and fifty," liable for only two days of road labor annually; and it authorized county commissioners to levy a road tax on landowners, including non-resident owners. The tax could be worked out in labor on roads at 75 cents per day. This legislation, however, was not mandatory since it gave commissioners the option of continuing under pre-vious enactments concerning roads. But an act of 1821, which seems to reflect a bias against absentee landowners, mandated two days of labor yearly for able bodied males, between eighteen and fifty, who were not owners of any real property or the renters of any dwelling house for more than a year. Owners of forty acres or less would work three days, with a jump to ten days for those who possessed from 480 to 640 acres. Persons having more than 640 acres would provide an extra day for each further 160 acres held. In addition, the commissioners were empowered to levy a road tax on landowners, but that on nonresidents could not exceed the levy on residents.[126] Before this act increasing the responsibility of landowners was adopted, an editor at Madison viewed road legis-lation as "calculated to pamper the rich, and oppress the poor." Compelling the poor, scarcely able to "keep their helpless wives and children from starving" to work as many days as "affluent" owners of thousands of acres being enhanced in value, was branded "very unequal and unjust." After passage of the 1821 act, Representative General Washington Johnston asserted that a number of citizens considered it "quite objectionable," charging that it put almost the sole burden for opening and repairing roads on landowners, particularly nonresidents. Johnston explained that a man owning $1,000 of intangible property would work only two days annually, while a nonresident owner of six thousand acres would owe thirty-seven days of labor, which at 75 cents a day would cost him $27.75; plus about $6.25 to pay the road tax on the land. Modest as these sums are, an eighty acre farm could then be obtained from the federal government for only $100.[127]

Neighborhood roads were important, but roads connecting settlements and towns were much needed. Early in 1820 the leg-islature authorized the location of about two dozen "permanent roads," largely in counties near the perimeter of the state from Richmond south, westward north of the Ohio River, thence up the Wabash Valley to the area of Terre Haute. Mainly in the eastern rather than western part of the state, some of the roads pointed toward the center of Indiana, where the permanent capital site was to be selected. Commissioners, usually three or four in number, were designated to determine their routes with the aid of county surveyors. Commissioners and surveyors were to be paid $1 and $2 per day respectively from private donations. If donations were not available, the service was not required. Once the routes were determined, the county commissioners were to have them opened, not exceeding seventy feet wide; and keep them in repair as for other roads, but none of them was to have any priority for support as Three Per Cent Roads.[128]

During the teens and early twenties Indiana began to receive a modest amount of money from the federal government to build roads and canals under the direction of the General Assembly. As part of a general quid pro quo, the state was to receive 3 percent of the proceeds from federal land sales within its borders. Late in 1818, shortly after having helped obtain the vast New Purchase area from the Indians, Governor Jennings over optimistically advised legislators that the fund made it within their power "to lay the foundation of a system of internal improvement co-extensive with the state," which, properly used, "will progressively effect the grand purpose, without exhausting the means of its progress, until it shall have been fully accomplished." But the executive stressed that until the permanent capital had been selected as a hub from which "substantial leading roads" could be made to "important points on the limits of the state" its expenditure would be "but limitedly advantageous, if not ultimately useless." Meanwhile, if invested in interest bearing stock it might soon yield $30,000 yearly for roads and canals in starting "a system" of internal improvements.[129]

As the year 1821 ended the legislature *prospectively* appropriated $100,000 from the Three Per Cent Fund for "laying off" and "opening" twenty-two "state" roads. Earlier in the year Indianapolis had become the site for the permanent capital, and settlers were moving into the New Purchase area acquired from the Indians three years earlier. Like the "permanent" roads in the act of 1820, the "state" roads had more mileage in the eastern than the western counties; and there was much overlap between the two networks. Various of the "state" roads had terminals at Indianapolis, but none of the "permanent" roads had extended to this point. The General Assembly named three commissioners for each road, and empowered them to locate their roads, divide them into segments not exceeding five miles, and contract with "undertakers" to open and clear them a width of forty-eight feet. Trees were to be removed at ground level, except for those "eighteen inches and upwards [in diameter]," which were to be "cut at the usual level of twelve inches." The "undertakers" could use gravel, stone, or timber from adjoining land to make the roadways equally good so far as possible; and at mile intervals they were to erect "a stone, post, or some good durable timber" giving distances to the terminal points. The assembly named Christopher Harrison, former lieutenant governor and rival of Jennings for the office of governor, as agent of the state to receive and distribute the Three Per Cent Fund.[130] Before the Jennings-Boon administration ended in December, 1822, Harrison announced that $32,629.46 had been received for the fund; and labor had begun on some of the "state" roads.[131] Five representatives, four of whom served counties bordering on the Ohio or Wabash rivers, protested that the $100,000 had been for roads alone, whereas the fund had been designated for both roads and canals. The representatives termed the appropriations to the roads "unequal" and "unjust" because the area served had been given more consideration than taxation, population, and prospects for future improvements warranted. The representatives contended that only speculators would benefit from the appropriations, despite the fact that contracts had to be for short segments and awarded only to resident citizens.[132] Some critics viewed it premature to appropriate a larger sum than the money on hand; others said the money was scattered over too many roads to achieve significant results; and still others complained that too much of the appropriation would be used to compensate commissioners, surveyors, and the state agent.[133]

The General Assembly also gave considerable attention to transportation via rivers. Since the larger rivers could be used to convey imports as well as exports, early settlements were predominantly on or near the Whitewater and its main forks, the Ohio, the lower Wabash, and the White and its main forks. Downstream traffic on these, plus numerous smaller streams, was principally by flatboats, a growing number of which floated to New Orleans and other points on the lower Mississippi in the teens and early twenties. These locally made boats, chiefly loaded with farm produce and lumber products, usually required a month or so to reach New Orleans.[134] Because steamboats were in their infancy, upstream traffic was largely conveyed by the slow and laboriously hand-propelled keelboats. The latter were advertised for sale at Vincennes in 1817, and two years later Thomas Emison sought freight for delivery to points above or below Vincennes. During the spring of 1822 an Indianapolis paper announced the arrival of two keelboats from Ohio and Virginia.[135] Meantime, steamboats began navigating the Ohio and Mississippi, causing excitement in Ohio River towns. In 1817 a Madison editor reported that the "Harriet" had passed there supposedly going "at the rate of twelve miles an hour!"[136]

The importance of river traffic for the Old Northwest had been emphatically recognized in the Northwest Ordinance of 1787. It mandated that "The navigable waters leading into the Mississippi and St. Lawrence, and the carrying places between the same, shall be common highways, and forever free" to its residents and citizens of the United States "without any tax, impost, or duty, therefor."[137] The increased use of waterways by flatboats and keelboats required consideration of which waterways were navigable, especially because numerous grist and saw mills were being erected on them. Early in 1820 the legislature declared hundreds of miles of fifteen of Indiana's rivers and streams navigable, in most instances up to certain mills. Owners could continue milling if they built locks or slopes around their dams adequate to maintain normal navigation. Owners destroying or injuring navigation were subject to a fine of from $10 to $500 for each offense, and individuals felling trees into navigable waters were liable for a penalty of not to exceed $3, unless the timber was removed within ten days. The county commissioners were given the power to regulate dams and slopes, but at times the legislature made concessions to millers.[138] As Logan Esarey stated regarding this legislation, exaggerating to emphasize his comment, "Almost every creek large enough to float a sawlog was opened, so far as a statute without an appropriation would effect it."[139] What such legislation accomplished is moot, but the obstacles to navigation arising from such obstructions as rapids and falls, snags and log-jams, rocks and sandbars, and changes from high to low water made parts of some rivers and streams always unnavigable; and all of them unnavigable from time to time.[140]

Rivers, however, posed dangerous hazards to transportation and travel by land. Various toll bridge companies were chartered and county commissioners were authorized to have bridges built, but it seems that none of any consequence was erected during the teens and early twenties. Rivers and streams were crossed on foot, on boats, on horseback or vehicles, with individuals and horses at times swimming across them.[141] Hence, ferries were essential, but they were mainly located on the larger waterways. An act effective in 1818 gave county commissioners power to regulate ferries. Unless particular needs were to be met, a ferry could not be commenced within a mile of one in operation. Keepers of ferries were to have a "good and sufficient" boat or boats, supply a "sufficient number of good and skilful ferrymen," transport persons and property from daylight to dark at rates set by the commissioners, give free passage to persons carrying public messages, and provide passage at night for double the day rate. A keeper who took more than the allowed compensation was subject to a penalty of up to $40. The extent to which ferries were recognized as important public utilities is evidenced from the exemption of persons necessarily employed for them from "personal" road labor as well as from militia and jury duty except in time of war or public danger.[142]

CHAPTER 2

THE ECONOMY, 1816–1850

WHEN INDIANA BECAME a state in 1816, as Alton A. Lindsey has aptly stated: "It was overwhelmingly natural—a freshly minted land." The somewhat nomadic and sparsely settled Indians had lived largely in harmony with the natural environment; and the French, English, and Spanish had made only negligible change in it.[1] As two scholars have noted "a magnificent yet forbidding wilderness of giant hardwoods" stretched across the state probably covering "nearly 20 million acres of what is now Indiana." Within this forested domain were scattered clearings and meadows as well as large prairies and sloughs located mainly in the northern third of the state. But "the great hardwoods dominated and overwhelmed as far as the eye could reach."[2] With statehood, however, roughly 80,000 settlers began the slow and laborious task of eliminating the forests and bringing them, the prairies, and wetlands under cultivation. Although the pioneers from 1816 to 1850 worked endlessly to remove the forests, it was their successors, not they, who destroyed most of the native forests. For the most part, however, the pioneers bypassed settling the wet prairies or other wetlands.[3]

For the pioneers, however, the state's greatest natural resources were its millions of acres of fertile and tillable soil, a climate suitable for agriculture, and its abundant virgin hardwood trees, not its mineral resources. For centuries this soil had been enriched by fallen leaves, dead and decaying timber, and the natural fertilizer of animals and other creatures. The soil of central and northern Indiana was generally more fertile than that of southern Indiana, however, there was much fertile and tillable soil in the lower Wabash Valley and scattered places elsewhere in the lower portion of the state.[4] Much the larger part of the state had approximately 160 to 180 days between the last damaging frost in the spring and the first such frost in the fall. Precipitation usually varied from a little below forty inches per year in most of the north to somewhat above forty inches in the south. Fortunately rainfall was normally considerably diffused among the four seasons.[5]

Agriculture was overwhelmingly the economic base of the pioneer economy. It was essential as a source of food and clothing, both essential for the survival of the pioneers. Moreover, from agriculture came the preponderance of items for the export trade without which the means for obtaining imports and paying for taxes and miscellaneous items would have been lacking. Agriculture, plus lumber to a lesser extent, provided the leading items on which both trade and manufacturing rested.[6] Dr. Buley has emphasized that "Life in the villages and country towns differed but little from that in the country; neighbors were somewhat closer and contacts more frequent, but the essentials of life were the same." Town dwellers also had gardens, cows, pigs, and chickens. "Some had log houses, many possessed unpainted frame houses, while a few lived in painted frames with picket fences; there were always a few substantial bricks for the local aristocrats. Hogs, dogs, and surface drainage took care of garbage and rainfall; little shanties with crescent-shaped ventilating holes constituted the sanitary disposal facilities." Though not suggested by Buley, doubtless the country dwellers, both those with and without "little shanties with crescent-shaped ventilating holes," had fewer odors permeating the atmosphere and penetrating their houses than the village and town dwellers.[7]

Indiana's geographical context had a large impact on how the economy developed and expanded. Save for small parts of northern Indiana, which drained to the Great Lakes via the St. Lawrence into the Atlantic Ocean, its rivers were within the vast Mississippi Valley that drained via the Ohio-Mississippi waterway into the Gulf of Mexico. So long as trade was principally by water, the natural draining greatly favored the Mississippi outlet over that by the St. Lawrence. Moreover, the elongated and generally very difficult to cross Appalachian Mountains, which stretched hundreds of miles from Maine to Alabama, formed a natural obstacle to east-west traffic between Indiana and the Atlantic Seaboard. Here there was no natural drainage outlet. Hence, until east-west railroads crossed this mountain barrier in the 1850s, the Ohio-Mississippi waterway was Indiana's most important artery for trade. This dependence fostered political ties with the southern slave states, while the desire to establish east-west trade over the mountains fostered ties with Ohio, Pennsylvania, New York, and other northern states. As Albert L. Kohlmeier discerningly emphasized in his *The Old Northwest as the Keystone of the Arch of American Federal Union: A Study in Commerce and Politics*, this concern about trade routes, plus a strong commitment to preservation of the Union, prompted Indiana politicians to vote at times principally with southern politicians and at other times principally with northern politicians.[8]

Hoosiers of the 1900s—mainly the products of an urban, commercial, and industrial society, with much division of labor—often mistakenly view the pioneer era as the good old days when life was for the most part simple and uncomplicated. Far more than these Hoosiers are aware, pioneer life was steeped in experience, knowledge, and understanding accumulated by their forebears during the two hundred years or so that settlements had slowly zigzagged from the Atlantic Seaboard over the mountains into the vast region drained principally by the Mississippi River. Here the immigrants found themselves more isolated and more on their own concerning food, clothing, shelter, and medical care than many of the families had been from which they came. To be sure, their experience, knowledge, and understanding was laden with myth, folklore, and superstition. Nevertheless, they were *generalists* who could do a variety of different things. The men were not only farmers but hunters, woodsmen, and tradesmen. The women were not only mothers and housekeepers, they raised and preserved much of the food; made wool and flax into clothing; administered medicine to the ill; served as midwives; and performed a number of important household processes.[9] Logan Esarey, in commenting about the labor performed by farm families, said: "The work varied with the seasons but there was no idle season for either men or women. The usual day's work for a man began at sunup and ended at sundown—'from sun to sun.' The women worked a few hours longer, since there was wool to pick, socks and stockings to knit and clothes to mend, and these were after-supper jobs." Esarey added: "We fret our lives away now for fear some 'youth' who weighs one hundred fifty pounds will be compelled by some hard-hearted taskmaster to do a few hours' work. In those [pioneer] days a boy of thirteen or fourteen hitched his team—oxen, horses or mules—to a wagon or plow and did a 'man's' day's work. Nor were the girls idle. The gospel of work was taught in church and school and practiced in the home. The Devil was always at the elbow of idlers, for the Devil had plenty of work for idle hands to do. Hard work and sanctity were closely akin but idleness and sin were twins."[10]

Selecting a home site and providing shelter for a family was a priority for new settlers. Congressman Ratliff Boon—who had come to Indiana several years before statehood, then served as legislator, lieutenant governor, and governor before becoming a congressman—in 1838 told fellow congressmen how he had settled in Indiana as a squatter with his family when his "nearest neighbor was a hostile Indian," and his "only shelter from the storm, and . . . protection from danger, was an open *camp* and the bark of the elm tree when spread upon the cold earth served both as my floor and my carpet."[11] Logan Esarey, who was born in Perry County on the Ohio River in 1873, doubtless got much of his information and ideas about pioneer life from relatives and others who had been participants in it. According to Esarey: "There was no agreement on what was the best site for a home." But "Soil, water, vegetation, drainage, roads, neighbors, hunting, 'lay' of land—each had its influence and rarely did two people agree on which was most important." Regardless of the choice "the first work was a camp to live in until some kind of a house could be built. The 'half-faced' camp was common. It was made of poles, usually with three walls, and covered with poles and brush." As Esarey well knew not all immigrants first lived in such camps. As a teacher and writer, he often generalized without allowing for exceptions to make basic ideas clear and better understood.[12] Professor Buley explained that the selection of a site for a home "was determined largely by availability of water, timber, streams, and quality of land. Springs were more plentiful among the hills, the timber furnished mast for the hogs as well as wood for buildings and fuel, and streams means of access in absence of roads. These considerations as well as those of health, accounted for early settlement of lands [in southern Indiana] now among the roughest and poorest in the region." With the Indians no longer a threat after 1814, Buley suggests, the "concentration of settlements around stations or blockhouses and stockades, so long the practice in the Kentucky settlements, was no longer necessary." But "Since the need for labor in girdling trees, planting, and clearing was pressing, a temporary shelter, or open-faced camp or lean-to, sometimes sufficed for the family the first year." After telling how such a shelter was constructed, Buley adds: "It was in such a home as this near Little Pigeon Creek, in Spencer County, that the Lincoln family spent their first winter in southern Indiana."[13]

Offering better shelter than the open-faced camp were "the more primitive types of log cabins," the building of which Buley describes in much detail. Some of these primitive cabins were made "of unfinished logs which frequently sprouted and covered the exterior with a growth of foliage, floorless and loftless, with one door and window, constructed without a nail, became the 'Hoosier Nests' of poetry . . . ." Then, as the family increased and conditions of life bettered, "improvements and refinements were developed and added until the simple log house became an abode of some comfort and convenience. Hewn logs replaced the round bark-covered timbers." If lacking, puncheon floors were added; and as the process continued: "A loft could be added and the capacity of the one room almost doubled. Sometimes a lean-to or annex would be built on one end or side, to serve as a kitchen, or else the original cabin became the annex when a more commodious dwelling was joined to one side or end." Built in a variety of ways, log cabins of one kind or another became and remained the dwellings of the preponderance of the Hoosier pioneers. As Buley observed their "furnishings . . . depended upon the means, tastes, and abilities of the settler."[14]

Preparing forested land for cultivation was as laborious and continuous a task as anything done by men and boys. In describing pioneer men as woodsmen and hunters as well as farmers, Buley emphasized the very great importance of the long rifle and the woodsman's ax to the frontiersman. The former "enabled him to protect his life, overcome his enemies, and feed his body," and the ax enabled him "to build his home, conquer the forest, and provide for his maintenance from the soil." With the small but invaluable ax the forests were denuded bit by bit. In Buley's words, "The settler might 'cut smack smooth' and have the job done once for all, or he might clear extensively, start his crops, and finish the job later. As a rule the underbrush and trees under 18 or 20 inches [in circumference?] were cut, and the larger ones girdled." Walnut, hickory, elm, and beech, if girdled while in full leaf, never leafed out again, but hackberry, ash, and sugar trees would leaf out again and shade the crops. Hence, some farmers set fire to them the ensuing winter, "and a several-acre 'deadnin' spouting flames heavenward at night was a sight to behold. If not fired, dead beech and sugar maples would begin to fall about the third year, but oak, poplar, and walnut would stand for several years." Plowing became easier if the larger roots near the surface were cut off "with the ax; German settlers as well as some Yankees went after them conscientiously with the mattock." As the fallen timber accumulated logs and limbs were piled and burned, especially in the spring or fall, often at neighborhood logrollings, so that the "smoke of burning wood piles permeated the settlements . . . ." Nonetheless, "years of backbreaking work with brush hooks, briar scythes, mattocks, and other grubbing tools had still to be spent." There were different methods used to remove the forests. But as A. L. Kohlmeier at times explained to students, having trouble determining the facts about some item, *even the pioneers left some stumps standing!* Regardless of the process, the pioneers normally had patches of *new ground* in successive stages of clearing.[15] But chop and clear as they did, the federal census of 1850 indicates that only 5,046,000 of the approximately 23,000,000 acres of Hoosierland had been cleared and put under cultivation.[16]

The initial plowing of newly cleared ground was a tough and difficult task. Buley concluded that the "typical plow" used in the West "was either the plain shovel or jump plow, or the old barshare or bull plow, which made no pretense of scouring." As Esarey explains, however, the shovel plow to become a jumping shovel plow had to have "an upright cutting bar or cutter passing down from the beam so that the point of the cutter was a half-inch lower than the point of the plow and immediately in front. The cutter was set slanting slightly to the rear so that it would cut small roots and jump the plow over others." But the heavy downward *jerk* that often came when the cutter hit a root could injure the plowman and make a spirited team of horses extremely hard to control. "The ideal outfit," Esarey observed, "was a 'philosophical' plowman and a yoke of heavy, patient oxen." At times new ground was plowed back and forth, and then cross plowed in the same manner. Blacksmiths made and repaired crude plows, and some of them produced newer and better plows. For instance, it was John Deere, a smithy, who introduced a much improved plow in 1837 that could be used in breaking prairie soil as well as that from cleared forests. It would also scour in prairie and in friable soils. By 1850 there were dry prairie areas, such as those near Vincennes and Lafayette; however, the draining, plowing, and cultivating of the wet prairies, mainly in northwestern Indiana, occurred principally in the last half of the 1800s.[17]

Corn, a very valuable crop Europeans found cultivated by the Indians, was the leading cereal. Wheat and oats were important, and lesser quantities of buckwheat, rye, and barley were grown. In 1840 Indiana produced 28,156,000 bushels of corn; 4,049,000 bushels of wheat; 5,982,000 bushels of oats; 49,000 bushels of buckwheat; 130,000 bushels of rye; and 28,000 bushels of barley. In 1850 corn output jumped to 52,964,000 bushels; wheat increased to 6,214,000 bushels; oats dropped to 5,655,000 bushels; buckwheat more than trebled to 150,000 bushels; rye plummeted to 79,000 bushels; and barley rose to 46,000 bushels. Corn was the staple among cereals while wheat overtook oats during the forties as wheat production expanded because more of the soil was becoming adapted to its growth, and wheat growing was stimulated by the opening of the Wabash and Erie Canal in 1843, establishing an all water route to New York City. At midcentury, Indiana produced 53.6 bushels of corn; 6.3 bushels of wheat; and 5.7 bushels of oats per capita respectively. Although one of the smaller states, Indiana ranked fourth in the production of corn; sixth for wheat; eighth for oats; tenth for buckwheat; eighteenth for rye; and eleventh for barley. Indiana had become an important part of the national granary for cereal crops.[18]

Corn was used principally as food for farm animals, farm families, and for conversion into whiskey. Once the ground had been plowed, the land was normally laid off into squares of roughly four or five feet with furrows made in one direction, then crosswise at right angles thereto. Several seeds of corn were dropped into the corner holes and covered by a hoe or some such item. The seed sown was overwhelmingly corn such as planted by the Indians or a minor modification thereof. Both yellow and white corn were grown, but mostly the former. As the corn grew it was cultivated in one direction and then crosswise with harrows, double shovels, and the like, leaving no untilled strip *between* rows. Normally planted in April or May, corn was usually "laid by" in July or August with harvesting beginning in September or October, and at times persisting into the early months of the ensuing year. The ripe corn was shucked or husked by hand and tossed into wagons or carts pulled by horses or oxen. Some farmers turned hogs into corn fields to "hog down" the stalks and eat the ears. Many farmers cut and shocked part of the stalks before they were ripe, then later husked the ears before feeding the fodder to horses and cattle. Still others jerked ears from stalks and piled them in some place such as a barn in preparation for a husking bee. While yields on very fertile land at times exceeded one hundred bushels per acre, yields of fifty to seventy-five bushels seem to have been more typical. By the 1840s drills and handheld planters were being used to seed the corn, somewhat improved varieties were being sown, and the harrows, double shovels, and other kinds of cultivators were also being improved.[19]

Wheat growing developed slowly among those farming newly cleared forested land. Buley noted that wheat grown on such soil might produce what looked like good grain, "but when baked into bread very potently affected the stomach. Even hogs, whose stomachs were arsenic proof, would not give such grain a second trial." Although an important food for families, wheat in contrast to corn was not generally used as feed for farm animals. It became important as a money crop for export from Indiana, which made its sale dependent on both flour milling and transportation facilities. Unlike corn, which could be preserved many months, wheat needed careful storage and delivery to market without undue delay to avoid its deterioration. Usually sown broadcast by hand in the fall, and tilled in or covered by harrows or drags, wheat was harvested during June or July. When ripe it needed to be harvested quickly. At first cut mainly with a sickle or scythe, the cradle was in common use by the thirties and forties. The cutting of wheat often was done by men and boys who specialized in this task, while others specialized in binding the wheat into bundles and putting them into shocks for curing and drying. The threshing—separation of the grain from the stalks—initially was done largely by having oxen or horses trample out the grain on a hard surface, or beating it out by hand with a flail. Horse-powered threshing machines, that could be moved from farm to farm, made their appearance by the 1840s but had modest use before 1850. Yields perhaps averaged between fifteen and twenty-five bushels per acre on most farms. Varieties planted included Red Blue Stem, Black Sea or Mediterranean, and Old Red Chaff.[20]

The sowing and harvesting of oats, buckwheat, barley, and rye were similar to that for wheat. Rye and barley, like wheat, were usually sown in the fall and harvested in summer. Oats were sown in the spring and buckwheat in midsummer and harvested before the fall frosts. These cereals did better on new ground than did wheat. In varying degrees the straw from them and wheat was used both to feed and bed farm animals. Some of the pioneers ate buckwheat cakes made from buckwheat flour, drank gin and whiskey made from rye, and beer made from barley. But whiskey from corn had no serious rival among liquors made in part from rye, buckwheat, or barley. Among these cereals oats were produced in greater quantity than the others, even exceeding wheat in output in bushels in 1840.[21]

Miscellaneous crops of varying significance were tobacco, flax, hops, and hemp. The growing of tobacco, usually in small patches, was doubtless increased because many settlers came from the Upper South. Pioneer families often had a small patch of flax from which they obtained fiber for spinning into linen; or, combined with homespun wool, the women made warm and durable clothing from the resulting linsey-woolsey. After the pretty blue flowers of flax had ripened, the seed from them could be sold to millers who made linseed oil from it. Hops provided an extract used in making beer. Hemp, from which rope and baggage were made, especially at shipping points on rivers, was a valuable but minor crop. Making rope at an elongated ropewalk was a laborious process. Using census data, Bidwell and Falconer indicate that Indiana produced 1,820,000 pounds of tobacco in 1840, which decreased to 1,045,000 pounds in 1850, and jumped to 7,994,000 pounds in 1860; 36,888 bushels of flax seed in 1850, which soared to 119,420 bushels in 1860; 585,000 pounds of flax fiber in 1850 plummeted to 97,000 pounds in 1860; 93,000 pounds of hops in 1850 slid to 28,000 pounds in 1860; but this source has no such data for hemp.[22] During the thirties there were dreams of profit from the cocoons of silkworms that lived on mulberry trees. These dreams, however, proved visionary. In 1840 a paper at South Bend gave twenty-two reasons why farmers in the United States should raise mulberry trees and produce silk.[23]

Travelers to or through Indiana observed clover, timothy, and grass in Indiana before it became a state in 1816. Native grasses of various kinds, on both forested and prairie soil, were in considerable supply. Hence, farm animals foraged on and were fed some of these grasses—decreasing the need for cultivated crops of clover and timothy to feed horses and mules in particular. The cultivation of clover and timothy spread across the state as settlements progressed and gained in importance in the 1830s and 1840s. Red clover, which added nitrogen to the soil, was sometimes included as crop rotation increased. Timothy resulted in hay for sale as well as feed on farms but it drained fertility from the soil. Hay production, according to the federal censuses, more than doubled in the forties, growing from 178,000 tons in 1840 to 403,000 tons in 1850, and up to 622,000 tons in 1860. But what part thereof was clover, timothy, native grass, or otherwise is impossible to determine.[24]

Vegetables, produced in town as well as in the country, constituted an indispensable part of the food consumed by the pioneers. The most consumed vegetable was doubtless the "Irish" potato. According to federal census returns Hoosiers produced 1,526,000 bushels of potatoes in 1840; 2,083,000 in 1850; and 3,867,000 in

1860. Per capita, this translates into an average of 2.2 bushels per person in 1840, 2.1 in 1850, and 2.9 in 1860. On this basis a family of ten—and many families were considerably larger—would have consumed over twenty bushels of "taters" each year. Other vegetables ranged from such root crops as sweet potatoes, turnips, parsnips, beets, and carrots. Above ground vegetables embraced beans, pumpkins, squash, cabbage, lettuce, lentils, peas, rhubarb, asparagus, celery, and melons. Most root crops could be "holed up" in the ground, covered with straw and dirt, and eaten as winter passed into spring. Cabbage could also be preserved by transforming it into sauerkraut. Properly stored, the time that squash, pumpkins, and even melons remained edible could be somewhat extended. Fully ripe peas, beans, onions, and lentils, well stored, could be preserved for at least several months. Some caves made good storage places, and as *cellars* were added, under the house or otherwise, many vegetables were preserved there for differing periods of time. Then there was the tomato or "love apple," viewed as a poison by some, that gained in favor during the thirties and forties.[25]

Fruits, berries, and nuts added variety and flavor to the diet. They could be cultivated or obtained from the wild. Fruits included apples, pears, peaches, cherries, plums, pawpaws, and persimmons. Berries ranged from strawberries, raspberries, blackberries, currants, mulberries, gooseberries, grapes, dew-berries, and cranberries to blueberries. Then there was the juneberry or shadbush that unofficially launched the annual succession of berries. There were walnuts, hickory nuts, butternuts, pecans, and hazelnuts. Birds, squirrels, and children in particular competed for the berries. Buley and Esarey both noted that the mulberries were generally full of bugs, but since the bugs were also full of berries it mattered little to the birds, children, or squirrels. Especially from the fruits and berries mothers and daughters made jams, jellies, preserves, applebutter, and cider. The Swiss at Vevay and the Harmonists at Harmonie were foremost among those who made wine from grapes. If Johnny Appleseed planted all the apple trees and apple seeds in Hoosierland attributed to him by folklore, he must have done his work by night as well as by day! Buley ob-

served that the grafting of fruit trees had been developed, however; Johnny Appleseed, who died and was buried at Fort Wayne
in 1845, "believed grafting to be 'against Nature,' consequently"
most of the fruit from his "seedling trees was of poor quality."[26]

Miscellaneous items in demand such as salt, sugar, honey, coffee,
and tea were imported to a considerable extent. Salt was indispensable for the flavoring and especially the preserving of various foods.
Since Indiana's salines produced only a modest amount of salt, much
used in preserving meats, salt was imported principally from other
states such as Virginia and from the West Indies. Maple sugar from
sugar trees, and sugar from sugar beets, were obtained locally, but
store or imported sugar was much desired. Some made tea from sassafras, spicewood, and other shrubs but again imported tea was desired. Indiana members of Congress, even those who sustained tariff
protection, at times sought to reduce or even eliminate duties on
sugar, salt, coffee, and tea. Buley concluded that "The honey of the
wild bee was almost as valuable to the settlers as ambrosia and nectar
to the gods." Buley explains that the "honey bee . . . came into the
woods from domestic hives. Unlike the housefly and rat, however,
which followed settlement, the bee, by reason of its swarming and migrating tendencies, was usually a hundred or more miles in advance of
the frontier, and the product of its labors, found on all sides, was one
of the most sought after treasures which the woods could yield."[27]

The pioneers were more dependent on meat, milk and milk
products, and eggs than on vegetables, fruits, berries, and miscellaneous items for their food. Their unusually hard and persistent
labor doubtless made the protein derived from meat, milk, and
eggs of much importance to them whether they realized the value
of protein or not. This was doubtless especially true at a time
when mothers frequently bore children annually during several or
even more years in succession. Meat included such varied items as
pork, beef, mutton, poultry, venison, rabbit, bear, squirrel, quail,
and fish. Dairy products included milk, cheese, butter, and cheese
in various forms, plus their use with other foods. Eggs were secured from domesticated chickens, ducks, geese, turkeys, and
guineas, and from wild turkeys and the like as well. As these comments indicate much of the meat was attained from the wild, and

this was probably especially true for immigrants during their initial years until they became established. Pork, potatoes, eggs, and milk were among the items on which the pioneers mainly relied. Esarey in particular has paid tribute to Mr. Hog as a source of food and William C. Latta has explained our large debt to Madame Cow and Miss Hen.[28]

The planting and harvesting of corn, wheat, and other grain crops were much hindered by various pests and diseases. Among the pests were birds, especially blackbirds, raccoons, bears, wild turkeys, deer, and squirrels. Since farm animals, particularly hogs and cattle, ran at large much of the time, unless fields were fenced crops were at their disposal. If fenced, they were often easily broken down or otherwise penetrated. The improvement of fences, erection of scarecrows, use of guns and dogs, and guarding of fields by men, women, and children lessened but did not eliminate losses. As noted in Barnhart and Carmony, a pioneer of Morgan County explained: "The squirrels and birds stole by day, the coons and bears by night, and so they kept the first settler anxious until his corn was safely cribbed." The squirrels and birds sought the tender sprouts, while the coons and bears preferred roasting ear time for their forays. The need for constant vigilance is expressed in the traditional jingle about planting corn:

One for the blackbird, two for the crow;
One for the cutworm and two to grow.

Latta says the Indians expressed the same idea thus:

If he come, he no come; If he no come, he come.

Latta explains that the Indians meant "that if many pests came there would be no corn, but if only a few [pests] came there would be at least some corn." Other pests infesting grain crops were the corn borer and army worm for corn, and, to some extent, the weevil, rust, and Hessian fly for wheat and other cereals. In addition, farmers sustained losses from too much or too little rain, late frosts or freezes in the spring, early frosts or freezes in the fall, hail storms, heavy winds, and the like.[29]

The principal farm animals were hogs, cattle, sheep, and horses. As described by Latta: "The livestock of the early pioneer period was very indifferent. The immigrants brought with them what they had and it was poor enough. The practice of allowing the stock to run at large throughout the year (work animals some-times excepted), shelterless and foraging largely for themselves, resulted inevitably in further deterioration in size and quality. Springtime especially after a hard winter, found many of the ani-mals in a famished and weakened condition and the less vigorous often died of sheer starvation and exposure." Nonetheless, by midcentury, although Indiana was one of the smaller states in area, it ranked third among them in hog production; thirteenth in cattle; fifth in sheep; and sixth in horses and mules. This output, based on corn and hogs as the basic elements, provided substan-tial diversification for agriculture and made Indiana one of the leading agricultural states as of midcentury.[30]

Hogs were the most numerous of the farm animals. According to the federal census returns of 1840 and 1850 Indiana had 1,624,000 and 2,264,000 hogs respectively. Regarding hogs Buley states: "Hogs of the 'razorback' variety could be brought along, obtained from the Indians, or sometimes be found wild in the woods. These long-legged, long-bodied, long-nosed creatures with short straight-up ears, were often known as 'elm-peelers,' 'wind splitters' or 'tonawandas'; they could do almost anything except climb trees. They were adapted to their environment, and ordinarily were left to forage for themselves." Latta explains: "Hogs multiplied rapidly and quickly adapted themselves to their wild surroundings. Wolves sometimes killed young pigs but the mature hogs, especially the males, were formidable antagonists. They sometimes became so vicious and dangerous that, in squads, they would even attack and kill a bear. It is said that these semi-wild hogs would shake down blacksnakes from bushes, spring upon rattlesnakes, and kill and eat these reptiles with impunity. These long-snouted, long-legged, slab-sided, razor-backed, and altogether sorry-looking specimens attained their growth at two or two and one-half years on forest products, which, when abun-dant, put them in condition for market. Sometimes, after being finished on corn a few weeks before Christmas, they weighed 200 to 250 pounds." Hogs were frequently driven to markets at Cincinnati and Chicago, and probably even as far as Baltimore. As the pioneer period advanced hogs were driven more often to markets at pork packing plants on the Ohio and Wabash rivers. Esarey paid merited tribute to Mr. Hog when he said: "We may sing the praises of all the heroes of Indiana from LaSalle or George Rogers Clark to the present, but the prosperity of our state through the century has depended upon Mr. Hog. In fat years and lean years, until his late unmerited humiliation . . . he has come up with his part, even though he does grunt about it considerably." Although many hogs were sold, the butchering of hogs after the winter season brought cold weather provided families with lard for use in cooking and bacon, hams, and other pork products as a very important part of their diet.[31]

Cattle, like hogs, provided food for families and export. According to the federal census returns Indiana had 620,000 "neat" cattle in 1840; 715,000 in 1850; and 1,069,000 in 1860. There is no separate listing for dairy cattle for 1840; however, the census of 1850 indicates 285,000 dairy cattle for Indiana and 363,000 in 1860. At midcentury Indiana ranked thirteenth among the states for the number of cattle. Latta has stated that "The family cow came with the early settler. She was a prime necessity from the start. That she could subsist most of the year on the scanty herbage of the forest, live through the winter on straw, corn-fodder, and a little ear corn, produce a calf every spring, supply milk for the family and sometimes also a little butter, is evidence of her hardiness and usefulness." Furthermore, "That she endured the cruelty of the treatment for hollow-horn, having her horns bored into with a gimlet and her tail split open at the switch and salt put in the incision, when her major trouble was a hollow 'insides,' and lived often unsheltered through the winter, sometimes with snow frozen on her pinched back, is a wonder." Latta concluded that "Prior to 1840 and even as late as 1850 in Indiana most of the cows must have been of so-called native stock." Meantime, there had been a "growing admixture of the blood of grade Shorthorn and Devon cattle, the two breeds first brought into the state." The federal census for 1850 reported 12,881,000 pounds of butter and 625,000 pounds of cheese for the Hoosier state, and that of 1860, 18,370,000 pounds of butter and 606,000 pounds of cheese.[32]

Sheep were important mainly for their wool, while mutton was a minor part of the meat diet of the pioneers. Frontier conditions were not favorable to the raising of sheep because of their killing by wolves, dogs, and the like; and their fleece was impaired in value by the thorns, briars, seeds, and other like impediments that became entangled in it. The federal census of 1840 counted 676,000 sheep for Indiana, jumped to 1,123,000 in 1850, and dropped to 991,000 in 1860. Wool production more than doubled in the forties, rising from 1,238,000 pounds in 1840, to 2,610,000 pounds in 1850, then slipped to 2,552,000 pounds in 1860. The wool was consumed principally at home rather than being exported. Latta observed that the "dictum that 'deep woods are not the proper abodes of sheep' seems to have been generally accepted by the early Indiana pioneers." Nevertheless, in 1850 Indiana ranked fifth in the country for the number of sheep. The Harmonists at Harmonie and the Shakers, north of Vincennes, drew attention from travelers who commented about their large flocks of sheep. Improved breeds of sheep apparently developed faster than those for hogs, cattle, or horses, with the Merino the most common. Those who understand the context and circumstances of pioneer life should not be surprised to discover that in this era the legislature appropriated more money for wolves destroyed than for the state library.[33]

Though farmers at times preferred oxen to horses for farm work, and especially for plowing new ground, horses were much more numerous than oxen. And horses were far more numerous than mules and asses combined. The federal census of 1840 listed 241,000 horses and mules, that for 1850 reported 321,000 and 550,000 in 1860, when Indiana ranked fifth among the states. Latta concluded that "The early immigrants must have brought horses having an infusion of Morgan, Conestoga, and Thoroughbred blood." Latta states that French settlers at Vincennes "had good horses which they obtained from the Indians who brought them from the Spanish settlements west of the Mississippi." Buley, however, comments that "Pioneer horses were of inferior quality—small, scrawny, and ungainly looking." He asserts that "Horses with a strain of thoroughbred blood brought in from Virginia and Kentucky were somewhat better, particularly for saddle purposes. Since much of the heavy work was done by oxen or even cows, no great interest was shown in the development of draft animals." Bidwell and Falconer assert that mule raisers "on the good grazing lands of Kentucky were in the habit of sending jacks into the farming districts of Ohio, Indiana, and other sections of Kentucky. The mule colts which were raised there in small numbers by individual farmers were purchased by the grazier at the age of about 6 months, and taken back and grazed in Kentucky," then at maturity sold to southern planters or eastern coal miners. The preponderance of Indiana's mules were probably in the southern counties of the state. The relative merits of horses, mules, and oxen for particular types of work must have been an important subject of discussion among pioneer farmers. The expression "steady as an ox" explains why pioneer farmers found various uses for this strong, sturdy, and steady animal.[34]

Chickens, ducks, and geese were raised throughout the pioneer era. According to Latta Miss Hen and her "Chickens must have come with the early settlers. They were doubtless of mixed breeding, but of the lighter kinds that could fly up into the lower branches of the trees to roost out of the reach of foxes and wolves. The hens chose their nests about the straw stack, in the stables, under bushes, in the fence corners, anywhere that promised 'biddy' the desired seclusion." Chickens, ducks, and geese provided both meat and eggs as well as down and feathers for items such as pillows and feather beds. As for the principal farm animals, little attention was given to flock improvement. Chickens, geese, and ducks roamed and foraged a wide area, even with occasional trips into or through cabins on their unpredictable journeys. The filth which they scattered everywhere earned them the title of barnyard or dung-hill fowls. Latta concluded that because of "their small cost and ability to shift for themselves and endure neglect, it is highly probable that practically every farm had poultry of some kind." Latta indicates that early statistics about the number of poultry in Indiana are lacking, but that in 1880 poultry numbered "nearly eight millions and the number of dozens of eggs produced was over twenty-eight millions." This suggests that poultry must have increased rapidly from statehood to 1850.[35]

In various ways pioneer agriculture was more like that of medieval and even ancient times than farming of the late nineteenth and early twentieth centuries. The large degree of isolation and self-sufficiency which prevailed, especially in newly settled parts of the state, made the family the basic unit, sustained and in part reinforced by the exchange of goods, labor, or money within neighborhoods. Men and women alike had to be *generalists,* knowing how to do many different things about obtaining food, clothing, and shelter. Hard and almost endless labor was required, not only by men and women but also by rather young children. Child labor was not illegal, and most children were much involved therein before they reached their teens. Although agriculture was the economic base for pioneer life, it is difficult to describe pioneer agriculture in a concise manner, but certain characteristics may be noted. First, pioneer agriculture was *diversified* regarding both crops and livestock. Within this diversification corn-hog production was much the leading element. Corn fed to hogs which became pork was in a real sense corn in another form. Second, pioneer farming was *extensive,* not intensive. Labor was spread among various chores, with a definite lack of time to care for crops and animals. Third, as previous pages have indicated, the *tools and implements used* were crude and often ineffective in plowing, cultivating, harvesting, and the like. Fourth, *land was in abundant supply* at low cost and much occupied by squatters without any cost. Hence, the soil was frequently mined with successive crops of corn so that its original fertility was soon gone, resulting in erosion of the top soil and gullies. Fifth, in a *pre-scientific period* there was much reliance on traditional practices that included a mix of folklore and moon farming. Thus, not much attention was given to improved breeds of livestock and better seed for crops. Given the context in which pioneer livestock existed, truly improved stock might not have survived the rigors and hardships that prevailed. Sixth, generally speaking, during roughly at least the first five to ten years most pioneer families of necessity emphasized *subsistence farming* to meet the basic needs for food, clothing, and shelter. Therefore, they had to develop surplus items that could be sold to others before they could have the means to obtain better farm animals, tools, buildings, and the like. Seventh, the pioneers *preponderantly farmed forested lands* that they or the Indians had cleared, in part because of their bias against farming prairie land. Farming the truly wet prairies, mainly in northern Indiana, was not obtained until later decades when newer and larger machinery and implements became available.[36]

Several approaches were made toward the improvement of agriculture between statehood and midcentury. First, a number of years were normally required before new areas were cleared of their forests, including the final removal of large stumps. Once this process was finished the soil could be planted and cultivated more carefully than previously, with less amounts of roots, weeds, and the like with which to contend. Second, the improvement that occurred in tools, drills, plows, reapers, and the like in the thirties and forties led to improvement in the planting, cultivating, and harvesting of crops. Third, as preceding pages have indicated, there was some improvement in seed used for crops and in breeds of farm animals as the pioneer period advanced. Fourth, as farmers became established and increased their production of crops and farm animals they gradually added bins, cribs, sheds, barns, and the like for better care and preservation of their harvests and livestock. Fifth, especially by the 1840s, there seems to have been some increase in the rotation of crops and in the application of manure, fertilizer, and straw to the land. Judged by standards of the late twentieth century, the progress that took place seems negligible. If viewed in the context of agriculture in the first half of the nineteenth century, however, the improvement made was probably more significant than commonly presumed.[37]

With agriculture the dominant part of the economy, it is not surprising that varied efforts were made for its improvement. Interest therefore was manifested by legislators and politicians generally, farmers here and there, many newspapers, county agricultural societies, and a State Board of Agriculture. A law of 1829 encouraged the formation of agricultural societies but it seems to have had negligible results. An ensuing law of 1835 made it the duty of each county board annually to take steps toward the formation of an agricultural society for its county until one was organized. Once organized the society could tax its members not less than 50 cents or more than $5 yearly. It could receive donations of land or other property for its use but could not hold real estate above the value of $500 "for a longer period than one year unless the same be used as farms or gardens for agricultural experiments or purposes." This act mandated the naming of a five member State Board of Agriculture for terms of five years by the governor. The board was to give instructions to county agricultural societies for the improvement of agriculture and publish and distribute reports from county societies relevant to its improvement. This board was to hold a state meeting annually, with delegates from county societies in attendance and devise plans and means to give "the best and most efficient impulse" for agricultural progress. Each county might appropriate up to $50 yearly to its society, but no state appropriation was made, not even for the costs of members of the state board.[38]

Nevertheless, the State Board of Agriculture made its first and only annual report to the legislature in January, 1836. The board commented: "In a considerable number of counties, societies have been formed and regularly organized. A portion of these have held agricultural fairs, which have been productive of the most happy and encouraging results. a [sic] few of the societies sent up delegates to the annual meeting of the State Society, and sent in their annual reports." In an optimistic mood the board observed: "In some counties, quite an agricultural revolution has been produced; and in all the local reports, are to be found items of cheering intelligence, or plans promising future usefulness." The state board advised legislators that it "would be pleased to see an agricultural, in connection with a geological survey of the state, as recommended by" Governor Noah Noble. It indicated the need for "an agricultural periodical suited to" the condition of agriculture in Indiana; for "an elementary book, affording a plain, comprehensive, and useful view of the science and practice of agriculture"; "an experimental farm and agricultural school." The board had named a committee to seek information and plans about how "improved breeds of cattle and other domestic animals" should be introduced to the state's farmers.[39]

Two committees, appointed by the state board, gave very interesting reports. One committee gave a rosy account about the culture of silk. It concluded "that there is nothing in the nature of our climate to prevent the introduction of Silk culture into Indiana . . . ." The first object of consideration, it said, "is the necessary food for the silk worm. This is the leaf of the Mulberry tree." Though silkworms had been found on the "native Mulberry," the "appropriate food of the Silk worm" came from the White Italian Mulberry and especially the new Chinese Mulberry, the latter being "remarkably easy of propagation and growth." An acre of Chinese Mulberry trees, one source estimated, would yield an annual profit of $205 for the initial twenty years, and $490 annually afterwards. The committee noted the "immense" foreign demand for silk; that most of the labor required would be done during five or six weeks annually; and the "whole [labor] can be performed by children, aged persons, &C." Modest as this sum seems to be, such a return would have been extremely attractive to pioneer farmers and their families. But, as noted earlier, the silk craze soon abated.[40]

The second committee strongly urged the establishment of an agricultural school. It asserted that previously agriculture had been regarded as "a mere manual operation, more simple than any other art, science, calling or profession," hence required "less of mental operation" than other pursuits. Although some farmers had sent their sons "to the best schools in the country," they had "come forth classical scholars" not having had "the first idea . . . imparted to their minds, calculated to raise in their estimation the vocation of agriculture." Therefore, "that which is wanting to secure the respectability, usefulness, and happiness of the agricultural community, is a school in which the science and practice of agriculture should be taught *professionally*. Not to *use* (rather than teach) the practice without its science, and use it only as a *footblock* by which the student hopes to reach the *sanctum sanctorum* of Greek and Latin classics." The committee asserted: "And you might as reasonably hope to make your son a finished Greek scholar, by apprenticing him to a blacksmith, as to teach him the love, the science, or the practice of agriculture, by an ordinary academical course of education." The committee suggested that there were medical, law, theological, music, and fine arts schools, but "there is not . . . in the whole world, what can be in strict propriety, called an agricultural school!" It recommended the establishment of an agricultural school, plus an experimental farm and gardens. Properly located, established and equipped, "the institution would soon rise above its current expenses, and by its own income, gradually diminish its original debt of erection." Furthermore, "No measure . . . requiring the same amount of expenditure, would equally promote our character abroad, or our prosperity at home."[41]

Although a number of county agricultural societies were formed in the thirties and forties, they generally had a short life. In 1847 a Senate Committee on Agriculture stated that there were no more than ten such societies in the state. Latta says that all county societies—save possibly that of Marion County, of which Indianapolis is the county seat—soon ceased to exist. He concluded that these societies had been "in advance of the time" because "farmers generally, were too fully occupied in clearing away the forest and improving their farms to engage in agricultural organization." Probably so, but possibly the impact of the depression which began in 1837 and persisted until roughly the midforties, combined with the collapse of the Internal Improvements System of 1836 in 1839, was an equally important factor explaining the early demise of the county agricultural societies.[42]

In his book entitled *The Old Northwest as the Keystone of the Arch of American Federal Union*, A. L. Kohlmeier emphasized the relationship between commerce or trade and politics for this region in the decades preceding the Civil War. Dr. Kohlmeier concluded that its commerce and politics were both much influenced by the geographical location and context of the Old Northwest. One basic influence stressed was the manner in which the Old Northwest sat astride the low-level continental divide between the Mississippi and Great Lakes-St. Lawrence drainage systems. As Kohlmeier observed, the section which became Indiana—save for modest portions of northern Indiana that drained into the Atlantic via the St. Lawrence River—drained southward via the Mississippi River into the Gulf of Mexico. A further major geographical factor of much importance, noted by Kohlmeier, was the elevated Appalachian Mountain barrier between the Old Northwest and the Atlantic Seaboard stretching southwestward from Maine to Georgia and Alabama. The best trade markets for residents of Indiana were on the Atlantic Seaboard, but this Appalachian barrier had no key river system draining through it from the Old Northwest to the Atlantic coast. For the most part this barrier was extremely difficult to cross by pioneer vehicles. These two geographical factors made Indiana principally dependent upon the Mississippi route for its exports and much of its imports as well. This tendency was increased because most of the pioneers were of southern extraction, and also because they settled overwhelmingly in southern and central Indiana which drained into the Mississippi outlet. Nevertheless, the desire to augment export and import trade with the eastern seaboard fostered sentiment for supporting the construction of a canal that would cross the Appalachian Mountains. The combination of geographical and trade considerations caused Hoosiers to be much interested in improving trade facilities with both the area to their south and that eastward over the mountains. Hence, as Kohlmeier concluded, because of considerations about trade and preservation of the Union of the states, "The support of the Old Northwest was now thrown on one side and now on the other but on most difficult occasions it was exerted for compromise." Thus, Indiana's geographical location, with much interest with trade to and from both the southern and eastern states, greatly influenced its votes in Congress and made preservation of the federal Union a matter of its vital interest.[43]

While agriculture supplied the principal economic base, commerce and manufacturing, based principally on farm produce, grew rapidly. Among the important farm exports were pork, whiskey, corn, wheat flour, and wheat. Other farm exports included wool, flax fiber, beef, mutton, tobacco, butter, cheese, and hemp as well as live hogs and cattle. Nonagricultural exports of considerable significance were furs and hardwood lumber. Exports of corn and pork exceeded those of wheat and flour.[44] Imports ranged from salt to sugar, drugs, clothing, spices, tea, chinaware,

furniture, iron, glass, nails, and farm animals. With the augmenta-
tion of population and the advance of subsistence farming, both
exports and imports advanced very much in the thirties and forties.
The value of exports exceeded that for imports, however. In addition, the bulk and weight of exports exceeded that of imports.[45]
From statehood in 1816 to midcentury the preponderance of exports from Indiana were conveyed by boats southward via the Mississippi outlet. By 1850, however, there had been a considerable
increase in the exports sent out via the Middle Atlantic states and
the St. Lawrence River. From the beginning there had been a significant part of the imports that had arrived from the northern and
eastern routes; and perhaps by 1850 the value of imports via the
northern and eastern routes exceeded those coming in via the Mississippi River.[46]

Drs. Buley and Kohlmeier both emphasized that salt was an
import of great significance to the pioneers. As explained by Buley: "Salt as an article of commerce occupied a much more prominent place than it does today. Although it might be dispensed with
for a while as an item of food for people and animals, it was indispensable for preservation and shipping of certain foodstuffs. Its
perishable nature, weight, and variable quality made it difficult to
handle and expensive to buy." Since Indiana's salines were only
modestly productive, salt came principally from southern Illinois
and southern Ohio, the Kanawha Valley of Virginia (now West
Virginia), and islands of the West Indies. Its importation grew
rapidly as meat packing expanded in the thirties and forties.[47]

Manufacturing, like trade or commerce, was based mainly on
agricultural produce. It is impossible to divide pioneer manufacturing into *separate and distinct categories*, however, it may be
roughly divided into three broad, even if somewhat overlapping
categories, as: (1) household processes or domestic manufacturing; (2) trades or crafts; and (3) the larger mills, workshops, pork
packing plants, liquor distilleries, and the like, which may be considered small or budding factories. The men, women, and children who did the manufacturing were largely generalists, and this
is particularly true for those engaged in household processes. All
three categories existed from statehood to midcentury, but the

household processes diminished in relative importance by not later than the 1840s. Nevertheless, as of 1850 all three categories had considerable importance concerning manufacturing. The household processes or domestic manufacturing mainly concerned the making of items regarding food, clothing, and shelter, much mandated by the substantial degree of isolation and self-sufficiency that prevailed. Hence, this part of manufacturing was produced overwhelmingly by families, plus cooperative efforts among neighbors. Household processes concerning food and drink included the making of such items as cornmeal, wheat flour, maple sugar, hominy, maple syrup, sassafras tea, applebutter, sauerkraut, jellies, jams, preserves, dried fruits, cider, whiskey, butter, cheese, and especially the slaughtering and curing of pork as well as beef and mutton to a lesser extent. Among household processes for the making of clothing and related items were carding, spinning, weaving, fulling, tanning, bleaching, dyeing, sewing, knitting, and quilting. From miscellaneous household processes were made such household utensils and furniture as brooms, brushes, tables, chairs, jars, dishes, lamps, looms, hand-mills, spinning wheels, chairs, beds, cradles, candles, soap, buckets, reels, and a variety of other items. Men and boys made nails, carts, forks, wagons, sleds, plows, hinges, rakes, shovels, harness horsecollars, singletrees, flails, ax handles, clevises, and other such items. Although the household processes generally peaked at about midcentury, many of them have persisted through the twentieth century though usually in modified form.[48]

Numerous tradesmen or craftsmen appeared as a simple division of labor developed. Individuals with a skill or preference for making certain items became tradesmen, specializing in one or more trades. At times they served as itinerant tradesmen who secured orders then later delivered items made for their customers. Villages and towns, with some compactness of settlement, naturally attracted a greater variety of tradesmen than did the country neighborhoods. The federal census of 1850 illustrates the variety and abundance of tradesmen in Indiana as of midcentury. According to it tradesmen making clothing products included 2,971 cordwainers (leather workers, especially shoemakers); 1,386 tailors;

1,280 harness and saddlemakers; 551 tanners and curriers; 218 hat and capmakers; 157 weavers; and less than 100 each of clothiers, spinners, dyers, furriers, and hemp dressers. Tradesmen concerning the preparation of food and drink embraced 1,683 millers; 363 butchers; 231 bakers; 179 brewers and distillers; and 56 barkeepers. Woodworking craftsmen, more numerous than metal workers, ranged from 7,907 carpenters; 3,679 coopers; 1,872 cabinet and chair makers; 1,691 wheelwrights (makers of wagons, wheels, carriages, etc.); 305 coach makers; 297 joiners; 263 sawyers; 194 ship carpenters; and less than 100 each of woodcutters, boatbuilders, shingle makers, agricultural implement makers, sash and blind makers, and fire engine makers. The less numerous but very essential metal craftsmen were represented by 4,679 blacksmiths and whitesmiths; 334 tinsmiths; 213 machinists; 126 molders; 107 iron founders; and less than 100 each of gold- and silversmiths, iron workers, toolmakers, plane makers, locksmiths, boilermakers, mold makers, and stove makers. Tradesmen associated with the building and furnishing of houses numbered 1,805 masons and plasterers; 543 painters and glaziers; 331 brick makers; 185 potters; 114 block and pump makers; and less than 100 each of basket makers, broom makers, chandlers, watchmakers, rope makers, brush makers, glue makers, clock makers, paperhangers, upholsterers, cutlers, and pianoforte makers. Among miscellaneous craftsmen were 1,591 boatmen; 599 teamsters; 436 millwrights; 374 printers; 251 drivers; 227 railroadmen; 149 barbers; and less than 100 each pilots, colliers, surveyors, bookbinders, limeburners, telegraph operators, pattern makers, jewellers, quarrymen, drovers, oil makers, and engravers. Most likely these data are considerably less than accurate, yet however viewed they illustrate the extreme decentralization of pioneer manufacturing.[49]

One of the most essential and versatile of the trades was that of the blacksmiths. They were jacks-of-all-trades and masters of many of them as well. As explained by Dr. Buley:

> The blacksmith was gunsmith, farrier, coopersmith, millwright, machinist, and surgeon general to all broken tools and implements. His forge was a center of social as well as industrial ac-

tivity. From soft bar iron, nails as well as horseshoes were forged as needed. Tires [for wagons, etc.] were hammered out, measured, welded, heated, and shrunk on the felly. Chains, reaping hooks, bullet molds, yoke rings, axles, bear and wolf traps, hoes, augers, bells, files, shears, locks, keys, adzes, plowshares, hackle teeth, bits, saws, and the metal parts of looms, spinning wheels, sausage grinders, presses, and agricultural implements were a few of the items either manufactured or repaired in his shop. In addition the master smiths created axes and rifles, and, if provided with foundry and machine facilities, stoves, skillets, kettles, pots, mills, threshing machines, and plows.

Baynard R. Hall, the first professor of the institution from which Indiana University evolved, in his recollections of life in Indiana during the 1820s, devoted an entire chapter to a Bloomington blacksmith whom he admired as an artisan, musician, and friend. The professor, who taught Latin and Greek, commented, "But let none suppose Vulcanus Allheart was a common blacksmith," for "No man in the Union could temper steel as my friend tempered; and workmen from Birmingham and Sheffield, who sometimes wandered to us from the world beyond the ocean, were amazed to find a man in the Purchase that knew and practised their own secrets." Consequently, "Neccesity led him to attempt one thing and another out of his line, till, to accommodate neighbours, (and any man was *his* neighbour) he made sickles, locks and keys, augers, adzes, chisels, planes, in short, any thing for making which are used iron and steel. His fame consequently extended gradually over the West two hundred miles at least in any direction." Despite some embellishments in these comments by Buley and Hall, the blacksmiths merit their accolades. The appropriate establishment of a properly equipped blacksmith shop at one of the state parks would be a very fitting memorial to the blacksmiths of Indiana from the pioneer era to those of the twentieth century as well.[50]

As of 1850 the factory system, though important, was in its infancy. The transition from household processes to trades and thence to mills, shops, packing plants, and the like of the factory system was not made in successive sequences. All three stages were contemporary; and it is impossible to say just when mills, shops, and plants of various kinds became small factories, but their numbers grew during the second quarter of the nineteenth century. Some had appeared during the preceding quarter. As Barnhart and Carmony observed: "Before 1850 a varying number of grist, flour, saw, paper, rolling, fulling, cotton, oil carding, and woollen mills had appeared. Scattered factories made bricks, barrels, steam engines, threshing machines, hats, nails, stoves, cigars, carriages, wagons, as well as sundry other articles of farm equipment such as plows and cultivators. Finally, some tanneries, distilleries, pork- and beef-packing plants, boatyards, iron and brass foundries, rope walks, and wineries were small factories.[51]

The aggregate value of manufactured products was only $18,725,423 in 1850, at which time Indiana ranked fourteenth among the states. The aggregate was reported from 4,392 establishments that employed 14,440 wage earners who were paid $3,728,844. Thus, there was an average of 3.28 workers per establishment, and the average yearly wage was $258.23 per wage earner. These data, from the federal census of 1850, are probably somewhat incomplete and inaccurate but perhaps generally indicative of trends and characteristics.[52] In 1860, 5,110 establishments employed 20,755 wage earners who were paid $6,145,667. Hence, per the census of 1860 there was an average of 4.06 workers per establishment who received an annual wage averaging $296.10.

At this time the leading element of manufacturing was flour and meal milling, which aggregated $17,337,950; with lumber second at $5,786,250; meat third at $3,354,754; and liquor fourth at $2,486,407. Lesser industries ranged from machinery at $1,414,465; textiles at $1,145,971; carriages and wagons at $1,108,144; and boots and shoes at $1,087,495. Wayne County, on the National Road, led all counties for the value of manufactured goods, followed in order by Jefferson, Dearborn, Floyd, and Vanderburgh all on the north shore of the Ohio River; then in order by Tippecanoe and Vigo on the Wabash River; followed by Allen at the headwaters of the Maumee River; then Marion, site of the state capital and on the National Road; with Madison near the National Road, and La Porte on Lake Michigan tied for tenth rank.[53]

Nevertheless, at midcentury a contemporary observer, perhaps Samuel Merrill, forecast that the "agriculture of the State will always, no doubt, be the most important consideration." This observer failed to realize how rapidly and thoroughly the emerging factory system of manufacturing would modify the economic order, but he wisely anticipated that the principal manufacturing centers would shift northward. He wrote: "There is no commanding position in the State at which even a tenth of the whole business will ever centre. Madison is at present the most important point; but other places on the Ohio River are not much behind it: while Indianapolis and Richmond in the interior, Fort Wayne, Logansport, Lafayette, and Terre Haute on the Wabash and Erie Canal, and South Bend and Michigan City in the north, expect soon to equal the present business of Madison. The railroads and other improvements now in progress, and the facilities that shall hereafter be afforded to the business men of the State, leave yet much in doubt as to the points which will, ten years hence, have precedence." Despite industrialization and augmented manufacturing, agriculture remained very basic in the state's economy, and the combination of agrarian, rural, and urban decentralization influences remained very basic in Hoosier politics through at least the first half of the twentieth century.[54]

In contrast to manufacturing, Indiana's minerals had only modest development before 1850. In the midthirties, as prosperity and internal improvement fever peaked, Governor Noah Noble recommended that the General Assembly consider both a geological and a topographical survey of the state. He said that "many indications and discoveries" showed that Indiana "abounds" in mineral deposits which would "never be perfectly developed" without the aid of geological science. The executive mentioned "iron, coal, marble, and gypsum" as examples of minerals in which apparently Indiana abounded. The House Committee on Education recommended both geological and topographical surveys. It stated that there were "strong indications of mineral wealth, such as iron, lead, zinc, copper, and even gold and silver" as well as "similar indications of the existence of gypsum, marble, and alabaster." And that stone coal existed in "great quantities," but neither the committee nor the governor mentioned possible gas and oil. The legislature adjourned without authorizing any survey, but it authorized the governor to correspond with the executives of Ohio and Kentucky to ascertain if they would cooperate with Indiana for a geological survey. Noble was further authorized to communicate with "one or more eminent geologists in the United States" concerning such a survey.[55]

When the General Assembly convened in December, 1836, Noble, not having secured the cooperation of Ohio and Kentucky, recommended that "a competent person" be named to make a geological survey of Indiana. A bill which Noble approved February 6, 1837, "authorized and required" the governor "annually hereafter to appoint and commission a person of talents, integrity, and suitable scientific acquirements as geologist for the state of Indiana . . . ." The salary was not to exceed $1,500 per year, plus $250 annually for necessary expenses. The individual named was "to make a complete and minute geological survey of the whole state commencing" in the vicinity of public works (internal improvements). At the beginning of each legislative session the geologist was to give legislators "a detailed account of all remarkable discoveries made and the progress of the work, accompanied with proper maps and diagrams, including a geological chart of the state." This position was to expire at the end of 1838 unless extended by the ensuing legislative session. Even before the legislature had convened, the possible appointment of David Dale Owen of New Harmony had been anticipated. He was appointed in March, 1837. William Maclure, known as the Father of American Geology, had already made New Harmony known as a center for geological research; and David Dale Owen was just beginning his outstanding career in making surveys for various states and the United States. Soon after his appointment Owen circulated a letter via the press offering to receive and analyze mineral samples without charge. He expressed special interest in obtaining specimens of fossils and rocks as well as ores from miners, well diggers, quarrymen, and engineers.[56]

During 1837 Owen worked the Wabash and Ohio river banks and sampled formations here and there as he zigzagged across the state. He spent most of his time in southern Indiana, then the most settled area, but visited such northern towns as Michigan

City, South Bend, and Elkhart. Walter B. Hendrickson, who has detailed Owen's career as a geologist for various states and the federal government, concluded that "in the first year of the survey Owen covered a thousand miles, all of it on horseback." In March, 1838, Governor David Wallace renewed Owen's appointment for that year during which he made detailed studies of various places to achieve more definite conclusions for his second annual report. Owen's conclusions about his 1837 and 1838 surveys, though incomplete, were significant achievements and particularly so when viewed in the context of geological knowledge as of that time. According to Hendrickson, interest in how geological surveying might suggest ways that mineral resources could contribute to the improvement of transportation facilities and advance manufacturing caused Owen "to work along utilitarian lines" in his surveying. Hendrickson indicates that Owen gave considerable effort to locate and evaluate Indiana's coal, iron, salt, and limestone resources. The coal resources were located as being mainly in the western half of the state from the Ohio River to some distance north of the National Road. But with less interest in and demand for coal, Owen for the most part centered his efforts on salt, iron, and limestone. Regarding limestone, he recognized its presence in much of southern Indiana, but he apparently gave modest consideration to the oolitic limestone which later became of great importance in Lawrence, Monroe, and Owen counties. Owen suggested that discovery of "'a good iron bank is of more intrinsic value to the State, than a mine of gold or silver.'" He had studied the Kanawha Valley of Virginia and mistakenly anticipated that the salt wells and springs of southern Indiana would perhaps achieve similar importance. And the pioneer geologist was unduly impressed with the promise of the counties of Parke, Vermillion, and Fountain for the manufacturing of iron. Owen noted that clay was available for the making of brick and other products, but his reports gave at best meager consideration to possible resources of gold, silver, zinc, and lead. Gas and oil seem not to have been sought for or noted.[57]

In December, 1838, Governor Wallace recommended that Owen's appointment be extended for a third year. Wallace said the results of Owen's examinations the past year had been "highly gratifying." The executive told legislators that "The counties of Vermillion, Parke, and Fountain appear to be peculiarly rich in stone coal and iron ore." He asserted that preparations were being made for the erection of an iron furnace in Vermillion; that "salt water, of the strongest kind, has been obtained" in Fountain; and that coal "'equal to the best bituminous coal of Pittsburgh, or, . . . any portion of the United States,'" per Owen's words, "has been taken from the banks of Sugar creek in Parke County." And since "the Wabash & Erie canal passes through the midst of them," the governor added, "what stronger assurances of permanent, substantial, and rapidly increasing wealth could be asked for by any people?" Sentiment against continuation of the geological surveying was considerable among legislators, but in February, 1839, an act for its continuation another year was approved. This act called for a detailed examination and analysis of mineral resources, a report of soil and its suitability for agriculture, the prospect for the manufacture of silk and sugar, the location of building materials for use in the internal improvement projects, and experimentation about the causes and remedy for milk sickness. The salary was continued at $1,500 for the year, plus $250 for costs. In March Owen was offered a third appointment which he declined. Several months later he became the principal agent to explore mineral lands for the United States. Indiana's pioneer geological surveyor thus began a long and successful career in making geological surveys for the United States and several states. With the Depression of 1837 advancing and the Internal Improvements System of 1836 tottering toward failure, the resumption of geological surveying was delayed until the 1850s. David Dale Owen again participated in geological surveying in Indiana in cooperation with his brother Richard Owen.[58]

Minerals, however, were not the state's greatest resources so far as the pioneers were concerned. Despite the easy availability of coal in many counties, it was not of a superior grade; it was dirty and had only limited use in heating buildings, fueling transportation, and in manufacturing. Both limestone and sandstone were used some to build houses and public buildings, but the widespread use of oolitic limestone therefor was largely delayed until the closing decades of the 1800s. Clay, found in many parts of the state, was used considerably in making brick, jars, and other pottery. Late in 1838 Governor Wallace advised legislators: "The manufacture of the first bar iron from our native ore, has been achieved by [citizens of northern Indiana]; the novel spectacle of Indiana glass will come next; in short, Mishawaka, South Bend, and their vicinity, bid fair to become, ere long, the Pittsburgh of Indiana." A year later the governor made similar predictions about the extent and richness of Indiana's iron ore, but experience soon proved that his predictions were visionary and unrealistic. As noted in the beginning of this chapter, Indiana's greatest natural resources for the pioneer era were its abundance of fertile soils, its climate suitable for agriculture, and its massive hardwood trees.[59]

While writing this chapter, the author frequently asked himself what were the principal roles that women and girls had in the pioneer economy and in pioneer life versus the roles that men and boys had. As this chapter has indicated, the pioneers, regardless of sex, had almost endless work to do, and a considerable variety of tasks were required of them. Only a cursory view is required to make it apparent that there were many tasks done largely or even entirely by women and girls, and many other tasks done largely or entirely by men and boys. The division of labor, rooted in custom and tradition, seems also to have developed from the *context and circumstances associated with pioneering in an agricultural economy.* For the most part women, often aided by girls, did a multitude of things associated with obtaining food, cooking, housekeeping, making of clothes, rearing children, and caring for the sick. Whereas men, aided by boys, built cabins and other buildings, cleared the forests, plowed and cultivated the ground, cared for the farm animals, did the harvesting and threshing, and the like. To be sure, there were variations and exceptions but such was the fundamental division of labor between men and women so far as farming—the principal—occupation was concerned. But there were tasks which significantly involved the participation and cooperation of men and women. For instance, butchering of hogs, making maple sugar, logrolling, making applebutter, and preparations for weddings.[60]

The division of labor between the sexes suggests that pioneer men were the "providers" for and women the "keepers" of the household. Members of the household might include parents, plus close relatives and up to ten or more children, part of whom may have belonged to a previous marriage or marriages. Presumably pioneer women desired a good loving husband, but a *good provider was essential for them and their crowded domain*. Men might become farmers, tradesmen, merchants, teachers, ministers, lawyers, or doctors; however, these and other occupations with few exceptions were closed to women. There is substantial truth in Buley's observation that "As for girls, they worked at home or 'helped' in the homes of neighbors, while waiting for marriage, the only recognized occupation for them." Early marriages and frequent pregnancies proved too much for many pioneer mothers. As stated by Buley, with a mix of discernment and embellishment: "All too many women lost their bloom with their teens, were tired out and run down by thirty, and old at forty. Tombstones in the churchyards bear testimony that many a wife died young, to be followed by a second who contributed her quota and labors, and perhaps a third who stood a good chance to outlive the husband."[61]

Hoosier women of the 1990s, a large majority of whom outlive their husbands as countless retirement centers illustrate, for the most part live lives of ease and luxury compared to the lives of pioneer women of Indiana. Were pioneer men less concerned about the circumstances and welfare of their wives than men of the 1990s? Did they love them less and abuse them more? These and similar questions may be unanswerable with any degree of accuracy. To the extent that they may be answered, they must be understood and viewed in the context of pioneer life in an agricultural society. It seems apparent that pioneer men and boys at family gatherings were usually served ahead of women and girls, and the former were not inclined to show much deference to the latter in terms of who walked ahead of the other or in assisting them in miscellaneous household duties in repayment for their considerable miscellaneous help with harvesting and other farm work. From scanning thousands and thousands of pages of pioneer newspapers the author has noted reports about husbands and wives who were reportedly unfaithful to their spouses or even abusers of them. The author's presumption is that the pioneers, regardless of sex or age, fundamentally had much the same mix of foibles, hopes, aspirations, weaknesses, and strengths as their counterparts of the 1990s. A strong impression—perhaps more a guess—is that overall pioneer men and women were more moral, more devoted, and more faithful to their spouses than their counterparts of the 1990s. An equally strong impression is that the hardships and abuses that men, women, and children suffered in the rather primitive context of pioneer life were less sustained from brutal and unfaithful spouses and parents than for men, women, and children of the 1990s. Pioneer Indiana was not a Garden of Eden; however, Hoosiers of the late twentieth century should be extremely cautious about fingerpointing directed at the pioneers concerning unfaithful spouses, neglectful parents, or acts of brutality regarding the Hoosier pioneers.

CHAPTER 3

POLITICAL PARTIES FOUNDED, 1822–1831

THE ELECTION of Governor Hendricks was unique among Indiana gubernatorial elections in that for practical purposes the winner was the unanimous choice of the voters. Jeffersonian Republican principles and sentiments yet prevailed, party organization had not emerged, and candidates sought office largely on the basis of local and personal considerations. Governor Jennings was ineligible for reelection since the constitution restricted a chief executive to a maximum of six years in any period of nine. In March, 1822, newspapers at Madison, where Congressman William Hendricks lived, stated that they had been authorized to announce him as a candidate for governor.[1] An Indianapolis paper, asserting that if true Republican principles were followed the people would "consider it an assumption for any man to proclaim himself a candidate for an office which is at the disposal of the people," invited information about the fitness of Hendricks and others for offices sought.[2]

Hendricks seemingly made no formal announcement of his candidacy, however, from early April various papers listed only him as a candidate.[3] During May he resigned his congressional seat, signaling his desire to become chief executive. How much campaigning Hendricks did is not known, but in June his candidacy was supported "'at a meeting of a number of respectable Citizens of the different townships in Ripley County.'" From western Indiana, where Jennings had traditionally had major opposition, came strong editorial support for the "'able, faithful, and energetic services'" of Congressman Hendricks as affording "'ample satisfaction that he will not be wanting, either in ability or energy, in the chair of state.'"[4]

The voters generously concurred that Hendricks merited election as chief executive. After the balloting on August 5 Editor Elihu Stout tersely commented: "We deem it unnecessary to give the votes for Governor, William Hendricks is elected without opposition." The speaker of the House of Representatives reported to the General Assembly that Hendricks had received 18,340 votes, with none for anyone else. Though there was apparently a negligible vote against the former congressman,[5] his amazing triumph reflected his enormous personal popularity as well as a significant fading of the rivalry between western and eastern counties that had existed from territorial days.

Ratliff Boon, of Warrick County in southwestern Indiana, easily won reelection as lieutenant governor. In February Boon forthrightly announced himself as a candidate. Observing that for the previous eight years he had sat in either the lower or upper house of the General Assembly of the territory and then the state, he presumed that the public could thereby judge his "claims and qualifications" for the office. By early May three rivals, all with legislative experience, became candidates.[6] Boon, however, was a strong plurality winner over William Polke of Knox County, the runnerup. Boon ran well throughout the state, further illustrating that east-west sectionalism had faded.[7]

When the General Assembly met in December it elected a treasurer and auditor. Early in the session Auditor William H. Lilly and Treasurer Daniel C. Lane requested that a joint committee of the House and Senate examine their official conduct. This committee, "after diligent examination," reported that their books and accounts had been kept "neat, correct and clerical." The committee found nothing about their conduct that rendered "the same in the least suspicious, or requires animadversion." Nonetheless, next day Samuel Merrill, who had represented Switzerland County in the three previous legislative sessions, rather than Lane, was named treasurer. Lilly, however, won a third term with only a few votes against him.[8]

The gubernatorial election of 1822 was the last election of the pioneer era in which a chief executive came from south-central Indiana; the last in which one of the architects of statehood was chosen governor; the last in which the new executive was inaugurated at Corydon; the last before presidential politics began to cast shadows over state politics; and the last before party organization began to emerge.

Although Governor Hendricks almost certainly could have won a triumphant reelection in 1825, in February of that year he resigned as chief executive to serve in the United States Senate. Meantime, Lieutenant Governor Boon had vacated his office and been elected as a congressman in August, 1824.[9] Hence, James Brown Ray, president pro tem of the Senate, and not Boon, succeeded Hendricks as governor. Ray, a youthful senator from Franklin County and a Brookville lawyer, had been chosen president pro tem at the 1823–1824 session. When the ensuing session commenced in January, 1825, he was reelected to this post notwithstanding an awareness that Hendricks might be elected to the federal Senate, that the office of lieutenant governor was vacant, and that Ray's senatorial term expired with the upcoming August election.[10]

Though elected to the Senate on January 12, Hendricks served as governor until February 12, the last day of the session.[11] Ray's eligibility to succeed Hendricks continued to be questioned, with Senate resolutions pro and con offered. Senator John Ewing proposed that a *prospective* president pro tem be chosen for the period between the August election and convening of the legislature in December. Ewing reported that Ray left the chair during discussion of this item and seemed eager to have the question resolved, but many senators opposed Ewing's proposal and the session ended with the matter unresolved.[12] Two days later—and two days after Hendricks had resigned—Ray officially became the "acting governor."[13]

Meantime, the gubernatorial campaign of 1825 had commenced. During the early months of the year Ray, Judges Isaac Blackford, Jesse L. Holman, and James Scott, of the Supreme Court, and Representative David H. Maxwell of Monroe County were indicated as candidates. By the end of March the real contest had narrowed to Ray versus Blackford.[14] Neither was a party nominee, but Ray had favored Clay in 1824 and Blackford had been an elector for Adams.[15] In May Ray forthrightly announced himself as a candidate, saying: "I have lived in this Western country *thirty years*—am a native—a republican—the friend of civil and religious liberty—to the freedom of the press, to law—have long been an open advocate for Internal Improvement—for domestic industry

—a friend to education—to freedom and to peace—to equal privileges—to my country, her interests, inhabitants and glory."[16]

The Indianapolis *Gazette* strongly supported Ray over Blackford.
During March it puffed Ray as a "distinguished gentleman" who had
located at the capital and was attending *"in person"* to his duties as governor. For him, its editor added, "Elevation instead of inspiring van-
ity, inclines him to humility and vigilance. With him the commonwealth is safe."[17] From time to time the *Gazette* shot barbs at Judge
Blackford emphasizing: the desirability of legislative experience for a
governor, that an incumbent should resign an office held before seeking another, and the importance of continuity for judges.[18] Blackford,
like Ray, was considered a capable and honorable man, but he already
had a "fat office" which he refused to give up while "greedily grasping after another."[19] The Brookville *Enquirer* "Expositor" staunchly
criticized Blackford for remaining on the Supreme Court while seeking another office, because if elected he would name his successor and
be *"exchanging* in a *merchantable manner,"* one office for another."[20]

But Judge Blackford had strong support, and Ray had his detractors. In June the *Indiana Journal* suggested that the contest
was between Ray and Blackford, and it urged that the character
and qualifications of each be examined without being "deluded by
fine stories, or extravagant puffs, even ingeniously made." Early
in July this paper published a slashing attack on Ray by "Candor"
who called him far inferior in character and qualifications than
many members of the Senate who had elected him its president
pro tem. "Candor" objected to Ray's pompous and visionary style,
and charged that he had become an advocate of the principle of
resignation even though a year previous he had made numerous
"stump" speeches seeking election to Congress while he was a
state senator. "Are you willing to prefer *sound* to *substance*, disposed to elevate a man possessing scarcely a single solid acquire-
ment to the most honorable, responsible, and dignified station in
the government of your state," "Candor" asked, "in preference to
the man of acknowledged talents, and merit worth?"[21] The Indianapolis *Gazette* charged that "high minded cuts at Col. Ray's
block-house birth" in Kentucky reflected "aristocratic hanker-
ings" on the part of his opponents. True he was "a self made man,

without the advantage of an eastern nativity or a collegiate course," but "a discerning people" had confidence in his talents and character. As the election neared the *Indiana Journal* declared its preference for Blackford on the basis of his qualifications and integrity. It asserted that his recognized qualifications had been evidenced by his appointment to the Supreme Court by the governor and Senate, and his near defeat of Hendricks in the legislative election for the United States Senate. The editor granted that Ray had performed his duties with considerable ability, and he stated that there was no *"dividing question"* [or issue] involved.[22]

Ray's eligibility to serve as chief executive between the election in August and the inauguration of a new governor in December became an important issue as the campaign advanced. Proponents of Blackford contended that Ray, even if elected in August, would not be eligible to serve between then and December.[23] When Secretary of State William W. Wick declined calling a special session of the Senate to consider this situation, a Richmond editor asserted that if Ray so served "it will be an usurpation, which should not be tolerated by the people of the state."[24] This editor further questioned Ray's eligibility by asking the governor for a certified copy of the register of his birth, the affirmation of relatives, or any document that would satisfy the public about his age. Statements and certificates appeared in the press, some asserting that Ray was not yet thirty, others that he had reached this age. Not convinced by these items, the Richmond editor claimed that when the assembly convened in January, 1825, Ray had told the doorkeeper, who took down the name, birthplace, and age of members, that he was twenty-eight as was well known by most of the members. But with the prospect of sitting in the governor's chair looming "he saw the necessity of growing two years older very suddenly; and, as the most feasible way, he did it on the door-keeper's book."[25]

At the voting on August 1 Governor Ray defeated Judge Blackford by a significant but not a decisive margin. Ray ran well in all parts of the state, but his strength was greater in the eastern than the western counties.[26] Despite its preference for Blackford, the *Indiana Journal* declared that it was "disposed,—as all good citizens ought at all times to be disposed,—to acquiese [*sic*] in the decision of the majority, and to support the administration, so far as we may approve its measures." The Vincennes *Western Sun*, though "disposed to acquiesce in the will of the majority—and bow with reverence to its mandates," asserted that "the people of Indiana might have selected a person in almost every respect better qualified" than the one chosen. "The stern integrity, exalted talents, and extensive acquirements of ISAAC BLACKFORD," it said, "would have given to our young state a character and a stand in the Union, which we fear she cannot attain under her present chief magistrate."[27]

Attacks on Ray's eligibility to serve as governor between the election and his inauguration in December continued. Papers at Indianapolis and Lawrenceburg insisted that his eligibility had ceased with the end of his senatorial term at the August election.[28] When the General Assembly convened on December 5, however, Ray had almost completed the term for which Hendricks had been elected. On the opening day of the session the Senate named Milton Stapp its president pro tem, and legislators were divided whether he should be recognized as governor until Ray was sworn in pursuant to his victory in August. But on this day the House, by a vote of 30 to 15, favored inviting Ray to address the legislature, thus declining to recognize Stapp as governor. Next day the Senate, by a vote of 11 to 6, decided not to ask the secretary of state to explain why he had not called the Senate into session to consider the situation.[29] Senator Dennis Pennington introduced a resolution expressing "great doubts do exist as to the eligibility" of Ray "as to age," and he unsuccessfully tried to have the committee that was to notify him of his election be instructed "to ascertain . . . evidence of his age," and report back to both houses. On the third day of the session Ray was inaugurated for a three-year term. Whether Ray was then thirty years of age is uncertain.[30]

During the first half of 1825 several men were considered candidates for lieutenant governor. An Evansville editor, in noting that a sixth man had entered the race, quipped: "Happy country! to furnish so many good men, who are *willing to serve the People*."[31] As the time for voting approached, Senators Samuel Milroy, Dennis Pennington, and John H. Thompson emerged as leading candidates. All three were experienced legislators, and Milroy and Pennington had been delegates to the Corydon Constitutional Convention.[32] Thompson was touted as the earliest legislator to propose that Congress grant relief to debtors for public land under the credit system.[33] Milroy, claiming that he ran at the solicitation of fellow citizens, stressed that he was a farmer, an advocate of internal improvements and manufacturing, and as one "nurtured amidst the storms and conflicts of the revolution . . . could hardly be otherwise than a Republican . . . ." He offered private concerns and travel outside the state as his apology for not "visiting the different counties, as is customary with aspirants to offices of distinction." "A Citizen of Knox" presented Milroy as a farmer of intelligence and integrity who would uphold the rights and interests of the people. "Men of this sort," "Citizen" added, "never court office—they have to be called to it—."[34] Weeks before the balloting, Thompson and Milroy resigned their Senate seats, which action was hailed as an example of pure republicanism whereby an officeholder vacated an office held before seeking another from the sovereign electorate. A Lawrenceburg editor called their resignations "a useful precedent in future elections." Chiding Pennington, who had not resigned his seat, this editor mused: "Would it be better to let go a certainty to catch at an uncertainty? That's the question."[35] Thompson defeated Milroy by a comfortable majority, with Pennington a poor third. Presidential politics may have influenced the outcome for Milroy, a Jackson elector in 1824, who ran well in counties which had favored Jackson while Thompson generally ran well in counties which had favored Adams and Clay.[36]

During 1825 the General Assembly elected three state officials. In January, William W. Wick, a Clay elector in 1824, was elected secretary of state by a modest margin over Enoch D. John on the sixth ballot. Robert A. New, so elected in 1816 and 1820, apparently did not seek a third term.[37] Late in 1825 Samuel Merrill was unanimously given a second three-year term as treasurer. William H. Lilly, auditor since statehood, won reelection for a fourth term by a modest margin over Benjamin I. Blythe on the fourth ballot.[38]

Fiscal affairs as well as politics were in transition during the 1820s. The chronic stringency and repeated borrowing of the early years of statehood yielded to debt liquidation and lower tax rates in spite of a significant jump in the cost of state government. This situation resulted principally from four considerations. Especially important is the fact that the levy on land had been raised and a poll tax added shortly before Hendricks became governor. Of even greater significance, the acreage of taxable land more than doubled and the number of taxable polls approximately doubled.[39] Moreover, economic recovery from the Depression of 1819 led to an upswing in the economy which brought prosperity as the twenties advanced. Meantime, state government continued its adherence to republican simplicity and laissez faire regarding governmental functions and services. Hence, in sharp contrast to the teens and early twenties, *tax revenue exceeded current costs* of state government.

The favorable prospect concerning state finances was well understood by Governor Hendricks. In his inaugural in December, 1822, he observed: "In the revenue of the present year [levied in 1822], we shall reap the first fruits from lands sold by the general government, within the limits of the state, since the first day of December, 1816." Hendricks recognized that each succeeding year would bring an increment in the taxable acreage. "This source of revenue," he noted, "will be continually growing, and is *that*, to which we may look with certainty, for the extinction of the state debt, and for the diminution of our taxes in the support of the government." Debt liquidation and reduced tax rates, not an increase in functions and services, was the immediate priority according to Hendricks.[40]

As the accompanying tables show, during 1822–1831 ordinary state expenditures were much higher than they had been for the period 1816–1822. Such expenditures averaged $33,136.56 during the Hendricks-Ray administration versus $23,396.40 for the Jennings-Boon administration.[41] This jump arose mainly from enlarged legislative and judicial costs. The former averaged $13,675.64 from $8,162.00; the latter to $7,359.94 from $4,229.05. Legislative costs rose principally because of a large gain in the number of legislators, a growth in local and special legislation, and additions to the legislative journals and laws resulting from two general revisions of the laws.[42] The formation of new judicial districts created the need for president judges for them, and in 1825 payments began for a prosecutor for each circuit.[43] Disbursements for the executive department, however, had only a meager gain. Expenditures for the legislative, judicial, and executive departments were mainly for compensation to their officials. Although not included in the reports of the treasurer, an aggregate of $25,774.16, or an average of about $2,863.79 yearly, was paid collectors of state revenue for collecting same.[44] There were gains in money spent for the state prison, the governor's contingency fund, and especially for miscellaneous items. Modest sums were paid for the militia and wolf scalps, and modest payments began for the state library in fiscal 1826–1827.[45] As for the teens and early twenties, the responsibility for education, care of the poor, roads and libraries, so far as provided at all, remained almost entirely with local government and individuals.

Liquidation of the public debt, begun during the last year of the Jennings-Boon administration, was nearly completed during the mid-twenties. Late in 1827 Governor James Brown Ray advised legislators that the state debt had been "extinguished," except that owed "the road and canal and seminary funds," payable at the pleasure of the state. Payments on money borrowed and interest thereon totaled $30,238.12, averaging $3,359.79 for the period 1822–1831. More than two thirds of these costs went for redemption of treasury notes and payment of interest on them. Most of the remaining payments were for principal and interest on loans from the Harmonists and the First State Bank.[46]

During 1822–1831, ordinary revenues increased so that they exceeded ordinary costs. They rose to an average of $29,403.68 versus only $22,447.96 for 1816–1822. Moreover, the tax revenue *retained at the treasury*—that remaining after the tax collectors were paid their percentage for collecting it—much more than doubled; averaging $25,774.19 versus only $12,808.92 for 1816–1822.[47] Even so, the large gain in population and taxable polls, and yearly gain in taxable land, soon made possible a reduction of tax rates. The tax levy for 1823 and 1824, the same as for the last

Ordinary Expenditures, 1822–1831

Fiscal Year	Legislative	Judicial	Executive	Collectors	Debt	Interest
1822–23	$ 9,160.43	$ 6,831.87	$ 2,017.65	$ 2,441.37	$ 481.43	$ 363.81
1823–24	14,769.92	7,249.23	3,050.00	4,588.60	660.10	1,196.75
1825	8,002.56	4,603.48	1,471.23	1,473.42	1,665.28	18,826.93
1825–26	10,279.74	7,656.84	3,152.80	2,521.51	588.23	6,937.75
1826–27	13,574.99	7,222.01	2,097.20	3,016.92	216.28	2,870.47
1827–28	14,019.06	6,881.78	2,482.53	2,684.11	309.15	42.41
1828–29	14,266.82	6,676.08	2,138.95	2,798.11	394.27	0.00
1829–30	15,377.23	7,877.81	2,361.05	3,134.06	1,026.08	0.00
1830–31	23,630.08	11,240.39	2,266.67	3,116.06	1,074.61	0.00
Total	123,080.83	66,239.49	21,038.08	25,774.16	6,415.43	30,238.12
Average	13,675.64	7,359.94	2,337.56	2,863.79	712.82	3,359.79

Ordinary Expenditures, 1822–1831

Fiscal Year	Prison	Militia	Library	Wolves	Miscellaneous	Total
1822–23	$ 4,693.53	$ 100.00	$ 0.00	$ 16.00	$ 70.00	$ 26,176.09
1823–24	3,614.76	125.00	0.00	112.00	232.59	35,598.95
1825	453.61	73.08	0.00	0.00	50.32	56,619.91
1825–26	1,055.28	125.00	20.00	0.00	1,202.07	33,539.22
1826–27	0.00	125.00	51.50	51.50	2,106.54	31,332.41
1827–28	315.04	80.25	175.38	400.00	1,021.04	28,410.75
1828–29	519.52	206.25	63.63	555.50	1,791.21	29,410.34
1829–30	507.32	154.86	113.12	636.50	1,212.64	32,400.67
1830–31	1,025.97	112.50	125.00	734.50	1,414.94	44,740.72
Total	12,185.03	1,101.94	548.63	2,506.00	9,101.35	298,229.06
Average	1,353.89	122.43	60.95	278.44	1,011.26	33,136.56

Ordinary Revenue, 1822–1831

Fiscal Year	Taxes Received	Taxes Paid Collectors	Prison	Miscellaneous	Borrowing	Total
1822–23	$ 27,126.35	$ 2,441.37	$ 0.00	$ 0.00	$ 0.00	$ 29,567.72
1823–24	50,984.49	4,588.60	0.00	0.00	5,550.00	61,123.09
1825	16,371.36	1,473.42	0.00	0.00	0.00	17,844.78
1825–26	28,016.81	2,521.51	0.00	0.00	0.00	30,538.32
1826–27	33,521.39	3,016.92	0.00	85.00	0.00	36,623.31
1827–28	29,823.51	2,684.11	0.00	23.04	0.00	32,530.66
1828–29	31,090.14	2,788.11	0.00	36.74	0.00	33,924.99
1829–30	34,822.94	3,134.06	0.00	50.77	0.00	38,007.77
1830–31	34,622.91	3,116.06	800.00	345.90	0.00	38,884.87
Total	286,379.90	25,774.16	800.00	541.45	5,550.00	319,045.51
Average	25,774.19	2,863.79	88.88	60.16	616.66	29,403.68

year of the Jennings-Boon administration, was 50 cents on taxable polls; $1.50, $1.00, and 75 cents respectively on first, second, and third rate land.[48] At the initial legislative session at Indianapolis, early in 1825, Governor Hendricks advised legislators that "the time has arrived, when we may safely lessen the burdens imposed on the community, for the support of the Government." The General Assembly responded by reducing the levy on land to $1.00, 80 cents, and 60 cents respectively per hundred acres of first, second, and third rate tracts while leaving that on polls unchanged.[49] Late in 1825, and again a year later, Governor Ray told members of the legislature that taxes could be lowered further, and he especially urged a decrease in the levy on polls. The House Ways and Means Committee recommended that the rate on polls be lowered to 37½ cents; and that on land to 80 cents, 60 cents, and 40 cents respectively per hundred acres of first, second, and third rate land. This reduction was approved by the legislature, effective for 1827, and it apparently remained in effect through Ray's administration.[50]

In taxing land consideration was given its location and quality, and miscellaneous exemptions were allowed concerning both land and polls. The revised code of 1824 stated that whether tracts were first, second, or third rate should "be ascertained by the comparative quality of the land in the county in which it is situate, its local advantages from contiguity to towns, navigable waters, or public roads, and by the quality of the greater portion of the tract" assessed. These criteria were repeated in the revised code of 1831. The principal exemption, which had existed from statehood, excluded land bought from the federal government from taxation for five years after its purchase. Both codes exempted the real and personal property of literary, benevolent, and religious societies and corporations from taxation. These codes and other legislation gave various exemptions from taxation to women, orphan children, paupers, insane persons, males over a certain age, and veterans who had served three months or more in the American Revolution. Some of these exemptions, however, applied to local rather than state levies.[51]

In spite of reduced levies complaints that taxes were too high persisted, but the reductions of 1825 and 1827 seem to have muted this criticism. In 1824 "A Citizen" declared that Indiana's tax system was "becoming too oppressive." During the summer of the next year Thomas H. Blake, a former legislator, in explaining to Henry Clay about the tax on land which Clay owned in Vigo County, commented: "The tax is very high and indeed so are the taxes of every kind in the State . . . ." But, Blake added, taxes were "diminishing" and would soon "be very little more than normal." One year later, "Joram" of Shelby County, after saying that farmers suffered great privations and difficulties in becoming established in a frontier society, complained that "taxes of every description of this State amount to the awful sum of 200,000 dollars, per annum." "Joram" objected that officeholders, doctors, lawyers, and others paid only modestly while farmers, the least able, bore the burden of taxation.[52] The commitment to frugality particularly applied to works of art. In 1826 a House committee opposed the expenditure of $1,000 for a portrait of Washington by Peale, asserting that state money "should be expended for the general good" and such an expenditure "would exceed the proper resources of the state, be confined in its effects to the seat of government, and [be] uncalled for by the people." A few years after General Lafayette of France visited Indiana in 1825 another House committee recommended against buying a portrait of him by an Indiana artist because the resources of the state would not "warrant an appropriation for the purpose of purchasing objects not immediately necessary for public use."[53]

Despite objections to the poll tax, it was continued in part because of its expediency. When enacted in 1822, James Brown Ray and two other representatives protested its "unjust and unequal" application. Especially in a republic, they said, persons should be taxed in proportion to property owned; and the "wealthy should be taxed for their luxury, their pride, their pomp, and privileges." In his first annual message to the legislature Governor Ray stated that the people often considered the head tax "a remaining badge of British vassalage," and he urged that it be lowered one fourth yearly until eliminated. "Many articles of pleasure and luxury," the youthful governor asserted, were more suitable for taxation "than the heads of freemen."[54] The regressive nature of the poll tax was noted by critics within and without the legislature.[55] But at the legislative session of 1829–1830, Representative John Dumont raised a key consideration when he suggested that if the revenue question were put to the people: "They will say whether expediency still requires a continuance of an odious poll tax; whether enough of those lands that have, by compact with congress, been exempt from taxation, are now released from that exemption, to make a repeal of the poll tax a politic and justifiable measure." In short, Dumont asked, should this tax be continued because it made adult male purchasers of federal land contribute to the costs of state government during the five years that their lands bought from the federal government were exempt from taxation.[56] Dumont might also have asked whether the poll tax should be continued because it made adult males, not purchasers of land, help pay the costs of state government.

The compact about the five-year exemption clause concerning land bought from the federal government continued in spite of efforts of the General Assembly to have it abrogated. At the legislative session of 1820–1821 the assembly sought termination of this item, contending that the change to cash sales for federal land in 1820 had ended the situation which made the exemption necessary. The House Committee on Public Lands, chaired by Congressman William Hendricks of Indiana, recommended termination of the exemption, arguing that it had been established, not to encourage land sales, but to avoid a possible clash between the state and federal governments if taxes on land became delinquent when purchased under the credit system while title remained with the federal government. A Senate committee, however, opposed ending the exemption. It noted that Indiana had voluntarily agreed to it, had not asked for abrogation of the donations, and that the exemption applied to all states carved from the federal domain.[57] Similar memorials of 1824 and 1831 were presented to Congress, but they were likewise unsuccessful. In none of the three memorials did Indiana offer to have the donations terminated if the exemption regarding land was also abrogated.[58]

Another proposal for enlargement of the tax base called for adoption of the ad valorem system of taxation. Under this plan both real and personal property, unless exempted, would be taxed at a uniform rate in proportion to its value. In 1826 meetings of citizens of Hamilton County expressed their preference for this system, and declared that they would not support candidates for the legislature unless they were committed thereto. Several candidates whose districts included Hamilton and adjoining counties made such commitment, including Calvin Fletcher and Elisha Long who won seats in the Senate and House respectively. Later that year Governor Ray advised the General Assembly: "No doubt, the ad valorem system is the most equitable, yet difficult to carry into effect. The time, however, may come, when it will be found the favorite one with us."[59]

In the late twenties and early thirties the ad valorem plan gained augmented consideration in the General Assembly. At the session in 1827–1828 a select committee of the House termed it "more equal, just and beneficial" than the current system. The committee thought it unfair for land to be the principal object of taxation, thus placing the heaviest tax burden on "the most industrious and laboring class" while the "capitalist and speculator" were nearly exempt therefrom. Emphasis was placed on the great inequality in the assessment of first, second, and third rate land from county to county, with some counties having much first rate land returning less acreage of such tracts than did other counties with a smaller amount of quality acreage. Doubtless anticipating the argument that the new plan would favor nonresidents over residents, the committee stated that the former generally owned "well chosen and valuable" tracts and would thus pay their just share of taxes.[60] Early in 1828 Representative Samuel Judah explained to his constituents why he opposed adoption of the ad valorem plan. "Some years hence I think it may do here," he said, "but not now. There is too much nonresident land—nor do I believe it would be right to tax improvements in a new country. I would rather tax laziness than industry. I would rather tax the speculator than the industrious settler." Two years later Representative John Dumont, who favored the plan, urged that the general principle of the ad valorem system be submitted to the people. They, he asserted, "understand as well as we can tell them, that an ad valorem system of taxation means a tax proportionate to the abilities of the people to pay—that a rich man will pay more and a poor man will pay less—and yet all will pay equal according as they are able."[61]

Perhaps in part because the ad valorem plan was not adopted, the basic system for assessing and collecting state tax revenue was not fundamentally changed.[62] Nevertheless, there was much concern that considerable of the assessed revenue was not being paid into the state treasury. In 1825 Treasurer Samuel Merrill reported data showing "an alarming increase" in the gap between taxes assessed and those collected for the years 1820 through 1824.[63] The previous year a prosecuting attorney had been named for each judicial circuit, and instructed to press suits against delinquent collectors. The following year the legislature directed these prosecutors to consider the records of collectors since statehood, and it offered them 20 percent of the revenue so collected as compensation for their efforts.[64] These and related efforts bore fruit for late in 1831 Merrill gave a very favorable report of state finances as the Hendricks-Ray administration ended. Merrill stated: "It is very gratifying to be able to state that there was but one delinquent out of sixty-three collectors for the year 1830. A few years since, the State Debt was nearly 30,000 dollars, and not one in ten of the collectors settled their accounts at the Treasury within the time prescribed to them by law. The debt has been paid—the taxes have been reduced nearly 50 per cent, and the ability and willingness to pay is evidenced by the delinquent lists of collectors, which in general do not exceed half what they formerly were in proportion to the sums collected."[65]

While the state's fiscal affairs were being stabilized, attention was given to codification of the laws and legislative reapportionment. Codification resulted in large part from a desire to make legislation less obscure, and to bring scattered laws about particular items into comprehensive acts. By the early twenties experience had shown the need for changes in the election code. The rapid growth of new counties complicated the process of legislative apportionment, and made frequent reapportionments desirable as the number of voters changed from county to county.

The Constitution of 1816 had provided that territorial laws, not inconsistent with the constitution, remain in effect until their expiration or repeal. In addresses to the first two sessions of the state legislature, Governor Jennings urged a general revision of the laws to adapt them to statehood, and also because they had become "obscure" from multiple amendments.[66] The legislature, however, did not authorize such a revision, but it enacted various laws concerning the change to state government and modified some territorial laws. General Washington Johnston, an experienced territorial legislator and official, published a useful summary of territorial laws for the period 1807–1814.[67] In his second inaugural in December, 1819, the youthful governor observed that immigrants from various states had brought with them a "great diversity of political maxims and opinions" as well as "prepossessions and prejudices," thus time, prudence, and perseverance would be necessary to "approximate towards an uniformity and stability in our public regulations." Two years later Jennings advised legislators that "the statute laws have become so obscure that a revision [of them] is considered important."[68] The legislature responded with an act which said that the uncertainty about the content of legislation and numerous defects in the statutes caused "much unnecessary public expense" and private loss from litigation. At a joint session of the Senate and House Benjamin Parke, federal district judge for Indiana, was elected to prepare a comprehensive and systematic code of the statute laws of the state. Parke was offered $200 in advance with $800 to be paid when the revision was submitted to the assembly. Parke, however, declined the appointment, saying that severe illness prevented his acceptance.[69]

At the legislative session of 1822–1823 there was considerable diversity of opinion whether to name a replacement for Parke or have a joint committee of the two houses prepare a code for review and approval by the assembly. Speaker General Washington Johnston advised his Knox County constituents that if the revision were made by the legislators the labor of Hercules would be light when compared with that of the General Assembly, and the session would be "prolonged some weeks." The *Western Sun*, edited by Elihu Stout, expressed chagrin and dissatisfaction at the effort of the Senate to have the revision made by the legislature.

It hoped that the speaker and the House would defeat this effort. Following considerable maneuvering and voting,[70] the legislators chose "a suitable person" to reduce all "acts and parts of acts" in force "into one consistent act" without changing their substance. The reviser was also to abridge all English statutes in aid of the common law which applied to Indiana's legislation. The reviser would be paid $200 in advance, plus whatever further compensation the next legislature deemed just upon receiving the revised code. The General Assembly, meeting in joint session, required seven ballots before it elected Governor William Hendricks as the reviser.[71] In submitting his revision in December, 1823, the governor explained why he had considered it necessary to make interpolations and changes in wording in combining relevant acts into a single act. Such modifications, he explained, were limited in number, generally not concerned about substance, and had usually been indicated so that the legislature could accept or reject them. Acts that were "general in their operation, and public in their character," the executive advised, should be included in the revised code but the "large mass . . . of private acts" should be listed only by titles. The governor, himself a lawyer, tactfully explained why he had not regarded it expedient to embrace British statutes in aid of the common law in his compilation. "The references to British law which are so frequently made in our courts of justice," Hendricks added, "are almost entirely to reports of judicial decisions and not to the acts of parliament." But he termed it "prudent" to include in the new code an act declaring which British statutes about the common law continued in force.[72] The legislature painstakingly reviewed the revision, the two houses effecting a division of labor whereby the general laws were considered and acted on as if they were new bills. Hence, the session became longer than any had been since statehood.[73] The new code was printed as a large and separate volume, with numerous private laws listed merely by titles, and it affirmed designated statutes of Parliament as part of the legislation to be in force.[74] Hendricks declined compensation for his services as reviser, commenting that if his services had "a favorable reception by the people" he would have "ample reward."[75]

During the last half of the twenties and early thirties there was considerable interest in reducing or even eliminating English statutes in support of the common law, and in making the laws more easily understood by the people.[76] Early in 1827 an editor at Richmond urged that the laws be reduced into a code, then let the laws be more stable and less changed at successive sessions. At the previous session he noted, a "great proportion" of the laws had been concerned with "subjects of a private or local nature," which should be delegated to "subordinate jurisdictions." Later that year Samuel Judah, lawyer and politician, asserted that the common law, and English statutes in its support, had been "founded in barbarism, nourished in ignorance and tyranny, and cherished by aristocracy and monarchy" and had become "a vast and confused mass of sayings and opinions, and rules, scattered through a thousand heavy volumes." Judah referred to the benefits which had accrued to France from the Napoleonic code and the [Livingston] code for Louisiana, both written.[77] In December, 1827, Governor James B. Ray announced to the legislature his "intention to present to a future Legislature, a code of laws, both *civil* and *criminal*, for its consideration," adding that "the responsibility and cost" would be his. The would-be Hammurabi became verbose in explaining that his contemplated code would reduce dependence on English statutes in support of the common law, make use of the French code of Napoleon and the Louisiana code, and "enable the governed to know what the law is, and to have it in their power to acquire that knowledge without much trouble or expense." A report from the House Judiciary Committee, made by Stephen C. Stevens, concurred with much that Ray had said. It asked why not reduce "the whole body of the laws," including so much of the common law, British statutes, and decisions of the chancery courts in effect in the state, "to a written text, so that every man may see, read and judge for himself, without having to recur to the antiquated decisions of English Judges?"[78] Two years later Ray reported to the legislature that the preparation of "a civil code of laws for the state" had not achieved "as great a state of forwardness as might be wished." Without an assistant, the governor said, the code could be completed before he left office;

with one "its progress might be greatly accelerated." The Senate judiciary committee, chaired by Stephen C. Stevens, responded to the governor's apparent bid for help with biting sarcasm. It bluntly reminded him that he had announced that the responsibility and labor for the code would be his. Hence, an appropriation of money for an assistant, the report jabbed, might be viewed as legislative interference. Moreover, the people looked to "his Excellency" for completion of the code; and if it "should meet their expectations, his Excellency will be amply rewarded in due time." This barbed comment suggests an awareness that Ray might not be able to complete the code, and it illustrates the low esteem which various legislators had for the executive.[79]

At the legislative session of 1830–1831, the last under Ray, the General Assembly revised the laws. The House concurred with a Senate resolution calling for a joint committee of five senators and five representatives to name subcommittees of the two houses, apportion legislation to them for their review, and employ clerks to assist in expediting the revision.[80] Several representatives protested that revision in this manner would unduly prolong the session and greatly increase the cost. The session, however, though the longest since statehood, was only slightly longer than the one that had completed the revision of 1824 based on a compilation received from Governor Hendricks.[81] The revised code of 1831, like that which preceded it, declared all laws and resolutions not specifically continued to be repealed; it published many local and private acts only by their titles; and it expressly recognized the customary dependence on English statutes in support of the common law.[82] To help make the code more easily understood, at the request of the assembly, the secretary of state prepared an appendix which offered concise explanations of a number of technical terms and phrases. Inasmuch as the revised code was published as a separate volume, the other laws and resolutions, termed special acts, were printed separately.[83]

Closely related to the revision and codification of the laws were efforts to improve miscellaneous items concerning elections.[84] The manner in which secret ballots were cast and counted remained substantially as inherited from the Jennings-Boon years.

In his only annual address to the legislature in December, 1822, Governor Ratliff Boon said legislation was needed about filling vacancies concerning congressmen, members of the legislature, and county and township offices; that existing laws had failed to impose any penalty on county clerks failing to forward county voting returns for governor, lieutenant governor, and congressmen; and that the assembly had not enacted a measure to determine how contested elections for governor and lieutenant governor should be resolved. The General Assembly responded with a law making the county clerk responsible for issuing writs of election for county and township vacancies in instances in which the offices of sheriff and coroner were vacant. It also made county clerks liable to a fine of $500—a large fine for that time—and removal from office by impeachment if county election returns were not forwarded regarding governor, lieutenant governor, and congressmen.[85]

Nonetheless, in December, 1825, Governor James B. Ray informed legislators that returns were apparently lacking from eleven counties regarding the vote for governor and lieutenant governor the previous August. It would be "of no avail to impose heavy penalties on Clerks" to make returns by mail, Ray stated, while "post masters, through whose hands these returns pass, are subject to no penalty whatsoever." He suggested that clerks be required to send one report of the election returns by a "special messenger" and another by mail. The assembly mandated clerks, within thirty days of the voting, to seal up and mail one copy of the returns to the speaker of the House in the presence of the postmaster, and obtain from the latter a certified statement giving the time and place when the returns were mailed. In addition, a certified statement of the vote was to be given to a representative or senator from his area for delivery to the speaker on or before the second day of the ensuing annual session.[86] Thereafter, there was considerably less delinquency than previously in forwarding such returns. But especially as rival political parties developed during the late twenties, editors complained of the delay in obtaining reliable data about the outcome of elections. Thus, as the decade ended, the legislature required clerks to mail, within ten days after they received the returns, a third set of returns to the secretary of state who was required to give the returns to an Indianapolis newspaper.[87] This action illustrates the large importance of pioneer newspapers, and especially those at the capital, in disseminating information to the people around the state. Inasmuch as newspapers copied much from other papers, this practice augmented the dissemination of information.

Meantime, consideration was given to how contested elections for governor and lieutenant governor should be resolved. The Constitution of 1816 had declared that these contests would be decided by a joint committee of the House and Senate, "formed and regulated in such manner as shall be directed by law." In December, 1823, Governor William Hendricks advised legislators that *"How, when,* and *where* the validity"* of election returns for governor and lieutenant governor "are to be tested and determined, ought to be regulated by law."[88] The troublesome questions regarding Ray's eligibility to serve as chief executive, both before and after his election on his own in 1825, apparently spurred the General Assembly to action. At the session of 1825–1826 there was a hassle concerning whether the joint committee to decide such contests should have an equal number from each house or have more representatives than senators. The assembly enacted a law which allowed any voter or candidate to contest such elections by making a statement in writing explaining the basis for the contest. It then became the duty of a committee, composed of seven members of the Senate drawn at random by its secretary, and seven members of the House drawn in like manner by its clerk, to review the evidence offered and decide the outcome.[89] This law was never called into use in the pioneer era.

Although the privilege of voting at county seat towns remained until the early 1840s, during the twenties the General Assembly considered whether it would be desirable "to confine" voters to their respective townships.[90] When this item was discussed in the House in 1829, an advocate of confinement asserted that it was essential to preserve the purity of elections. Balloting at county seats, he stated, created crowds and confusion, enabling many aliens, nonresidents, and vagrants, unknown to election inspectors, to vote at the expense of the rights of citizens. Moreover, for many counties it had become "almost impossible" to receive the ballots within the hours prescribed by law. Representatives favoring voting at county seats contended that the practice did not threaten the purity of elections, and that it enabled citizens to economize their time by the opportunity afforded to do necessary business at the county capitals. The strong attachment to county government is suggested by the argument that the people would not surrender this practice, and that it was guaranteed to them by the state constitution.[91] Some citizens doubtless preferred voting at county seats to partake in the "treating" often provided by candidates. Though contrary to law and at times denounced by citizens, treating seems to have been fairly common and probably increased during the twenties as political parties emerged and county seat towns grew in population.[92]

Perhaps more important than revisions of the laws and modifications of the election code were legislative reapportionments in 1826 and 1831. The more than twofold jump in population during the twenties, the northward sweep of settlers into Central Indiana, and the continued increase in the number of counties made desirable frequent regrouping of representative and senatorial districts.[93] It will be recalled that the state constitution mandated reapportionments at five-year intervals, stating that representation was to be given in proportion to the number of qualified voters. With the rapid growth of population in the twenties, the General Assembly had either to augment the aggregate of legislators or enlarge the number of voters embraced in both representative and senatorial districts.

In addressing the General Assembly early in 1825, Governor Hendricks called attention to the constitutional provision for an enumeration of voters preparatory to a new legislative reapportionment. Hendricks stated that the gain in land subject to taxation would more than offset the cost of an enlarged representation. The enumeration, taken in 1825, indicated about 37,377 voters in the state.[94]

The reapportionment of 1826 was apparently based upon the same formula in distributing representatives and senators as had been used in the legislative apportionment five years earlier. Hence the guideline was probably one representative and one senator per 700 and 1,800 voters respectively.[95] The total of representatives rose from 43 to 58 and that of senators from 16 to 21 for the new versus the previous allotment.[96] The House tried to check the increase of legislators among the fifty-three counties by enlarging the ratio of voters to lawmakers, but the Senate blocked this attempt.[97] The respect for county lines, combined with the gain in the number of counties from 37 to 53 between 1821 and 1826, made inevitable considerable diversity in the total of electors from district to district. Although no county was divided, as Warrick had been in the former apportionment, an interesting precedent was established whereby Fayette and Union received one representative each *plus* an additional representative which *alternated* or *floated* between them. The more populous counties, located mainly in the eastern half of the state, got from two to four representatives; a number of counties secured their own representative; and various representative districts embraced two and in one instance three counties. No county obtained more than one senator, but generally two, three, or four, and for one district five counties were joined to form senatorial districts. The legislative apportionment of 1826 increased the voting power of legislators from Central Indiana, but political dominance remained with members from Southern Indiana. Of the fifty-eight representatives, approximately forty represented counties of Southern Indiana, seventeen counties of Central Indiana, and one the voters of Northern Indiana. Despite the usual inequality in the number of voters represented from county to county, it seems that representation was rather evenly distributed among these three areas of the state.[98]

The extremely rapid upward surge of population during the last half of the 1820s posed difficult decisions regarding the legislative reapportionment of 1831. The state enumeration of 1830 recorded an aggregate of 65,359 voters. This growth occurred mainly in Central Indiana but throughout the state the western counties gained more electors than the eastern ones. Late in 1830 Governor Ray suggested to the General Assembly that the "prodigious" growth in population for the five preceding years made inevitable an increase in its membership. The governor, however, recommended against too great a gain in members in part because of the added cost. He urged "leaning to a system of compromise" rather "than too close an adhesion to exact numbers" in forming legislative units to maintain separate districts for as many counties as possible.[99]

By 1831 "leaning to a system of compromise" had become established practice in making legislative reapportionments. With an increase to sixty-three counties, the House of Representatives tried to check the increase in lawmakers by proposing 1,000 voters per representative and 2,600 voters per senator as the guideline for legislative districts. The Senate, however, held out for fewer voters per unit.[100] The number of representatives rose from fifty-eight to seventy-five and that of senators from twenty-one to thirty compared to the reapportionment of five years earlier. The legislative apportionment of 1831, like all previous ones save that of 1821, did not split any county in forming legislative districts. Moreover, as for all previous apportionments, no county got more than one senator. Most senatorial districts consisted of two or three counties, but one included five. A majority of the counties also obtained one representative, a number were given two, and Dearborn and Wayne received three and four respectively. In various instances two counties were embraced in representative districts, and one district contained three. The inequality of legislative districts is illustrated in that several counties, which were given two representatives, each had its own senator as did Dearborn and Wayne with their three and four representatives. An innovation, never before used, resulted in Montgomery and Clinton counties having two representatives jointly, perhaps because Clinton alone lacked enough voters to justify a representative on its own, while Montgomery plus Clinton merited more than one representative. There were a few floats regarding representative districts. One of the *floating* representatives *floated* between two districts, thus representing Daviess and Martin counties combined for two years; and Knox County, which had two representatives of its own for three years of the apportionment period. The reapportionment of 1831 marked a substantial erosion of the political dominance which Southern Indiana had enjoyed from statehood. Members of the House were distributed approximately so that of the seventy-five representatives Southern Indiana controlled the votes of thirty-eight members, Central Indiana of thirty-five members, and Northern Indiana of two members. Nonetheless, the voters of Central and Northern Indiana seem to have averaged fewer voters per representative than did those of Southern Indiana.[101]

While the reapportionment of 1831 was in progress, eleven members of the House protested against a bill which had passed this body. They cited various examples of proposed districts in different parts of the state which they contended were flagrant examples of inequality contrary to the constitutional provision for representation proportional to the number of voters. Some legislators, the protesters averred, would receive more than double or even triple the voice of other members. The majority of the representatives, however, contended that neither "the letter or spirit of the Constitution" could be construed to give "the same precise ratio" for every district. Various of the alleged inequalities were explained and the conclusion offered that "Upon the whole . . . a bill combining equality and justice more than this, cannot be presented to this House."[102] Representative John Zenor, of Harrison County, who voted against the final reapportionment, advised a correspondent that "there was so great a variety of interests clashing together that it was impossible to procure a fair apportionment." "A Citizen of Marion County" complained that once again Marion County had been denied its proper voice in the General Assembly.[103] Such complaints suggest that as reapportionments were made some political oxen were fattened and others were gored.

Meantime, during the twenties two interim or partial apportionments were made for various counties of Central and Northern Indiana. As statehood began the legislature had established the precedent that as new counties were organized their residents would continue to vote for senators and representatives in existing legislative districts. Hence, as new counties were carved from old ones, legislators often represented a mix of parts of both new and old counties.[104] But as counties were established in the large area known as the New Purchase, acquired from the Indians in 1818, representation was needed for its residents. At the legislative session of 1821–1822 seven new counties were added, carved overwhelmingly from the New Purchase.[105] An editor at Indianapolis objected that the legislature had declared that such residents would not have representation in the General Assembly for four years, yet would be subject to payment of the poll tax. Calling taxation without representation unconstitutional, he stressed that individuals were not obligated to pay this tax. Some months later a committee, representing citizens of Marion County, emphasized that taxation without representation had been the cause for which Americans had "spilt" their blood to win freedom from England. Nevertheless, the committee recommended that "in the spirit of true patriotism" that the tax be paid for 1822 then "rely on the sympathy and justice of the ensuing legislature for redress." This committee insisted that the state constitution did not prohibit apportionments at other than five-year intervals.[106]

When the legislature met in November, 1822, Governor Ratliff Boon noted that "several new counties" had been organized from parts of the state not included "within the original counties . . . ." His further remarks suggest support for an interim apportionment concerning these counties. Despite the objections of some legislators that such an apportionment would be unconstitutional, both houses, by large majorities, approved three additional representatives and one senator, principally for counties within the New Purchase.[107] At the session of 1827–1828 a House committee contended that as the population of Northern counties increased representation should be increased to them, according to the Ordinance of 1787 and the intent of the Constitution of 1816, without waiting for a five-year general apportionment. The next session added five representatives and two senators for various new counties of Central and Northern Indiana.[108] Seven senators from Southern Indiana protested this action as giving these counties a larger voice in the legislature than they deserved. The interim apportionment of 1823 may have hastened the removal of the capital to Indianapolis, and that of 1829 apparently strengthened support for a state financed system of internal improvements.[109]

As the population increased and pressed northward during the twenties the permanent state capital was established near the geographical center of the state. In asking Congress for donation of a township of land as the site for such a capital, the territorial legislature had deemed it "good policy that every State should have its seat of government as nearly central as the local situation of the country will permit," but noted that this could not be done until the Indian title had been extinguished from the area. Congress, however, granted only four sections; and specified that the capital must be located "under the direction of the legislature" on land thereafter acquired from the Indians in advance of the sale of the surrounding federal land.[110] At the constitutional convention at Corydon in 1816 local residents gave a bond for $1,000, which apparently contributed to the mandate of the new constitution that "Corydon, in Harrison County shall be the seat of Government of the state of Indiana, until the year eighteen hundred and twenty-five, and until removed by law." The understanding about this bond and concerning state use of buildings at Corydon while the capital remained there are uncertain, but only a modest part of this sum was paid the state while the capital remained there.[111]

Steps toward transfer of the capital to the central part of the state began soon after statehood. Late in 1818 Governor Jonathan Jennings advised legislators that expenditures from the Three Per Cent Fund, for building roads and canals, would be of limited value or even useless until the permanent capital had been located as a hub for roads from there to important points on the perimeter of the state. A year later, after federal ratification of treaties which cleared the Indian title to a vast area in the middle of the state, Jennings suggested to the legislature that this extinguishment and the progress of land surveys required early location of the future capital.[112] The legislature named a commission of ten men, none members of the General Assembly, and gave them authority "to select and locate" such a site. Pursuant to this legislation the executive set May 22, 1820, for their initial meeting at "the house of William Conner, on the west fork of White river" from which they were to view possible sites.[113] After examining both sides of White River southward to the bluffs at Waverly, the commission chose a site, on its east bank, below Fall Creek. In reporting to the next legislative session the commissioners noted that the place chosen had the advantages of fertile soil, was on a navigable stream, and was near the "political centre" of the state. Commissioner Tipton commented in his journal that the place selected was dry, with good soil, but with scarce timber.[114] An editor at Madison quoted Commissioner Joseph Bartholomew as saying the site chosen "is as nearly central as any that could be selected; and perhaps, unites as many natural advantages as any spot of ground in the western country; being a high, dry, rich and well timbered piece of ground, surrounded by an immense tract of country of first rate land, abounding with the most excellent and durable streams for mills and other machinery of every description." An editor at Vincennes touted the location, saying: "The surrounding country is luxuriantly fertile, pleasant and healthy; excelled by none west of the Alleghany mountains." Still another editor observed that neither the official journal nor that kept by Tipton mentioned the "probability that the capital would become a point on the National Road," but added that most likely "the commissioners had this possibility in mind."[115]

Having located the permanent capital, it became desirable to sell lots to obtain revenue for construction of public buildings. In November, 1820, Jennings optimistically told the General Assembly that "with timely care and prudent management" the capital donation would "in due time produce ample resources, without resorting to taxation, to meet the expenditures necessary for the erection of all public edifices of state character." The legislature named three commissioners to lay out a town on a plan considered "advantageous to the state and to the prosperity of said town having specially in view the health, utility and beauty of the place." After platting the town the commissioners were to sell as many lots as they deemed expedient at public auction for the "best price" offered, except that every odd numbered lot would be reserved from sale. Buyers were to pay one fifth of the cost in cash, plus the remainder in four equal annual installments. The proceeds from sales were to "constitute a fund for the special purpose of erecting the necessary public buildings of the state." The responsibility for receiving payments and otherwise serving as a fiscal representative of the state was given an agent, named by the General Assembly for a term of three years.[116]

The legislature decided that the new town would "be called and known by the name of Indianapolis." Who suggested this name remains uncertain, but it evoked scathing sarcasm from a Vincennes editor who asserted:

> One of the most ludicrous acts, however, of the sojourners at Corydon, was their naming the new seat of state government. Such a name, kind readers, you would never find by searching from Dan to Beersheba; nor in all the libraries, museums, and patent-offices in the world. It is like nothing in heaven nor on earth, nor in the waters under the earth. It is not a name for man, woman or child; for empire, city, mountain or morass; for bird, beast, fish, nor creeping thing; and nothing mortal or immortal could have thought of it, except the wise men of the East who were congregated at Corydon. It is composed of the following letters:
> I-N-D-I-A-N-A-P-O-L-I-S!
> Pronounce it as you please, gentle readers - - - you can do it as you wish - - - there is no danger of violating any system or rule, either in accent, cadence, or emphasis - - - suit your own convenience, and be thankful you are enabled to do it, by this rare effect of the scholastic genius of the age. For this title your future capital will be greatly indebted, either to some learned *Hebraist*, some venerable *Grecian*, some sage and sentimental *Brahmin*, or some profound and academic *Pauttowattimie*.

Similar sarcasm was added in an ensuing issue of the Vincennes paper, but the name became as durable as the location of the capital.[117]

Indianapolis was platted during 1821. Of the three commissioners named to lay out the town, apparently only Christopher Harrison, Indiana's first lieutenant governor, served, but the ensuing legislature legalized his acts as if they had been done by a majority of them.[118] Harrison engaged Alexander Ralston, a Scotchman who had helped plat the federal capital at Washington, and Elias P. Fordham, an Englishman from Birkbeck's settlement in southern Illinois, to do the surveying and platting. The basic design for the town seems to have been contributed by Ralston.[119] The original plat covered only a mile square, leaving three fourths of the capital donation for subsequent development. This mile square, bounded by what is yet known as North, East, South, and West streets, was principally platted along the early middle western grid system with north and south and east and west streets running at right angles. But the grid pattern was significantly modified in three respects. In place of a central square the plat called for a Governor's Circle, carved from the four central squares or blocks. Only two streets directly connected with this Circle, Meridian which divided the prospective town from north to south and Market which did likewise from east to west. From the corners of these central squares to the four corners of the land donated for the capital were four diagonal streets which, along with Meridian and Market, provided convenient access to the center from outside the donation. The grid pattern was also modified in the southeastern section because of the meandering of Pogue's Run and the swampy area along its banks. Many streets were named after states of the Union, but the widest one, which ran east and west just below Market, was called Washington. A short distance west of the Governor's Circle, a square, suggested as a site for a state house, faced Washington, while a similar distance east of the Circle another square, designated for a courthouse, likewise fronted Washington. Across Market from the proposed courthouse was a half square suggested for a market site, and another half square was so listed along Market at the west end of town. Three of the outlying squares, traversed by the diagonal streets, were earmarked for religious purposes. Although the platted area did not border on the West Fork of White River, the unplatted portion of the donation included land on its western side. Ralston reportedly observed that the plat "would make a beautiful city, if it were ever built."[120]

Notice was given that the initial sale of donation lots would commence October 8, 1821. The town was advertised as being in the center of the state, located on a high and dry plain of several miles in extent near the West Fork of White River, "perfectly free from inundation, marshes and ponds." According to the announcement, the beauty and fertility of the site and surrounding area made it "probably the best body of land in the state." Moreover, "The plan of the town," was "calculated to ensure the health comfort and convenience of its inhabitants," and "Good wholesome water may be had at the depth of 26 feet, in any part of it, in a sandy stratum." Though the capital site was an isolated outpost, poorly connected with the settled portions of the state, a positive note was struck with the suggestion that "It is confidently expected that the great National turnpike" from Washington to Missouri will pass through Indianapolis as well as the capitals of Ohio and Illinois. Pursuant to legislative direction, lots would be sold to the highest bidders, with one fifth of the purchase price in cash and the remainder in four equal annual installments.[121] During the initial sales in October 314 lots were sold for an aggregate of $35,595.75, with $7,119.25 in cash received for the Indianapolis Fund for an average of $113.33 per lot.[122] Modest as this sum was, at that time land near the capital could be bought in eighty-acre tracts for a cash payment of only $100. Additional lots were sold, both within and without the platted part of the capital donation, so that by late 1831 the revenue from sales of lots, plus modest revenue from rentals and sale of timber, aggregated $43,714.75 according to Treasurer Samuel Merrill.[123] The yield would doubtless have been significantly larger, but many lots were forfeited in spite of relief legislation allowing additional time to complete payments and the option of transferring sums paid on forfeited lots to those retained. Late in 1826 Governor Ray told the legislature that 165, or more than half of the lots purchased in 1821 for a total of $17,506.25, had been forfeited.[124]

The location of the permanent seat of government, and the advent of settlers to the capital and vicinity, made local government essential. The General Assembly provided for the beginning of government for Marion County, effective April 1, 1822. Legislation usually named individuals to locate the county seat, but in this instance the law designated the courthouse square, as reserved on the Ralston plat, as the site. With the organization of county government, civil townships were created but town government for Indianapolis was delayed until the early 1830s.[125] County government and the anticipated early removal of the capital to Indianapolis required some arrangement for housing county and state officials. A very interesting and commonsense feature of the statute creating Marion County appropriated $8,000 from the Indianapolis Fund toward the erection of a two-story brick courthouse which was to be available for the use of the General Assembly, state Supreme Court, and the federal district court until a state capitol was constructed. This brick courthouse was to be begun within one year from the establishment of county government and be finished within three. This structure apparently cost the Indianapolis Fund at least about $15,000. In 1826 a legislator described the Marion County courthouse to his wife as "much the handsomest public building in the state."[126]

Plans for removal of the capital to Indianapolis were effected at the legislative session of 1823–1824, the last held at Corydon. Early in January, 1824, Calvin Fletcher commented in his diary that Bethuel F. Morris—then Indianapolis agent—had returned from Corydon with "flattering reports" that the legislature would move to Indianapolis "next year," exciting Indianapolis "citizens to a very high pitch."[127] The assembly provided that Indianapolis should become and remain the permanent seat of state government from and after January 10, 1825. Persons required by the constitution or legislation to reside at the seat of government were to locate their offices in the new capital by this date, at which time the ensuing legislative session would convene. State Treasurer Merrill was authorized to sell at auction to the highest bidder state furniture which could not be advantageously removed, and generally to superintend the removal of all records, documents, and other state property "previous to" the convening of the legislature. The act removing the capital from Corydon to Indianapolis squeaked through the Senate by the narrow margin of 9 to 8, but it was supported in the House by a vote of 25 to 17. Representatives Dennis Pennington and John Zenor, representing Harrison County of which Corydon was the county seat, protested the removal as contrary to both the intent and letter of the state constitution. Postponement of convening the assembly from the first Monday in December to the second Monday in January, they insisted, "annihilates the notion of annual sessions" as "fixed" by the constitution, substituting legislative discretion based on expediency in its stead.[128] Although the removal was not officially effective until January 10, 1825, the delay in the start of the annual session until this date and the actual removal of at least most of the state records, property, and offices before the end of 1824 seems to have been contrary to the spirit of the constitution which had stated that Corydon should remain the capital until the year 1825 and until removed by law. In August, 1824, the Indianapolis *Gazette* reported that the new courthouse could be completed and ready for the assembly by October 1, and in any event would be finished by November 1, hence those who were expecting and hoping that another session would have to be held at Corydon were expecting and hoping in vain. The editor jabbed that from the number of public houses opened or about to be started there was no hesitation in saying that "members of the legislature and others will be at least, *as well* accommodated as they have ever been at Corydon." In November, 1824, Merrill sold state furniture and other items at Corydon and began the well-known removal of selected state records and property to Indianapolis by wagon, taking ten days to make the trip of about one hundred twenty-five miles to the new wilderness capital.[129]

In his address to the initial legislative session at Indianapolis early in 1825, Governor William Hendricks looked to the Indianapolis Fund to pay for needed public buildings. "Public faith stands pledged," he said, for commencement of "the public buildings contemplated on the Circle and the State House Squares . . . as soon as practicable." He asserted that such a policy would serve the interests of the state and purchasers, afford strong inducements for completion of payments, decrease forfeitures, and increase the means to finish the buildings. The assembly, however, merely appropriated $1,000 from the fund to build "a substantial brick house for the residence of the treasurer of state, to contain the offices of the treasurer and auditor, and a fire-proof vault for the better security of the funds and records of the state" under the direction of the treasurer.[130] Two years later an appropriation, not to exceed $500, was made for a modest brick structure as an office for the clerk of the Supreme Court; and $4,000 was set aside "to erect on the Governor's Circle . . . a suitable house for the residence of the Executive," both buildings to be financed from the Indianapolis Fund. Additional appropriations soon increased the total for the governor's house to roughly $6,700.[131] In 1828 the General Assembly reserved two lots next to the Circle as "a garden and stable lot" for the governor's use. At this time the Indianapolis agent was asked to have the lot on the Circle "on which the Governor's House is built, properly graduated, and enclosed with a temporary rail fence" by May 1. The house for the executive was a two-story brick structure about fifty feet square, with an attic and basement.[132] But no governor took up residence on the Circle, and it was used for various state offices. In the late twenties and early thirties there was consideration of converting the building into a state house and perhaps using the state house square as a site for a gubernatorial residence. About the time Ray ended his administration late in 1831, the legislature decided to build a capitol on the square which presumably Ralston had designated for it in his plat of 1821.[133] Meanwhile, the chief executive apparently received $200 annually as an allowance toward his own housing.[134]

Although no governor ever lived on the Circle, it is remarkable how central the capital site was located and how closely Indianapolis developed much as platted. The site for the permanent seat of state government won general acceptance, freeing Indiana from disturbing rivalries which other states had about location of their capitals. Indianapolis grew slowly throughout the pioneer era. The basic street pattern extended as the town grew and continued largely unchanged until the last quarter of the twentieth century. Indianapolis soon became the hub for an emerging network of roads to the borders of the state, and by 1860 had become the largest city of the state. Those who established the permanent capital in an isolated wilderness exhibited much common sense and a concern for the best interests of the state's residents.

The nearly seven years from early 1825 until late 1831 while Ray served as governor were years of significant political transition. By the mid-1820s a new generation of politicians had largely succeeded the founding fathers of the state. The increased representation of Central Indiana counties in the General Assembly during the last half of the twenties and early thirties brought new leaders to politics and diminished the power previously exercised by the counties of Southern Indiana. Moreover, with the presidential election of 1824–1825, political parties, initially based on presidential preferences, began to emerge. During Ray's tenure citizens and legislators increasingly thought of themselves as National Republicans (Adams-Clay men) or Democratic Republicans (Jacksonians). Hence, presidential preferences and party ties began to influence state elections and legislative deliberation. Accompanying the development of parties was the popular election of presidential electors, a trend toward the use of delegate conventions to nominate candidates for office and select party officials, increased campaigning for office, and the development of intensely partisan newspapers. With prosperity advancing as population and economic resources increased, Hoosiers caught the internal improvements fever, causing them to seek federal aid by way of land and/or money for roads and canals. In such a context state and federal politics, heretofore not closely interlocked, became more intertwined.

Given the political transition of the period, even an able and veteran politician might have had rough sledding. For the immature Ray, who completed Hendricks' term despite concern about his right to do so and won election amid doubt whether he was of adequate constitutional age, the hazards were great. The youthful governor professed neutrality between Jackson and Adams for president, but he practiced deception with leaders of both parties. When faced with opposition from legislators he at times tactlessly appealed over their heads to the sovereign people. In communications he was frequently verbose, pompous, contentious, and lacking in civility. These characteristics help explain the continuing squabbles and feuds which decreased his popularity among legislators and among voters as well. No pioneer governor completed his term so thoroughly discredited and so much a political *has-been* as James Brown Ray.

Controversy dogged Ray throughout his tenure as chief executive. Even before questions about his right to complete Hendricks' term and whether he was old enough to be elected governor were resolved in his favor, Ray wrote President John Quincy Adams seeking a federal appointment to help extinguish Indian claims to land within Indiana. Less than three months after inauguration for his first term, the youthful and ambitious governor sought the support of the secretary of war for being named "*One* of the commissioners" to negotiate a treaty "to effect the extinguishment of the Indian title to Land within" the state. In May, 1826, the secretary wrote Ray, John Tipton, and Lewis Cass of their appointment as "Commissioners to Treat" with the Miami, Potawatomi, and "any other Tribes claiming lands" in Indiana.[135] Two months later an editor at Vincennes advised Ray to read that part of Indiana's constitution which prohibited a governor from "holding any office under the united States" while serving as its chief executive.[136] Nevertheless, during parts of September and October Ray participated in the negotiation with the Indians at Wabash, Indiana, which resulted in a significant cession of land.[137] Since Ray never left the state, unlike Jennings in 1818, there was no need to make temporary transfer of his office to the lieutenant governor.

Nonetheless, when the General Assembly met on December 4, 1826, a number of legislators questioned his right to continue as governor because of his service as a commissioner to treat with the Indians. When the House considered a resolution of the Senate that the two houses tell Ray of their readiness to receive communications from him, Representative Merit S. Craig presented a resolution declaring it the opinion of the House that Ray had "forfeited" his right to serve as governor by acting as a commissioner for the United States. Craig's resolution asked the Senate for its opinion regarding this question.[138] While this resolution was pending, the House invited Ray to lay before it any "papers, documents or other evidence" pertaining to his role as a federal negotiator. In a brief response—especially brief for Ray—he said he had nothing to communicate regarding this item, but asserted that he had followed "precedent and example" and was unaware of having done anything incompatible with his role as governor. If he had erred, he had done so "with the fathers of the republic, the first patriots of the age, and in attempting to do good, and advance the highest interests of our beloved country."[139]

The House spent much time discussing Craig's resolution.[140] Though not always agreeing concerning details, advocates argued that Ray had violated the state constitution by concurrently holding state and federal offices; and by simultaneously occupying two lucrative positions. Representative Benjamin Hurst, of Harrison County, declared it was time to let the president know that "he should not interfere with the Executive of this state." If we were to be subject to the president on every occasion, Hurst declared, "it would be better we were governed by a monarch, and return to our former allegiance under Great Britain." Supporters of the governor contended that he had not held a federal office in the proper meaning of that term; that if Ray had violated the state constitution, then the legislature had and was admitting and employing members in violation thereof; and that the precedent set by Jennings in 1818 had been approved by the legislature, some of whose members had helped write the constitution, and also by the people. Representative Joseph M. Hays, from Parke and Vermillion counties, noted that Ray had been "praised and eulogised by almost every tongue, for the very important services he had rendered to his state in this transaction." Some lawmakers insisted that the General Assembly had no authority to declare the executive office vacant, while various supporters and opponents of Ray agreed that only by impeachment by the House and conviction in the Senate could a governor be removed.[141]

On the fourth day of the session, Craig's resolution was defeated by the close vote of 31 to 27. By this tally the House then joined with the Senate in inviting Ray to address the legislature. Before this message was received, however, the Senate by a count of 15 to 5 tabled a resolution which stated that if any governor, lieutenant governor, or legislator had or should accept an appointment from the United States, for any public duty involving pay, such acceptance should be regarded as a "vacation" of office to be filled as if a "formal resignation" had been filed.[142] In his message Ray was silent about the question of the constitutionality of his service as a federal commissioner. But he pointed out that between two and three million acres of unusually fertile land had been secured from the Indians in the area north and west of the Wabash River. The governor also noted that the treaty obtained offered a favorable prospect for a federal land grant "for making" a road across the state from the Ohio River to Lake Michigan via Indianapolis.[143] Ray's service as a federal commissioner to negotiate with the Indians was doubtless popular with many politicians and citizens, while the vote against him in the Senate, and especially in the House, was probably based more on personal disapproval of him as chief executive than on significant constitutional and related scruples about his service as a federal commissioner to treat with the Indians.

At the session which considered Ray's right to continue as governor, despite his service as a federal commissioner, the House investigated how state offices had been conducted. On January 12, 1827, without a roll call vote, it approved resolutions requesting complete information from the auditor and treasurer about payments to Governor Ray regarding salary, house rent, and specific appropriations from the time he became the executive in February, 1825, to January 1, 1827. The treasurer was also asked for a full statement of the sums he had paid "in advance to officers" of state within this period, plus their names. In addition, he was to report the names and amounts paid "members of the present House" from the treasury in "anticipation of their services" as members. Next day, by an overwhelming vote of 45 to 11, the House approved the appointment of a committee to consider and report whether the governor, secretary of state, auditor, and treasurer had "been in the habit of absenting themselves" from the capital; and who performed their duties in their absence. The governor was to provide information showing the sums he had "actually paid" for house rent and to whom it had been paid. The committee was to inquire how civil and military commissions had been prepared and issued in the absence of the governor and/or the secretary of state. The auditor was to give the names of the county collectors of state revenue who were delinquent, the sums due from them, and explain why suits had not been brought against all delinquent collectors. In addition, he was to explain why tract books, showing land bought of the federal government, had not been made available to the collectors. The committee was to review, if it was consistent with the constitution, legislation, and public policy, for the duties of the auditor to be performed by the treasurer; and then submit a bill indicating their proper duties.[144]

The statements submitted by the state officials afforded convincing evidence of the casual and informal manner in which official duties had frequently been performed. William H. Lilly, auditor since statehood, said it was not possible for him to name the times he had been absent from the capital. While the government was at Corydon, he said, "he was seldom absent except on short visits," however, after removal of the capital to Indianapolis, he had been away from February to June, 1825, to visit his family in Kentucky when he had been detained by "extreme" illness. From February to May in 1826 he had been gone to bring his family to Indianapolis, but his return had been "delayed by the sickness of his child." During May, 1826, "Tim Gallitin" reported facetiously a rumor that Lilly had gone to Greece "to die in the cause of liberty, or live and reap the well earned honors of the brave." "Tim" claimed that since Lilly was not a citizen of Indiana, his office had been vacated and should be filled by the governor.[145] Treasurer Merrill detailed a number of absences from the capital since he assumed office in 1823, usually for one or two weeks and often including state business. His longest time away had been from May 8 to July 20, 1826, when he visited his parents in Vermont whom he had not seen for ten years. On this trip he had paid "Mr. Rapp" at his residence near Pittsburgh the money the state had borrowed of him, thereby saving the state $217 in interest.[146] Although Secretary of State William W. Wick had been in office only about two years, he professed an inability to be precise about his absences. He had usually been gone about four or five weeks attending circuit courts, and was away two or three weeks during negotiation of the late treaty with the Indians.[147] Governor Ray seems not to have reported his absences, but they were probably usually of short duration and infrequent except for roughly the two months he served as an Indian commissioner and whatever time he spent campaigning around the state seeking election as governor in 1825.

The auditor, treasurer, and secretary explained who conducted their duties during absences. While at Corydon, Lilly said, if there was business to be done "Mr. Jennings usually went into his office and did what was wanting." At Indianapolis, when gone, his work had been performed by Merrill and Judge Bethuel F. Morris, but "The most they did was to enter the issue of warrants on the register, and proper vouchers were always placed on file." For this aid neither Merrill nor Morris "expected or received compensation."[148] Merrill reported that in his absences Lilly and others had served on his behalf, but some departures had been at times "when no business was necessary to be done," and the "treasury was generally empty," hence no deputy had been employed. He never gave compensation to those who helped him, but for some of them he had given "a similar attention to their concerns" on occasion.[149] Wick asserted that when away his work had been done by John N. Wick, "a regularly authorized deputy" indentured to him by Calvin Fletcher, his guardian. Merrill and others had also aided him at different times, but no compensation was indicated for them. Wick described the addition of new and unanticipated duties to his office by the assembly, without an increase in pay, as "in the nature of a fraud" or like selling "real estate with an incumberance thereon unknown to the purchaser." So long as the compensation remained inadequate, his work would at times be performed by a deputy. Wick stated that absences during court sessions to pursue his practice of law were to enable him to add to his "salary a sufficiency" to enable him to "eat the bread of honesty and independence, and provide for a helpless family."[150] The salary of $400 per year which the secretary, treasurer, and auditor each received was modest, even for the pioneer era.[151] On the other hand, the duties involved did not require full-time service.

Information supplied by the auditor and treasurer detailed state expenditures to Governor Ray for salary and house rent. Their reports, particularly that of the treasurer, charged the governor with irregularity in the manner that he obtained payments for these items, and of applying $50 for house rent that had been appropriated for salary. They also indicated that the executive had drawn his salary as governor while serving as a federal commissioner to treat with the Indians.[152] Ray branded the legislative probing concerning payments for house rent "inquisitorial," and he bristled at the manner in which Lilly and Merrill explained such items. The governor insisted that "house rent, &c." had hitherto been understood in part to include the cost for the inevitable damage to furniture in the house of the governor arising from hospitality bestowed as well as for rent itself. After reviewing money received for "house rent, &c.," Ray stated that it had been less than his "losses and sacrifices" arising from the lack of suitable accommodations for the governor.[153]

Treasurer Merrill detailed various sums he had advanced to state officials. Payments were noted on behalf of the governor, secretary of state, auditor, adjutant general, members of the Supreme Court, some circuit court judges, and certain legislators. Merrill was emphatic that these sums had always been from his personal money, had usually been for short periods in advance of state payment soon due, and had been without loss to himself or the state. Included in his listing of loans were ten members of the current House, plus three additional members who had repaid him. The sums ranged in amount from $2.75 to $40, but only three loans were in excess of $10.[154]

Secretary Wick explained the practice regarding the issuance of commissions. He noted that during 1826 over 900 military commissions had been issued, about 1,000 civil commissions, 45 pardons and remissions, 100 writs of election, 100 resignations, and a few demands for fugitives from justice, making not less than 2,250 executive acts issued and recorded for the year. According to the secretary, such business had increased at least 700 percent since the early years of statehood. Civil and military commissions had been presigned by the governor and at times by the secretary. When circumstances warranted, others had completed and delivered them.[155]

The auditor gave information concerning balances due from county collectors of state revenue and the use of tract books. Revenue due was listed by counties for each year since statehood, plus information about suits against delinquent collectors. The auditor suggested that he had explained the difficulties in completing tract books in another communication, but added that they had been completed for most counties and those lacking would be supplied during the ensuing summer.[156]

The conclusions of the select committee concerning its inquiry were more in defense of than criticism of the manner in which state affairs had been administered. As regards the absences of the governor, secretary, and treasurer from the capital, the committee observed "that no inconvenience has resulted, or possibly could result from the absence of either of those officers; but in some instances on the contrary, the state has been benefited."[157] Emphasizing that the constitution, legislation, and public policy required that the treasurer and auditor be "distinct checks upon each other" to prevent fraud or collusion, the committee was emphatic that it could not "recognize the blending the duties of those offices as legal or admissible." But it did not know of any wrong that had been done or injury suffered therefrom by the state, "only that it is a bad precedent and ought not further to be indulged in."[158] Governor Ray, the committee decided, had drawn money from the treasury without a warrant, but "he very seldom, if ever, drew more than was actually due to him," and the "apparent overdrawing" had been promptly rectified when discovered. Merrill's advances to officials had "originated in good motives," and as "connected with the collectors [of state revenue] have generally be beneficial to the state." Nonetheless, "the precedent is a bad one and ought not to be continued."[159] The committee reported that "it has been the established custom from the organization of our state government, for the Executive to sign blank military commissions and leave them in the secretary of state's office." This practice was believed to be that which prevailed in sister states and for the federal government, and "from this custom, of itself, no inconvenience can result." Although the committee noted that civil commissions involved discretion by the executive or another official, it did not condemn the practice concerning them which Wick had described.[160] Warm approval of tract books was expressed, with at least implied criticism that the auditor had been lax in obtaining and delivering them to the counties. On the other hand, satisfaction was expressed for the "vigilance" of the auditor "in relation to balances due the state for taxes."[161] The committee asked that its report and related documents be printed in the journal and the committee be discharged, which requests the House approved.[162]

The House investigating committee apparently produced no convincing evidence of fraud. Merrill, apparently more involved in the blending of duties than any other official, explained to the committee that "the business necessary to be done in many public offices during certain periods of the year is so trivial, that the holders of these offices must occasionally become careless." Hence, "persons who come to do public business, may occasionally not find the proper officer at home." Merrill said the aid given the secretary, auditor, and adjutant general had been done openly. Many citizens were doubtless pleased by the accommodations performed by Merrill. Legislators, judges, and others who received the advance payments probably gave little thought to possible abuses from them. About the time the House investigation was completed, a Lawrenceburg editor asserted that it was "a fact, known to many, that the Treasurer of State has, at different periods, been, in *reality*, the Secretary and the Auditor of State, and some times Governor." The editor jabbed that a "man so useful . . . surely could attend to two offices at all times" with "a considerable saving annually to the state." An Indianapolis editor, strongly supportive of the governor, observed that the auditor had escaped with a "slight reprimand" regarding his duties being performed by the treasurer during his absences; cast aspersions and raised doubts about the propriety of Merrill's conduct; and boasted that the governor had emerged from "the fiery ordeal of investigation . . . like gold from the crucible, purer from the hands of the refiners," at least so far as the people were concerned.[163]

The investigation of state officials stirred a smouldering controversy between Governor Ray and Treasurer Merrill. Why and when it started is uncertain. In June, 1827, Merrill, asserting that he was responding to attacks against him that "must have been approved" by Ray, declared that he had "long believed" the governor "destitute of principle and all sense of propriety becoming" a chief executive. Merrill charged Ray with: having repeatedly drawn money from the treasury in an improper manner, and retaining "other money . . . he has no right to"; seeking personal gain "by promising favors at the expense of the state"; taking the oath of office for governor, after "for years" having stated his age as less than required to hold the office; frequently interfering with legislative elections by "electioneering for, and against different persons"; engaging in "the most barefaced fraud, falshood [*sic*] and oppression" concerning property sales, debts, and efforts "to ruin persons opposed to him," and of using his office as Indian commissioner to sell his property to the United States at "five or six times its value."[164] Ray's retort was more of an attack on the treasurer than a defense of himself. He termed Merrill's charges against him *"six poisoned daggers"* at his breast, and labeled the treasurer "the organ of a faction [against him], *a slanderer and a coward"* who hated "republican principles." "You was one of those men," Ray said, "who secretly opposed my election for Governor, whilst you pretended friendship to my face, and afterwards felt unwilling to submit to the decision of the majority." Editorials and communications in support of Ray appeared in the *Gazette* from time to time through the remaining months of 1827.[165] In August Merrill published a twenty-four page pamphlet which both repeated and expanded his charges against the governor with a variety of items offered in their support. The treasurer's criticisms, however, seem to have been overstated and the evidence offered in their support too unconvincing to sway the voters to repudiate Ray.[166] In September, Calvin Fletcher wrote his brother that he had "been on the best of terms with the contending parties" and had "declined" attaching himself to either side. At this time Samuel Milroy, an experienced politician commenting about the dispute to John Tipton, said: "I do not understand its origin, or its object, and am willing to stand aloof—."[167] If Merrill was trying to prevent Ray's reelection as governor in 1828, as seems likely, he failed. Whatever its origin and objective the controversy or feud appears to have been mainly a personal one between the treasurer and the governor rather than one between rival party elements.

While the Ray-Merrill controversy boiled, speculation about gubernatorial candidates for 1828 grew. With the election of a governor and president in the same year for the first time since 1816, and political parties emerging based on preferences for president, it was uncertain whether presidential politics would have a significant impact on the race for chief executive. During the last half of 1827 and early weeks of 1828, Judge Isaac Blackford, Israel T. Canby, William Graham, Congressman Jonathan Jennings, Samuel Milroy, Harbin H. Moore, James Rariden, and Lieutenant Governor John H. Thompson were among those considered as possible contenders against Ray who sought reelection.[168] Canby, a physician and a member of the Jackson State Conventions of 1824 and 1828, for a time appeared to be at least the consensus favorite of the Jacksonians. Several days after the 1828 convention adjourned, Jordan Vigus wrote John Tipton: "For Gov. Doct Canby is nomenated by the Jackson partey." The Vincennes *Western Sun*, however, edited by Elihu Stout who had been a delegate to the convention, called Canby a "decided Jacksonian" but declared that he "was *not* brought out by the Jackson convention"; and asserted that unexpected "private occurrences, beyond his control . . . have compelled him to decline holding a poll."[169] With Canby's withdrawal, Lieutenant Governor Thompson, an Adams man, apparently became the leading rival against Ray until early April.[170] By May, Harbin H. Moore, who had served as speaker of the House at the last two legislative sessions and had been a delegate to the Adams State Convention in January, became a candidate.[171]

Meantime, while trying to obtain support from both Jacksonians and anti-Jacksonians, Ray had been trying to ride two horses at the same time. Early in May the Jackson State Committee instructed Henry S. Handy to ask Ray if he would become the Jacksonian candidate for governor, with support from Jacksonian leaders, if an Adams man entered the competition. Ray responded that he had favored Clay in 1824, with Jackson as his second choice. But Adams had been elected; the *"measures"* of his administration had been good, especially for Indiana; and he had "determined to occupy *neutral ground."* His recent correspondence

with Jackson, however, had convinced him that the same measures would prevail in a Jackson administration. The governor expressed enthusiasm "for a *concentration* of the *whole* force" of the
Jacksonians in his favor. But Ray insisted that neither the letter he
received nor his reply be published "*before* the election" since that
course would weaken the cause "thousands in number."[172] But in
mid-June Augustus Jocelyn, a pro-Adams editor at Brookville,
published an interview that he had had with Ray which set off a
political bombshell. According to this editor, Ray agreed that the
Adams administration had been "constitutionally instituted and
organized"; said he never believed "the charge of corruption, bargain and sale" levied against Adams and Clay; and concurred that
the opposition to the administration had been "an outrageous and
violent faction" which "by every lawful means" should be opposed
as the duty of all men.[173]

The comments attributed to Ray incensed the Jacksonians, and
Canby again entered the race against him about a month before
the election. At a meeting on June 28 the Jackson State Committee decided that its invitation to Ray in May and his response to it
should be released to the Salem *Annotator*, plus an explanatory
statement by Handy indicating why the committee had concluded
that Ray supported the election of Old Hickory.[174] On July 5
Canby addressed the electorate emphasizing that he had sustained
Jackson in 1824, thought him "pre-eminently qualified," and believed that protection to national industry and federal aid to internal improvements were national measures which had strong
national support. The *Annotator* said Canby's withdrawal in February had not been for fear of the outcome, but to do necessary
business which had taken less time than anticipated.[175] In mid-
July Ray made a lengthy and meandering reply to accusations
against him. Adams and Jackson, he said, were both "great men,"
and he had "written favorably of them both." He would "be governed by *measures* and not *men*," and claims that he had promised
to vote for either of them were branded "*base forgeries.*" He considered both men committed to the key measures of tariff protection and federal support of internal improvements. Although he
had favored Jackson in the House election of 1825, he thought

Adams had been constitutionally elected. Ray denied that he had called the Jacksonians "an outrageous and violent faction" at Brookville, and insisted that the editor who had so quoted him had since admitted that he had not asked "any such a question." He emphasized that his response to the Jacksonian leaders in May had been with the explicit understanding that he would continue "on *neutral* ground," unless the Adams men "drew the line" and supported a party rival against him. Ray advised that in voting for a governor it should not be asked whether he is for Adams or Jackson inasmuch as "the Governor has nothing to do in making a president" other than voting with the people at the polls.[176]

Ray gained reelection, but as the first governor to be only a plurality victor. He won at least a plurality in thirty-two counties, securing 15,131 votes; on this basis Canby carried sixteen counties for 12,251, and Moore nine counties with a total of 10,898. Ray's strength was widely diffused, and especially strong in counties of or near the Whitewater Valley. Canby's support was mainly from southern counties, plus three on the Wabash River from Terre Haute north, while Moore did well in counties scattered around the border of the state. Ray ran well in a number of counties that Jackson carried in the ensuing November, and likewise in a number of them that went for Adams.[177] For the initial time party voting for governor was significant, but local and personal preferences remained strong. After the election the incumbent governor appropriately claimed that he "was *not elected* by the friends of either side in a *party* controversy."[178]

The race for lieutenant governor was closely contested between Milton Stapp, of Jefferson County, and Abel C. Pepper, of Dearborn County. Early in June the *Indiana Journal* termed Pepper a "decided friend" of Jackson, and Stapp likewise "of the present Administration." Both had served in the General Assembly.[179] Stapp defeated Pepper by 633 votes, winning nearly all the counties that went for Adams and nearly half of those that supported Jackson in the November voting. Since Jackson defeated Adams by several thousand votes, it is reasonable to conclude that Stapp, an Adams man, was elected by obtaining the preponderance of the voters who preferred Adams, plus a significant part of those who supported Jackson. Stapp's margin might have been larger, but his preference for Madison as the southern terminal of the Michigan Road apparently cost him votes from the southeastern counties.[180]

During the pioneer era when Hoosiers voted for a governor and president in the same year, the ensuing General Assembly chose a treasurer and auditor for three years and a secretary of state for four years. Prior to the convening of the assembly in December, a Lawrenceburg editor observed that "some stir is made among the good folks of our state about the loaves and fishes" concerning these offices.[181] Shortly after the legislators convened, Samuel Merrill was elected treasurer for a third successive term by the nearly unanimous vote of 74 to 4 on the initial ballot.[182] Since Auditor William H. Lilly had died in February, the governor had appointed Indianapolis agent Benjamin I. Blythe to finish his term. In the balloting for a new term, for two ballots Blythe had a slim lead over Morris Morris, but Morris won election on the next ballot.[183] For secretary of state James Morrison defeated William W. Wick on the first ballot by a modest margin. Wick's blunt responses to the committee investigating state offices at the previous session may have led to his defeat.[184]

With the death of Auditor Lilly in 1828, all state executive officials in office when statehood began had been replaced. But in the judicial department for practical purposes Judges Isaac Blackford, Jesse L. Holman, and James Scott had constituted this court from statehood. The trio had been enthusiastically reappointed in December, 1823, for terms expiring in December, 1830.[185] Some weeks before the legislature convened late in 1830, reports and accusations circulated that Governor Ray was trying to *bargain* appointments to the court in such a manner as to enhance his prospect for election to the United States Senate.[186] In spite of these charges the governor declined to make nominations for their successors before the expiration of their terms. On December 27, which Senator Dennis Pennington considered the last day for the terms of the incumbents, he offered a resolution recommending them "as suitable persons" for reappointment; and proposed that they be nominated for new terms. This resolution was laid on the table, but on January 8, with names of the incumbents deleted, by a vote of 19 to 3, the Senate asked the executive to submit nominations.[187] Several days later the governor submitted a joint or package nomination of Judge Blackford, plus Senators John T. McKinney and Stephen C. Stevens. He admonished the Senate that his nominations had been delayed because it had earlier encroached upon his *"nominating power"* by advising him to nominate Blackford, Holman, and Scott. "If the State is to be without a Court," Ray jabbed, "it will be because the Senate refuse to confirm the [this] nomination."[188]

Ray laid down the gauntlet, but the Senate responded with vigor. On the day the package nominations were made, the Senate in secret session, with McKinney and Stevens absent, voted on the nominees one by one rather than all at one time. After confirming Blackford by a count of 21 to 0, the Senate rejected McKinney 15 to 6, and Stevens 13 to 8. It also named a committee which soon presented a report castigating the governor for lack of civility in his communication with the Senate, and blasted him for not making nominations soon enough to allow the Senate time for adequate consideration of them. The report also admonished the governor that it was his duty to make another nomination, or the onus of not having a court would be upon him.[189] The governor immediately informed the Senate that after "maturely reconsiderating" the situation he could not see any more "judicious nomination" than the one previously made. Ray asked that the rejection of McKinney and Stevens be reconsidered; and the Senate, voting in secret ballot with the nominees absent, reluctantly approved them by the narrowest possible margin of 11 to 10.[190]

Ray obtained approval of his nominations, but his role regarding them is a serious blot on his administration. Before adjournment the Senate unanimously thanked Holman and Scott "for their past services," and affirmed "That the great weight of moral character, stern integrity, legal ability and faithful services," which characterized their role as judges, "well deserve the approbation of the people of this state." On the eve of adjournment Senator John Watts explained that he had been "one of the earliest and warmest friends" of the governor, then condemned Ray for trying to parlay Supreme Court nominations to advance his prospect for election to the federal Senate. Watts argued that the appointments of McKinney and Stevens at least violated the spirit of the state constitution. Moreover, Watts bluntly asserted, McKinney "did not possess the superior qualifications required for so important a station," and he expressed "a want of confidence in the integrity & moral character of" Stevens.[191] The extent to which Ray abused his office as governor to obtain election to the United States Senate, and the extent to which some senators used the situation to embarrass Ray, is uncertain. Nevertheless, whatever Ray's role his chance to become a member of the United States Senate was not enhanced. When the General Assembly elected federal senators in December, 1830, December, 1831, and December, 1832, the only votes recorded for Ray were two votes on one of the ballots in the latter year.[192]

Ray, however, was not the first to involve members of the Supreme Court with politics. Blackford, Holman, and Scott had either sought or allowed their friends to support them for other offices while they were members of the court. For instance, Judge Scott had been the runnerup to Senator Waller Taylor when he won reelection in 1818; Judge Holman had been second to Senator James Noble when he was reelected in 1820; Judge Blackford had almost defeated Governor William Hendricks in 1825, and was a runnerup to Noble in 1826. All three judges had been electors for Adams in 1824, Scott opposed Jonathan Jennings for election as a congressman in 1822, and Blackford provided Ray tough competition during the contest for governor in 1825. But as political parties advanced during the last years of the twenties, judges of the Supreme Court were much less involved in possible election to other offices. In 1828 no member of the court served as an elector for either party.[193]

While the controversy brewed about appointments to the Supreme Court, a majority of the senators waged a petty vendetta against the governor. In 1827 Ray had promised to prepare a code of laws for the state, based on the civil code of Louisiana, without cost to the state, but his promise remained unfulfilled.[194] Since the House and Senate were engaged in revising the laws of Indiana, this gave the Senate an excuse for asking the governor "to place in the State Library . . . the Louisiana civil code, . . . understood to be in your hands." This request was made after the Senate's committee concerning revision reported that it had no need for this book.[195] The governor responded to this request amid quibbling about when he had received the book; if he or the state had paid postage on this or similar items; and if the book belonged to him or the State Library. Ray stated that no one had ever asked him for the book; that books charged to other officials, including senators and Supreme judges, had not been called for publicly; and that he had been so called to excite "a suspicion of his moral honesty." He asserted that the Senate might be trying to defeat his making a code. As the session ended Ray, in a lengthy and disorganized letter, asked if the people could applaud the patriotism and economy of senators who, "for the sake of arraying their names against the Executive, uselessly spend their money and stigmatize their government, in a *petty* and *unnecessary* wrangle about a *law book?*"[196] Justified as this comment was, Ray's meandering harangues and heated comments with legislators contributed to this, for its day, costly and ridiculous vendetta against the executive.

While politicians and voters were dividing into political parties, they maintained a broad consensus about the need to improve transportation facilities. The opening of trails and roads continued to be emphasized, but there was an enlarged concern about trade routes to and from Indiana. The extremely rapid gain in population, and its spread northward; the swelling surplus of farm produce for exports; the expanding trade of merchants; and the rising prosperity, from the mid-1820s, intensified this concern. Indiana remained overwhelmingly dependent upon the Mississippi artery for its imports as well as its exports, but there was a growing desire for the development of east-west trade. The higher prices usually paid for exports in eastern markets, the opening of the Erie Canal in 1825, the beginning of canal construction in Ohio during this year, and the permanent location of the National Road across the state in 1827 whetted this desire. Indiana's geographical location as an inland area, sitting astride portages connecting the Mississippi and St. Lawrence drainage basins, was a key factor in stirring concern about improved transportation facilities. The short portage between the Wabash and Maumee rivers offered the promise that a canal connecting their navigable portions might become the connecting link in a chain of waterways reaching through the interior of the continent from New York to New Orleans.

Though roads and trails were much extended, they remained little improved and often became worse with use. The principal effort was on cutting and opening roads through the wilderness and then keeping them open. Travelers meandered around obstacles, frequently unable to determine the main path from tributary ones. The conditions of travel were much as they had been in the teens and early twenties, hence during the greater part of the year roads alternated between mud and dust.[197] According to a story of the pioneer era, a citizen of Ohio who had visited Indiana about 1825 was asked "whether he had been pretty much through the State." In response, "He said he could not tell with certainty, but he thought he had been pretty nearly *through* in some places." During the autumn of 1822 a traveler between the Ohio Falls and Vincennes, following several days of rain, found the roads "almost impassable, even on horseback." In the fall of 1829 an editor at Madison, who had been to Vevay, reported washouts from heavy rains and fallen trees across the road, causing him to conclude that it would be difficult if not impossible to make the trip on this road by wagon. About the 1820s Oliver H. Smith, traveling near where Greenfield was later located, was riding his horse "through the mud and water, up to the saddleskirts" when he encountered John Hager and his team of four oxen enroute with freight from Cincinnati to Indianapolis proceeding "at the rate of a mile an hour—the wheels up to the hubs in mud."[198] In the Age of Mud—which extended far beyond the pioneer era—winter freezes were often a boon to travelers and freighters alike. In February, 1831, a capital city editor, after noting that the ground had been hard frozen since mid-December and covered with snow, added: "The roads have consequently been unusually good, and the travelling very fine." Such weather, as Calvin Fletcher observed a couple of years earlier, was excellent for sleighing.[199]

In these circumstances travel was slow and at times hazardous. During May, 1824, it took Calvin Fletcher and others five days via horseback in going from Indianapolis to Fort Wayne, a distance of about 120 miles. Proceeding from the Summit City to his native Vermont, where he spent over a week with his parents, Fletcher arrived back in Indianapolis on August 8. The journey, via horseback, canoe, packet, steamboat, wagon, and stage had, his wife noted, taken eighty-two days. Several years later Mrs. Fletcher joined her husband on a month's trip to Ohio, traveling an estimated 400 miles by horseback. The journey was made in June, Mr. Fletcher explaining that the roads were too bad to allow travel via wagon.[200] Early in 1829, after a long cold spell during which the roads had apparently become frozen, an Indianapolis editor observed that two men had arrived from Connersville, "a distance of 58 miles, in a day." In an "ordinary state" of the route, "40 miles might be considered a good days travel." The initial stage between Madison and Indianapolis, commenced in 1828, required four days to make the roughly ninety miles between them. During the fall of the preceding year Congressman-elect Oliver H. Smith and Senator James Noble left from near Cincinnati via horseback and seventeen days later "dismounted at the Indian Queen hotel" in Washington for a new session of Congress.[201] Crossing flooded streams, either by horseback or boat, could be especially dangerous. Early in 1828 William G. Lowry, a Presbyterian missionary, lost his life in a crossing by canoe. Even travel via ox team was not always safe. In August of this year a Dearborn County man, while driving around a fallen tree in the road, "struck an old tree and broke the top off, which, falling upon him in the wagon, killed him instantly."[202]

The responsibility for locating, maintaining, and vacating local roads rested with local officials. State legislation gave this authority, with guidelines and limitations, largely to county commissioners. The revised code of 1824 made males ages twenty-one to fifty inclusive subject to three days of labor on roads annually. Such males who were resident landowners were liable for additional days up to a maximum of ten, rising somewhat as the acreage owned increased. Nonresidents who owned 160 acres or more, were required to donate four days yearly without regard to the acreage owned. Residents could avoid labor by paying 50 cents for each day not performed but owed. Nonresidents could avoid labor by providing a substitute worker or paying 75 cents per day in lieu of labor. Road work was done under the direction of supervisors named by the commissioners. The revised code of 1831 reduced the labor required of males, ages twenty-one to fifty inclusive, to two days yearly, but it levied a road tax on all landowners at one half of the state levy on land. Both the two days of labor and the road tax owed could be satisfied by work in person or by a substitute at the rate of 50 cents per day. An individual who supplied "a plough or wagon, with a pair of horses or oxen and driver," received three days credit for each day worked.[203] Both codes provided that: supervisors, when circumstances made it necessary, could call for labor above that normally required; labor was to be performed on state as well as local roads; persons above fifty, and others exempted by state law or by the county commissioners, were excused from road labor; for the erection of signposts at principal forks, giving direction to travelers; and made special provision regarding how and by whom streets of towns were to be improved.[204]

Starting in 1822 the opening of roads was in part financed from the federally supplied Three Per Cent Fund.[205] The appropriation the previous year had included twenty-two roads, and by December, 1831, this aid had been allotted for about fifty roads connecting the principal towns and settled portions of the state. The largest sum expended on any road was $8,506.96, but most of them had received $1,000 or less. By this time $111,022.69 had been spent, all but a modest part for roads.[206] The expenditures were apparently used mainly to cut and open roads through the forests. An 1823 notice, inviting "Road Cutters" to submit proposals for the road from the Ohio line via Brookville to Indianapolis explained: "Said road will be required to be cut and cleared out 48 feet wide; all timber 12 inches and under, with all the old logs, to be taken out of the road; the trees, 6 inches and under, with all the under brush, to be cut level with the ground; all over that size to be cut within 12 inches of the ground. Said road to be let out in sections of five miles each." Next year the three commissioners for this road sought additional proposals, saying: "All timber of two feet and under in thickness, to be cut and cleared out of the road—the stumps to be cut not exceeding 18 inches in height." The road was to "be causeway'd in the worst places sixty rods [in length] and fourteen feet in width."[207] Various criticisms were made concerning how the fund was distributed. In December, 1825, Governor Ray, after telling the General Assembly that about $40,000 had been due the fund when the $100,000 had been appropriated on a prospective basis, asked whether: large sums had been paid numerous commissioners for services which could have been rendered by one third the number at one third the cost; a number of the roads were "not entirely useless to the public, and . . . altogether impassable by a second growth"; the fund should be used for canals as well as roads; and whether appropriations should be made for sections of the state settled since 1821. Others voiced similar criticisms.[208] An act of 1829 cut costs for road commissioners by reducing their number from three to one. A year later the General Assembly earmarked $400 for distribution to each county for specified roads, rivers, and bridges on a priority basis. Once these priorities had been fulfilled, the residue could be used as directed by county boards. Its distribution in this manner did not result in good roads, but it was a boon to many individuals in making payments for taxes, land, and other obligations.[209]

As roads became more numerous and population grew there was increased need for bridges and ferries. The earliest bridges were doubtless made of wood, and erected over small rivers and streams. During the twenties, as for the teens, the legislature authorized their building under the supervision of county commissioners, and frequently by individuals as toll bridges.[210] Nonetheless, Oliver H. Smith, in his recollections published in the 1850s, asserted there "were no bridges over any of the streams" in the mid-twenties. While this was true for practical purposes, small bridges had apparently been built at various places. Early in 1825 the legislature authorized the commissioners, named to open a state road from Mauk's Ferry to Indianapolis, to pay William

Rodman up to $319 from the Three Per Cent Fund for extending a bridge over the "Muscatituck River" from 160 to 190 feet in length, plus improvements made.[211] In 1830 a subscription bridge was in process of construction over Tanner's Creek, near Lawrenceburg.[212] Three years earlier a "floating bridge," which had been "thrown" across the Ohio River at Lawrenceburg during the winter, had been swept away by a high rise in the Ohio River.[213] With bridges generally unavailable, ferries grew in number and continued to be regulated by the state as an extremely important public utility, much as they had been from statehood.[214] Preponderately privately owned, they were sustained by tolls charged for transporting passengers and freight, and owners often touted their service and location. In 1822, three years before Indianapolis became the capital, a ferry there was reported as having a "good boat" for transporting passengers and freight over White River; and a "small craft" to take "footmen" across. In 1828 a ferry at Lawrenceburg was advertised as being well located for travel between portions of Indiana and Ohio with the Kentucky Bluegrass area. "Passengers," Arthur Vance promised, "may always rely on a speedy, safe, and commodious conveyance." Vance claimed that the road between Lawrenceburg and Indianapolis was "better" than that from Brookville to the capital.[215]

The growing need for transportation by land stimulated interest in turnpikes. In 1826 citizens of Madison talked about a possible turnpike from there to Indianapolis.[216] At this time an editor upstream at Lawrenceburg urged local citizens to consider "'*A Turnpike Road from Lawrenceburgh to Indianapolis.*'" He asserted that the utility of such a road could not be questioned, nor its practicability. Lawrenceburg, the editor asserted, was the most commanding point in the state for trade extending west. Moreover, located between Cincinnati and Vevay, it was the most convenient point for emigrants from the east to central Indiana. The editor, perhaps with Vevay and Madison in mind, claimed that Lawrenceburg was the same distance from the capital as one or two points downstream. He anticipated that citizens of Madison would establish a turnpike to the capital, but said such a road would do very little injury to one from Lawrenceburg to Indianapolis. These comments were extremely overoptimistic about the prospects for turnpikes in Indiana, but they illustrate the rivalry among river towns for transportation facilities to the interior.[217] Early in 1828 the legislature authorized the incorporation of the Indianapolis and White Water Turnpike Company to make "an artificial clay turnpike road, which shall be made solid durable and graduated" from its center, with good bridges over all rivers and streams except the East and West forks of the Whitewater.[218] Late in 1829 Governor Ray, in one of his more visionary statements, anticipated the building of turnpikes intersecting the about-to-be-established Michigan Road, plus turnpikes from the capital radiating to all sections of the state.[219] By the time Ray left office in December, 1831, several additional turnpike incorporations had been authorized but none had begun more than limited construction, if any.[220] The preamble for the Indianapolis and White Water Turnpike Company, which asserted that the state road from the capital to Brookville had been "so imperfectly constructed as to be frequently impassable," doubtless applied to roads generally. Making turnpikes that afforded good roads throughout the state, or even a significant part of them, however, was much beyond the means of the Hoosier pioneers.[221]

Meantime, two of the most important thoroughfares of early Indiana, the Michigan and National roads, had their genesis in the twenties. In 1818, soon after statehood, Congressman William Hendricks considered it of the "utmost importance" that a military road be made from the Falls of the Ohio to Lake Michigan. As the result of a treaty which Lewis Cass, John Tipton, and Governor Ray made with the Potawatomi in 1826, Congress granted Indiana a right of way of one hundred feet and one section of land for each mile of a road from some point on the Ohio River via Indianapolis to Lake Michigan.[222] Early in 1828 the General Assembly accepted the grant, and named three commissioners to: select the site on Lake Michigan *within Indiana*, which they deemed "most eligible" for a harbor and commercial town; and locate and survey the "most eligible route" from this site to Indianapolis. When the legislature convened in December, the commissioners reported that starting in May they had run a random line to the lake, found no site "altogether suitable," but chose the mouth of Trail Creek as "the most eligible" place within the state. They then ran a line, of about seventy-three miles, across the Kankakee River toward Indianapolis, but found at least forty miles of this route "low and swampy" so that their horses got stuck "in the marshes several times in each day's travel." Convinced of the "impracticability of constructing a road . . . between the lake and the Wabash," during the fall they returned to the lake and marked an indirect route from there to the Wabash River via "the southern bend of the St. Joseph" River, which they termed navigable from the lake to the mouth of the Elkhart River "about twenty-five miles above the southern bend." The commissioners called the "site at the southern bend of the St. Joseph, and the adjacent country, the most desirable situation to be found north of the Wabash." A "Citizen of Carroll County," almost certainly Tipton who had recently moved the Indian agency from Fort Wayne to Logansport, contended that the entire proceeds of the Michigan Road donation would not yield revenue enough "to make a road over the Kankikee ponds" toward the lake. He urged that the road be routed north, passing east of the "Kankikee ponds" to the mouth of the St. Joseph River in Michigan. A road over this route, "Citizen" asserted, would cost less than half that over the ponds and be worth double that via "Yellow river and Kankikee."[223]

Meantime, intense rivalry had developed, especially about where the southern point on the Ohio River should be located. At the legislative session of 1827–1828, these towns were among points voted for by members of the House: Lawrenceburg, Aurora, Rising Sun, Madison, Falls of the Ohio (Jeffersonville), New Albany, Mauckport, Mouth of Blue River, Horseshoe Bend (Leavenworth), Fredonia, Evansville, and Mount Vernon.[224] The impasse continued through the next session, but early in 1830 the General Assembly established the route from Madison via Greensburg, Indianapolis, Logansport, and South Bend to the mouth of Trail Creek. An Indianapolis editor appropriately commented: "So ends this distracting question; which for three years has been so fruitful a source of legislation."[225] Why Madison prevailed over its rivals is uncertain, but locating the road from Indianapolis to Madison via Greensburg, instead of by the more direct way via Columbus and Vernon, perhaps resulted from a desire to make the Michigan Road also advantageous to residents of Lawrenceburg and the surrounding area.[226]

With the Michigan Road located, the General Assembly, over vigorous objection from Governor Ray, named Noah Noble commissioner to let contracts for its "opening" from Madison to Logansport. Contractors were to open the road one hundred feet in width by clearing and cutting "all the logs, timber and underbrush, leaving no stump more than one foot above the level of the earth"; and grub a thirty-foot width in the center in the same manner as was required for the Cumberland Road. Since none of the donated land had been sold, Noble was instructed to give contractors scrip redeemable from proceeds after sales would begin. During July, 1830, Noble let contracts for all of the 163 miles between Madison and Logansport for an aggregate of $62,135.85, hence at an average of $381.20 per mile.[227] No contracts were let during 1831. However, William Polke, as commissioner to sell the land granted, obtained about $49,000 for the sale of 29,761 acres at an average of $1.65^1/$_2$ per acre. Hence, as Ray left office in December, 1831, considerable progress had been made toward "opening" the Michigan Road from the Ohio River to the Wabash River at Logansport.[228]

While the Michigan Road was financed by a federal land grant, the National Road was both financed and constructed by the United States. Started at Cumberland, Maryland, in 1811, seven years later it reached Wheeling, Virginia, on the Ohio River below Pittsburgh, having been constructed through the mountains of southwestern Pennsylvania. Indiana claimed that its extension through Ohio, Indiana, and Illinois to the Mississippi was owed on the basis of the Two Per Cent Fund agreed to when they became states.[229] Early in 1821 the General Assembly asked that the site of the permanent state capital, Indianapolis, be established as a point on the road. From the mid-twenties the General Assembly enacted a series of memorials urging appropriations for its extension across the state, some of which asked for its continuation to the Mississippi River.[230] During 1827 Jonathan Knight located the line of the National Road from the Ohio border via Richmond, Indianapolis, and Terre Haute to the Illinois border, a distance of approximately 150 miles.[231] As President Adams left office in March, 1829, Congress appropriated $50,000 to open the roadway eighty feet wide through Indiana. During June, Homer Johnson and John Milroy, superintendents for the opening, let contracts for grubbing a strip thirty feet wide in the center of the roadway for all but about seven miles of the line for a cost of $16,597; and contracts for "cutting and removing the timber" from the remainder of the roadbed the same distance was let for a total of $17,292.[232] In 1830 Congress appropriated $60,000 for opening, bridging, and grading the road, starting at the capital and progressing both east and west toward the borders. In 1831 an additional $75,000 was granted, with the same injunction about how construction was to proceed.[233] Already new towns were being founded on the road, especially east of Indianapolis. Though this road was only in its early stage of construction, travelers on it were hampering its progress.[234]

Land travel was important, but trade to and from Indiana moved largely on rivers. After mentioning the Ohio, Wabash, and White rivers in his annual message to the General Assembly in 1826, Governor Ray observed: "Upon these water courses with many others of less magnitude, rest the hopes of the merchant and the agriculturalist at present, in common swells of water to export the accumulating surplus produce of the country to a *southern* market."[235] Because of the Appalachian barrier to the east and the fact that most of the settlers lived within the area drained by the tributaries of the Mississippi, throughout the period 1816–1850 the preponderance of imports and exports were conveyed upon this river system.[236]

The overwhelming proportion of farm produce, lumber, and other exports floated southward on flatboats. Varying in size and shape, hundreds, perhaps even thousands, were unloaded annually along the Mississippi and especially at New Orleans.[237] Most numerous on the Ohio, Wabash, and the two forks of White River, they descended lesser streams as well. They were usually put afloat during spring and fall rises of the rivers. A Vincennes paper reported in June, 1826, that so far that spring more than 152 flatboats had already gone down the Wabash, with many doubtless having passed unnoticed. In June, 1828, a Bloomington paper announced that 300 of them had passed out of the East Fork of White River into the Wabash below Vincennes, since the start of that year. Flatboats were said to be passing Lawrenceburg daily in the fall of 1830, at times four or five being visible as they went by.[238] Traffic on the Ohio and lower Wabash included boats from other states. Unable to return their boats upstream, flatboatmen often walked at least part of the way home and as steamboats became more common increasingly they used this mode of travel. Regardless of how the journey home was made, flatboat trips normally required a minimum of several weeks to complete.[239]

While imports of salt, manufactured goods, iron, and other items were received principally via the Mississippi-Ohio river route, imports also arrived from the Ohio River above Indiana. The upstream traffic was mainly by keelboats and steamboats, while much of that from the upper Ohio was also by flatboat. As steamboats replaced keelboats on the larger rivers the latter largely receded to portions of these rivers which were difficult to navigate and to smaller streams not suitable for use by the former.[240] With the advance of steamboats the cost of imports and the time for conveying them was much reduced.[241]

Steamboat traffic on the Wabash River became significant during the twenties. In May, 1823, an editor at Vincennes welcomed the "Florence" from Louisville, as the first example of navigation on "the Wabash with a craft propelled by steam," and "as the harbinger of more prosperous days." The "Florence" proceeded upstream to Terre Haute, and reportedly returned from there to Vincennes in nine and one half hours.[242] About this time the next year, the "Plough Boy," also from Louisville, made stops at Vincennes and Terre Haute.[243] Several steamers arrived at Vincennes during March and April, 1826. One of them, the "American," was said to have continued upriver to Lafayette, "without meeting with any obstruction, the navigation being perfectly safe, and easy." At the site of the Tippecanoe Battle Ground "'sons of the

forest,'" who were taken aboard, "appeared to manifest much sur-
prize at the velocity with which the boat ascended the stream."[244]
Early in 1830 two packets, the "Tippecanoe" and "Highlander,"
were advertised as offering passenger and freight service for Vincennes, Terre Haute, Lafayette, and other landing places for the
entire season.[245] Although Lafayette was viewed by some as the
head of steamboat navigation on the upper Wabash, in the spring
of 1830 "A Citizen of the Upper Wabash" announced that the
"Paragon" had ascended the river to the mouth of Rock Creek,
fifteen miles beyond the site of the "memorable" Battle of
Tippecanoe. "Citizen" termed Delphi the head of navigation, and
he asserted that the captain of the "Paragon" had reported "the
river above Lafayette, so far as he ascended, equally safe for steam
boat navigation as below."[246] In February, 1831, a correspondent
advised John Tipton about plans which he hoped would make the
"Indiana Hoosier" the "first" steamer to ascend the Wabash to
Logansport.[247] Meantime, steamboat navigation had commenced
on the Vermillion River, tributary of the Wabash, which reached
northward from Terre Haute, before bending into Illinois. During May, 1828, a paper at Terre Haute reported that the "Cincinnati" had discharged some of its freight there and then headed
"for Eugene upon [the] Vermillion" River.[248]

During the late twenties several efforts were made to get a
steamboat up the West Fork of White River to Indianapolis.
Noah Noble was instrumental in some of these efforts, which
were well publicized by the *Indiana Journal* whose editor was
quite friendly to him.[249] When the "Triton," from Louisville, got
within fourteen miles of Spencer in April, 1828, this editor said
there was little doubt but that steamboats could navigate White
River, "when well filled with water," to Indianapolis. In December, 1829, the "Victory" arrived at Spencer; and in April, 1830,
the "Traveller" reached this point. Both captains were too prudent to make a try for the capital, apparently in part because of
low water. According to the captain of the "Traveller," up to
Washington the river could be navigated whenever the Wabash
was navigable, and obstructions were not numerous until above
the mouth of the Eel River. Between there and Spencer snags and

logs made navigation more difficult.[250] Finally, early in April, 1831, the "General Hanna" arrived at the capital towing "up a heavily loaded keel boat." General Hanna and Company had purchased the steamer for "conveying stone from some distance below . . . for the building of bridges on the Cumberland Road . . . ." The editor of the *Indiana Journal* declared: "No event is recollected, since the first settlement of this town, which produced a higher excitement than . . . the arrival of this steam boat." Citizens lined the river bank, a salute was fired with a cannon, and the steamboat had to make a second excursion to accommodate all the "ladies and gentlemen" who wished a ride. A committee of local citizens resolved that the boat's arrival was "a fair and unanswerable demonstration of the fact that our beautiful river is susceptible of safe navigation for steam vessels of a much larger class than was anticipated by the most sanguine." The owners and officers of the "General Hanna" were invited to "partake of a public dinner" with the citizens of Indianapolis, but Robert Hanna explained that prior arrangements made it necessary to leave "for the Bluffs" without "the pleasure of partaking" of the dinner with his fellow citizens. Quite likely, concern that a decline in the water level would cause his boat to become stranded enroute downstream shortened the stay at the capital.[251] Until 1831, with perhaps a few exceptions, steamboat traffic was apparently limited to the Ohio, Wabash, East Fork of White, and Vermillion rivers, with it principally confined to the Ohio and to the Wabash to a lesser extent.

Despite the large dependence on rivers for imports and exports, the latter mainly via flatboats, only modest labor and money was spent on their improvement. Numerous laws were passed declaring portions of rivers public highways, often up to a fork in the river or a mill site. On streams so declared dams for mills were usually prohibited, unless suitable provision was made for passage of boats. Streams such as Laughery Creek, Big Sand Creek, Blue River, Lost River, Big Indian Creek, Busseron Creek, Salt Creek, and many other small rivers were so declared on behalf of the downstream traffic by flatboats.[252] This legislation, however, was powerless to remove sandbars, fallen trees, rapids, rock ledges, and other natural obstructions.[253] Though the Three Per Cent Fund had been specified for roads and canals, small sums were spent from this source on various rivers through 1831. The report of the agent for this fund indicated that of the $119,536.08 appropriated by this time that $6,725.86 had been earmarked for rivers, but only $1,872.34 had been spent on them.[254]

Meantime, Indiana had made its first but unsuccessful attempt at canal building. In 1805 the territorial legislature had chartered a company to open a short canal around the Falls of the Ohio River on the Indiana shore opposite Louisville. There the rocks and ledges presented the most serious obstacle to navigation of the Ohio-Mississippi waterway from Pittsburgh to New Orleans. Many boats passed over this obstruction in safety, but as the water level lowered the passage of boats became difficult and dangerous, and at times impossible.[255] The initial legislative session after statehood charted another company to dig such a canal, and the next session liberalized its charter. This legislation authorized the Jeffersonville Ohio Canal Company to raise $1,000,000 in stock in units of $50, $100,000 of which could be raised by a lottery. One fourth of the stock could be purchased by the state.[256] By the spring of 1819 some revenue had apparently been raised from stock subscriptions and the lottery. According to a local paper at noon on May 3, 1819, directors of the company commenced the digging amid cheers and huzzas, and a large number of workers took over and "the work progressed with a spirit never surpassed." In anticipation of this event John Francis Dufour, of Vevay, had been sent a check for $15 with a request that he send a cask of wine so there could be "a little wine of domestic manufactory to drink on the occasion . . . ." But there was not *enough revenue*, and perhaps not *enough spirit* as well, to dig the canal for a distance of about two and a half miles. Late in 1820 a House committee reported that information from the secretary of the company showed that its revenue had aggregated only $14,933.09. Cash obtained from individuals included $2,536 from managers of the lottery, with $5,000 of stock paid for by the state and the remainder from individual purchasers of stock. Only $13,660.37¼ had been spent by the company.[257] Nonetheless, at the last legislative session at Corydon in 1823–1824, Governor William Hendricks and Three Per Cent Agent Christopher Harrison were named commissioners to seek means to commence and complete a canal on the Indiana side of the river. If they could borrow money sufficient to build it, at interest not to exceed 6 percent—including borrowing from Congress and other states— they were to pledge the revenue to be derived from the canal and the Three Per Cent revenue, beyond that already appropriated, for payment of the interest. A report of the two commissioners in January, 1825, though cautiously worded, made it clear that their efforts had been unavailing. During this year, however, efforts to obtain a canal on the Kentucky side of the river culminated in the chartering of the Louisville and Portland Canal Company which, aided generously by congressional appropriations of money, completed and opened a canal around the Ohio River Falls in 1830.[258]

Meantime, starting about 1825 numerous citizens and politicians increasingly caught a serious, persistent, and incurable case of internal improvement fever. How this developed—and how it ultimately led to fiscal insolvency for several years in the 1840s— are developed at length in subsequent chapters.[259]

CHAPTER 4
BANKING AND INTERNAL IMPROVEMENTS, 1831–1837

STATE GOVERNMENT and politics entered a new era during the 1830s. A rapidly growing population, an expanding economy, advancing prosperity, and an enlarging fiscal base led to state sponsored systems of banking and internal improvements. Party rivalry between the Jacksonians (Democratic Republicans) and anti-Jacksonians (National Republicans) became more involved in state politics than during the twenties. With Governor Ray ineligible for reelection, another would succeed him in December, 1831. Although General Jackson had easily triumphed over President Adams in 1828, his opponents retained the upper hand in state government.[1] Hence, party politics became considerably involved in the gubernatorial election of 1831.

Before the end of 1830 two National Republicans were in the race to succeed Ray. Early that year Israel T. Canby, defeated Jacksonian candidate for governor in 1828, wrote John Tipton that Noah Noble and (Lieutenant Governor) Milton Stapp were "avowedly candidates for Governor and in about a year we propose starting a third of different complexion." In November, 1830, the *Indiana Journal* reported Noble and Stapp as the only known candidates. In February this National Republican organ explained that both men had requested that they be announced as candidates for governor. A few weeks later, also by request, the *Indiana Journal* announced James Scott, former judge of the state Supreme Court, for the same office.[2] These three men had informally become candidates, but none was the nominee of a political party. Noble and Stapp were National Republicans and Scott, who withdrew before the August voting, was apparently the same.[3]

Although tardy in getting a candidate in the race, the Jacksonians were willing to give their followers help in selecting their aspirant for chief executive. In December, 1830, a Jacksonian legislator advised Tipton that "a large portion of the members of the Legislature & officers together with other Jackson men" had consulted and "unitedly nominated" him for governor and James G. Read for lieutenant governor. Why Tipton, then federal Indian agent at Logansport, failed to accept the nomination is uncertain.[4] Less than three months before the voting in August, the *Indiana Democrat* asked editors throughout the state to "please announce Judge Read" for governor. The *Indiana Journal* attributed Read's candidacy to a caucus of Jacksonians, and denounced the Jacksonians for injecting presidential politics in the election of a governor. After insisting that there was no difference between the parties regarding essential items the *Indiana Journal* stated that the three men already in the race had been canvassing without regard to party with the support of leading Jacksonians.[5] With Jackson's strong popularity among voters, political expediency prompted Democratic Republicans to encourage and National Republicans to discourage voting along party lines in the election of a governor.

Although Lieutenant Governor Stapp remained in the contest, the competition narrowed largely to that between Noble and Read. They were able and experienced candidates, and Noble was apparently as much an anti-Jacksonian as Read was a Jacksonian. Noble had been contract commissioner for the Michigan Road since early 1830, and Read became receiver of the Jeffersonville Land Office about the time he became the Democratic Republican candidate for chief executive. Both men retained these offices while they campaigned for governor.[6] During May the rival candidates issued circulars concerning their political views. Noble advocated "a judicious application" of the state's resources "in improving natural, and making artificial avenues" for conveying "surplus produce to market." But with means limited and drawn from taxes, Noble said priority should be given projects of first importance. Read asserted that internal improvements "essential to the defence or commerce of the nation, should . . . be constructed by the general government," with "local improvements" for construction by the states with the aid of federal surplus revenue. Noble strongly supported recent tariff legislation as beneficial to agriculture and all branches of industry. Read affirmed himself an "advocate of a moderate and efficient tariff for the protection of the domestic industry," which the federal government had power to enact. Noble presumed that "integrity and qualifications" were the "only needful passports" for election, and declared that he looked "to the people *all* & not to party discipline" for his support. Read asserted that he "decidedly approved" the existing federal administration, but he did not explicitly ask for support on the basis of party.[7] An address of the Jackson State Central Committee, however, thundered out a call for the election of "a Governor and Lieutenant Governor, Representatives in our State and national Legislatures, who will speak our language and advocate ably and zealously our principles and interest."[8]

A considerable amount of political rhetoric characterized the contest between Noble and Read. Jacksonians accused Noble of combining electioneering with the performance of duties as contract commissioner for the Michigan Road, while friends of Noble attacked Read for campaigning while holding a federal appointment as receiver of the Jeffersonville Land Office. Read and various of his supporters were described as an elite of federal officials drawing fat salaries. Both men were said to have been more favorable to the Wabash and Erie Canal while campaigning in northern counties than when speaking in those of the south. Noble reportedly deprecated party voting in areas where Jackson was popular, but sought support as a friend of Clay in other places. Read was pounced upon for a handbill circulated on his behalf by postmasters, but he claimed that this had been done without his knowledge by a supporter unaware that it was contrary to postal regulations. Noble denied that he had sold a black woman into slavery after she had gained freedom, but admitted that he had sold her as a slave on behalf of his father-in-law.[9]

At the voting in August Noble defeated Read by a modest plurality, and probably would have won by a considerable majority had Stapp not been a candidate. Noble ran well in the eastern counties of Central Indiana and those on or near the Whitewater Valley, plus counties on or near the Wabash from Vigo to Allen. Read exhibited much strength in the central and western counties of Southern Indiana, including all the counties on or near the Wabash River. Stapp won a majority in Jefferson, his home county, and a plurality in two other counties. Noble generally ran better in counties that preferred Adams and Read did the same in those which had preferred Jackson, but Noble's victory included significant support from Jacksonians.[10]

With Lieutenant Governor Stapp in the contest for governor, various men were mentioned as possible successors to him.[11] Some Jacksonian leaders apparently expected Amos Lane of Dearborn County to be paired with Read for lieutenant governor. But Ross Smiley of Union County, who had been a Jackson elector in 1828, refused to give way and Lane withdrew as a candidate.[12] The August voting indicates that David Wallace and James Gregory were respectively paired with Noble and Read. Wallace, like Noble, was only a plurality winner, with Smiley second and Gregory a distant third.[13]

The outcome of the state election favored the National Republicans. Although the new governor and lieutenant governor were National Republicans, and this party retained its upper hand in the legislature, the Democratic Republicans elected Indiana's three congressmen.[14] The pro-Clay *Indiana Journal* and pro-Jackson *Western Sun* agreed that the outcome had not been a test of party strength concerning presidential politics. The *Western Sun* wryly observed: "It is a remarkable fact that with a large majority of the state in favor of Jackson, there has at all times been a majority of Adams and Clay men in our Legislature." Its editor insisted that "The state is as decidedly Jacksonian as ever it was."[15] By running a strong and popular candidate, while contending that presidential politics had no place in gubernatorial elections, the National Republicans had defeated their more numerous rivals.

When the legislature met in December, Treasurer Samuel Merrill and Auditor Morris Morris were elected to new three year terms. The *Indiana Journal* called them "faithful and competent," and doubted "whether their places could be better supplied." On the initial ballots Merrill was elected to a fourth successive term by a near unanimous vote, and Morris to a second term by about a three to two vote. At the ensuing session, however, the assembly passed over James Morrison for reelection to a four year term as secretary of state, and chose William Sheets by more than a two to one margin.[16]

By winning reelection in 1834 Noah Noble's tenure as chief executive extended from December, 1831, to December, 1837. His reelection and the continued upper hand of the National Republicans (Whigs, starting in 1834) in the legislature was remarkable because Jackson trounced Clay in the presidential election of 1832 as he had Adams four years earlier. Though party lines were hardening, the division mainly concerned presidential politics. So far as state issues were concerned—and especially the key issues of banking and internal improvements—a substantial consensus existed between the Democratic Republicans and their National Republican-Whig rivals.

The Democratic Republicans commenced their campaign for governor in 1834 months earlier than they had in 1831. In August, 1833, the *Indiana Democrat* said many people had expressed the need for a state convention to make nominations for governor and lieutenant governor, and select delegates to the party's national convention to name candidates for president and vice president. Alexander F. Morrison, its editor, asserted that "the paramount interests" of the country and "success in elections demand concert of action" which could best be secured by selecting "delegates from the bosom of the people . . . ." After reporting that his suggestions apparently had met "the decided approbation of the Democratic party throughout the state," Morrison issued a call for a state convention at Indianapolis, December 9, 1833. The editor expressed the hope that party members from every county would select delegates to the convention.[17] The *Indiana Journal*, staunchly National Republican and pro-Noble, lambasted the convention as the work of designing men hungry for patronage. Such a course had never been pursued in the state, it said, as it argued that a governor should be elected on the basis of merit without regard to presidential preference. "Indianian," who claimed to be a plain mechanic, contended that "the political aristocrats" disliked giving the people a voice in selecting candidates. "Indianian" charged that the Jacksonian candidate had been defeated in the previous election for governor through the use of secret committees and "management" by leaders devoted to Clay.[18] For the

Democrats a state convention was an attempt to augment party loyalty, and unite Jacksonians in support of their candidate for governor. For the National Republicans placing emphasis on merit without regard to party was an effort to secure a significant part of the Jacksonian vote.

According to the *Indiana Democrat*, delegates from about forty counties were seated at the "Democratic Republican" convention that met December 9. The convention decided that the vote of each county would be the same as its representation in the House of Representatives, except that each county would have at least one vote. It further decided that voting would continue until its nominees achieved a majority of the vote. On the second ballot James G. Read, the party's candidate three years before, won nomination with 50 of the 72 votes cast. David V. Culley, of Dearborn County, secured 43 of 70 votes cast to obtain nomination for lieutenant governor over Ross Smiley on the second ballot. On the motion of Jacob B. Lowe of Monroe County, who had been the runnerup for governor, the convention "*unanimously*" resolved to "use all means to procure harmony, and promote the elections of the persons" nominated regardless of personal preferences.[19] The *Indiana Democrat* proclaimed that the convention system had been "established upon so firm a basis, that our opponents can no longer indulge the vain hope of overturning it." The *Wabash Courier*, an opposition paper, claimed that about two dozen counties had been totally unrepresented in the convention, which had been "concocted" by a few politicians. It asserted that in several counties the people had had no more to do with the selection of delegates than had the man in the moon. Paris C. Dunning, from Monroe County, wrote Noah Noble that he thought he could not support Read, and that the manner in which his nomination was procured satisfied him "of the impropriety of Conventions" for the nomination of state officers because in them it is "merely accidental" if the voice of the majority is heard.[20]

Meantime, Governor Noah Noble and Lieutenant Governor David Wallace were presumed to be candidates for reelection.[21] Both were National Republicans, but as in 1831 they did not run as party candidates. Early in 1834 Noble proposed to Read that they either campaign together or else both stay home and attend to public and personal affairs. In April they announced an agreement to return to their "homes and business" as soon as each had completed certain campaign visits. This agreement was soon amended and seems to have been largely ignored by both candidates.[22] In separate circulars the rival candidates expressed strong support for a general system of internal improvements, but neither commented about the Second State Bank then being established. After observing that Read had disclaimed seeking votes on party grounds, Noble emphasized that this was the principle on which he wished to be reelected and which he had practiced in appointing over ninety persons, more than half of whom had been of the party opposite to him.[23] Nevertheless, both candidates were accused of seeking support on the basis of presidential preferences. Read was labeled as a caucus or convention candidate, and correctly identified as a Jacksonian officeholder. Noble was charged with wooing votes from Democrats who favored Richard M. Johnson of Kentucky for president. Democrats mocked claims that more than half of Noble's appointments had gone to members of their party. Jacksonian postmasters were accused of having delayed mail favorable to Noble. Read was said to have made speeches against as well as for the Wabash and Erie Canal.[24]

At the voting in August Noble won reelection by a decisive margin. Read won only eighteen of the sixty-nine counties, located mainly in the central and especially western counties of Southern Indiana not likely to fare well in a system of internal improvements. Wallace defeated Culley by an overwhelming margin of nearly two to one. The *Indiana Democrat* commented that the friends of Jackson, with their usual magnanimity, had elected a governor and lieutenant governor from their rival party.[25] The *Indiana Journal* agreed that many Jacksonians had voted for Noble and Wallace, but it insisted that the result demonstrated that it would be difficult for the Democrats to carry Indiana for Van Buren in 1836. The *Western Sun* attributed Noble's reelection to his personal popularity, the lack of opposition to his policies which had generally been wise, and the unbroken custom of reelecting an incumbent governor. Nonetheless, this staunchly Jacksonian organ declared that Indiana was "Democratic to the core" and would remain so.[26]

The Whigs, as the successors to the National Republicans, retained their usual upper hand in the General Assembly. Even so, at the session of 1834–1835 near unanimity prevailed in the election of a treasurer and auditor.[27] Early in 1834, after Treasurer Samuel Merrill had resigned to become president of the Second State Bank, Governor Noble had given Nathan B. Palmer, a Democrat, a recess appointment to complete Merrill's term. About nine tenths of the members of the assembly had recommended Palmer as "eminently qualified" to become treasurer. The *Indiana Journal* heralded this action as evidence that Noble was performing his duties unaffected by party feeling. Editor Elihu Stout of the *Western Sun* "rejoiced" that the governor had named a Jacksonian to this office, but objected that the "no party Governor," though elected by Jacksonians, had named no more than two other Jacksonians to offices.[28] When the legislature met in December Palmer was elected to a three year term by close to a unanimous vote; and Morris Morris, incumbent auditor and Whig, won reelection to a third term by an even nearer unanimous vote. These elections by the General Assembly illustrate that party cleavage had not become rigid in such elections.[29]

While Noah Noble was governor the revenue from taxation easily met the ordinary costs of state government. The rapid gain in taxable property and polls caused a swelling of the yield from tax levies. Apparently most of the costs for the state prison and a significant part of the cost of the first state capitol were also paid from tax revenue. The administrative system for assessing and collecting taxes remained largely as it had been in the teens and twenties. But a fundamental change occurred which expanded the tax base with the adoption of the ad valorem system whereby property generally as well as land was taxed.

Ordinary expenditures averaged $50,130.83 under Noble versus $33,136.56 for the years 1822 to 1831.[30] Legislative costs were nearly doubled those for the executive and judicial departments combined, and judicial costs were more than four times those for the executive branch. Legislative costs averaged $25,003.93, a

Ordinary Expenditures, 1831–1837

Fiscal Year	Legislative	Judicial	Executive	Taxes Paid Collectors	Contingent	Debt
1831–32	$ 20,787.76	$ 8,660.52	$ 2,596.72	$ 3,669.28	$ 836.35	$ 5.00
1832–33	22,886.71	11,222.04	2,450.00	3,668.22	794.62	4.00
1833–34	22,785.44	10,845.03	2,750.00	3,281.34	939.35	0.00
1834–35	24,737.71	10,728.17	1,800.00	4,008.34	774.45	27.00
1835–36	25,422.19	12,874.25	2,700.00	4,615.06	1,047.62	0.00
1836–37	33,403.80	13,099.51	2,999.00	5,799.35	1,017.52	0.00
Total	150,023.61	67,429.52	15,295.72	25,041.59	5,409.91	36.00
Average	25,003.93	11,238.25	2,549.28	4,173.59	901.65	6.00

Ordinary Expenditures, 1831–1837

Fiscal Year	Prison	Militia	Library	Wolves	Miscellaneous	Total
1831–32	$ 1,985.09	$170.71	$ 100.00	$ 794.50	$ 1,454.38	$ 41,060.31
1832–33	877.25	100.00	248.37	816.00	1,765.44	44,832.65
1833–34	2,856.62	125.00	100.00	751.50	2,178.08	46,608.36
1834–35	3,085.01	87.10	200.00	606.50	2,621.05	48,675.33
1835–36	1,573.54	192.00	100.00	512.50	6,026.72	55,063.88
1836–37	874.62	208.33	301.29	412.50	6,428.53	64,544.45
Total	11,252.13	883.14	1,049.66	3,893.50	20,474.20	300,784.98
Average	1,875.35	147.19	174.94	648.91	3,412.36	50,130.83

sum larger than the average for all ordinary expenditures during the early years of statehood. The enlarged legislative costs arose principally from a gain in the number of legislators and additional public printing. The legislative reapportionments of 1831 and 1836 greatly increased the number of legislators. With the gain in legislators, county officials, and judges more copies of the annual session laws and legislative journals were needed. As lawmakers gave increased attention to important topics such as internal improvements and banking, volumes of session laws and journals expanded in size.[31] Expenditures for the state prison averaged $1,875.35 per year.[32] There were gains in most other expenditures, and the money spent for wolves destroyed was more than treble that spent on the state library. Since collectors of state tax revenue were apparently allowed 9 percent of such revenue for collecting it, an average of roughly $4,173.59 was paid them annually.[33]

The ordinary revenue to meet these expenditures averaged $51,527.80 as against $29,403.68 for the period 1822 to 1831.[34] Until 1836 tax revenue came almost entirely from levies on land and polls, with land apparently levied at 80, 60, and 40 cents per one hundred acres of first, second, and third rate tracts respectively; and a levy on polls of 37$^1/_2$ cents per head.[35] When the ad valorem or general property tax became effective in 1836, land and other property, unless exempted, was levied at 5 cents per $100 of valuation. For the year 1837, however, this levy was tripled to 15 cents per $100 of valuation, with one third of the levy earmarked to pay interest on the internal improvement debt during the ensuing year. When the general property tax became effective in 1836, the levy on polls jumped from 37$^1/_2$ cents to 50 cents.[36] As for the period 1822–1831, ordinary revenues exceeded ordinary costs.

The adoption of the ad valorem tax was the most basic innovation in the tax base for the pioneer era. Given considerable attention at legislative sessions from the mid-1820s, it gained support from legislators during the first half of the thirties.[37] The debate pro and con its adoption rested on much the same arguments throughout this decade. The House Ways and Means Committee

Ordinary Revenue, 1831–1837

Fiscal Year	Taxes Received	Taxes Paid Collectors	Prison	Miscellaneous	Total
1831–32	$ 40,769.85	$ 3,669.28	$ 0.00	$ 937.18	$ 45,376.31
1832–33	40,758.10	3,668.22	700.00	106.82	45,233.14
1833–34	36,459.39	3,281.34	700.00	118.28	40,559.01
1834–35	44,537.13	4,008.34	700.00	44.03	49,289.50
1835–36	51,278.45	4,615.06	700.00	603.69	57,197.20
1836–37	64,437.23	5,799.35	700.00	575.06	71,511.64
Total	278,240.15	25,041.59	3,500.00	2,385.06	309,166.80
Average	46,373.35	4,173.59	583.33	397.51	51,527.80

at the 1832–1833 session contended that because of "the great diversity in the progress of improvements in the State," the general property tax would "throw nearly the whole burthen of sustaining the revenue of the state upon the old counties." If the new mode was adopted, the committee predicted that public opinion would call for an end to the unpopular poll tax, the replacement for which also would be paid chiefly by citizens of the older counties. Furthermore, the ad valorem system would discourage needed improvements in agriculture and manufacturing and favor non-resident owners of land who failed to add improvements over residents who added them. But the committee added that "in a few years the denseness of our population, and the sameness of improvements throughout the State, will present a more propitious season for a change in our revenue system." Representative Richard W. Thompson, from Lawrence County in southern Indiana, wrote Governor Noble that the people of his area were "most violently opposed" to the ad valorem plan. They believed, and Thompson concurred, that fiscal burdens would "be *unequally* increased upon the farmer of the old counties." Thompson urged delay until the ownership of property and land was equalized between newer and older sections of the state. If the next legislative reapportionment should give northern legislators a majority in the assembly, Thompson asked, "what will be *our* condition when the money, paid by our industry, is attempted to be appropriated?"[38]

Advocates of the general property tax emphasized its fairness and the desirability of taxing personal property as well as real estate. After his reelection in 1834 Governor Noble advised legislators that the tax system was "creating discontent, on the ground that its exactions are oppressive to the land holders . . . ." Suggesting that "the burthen of taxation should be distributed equally, and levied from capital actively employed, from real and personal estate, in proportion to the productive quality of each," the executive added that he had always regarded the ad valorem plan as more equitable than specific levies on land. Noting that the disparity in the value of property in older versus newer counties was perhaps less than had been supposed, he recommended that "every description of property" that might be taxed be valued as a possible step toward the ad valorem plan. Early in 1835 the assembly provided for such an evaluation. According to an Indianapolis paper, "This law was considered by many as an entering wedge to the general system of [internal] improvement contemplated at the next session."[39]

The first state levy under the ad valorem plan was adopted at the 1835–1836 legislative session, at which time the Internal Improvements System of 1836 was approved. Governor Noble advised legislators that apparently "the disparity anticipated in the value of real estate in the old and new districts of the state, does not exist." Observing that some citizens objected to the number of items valued for taxation, Noble suggested that a law could be "shaped" to remove such objections, "particularly when they see that the tax upon land will be reduced in proportion" to that charged property heretofore not subject to levy. Noble emphasized that there was no adequate reason "why capital invested in town property, bank stock, merchandize, or money at interest, should not be subject to the same rate of taxation as an equal amount invested in land."

As already noted, the general property levy was set at 5 cents per $100 of assessed valuation for 1836; and treble this rate for the ensuing year. Both real and personal property were to be levied at actual or real value. Consideration was to be given to fertility of the soil and location of the land as regards such items as roads, canals, railroads, towns, villages, and navigable rivers. Taxpayers were to give a "fair and true valuation" of their personal property, but if the assessor was not satisfied with their evaluation he was to value "same at its full cash value, according to the best of his knowledge and information." Moreover, all property taxed, whether personal or real, was to be assessed at the same rate in proportion to its value.[40]

The adoption of the general property tax made it essential for the General Assembly to spell out which property was taxable and which was not. It indicated that real property embraced lands and town lots, plus buildings and improvements thereon, while personal property included "household furniture, all monies on hand, also all monies loaned at interest, goods, chattels, public stocks, and stocks in monied corporations." A major exemption, mandated by compact with the federal government at the time of statehood, excluded lands sold by Congress from levy for five years subsequent to their sale. Other real estate exempted was that used by: religious societies for a meeting house or burial ground; common schools, academies, seminaries, and colleges; county and state libraries; hospitals, almshouses, and houses of correction; and that used for county purposes. Libraries and philosophical apparatus used by or belonging to an incorporated society, academy, or college for the promotion of science was also tax free, as were stocks owned by the state, charitable, or literary institutions. For each taxpayer $100 of personal property was exempted, while a widow and orphan children were allowed twice this sum. For every family wearing apparel and beds and bedding, not exceeding two beds per family, were free from levy. Veterans of the American Revolution, who had served at least three months in the land or naval forces in the cause of independence from England, were exempted from the poll tax, and levy on personal property, and from taxation on up to 160 acres of land. Other legislation excused those who had purchased state owned land on credit from levy until it was paid for, and gave county boards the authority to exempt males from payment of the poll tax if unable to pay the tax or on account of bodily disability regardless of their age.[41]

The augmented tax base arising from the increased population and wealth of the 1830s helped set the stage for an advance in pay to state officials. In the two decades since statehood duties performed by public officials had expanded and living costs had increased, but salaries for the higher judges and executive officials as well as per diems to legislators had remained unchanged.[42] Some officials, however, such as the secretary of state, treasurer, and auditor had received supplemental payments for specified services as additions to their regular salary.[43] A major concern was the urgent need to raise the compensation for circuit and Supreme judges. In his second inaugural in 1834 Governor Noble observed that many justices of the peace earned more than $1,000 annually, while the higher judges, who decided "matters involving life, liberty, and fortune," received only $700. The latter sum, Noble stressed, was "entirely insufficient" to enable judges to support their families or buy books essential to the performance of their duties. When Charles H. Test resigned as president of a circuit court in 1836, he advised the governor that bad health and "a salary quite too small" had induced his decision. Shortly thereafter Stephen C. Stevens withdrew from the Supreme Court, and Noble informed the next assembly that this action had resulted because the office "would not support his family."[44] Newspapers from both parties advocated augmented compensation to public officials. The Indianapolis *Indiana Democrat* urged that judges on the Supreme Court be paid at least $2,000 annually. Its editor reported that Charles Dewey had reluctantly become the successor to Stevens "after the repeated and urgent solicitations of the bar." Early in 1837 the legislature raised the salary of the governor to $1,500 yearly, that of the Supreme judges to the same amount, and the presidents of circuit courts to $1,000. The per diem for members of the General Assembly was upped to $3 per day of attendance at sessions, plus $3 for every twenty-five miles traveled by the "most usual road" in going to and from sessions. The judicial increases were effective from passage of the act, that for the governor at the end of the incumbent's term, and that for legislators from the ensuing August election.[45]

From 1831 until 1837 there appears to have been no more than modest criticism regarding the cost of state government. But the three-fold increase in the property levy for 1837 over that for the preceding year, augmented concern about the fiscal implications of the Internal Improvements System of 1836, and the panic commencing in May, 1837, led to mounting protest. As previously noted, half of the jump in the property levy for 1837 was earmarked for payment of interest due on the internal improvement borrowing for the ensuing year. In March, Enoch D. John, a close acquaintance of the governor, wrote from Lawrenceburg telling the executive that "The People (the rabble & Demagogs) are in arms against taxation & our general Improvement Sistem[.]" Contending that unless the system was changed "the whole System falls," John urged that "The Works Should be class'd & the Most important Shoved ahead & others kept back." The Indianapolis *Indiana Democrat* charged Noble with using the system to enhance his election to the United States Senate, and pounced on him for not having recommended to the General Assembly "a prudent and economical plan" that could have been implemented "without ruining the people and the State." The Indianapolis *Indiana Journal* admitted that classification might have been a good plan, but asked, "Would not a resort of that kind, at this time, endanger the whole system?" Another editor explained that the property levy for 1836 had been so low that a deficit had resulted, and it pointed to payments for the new capitol and increased salaries as having made necessary an added levy. This organ considered 5 cents for $100 of property valuation a small price to pay for the enormous advance in wealth, population, and glory anticipated from the System of 1836. Classification of the public works, the editor insisted, had been "broached for no other purpose than that of influencing the coming gubernatorial election; and as soon as that is over, we shall hear but little said on that subject."[46] Partisan politics had much to do with the mounting criticism of taxes and the improvement system, but the disaffection was deeper than mere campaign rhetoric.

The increase and northward spread of population during the thirties led to a special apportionment for counties of northern Indiana. The general apportionment of 1831 had distributed thirty senators and seventy-five representatives among sixty-three counties. In December, 1833, Governor Noble told legislators that in "several instances" the great increase in population and inequality among districts had resulted in special apportionments. He urged an additional senator and three more representatives for various counties of northern Indiana.[47] The *Indiana Journal* lashed out at Representative John H. Thompson, from Clark County on the Ohio River, who, it said, agreed that additional representation was needed but argued that special apportionments were contrary to the state constitution. Representative David Kilgore, from Delaware County and part of the area seeking further representation, contended that special apportionments could be made at any time. He said some gentlemen insisted on more polls for new counties than the apportionment of 1831 had required for old ones. Kilgore asserted that Thompson was from the portion of the state that had "always opposed the north in her projects of internal improvements."[48] The General Assembly concurred with the governor and added one senator and three representatives for several northern counties.[49]

In preparing for the general apportionment of 1836, Governor Noble advised the legislature of two key problems in making a fair apportionment. One was the "great disparity in the size and population of the counties," and second was the reluctance to reduce the number of members which might "be necessary to [achieve] a just and equal apportionment." Noble further advised that any material increase in the number of lawmakers might "lessen the usefulness and business capacity" of the legislature. The members, however, disregarded this counsel and established forty-seven senatorial and 100 representative districts and apportioned them among seventy-six *organized* counties.[50] Of the *organized* counties, many of them received one representative, a number received two, Rush obtained three, and Dearborn and Wayne were each given four. In several instances two or three organized counties were combined and given one representative jointly. The *paper* districts, for senatorial as well as representative purposes, were attached to legislative districts comprised of one or two organized counties. For the organized counties, only Wayne gained two senators. Many counties received their own senator, and some senatorial districts embraced two or three organized counties. The paper county of Jasper was divided for both representative and senatorial purposes, but no organized county was so divided. The paper counties were located in generally sparsely settled parts of northern Indiana.[51] There were glaring inconsistencies between the voice some counties gained in the House versus that for the Senate. Counties which seem to have gained less representation in the House than they should have received, at times appear to have been given generous representation in the Senate. By the use of a number of "floats" various counties gained extra representation in the House for stated years, again perhaps frequently in recognition of their being otherwise shortchanged. With the large increase in the number of legislative districts over that given for 1831, many incumbents could seek reelection in the same or but little changed districts they already represented.[52] The apportionment of 1836 was significant in that for the first time members of the House from Central Indiana had more voting power than members from Southern Indiana.[53]

Several changes were made in the election code during Noble's tenure as chief executive. The continued failure of the secretary of state to receive a certificate of the county vote for governor and lieutenant governor from some circuit court clerks resulted in a law mandating clerks to forward such a certificate to the speaker of the House in addition to one already due the secretary of state. But this neglect persisted and a further enactment required the secretary of state to inform local prosecutors concerning negligent clerks as a basis for suits against them.[54] As population thickened there were suggestions that further polling places be opened, that voting be extended over more than one day, and that individuals be required to vote in the township in which they resided.[55] The attempt to "confine voters" to their own townships—and thus prohibit voting at county seats—failed as did that to allow more than one day for an election, but an 1834 law authorized county boards to "open an additional place of holding elections at the county seat, or in any township in the county, where the votes usually polled exceed eight hundred." An unsuccessful effort was made to make the act of knowingly giving an illiterate person a ballot containing a name other than that represented to him punishable by fine or otherwise. The last legislature under Noble required that elections by the General Assembly for United States senators and other officials, except for the secretary, treasurer, and auditor as well as president judges of the circuit courts, be viva voce.[56]

Two vacancies on the Supreme Court gave Noble a decisive role in selecting replacement judges. Early in 1836 Judge Stephen C. Stevens resigned from the state's highest court effective March 1.[57] When the General Assembly met in December the governor told legislators that the judge had resigned because the office "would not support his family." Noble explained that no one sought the office and "most of the senior members of the Bar" had been offered an appointment, but all of them had rejected the offer. Then "at the urgent request of the Bar" a "distinguished individual" had accepted a recess appointment with the reservation that he could surrender the office at his pleasure. Thus Charles Dewey became a member of the court on May 30. In January, 1837, by a vote of 43 to 0, the Senate approved the governor's nomination of Dewey to complete the final year of Stevens' term.[58] Although Dewey was a Whig, the *Indiana Democrat* viewed his acceptance "as a sacrifice of private interest to the public good." Its editor asserted: "A better appointment could not have been made." The pro-Whig *Indiana Journal* said Dewey had accepted after "the urgent and unanimous solicitation of the members of the bar, at a great sacrifice of personal interest." The sacrifice, however, was somewhat lessened because early in 1837 the General Assembly raised the salary of Supreme judges from $1,000 to $1,500 annually.[59] Nevertheless, following the death of Judge John T. McKinney in March, 1837, the governor again had considerable trouble obtaining a successor. Miles C. Eggleston may have indicated acceptance and then changed his mind.[60] Former Judge Stevens, saying that he was writing at the request of Eggleston, Joseph G. Marshall, Jeremiah Sullivan, and others, offered to return to the court if the governor wanted him to do so. But Sullivan, who may at first have declined appointment, began a recess appointment in May to complete the last year for which McKinney had been chosen.[61] As Noble's term ended in December, 1837, the Supreme Court consisted of three well qualified judges: Dewey, Sullivan, and Isaac Blackford, the latter having served since 1817.

Meanwhile the efforts to develop the economy during the thirties resulted in the abandonment of economic laissez faire as state government tried to hasten economic development through heavy participation in banking and internal improvements. From the death of the disreputable First State Bank in the early twenties until the establishment of the Second State Bank in 1834, the commonwealth was without chartered banks except for the apparently intermittent existence of the Farmers and Mechanics Bank of Indiana at Madison. But a circulating medium was not lacking, thanks to the widespread use of notes from banks of other states and especially those from the Second United States Bank which had branches on the Indiana border at Cincinnati and Louisville. Late in 1833 Treasurer Samuel Merrill, speaking of this national bank, which had opened in 1817, stated that through it "our citizens have been extensively supplied with capital, which they much needed, and which they could not, in those times procure elsewhere on any reasonable terms."[62]

The movement for another state bank gained momentum in the late twenties and early thirties. With the passage of time and arrival of numerous additional settlers, the memory of the discredited First State Bank had waned. An expanding economy and population base amid developing prosperity provided a growing need for banking facilities. Moreover, as the number and aggregate of various special funds increased, legislators were concerned about their safekeeping and how to increase their proceeds. At the legislative session of 1827–1828, a state loan office was created under the supervision of the state treasurer.[63] During the session of 1829–1830, a representative proposed that a select committee consider the expediency of establishing a state bank at Indianapolis with three or four branches elsewhere, its stock to be based "upon the capital of the seminary, school, and canal and such other disposable" funds controlled by the legislature. In the Senate John Sering proposed that a bank, based upon the capital of certain funds, "would greatly aid the state in a proposed system of internal improvements . . . ". According to an Indianapolis paper, the bank proposed by Senator Sering was to be capitalized at $2,000,000, with half of the stock owned by the state and half by individuals. The bank would be located at the capital, with branches at other points. These efforts were premature, as was a further effort by Sering at the ensuing session.[64] They are, however, significant because they show that the movement for another state bank predated Jackson's veto of the effort to renew the charter of the Second Bank of the United States in 1832.

But a state bank, with branches, was not the only alternative suggested for obtaining an expanded circulating medium. Although a branch of the Second United States Bank had never been opened in Indiana, at its session in 1831–1832 the General Assembly memorialized this bank for one or more branches within the state. While this memorial was under consideration, a select committee chaired by Senator Sering contended that such a branch would stimulate commerce; aid the mechanic and manufacturer;

enlarge capital for buying and transporting surplus produce of the
country; and deter the circulation of notes from local banks of
other states, thus checking the evil of a depreciated currency. The
committee viewed the banking article of the Constitution of 1816
as intended to prevent such currency from banks under legislative
authority, and it presumed that congressional legislation superseded the state constitution regarding currency of the United
States. One representative, Marinus Willett of Rush County,
lodged a protest against the memorial. The contemplated federal
branch, he argued, would violate both the spirit and letter of the
state constitution. Moreover, it would also aid a secret, monied
corporation and foster "an undue aristocracy in the country."[65]
Nicholas Biddle, the bank's president, acknowledged receipt of Indiana's petition and another one signed by "many members of the
Legislature" recommending Indianapolis as a proper site for a
branch. Three men from the Lafayette area asked Senator John
Tipton to support a branch at that Wabash River town.[66] A recharter of the Farmers and Mechanics Bank of Indiana was another alternative which seems to have been contemplated by some, however, this institution liquidated its business following the expiration
of its charter at the beginning of 1835.[67]

Any prospect that a branch or branches of the Second United
States Bank might be opened in Indiana was blasted by Jackson's
veto, July 10, 1832, of a bill to renew its charter. The veto augmented the need for banking facilities and served as a boon for
another state bank. In addressing members of the General Assembly in December, 1832, Governor Noble referred to the pecuniary embarrassments which citizens generally were experienc-
ing. He told legislators that "among the remedies spoken of, to
prevent the further aggravation of the evils of a decreasing circulation, to mitigate the existing distress, the establishment of a
State Bank and branches seems to be concentrating the largest
share of public attention." The plan for a bank, as he understood
it, called for a capitalization of perhaps $800,000 with ownership
divided equally between the state and individuals. The public
stock would be purchased through a thirty year loan at 5 percent
interest that would be repaid from dividends.[68]

Substantial support for a new state bank existed among both Jacksonian Democrats and National Republicans. The staunchly pro-Jacksonian Indianapolis *Indiana Democrat* suggested that states as well as individuals might justly seek gain from banking. "We may as well pay interest into the state treasury, and reduce our taxes thereby," the editor observed, "as to pay it to eastern capitalists and foreigners. A portion of the stock can be taken by the state, and a portion by individuals." Anticipating the early demise of the national bank, the *Indiana Democrat* regarded a state bank as "the best possible substitute." Its charter should be very carefully drawn, with proper restrictions, but the fact that one state bank had failed did not mean that another, under different circumstances, would have a similar fate. The pro-National Republican Indianapolis *Indiana Journal*, while endorsing a state bank and branches, vigorously attacked Jackson's bank policy. "If the President had signed the bill re-chartering the bank of the United States," its editor stated, "the clamor which pervades the western country for the establishment of state banks would probably not have been heard." The editor asserted that the anticipated withdrawal of the circulating medium of the national bank would greatly reduce the price of property and produce sacrifices which could have been avoided.[69] There were manifestations of popular support for a bank and branches from various parts of the state, but although a bank bill passed the House by a considerable majority at the session of 1832–1833, it failed in the Senate by a narrow margin.[70] Senator Calvin Fletcher, rather than vote for a bill which he viewed as creating a principal bank and branches as "in effect, separate and independent corporations, such as are not authorized by the provisions of our constitution," resigned from the Senate because of his inability to support a measure which he believed most of his constituents wanted him to sustain. Writing from Washington before he could have known that the legislature had adjourned without chartering a bank, Senator John Tipton told Fletcher that he concurred with him in the "opinion that a state Bank with 9 or even 5 Branches will be a curse to the state, and the people will see it when it is too late."[71]

The bank question became a basic issue in the state election in August, 1833. After adjournment of the General Assembly, the

Indiana Democrat vigorously urged the governor to call a special session of the assembly to expedite the founding of a state bank and branches. It reported meetings in which many citizens expressed approval of the proposed bank, at times also urging a special session of the legislature. The *Indiana Journal* believed that a large majority of the people wanted a state bank, but added that many of them considered it unwise to have a session prior to the election with the same legislators present as had failed to approve one at the regular session. As time passed without a call for a special session, the *Indiana Democrat* urged voters to elect legislators who would support a state bank.[72] Following the August election the rival party organs at the capital continued their support for a state bank. In listing about a dozen banks around the country which had been selected to receive deposits of federal money, the *Indiana Democrat* gleefully suggested that the State Bank of Indiana might as well be added to the list "as there is no doubt such an institution will receive a charter during the coming winter." When the General Assembly convened in December, Governor Noble neither recommended nor opposed a bank but told legislators that presumably they had "come prepared to speak the public sentiment and to act upon it advisedly." If members opted for a bank, the executive urged that it be safeguarded from political influence, from abuses of directors and employees, and from loss of money on the part of the public.[73]

Proponents of a state bank had decided majorities in both houses for the 1833–1834 legislative session. Early in the session the Senate received a report from Treasurer Samuel Merrill offering information and evaluations about banking, pursuant to its resolution of the previous session.[74] Although Merrill stated that he had not had any experience in banking, he exhibited much understanding about banking in western states. He noted that about seventy-six of eighty-five banks founded in Ohio, Kentucky, Tennessee, Indiana, and Illinois prior to 1830 had failed, explaining that those which had survived had largely ceased doing business of importance. According to Merrill, these western banks had been principally created "to *borrow* and not to *lend*"; their "floods of circulating paper" had impoverished the community, often causing personal and real property to depreciate to one fourth its former value. Banks had been located where not needed, mainly managed "by persons, whose confidence was in exact proportion to their lack of experience," and loose business practices had prevailed.[75] Merrill estimated that $300,000 might be obtained from special funds for investment in bank capital within five years, plus perhaps an equal amount in an additional five year period. The treasurer bluntly advised against investing these funds in state stock, because "the experience, regularity and caution necessary to succeed in banking, cannot always be expected from the Legislature." Despite this jeremiad, Merrill granted that the "wisdom of the Legislature" might devise a plan for a bank free of most of those evils, and he offered suggestions for consideration if one was chartered.[76] Various of his suggestions were incorporated in the charter which passed the House by the overwhelming vote of 49 to 24 and the Senate by the comfortable margin of 18 to 11, winning substantial support from Jacksonians and anti-Jacksonians alike.[77] Within both houses, however, there was much sentiment for reducing the number of branches.[78] United States Senator John Tipton wrote Calvin Fletcher that he had decided that a state bank should be established. Tipton predicted that the federal deposits would not be returned to the national bank and that this bank could not be rechartered.[79] A few years later Governor Noble asserted that establishing the state bank had been "rather a matter of necessity than choice; and that necessity grew out of the discontinuance of the late National Bank."[80] Certainly Jackson's successful opposition to the Second United States Bank fostered chartering of the Second State Bank.

The charter of the new state bank was drawn with considerable care and foresight.[81] This lengthy document authorized the immediate opening of ten branch banks, plus another after the expiration of one year and a twelfth at the end of three years. The charter was valid until January 1, 1857. The authorized capital was set at $1,600,000 or $160,000 for each branch, to be owned half by the state and half by individuals. Shares were in units of $50, with subscription payments due in specie. Individual subscribers had to pay $18.75 per share as down payment, and the remainder in two equal annual installments. The state was required to make a down payment of $50,000 on its stock for each branch, with the residue payable in two equal annual installments. Borrowing up to $1,300,000 was authorized to pay for all public stock and cover loans to individuals as an advance for payment of their two installments. In obtaining shares preference was to be given residents over non-residents, individuals over corporations, and small buyers over large ones. As the number of shares individuals held increased, the voting power per share decreased.[82]

The management and control of the bank was a partnership between the state and individual stockholders. Its leading officer was a president, elected by the General Assembly for five years. Enormous power was given a state bank board composed of four directors named by the assembly, who served four year terms on a rotating basis, plus one elected annually by each branch bank board. The president chaired meetings of the state board, voted in case of a tie, called special sessions when he deemed them desirable, and transacted business normally pertaining to this office. Among the powers conferred on the state board were: the examination, without warning, of each branch at least every six months by one or more of its members; the prescribing of bylaws and uniform accounting procedures for the branches; the obtaining of monthly reports of banking transactions and trial balances from the branches, with a complete settlement of accounts not less than twice yearly; and the suspension or closing of branches for insolvency or mismanagement. The state board was authorized to appoint a cashier and such other officials and employees as needed. The day to day operations of the branches were under the direction of local boards. These branch boards included three members named annually by the state board, and from seven to ten members elected yearly by private stockholders. Branch directors chose a cashier and appointed other officials and employees as needed.[83]

Both the General Assembly and the governor had much control over the bank. The president and four members of the state board were subject to recall by the assembly. No branch could be opened by the state board beyond the twelve authorized in the charter, nor could the stock of any branch be increased, save with legislative approval. Both the state and branch boards were mandated to give detailed reports to the legislature annually, and if the condition of the bank seemed unfavorable this body could appoint an agent to investigate the institution. If the evidence from the examination warranted, or if the governor had reason to believe that the charter had been violated, he was to have suit entered against the bank. No amendment could be made to the charter, unless approved by the General Assembly.[84]

Several significant restrictions and safeguards were enjoined upon the bank by its charter. The note issue could not exceed twice the actual capital paid in, nor could debts due exceed the same. The loan and discount rate could not exceed 6 percent per annum, compounded in advance. Its notes for circulation must be in units of not less than $5, and its charter was to be forfeited if it failed to pay specie for its paper. The bank was forbidden to deal in real estate, except as required for transaction of its business or to dispose of that received in payment of debts. Although the stockholders of each branch retained their earned dividends, in case of failure to meet obligations the stockholders of all branches were liable therefor. Key state officials could not hold important positions with the bank, and certain bank officials were ineligible for a seat in the legislature. Branch directors allowing debts due their branch to exceed twice its paid in capital were personally liable for the excess loaned, while in case of fraudulent insolvency they were personally liable for losses suffered by creditors and stockholders.[85]

Various features of the bank's charter are worthy of note. In contrast to the First State Bank, the Second State Bank was a partnership between the state and private stockholders. Inasmuch as the stockholders of each branch retained their dividends, while all stockholders were mutually liable if any branch failed, there was a strong inducement in favor of success and against failure. The establishment of *equal branches throughout the state, without any central or parent bank over them*, was especially suited to the decentralized economy of the day. The provision for early addition of two branches for northern Indiana exhibited both foresight and a sense of fairness concerning this least developed section of the state. The levy of twelve and a half cents annually on each share of private stock toward the support of common schools, combined with the promise that all profit from state stock above its cost would be likewise applied, reflected the growing concern about public support of elementary education.[86]

Steps were taken at once toward organization of the new bank. Immediately after approval of the charter the General Assembly elected Samuel Merrill its president and named the four public members of the state bank board, including Calvin Fletcher.[87] In mid-February the president and these directors located the ten initial branches and named commissioners to take private stock subscriptions for each branch. Four branches were located on the Ohio River at Lawrenceburg, Madison, New Albany, and Evansville. Three were placed at Vincennes, Terre Haute, and Lafayette on the Wabash. Of the remaining branches, those at Richmond and Indianapolis, like the one at Terre Haute, were on the National Road, while the branch at Bedford was the only one within the interior of southern Indiana.[88] Thus seven branches were located on the Ohio and Wabash rivers, and eight of the total were situated around the perimeter of the state from Richmond southward around to Terre Haute. The Lafayette unit was the only branch located north of the National Road. The largest of these towns, New Albany and Madison, were mere villages of a few thousand residents.

Before the bank could open, down payments *in specie* had to be made for both state and private stock subscriptions. By mid-May individuals had taken all of the $80,000 of private stock for each branch. During the summer the Wabash and Erie Canal Fund Commissioners borrowed $500,000 to enable the state to make its down payment. When the state bank board met on November 17, down payments had been completed on individual stock for all branches, local stockholders had named branch bank officials, and each branch board had named its delegate to the state board. At the November meeting the state board subscribed for the state stock.[89] Two days later the governor declared the bank ready for business. In addressing the legislature early in December Governor Noble reported: "The State Bank has just commenced operations under very favourable circumstances. The stock in all the branches authorized, was subscribed by individuals, and the instalment paid as required by the charter."[90]

The Second State Bank enjoyed much success amid the peak prosperity of the midthirties. President Merrill, in a report to legislators at the end of its first year, asserted that "The operations of the several branches present, on the whole, a state of prosperity wholly unequalled in institutions and a community circumstanced like ours." Merrill noted the "highly prosperous" status of agriculture and the rapid withdrawal of the paper of the national bank, which had previously been the state's "chief circulation," as among the "most favorable auspices" encouraging the bank's success. A House committee, chaired by Richard W. Thompson of Lawrence County, oozed optimism in viewing the bank as more safe and prosperous than anticipated by its friends. Stating that the demand for its notes had exceeded their supply, the committee observed that they were as much sought for "in the neighboring States, and in the eastern and southern cities, as the paper of any other western State Bank."[91] According to President Merrill the bank returned a dividend of 3 percent for its initial year, 9 percent for its second, and 8 percent for the third year.[92] The rapid expansion of the business of the Second State Bank and its very strong financial position is indicated by the table which follows.

DOCUMENT C.[93]
Table showing the Capital, Discounts, Circulation and Specie of the Bank at different periods.

Date	Capital	Discounts	Circulation	Specie
Jan. 1, 1835	$800,000.00	$529,843.75	$456,065	$751,083.29
April 4, 1835	800,000.00	1,085,261.87	879,000	632,800.80
July 11, 1835	800,000.00	1,228,224.82	1,186,795	723,584.47
Oct. 3, 1835	800,000.00	1,496,638.24	1,361,430	700,201.85
Jan. 9, 1836	1,279,857.78	2,304,683.19	1,981,650	874,340.25
April 2, 1836	1,279,935.90	2,768,384.56	2,101,065	995,463.09
July 9, 1836	1,279,921.88	2,776,905.87	2,057,300	1,096,820.28
Oct 3, 1836	1,310,000.00	2,747,155.57	1,834,310	997,118
Jan. 7, 1837	1,782,813.50	3,914,933.53	2,157,595	1,236,164.35
April 1, 1837	1,824,921.88	4,314,825.13	2,498,960	1,177,776.96
July 8, 1837	1,845,000.00	3,821,561.12	2,475,385	1,112,719.44
Sept. 30, 1837	1,845,000.00	3,562,491.67	2,378,075	1,158,887.72
Dec. 23, 1837	1,900,687.50	3,520,163.35	2,288,458	1,291,265.42

The above is extracted from the "General Statement of the State Bank of Indiana and Branches." S. MERRILL Jan. 23, 1838. The prosperity of the midthirties created a demand for new branches, increased bank capital, and amendments to the charter. In November, 1835, Governor Noble proclaimed the opening of the eleventh branch at Fort Wayne.[94] A number of additional branches were sought, but none was opened while Noble was chief executive.[95] In December, 1837, as Noble's administration ended and seven months after the onset of the Panic of 1837, the state bank board considered "The inexpediency of creating new branches, . . . is so apparent, that few are disposed to object to the delay."[96] Meantime, in 1836 the charter was amended to permit the state bank board to allow any branch to increase its capital to $250,000, the increase to be raised entirely by private subscriptions of stock. The state, however, could subscribe for half of the increase if it so desired. At the same time the state bank board was authorized to allow the branches or any of them to have both debts owed by and debts owed to them to be raised from twice its capital to an *average* of two and one half times its capital. This allowed an expansion of credit at busy season provided there was a corresponding contraction of it at other times.[97] As Noble completed his administration the Second State Bank had been established on a solid and successful foundation. Though not without its critics, especially after the beginning of the Panic of 1837, it had substantial bipartisan support both within and without the legislature.

Meanwhile, during the thirties there were continuing efforts to improve transportation facilities by opening and repairing roads and to a lesser extent by restricting man-made obstructions to navigation of rivers. The growth of population, which had more than doubled in the twenties and nearly doubled in the thirties, increased the need for these efforts. The rapid spread of population over central Indiana, and to some extent northern Indiana, enhanced this need. And the substantial rise in the volume of agricultural produce and manufacturing goods augmented the demand for country roads and navigable rivers. Furthermore, the attempt to develop a basic network of canals, railroads, and turnpikes, via the Wabash and Erie Canal and the Internal Improvements System of 1836, stimulated the need for facilities tributary to this anticipated network.

With increased use roads often became worse rather than better, especially during rainy seasons or winter and spring thaws. As travelers dodged stumps, rocks, mud holes, ruts, ponds, and other obstructions, it was frequently difficult or even impossible to determine which was the correct route. Roads through prairies lacked some of these obstacles, but they often led through swamps and ponds that were at times impenetrable. When Hugh McCulloch reminisced about his initial visit to Indianapolis in the spring of 1833, he observed that "nothing had been done to the streets except to remove the stumps from two or three of those most used. There were no sidewalks, and the streets most in use, after every rain, and for a good part of the year, were knee-deep with mud." Describing the capital as an "almost inaccessible village," McCulloch asserted that "Upon none of the roads were wagons in use, even for carrying the mails, except those from Madison and Terre Haute to the capital. From all other points it could only be reached by those who travelled on foot or on horseback." On proceeding to Delphi he approached this town on a "country road" that "ran through sloughs which must have been at times bottomless, and over brooks . . . too deep to be forded after heavy rains . . . ."[98] Calvin Fletcher used his diary to comment about "Mud so deep" in the capital city that he "could scarcely [*sic*] get from street to street," and of nearly impassable roads during trips out of Indianapolis. He recorded the danger to his life from being caught in a storm or being dumped from a horse in crossing a swollen stream. Of one such crossing Fletcher commented: "I was in a great peril but by a good Providence I was preserved." When a Logansport editor reported that the Michigan Road was in "a most pitiable condition," a wag suggested it be converted into a canal by the addition of a towpath.[99]

As previously the responsibility for opening and maintaining roads rested largely with local officials and citizens. Pursuant to the revised code of 1831 county boards annually divided their townships into one or more districts, then the voters in each township elected road supervisors for these districts. Unless exempted, males from twenty-one to fifty donated two days of personal road labor yearly. Owners of land, nonresidents included, were each year charged a road tax equal to half the state levy. Landowners could work out their tax, at the rate of fifty cents a day, either in person or through a substitute. Each day's labor at the request of the supervisor that included a plow or wagon with a team of oxen or horses counted as three days. Anyone failing to perform labor owed was subject to a fine of fifty cents for each day missed. If work was needed beyond that resulting from personal labor and the road tax, the supervisor was to obtain it from owners of land in proportion to the road tax levied on them. Supervisors were paid seventy-five cents per day, but they worked out their two days of personal labor at the fifty cent rate. If a supervisor failed to erect and maintain a post at the fork of a road, indicating the way and distance to important places, he was subject to a fine of five dollars. With the transition to the ad valorem tax plan in 1836 the two days of personal labor were retained. Compared with the road legislation of earlier years, that of the 1830s increased the burden on owners of land and reduced the personal labor of adult males.[100]

The location and relocation of state roads was a costly and time consuming task of legislative sessions. In the midthirties a House committee asserted that from statehood "more of the time of the legislature has been occupied on the subject of roads, than that of any other one object of legislation." This committee observed that "a very large proportion of the petitions praying the legislature to locate state roads, are predicated on the hope of obtaining a part of" the Three Per Cent Fund for their support.[101] During the twenties and early thirties several dozen state roads had been designated Three Per Cent roads, each receiving an appropriation to be spent under a commissioner or commissioners named by the General Assembly.[102] A contemporary observed that some of these roads had become "a great convenience both to the citizens of the state and to travellers and emigrants, while others have been suffered to go out of repair, and are now useless." How best to use the Three Per Cent Fund gained importance during the thirties, the decade for peak sales from Indiana land offices. Whereas the aggregate yield from the fund had been $119,294.32

at the end of 1831, by late 1837 the total had soared to $438,100.61. The revenue from this source while Noble was governor exceeded the tax revenue collected for the ordinary costs of state government.[103]

Although the General Assembly continued to locate state roads, the use of Three Per Cent revenue was placed mainly under county boards. Legislative appropriations in 1831, 1833, 1836, and 1837 gave each county $400, $500, $2,000, and $2,000 respectively of this money. These enactments, however, frequently required that designated roads, bridges, and rivers have priority in the expenditures.[104] An act of 1832 gave county boards much autonomy in *relocating* state roads in an effort "to prevent useless and expensive applications to the General Assembly" about changes in routes.[105]

Governor Noble and various legislators objected to the widespread diffusion of the Three Per Cent Fund. After his reelection in 1834 Noble protested that the fund had been "frittered away" on "detached portions" of numerous roads with only temporary improvements obtained. If its revenue from the beginning had been concentrated on "a limited number" of well selected thoroughfares, the governor asserted, "a number of well improved roads" could have been achieved. Noble and some legislators recommended that a large sum be borrowed in anticipation of Three Per Cent revenue for use in improving a basic network.[106] The imperfect results achieved by the federal government in building the National Road across Indiana, despite large expenditures on it, suggests that concentration of Three Per Cent revenue on "a limited number" of roads would almost certainly have not resulted in a "well improved" network. A House committee observed that its appropriations were important in enabling citizens "to pay into the public treasury the revenue wherewith they are charged." The committee also considered these disbursements "well calculated" to allay objections against the proposed state system of internal improvements and to indicate to "all reasonable persons, that no part of the state is entirely left unprovided for."[107] This decentralization of expenditures perhaps prompted the legislature to abolish the Three Per Cent agent and transfer his duties to the treasurer of state.[108]

While the federally supplied Three Per Cent Fund was being diffused, Congress gave much aid for construction of the National and Michigan roads which crossed Indiana, intersecting at Indianapolis. Commenced at Cumberland, Maryland, in 1811, and often projected to the Mississippi at St. Louis as its western terminal, not until 1827 was the route of the National Road established through the state via Richmond, Indianapolis, and Terre Haute. From 1829 through 1838, when federal aid ended, Congress appropriated an aggregate of $1,085,000 or roughly $7,233.33 per mile for the approximately 150 miles of this segment.[109] Under the direction of federal officials, the money was spent for right of way, removal of timber, grubbing stumps from a center strip, erecting culverts and bridges, and applying stone and gravel. Although doubtless the best constructed road in the state for the pioneer era, in seeking an appropriation of $500,000 for its improvement in 1838 the General Assembly claimed that it was "in such [a] situation, as to be in a great measure impassible [sic], even by the mails of the United States."[110] By this time, however, federal largesse for the National Road had ended; and Congress had turned over that portion of the road in Maryland, Virginia, Pennsylvania, and Ohio to those states. Meanwhile, the Indiana segment had been used, even as its construction and repair continued, by teamsters, stage owners, and citizens generally. It had been a boon to towns and settlements along its route, and many emigrants to central and northern Indiana traversed this national thoroughfare.[111]

The Michigan Road became an important north-south road, stretching from the Ohio River to Lake Michigan. Financed by a federal grant of one section of land for each of its approximately 264 miles, in 1830 the legislature named Noah Noble a commissioner to supervise its opening from Madison to the present site of Michigan City via Versailles, Napoleon, Greensburg, Shelbyville, Indianapolis, Logansport, and South Bend. With Noble's elevation as governor, William Polke became commissioner and completed its opening.[112] The approximately $252,000 obtained from the federally donated sections was mainly spent on cutting and removing timber, grading the roadways, bridges, and some application of stone and gravel.[113] This road, however, was little if any better than other state roads.[114] As was the National Road, it was much used for travel and by persons settling in central and northern portions of the state.[115] Even before Noble left office, the process of turning the road over to local maintenance had begun.[116]

Meantime, there was rising interest in turnpikes. A turnpike, often called a macadamized road, suggested a highway from which timber, including stumps, had at least largely been removed; the right of way considerably graded; some bridges added; and a significant amount of stone or gravel applied.[117] Charters to private companies for building turnpikes had been granted before Noble became governor, but their number increased during his tenure. According to these charters, construction and maintenance costs would be covered by tolls collected from users. If even one such turnpike was completed and put in operation, either before or during the thirties, evidence thereof has not been found by this author. Two state sponsored turnpikes, however, were commenced as a part of the System of 1836.[118]

As trails and roads spread over the state, crossings of rivers became more numerous, frequently forded without ferries or bridges. The revised code of 1831 empowered county boards to locate ferries and license persons in charge of them. It required ferry keepers to have an adequate boat or boats and a sufficient number of skilled ferrymen to provide service "from day-light in the morning until dark in the evening, so that no unnecessary delay may happen to persons" using them. Toll rates were set by county boards, with the night charge twice that for day service. River banks were to be maintained sufficiently low to be passable for horses and loaded wagons. For unnecessary delay in providing passage by daylight, a keeper was subject to a fine of up to $100.[119] As this legislation indicates, ferries were public utilities of substantial importance. In 1834 the Washington County Circuit Court held a ferryman liable for the loss of salt and other items at his ferry over the "Muscattituck" River because a wagoner's loss had resulted from a broken chain on account of negligence by the keeper. Further evidence of the public utility nature of ferries is suggested by the provision in the 1831 code exempting necessarily employed ferrymen from road labor for personal service, jury service, and militia duty except in time of public danger or war.[120] A number of bridges were built in the thirties. The revised code of 1831 empowered county boards to use donations or subscriptions to finance them. A board could arrange for an individual or individuals to erect a toll bridge.[121] The General Assembly also chartered private companies to erect toll bridges, often over the larger streams; designated modest sums for bridges from the Three Per Cent Fund; and provided for bridges on the Michigan Road from revenue obtained by sale of the federally granted land for its opening.[122] Congress appropriated money for bridges which were erected on the National Road, including one over the East Fork of the Whitewater at Richmond and the West Fork of White River at Indianapolis.[123] Consideration was given to a bridge across the Ohio River at Louisville by joint effort of Kentucky and Indiana, but this attempt was premature.[124] A private company, which included John Tipton and Calvin Fletcher as stockholders, opened a bridge over the Wabash at Logansport in 1838, but it was poorly constructed and became a costly venture for Fletcher.[125]

Despite the continued badness of the roads a stagecoach network rapidly developed. Stage lines usually depended on revenue from federal mail contracts as well as that received for conveying passengers and light freight. The initial stagecoach line in Indiana was almost certainly that started in 1820 by a mail contractor on the Great Western Mail route between Louisville and St. Louis via Vincennes.[126] According to a postal announcement in 1826, the former territorial capital had twice weekly mail by stagecoach from both Louisville and St. Louis. A weekly mail then extended to Terre Haute and Crawfordsville on the north, to Princeton, New Harmony, Mount Vernon, and Evansville on the south. Two years later another advertisement announced thrice weekly mail via stage to and from Louisville and St. Louis. An editor, after noting that mail would be "conveyed in four horse stages," proudly asserted that henceforth "the Eastern mail will be but ten days in its passage from Washington City," adding "Who could have anticipated this ten years ago?"[127] In 1828 a mail stage began between Madison and Indianapolis, apparently providing the first such service between the capital and an Ohio River town.[128]

By the late 1830s a stage network had spread over settled areas of the state. Indianapolis, its principal hub, developed at least intermittent connections with towns around the perimeter of the southern half of the state, including Richmond, Brookville, Lawrenceburg, Madison, Jeffersonville, New Albany, Leavenworth, Evansville, Vincennes, and Terre Haute. Stage lines operated on the Great Western Mail route through Vincennes as well as on the road from Evansville via Vincennes, and Terre Haute to Lafayette and Logansport. By 1837 Logansport had stage connections with Indianapolis, Lafayette, Fort Wayne, Goshen, and Monticello.[129] Already Indianapolis was viewed as an important crossroads for transportation. A local editor boasted that travelers would find "conveyances at this place, to almost any point of the compass."[130]

As stage travel became more common it also became faster. Although the announced schedule for the trip from Indianapolis to Madison in 1828 called for four days of travel on this approximately ninety mile route, four years later the suggested time was only two days. In 1836, if the advertised schedule was met, a student attending Indiana College could leave Indianapolis early in the morning and arrive at Bloomington, some fifty miles distant, that evening. From this point "speedy passage" was available to Louisville or Leavenworth.[131] Travel cost per passenger often varied from a few to several cents a mile. Proprietors described their coaches as good or improved, horses as good or fine, fares as moderate, and scenery along the way as attractive. Drivers were said to be experienced, sober, and careful.[132] Nonetheless, serious accidents occurred. Congressman John Test and his wife were injured in an accident near Lawrenceburg, while a driver lost his life in an upset west of Paoli.[133] Early in 1838 the legislature provided penalties against owners failing to equip their stages with two good lamps, and for drivers who neglected to keep them lit at night when the road could not be "distinctly seen" from the driver's seat. A driver guilty of intoxication "to such a degree as to endanger the safety of the passengers" was to be fired. Drivers were subject to fines if horses were left untied or unattended while passengers were aboard, and likewise for racing horses to pass or keep from being passed by another stage.[134]

While a stage network became a reality, a network of railroads was anticipated. After visiting the capital late in 1831 when the legislature was in session, Samuel Milroy wrote John Tipton that "the Rail Road favour [fever], appears to be giting up—."[135] So it was, for that session chartered eight private railroad companies, the first in the state, and a number of charters followed as the thirties advanced. These companies were given generous terms regarding right of ways and rates for tolls. The proposed lines were mainly intrastate routes, usually having at least one terminal on an important waterway, particularly the Ohio or Wabash river.[136] Some of them promised rail connection with distant markets. What became known as the Baltimore and Ohio, to link Indiana with the Atlantic at Baltimore, was such a route. Another line contemplated terminals at Charleston, South Carolina, and Lake Michigan. The Lawrenceburg and Indianapolis Railroad Company, later loaned money pursuant to the System of 1836, was viewed as part of this line.[137]

Railroad construction possibly began at Shelbyville in 1834 on a segment of the proposed line connecting Indianapolis and Lawrenceburg. According to a local paper, here on July 4 "a car, drawn by one horse," transported at least six hundred persons two and a half miles between 10 a.m. to 6 p.m. with "the greatest eagerness evinced to ride." What the "car" was like is not known, but it almost certainly ran on track made of wood. About one year later there was another celebration and "commencement" of the Lawrenceburg and Indianapolis Railroad at Lawrenceburg with an estimated four or five thousand in attendance.[138] Indiana's first successful railroad, however, was the one begun at Madison in 1836 as part of the internal improvement system of that year.[139] When Noble's term ended Indiana had a *paper network* of railroad lines, but none was in operation. About this time Jesse L. Williams, the state's principal engineer, advised the internal improvement board that for railroads constructed by the state it would probably be "best for the state to furnish the motive power, leaving the cars for the conveyance of freight and passengers, to be furnished by individuals or companies," with the state collecting tolls for use of the road and motive power.[140]

In the absence of good roads, railroads, or canals, Indiana's swelling volume of exports and imports were transported mainly on rivers. Numerous streams had already been declared public highways by legislative fiat, and additional rivers were so designated in the thirties. Among them were Big Raccoon Creek from its mouth to Grimes' Mill in Putnam County, Yellow River from its junction with the Kankakee to Plymouth in Marshall County, and Banbango Creek from its mouth to its main forks in Elkhart County.[141] The purpose of this legislation continued to be to prevent dams and other artificial obstructions from seriously interfering with downstream passage of flatboats. Generally speaking, dams for grist and other mills were permitted provided passage was not obstructed.[142]

Flatboat traffic, which mainly floated into the Ohio and thence down the Mississippi, greatly increased during the thirties. According to a Vincennes editor, apparently reporting concerning the first half of 1836, by late June of that year an estimated eight hundred flatboats had passed there from the upper Wabash, while an equal number had poured out of White River into the Wabash below Vincennes. The editor estimated that the value of freight carried ranged from $1,000 to $8,000 per boat. A local historian has concluded that for "each shipping season" as many as one hundred boats drifted by Eugene, located on the Big Vermillion above its junction with the Wabash. A pioneer resident of Morgan County calculated that an average of about fifteen flatboats per year left this interior county between 1829 and 1853 via the West Fork of White River. Flatboats descending Indiana rivers doubtless annually numbered in the thousands in the thirties.[143]

While exports were conveyed largely by flatboats, imports arrived mainly by steamboats and keelboats. The Ohio-Mississippi waterway was the chief artery for this traffic. By the 1830s steamboats had principally replaced keelboats on the Mississippi, Ohio, and other large rivers.[144] Steamboats on the Ohio and Wabash served a number of river towns which became depots for goods transported by wagon throughout southern and central Indiana.[145]

Numerous steamers plied the Wabash past Vincennes to Terre Haute, and to a lesser degree to Lafayette and occasionally beyond. In August, 1832, the "Vincennes," said to have a capacity of one hundred and fifty tons and proclaimed the "first one built and launched upon the Wabash river," began her career at Vincennes amid "the cheers of hundreds of pleased and anxious spectators."[146] In the spring of 1836 a Vincennes editor stated that at least two hundred steamers had arrived at that place the past season, and that thirteen had arrived in a recent week. According to this editor only a few years earlier the arrival of a steamboat had been a novel sight, but arrivals had become daily occurrences.[147] Steamboats were at times used on the Maumee and St. Joseph (of Lake Michigan) rivers, and on the lower reaches of various tributaries of the Ohio and Wabash such as the Big Vermillion.[148]

Attempts to improve navigation of the Wabash received a high priority from the Indiana legislature because it drained about two thirds of Indiana, one sixth of Illinois, and a bit of Ohio.[149] If made truly navigable to Lafayette, with completion of the Wabash and Erie Canal to that point, Hoosiers would have all water outlets to New York City and New Orleans. At the legislative session of 1833–1834 a House committee noted the "almost unequalled fertility" of the Wabash Valley and estimated the value of its export staples as "at least $550,000 *annually*." The committee, however, stated that steamboat traffic was much restricted because of "formidable obstacles" to navigation just above and below the mouth of White River, causing upstream residents to suffer an "immense tax" in using "Indiana's nobles[t] stream."[150] Rebuffed in efforts to secure federal aid for improvement of the Wabash, in 1834 Indiana appropriated $12,000 for this purpose if matched by a like sum from Illinois. Two years later $50,000 was appropriated for the river's improvement, between Vincennes and its mouth, as part of the Internal Improvements System of 1836, but no significant improvement resulted from these appropriations.[151]

Meantime, Hoosiers successfully sought federal aid for development of a harbor at Michigan City, the northern terminal of the Michigan Road. In one of its requests the General Assembly called Lake Michigan "the Mediterranean of North America," and declared that Michigan City was "becoming, if not already, the Grand commercial Emporium of Northern Indiana." Claiming that Indiana had received less than its share of federal aid for harbors, the legislators "presumed" that $100,000 would not be too much to grant Indiana since millions were being given Michigan, Ohio, Pennsylvania, and New York for this purpose.[152] In 1836, 1837, and 1838 Congress appropriated $110,733.59 for construction of a harbor at Michigan City.[153] As the only truly established town on Indiana's southern shore of Lake Michigan, the future of Michigan City seemed promising with these appropriations.

Indiana's general efforts to improve transportation facilities were on a larger and more varied scale than for the teens and twenties. Nonetheless, transportation facilities remained primitive. Especially needed, however, were through trade routes connecting Indiana with states of the Atlantic Seaboard. The first major effort to achieve such connections came in the thirties with the commencement of the Wabash and Erie Canal in 1832 and the launching of the Mammoth Internal Improvements System of 1836.

While Indiana established the Second State Bank on a solid base, in 1836 she commenced a system of internal improvements on a fragile and shaky foundation. By the early 1830s many citizens had caught the internal improvements fever in a virulent form. As prosperity increased, accompanied by rapid growth in population and the economy, a basic network of canals, railroads, and turnpikes was viewed essential to carry Indiana's expanding exports and imports from and to the state. Numerous politicians and voters alike persuaded themselves that a system of internal improvements could be financed through long term loans paid for largely, if not entirely, by revenue generated by the resulting canals, railroads, and turnpikes. For such a system to be effective, a canal connecting the navigable waters of the Wabash and Maumee rivers was considered a necessity. With the opening of the Erie Canal in 1825, the addition of the proposed canal would make possible transportation by water between Indiana and New York via Lake Erie, the Erie Canal, and the Hudson River. In 1827 Congress offered Indiana five sections of land to aid it in constructing such a waterway. Indiana accepted this offer, agreed to begin the canal within five years and finish it within twenty. Its commencement in 1832 fostered the launching of Indiana's system of internal improvements four years later.[154]

At the legislative session of 1831–1832, the three Wabash and Erie Canal Commissioners, whom the assembly had named earlier, urged an immediate start of the digging. Although Ohio had not yet ratified the compact which Indiana had negotiated with her in 1829, whereby the Buckeye State would build the portion of the canal within her border, the commissioners were optimistic that she would complete her segment. The estimated cost of the canal from the Ohio line to the mouth of the Tippecanoe River, a distance of about 111 miles, was set at $1,100,000 or $10,000 per mile. An aggregate of $756,000 was predicted from the sale of the federal donated canal lands, at an average of $2.10 per acre, leaving $344,000 to be obtained from tolls and other revenue from the canal. If prosecuted with reasonable dispatch, the commissioners asserted, the canal could be built without benefit of tax revenue.[155]

Early in 1832 the General Assembly crossed the Rubicon and instructed the commissioners to contract for the thirty-two miles of the middle division or summit section astride the portage between Fort Wayne and the forks of the Wabash at Huntington. A board of three members, known as the Wabash and Erie Canal Fund Commissioners, was empowered to borrow up to $200,000 to launch the canal. The aggregate of contracts, however, was not to exceed the cash available from the sale of canal tracts. For the repayment of loans with interest, the assembly "irrevocably pledged and appropriated" all proceeds from the canal lands and the canal, the sufficiency of which the state "irrevocably" guaranteed. The canal bill passed the House by a margin of 42 to 31, and the Senate with a vote of 18 for and 12 against. The negative votes came entirely from counties south of the National Road, plus some opposition votes from Wayne and Marion astride the road. Proponents and opponents alike included both Jacksonians and anti-Jacksonians, with division being more along sectional than political lines.[156]

Canal proponents enthusiastically celebrated their victory. Austin W. Morris, of Indianapolis, advised Senator John Tipton that the evening the bill passed the "doings" included "illuminating, firing of guns, the cannon and every thing else down to Indian crackers," plus "*some* wine drank" and a parade to the governor's house. Exuberant celebrations were likewise held in towns along the route for the canal.[157] On February 22 a symbolic start was made at Fort Wayne amid pageantry and oratory, a parade featuring a float representing a canal boat, and an illumination by candlelight in the evening. According to a Logansport paper, at the groundbreaking ceremony, Jordan Vigus, a canal commissioner and grand marshal of the day, proclaimed: "I am now about to commence the *Wabash & Erie Canal*, in the *name* and by the *authority* of the *State of Indiana*." The initial contract was not let until March 1, and only a modest amount of clearing, grubbing, and excavating was done during 1832. Meantime, the Wabash and Erie Commissioners, at times referred to as the contract commissioners, employed Jesse L. Williams, who had been an engineer for canals in Ohio, as the principal engineer for the canal at a salary of $1,800 annually.[158]

Year by year construction inched westward from Fort Wayne along the north side of the Little Wabash. This area was largely wilderness and mainly inhabited by Indians, and laborers were in short supply. One of the canal commissioners went to New York, at times advancing money to prospective workers, obtaining both Irish and Germans to help dig the canal. Laborers were also sought along the Ohio River and within southern Indiana. The Irish became an important part of the labor force, often living in crude shacks, toiling and drinking, and at times fighting among themselves.[159] As contracts were let for construction beyond Huntington, the borrowing was considerably increased. In 1834 the assembly authorized $400,000 of additional borrowing and omitted the restriction that the total of contracts let could not exceed the revenue secured from the sale of canal tracts. On July 4, 1835, the middle or summit section was officially opened for navigation, prompting a Fort Wayne or Summit City editor to proclaim that "Canal navigation in Indiana has now fairly commenced." When the legislature convened in December, the governor referred to this observance as the day on which "our citizens, in assembled thousands, witnessed the waters of the St. Joseph mingling with those of the Wabash, uniting the waters of the northern chain of Lakes with those of the Gulf of Mexico in the south."[160]

As the digging crept down the Wabash Valley, it was deemed desirable to extend the western terminal beyond the Tippecanoe River. In 1834 the canal commissioners, after emphasizing that the interests of the state would before long demand extension of the canal "to some point where canal and steamboats can at all times meet," recommended its construction a short distance farther to Lafayette as the place for "the great mass of steamboat business" on the Wabash River. If this were done, the commissioners advised, the canal should be taken over the Wabash between Logansport and Delphi. Moreover, if brought to the southern side of the Wabash, the canal would afford better connections with other contemplated projects and thus serve many more Hoosiers.[161] In 1836 the decision was made to take the canal over the Wabash River in the pool of a dam several miles north of Delphi.[162] Of more importance, in framing the state system of internal improvements in this year provision was made to extend the Wabash and Erie down the Wabash Valley to Terre Haute and thence southeast to the Central Canal. Inasmuch as the Central was projected to run southward to the Ohio at or near Evansville, it and the Wabash and Erie Canal *promised* continuous navigation between the Ohio River and Lake Erie.[163]

Although the chief object of the Wabash and Erie Canal was to open a waterway to the East, construction lagged on the route between Fort Wayne and Lake Erie. Because much of the canal would be in Ohio, in 1829 Indiana and its eastern neighbor negotiated a compact whereby Ohio would construct and operate the portion within its borders. This compact, however, was not mutually ratified, but another compact in 1834 was so ratified. It provided that the Buckeye State would complete its segment by March 2, 1847. Ohio also promised that it would not charge Hoosiers or other users of the canal higher rates than required of its own citizens, nor more than charged on its principal canals. On its part Indiana conveyed to Ohio the federal land grant of five sections per mile of the canal to help finance its construction. Hoosiers were disappointed regarding Ohio's delay, at times accusing her of stalling to divert traffic to her own improvement system.[164] Nonetheless, in the spring of 1837 Indiana contracted for the digging of the canal to the Ohio border, and by the end of the year the Buckeye State let contracts for its segment.[165]

From 1832 to 1837 inclusive, the digging of the Wabash and Erie Canal proceeded more slowly and was more costly than anticipated. Though far from complete, by late 1837 Indiana had already spent almost $1,320,000 on it and had floated loans totaling $1,327,000, while proceeds from land sales had netted only $250,886.41.[166] Moreover, the impact of the Panic of 1837 remained to be seen, and accusations of favoritism and corruption on the part of canal officials had become serious. In the fall of 1835 federal Senator John Tipton privately stated that "some of the commissioners and engineers have made speculations at the expense of the state and of individuals," but he justified his not publicly exposing them on the grounds that a state system of internal improvements was about to begin and if such conduct became "known to all the people, it would destroy public confidence and do much *mischief at this time.*" Next year the state Board of Internal Improvements announced the "defalcation" of former Commissioner David Burr in the amount of $21,344.59 for which he had "failed to give any satisfactory explanation."[167] Nevertheless, at the end of 1837 Governor Noble announced that navigation was open between Fort Wayne and Peru, and would be extended to Logansport the ensuing spring, for an aggregate of seventy-six miles. Noble too optimistically predicted that "within two years . . . canal boats may pass from the Lake to Lafayette, thus realizing the great object which has so long engaged the attention and solicitude of the State."[168]

The expectation that the Wabash and Erie Canal would add the needed link for continuous water transportation between New York City and New Orleans stimulated internal improvement fever among Hoosiers. The rosy optimism that a system of internal improvements could be achieved, with moderate or perhaps even no use of tax revenue, was founded on three basic suppositions. The first was that a transportation network could be financed by long term borrowing of millions of dollars at modest rates of interest. A second was that the cost of the resulting canals, railroads, and roads could be paid, if not entirely then at least largely, from the revenue derived from them. An additional supposition was that the resulting transportation network would hasten the growth of population and wealth. Even if moderate taxation became necessary to liquidate the millions borrowed, the levy therefor would be a small price to pay for the economic benefits gained. *Faith* in these *suppositions* was the *cornerstone* on which the Internal Improvements System of 1836 was fabricated.

These basic suppositions were openly and freely discussed. According to Calvin Fletcher, the fund commissioners who went east in 1832 to borrow money for launching the Wabash and Erie Canal were dazzled with what they heard about monied affairs and banking. After commenting that a loan was obtained "on terms surprisingly good for the State," Fletcher observed that "the whole *areana* [*sic*] of the monied operations of the world" had been disclosed to the commissioners. The "vast hidden resources" of the states, "which only required banking institutions to bring them fourth," were said to have been laid before them in an artful manner.[169] At the beginning of his second term in 1834, Governor Noble advised legislators that public opinion had become "more decidedly" in favor of internal improvements to transport surplus production to market, increase the rewards of industry, and enhance the value of property. Asserting that "the beneficial policy of engaging" in such improvements had been "frequently and clearly demonstrated," Noble suggested that with any amount of capital available at 5 percent interest or less "no good reason can be assigned why we should longer hesitate to follow the successful examples of other States." New York, Pennsylvania, and Ohio had "enriched their citizens" by throwing money into circulation for labor, materials, and subsistence, while their completed works had repaid these states and their people "many fold" through higher prices and increased productivity. Becoming philosophical, Noble proclaimed: "The actual wealth of a state or nation, does not consist of the sums hoarded in the Treasury, but in the wealth of the citizens and their ability to pay whenever the exigencies of the Government make contributions necessary. The Treasury of a well managed Government, is the pockets of the people, in which something should be placed by wise legislation, before much is required."[170]

Before an improvement system could be commenced, however, difficult decisions had to be made. Of fundamental importance were questions about which projects would be included; how much borrowing should be authorized to finance their construction; and whether particular works should be built as canals, railroads, or turnpikes. Since the Wabash and Erie Canal was looked to as the outlet to the East, junctions with it were essential. Because a sizeable majority of Hoosiers lived in the southern half of the state, political realism required much attention to their preferences. Hence a canal down the Whitewater Valley received a high priority in discussions about projects to be embraced.[171] The General Assembly probably would have adopted a system at its session in 1834–1835, but for the inability of legislators to agree regarding which works should have priority. While the session was in progress, the pro-Jacksonian *Indiana Democrat* stated: "We have never witnessed, in our ten year's experience of legislative matters, in Indiana, so much interest manifested on any other question." The rival Whig organ advocated that Indiana "embark with spirit in the great cause of internal improvement[.]" After the assembly adjourned Treasurer Nathan B. Palmer advised Senator Tipton that "A decided majority appeared to be in favor of entering into a general sistem [*sic*], but the rock upon which they split, was the details of the bill." Governor Noble wrote an engineer that adoption failed because of "the absence of such facts and information as seemed indispensable" to make relevant decisions. Consequently the assembly had mandated surveys about the feasibility and cost of various canal, railroad, and turnpike routes with the information gained to be submitted to the ensuing session.[172]

During 1835 the movement for a state internal improvement system gained momentum. According to Calvin Fletcher, he and Jesse L. Williams, principal engineer for the Wabash and Erie

Canal, met and concluded that $7,000,000 could safely be spent for appropriate projects, especially canals. Following the August election Fletcher had a leisurely discussion with Governor Noble at which they agreed that canals should be emphasized. Noting their concern that too many projects might be attempted, Fletcher observed: "We are fearful that unless all can be undertaken none will be accomplished." Immediately after the August election the *Indiana Democrat* urged that differences about preferences be avoided, for "In due time a system of internal improvement will be extended to every portion of the state, if we are only judicious in the commencement." In the beginning, "The only question should be how few should be the objects, that first receive our favorable regard." The *Indiana Journal* asserted that "Our state needs nothing but outlets, by means of canals and rail roads, to make her a populous, wealthy, and influential member of the confederacy." Its Whig editor reported that from his mingling with the people he had "found them prepared for the commencement and energetic prosecution of a liberal and judicious system of internal improvements."[173] During the fall both of these papers published a series by "H," who was Jesse L. Williams, that stressed Indiana's great suitability for canals with railroads and turnpikes to supplement them. "H" emphasized that strong popular sentiment for a system would avail nothing "so long as there exists so much diversity of opinion" about "the particular measures" to be adopted. There must be, "H" insisted, sacrifice of sectional interest for the public good, harmony about details, and concentration of effort.[174]

Reports concerning engineering surveys of various possible canals, railroads, and turnpikes, made during 1835, were presented to the General Assembly when it convened in December. For the most part the surveys favored canals over railroads, and railroads over turnpikes. Chief Engineer Jesse L. Williams observed that the Wabash and Erie Canal must form the outlet for the trade of "the greater part of Indiana and a portion of Illinois." He also said there was "every reason to believe" that Indiana had "valuable mineral resources" which, when fully developed, would add much to the wealth of the state.[175] Governor Noble's lengthy comments to legislators indicated that the surveys had been hurriedly made, hence were not as reliable as might be desirable. Nonetheless, he emphasized that they confirmed his previously expressed views in favor of a system. The governor advised legislators that they "may safely expend the amount of ten millions without calling on the present or future generations for the payment of any portion of the principal under the process of taxation. But, to sustain an enterprise of such magnitude, a suitable provision should be made for the payment of the interest on the capital . . . until the work shall be finished." To pay such interest, the executive declared, would mean that "he who now pays one dollar [in state tax] would have to pay the further sum of fifty cents each year." Noble asked, "will our citizens cheerfully pay the small additional tax? Or, . . . , should the state, by a wise policy, open a market with increased prices for produce, and wages of every kind, will they pay a cent or two for each additional dollar thus put into their pockets? Of this you can best determine." The governor recommended that the system embrace "canals, railways and turnpikes, each having a beginning, connection with, or termination at the Lake [Michigan], the Wabash canal, or the Ohio river; the Wabash canal constituting the main artery or trunk of the plan." He preferred canals over railroads or turnpikes "on the ground that canals are cheaper, more permanent, and better adapted to the convenience and habits of the people, and to the character and products of the state." The *Indiana Democrat* rejoiced that the governor was "acting with the Editors of the Democrat, in his recommendation of a system of Internal Improvement, to the extent of *ten millions of dollars*."[176] The Wabash and Erie Canal Commissioners contended that for Indiana "the cheapness of freights on Canals, render them the best mode of internal improvement for an agricultural people. They are made, kept in repair and navigated, by the common labor and means of a country, their uses are general . . . ; as the expense of horses and boats are within the means of persons of moderate capital; the moneys paid for freights are widely diffused, and returned often in exchanges among the people; [and] they enliven and give a greater degree of activity to the business of a country than can be done by any other kind of public improvement." The commissioners predicted that within ten years after its completion the Central Canal would yield $62,850 annually from the water power it created, with a potential of yielding $125,700 therefrom following ten years from its completion—"a sufficient sum to pay for all the repairs which this line would require." Canals "through the eastern, centre, and western divisions of the state," the commissioners stated with assurance, would become profitable from tolls; and within a few years after their completion they "would amply repay the cost of their construction."[177]

Amid such rosy enthusiasm and optimism, the Internal Improvements System of 1836 easily won approval in the legislature. The bill passed the House by the lopsided majority of 56 to 18, and the Senate by the considerable majority of 19 to 12. The Whigs had dominance in both houses and were mainly responsible for its passage, but it received substantial Democratic support. The negative votes came mainly from counties on or near the Ohio River, plus that from various counties immediately north of them. Legislators from scattered counties in the remainder of southern Indiana and likewise from central Indiana also voted against adoption of the system.[178] John B. Dillon, a contemporary observer and Indiana's earliest historian of note, correctly observed that it did not "grow out of a new and hasty expression of popular sentiment. For a period of more than ten years, the expediency of providing, by law, for the commencement of a State system of public works, had been discussed before the people of the State by governors, legislators, and distinguished private citizens."[179]

Adoption of the system was widely hailed and celebrated with exultation. After the improvement bill had passed both houses, but before they had agreed on its final version, the *Indiana Journal* announced that "On Saturday night Indianapolis was most brilliantly illuminated as a manifestation of joy for the passage of the bill." Its Whig editor predicted that its enactment would "immediately elevate the character of our state to a point which otherwise it would not have attained for a score of years," so that "many of the present generation will live to see Indiana the third state in the confederacy." The rival *Indiana Democrat* boasted that

"The citizens of Indianapolis consider themselves one hundred per cent. richer than they were but one week since," and even added kind words for Governor Noble along with the hope that "all party feeling may be swallowed up in an earnest desire" toward promoting the state's honor and glory. Calvin Fletcher described the "splendid illumination" at the capital. "Every house in [*sic*] Washington St. was illumined & most off[ices on] the street my office with the rest," while some of the legislators who joined in the jollification "got a little *drunk,*" Fletcher confided in his diary.[180] Editor Elihu Stout of Vincennes reported that approval of the system had "been received with every demonstration of joy and gladness; by illuminations, bonfires and addresses, in almost every town and village from Lafayette to Evansville." Stout expressed confidence that the same feeling had been manifested throughout the state. At the infant village of Peru "the expression of general joy was manifested by the symultaneous glow of light from every house, hamlet, and shantee, within the town and vicinity, presenting one of the most beautiful illuminations . . . ever witnessed." With sentiments doubtless echoed in similar vein in other villages, it was wistfully observed that "From a spot where but twelve months ago, little else was to be seen save the dense wilderness and the red man of the forest, now sending forth streams of vivid light from at least one hundred good houses, accompanied with the cheer of civilization, none could fail to foster and cherish the most lively hopes, for the future prosperity of a town so flourishing as Peru, on an occasion like this."[181]

The System of 1836 embraced canals, railroads, and turnpikes, but the largest appropriations were for canals. The projects and the sums earmarked for them were as follows:

1. The Whitewater Canal, from the west branch of the Whitewater River as far above the National Road as feasible, down the valley to Lawrenceburg on the Ohio River, to be joined with the Central Canal, by a canal if practical, otherwise by railroad. $1,400,000 appropriated.
2. The Central Canal, from the most suitable point on the Wabash and Erie Canal between Fort Wayne and Logans-

port, to Evansville on the Ohio River via or near Muncie, down the West Fork of White River through Indianapolis to its junction with the East Fork, thence to Evansville by the most practical route. $3,500,000 appropriated.

3. Extension of the Wabash and Erie Canal from the mouth of the Tippecanoe River down the Wabash River to Terre Haute, thence across to the Central Canal at a point between Eel River and Black Creek. $1,300,000 appropriated.

4. A railroad from Madison on the Ohio River to Lafayette on the Wabash River, by way of Columbus, Indianapolis, and Crawfordsville. $1,300,000 appropriated.

5. A macadamized turnpike from New Albany on the Ohio River to Vincennes on the Wabash River, via Greenville, Fredericksburg, Paoli, Mount Pleasant, and Washington. $1,150,000 appropriated.

6. A resurvey of the route from Jeffersonville on the Ohio River to Crawfordsville, by way of New Albany, Salem, Bedford, Bloomington, and Greencastle for a railroad if practical, otherwise for a macadamized turnpike. $1,300,000 appropriated.

7. Removal of obstructions to navigation of the Wabash River from its mouth to Vincennes. $50,000 appropriated.

8. A survey during 1836 for a canal if feasible, otherwise a railroad, from or near Fort Wayne to or near Michigan City on Lake Michigan via Goshen, South Bend, and if practical through La Porte. No appropriation, but the faith of the state was irrevocably pledged to start construction within a decade and its ultimate completion.

9. Purchase of stock in the Lawrenceburg and Indianapolis Railroad to a maximum of $500,000.[182]

The *authorized* appropriations aggregated $10,500,000, plus a deferred commitment of an undetermined sum for a canal or railroad between Fort Wayne and Michigan City. The next legislature, however, detached the projected extension of the Wabash and Erie Canal west of the Tippecanoe River via Terre Haute to the Central Canal from the system and made it a charge against the Wabash and Erie Canal Fund. This separation probably resulted from a hope that Congress would grant Indiana five sections of land for each mile of the canal from the mouth of the Tippecanoe to Terre Haute.[183] For punctual payment of interest and ultimate repayment of loans the state pledged and appropriated the canals, railroads, and turnpikes which constituted the system as well as the proceeds from tolls and rent of water power arising from them, "The sufficiency of which . . . the State of Indiana doth hereby irrevocably guarantee."[184]

The responsibility for directing and supervising construction of the system was vested in a nine member Board of Internal Improvement. Members were named by the governor for three year terms, subject to the approval of the Senate. In nominating persons the executive was to "have regard to the local situation of the nominee, so that each work may be represented in said Board by a suitable person residing as near as practicable thereto." The board was empowered to put any or all of the projects under construction and make minor changes in routes, "having regard always to economy and the most profitable and early receipt of tolls." Board members were paid $2 per day of actual service, plus an allowance for travel and contingencies.[185] At the initial meeting of the board at Indianapolis on March 7 David H. Maxwell, of Bloomington, was elected its president. By December, 1836, contracts had been let on six of the system's projects, aggregating $2,073,362.07, but since payments for the projects totaled $8,956 apparently only modest construction had been achieved. Near the end of 1837 the board explained that contracts let had been less during that year because of the high price of labor. But far more construction had been achieved than for the previous year since payments for the construction aggregated $1,162,176.74. The largest payments had been for the Madison and Indianapolis Railroad, followed in the order named by those for the Central Canal, the Whitewater Canal, New Albany and Vincennes Road, the Crosscut Canal, and Crawfordsville Road.[186]

Efforts to add significant additions to the System of 1836 and other efforts to have the works *classified* and completed on a priority basis according to their class failed at the legislative session of 1836–1837. As the session began Governor Noble admonished legislators that Indiana had "staked her fortunes" on an enterprise "from which there is no retreat that would be either safe or honorable." In noting that citizens in some parts of the state felt unaccommodated by the system, Noble stated that it would seem good policy to "quiet" their claims and unite their "interest and feeling" with other parts of the state.[187] But when Robert Dale Owen, a Democrat from Posey County, presented a bill to accommodate the unaccommodated it failed to pass. Owen considered the anticipated $1,500,000 in surplus revenue from the federal government "our Godsend" to "heal rankling wounds, and sooth justly irritated feelings." If, he said, the system is safe, as adopted, it would be "much more safe by enlisting the feelings of hundreds of thousands more . . . ."[188] A proposal by Representative George H. Proffit, Whig from Pike and Dubois counties, that a select committee prepare a bill appropriating $1,610,000 for two railroads and eight roads also failed.[189] A proposal of Senator John Dumont, a Whig from Switzerland County, that the Committee on Canals and Internal Improvements consider the expediency of constructing "one to three of the most prominent public works as speedily as practicable," with all other works suspended until these few were in at least an advanced state, plus "prospectively" extending the system to provide for the unprovided areas of the state was adopted. The committee, however, quickly reported that such legislation would be inexpedient.[190] Later Dumont vigorously supported a bill by Senator Samuel Milroy, a Democrat from Carroll and Clinton counties, which proposed to divide the works into three classes with those in the first class having priority, followed respectively by works in class two and then class three. Dumont said he had voted against the system "because it was too heavy, too bulky—more than the times required, and more than the people could bear." Unless classification were adopted, Dumont contended, a "paralytic blow" would be given the system from which it would be long in recovering.[191] Representative Benjamin Ferguson, a Whig from Clark County, predicted that it would require

$50,000,000 to complete the works as projected in the system. He viewed classification as the only means to save the state from bankruptcy.[192]

Even senators who had voted for the System of 1836 had become much concerned about its ultimate cost. In December, 1836, Governor Noble had advised legislators that some parts of the state felt unaccommodated by the system as adopted. The Senate responded by instructing its Committee on Canals and Internal Improvements "to inquire into and report to the Senate what additional public works are necessary to extend equal benefits to every part of the State, particularly as relates to" the area "north and west of the Wabash river." In its report, early in 1837, the committee asserted: "The last legislature authorized the commencement of a system of internal improvement, which in the opinion of the committee embraces, all the principal divisions of the State, and includes a sufficient number of works to accommodate most of its great interests." The committee estimated that it would cost an aggregate of *$18,367,741* to carry the system, and the Wabash and Erie Canal through 1842. With the National Road as a dividing line, it suggested that works north thereof would cost $9,003,047; those south of the road $9,304,691. By the end of 1842 an estimated $2,696,381 would be spent on the canal, the remainder on works in the system. The committee commented that "no great section of the state" had been "overlooked, and perhaps the only consideration which could have justified a prudent statesman in advocating so extensive a system, was that the cheerful cooperation of all portions of the country might be obtained in its support." Concerning costs, the senators projected that interest on the debt, for the canal and the system, would be $50,000 for 1837, $108,000 in 1838, $252,000 in 1840, and skyrocket to $420,000 for 1842. On the revenue side, it was supposed that income from the works, above the costs of repairs, would start at $15,000 in 1840, rise to $80,888 in 1841, and jump to $120,000 for 1842. If an anticipated distribution of $1,500,000, from federal surplus revenue, were invested in loans on real estate at 8 percent yearly, then

$120,000 annually would be available from this source. If, in addition, a special tax of 5 cents per $100 of taxable property were levied during 1837 through 1840, plus double this levy for 1841 and 1842, at the end of 1842 the difference between estimated costs and income should end with a deficit of $36,338. Hence, "after that period no very great increase of taxation will be required." But these data presumed that there would be no enlargement of the system; made no provision for any payments on principal; assumed that the $1,500,000 would be received, invested and yield as suggested; and also that the Wabash and Erie Canal would be navigable for trade between Lafayette and Lake Erie by late 1840. Moreover, the report indicates that there was no presumption that all of the works in the system would be completed by the end of 1842. In addition, it presumed that the taxable property of the state would increase in value from $85,800,000 in 1837, to $114,199,800 in 1840, and rise to $138,181,758 for 1842. The committee's estimates and projections, however, were made about four months before the bank panic of 1837 commenced. No wonder the committee declared that "in their opinion, any further enlargement of the system of internal improvement at the present session, is inexpedient, and would lead to a prostration of the credit of the State, and an abandonment of the works already commenced . . . ."[193] Soon after the session adjourned, the *Indiana Journal* observed that the great issue of the session had been extension or nonextension of the system, and save for two or three surveys, which would cost but little, the opponents of extension had won. This Whig organ did not suppose the existing system perfect, commented that some additions might later be proper, and complimented members who voted down additions of much interest to their constituents.[194]

With the chartering of the Second State Bank in 1834 and the adoption of the System of 1836 Indiana abandoned economic laissez faire and crossed the Rubicon. The Second State Bank had been carefully established on a sound foundation, and it was profitable to state and private shareholders from its beginning. But the System of 1836 rested on a weak and fragile foundation from its adoption. The legislative session of 1836–1837 wisely declined to add works to the system, but it also declined to classify the works in the system, so that a few of them could be completed or nearly so, and likewise for a few others until all had been finished. Whether the System of 1836, or at least a substantial part of it, could have been completed had prosperity continued several more years is a moot question. But the impact of the Panic of 1837, commencing in May and followed by disruptions in financial markets, reduced the prospect for a successful return across the Rubicon.

CHAPTER 5
DEPRESSION AND DEBT, 1837–1843

WHILE DAVID WALLACE and Samuel Bigger were governor from 1837 to 1843, the Whigs achieved the zenith of their domination over state politics. They maintained uninterrupted control of the offices of governor, lieutenant governor, and auditor; they enjoyed a majority in the Senate at every annual session of the General Assembly. At the sessions in 1837–1838, 1838–1839, and 1840–1841, they also had a majority in the House of Representatives. Members of the Board of Internal Improvement, fund commissioners, and directors of the state and branch bank boards were largely Whigs. This Whig dominance of state politics represents the culmination of National Republican-Whig control which had persisted from the mid-twenties.[1]

Although Governor Noah Noble was ineligible for a third term in 1837, the political situation strongly favored the election of a Whig as his successor. The popularity of Noble; the landslide vote for Harrison, Indiana's territorial governor, for president the previous year; and the unpopularity of Van Buren as Old Hickory's successor as president all augered well for Whig success. Concern about the ultimate cost of the System of 1836 was tempering the rosy optimism about its completion, but strong desire remained to push forward to achieve its anticipated benefits. The Panic of 1837, which began in May, caused no widespread distress prior to the election in August; and the Second State Bank, aided by the general suspension of specie payments, continued as a strong and prosperous institution.

Long before August, 1837, Lieutenant Governor David Wallace seemed to be the heir apparent to Noble. After he had tea with the Calvin Fletchers in July, 1835, Fletcher commented in his diary that Wallace "no doubt will be our next executive . . . ." Born in western Pennsylvania in 1799, the Wallaces lived in Ohio about a decade before David became a cadet at the West Point Military Academy from which he graduated in 1821. After teaching at the

Academy for a year, Wallace took up residence at Brookville, Franklin County, Indiana. He studied law in the office of Judge Miles C. Eggleston, and was soon admitted to the bar. In 1824 he married the daughter of Congressman John Test, and about this time became a member of Test's law firm. Elected to the House of Representatives in 1828, 1829, and 1830, he gained election as lieutenant governor in 1831 when Noble became governor. He won reelection with Noble in 1834. Meantime, about 1832 the lieutenant governor and his family moved northwest across the state to Covington, in Fountain County on the Wabash River.[2]

The Democrats, with party strength at low ebb, failed to find a viable candidate against Wallace. In November, 1836, the party's state central committee called for a state convention at Indianapolis on January 8, 1837, to nominate candidates for governor and lieutenant governor. Less than a month later the committee withdrew its call, and the campaign was completed without a state convention for either party. The *Indiana Democrat* considered a convention much the best way to achieve "important political results," but it reflected a defeatist mood by saying that the recent presidential election rendered "it quite probable, that His Half Excellency will be made a Whole Excellency at the August election." This Democratic organ asserted that the people seemed to be submitting to the dictation of Governor Noble and the Central Junto of the Whig party.[3]

During the early weeks of 1837 Wallace seemed the only candidate for governor. Late in January the pro-Whig *Indiana Journal* announced that it had been requested to announce Wallace as a candidate. The *Indiana Democrat* sarcastically observed that Governor Noble, with the advice of the Whig Central Junto, had appointed David Wallace, "*a West Point Politician*," as the next governor. The editor said Democrats had not the slightest disposition to run a party candidate for chief executive, but asserted that they wanted a man of talents, "not a jay bird, a mere talking parrot . . . only taught to repeat the lessons of the Junto."[4] Meantime, "Many Indianans," claiming that numerous of them were Harrison men, suggested that Samuel Milroy, a prominent Democrat from Carroll County, was well qualified to be governor. Milroy was described as one who had helped write the Constitution of

1816, and had filled important public trusts with marked public approval. "Citizen" offered no objection to Milroy, but deemed Gamaliel Taylor, of Jefferson County, a "staunch old Democrat" who would serve the people better than anyone who had been mentioned for governor.[5] The *Indiana Democrat*, doubtless to stir division among Whigs, encouraged support for such a Whig as Amaziah Morgan.[6] By late April Gamaliel Taylor and John Dumont, a Whig from Switzerland County, became candidates, but several weeks before the voting Taylor withdrew. The *Indiana Democrat* said Taylor withdrew because the "party question" had been raised against him. Hence, to prevent party excitement and enhance the success of a classification candidate he had dropped out in favor of Dumont.[7]

What policy to follow regarding the System of 1836 overshadowed all other campaign issues. Wallace argued for simultaneous completion of its projects, saying this understanding had been essential for legislative approval of the system; and good faith required their concurrent construction. If the works were classified, Wallace said, when the priority projects were completed their friends would unite with opponents of the system, cry out against high taxes, hence some works would be abandoned. He asserted that the increased population and higher prices, arising from the system, would enable taxpayers to pay levies against them without fiscal ruin and bankruptcy.[8] The *Indiana Journal*, a vigorous supporter of Wallace and simultaneous construction, emphasized that completion of the system would enrich rather than impoverish the state. This leading Whig organ termed the ensuing gubernatorial election the most important ever held in the state, one that for weal or woe would decide the future destiny of the state. If the system was not completed, the editor predicted that farmers of Marion County, if able to sell their produce at all, would have to sell it for a song. But, if completed, "They can either send their produce . . . to New Orleans or to New York, by way of the Lakes. One or the other of these markets will always furnish ready sales at fair and liberal prices."[9]

Dumont and the *Indiana Democrat* emphatically supported classification. Dumont, who had voted against adoption of the system, contended that it would never have been approved had it been openly and fairly debated by legislators. Simultaneous completion, he contended, would cause excessive taxation; however, with classification, and key projects first finished, the revenue from them would help finance the remaining items in the system. Additional works could then be added without taxation and financial ruin.[10] Following Taylor's withdrawal the *Indiana Democrat* declared that there remained only two candidates: "The Hon. John Dumont, the advocate for classification, and the opponent of high taxation and Mr. Wallace, the opponent of classification and the advocate of high taxes."[11]

Issues other than internal improvements had a lesser role in the campaign. The *Indiana Democrat* portrayed Wallace as a youthful, inexperienced, unqualified, and pliant tool of Governor Noble and the Whig Central Junto.[12] After reporting that friends of Wallace had called Dumont a drunken "sot and pot-house wallower," this Democratic paper claimed that it had never alluded to the "well founded" reports of Wallace's "ill-treatment of his former spouse," to "his daily habit of resorting to groceries," or to "his derelictions in private life." The editor asserted that "Mr. Wallace drinks two glasses of grog to Mr. Dumont's one."[13] A New Albany paper said the Whig press was going full blast for Biddle's national bank in an effort to rally Whigs to Wallace over Dumont who had entered the race contrary to the mandate of the Whig Central Junto.[14] As the campaign ended the *Indiana Democrat* sought votes for Dumont as "The People's Candidate" against "The Speculators' Candidate," Wallace.[15]

Wallace's victory was apparently never in doubt. Shortly before the voting Edward A. Hannegan, who had served four years as a Democratic congressman, advised Senator John Tipton that La Porte County would give a "united vote" for Wallace. The balloting in August gave a thumping victory to Wallace who carried fifty-two of the eighty-one counties, with 46,067 votes for Wallace to 36,915 for Dumont. Counties favoring Dumont were overwhelmingly located in the southern half of the state, especially those not favorably located to share significantly in the benefits anticipated from the System of 1836. Since Wallace won about 55.5 percent of the vote, with the system as the key issue, his triumph indicates an endorsement of its simultaneous construction over classification. In the 1850s, Oliver H. Smith, a staunch Whig as of 1837, observed that in advocating classification "Col. Dumont was clearly right, but the majority went with [Lieut.] Gov. Wallace."[16]

The Whigs scored an even greater victory in the contest for lieutenant governor. For a time David Hillis, a Whig from Jefferson County who had voted for adoption of the system, and Abel C. Pepper, a Democrat much experienced in Indian affairs, were the principal candidates.[17] In June Pepper, probably sensing certain defeat, withdrew; and Alexander S. Burnett, a former legislator and merchant from Floyd County, replaced Pepper for the Democrats. Hillis swamped his rival, gaining over two thirds of the vote and sixty-four counties to seventeen for Burnett who won his counties mainly in the same parts of the state that Dumont had.[18]

Although Whigs considerably outnumbered Democrats at the ensuing legislative session, the General Assembly reelected both Treasurer Nathan B. Palmer, a Democrat, and Auditor Morris Morris, a Whig. For some time the *Indiana Democrat* had lambasted the Morris family, claiming that it had for too long received more money than due it from the state treasury. This lambasting apparently injured Palmer's reelection prospects, but in December, 1837, he gained a second term by a modest majority; and Morris gained a fourth term by a somewhat larger majority.[19] Meantime, at the previous session, which also had a considerable Whig majority, William J. Brown, a Democrat, had defeated incumbent William Sheets, who was completing his initial term as secretary of state.[20]

Questions and concerns about the Wabash and Erie Canal and the System of 1836 overshadowed all other issues during Wallace's only term as governor from December, 1837, to December, 1840. In his inaugural the new executive viewed the "magnificent system of State Improvement" which the legislature had "so laboriously matured" the settled policy of the state. He disagreed with those who considered that it would "inevitably involve us in debts beyond our abilities to pay"; and lead to "the worst of all evils—oppressive and ruinous taxation without even the hope of relief or mitigation." Classification, he emphasized, would cause "a division of friends—the clashing of adverse interests," and "the utter prostration of the whole system." Wallace offered data which indicated that the extremely rapid growth in population and fiscal resources would, in his opinion, be adequate to finance the system. Nevertheless, he proposed a modified plan of simultaneous construction so as "to concentrate the means of the state on portions of each work at the same time, commencing at the most profitable and commercial points" and completing these portions before other portions are started so "the State may be realizing something from them" while "finishing the remainder." He recommended "strict economy" and scrupulous accountability regarding all expenditures.[21]

In his final address to the legislature on the day preceding the inaugural, Governor Noble advocated at least a modified form of classification. He explained that the great disparity in the length, cost, and time required to complete the various works made "evident" the "impolicy of their simultaneous completion." Increased appropriations should be given to works in a state of "forwardness," he said, "without discontinuing expenditures elsewhere" so that on finishing those expedited "all our effective means and force" could be applied to those that remain. Moreover, if necessary, additional time should be allowed to complete the system.[22]

At the legislative session of 1837–1838, both the internal improvement board and the fund commissioners gave ominous signals of fiscal disaster ahead. The board explained that the rise in the cost of labor and the desire not to draw too much labor from the expansion of agriculture had been an important factor in its decision to let only a few new contracts during 1837. Nevertheless, it affirmed its "undiminished confidence" in the state's ability to finish the system as adopted.[23] In another report the board informed legislators that from December 1, 1836, through November 30, 1837, a total of $1,617,973.94 had been spent on the system and the Wabash and Erie Canal.[24] The fund commissioners announced that they had been required to pay 10 to 11 percent as a premium to secure specie for payment of interest due July 1, 1837, on improvement loans. They also reported that the Cohens of Baltimore had failed while owing the state $298,000 on bonds purchased from them in 1836. In a related report the commissioners explained that heretofore interest due on bonds for internal improvements had been paid from bonds bought. They noted that as of December, 1837, an aggregate of $3,827,000 had been received from bonds purchased for this purpose.[25]

Meantime, prospects seemed promising that the Wabash and Erie Canal, begun in 1832, would ere long be connected with Lake Erie, opening trade via water to New York City. As Governor Noble left office in December, 1837, he predicted that within two years boats would navigate the canal from Lafayette to Lake Erie. A short time later the improvement board reported that the canal would be navigable between Fort Wayne and Logansport by the spring of 1838, and that it was under contract from Lafayette to the lake. Board members, however, were concerned that the segment in Ohio, immediately east of the Ohio border, had been contracted for a size smaller than the sixty foot width and six foot depth specified between Fort Wayne and the Ohio border.[26]

As Indiana's trunk line to the East moved toward completion, an effort was made to secure extension of the federal land grant to help finance continuation of the canal down the Wabash Valley to Terre Haute. Late in 1837 the board asked Congress to confirm five sections of land for each mile required to extend the canal to this point. It reminded this body that the United States had promised a grant of land for each mile of canal connecting *navigable points* on the Wabash and Maumee rivers. Although the board had "supposed" that the mouth of the Tippecanoe River would be the western point, it had become necessary to take the canal to Terre Haute. The legislature adopted a resolution seeking federal approval of a grant for this purpose.[27]

Prosecution of the system and canal pressed forward during 1838. After the General Assembly convened in December, 1838, the fund commissioners reported that an aggregate of $4,300,000 in bonds had been sold on behalf of the system and $1,327,000 in bonds for the Wabash and Erie Canal, from their commencement. The interest on the $5,627,000 so borrowed would be $287,169.25 during 1839, yet almost no revenue had been obtained from the improvement projects.[28] Without exaggeration

Governor Wallace told legislators: "we have our hands full—full to overflowing!" Even so, he insisted that "Indiana is still safe, and that she must and will ultimately triumph."[29] Counting some of his chickens before the eggs had been hatched, even before some had been laid, Wallace presented data suggesting that Indiana could count on $4,383,623 from proceeds of Wabash and Erie Canal acreage and surplus revenue from the federal government. Presuming that at least $4,000,000 was the minimum from these sources, Wallace stated that, invested in bank stock or loaned upon mortgages, this sum would yield not less than 8 percent or $320,000 annually. This return, plus $180,000 per year from taxes or proceeds from improvements, would pay all the interest on the anticipated debt of $10,000,000, without raising state tax levies.[30] The governor objected to the continued scattering of improvement appropriations in an unconnected manner, and emphasized the need to adopt "concentration" as proposed in his inaugural. He also recommended that the Board of Internal Improvement be reduced from nine to three members, and that the engineering corps be organized so that but one corps be assigned each work.[31] The governor vigorously urged that the Wabash and Erie Canal be extended to Terre Haute. He asserted that neither at Lafayette nor Covington, where the governor had lived, was the Wabash River navigable "for several months in the year," and that "under precisely similar circumstances" Ohio had been given land to make Lake Erie the eastern terminal.[32]

The fund commissioners offered an optimistic view about the debt owed by the Cohens, but Treasurer Nathan B. Palmer gave sobering comment concerning payment of interest on the improvement debt. The commissioners detailed bonds, stocks, and other property obtained from a compromise with the Cohens, and predicted that it would "ultimately indemnify the state against any loss" from this source. Palmer pointedly warned that the construction of the works must shortly be directed toward producing "from other sources than taxation, an amount sufficient to cover some considerable portion" of the rapidly accumulating interest on the improvement debt. Otherwise, "neither the treasury, nor the ability or patience of the people will be able to bear the overwhelming load of interest, for the payment of which the public faith is sacredly pledged."[33]

At the session of 1838–1839, the legislature emphasized efforts to cut expenditures and find revenue to pay interest on the debt for the system and canal. The Board of Internal Improvement was reduced from nine to three members, and asked to concentrate construction on works or portions of works most useful to the state which promised revenue upon their completion. The board could not spend more than $1,500,000 in any year, and economy was to be practiced to the fullest extent possible. With the consent of contractors, it could cancel, transfer, or increase contracts from one work to another. In a related measure the fund commissioners were reduced from three to two.[34] To gain additional money to pay interest in the short run, the entire levy of 30 cents per $100 of assessed general property for 1839 was earmarked for this purpose. In the desperate hope of subsequently gaining money to help pay this interest, the General Assembly authorized the Second State Bank to increase its capital stock by $5,000,000 during 1839 to 1844, with permission to add four additional branches to the existing eleven.[35] Despite these efforts to shore up a worsening fiscal situation, the legislature appropriated an additional $400,000 for completion of the Madison and Indianapolis Railroad to Indianapolis. Shortly before the legislative session had commenced there had been a celebration of the start of railroad operation on the seventeen miles of this line from the top of the hill at Madison to Graham's Fork. Some weeks before this observance Calvin Fletcher had predicted that the "Madison road railroad will one day be a great thro-fare."[36]

The new Board of Internal Improvement held its initial meeting March 4, 1839, and elected former Governor Noah Noble its president. In December the three member board reported that it had found $3,410,111 in contracts outstanding, "scattered over seven distinct lines, and at some eighteen different points—one-third of them unconnected with others . . . ." Contracts for the system totaled $2,803,378, that for the Wabash and Erie Canal $606,733. The board explained that it had been unable to achieve significant concentration because of the scattered nature of existing contracts; the limit of $1,500,000 on its annual expenditures,

at which rate it would require more than two years to pay off outstanding contracts; the restriction against any reduction in original appropriations for the system, and the necessity to secure approval of contractors to alter contracts.[37] Meantime, in early
August word arrived that the Morris Canal and Banking Company had suspended payment on nearly $2,000,000 of internal
improvement bonds and $1,000,000 of bonds for increase of the
capital of the Second State Bank. With this catastrophe and the
deepening of the depression during the summer, under date of
August 18 Noble, as president of the board, informed contractors
that money was not available to meet the August payment due
them and it would be postponed, "perhaps for several months."
He advised contractors to decide for themselves whether to continue their operations.[38] Then on November 18 the board mandated that "the Public Works be immediately suspended" except
for the Wabash and Erie Canal from Lafayette to the Ohio line;
dams on other works yet to be preserved; on the Whitewater
Canal at Lawrenceburg, and the bridge at Harrison.[39]

A short time before the suspension order, the fund commissioners gave a detailed and revealing report about the state debt.
They reported that bonds issued for the System of 1836 had
totaled $5,932,000; that revenue for its construction had aggre-
gated $6,156,271.62; and that expenditures therefor had
amounted to $3,840,813.12³/₄, leaving an unexpended balance
of $2,315,458.49¹/₄. Only $78,000 of the revenue had come
from taxation, with none indicated from any of the works, while
$405,962.44 had been spent for interest on the bonds. The
commissioners optimistically explained that if all the money due
and owing the fund for the system was paid, and all pending
debts against it were paid, there would be an additional balance
of $589,542.70 in its favor. The commissioners admitted that
not all of their data were precise, and that debts from "moneyed
institutions" might be an "ultimate loss." Roughly $1,800,000
of the current debt indicated seems to have been considered of
this doubtful category. Bonds bought for the Wabash and Erie
Canal aggregated $1,727,000; revenue received for its construc-
tion amounted to $2,056,989.75¹/₂; and expenditures totaled

$1,750,203.46½ including $252,123.39 for interest, leaving a balance of $306,786.29. Proceeds of $274,304.71 had been obtained from sale of canal lands as part of the revenue to build the canal, but only $5,023.95 had been secured from tolls. Sums due and owing the canal fund, more than half owed by the questionable Morris Canal and Banking Company, minus items pending against the fund, provided an additional balance of $1,146.65 to it. However these sums are interpreted, Indiana was indebted for *principal of and interest on* at least $7,659,000 in bonds, for which the fund commissioners calculated the annual interest at $388,950.[40] To liquidate this obligation the faith and honor of the state had been pledged, yet the state was in the midst of a severe depression, without any revenue from items in the system, and only negligible revenue from the Wabash and Erie Canal which remained to be completed to Lake Erie. The exact amount of the state debt for the system, the trunk line canal, and *related obligations* seems impossible to ascertain. A House committee, all of whose members were Democrats, estimated such debt at $13,148,452.09, which might be somewhat inflated.[41] Whatever the sum, apparently at least $3,500,000 was ultimately lost from bonds sold to finance internal improvements for which the state failed to receive the principal therefor.[42] Modest as these sums may seem to Hoosiers of subsequent generations, in the context of the rural and undeveloped economy of pioneer Indiana they were extremely large and their fiscal impact was burdensome. The context is better understood when it is realized that for the period 1831–1837, when both the Wabash and Erie Canal and the System of 1836 were commenced, state tax revenue averaged $51,546.94 annually.[43]

In its annual report in December, 1839, the Board of Internal Improvement offered an apologetic but illuminating commentary concerning causes for the downfall of the system. It emphasized four items. First, the cost of labor and provisions, which though correctly estimated at the outset, had, with few exceptions, cost "20 per cent. higher" than had been anticipated. Second, it had been appropriately presumed that bonds could be bought at a low rate of interest in the European market, but the "large and unexpected demand" for bonds from this source had caused a rise in the rate of interest, which reduced the value of and demand for state bonds, thus preventing Indiana and other states "from proceeding with their works." Third, "various expedients" to find revenue for payment of interest from other than "the ordinary resources" (taxation), had failed. In particular the effort to obtain revenue for this purpose from Indiana's share of federal surplus revenue had had only modest success. And there had been the unsuccessful effort to increase the capital of the state bank, possibly by $10,000,000, from which the state might have realized dividends of $1,000,000 toward payment of interest on the improvement debt within a decade. Fourth, the state had "divided her resources and energies among too great a number of objects," and it would have been "better policy from the beginning to" have directed "our means to the completion of a part of the works" before proceeding with others. Without using the words "simultaneous construction" the board asserted that this policy may have been "our greatest error."[44] This commentary was silent regarding the role the sale of bonds on credit and possible fraud and corruption might have contributed to the debacle. The House Committee on State Debt emphasized two primary causes for the system's downfall. First, contrary to law all bonds for internal improvement had been sold on credit to institutions of doubtful solvency. Second, that to "The great anxiety to commence the system and urge it forward, before the people of the State should become acquainted with its extent and the burdens it would bring upon them, is to be attributed the embarrassed and deranged condition of the financial affairs of the State."[45] Despite the varied causes given for the downfall of the system, by the end of 1839 hindsight made it abundantly clear, to many Whig and Democratic legislators alike, that it had been commenced on a weak and unsafe fiscal foundation.

The year 1839 also brought distressing news about the Wabash and Erie Canal. Governor Noble's prediction that it would be navigable from Lafayette to Lake Erie by the end of that year had proved premature. The improvement board reported that Indiana's 144 miles, from Lafayette to the Ohio line, could be made navigable by June, 1840. The board explained that despite assurance from Ohio that its portion would become navigable during 1840, a change in the route, immediately east of the state line, had caused a further delay of "some time to come" in its completion. In December, 1839, Governor Wallace told legislators that "every foot" of the canal would remain "almost valueless" until the canal was connected with Lake Erie. The General Assembly appealed to Ohio to do justice to Indiana, by speeding completion of the link next to the state line and building it the same width and depth as between Fort Wayne and the border as well as for most of the canal within the Buckeye State.[46]

When the legislature met in December, 1839, Wallace described the state's acute fiscal crisis. He indicated that it would require about $425,000 during fiscal 1839–1840 to pay interest on bonds for the system and trunk line canal. The governor noted that the state owed contractors $706,559 on improvement projects, plus $641,200.17 to the State Bank for money advanced for such costs. He suggested that perhaps the debt owed the bank could be delayed a few months, but, if necessary, he would sanction an issue of scrip to pay contractors immediately. Wallace asserted that it was "necessary" to extend the tax levy for 1839 of 30 cents per $100 of property for 1840, earmarked to help meet the interest on the state debt. He recommended that "as means can be procured" that provision be made against dilapidation of unfinished works so that some could be completed and others finished to points where they would be useful.[47] The improvement board hoped that one project approaching completion could be resumed in the spring of 1840. It also observed that citizens were disposed to organize "private associations" to continue construction of "several of the advanced improvements, without calling upon the state for money," and recommended that these associations be encouraged with appropriate restrictions.[48]

The General Assembly, which began in December, 1839, had a modest Whig majority in the Senate and a large edge for Democrats in the House.[49] To pay contractors it authorized a maximum of $1,500,000 in state scrip, acceptable in payment of state taxes and redeemable at the pleasure of the state, provided money for this purpose could not otherwise be found without the further sale of bonds. Contractors, willing to suspend operations until the legislature authorized their renewal, were to be paid the 10 percent usually retained until contracts were completed. Contractors willing to relinquish their contracts were to be reimbursed for costs from preparations made for their prosecution. No provision was made for continuing any work, but small sums could be spent "to protect, or save from dilapidation or waste, any portion of the public works." Contracts for the Wabash and Erie Canal were exempted from this legislation, which asked that it be continued "as fast . . . as can be done with its own legitimate funds."[50]

A majority of the House Ways and Means Committee considered an increased tax levy desirable, but House Democrats disagreed. The committee proposed an increase in the poll tax from 50 cents to $1, and a rise in the levy on property to 40 cents per $100 of assessed valuation—10 cents higher than that for 1839, and this amount larger than had been urged by Wallace.[51] In wrangling between the House and Senate concerning the levy for 1840 the poll tax remained *unchanged*. But the property tax was *reduced* to 15 cents per $100 of taxable property, with only one third of it set aside for interest on the improvement debt.[52] The Board of Internal Improvement was reduced to two members, with Noah Noble continued and Chief Engineer Jesse L. Williams as a new member. The board was "forthwith" to discharge all assistant engineers, and all other persons not "absolutely necessary" in preserving improvement projects. The number of fund commissioners was unchanged, with Milton Stapp remaining and Nathan B. Palmer, state treasurer and a Democrat, as the new commissioner. The staunchly pro-Whig *Indiana Journal* insisted that Democrats in the House had sabotaged the tax bill in an attempt to force two or three key appointments to particular Democrats.[53] Whatever the motivation the levy approved was utterly inadequate, and increased the possibility that the state would be unable to pay the interest on the improvement bonds during fiscal 1840–1841.

The breakdown of the system in 1839 set the stage for the gubernatorial election of 1840. During 1839 various Democrats were mentioned as possible candidates, but none emerged as the party favorite.[54] As the year ended the key question for the Whigs was whether Wallace should be renominated. The *Indiana Democrat* insisted that the governor could be defeated more easily than any other Whig. The *Indiana Journal* preferred Wallace, but promised to support any Whig devoted to Whig principles, "unless he should be in favor of stopping entirely our public works." It asserted that "very few" wanted "the entire and final stoppage" of the public works, while "still fewer" desired that "*all*, or even any considerable number of them, should be simultaneously progressed . . . ."[55] Despite its support for Wallace, this leading Whig organ noted that some Whigs preferred Jonathan McCarty, Charles Dewey, Thomas H. Blake, or Joseph G. Marshall. Meantime, Governor Wallace reminded Samuel Judah that the previous winter he had "intimated" to him that he would "cheerfully step aside" if the Whigs could unite on someone else. The governor suggested that Jonathan McCarty was "formidable on the stump," and had "nothing to do with our internal Improvements," so on this issue McCarty could occupy the same ground as the opposition would doubtless take.[56]

At the Democratic State Convention at the capital on January 8, Samuel Milroy was named chairman of the committee to nominate candidates for governor and lieutenant governor. When he announced that the committee recommended Tilghman A. Howard and Benjamin S. Tuley respectively for these posts there was, according to the proceedings, "an enthusiastic burst of applause that was prolonged for several minutes before the question could be put." Several delegates from the Seventh Congressional District, which Howard represented, explained that the congressman had authorized them to say that he earnestly wished that his name not come before the convention, and that they joined with him in the hope that he would be permitted to remain as a congressman. Nonetheless, there arose shouts of "'Howard! Howard! No one but Howard!'" The nominations were approved with "shouts of applause, which shook the walls of the Capitol." The president and secretaries of the convention were asked to communicate with the congressman, attending his duties at Washington, "and request him in the name of this Convention and of the people of Indiana" to accept his nomination.[57]

At the Whig State Convention at Indianapolis on January 16–17, the first such convention for the Whigs, Caleb B. Smith chaired its nominating committee. The proceedings note that when Smith on behalf of the committee "unanimously" recommended Samuel Bigger and Samuel Hall respectively for governor and lieutenant governor that the nominations were "received amid loud and enthusiastic cheers." The address of the convention comments that "after much consideration" the delegates had united in support of Bigger and Hall.[58] The *Tri-Weekly Journal* reported that Bigger accepted the nomination in a very appropriate address, and that Governor Wallace exhorted the delegates to "go home and give the nominations their whole and most energetic support." Its editor asserted that the governor's friends had given him up with "the utmost difficulty," from the conviction that his identity with the system might endanger the success of General Harrison as the party's presidential nominee.[59]

Bigger and Howard, both lawyers, were able and respected men. Neither had voted for or been closely linked with the System of 1836. Bigger, born near Cincinnati, Ohio, in 1802, moved to Liberty, Indiana, in 1829 but soon settled at Rushville. He served in the legislature two sessions as a representative from Rush County, then as a circuit judge from 1836 until soon after his nomination for governor. Howard, native of South Carolina born in 1797, arrived at Bloomington, Indiana, about 1830, and moved to Rockville a few years later. As a resident of Tennessee in 1828 he had voted for Old Hickory as a Jackson elector. From 1833 until 1839, when elected a congressman, he was federal district attorney for Indiana.[60] The *Tri-Weekly Journal* termed Bigger a man of "strict political and moral integrity," and observed that he had won first honors in graduating from Ohio University. The *Western Sun* called Howard "a man of strict integrity, honor, independence and talents," superbly qualified to be governor.[61] The Whig editor of the *Tri-Weekly Journal* quipped that "The Local Focos have nominated their *big* man for Governor; but the friends of Harrison have nominated a *Bigger*."[62] Samuel Hall and Benjamin S. Tuley added geographical spread to their respective tickets. Hall, of Gibson County, had twice represented his county in the House of Representatives, and had been an original member of the Board of Internal Improvement. Tuley, of Floyd County, had never served in the legislature. In an effort to link him with the system the *Indiana Journal* contended that his "*storehouse*" had been "*illuminated on account of the passage of the Internal Improvement Bill.*"[63]

What to do about the System of 1836 was the dominant issue in the contest between Howard and Bigger. The address of the Democratic State Convention, reported by Robert Dale Owen, argued that "EXTRAVAGANT SPECULATION" and "a recklessly extended SYSTEM OF CREDIT" had been the one great cause for the existing commercial distress. During the ascendancy of the Whigs, formerly known as Federalists, the address charged, Indiana had undertaken to construct on credit a system whose cost was originally estimated at $16,000,000, for which the price tag had jumped to $25,000,000, yet not one work had been completed. Though admitting that the bill had been adopted and carried forward with bipartisan support, the address asserted that for its "original projection . . . and for its entire management, the whigs are, and of right ought to be, strictly responsible." Prudence called for stringent economy and retreat, not abandonment of the system, nor could there be any retreat from the Jeffersonian principle for the honest payment of debts and the sacred preservation of public credit. If this caused heavy taxes, the blame should rest on those who incurred the debts; and putting off tax burdens to the next generation was termed untenable and dishonorable. What should be done with the unfinished projects was considered the particular province of the legislature to decide.[64]

While the Democratic address emphasized state over national issues, the Whig address principally stressed national issues and lauded General Harrison. Reported to the convention by Richard W. Thompson, it charged that the Jacksonians, by fostering state banks and state internal improvements over a federal bank and federal internal improvements, along with related policies, had caused the widespread prosperity of 1836 to be replaced by general distress. A "great revulsion in the currency," attributed to the Jacksonians, had produced the suspension of specie payment by

banks, the suspension of most internal improvements, unemploy-
ment, the inability to pay both public and private debts, and other
ills. The sudden change from prosperity to distress had resulted
from "the ignorance and quackery" and the "extravagance and
corruption of *Martin Van Buren*" and Democratic officeholders.[65]
    Bigger commenced campaigning weeks ahead of Howard. In
March the *Indiana Democrat* asserted that Bigger had retained his
position as president judge of a circuit court to gain money from
the state to pay the cost of his campaign. Bigger resigned his judgeship, effective March 29, and by the end of April had addressed voters at Vincennes.[66] Though Howard had quickly accepted his nomination, near the end of March, despite solicitation from friends to
the contrary, he averred his intent to continue his congressional duties to the end of the session.[67] Perhaps because the session became
an extended one, he apparently left Washington early in June.[68] On
June 27 he spoke at Indianapolis, probably making campaign talks
in southeastern and central Indiana enroute to the capital.[69]
    The rival candidates expressed their views about policy regard-
ing the system. In a speech at Madison Bigger was reported as
having said that as a judge he had "taken no part in the strife"
which had developed concerning the system, but had "ever been
opposed to it, as too large for the then, or present resources of the
State." The suspended works should be preserved from dilapidation or ruin as soon as possible, "*without burthening the people with
additional taxes*," and those nearest completion which promised
the most revenue should gradually be prosecuted. Doubtless
seeking votes by riding on Harrison's coattails, he told his Madison audience that they must choose between "General Harrison
and . . . General Ruin."[70] Soon after learning of his nomination,
Howard expressed his views about the system in a letter to a
Whig state senator from southern Indiana. He had favored commencing a system of improvement and prosecuting it in a manner
to render it productive as the work progressed, but had "considered the system established, too large, and so expressed myself."
Hence, "From the time the system went into operation I was a
classifyer, as is known to my friends generally." If elected governor, the people must not expect him to sanction "prosecution of

the public works in the manner in which they have been prosecuted from the commencement," nor any law authorizing state
bonds "for loans prior to the receipt of the money to be given for
them." In any event, "the legislature should never borrow a dollar until they have provided means to pay the interest." Howard
said the choice ahead was between evils, since "almost the whole
community" had gone astray a few years earlier and the state as
well as the people had "engaged in extravagance and . . . folly." In
March, while yet in Congress, Howard urged that the "canvass
may be conducted without angry disputation." In a statesmanlike
manner he suggested that "The question now is, not WHAT
HAS BEEN DONE, but WHAT SHALL WE DO?"[71] As the
campaign ended the *Indiana Democrat* reported that Howard was
advocating "That each of the public works shall be disposed of to
companies, with a guaranty that they shall be finished." And, if
not, "that the works shall be classified *by the Legislature*, subject to
the approval of the *people*, at the ballot box." The editor of the *Indiana Democrat* suggested that some works could be disposed of to
private companies and others progress by the state through classification.[72]

   While Howard and Bigger perhaps traveled the high road,
their partisans used political rhetoric. The *Indiana Democrat* described Bigger as a man of high moral and intellectual attainment,
but one who in every way had aided those who had ruined and
prostrated the state. "Backwoodsman" lambasted the Whigs for
mismanagement of the system, whereby $3,000,000 had been
squandered for a "patch-work of uncompleted public works,"
while annual state expenditures had soared from only $30,000 in
the last year of Ray's administration to over $600,000 yearly.[73]
Whigs argued that Howard, despite his statement otherwise, had
supported the system as adopted and had been slow in endorsing
classification. The *Indiana Democrat* contended that Noah Noble
and his "sanctified coadjutor," Jesse L. Williams, were using their
official power and the people's money as members of the Board of
Internal Improvement to spread the word that Howard was entirely opposed to all parts of the system and would veto any legislation to carry the works forward. After the election the *Indiana*

Journal asserted that in places where expedient Howard had urged early completion of the most useful works, but spoken against the same in the southwestern part of the state to gain votes there.[74]

The state election in August yielded a sweeping triumph for Bigger, who obtained 62,932 votes against 54,274 for Howard. Both men carried scattered counties in southern, central, and northern parts of the state, with Bigger winning fifty-six counties as opposed to thirty-one for Howard. Bigger ran well in counties of the Whitewater Valley, while Howard gained most of the counties in south central Indiana. Party lines were closely drawn as Hall defeated Tuley by close to the same margin, and carried much the same counties as Bigger had over Howard. In the legislative races the Whigs won lopsided majorities in both the House and Senate, giving them unprecedented control of the General Assembly.[75] Harrison's popularity among Indiana voters, as demonstrated in the presidential contests of 1836 and 1840, seems to have been an important factor in causing this Whig triumph. But Van Buren's unpopularity as Harrison's rival possibly hurt Howard more than Harrison's popularity aided Bigger. Moreover, Bigger campaigned for a longer period than Howard, and the former's views about the system probably were considered by many voters as affording more prospect for its ultimate completion, or at least for more parts of it, than the views of Howard. Whatever the reasons, the state election of 1840 represents the high tide of National Republican-Whig domination of state politics which had its beginning in the middle twenties.

When the General Assembly met in December, 1840, it had the responsibility of electing a treasurer, auditor, and secretary of state. With party lines hardening and lopsided control of both houses by the Whigs, the prospect for reelection of Treasurer Nathan B. Palmer and Secretary William J. Brown, both Democrats, was unfavorable. Auditor Morris Morris, a Whig, was concluding his fourth term.[76] When the elections occurred on December 11, George H. Dunn, a Whig, easily defeated Palmer on the initial ballot. William Sheets, a Whig who had served as secretary from 1833 to 1837, defeated several rivals to become secretary of state again. Auditor Morris won a unprecedented fifth term on the second ballot, with William T. Noel, a Whig, his strongest rival. Apparently neither Dunn, Sheets, nor Morris obtained anything like all of the Whig vote.[77] Calvin Fletcher, a Whig, opposed Dunn's election, not that he thought him dishonest but "had not firmness to risist [sic] temptations which would be presented." The *Indiana Democrat* commented: "*Rotation in office! Rotation in office!* that darling whig doctrine, is all a sham. Morris Morris, who has been Auditor *for twelve* years is to be Auditor three years longer. Messers Brown and Palmer are *proscribed.*" It accused the Whig leaders of monopolizing the offices, so that "the *little whigs*, with the democrats, are to be proscribed."[78]

Although Samuel Bigger had not been closely associated with the System of 1836, it was his misfortune to be governor while Indiana sank into fiscal insolvency following its breakdown. Shortly before Bigger became governor in December, 1840, the internal improvement board, consisting of former Governor Noah Noble and Chief Engineer Jesse L. Williams, offered a pessimistic picture about prospects for the system. After observing that the state had "exhausted her former means upon so many objects, leaving all in an unfinished and unproductive condition," the board confessed its "inability to present a plan for going forward" but repudiated "every suggestion, for an abandonment of the enterprise." Since to "surrender all that has been done would end in ruin to the State," there was "no escape but to go onward until the advanced and more profitable lines are completed. Such a course, only can ameliorate the burden of taxation, to our citizens." By spending an additional $2,000,000, the board suggested, "over 400 miles of the forward and most valuable works" may be completed; and "render available an investment of some four millions now unproductive, and which cannot otherwise contribute to the relief of the tax-paying community." With a further expenditure of $1,500,000, "100 miles more may be completed." Unable to indicate where such money might be secured, the board suggested that private enterprise be "permitted to construct [or complete] one or more of the best works for our bonds," under proper safeguards. Without using the word classification, Noble and Williams indicated that it would be preferable to either abandon the system or its simultaneous construction.[79]

The extremely embarrassing fiscal situation was forcefully spelled out by Treasurer Nathan B. Palmer. According to his annual report, at the end of October, 1840, the entire state debt, both funded and unfunded, aggregated $13,667,433. He itemized it as follows:

1. State bonds sold for the Wabash and Erie Canal $1,727,000

2. Other internal improvements bonds, sold prior to October 31, 1839, and heretofore reported to the legislature $5,932,000

3. Bonds entrusted to the Morris Canal and Banking Company in 1838, to be exchanged for other bonds, which have been withheld and disposed of by said company, which it alleges its inability to return or account for $300,000

4. Other bonds sold to Morris Canal and Banking Company in 1839, not before reported $190,000

5. Bonds sold in fall of 1839 to banks in Buffalo, New York $282,000

6. Bonds sold and delivered to the company at Madison for Madison and Indianapolis Railroad Company $221,000

7. Bonds issued to Lawrenceburgh and Indianapolis Railroad Company $221,000

8. Bonds issued to [State] Bank for advance of fourth installment surplus revenue $294,000

9. Bonds on account of the State Bank "(including Mr. Merrill's $1,000,000 loan)" $2,390,000

10. Unfunded debt due branches of State Bank, for advances on public works in 1839, about $692,433

11. Treasury notes issued prior to this date $1,284,000

12. Unpaid claims for operations on Wabash
    and Erie Canal, the present year [1840] $84,000
13. Unpaid claims on public works for
    operations previous to 1840, to be $50,000
    paid by further issue of treasury notes,
    estimated at 50,000 $13,667,433

Palmer reported that $7,219,000 in bonds had been issued for the system, $1,727,000 for the Wabash and Erie Canal, and $221,000 for the Lawrenceburgh and Indianapolis Railroad—making an aggregate of $9,167,000 for internal improvements. The principal on more than one third of these bonds, or $3,559,791.34 of them, had not yet been received. The treasurer took a dim view about when, if ever, more than a modest amount of this unreceived principal at most would ever be paid the state. He emphasized that other means than this source must be found to pay interest on the bonded debt and to liquidate the unfunded debt, principally for the system but partially for the trunk line canal, which totaled $2,110,433. Especially startling was Palmer's calculation that it would require $723,371.65 to pay all the interest due during 1841 on the entire state debt. He considered only $195,000 of this sum available from existing sources, leaving $528,371.65 yet to be obtained. Doubtless convinced that taxes had to be increased sharply, if interest payments were continued, Palmer, a Democrat, admonished that the "honor and credit of the State" and "her character and all that is dear to Indiana, require and demand that undoubted provision should be made to meet this sacred obligation" on a permanent basis.[80]

In his inaugural on December 9, Samuel Bigger stressed items about internal improvements. "The question of paramount importance" he said, is "what shall be done with our public improvements?" After noting that over $5,600,000 had been spent on nine different works in the system, "many portions of which are nearly ready for use," Bigger added that it would take about $14,000,000 to finish the entire system. The new executive admitted that the system was prostrate, and he asserted that its "simultaneous prosecution," as originally intended, "would be the extreme of folly." But its "entire abandonment . . . would scarcely be less ruinous . . . leaving us to discharge the interest, and finally, the principal, without any prospect of remuneration." The governor recommended that the works be protected from injury and decay, then as means become available complete those that require the least cost and promise the greatest revenue and most advantage to the state. Thus, via classification.[81] Although doubts were expressed about the wisdom and expediency of selling the works, Bigger suggested that if "responsible companies can be induced to take the works . . . with proper conditions and restrictions, the State can well afford to grant [them] the most liberal terms of payment."[82]

The governor expressed great concern about payment of the interest on the state debt during 1841. He reminded legislators that the tax levy for 1840, greatly reduced from that of 1839, would "fall far short" of paying such interest. Concerning this reduction Bigger acidly commented that men seeking "present popularity, may risk such a course"; but the "real issue" was not "merely the reduction of taxes," but the question of "Shall the faith and character of the State of Indiana be sustained?" With apparently a barb at House Democrats who had supported the reduction, Bigger added that if this situation was repeated, the conclusion would be regarded that it was "the solemn determination of the State, that she will not pay her debts." And this would "affix a stain on the character of her citizens that could never be effaced, and would render our name a reproach and a by-word." But because much individual indebtedness remained to be paid, it might be "inexpedient to resort to full taxation" until the year 1843.[83]

The governor observed that some people thought payment of the state debt to be "almost impossible." But putting on his Whig hat he optimistically contended that if a pending plan for distribution of federal land sales among the states was adopted, then Indiana could "safely" expect to receive $30,000,000 from the distribution. With such a sum Indiana could pay "her current debts," use it as security for "judicious works of [internal] improvement," lighten taxes, and have "the means for the most liberal provision for the benefit of common schools, and the general promotion of education." These remarks, heavily laden with Whig rhetoric, were based on unrealistic presumptions.[84]

A few weeks after Bigger's inaugural address, Milton Stapp, as perhaps his last significant act as a fund commissioner, paid the semiannual interest on the debt due January 1, 1841. Calvin Fletcher reported on good authority that Stapp had "hypothicated 1/2 million bonds to pay our January [1] interest." Fletcher commented: "So we are going more deeply in debt & this process must soon terminate with utter ruin & insolvency of the state." A short time later he predicted that "a number of states" will "fail paying the July interest due England on the state bonds."[85]

At the legislative session of 1840–1841 the Whigs had overwhelming majorities in both houses of the General Assembly.[86] In the Senate a committee, whose chairman and most members were Whigs, strongly supported classification. In reporting for the committee, Chairman James H. Cravens of Ripley County, stated that it could scarcely conceive of a greater political calamity than renewing "the old plan of a simultaneous prosecution of all the works." The committee submitted a bill which proposed that the Whitewater Canal be put in the first class, the Madison and Indianapolis Railroad in the second, and the other works in the third. All unfinished portions of works in the third class should go to private companies, and their finished portions as well, provided the requirement that profits from them must go toward liquidation of the public debt could be removed. The report also called for tighter control over actions of the fund commissioners and internal improvement board by the legislature.[87] The House Committee on Canals and Internal Improvements, comprised entirely of Whigs, also favored classification. The report of a majority of the committee by its chairman, Caleb B. Smith of Fayette County, asserted that the system as adopted in 1836 had been larger than its friends desired. The majority declared that "simultaneous prosecution of all [its works] would meet with no favor from any quarter." But through "a judiciously modified" plan of classification the state could finish all the works in the system.[88] The minority report of two Whigs from another House committee insisted that only one or two works be resumed to test whether the result would warrant further construction on other works.[89]

A bill classifying works in the system passed the legislature early in February. It put the Whitewater Canal, between Brookville and Connersville; the Madison and Indianapolis Railroad, from Vernon to Edinburgh; and the Grand Rapids of the Wabash River, below Vincennes, in the first class. The sum of $150,000 was appropriated for construction on the canal, $100,000 for the railroad, and $50,000 for improvement of the rapids. These appropriations, however, were subject to money being obtained from the suspended debt, *if money from this source remained after*: first, the state's outstanding treasury notes had been paid; second, interest owed on the public debt for 1841 and 1842 had been paid; and third, the state's outstanding hypothecated bonds had been redeemed—making the appropriations worthless. All other items were termed second class. This act authorized corporations or individuals to complete unfinished portions of works—and "enjoy the use and profit" from them. Within a ten year period the state could take over such works by paying the amount corporations or individuals had spent on them, plus interest thereon at 6 percent.[90] A related act allowed counties on the line of the Madison and Indianapolis Railroad to levy 5 cents per $100 of taxable property, for the years 1841 through 1845, to gain revenue toward its construction.[91] To save money and secure as much as possible from the suspended debt, the assembly reduced the fund commissioners from two to one, and gave the single commissioner broad authority "to take charge of, collect, settle, and receive the suspended debt due, and other property belonging to the state . . . ." The commissioner could employ legal counsel, make compromise settlements, travel anywhere within the United States, or go to Europe if need be in performance of his duties. If necessary to pay interest on the debt or redeem treasury notes due, he could sell new bonds or hypothecate those already hypothecated. A supplemental act provided that such bonds could not bear more than 7 percent interest.[92] Immediately upon passage of this legislation the General Assembly elected Noah Noble the new commissioner.[93]

Obtaining money to pay interest on the public debt for July 1 and thereafter was the most difficult problem facing the legislative session of 1840–1841. The Whig dominated session raised the state levy, which had been 15 cents per $100 on taxable property and 50 cents on polls for 1840, to 40 cents per $100 on such property and 75 cents on polls for 1841. Moreover, whereas only 5 cents of the levy on property for 1840 had been earmarked to pay interest on the state debt, all of the property levy for 1841 was so designated but with the proviso that if the tax on polls failed to cover the ordinary costs of state government the balance needed would be taken from the levy on property.[94] In a further effort to secure additional money to pay interest on the internal improvement debt, the legislature required that the sinking, surplus revenue, college, saline, and state bank (school tax) funds "be drawn in and invested in bank stock" on behalf of the state.[95] A significant gain in revenue was also anticipated in the assessing and collecting of taxes, which were expected to increase the amount of property assessed and decrease the cost of collecting taxes due.[96] Other enactments tightened regulations about the collection of tolls and water rents from internal improvements, required receipts and expenditures concerning internal improvements to be accounted for by both the auditor and treasurer, and prohibited the further issue of bonds to prosecute any work in the System of 1836.[97] Although these acts of the Whig dominated session of 1840–1841 proved quite inadequate to meet the interest on the state debt for July 1, 1841, or convince creditors that with concessions this and other payments would be met, its efforts were more significant and honorable than those of the previous session when the Democratic controlled House had caused the tax levy for 1840 to be less than that for 1839.

Fund Commissioner Noah Noble made valiant but unsuccessful efforts to pay the semiannual interest due July 1. While in New York City the "months of March and April passed," he later reported, "without realizing any thing" from the suspended debt. He found the bond market so depressed that he doubted whether he could sell Indiana bonds, even at the 7 percent interest authorized by legislators. Back in Indianapolis by May, Noble conferred with state officials and tried in vain to get the needed money from branches of the Second State Bank. Meantime, Rothschild and Sons, through whom much of the interest was paid, appealed to President Harrison to help prevent Indiana from defaulting. On learning of the appeal, Governor Bigger wrote Noble, who had again left for New York City, expressing his view "that if the interest is not paid in July the credit of the State is irretreviably [*sic*] gone." If not paid, there would be "little hope" of reviving payments, and probably a repudiation of the suspended debt, "no matter how *innocent* the present holders may be." The governor gave his impression "that if we can weather the storm to the end of the present year, we can then sustain ourselves." Hence, perhaps before creditors would "pertinaciously insist upon their pound of flesh, and thus destroy all at a single blow," they would accept payment for the July interest in 7 percent bonds. But Noble was unable to make collections from the suspended bonds, and secured only about $30,000 of the 7 percent bonds. Hence, Indiana defaulted on the payment of interest for internal improvements bonds due July 1, 1841.[98] Next day, while yet in the East, Noble explained his unsuccessful effort to make this payment, and repeated his offer to pay in 7 percent bonds. Before learning of the default on interest, Philip Mason, a Whig who had succeeded Noble on the Board of Internal Improvement, wrote Noble that he did not expect the payment to be made. If not, he said, with almost precise accuracy, "we will be unable to pay one cent for the next six years."[99]

When the General Assembly met in December, Governor Bigger appropriately advised legislators that they had "met under peculiarly trying circumstances." After noting that there was "some difficulty in ascertaining the exact amount of" some items in the state debt, he detailed them as aggregating $15,088,146, all of which seems to have resulted from internal improvement costs, save $1,390,000 in bonds for establishing the Second State Bank. Of this total, $3,381,000 was indicated as the suspended debt for which no principal had been received. The governor frankly stated that the "simultaneous prosecution" of large and expensive works included in the system had been a prominent cause for the "present embarrassments." Moreover, two "great errors" had been committed in the construction of the system. First had been the payment of most of the interest from borrowed money, hence the people did not realize how much "extravagant expenditures" were accumulating. "The second error was selling bonds on credit," resulting in some who had bought them not paying the principal as promised.[100] Thus, "for some time to come" the state would lack "the means to discharge the interest on the whole of our public debt." Bigger explained that the further sale of bonds, at their low price, would make the total debt unbearable; and that "for several years" the tax revenue would nearly all be paid in treasury notes, unacceptable by bondholders for interest. But disavowing repudiation of the state debt and abandoning of the System of 1836, the executive urged that the state "collect all her scattered means" and try to make some of the "most valuable works" become profitable. By husbanding resources, as wealth and population increased, Indiana would become able to "pay her debts, and finally redeem her sunken credit."[101] Senator Ebenezer M. Chamberlain, a Democrat from northern Indiana who had voted for adoption of the System of 1836, called Bigger's address "rather an extraordinary document," one generally well spoken of by men of both parties. After claiming that the governor and his fellow Whigs had admitted that "Indiana is a ruined State," Chamberlain protested the failure to admit that the Whigs, by mismanaging the state's interests and finances, had *"done it."*[102]

In contrast to the legislative session of 1840–1841, when the Whigs had overwhelming majorities in both houses, at the 1841–1842 session the Democrats had a modest majority in the House but the Whigs retained a majority in the Senate.[103] On the second day of the session, the Senate adopted a resolution the preamble of which declared it to be "notorious" that some who had borrowed money to prosecute the system had "been guilty of gross negligence . . . whereby great loss" had been sustained by the state; observed that it had been "surmised" that one or more officials had "been guilty of fraud in the sale of bonds"; charged that commissioners to superintend the various works had "been guilty of gross mismanagement and of wasteful and unnecessary expenditure of the public money," with rumors that one or more commissioners had "fraudulently" made expenditures "for private ends"; and related charges. About two dozen persons were cited to appear before the bar of the Senate on the third Monday of December to answer questions under oath about such matters. A committee of five, embracing three Whigs and two Democrats, was named to conduct the investigation.[104] Next day the House resolved that a committee of nine members be named to investigate how bonds to finance the system had been obtained and disposed of. This committee was given "power to send for persons and papers," and it was required to report "all the evidence detailed before them." The House committee consisted of five Democrats and four Whigs.[105] Both committees made lengthy reports which included much testimony from persons who had appeared before them. The committees agreed that there had been great laxity in how matters had been handled, and that some actions had been illegal. Only a few matters went to court, and some of the suits were won by defendants. The Senate committee commented concerning "the difficulty of distinguishing between those evils which are properly attributable to the legislation under which these officers have acted, and the consequences of their negligence or malconduct." It also understandably stressed that it could not pretend that its "statement of what appears to be fact, is always correct." There was considerable consensus among members of the committees regarding the performance of particular individuals, but some Democrats objected that certain Whigs had been treated too gently.[106] Senator Chamberlain, minority member of the Senate committee, put on his Democratic hat and charged that the committee had been too generous to Noah Noble, and had tried "to whitewash . . . His Dictatorial Highness" Jesse L. Williams. The northern Indiana Democrat asserted that a loan obtained by Merrill, president of the State Bank, had been one "by which we were swindled out of a million of dollars, as quick and as easy as ever a professor of the black-art played a trick of juggling." He sarcastically called Merrill "Our profound Financier, the Biddle of Indiana . . . ." Chamberlain jabbed that Merrill had been let off "by merely ranking him among the biggest fools that have ever given the world specimens of western financiering." Dr. Isaac Coe and Milton Stapp were branded "stars of first magnitude, in this galaxy of worthies" who had been "chosen and sustained by the Whig party," each of whom he considered "justly liable on their bonds" for not less than $100,000.[107]

Even a cursory examination of these reports affords convincing evidence that laws about the system had fostered loose practices and wasteful expenditures. Democrats as well as Whigs were responsible for such legislation, but since the Whigs had been much the dominant party, and most of the officials who bought the bonds and prosecuted the system had been from their ranks, the onus for its downfall and the fiscal debacle which ensued mainly fell upon them. This responsibility, perhaps more than any other factor, contributed to the gradual transfer of power from the Whigs to the Democrats during the first half of the forties.

As the preceding pages have indicated, when the General Assembly met in December, 1841, the System of 1836 was in shambles. Millions were owed on a bonded debt for it and the Wabash and Erie Canal, and the annual interest on this debt was several times the aggregate yearly average of the ordinary costs of state government. Not one work in the system had been completed, and the revenue from the finished portions was *insufficient even to maintain them from ruin and decay*.[108] Moreover, Indiana was in the depth of a depression which did not yield to prosperity until the middle forties. Following the default on interest due July 1, 1841, the basic question was whether Hoosiers *could* and *would* pay this bonded debt and the interest on it. Throughout the early forties there were assertions that Indiana would pay principal and interest in toto, even if it took years to make full payment. At the same time, there were proposals that at least the suspended debt be repudiated; that perhaps the state could somehow buy up the bonds at their low market price, thus redeem them at far less than their face value; that perhaps at least a substantial part of the debt might be assumed by the federal government, or be liquidated by federal distribution of proceeds of land sales from the public domain; and that a "compromise settlement" should be effected with the creditors. As these and other proposals were considered, protestations persisted that Indiana's honor and fair name must not be tarnished by repudiation of money owed or by any dishonorable action. Moreover, several successive legislative sessions failed to take actions which indicated a determination to honor the state's obligation to pay principal and interest owed.[109]

At the session of 1841–1842, the House Ways and Means Committee, dominated by Democrats, concurred with Bigger that Indiana could not at once resume payment of interest on the bonded debt for internal improvement. In a report dripping with sarcasm and laden with partisan jabs, the committee declared that a tax high enough to pay this interest would put burdens upon "citizens equal to those imposed upon the serfs of Russia, and place them upon an equality with the peasantry of England or France." Under no circumstances would the people "consent to such unreasonable and oppressive levy," which view former legislatures had seemingly recognized. Moreover, even in the system's heyday, its friends (the Whigs) had "never *dared* to levy a tax to meet the [entire] interest on the internal improvement loans." The committee recommended a levy of 20 cents on each $100 of taxable property, which, if continued for succeeding years, would "meet all the necessary expenditures of the State government and gradually . . . absorb the outstanding treasury notes." The committee emphasized that no higher levy would be necessary, hence "the idea of onerous taxation may be removed from the minds of the people." "Nothing can operate so injuriously to any country," the committee pontificated, "as the belief that its citizens are liable to be oppressed by taxation." A bill submitted by the committee recommended a levy of 50 cents on each taxable poll as well as the 20 cents on each $100 of taxable property.[110]

At its session in 1841–1842, the General Assembly made no provision for payment of interest on the bonded debt for the System of 1836. It approved the recommendation of the Ways and Means Committee, and made the annual levy 20 cents on each $100 of taxable property and 50 cents on taxable polls, with half of the property levy set aside for redemption of treasury notes. The treasurer was authorized to "appropriate any available funds" to liquidate treasury notes or "other liabilities of the State." *Thus, the legislature made payment of the unfunded or domestic debt its priority, and turned its back on the semiannual payments of interest on the bonded debt.* This legislation was devoid of any commitment toward ultimate payment of the interest and principal of the bonded debt which the state had pledged when the System of 1836 was approved. It lowered the levy on property for 1842 to half what it had been for 1841, and decreased the tax on polls by one third.[111] The signal it sent bondholders was chilling and extremely negative. A related act made treasury notes in units of $5 acceptable "in payment of all public dues" except for trust funds, money for schools, and sales of Wabash and Erie Canal lands. This enactment gave these notes wide acceptance, and encouraged payment of taxes owed in them.[112]

The 1841–1842 session also turned its back on any effort to complete the System of 1836. The legislature offered all or any of its works to private companies. Such companies, properly organized, were to be given all the rights the state had regarding tolls, water rents, right of way, and continuation of their construction. A company approved to continue a work, by giving the state bonds equal in value to the cost of the part already finished, would obtain title thereto. Even if a company did not obtain title to a segment taken over, as soon as it completed ten additional miles of line contiguous to the segment, it could operate it and share in its proceeds. Counties were empowered to buy stock in these companies, while the net proceeds of state owned segments were to be invested in companies continuing them. After twenty years had passed the state could buy out companies, and resume control of works by paying companies what they had spent for construction, plus interest at 6 percent. As many companies might be organized as required to complete the system. This law terminated the internal improvement board, fund commissioner, and principal engineer, and it provided agents and commissioners to preserve works remaining in state hands. Provision was made for election of a state agent, by joint vote of the assembly, to perform what had been the duties of the fund commissioner, except he could not "execute, sell, deliver or hypothecate state bonds for any purpose." This agent was authorized to dispose of all debts due the state for the system, and all property and securities held by the state on account of bonds sold, on such terms as he deemed for the interest of the state. In addition, he was to settle or "compromise" the suspended debt or any of its parts.[113] A companion act empowered the agent to bring suits or make compromise settlements as seemed warranted by the testimony collected by the Senate and House investigating committees, and asked him to report to the next General Assembly about these and related matters. When the legislators met in joint session, Michael G. Bright, a Democrat from Madison, was elected state agent on the initial ballot.[114]

The act authorizing private companies to take over works in the system passed the House by the decisive margin of 54 to 33, and the Senate by the considerable edge of 29 to 19. The negative votes were preponderantly from Democrats, yet in both houses Democratic votes were essential for passage.[115] Twenty-two members of the House, including nineteen Democrats and three Whigs, protested the approval given private companies. They objected that the measure gave away, without any consideration, works which had cost the state over $6,000,000; that it bestowed "exclusive privileges," involving banking powers and related privileges, on "irresponsible, soulless, and mercenary" corporations; and violated the great American principle of equal rights by its "prospective bestowment of exclusive privileges on associations or companies of men."[116] Representative Marshall S. Wines, a Democrat from Allen County who presented the protest from members of the House, advised constituents that many votes were gained for passage by the argument of proponents that the companies would purchase the state bonds in order to own "all the public works" so "by these means the State would get out of debt"; and that several votes were secured along the line of the Madison and Indianapolis Railroad because of the expectation its "early and certain completion" would follow. Wines scoffed at the idea that such companies would ever buy any state bonds. Instead he predicted that Indiana might be "'shingled over'" with as many as one hundred corporations, which while failing would "remunerate themselves by frauds practised on the community" prior to their demise. Both Wines and Representative William B. Mitchell, a

Democrat from Elkhart County, bitterly objected that northern Indiana would have to pay much of the debt which had been largely created for the purpose of developing transportation facilities in the southern area of the state.[117]

Indiana was not "shingled over" with corporations to complete portions of works, and apparently no company ever bought any of the bonds which the state had purchased for their construction.[118] In June, 1842, Governor Bigger proclaimed the organization of the Madison and Indianapolis Railroad Company to finish this line from Griffiths, in Jennings County, to Indianapolis; and two months later he proclaimed the organization of the White Water Valley Canal Company to finish the Whitewater Canal from the National Road down the West Fork of the Whitewater River past Brookville to its terminal at Lawrenceburg on the Ohio. Then in October, 1843, Bigger proclaimed the establishment of the Wabash and Eel River Canal Company to complete the western part of the Cross Cut Canal, to link the Wabash and Erie Canal at Terre Haute and the Central Canal near Newburg in Greene County.[119] In addressing the General Assembly in December, 1842, the governor told legislators his understanding that the Madison and Indianapolis Railroad and the White Water Valley Canal companies were being "prosecuted with energy and spirit, and strong hopes are entertained of a successful termination." In his final message to the legislature a year later, Bigger observed that the Wabash and Eel River Canal Company had been established "under very favorable circumstances"; and he expressed his understanding that the Madison and Indianapolis Railroad and the White Water Valley Canal companies had prosecuted their work "with a zeal and determination which promise fair for their completion."[120] But, as far as the author has discovered, private companies for completion of works in the system for the most part met with either failure or limited success.[121]

Meantime, the legislature had commenced surrendering works to local control and maintenance. Early in 1842 it authorized the commissioners of Vanderburgh County to assume control of the segment of the Central Canal between Evansville and the Feeder Dam on Pigeon Creek, keep it navigable, and collect tolls from its use. If they so desired the commissioners of Warrick County could participate with those of Vanderburgh County in the control and operation of this short segment of the Central Canal. At the next session of the assembly the Jeffersonville and Crawfordsville Road was put under the supervision of the commissioners of the counties through which it passed in accordance with existing legislation. When desirable the commissioners could have toll bridges erected with the revenue from them for the county or counties involved.[122] Thus, while some works were being transferred to private companies as Bigger's term ended, other works were being surrendered to local control.

The legislative session of 1842–1843, the last under Governor Bigger, had a Whig majority in the Senate and a Democratic majority in the House.[123] Shortly before the session commenced, Auditor Morris Morris reported that it would require $609,289.35 to pay interest owed on the bonded debt for the System of 1836 and the Wabash and Erie Canal during the ensuing year. To pay this interest by taxation, Morris explained, would require a levy of 65 cents per $100 of taxable property, besides a levy of 5 cents per $100 on such property to meet the ordinary costs of state government. These levies, the auditor estimated, would require from taxpayers an "average [of] about five dollars and fifty-four cents for internal improvement purposes, and about one dollar for the ordinary expenses of the government."[124] In his annual address to the legislature, Bigger expressed the view that Indiana could not meet all its current obligations to creditors, but he expressed his confidence that in time Indiana would discharge its obligations and avoid the "lasting infamy" of repudiation. The Whig executive made no recommendation concerning the tax levy for 1843, and the legislature continued that for 1842. Hence, the levy remained at 20 cents per $100 of taxable property, with three fourths of the levy reserved for redemption of treasury notes.[125] In his final message to the legislature in December, 1843, Bigger told legislators that the public debt remained about the same as it had been two years earlier, when he reported it as $15,088,000. The debt had been reduced, mainly by liquidation of treasury notes in payment of taxes; but the accruing interest had added to the amount owed creditors on internal improvement bonds. Bigger again made no recommendation regarding a tax levy for the ensuing year, but he asserted that "the worst is past" and repeated his opinion that in time Indiana could and should meet its obligations and avoid the disgrace of repudiation. Nevertheless, the outgoing governor frankly admitted that "The system of state improvements, from which so much was anticipated, has failed, involving the State in a debt beyond her immediate resources."[126]

While the General Assembly was abandoning the System of 1836 construction of the Wabash and Erie Canal continued westward down the Wabash Valley. When construction stopped on the system in 1839, the canal was expressly exempted from this mandate.[127] Moreover, having been commenced in 1832, it had not been a part of the system but the latter had principally been tributary to the canal. Three factors in particular explain the favored status given the Wabash and Erie Canal. First, it was anticipated as a much needed trunk line for trade between Indiana and the Atlantic Coast via Lake Erie, the Erie Canal, and the Hudson River to New York City. Second, in contrast to the system, it was financed in significant part by a federal land grant of five sections of land for each mile of canal. Third, it was expected to yield substantial revenue from tolls on traffic and to a lesser extent from the renting or leasing of water power.

Construction of the Wabash and Erie Canal continued during the forties, but its financing was amid straitened circumstances. Under date of December 11, 1840, the fund commissioners reported that from the start of construction a total of $2,078,582.21 1/2 had been spent on the canal between the Ohio line and the Tippecanoe River. Receipts, however, had aggregated $2,063,665.24 1/2, leaving a deficit of $14,916.97 in the Wabash and Erie Canal Fund. But the actual deficit seems to have been much larger than this sum. The commissioners explained that the fund owed obligations amounting to $326,277, with items owing it of $311,360.03, thus the deficit of $14,916.97. Among items owed the canal fund, however, was $152,275.80 from the *disreputable Morris and Canal Banking Company*.[128] Moreover, the annual report of the Board of Internal Improvement for 1839–1840 noted that the proceeds secured from sale of canal lands had been insufficient to pay contractors the sums owed them, hence "$86,587 47 [was] due them and their creditors." The board recommended that these contractors be paid in treasury notes, as had been done for obligations due contractors when the system had been suspended.[129] The General Assembly, however, provided that certificates the board had given for sums owed canal contractors be made receivable for purchase of canal lands, making this debt a charge against the canal lands rather than the state treasury.[130] Noah Noble, from the internal improvement board, estimated that costs of the Wabash and Erie Canal, from the Ohio border to the Tippecanoe River, had aggregated $1,843,114 to November 1, 1840; and he predicted that when finished this 129³/₄ mile segment would cost a total of $2,056,634.[131] As the above items suggest, different sources calculated canal costs in different ways but however calculated henceforth the canal was expected to look, at least principally if not entirely, to the proceeds from sales of canal lands, tolls from traffic conveyed, and revenue from the renting or leasing of water power.[132]

The straitened financial status of the trunk line canal to the East was augmented because Ohio had not yet finished its part of the outlet to Lake Erie. Shortly before Bigger became governor in December, 1840, the improvement board advised legislators that the Wabash and Erie Canal was "fully ready for navigation" for the 140 miles "from the State line to Lafayette," but completion of the Ohio portion to the lake "cannot be anticipated earlier than the spring of 1842." The board called Ohio's delay "incompatible with her general character for enterprise and public spirit" and "injurious and unjust towards her sister States"; and urged Ohio to make "one determined and vigorous effort . . . for the immediate completion of this important thoroughfare."[133] The Hoosier legislature asked the governor to express to the executive of Ohio Indiana's "deep interest" in having the entire canal navigable by the end of 1841. In a lengthy letter to his Ohio counterpart with irritation evident, Bigger indicated that Ohio's segment, though "commenced early in 1837 cannot be completed until near the close of the year 1843," thus requiring "nearly seven years" to build its eighty miles of canal.[134]

As Ohio's part of the canal neared completion, Hoosier antici-
pations grew. Late in 1841 the improvement board forecast "a
perfect outlet to Lake Erie" by August 1, 1842. During the summer of 1842 a Vincennes paper quoted a Toledo editor who announced that boats had passed from the almost finished canal into
Lake Erie. "The Wabash and Erie Canal," the Ohio editor exu-
berantly proclaimed, "is but one of the links of a vast chain of inland water communication, of more than three thousand miles in
extent. East it has two points of termination, the city of New York
is one, and Montreal the other.—New Orleans is the Western. It
is the connection by water, of the Gulf of Mexico and the Gulf of
St. Lawrence; and at New York, the broad Atlantic."[135]

The Wabash and Erie Canal was at last open for navigation
from Lake Erie to Lafayette in April, 1843, eleven years after the
digging had begun on the "summit section" at Fort Wayne. A gala
celebration was held there on July 4. Accompanied by bands, including a German band in uniform, the celebrants assembled on
Thomas Swinney's farm for a barbecue, speeches, and toasts.
Lewis Cass of Michigan, who had helped clear the Indian title
from the area through which the canal passed, the principal ora-
tor of the day, voiced the expansionist sentiments of Manifest
Destiny. Hoosier Senators Albert S. White and Edward A. Hannegan; Henry W. Ellsworth; and Governor Ethan Allen Brown,
of Ohio, added to the oratory. Messages were read from Martin
Van Buren, Henry Clay, Richard M. Johnson, Daniel Webster,
and others. Visitors arrived by horseback, wagon, and canal boat,
the boats reportedly extended in double tier along the canal
through the town, with participants estimated from at least eight
to fifteen thousand.[136] A correspondent of the Lafayette *Journal*
commented that "Although the laborious sons of Erin have done
so much to consummate this second union of the Lake with the
Mississippi, whose rites were consecrated on the 4th at Fort
Wayne, yet, there was nothing to characterize the scenes as 'an
Irish wedding'"; but "'all was merry as a marriage ball.'"[137]

The Indiana segment of the newly opened canal rested on a
fragile financial basis. The state auditor reported that
$2,671,434.35 had been spent on it, from the Ohio line to the

Tippecanoe River, from its start to November 1, 1843. Proceeds from this part of the canal, however, had been only $692,087.23, or almost $2,000,000 less than costs. The proceeds had preponderantly come from sales of the 325,041.14 acres which Congress had donated to aid in its construction. All but a negligible amount of this acreage had been sold and most of the anticipated revenue from the sales had also been obtained, while only $46,870.38 had been secured from tolls and rental of water power during 1843.[138] Moreover, during the years 1840 through 1843, construction and maintenance costs had principally been paid by issues of treasury notes and canal scrip. Repair and maintenance costs were considerable in part because many of the canal's early wooden structures were much decayed and in need of repair or replacement.[139] And interest on the bonded debt of $1,727,000 for the canal east of the Tippecanoe River had been accumulating at the rate of about $87,350 annually since the suspension of interest payments on July 1, 1841.[140] If the completed part of the canal was to become a self-liquidating venture, a large increase in canal tolls had become indispensable.

When construction began on the Wabash and Erie Canal in 1832 the junction of the Wabash and Tippecanoe rivers, about fourteen miles above Lafayette, was established as its western terminal. Four years later the System of 1836 included an appropriation of $1,000,000 to extend the canal to Terre Haute. The legislature soon appropriated money for extension of the canal to Lafayette but Hoosiers saw the possibility of persuading Congress to extend the grant of five sections of land per mile of the canal to Terre Haute, and Congress agreed to this in 1841. Considerable progress had been made toward extension of the canal to Terre Haute when Bigger left office in December, 1843. But these developments are a prelude to the larger account of how and why the canal was ultimately completed to Terre Haute in 1849, and then completed and opened for navigation to Evansville, on the Ohio River, in 1853. Hence, they are discussed in the ensuing chapter.[141]

While Indiana's system of internal improvements precipitated a catastrophic fiscal debacle, the ordinary costs of state government more than doubled. These costs for 1837–1843, as the accompanying tables show, averaged $113,591.27 per annum versus only $50,130.83 for the years 1831–1837.[142] The enlarged costs arose principally from five sources. First, the legislative apportionments of 1836 and 1841 greatly expanded the number of legislators. Second, the growth in the number of judges and prosecutors as new judicial districts were added as population increased and spread northward.[143] Third, there were significant percentage increases in pay to judges, legislators, and the governor. Fourth, the substantial attention which legislators gave questions about internal improvements and banking added costs by lengthening sessions and expanding legislative journals and laws to be published.[144] Fifth, there was a considerable increase in costs regarding the state prison. The principal expenditures for the most part were for the same items as from the early years of statehood.[145] For the first time money spent on the state library exceeded that for premiums on wolf scalps. Modest payment was made for the state's initial geological survey, and a small sum for the deaf and dumb suggests the start of state money for benevolent purposes.

The jump in ordinary costs, and the use of most tax revenue for internal improvement costs, made an increase in tax levies essential. When the ad valorem or general property tax was first levied in 1836, it was but 5 cents per $100 of taxable property and the levy on polls was 50 cents each. As shown in the accompanying tables, higher levies were enacted for the period 1837 to 1843, with parts of the taxes set aside for internal improvements.[146] The revenue table which follows indicates that all but a small portion of the state revenue, which averaged $261,475.23 yearly, versus $51,527.80 for the period 1831–1837, came from taxes. In contrast to the previous years from statehood, most tax revenue was spent for internal improvements rather than ordinary costs. It *seems* probable that *roughly* $887,366.72 of the aggregate tax revenue went to pay interest on the bonded debt for the System of 1836 and the Wabash and Erie Canal and especially for redemption of treasury notes issued to contractors after suspension of the payment of interest on the bonded debt for internal improvements in 1841.[147] Auditor Morris Morris estimated that the levies

Ordinary Expenditures, 1837–1843

Fiscal Year	Legislative	Printing	Judiciary	Executive	Taxes Paid Collectors	Debt
1837–38	$ 43,412.68	$18,321.67	$ 21,194.36	$ 3,297.60	$14,816.97	$ 5.00
1838–39	42,562.12	17,798.93	16,405.12	2,716.66	14,725.95	4.00
1839–40	45,052.17	12,457.81	21,804.19	3,850.00	28,219.23	0.00
1840–41	38,092.59	12,876.28	21,004.79	3,559.55	8,445.04	27.00
1841–42	33,826.39	8,646.35	19,872.04	8,349.81	19,871.52	0.00
1842–43	39,842.28	10,895.77	26,992.42	5,550.00	12,086.64	0.00
Total	242,788.23	80,996.81	127,272.92	27,323.62	98,165.35	36.00
Average	40,464.70	13,499.46	21,212.15	4,553.93	16,360.89	6.00

Ordinary Expenditures, 1837–1843

Fiscal Year	Prison	Militia	Library	Wolves	Contingent	Specific Appropriations	Miscellaneous	Total
1837–38	$1,022.86	$75.00	$591.45	$443.50	$1,212.38	$6,962.44	$1,010.00	$112,365.91
1838–39	1,065.36	190.25	437.50	335.00	1,059.66	8,369.18	2,870.29	108,540.02
1839–40	19,651.69	125.00	400.00	78.50	671.09	6,251.97	1,946.30	140,507.95
1840–41	1,655.23	150.00	562.07	10.00	823.61	8,528.03	1,344.64	97,078.83
1841–42	5,043.40	176.63	448.93	1.00	1,370.16	3,100.96	1,097.37	101,804.56
1842–43	17,222.12	225.00	811.21	4.00	1,737.15	4,645.41	1,238.39	121,250.39
Total	45,660.66	941.88	3,251.16	872.00	6,874.05	37,857.99	9,506.99	681,547.66
Average	7,610.11	156.98	541.86	145.33	1,145.67	6,309.66	1,584.49	113,591.27

Ordinary Revenue, 1837–1843

Fiscal Year	Taxes Received	Taxes Paid Collectors	Borrowing	Prison	Miscellaneous	Total
1837–38	$ 164,633.08	$14,816.97	$0.00	$ 0.00	$ 682.50	$ 180,132.55
1838–39	163,621.71	14,725.95	0.00	0.00	365.99	178,713.65
1839–40	313,547.02	28,219.23	0.00	18,100.00	204.98	360,071.23
1840–41	168,900.94	8,445.04	0.00	0.00	355.97	177,701.95
1841–42	397,430.54	19,871.52	0.00	0.00	273.89	417,575.95
1842–43	241,732.88	12,086.64	0.00	0.00	836.53	254,656.05
Total	1,449,866.17	98,165.35	0.00	18,100.00	2,719.86	1,568,851.38
Average	241,644.36	16,360.89	0.00	3,016.66	453.31	261,475.23

for internal improvements cost taxpayers an average of $1.03³/₅ annually for the years 1837 through 1840.[148]

During the Wallace-Bigger administrations there was much discussion pro and con over increased pay to state officials. Since this compensation comprised a substantial part of the costs of state government, reducing pay was an inviting target for those who sought lower tax levies. Early in 1837—during the final year of the Noble administration and months before the Panic of that year began—the legislature had raised the salary of the governor, Supreme, and circuit judges to $1,500, $1,500, and $1,000 respectively. At the same time the per diem of legislators was increased from $2 to $3, with an additional $3 allowed for every twenty-five miles of travel to and from the capital by the most usual route.[149] During the depression the *Indiana Democrat* vigorously defended a further increase in the salary of circuit court judges. Its editor asserted that from their salary of $1,000 annually they had to pay travel costs and, unless they had other means, also sustain their families and buy their libraries. He said that if meager salaries caused men of talent to leave the bench that "little *bush whacking pettifoggers* who . . . degrade the halls of Justice" would take their place. Already, the Democratic editor added, the western country was so cursed. While the depression persisted, this editor advocated compensation sufficient to attract competent men to hold office. Judges in particular should be well paid because the "practice of able lawyers is worth much more than the salary paid to a judge." In 1841 the pro-Whig *Indiana Journal* reported that various members of the Senate advocated "that all salaries, particularly of the Executive and Judicial officers, should be increased."[150]

Unsuccessful efforts were made to reduce per diem to lawmakers. In December, 1840, Governor Wallace urged reduction of legislative costs by greatly curtailing the number of legislators, but he did not suggest a reduction of per diem. The *Indiana Democrat* advocated reducing per diem to $2 or even $1.50, explaining that with excellent boarding available in Indianapolis at $3 a week there was no reason to pay legislators $21 weekly! This paper suggested that if per diems were halved and pay to circuit

Indiana Tax Levies, 1837–1843

Year	Levy per $100 property owned	Poll tax
1837	15¢ per $100: ordinary costs state government 5¢ per $100: for internal improvements Total tax per $100: 20¢	50¢
1838	15¢ per $100: ordinary costs state government 5¢ per $100: for internal improvements Total tax per $100: 20¢	
1839	20¢ per $100: ordinary costs state government 10¢ per $100: for internal improvements Total tax per $100: 30¢	50¢
1840	10¢ per $100: ordinary costs state government 5¢ per $100: for internal improvements Total tax per $100: 15¢	50¢
1841	40¢ per $100: for internal improvements If poll tax not enough to pay ordinary costs, money needed may be taken from levy on internal improvements. Total tax per $100: 40¢	75¢
1842	10¢ per $100: ordinary costs state government 10¢ per $100: redemption of treasury notes 2 mills per $100: Deaf and Dumb Asylum Total tax per $100: 20¢ and 2 mills	50¢
1843	5¢ per $100: ordinary costs state government 15¢ per $100: redemption of treasury notes 2 mills per $100: Deaf and Dumb Asylum Total tax per $100: 20¢ and 2 mills	

court judges were doubled that thousands of dollars would be saved and justice be much better served.[151] At the legislative session of 1841–1842, Senator Robert C. Gregory, a Whig, doubtless with tongue in cheek, proposed that per diem be slashed to 25 cents a day, with legislators required to come to the capital on an old gray horse not worth more than $10. And members should bring at least one month's provisions in a tow bag, along with an old case knife, prepared to eat their meals together on the steps of the capitol, ready to resume business at any moment. Representative James P. Millikan, a Democrat, proposed that a committee consider the expediency of paying $3 per diem for the first thirty days of a session, $2 for the next thirty days, and $1 for any additional days.[152] At the session of 1842–1843—the last before the gubernatorial election of 1843—the Democratic controlled House passed a bill to lower per diem to $2, but the Senate rejected this bill.[153]

Meantime, at the 1840–1841 session pay to the treasurer, auditor, and secretary of state had been reduced. The treasurer and auditor reported to the House that their salary was $400 per annum, the secretary that his salary was $600, but all three indicated receipt of additional sums for other duties that more than doubled their official salary. A select committee of the House recommended that each official be paid "a certain salary" plus clerk hire. It observed that the treasurer occupied "a residence, the property of the State, designed for that purpose."[154] The General Assembly responded by raising the salary of the treasurer and auditor to $1,000, with an allowance of $400 for clerk hire; and a salary of $800 for the secretary, plus $300 for clerk hire. These salaries and allowances were to be "in full compensation for their respective services" as required by law.[155]

Compensation to officials developed strong partisan overtones at the session of 1842–1843, which immediately preceded the gubernatorial and other elections of 1843. The partisanship was encouraged since the Democrats controlled the House, and the Whigs the Senate. The *Indiana State Sentinel*, staunchly Democratic, insisted that officeholders who never worked in the broiling sun of a long summer; or during storms of rain, wind, or hail; and "have nothing to do but to hang at the public teat and suck, suck, suck!," should lighten the burden "of the toil-worn farmers, by reducing their own salaries!" Officeholders were pictured as working short hours at labor which soiled their fingers, while farmers toiled early and late throughout the year, risking crop failures and lacking time to gad about in silks and broadcloths.[156] Senator Nathaniel West, a Democrat from Marion County, introduced a bill to decrease the salary of the governor and treasurer to $1,000 each, the salary of the auditor and secretary of state to $600 each, and the per diem of lawmakers to $2.[157] The finance committee of the Senate, consisting of six Whigs and three Democrats, strongly opposed the reductions proposed by West. "Illiberal and incompetent allowances will not secure the services of competent and vigilant officers," it asserted. But ample compensation enabled "the poor man as well as the rich" to hold office, while meager pay "secures to the wealthy a monopoly of all offices; and . . . secures all the higher state offices to the wealthy living at, or near the seat of government . . . ." An adequate salary for judges, the committee stressed, is important for as wealth, trade, civilization, and the arts advance "judicial questions multiply, not only in number, but in complication and interest; and the benign influence of the judiciary is the more felt and the more needed." The committee said Indiana ranked tenth in population among the twenty-six states, but the Hoosier governor had a salary $1,009 less than the average, and below that for the executives of Ohio, Michigan, Illinois, and Kentucky. Pay to Supreme Court judges was about $585 below average, that for circuit judges $645 below; and only one state paid circuit judges less than Indiana. The treasurer, auditor, and secretary of state, whose compensation had been lowered in 1841, were considered underpaid compared to what most states paid. The committee noted that the postmaster of Indianapolis received $177 more per annum than either the governor or Supreme judges of Indiana; while postmasters at Madison and Vincennes secured more pay than Indiana's circuit judges. The per diem of $3 allowed legislators was 8 cents under the average for the states; the same as in Ohio, Michigan, and Kentucky, but less than for Illinois and seven southern states. The Senate approved the unanimous recommendation of its committee that no legislation be enacted regarding per diems or salaries.[158] The House Ways and Means Committee, comprising four Democrats and three Whigs, supported reduced compensation largely because of deflated prices resulting from the depression. After observing that farmers, from whom the main support of state officials comes, were obtaining no more than "one half for all the products of their farms" than that received in 1838, the committee declared that justice required an easing of tax burdens. Reduced pay, it said, would not be unjust to officeholders "because 50 cents in fees now is worth quite as much in the purchase of all the necessaries of life as one dollar was five years ago." The House Committee on Public Expenditures recommended passage of a bill to reduce salaries of the treasurer, auditor, and secretary of state, with elimination of their allowances for clerk hire. The deflation of prices and the contention that their duties had decreased was offered as the basis for such reduction. Despite the agitation pro and con, the per diems of legislators and salaries of state officials were unchanged by the legislative session of 1842–1843.[159]

Meantime, during the Wallace-Bigger years the ad valorem or general property tax became firmly established. From statehood until 1821, for practical purposes all state tax revenue had come from taxes on land. From then to the levy of general property taxes in 1836 the poll tax supplied considerable part of the tax revenue, but its relative importance declined thereafter. This broadening of the tax base, along with a rapid gain in the polls and property subject to levy, made possible a several fold jump in revenue for 1837–1843 over that for the preceding six years under Governor Noble. From statehood the assessing or listing of property had been by one or more assessors or listers named by the county boards, while the collection of state tax revenue had been by the county sheriff or another person named by the board.[160]

Three concerns in particular led to important changes in the assessing and collecting of taxes during the early forties. The need for money to help finance internal improvements stimulated these changes. The principal concerns were that much property and many polls escaped taxation, that great inequalities and inconsistencies existed in assessments from county to county, and that property not on or near internal improvement projects paid the same rate as those on or near them. During the late thirties Governor Wallace had discussed these concerns in messages to legislators.[161] In his inaugural in December, 1840, Governor Bigger asked legislative consideration of "the unequal assessments of real estate in the different counties, with a view of providing for their equalization." He declared that "counties which are to reap the advantages to be derived from the public works" should pay an increased portion of the tax revenue.[162] The defects, however, mainly concerned the assessing rather than the collecting of taxes. Treasurer Nathan B. Palmer and Auditor Morris Morris agreed that for some years the tax revenue had generally been promptly and faithfully collected. But Morris "doubted whether, in any state the assessments, including the valuation of property, is worse done than in Indiana."[163] At the legislative session of 1838–1839 a House committee had recommended that "a state board of assessors, or district boards" be established to "equalize taxation" among the counties. The Ways and Means Committee submitted a bill for a state equalization board, but it was not approved.[164]

At the session in 1840–1841, however, with Whig majorities in both houses, significant modifications were made in the assessing and collecting of taxes. Auditor Morris, responding to a request of the House that he suggest legislation to make the system more equitable and less expensive, submitted a package of seven bills.[165] Several of his proposed changes were enacted into law by the General Assembly. The new law required that county boards name one suitable county resident as an appraiser to make an *initial appraisal* of real estate, and list its true and full value after viewing the land and its improvements. The county auditor, rather than the county clerk, was required to prepare the yearly tax duplicate; the county assessor was to assess all property, both personal and real; and the county treasurer, not the sheriff, was to collect the state taxes. These three officials were elected by the voters of the counties. Both county and state boards of equalization were established, but county boards had already existed. The assessments for 1841 were to be made under the old legislation, with the new law followed as far as practical, thus affording the appraisers time to complete their valuations of property in anticipation of the assessment for 1842. By this time the newly elected auditors and assessors would be in place. But the collection of the revenue for 1841 was to be under the new legislation, which required treasurers to meet taxpayers on stated days at township voting places, after which payment would be received at the county seats until a certain time.[166]

The new tax code of 1841 illustrates the all-inclusiveness of the general property tax, first levied only five years previously. It declared all land taxable which had been purchased from the general government for five years or more; all land the state had sold re-

garding the Wabash and Erie Canal, Michigan Road, the seminary [Indiana University], and the salines; and reservations to
both Indians and whites resulting from federal treaties. With
some limitations, personal property, both tangible and intangible,
was declared taxable, ranging from such items as household furniture, cash and current bank notes on hand, stock in corporations, notes, and bonds, to bills of exchange. Land exempted from
taxation included the public domain belonging to the United
States, and acreage sold therefrom for five years subsequent to its
sale, plus improvements. Generally speaking land owned by religious societies for church or burial grounds; for educational purposes; for state and county libraries; for purposes of county government; and by hospitals, almshouses, and houses of correction
were excluded from taxation. The acreage exempted varied from
a maximum of ten acres for churches and burial grounds to 320
acres for county poor farms and manual labor schools or colleges.
Personal property excluded from taxation embraced that belonging to hospitals, almshouses, and houses of correction; stock
owned by the state or by literary and charitable institutions; the
personal property of a widow and children, not exceeding $200 in
value; and the necessary beds and bedding, not over two per family, and clothing for the family. As regards the poll tax, males
above fifty years of age were freed from this levy.[167]

Although the revised tax legislation apparently resulted in improved administration and increased revenue, the item about a
state board of equalization was repealed before it became effective. In September, 1841, "Veto," perhaps a Democrat from Knox
County, charged that this innovation had been obtained by "bam-
boozling" southern legislators or by treachery of aspirants who
wished to become speaker of the House. "Veto" argued that since
southern Indiana land was less valuable than other land that
northern members of the state board would insist on lowering
valuation of land in their area, thus adding unfairly to the tax burdens in the south. During August Robert Dale Owen had called
the plan for the state equalization board "absurd" and "mon-
strous" and asked for its repeal. "We *must*," he said, "trust something to our county officers."[168] In November Auditor Morris

staunchly defended the new law, claiming that it had saved the people $20,768.18 in collecting the revenue of 1841. Morris emphasized that the state board was "*not* to increase the aggregate valuation of the State, but to distribute that valuation fairly between the different counties."[169] When the assembly met in December, the Democratic controlled House quickly passed a bill to abolish the state equalization board. Representative John Hendricks, a Democrat from Shelby County, said his constituents authorized him to say that if the state board increased their taxes even one "picayune" it would not be paid. Early in January the Senate laid the abolition bill on the table.[170] The Whig dominated Senate called the state equalization board "one of the most essential features in the new revenue system," and predicted that it would have "popularity amongst the tax-payers, as fast as it is understood." A bill to reorganize this board, recommended by this committee, passed the Senate by the narrowest possible vote, but the House immediately rejected it by a close vote.[171] Following defeat of the reorganization bill the Senate approved a bill to repeal the state equalization board by a slender margin, and the House quickly passed it by almost a two to one margin.[172] Although Democrats were largely responsible for this outcome, a number of Whigs supported the action and a lesser number of Democrats opposed it. The centralizing trend, represented by the state equalization board, was doubtless opposed by many on principle; however, its abolition seems to have owed as much to Democratic partisanship as to commitment to principle.

Meantime, while the System of 1836 became a heavy liability for the Whigs, the substantial success of the Second State Bank did not yield them an offsetting credit. Established in 1834, the bank, like the system, had been enacted by significant bipartisan support. But as for the system its management and operation had been mainly by Whig officials. During 1834–1836, peak years for economic prosperity, the bank became a profitable institution.[173] During the years 1837–1843, however, three major storm clouds hovered over it. First, was the Panic which began in 1837, followed by the depression of the late thirties and early forties. Second, was its suspension of specie payment in May, 1837, making its charter and continuation subject to the discretion of the General Assembly. Third, was the state's heavy borrowing from the bank to finance the system, which prompted the legislature to seek revenue from the bank in ways that violated desirable banking practices. As these storm clouds swirled, the bank came under much criticism, especially by Democrats.

The first severe test that the Second State Bank experienced began in May, 1837. Late in the preceding year Governor Noah Noble had called attention of legislators to the "perplexing and deranged condition of the currency and unsettled state of the money market in the Atlantic Cities," which had caused Indiana's internal improvement bonds to be sold on less favorable terms than previously. During 1836 and early 1837 Calvin Fletcher frequently commented in his diary about unsettled markets, pecuniary pressure, business and bank failures, excessive speculation, and widespread reliance on credit.[174] On May 13, 1837, various merchants of Indianapolis met, exchanged ideas about the economic situation, and resolved to make proportional payments on items due eastern creditors. Two days later merchants met again, discussed the "approaching crisis," and agreed to further meetings weekly.[175]

While local merchants pondered the financial situation, the state bank board convened at Indianapolis on May 17. As Fletcher, Hugh McCulloch, James F. D. Lanier, and other members convened, news arrived of bank failures in New York, Mississippi, and Louisiana, with more failures anticipated. Since the bank had about $1,200,000 of deposits from banks of other states, and about this sum in federal deposits for which transfer drafts were pending, the bank was vulnerable to the depletion of its large specie reserve.[176] Next day messengers from the Lawrenceburg and Madison branches brought news of a general suspension by banks in the eastern cities and Cincinnati. Of particular concern was the information that within "a few hours after the suspension in Cincinnati" all paper of the branches had been "bo't up & sent by runners to Lawrenceburg & to the other branches" for redemption. Upon arrival of the runners at Lawrenceburg, the branch had "prudently shut her doors"; while the Madison branch had closed before their arrival there. The day this news arrived members of the board met with Governor Noble and Nathan B. Palmer, state treasurer. Samuel Merrill, president of the bank, posed the basic question whether to "Let our specie be drawn out by Banks that owe us when they have closed their doors?" Suspension of specie payment would be contrary to the arrangement for federal deposits as well as make the charter subject to forfeiture. "After a most solemn diliberation [*sic*] in which the Governor & Treasurer both took part," Fletcher confided to his diary, "we agreed to permit each branch to suspend if it thought best and messengers were dispatched to each branch."[177] Save for this decision, "citizens of other states would draw from us every dollar of our specie," President Merrill asserted in a circular to the people of Indiana. Merrill stated that there was no cause for alarm, adding that the bank had "upwards of a million" of specie in its vaults. He pledged, on behalf of the board, resumption of specie payment "the hour" neighboring banks did so. Apparently all branches quickly suspended.[178]

The suspension received significant public and bipartisan support. On May 19 Merrill addressed a meeting of citizens at Indianapolis in which he explained the reasons for the suspension and stressed the "perfect solvency" of the bank. Lanier, a member of the board representing the Madison branch, described the "extraordinarily flourishing condition" of the Second State Bank. It had, he said, "more specie in its vaults than any other banking institution in the United States, in proportion" to its capital. The meeting approved a resolution, reportedly adopted almost unanimously, approving the suspension. Other resolutions promised support to the branches, expressed confidence in their ability to meet their obligations, and recommended an early convening of the legislature.[179] In the afternoon a meeting of merchants, at the countinghouse of Nicholas McCarty, "unanimously" sustained the suspension; and promised to receive paper from the branches at par in payment of debts due them.[180] "Many Citizens" thought there was "cheerful acquiescence among all the people" for temporary suspension, but objected that a legislative session would cost at least six to ten thousand dollars and cause "exaggerated accounts" of the bank's actual condition.[181] The *Indiana Journal* and

Indiana Democrat, rival party organs at the capital, both endorsed the suspension of specie payments. The latter paper said that no "other safe course could have been pursued," otherwise specie would have been drained from the West to the East, with notes of eastern banks of uncertain solvency replacing the lost specie. The Democratic editor called the bank one of the most solvent institutions in the country.[182]

As the suspension continued for weeks and months, however, the Second State Bank came under vigorous criticism, especially by Democrats. In June the *Indiana Democrat* doubted Merrill's skill as a banker, and insisted that the bank should be *extending* in place of *reducing* its loans. A few months later this Jacksonian organ charged that "by *shaving* the public" stockholders of the bank were reaping large profits.[183] The editor said he was uncertain whether the bank had forfeited its charter, but he was "fully convinced that it has forfeited public confidence." Meetings were recommended for all counties to elect delegates to a state convention to consider whether the charter had been forfeited. If so, attention should be given to "what additional restrictions ought to be put upon the bank." Inasmuch as suspension was contrary to its charter, amendments could be exacted as the price of its continuation.[184]

In December, 1837, retiring Governor Noah Noble staunchly defended the suspension of specie payments. Had members of the state board not recommended "an immediate suspension to the Branches," Noble advised legislators, they would have been "faithless to their trust" and have acted contrary to the public interest. President Merrill explained that the bank had protected its large sum of specie, reduced its loans, and decreased its holding of the paper of other banks. In his inaugural as the new governor David Wallace neither discussed the suspension nor made any recommendation about the bank.[185] Although the chairman and most of the members of the judiciary committee in the House were Whigs, Chairman Samuel Judah reported that a "very decided majority" agreed that the charter was "subject to forfeiture," but because the bank was "necessary for the public prosperity" all agreed with "the propriety of not enforcing a forfeiture" and extinguish it. Judah reported that a minority of the committee opposed amending the charter, while a majority viewed amendments as outside their assignment.[186] In the Senate a bare majority of its judiciary committee, including four Democrats and one Whig, declared suspension an "incontrovertible" fact. The majority of the members, however, viewed suspension as best for the people and the bank, opposed forfeiture of its charter, but wanted the charter "tendered back to the bank, with such amendments as time and experience" indicated for the public good. A minority of the committee, comprising three Whigs and one Democrat, argued that the bank was not limited to the express terms of its charter but had authority "to exercise certain powers, necessarily inferred from her existence, and essential to her perpetuity as a financial institution," hence had not violated its charter by suspension.[187]

The General Assembly declared that suspension had been "justifiable and necessary" in the existing circumstances. This body mandated the state bank board to require every branch to resume payment of specie within thirty days after resumption in the Atlantic cities and simultaneously with banks of Ohio and Kentucky. Both houses approved this action by large majorities.[188] Meantime, Dr. Isaac Coe had been a delegate to a bank convention that convened at New York City on November 29, 1837. This convention deemed it premature to fix a date for resumption of specie payments, but at its adjourned meeting in April, 1838, the first Monday in January, 1839, was established as the time for resumption. James F. D. Lanier and John Law, delegates for the Second State Bank at the adjourned meeting, voted for the date approved after having voted in vain for earlier dates, including May 10, 1838.[189] The Second State Bank, however, continued to encourage resumption as soon as adequate consensus for resumption was obtained. In December, 1838, President Merrill reported that "a general resumption was . . . finally effected by the banks in the Eastern, Western, and Middle states on the 13th August [1838] last with but little inconvenience to our citizens or to the bank."[190] On that date Calvin Fletcher had commented: "This day all our br[anch] Banks commence specie payments which were suspended in May 1837 thro out the union." He rejoiced for the resumption, which he presumed all states but Mississippi and Louisiana would participate in; however, "for the next 2 years" he expected "to see the greatest pressure we have yet endured."[191]

With the deepening of the depression in 1839, the Second State Bank again suspended specie payments during the fall of that year. In October the *Indiana Journal* reported bank failures in the East, and presumed that western banks would have to do likewise or be drained of their specie and perhaps even fail. Its Whig editor predicted the downfall of the existing banking system, then people would discover that "State institutions and not individual corporations" were best for banking. "The former," he added, "will always command the confidence of the people while the latter never can, no matter how solvent and safe." The rival *Indiana Democrat* anticipated resumption of suspension as "a glorious thing for the people and the country," offering a chance to root out existing evils and replace unsound and swindling banks with safe and sound ones.[192] When the state bank board met in mid-November, it had reports that there had been "a partial suspension" in some branches "so far as relates to foreigners & brokers." The board, however, "concluded not to recognize any suspension," but left each branch free to chart its own course.[193] Apparently all branches "suspended" about this time; however, during the late thirties and early forties there appear to have been *partial suspensions* and *partial specie payments* during times of so-called general suspensions.[194]

As the depression persisted, suspension became protracted. In December, 1840, Samuel Merrill, president of the state bank, reported that "Since October, 1839, most of the banks in the middle, southern and western States, have not paid specie on their notes as usual."[195] In January Merrill presided over a bank convention at Louisville. Delegates from Indiana, Ohio, and Illinois attended, but it failed to establish a date for resumption.[196] Soon after the state election in August, which gave Democrats a majority in the House and greatly narrowed Whig control of the Senate, the *Indiana Democrat* asserted that the bank violated its charter every hour it failed to redeem its notes in specie. "What would become of the farmer or laborer," its very partisan Democratic editor inquired, "were he thus to set the laws at defiance?" A short time later this editor urged that the General Assembly force an *"immediate and unconditional resumption of specie payments"* upon the bank.[197] The *Indiana Journal* appropriately asked whether its Democratic rival was aware that if Indiana banks resumed before those of Ohio and Kentucky that their specie would be withdrawn for the benefit of banks and brokers elsewhere. It also emphasized that the bank was ready and willing to resume, and was continuing to seek cooperation of banks in other states to this end. The Goshen *Democrat*, an important and vigorously Democratic organ in northern Indiana, agreed that resumption should be compelled but opposed destruction of the bank because its interests and those of the state were interwoven.[198] Early in December, 1841, Merrill declared that "general resumption of specie payments, under favorable circumstances, would, with prudent management, do much to restore public confidence." Perhaps to assuage legislative and other critics, he announced that at its last meeting the state bank board had set August 1, 1842, "for the resumption of specie payments, and other Banks in neighboring States have been notified and requested to co-operate." If resumption could be commenced sooner, Merrill added, "the Bank will unite in the effort."[199] In a joint resolution approved January 31, 1842, the General Assembly mandated resumption for not later than June 15, 1842. If, however, banks of the four neighboring states failed to resume specie payments, Indiana banks were to be exempt from this mandate.[200] As June 15 approached the state bank board concurred with this date for resumption by branches of the state bank. In December Merrill reported that "resumption of specie payments commenced on the 15th of June, and has since been, and will be, maintained."[201] But for at least a few branches resumption at first had not been in toto.[202] So ended the "general suspensions" which had been in effect for most of the five years plus from May, 1837, to June, 1842.

The ability with which the Second State Bank survived the financial upheaval of the late thirties and early forties, while paying substantial dividends to state and private owners, greatly enhanced its reputation. In recounting bank failures in the Old

Northwest, William Gerald Shade concluded that "Only the State Bank of Indiana came through the period with its reputation intact." And R. Carlyle Buley, in his two-volume opus on the Old Northwest, declared that "Its record stands out in contrast with most of the flimsy banks of the day."[203] These accolades have much merit; nonetheless, the much praised bank suffered from undesirable practices, particularly at the hands of directors, other stockholders, and officers. Samuel Merrill, its president from the beginning in 1834 until 1843, mingled criticisms with his defense and support of it. In his report for 1837–1838, Merrill noted that about 40 percent of all branch loans had been to stockholders, with over half of this total to a small number of bank directors.[204] In his next yearly report, the president observed that stockholders too often wanted to procure loans rather than dividends; and that borrowers constantly sought to turn temporary loans into long ones, making it necessary for the bank to decrease its circulating paper as well as its loans to others.[205] In December, 1840, Merrill gave emphasis to his comment that "There have been almost no difficulties in managing the bank, which have not arisen mainly from the purchase of stock by persons with the expectation of borrowing money on more favorable terms than could be allowed to others." Two years later the president asserted that "The *large loans*, the *long loans*, and all *special favors*, to directors and stockholders, have been not less injurious to the borrowers than to the Bank." The branches at Lawrenceburg and South Bend, he explained, were in "difficulty from the large debts of those who are, or have been, stockholders." Thus, "it is much to be regretted that they cannot also perform the proper duties for which they were established." Late in 1843 Merrill explained that the Lawrenceburg branch whose "officers, directors, and stockholders were accommodated with large loans, many of which were suffered to continue for long periods without any material reduction," had been suspended by the state bank board.[206]

Early in 1838 a bipartisan committee of the House of Representatives, comprising two Whigs and two Democrats, vigorously criticized the manner in which the bank had been operated.[207]

The committee insisted that the bank had been established for the public good, but had been subverted for private advantage and profit with the support of even its president and the state bank board.[208] The institution should be reclaimed and brought under state control to provide "for the State a sound and convenient circulating medium, and of furnishing to our enterprizing citizens additional capital at 6 per cent. interest." Its officials should "secure to the public at all times, a fair proportion of specie for the discharge of the liabilities of the bank, and . . . prevent all those expansions and contractions, which all admit to be so ruinous."[209] Moreover, Indiana's banking capital was much too low. The eleven existing branches should have their capital increased by $100,000 each, and further increased "in proportion to the wealth and business of the State"; and new branches should be established.[210] As for the existing branches, "improper advantages" had been "given to directors and stockholders" at the Lafayette, Indianapolis, and Lawrenceburg branches. The committee, however, was "happy to state that the answers of the Terre Haute, New Albany, Madison and Fort Wayne Branches . . . show that the officers of those Branches understand their business, and do not dread investigation." The branch at Richmond had "been managed with great prudence and moderation . . . ."[211]

As adverse criticism of the Second State Bank continued, at its session in 1841–1842 the General Assembly named an agent to make a thorough examination of its performance. The Senate, heavily dominated by Whigs, proposed such an appointment. The Senate expressed its preference for Tilghman A. Howard, defeated Democratic candidate for governor in 1840, to become this agent. The House, however, heavily dominated by Democrats, insisted on the naming of Nathan B. Palmer who had voted in favor of chartering the bank prior to his serving as state treasurer from 1834 to 1841; and the Senate deferred to its preference.[212] The resolution naming Palmer instructed him "faithfully and impartially" to make a careful and detailed examination of the operation of all branches. Palmer was also invited to propose changes regarding the bank "of importance to the interests of the institution or the State."[213] This bipartisan consensus for such an examination, and Whig approval for a Democrat as the agent, strongly suggests that legislative friends of the bank hoped that partisan and other criticism of it would thereby be muted.

Palmer's report about the bank, submitted late in 1842, was supportive of it but extremely critical of how it had been managed. As Palmer began his report he emphasized that the existing "cash means of the Bank amount to over half the immediate cash liabilities of the institution, which may be regarded as a very safe and healthful condition for seasons of ordinary confidence and prosperity, but in the present disastrous condition of things [the continuing depression], both in relation to confidence and business, it will require much foresight and prudence to carry the Bank safely through."[214] The "large accommodations to favorites and men of influence, rather than of responsibility," Palmer asserted, had perhaps been the most injurious of the errors suffered by the bank. Many had become stockholders, lacking spare capital, then as "mere borrowers," had been favored, especially in some branches, "leaving unpaid large amounts of paper of questionable character."[215] Of $2,606,526.48 owed the bank in discounted notes and bills of exchange, Palmer reported that more than one fourth, or $702,526.89 of this aggregate, was either under protest or in suit. He estimated that $533,083.33 of the latter sum would be lost to the bank, which, plus other losses, would bring the total to $642,188.61 or close to one fourth of its discounted notes and bills of exchange receivable.[216] Palmer explained that the state owed the bank $930,047, apparently from advances for internal improvements, which he considered "dead weight upon the Bank . . . not likely soon to be convertible, so as to afford aid to the Bank or the community." This large private and public debt to the bank Palmer viewed as a reduction of an equal amount in its capital and ability to do other business. His view that the business of the bank would be modest for a period of time prompted Palmer to conclude that a substantial reduction of capital, by its surrender in payment for such indebtedness, would be beneficial to the bank, the state, and private debtors.[217]

Included with Palmer's report were evaluations of each branch and lists of persons indebted to the thirteen branches. Generally speaking those at Evansville, Fort Wayne, Madison, New Albany, Richmond, Terre Haute, and Vincennes fared better than the branches at Indianapolis, Lafayette, Lawrenceburg, and South Bend; and in some respects better than the remaining branches at Bedford and Michigan City. Because of its reckless management and embarrassed condition, Palmer recommended that the branch at South Bend "immediately be put in liquidation." Although the Lawrenceburg branch had suffered from "too much scheming and favoritism" to directors and other stockholders as well as misconduct on the part of some officers, in lieu of its recent improvement in management and financial condition its closing was not recommended. The Indianapolis branch, Palmer stated, had been "conducted with considerable skill and ability, so far as money-making was concerned," but had "greatly erred in the practice of favoritism, and exorbitant loans and large debts." Its losses were expected to be considerable. Sundry examples of favoritism to officials, directors, and others were detailed.[218]

During the early forties Calvin Fletcher offered blunt criticisms about the Indianapolis branch bank. While a member of the state bank board in 1840 he expressed concern about "great omissions of duty" and "a corruption" which seemed to be creeping into this branch. He helped secure the election of directors in order to weaken the influence of "a majority of the directors & the heaviest stockholders" who wished "to use the bank." Fletcher branded Benjamin I. Blythe "an ignorant dangerous director." He commented that Blythe's model was Nicholas McCarty, and "to expand [and] use borrowed capital is the order of the day with them both."[219] As a member of the branch bank board at the capital in 1842, Fletcher complained about personal accommodations and "peculations" by its officers. He lamented that "former directors & well wishers" of the branch "had become insolvent & debters" to the institution "they had for years pretended to oversee & direct."[220] Early in 1843 Fletcher praised Palmer's report about the Second State Bank, and commended him for publishing the names of persons indebted to it. He hoped such publication would be repeated, adding: "There are other uses of a bank than loaning for accommodation."[221] At times Fletcher's evaluations are harsh, about himself as well as others, but his diary adds convincing evidence that criticism of the bank was not entirely political rhetoric.

Samuel Merrill, while admitting problems and abuses regarding the Second State Bank, was its staunch, vigorous, and generous defender. Near the end of 1842 President Merrill asserted that the bank had earned an average profit of about 12 percent for its first six years, $9^1/_3$ percent the seventh year, and nearly 7 percent for 1841–1842. The bank president explained that the suspension of specie payment in 1837 had "made it apparent that the currency was too much expanded, and that to become sound again the wrong steps must be retraced" and the state bank board had "kept this object steadily in view." Merrill gave much credit to this board for the fact that "amidst so many wrecks, the Institution has passed safely through the late crisis [suspension of specie payment], and that its capital and credit, as a whole, are yet unimpaired . . . ."[222] As the Bigger administration ended in December, 1843, Merrill declared that despite the depreciation of the stock of the bank that for the preceding nine years no other property in the state had "maintained so steady a value and produced so certain an income." He submitted data showing that for its first nine years, 1834–1843, it had earned "profits" for the state averaging $91,492. This sum approached the average yearly cost of ordinary state expenditures for these years.[223] In January, 1843, Merrill gave this capsule of its achievements:

> The course pursued by the Bank, has maintained its honor with the General Government, by paying its whole deposite claim of $1,427,887; it has checked the contraction of new debts; hastened and facilitated the collection of old debts; given to the farmer prices for produce, far above what can be paid in the present currency; it has maintained the honor of the State, so far as it could be done, by paying regularly the interest on the State bonds sold for Bank capital; it has, by its operations, and that of the Sinking Fund, yielded a clear profit to the State, of 750,000 dollars; and the institution now stands on a safe and firm basis, no matter what prejudiced individuals may say to the contrary.[224]

From 1835 to 1839 three new branches were added to the Second State Bank which had commenced late in 1834 with ten branches. Its charter, however, permitted the addition of an eleventh branch after the lapse of one year, and a twelfth following three years.[225] In May, 1835, the Indianapolis *Indiana Democrat* reported that the eleventh branch had been located at Fort Wayne. This Democratic organ announced that private stock subscriptions for it would begin July 4, and soon noted that its stock had been promptly subscribed. "An institution of this kind," the editor asserted, "will be of immense advantage to the northern part of the state." Under date of November 17, 1835, Governor Noble proclaimed the new branch organized and ready for business.[226] Shortly after the Fort Wayne bank began, a meeting of citizens at South Bend solicited the legislature to permit location of the twelfth branch there after passage of only two years. During 1836 and 1837 two separate committees visited northern Indiana on behalf of the state bank board regarding where the twelfth branch should be located. South Bend, La Porte, and Michigan City all had advocates, but lack of consensus and hesitation about adding another branch while suspension of specie payments continued delayed a decision about which site to choose. Early in 1838 the state bank board selected South Bend, and private stock subscriptions began there in June. By proclamation of the governor it was authorized to start business on November 14, 1838.[227] Meantime, the charter had been amended to allow several additional branches, and the state bank board located the thirteenth branch at Michigan City at the same time it located one for South Bend. Isaac C. Elston had desired such a location as early as 1835. The thirteenth branch opened for banking early in 1839.[228] No additional branches were ever established, though others were authorized and subscriptions were commenced for some of them.[229]

While three new branches were being added to the Second State Bank amendments were made to its charter. According to the charter, valid until January 1, 1857, amendments required concurrent approval of the General Assembly, all branch bank boards, and the state bank board.[230] In December, 1835, a little

more than a year after the bank had commenced, Governor Noble advised legislators that the time was "not far distant" when the
bank's capital would be "entirely insufficient for the rapidly increasing business and population of our state." The House committee concerning the bank viewed Indiana's bank capital "very
small" compared to that of other states. It suggested that the capital of the state bank could be "extended to *four* or *five* millions of
dollars." It also urged that the branches be allowed to extend their
loans to an *average* of "*two and a half* times" the aggregate of paid
in capital—rather than twice the same according to the charter.
The committee explained that this would permit loans to expand
with increased demand during the fall and winter, then contract
with decreased demand for loans during the spring and early summer.[231] Early in 1836 the General Assembly gave its approval for
increasing the capital of each branch from $160,000 according to
the charter to $250,000. It also approved allowing branches to
make loans *averaging* two and a half times their paid in capital, but
never to exceed three times this ratio. The branch bank boards
and the state bank board soon concurred with these two amendments—added during the peak of prosperity immediately preceding the Panic of 1837.[232]

As the financial crunch from the System of 1836 became more
ominous during the late thirties, efforts were made to secure revenue from state stock in the Second State Bank to help pay interest on internal improvement bonds. In the summer of 1838 Jesse
L. Williams suggested that increasing state capital in the bank was
one way to finance completion of the System of 1836.[233] When
the legislators assembled in December, Governor Wallace gave
them a fanciful and meandering account of how Indiana could
augment state capital in the bank by at least $4,000,000 and gain
"not less than . . . 320,000 dollars per annum" toward payment of
interest on internal improvement bonds. Samuel Merrill, president of the bank, agreed that state stock "might be considerably
increased with safety to the bank and profit to the state," but he
left the size of the increase for the "wisdom of the Legislature" to
determine.[234] The legislature approved borrowing $1,500,000 for
additional state stock during 1839, plus annual increments of

$700,000 for 1840–1844 inclusive. At the same time the lawmakers gave approval for the establishment of four additional branches.[235] Apparently both the branch boards and state board concurred with these amendments to the charter, however, neither was ever implemented.[236] At New York City in April, 1839, Merrill negotiated a loan of $1,000,000, to be paid in ten equal monthly installments by the Morris Canal and Banking Company starting September 1, 1839. But about the time that the state was forced to halt construction of the System of 1836, the creditor reported that payments could not be made according to the agreement effected. Merrill returned to New York City and obtained collateral security from the delinquent company which he said would "insure the payment of the whole amount." The state bank apparently lost about $1,000,000 thereby, and Merrill's reputation was damaged.[237]

Ironically, both state and private stock in the bank were soon decreased rather than increased. With considerable state and private indebtedness owed the branches, they were limited in making new and better loans that would increase their dividends. Late in 1842 the state owed more than $1,000,000 to the branches. Michael G. Bright, who made a thorough examination of the branches earlier that year, concluded "that for the present, and for some years of the future, the capital stock is much larger in most of the Branches than is useful to the Bank or the community." He recommended that state and private stock be decreased in such a way as to reduce the money owed the branches.[238] The House committee concerning the bank offered similar comments and recommendations. Early in 1843 the legislature authorized the state treasurer to surrender $437,450 of state stock in branches willing to pay for it, "one fifth in bankable funds," and the residue in state paper issued on account of its indebtedness to the branches. The act included safeguards concerning how private indebtedness could be liquidated by surrender of stock held.[239] During 1843, $437,450 of state and $151,899.89 of private stock were surrendered in this manner.[240] At this time the aggregate capital of the thirteen branches totaled $2,136,272.25, only $885,716.27 of which was owned by the state.[241]

The success attained by the Second State Bank from 1834 to 1843 was remarkable. Despite the limited economic base for effective banking, the meager understanding and experience which existed about banking, the impact of the Panic of 1837 and ensuing depression which destroyed the preponderance of western banks, and its close and costly association with the System of 1836, the bank made large and significant contributions to the as yet principally undeveloped economy of the pioneer state and its people. Commenced more by Democratic than by Whig support, it was more sustained and administered by Whigs than by Democrats. Thus, the Whigs more than the Democrats were responsible for the unusual and outstanding record of the Second State Bank. But as the Whigs were soon to learn major responsibility for its success never offset their major responsibility for the failure of the System of 1836.

Meanwhile, the Whigs had probably gained an advantage from the legislative apportionment of 1841. The enumeration of white males above twenty-one, made in 1840, indicated an aggregate of 121,169 such persons.[242] When the legislature met in December, outgoing Governor Wallace recommended that the number of senators be reduced from the existing forty-seven to thirty, and that of representatives from 100 to sixty. The governor declared that such a reduction "would greatly contribute to curtail the onerous expense" of the legislative department "without jeopardizing . . . any of the great interests of the State." His experience, he said, taught him that the decrease would result in the transaction of "more business in a less time—far better—and more to the satisfaction of the people" than by a Senate of fifty and a House of 100 (the maximums set by the Constitution of 1816). The pro-Whig *Indiana Journal* viewed "the great expense" of the current large representation; the embarrassed fiscal situation of the state; and the example of adjoining states, having "more than twice the population and but little more than one half the representation," as "powerful arguments" for a reduction. The editor, however, aptly observed that the "difficulties of apportioning the Senators without legislating some of the present members . . . out of office, and the necessity of depriving some of the smaller counties of the full representation in the House, which they now enjoy, are *arguments* of a local and personal nature not easily to be satisfied by logical demonstrations."[243] Senator Charles H. Test, a Whig from Wayne County, approved reduction, but considered a decrease to forty senators and eighty representatives more practical than the numbers proposed by Wallace. With the state "on the verge of bankruptcy," Test said, economy dictated a reduction that would save thousands annually. He concurred with the governor that fewer legislators would expedite and improve legislative business. To northern senators who argued that fewer legislators would make districts too large, Test contended that interests often varied as much within counties as within districts. He noted that the state constitution required representation based on "the *number of polls* and not the *extent of territory*." Moreover, the constitutional limit of fifty senators made it impossible to apportion senatorial districts except by "attaching counties to the districts of Senators already elected . . . ." For years, Test explained, new counties had been attached to the legislative districts of incumbent senators. Senator William Berry, a Democrat from Monroe County, combining wit with wisdom, observed: "All are willing for reduction, provided their respective counties and districts can be made to retain their present number of Representatives, which . . . in many parts of the State, would be utterly impossible."[244]

At the legislative session of 1840–1841, when the Whigs had their peak control over the General Assembly, the Democrats were given negligible membership on key committees regarding apportionment. The Senate, despite the constitutional mandate that representation be proportional to the number of voters, instructed its committee on apportionment to consider votes cast at the state and presidential elections of 1840, in which the Whigs had fared unusually well.[245] The apportionment bill passed both houses by overwhelming majorities. Though supported preponderantly by Whigs, more Whigs than Democrats voted against passage.[246] Local and personal considerations probably influenced some of the negative votes, and others may have opposed passage because they thought the number of legislators too large.[247]

The apportionment of 1841, by providing fifty senators and 100 representatives, was the first to reach the maximum allowed by the Constitution of 1816. This reapportionment included eighty-seven *organized* counties, and only one *paper* county. No county was divided in distributing representatives, but two, three, and even four of them were joined to form districts. Even so, many of the organized counties got a single representative, some gained two, but only Wayne and Dearborn in the White-water Valley got three each. In a number of instances two or more counties were combined to give an extra or a "floating" representative. Thus, Montgomery and Putnam, each having two representatives, shared a "float" so that Montgomery gained a third representative in 1841, 1843, and 1845, with Putnam having it in 1842 and 1844. Counties that were not contiguous at times shared floats. The respect for county lines made for much diversity in the representation among counties. The enumeration of 1840 reported 2,178 voters for Shelby, 702 for Dubois, 1,323 for Hancock, and 1,349 for Madison—yet each obtained one representative. Moreover, Hancock gained a floating representative for 1841, 1843, and 1845, while Madison had one for 1842 and 1844. Starke, the only paper county, was attached to Fulton and Marshall for representative purposes; and to Benton, Jasper, Pulaski, Warren, and White for a senatorial district. No county was divided in forming senatorial districts, but at times two, three, four, or five organized counties were united. Various counties got their own senator, but only Wayne obtained two. There were no floating districts for senators, however, much diversity existed in the representation given counties. Vermillion with 1,649 voters and Ripley with 1,696 voters, each secured a senator as did Shelby with its 2,178 voters. The legislators from Shelby protested that their county had been shortchanged. It is possible that Shelby was discriminated against because it had supported Democrats for governor and president in 1840, while Hancock and Madison may have been favored for having voted for Whigs in those elections.[248] Since the apportionment of 1836 had included forty-seven senators, one third of whom were elected yearly, most existing senators had one or two years yet to serve. The apportionment legislation of 1841 provided that when an incumbent senator resided in a "newly formed district" that no election in such district would be held until the term of the incumbent expired. This arrangement was conducive to misunderstanding such as developed in Posey and Vanderburgh counties.[249] The only modification of the 1841 apportionment which has been noted was an act that gave Brown and Monroe one representative each, effective in 1844, whereas previously they had elected two representatives jointly.[250]

The apportionment of 1841 seems to have distributed members of the House of Representatives more equally among Southern, Central, and Northern Indiana than among the counties of the state. Based on the number of voters within their areas, it seems that Southern Indiana got somewhat fewer representatives than its number of voters justified; that Northern Indiana got somewhat more representatives than justified; and Central Indiana got about the number of representatives to which it was entitled. Moreover, population and political control were continuing their northward march, with Central Indiana retaining the plurality of representatives it had first achieved in 1836.[251]

While legislative apportionments were made at five year intervals throughout the pioneer era, codification or revision of the laws was less frequent and at irregular intervals. The initial code of 1823–1824 had been prepared by Governor William Hendricks; the second, approved in 1830–1831, by a joint committee of the House and Senate.[252] At the legislative session of 1834–1835, Senator Elisha Embree, a Whig from Gibson County, introduced a bill for condensing, arranging, and simplifying the laws. The *Indiana Democrat* reported that Embree asked that this also be done for the common law. Its editor stressed that such would be desirable for "As the common law now stands, it is as vague as if it had never been written . . . ." "Our government," the editor asserted, "is widely different from that from which we derive our principal legal rights."[253] Shortly after the legislature convened in December, 1836, the *Indiana Democrat* explained that a revision of the statute laws was needed because they were scattered through many volumes making it difficult for recent immigrants, "who comprise one half of our population," to know their content. Early in 1837 the legislature named the three judges of the Supreme Court to "revise, alter, amend, abridge, enlarge and model" the state's laws into a comprehensive and systematic code.[254] In December, 1837, Governor Noah Noble reported that the judges had made "some progress" toward revision, and he recommended that they be given time for its completion. The General Assembly, however, decided to make the revision. It selected a joint committee of the House and Senate, which effected the revision with the aid of subcommittees and clerks. This work progressed slowly, resulting in the longest legislative session since statehood.[255] The *Indiana Journal* expressed its concern that the revision would lack desirable quality. Possibly legislators shared this concern for they asked the state treasurer and secretary of state to have all general laws and resolutions, omitted from the revision, "printed with the revised acts." A few years later Charles H. Test, a lawyer, declared that the code of 1838 was inferior to those of 1824 and 1831. The code of 1838, he said, "was full of inaccuracies—and almost as difficult to be understood as the laws of Caligula . . . ."[256] The new code made explicit that Indiana's legal system was based upon the common law.[257]

Even before the code of 1838 was published legislators were apparently concerned that their revision would be less satisfactory than desirable. Early in 1838 they asked Isaac Blackford of the Supreme Court to collect "all the general statutes of this State, arranged under proper heads, and submit the same to the Legislature on or before another revision may be necessary," with his suggestions about "alterations and additions" deemed necessary. The next session renewed this request, but directed it to all three of the Supreme judges.[258] In December, 1840, however, the judges reported that they had been "so constantly engaged" in business of the court that they had "not been able to commence the revision," nor had they any hope that a revision could be done within a reasonable time. The General Assembly then authorized Governor Samuel Bigger to submit a revision of the laws, plus amendments and alterations thought proper, by December, 1842.[259] When the legislature met in December, 1841, Bigger reported "the undertaking most arduous and difficult." He said there were "three prominent defects in the statutes." Thus, provisions about the same subject were often found in different acts; sections of laws often contained unrelated items, and were so long and intricate as to be "almost unintelligible"; and they had glaring defects, omissions, and contradictions. The governor proposed that "all matters touching the same subject, and nothing more" be systematically combined under the same title. Since "much labor" was required, the executive desired assistance for the revision. The General Assembly named Treasurer George H. Dunn, a Whig and lawyer as was Bigger, to aid the governor.[260] When submitting their code in December, 1842, the governor and treasurer told legislators that it had been "a work of immense labor." They said they had tried not to make material changes in the laws, but had sought "to make the law consistent with itself." They proposed "numerous additions" to improve the code for legislative consideration. The revision of 1843, organized into major parts, chapters, articles, and sections, was seemingly accepted by the legislature with modest exceptions.[261] As for the three previous codes, continued reliance on English common law as part of Indiana's legal system was expressly reaffirmed.[262]

The revised codes of 1838 and 1843 left legislation about local, state, and presidential elections much as they had been in the thirties. Hence, they were by secret ballot, supervised by an inspector for each township chosen by local voters. The inspector named two judges and two clerks, from voters of the township, to assist in conducting the election. Despite the development of political parties since the midtwenties, the inspector was not required to give representation to both Whigs and Democrats in selecting judges and clerks.[263] After the state and presidential elections of 1840, "A Voter of Old Knox" sarcastically thanked an inspector for his "honor[a]ble and very gentlemanly conduct" in having named both "Judges and Clerks out of our Whig ranks at the last two elections." Writing as if he were a Whig, though perhaps a Democrat, "A Voter of Old Knox" stated that this has been done "after some of the Locos [Democrats] told you it was not fair. But go on, Squire, the end will justify any means; it is right to do evil, that good may come. All that I am afraid of is that some of our silly Whigs may think it not quite right, as some of them are talking about it already."[264]

Determining which ballots were valid was at times difficult. If two or more ballots were folded together, all were to be rejected. If more persons were voted for concerning a particular office than were to be elected, only this portion of the ballot was to be rejected. But no ballot was to "be lost for the want of form" if the local judges could "determine to their satisfaction" the person voted for.[265] At the state election in August, 1842, Henry Shoemaker apparently submitted a ballot consisting of three pieces of paper folded within a fourth larger piece, when he voted in Smithfield Township, DeKalb County.[266] The local judges rejected his ballot, and its counting or not counting became important when the returns for state representative from Steuben and DeKalb counties showed 360 votes each for Madison Marsh, a Democrat, and Enos Beall, his Whig rival. According to the law the sheriffs of the two counties cast lots, which Beall won, and they gave him a certificate of election. When the General Assembly met in December Beall was seated as a member of the House, which had a modest Democratic majority. Meantime, Marsh learned about Shoemaker's rejected ballot and asked that it be counted for him, making him rather than Beall the elected representative. The House election committee, comprised of four Democrats and three Whigs, reviewed sworn testimony pro and con the validity of Shoemaker's ballot. It also considered the claim by Beall that illegal votes had been cast for Marsh so that with or without the rejected ballot he had won the election; and the claim by Marsh that illegal votes cast for Beall made him, not Beall, the winner regardless of the rejected ballot. A majority of the election committee, seemingly voting along strict party lines, argued in favor of seating Marsh. The majority contended that the evidence showed that the inspector where Shoemaker voted had given him both the ticket and the knife used to cut the piece with Marsh's name on it, accepted his ballot without protest, and then rejected it after Shoemaker had left. The majority also argued that the question about the rejected ballot was the only item which had been properly contested.[267] A week after the session began, voting along strict party lines, the House voted 52 to 45 that Beall was not entitled to his seat; and then by the same party division and count that Marsh was entitled to it.[268] The *Indiana Journal*, staunchly pro-Whig, branded Beall's ejection "by a strict party vote" an affair "of almost unparalleled infamy and political villainy."[269] It seems evident that Marsh owed his seat to the Democratic majority in the House. Had the situation been the reverse, doubtless Beall would have retained his seat. As this disputed election indicates, party rivalry had become intense by the early forties. In this instance the rivalry was especially keen inasmuch as the legislative session was expected to elect a successor to Senator Oliver H. Smith, a Whig.[270]

While voters continued to have the privilege of voting at their county seat, this practice came under increasing criticism. At the legislative session of 1840–1841, the House adopted a bill to "confine" voters to their townships by the substantial margin of 55 to 39, but the Senate rejected it by the decisive margin of 27 to 18.[271] Senators favoring the bill argued that it would reduce fraud and corruption, and thus increase the purity of elections; make it harder for "foreigners" and persons under age to vote illegally; discourage excitement and mob action by scattering voters over the county; and leave 364 days when persons could visit the county seat for business and otherwise. They emphasized that there was better knowledge at the township level about who was and who was not qualified to vote than at the county seat. Senators against the bill contended that election days were days of liberty, hence confining voters to townships would abridge their liberties and privileges; since there had been no fraud, corruption, or mob violence of any consequence associated with balloting at county seats, legislation should not be passed in anticipation of possible evils; voting at the county seat enabled some to vote while absent from their townships; and many people preferred combining business and other matters with voting at the county seat. Senator Charles H. Test, a Whig, considered the county seat "the proper place to vote." "There," he said, "were men of intelligence, there were the newspapers, there was the county seminary, and the best information was to be obtained there." Samuel W. Parker, another Whig, responded to Test that "He had been at a county seat for the greater part of his life, but he had never come to the conclusion that it was a great Lancasterian school to teach people to vote."[272] Support for and opposition to confining voters to their townships was bipartisan, but no general law therefor was passed during the Wallace-Bigger administrations. The legislature, however, enacted laws which confined voters in designated counties.[273] Though apparently not common, at times individuals even voted in counties other than that of their residence. Robert Dale Owen frankly admitted having voted in Harrison County, rather than in Posey where he lived, at the state election in August, 1843. He asserted that the local election board invited him to vote; and he did, voting for the Whig candidate against him for a congressional seat instead of himself.[274] While at Madison on November 7, 1836, Calvin Fletcher confides in his diary: "I went with Mr. Sullivan & offered to vote the Harrison ticket but I was refused."[275]

During the late thirties and early forties, as during the pioneer period generally, the treating of voters seems to have been common despite legislation forbidding it.[276] In the state election of 1838, Samuel Judah and Jonathan P. Cox, rival Whig candidates for state representative from Knox County, were both convicted of having treated voters. Cox, whom Judah defeated, asked Judah to intercede with the governor on his behalf. This Judah did, advising Governor Wallace that the case against Cox was "precisely like" his own which he also called "to the attention and favour" of the executive. Early in 1839 both men were pardoned. Judah, elected to the House in 1838, 1839, and 1840, served as its speaker at the session of 1840–1841.[277]

Significant changes occurred in the membership of the Supreme Court during the years 1837 through 1843. In 1831

Governor James B. Ray had refused to renominate Jesse L. Holman and James Scott, who had served from statehood, and had forced the Senate to give reluctant approval of Stephen C. Stevens and John T. McKinney as their successors. But Isaac Blackford, who had served since 1817, was renominated and unanimously approved.[278] In March, 1836, Judge Stevens resigned, apparently explaining that his judgeship "would not support his family."[279] Governor Noble had much difficulty finding an individual he thought competent to replace Stevens. Unless more appropriate compensation were paid Supreme judges, Noble asserted, "those of the highest attainments will be driven from the Bench, and seats there will only be accepted by those who have not talents to live by the practice." The governor persuaded Charles Dewey, whom he called "a distinguished individual," to succeed Stevens. Lawyers and prominent leaders in both major parties approved Dewey's elevation to the Supreme bench. The *Indiana Democrat* termed his appointment "a sacrifice of private interest to the public good," adding that "A better appointment could not have been made." The ensuing legislative session jumped the salary of Supreme judges from $1,000 to $1,500 per annum.[280] This increase, large for its day, was perhaps the consideration which persuaded Dewey to make the appointment more than temporary.

The death of Judge McKinney in March, 1837, ended the service of the two justices whose appointment Governor Ray had coerced. Ironically, with the jump in salary, former Judge Stevens indicated his willingness to resume the bench. But he also expressed a preference for the naming of Jeremiah Sullivan, who was named to replace McKinney, making Blackford, Dewey, and Sullivan the judicial triumvirate whose terms ended in January, 1838.[281] Governor David Wallace nominated all three for reappointment. Dewey and Sullivan were Whigs, but Blackford had deserted this party and become a Democrat. Nonetheless, the Senate, which had a decided Whig majority, confirmed Blackford and Dewey without a dissenting vote. For reasons not clear because of opposition from both Whigs and Democrats Sullivan gained approval by a vote of only 25 to 20.[282] In a three volume study of Indiana lawyers and courts, Leander J. Monks declared: "Judges Sullivan, Dewey and Blackford undoubtedly constituted the best court that sat under the old Constitution, if indeed it has been excelled in the history of the state." They "made a team which for excellence was recognized not only in every state in the Union, but even in England." This evaluation is generous, but these justices formed a very able court at a time when cases coming before it were more numerous than they had been since statehood.[283]

CHAPTER 6

REPUDIATION, 1843–1850

SIGNIFICANT CHANGES OCCURRED in state politics during the 1840s. From the emerging formation of rival political parties in the mid-twenties, the National Republican-Whig party had *dominated state politics.* The Whig party had reached its peak strength over state government in 1840 when it elected Samuel Bigger governor by a large margin and won both houses of the General Assembly by overwhelming majorities. But in 1841 and 1842 the Democrats won control of the House of Representatives, and in 1843 they elected James Whitcomb as the first Democratic governor and gained majorities in both houses of the General Assembly. Thereafter the Democrats slowly increased their control of state politics, reelecting Whitcomb in 1846 but not until 1848 did they again win majorities in both houses of the legislature. As the forties ended the Democrats gained lopsided majorities in both houses of the legislature, elected Joseph A. Wright as the second Democratic governor, and obtained overwhelming control of the Indiana Constitutional Convention of 1850–1851. Although party rivalry and organization had considerably developed by 1840, both increased in the forties.[1]

As the year 1842 ended the state election in August, 1843, seemed likely to favor the Democrats. Not only had no project in the System of 1836 been completed, but for practical purposes it had been abandoned by the state. In the fall of 1842 Auditor Morris Morris reported that Indiana owed $10,307,028 on her *bonded debt for the system and the Wabash and Erie Canal.* He explained that the unpaid interest on this debt was accumulating at the rate of $522,570 per year, a sum approximately four and a half times the aggregate of ordinary state expenditures per annum for the Wallace-Bigger administrations.[2] The depression had not yet run its course, and the Second State Bank had been weakened by its close association with the system, its prolonged suspensions of specie payment, and favoritism to stockholders and directors. Although the system and bank had been bipartisan measures, the Whigs had been in power and the Democrats blasted them for the ills associated with its management.

During the closing months of 1842, the renomination of Governor Samuel Bigger was widely anticipated by the Whigs. The *Indiana Journal*, leading Whig organ of the state, staunchly defended his administration, making evident its support for the renomination of Bigger and Lieutenant Governor Samuel Hall.[3] As the year ended the *Indiana Journal* asserted: "Our present worthy and most popular Governor is every where already re-nominated by acclamation."[4] Meantime, various persons were mentioned as possible nominees of the Democrats. In September, 1842, the Delphi *Oracle* recommended consideration of Samuel Milroy, who had helped frame the Constitution of 1816 and served in both houses of the legislature, for governor; and Congressman Andrew Kennedy, the only Democrat among Indiana's congressional delegation, for his running mate. In conveying this information the *Indiana State Sentinel* named Nathaniel West, James Whitcomb, Robert Dale Owen, and Nathan B. Palmer as prominent Democrats who had been suggested for governor. Declaring that the Democracy of Indiana believed "the State has been under federal [Whig] control long enough," this leading Democratic paper stated that no matter how many candidates the Democracy would unite to a man in support of the nominee of its state convention.[5] The Goshen *Democrat* preferred General Samuel Milroy, that "old veteran and upright Democrat," for governor, but pledged acquiescence in the decision of the state convention. For lieutenant governor, it could "most cheerfully go hammer and tongs" for Andrew Kennedy, the Delaware County blacksmith. In contrast to the twenties and thirties, when Democrats often emphasized personal loyalty to Andrew Jackson, this northern Indiana party organ declared: "'Principles and not men,' should be our motto. Under this sign we conquer."[6]

Apparently neither Democrats nor Whigs had yet established continuing party organization at the state level, but both presumed nominations via state conventions. Early in 1842 an Indianapolis meeting of Democratic legislators and citizens named a

State Central Committee for their party. In September this committee recommended that county conventions name delegates to a state convention at Indianapolis, January 8, 1843.[7] In November, 1842, the *Indiana Journal* deemed a convention "indispensable," and warmly seconded the proposal of the Richmond *Palladium* that a Whig convention convene at the capital on January 17. Possibly concerned that Whig disaster might be impending, its editor stressed the need for "concert, organization and harmony in EVERY county and township in the State." Editorial brethren were urged to support the party with the admonition: "Indiana must roll back the current of defeat and start the ball once more! Onward, then, onward to the rescue!" Whig papers around the state concurred with the January 17 date and county conventions named delegates thereto.[8] Meantime, the *Indiana State Sentinel* announced its understanding that since January 8 would be a Sunday, the Democratic State Convention would convene on January 9.[9] Despite the intense party rivalry, Whigs and Democrats cooperated in making the room in the capitol where the House of Representatives met available for the party conventions.[10]

The manner in which the Democrats completed their convention on January 9 suggests that some key decisions had been made in advance. Ethan Allen Brown of Dearborn County, who had been governor of Ohio, was named president to preside over its deliberations. Among its twelve vice presidents were two veterans of the American Revolution, who were given seats to the right and the left of the president. The number of delegates and the counties represented is uncertain, but "all democrats present" were invited to sit as members. Each county, with some exceptions, was given the same voting power as it had in the House of Representatives. After the convention organized, Reverend John S. Bayless, a local Methodist minister, "addressed the Throne of Grace in humble prayer." A committee, having one member from each county, was asked to make nominations for governor and lieutenant governor. It proposed James Whitcomb, of Vigo County, and Jesse D. Bright, of Jefferson County, respectively for these offices; and its recommendation was accepted "by acclamation." Both nominees addressed the convention, and accepted their nominations with thanks. A State Central Committee was named, directed to encourage the establishment of county committees, and do all other matters for "advancement of the democratic cause in the State."[11]

The committee named to prepare an address concerning state policy castigated the Whigs and asked that the Democrats be entrusted with the offices of state government.[12] The address asserted that from the beginning of parties in the twenties the party known as Whig had "had an almost unrestrained control" of state politics. It emphasized that no Democrat had ever been elected governor, despite the fact that the "decidedly democratic" people had sustained Jackson from 1824 through his second term. And that the Whigs had always had a majority in the Senate; likewise in the House, with two or three exceptions. No Democrat had ever been auditor of state, only one had been treasurer of state, and only two had been secretary of state. Moreover, the president and cashier of the Second State Bank had always been Whigs; a majority of the members of the state bank and internal improvement boards also had always been Whigs; and Whig fund commissioners had negotiated the internal improvement bonds.[13] Hence, the Democrats asked, was it not evident that "the whole responsibility of the management" of state affairs "must rest upon the shoulders of the Whig leaders?" Thus the Whigs were considered responsible for: the breakdown of the System of 1836; its enormous debt of $13,000,000 which had been lost from deception, fraud, and peculation; the augmented taxes arising from this debt; and the abuses associated with the Second State Bank.

With such a record, the Democratic address insisted, a "change" in state politics had become imperative. "Try us," it said with wry humor, for "we can surely do no worse for the people than has been done by our opponents." "We repudiate no honest debt," the address affirmed, but we "are decidedly in favor of first arranging our domestic debts, and then taking such steps as will ultimately cancel our foreign obligations, as our means and abilities may present themselves, without additional burdens to those of a people already bearing as much as they are able to bear." Reviving business, improved markets for produce, "a skilful negotitation [sic] with our creditors," "the help of posterity," and the development of the state's vast resources were suggested as the means for extricating the state from its vast debt for internal improvements. The address was vague about policy toward the Second State Bank, but it credited the Democrats with having compelled it to resume specie payment. It also indicated that "the people" could "introduce other radical reform" of the bank if they so desired. In an attempt to sharpen the distinction between Democrats and Whigs, the address declared: "The people of Indiana are naturally Democratic. They cherish no fond regard for aristocracy, either in the shape of men or corporations." Further, the people ask for a state revenue to "defray our State expenses without creating a State debt, and such reduction of salaries and fees as will insure competent men in the public trusts." If the Whigs won, there would be "four years longer" of the difficulties into which they had dragged the once flourishing state. But if Whitcomb and Bright were elected, and supported by a legislature willing to execute the will of the people, "a salutary reform will be experienced in the government of the State, and an improvement in the condition of the people [will] be felt throughout the length and breadth of the land."

The Whig State Convention on January 17, 1843, was also a one day meeting for which important decisions had apparently been made in advance. Dennis Pennington, veteran legislator from Harrison County, was elected its president. The number of delegates seated and the counties they represented is uncertain. After convention officials were named, Reverend Phineas D. Gurley, of the local First Presbyterian Church, offered prayer. Counties having members in the convention were given representation on a committee to propose nominees for governor and lieutenant governor. Committees were named to prepare an address to the people of the state indicating the political views of the party, draft resolutions regarding such views, and propose members of a Whig State Central Committee. The nominating committee "unanimously" recommended the renomination of Samuel Bigger for governor and that of John H. Bradley for lieutenant governor. There seems to have been no disruptive rivalry regarding either nomination. The convention sought to increase party organization and campaigning. It named a Whig State Central Committee, and recommended "the formation of Whig clubs throughout the several counties and towns" of the state. After deeming it "niggardly in politics as [in] religion to 'muzzle the ox that treadeth out the corn,'" the delegates "*unanimously*" resolved that for succeeding campaigns that all candidates, not just those for governor and lieutenant governor, be invited "'without money and without price' to make our houses their hotels—our tables, cellars, pantries, beds and barns, their places of refreshment, so that they may go on their way rejoicing—and at all suitable times and occasions we pledge ourselves to cooperate with them in fighting the good fight—keeping the faith, and finishing our course with glory."[14] Such aid and hospitality in kind concerning political campaigns probably exceeded in value the contributions given them in money during the pioneer era.

The address of the Whigs to the people of the state blamed Jacksonian policies of the previous twelve years for the change from prosperity to depression,[15] and the ills concerning the System of 1836 and the Second State Bank. It admitted that "pecuniary embarrassments of an almost unprecedented character" existed; that farm produce was rotting in "barn yards" or if sold was paid for in "miserable depreciated currency, liable to become entirely worthless" to the seller; and that the state debt was "about fifteen millions of dollars and increasing over a half million" dollars annually. Only by adopting and implementing "proper measures by the General Government," the Whigs contended, could prosperity be restored and state government resolve its fiscal problems. According to the Whig address, in 1832 the "National government" had changed its policy toward internal improvements, and had "entirely repudiated" the doctrine that the general government could use the people's money to bind together the interests of the country with transportation facilities and provide the means for national defense. The states had been told that "they alone should make their own roads and canals," hence Indiana had commenced its system of internal improvements. In addition, at this time, the Second United States Bank, which had provided a sound circulation always convertible in specie, had been refused a recharter; and thus "became the victim of political warfare." With the destruction of this bank, "local Banks were ushered into existence with more than magic rapidity. Their issues soon covered the land as leaves the earth in autumnal seasons. They soon became worthless, and . . . the earnings of toil perished in the hands of the people!" Consequently "during the few years past" in exchanging local money for "City par funds" Hoosiers had spent an amount sufficient "to have paid the interest on our State debt, which [amount] would have been saved to us had a national currency been in existence." Furthermore, the president's veto of a bill in 1832 to distribute federal surplus revenue from land sales to the states had cost Indiana "over three millions of dollars as her distributive share up to 1838." Instead, this surplus had been deposited in local banks and caused that "wild spirit of speculation and visionary enterprises among individuals and States," resulting in "two hundred millions of indebtedness of the States, and the insupportable embarrassments of our people." Whereas, had distribution prevailed, and offsetting revenue been obtained by increased tariff duties, paid mainly by the rich on luxuries, Hoosiers would have been relieved of heavy tax burdens. Moreover, higher tariff duties were essential to increase prices for farm products and stimulate manufacturing based on them. The Whig address offered a fourfold program to resolve Indiana's economic and fiscal woes. It called for: adequate revenue with fair protection to industry; a sound national currency, regulated by national authority [apparently by a national bank]; equitable distribution of the proceeds of land sales among the states; and an amendment to the federal constitution limiting a president to a single term of specified years. These measures were termed essential to "western interests" as well as for those of the country generally. With an inference that the Democrats might adopt measures for "practical or open repudiation" of the bonded debt for internal improvements, the Whigs emphatically declared that they would "not taint their proud name with a deed so foul"; and the world could depend upon their doing all that could be done "to preserve, forever, the fair fame, by vindicating the honor of Indiana." But the Whigs, like the Democrats, were not explicit about what steps they would take to liquidate the bonded debt for internal improvements.

As would be expected, editorial comment about the gubernatorial nominations generally followed party lines. The editors of the *Indiana State Sentinel* reported that so far as they had heard the nominations of Whitcomb and Bright "meet with universal approval." They said that for twelve years the people had been "fleeced and *soaped* quite enough" so that the people had "decided on a *change*"; and they would not forget that "federal whigs" had "held supreme sway for years."[16] The Goshen *Democrat* declared that "a better span of horses were never harnessed together"; the Fort Wayne *Sentinel* called the nominees in "every way qualified" for their high stations; and the Madison *Courier* said that the people of Jefferson County, regardless of party, were "proud and happy to give so efficient a son" as Bright to state service.[17] The *Indiana Journal* sarcastically asserted that Whitcomb had been "a prime mover, and a voter in favor of the awful and horrible federal-Whig-Bank-Biddle-Stapp-Noble-Fund-Commissioner System of Internal Improvements!" In addition, he had been "an original Indiana State Bank man!" Bright was termed "a *National Bank*" man; and charged with having been associated with some unsavory aspects concerning the System of 1836, especially regarding the Madison and Indianapolis Railroad. This Whig organ considered it "farcical in the last degree" that the Locofoco candidates might be successful. Indiana, it said, "is thoroughly whig"; and Samuel Bigger "is the sword and shield of this goodly hoosier commonwealth."[18]

Even before the Whigs nominated Bigger and Bradley, the *Indiana State Sentinel* viewed them as prepricked nominees. It said there was little need for a Whig State Convention because "the whole matter has been settled in caucus by the Indianapolis junto." Its Democratic editors granted that Bigger was very clever and a gentleman, but a man of more enlarged views, energy and decision, and moral courage was needed as chief executive.[19] As expected, the *Indiana Journal* expressed its delight with the Whig nominees. On the day the convention met it commented: "The vestal fire that has never been extinguished, has been replenished upon our altar, and the same spirit has gone abroad which in 1840, led on the Hoosier phalanx to conflict and to glory." While the *Indiana State Sentinel* declared that "the sun of whiggery is about to set," the *Indiana Journal* placed the "flag" of Bigger and Bradley at its masthead with the forecast that it would "wave there, in honor and in triumph."[20]

Whitcomb and Bigger were both capable individuals. The former was born in Vermont in 1795, and the family had lived near Cincinnati for a time. After graduating from Transylvania University at Lexington, Kentucky, Whitcomb was admitted to the Kentucky bar in 1822. Two years later he arrived at Bloomington, where he practiced law and served as prosecuting attorney of the Fifth Judicial District for a few years. From 1830 to 1836 he was a member of the state Senate, voting against chartering the Second State Bank in 1834 and for adoption of the System of 1836. In the latter year Whitcomb became the commissioner of the General Land Office, continuing as such to the end of the Van Buren administration. Returning to Indiana in the fall of 1841, he took up residence at Terre Haute and began the practice of law there.[21] Whitcomb was the first bachelor as well as the first New Englander to become governor of Indiana. The *Indiana State Journal* asked the ladies of Indiana to consider whether a "stern and inflexible bachelor" should be so elected. Whitcomb was described as a man who had "rubbed" against the president, mingled with "foreign plenipotentiaries," had had "season tickets to grand levees," and was very familiar with gold spoons and silver forks. But, the Whig editor asked, "Has he a heart, ladies? and should he preside over the destinies of this chivalrous commonwealth *without* one?" The editor averred that no such gentleman should be Indiana's chief executive. The *Indiana State Sentinel* assured the ladies that Whitcomb was not one of those "crusty old bachelors," hence, if elected, "some Hoosier maiden" would soon be found at the governor's residence.[22]

Soon after the nominations of Whitcomb and Bright, the *Indiana State Sentinel* published puffy accounts about them. It presented Whitcomb as a man of high intellect, a friend of education, and as one who had reluctantly voted for the System of 1836 in response to "instructions" from constituents who overwhelmingly urged him "to go for the bill." It credited him as having been a powerful force in obtaining the federal grant of land for extension of the Wabash and Erie Canal to Terre Haute. The *Indiana State Journal*, however, insisted that Whitcomb had been among the Democratic leaders who obtained adoption of the system, knowing that its actual cost was expected to aggregate $16,000,000; and then even sought to have projects costing $2,000,000 added to it.[23]

Questions about responsibility for the system and its fiscal consequences overshadowed all other issues during the gubernatorial campaign. In March and April the *Indiana State Journal* published a series which contended that the Democrats had been at least as responsible for commencing the system as the Whigs, had had a prominent part in its management, and that credit for investigations exposing its corruption belonged almost entirely to the Whigs. In a much longer series the *Indiana State Sentinel* admitted that the system had not been "*a strict party measure*," which at first had been "popular with a majority of the people," but its extravagance soon alarmed Democrats and some Whigs. Then, after the Democrats failed to obtain its construction via classification rather than by simultaneous construction, "the System became emphatically a [Whig] *party measure*."[24] A Whig editor from western Indiana asserted that a candid and honest man would "admit that it [the system] was not a party measure at all— that it was the work of the *People at large*, through their Representatives . . . and that it was hailed by *all* parties as a great and glorious act of State policy."[25] After indicating that the state's bonded debt for internal improvements aggregated $12,129,338, a Democratic editor of northern Indiana declared: "Were all the wealth of the State brought to the hammer at fair prices, one dollar in every eight would be taken to pay her debt." In place of augmented transportation facilities and augmented wealth, Indiana had half "finished canals," "detached portions of rail road," "dilapidated bridges," and straggling frog ponds here and there. This editor lambasted the Whigs, saying: "For twelve long years have the Whig party had possession of Indiana. They found her in her virgin beauty, the pride of the Western forests. Her hardy yeomanry were free and independent. Her rich soil teemed with valuable products, and the husbandman received a rich reward for his toil. But they beggared her—they ruled and they ruined her—

they piled a debt monntain [*sic*] high upon her—they crushed her energies—they sapped her credit, and they gnawed like hungry dogs at her vitals."[26]

Partisans disagreed about how the approximately $10,307,028 of bonded debt for internal improvements could *ultimately* be liquidated. From the initial default in payment of interest due July 1, 1841, unpaid interest had accumulated at the rate of about $522,570 per annum.[27] Bigger noted three alternatives for disposition of this debt: repudiation, use of federally distributed proceeds of sales from the federal domain, and state taxation. He repudiated repudiation but claimed that several million dollars might be obtained if federal distribution of land proceeds were adopted, thus greatly reducing the amount that would be required by taxation.[28] Whitcomb apparently suggested that if he were elected the debt would be paid, the honor and credit of the state redeemed, and the people furnished with means to pay their debts. The *Indiana State Journal*, after saying Whitcomb had opposed distribution and made pledges inconsistent with repudiation, asked him how he would liquidate the bonded debt.[29] Failing to obtain such a statement, it commented: "Of all the demagogues extant he is at once the most unscrupulous and pointless." It contended that Indiana was due $8,000,000 from her share in the proceeds of the federal domain, and asked: "Are we rich enough to throw it away?"[30] The *Indiana State Sentinel* said the prospect that "the Swindling Coon Party are to be overthrown in this State, and honest men put in their places," had caused Indiana's credit to rise "in the New York market no less than five per cent." Linking better times with the prostration of "Coon Whiggery," this Democratic organ declared that "As Federalism sinks, the country rises."[31] Both Bigger and Whitcomb probably presumed that the bonded debt would ultimately be scaled down by a compromise with the creditors, leaving the residue to be paid overwhelmingly from state taxation.[32]

The Second State Bank seems not to have been a major issue in the gubernatorial election of 1843. Both candidates had voted against its charter in 1834,[33] but meantime it had performed useful services to the state and many citizens while yielding considerable in dividends to the state and individual stockholders. As governor, Bigger had supported the bank and viewed its prosperity important to the public welfare. No campaign statement by Whitcomb about his policy regarding the bank has been found, but its seems that he favored its continuation.[34]

Whigs and Democrats alike made generous use of political rhetoric as the campaign advanced. The *Indiana State Journal* stated that Bright, the Democratic nominee for lieutenant governor, should resign as state senator, for if elected he would hold two offices. The *Indiana State Sentinel* retorted: "why don't *BIGGER* resign *his* office?" Suggesting that the incumbent governor was neglecting his duties while "stumping over the State, *coaxing* the people to re-elect him," the *Sentinel* jabbed that "What is sauce for the goose is sauce for the gander."[35] Moreover, the governor's house had been finely furnished with the people's money, and Bigger would receive a handsome sum for revising the laws as well as his salary as governor. In addition, Bigger was controlled by a Whig clique at Indianapolis that supported high salaries, high taxes, life offices, and profuse expenditures to win elections. The Whigs, the *Sentinel* added, had "been hanging to the public teat for twelve or fifteen years."[36] The *Indiana State Journal* asserted that Whitcomb had "held a fat office" with a salary of $3,000 for six years, while "honest Sam Bigger" had held his office for only two years with half the salary that for years had enriched Whitcomb's pockets.[37] The *Journal* charged that Whitcomb had privately told a fellow Democrat that to control the vote of the people: "'GIVE THE PEOPLE PLENTY OF WHISKEY, AND STIR THEM UP WITH A LONG POLE, AND THEIR VOTES ARE CERTAIN.'"[38]

Issues regarding slavery and religion surfaced during the campaign. The Liberty party, making its first appearance in a gubernatorial campaign, nominated Dr. Elizur Deming, of Tippecanoe County, for governor; and Stephen S. Harding, of Ripley County, for lieutenant governor. The *Indiana State Sentinel* quipped that "we Hoosiers are likely to have a Black Governor when the abolitionists shall be strong enough to elect him."[39] Some Whigs were alarmed that Quakers and other members of the Liberty party might defeat Bigger. The *Sentinel* stirred the political waters by calling Deming "a pleasant speaker, and a man of decided ability"; and by charging that the Whigs were trying to get Deming "*off* the track" for the "glory of Henry Clay, a slave holder." It also labeled Bradley, the Whig candidate for lieutenant governor, "a Dandy Coon Abolitionist." The *Indiana State Journal* asserted that the "highest compliment" the Democrats had paid Deming was "the presumption that he is an Ass, and the highest respect which they entertain for him, is the hope that he may become their tool."[40] In the closing weeks of the campaign, the *Sentinel* charged that Bigger, a Presbyterian and member of the Wabash College Board of Trustees, had belittled Methodists regarding their lack of competence to contribute to higher education; been partial to Wabash College; and had insulted Reverend Matthew Simpson, president of Asbury University. After the *Sentinel* contended that the Whigs were "blackguarding" Whitcomb because he was a Methodist, the *Indiana State Journal* published an appeal by the Whig State Central Committee to Methodists and the public denying this contention. In so doing it further stirred the controversy by saying that it needed to "be advised" whether "Mr. Whitcomb is a member of any church." This quibbling regarding religion gave birth to the much repeated story that the controversy caused the "Amen corner" of the Methodist church to vote against Bigger, thus preventing his reelection. While an interesting story, the evidence in its support seems unconvincing.[41]

As the voting approached on the first Monday in August, the incumbent Whigs appear to have been less confident than the Democrats. "Remember," the *Indiana State Journal* admonished, "ONE VOTE has decided many a contest."[42] The rival political organs at the capital exhorted the party faithful to vote, and see to it that even the sick also voted. Party members were urged to get lists of legal voters, make certain that ballots were correct concerning persons to be supported, guard against illegal voting, and carefully watch the casting and counting of votes.[43] As returns were received from scattered counties, it became apparent that a political upheaval had occurred. "CROW, CHAPMAN, CROW," the Fort Wayne *Sentinel* exulted: "Indiana is redeemed —regenerated. We hope yet to see her restored to prosperity."

The Chapmans of the *Indiana State Sentinel* crowed: "For the first time since the organization of the State Government, INDIANA is DEMOCRATIC." The "best Generals of Whiggery" and its entire army had been defeated, the crowers added, and a "New Era" in Indiana's political history had commenced.[44] Whitcomb defeated Bigger by the modest margin of about two thousand votes. The Democrats won a considerable majority in the House of Representatives, and a narrow margin in the Senate. Though not a landslide, it gave Democrats a sweeping victory.[45] Among items to which contemporaries attributed this outcome were: defections of more Whigs than Democrats to the Liberty party, loss of Methodists' votes because they felt Bigger had been unfair to them and partial to Presbyterians, apathy and division among Whigs, the preference of voters of foreign birth for the Democrats, and a transition in political sentiment in favor of Democratic policies.[46] A Whig paper viewed "*the great ignorance of many of the People!*" to be "the *great cause*" for the defeat. It declared that two thirds of the well informed people were Whigs, but among backwoods settlements and the ragamuffins of cities "seventenths of them" were Democrats. The *Indiana State Sentinel* denounced such comment as "ridiculous twattle," adding that "many a fool had learnt to read and write, who in most other items of knowledge did not know B from a bull's foot." The *Sentinel* insisted that "there is an essential difference between *illiteracy* and *ignorance*," and that "many men who can neither read nor write . . . are far better qualified in point of political knowledge to exercise the right of suffrage than many who can."[47] While the foreign vote, largely German and Irish, apparently favored the Democrats,[48] it seems that the Liberty party drew more votes from Whigs than from Democrats.[49] Whatever the mix of influences, the Democratic sweep suggests a significant change in favor of the Democrats. But this perhaps resulted as much from dissatisfaction with the Whigs as from a preference for the Democrats. Having been the party mainly responsible for adoption of the System of 1836 and for its prosecution and financing, the blame for the fiscal crisis resulting from its collapse fell principally upon them.

When the General Assembly met in December, 1843, it had trouble deciding *which Democrats* should succeed *incumbent Whigs* as state treasurer and auditor of state. Even though the Democrats had a majority of about twelve members on joint ballot of the two houses, lack of consensus among them gave Whigs and minority Democrats an opportunity to control these elections. Soon after the August election the *Indiana State Sentinel* announced Nathan B. Palmer as a candidate for treasurer. Since Palmer had earlier filled this office "with great efficiency," only to be ousted "during the Hard Cider *flurry*" in favor of a Whig, the Chapmans of the *Sentinel* considered his resumption of this post an act of justice to him. Dr. Ellis of the Goshen *Democrat* clamored for the political scalps of three Whig incumbents. Starting with Samuel Merrill, president of the state bank, Ellis urged: "Throw him over, and let an honest man, like Nathan B. Palmer, reign in his stead." Then, Ellis proposed, make Treasurer George H. Dunn "take the next leap, and close upon his heels, walk up that old sinner, whose brow is wrinkled in the service of Whiggery, Morris Morris, Auditor of State," and let him take "the plunge" along with "all the princes of the Royal Blood." Objecting that justice had not been given northern Indiana concerning offices, Ellis requested that the new auditor come from that area.[50] The Fort Wayne *Sentinel*, also a Democratic paper, contended that the election meant that people expected the offices to be filled with "new men of ample qualifications from amongst the thousands to be found *out of the* City of Indianapolis . . . ." This barb brought agreement between the rival party organs at Indianapolis. The *Indiana State Sentinel* called such criticism "unfair, ungenerous and unjust in the extreme"; the *Indiana State Journal* viewed prejudice against officials from either party "*merely because they reside*" at Indianapolis as "unjust and unwise; nay, intolerant and despotic."[51] In the election of a treasurer, George H. Dunn obtained a plurality of the votes on all but a few of the first twenty ballots, however, on the twenty-second ballot Royal Mayhew, a Democrat from Shelby County, was elected. In the voting for auditor of state Morris Morris had a plurality on the two initial ballots, but Horatio J. Harris, a Democrat from Carroll County in northern Indiana, won election on the tenth ballot. From the nature of the voting, ballot by ballot, and the comments of Calvin Fletcher, it appears that Mayhew and Harris won by obtaining a significant minority of Democratic votes and at least nearly all the votes of Whig legislators.[52] Prejudice against electing residents of Indianapolis may have been an important influence in their election.

No Indiana governor had faced so vexing and burdensome a fiscal debacle as that which existed in December, 1843, when James Whitcomb became the first Democrat to be elected governor. The System of 1836, which should have been largely finished, had been suspended in 1839. None of its projects had been completed, a few items had been transferred to private companies, and a few had been turned over to local governments. Several months earlier, the Wabash and Erie Canal, commenced in 1832, had been opened for navigation from Lafayette to Lake Erie; and its extension to Terre Haute was in progress. But the failure to finish tributary feeders to the canal, projected in the System of 1836, reduced its importance and lessened anticipated revenue from tolls.[53] Shortly before Whitcomb became governor, Auditor Morris Morris reported that the bonded debt for the System of 1836 and the Wabash and Erie Canal aggregated $11,901,000, on which unpaid interest was accumulating at the rate of $649,950 per annum. This interest alone was more than five and one half times the yearly ordinary costs of $113,591.27. Moreover, roughly $3,000,000 of this bonded debt was for bonds from which the principal thereof had not been received.[54] Deciding whether to pay the piper millions of dollars, plus accruing interest, for transportation projects largely unrealized, severely tested the willingness of Hoosiers to *sacrifice* to pay bondholders the principal and interest thereon in full as they were pledged to do. Their will was weakened because the principal had not been received for more than one fourth of the debt owed as well as from concern about favoritism and corruption in obtaining and expending the millions owed.[55] Moreover, Indiana was then a rural and agrarian society in its pioneer stage, with a population of perhaps about three quarters of a million, and its principally undeveloped economy was just emerging from the harsh depression of the late thirties and early forties.[56]

During the early forties several alternatives were discussed regarding how the principal of the internal improvements bonds, plus accrued interest, might be liquidated. Five alternatives in particular were considered: (1) pay principal and interest in full; (2) repudiate at least the bonds for the suspended debt from which the state had not received any of the principal; (3) buy up as many of the bonds as possible at their low market price, thus redeeming them far below their face value; (4) use revenue from federal distribution of proceeds from the sale of land from the federal domain; and (5) make a compromise arrangement with the creditors whereby the money owed would be reduced. Generally speaking, items two through five presumed that the debt not so liquidated would be paid from taxation. The first alternative was expressly and strongly urged by Governor Bigger in his inaugural and again in his annual message to the General Assembly in December of 1841 and 1842.[57] During 1841 both the pro-Democratic *Indiana State Sentinel* and the pro-Whig *Indiana State Journal* supported this alternative.[58] In January, 1842, Representative Edward A. Hannegan asserted that if repudiation developed then "loss of fame, of honor and of credit—of all that is valuable in reputation, to States and individuals" would follow.[59]

Nevertheless, despite such affirmations about complete payment of the bonded debt, after the default on interest owed July 1, 1841, no further interest was paid until July 1, 1847. Instead, at the legislative session of 1841–1842, the General Assembly had *reduced* the state levy on property from 40 cents per $100 of taxable property to only 20 cents; and it made payment of the unfunded or domestic debt a priority over liquidation of the funded or bonded debt on internal improvements.[60] While Bigger was governor, 1840–1843, it seems that Democrats were more inclined than Whigs to repudiate the suspended debt of roughly $3,000,000. Senator Ebenezer M. Chamberlain, a Democrat from Elkhart County, pressed for its repudiation at legislative sessions under Bigger, but none of the bonded debt was then repudiated.[61] It also seems that Democrats were more favorable than Whigs for trying to buy up internal improvement bonds at a low price as a means of redeeming them. This alternative was likewise not approved, but in 1842 the House Ways and Means Committee, dominated by Democrats, anticipated that the bonds might sink as low as ten cents on the dollar. Hence, it proposed, it would require only $1,300,000 "to redeem all our out standing bonds" and relieve citizens from "apprehensions of State insolvency and oppressive taxation."[62] Whigs, however, were far more supportive than Democrats for seeking revenue from federal distribution of proceeds from sales of the public domain. But the revenue so received during the forties was modest.[63] When the idea of effecting a compromise with the bondholders was first publicly proposed is uncertain. In the summer of 1842 the publishers of the *Indiana State Sentinel* suggested: "We believe, if we had the authority, we could arrange a plan to settle the principal and interest of our debt, without taxing the people a dollar in cash." As this year ended the *Indiana State Journal* expressed the hope that the legislative session of 1842–1843, without regard to party, would "make some provision for the benefit of our creditors abroad." This Whig organ asserted that because of the embarrassed and appalling condition of state finances that "our creditors are prepared to expect the *less* from us, on these accounts, and to extend towards us the more charity and forbearance," but they would not acquit us "of dishonor if, because we can do but little, we refuse to do anything." As noted earlier in this chapter, the address of the Democratic State Convention in January, 1843, looked to "a skilful [sic] negotiation" with creditors as part of the process by which the bonded debt for internal improvements could be liquidated.[64] Moreover, in December, 1843, departing Governor Bigger and incoming Governor Whitcomb both advised legislators that Indiana was then unable to pay the interest owed on this debt.[65]

The continued default regarding interest on the bonded debt caused much apprehension among bondholders. Soon after the initial default on July 1, 1841, Rothschild and Sons of London protested that interest had not been paid on the $3,600,000 of bonds payable through them. This firm explained that bondowners were daily seeking payment thereof, and it admonished that only by "full payment" as promptly as possible could the "injustice" suffered be repaired.[66] In March, 1842, after the legislature had adjourned without providing for payment of interest, about four dozen English bondholders sent a caustic remonstrance to Governor Bigger and the people of Indiana. They suggested that if Indiana had "imprudently" incurred excessive debt or "indiscreetly entrusted" bonds to fellow countrymen who sold them without paying the state the principal for them, that "these circumstances" were "no justification or excuse" for not fulfilling the obligation due them. The letter transmitting this remonstrance asserted that in "many instances . . . great inconvenience" had resulted for lack of dividends relied upon "as a certain source of income." "Every honest and wise people," the English creditors averred, "will cheerfully make . . . and submit to the sacrifices necessary, for the preservation of its credit and the redemption of its faith solemnly pledged." Indiana's failure to make any provision concerning the claims of bondholders was castigated as "the first instance in the history of the world, in which any legislative assembly, representing the People of a sovereign State, had deliberately refused to recognize its obligations . . . ."[67]

Early in 1843 a caustic memorial was received from American bondholders. It declared that nonpayment of interest for two years had caused "great inconvenience and loss" to "many widows, orphans, and aged persons" who "had their whole means of support invested in these *supposed* securities . . . ." Numerous creditors, the memorial emphasized, had "been compelled to sell their bonds at the most enormous sacrifice to raise small sums of money, and some have been driven to subsist on charity." The American bondholders bluntly asserted that any state could "as readily pay the whole annual interest due from it as can the inhabitants of this city [New York] pay their taxes, which this year amount to rising eighty-four cents on each one hundred dollars of the assessed value of real and personal estate." If any state considered it too burdensome to pay all the interest due, the memorial suggested, "it would redound much to its credit, and go far towards satisfying the wretched and impoverished creditor" if half were paid as it became due, "with the assurance of the residue at some future period." In any event, honor, equity, and justice required that every creditor be paid "in the same ratio" as payments were made on the interest and principal of treasury notes.[68]

Criticism that Hoosiers were extremely lax in meeting their obligations to bondholders aroused strong resentment. After the New York *Express* was quoted as saying that "the very whiskey drunk in Indiana and Illinois is drunk in quantities sufficient to meet the interest on their debt," Governor Bigger protested "in the name of the whole people of Indiana . . . against that indiscriminate censure and reproach which place those who have become unable, by unavoidable circumstances, to discharge their just liabilities, on the same level with the wilful repudiator."[69] Dr. E. W. H. Ellis, editor of the Goshen *Democrat*, responding to a report that the New York *Tribune* had charged that Whitcomb's election meant that the state debt would be repudiated, lashed out that the *Tribune's* editor, "pampered in luxury, knows nothing of the privations of the West." Ellis then lectured the Whig critic: "Let him go with us to the log cabins—not such as graced our Eastern cities in 1840, but to the real cabins, which our hardy settlers occupy. —Let him sit down on the rough bench and look around at the furniture of that humble cabin, the puncheon table, the humble bed, the little shelf of crockery—the whole value of the furniture not exceeding twenty dollars—let him sit down at the frugal meal, at which the dandy fops of the East would turn up their noses. Let him look out upon the dense forest, and see what years of toil are undergone before comfort and ease shall reach that wilderness habitation—and then ask himself the question, whether the people of Indiana are able to bear the high taxation he urges." Ellis insisted that "Many and many is the man who does not handle five dollars of money in a year . . . . Our taxes are now light, yet not one man in ten has the money to pay them; and yet are we to be stigmatized by this organ of whiggery as knaves and scoundres [*sic*] because we do not quadruple them?"[70] The *Indiana State Sentinel*, in commenting on the observation of an unnamed New York paper about the poor prospect for even ultimate payment of the debts of various western states, retorted: "Indiana will have as much as she can conveniently do, to redeem her Scrip, for the coming four years; and every body knows that the older a debt becomes, particularly for a 'dead horse,' the harder it is to pay—particularly so when we know that we got cursedly shaved in the original purchase."[71]

When James Whitcomb was inaugurated governor in December, 1843, he asserted that he could not submit "specific recommendations" concerning the bonded debt for internal improvements. He said, however, that he cherished "the hope, that with slowly returning prosperity, an arrangement may yet be made touching all claims that are just and equitable, and comporting with the honor and dignity of the State." These words doubtless meant different things to different individuals, and they were perhaps intended to encourage negotiations toward a compromise settlement with the bondholders. But a year later, in his first annual message to the General Assembly, Whitcomb gave vigorous support for a compromise. He estimated the aggregate bonded debt for internal improvements at $12,218,000 including $10,828,000 on which unpaid interest was accumulating at the rate of $543,120 annually. Whitcomb told legislators that the "great mass" of citizens were "willing—nay, anxious—to meet all our just obligations." With them, the governor added, "it is not a question of inclination but of ability." Further study, Whitcomb said, confirmed his previously expressed opinion "that it is beyond our power to meet our liabilities."[72] In presenting a communication about the debt from English bondholders, the executive recommended that one or more commissioners be appointed to receive such communication "in the hope of making an arrangement as to all our just debts, which, while it will bring the subject within our means, will save the honor of the State, and be satisfactory to our creditors." But no settlement should be binding until approved by the legislature, "or what is perhaps better, until confirmed by a direct vote of the people." The executive expressed the hope that creditors would "see their own interest in an early adjustment of this matter, before the present anxiety of the people to discharge this debt is succeeded by apathy and despair." A proper settlement would infuse confidence in the community, improve individual credit, encourage immigration, and hasten the improvement of the country.[73] Although the Ways and

Means Committee of the Whig dominated House reported a bill giving State Agent Michael G. Bright authority to negotiate with bondholders, the House passed the bill with Governor Whitcomb assigned this role. The Senate, however, equally divided between Whigs and Democrats, failed to approve the bill and no commissioner was named.[74]

The legislature received various proposals regarding a compromise with bondholders, but none was adopted. Senator John D. Defrees, a Whig from St. Joseph County, obtained appointment of a select committee to consider the feasibility of exchanging existing bonds for new ones covering them, accrued interest, and interest for one year in advance, bearing 3 percent interest annually and redeemable after twenty-five years. Reporting as chair of the committee, Defrees stressed that with wealth and population increasing rapidly that a levy of 30 cents per $100 of taxable property, plus $1 per poll, would cover both ordinary state expenditures and finance his proposal. "We have reason to believe," the report stated, that our creditors "would avail themselves" of such an arrangement, which "was certainly not beyond the ability of our people." A majority of the committee, including a Whig and two Democrats, dissented from this report; and the bill submitted with it failed in the Senate.[75] Representative Frederick Leslie, a Whig from Harrison County, asserted that it was understood that an adjustment could be made with bondholders by converting existing bonds, plus 3 percent per annum on principal and interest due, plus 3 percent added for interest due for the ensuing four years, to new bonds redeemable at the pleasure of the state; with interest on the new bonds at 3 percent, commencing four years after their issue. Leslie strongly urged this arrangement, suggesting that a levy of 25 cents per $100 on taxable property and a poll tax of 75 cents would finance it, meet all ordinary state expenditures, and absorb all outstanding treasury notes within four years. The House tabled this plan by a vote of 64 to 33.[76]

The legislative session of 1844–1845 made no provision for payment of any interest or principal on the bonded debt for internal improvements. The Whig dominated Ways and Means

Committee presented data indicating that at the current rate of taxation it would take until January 1, 1853, to liquidate the principal and interest on the domestic or unfunded debt of $1,528,032. William Herod, a Whig and former congressman, in reporting for the committee, explained that with people "already complaining of their burthens, and not without cause," imposing "additional taxes sufficient to meet the interest [on the bonded debt for internal improvements] annually, and finally the principal of this unfortunate debt, would be but to retard, if not defeat, its final payment."[77] Joel Vandeveer, a Democrat on the committee, offered data suggesting that the domestic debt could be liquidated by January 1, 1850, without any increase in the tax levy. By this time, he stated, the bonded debt, plus unpaid interest, would aggregate $15,716,080. This sum, Vandeveer declared, could only be discharged by "an additional and oppressive tax . . . for several generations to come." Vandeveer contended that the debt had been illegally contracted; that the bonds had passed to persons who paid less than face value for them; and that money, compared to property, had become worth three times what it had been when the bonds were sold. Hence, he strongly advised contractors to make an arrangement for funding the aggregate debt at about twenty-five cents on the dollar. If this were done, at the existing tax levy, the payment of interest could begin in 1847, with the bonded debt liquidated by January 1, 1862.[78]

When the General Assembly convened in December, 1845, more than four years had passed since Indiana had defaulted on interest due on its bonded debt for internal improvements, July 1, 1841. Meantime, no payment had been made on either its principal or interest, with unpaid interest accumulating at close to $550,000 annually. Despite this mounting debt, the state tax levy for the years 1842, 1843, 1844, and 1845 *averaged* less than it had for the years 1838, 1839, 1840, and 1841.[79] Whether Hoosiers *could* have paid the bonded debt, principal and interest, in toto, had not been tested. By the mid-forties Indiana was drifting toward repudiation of a significant portion of its debt for its failed mammoth system of internal improvements.

During 1845 Charles Butler, representing persons owning most of the bonded debt, spent considerable time in Indiana to negotiate a compromise settlement.[80] In May he attended a meeting at Terre Haute at which delegates from a dozen counties deliberated how to obtain completion of the Wabash and Erie Canal to the Ohio River at Evansville. The proceedings of this convention indicate much cooperation between Whig and Democratic politicians as well as between them and Butler regarding the canal and the bonded debt. In addressing the convention Butler asserted that only by restoring public credit and paying the debt could prosperity be achieved and immigration again be augmented. The agent for the owners of many bonds emphasized that character and debt paying, for states as well as individuals, went together; that the bondholders "most unquestionably" expected the debt to be paid; and that the bonds were held, not by wealthy bankers like the Rothschilds and Barings, but principally by "thousands, who are this very day suffering for the want of the accruing interest." Butler "regarded the immediate and judicious prosecution" of the canal to Evansville "the chief means for payment" of the bonded debt for internal improvements. He viewed such a canal as second in importance to the New York and Erie Canal in his home state. He expressed his belief that if Indiana would pay a portion of the bonded debt by taxation and otherwise, then the bondholders would take "*the revenues of this canal for the balance*." Butler suggested that by economic and judicious legislation, Indiana could pay 2 percent interest annually on the entire debt to bondholders, "*without adding one cent*" to the existing tax levy. Moreover, if Indiana exhibited "a disposition and exertion to meet" its debts, the bondholders would probably loan money for extension of the canal to Evansville.[81] The convention unanimously adopted a report which predicted that with completion of the canal to Terre Haute by 1850 that at least $400,000 would be received from tolls for that year. It likewise approved a resolution declaring that the canal could be completed from Terre Haute to Evansville, by the means within the control of the state, and "without resort to taxation for that purpose."[82] As far as

Butler and the delegates were concerned, payment of the bonded debt and opening of the Wabash and Erie Canal to Evansville would be Siamese twins.

In addressing the General Assembly in December, 1845, Governor Whitcomb sought to rally support for a compromise settlement with the bondholders. He observed that there had been "abundant harvests" and "returning prosperity" during the year, but Indiana remained unable "to fully meet its obligations." The governor noted what had been said at Terre Haute about using the canal to pay part of the interest and principal on the bonded debt. Without naming Butler, Whitcomb told members of the assembly that a representative of the bondholders was at the capital and would soon communicate "a liberal arrangement" for legislative consideration. He expressed his faith "that the people will cheerfully submit to the necessary burthen" to save the honor of the state, resuscitate its credit, increase immigration, add to the value of property, restore confidence, and improve individual credit. These benefits, the executive added, would "more than compensate" the people "for their outlay." Moreover, the governor declared, "It is a great moral question, in the adjustment of which, all mere party and local considerations should be merged."[83] After the message Butler wrote his wife: "it is only by addressing myself to the conscience of the people, stirring that up, and bringing that to bear that I stand the slightest chance of success . . . ." Though "backed up by a few good and strong men of both parties," none dared "take the responsibility in the Legislature of advocating payment. The Governor, even though he went very far for him, yet dare not use the word *pay* or *tax*." Nevertheless, the agent viewed the message "a great triumph" amid indications that were encouraging.[84]

Soon after his message, the governor referred a letter from Butler concerning a compromise settlement of the bonded debt for internal improvements to the General Assembly for its consideration. In presenting his compromise proposal, Butler made several points: (1) he represented "holders of a large amount" of the bonded debt on which interest had not been paid for five years; (2) the bondholders did not doubt the intent of the people to pay their debts "to the uttermost farthing" as soon as they were able; (3) his clients "never contemplated or authorized any proposals" embracing "less than the eventual payment of their just claims for the entire . . . principal and interest" on their bonds; (4) if immediate payment in full was too burdensome, part should be paid soon and the remainder as ability increased from returning prosperity and an augmenting tax base; (5) he protested the priority given liquidation of the domestic or unfunded debt over payment of interest due bondholders as unjust and in violation of prior obligations and the pledged faith of Indiana; and (6) he asserted that the bondholders represented were principally aged and retired persons, including widows, who had sustained serious loss of income relied upon for their support. The agent noted that for 1841 the state had levied 40 cents per $100 on taxable property, plus 75 cents per poll; yet, according to the auditor's record "in no year before or since, has the revenue been paid in with greater promptitude" than for that year. After suggesting that the ability of people to pay had since "increased largely," Butler stated that none would deny "that the people of any of the western States could now pay a tax of four mills [per dollar of taxable property or 40 cents per $100 of taxable property] with more ease than they could then pay half that sum . . . ." After observing that for several years the value of taxable property had increased an average of nearly $5,500,000 per annum, he forecast that its average increase for the ensuing ten years would be at least $6,000,000. This swelling property tax base, the augmenting revenue from the poll tax, and receipts from the Wabash and Erie Canal, Butler indicated, afforded an adequate basis for an appropriate settlement with the bondholders.[85]

The General Assembly established a joint committee of the House and Senate, consisting of twenty-four members, to review Butler's letter regarding a compromise debt arrangement.[86] At the invitation of the committee Butler met with it and submitted his "First Proposition" regarding eventual payment of principal and interest on the bonded debt for internal improvements of $11,090,000 in two phases: During the initial phase: (1) for the unpaid interest on the bonds from the initial default July 1, 1841, to July 1, 1846, the state would issue certificates therefor to be paid on January 1, 1851, or then be added to the principal of the debt in stocks bearing 5 percent interest; (2) from July 1, 1846, to

January 1, 1851, Indiana would pay 3 percent interest on the debt of $11,090,000, relying on state revenue for two thirds of the interest and receipts from the Wabash and Erie Canal for the other third. Beginning with phase two on January 1, 1851: (1) any deficiency in the payment of the 3 percent interest due from July 1, 1846, to January 1, 1851, would be funded and added to the principal of the debt; and the same for any interest still owed for the period July 1, 1841, to July 1, 1846; and these additions to the principal would also bear interest at 5 percent; (2) and three fifths of this 5 percent interest would thereafter be paid from state revenue; and two fifths from proceeds of the canal, but with the understanding that the state would "take measures" to complete it "to the Ohio river, within the ensuing three or four years . . . ." The agent for the bondholders presumed that a state levy of 30 cents per $100 of taxable property and 75 cents for each poll would fund his proposal for 1846 to 1851, and finance other state expenditures. For the period starting January 1, 1851, Butler presumed continuation of the same levy on polls, but an increase of the levy on taxable property to 35 cents per $100.[87]

Butler advised his wife that by December 24 he had had four meetings with members of the joint committee or "the Sanhedrim" as he called it. During these meetings some members questioned his authority to act for bondholders, and strong support was expressed for repudiation of the suspended debt. Before meeting with the committee, the agent viewed his "foes" on the committee "the strongest, not in numbers, but in power." After his second meeting he wrote that Governor Whitcomb and Lieutenant Governor Bright "go in for me strong, head and shoulders, and now I have a strong team, indoors and out." At this stage friends of the public credit considered "the House safe," with "the only difficulty" in the Senate. After the fourth meeting, Butler thought he had "made one or more converts" at each meeting.[88] Nevertheless, on December 25, Christmas Day, the committee had morning and afternoon sessions, with Butler absent, and tersely "*Resolved*, That Mr. Butler be informed that this committee are unable to accede to the proposition heretofore submitted by him to said committee." But the committee "requested" Butler "to make any further proposition to said committee which he may desire to make, at his earliest [*sic*] convenience."[89] Next day the agent submitted his "Second Proposition," which he hoped would "be accepted." But he told his wife: "I do not know that anything satisfactory can be done; and if it goes on, the danger is that it will be worse than it now is." In submitting this second proposition, Butler reemphasized that he was not "at liberty to . . . consent to any arrangement, which shall embrace less than the eventual payment of the just claims of the Bond-holders for the *entire . . . principal and interest of the Bonds in their possession*," with 5 percent interest on the principal. Starting on January 1, 1847, the state would pay 2 percent interest on the principal of the bonded debt of $11,090,000 until January 1, 1853. As of 1853 half of the unpaid interest on the principal for the years 1841 to 1853 would be added to the principal. In addition, 1/2 percent of the unpaid interest for the period 1847 to 1853 would also be added to the principal. Then, commencing in 1853, half of the 5 percent interest would be paid from taxation, and the remaining half, "computing from first January, 1841, shall be chargeable against, and paid out of, the revenues of the Canal, and shall not otherwise be chargeable against the State." This proposal presumed that "the Canal would be speedily completed in its full extent to the Ohio River." Since this item made "reliance" on the canal the source for "payment of one-half of the back and accruing interest," Butler suggested that bondholders who subscribed money for its completion be given appropriate priority in repayment therefor from proceeds of the canal.[90]

During the evening of December 26, Butler discussed his second proposition with members of the joint committee. Friends of the canal and of public credit, he reported to his wife, had not dreamed that his amended proposal would be "so liberal and fair —and they were overwhelmed, whilst the enemy scattered in every direction." By the next day these friends were "in a perfect glee—as though the question were now settled, Indiana redeemed and the canal finished. They already talk of illuminations, bonfires and cannon, but I tell them to keep cool, the battle is yet to be fought." And indeed it was.[91]

On January 3, 1846, the joint committee introduced a bill in both houses concerning a settlement of the funded debt and completion of the Wabash and Erie Canal to Evansville.[92] On January 8 and 9 the state conventions of the Democrats and Whigs respectively adopted resolutions which Butler considered favorable to a debt settlement.[93] As the bill made its way toward passage, Butler became concerned because some of his friends gave him "a great deal of trouble" as they quarrelled "about the details" and kicked "out of the traces." Democrats in the House considered adding a proviso to the bill making it subject to the approval of the people at the ensuing August election. Such a referendum, the agent feared, "would forever destroy the hopes of the bondholders . . . ."[94] At this juncture Butler made a major concession and agreed that *half of the principal* as well as half of the interest could be paid from revenue of the canal. The House approved this substantial concession by the overwhelming count of 82 to 7 on January 14.[95] Next day the House passed the bill by nearly a two to one margin of 61 to 33. Even so, Butler feared that the bill would be "killed in the Senate . . . by the *unreasonable* and absurd notions of some Senators and the shameful conduct of others."[96] While the Senate considered the measure Butler initially opposed then agreed to an item that the bill would not become effective unless at least half of the bonded debt was surrendered according to its terms. He also agreed to an increase in state control over the trustees who would administer the canal.[97] Then on January 17 the Senate passed the bill by a vote of 31 to 15 or slightly more than a two to one margin.[98] In both houses Whigs and Democrats alike gave majorities for passage, but a larger proportion of Whig than Democratic legislators sustained adoption.[99]

The Butler Bill of 1846 made payment of the bonded debt for internal improvements and completion of the Wabash and Erie Canal to Evansville Siamese twins, as had been projected by the canal convention at Terre Haute the previous May. Half of the principal and interest at 5 percent was to be paid from state revenue; the other half, at 5 percent, became a charge against revenue from the Wabash and Erie Canal *without further obligation from the state*. The principal and interest to be paid in two stages, the first starting January 1, 1847, and the second beginning January 1, 1853, in a manner much like that suggested by Butler's second proposition, but with revenue from the canal preponderantly anticipated only during the second stage. For the measure to become effective, at least half of the bonded debt must be surrendered; and at least $2,250,000 in stock had to be subscribed for extension of the canal to Evansville. If these requirements were met, the canal would be vested in three trustees—two of the trustees to be elected by bondholders, both of whom had to be American citizens and one had also to be a resident of Indiana, and the third trustee to be named by the General Assembly, or by the governor on an interim basis between its sessions. Subscribers to the advance of $2,250,000 for finishing the canal to Evansville were given considerable priority over nonsubscribers in payment of obligations against its revenue. The canal was to be completed within four years.[100]

The rival political organs at the capital and various papers around the state supported the First Butler Bill of 1846. As the legislative session which approved it began, the pro-Whig *Indiana State Journal* insisted that Indiana had pledged "the plighted faith of the State of Indiana, for the payment of principal and interest." "Violated public faith, and not the Roman arms, destroyed Carthage," its editor exhorted, and *"Punic faith"* was all that was left of the once wealthy and powerful republic of Carthage. Later the *Journal* contended that the debt had been created "with the wishes of an overwhelming majority of the people"; hence it "must be discharged by the whole *People.*" Thus, the debt question was "above all mere party, local, or personal considerations." Upon the bill's passage by the General Assembly, the Whig editor declared that "Indiana will again resume her stand among the honored debt-paying States," if its provisions were carried out in good faith by the state and its creditors.[101] The pro-Democratic *Indiana State Sentinel* claimed that the bondholders, seeing the Democrats "favorably disposed towards an arrangement," had sent an agent to negotiate about the debt. Its editor charged that through "incompetency and mismanagement" of Whig fund commissioners that $4,000,000 had been lost from bonds sold for which "no consideration" had been obtained. But during a "gloomy period" Whitcomb had taken the lead and recommended an arrangement with the creditors. "We called upon Hercules," the editor proclaimed, and "He responded to the call." The *Sentinel* warned bondholders that "the very best proposition ... Indiana will ever submit to" had been made. It predicted that the canal would be "immensely profitable" to those who took it over. As "a great connecting link, between the cities of New Orleans and New York," unless "canals be superseded entirely by Railways," in no distant day it would be replaced with "a double width canal ...." While these remarks were perhaps designed to encourage approval by bondholders, the assurance that a levy of only 25 cents per $100 on taxable property and 75 cents per poll would be the "highest point" required to finance the settlement was doubtless intended to foster Hoosier support for it. The *Sentinel* reported that with "two or three unimportant exceptions" Indiana newspapers "of both parties" generally approved the First Butler Bill.[102]

Before Butler left Indiana for the East and England, he advised certain legislators and other friends of the arrangement that Indiana had not met what the bondholders had hoped for or had the right to expect. Nonetheless, he asserted, it "is honorable to the State of Indiana, and will I trust be accepted by the Bondholders ...."[103] In a communication to the legislature, the agent said Indiana had met its obligations on very favorable terms. "The state, not having the ability to give a whole loaf, to a suffering bondholder," Butler observed, "does offer to him half a loaf certain, and makes a provisional arrangement for the other half." To bondholders he explained that the terms of settlement had been affected by the belief of legislators that they had been defrauded in the sale of bonds, the impact of the depression, and the dismal outcome of the state's internal improvement program. Hence, the item that only half of the principal and interest would be paid from taxation, had been essential because "'in no other form could the bill have passed the House of Representatives ....'" Butler gave favorable estimates about anticipated trade on the revenue from the canal, asserting that it was "second only to the

New York and Erie Canal."[104] Perhaps Butler overestimated revenue from the canal, both to make the "provisional" half loaf more palatable to the bondholders, and to encourage them to participate in its completion to the Ohio River at Evansville.[105]

When the General Assembly reconvened in December, 1846, no bonds had been surrendered pursuant to the Butler Bill of the previous session.[106] Butler, who had conferred with bondholders in the United States and England, returned to Indiana with the news that English bondholders had instructed him to seek a reduction in the subscription required for completion of the canal to Evansville and additional security for the money advanced therefor. In his annual message to the legislature and also in his second inaugural, Governor Whitcomb emphasized that both fiscal and economic conditions had improved during his first term. He noted that the English bondholders accepted the principle of charging half of the principal and interest to the canal, and his impression that "the great majority of our citizens is also decidedly in its favor." Whitcomb asserted that there was well grounded hope for an agreement "substantially as proposed by the bill of last session," which, if achieved, would sustain "the whole arrangement, principal and interest," without raising taxes.[107] Butler told legislators that if the subscription for completion of the canal to Evansville was reduced to $800,000, with appropriate preference given subscribers over nonsubscribers for revenue from the canal, that "few, if any of the bondholders" would fail to surrender their bonds. On this basis, he suggested, an arrangement could be effected within "a few weeks, and at an early day in the approaching summer, the work upon the Wabash and Erie Canal will be put under contract."[108]

After much debate and vigorous opposition the Second Butler Bill passed both houses of the legislature by bipartisan majorities. The House passed it on January 16, 1847, by more than a two to one margin, with 70 votes for and 30 votes against passage. Nine days later it passed the Senate by a much closer vote of 24 to 18.[109]

The thirty members of the House who voted against passage of the Butler Bill, including an equal number of Democrats and

Whigs, protested its approval. They argued that since it did not cover the entire debt, the state would have to make provision later for bonds not surrendered, "or be branded forever with the foul disgrace of *repudiation.*" They considered the money bondholders would advance to complete the canal to Evansville insufficient to extend it "any further than to Terre Haute, or at farthest to Point Commerce" in Greene County. The increased priorities the new law gave bondholders who so advanced money, they said, gave advantages to wealthy bondholders, including speculators who had bought bonds at a low price, at the expense of money to poor and needy bondholders, including widows and orphans. Moreover, giving such an advantage or priority was termed an express violation of previous legislation in which the state had pledged its good faith to all bondholders.[110] The Butler Bill of 1847 made significant changes in the Butler Bill of 1846. First, it lowered the amount of money which must be advanced for extension of the canal to Evansville from $2,250,000 to only $800,000. Second, it gave increased priority to subscribers of this fund over nonsubscribers in payment of revenue from the canal. Third, it indicated circumstances which would allow six years for the canal's completion to Evansville. Fourth, it included an ultimatum to bondholders that Indiana "would make no provision whatever hereafter, to pay either principal or interest on any internal improvement bond or bonds" unless surrendered for certificates according to the compromise legislation. The Butler Bill of 1847, like the Butler Bill of 1846, reaffirmed that the compromise would not be effective unless at least half of the bonded debt was surrendered for certificates. Moreover, the key provision that half of the principal as well as half of the interest would be a charge against the canal, without further obligation from the state, was also reaffirmed.[111]

Representative G. Burton Thompson, a Whig from Perry County who voted for the Butler Bill of 1847, probably expressed views similar to most of its proponents. Before he voted Thompson declared that the bill was "not in all respects" what he desired, but under its provisions "we can so manage as to extinguish one half of the State Debt with the canal, and all its lands and other appurtences [*sic*]; the other half we can endure for a while, pay the interest thereon yearly, and ultimately the principal. Should we hesitate? I think not." Thompson compared Indiana's situation to "that of a Probate court settling an insolvent's estate, and advertising for creditors to come within a certain time to draw their due proportion, else all assets will be paid to more diligent creditors, to their exclusion." The southern Indiana legislator accurately asserted that the bill about to be voted on "is not a Whig or Democrat measure—it alike derives its paternity from each. Be it said to the credit of this Hall, it is no party question. A majority of each party manfully comes up to its support." Thompson appealed for a united effort to alert bondholders that "we have done the best in our power; . . . and they are obliged to fall in and accept our terms; and if any are so unwise as not to accept, their bonds will not be worth a groat . . . ." After explaining that he had in vain warned that "inevitable disgrace and ruin" would follow from the System of 1836, Thompson declared that it was time "to shoulder the responsibility, and if possible, to redeem our State from the wreck and havoc others produced. Let us pass the bill, and our constituents and our consciences will approve of it, and Indiana may again become what she once was, the pride of the West."[112]

Was the settlement of Indiana's bonded debt for internal improvements, by terms of the Butler Bill of 1847, consistent with the state's obligations and pledged faith to the bondholders? Jacob Piatt Dunn staunchly contended: "It is a perversion of language to speak of this settlement as 'repudiation,' as has been done." Logan Esarey, however, concluded otherwise. "One could not fail to agree with Butler," he wrote, "that the State was able to meet all its obligations honorably, except for two reasons. These were, first, the demoralized condition of the currency, and second, the leadership of a clique of oily politicians." Esarey suggested that a "State levy of 70 cents [per $100 of taxable property] would have paid principal and interest." "No one," Esarey stated, "will for a moment contend that the bondholders would have preferred the arrangement of 1847 to the payment of the bonds according to their tenor."[113] From a legal and contractual point of view the settlement arising from the Butler bills was explicitly contrary to Indiana's pledged faith irrevocably guaranteeing payment of principal and interest on bonds sold for construction of the Wabash and Erie Canal and the System of 1836.[114] Indiana's modest tax levies during the returning prosperity of the forties, compared to those for the depression years of 1839 through 1841, afford convincing evidence that lack of will, not lack of ability, caused Hoosiers to repudiate much of their bonded debt for internal improvements.[115]

During the fiscal years 1843 through 1850, Indiana financed the ordinary expenditures of state government, largely liquidated the unfunded debt for internal improvements, and in 1847 resumed payment of interest on the funded debt for internal improvements. In his inaugural as governor in December, 1843, James Whitcomb declared that "lured by the flattering guise of credit" consumption had exceeded income, hence extraction could be achieved only "by the joint aid of industry and economy." The new executive admonished that it was desirable to "seek the ancient land marks of frugality and republican simplicity from which too many have unwittingly strayed."[116] Several weeks earlier Calvin Fletcher had written the governor-elect about the "weighty duties" soon to devolve on him. Fletcher observed that Whitcomb would "enter upon the administration of the state government under most perplexing difficulties, as it relates to individual and public indebt[ed]ness & I might say insolvency. A people so involved," Fletcher advised, "have neither the inclination nor the ability to make proper efforts to discharge any portion of their present liability much less the public debt—which in good faith should be paid, nor can you bring them to that condition till you relieve them from individual embarrassment."[117] A desire to allow individuals time to reduce their debts seems to have been an important influence in maintaining low tax levies for the years 1842 through 1845.[118]

As the accompanying tables show, during 1843 to 1850 ordinary expenditures remained modest. They remained so principally because of a decrease in the length of legislative sessions, and a reduction of salaries and per diems to state officials.[119] Ordinary expenditures averaged $142,464.25 versus $113,591.27 for

Ordinary Expenditures, 1843–1850

Fiscal Year	Legislative	Stationery and Fuel	Judiciary	Executive	Taxes Paid Collectors	Prison	Militia
1843–44	$ 38,967.04	$ 12,959.15	$ 23,111.05	$ 3,102.04	$ 12,446.05	$ 4,804.13	$ 227.12
1844–45	31,792.07	2,156.71	22,149.74	4,300.00	13,598.98	11,320.44	200.00
1845–46	32,620.41	2,111.69	21,877.97	2,000.00	14,693.14	4,649.11	791.81
1846–47	37,017.92	3,093.36	21,622.12	9,101.18	18,099.78	21,049.30	1,438.51
1847–48	40,606.77	4,429.10	20,891.15	3,550.00	20,719.00	5,953.33	862.61
1848–49	36,469.76	3,416.36	22,298.67	4,496.66	22,182.51	27,793.18	1,444.34
1849–50	43,084.67	2,453.13	19,705.81	5,877.93	22,781.50	16,542.53	618.92
Total	260,558.64	30,619.50	151,656.51	32,427.81	124,520.96	92,112.02	5,583.31
Average	37,222.66	4,374.21	21,665.21	4,632.54	17,788.70	13,158.86	797.61

Ordinary Expenditures, 1843–1850

Fiscal Year	Library	Wolves	Benevolent	Contingent	Specific Appropriations	Miscellaneous	Total
1843–44	$382.56	$2.00	$1,168.75	$1,138.62	$7,041.38	$1,211.68	$106,561.57
1844–45	472.57	2.00	2,797.87	1,232.70	4,890.86	6,610.32	101,489.26
1845–46	438.55	0.00	13,623.09	319.73	6,240.90	207.22	99,573.62
1846–47	1,558.07	3.00	44,813.36	619.30	11,193.18	278.83	169,887.91
1847–48	1,090.16	0.00	37,016.73	323.70	3,705.08	871.63	140,019.26
1848–49	751.99	0.00	61,847.89	842.12	1,202.62	3,407.94	186,154.04
1849–50	964.81	0.00	73,762.34	1,765.30	3,114.29	2,857.91	193,236.33
Total	5,658.71	7.00	235,030.03	6,241.47	37,388.31	15,445.53	997,249.80
Average	808.38	1.00	33,575.71	891.63	5,341.18	2,206.50	142,464.25

the six previous years.[120] Except for significant sums spent for benevolent and correctional institutions, the aggregate expenditures would have been noticeably lower than for the six previous years. Moreover, apart from benevolent and correctional items, expenditures were preponderantly for the same items as they had been from statehood, with legislative costs the largest of all and those for the judiciary second in rank.[121] Executive salaries, which had always been a small part of the total, averaged slightly less than they had been under Governors Wallace and Bigger. Payments for wolf scalps nearly vanished, but money for the State Library reached its peak for the pioneer era. The Mexican War prompted a new high in militia costs. Missing from this table of ordinary expenditures—as for all such preceding tables—are items spent for education.[122]

The expenditures on behalf of the blind, deaf and dumb, and the insane, generous in the fiscal context of the forties, reflected humanitarian concern for these unfortunate individuals. Heretofore, their care, so far as provided, had been by relatives, other interested persons, and local officials.[123] The wretched condition of the insane attracted public concern. During 1835 Calvin Fletcher lamented the death of his once "esteemed worthy friend," John Hays, who had "burned [to death] at Greenfield while confined in Jail for insanity."[124] Early in 1842 a committee of the House of Representatives branded "absolutely intolerable" the status of the insane, many of whom were "*imprisoned for life* . . . in some filthy cellar or out-house," while others roamed the country nearly nude, destitute of proper food, and exposed to inclement weather. The committee insisted that proper treatment of the insane required the "establishment of a Lunatic Asylum" with appropriate facilities and trained physicians to care for them. The House committee observed that although Indiana had been "shamefully squandering" millions on internal improvements, as yet "not one cent" had been spent on asylums for the deaf and dumb, the blind, "or the still more unfortunate class, who have been deprived of Reason."[125] After James McLean and William Willard demonstrated that the deaf could be taught, and William H. Churchman did likewise for the blind, in the midforties the state established institutions for them.[126] As the decade ended Governor Joseph A. Wright told legislators that Indiana, in proportion to its population, was educating, "free of all expense," 33 percent more deaf mutes than any other state. He also asserted that 90 percent of those "placed in the Insane Asylum within six months after" their attack, had been cured; and that for those so admitted within one year after becoming insane, 80 percent of them had been cured.[127] The achievements of three benevolent institutions can easily be exaggerated, but their development in the forties represents a major expansion of the role and ordinary expenditures of state government—nearly a decade before state tax support for education became established as a responsibility of state government.

The large increase in prison costs apparently resulted from necessity tinged with humanitarian impulse. In 1840 the House Committee on the State Prison described the prison opened in 1822 as in "a wretched condition," with inmates suffering from filth, poor and inadequate food, unduly severe punishments, overwork, inadequate care of the sick, neglect of education, and want of "moral and religious instruction." The committee branded the leasing of the institution to the highest bidder to be "the most ill advised and pernicious" of any practice in the United States. The "cause of humanity," it said, demanded that the prison be managed by the state.[128] But a subsequent House Committee on the State Prison concluded that "the embarrassed situation of the financial concerns of the State" made "impolitic" the recommended change. At the session of 1840–1841, the legislature retained the leasing system, appropriated $4,000 for improvement of prison facilities, and authorized the governor to appoint a physician and a chaplain for the prison.[129] During June, 1842, however, Samuel Wort, prison visitor, examined the existing facilities, and urged that no further improvements be made at the "crowded, filthy, illy-constructed" prison situated on about an acre of land within Jeffersonville. Wort reported that there were 113 convicts at the institution, and he predicted that the number would exceed 200 within a decade.[130] After a second visit in November, Wort recommended consideration of locating a new prison "towards the central part of the State," with sufficient land for the employment of prisoners in manufacturing rope and bagging as well as in raising their own provisions. If located near the "knobs, abounding in good tan bark," leather could be obtained for making shoes and saddlery. So located, and built with prison labor, within fifteen years the state could be "fully remunerated" for its cost; and have a prison "both honorable and profitable" to the state.[131] When the legislators convened in December, Governor Bigger told them that his inspection of the prison during the summer had convinced him that it could not be managed properly in its cramped and poorly constructed quarters. Bigger recommended early location of a new prison, near Jeffersonville, but neither he nor Wort proposed that leasing be ended. The General Assembly authorized the governor to buy from ten to twenty acres outside the city limits of Jeffersonville. It appropriated $1,000 for the site; asked the executive to arrange for construction of a new prison, sufficient for 200 inmates; and appropriated $5,000 for its construction.[132] In February, 1843, the legislature commended Bigger for the manner in which he had performed these duties, and it urged speedy construction of the new prison, declaring that only "a slight mitigation of the enormous evils" borne by prisoners could be obtained in "such a *calcutta hole*" as the existing prison. In a further report this committee expressed its "unanimous" view that a system should be adopted whereby "the future control and profits" of the prison should accrue "exclusively" to the state.[133] Although construction began in 1842, not until 1847 were all of the inmates moved from the "calcutta hole" to the new prison. Meanwhile, in 1846 Dorothea L. Dix, nationally known reformer, visited both the old and new prisons. She described the "lodging cells" of the old prison as "worse beyond all comparison than any cells I ever saw allotted to human creatures." "They are," she added, "horribly disgusting, filthy and wretched." Dix called the workshops of the new prison good, except those for making hemp, but she explained that the "absence of air passages *in the cells*" would make them "as bad if not worse than those . . . occupied in the old prison . . . ."[134]

While ordinary expenditures from 1843 to 1850 rose only moderately over those for the years 1837–1843, revenue from taxation increased tremendously. Tax revenue plus modest other ordinary revenue averaged $381,310.34 annually versus an average of $261,475.23 for the six preceding years. As the accompanying table illustrates, this revenue came overwhelmingly from taxation.[135] Receipts from prison rent and sale of the old state prison ranked a very low second; revenue from borrowing and other sources was quite modest. As the table regarding tax levies indicates, apart from small levies for benevolent purposes, the levies for 1844 and 1845, the two initial years of the Whitcomb administration, remained the same as they had been for the last two years of the Bigger administration—being 20 cents per $100 of taxable property and 50 cents per poll. The 5 cent increase in the property levy and the 25 cent jump in the poll tax starting in 1846 were connected with the compromise settlement with the bondholders. But with all the special levies included, the peak levy of 1850 was significantly less than that of 1841 had been and roughly the same as for 1839.[136] The tax levies during the increasing prosperity of the last half of the forties, when compared to those of the depression years of the late thirties and early forties, afford convincing evidence that Hoosiers made no unusual effort nor any significant sacrifice to pay the entire bonded debt for internal improvements as the General Assembly had pledged would be done.

As tax revenue soared upwards, principally because of an expanding amount of taxable property and polls, criticism persisted that property was not being assessed in an equal and fair manner. The assessing and collecting was done by local officials, much as provided by legislation of the early forties.[137] Personal property was reassessed yearly, and real estate at five-year intervals such as 1841 and 1846.[138] All property was to be assessed at its actual value, but much intangible property, and especially stocks, escaped taxation. Auditor Douglass Maguire reported that all kinds of property assessed for 1847 increased in value versus that for the previous year, except for stocks whose value decreased. Maguire asserted that so far as he knew "not a cent of taxes" had ever been paid on the four or five hundred thousand dollars of individual stock for the Indianapolis and Madison Railroad Company, which

Ordinary Revenue, 1843–1850

Fiscal Year	Taxes Received	Taxes Paid Collectors	Borrowing	Prison	Miscellaneous	Total
1843–44	$ 248,921.07	$ 12,446.05	$ 0.00	$ 0.00	$ 456.12	$ 261,823.24
1844–45	271,979.78	13,598.98	0.00	0.00	334.58	285,913.34
1845–46	293,862.90	14,693.14	0.00	0.00	401.95	308,957.99
1846–47	361,995.62	18,099.78	0.00	0.00	537.82	380,633.22
1847–48	414,380.17	20,719.00	0.00	0.00	665.20	435,764.37
1848–49	443,650.22	22,182.51	0.00	24,620.14	310.85	490,763.72
1849–50	455,630.02	22,781.50	14,476.50	11,145.42	1,283.08	505,316.52
Total	2,490,419.78	124,520.96	14,476.50	35,765.56	3,989.60	2,669,172.40
Average	355,774.25	17,788.70	2,068.07	5,109.36	569.94	381,310.34

Indiana Tax Levies, 1844–1850

Year	Tax per $100 owned	Poll tax
1844	15¢ per $100: redemption of treasury notes 5¢ per $100: ordinary costs of state government 1¢ per $100: Insane Asylum 2 mills per $100: Deaf and Dumb Asylum Total tax per $100: 21¢ and 2 mills	50¢
1845	15¢ per $100: redemption of treasury notes 5¢ per $100: ordinary costs of state government 1¢ per $100: Insane Asylum 5 mills per $100: Deaf and Dumb Asylum 2 mills per $100: education of the blind Total tax per $100: 21¢ and 7 mills	50¢
1846	25¢ per $100: ordinary costs of state government 1¢ per $100: Insane Asylum 5 mills per $100: Deaf and Dumb Asylum 2 mills per $100: education of the blind Total tax per $100: 26¢ and 7 mills	50¢
1847	25¢ per $100: for state purposes 1¢ and 5 mills per $100: Deaf and Dumb Asylum 1¢ per $100: Insane Asylum 1¢ per $100: education of the blind Total tax per $100: 28¢ and 5 mills	75¢
1848	25¢ per $100: for state purposes 2¢ and 2$^1/_2$ mills per $100: Deaf and Dumb Asylum 1¢ and 7$^1/_2$ mills per $100: Hospital for Insane 1¢ per $100: education of the blind Total tax per $100: 30¢	75¢
1849	25¢ per $100: state purposes 2¢ and 2$^1/_2$ mills per $100: Deaf and Dumb Asylum 1¢ and 7$^1/_2$ mills per $100: Hospital for Insane 1¢ per $100: education of the blind Total tax per $100: 30¢	75¢
1850	25¢ per $100: for state purposes 3$^1/_2$ mills per $100: cost of Constitutional Convention 2¢ and 2$^1/_2$ mills per $100: Deaf and Dumb Asylum 1¢ and 7$^1/_2$ mills per $100: Hospital for Insane 1¢ per $100: education of the blind Total tax per $100: 33$^1/_2$¢	75¢

yielded "large dividends" to subscribers. The auditor viewed it "rather remarkable" that in many counties less land was assessed in 1847 than had been assessed in 1846, and "strange" that the assessed value of tracts on opposite sides of county lines varied greatly.[139] Whitcomb and others expressed similar views about the unequal assessment of land and the grossly incomplete assessment of intangible property.[140] For the most part county treasurers paid taxes collected to the state treasury on time, but Auditor E. W. H. Ellis reported that delinquency among taxpayers averaged about $31,028.11 annually for the years 1844 through 1848.[141] The continued criticism about the assessing of property led to legislation in the early fifties which emphasized that all kinds of property should be assessed at its "true cash value," and established congressional district boards to review and equal assessments among counties, with a state review and equalization board as the final authority in determining county assessments. Ironically, this state board was established under Democratic auspices, whereas in the early forties Democrats had been mainly responsible for killing such a board.[142]

Meanwhile, during 1843–1850, *considerably more than half of the tax revenue collected* was used to pay principal and interest arising from the Internal Improvements System of 1836 and the Wabash and Erie Canal. Since ordinary revenues aggregated $2,669,172.40 against $996,921.99 for ordinary expenditures, revenues exceeded expenditures by $1,672,250.41. The fiscal context of this period makes it reasonable to presume that the surplus tax revenue was overwhelmingly used for payment of interest and principal on debts owed because of the System of 1836 and the canal. These items in particular were apparently paid for from this surplus of tax revenue.[143] Early in the 1850s the House Ways and Means Committee issued a comprehensive report about state finances, and reported that during 1843–1850 a total of $830,265 had been spent on the domestic or unfunded debt for the redemption of $1,500,000 of treasury notes which had been issued under the act of 1842 to pay sums owed contractors for construction costs for the System of 1836 and the canal. And the sum of $639,269 had been required for payment of interest on the bonded debt for internal improvements, per the Butler Bill of 1847, from July 1, 1847, to July 1, 1850, inclusive.[144]

Some of the bondholders, however, declined to surrender their bonds for certificates according to the Butler Bill of 1847. Of the $11,048,000 in bonds outstanding when this bill was adopted, bonds valued at $8,133,000 were surrendered by July 1, 1847, when the state began paying interest on them. By August, 1850, bonds aggregating $9,563,000 had been exchanged for certificates, leaving those valued at $1,485,000, or 7.43 percent of the total unsurrendered.[145]

Several influences made possible the restoration of solvency and stability to Indiana's state finances at mid-century. First, the rising prosperity from the mid-forties, which gave a stimulus to the rapidly advancing economy and population, augmenting the tax base and the flow of revenue therefrom despite moderate tax levies. Second, the strong trend away from efforts to develop the economy through state participation in banking and transportation facilities, left this responsibility principally to private enterprise as the forties ended. Third, by 1850 the unfunded or domestic debt had been preponderantly liquidated. Fourth, and perhaps most important of all, the Butler Bill of 1847 had made the revenue of the Wabash and Erie Canal, not the state treasury, responsible for payment of half of the interest and principal of the bonded debt for the system and canal. In addition, it had given the state until January 1, 1853, before it would have to pay the full 5 percent interest due on its half of the bonded debt. The achievement of fiscal solvency and stability had been obtained by substantial bipartisan cooperation between Whigs and Democrats. But the boon given state finances by the compromise debt settlement, forced upon the bondholders, caused heavy losses to an unknown number of bondholders.

While state finances regained solvency and stability, the Second State Bank renewed its strength and became increasingly prosperous. Though largely controlled by Whigs before the Democratic triumph of 1843, thereafter Democrats had a greater role in its management. The rapid increase in the state's wealth, the large growth in population during the forties, the restoration of fiscal solvency, and returning prosperity afforded the best context for successful banking since statehood. Nevertheless, considerable opposition existed against the bank, and especially during the last half of the forties there was rising sentiment for free or general banking.

Even before their triumph in 1843, Democrats gained an increased voice in the management of the Second State Bank. Early that year the General Assembly named three Democrats as its representatives on the powerful state bank board.[146] After the election in August, there was much discussion among Democrats regarding a successor to Samuel Merrill, the bank's president from its beginning, whose term would expire during the ensuing legislative session. The Goshen *Democrat* at once admonished: "Throw him over, and let an honest man, like Nathan B. Palmer, reign in his stead." On the other hand, the Vincennes *Western Sun*, after asserting that banking and Democracy were completely antagonistic and at war with cardinal principles which Democrats had proclaimed during the late campaign, urged that the best and most honorable Whig be elected its president and then "keep an eye on him" for no "true Democrat" should accept the office.[147] The Greencastle *Patriot* preferred that Whigs manage the bank. But if they failed to "do so fairly, according to law, then knock it in the head at once . . . ." If, however, a Democrat must be elected, "take one like Thompson's dog, fit for nothing else." The Madison *Courier* said it would be inconsistent and bring trouble to the party to put a Democrat at the head of the bank.[148] Some Democrats, doubtless motivated in part by hunger for patronage, argued that a Democrat should replace Merrill as a step toward the bank's reform and purification. Soon after Whitcomb's election the *Indiana State Sentinel*, an often vigorous critic of the bank, commented that it had "been recently improved in its condition." Part of the improvement was attributed to the "salutary effects" of the "searching examination" which Democrat Nathan B. Palmer had made of its management the previous year. If "monopolists, favorite families, *cliques*, and the mad party [Whig]," under whose "exclusive care" it had been, were driven out the bank might become "useful to the community." If the bank became justly administered, the editor averred, "we shall not be backward to declare our approval." An anonymous Democrat, who insisted that whether a Whig or Democrat served as president the Democrats would be held accountable, advocated that "an *Anti-Bank*" Democrat such as Ebenezer M. Chamberlain be chosen to succeed

Merrill. If anything remained of the bank, after being "purged of corruption and abuses," it could be preserved and fostered. But since it suffered from "*total depravity,*" it could be saved "by *grace* alone."[149] With the "ascendancy" of the Democrats, the New Albany *Democrat* asserted, the people would hold Democrats responsible for correcting existing evils. Moreover, since the people owned half or more of the stock of the bank, with all branches under Whig control, it was the "imperative duty" of the new administration "to select some good, honest, and capable democrat to preside over the State Bank of Indiana." The *Grant County Herald* suggested that to think that since the bank had always been under Whig dominance that it should remain so was "a poor way to carry out reform." With "*honest* management" it could be made useful to the community. The Goshen *Democrat* charged that the Whigs had used the bank "as a political engine" to sustain their falling fortunes, but termed it folly and preposterous for Democrats to elect a Whig as its president.[150]

Various Democrats were proposed to replace Merrill as president of the Second State Bank. In addition to Palmer and Chamberlain, mentioned above, James Morrison, Alexander J. Burnett, and James White were among those recommended.[151] Soon after the state election in August, 1843, Calvin Fletcher expressed concern that Merrill's interest in winning reelection was causing him to seek "new friends at the sacrifise of old ones." Since the House had fifty-five Democrats and forty-five Whigs, and the Senate twenty-six Democrats to twenty-four Whigs, even if all the Whigs voted for Merrill significant support from Democrats was essential for his reelection.[152] On January 3, 1844, on three successive separate ballots the House gave its majority to Morrison while the Senate gave its majority to Merrill. To end the impasse, the two houses met and voted jointly. On their initial ballot Merrill led Morrison by one vote, with ten votes "scattering"; but on the fourth tally Morrison won election, gaining seventy-seven votes against sixty-seven for Merrill, with two votes scattering.[153] James Morrison for the most part served the bank ably and well. In 1848 he gained reelection to a second five-year term, defeating Daniel Mace, a fellow Democrat, on the initial ballot. According to the *Indiana State Journal*, Whig legislators, much outnumbered by Democrats, did not sponsor a candidate and "generally voted for Judge Morrison, believing him to be the best qualified for the place."[154] When Morrison was defeated for reelection in 1853, by fellow Democrat Ebenezer Dumont, the state bank board adopted resolutions commending his role as the bank's president. At this time, Calvin Fletcher, who had lamented Morrison's election in 1844 when he had termed him "a man of bad temper [and] malicious habits" who was "unfit for the place," added "remarks commendatory" of the retiring president.[155] Although Democrats gained increased representation on both branch and state bank boards while Morrison was the bank's president, it appears that most board members were usually Whigs.[156]

When Whitcomb became governor late in 1843, the Second State Bank was suffering from its weakened status of the early forties. President Merrill reported that profits for 1842–1843 had been less than for any year except the first. He noted that the branch at South Bend had had no profit; and the branch at Lawrenceburg, after prolonged controversy, had been suspended.[157] For the year ending in November, 1843, the capital of the bank, chiefly that owned by the state, had been reduced nearly $600,000, lowering its aggregate capital to $2,136,272.25. Specie on hand, however, amounted to $965,226.85, having increased almost $154,000 over the previous November. But the "suspended debt" of the bank—owed it by delinquent borrowers, including directors and others—aggregated $707,939.66, thus greatly curtailing its ability to accommodate other borrowers. Nevertheless, in June, 1842, the bank had successfully resumed specie payments for its notes.[158] The capital of the bank declined slightly for a time after Whitcomb became governor, but its total stock continued remarkably stable at roughly $2,100,000. As the forties advanced the proportion of stock owned by the state rose, and by 1850 the state once more owned about half of the stock. By this time the suspended debt had dropped to $270,213.77, increasing the bank's capacity to accommodate new borrowers; and the specie on hand had jumped to approximately $1,400,000. Inasmuch as the bank's circulation of its notes was limited to an average of two and one half times its capital, this large specie reserve enhanced its very favorable reputation.[159]

The dividends of the Second State Bank also increased significantly during the last half of the forties. The dividends for all branches averaged 6.80 percent for the year ending in November, 1844; and 10 percent for the year ending in 1850. With the reinstatement of the Lawrenceburg branch in 1844, the ten original branches established in 1834, plus the three new ones commenced in the late thirties, all remained in operation.[160] As a member of the state bank board for meetings in May and November, 1845, Calvin Fletcher observed "a general prosperity" in its branches and concluded that "The Bank as an institution seemed to be in a healthy state." Early in 1846 the pro-Whig *Indiana State Journal* pronounced the bank "sound beyond all controversy." It said the *Bankers' Weekly Circular*, of New York, had commented that "Such an accumulation of specie funds would seem to be unnecessary for a bank in such credit as the State Bank of Indiana."[161] Soon after the Indiana Constitutional Convention of 1850–1851 convened, Cashier James M. Ray informed delegates that the bank had earned the state "at least, the sum of one million of dollars" for the benefit of common schools. The cashier asserted that the bank had furnished "a sound currency for the business of the community" in spite of "disastrous revulsions in financial affairs" since its opening in 1834. And such contributions had been achieved in contrast to the generally dismal record of both state and private banks in other states, Ray suggested.[162]

As the state advanced in wealth, population, and prosperity during the late forties, four new branches of the Second State Bank were authorized. At the legislative session of 1847–1848, in which Whigs and Democrats had equality in the Senate but the Whigs had a slight edge in the House, such authorization was approved by the General Assembly. The preponderance of Whigs favored and most Democrats opposed passage, but Governor Whitcomb vetoed the bill saying that he needed more time to obtain relevant information about the matter which could then be given the "mature deliberation" it deserved at the ensuing session.[163] Early in the next session, which had Democratic majorities in both houses, the same or at least a similar bill was adopted by the General Assembly and Whitcomb signed it into law. Whig votes were largely responsible for its passage. Three Democrats on the House Committee on the State Bank protested that four new branches were not needed. They suggested that such new branches would augment the bank's stock by $640,000 and allow a circulation of $1,600,000 more of its paper. The protesters emphasized that the bank would soon be seeking a renewal of its charter, thus four new branches would increase the number of persons indebted to it and impair the independence of the legislature regarding a new charter.[164] The state bank board endorsed the proposed amendment to the bank's charter, with a recommendation that it be approved by the branches, but their unanimous consent was not given and the amendment failed.[165]

Meantime, during the depression of the early forties the Second State Bank had gained the privilege of issuing small notes. The charter of 1834 prohibited the issuance of notes for less than $5, and it reserved to the legislature the right to prohibit the issue and circulation of notes for less than $10 after a lapse of ten years.[166] But as the thirties ended, the large circulation of small notes of various size from other states; the efforts to increase dividends to help the state meet augmenting interest on the internal improvement bonds; and the deepening depression fostered sentiment for issuing notes in units of less than $5. At the legislative session of 1839–1840, in which the Whigs had a modest edge in the Senate and the Democrats a sizeable margin in the House, bills authorizing small notes were considered but not adopted. The *Indiana Journal* estimated that Indiana had almost $1,000,000 of such notes from other states, "not a dollar of which can be redeemed in specie in this State." Allowing the bank to issue small notes, this Whig paper suggested, would provide "a specie convertible circulation" to replace the "foreign trash" flooding the state. The *Indiana Democrat* called it "folly" to authorize small notes at a time when other states were reportedly taking measures to expel them from their circulation. Between specie and small notes, the Democratic editor added: "Whigs might say small notes. Democrats would say specie."[167]

The huge Whig majorities in both houses at the legislative session of 1840–1841 offered a favorable prospect for the issuance of small notes. Governor Wallace advised legislators that an early increase in the capital of the bank, payment of the state debt to it, and "authority for a limited period" for the bank to issue small notes would "materially" aid the state in meeting its fiscal crisis.[168] The General Assembly proposed an amendment to the bank's charter authorizing the privilege of issuing up to $1,000,000 of notes in units of less than $5 but not under $1. If issued, the bank would pay the state 1 percent on the amount of such notes. A related measure prohibited the issue of small notes by individuals or corporations, other than the Second State Bank. This act also declared small notes, except those of the Second State Bank and chartered banks of other states, void for payments owed.[169] Although this legislation was not approved entirely along party lines, the Whigs were largely responsible for it.[170] After attending a meeting of the state bank board, Calvin Fletcher predicted that the board would refuse to concur with the proposed amendment for small notes.[171] New legislation, however, approved in February, 1841, extended legislative authorization for small notes to January 1, 1846. Furthermore, apparently to placate members of the state bank board, it provided that because of the "trouble and responsibility" of "managing and collecting" certain funds, the bank would not be required to pay the 1 percent tax on small notes issued.[172] The state and branch bank boards quickly accepted the modified terms for insurance of small bank notes. Late in 1841 President Merrill reported that $412,000 of small notes had been issued by the Second State Bank, with about three fourths of them probably in circulation. These notes, Merrill said, had "in most parts of the State, expelled the small notes of other States, and they will form a basis of home circulation for the Bank of more value than was anticipated."[173] At the next annual legislative session, however, Democrats vigorously attacked the conversion of the principal of special state funds into state bank stock, and such conversion was virtually ended. The law regarding this item expressly stated that the privilege of issuing small notes remained valid only so long as they were redeemed in specie upon demand.[174]

At the legislative session of 1844–1845, legislation was considered for extension of the issuance of small notes beyond January 1, 1846. Acting on behalf of the state bank board, President James Morrison asked the legislature that the authority for issuing small notes to a maximum of $1,000,000 be extended through the life of the bank's charter. Morrison said the board favored this extension because public sentiment favored their continuation; the circulation of small change specie, contrary to the anticipation of many, had not been expelled by the small notes; the circulation of "foreign" small notes, of a doubtful and dangerous character, had largely been driven from the state; and the public had confidence in the small notes of the bank. If continuation were not permitted, Morrison suggested that the branches would be compelled to begin their contraction. In the Senate, equally divided between Whigs and Democrats, a bill granting continuation of small notes squeaked through by a narrow margin. In amended form it passed the House by a large majority, but the two branches were unable to resolve differences involved and approval for continued issuance of small notes was not renewed.[175]

When the legislators reconvened in December, 1845, Morrison advised them that a careful examination of existing legislation about small notes had convinced him that the privilege given was "a continuing one, until repealed by the General Assembly." Nevertheless, the state bank board would be grateful to have the privilege renewed. The legislation concerning small notes was vague enough to make Morrison's interpretation plausible.[176] The *Indiana State Sentinel* charged that the bank president had "Grown great, like Caesar, upon the meat he has fed on," until he "claims, as a sort of prescriptive or 'vested right,' what a year ago he prayed from the legislature as a boon of favor." The "hardest thing in the world," the *Sentinel* observed, was to regain privileges granted corporations. And if a paper currency expanded unchecked, the revulsions from which the country had not yet recovered would return. The editor deemed the "future ascendancy of the Democratic party" at stake in the outcome of this question. The Goshen *Democrat* contended that the bank wanted its privilege made permanent so that "the pockets of the people may be crammed with the dirty rags, instead of the pure white coin [silver] of the nation." Rather than yield to the privilege claimed, the Goshen editor declared, "chain the tiger while it is young—keep it in subjection, and . . . when its career of intrigue and oppression and outrage has been run, let it die the death of a dog, and be consigned to merited oblivion, 'unwept, unhonored and unsung.'"[177] The *Indiana State Sentinel* took a swipe at Morrison by expressing its disappointment that "a professed Democrat" would not only tolerate rottenness in the bank but even "connive at an extension of its privileges, and of its means of further corruption, by the continued issue of shinplasters." Nonetheless, the *Sentinel* added the $660,536 of small notes could remain "*afloat, if the people choose to hold them.*" The New Albany *Democrat* urged that any Democrat who voted to extend the privilege "be branded as a *traitor* to the principles of his party, and be hurled from the ranks."[178] Although the General Assembly neither approved nor disapproved the continued issue of small notes, their circulation persisted. While the support for small notes had been predominantly Whig, the Democrats failed to legislate against the privilege when they gained dominance of both houses of the legislature in the late forties.[179]

Although the Second State Bank continued to issue small notes and became prosperous, its monopoly of *authorized* banking came under increased criticism as the forties advanced. A "No Bank" element had persisted from statehood, and support for free or general banking, subject to designated restrictions, gained strength from about the late 1830s. The unsavory practices and abuses of the First State Bank during the teens and early twenties had fostered a "No Bank" element. A meeting of citizens of Washington County in 1819 declared banking destructive of their "rights as a Republican people," and called it a system which would "ultimately terminate, if not checked, in the subversion" of their independence. They called banking, as it had been conducted, "a species of fraud and swindling, in which the interests of the many has been sacrificed to the benefit of the few." Two years later sundry citizens of Washington County petitioned the legislature "for the abolition of banking . . . ."[180] In 1820 "Corn Planter" urged that the First State Bank and other "banking associations

. . . which tend to amass the capital of the community, destroy fair dealing, and monopolise the credit and trade of every body else" be abolished. At Fourth of July toasts later that year one of them termed "The Banking System—the swindler's God; the honest man's Devil."[181] During the early forties the *Indiana State Sentinel* advocated the "banishment of bank paper" and reliance on a metallic currency based on silver and gold. Several years later the *Sentinel* insisted that banks "create no capital, but simply accumulate and control that which already exists." This paper branded it "folly" to conclude that "without the aid of banks, business would cease . . . ." Properly managed they may facilitate business, but "it is doubtful whether their services are worth what they cost to the community."[182] The Fort Wayne *Sentinel*, vigorously Democratic, tersely asserted: "The banking system is after all nothing but a scheme to enable rich men to speculate at the risk of the poor ones."[183]

In contrast to the "No Bank" element, proponents of free or general banking encouraged the growth of banks. On the eve of the legislative session of 1838–1839, the Indianapolis *Indiana Democrat* vigorously contended that free banking would not be contrary to the Constitution of 1816. This Democratic paper argued that the acquisition of property was a natural right which could not be denied individuals. Therefore, property might be acquired from banking as well as from farming, a trade, or a profession. The legislature, however, could and should establish needed regulations concerning the total of notes issued, the specie reserve for them, and to prevent fraud and dishonesty. Moreover, the *Indiana Democrat* elaborated, private banking had existed in and been regulated by the legislature since before statehood. The banking article of the Constitution of 1816 was interpreted to mean that the legislature could not grant certain *corporate rights* in conflict with its provisions.[184] This editorial was perhaps an opening salvo toward consideration of free banking by the legislature. Soon after the session convened in December, Robert Dale Owen, a Democrat, obtained House approval of a resolution asking the Committee on the Judiciary to inquire "whether a general banking law, or bank restraining law," such as in force in New

York, could "be passed by this legislature, without a violation, direct or indirect," of the constitution of Indiana; and, if so, consider its expediency and report "by bill or otherwise."[185] On January 1, 1839, Samuel Judah, a Whig and chairman of the committee, submitted a bill for the regulation of private banking. The report which accompanied the bill emphasized much the same premises and views as had been expressed by the *Indiana Democrat*. The report noted that James Noble had submitted the article to the Corydon Constitutional Convention of 1816 which had adopted it. Then shortly after that Noble had gone into private banking with one of his brothers and an individual, currently serving in the House of Representatives (Robert Hanna), who also had been a member of the convention. In addition, Judge Benjamin Parke, another member of the convention, had soon engaged in private banking. With such precedents, the committee could not believe that members of the constitutional convention "intended to prohibit, or . . . considered that they had prohibited, private banking, or the formation of banking companies by individuals."[186] Representative Owen also argued that private banking was a right which could not be taken from individuals, though it was subject to appropriate legislative regulations. Free banking, Owen asserted, was founded on that "good and useful . . . principle of free competition. It grants to all certain general rights—to none exclusive privileges. And it reguards [*sic*], as every banking system ought, the security of the people first, and the profits of stockholders afterwards." The Democratic legislator correctly predicted that the bill for free banking would fail, and likewise that it would gain favor with the people and be adopted "before many years" pass.[187]

Although free banking was not adopted until the early 1850s intermittent bipartisan support for it persisted. In the fall of 1839, the *Indiana Democrat* asserted that if the legislature had enacted a free banking law and a state land lottery "a suspension of public works [in the System of 1836] would not have taken place." In his annual message to the General Assembly in December, 1840, Governor Wallace observed that "The most skilfully conducted banks in the world, are said to be those of Scotland." Two years later Calvin Fletcher expressed the opinion "that private banking has not had a fair experiment & will in the end prevail. It can be conducted by one individual as well as another without charter or special enactments."[188] Perhaps the growing strength and prosperity of the Second State Bank from about the middle forties slowed sentiment for free banking, however, the increasing emphasis on private rather than public enterprise for advancing the economy doubtless helps explain why legislation in favor of free banking was mandated by the Constitution of 1851.[189]

The gubernatorial and legislative elections in August, 1846, were crucial for Whigs and Democrats alike. Whitcomb had become the first Democratic governor in 1843, but as yet the Democrats had not *established* their control of both legislative houses.[190] Hence, a Whig victory would give them an opportunity to regain control of state government, which they had dominated from 1834 to 1843. Various men were mentioned as the prospective Whig nominee for governor. In September, 1845, a Lafayette editor named former Governor Samuel Bigger, ex-United States Senator Oliver H. Smith, and Congressman Samuel C. Sample as acceptable to Whigs. A Richmond editor viewed all three as good men, any of whom would gain the full Whig vote of the Whitewater Valley. The next month the *Indiana State Journal* listed Bigger, Sample, Joseph G. Marshall, Godlove S. Orth, Johnson Watts, Henry S. Lane, Richard W. Thompson, John H. Bradley, and others as under consideration by the Whigs.[191] In October Smith withdrew his name from consideration.[192] By this time Orth was actively seeking the nomination. After Lieutenant Governor Jesse D. Bright defeated Marshall for election to the United States Senate in early December, and Marshall loomed as the probable Whig nominee for governor, Orth agreed to be his running mate as lieutenant governor if given a unanimous nomination and Marshall would "pledge himself to canvass the state."[193] On the eve of the Whig State Convention in January Representative G. Burton Thompson, of Perry County, asked friends not to think of him for lieutenant governor because a gentleman from "the Southern part of the State" will be the candidate for governor, hence the second on the ticket should come from central or northern Indiana.[194]

Meanwhile, it seemed uncertain whether Governor Whitcomb or Lieutenant Governor Bright would be the Democratic nominee. The *Indiana State Journal*, apparently to sow discord among Democrats, quoted a Democratic paper which wanted Democrats to choose "a new man, fresh from among the people—one not connected with any junto or clique," who would not use the office of governor as "a stepping stone for higher stations . . . ." This Whig paper charged that at the previous legislative session Bright had cast his vote to postpone the election of a United States senator "with the express understanding" that he would be the Democratic nominee for governor in 1846.[195] As Democrats held county conventions in anticipation of their state convention in January, some counties expressed a willingness to support either Bright or Whitcomb but some of them expressed a preference for Whitcomb. With Bright's election to the federal Senate in December, Whitcomb's renomination appeared certain.[196]

The Democratic State Convention met at Indianapolis on January 8, 1846, the thirty-first anniversary of Jackson's defeat of the British at New Orleans during the War of 1812. The proceedings indicate that delegates were in attendance from nearly eighty counties, but since "every Democrat" present was "requested to act as a delegate" from his county it is uncertain which delegates had been named by county conventions. The renomination of Whitcomb for governor was "adopted by acclamation." A committee of one person from each county reported Paris C. Dunning, of Monroe County, as its "unanimous choice" for lieutenant governor; and the convention "enthusiastically" concurred. Although there were neither presidential nor congressional elections at stake, the Democratic convention gave more emphasis to national than to state issues. The platform disavowed "all sentiments or action looking towards the repudiation of the honest debts of the State"; and it approved efforts "to adjust and arrange those debts," within the acknowledged means of the state, "at the earliest practicable period." The Second State Bank was neither endorsed nor condemned, but the Democrats asked that no banking or other company be incorporated unless stockholders were made "individually liable for the debts of such company." In their address the Democrats presented themselves as defenders of natural and God-given rights of all people, regardless of birth, family, or wealth. They claimed to be the true heirs of the American Revolution, and of Thomas Jefferson. The Whigs were described as *professing* similar views, while *adopting* measures favoring the few and seeking to establish "an aristocracy of wealth." Presumably to woo German and Irish voters, the Whigs were accused of wanting to limit "suffrage to the *native born*," while taxing the property of all. The years 1836 to 1841 were called the "dreadful epoch" when much "embarrassment and ruin" had been suffered. But the Democrats had determined to change things, and since 1843 prosperity had been revived, state costs drastically reduced, public confidence restored, and a proposed settlement effected with bondholders.[197]

The Whig State Convention met at Indianapolis January 9, 1846, the day following that of their rivals. Every Whig "present from any portion of the State" was invited to participate in its deliberations. Possibly the attendance was disappointing for the *Indiana State Journal* does not list the delegates seated or the counties represented, but it explains that "notwithstanding the almost impassable state of the roads, a large portion of the State was represented." Former Governor David Wallace, president of the convention, reminded delegates of glorious triumphs achieved against Andrew Jackson despite great odds; and asserted that only want of union, harmony, energy, and patriotism would prevent victory again. Wallace said legislative records showed that Whitcomb had shared in the "paternity" of the System of 1836, while Dunning had loudly denounced classification and "battled manfully and most efficiently" for preservation of the system. With such nominees, Wallace supposed that "the croaking cry of ruin and extermination" to all who had helped begin or sustain the system would no longer be heard. The Whig platform declared that the party should contend for its principles, and adhere "to its separate and distinct organization," while seeking the cooperation of all who sought the good of the country. It asserted that Whitcomb had "not redeemed the *promise* made when a candidate in 1843" that he would suggest a plan regarding the state debt for reestablishing the public credit. The Whig platform pledged the delegates to "sustain their" legislators, "now or hereafter, in any honorable and just settlement of the public debt . . . within the means and ability of the people of Indiana." The Whig convention asked a committee, consisting of one person from each county named by its delegates, to propose "suitable candidates" for governor and lieutenant governor. Before this committee reported Godlove S. Orth requested the convention to consider his name "*entirely withdrawn*" concerning the nomination for governor to enable delegates "to arrive at a more speedy and harmonious conclusion." The word that the nominating committee proposed Marshall for governor and Orth for lieutenant governor was responded to with "three loud shouts of approbation." During the convention such Whig leaders as Dennis Pennington, Thomas H. Blake, Robert Hanna, Henry S. Lane, and Milton Stapp appealed to delegates for adherence to Whig principles, harmony, and support of the nominees.[198]

Rival party editors at the capital viewed the conventions and their nominees for governor with inflated rhetoric. The *Indiana State Sentinel* proclaimed the Democratic meeting "one of the most enthusiastic," but called the Whig gathering "one of the most depressed" ever witnessed. Whereas Whitcomb had been nominated "by acclamation, without a single dissenting voice," the Whigs, "full of doubts and fears, finally agreed upon Mr. Marshall, because such men as O. H. Smith and Ex-Governor Bigger would not subject themselves to the odium" of certain defeat. The *Indiana State Journal* said that neither convention had been "as numerously attended as heretofore," yet that of the Whigs had exceeded that of the Democrats. This premier Whig organ of the state asserted that because Whitcomb had failed to redeem the promises made to the people in 1843, "it was pretty well understood, that they intend trying Mr. Marshall the next three years." Both Whitcomb and Marshall had strong qualifications, prompting Logan Esarey to say that "it would be difficult to point out a campaign in which two cleaner men contended for the office of governor."[199] Despite conflicting victory forecasts, about three weeks after the conventions Orth confided to Schuyler Colfax that "a majority of the voters of Ind are against us, especially on general policy." "If anything beats us," the Whig nominee for lieutenant governor suggested, it probably would be the recently approved Butler Bill of 1846—which Orth had voted against in part because he thought it would be of advantage to Whitcomb.[200]

The question of responsibility for and settlement of the huge debt for internal improvements was a major issue in the campaign. The *Indiana State Journal* asserted that Marshall had been defeated for membership in the legislature which adopted the System of 1836 because of "his avowed opposition to it." At the ensuing session, the Whig editor added, Marshall had opposed any additions to the system. Hence, unlike his competitor, he had no part "in fixing that incubus upon the rising prosperity of Indiana."[201] Moreover, Whitcomb, despite his promise in 1843, had failed to submit a plan for settlement of the internal improvement debt. The recently approved Butler Bill, the *Journal* said, had been proposed by the bondholders, then merely approved by Whitcomb.[202] The claim that Democrats had reduced state expenditures by $22,000 annually was pronounced untrue; and Whitcomb was charged with "humbugging the people" about having taken a voluntary reduction in his salary.[203] A Whig paper at Bloomington argued that Jesse L. Williams, not Whitcomb, merited the credit for extension of the federal land grant for extending the Wabash and Erie Canal to Terre Haute from the mouth of the Tippecanoe River.[204] Various Democratic organs hailed the Butler Bill of 1846 as a great achievement of the Whitcomb administration.[205] The LaGrange *Democrat* emphasized the oft-repeated cry that the Whigs had "plunged Indiana upon the very verge of bankruptcy and ruin!" But Whitcomb and associates had "not only stopped the debt from increasing . . . as it did every year under Whig rule, but have placed the whole debt in a fair way of adjustment," hence Whitcomb should be sustained.[206]

Charges and countercharges developed concerning the personal characteristics of the gubernatorial rivals. Whigs described Whitcomb as scheming, evasive, cunning, and as an opportunistic politician who obtained offices as steppingstones to other positions. In contrast, they presented Marshall as a statesman who rose above party rancor and partisan aggrandizement.[207] Whitcomb, critics said, might be qualified "to figure in a drawing room, or to read French and Italian," but his ineptness and weakness had been revealed by the delay and mismanagement involved in getting Indiana volunteers organized for service in the Mexican War.[208] The incumbent governor was accused of insisting upon the appointment of unqualified Democrats to the state Supreme Court to replace experienced and able Whigs;[209] of telling the voters in 1843 that one term was enough for any man to serve as governor, and pledging that if elected, he would serve but one term;[210] and of having received $500 from the state for legal services which he had failed to render.[211] The *Indiana State Sentinel* stated that Marshall had defended the issue of small notes by the Second State Bank; and had defended legislation "for placing the sacred funds of the State, devoted to the cause of education, under the management of the Bank!"[212]

Rising concern about slavery gave the Liberty party a larger niche in the state election of 1846 than it had had three years previous. About June, 1845, the Brookville *Franklin Democrat* announced Stephen C. Stevens as the nominee of "the Abolition party for Governor," and Stephen S. Harding its nominee for lieutenant governor. This Democratic paper noted that both men had begun their practice of law at Brookville and said: "The ticket is as good as the Abolitionists could raise; the candidates are said to be speakers."[213] The Liberty party alarmed the Whigs more than the Democrats. Soon after his nomination for lieutenant governor, Orth suggested that especially "among the *liberty* voters," he would insist that the United States was entitled to and must have Oregon "to regain the political ascendancy of the Free States . . . ." The *Indiana State Journal* asserted that Orth was not an abolitionist, but it explained that when Marshall had inherited slaves from his father, a resident of Kentucky, he had immediately given "them their freedom." "How different," the *Journal* jabbed, "from the course pursued by Jesse D. Bright, who is now a Slaveholder."[214]

Both Whitcomb and Marshall were apparently slow in taking their campaigns to the voters. In March John D. Defrees, Whig

editor of the *Indiana State Journal*, emphasized that Whigs had relied too much on "large mass-meetings," and he appealed for
party organization "so minute as to reach every school district in
the State." Defrees said that the Democrats, though a minority,
triumphed because "they don't forget to be at the polls on an election day." He urged Whigs to select their best and strongest candidates, unite behind them, and support regular Whigs over independent Whigs whom Democrats encouraged to run to divide
the Whig vote. In April the Whig editor expressed concern about
the "great apathy" among Whigs concerning the election "so near
at hand."[215] He also explained that he was unaware when Marshall
would leave his business to commence "canvassing the State," but
presumed it would be some time in May.[216] Then in May Orth declined to canvass the state for lieutenant governor, on the ground
that the success of Whig principles and justice to himself demanded his decision.[217] A few weeks later the Whig State Central
Committee, of which Defrees was secretary, announced that after
"mature consideration" it had "unanimously agreed" upon
Alexander C. Stevenson, of Putnam County, to replace Orth.[218]
When and where campaign talks began is unclear, but early in
June Marshall and Whitcomb addressed voters at the Marion
County Courthouse at Indianapolis. After a speaking tour in
northern Indiana in June, Marshall and Stevenson addressed "a
large number" of citizens at Danville on the Fourth of July.[219] The
apathy, which Defrees expressed concern about in April, seems to
have made the campaign lackluster. On the eve of the voting on
August 3, Calvin Fletcher observed: "The approaching election
on Monday makes no stir all is quiet. The candidates scar[ce]ly
known. Little if any intere[s]t felt."[220]

   The official election returns were slow in reaching the Hoosier
capital. A month and a half after the voting, the *Indiana State
Journal* reported that the official returns "had not yet been received at the office of the Secretary of State."[221] The official count
for the ninety counties showed fifty-eight for Whitcomb, thirty-
two for Marshall, and none for Stevens. Whitcomb obtained
64,104 votes; Marshall, 60,138 votes; and Stevens, 2,301 votes.
Whitcomb carried the preponderance of the hill counties of

south-central Indiana, and won most of them on or near the line of the Wabash and Erie Canal from the Ohio border to Evansville. Marshall beat Whitcomb in a large majority of the counties in or near the Whitewater Valley, the southeastern counties of the state, and in most counties intersected by the National Road. The Liberty party gained a large percentage increase in its vote over that of 1843, but its greatest strength was in the same five counties of central and east-central Indiana as for the election of 1843.[222] The election returns seem to indicate considerable personal popularity for Governor Whitcomb, and widespread approval for his efforts to lower the cost of state government and the compromise settlement concerning the internal improvement debt. But the fact that the Whigs gained a significant majority in the House, giving them a majority on joint ballot of the two houses, shows that the Whigs remained a strong opposition party.[223]

With their majority on joint ballot of the General Assembly, the Whigs were able to elect their men as treasurer and auditor. When the legislature convened in December, Samuel Hanna, a Fort Wayne businessman, was elected treasurer over Royal Mayhew, the Democratic incumbent. In the voting for auditor, Douglass Maguire, pioneer editor and devoted advocate of National Republican-Whig principles, won over Horatio Harris, the Democratic incumbent.[224] The voting for these men was doubtless overwhelmingly along party lines, but it was not completely so.[225] Meantime, early in 1845, the preceding session at which Whigs also had a majority on joint ballot, they had elected John H. Thompson, a Whig, as secretary of state to replace incumbent William Sheets, another Whig.[226] Thus as party lines hardened, Whigs shared in the state offices.

Meanwhile, at the legislative session of 1845–1846, the regular five-year reapportionment of legislators had been enacted. According to the enumeration of voters, made in the spring of 1845, there were 155,409 voters in the ninety counties of the state.[227] As for the reapportionment of 1841, an unsuccessful attempt was made to reduce the number of legislators. The *Indiana State Sentinel* urged that both senators and representatives be reduced by one third, as consistent with the "system of economy" which Democrats had introduced with the Whitcomb administration. When the General Assembly met in December, Governor Whitcomb asked members to consider whether the membership of both houses could "be reduced without disadvantage to the public service." He suggested that money could thereby be saved, and that more "mature and dispassionate legislation" would probably result.[228] The *Indiana State Journal*, which had advocated a reduction in the members of both houses five years earlier, commended the question to "the attention of Legislators" without expressing an opinion pro or con.[229] The select committee of the House concerning reapportionment, which included six members of each party, was instructed to establish districts "according to the number of polls" in the counties. An apportionment bill passed the Senate, which had twenty-five Democratic and twenty-five Whig members, 27 to 22; and it then passed the House, which had fifty-six Democratic and forty-four Whig members, 49 to 43. The new apportionment of 1846 probably favored Democrats over Whigs inasmuch as in the House forty-eight Democrats and only one Whig voted for passage, while thirty-nine Whigs and but four Democrats opposed its approval.[230] The respect for county lines emphasized, in apportionments from statehood, persisted in this reapportionment which, as Leon Wallace has stated, "almost defies understanding, description, or analysis."[231] In dividing 100 representatives among seventy-three districts, fifty-eight of the ninety organized counties obtained one or more representatives; most of the remaining districts included two counties each, with one or more representatives; and one such district included four counties, having only one representative. For the fifty senatorial districts, twenty-three counties obtained their own senator; fifteen districts combined two counties each; ten districts, three counties; and two districts, four counties. For both representative and senatorial districts, only contiguous counties were joined. Apparently intended to reduce inequality among districts, a practice first used in 1826, was the use of "floats" whereby designated districts gained an additional representative for one, two, three, or even four years of the new apportionment. As Wallace observed, in 1846 "'Floats' reached their high tide in this act, involving thirty counties and thirty-nine representatives." Nevertheless, much inequality of representation prevailed.[232] With 155,409 voters, per the enumeration of 1845, an ideal representative district would have had 1,554 voters; an ideal senatorial district, 3,108 voters. The apportionment of 1846, compared to that of 1841, showed a continued but modest advance of political power northward toward the Michigan border. Both Southern and Central Indiana suffered small losses in the House.[233] A comparison of the apportionment of 1846 with that of 1841 suggests that most senatorial districts remained unchanged—apparently allowing holdover senators to complete their one or two remaining years in districts drawn five years earlier.[234]

Although the Constitution of 1816 mandated apportionment of legislators at five-year intervals, revision of the laws was made at the discretion of the General Assembly. General revisions had been made in 1824, 1831, 1838, and 1843, but no further revision occurred until that of 1852 as mandated by the Constitution of 1851.[235] The election code, as provided by the revised code of 1843, largely remained in effect during the remainder of the forties.[236] The large increase in population, however, led to laws authorizing and at times mandating an "additional place" for voting in townships scattered around the state.[237] Since the Constitution of 1816 merely limited voters to casting their ballots within the county of their residence, numerous citizens voted at their county seat. During the early 1840s various laws "confined" voters to the township of their residence.[238] Then in 1845 the legislature mandated that ballots must be cast in the township of residence. The *Indiana State Sentinel*, leading Democratic organ of the state, welcomed this restriction. It said: "This [act] will give the township committees a sure chance to detect frauds, should they be attempted." It then exhorted: "Begin to organize *now*. We shall have no child's play in August." On election day, August 4, 1845, Calvin Fletcher commented: "Heretofore any one residing in any township in the county [Marion] could vote at Indianapolis." Under the new legislation, Fletcher explained: "instead of one half or more of the votes being given here [at the county seat] there will not be more than a 1/5. Our streets are clear & not but very few in town."[239] At the ensuing legislative session the House concurred with its committee on elections that there was no need to modify the confining of voters to their townships. Nonetheless, as often happened in the pioneer era, special enactments permitted voters in some townships to vote in other townships. Rivers and other physical features were often involved in these exceptions. But the Constitution of 1851 expressly confined voters to the "township or precinct" in which they resided.[240] A change in the state election code was also made regarding the time for choosing presidential electors. Until the forties the states elected their electors at different times, hence Hoosiers learned of such elections in some states before they themselves went to the polls. At least three times in the thirties and forties the General Assembly urged that a uniform date be selected for all states to make this choice.[241] In 1845 Congress mandated the first Tuesday after the first Monday in November for choosing presidential electors. Three years later, the legislature modified Indiana's election code accordingly in time for the presidential election of 1848.[242]

While the election code remained much the same, the state Supreme Court underwent its second major shakeup of the pioneer era. When Whitcomb became governor in 1843, the court included Isaac Blackford, a member from 1817, and Charles Dewey and Jeremiah Sullivan who had been named by Governor Wallace.[243] With their terms ending on January 28, 1845, during the legislative session of 1844–1845, Whitcomb made repeated efforts to replace Dewey and Sullivan, both Whigs, with Democrats. After talking with the governor about "the supreme judges," Calvin Fletcher concluded that the executive "will be governed by the democratic Senators" regarding possible changes.[244] On January 10, as the session neared its close, Whitcomb nominated Democrats William W. Wick and James Morrison in lieu of Judges Dewey and Sullivan, with Judge Blackford nominated for reappointment. The Senate, equally divided between Democrats and Whigs, unanimously confirmed Blackford, however, Wick and Morrison were both rejected by a vote of 28 to 22.[245] The next day the governor nominated Charles H. Test and Andrew Davidson, who were rejected by margins of 34 to 16 and 30 to 20 respectively. On January 13, the last day of the session, Democrats Ebenezer M. Chamberlain and Charles H. Perkins were nominated, and rejected 29 to 21 and 31 to 19 respectively.[246] Despite these three successive defeats, as the session was closing Whitcomb emphasized that he was "strongly impressed" with the qualifications of Wick and Morrison, and resubmitted their nominations which were rejected by a tally of 24 to 19. Before adjournment the Senate tabled a resolution proposing the reappointment of Judges Dewey and Sullivan by a count of 21 to 20.[247]

The rival party papers at Indianapolis reacted to the judicial impasse in a very partisan manner. The avidly pro-Whig *Indiana State Journal* noted that Whitcomb's inclination "to ostracise" Dewey and Sullivan had not been supported by all of his political friends. Its editor urged the governor to renominate the old judges "rather than fritter away his own reputation, and *test* the patience of decent men even of his own party, by such a miserably proscriptive policy." The equally avid pro-Democratic *Indiana State Sentinel* responded that Whigs were trying to kick up "a great fuss, because the Governor nominated Democrats instead of Federalists" for the Supreme bench. Had the nominations of Wick and Morrison been confirmed, the *Sentinel* declared, "Indiana would have had an abler Supreme Court than she ever had before."[248]

Perhaps to buy time to gird himself for the next round with the Senate, Whitcomb gave Dewey and Sullivan interim appointments effective until the end of the next annual legislative session. Following the start of the session of 1845–1846, the *Indiana State Sentinel*, after reporting that Whigs were saying that politics should have nothing to do with judicial appointments, snorted: "Can any one remember *any Democrat* that the Whig leaders thought qualified for office? If so, just name him! We'll give the whole range of our history and one week to do it in." The Vincennes *Western Sun* presumed that the governor would again nominate Democrats for the Supreme Court. "Selecting democrats for judges," it said, "is not so criminal a matter after all!"[249] Whitcomb nominated Democrats Thomas L. Smith and Samuel

E. Perkins, to replace Dewey and Sullivan. The *Indiana State Sentinel* termed the nominees "as good as any that can possibly be named, and *better* than some." But the Senate, again divided equally between Whigs and Democrats, rejected Smith 28 to 22 and Perkins 26 to 24.[250] Whitcomb then gave interim appointments for the ensuing year to Dewey and Perkins. The *Indiana State Journal* proclaimed that Judge Sullivan, generally recognized for his "moral character, fitness of temper, gentlemanly deportment, and legal acquirements," had been "*proscribed*" in favor of a young Democrat about thirty-three years of age without "any eminence in his profession" and unknown as a lawyer outside "his own immediate neighborhood." Dewey, however, had escaped proscription because he had "warm personal friends" among Democrats whose wishes could not be slighted with impunity.[251]

When the legislature convened in December, 1846, Whitcomb renewed his prolonged effort to replace Whigs with Democrats for the Supreme Court. For the third time the executive nominated Perkins for a regular term. With the Senate consisting of 26 Democrats to 24 Whigs, Whitcomb obtained a regular appointment for Perkins by a vote of 33 to 17. Whitcomb for a second time sought confirmation of Thomas L. Smith to replace Dewey, but Smith was rejected by a count of 26 to 22. Several days later Whitcomb again renominated Smith, and he was rejected 15 to 14.[252] Nonetheless, the governor gave Smith an interim appointment, thus depriving Dewey of his seat on the bench. The *Indiana State Journal* contended that while campaigning for reelection in 1846 Whitcomb had "assured the people" that his nomination of Dewey and Perkins had been "a compromise between the parties" with the promise that both would be renominated at the forthcoming legislative session. Dewey claimed that the interim appointments given him and Sullivan early in 1845 had been "implied pledges" that they were to be nominated for regular terms at the ensuing session. Dewey insisted that before accepting his second interim appointment Whitcomb had given assurance of "his unqualified intention" to nominate him at the next session.[253]

After three years of partisan wrangling, at the legislative session of 1847–1848 Whitcomb obtained a Supreme Court consisting of three Democrats. The Senate, equally divided between Whigs and Democrats, confirmed the nomination of Thomas L. Smith by a vote of 26 to 22, with two Whigs joining with Democrats to give Smith a regular seven-year appointment.[254] Judges Dewey and Sullivan, however, were better qualified than Perkins and Smith who replaced them. The three year struggle, in which some Democrats also frequently opposed Whitcomb's nominations for the Supreme bench, seems to have resulted from Whitcomb's putting partisanship above merit and the public good concerning members of the Supreme Court. Had the political tables been reversed, a Whig governor would have perhaps acted in a somewhat similar manner. Whether so or not, Whitcomb's use of interim appointments to obtain judges, opposed in significant part by Democratic senators, was a blot on his gubernatorial administration.[255]

Despite considerable political wrangling between Democrats and Whigs regarding some items, they generally cooperated in efforts to improve and diversify transportation facilities. The returning prosperity from the mid-forties, combined with a rapid growth in population, agricultural output, manufacturing, trade, and wealth, intensified the need for better transportation facilities. Particularly desired were ways of augmenting trade to and from the Atlantic Seaboard. But the insolvency resulting from the internal improvements debacle, and burdensome debt inherited from that debacle, ended significant state support for developing transportation facilities in favor of a return to economic laissez faire and reliance on individual enterprise.

Meanwhile, although construction of the System of 1836 had been suspended in 1839, the Wabash and Erie Canal had been opened for navigation, from Lafayette to Lake Erie, in 1843; and its extension to Terre Haute had commenced. Two years later Congress offered Indiana half of the unsold federal land in the Vincennes land district, plus half of a five-mile strip in width on both sides of the canal, to help finance its completion to Evansville on the Ohio River. The completed waterway was to be free of tolls or other charges for persons or property in the service of the United States. Early in 1846 the General Assembly confirmed the selection of nearly 800,000 acres of land pursuant to this offer, and also confirmed continuation of the canal to the Ohio River.[256] By July 31, 1847, when the governor ceded the Wabash and Erie Canal to three trustees, according to the compromise debt legislation of 1847, for practical purposes it had been completed to Coal Creek in Parke County, 189 miles from the Ohio border. The immediate priority of the trustees was to finish the canal to Evansville as quickly as possible. But their basic responsibility was to obtain, if possible, sufficient revenue from the artificial waterway to pay half of the bonded debt thrown upon it by the compromise settlement. Late in 1847 the trustees reported that $5,855,850 had been so charged against the canal for bonds surrendered and interest due on them from 1841 to January 1, 1847. The surrender of additional bonds, plus interest owed, was expected to raise the total charge to $9,375,375 by January 1, 1852. This huge sum, however, did not include the estimated $1,910,371 anticipated to complete the canal to Evansville or provision for repayment of somewhat over $800,000 advanced by bondholders toward its completion.[257]

While it had taken the state a little more than fifteen years to open the canal the 189 miles from the Ohio line to Coal Creek, under supervision of the trustees it was extended the additional 186 miles to Evansville in less than six years. The state, however, had done considerable work on sections of the canal below Coal Creek. Principal Engineer Jesse L. Williams submitted a plan for finishing the canal to Evansville by July 1, 1851.[258] Contracts called for its completion to Terre Haute by November 1, 1848; but this thirty-seven mile section was not open until October 25 of the ensuing year, "on which day two boats arrived, one of which was from Toledo." In spite of floods, cholera, difficult crossings of both East and West forks of White River, and increased labor costs its construction was nearly finished to Evansville by the fall of 1852. Heavy floods and breaches in the canal delayed the opening until September 22, 1853, when the "Pennsylvania" reached Evansville as the first through boat from Toledo.[259]

Indiana's costly and long sought trunk line connecting with the eastern coast quickly became a financial disaster for the bondholders. Its revenue from tolls and water rents rose annually from 1846 to a peak of $187,392.15 in 1852, then began a downward slide in 1853 concurrent with its opening to the Ohio River. Even the peak revenue for 1852 was much less than half that which had been forecast in the mid-forties, and the revenue from tolls and water rents plummeted to $63,996.44 and $48,278.10 for 1858 and 1859 respectively.[260] In 1857 the participating bondholders memorialized the General Assembly, asserting that the extensive system of railroads which the state had authorized had been "*the single and sufficient cause of the lamentable decline*" in revenue from the waterway. Viewing this railroad development a "violation of the *spirit* as well as the *letter*" of the settlement whereby they had received the canal in trust, the creditors considered the state liable for the debt charged against the canal.[261] Late in 1858 another committee representing bondholders asked the trustees to suspend any part or all of the canal immediately if revenue for its maintenance proved inadequate. After observing that because of "railroad competition" that the line below Terre Haute had yielded meager revenue for its maintenance and had taxed the trust fund nearly $150,000 for repairs, the committee urged the trustees to dismiss all officials on this part of the canal and prepare for its closing.[262] Lacking positive action from the General Assembly to these appeals, in 1859 the trustees contracted operation of the canal, from the Ohio line to Evansville, to three groups of individuals for its maintenance and operation. For practical purposes the canal below Terre Haute was thereby abandoned, but private enterprise sustained navigation of sorts, much of it local, on the line north of Terre Haute to 1874.[263]

Meanwhile, from the late fifties the General Assembly had indicated its unwillingness either to resume control of the canal or assume any responsibility for the debt which had been made dependent on revenue from it. The state conventions of both major parties vigorously supported this policy.[264] In 1870 the creditors again memorialized the legislature, contending that Indiana was both liable and easily able to pay the debt which rested on the canal.[265] To this appeal Governor Conrad Baker recommended, and two successive legislative sessions proposed, amending the constitution to prohibit any payment on this debt. In 1873 the electorate, by a vote of 158,400 to 1,030, overwhelmingly made this prohibition the first amendment added to the Constitution of 1851.[266] The following year a suit on behalf of the creditors resulted in the sale of the canal on their behalf, but only a modest portion of the debt was ultimately paid therefrom.[267]

It is a moot question whether the bondholders who received the canal according to the compromise settlement of 1847 gained or lost thereby. Had there been no compromise arrangement, what their situation would have been is perhaps even more moot. In 1872 the legislature provided for payment of the principal and interest due on 191 bonds valued at $191,000, which had not been surrendered. By 1875 all but thirty of these bonds had been redeemed.[268]

While the Wabash and Erie Canal failed to become the anticipated trunk line to the East Coast, travel on common roads remained bad and at times became worse as their use increased. In March, 1842, Calvin Fletcher noted that high water had made "Roads impassable." During November of that year, after reporting "an abundant fall of snow," the *Indiana Journal* commented: "winter has set in. Good bye, sunshine and good roads." At the beginning of 1844 a Vincennes paper stated: "For the last few days, we have had winter.—The roads are almost impassable, and the mails somewhat irregular."[269] In March, 1845, Fletcher recorded that the "Waters [are] so high the stages can't come in or go out." In May of the ensuing year "high waters prevented many" members of the state bank board from attending a meeting at the capital. During March, 1847, Fletcher observed: "The roads were never worse so bad that some of our merchants walked to Edinburgh a foot." In March of the next year a Goshen paper humorously declared: "Old Hascall arrived the other day from Fort Wayne, having come through mud up to his shirt collar. He saw several travellers sinking in the soil and trying to dig out their horses."[270] In September, 1838, an Indianapolis editor termed Washington Street, the route of the National Road through the capital, "nearly impassable" from accumulating obstructions. Delays in macadamizing this street were said to offer "a fair prospect of wading through the mud, falling into ditches, and breaking our shins against the logs and rails, during the next winter." Several weeks later another capital paper announced that a lady had been injured in a stage upset on Washington Street, nearly opposite the courthouse. Calling it "a disgrace to our towns that ruts &c. should be suffered to remain in our streets deep enough to over-turn a stage," the editor wondered: "Cannot our town authorities at least keep *such* places filled."[271] Late in 1851 an Indianapolis ed-itor facetiously remarked: "The ice is out of the Michigan Road, and navigation is again opened. With four horses and a mud-scow, the trip to Logansport can be made in a little over 36 hours." Part of this road north of Plymouth had become a cor-duroy road, but in February, 1859, a local editor declared: "Of all the rough roads it has been our misfortune to travel over, this is certainly the very roughest. It has been said that 'Jordan is a hard road to travel,' but that saying was surely invented before any body had passed over this road."[272] Loss of life at times resulted from travel on roads. In the summer of 1839, a man in a "com-mon wagon" passed a stagecoach on the National Road east of In-dianapolis. Apparently while standing in the wagon, swinging his hat and exulting over his triumph, he fell; and his runaway horses dragged him on the ground mutilating his body and causing in-stant death. Four years later, a man suffered a "dislocated" neck when thrown from a cart by a runaway horse, causing almost in-stant death. Early in 1847, the driver of a stage to Bloomington lost a horse by drowning in an unsuccessful effort to cross Pogue's Run as he left Indianapolis.[273]

From the late thirties until mid-century responsibility for lo-cating, changing, and maintaining roads principally rested on local officials, males subject to road labor, and landowners. The revised code of 1838 gave county commissioners the "authority to make and enforce all orders necessary" for establishing or chang-ing roads within their respective counties.[274] All males "between the ages of twenty-one and fifty years," unless exempt by law or by their county board, were required to work on the roads two days annually. Men furnishing "a plough or wagon, with a pair of horses or oxen and driver," would receive credit for three days of labor for each day worked. All owners of real estate, explicitly including nonresident owners, were required to pay an annual road tax on their land of one half of the state levy thereon. The tax owed, however, could be met by road labor at the rate of seventy-five cents per day. Moreover, an individual could meet his obligation for either labor or taxes by hiring a "satisfactory substitute" to work in his stead. The county commissioners established road districts, the voters in each township elected road supervisors for their township, and road labor was performed under the direction of the supervisors. If a supervisor failed to maintain guide posts "at the forks of every road," with a "legible inscription, directing the way and mentioning the distance to the most remarkable place on each road," he was subject to a penalty of five dollars.[275] Any person found guilty of unnecessarily obstructing use of a road was subject to a fine of not exceeding ten dollars. If an individual was found guilty of intentionally demolishing or defacing a guide post, he was to pay ten dollars for every such offence. An individual found guilty of "horse racing along or across" a public bridge or road, or of "shooting at a mark along or across" either of them was subject to a fine of up to three dollars. Supervisors were empowered to use proceeds from certain fines to buy "ploughs, scrapers, crowbars, hammers, and other necessary implements."[276] The use of these items, along with plows and wagons and teams of horses and oxen, illustrate the intensive use of human and animal labor in opening and maintaining pioneer roads. No wonder these roads or trails were at times impassable, and often were muddy or dusty as the seasons came and went. The revised code of 1843 also required two days road labor by adult males, unless exempted; and its performance under supervisors elected by voters of their respective townships. But the road tax was to be set at not to exceed 10 cents per $100 of taxable real estate at the discretion of the county commissioners.[277] The code of 1852 also had almost the same items about road labor required by adult males. But it provided that a road tax of not less than 5 or more than 25 cents would be levied on each $100 of taxable and personal property by the respective township trustees, if the majority of the voters of the township asked for a road tax.[278]

As the preceding pages indicate, males who owned taxable property contributed more to the opening and maintaining of roads than those who owned no property. Late in 1843 a House committee on roads called it "highly inexpedient, unjust and anti-democratic" to repeal the authorization for county boards to levy a road tax on real and personal property. After saying that property owners in particular benefited from improvements in transportation, the committee asserted that it could "see no hardship in requiring the owners of real and personal property to pay a road tax"; moreover, the committee declared that if ground for complaint existed, "it might come with better grace from those who own no property" but are compelled to do road labor. The House concurred with the report of its committee. Although nonresidents who owned taxable property in Indiana were subject to the same tax for roads as were residents, they could not be taxed at a higher rate than the latter. Thus it was that in 1842 Governor Samuel Bigger vetoed a law because it called for a road tax on nonresidents of Gibson and Pike counties without any such tax on residents. As Bigger noted an irrevocable item in the Northwest Ordinance of 1787, which Indiana had agreed to at statehood, expressly forbade taxing nonresidents higher than residents.[279]

With continued growth and expansion of population and an increasing network of roads, numerous additional bridges and ferries were needed. The revised codes of 1838 and 1843 empowered county boards to have bridges erected over watercourses whenever "the public convenience" required them.[280] The revision of 1838 provided that bridges could be financed by donations, subscriptions, and local road funds. If adequate means could not be "obtained by donation or taxation without oppressing the people," a county board could contract with an individual or individuals to build toll bridges. The code of 1843 indicated that if the ordinary road tax and labor of a road district was not sufficient to build a needed bridge that the county board could tax other districts or parts of districts for its construction. A bridge of "general importance" could also be supported from the county treasury and by individuals performing road work or paying road tax early with credit toward reduction of same for that or subsequent years. As for the preceding code, if a needed bridge could not be "erected by public means or donations," the county board could have it built by a individual or individuals as a toll bridge. Both codes made toll rates subject to the approval of county boards, and they reserved the right of a county to purchase such bridges by reimbursing costs plus 10 percent. The second code also allowed a township or road district in which a bridge was located this repurchase option. Although these codes encouraged the building of public bridges, the General Assembly frequently authorized companies and individuals to construct toll bridges with varying terms regarding toll rates.[281] Similar provisions about financing and building bridges were embraced in the revised code of 1852, however, they were to be constructed under the direction of township trustees rather than county boards.[282] Heavy reliance on local units of government for maintenance of common roads and erection of bridges was typical of the pioneer era, especially during the 1840s. As a Senate committee regarding roads noted in 1843, in opposing aid for a bridge "across Indiana Kentucky creek," "the impoverished state of the finances in Indiana" made such aid inexpedient.[283]

The revised codes of 1838 and 1843 likewise empowered county boards to establish and regulate ferries.[284] An owner of land on either side of a river could obtain a license to commence a ferry by application to the county board. No ferry could be opened within a mile up or down stream from an existing ferry, unless the "public convenience" made one desirable because of a road crossing, a village or town, or an intervening creek or ravine. If an adjacent landowner failed to establish a ferry at a site where "public convenience" required one, another individual or individuals could do so. Ferrykeepers were to pay a fee, assessed by the county board, varying from $2 or $3 to $50 yearly for the privilege of operating a ferry. But on streams, normally passable without a ferry, a fee could be waived. The county boards also "fixed" the tolls which each keeper could charge. Keepers were obligated to provide adequate boats and skilled ferrymen; maintain the banks of streams low and suitably passable; give prompt service from daylight until dark; and "at any hour of the night . . ., except in cases of evident danger," to give passage for double the day rate. The revised code of 1852 regarding ferries was similar in content to those of 1838 and 1843. Although many bridges were public and free, ferries were generally privately owned and operated for toll. Ferries, however, were less frequently authorized directly by the General Assembly. And though they were opened over small streams, they were often the only means of crossing large rivers.[285] If before 1850 any bridge was built over the Ohio River, between Indiana and Kentucky, or over the Wabash River, between Indiana and Illinois, this writer has not found convincing evidence thereof.

Bridges and ferries, like grist mills, were important public utilities for the pioneers. The revised code of 1843 illustrates the importance attached to them. Its criminal code made persons responsible for toll bridges and ferries liable for a fine of up to $40 for: demanding or receiving more than the established toll for passage; neglecting to keep bridges or ferries in good condition, or failing to keep their approaches adequately passable; and insufficient attendance for service during the day.[286] Keepers of ferries were required to give free passage to public messengers and expresses; including items regarding the militia, except in times of peace, unless during an insurrection. Ferrykeepers were required to give bond for $500, conditioned on their performance of duty according to law. Individuals who obstructed ferryboat landings with steamboats, keelboats, flatboats, or otherwise were subject to be fined. Unlicensed persons who provided ferry service, within two miles of a public ferry, were subject to payment of a tax as for licensed ferries as well as a fine. Persons necessarily employed with ferries were exempt from personal road labor, jury duty, and militia service, except in time of public danger or war.[287] Anyone damaging a public bridge was subject to payment of treble the cost of the damage caused. Road supervisors were authorized to post, in large letters on both sides of bridges, the warning: "'ONE DOLLAR FINE FOR RIDING OR DRIVING ON THIS BRIDGE FASTER THAN A WALK.'"[288] Similar provisions concerning bridges and ferries were included in the codes of 1838 and 1852. But ambiguities and inconsistencies in the laws, combined with miscellaneous exceptions for various counties, make uncertain what legislation actually applied in particular situations.[289]

Proceeds from the federally supplied Three Per Cent Fund, used to improve roads, build bridges, and remove natural obstructions to the navigation of rivers, plummeted during the forties. Late in 1837 Agent Nathan B. Palmer reported that since statehood Indiana had received $438,100.61 and spent $401,354.20 from the fund. This left a balance of $36,746.41 unexpended, but legislative appropriations aggregating $177,528.32, for practical purposes entirely to counties of the state for roads, bridges, and rivers, with emphasis on roads, remained outstanding. Palmer estimated that it would take at least three years for accruing revenue to equal unmet appropriations. By late 1843 these appropriations had been reduced to $84,036.42.[290] Although apparently no new appropriations were added after 1837, as of 1850 most of the appropriations outstanding as of 1843 remained unliquidated.[291]

Two factors largely explain why revenue to the Three Per Cent Fund tumbled during the forties. As public land sales slid downward after their peak in 1836, their proceeds diminished and remained modest.[292] Then, when the state suspended payment of interest on its internal improvement bonds in 1841, the federal government, which held such bonds in trust for some Indians, began withholding accruing proceeds to pay interest on them. Late in 1875 the state treasurer explained that in a settlement between the state and federal government, involving state claims against the government because of the internal improvement bonds, that $108,208.59 of the Three Per Cent Fund had been "temporarily" withheld and credited to the state toward interest on the bonds. In 1875 the state auditor reported that the balance in the fund had been $32.13 since 1854, when "the last distribution" had been made to the counties.[293] During the forties Indiana unsuccessfully renewed its effort to obtain proceeds for the fund which it claimed were due because of land within Indiana which had been sold from the land office at Cincinnati.[294]

Meantime, by the mid-thirties the use of blocks or planks of wood to improve roads had been considered. In January, 1835, "Indiana" urged the legislature to authorize the use of "timbers" or planks for "repairing bad places in the state roads." He recommended the track road system whereby a single or double set of timbers were laid lengthwise of the road in contrast to the "old plan of cross-laying" them. "Indiana" suggested that legislators provide for "a single or double set of tracks, from Lake Michigan to Madison, or some other point on the river," with the work being "done first on the worst places." Some weeks before the assembly convened in December, 1836, "Tullius" explained that wooden turnpikes, believed to be "a Russian plan," had been successfully tried in Great Britain, where "such blocks have lasted, in streets, without repair, for *twenty* years . . . ." Such a road, "Tullius" suggested, *combines the advantage of a rail road and a M'Adamized turnpike*; for locomotives can move upon it almost as rapidly as on iron rails." Hence, "the farmer, so far from being prevented, as on a railway from employing his own wagon or other conveyance, may carry to market, on such a road, with a single pair of horses or a single yoke of oxen, a load which it would require two if not three pair or yoke to drag over our common roads . . . ." A wooden turnpike twenty feet wide, paved with wooden blocks nine inches square, "Tullius" estimated, could be built for about $5,650 per mile or a "little more than one half of the cost of covering with stone a Macadamized road." At the ensuing legislative session, Representative Robert Dale Owen unsuccessfully proposed that the state experiment with a "wooden turnpike" on a small scale during the next summer. The same session empowered the Madison and Napoleon Turnpike Company to construct a clay, macadamized, "or wooden turnpike" between these two towns.[295]

Late in 1837 Engineer Julius W. Adams told members of the Senate that roads made of wooden blocks had "long been in use in Russia," and had recently been tried in the United States. Adams explained how wooden blocks could be used on the 171 miles of the Michigan Road from Indianapolis to Michigan City to make a highway that would have "a decided advantage" over one built of stone. But his estimate that it would cost an average of $14,616 per mile, or a total of nearly two and one half million dollars, to complete the entire distance in a proper manner, doubtless numbed support for such a project.[296]

About 1845 Hoosiers caught the plank road fever which persisted about a decade. The emphasis was on roads made of planks of wood, to be constructed by private companies which would operate them as toll roads. During 1845 the Richmond *Palladium* commented favorably regarding a suggestion that Congress surrender the National Road across the state to Indiana so that the General Assembly could charter a company to begin its planking. That same year efforts were launched for a plank road from Fort Wayne to Lima, in LaGrange County, near the Michigan border.[297] Principally advocated as an alternative to the unimproved and wretched local roads, and as feeders to canals, rivers, and railroads, proponents asserted that plank roads would advance the prosperity of their communities; expedite stage travel and make delivery of the mail more regular and faster; could be built for less money than required for good macadamized roads; make it possible for horse drawn wagons to convey at least two and possibly several times the load on them than on common roads; and could be financed by local capital and built by local labor.[298] The *Indiana State Journal* quoted the author of a manual concerning plank roads who termed them the "'*Farmer's Railroads.*'" In 1847 an editor at Logansport urged the planking of the Michigan Road from there to Indianapolis in preference to the construction of a railroad to the capital. If "a railroad" were substituted for a plank road, the editor observed, "we may all grow gray before we see it completed."[299]

The construction of plank roads in Indiana began about 1848. Charters for special companies to build them were authorized by both special and general laws, and by 1850 plank roads were projected for all parts of the state. Despite differences from charter to charter, certain generalizations apply to many of them. Capital was authorized in modest amounts, often in units much less than $50,000, and often in shares of $25. Only a fraction of each share was normally due at the time of its subscription, with the remainder to be paid at intervals. Moreover, stock could be paid for in labor, land, or other property as well as in cash. Charters indicated at least the approximate route for the roads to be planked, however, they often stated that parts of routes could be of some hard surface other than plank. Directors and officers were frequently made liable in their personal capacity for debts above the amount of stock which had been paid for. At times tolls were fixed at stated rates, at other times tolls were set by companies subject to restrictions. If plank roads were not commenced within a certain time, or finished within a stated period, they were in many instances subject to forfeiture. The General Assembly frequently expressly reserved the right to alter or repeal charters.[300]

For the most part plank roads were poorly constructed and built of varying widths and in different ways. Frequently pieces of wood, called sleepers, stringers, or sills were laid down, three or four feet apart, parallel to the roadbed. Planks three or four inches thick, commonly about eight feet wide, were then laid crossways over the sleepers. Ditches were dug along the sides of the road to provide drainage and help dry out the road and planks.[301] Late in 1850 Governor Joseph A. Wright advised legislators that four hundred miles of plank roads had been completed "the past season," costing from $1,200 to $2,500 per mile, "with some twelve hundred miles additional surveyed and in progress." Early in 1853 Wright reported that the state had about "1,200 miles of plank roads" in operation, but the actual mileage planked may have been less than these totals.[302] With roads generally poorly constructed, planks were often wet and muddy, and wore out or broke within a few years, making them dangerous for persons and horses. Because they were largely local roads, limited traffic kept tolls modest, making revenue inadequate for their proper maintenance. As roads became dilapidated, they doubtless soon became abandoned, frequently before subscriptions of stock had been paid in full. By the middle fifties plank roads had for the most part already been abandoned, and the railroad fever had replaced the plank road fever among Hoosiers.[303]

Meantime, from the midtwenties railroads had been considered. In the last half of that decade Governor James Brown Ray advocated a railroad in preference to the Wabash and Erie Canal, and he supported the building of various railroad lines within and to Indiana.[304] Early in 1832 the General Assembly authorized charters for eight private companies to construct railroads, five of which anticipated terminals on the Ohio River, the state's principal outlet for southern markets. Three of these five lines projected northern terminals at Indianapolis, with the other two ending at Lafayette on the Wabash River via Indianapolis. Of the three remaining lines, one proposed to connect Lafayette with Michigan City, on Lake Michigan; another to link Indianapolis with Harrison, on the Ohio border near Cincinnati; and still another to extend from Richmond to the Miami Canal, between Dayton and Cincinnati, Ohio.[305] In July, 1834, one of these companies had a celebration at Shelbyville regarding construction of its line from Lawrenceburg to Indianapolis. In the absence of a locomotive, celebrants were given rides on a track apparently built of wood in a car drawn by horses.[306] Additional charters were approved during the ensuing decade, but the priority given canals over railroads in the Internal Improvements System of 1836, followed by the depression of the late thirties and early forties, gave the former the edge over the latter until about the midforties.[307] With railroads a novelty, there was uncertainty who should supply the vehicles for transportation of passengers and freight. In 1837 Jesse L. Williams, principal engineer for the Board of Internal Improvements, suggested that for railroads "constructed by the state, it will probably be best for the state to furnish the motive power, leaving the cars for the conveyance of freight and passengers, to be furnished by individuals or companies," with toll charged for the motive power and use of the road. A common feature of early charters authorized companies to decide what motive power and vehicles would be used and who should own and control same. Company ownership and control apparently prevailed on pioneer railroads as they were completed.[308]

During the last half of the forties, amid reviving prosperity, increasing population, and augmenting wealth, the legislature approved a flurry of additional charters. By 1850 Indiana had a *paper network of railroad lines*, scattered over the state, probably aggregating at least three or four thousand miles. These projected lines were principally tributary to waterways, especially the Ohio River, Indiana's leading artery for imports and particularly exports. Various lines contemplated terminals on the Wabash and Erie Canal, a lesser number on Lake Michigan. Quite a few routes presumed terminals at Indianapolis or passage through the capital, as the hub for railroads forecast by Governor Ray. A number of lines were projected to connect with railroads at the Illinois, Michigan, and Ohio borders; at times as links which would ultimately connect with large cities on the Atlantic Seaboard.[309] As early as 1827 Governor Ray had urged citizens of Marion County to solicit extension of a railroad, planned from Baltimore to the Ohio River, westward to the Mississippi. Late in 1849 Governor Paris C. Dunning chaired a meeting at Indianapolis, addressed by Asa Whitney, which endorsed his project for a railroad westward to the Pacific Ocean.[310] Charters varied regarding details, but they were generally explicit about the amount of capital stock authorized; principal points on the route approved; the use of portions of existing state and county roads as roadbeds, under certain restrictions; time allowed for beginning and completing construction; and possible connections with other railroads. Stock, normally in units of $25 or $50, could be paid for in labor, land, and property as well as cash. A modest payment, often of only $5, was required in advance, the remainder payable at intervals. Companies were given much autonomy concerning tolls charged, especially until construction costs were recovered. Charters commonly provided that, if companies thought necessary, they could increase their capital or have further time to start or finish their routes. Moreover, these liberal charters were often amended, some of them several times, as legislators welcomed and encouraged the movement toward railroads financed by private enterprise.[311]

Indiana's first real railroad, opened to Indianapolis in 1847, connected the capital with Madison 86 miles distant on the Ohio River. One of the eight charters approved in 1831–1832 had called for a railroad linking Madison with Lafayette, on the Wabash River, via Indianapolis. A groundbreaking ceremony occurred at Madison in 1835, with construction beginning in earnest the next year when such a railroad was adopted as a key project in the state financed System of 1836. Its construction up the steep hill above Madison proved extremely costly, and in 1838 the legislature changed the route north of Indianapolis to a macadamized road.[312] Five years later, while the state slowly extricated itself from the fiscal insolvency resulting from the internal improvements debacle, the line, not yet finished to Columbus, was turned over to the Madison and Indianapolis Railroad Company.[313] According to Calvin Fletcher's diary, on October 1, 1847, the line "was so far completed that the carrs from Madison on the Ohio came in . . . full at 3 P.M." Governor Whitcomb delivered an address to the assembled curious, "not one in 15 [of whom] had ever seen a steam carr," hence for the most part "the multitude were stairing at the Iron Horse" instead of hearing the executive who "opposed high toles [tolls]." Henry Ward Beecher, then leaving Indianapolis after eight years as minister of the Second Presbyterian Church, departed on the return trip to Madison. In a letter to a friend Beecher explained that on boarding the train he found that "'the car was no car at all, a mere extempore wood box, used sometimes without seats for hogs, but with seats for men; of which class I (oh! me miserable!) happened to be one.'" But hogs were not the only animals transported on the new railroad. In 1839 Fletcher commented in his diary that when he and Governor Noah Noble took the train from Vernon to Madison that "One traveller . . . put his horse aboard. This I disliked but in order to make the work popular it had to be done."[314]

Until mid-century railroad construction was almost entirely limited to the southern half of the state and mainly tributary to the Ohio River at Madison. By the end of 1850 Indiana reportedly had 228 miles of completed railroads, but as the year ended Governor Joseph A. Wright informed legislators that the state had 212 "miles of railroad in successful operation; of which one hundred and twenty-four were completed the past year."[315] The 86 miles of the Madison to Indianapolis line was easily the premier railroad at this time. A lateral from it, extending 16 miles to Shelbyville from Edinburgh, plus extensions 20 miles from Shelbyville to Rushville and 27 miles from Shelbyville to Knight-stown, had been opened.[316] The initial 35 miles of the New Albany and Salem line connected these towns.[317] In central Indiana 28 miles of the Indianapolis and Bellefontaine Railroad had been completed between the capital and Pendleton.[318] Part of a railroad, commenced at Jeffersonville toward Columbus, had apparently been completed.[319] Various other lines were under construction, and early in 1853 Governor Wright told legislators that the state had over eight hundred miles of lines in operation. By 1855, when plank roads were fast disappearing, Indiana reportedly had 1,406 miles of railroads; and the aggregate jumped to 2,163 miles in 1860, including connections with lines eastward to the Atlantic Seaboard.[320] Although railroads had only a modest impact on Indiana before 1850, their unusually rapid advance during the ensuing decade diminished pioneer isolation and self-sufficiency and became a principal influence fostering increased trade, agricultural output, industrialization, and urbanization. By the end of the fifties, competition from railroads was hastening the demise of the Wabash and Erie Canal. At least as early as 1856 Jesse L. Williams, chief engineer for the Wabash and Erie Canal trustees, had read the handwriting on the wall. He observed that earlier some had "entertained [the idea] that lateral [rail]roads running from the interior of the State to the Canal at various points, would rather aid than impair the Canal traffic. But these roads are now connected with extended lines of corresponding guage [sic], running eastward to Lake Erie, and southward to the Ohio River, forming by this means, in effect, parallel and competing lines from nearly all the chief commercial towns on the Wabash, to Cleveland, Detroit, Cincinnati and Louisville, as well as Toledo." "The most active and general competition," Williams explained, "is from the Toledo, Wabash and Western Road, meeting the canal . . . at every town, and transversing the entire valley to Attica" on the Wabash River. Williams asserted that when the trust was established, per the Butler Bill of 1847, it had been assumed that the canal would not be threatened by competition from railroads. The only competitive transportation that had been anticipated had been that from "the Wabash River." But, he

added: "The River competition has been in great measure overcome." Williams then recognized the superiority of railroads over
the canal when he said: "But for the introduction of the system of
railways, presenting a new, and in many respects, better mode of
transportation, possessing the advantage of steam, the great rev-
olutionizer in the world's business, as a motive power, the Wabash
and Erie Canal would have continued the channel of trade, as
originally designed by the Legislature, for one half of the State,
and justified the reliance placed upon its completion, as a successful financial measure." Williams concluded that either the
canal or railroads could serve the area, but both systems could not
exist simultaneously as profitable enterprises.[321] Although the
System of 1836 had emphasized canals over railroads, within less
than a quarter century the railroads had triumphed over canals so
far as Indiana was concerned.

CHAPTER 7

EDUCATION, 1816–1850

EDUCATION DEVELOPED SLOWLY in pioneer Indiana, especially that under public auspices. Of necessity the pioneers gave high priority to meeting their basic needs for food, clothing, and shelter. At least until the 1830s they lived mainly in sparsely settled areas; hence, many neighborhoods had too few, if any, parents willing to help finance either a private, denominational, or public school. Numerous families viewed education principally as the responsibility of parents or their respective religious denominations. The depression of 1839, which persisted into the early 1840s, combined with the impact of the debacle arising from the failure of the Internal Improvements System of 1836, hampered and delayed the advance of education, whether private, denominational, or public. Elementary education was extremely decentralized within congressional townships and the school districts into which they were divided. Money for support of public common schools, however, was at times, perhaps frequently, applied to the support of private and denominational schools. Throughout the pioneer era the emphasis was decidedly on common schools rather than seminaries or colleges.[1]

The forty-three delegates who drafted Indiana's first state constitution at Corydon in 1816 established a high ideal for education. They declared: "It shall be the duty of the General assembly, *as soon as circumstances will permit* to provide, by law, for a general system of education, ascending in a regular gradation, from township schools to a state university, wherein tuition shall be gratis, and equally open to all." No tax support was mandated to achieve this ideal, but the proceeds from section 16 in every congressional township, donated to Indiana by Congress, were to be used for the support of common schools. Money individuals paid for exemption from militia duty and fines collected for violation of penal laws was reserved for the support of a seminary in each county.

Though not noted in the constitution, at statehood Congress granted Indiana an additional congressional township of land, with the proviso that it, and another such township previously granted, be used to sustain a seminary of learning. The new constitution proclaimed that "Knowledge and learning generally diffused, through a community," was "essential to the preservation of a free Government . . . ."[2]

At the initial state legislative session, 1816–1817, the General Assembly enacted a law *"to prevent waste on lands reserved for the use of schools and salt springs."* The county commissioners were "directed" to name "some fit person" as superintendent of the school section for each congressional or survey township. The superintendent was to lease land on the school section for the benefit of the residents of its township for any term not exceeding seven years. He was to take bond for proper performance of the lease and the preservation of the timber thereon. Each lessee was annually to set out twenty-five apple and the same number of peach trees, but the number of such trees should never exceed one hundred for each variety. Whenever twenty householders of a township indicated, "by petition or otherwise," that they wished to organize a school, it became the duty of the county sheriff to call for an election of three township trustees for terms of three years. So elected, the three trustees would have "full power to make all such bye laws, rules and regulations . . . necessary for the purpose of encourageing and supporting [a] school or schools in said township . . . not inconsistent with the constitution and laws" of Indiana. After township trustees were elected, the duties of the superintendent passed to them. Net proceeds from leases on section 16 land, and fines paid for breach of contract or injury to a school section, went to the county treasurer. These monies were subject to transfer to the three trustees of the township from which they were collected for the establishment of a school or schools.[3] An act of 1819 authorized the township trustees to use money acquired from the renting of land in section 16 for this purpose. It also made it the duty of teachers to report under oath or affirmation the number of scholars taught. But no money could be used for any scholar "learning any other than the English language," nor for any student residing outside the township.[4] If any schools were established pursuant to either of these laws, they were probably very limited in number.

Early in 1821 the legislature named a committee of seven men, none members of the legislature, to draft and report a bill to its next session, "providing for a general system of education ascending in a regular gradation from township schools to a state university wherein tuition shall be gratis and equally open to all and particularly to guard against any distinction existing in any of the said institutions between the rich and the poor." The preamble to the joint resolution naming this committee asserted that members of the General Assembly "are deeply impressed with the importance of knowledge and learning being diffused through the rising generation of the state of Indiana . . . ."[5] In December, 1821, three members of the committee submitted a report, "shewing the grounds of calculation upon which" a bill for a general system of education might be drafted. Calculations were offered concerning a state university and county seminaries, but the report principally considered the prospects for common schools or elementary education.[6]

The committee declared that at most only meager taxation would be required to finance common schools. It estimated that Indiana had about 950 congressional townships, each with about 640 acres.[7] If this acreage were sold on credit, with interest received annually added to the principal, in "six years, a sufficient dividend may be made to maintain a school in each school district, for the term of 3 months in each year, out of the public money alone."[8] The committee recommended that each township be divided into "four district schools," which, if properly located, no children would live "but little more than one mile and one half" from their school.[9] If section 16 land was sold at $3.50 per acre at the end of six years the proceeds, plus interest on unpaid principal, would make $47.67 annually for each of the state's 3,800 district schools. This sum would pay a teacher for three months;[10] and whenever a majority of the voters of a district approved, a tax could be levied sufficient to erect suitable buildings and maintain a school for whatever period they desired.[11] These data assumed that sections 16 would be sold through a state land office, with the proceeds divided equally among the 950 townships.[12]

The committee emphasized the need for competent teachers. It proposed that in counties where schools had been established "a board of inspection" examine prospective teachers and certify those deemed qualified. Moreover, it suggested that at least one inspector visit each school twice every session. No one was to be "considered a competent teacher . . . unless he be of good moral character, and well versed in reading, writing, arithmetic, English Grammar, Geography and surveying." Such competence was termed "indispensible to a good English education." Qualified teachers were especially important for the common schools because "few persons will feel themselves able to educate their sons at the University . . . ." Township schools should "become nurseries of teachers, for the wide extent of country yet to be settled." Unless certified teachers were employed, their pay would not be drawn from the township fund.[13]

In 1824 the last legislative session at Corydon enacted the most comprehensive law yet about common schools.[14] If three householders or freeholders called a township meeting, and at least twenty such persons were present, the meeting could elect three trustees as the corporate board concerned with schools within the township. The proceeds available from section 16, plus donations received, were vested in the township trustees. Within a month they were to divide the township into the "number of school districts" needed and name three sub-trustees for each district. The respective trustees then called meetings of freeholders and householders to determine "by *ayes* and *noes* in writing" if they would "support a public school for any number of months," but not less than three months annually. If a majority voted for a school, the sub-trustees selected "a site suitable for a school house, as near the centre of such district as possible, taking into view the convenience to water, fuel, and health . . . ."[15]

At a subsequent meeting, set by the district trustees, the "building of a suitable school house" should begin. It could be constructed "of brick, stone, hewn timber, or frame" according to a majority vote of the residents. The schoolhouse was to be large enough to accommodate "as many pupils, as may probably at any time attend such school . . . ." The district trustees superintended the construction, with every "able bodied male" freeholder or householder, twenty-one or above, liable for work thereon one day per week until its completion, or to pay 37½ cents for each day not worked. This labor could also be satisfied by providing a "sufficient substitute" or by donating "plank, nails, glass, or other materials" needed for the building. The schoolhouse was to be made "comfortable [for] the teacher and pupils; with a suitable number of seats, tables, lights and every other thing necessary" for their convenience. The school should be "forever open for the education of all children within the district without distinction."[16]

After completion of the building, the district trustees called another meeting of "the inhabitants" to decide whether they would "suffer any portion of the tax for the support of such school to be raised in money" as well as in labor and material. If a money tax, the meeting decided its levy and the term for which to employ a teacher. Then the district trustees employed a teacher on "the most advantageous terms" possible, contracting to make payment in articles and otherwise at the end of the term. No teacher could be employed unless the "township trustees" had examined and certified his qualifications, "particularly as respects his knowledge of the English language, writing, and arithmetic"; and also had concluded that he would be "an useful person to be employed as a teacher in said school." It became the duty of the teacher to keep and report the attendance record of all students. The clerk of the township trustees then distributed revenue from section 16 to schools within the township with respect to the length of the term and days the pupils had attended.[17] At the next legislative session in 1825, the first at Indianapolis, the General Assembly directed the district trustees to list and value taxable property within their district. If necessary to fulfill the contract with the teacher, such property could be taxed annually not to exceed "one fourth per centum on the valuation."[18]

The legislation about common schools in the revised laws of 1831 much resembled that of the 1824 law.[19] In congressional townships not having elected township trustees, the county board was to provide for the election of three trustees for terms of three years by the voters therein. The township trustees were then to divide the township into a sufficient number of school districts to accommodate the residents and name three sub-trustees for each district. Within thirty days the district or sub-trustees were to call a meeting of the freeholders and householders of their district. If at this meeting a majority of those present agreed by written vote to support a school at least three months in the year, the district trustees were to locate the school as near its center as possible, considering "its convenience to water, fuel, and its healthiness . . . ." When the site was located, the district trustees called another meeting to obtain majority agreement as to whether the schoolhouse would be built of "brick, stone, hewn timber or frame . . . ." These trustees then superintended its construction. Until its completion every able-bodied male, twenty-one or older, being either a freeholder or householder, was liable for one day of work each week until the building's completion, or they could provide a "sufficient substitute," or pay 50 cents for each day not worked.[20] Then the district trustees called a meeting of the voters of the district "at such school house," to determine whether they would "suffer any proportion of the tax, if any tax be necessary" for its support, to be raised in money. If so, "what proportion," and when a teacher would be employed. No one, however, was to be taxed on property unless such person "wishes to and does participate in the benefit of such school fund." The local trustees were to employ "a teacher on the most advantageous terms" possible, contracting to pay in "articles, and otherwise" according to the decision of the residents. No one could be employed as a teacher "until he" produced a certificate from the township trustees attesting that they had examined "his qualifications, and particularly, as respects his knowledge of the English language, writing and arithmetic"; and that they believed "he" would be "a useful person" for the school. The teacher's record of the attendance of pupils became the basis for distributing revenue from section 16 among schools within the township. If necessary to pay the teacher, a tax not exceeding 25 cents a year per $100 of taxable property could be levied by the township trustees.[21]

Elementary or common school education—so far as it existed before the early thirties—was overwhelmingly under family or religious auspices. But according to the laws of 1817 and 1819 pub-

lic common schools could be established in any of the approximately 950 congressional townships within the state, supervised
by three township trustees elected by its voters, provided an adequate number of voters approved their establishment. The revised
codes of 1824 and 1831 empowered township trustees to divide
their townships into an appropriate number of school districts;
however, they transferred the establishment and supervision of
such schools to three sub-trustees named by them for each district. For the most part the key items in the codes of 1824 and
1831 were not drastically modified before 1850.[22] Most likely the
number of common schools, supported by public revenue, increased as a result of these codes.

Efforts to extend and strengthen public common schools increased in the 1830s and 1840s. Four factors in particular stimulated these efforts. The population of Indiana considerably more
than doubled during the 1820s, almost doubled in the 1830s, and
in the 1840s gained more than twice the aggregate as of 1820.[23]
Hence, many neighborhoods, villages, and towns became more
densely settled and added to the number of taxpayers and would-
be students in many school districts. Second, as the decades passed,
numerous families overcame some of the most severe hardships
and privations of pioneer life, and thus became more able and willing to support public schools. Third, from the mid-1820s until
1837 there was a considerable upsurge in the economy, followed
by another and stronger upsurge during the last half of the 1840s.
Fourth, as the following pages indicate, the view was increasing
that common schools, supported in part by the state and in part by
local school districts, and open to all without payment of tuition,
afforded the most effective way to provide elementary education.

During the 1830s and 1840s legislation about public common
schools much resembled that in effect in 1831. The legislature established the process and criteria for their establishment and
maintenance. Generally speaking, before schools could be opened
the voters of a congressional township elected three trustees.
They divided the township into school districts as seemed desirable—later making changes and additions in them. Each district,
however, elected three sub-trustees who were responsible for

opening and managing its school. The district trustees had the major authority for erecting and repairing schoolhouses, selecting the teacher, and arranging for his pay in money or otherwise. Terms varied considerably in length but perhaps averaged about three months. Pay to teachers was apparently roughly $15 per month for males, and several dollars less for females. In making their decisions, both district and township trustees were often directed by the votes and preferences of those who elected them. *School districts, not congressional townships, were the key unit for public common schools in the 1830s and 1840s.* In the context of pioneer life and attitudes, it could hardly have been otherwise.[24]

From 1830 to 1850 common schools were established and maintained with modest, or at times with no, payment of tax in money. Taxes levied for schools generally could be paid by donating land, a building, building materials, seats, fuel, or labor as well as in money. Some laws exempted persons from paying any tax if they did not have children in attendance. With short terms and meager pay to teachers, maintenance costs requiring taxes were quite modest once a school was established.[25] Starting in the 1820s various funds, endowed and otherwise, were established, but the proceeds therefrom were rather limited prior to 1850. The so-called Congressional Township Fund in some ways hindered the development of common schools. Each township had its separate fund, but proceeds varied significantly from township to township. As Superintendent William C. Larrabee reported in 1853: "In one township the school section happens to be valuable, and sells for a large sum; in another it is worthless. In one township the section falls on the prairies of the Wabash, where the soil is the richest ever shone on by the sun or wet by the dews of heaven; in another it falls in the swamp or a lake, or on a rocky bluff, where six grasshoppers could not find a living. In one township the fund would support, without a tax, schools all the year; in another there would be little, if any, fund at all." If there had been only one Congressional Township Fund, its proceeds could have been divided so that all school districts would receive the same annual distribution per student enrolled. Such a distribution would have been more equitable. Moreover, it probably would have made citizens realize sooner the importance of having a significant tax levy to strengthen common school education throughout the state.[26]

Governor Noah Noble strongly encouraged the increasing interest in public common schools which developed in the 1830s. In his first inaugural, December, 1831, he asserted: "That our free institutions may be perpetuated, it is not enough that we provide a few who arc qualified to sit in the councils, or guide the helm of state—we must commence at the fountain of power, with the great mass of the people, to cultivate and enlighten the public mind, by a diffusion of the benefits of education." A year later, Noble told legislators that "not less than one hundred thousand children, of suitable age" lacked common school education. To begin to pay the debt owed such children, he recommended that any surplus in the state treasury annually be appropriated "among the schools that may be supported by tax or contribution, six months in the year . . . ." Noble further recommended that individuals who "contributed in money or labor, one dollar and upwards" for the benefit of schools be excused from "his delinquencies" regarding militia duties for "that year." Neither of these proposals seems to have been enacted into law.[27]

A meeting of influential citizens at Madison in 1833 indicates that support for district or neighborhood schools, sustained by residents thereof, was growing. On September 3–4 of that year the Association for the Improvement of Common Schools in Indiana had its initial meeting there. The new association declared: "Few subjects of vital importance to society in all its relations, have received as little attention, or has been as little understood as *primary education*." It attributed this situation to the "incessant labour necessary to subdue the forest and the soil"; "sparseness of population"; the "heterogeneous character" of the people, embracing "natives of every soil and every clime—with all of their diversities"; but the greatest difficulty was the "*want of competent teachers of good moral character and respectability* . . . ." Although the association gloried "in forming a *christian* institution," it called it a "fact" that "the cause of education is most flourishing where the salutary provision for public schools is embraced." The importance of these statements is increased because the meeting was attended by leading citizens who were a mix of Democrats and Whigs, natives of northern and southern states, and representatives, of members and ministers, from at least the Presbyterian, Methodist, and Baptist denominations.[28]

As support for common schools increased, the desire for better qualified teachers also increased. Before the Association for the Improvement of Common Schools in Indiana adjourned its meeting at Madison, it "highly" approved the efforts of its board "to establish a Manual Labor Seminary to educate [Common] School Teachers."[29] In December, 1833, Governor Noble advised the General Assembly that the "want of competent teachers to instruct in our township schools is a cause of complaint in many sections of the state; and it is to be regretted, that in employing transient persons from other states combining but little of qualifications or moral character, the profession is not in that repute that it should be." The governor asked the legislators to consider two ways to obtain better teachers. First, by "establishing, on the manual labour or some other plan, one or more seminaries for the preparation of young men" as teachers in the common schools, with the interest from the Saline Fund applied for their support. Second, by connecting "a preparatory department," based on the manual labor system, with the Indiana College. If either plan was adopted, its benefits were to be extended equally to "young men" from all counties.[30] The legislative session of 1833–1834 chartered the Indiana Teachers' Seminary at Madison and the Wabash Manual Labor College and Teachers' Seminary at Crawfordsville—later known as Wabash College. As noted later in this chapter, various of the colleges chartered in the 1830s and 1840s helped prepare teachers for the common schools.[31]

As Hoosiers succumbed to the internal improvements fever in the mid-1830s, their interest in establishing and strengthening public common schools seems to have ebbed a bit. When Governor Noble ended his first term in December, 1834, he counseled legislators that there would be "a greater certainty of success" for establishing such schools by adapting "our legislation to the peculiar situation and circumstances of the people . . . than by adopting at once the most perfect system that has been devised in other States . . . ." And "even their prejudices ought to be regarded, so far as not entirely inconsistent with the great object to be accomplished."[32]

Between 1837 and 1839, however, the movement on behalf of public common schools was renewed with vigor as evidenced by the meeting of three state conventions which vigorously explained the need for them. The first convention met at Indianapolis on January 3–4, 1837, several months before the start of the bank panic of that year. Apparently at least two hundred fifty individuals from scattered parts of the state, calling themselves "friends of Common Education," attended. A roll call of members indicates that prominent Whigs and Democrats, natives of both southern and northern states, and leaders from the Presbyterians, Methodists, and Baptists were there. Governor Noble was its president; and Andrew Wylie, president of Indiana College, and Judge Isaac Blackford of the Indiana Supreme Court were vice-presidents. President Wylie delivered an address on "common education," following which the convention resolved "that a good common education has the highest claims upon our attention, inasmuch as it lays the surest foundation for civil liberty, social order and private happiness." Dr. Wylie was thanked for his "excellent address," and upon request of the convention he provided a copy so that it could be published.[33]

The "friends of Common Education" sent a memorial to the legislature asking for important changes in legislation about common schools. First, they requested the General Assembly to elect, by joint ballot, a Board of Public Instruction, comprised of a member from each judicial district of the state. Each member would "superintend the general interests of common education" within his district. He would also appoint "a board of examiners" for each county of his district to examine and license common school teachers. This board would report annually to the state member who named it about the "condition of the schools" in its county. The Board of Public Instruction would meet annually, more often if it were thought desirable, "and lay before the Legislature . . . such suggestions as they may deem important to the advancement of the general interests of education." Second, the reports of the county board of examiners were to indicate the number of townships within their county; number of school districts in each township; number of children in each district "between 5 and 21" years of age; number of children in school the previous year; number of months the school was taught, and whether "by male or female teachers"; the "wages paid; and the amount of public money expended." Third, "after a given time, no teacher," unless licensed by the county examiners, could benefit from legislation about collection of debts due teachers. Fourth, all of the federal surplus revenue anticipated for Indiana, "should be devoted exclusively to education," with half going for the support of district schools and the other half for county seminaries. Fifth, "each school district should be required to have a school at least four months in the year, taught by a teacher who has been examined and approved by the proper board of examiners as to his moral character, and his ability to teach reading, writing, English grammar, geography and arithmetic . . . ." But "no district should receive their portion of the public money unless" they had a school for at least four months the previous year. Sixth, school money "should be apportioned" to districts according to their number of children "between 5 and 20" years of age.[34]

The committee gave the General Assembly five reasons for proposing these changes in the laws about schools. First, the existing laws "you have by your own legislation declared to be inadequate . . . ." Second, the system proposed had been demonstrated "to be the best ever tried"; and "its leading principles" were in effect in Prussia where common school education was "more generally diffused than in any other country in the world." Third, "the expense of the proposed system would be comparatively trifling." Fourth, using the state's share of federal revenue to support common schools and county seminaries, "would be the wisest policy our Legislature can pursue" because such schools "are necessary for the education of our future statesmen, our lawyers, our physicians, our divines, and our teachers.—Without them, ignorance, the fruitful mother of crime and poverty, will fill our State with her offspring." Fifth, although the convention expressed great admiration for "the magnificent system of Internal Improvements," commenced "with so much spirit," it declared that "the future glory of our youthful State will depend more upon the intelligence and morality of the people . . . than the improvement of our roads or the construction of our canals."[35]

In a circular to the people of Indiana, the convention emphasized "the advantages of a good common education" to its youth. Such an education, it declared, promoted physical well-being, "vigor of the cultivated mind," "personal happiness," "happiness of the domestic circle," "social relations," "civil liberty," "political prosperity," and "infinitely more important, man's eternal welfare . . . ." "The *means* of acquiring this all important treasure," are either available or soon attainable. But two principal "hindrances" prevented speedy establishment of a good common school system. One was "The scarcity of well qualified teachers of common schools." Most "young men of enterprise" find more lucrative employment in almost any lawful business. Another hindrance was the "Apathy in relation to the real value of a good education . . . ." To obtain good common schools, citizens were urged to exchange ideas about education in township or neighborhood meetings and in county conventions. The latter were urged to appoint delegates to represent them at "the next State Convention," so that it could act more "advisedly, or with a more accurate knowledge of the wants and wishes of the whole people."[36]

As the four preceding paragraphs indicate, the State Education Convention of 1837 launched a vigorous and comprehensive appeal for improving and extending public common schools. Had there been no fiscal debacle from the Internal Improvements System of 1836, would such schools have been much improved and greatly extended by 1850? Probably not. To have achieved this, *especially in the pioneer context*, something far more important than money was essential. The greatest need was the development of a significant consensus in favor of a statewide system of public common schools. Three key elements thereof were yet to be achieved. First, the belief that education was important and desirable for all children throughout the state. Second, that these schools should and must be supported by taxpayers, whether they sent children to them or not, because of the benefits to society arising from their education. Third, that such a system of public schools could not be adequately sustained so long as public money was also used to support a variety of schools under private or denominational auspices. About a decade later the necessity for such a consensus was forcefully and skillfully set forth and defended by Caleb Mills, a key founder of Wabash College, in six annual messages.[37]

Before the State Education Convention of 1837 adjourned it took steps to encourage continued emphasis on the need for improving and extending public common schools. It asked editors of "public journals" to publish its proceedings, and "devote a part of their columns to the object of a common school education." It also requested "ministers of the gospel . . . to deliver addresses or sermons" concerning education on the second Sabbath of July. Even more important, it named a committee to plan "a convention of the friends of education" at Indianapolis in December following, when the annual legislative session would be in progress.[38] Pursuant to these plans friends of education held a second State Education Convention at the capital on December 26–29. But with the Internal Improvements System of 1836 hovering on the brink of fiscal disaster, the time was not favorable for legislative emphasis regarding improvement of public common schools. Attendance at the convention seems to have been modest, perhaps partly in the hope that leaders among the friends of education could speak to the legislators more effectively and with less diversity of view than many individuals could have done. Andrew Wylie, president of Indiana College, and Elihu Baldwin, president of Wabash College and a Presbyterian minister, each gave an address about education. The convention, "impressed with the extreme importance of educating competent common school teachers," suggested that the legislature instruct "the trustees of the Indiana college to establish a normal [school] professorship for the training and preparing of such teachers, the tuition to be free." It also endorsed a report concerning how best to promote "moral education in common schools," which recommended "use of the scriptures of the Old and New Testaments in the common schools of the State in connection with other such books as are now in common use, calculated to promote the morals of the young and rising generation."[39] Emphasis on "moral education" and concern whether it could be emphasized in public schools may have increased as sentiment for public schools increased.

A third State Education Convention met at Indianapolis, January 2–4, 1839. At this time the state was almost bankrupt, with suspension of the System of 1836 only months away. The convention's memorial to the General Assembly declared "the fund furnished by the munificence of the General [Federal] and State Governments" ample for the support of common schools. Existing school legislation, however, was branded "very imperfect." Particularly needed was a superintendent of common schools to collect data about "the number and character of the common schools in Indiana," plus "such other . . . information" as would "enable our Legislature to correct the defects of our common school system." The memorial asserted that education was rapidly advancing in Kentucky and Ohio because of "the assistance . . . of an active and intelligent superintendent of Common schools." In 1843 the legislature named the state treasurer ex-officio superintendent of common schools. But not until the early fifties was the office of state superintendent of common schools established as a separate office. The convention of 1839 also adopted a constitution providing for the organization of annual conventions to foster the improvement of education in Indiana. Any citizen in the state could become a member of the contemplated "Education Convention." According to this constitution, members of county conventions would elect delegates to the annual state conventions. A central or state correspondence committee, named by the president of the state convention subject to its approval, would obtain data from every county concerning its "number of children, number of schools, kind of teachers, how, and how much paid, amount of school fund, how invested," plus related items for a report to the next state convention. At each annual convention the president would name a committee of three to suggest needed changes in the laws about schools. If such amendments would be approved by the convention, they were recommended to the legislature for passage. The convention also appointed a committee to report to the next annual convention regarding books "in spelling, reading, Arithmetic, Geography, and Grammar," which might be recommended by the convention for general use in the schools.[40]

The two State Education Conventions of 1837, and that of early 1839, launched significant and thoughtfully organized movements for the establishment of a statewide system of common schools under public auspices. This was a nonpartisan endeavor, participated in by prominent Democrats and Whigs; ministers and laymen from the Presbyterian, Methodist, and Baptist denominations; leaders in education; lawyers; and miscellaneous citizens. Roman Catholics; Quakers; strict adherents to certain elements among the Presbyterians, Methodists, and Baptists; and others were overwhelmingly nonparticipants. In 1839 Indiana abandoned its disastrous Internal Improvements System of 1836—then paid neither interest nor principal on its bonded debt therefor until July, 1847. This debacle, and the depression of the late 1830s and early 1840s, seem to have been the major influences causing nearly a decade to pass until another education convention met in 1847. During the late 1840s the movement for strengthening and extending public common schools was renewed with vigor and determination. Its fruition was obtained in the drafting of the Constitution of 1851. Like the movement in the last half of the 1830s, that of the last half of the 1840s seems to have had significant support from all regions of the state, from both Democrats and Whigs, from persons of southern as well as northern origin, and among at least the Presbyterians, Methodists, and Baptists.[41]

In December, 1846, following his reelection to a second gubernatorial term, James Whitcomb, a Democrat, emphasized the great need for common schools, but he was silent as to how they should be financed. He advised legislators that with "all citizens . . . regarded as politically equal," to protect their "full share of political rights" they "must be armed with at least an elementary education" and know how to read and write their mother tongue. Hence, "it is a sacred *debt* which we owe to every son and daughter of Indiana, however poor they may be, to place them upon an equality with their more favored associates, as to the means of acquiring a common school education." He regarded existing laws about schools "vague and conflicting," and proposed that items be adopted from other states which had produced "happy results." The governor called for the appointment of a state superintendent to supervise common schools and the various school funds.[42]

Royal Mayhew, state treasurer and ex-officio superintendent of common schools, presented the 1846–1847 legislature a dismal picture of public common schools. From incomplete reports from sixty of the ninety counties, Mayhew estimated that established funds for their support aggregated $2,019,288.40. He concluded that Indiana had about 350,000 children of school age, roughly 64 percent of whom had been without "any benefit of common school instruction" the preceding year. Rejecting the view that there was something "radically wrong" with legislation concerning common schools, Mayhew asserted that "a few slight amendments, with some supplemental enactments," and the election of a proper superintendent of "common schools" was all that was required "in the way of legislation." An elected superintendent—who was concerned only with items regarding public education—and who would visit and aid local school officials, give public talks about education, and generally supervise the common schools was deemed "of most vital importance." In a gingerly manner Mayhew urged consideration of a state tax to help finance district schools, plus "an equal amount" by the districts to make them eligible to obtain tax money from the state.[43]

Shortly before Whitcomb's message to the General Assembly, Caleb Mills, a professor at what became known as Wabash College, addressed the first of six messages about Indiana's continuing neglect of common schools to its citizens and politicians. Using the pseudonym "One of The People," he declared: "The true glory of a people consists in the intelligence and virtue of its individual members, and no more important duty can devolve upon" the legislature "than the devising and perfecting a wise, liberal, and efficient system of popular education." A proper system of education, Mills proclaimed, would "benefit every part of the State, improve every class of community, give permanency to our civil and religious institutions, increase the social, literary and intellectual capital of our citizens, and add materially to the real and substantial happiness of every one." The professor termed it "humiliating . . . that *one-seventh* part of the adult population of a great and flourishing State is not able to read the charter of her liberties, or the votes they cast in the exercise of their election franchise!" "Shall we dig canals and build railroads to transport the products of our rich soil to market, and leave the intellect of the rising generation undeveloped and undisciplined" he asked. "Is matter more valuable than mind?"[44]

Mills gave a litany of reasons for the low esteem of the common schools. He declared: "We have *borrowed* millions for the physical improvement of our State, but we have not *raised* a dollar by *ad valorem* taxation to cultivate the minds of our children." Common schools were "deficient in number" because of "the want of the necessary means to sustain them." Moreover, in their support, "the poor have been burdened and the rich exempted from contributing their due share." "Shall the rich man's neighbors and tenants bear the whole burden of sustaining schools, which . . . will pecuniarly benefit him more than the parents of the children taught in them?" Mills asked. He predicted that a tax of 10 cents per $100 of taxable property would yield $118,500 annually, which, plus proceeds from school funds, "would secure to the youth of Indiana a blessing, of which they have been hitherto deprived, a *free school*."[45] According to "One of The People," some of the causes for the "inefficiency of character" regarding the common schools were the "want of competent teachers, suitable school books, a proper degree of interest in the community on the subject, adequate funds, and the method of procuring such funds." Mills strongly recommended county superintendents of schools to examine teachers; visit schools; and report to the state superintendent about the number of children of school age, the number in school, conditions of the schools, use of public funds, "and such information and suggestions as may occur to them in the discharge of their duties."[46] Mills said that "religion and learning" caused "the wide difference in the character and condition" of communities throughout the state. Religion, he added approvingly, "is happily protected from legislative interference and State control, . . . and the latter must be fostered and sustained by liberal and enlightened legislation, or it will never flourish."[47] Such basic concepts and ideas from Mills are repeatedly emphasized in scattered portions of his six messages.

The legislative session of 1846–1847 gave significant support to the growing interest in improving and extending common school education. On January 8, 1847, the House recommended that "the friends of education" hold "a State Common School Convention at Indianapolis, on the fourth Wednesday of May . . . for the purpose of consulting and devising the best course to be pursued to promote common school education in our State." Next day the Senate adopted a similar resolution.[48] Less than three weeks later, "a meeting of the citizens of Indianapolis, friendly to the cause of Common School Education," chaired by Calvin Fletcher, named a committee of five members to make plans for the State Common School Convention in May. Two days later Henry Ward Beecher, chairman of the committee of five, reported resolutions "which were unanimously adopted" by those present. Pursuant to their resolutions "all persons friendly to the cause of common school education" were cordially invited to attend the state convention. In addition, "literary associations engaged in the promotion of education, and voluntary assemblies of the citizens" were asked to send delegates. A committee of three was appointed to arrange for the "entertainment of the delegates." A committee of seven was named to promote attendance at the state convention, prepare a circular setting forth the objects of the convention, and solicit data about the "condition of common schools in each township of the State, so far as it can be obtained." The Indianapolis friends of education exhorted: "Let not Indiana be behind her sisters"; and let the school teachers, attorneys, ministers, and "all who have influence . . . see that this convention is well attended, not doubting that the result will be the adoption of a system of common school education, at the next session of the legislature, that will add to the glory and honor of our beloved State."[49]

On the eve of the common school convention, the *Indiana State Journal* emphasized its unusual importance. This leading Whig paper of the state commented: "We would ask what more important meeting has ever taken place than the one at hand . . . . It is the laying the very corner stone of the durability of the republic; the commencement of a system of free schools, by which every child in the State is benefitted upon an equality—can read its own destiny and the design for which it was sent into the world . . . ."[50] The convention met May 26–28 at the capital. Governor Whitcomb was its temporary chairman, and Isaac Blackford, senior member of the Indiana Supreme Court, served as permanent chairman. Calvin Fletcher indicates that he had Blackford, reluctantly supported by some, nominated because "It seems the Methodist College at Greencastle [Asbury] was afraid of the college at Crawfordsvill[e] [Wabash] & the college at Bloomington [Indiana College] afraid of both." Moreover, "There were many elements existing to make the various sects jealous of each other[.]" The *Common School Advocate* reported that three hundred fifty delegates attended the convention, but the actual number was probably considerably less. The convention named a committee of five, chaired by Ovid Butler, to prepare business for the convention.[51]

During the three day session there was vigorous discussion concerning school legislation. Should the General Assembly enact a desirable general law, which would be in effect throughout the state, without a popular vote for or against? If such a law were submitted for a popular vote, should it become effective statewide if it gained a majority of the popular vote, or only in the counties which gave majorities for it? There seems to have been a consensus that any "vote for or against the adoption of the school law should be taken on some day other than the day of the annual election." A committee of seven persons was named and charged with preparing and circulating an address to the people indicating the kind of legislation needed for improvement of the common schools. In addition, a committee of three was named to prepare and submit a proposed law to the governor and General Assembly at its ensuing session.[52]

The address to the citizens of Indiana by the committee of seven was a blunt and devastating indictment of common schools as they existed. Schoolhouses, where any had been built, were "miserable structures." Despite "many worthy exceptions," the teachers were "miserably qualified for their high stations." For numerous school districts there was "at least a limited impression that if a man has failed in every thing else and is fit for no other occupation, he will nevertheless do for a school teacher." Hence, as revealed by the federal census of 1840, "one-seventh of our population, that is 38,100, over twenty years of age, could neither read nor write." According to data from a recent report of the state treasurer as ex-officio superintendent of common schools, Indiana had about 350,000 children of school age between five and twenty-one. Approximately 129,500 or 37 percent had apparently attended school "for a small part of the year." Thus 63 percent, or 220,500 children, had been "without any benefits of Common school instruction!!" The Common School Fund aggregated about $2,000,000, but if loaned at 7 percent interest, with costs subtracted, the yield per year for 350,000 students would be about 34 cents per scholar yearly—therefore, "too small to command attention and to awaken that interest, which the subject demands."[53]

The committee of seven gave emphasis to five elements viewed essential to making common schools what they ought to be. "It is of vital importance," the committee asserted, "that our Common Schools should be *free*," free to rich and poor alike, with costs shared by townships and state taxpayers in such a way that makes taxes from the state used "as a *lever*, to raise the additional sum needed, to excite an interest in the [local] people, and urge them to action." Second, the committee presumed it would "be absolutely necessary" to increase money by taxation to maintain a system of common schools. On the assumption that Indiana had 350,000 youth of school age, and 7,000 school districts averaging fifty children, it would require $283,500 to pay "the wages" to teachers for three months of the year. On this basis if males were paid $15 and females $10 per month, it would cost 81 cents per scholar. This assumption included ten or twenty more pupils per teacher than desirable, making $163,500 additional to be raised by taxation. Nonetheless, the committee anticipated that the annual increase in revenue from taxable property and polls for years to come would make it possible to finance common schools by an annual levy of 13 cents per dollar of taxable property. The committee proclaimed: "Then let the schools, based upon such a foundation, be perfectly free, as the dew of heaven, to rich and poor, without the least recognition of pauperism or charity."[54]

Key elements three and four concerned the caliber of the schools and the necessity for qualified teachers. The common schools had to "be *elevated* [in quality] so that all will feel an interest in them," because "a school not good enough for the rich, will not excite much interest with the poor." Further, "A suitable standard of qualification should be erected for teaching, and a compensation given accordingly." "Nothing," the committee noted, "has more tended to degrade our Common Schools, than the want of well qualified teachers." The average pay for male and female teachers was estimated at $12 and $6 per month respectively or "about the price of day laborers who pay nothing for education." The committee declared: "Not the warriors or legislators, but the school teachers of old Greece and Rome, perpetuated for generations the majesty of their institutions, and bequeathed to them an undying glory."[55]

The fifth element needed to make the common schools what they ought to be was "an able and zealous [State] Superintendent of Common Schools . . . ." This official should generally "have charge of the interests of Common Schools" throughout the state, and keep abreast of ways of improving schools, receive information and reports from local officials, and offer ideas and suggestions to them for improvement of their schools.[56]

The committee of seven insisted that there were no "serious obstacles" to making Indiana's common schools what they ought to be. Obstacles "of the most formidable character" had resulted from "serious misfortunes" arising from the internal improvements debacle. But with the "arrangement" for liquidating the debt therefrom, "the vast productions of our numerous vallies and prairies, unsurpassed for fertility and resources"; the expanding canals and railroads; and an increase of $3,500,000 annually in taxable wealth—"who will say that Indiana is so miserably poor, or so contemptibly ignorant, or utterly destitute of enterprise, that she cannot have a well digested and efficient Common School System, that will nobly elevate the mass of the rising generation, where they can meet the demands of their country and their God upon them?"[57] Unless "immediate and efficient measures" were taken to improve and extend common schools throughout the state, the committee predicted that by 1860 the state would have "60,000 voters, and 50,000 mothers" unable to read or write, and hence, would have "elements for mobs, for repudiating State debts, for filling our penitentiary, poor houses, and jails!" The committee said that three months of education in "private schools cost about five times more than [three months] in the Common Schools." Thus, all the 350,000 school children of the state could be educated in public common schools as cheaply as one fifth of them could be educated in private schools. Therefore, public schools, sustained by a mix of state and local revenue, provided the best and least costly way to impart elementary education to the youth of the state.[58]

Before the General Assembly convened on December 6, 1847, the *Indiana State Journal* commended the address of the committee of seven to the people of the state. The address, it said, "has been published by several papers without the State, but has not received that attention it merits from the Press in our own State." This leading Whig paper asserted that if legislators needed "any incentive to action . . . it will be found in the facts set forth by the committee." In quoting from that part of the address, which contrasted conditions of life in Indiana with those in the older and more developed states, the editor asked who could not recall "many instances of orphan children of highly intelligent parents, being raised in ignorance because of no adequate provision being made by the State to educate the rising generation."[59]

Shortly before the legislature convened the committee of three, named by the education convention in May, completed a bill for improving and extending common schools. The committee said it had "not attempted a complete revision of the school system" but had tried to add "such provisions" as would give "life and energy" to the system. It proposed a state tax of six tenths of a mill per dollar of taxable property, rising one mill per year until it became one cent per dollar of taxable property. Such a levy, plus revenue from a township tax and the school funds, would annually probably maintain a free school for "at least 4½ months." The cost of a well regulated system of common schools would "probably [be] less than half the expense of private schools." If necessary "a great majority" of the large property owners would make "temporary sacrifices" to sustain common schools, which would increase prosperity and wealth and distribute it more equally around the state.[60]

The committee's bill called for increased centralization in the administration of common schools. At the township level it recommended that township and school district trustees be reduced from three to one, thereby saving $28,572—enough to pay the cost of having county superintendents. Teachers would be required to make their report about the number of students enrolled before they could be paid. If district trustees failed to make reports or spent money contrary to law, they were subject to penalties. If a county superintendent failed to make a report about his county to the state superintendent, his county would not get its share of state funds, and he would be subject to a heavy penalty. The county superintendents would visit schools; "organize a board for the examination of teachers"; give "addresses in all the townships"; advise school officials and teachers; and be "the medium of communication between the State Superintendent and all township and district officers." A state superintendent of common schools, elected by the voters, would visit all counties; give addresses; instruct school officials; distribute school funds; devise means to establish school libraries and institutes for teachers; and suggest needed changes in the school laws and funds. To encourage "united effort and uniformity" regarding common schools, the county superintendents in each congressional district would constitute a board of education to consult on and decide difficult issues. To promote further "uniformity," a State Board of Education, with one delegate from each congressional district, would "do much in producing harmony, in selecting the most suitable text books—devising the best plans for school houses—providing for school libraries—in establishing teachers' institutes."[61]

The State Board of Education would, "at wholesale" cost, buy books for the district libraries as "suited to the wants of the schools." These libraries would "enable the scholars to improve their leisure hours in the acquisition of useful knowledge, and to form in the morning of life, a habit of reading, which will cheer them in the vale of years." Moreover, "By placing in the hands of children, well selected books, we shall save many from the fascination and demoralizing influence of the miserable trash which is now so eagerly sought, called 'light reading.'"[62]

Although the committee of three declared that its bill did not propose a complete revision of the common schools system, it did propose two basic changes. First, it called for a large increase in administrative supervision by county and state officials. Second, it asked for a large increase in tax support at both state and local levels. It appears that such taxes were to be paid entirely in money, hence, apparently with considerably less control by district and township officials; and a significant reduction in tax levies paid in labor, building items, fuel, and the like. In submitting its bill to the General Assembly, the committee urged that body to enact legislation about common schools and submit it "to the people for their approval or rejection." It hoped the General Assembly would agree with the convention of the previous May "in the belief that the time for action has come—that the present is an important era, in our history. Universal education is essential to full success of sound Democratic principles—to the stability of our free government." The committee wisely emphasized that the development of secondary and higher education was much dependent on how education developed at the elementary level. It declared that an efficient system of common schools, "accessible to all . . . is not only of the greatest moment to the whole mass of the people, but it will prove the grand basis of the higher Seminaries, Colleges, and Universities of the State."[63]

In his second message to the legislative session of 1847–1848 Caleb Mills reemphasized his vigorous support for a statewide system of public common schools. He advised legislators: "There is no topic which presents stronger claims on your notice, or calls more imperatively for wise, efficient, and prompt action than this." "Our present system," he declared, "approaches about as near to a perfect one, as the first steam-boat on the Hudson, did to the floating mansions that now navigate the father of waters [Mississippi]."[64] From the federal census of 1840 Mills concluded that residents of Indiana "are the most ignorant of the *free States*, and are far below even some of the *Slave States*. *One-seventh part* of our adult population are unable to read the word of God, or write their names. Some of our counties are enveloped in a thicker intellectual darkness than shrouds *any State in the Union.*"[65]

Professor Mills was emphatic that "there is but one way to secure good schools, and that is to pay for them." He admonished: "*it is the duty of the state to furnish the means of primary education to the entire youth within her bounds.*"[66] He urged that the many separate Congressional Township Funds be merged into a single Congressional Township Fund in which all residents would "share in the educational funds, according to the number of children, irrespective of all other considerations." To pay for common schools Mills recommended a state tax of two mills per dollar of taxable property distributed among the congressional townships according to their "number of children between certain ages." He asked that residents of these townships be authorized to levy a tax of one mill per dollar of taxable property, to be added to the state support for schools.[67]

Once the essential "pecuniary means" were secured Mills stressed that "the proper education" of youth required "*comfortable and convenient school houses, competent teachers, suitable school books, and efficient supervision . . . .*" He complained about the impure atmosphere, extremes of heat and cold, and of light and shade, and the "*torture of backless seats*" common to schoolhouses. Further, "Many a farmer makes ten fold better provision for the comfort of his *cattle*, than has been made by scores of [school] districts for the comfort of the rising generation, in acquiring that education which shall prepare them to discharge the duties of *American citizens.*" But "make the profession of teaching as lucrative and honorable as the other professions, and there will be no lack of noble and generous youth to fill it."[68] Mills staunchly opposed making the state superintendent of common schools a separate office. He suggested that the treasurer of state should continue as ex-officio state superintendent. Mills much preferred that common schools be supervised by county superintendents, elected for terms of three years, and paid sufficiently "to command the services of competent men." Indiana, the Wabash College professor said, was too large for a state superintendent to keep in touch with local school officials and citizens. Moreover, whether chosen by the governor, the legislature, or the people, partisan politics would intrude. Even worse, "thousands" would immediately ask if he is a Presbyterian, Methodist, or Baptist, or of no denomination, hence, with a bias and preference for the group to which the inquirer belonged.[69] Mills wrestled with the question of the role of religion in the common schools. He observed that "however diversified may be our religious sentiments, there is a strong and prevailing impression in society that the great principles of the Bible, are inwrought in, and inseparable from, the civil institutions of the land." To this he added: "The Bible is too deeply enthroned in the hearts of the people, to be excluded from our common schools, and other institutions of learning." Mills noted, with regret, that "prominent and influential individuals in leading denominations" advocated "distribution of the school funds among the different sects, according to their number"; or urged "the withdrawal of their denomination from the [public] common schools to establish and sustain parochial schools under the pretext that the Bible, whose claims as a standard of morals, have been recognized in various ways, in our civil policy, cannot be used in our common schools without interfering with the religious belief of citizens . . . ." He then commented: "If the plough-share of sectarian bigotry, must be driven through our common schools, it should be distinctly understood, by the advocates of such measures that the legitimate result of the policy, will be to sunder some of the strongest ties that bind our social and political fabric, and loosen the very *keystone* of the arch of our present happy Union."[70]

Mills emphasized three items. First, state and local tax money should be used only for the support of public common schools. Second, morality and religion could and should be discussed and sustained in such schools. Third, if state and local money were made available to denominational and private schools, it would be very dangerous to the "social and political fabric . . . ." Mills, however, was unclear about how morals and religion should be sustained in public common schools. A century and a half later, a satisfactory and general consensus about this very important item has never been attained.

At the legislative session of 1847–1848 Governor Whitcomb and the General Assembly gave a timid response to the recommendations of the education convention and Mills for improving and extending public common schools. The governor said: "it is much to be regretted" that because of obligations to creditors, for bonded debt for internal improvements, and benevolent institutions, "we are unable by legislation, to afford such immediate and substantial aid" as would be desirable if the state's finances were more flourishing. The House of Representatives passed a bill embracing various items desired by the convention and Mills, but the Senate rejected it. The legislature, however, approved a law asking voters of the state, at the general election on the first Monday in August, 1848, to respond for or against "a law by the next legislature, for raising by taxation, an amount which added to the present school funds, shall be sufficient to support free common schools in all the school districts of the state not less than three nor more than six months each year."[71]

Before the legislature adjourned it called for another education convention, which met at Indianapolis on May 26, 1848. The attendance was modest. Reports were received about school libraries and common schools. Judge Amory Kinney was appointed "to go thro the state & deliver addresses" on the importance of free schools prior to the August referendum. Calvin Fletcher feared that if the vote were against free schools that "every demagogue will feel instructed to vote against any system of common schools for the next 15 years . . . ." After the convention adjourned, a committee chaired by Fletcher made an urgent appeal to the press of the state for its cooperation and assistance in convincing the people of "the superior advantages of the 'Free School System,' over every other plan devised to educate the whole people . . . ." The communication from this committee appeared in many papers throughout the state.[72]

The referendum in August, 1848, asked voters to indicate whether they wanted the next legislative session to enact a law for the support of "free common schools" throughout the state. If so, were they willing that the schools be supported by taxation sufficient for their operation not less than three or more than six months annually? If so established, the schools would be free of any tuition or admission fee for all youth of school age. In his third address, directed to the legislative session of 1848–1849, Caleb Mills gleefully noted that fifty-nine of the ninety counties, "embracing the most intelligent in the State," gave majorities for "Free Schools," whereas thirty-one counties, of which "*twenty* are below the general average of adult intelligence," gave majorities "against them." Of the 140,410 votes counted, 78,523 voted for and 61,887 voted against free schools on the basis suggested. There was, thus, a majority of 16,636 for free schools. Richard G. Boone noted that the forty-seven counties—located north of an east-west line along the southern boundary of Marion County—gave a majority of 18,270 favorable votes, whereas the forty-three counties south thereof gave a majority of 1,634 negative votes.[73]

What elements favored and what elements opposed the free school referendum of 1848? This question needs much careful study, but the author adds his *impressions* gained from a variety of sources. Since the Democrats overwhelmingly dominated state politics, it seems evident that approval would not have been obtained without significant support from them. Perhaps, however, a larger percentage of Whigs than Democrats voted for free schools. It appears that considerable support came from Presbyterians, Methodists, and Baptists, perhaps in that order, with Roman Catholics, Quakers, and miscellaneous groups largely in opposition. Probably voters of southern origin gave a smaller proportion of their votes for approval than did those of northern and European origin. But some voters of southern origin, more numerous south of the National Road, where public common schools had generally been established longer, perhaps saw no good reason to help establish schools on a statewide basis. Persons of meager, moderate, or considerable wealth doubtless included voters both for and against; and likewise for voters lacking a family. Most likely the same occurred among illiterates.[74]

Although a significant majority of the voters in the referendum of 1848 favored a state tax levy in support of free schools in every school district, a substantial minority voted contrary thereto. In his address to the General Assembly in December, 1848, Governor Whitcomb was silent about this item. The legislature responded by enacting a comprehensive law in favor of free common schools on a statewide basis. According to the law of 1849 owners of taxable property would pay 10 cents per $100 of taxable property owned, and persons liable for a poll tax would pay 25 cents therefor annually. The state revenue gained from these two levies, plus that from state-owned school funds, would be distributed among the school districts of the state. Because districts varied much in what they obtained from the separate Congressional Township Funds, the state revenue would be distributed as nearly as possible to give each school district the same total per student enrolled. Congressional townships with large funds would share their revenue with townships having small or even no township fund. Voters of a school district, if they desired, could levy an additional tax, not exceeding 15 cents per $100 of taxable property, for use in building or repairing schoolhouses, fuel, furniture, books, and other apparatus or to extend the school term beyond three months. Local taxes could be made payable in money, labor, or various items. All schools were to continue for at least three months and be taught by "legally qualified teachers . . . ." No provision was made for county superintendents, and the state treasurer was to continue ex-officio as superintendent of common schools. Three trustees were retained for each congressional township, but the district trustees were reduced from three to one. In districts in which schoolhouses had been erected and schools established "by private liberality," the township trustees were authorized "to recognize the same as a public school," and make a "just and equitable" allowance thereto. The law of 1849, however, would become effective only in counties giving a majority for its adoption. Counties rejecting the law at the election in August, 1849, would vote annually for or against adoption until approval was achieved.[75]

From rather convincing evidence Caleb Mills concluded that sixty-one counties adopted the school law of 1849 and the other twenty-nine counties rejected it. Of the 142,391 votes cast, 79,079 voters approved the law and 63,312 opposed it, making a majority of 15,767 in its favor. Save for the county option provision, the 1849 law would have become effective in all ninety counties. Since the vote in 1849 was pro or con a law with many details, it is uncertain how many voters cast votes against the law in the hope of having it replaced by a better one. It is likewise uncertain how many voted for it, despite objections, considering it an improvement or perhaps the best law that could then be attained. The plan to equalize proceeds from Congressional Township Funds perhaps increased votes in counties having no or modest funds and had the reverse effect in counties having larger than average Congressional Township Funds. Mills viewed this item as "*emphatically* the crowning excellence" of the 1849 law. But to him its "most objectionable feature" was the "ridiculous and absurd" provision for its approval on a county-option basis. Free public schools, Mills insisted, "must take effect in virtue of a general vote and not a local approval."[76]

As of 1850 Indiana had made only modest progress toward establishing public common schools. During the last half of the 1840s probably less than half of the youth between ages five and twenty-one attended such schools for as much as three months in a year. Numerous of these schools were private or denominational schools, recognized and in part financed from taxes and proceeds from public school funds, hence not public schools as advocated by Caleb Mills and others. At midcentury the basic decisions about establishing and operating public common schools were made in part by residents of congressional townships and mainly by residents of the thousands of school districts into which the townships were divided. Such schools were neighborhood schools, largely within walking distance for pupils, but no law compelled parents to send their children to them. Teachers were generally poorly prepared and poorly paid. They were principally males, but the proportion of females was increasing. The latter were usually paid at least one third less than males, whose pay perhaps averaged roughly $15 a month. School buildings and facilities were very inadequate. The curriculum varied, often depending upon the qualifications or lack thereof of the teachers. Considerable emphasis was given to reading, writing, and arithmetic, and at times to geography, history, grammar, spelling, and other subjects. The tradition that most schools were "blab" schools, with students reading out loud as they prepared their lessons, seems to be a myth. The same seems to be true for the tradition that portrays pioneer teachers as extremely severe in punishment for trivial misbehavior. There is much wisdom in Logan Esarey's comments to students that it is possible to describe a pioneer school but it is impossible to give an accurate description of pioneer schools generally. Nevertheless, thanks in significant part to the public sentiment resulting from the educational conventions of the 1830s and 1840s; the annual messages of Caleb Mills, 1846–1849; and the school referendum of 1848, the delegates who drafted the Constitution of 1851 included the unqualified provision that "it shall be the duty of the General Assembly . . . to provide, by law, for a general and uniform system of Common Schools, wherein tuition shall be without charge, and equally open to all."[77] This mandate resulted in the school law of 1852, which as Richard G. Boone correctly concluded, made changes that "were really revolutionary."[78]

From statehood until 1850 secondary education was mainly at seminaries and academies or at similar institutions with various names. These institutions were conducted principally under private or religious auspices. Nevertheless, the Constitution of 1816 mandated that sums paid for exemption from militia service and fines paid for violations of penal laws be used to support a seminary in the county in which they were collected. Such revenue, fees paid by students, and donations were the principal sources for the modest support of county seminaries.[79] In 1818 the legislature asked the governor to name a trustee for each county to have charge of its seminary fund. The revised code of 1824 authorized the voters of a county, at any regular election, to elect three trustees to replace the trustee named by the governor. The three trustees could buy and hold property as a site for a seminary, have a building erected thereon, and open a seminary. County seminary money not used for such purposes was to be loaned at 6 percent interest per annum to gain revenue for support of the county's seminary. This law restricted the terms of trustees to three years, unless reelected. The revised code of 1831 had provisions much like that of 1824.[80] County seminaries, however, were often established by special laws with considerable variation in the number of trustees and other details. From 1825 to 1850 county seminaries were opened in more than half the counties, but various of them closed before midcentury. They were more common in the earlier settled counties of southern and central Indiana than in the later settled counties of northern Indiana.[81] County seminary funds were for the most part poorly managed. In 1834 Governor Noah Noble advised legislators that in "some instances" such funds had been "entirely squandered and lost." In 1845 the state treasurer, acting as superintendent of common schools, reported that fifty-nine counties had seminary funds aggregating $40,687.87 and had grounds and buildings worth $50,617.47—for an average of about $690 and $850 respectively per county. According to Boone, who doubtless saw some of the county seminary buildings, they "were generally substantial two-story structures, well built . . . with three or four rooms, and, for the time and conditions, conveniently arranged."[82]

The county seminaries varied greatly regarding the number of students and the level of instruction, which ranged from classes for children only four or five years of age to courses of study equaling those offered at the colleges and universities. Boone concluded that "for most counties . . . the seminary provided both elementary and secondary instruction." Students were, for the most part, residents of the county in which the seminary was located, but some of the seminaries with well-known and respected teachers drew pupils from other counties and even from other states. Among such teachers were John I. Morrison and Samuel K. Hoshour. Enrollment at county seminaries was modest, but in some counties attendance exceeded one hundred for various terms. At times seminary buildings were used for religious meetings, political discussions, lyceums and debates, and sessions of county courts. By midcentury, however, the county seminaries had become unpopular; and the Constitution of 1851 mandated that they be sold, with their proceeds going for the support of public common schools.[83]

Various colleges and universities were founded before 1850, most of them by religious denominations. Those not so founded were much influenced by religious practices and beliefs. In 1804, four years after Indiana Territory was created, Congress donated a congressional township of land for support of a seminary of learning. Two years later the territorial legislature chartered Vincennes University. The charter urged the trustees "'to use their utmost endeavors'" to persuade the Indians to send their children to the university, and it asked that the education of women be started as soon as funds would permit. The legislature approved a lottery of $20,000 to gain money for the university, and it appropriated the proceeds from part of the donated township for its support. Neither source yielded much revenue, but in 1810 Reverend Samuel Scott, a Presbyterian minister, became the first professor. Until 1825 Vincennes University had meager enrollment, with instruction at irregular intervals. Apparently neither Indians nor women enrolled, and its modest curriculum was far less inclusive than its charter had suggested. In 1825 the legislature declared that the board of trustees had lapsed and designated the proceeds from the remaining part of the congressional township for the infant Indiana State Seminary. During the 1830s a board of trustees was revived for Vincennes University, a revival that initiated a tangled and prolonged controversy between it and the Indiana College, successor to the Indiana State Seminary, for proceeds from the congressional township. Despite this loss, Vincennes University resumed operation.[84]

The Constitution of 1816 envisioned a state university as the capstone of a general system of education. When Congress approved statehood for Indiana, it authorized a second congressional township of land for support of higher education. This township was located at the edge of the infant village of Bloomington. Proceeds from these two townships, plus tuition paid by students, were the leading sources of revenue prior to 1850.[85] When classes began at the Indiana State Seminary is uncertain, but probably in 1825.[86] Baynard Rush Hall, a Presbyterian minister and recent graduate of Princeton Theological Seminary, was its first professor. About a dozen boys enrolled the first year, apparently including Joseph A. Wright, later the state's governor. Enrollment gained slightly the second year and rose to about twenty students for the third year. Apparently only Greek and Latin were taught during the first two or three years. In 1827 John H. Harney, of Kentucky, a recent graduate of Miami University, Ohio, became the second professor, teaching mathematics, natural and mechanical philosophy, and chemistry. The next year the institution was renamed Indiana College by an act of the General Assembly. That same year Andrew Wylie, a Presbyterian who had been president of Washington College in western Pennsylvania, became its first president. He continued as such until his death in 1851. In his inaugural address in 1829, the president noted the importance of a college for the education of lawyers, doctors, and ministers—and its advantages to farmers. Especially during the pioneer era, now and then there were both faculty squabbles and public charges of sectarianism at the institution. In 1838 Indiana College was renamed Indiana University.[87]

Late in 1848 the board of trustees, in a report to the General Assembly, indicated the modest status of Indiana University at midcentury. This report lists Andrew Wylie as president and professor of Moral Philosophy; Theophilus A. Wylie, professor of Natural Philosophy; Daniel Read, professor of Languages; Alfred Ryors, professor of Mathematics; David McDonald and William T. Otto, professors of Law. M. M. Campbell was listed as principal of the Preparatory Department. Student enrollment, including the Preparatory Department, had been at a low of sixty-four in 1840, and at a peak of 198 in 1846. There had never been more than thirty-one students from other states, and the current year had only nineteen such students. Generally speaking the students were "of more mature years, than those of Colleges in the older States." Most students lodged and boarded in private homes at a cost of "from $1 00 to $1 50 per week." Some students, who lived at the University Boarding House under faculty supervision, furnished their own table and employed their own cook at "from 50 to 75 cents per week" per student. "The discipline," the trustees emphasized, "is intended to be strictly parental, and to accomplish its effect, by appealing to the better principles of the heart, avoiding, if possible, severe and disgraceful punishments; students are treated as reasonable beings and gentlemen," but "immoral, disorderly, or dishonorable conduct, or habitual negligence of duty, or want of preparation, is always sufficient reason for directing a student to leave the University." In the college curriculum students entered as freshmen, followed by sophomore, junior, and senior years, "attending three recitations in a day." The university owned property valued at $23,550, including the main "College edifice" valued at $12,500; the Boarding House at $3,000; and the library at $2,500.[88]

In closing its report the board of trustees emphasized the importance of the university to citizens of the state. Despite its meager financial base, the trustees asserted "that no other College or University in the West, resting on a similar foundation, is at this time, in a condition of higher prosperity than our own State University, either in regard to the number of students or extent and thoroughness of the course of instruction." The board estimated that "near one hundred youth from Indiana, at an expense annually, of from $200 to $500," were pursuing studies elsewhere than in Indiana. Colleges, however, were not for the rich alone; moreover, most students in American colleges were "aspiring young men from the middling, and even from the humble walks of life; many of them having by their own efforts procured the means of their education." To them "it is of the utmost importance, that there should be in our midst, provision for the highest instruction, in every department of human knowledge." The trustees commended the framers of the Constitution of 1816 for their wisdom in presuming that "Common Schools and Colleges go together, . . . [and] flourish in the same soil and harmonize in the same system." They also declared that "Indiana University has no rivalry with any other Institution in the State. She sends cordial greeting to every Institution of sound learning belonging to whatsoever party or sect. There is room for all, and work for all."[89]

At least five colleges and universities, founded by religious groups, had their beginnings prior to 1850. In 1827 John Finley Crowe, a Presbyterian minister at Hanover, became a teacher of a classical preparatory school for boys and young men, particularly for those wishing to be ministers. Soon chartered as Hanover Academy, in 1833 it was chartered as Hanover College under Presbyterian auspices. The first president of the college was James Blythe, a Presbyterian from Kentucky. For about a decade Hanover College experimented with the manual labor fad. Students worked at farming, carpentering, cooperage, printing, rail splitting, and similar tasks. During the pioneer era it drew a significant number of students from southern states. In the 1840s an unsuccessful effort was made to move the institution to nearby Madison, then one of the largest and most rapidly developing towns of the state. Of existing Indiana colleges and universities founded under religious auspices, the roots of Hanover College are the oldest.[90]

Wabash College commenced under Presbyterian auspices, tinged with Congregationalism. Opened in 1833 as an academy, Caleb Mills was its initial professor. In 1833 it was chartered as the Wabash Manual Labor College and Teachers' Seminary. As Boone has noted, in its early years it sought to provide "scattered churches with ministers trained for the pulpit—a native ministry"; and "as a school for the preparation of teachers, it was one of the earliest in the State, or even in the Northwest." Wabash College early established a strong foundation for liberal and classical studies. Its experimentation with the labor system was meager and of short duration. From its beginning to the present, Wabash has remained a college for men only.[91]

Although the Methodists were more numerous than the Presbyterians they placed somewhat less emphasis on a college educated ministry. While Indiana University was known as Indiana College, Methodist leaders contended that its board was dominated by Presbyterians and asked for increased Methodist representation thereon. How much failure to gain such representation led to the chartering of Asbury University, at Greencastle, in 1837 is uncertain. Reverend Cyrus Nutt a short time before had opened a preparatory school in Greencastle under Methodist auspices. Reverend Matthew Simpson was inaugurated as Asbury's first president in 1839. In its early years Asbury gave considerable emphasis to the education of ministers and teachers of common schools. It seems to have been less fully committed to liberal and classical study than Wabash College. Asbury added a department of law in 1846. Two years later it adopted the Indiana Central Medical College, at Indianapolis, as a branch of the university.[92]

The Baptists, more numerous than the Presbyterians, were slower than the Presbyterians in establishing a college. Many Baptists saw no real need for a college to educate ministers, and some of them opposed having a paid ministry. They had even less representation on the board of trustees for Indiana College than the Methodists. In 1834 Jesse L. Holman, former state Supreme Court judge, and others established the Indiana Baptists Manual Education Society. Three years later the Indiana Baptist Manual Labor Institute opened at Franklin, but the manual labor part was limited in practice and duration. Women were admitted in 1842. In 1844 it was rechartered as Franklin College, after which emphasis on liberal and classical education increased.[93]

Notre Dame and Earlham College also have roots in the pioneer era. In 1842 the Reverend Edward Sorin, superior-general of the Congregation of the Holy Cross, founded the University of Notre Dame near South Bend. In 1844 it was chartered as the University of Notre Dame and soon became the leading university of the state under Roman Catholic sponsorship.[94] In 1838 the Indiana Yearly Meeting of Friends (Quakers) commenced a Friends' Boarding School a short distance west of Richmond, which combined manual labor and education. In 1859 it was chartered as Earlham College.[95]

In 1849 Governor Paris C. Dunning told legislators that the state's colleges and universities had never "enjoyed so great a degree of prosperity . . . ." Despite this optimism, however, they were modestly attended. According to Dunning, Asbury had 295 students, Indiana 197, Hanover 183, Wabash 148, and Franklin 145, for an aggregate of 968 students. As these data suggest, higher education was then overwhelmingly under religious auspices.[96] Despite the fact that Caleb Mills insisted on public support for common schools, he vigorously opposed it for education above this level. In his second address to the legislature in 1847, Mills declared: "The State can not manage colleges any better than she can canals and railroads . . . ." He recommended that the board of trustees for Indiana University be dissolved and replaced by a board known as "Regents of the University." The regents should "consist of at least sixteen members, two from each of the several denominations engaged in promoting collegiate education and the remainder from other portions of the community, who have not yet embarked in such an enterprise." The regents would "have charge of the University funds, and disburse the income of these funds, equally to those colleges which would comply with the conditions of the disbursement." Participating institutions "would adopt a course of study substantially equivalent" to the one prescribed by the board of regents. "Such an Union of affiliated institutions," Mills said, "would be a glorious realization of the idea of an University."[97] In subsequent addresses Mills modified some items, but his key recommendation remained—destroy Indiana University and divide its proceeds among colleges and universities sponsored by religious denominations and private individuals. In his fifth address, to the Constitutional Convention of 1850–1851, Mills contended that since his plan contemplated "no *perversion* of funds, no *alienation* of State control of the grant [of two congressional townships for the support of higher education] and involves no *constitutional* objection and impairs no *vested* right, it is conceived that no valid reason exists in the way of its adoption." Mills told the delegates: "No fact in the history of education has been more clearly demonstrated and firmly established than this, *that all literary institutions of a higher grade than common schools are best conducted by private enterprise, and flourish better under the supervision of voluntary associations than under any oversight and care the State can exercise.*"[98]

Caleb Mills was not the only prominent citizen who wanted to destroy Indiana University. In 1840 Calvin Fletcher confided in his diary: "Cooper agent for Asbury College called & wished me to appear at auditors office with Messrs. A. W. Morris[,] Good (preacher)[,] Wilkins[,] &c to advise whether the officers of the college should join with the Hannover & other colleges in destroying the Bloomington University & divide the funds." Fletcher's diary for the next day includes this comment about the meeting: "Called at the place as requested by Mr. Cooper—all present as above. I gave my objections: I It was unconstitutional 2d antichristian 3d Bad policy as it would awake to a greater vigellence the infidel spirit at Bloomington 4 a quarrel in the distribution of the funds 5 It would unite Infidelity 6 the Asbury College is now poor but in good repute & it should Keep so and grow up by degrees not suddenly." Why Mills expressed opposition to withdrawal of money from school funds and taxation for the benefit of denominational common schools, yet urged the distribution of the Indiana University Fund among colleges and universities, sponsored by religious groups, is baffling.[99] If the latter was appropriate and constitutional, why was not the same policy equally appropriate and constitutional for common schools? Mills wrestled with the proper role of morality and religion as regards common schools. Neither, he insisted, should be excluded, either from common schools or other institutions of higher learning. Mills was correct in his view that neither morality nor religion should be so excluded; however, he was seemingly uncertain how this could be achieved. A century and a half later the citizens of Indiana have not yet attained anything like a consensus about this very important question.

CHAPTER 8

JACKSONIAN CONSTITUTION OF 1851

THE CONSTITUTION OF 1816 *continued unchanged* until replaced by a new constitution in 1851. It afforded each generation at least two opportunities to amend or revise its fundamental document. It mandated that every twelfth year the voters indicate whether they favored calling a convention to amend or revise the constitution. If "a majority of all the votes given" at a referendum favored a convention, it became the duty of the next General Assembly to provide for the election of delegates thereto and establish the time and place for their meeting. The law therefor, however, had to be supported by a majority of all members of both houses. Whether a referendum could or could not be held at other than twelve-year intervals was not explicitly stated in the first constitution. But its bill of rights declared that "the people . . . have at all times an unalienable and indefeasible right to alter or reform their Government in such manner as they may think proper."[1] Three factors help explain why the Constitution of 1816 was *never amended*. First, this constitution, which included liberal Jeffersonian principles, was widely respected and supported by voters and politicians. Second, it was a concise document, emphasizing basic principles with few restrictive details, thus leaving the legislature much discretion in adapting laws to changing circumstances. Third, amendments could not be added without the considerable expense of calling a constitutional convention.

Referendums held in 1823, 1828, and 1840 revealed only limited desire for a constitutional convention.[2] Three amendments in particular were proposed for their consideration. They were: have biennial rather than annual sessions of the legislature; abolish the two associate judges of the circuit court of each county; modify the requirement that all impeachment trials of civil officials must be by the Senate so that local officials would be impeached by the circuit court or some other plan. In 1823 "Junius" argued that these three changes would save "ten or twelve thousand dollars" yearly and make "a permanent improvement in our system of government." He asserted that annual sessions spent much time repealing laws of previous sessions, whereas biennial sessions would enact laws "equally as wholesome and salutary, and more permanent . . . ." This anonymous correspondent termed the two associate judges, who served with a president judge to constitute the circuit court, "supernumerary officers" who hindered justice and should be "pruned from our judiciary as unprofitable branches." The impeachment of local officials such as a justice of the peace, which might take the Senate a week at a cost of $1,000, "Junius" said, should be determined locally.[3] During the initial referendum in 1823, there was some discussion about the restoration of slavery which had been prohibited in the Constitution of 1816. Some historians have unduly magnified this possibility. The *Indiana Gazette*, printed at Corydon, the capital, declared: "It cannot be true that a majority of our citizens would desire the introduction of slavery." A paper at Vincennes, where slavery had existed, opposed changing the "*fair* complexion" of the existing constitution for "a *black one*."[4]

Only one of the three referendums was held at a twelve year interval. The *Indiana Gazette* branded the referendum of 1823 "unconstitutional." How, it asked, "can a judge of election, who swears to support the constitution . . . open a poll for a convention without permitting *perjury*?" But this referendum, just seven years after statehood, called by a legislature which included five members who had helped draft the constitution, suggests that early legislators presumed that a referendum could be held at other than twelve year intervals.[5] This question continued to be discussed pro and con, with Whigs more inclined than Democrats to restrict referendums to these intervals. In recommending the referendum of 1849, which resulted in the Constitution of 1851, Governor James Whitcomb spoke for the view that prevailed when he said: "But by securing to the people the privilege of voting upon the question every twelfth year, their power to exercise that right in any other year for which their representatives should make suitable provision, was not taken away."[6]

Sentiment for calling a constitutional convention gained momentum as the forties advanced. Four factors in particular help explain this development. First, and perhaps most important, was the catastrophic impact of the fiscal crisis which arose from the breakdown of the System of 1836. As the nonpayment of interest on the millions of this internal improvement debt accumulated at the rate of several hundred thousand dollars annually, from 1841 to 1847, there was strong and persistent demand that the constitution be amended to add severe restrictions against the power of the legislature to create a state debt. Second, from statehood there had been considerable and continuing support for biennial in lieu of annual sessions of the General Assembly, plus strict limitations against its passage of local and special laws. The financial crunch of the forties fostered augmented desire for these changes to reduce the cost of state government. Third, because of the internal improvement debacle and the growing desire to end the monopoly of banking within Indiana by the Second State Bank, there was a strong trend for a return to economic laissez faire. The augmenting population base and expanding economy amid the returning prosperity from the mid-forties afforded a favorable context for this return. Fourth, during the 1840s Indiana came increasingly under the sway of Jacksonian Democracy with its emphasis upon individual rights, popular election, restrictions of legislative bodies, and private enterprise. The Constitution of 1851 incorporated a variety of items reflecting these four factors.[7]

The referendum of 1846 came as the above items were augmenting sentiment for revision of the Constitution of 1816. Early in 1846 the Senate, equally divided between Whigs and Democrats, approved a constitutional referendum by a count of 33 to 14, with most Whigs and Democrats overwhelmingly for passage. The House, which had a Democratic majority, tabled the Senate bill but adopted a similar one without a roll call vote. The Senate then endorsed the House measure 31 to 14, with party division much as for its defeated bill.[8] At the state election in August, seventy-nine of the ninety counties gave 34,192 votes for and 30,394 votes against a convention. When the General Assembly convened in December, Governor James Whitcomb advised members that "less than one-half of the number of voters who had . . . voted upon other questions" had participated in the referendum. The governor, newly reelected, neither recommended nor opposed calling a convention. At this session the Democrats had a slight majority in the Senate, but the Whigs had a majority in the House.[9] Various resolutions, bills, and committee reports were considered, but as adjournment neared, the Senate, by a vote of 24 to 22, approved the calling of a constitutional convention. The House, however, by the decisive count of 58 to 37, rejected a call. In the Senate calling a convention was supported by the preponderance of Democrats, and opposed by the preponderance of Whigs; in the House the preponderance of Whigs supported rejection, with Democrats preponderantly against this action.[10] Several Whig representatives granted that there were defects in the constitution, admitted that they differed among themselves about a convention at other than a twelve year interval, but they agreed that since "*less than one half* of" those "who . . . voted upon *other* questions" had favored a convention one could not be called because a "*constitutional majority*" had not been cast for it. Senator Godlove S. Orth questioned whether it would be consistent with the constitution to call a convention since less than half of those who had voted at the election of August, 1846, had favored such a call.[11]

At the election in August, 1848, the Democrats, for the first time since they won majorities in both houses five years earlier, again won majorities in the House and Senate. Early in the session of 1848–1849, Senator John I. Morrison, a Democrat, offered a bill for a referendum about a constitutional convention. The Senate adopted his bill by the overwhelming tally of 34 to 12, and the House concurred by the close to unanimous vote of 80 to 2.[12] The enlarged Whig support for a referendum seemingly reflected growing Whig approval for a new constitution, but may have resulted in part because some Whigs believed that they could gain a constitution more to their liking by sustaining rather than opposing the movement therefor. Official returns for all ninety counties from the election in August, 1849, indicated that 81,500 voters favored and 57,418 opposed a convention. An aggregate of 138,918 votes were cast concerning the referendum, and 147,290 votes were given for governor. Only eighteen of the ninety counties gave a majority against a convention. These counties were principally in Southern Indiana, however this area as well as Central and Northern Indiana counties gave majorities for calling a convention.[13] A few months before the vote on the referendum the *Indiana State Sentinel* asserted: "there is not a newspaper in the State which now openly opposes a convention, while the most of them, of all parties, are very decidedly in favor of one." In December, 1849, Governor Paris C. Dunning advised legislators that it had become their "plain" duty to provide for the election of delegates to a constitutional convention. He urged that delegates be apportioned so as to "insure to the people of the State, irrespective of parties, a full and fair representation" in the convention.[14] After much discussion the Senate, without a roll call vote, adopted a bill for popular election of 150 delegates in August, 1850, to convene at Indianapolis on October 7, for a revision of the Constitution of 1816. The House amended the Senate measure, then passed it 54 to 38, with most Democrats and most Whigs for passage. Any voter was declared eligible to be a delegate.[15]

Despite suggestions about bipartisan election of delegates, mainly advocated by the minority Whigs, delegates were largely chosen along party lines. A correspondent of the Fort Wayne *Times*, a Whig organ, urged election on a bipartisan basis. To this, the Fort Wayne *Sentinel*, staunchly Democratic, snorted that Whigs "strongly deprecate party lines—in places where they happen to be in a hopeless minority." About the first of March the Democratic State Central Committee recommended that county conventions nominate "a full ticket, embracing delegates" to the convention.[16] Of the 150 delegates elected in August nearly two thirds were Democrats, slightly more than one third were Whigs. They were generally representative citizens with much and varied political experience, and the rural and agrarian context of the pioneer economy is reflected by the variety of their occupations. Although for the most part their formal education had been very limited, in discussing items before the convention various of them drew from writers and political experience concerning the Greeks, Romans, western European countries, and the United

States. Seventy-four delegates were natives of free states, including only thirteen from Indiana; seventy of slave states; and three each from Ireland and Scotland. Of those who reported their age, the youngest was twenty-three, the oldest seventy-two; and about two thirds of them were in their thirties and forties. Although overwhelmingly of American birth and English background, they had varying degrees of German, Irish, Scottish, Dutch, and French ancestry.[17]

The constitutional convention opened Monday, October 7, 1850, with 143 delegates in attendance. Judge Isaac Blackford, member of the Supreme Court from 1817, administered the oath of office to them in the room in which the House of Representatives met. George W. Carr, a native Hoosier and veteran legislator, was elected president of the convention on the initial ballot, receiving 132 votes, with none against him. During the first afternoon William H. English, a Democrat, was elected principal secretary on the third ballot.[18] Next morning three assistant secretaries were elected, and a sergeant at arms and doorkeeper were appointed. These officials were apparently all Democrats, perhaps named according to informal understandings among Democratic delegates. Harvey Fowler, an experienced stenographer from the federal capital, became stenographer by selection of the governor pursuant to prior legislative request.[19] Milton Gregg, a Whig, sought rejection of Fowler, claiming that a stenographer would needlessly increase discussion, prolong the session, and be too costly.[20] Seemingly the convention did not open with prayer, but at the request of the convention its secretary arranged with the clergy of Indianapolis to offer prayer at the beginning session of each day, a practice that began on the fourth day.[21] The convention considered the rules of the House of Representatives as its basic rules, until other rules were adopted. As the second week commenced, the convention adopted rules generally similar to those of the House. Perhaps largely because 150 delegates were crowded in quarters used for 100 representatives, smoking within the hall and its galleries was prohibited.[22]

More discussed than the rules was the question of how 150 delegates should proceed in drafting a new constitution. Considerable discussion ensued regarding whether there should be a mod-

est or large number of committees to review and report recommended items to the convention. After adoption of James G.
Read's proposal that the president name a committee "'to report
a plan for the business of the Convention,'" President Carr
named him and twenty-two other delegates to propose such a report. On the fifth day of the convention Chairman Read submitted a plan calling for twenty-two standing committees to receive,
review, and recommend items for inclusion in the new constitution, subject to the approval of the delegates. These twenty-two
standing committees were approved and they recommended most
of the items which were incorporated in the new document, but
some items were reviewed and proposed to the convention by select committees.[23]

While some of the delegates preferred only modest changes in
the old constitution, most members, Whigs as well as Democrats,
supported substantial revision. On the third day of the convention
David Kilgore, a Whig, proposed that the convention "recommend to the People of the State the present Constitution" and
"adjourn *sine die*." His proposal was immediately tabled by the
overwhelming vote of 126 to 11. About three weeks later, Kilgore
asked that the standing committees be discharged from the items
referred to them; and the convention "take up the old Constitution, article by article and section by section, and adopt, amend,
or reject the same and make such additions thereto, as may be
deemed proper." This item was disapproved by the decisive count
of 91 to 39. The votes for and against Kilgore's proposals were bipartisan, and they were rejected without discussion.[24] During November James Ritchey, a Democrat, asserted that there were "very
few prominent objections to the old Constitution," hence perhaps
not more than a half dozen amendments were required to satisfy
the people. If "this body shall lose sight of the old land-marks of
experience, which have obtained in the State government for the
last thirty odd years," Ritchey stated, he would seek rejection of
the new document "so that we may, at least, get back under the
wholesome influences of the old Constitution." James Rariden, a
Whig, said there were "many provisions" in the constitution he
would like to have changed, but he had "voted against a call of the

Convention; and have said from the beginning that the closer we stick to the old barque, the better will I and my constituents be satisfied with the results of our labors."[25]

In drafting the Constitution of 1851, the delegates responded to widespread demand for major limitations on the General Assembly. Among them were: (1) less frequent and less lengthy legislative sessions; (2) restrictions on how laws were enacted; (3) make laws of general application, and prohibit local and special legislation so far as possible; (4) and efforts to reduce the number of legislators and make legislative reapportionments fair and equitable. Although the delegates agreed, by a vote of 124 to 0, that the "legislative authority" of the state was vested in the General Assembly they hemmed in and limited this authority with sundry restrictions and prohibitions. As this process continued Jacob Page Chapman declared: "Almost the entire weight of this Convention seems to be directed against the legislative department, as if, in that department alone, originated all the evils of government." The former editor of the *Indiana State Sentinel* said the people were "right as to the bad character" of past legislation, but "they certainly never designed for a moment to destroy the legislative branch of government; they only wish to reform and correct it."[26] Most items about the legislature were proposed to the convention by the Committee on the Legislative Department, chaired by Michael G. Bright, a Democrat, and most of its members were Democrats. But the Committee on Special and Local Legislation and Uniformity of Laws proposed the restrictions about local and special legislation. This committee was chaired by John S. Newman, a Whig, and most of its members were Whigs.[27]

Soon after the constitutional convention began, the delegates, by close to a unanimous vote, decided in favor of biennial sessions of the General Assembly. A resolution to instruct the Committee on the Legislative Department to report an item mandating biennial meetings was adopted by the extremely lopsided vote of 124 to 5. An effort to amend the instruction in favor of triennial sessions failed, but forty-three delegates voted in favor and eighty-three delegates prevented its adoption.[28] Apparently far more delegates favored triennial than annual sessions. James G. Read, a Democrat, who offered the amendment for triennial sessions, then supported biennial sessions. Read said that if the question were referred to the people "nine-tenths of them would be in favor of biennial or triennial sessions." He noted that most of the states which had recently drafted new constitutions had opted for the biennial plan. Hiram Allen, a Whig who had also preferred triennial sessions, stated that if the "miserable system of local legislation" were abolished, and the election of various state officials and judges were taken from the legislature and given to the voters, then legislative sessions every other year could perform their duties "in less time" than under the existing system of annual meetings. Elias Murray, a Whig, concurred with much that Read and Allen expressed. He emphasized that "frequent elections . . . kept men in a constant turmoil." Moreover, with annual sessions the laws were "continually fluctuating" and people, not knowing what the laws were, "did not know when they had violated them." Two Whig delegates, Othniel L. Clark and Horace P. Biddle, vigorously advocated retention of annual sessions. Clark stressed that yearly sessions were essential to supervise state government and control abuses. "It was a proverb in free government," Clark said, "that 'where annual sessions end, tyranny begins.'" If meetings were biennial, Clark argued, frequent special sessions would "cost as much as the regular sessions." Biddle declared himself "emphatically" for annual sessions. With biennial sessions, he said, "the Legislature would just do twice as much business in a session." Moreover, "the people would not like to suffer under the effects of bad laws for so long a period as two years." Biddle suggested that the remedy for hasty legislation was a "hasty method" for its correction. Biddle insisted that frequent elections and frequent legislative sessions were necessary, until voters, comprised of people from every part of the Union and also from every portion of the world, "should all become wholehearted Hoosiers."[29] The delegates decided that the change to biennial sessions would begin on the first Thursday after the first Monday in January, 1853. Heretofore, unless advanced by a call of the governor, sessions had commenced on the first Monday in December. John B. Niles, a Whig who proposed this change, said starting sessions on Monday made "the Sabbath" a day "devoted to exchanging salutations, electioneering, and holding caucuses . . . in conflict with the prevalent feelings and opinions of our people." "Within a very few years," Niles forecast, individuals from any part of the state could leave home "on or after Monday, and be in Indianapolis before Thursday . . . ." By commencing on Thursday, legislators could spend the "holydays" associated with Christmas with friends according to respected custom. Other delegates spoke in favor of Thursday, usually for somewhat the same reason.[30] Some delegates, however, preferred starting sessions on Monday. John Pettit, a Democrat, urged beginning on Monday as "done by Congress, by the Legislature of Ohio, and nearly all the State Legislatures in the Union." He believed that "to do a good week's work, it was always necessary to commence Monday morning . . . ." If meeting on Monday would cause the desecration of the Sabbath, "for the last thirty-four years, have the devotional feelings of the people living at the seat of Government been disturbed." Othniel L. Clark and John S. Newman, both Whigs, also preferred Monday to Thursday. Newman considered the first Monday in December as best fitting the "particular habits" of the people in doing their business. Sessions starting in January, he noted, might not end by the time many legislators wanted to be "home to attend to their spring business."[31]

As October ended the Committee on the Legislative Department reported a section with no limit on the duration of sessions. It also provided that compensation for legislative service be "fixed by law," with no increase effective at the session which approved it. James G. Read, a Democrat, tried to have pay limited to not over $1.50 per day after the first fifty days. Otherwise, he said, "biennial sessions . . . would be protracted for three or four months." Daniel Kelso, a Democrat, sarcastically asserted that if Read is "a living witness" that a legislature can do as much in fifty as in one hundred days, then "he ought . . . be embalmed when he is dead, [great laughter,] for he is the first and the last man that has ever made such a wonderful discovery." The matter of pay, Kelso suggested, "can safely be left to the Legislature and the people themselves." Read's proposal was tabled by a vote of 64 to 48.[32] Read later offered an amendment to limit per diem to

$3 for the first sixty days of a session, then only $1.50 for the remaining days. Read noted that all western states, which had of
late adopted new constitutions, had with perhaps one exception,
"adopted similar restrictions." Moreover, with laws to be general,
and local legislation prohibited, there would be "no necessity for
long sessions of the Legislature." If the convention refused to reduce the number of legislators, Read predicted that the costs of
sessions "would be nearly doubled." Thomas Smith, a Democrat,
said "it takes considerable time to legislate for a great State." He
asked the delegates "whether they believe that legislation for all
future time can be done in six weeks out of every two years?"
Smith predicted that "in less than thirty years—the reports made
to the legislature, and the documents they will have to overlook
and investigate, will be such that no sensible set of men can do it
in six weeks." Though willing to restrict sessions to ninety days,
Smith would leave compensation for legislative discretion.
Read's second proposal was adopted by a vote of 66 to 56.[33] Despite this approval, the question of length of sessions and compensation for legislators persisted. The logjam concerning these
items was resolved by a compromise suggested by Robert Dale
Owen, a Democrat. He proposed that the Committee on the
Legislative Department be instructed to make a report leaving
compensation to legislative discretion, with regular sessions limited to sixty days and special sessions to forty days. Joseph Robinson, a Whig, asserted that emergencies might make some long
legislative sessions essential, and reducing per diem after a stated
time "partook of some of the efforts of the stump demagogue."
Robinson observed that the "Convention was the last body in the
world that should prescribe to another legislative body the duration of its sessions." For although this was the "twelfth week of
their labors" they were as yet scarcely able "to see the end of
their labors." Owen's proposal was adopted without change by a
count of 66 to 45. When the Committee on the Legislative Department reported the section back to the convention as instructed, the delegates approved the items about compensation
and length of sessions by the very large margin of 82 to 29. But
the Committee on Revision, Arrangement and Phraseology, for

some reason not apparent, changed the limit on regular sessions from sixty to sixty-one days.[34]

The convention also gave considerable time to the consideration of how laws should be enacted. Soon after it met, Alexander C. Stevenson, a Whig, asked that the Committee on the Legislative Department be instructed to report items requiring a majority of *all members* of both houses to pass legislation, with the vote thereon recorded in their journals. "One of the greatest evils which had oppressed the State was too much legislation," Stevenson said. He explained that he had seen "bill after bill" passed "by the votes of ten or twelve men, at the close of a session" after many members had gone home, resulting in laws "manifestly injurious and against the will of the people." Benjamin Wolfe, a Democrat, reported that on adjournment day in 1847 only twenty members of the House had been present. If the yeas and nays had been demanded for passage of bills, members "would have been compelled to remain and discharge the duties required of them." Jacob P. Chapman, a Democrat, agreed that some such "rule" was needed "to do away with" the evil of "'hasty legislation.'" Alvin P. Hovey, a Democrat who later became governor as a Republican, declared: "Any law that cannot receive more than one-half the votes of the Senate, must be of doubtful policy and should not be adopted." Various delegates strongly opposed Stevenson's proposal. Daniel Kelso, a Democrat, termed it "bad policy" to require passage by majority vote of all members. With eight or ten members absent for sickness or otherwise, he said, "the advantages of important legislation might be lost to the State." Othniel L. Clark, a Whig, contended that a restriction "would enable a factious minority in the Legislature to defeat the will of the majority"; and lead to emergencies "when it would be absolutely necessary that something should be done—when it would be fatal to stand still." On motion of Kelso, Stevenson's proposal was amended merely to have the Committee on the Legislative Department *inquire* in the matter. This committee reported in favor of including an aye and nay vote in the journals concerning passage of legislation, but said nothing about majority approval of all members in both houses. Later, on motion of William Steele

Holman, a Democrat, the convention, by a count of 78 to 40 mandated majority voting and approved the item about recording such votes in the journals.[35]

Another item, sponsored by Alexander C. Stevenson, that "'Every law shall embrace but one subject which shall be expressed in the title'" evoked vigorous debate. Proponents contended that this restriction was essential to prevent logrolling, whereby items combined together passed that would have failed if voted on alone. James G. Read, a Democrat, said: "Common sense dictates that the title of a bill should express precisely and distinctly what follows in the sections of the bill." Other states were said to have adopted this provision. But John Pettit, a Democrat, predicted that such a requirement would "cause more litigation than all the other provisions of the Constitution put together." Michael G. Bright, a Democrat, emphasized that the title of a law "is no part of the law." He objected to the proposal because "many subjects are sometimes necessarily embraced in one object." Stevenson's proposal was adopted by the overwhelming vote of 105 to 21, but amended so that if a law included something not expressed in its title only this part of the law would be void.[36]

While discussing the limiting of bills to one subject, a proposal was offered that all bills and joint resolutions "be plainly worded, avoiding as far as may be practicable the use of technical terms in the Latin or any other than the English language." Alexander F. Morrison, a Democrat who offered this item, wanted the laws made "so plain that every man can interpret them for himself, without the aid of a law dictionary" or a lawyer. John B. Niles, a Whig and a lawyer, deemed it wise, whenever possible, "to use simple, plain, old Anglo-Saxon household words." But "excluding Latin words," Niles explained, "would only introduce endless confusion instead of securing simplicity." Niles noted that "The word subpoena is Latin in form. The word action is Latin with the simple addition of the letter n. There is an hundred times more difficulty in understanding the word Action as a legal term than in understanding the word subpoena. Both words are convenient, appropriate and useful." Beattie McClelland, a Democrat and a farmer, observed that "the farmers have to pay the cost of a great many of these Latin phrases." McClelland thought it inconceivable that lawyers and judges would admit that they do not understand the meaning of Latin terms. "And if they do understand them," he asked, "is the English language so meagre, so poor that words cannot be found to express those ideas?" Daniel Read, a Democrat and professor at Indiana University, suggested that as "a Professor of Latin" he did not feel "called upon to defend the Latin of the law books." He suggested that the English language included words "which have gone through with the forms of naturalization, and those which are dwelling among us as mere foreigners, and have not yet been recognized as liege citizens." Read said the word constitution was "nothing but a Latin word, naturalized by the addition of the final letter." Read named various commonly used words which had been "naturalized," and voices responded in favor of striking them out! The Latin professor said "the phrase *ex post facto* . . . could not be safely displaced." Read explained: "We take in foreign words, grant them a domicil among us, and at length adopt them as citizens." Since Morrison's proposal was adopted by a vote of 109 to 21, it seems that Erastus K. Bascom, a Democrat, voiced the sentiment of the preponderance of the delegates when he exclaimed: "Sir, I care not how many words are requisite, I want language employed that men who are not versed in law can understand . . . . I am not in favor of compelling an honest and plain citizen, who understands nothing about legal phrases, to travel up to the county seat and pay a lawyer five dollars to explain a provision of the law. The whole system requires changing." The section, however, was at once amended, by a count of 98 to 25, which added a proviso giving the legislature the option of publishing the laws in German and French "for the benefit of those who cannot read English." This section, with the proviso attached, was approved and referred to the Committee on Revision, Arrangement, and Phraseology.[37]

The most important effort of the convention to restrict and reduce legislation was that made to prohibit most of the local and special legislation that had persisted from statehood. In December, 1848, Governor James Whitcomb had told legislators that "while the amount of our general legislation has for the last five years remained nearly stationary, that of local and private character has, within the same period, advanced more than three hundred and fifty per cent." To remedy "this growing evil," Whitcomb recommended a threefold approach. First, the adoption of laws general and uniform throughout the state, "under which more appropriate tribunals should be clothed with the necessary powers to afford the relief now sought for by means of most private and local statutes." Second, by an amendment to the constitution "expressly prohibiting the action of the General Assembly on specified subjects of a local and private character." Third, that such amendment mandate that the General Assembly "confer from time to time upon county boards, or other subordinate functionaries, the requisite powers." This remedy, the governor asserted, had been conferred in the constitution which the state of New York had adopted in 1846.[38] On November 8, the Committee on Special and Local Legislation and Uniformity of Laws, chaired by John S. Newman, a Whig, reported an article "for insertion" in the constitution. It enumerated nineteen items concerning which "all laws . . . shall be general and of uniform operation throughout the State."[39] Before this article was adopted, various amendments were approved, and on January 24 it was adopted by the overwhelming vote of 116 to 13.[40] Alexander C. Stevenson, a Whig, had tossed the fat in the fire by proposing that the legislature be authorized to confer "powers of a local legislative, and administrative character" upon county boards. Newman's committee recommended that this item be tabled, which it was. Later, however, it was revived and passed second reading by a count of 69 to 57. On its third reading the words "legislative and" were deleted by a vote of 86 to 43 pursuant to an amendment sponsored by John Pettit, a Democrat. So gutted, this item became a part of the new constitution.[41]

As the foregoing indicates, the delegates were overwhelmingly in favor of prohibiting the General Assembly from passing local and special laws about sundry items but were largely against authorizing the conferring of power to make local laws on county boards. In proposing that the General Assembly might confer local legislative as well as administrative power Stevenson had stated that his "object was to give to a county board legislative power in small and local matters." Newman responded that conferring this power upon county boards would run the risk "of doing what would be more dangerous than for the Legislature to retain the power to legislate for local or special purposes." Newman thought it "greatly preferable" that the legislature enact a general law "to be adopted or not by the county board, as the exigencies of the particular county might require." James W. Borden, a Democrat, "supposed" that the legislature would be restrained from "passing local laws." If so, Borden asserted, "then this power of local legislation could not be exercised by the State; and he knew of no better tribunal" upon which "local legislation could be more properly conferred—than the county board." Borden endorsed "the doctrine of Thomas Jefferson that everything that could be done in the county ought to be done there, and not entrusted to the legislature." He also noted that "Many of the new States had adopted this system." Another Democrat, Jacob P. Chapman, hoped that county boards would be given something like municipal status such as for city governments, with the legislature marking out "boundaries within which these county boards should legislate." Chapman considered it "best to bring legislation as near to the people as possible—to let men govern themselves as much as possible." David M. Dobson, a Democrat, explained that work regarding fences and roads cannot always be done at the same time in all parts of the state; that people in part of the state "want their hogs, and sheep, and cattle, to run at large," while they should be kept in enclosures in other parts of the state; and the "people of the south, having different manners and pursuits, and being surrounded by different circumstances, require, in many respects, different laws from those of the people of the north." But John Pettit, a Democrat, insisted that legislation should be "uniform, so that wherever the Indianian sets his foot, he might be governed and protected by the same laws, and liable to the same obligations." Pettit predicted that if you had "a little Legislature of three men in each county," then in "less than five years . . . you will have a conflict between your sovereign Legislature and the legislatures of your counties." He said: "All that you need in a board of commissioners is power to administer the laws as the Legislature shall make them." David Wallace, a Whig and former governor, agreed with Pettit. He asserted "that the laws that shall govern, and regulate, and control, and give power, if you please, to these counties, *shall be uniform*." But, Wallace said, if you give legislative power to the counties "you will have ninety different laws, perhaps, in ninety different counties in the State." It seems unusual that the convention, in which about two thirds of the delegates were Democrats, was unwilling to authorize the General Assembly to confer power to make local laws upon county boards.[42]

The convention discussed at length how many legislators there should be and how they should be apportioned. The Constitution of 1816 had launched statehood with ten senators and twenty-nine representatives, with fifty senators and one hundred representatives the maximum. It also mandated legislative apportionments at five year intervals, with both senators and representatives to be apportioned to counties and districts according to their number of white male voters.[43] As October ended Michael G. Bright, a Democrat, reporting for the Committee on the Legislative Department, suggested that the House should have not less than sixty or more than seventy-five members, with the Senate to have not less than one third or more than one half the membership of the House.[44] Early in December, after a number of votes were taken, the delegates agreed, by a tally of 64 to 58, that the number of senators should never exceed fifty and the number of representatives not over one hundred members. Despite efforts to amend this section it was adopted by a vote of 73 to 47, then passed by the same vote to become part of the new constitution.[45] A few days later William C. Foster, a Democrat, reported two sections concerning reapportionment on behalf of the Committee on the Elective Franchise and Apportionment of Representation. One section called for "an enumeration . . . of all the white male inhabitants above" twenty-one years of age at six year intervals. Another section stated that the number of senators and representatives would then "be fixed by law and apportioned among the several counties according to the number of" such males in each. These sections were adopted without change, also without a roll call vote, and they became a part of the new constitution.[46] An additional section regarding apportionment evolved from the Committee on the Legislative Department. As submitted by this committee, when more than one county comprised a legislative district it "shall be composed of contiguous counties; and no county for representative purposes shall ever be divided." As this item moved near a decision, by a vote of 67 to 54 it was amended to make the section apply only to senatorial districts, thus leaving the General Assembly the discretion to divide counties for representative districts. So amended, it became a part of the new constitution.[47]

The report of the Committee on the Legislative Department about the number of legislators touched off a lively debate on October 30. Some delegates argued for a reduction as a way of reducing the costs of government. George G. Shoup, a Democrat, suggested that about thirty senators and sixty representatives "would better subserve the interests of the State than any other." Shoup declared that "a small number will suit the people of the State, because they wish to economize the public expenditures, and a difference of two hundred dollars per day, or of but one hundred dollars per day, in the cost of legislation, would amount, in the course of years, to a vast aggregate." Various delegates argued that if there were fewer legislators better men would be elected, and they would pass better legislation in less time. Christian C. Nave, a Democrat, contended that the increase to fifty senators and one hundred representatives had "proved a curse rather than a blessing." If two or three counties formed a "representative district," the voters would have a larger area from which to select men to represent them; and fewer representatives "will be able to do more business in less time." Nave suggested that "the larger the number of Representatives the greater will be the amount of legislation," and the difficulty of understanding and administering the laws. Alexander C. Stevenson, a Whig, preferred twenty-five senators and seventy-five representatives. He stated that the rights, liberties, and interests of the people "depend more upon the ballot box and . . . universal suffrage, and single representative districts, than upon the number of representatives." If all men are allowed to vote, Stevenson said, "all men will be equally represented." Advocates for maintaining the existing fifty senators and one hundred representatives, or a close approximation thereof, emphasized the need to make government close to the people, and give many counties of the state an opportunity to have their interests and needs protected. Jacob P. Chapman, a Democrat, explained that "as a republican, I declare I am opposed to a small representation upon *principle*." Samuel Pepper, a Whig, viewed fifty senators and one hundred representatives "about right." With the state "increasing rapidly in wealth and population," he asked, why "reduce the number of our representation below the standard which has been deliberately fixed by the people, and acquiesced in for so long a time?" Pepper warned "against stifling the voice of small counties," and he explained that the support of "thinly settled districts" might be essential to obtain ratification of the new constitution. In legislation, Pepper emphasized, economy was "only an incidental consideration, and far below that of a fair and full expression of the popular will when the whole people desire a voice in saying who shall make the laws that are to protect their lives, liberty, and property." Erastus K. Bascom, a Democrat, urged "that every part of the State should have a full representation." Bascom called it "humbug" to pretend "that a few men can better transact business, in a deliberative body, than a larger number." He stated that "The larger counties will take the smaller counties under their wings and arrogate to themselves, and swallow up the whole of, the business of legislation." Bascom asked for an "apportionment by which the voice of every county shall be heard."[48] Most of the discussion about the number of legislators occurred on December 5, 6, 7, and 9. It covered much the same ground as that considered in October, with repeated efforts to obtain at least one or two thirds of a vote for each county.[49]

Determining how legislators should be apportioned and on what basis also aroused considerable debate. John Pettit, a Democrat, declared: "It is so many people that I want represented, and not fields, and fences, and hedges, and ditches, and mountains, and valleys." If you give a representative to a county having two thirds of the representative ratio, Pettit insisted, "you will make two men in one place equal to three men in another place." Alexander C. Stevenson, a Whig, agreed with Pettit that representation should be based on population and not property. If based on property, he said, "the wealthy counties would undoubtedly have greatly the advantage," but if based on population "the number that may constitute the Legislature, whether great or small, can have no injurious effect." Alexander F. Morrison, a Democrat, argued that basing representation on anything other than population would violate "every well-settled and correct rule of legislation—every republican right." Regardless of his county of residence, "Every man should have an equal voice in the councils of the State."[50] Daniel Kelso, a Democrat, asked that "the House of Representatives shall consist of one member from each organized county in the State." James Ritchey, a Democrat, contended that if "you lessen the number of representatives, you give to the large counties [in population] almost the exclusive privilege of making laws for the State." James W. Borden, a Democrat, wanted every county to have at least one representative. He said that a member of the Corydon Constitutional Convention had told him that this had been its intent. Borden noted that several states gave each county at least one representative, and that every state had at least one representative in Congress.[51] Nevertheless, both the old and new constitutions mandated that senatorial and representative districts be proportional to the number of voters represented.[52]

The decision that counties could be divided into single legislative districts, if they had more than one representative, was an innovation. Alexander C. Stevenson, a Whig, sought to have single districts mandatory for both senatorial and representative districts. He suggested: "It is only by single districts that a just accountability can be secured from the representative to the constituent." James W. Borden, a Democrat, thought single districts desirable, but he would leave the legislature the discretion of making the division or delegating the same to the county boards. Another Democrat, Christian C. Nave, pounced on the idea as "proposterous [sic]." Schuyler Colfax, a Whig, gave strong support for single districts, noting that the federal government had them for congressional elections. John Pettit, a Democrat, stated that "single representative and senatorial districts" would give each "voter the same power and influence in the legislative department of the government wherever he may live." The delegates declined to make single districts mandatory, but made them discretionary with the legislature for counties obtaining two or more members of the House.[53] Another suggested innovation was curtly rejected. While discussing the number of legislators, Thomas Smith, a Democrat, declared his willingness to "dispense with the Senate" and have but "a single legislative branch." He preferred one hundred representatives because he thought "Representatives should be diffused over all parts of the State." In December another Democrat, Christian C. Nave, proposed that the Senate be abolished. He asked, why should we "continue this aristocratic body in the organic law of the State? a feature opposed in principle to our republican habits—a badge of tyranny borrowed from our mother country, Great Britain." When constitutional conventions have been framed, Nave noted, "those delegates have invariably met and transacted their business in one body." Nave viewed "organic laws" more important than "statute laws," and he concluded there was "no necessity for a Senate . . . ." Nave's proposal was immediately tabled.[54] Later, when Nave commended David Wallace, a Whig, who as governor in 1840 had recommended that the Senate be diminished to thirty and the House to sixty members to reduce the cost of legislation, the former governor explained that his recommendation had been "entirely disregarded." To the applause of delegates Wallace asserted: "I believe the people themselves will always say—that if there is any one burthen which they will more cheerfully shoulder than another, it is that which compels them to pay for representation." Wallace apparently overstated the cheerfulness of the Hoosier pioneers in this respect because the modest compensation they paid legislators never manifested such cheerfulness from the electorate.[55]

While the delegates made major changes and imposed various limitations on the legislative department, they spent less time concerning and made only moderate changes in the executive department. When Chairman Alexander F. Morrison made the initial report for the Committee on the Executive on November 1, he submitted twenty-five sections for consideration of the delegates. The initial section stated: "The executive power shall be vested in a Governor, who shall hold his office for—years. A Lieutenant Governor shall be elected and hold his office for the same term of time." According to the Constitution of 1816 governors had been elected by the voters for terms of three years, with eligibility to serve no more than six years in any period of nine years. The lieutenant governor was likewise elected and limited.[56] Near the end of December the convention, by a vote of 52 to 41, decided that governors would serve four year terms. Thomas Smith, a Democrat, then moved that the executive be limited to four years in any period of eight, thus making immediate reelection impossible. Alexander F. Morrison, a Democrat, protested, saying: "There was no stimulant to the proper discharge of duty so potent as the desire of the approbation of the people. He could see no good reason why a man who had discharged the duties of his office properly should be made ineligible." Smith retorted that he would have no objection to eligibility for a second term if the term were two years, but "four years was long enough for any man to hold an office." Smith's amendment was adopted by the overwhelming vote of 69 to 35, and the section was engrossed for third reading. The next day an effort to change the term of the governor to two years, with eligibility for serving four years in any period of six years, was killed by the narrow margin of 55 to 53. James W. Borden, a Democrat, viewed giving the executive a four year term "very much like reforming backwards." He had supposed terms of officials would "be shortened, and not increased." Grafton F. Cookerly, a Democrat, thought it would be "strange" to elect a governor for two years while electing senators for four years. The section, making both the governor and lieutenant governor eligible to serve four years in any period of eight years, was adopted by the count of 63 to 44 and referred to the revision committee.[57]

Meantime, an unsuccessful effort had been made to eliminate the office of lieutenant governor. Daniel Mowrer, a Democrat, proposed that the Committee on the Executive be instructed to consider the expediency of abolishing this office, with the president of the Senate to "act as Governor *pro tem.*," and fill any vacancy until a governor is elected. A few weeks later, while discussing officers of the Senate, Mowrer and James G. Read, also a Democrat, both advocated termination of the office of lieutenant governor. Read would have "the Senate elect a President, as the House of Representatives do." But another Democrat, Hezekiah S. Smith, asserted that one consideration which induced the calling of the convention had been "that every officer of the State should be elected by the people. Not only the Governor, but every other officer, being the immediate servant of the people." Therefore, he opposed having the president of the Senate, rather than the lieutenant governor, succeed the governor. Smith estimated the cost of having a lieutenant governor at "Perhaps seventy-five dollars a year." When Benjamin R. Edmonston, a Democrat, moved that the office be abolished, his amendment was rejected by the decisive vote of 86 to 17.[58]

The convention for the most part gave the governor about the same power and authority as he had had under the Constitution of 1816. It, however, made some changes concerning his role regarding pardons and the veto of legislation. The Constitution of 1816 had given the governor "power to remit fines and forfeitures, grant reprieves and pardons, except in cases of impeachments." On November 1, the Committee on the Executive reported a section, giving the governor power to "grant reprieves, commutations and pardons after convictions" for all offences except treason and cases of impeachment, subject to legislation about "the manner of applying for pardons." This section mandated the governor to report at each session every "reprieve, commutation, or pardon granted, and the reasons therefor."[59] Prior to receipt of this report, Thomas W. Gibson, a Democrat, commented: "No prerogative of the Governor's office has been more abused than this. I allude to no person in particular; I am speaking of all the Governors, without distinction." James G. Read, a Democrat, agreed with this comment, but he asserted: "had I been in the Governor's place for the last twelve years, I might have granted as many pardons as the Governors have." David

Wallace, a Whig who had been governor from 1837 to 1840, agreed with Read "that there is no power so difficult and delicate to exercise as the pardoning power." Wallace considered it desirable to "lighten the responsibility of the Governor in this respect." The former executive suggested that fines and forfeitures had been remitted "to a questionable extent." Various delegates urged that the pardoning and related powers of the governor be shared in some respects by judges of the circuit and or Supreme courts. As discussion of this section continued such criticisms as already noted persisted.[60] Amid this discussion David M. Dobson, a Democrat, emphasized that he "had always supposed that it was the business of the Legislature to make laws, and the business of the courts to decide cases arising under them, and to do nothing else." The pardoning power belonged to the executive, as it was in the federal constitution, Dobson insisted. In short, the judiciary should "decide what the law is" and the executive should "enforce the execution of the law." As adopted the section about pardons and related items was much like it had been under the old constitution, except the governor had to report the names of persons involved and actions taken concerning them to the legislature, and the General Assembly had the *option* of naming a council of state officials whose advice and consent would be necessary regarding pardons. These items were approved, and the section adopted, without votes thereon being recorded.[61]

After discussion, mainly along partisan lines, the convention retained the suspensive veto. The Constitution of 1816 had required *a majority of all members* in both houses to override a veto, with the yeas and nays recorded on their journals. If the governor neither signed nor vetoed a bill "within five days (Sundays excepted)" after receiving it, the bill became a law as if he had signed it. But if adjournment of the session prevented "its return . . . it shall be a law, unless sent back within three days after their next meeting." On October 31 majority and minority reports were received from the Committee on the Legislative Department. The majority report, dominated by Democrats, proposed that vetoes could be set aside "by a majority of two-thirds of each house present"; the minority report, dominated by Whigs, by "*a majority of all the mem-*

bers" of the two houses. Both the majority and the minority approved the five day and three day items as in the existing constitution. Next day the Committee on the Executive, also dominated by Democrats, recommended that vetoes could be set aside "by *a majority of all the members*" of the two houses. But if the governor failed to sign a bill within five days from its presentation to him, then it "shall be a law, unless the general adjournment prevents its return; in which case it shall be a law."[62] Several weeks later the section reported by the majority of the Committee on the Legislative Department was tabled, and the delegates made the section from the Committee on the Executive the basis for its consideration.[63] Two ardent Whigs, James Rariden and Horace P. Biddle, contended that bills adopted by the legislature should become laws unless the governor's veto was overridden by the legislature. They opposed having laws killed because the executive kept them in his pocket for more than five days. Rariden said he had never seen "the time when there was not older and better men in the Legislature than" those who became governor. In a lengthy speech, Biddle argued that vesting all legislative power in the legislature, all judicial power in the courts, and all executive power in the executive was "the great fundamental idea" in all American constitutions. Biddle asserted that all "history shows us that the Executive continually encroaches upon the other departments, and destroys the true balance of government. It is the serpent of free governments." The veto, Biddle commented, "is an unnatural plant to free soil. It was transplanted to America from a crown, and far better does it become a monarchy; but even there it has died out." Democrats John Pettit, Robert Dale Owen, and Daniel Read defended the veto power of the governor. Pettit contended that the veto had helped preserve liberty, reduced ill advised legislation, and guarded against waste and partiality. Owen's views were similar to those expressed by Pettit. Owen said the veto power of the governor had a "democratic," not a "kingly" origin. Read called "excessive legislation" the "great vice of republics," and he termed the veto "a shield, and not a sword." Daniel Kelso, a Democrat, approved giving the executive a suspensive veto—subject to override by a majority of the members of both houses. He said: "it is easier to corrupt one man, than it is to corrupt an hundred."[64] As the discussion continued it became apparent that most of the delegates supported the suspensive veto, and they also wanted to compel the governor to give his objections to bills he declined to sign. Thus, the delegates provided that *a majority of the members* in both houses could override a veto. But if a bill presented to the governor was not signed and returned "within three days, Sundays excepted, . . . it shall be a law, without his signature, unless the general adjournment" prevents its return to the General Assembly. If a bill's return was so prevented, "it shall be a law, unless the Governor, within five days next after such adjournment" file it, "with his objections thereto" with the secretary of state who would lay it before the next session of the General Assembly. Moreover, no bill could be presented "within two days next previous" to the final adjournment of a session.[65]

Meanwhile, the Committee on State Officers other than the Executive and Judiciary submitted sections regarding the treasurer, auditor, and secretary of state. Its report, the first of such reports from the standing committees, called for their election by the voters of the state, for terms of two years with eligibility limited to four years in any period of six years.[66] All three officials had been elected by joint vote of the General Assembly under the Constitution of 1816, but the delegates generally presumed that they would be chosen by the electorate. There was, however, considerable disagreement whether they should serve for two or four years, and be eligible for indefinite reelection. Initially the delegates, by the substantial margin of 76 to 56, approved a four year term for the secretary. But immediately it became apparent that there was much sentiment for short terms and against indefinite tenure. William C. Foster, a Democrat, stated that "rotation in office . . . was a good democratic doctrine, but the worst of it was, it was seldom carried out." Foster suggested that "all administrative officers" be elected for a "certain term" and be ineligible for reelection. Samuel Hall, a Whig, asserted that "There is nothing more corrupting than money," for which "The only safe remedy is, strict accountability, short term of office, and ineligibility." If you keep a man in office for a long time, Hall said, he becomes dependent upon it for his support, is rendered incapable of "following any occupation," and thus "becomes a mere drone in the body politic." James G. Read, a Democrat and chair of the committee that made the report, declared: "The more frequently these elections came before the people the more faithfully would the incumbents . . . administer their necessary duties." David M. Dobson, a Democrat, emphasized that "because the Treasurer controls, annually, some eight hundred thousand dollars of the public money—which in four years amounts to nearly two millions—," he was "not willing that he should have so long a term as four years." The treasurer "might not venture anything wrong for the first, second, or third years," but in the fourth he might venture into a "well matured" speculation. Democrat John Pettit urged that the governor, lieutenant governor, secretary, treasurer, and auditor all serve four year terms. If you tell an incumbent that no matter "however faithful and competent" he might be that he cannot be reelected, Pettit suggested, this would tend to "produce a stupor, lethargy, negligence, and want of readiness to serve the people" that ought not be tolerated. He added: "the prospect of a re-election . . . is often the greatest incentive of the faithful discharge of the proper functions and duties of" an office. Johnson Watts, a Whig, argued that short terms would prevent a "poor man, however competent, from competing with his more wealthy neighbor" because of the expense of canvassing the state. Moreover, "no poor man, whatever his abilities," would risk the cost of seeking an office for a short term.[67] After several days of debate the delegates approved, by the decisive count of 90 to 7, that the secretary, treasurer, and auditor should serve two year terms, with eligibility for four years in any period of six years.[68]

The delegates made generally modest changes in the judicial department as they had for the executive branch. In both instances the increase in popular election of officials was a major change. On November 7, one month after the convention began, the Committee on the Organization of the Courts of Justice, chaired by John Pettit, a Democrat, submitted three reports for review regarding the judicial department. The principal report, save for its augmented emphasis on popular election of judges, closely resembled the judicial article of the Constitution of 1816 with its emphasis on vesting the judicial power of the state in a Supreme Court, circuit courts, and local justice of the peace courts. One of the other reports called for the election of an attorney general as a state official, and the election of a prosecuting attorney for each judicial circuit. The other minority report asked that there be five members of the Supreme Court, all to be elected by the voters of the state, whereas the principal report made each judge elected by voters in separate districts. This report also asked that the clerk of the Supreme Court be elected by the voters of the state, not by the court as proposed in the principal report.[69]

The convention made two important changes about the number of Supreme Court judges and how they would be chosen. The Constitution of 1816 had provided for three judges, to be named by the governor with the approval of the Senate. Christian C. Nave, a Democrat, moved that there be from three to five judges, each elected by the voters in separate districts, with the number of judges left to the discretion of the legislature. Delegates were divided whether the number should be increased, but with modest discussion approved Nave's proposal by the substantial majority of 67 to 40.[70] John Pettit persistently urged that the Supreme judges be elected by all the voters of the state. Each judge on the court, Pettit said, "represents the whole people of the State." Pettit asserted: "It is a mockery to tell me that you will elect a man in one district who is to administer laws for the whole State. As well might you elect a Governor by the votes of one district. As well might you elect a Circuit Judge, not by the votes of his circuit, but of the county in which he lives. Who would tolerate the idea?" These remarks were made after Pettit's amendment therefor had been tabled by the decisive margin of 75 to 47. But after Pettit's renewed appeal for electing the judges by all the voters, the delegates, by a 66 to 57 vote, asked his committee to make the change he had vigorously supported. So amended, this section passed by a count of 81 to 49.[71] It provided for from three to five Supreme judges, elected by the voters of the state, for terms of six years with no restriction against reelection. There were, however, to be as many judicial districts as judges, with each a resident of one of them.[72]

The principal report of the Committee on the Organization of the Courts of Justice also suggested that the Supreme Court name its clerk, sheriff, and the reporter of its decisions. But no member of the court could serve as its reporter. A minority report, which Pettit and two other members submitted, recommended that the clerk be elected by the voters of the state. "The office of clerk of the Supreme Court," Pettit said, "is a very important and lucrative one, and I hope that the clerk, like the judges, may be put before the people to be elected." William McKee Dunn, a Whig, considered it "very unnecessary to trouble the people with the election of the Clerk of the Supreme Court." With so many officers being made "elected by the voters," Dunn said, "the ballots at some of our general elections will be near a yard long." On motion of Pettit the delegates approved popular election of the clerk, then passed this item without a roll call vote.[73] Beattie McClelland, a Democrat, moved that the sheriff of the Supreme Court be elected by the voters of the state, rather than by its judges, but this section was quickly tabled and left unchanged.[74] The principal report from the Committee on the Organization of the Courts of Justice made the reporter of Supreme Court decisions an appointee of the court, with the proviso that no judge of the court could serve as such. McClelland proposed that the reporter be elected by the voters of the state. David Kilgore, a Whig, responded: "Oh no! That is a little too democratic. A little democracy is well enough, but that is going too far. It is buncombe up to the very hubs." McClelland's proposal was rejected by a count of 66 to 56. The convention, however, left this item for legislative discretion by passing a section requiring it to pass a law for speedy publications of the court's decisions, with the proviso that no judge of the court could serve as a reporter.[75] Elias S. Terry, a Whig, obtained approval for his resolution that the Committee on the Organization of the Courts of Justice consider the expediency of inserting constitutional provisions for an attorney general and a prosecuting attorney for each judicial circuit. As a member of this committee he submitted a minority report to make these offices mandatory, but his proposal was rejected.[76] Henry P. Thornton, also a Whig, unsuccessfully sought to have the office of attorney general required by the constitution. He suggested that this official could also serve as reporter for the Supreme Court. Thornton argued that "extravagant fees" had been paid lawyers who defended the state in court, including one thousand dollars paid two lawyers "for simply saying that the suit should be dismissed."[77]

The circuit courts were an extremely important part of the pioneer judicial system. The Constitution of 1816 had provided for three judicial circuits, with others to be added when the legislature deemed them desirable. The voters of every county elected two associate judges, and the General Assembly in joint ballot elected a president judge who rode the circuit from county to county serving with the associate judges in his circuit. All these judges were chosen for seven year terms with no limitation about additional terms. The Committee on the Organization of the Courts of Justice, in its principal report, suggested that the voters of each judicial circuit elect a judge who would hold court at least three times annually in each county thereof. He would serve for six years, with no restriction on reelection. Nothing was said about associate justices for each county. At least twenty circuits were suggested, leaving the legislature the authority to increase them as needed.[78] The delegates left the number of judicial circuits and terms of court annually to legislative discretion by leaving them unprovided for. But they approved the items about how judges should be elected and their tenure. Some efforts, however, were made to restrict their term to four years and to prohibit unrestricted reelection.[79] Especially vigorous attempts were made by William Steele Holman, a Democrat, and others to have the circuit judge also serve as the probate judge. Holman, who had been a probate judge, branded the probate system since statehood "supremely objectionable" and "a crying evil" of the judicial system. Holman admitted that perhaps most probate judges were honest, but "competency as well as honesty" was needed, and this made necessary "a competent salary for" the judges. Alvin P. Hovey, a Democrat, agreed that probate judges were "generally honest and upright," but few of them "make any pretensions to legal acquirements . . . ." The state had refused to pay them "anything like a fair compensation" and "they . . . do what they think is right, but every lawyer knows that there is more fraud and rascality, and more wrong done in these courts to the helpless, the widow, and the orphan, than has been perpetrated in all other courts put together." David Kilgore, a Whig, asserted that the probate system "is calculated not only to unsettle land titles, but to tolerate frauds of the most abominable character." But despite such calls for reform of the probate system, it was left for the legislature to deal with as one of the "inferior Courts" it might establish.[80]

Although Elias S. Terry, a Whig, was unable to have the office of attorney general inserted in the new constitution, his effort to have a prosecuting attorney required for each district of the circuit courts was approved. Thus, the new constitution mandated a prosecuting attorney for each circuit court, to serve terms of two years, and be elected by the voters of the circuit. An amendment to require such an official for each county was tabled by the decisive vote of 93 to 23.[81]

The justice of the peace courts were continued much as they had been under the Constitution of 1816. The Committee on County and Township Organization, chaired by Thomas Smith, a Democrat, recommended that "a competent number of justices of the peace" be elected by the voters of each township for terms of four years. No limitation was suggested regarding reelection. An amendment offered by James W. Borden, a Democrat, that there be three justices for every township, with one elected annually, was rejected without a roll call vote. The provisions regarding the number of justices, their terms, and eligibility for reelection were approved as recommended by the committee with the near unanimous vote of 114 to 1.[82]

As the convention neared adjournment, Samuel Frisbie, a Whig and a lawyer, and William C. Foster, a Democrat and a physician, introduced separate resolutions asking that all white, male voters "of good moral character" be "permitted" to practice law in any of the courts of the state. On January 27, as the convention neared adjournment, James W. Borden, a Democrat and a merchant who was chair of the Committee on the Practice of

Law and Law Reform, submitted such a section for consideration by the delegates.[83] Daniel Kelso, a Democrat and a lawyer, spoke to this item with tongue-in-cheek, saying: "The more pettifoggers we can get into our courts, the more money your good lawyers will make. I am quite willing that every man should practice law. And if there are not enough men to break down the bar by their practice, let the women have a chance at it, too." He suggested that this matter should be left to the "wisdom and judgment" of the legislature. Foster observed that when he arrived in Indiana "many years ago, no one was permitted to practice medicine," unless a university graduate or licensed by medical institutes of the state. But the law had been repealed, and "now every one could practice in the medical profession, no matter of what grade, regulars, Homoepathists, Thompsonians, or Allopathists." Moreover, the former custom that divinity students not only "receive an education in divinity, but . . . reside for some years at a theological Seminary or university" was no longer required. In other states, Foster explained, "the practice of the law had been thrown open to all persons of good moral character." Viewing medicine, divinity, and law as "the three liberal professions," he urged that law "like medicine and divinity" be made open to all. Amid laughter, Kelso asked for a direct and unencumbered vote on this question "so that all the quacks that cannot make a living by practicing medicine may resort to the law, and thereby save themselves from becoming paupers and chargeable upon the county." After such comments had been exchanged, the section was adopted by the overwhelming vote of 84 to 27. This constitutional provision, in effect until 1972, became a hindrance to the improvement of the caliber of Hoosier lawyers. Thus, as Logan Esarey used to say to students, in his subtle and amusing manner, for a long time "good moral character" was the same basic requirement for Indiana lawyers and saloon keepers![84]

While the delegates revised the *structure or machinery* of state government and *how it should be operated*, they also gave much time to establishing guidelines concerning *what government should and should not do*. Various delegates, Whigs as well as Democrats, emphasized the need for strict limitations on state debt and a return to economic laissez faire. Daniel Read, a staunch Jacksonian Democrat and a professor at Indiana University, commented: "If there is a single proposition settled beyond all manner of controversy, . . . it is this, that government should not in its own capacity, nor by a partnership with individuals, become an agent in business operations, except so far as required for the mere purposes of government." "Government, sir," Read said, "has no capacity to make canals, to construct turnpikes or railroads, deal in stocks, or to enact the banker." As often as the state becomes "entangled in any such operations, it . . . is sure, sooner or later, to be cheated, plundered, victimized." According to Read, "Business, when left open to private enterprise, regulates itself. Competition soon reduces profits to a just standard." Another Democrat, Robert Dale Owen, declared: "One generation of men have no moral right to contract a public debt so vast that the next generation, and perhaps that which follows it, shall be loaded down with taxes, to discharge the interest and repay the capital." John B. Niles, a Whig, expressed the opinion "that all works of real importance can be effected by means of individual or associated wealth and enterprise." Niles explained: "I hold that a government should confine its operations as far [as] possible, within its own necessary and appropriate sphere—throwing its protection over all alike—encouraging every useful enterprize, but leaving to the people, in their private capacity, whatever they are capable of doing." Niles commented: "The history of our own attempt to make ourselves rich and prosperous, by borrowing money to improve the State, is but too fresh in all our recollections." Another Whig, William McKee Dunn, termed experience "a hard school" whose "lessons are not easily forgotten. The people of Indiana have learned a lesson in this school that will not be forgotten for many generations yet to come. Whatever other follies they may commit there is but little danger of their recklessly running into debt." But James Rariden, also a Whig, though he agreed that Indiana had "acted imprudently, extravagantly, and unwisely," emphasized that they who "come after us are our debtors, and not we theirs . . . ." Rariden explained: "We found this whole country a wilderness, and we shall leave it a paradise, except the debt upon it. Let posterity give us credit for what we have done—for our railroads, our canals, our fine meeting houses, and seminaries of learning, and private dwellings, and all the other accompaniments of the highest civilization and internal facilities, . . . without taking into account the enhanced value we have given to the soil."[85]

On October 26, the Committee on State Debt and Public Works, chaired by Samuel Hall, a Whig, reported an article the second section of which authorized the General Assembly to contract debts, to repel invasion, suppress insurrection, and provide for the public defense if hostilities threatened. Debts were also allowed "to meet casual deficits or failures in the revenue, for the purpose of paying the interest on the State debt; but such debt" could never exceed $100,000.[86] The delegates struck out this sum, and they provided that this debt must never exceed "'The amount of such deficit.'" So amended, it passed by the thumping margin of 111 to 6.[87]

Meanwhile, consideration had been given to a third section which prohibited any debt, other than for "the purposes mentioned" in the second section unless accompanied by a tax levy sufficient to pay the principal and interest thereon within twenty-five years. The levy therefor would become effective only if approved by "a majority of all the votes cast for or against it" at a general election. By a count of 65 to 53, this section was amended to provide that no state debt could be contracted "except for the purposes mentioned" in the previous section as approved.[88]

The strong sentiment for economic laissez faire helped generate a long and meandering debate about banking. As noted in an earlier chapter, by the forties there was growing support for free or general banking. But there continued to be a considerable no bank element. The Second State Bank, roughly half owned by the state, had become strong and profitable.[89] On November 5, Allen Hamilton, a Whig who chaired the Committee on Currency and Banking, reported various proposals about banking for *consideration* by the convention. In submitting this report Hamilton explained that at first "he did not entirely approve of it, nor did a majority of the committee." Nevertheless, it was "submitted in the belief that it will more nearly meet with the approbation of the Convention than any other proposition which would be agreed upon by a majority of the committee." Two proposals were termed majority reports. One called for free banking, subject to several restrictions. The second merely stated: "'The State shall not be a stockholder in any bank, after the expiration of the charter of the present State bank.'" Three reports were labeled minority reports. One of them authorized establishment of a State Bank and branches, after expiration of the charter of the Second State Bank, subject to restrictions, including one which prohibited the state from owning stock therein. A second minority report, submitted by Franklin Hardin, a Democrat, prohibited banking unless the majority of all votes cast at a general election gave the legislature power to grant charters or pass a general banking law; and then only if the ensuing legislation was likewise approved by a majority of all votes cast at a general election. A third minority report signed by John P. Dunn and Johnson Watts, the former a Democrat and the latter a Whig, presented a hodgepodge of restrictions which, if approved, seemingly might have made establishment of banks impossible.[90] As the various reports and related items were discussed, it became apparent that the delegates were divided among those who opposed all banks, those who approved free or general banking, and those who preferred a State Bank and branches.[91] Some of the delegates who preferred a State Bank explained that they wanted such an institution much modified from the Second State Bank. And some who advocated free banking urged significant restrictions as a prerequisite therefor. Soon, it became apparent that a significant majority of the delegates agreed that banks were essential, and various of them contended that Indiana needed a considerable increase in capital invested in banking. Part of those who wanted augmented capital argued that free banks and a State Bank and branches could not coexist, but other proponents of banks contended that coexistence was both possible and desirable. The prolonged and comprehensive discussion of banking nearly all occurred during January.[92] Meantime, the decision of the convention that the state could not borrow money, except to meet casual deficits and pay interest on the state debt, made it impossible for the state to purchase stock in a

State Bank and branches after the expiration of the charter of the Second State Bank.[93]

But so long as the issue was free banking versus a State Bank and branches, with both systems entirely owned by private capital, the no bank men could prevent the adoption of either system by voting against first one side and then the other. On January 3, Chairman Hamilton, a Whig, appealed for compromise "on some middle ground" for the authorization of both free banking and a State Bank and branches, both wholly owned by private capital. He suggested that more banking capital was needed, and the two systems could well exist together. Hamilton wanted appropriate safeguards required of all banking, and he would leave some discretion to the legislature. Will the decision about the state's currency "be one of our own formation," Hamilton asked, "or will we take it from institutions formed by surrounding states?" Six days later Schuyler Colfax, a Whig who favored free banking, moved the adoption of a section authorizing both free banking and a State Bank and branches, on much the same terms as Hamilton had suggested, but his amendment was tabled by a tally of 90 to 47.[94] Then on January 14 Colfax commented that perhaps "all hopes of a compromise upon this question are now gone." He explained: "So closely divided are the free bank and State Bank parties, that the no bankers have upon every vote the balance of power, and they use it very impartially to cut the throats of both systems." Colfax noted that "but a few minutes since" the "State Bankers" had "applauded over a victory won over the free bankers by the aid of the anti-bank delegates." He warned that before permitting "all the banking privileges of this great State by a single institution" the free bankers, aided by the no bank men, would require restrictions that would make the bill holder "under such system safe beyond all peradventure." The Colfax "compromise" was offered as an amendment to an amendment which proposed the kind of restrictions which were expected to make the bill holder safe "beyond all peradventure." His amendment was then adopted by the large majority of 86 to 52, then the restrictive amendment, so amended, was adopted by the vote of 79 to 57. During the ensuing week the delegates completed their consideration of items regarding banking. As adopted, the General Assembly had the discretion of enacting either free bank or state and branch banking, or the two systems concurrently, or no banking.[95]

While the delegates had much difficulty agreeing on provisions about banking, they were for the most part agreed that the state should give increased support to public education. Their concern, however, principally involved common school or elementary education. On December 11, about two months after the convention began, John I. Morrison, a Democrat, submitted a report from the Committee on Education. This report called for "a general and uniform system of common schools, wherein tuition, as soon as circumstances will permit, shall be gratis, and equally open to all." Various special funds, including that for the support of county seminaries, were to be combined into a "perpetual" fund for the support of common schools. To provide "efficient and well qualified teachers" for the "common schools," it would be the "duty of the General Assembly" to establish "a normal school" at the state university. The county seminaries were to be abolished, and the money from their sale added to the Common School Fund. No provision was indicated for secondary education, but the proceeds from the University Fund, derived from land granted by the federal government, were to remain "inviolate" and be applied to the maintenance of the state university.[96] When section 1, about the duty of the General Assembly to establish a general and uniform system of common schools, came up for discussion James R. M. Bryant, a Whig, explained that the "'as soon as circumstances will permit'" phrase, from the old constitution, had been inadvertently included. These words were deleted, and the section was adopted without a roll call vote.[97] Section 4, which detailed the funds to be combined into the Common School Fund, was made a part of the constitution by a vote of 112 to 8.[98] Morrison's proposal that the voters elect a state superintendent of public instruction for terms of two years, despite substantial objection, was adopted. Daniel Read, a professor at Indiana University, hoped that one of Indiana's "ablest men" would become superintendent and "do for Indiana the same work which Mann, Barnard, Mayhew, and others, have done for their respective States." John I. Morrison declared that the "very salvation" of Indiana's "educational system" depended upon such an official. Morrison explained: "it must be confessed that Indiana is much behind many of her sister States, in educational statistics. The startling facts revealed by the late census [1850], that we have upwards of seventy thousand persons in our midst, over twenty-one years of age, unable to read and write, shows that more efficient measures should be adopted in order to save the youth of the State, thousands of whom are now growing up without any opportunities of instruction from swelling this list at a succeeding census."[99]

The high priority given common schools was in sharp contrast to that given higher education. Section 2, regarding a "normal school" at Indiana University, was quickly tabled and then ignored.[100] Section 3, which proposed that the University Fund "shall forever remain inviolate" for use of a state university, was likewise quickly tabled by the extremely close vote of 62 to 61. But immediately John Pettit, a Democrat, introduced section 12, which asserted that "All trust funds . . . shall be faithfully applied to the purposes for which the trust was created."[101] Shortly after the convention began, Joseph Ristine, a Democrat, had obtained approval of a resolution instructing the Committee on Education to enquire into the "expediency of abolishing the present county seminary system, and also of the State University," with the constitution amended "to compel" the legislature to sell their properties and "apply the proceeds thereof to the use of common schools." As the discussion of section 12 continued, Indiana University was both strongly attacked and strongly defended. Erastus K. Bascom, a Democrat, hoped that use of the University Fund could be left to the discretion of the legislature "so that the fund may not be expended in keeping a few professors in office, doing nothing." But he was "willing to sustain the institution so long as it performs its work aright." Another Democrat, George G. Shoup, suggested that Indiana had a "number of colleges" supported by "individual enterprize" which were "all in a healthy and prosperous condition." Since some of them could not "be surpassed, East or West," there was no "great necessity for a State University," Shoup said. "To educate the children of our State to that of a common school education, is all that we can hope to accomplish at the public expense," he asserted. Beattie McClelland, a Democrat, contended that Indiana University was only "free to those children whose parents are able to pay their board at Bloomington"; and he did not "want this institution to be kept up for foreign students, students coming from other States, when we have so many poor young men in our own State unable to pay their way so as to derive any benefit from this institution."[102]

The university, however, was not without its advocates. Daniel Read, a Democrat and professor at the university, reported that the University Fund yielded some $4,000 yearly, none of which was derived from any gift of the state. Rather than leave the fund to the discretion of the legislature, Read said it would be "better —far better" to strike down the institution at once. From this fund, Read stated: "You have an institution of learning, with suitable buildings, organized with different departments of instruction," which had an average of 180 students for the previous seven years, of which "sixty, from different counties, receive their tuition free of all charges." The professor noted that among the delegates in the convention and members of the legislature "you find those who have received their education in the University. You cannot go into any body of men, whether professional, political, or literary, in this State, in which you will not find the sons of your University." Read commended the colleges of the state supported by religious groups. "There is room and work for all," he said. "Besides, the State University—not claimed as its own by any denomination—is needed to fill precisely the ground which it occupies." James R. M. Bryant, a Whig, asserted that the framers of the existing constitution in providing "for a general system, ascending in a regular gradation from township schools to a State University" had given "us the germ of a perfect system." Bryant declared: "You might as well attempt to establish a planetary system, without a sun and centre, as to expect that the lower grades of education can flourish, whilst the higher are neglected, or discarded." And "Those who hope to assist common schools by the abolition of colleges," Bryant warned, "are mistaken—sadly mistaken."[103] As the convention neared its adjournment, a motion of Hiram Allen, a Whig, to instruct the Committee on Education to report in favor of seeking the assent of Congress to give the General Assembly "power to convert the State University trust fund to common school education," was defeated by the close vote of 64 to 58. Since the Constitution of 1851 makes no mention of Indiana University, the constitutional basis for its trust fund, derived from the sale of land donated by the federal government, rests with the section about trust funds, offered by John Pettit, which was adopted by a count of 73 to 48 following the defeat of Allen's amendment.[104]

While the delegates were strongly for an increase in financial support for common schools, they were vigorously opposed to further immigration of blacks to the state. Near the end of October, the Committee on the Rights and Privileges of the Inhabitants of the State, chaired by Robert Dale Owen, a Democrat, reported four sections for the consideration of delegates. The three initial sections proposed positive safeguards about personal rights and privileges. But the fourth section mandated the first legislative session, after adoption of the new constitution, to "pass laws prohibiting *Negroes* and *Mulattoes* from coming into or settling in this State; and prohibiting any negro or mulatto from purchasing or otherwise acquiring real estate hereafter."[105] This section ignited a discussion about blacks and mulattoes which reflected the intense prejudice against them and vigorous opposition of the large majority of Hoosiers to their presence in the state. As the discussion continued for several days during November, it became evident that the majority of the delegates also wanted to persuade the blacks and mulattoes within the state, numbering 11,262 according to the federal census of 1850, to leave Indiana. But a minority of the delegates insisted that there were various rights and privileges which blacks and mulattoes were entitled to, though apparently no delegate asked that they be given the same rights and privileges granted whites.[106]

The discussion about section 4 during November illustrates the intensity of the mind-set against blacks and mulattoes, and also the limited degree of rights and privileges which some delegates considered them entitled to. John B. Howe, a Whig from LaGrange County, urged that the entire section be deleted. The Whig delegate from the most northern part of Indiana contended that the section "is not only opposed to the fundamental principles of liberty, justice, and equality, but . . . it is in defiance of the Constitution of the United States itself." He contended that since blacks were recognized as citizens in some states, then, under the federal constitution, they had rights which other states must respect. Howe observed that "a majority in a republic" can "inflict as much injustice and oppression upon the minority, as a despot on his throne upon his subjects." Such a provision, Howe explained, "might suit the genius of a despotic government, but it does not suit the *free governments* of the Anglo-Saxon race." Milton Gregg, a Whig from Madison in southern Indiana, wanted to replace the section with one stating "'all men are born equally free and independent,'" and thus have the basic rights of "'enjoying and defending life and liberty, and of acquiring, possessing, and protecting property, and pursuing and obtaining happiness and safety.'" If "You take away from any man, . . . white or black, the power to acquire and possess property," Gregg suggested, "You remove from him all hope of ever acquiring a little spot of earth that he can call his own, and upon which he can erect his hut, to protect his wife and his little ones from the peltings of the pitiless storm." The proposed policy, he added, would "legislate the colored population among us into pauperism and crime, instead of making them good and useful members of the community in which they live." Gregg commended the blacks of Madison, many of whom he knew, for their "sober and industrious habits," high moral character, and their "regard for truth and veracity" that "might well serve as models for others in higher life." He said since they had been brought from Africa "in chains" against their will, "we are bound by all the dictates of humanity, to afford them shelter and protection, or furnish the means to carry them back to their own native home in Africa." Still another Whig, Schuyler Colfax of South Bend, stated: "I shall not deny, that the black race of this country is debased, that as a class they are inferior to the

whites, that they are poor, weak, and to some extent degraded."
But "The same God who made you and I, deemed it expedient in
his wisdom, to create them also." Colfax stated that he neither
asked nor expected any "extension of their privileges, but we ask
you to treat them with humanity, and not to crush them as you
would vermin out of your sight." Nonetheless, the Whig delegate
hailed the colonization movement to return the "black population" to their native Africa so that "civilization and Christianity
will illumine its dark interior." As the views and comments of
Howe, Gregg, and Colfax indicate none of them urged full citi-
zenship and equality for Indiana's black population.[107]

But there was significant difference between the views of the
three Whig delegates and that of many other delegates. William
C. Foster, a Democrat from Monroe County, wanted a provision
in the constitution providing that "'any free negro or mulatto
hereafter,'" trying to settle in the state would be "'punished by
confinement in the county jail, or being farmed out to the highest bidder for the term of six months, and the proceeds donated to
the Colonization Society, in trust for the benefit of those negroes
in this State who are willing to emigrate to Liberia.'" Illinois had
already "forbidden" blacks to enter her borders, and Ohio would
"unquestionably do the same," Foster said, and "Unless we protect ourselves, the result will be, that Indiana will be the great
refuge of all the worthless, the halt, the maimed, and the blind negroes that are to be found in the Southern States." He added:
"We cannot therefore be charged with inhumanity in preventing
our State from being overrun with these vermin—for I say they
are vermin, and I know it. [Laughter.]" Foster said he knew "from
Holy Writ that the negro race, whether they belong to the same
race as we do or to a higher order of animals, are under the ban of
Heaven—a curse that was pronounced upon them by Almighty
God still remains upon them." James Rariden, a Whig from
Wayne County, claimed that there was "a higher law" regarding
"the negro population, than the Constitutional law; a feeling of
pride that elevates the white man above the black man." If blacks
persisted in coming to Indiana, Rariden wanted the legislature to
have the power to require that "they should be sold or appren-

ticed, till the amount of their wages should be sufficient to send them to Liberia." John Pettit, a Democrat from Tippecanoe County, insisted that "no two distinct races" can live together harmoniously. Pettit stated that he would vote to prevent blacks from coming to the state, but if those here and their descendants were allowed to remain, he wanted to encourage them to acquire property. He explained that if a body of men "so entirely disfranchised as to have no interest in the harmony, well-being, and prosperity of the community"; paying no taxes and having no stake in the country, "fires may rage in your towns and villages, without an effort, on their part, to save your property." But, "if you induce them to acquire property beside you, they will always . . . be ready to contribute their aid in the protection of your property. They would then have an inducement to aid in suppressing riots and disorders; you would make them better citizens and safer neighbors." Joseph Robinson, a Whig from Decatur County, declared that "in the eyes of the great Creator of the Universe," the blacks and mulattoes "are as good as we are." Had they "voluntarily obtruded themselves upon us, . . . then might gentlemen stand up and talk here about the line of separation, and about their being brutes and below the level of civilization." But since "we have torn them from their families and chained them here in servitude, . . . I do think that it comes with an ill grace from any member of this Convention, to talk about a distinction which God himself does not recognize." Robinson said "the two races can never live together," and he hoped they could never mix or amalgamate. Though willing to prohibit their further immigration and holding of property, the Whig delegate asserted that "it would be an act of injustice and inhumanity . . . wholly beneath a Christian people" to say to a man who had honestly acquired his property, paid taxes, cleared the land, and improved the country that "'we will now take from you these rights.' Sir, I think we ought to get along with as many of this class of people we have now got, in the best way we can."[108]

As the preceding paragraphs indicate there were significant differences among delegates about what should and what should not be done regarding blacks and mulattoes. It seems that no delegate advocated full equality of rights and privileges, nor was there any consensus about what rights and privileges should be safeguarded. Before, during, and after the November discussion about blacks and mulattoes, memorials were received about restrictions desired and rights favored for them. Restrictions sought included: prohibition of their further settlement in the state, deny them suffrage, prevent them from testifying against whites, and appropriate money for their "gradual" colonization. Rights sought embraced: give blacks the same rights and privileges enjoyed by whites, allow testimony in courts of justice, permit acquisition and holding of real estate, and continued immigration to Indiana. The request for "same rights and privileges" probably meant different things to various individuals, but likely included the right of suffrage and access to education in some of the memorials. Part of the petitions for additional rights came from "people of color" or blacks, but regardless of the source it seems doubtful whether they had much effect upon the decisions of the delegates.[109]

As the November phase of the discussion neared its conclusion, Phineas M. Kent, a Democrat from Floyd County, asked that section 4, as reported by the Committee on the Rights and Privileges of the Inhabitants of the State, be referred to a select committee of one from each congressional district "with instructions to inquire into the best means of ultimately separating the white and colored races in Indiana; and also into the expediency of incorporating in one article all Constitutional provisions relative to negroes and mulattoes, and submitting the same separately to the people." Kent's proposal and related items were considered at length on November 18, 19, and 20, on which date the delegates agreed by a vote of 74 to 48 to refer section 4 to a select committee as suggested by Kent. Then the instructions, as proposed by Kent, were rejected by a tally of 63 to 60. Some efforts to instruct the committee for particular items were then either rejected or tabled; and a resolution of Robert Dale Owen that "all sections heretofore reported to this Convention relative to negroes and mulattoes" were referred to the select committee chaired by Kent.[110] On January 13, some seven weeks later, the select committee, composed of five Democrats and five Whigs, submitted six sections and recommended "their passage." The delegates briefly renewed this discussion about blacks and mulattoes, covering much the same items they had in November, but with increased emphasis on colonizing them in Africa or elsewhere.[111]

The six sections were approved with some modifications. Section 1, stating that "No negro or mulatto shall come into and settle in this State after the adoption of this Constitution," was adopted by a count of 91 to 40. Democrats sustained exclusion by more than a three to one margin, Whigs by about one and a half to one.[112] Section 2, making contracts with blacks who entered illegally void; and subjecting persons who employed or encouraged them to remain in the state subject to be fined for from $10 to $500 was adopted by a tally of 78 to 59.[113] But the third section, mandating an annual appropriation, of an unspecified sum, "for the gradual colonization of negroes and their descendants" in the state at the time of the adoption of the new constitution was modified. An amendment, approved without a roll call vote, provided that fines collected for violation of legislation concerning the sections adopted be used to colonize such blacks and mulattoes in the state as were willing to emigrate. So amended the section was adopted 100 to 32. Democrats supported this item by a little more than a four to one margin, the Whigs approved it by just over a two to one edge.[114] Section 4, denying blacks the right to acquire or have any interest in real estate, "otherwise than by descent" after 1860, was tabled and thus defeated by a vote of 77 to 54.[115] Section 5, mandating the General Assembly to pass laws carrying out the provisions of the sections adopted, was approved without a roll call vote.[116] Section 6 made the adoption of the sections subject to approval of the voters, voting on it as an item separate from the constitution, was adopted 80 to 54.[117] These provisions, imbedded in the Constitution of 1851 by the overwhelming endorsement of the voters, plus exclusion of blacks and mulattoes from suffrage and the militia, reflect the approximate peak of antiblack sentiment, prejudice, and discrimination in Indiana.[118]

Deciding how the constitution could be changed caused much less discussion than that about the status of blacks and mulattoes.

On January 16, the Committee on Future Amendments to the Constitution submitted two sections whose passage it recommended. Section 1 empowered the General Assembly, by a two-thirds vote of all members in both houses, to recommend the calling of a constitutional convention. If a majority of the voters taking part in the next general election favored a convention, the ensuing legislative session was required to "call a Convention for the purpose of revising, altering or amending" the constitution. Section 2 authorized the General Assembly, by a vote of a two-thirds majority of all members of both houses, to initiate suggested amendments. If at the next regular legislative session both houses concurred therewith, by a majority vote of all members of both houses, such amendments would be submitted to the voters for their approval or rejection at the next general election. If a majority of all participating voters approved the amendments, they became "a part of the Constitution."[119] About one month earlier, James G. Read, a Democrat, had offered a plan very similar to section 2 as reported by the committee. In discussing Read's proposal, Alexander C. Stevenson, a Whig, commented that it would "take this Convention at least four months" to "remodel the whole Constitution." But had there been a provision of the kind Read proposed "in the old Constitution, the necessary amendments might have been made with a very trifling expense." Stevenson explained that there was "a similar provision in the Constitution of the United States," and such a provision had "been adopted by a number of the States." Read commented that if the existing constitution had had such a provision, the state would not have had to spend "some eighty thousand dollars" in the calling of this convention. Robert Dale Owen, a Democrat, agreed with Read and Stevenson that "some such provision" should be adopted, however, he strongly opposed Read's restriction that the legislature could submit amendments only at ten year intervals. Christopher C. Graham and James W. Borden, both Democrats, strongly opposed empowering the General Assembly to propose amendments. Graham suggested that a referendum concerning a constitutional convention be held at ten or fifteen year intervals, while Borden proposed every tenth year.[120]

When sections 1 and 2, as reported by the committee, came up for discussion they were quickly resolved. Section 1, concerning a constitutional convention, was immediately tabled without discussion and without any roll call vote thereon. Section 2, regarding amendments being proposed by the General Assembly, was stricken out per an amendment offered by Stevenson and Owen. In its place, their amendment proposed that a majority vote of the members of both houses, rather than a two-thirds vote, be required to initiate amendments. It also omitted the item that amendments be voted on separately, and the one against considering new amendments while other amendments were pending. The Stevenson-Owen amendment was approved by a count of 78 to 48, then adopted, without change, as part of the constitution by a vote of 77 to 45.[121] But the next day the convention, without a roll call vote, approved a new section which included the two items that had been deleted, then adopted it as part of the constitution by a count of 100 to 24.[122] Various delegates made unsuccessful efforts to have an express provision for calling a constitutional convention adopted, and some delegates desired this as the only way to make changes in the constitution. John Pettit, a Democrat, appropriately reminded the delegates that "All experience shows us that the people of the several States of the Union will amend the Constitutions of their States whenever and in whatever mode they see fit."[123] Thus, while the Constitution of 1816 made no express provision for change except by a constitutional convention, the Constitution of 1851 made no express provision for change except by amendments proposed by the General Assembly and approved by the voters at a general election.

A few days before adjournment on February 10, the convention mandated that the new constitution, if adopted, become effective November 1, 1851. It also mandated that the article about black exclusion and colonization be voted on as a "distinct proposition," with no other part so submitted.[124] Although there had been far more Democratic than Whig delegates, the Constitution of 1851 resulted from considerable bipartisan input and support. The Indianapolis *Indiana State Sentinel*, leading Democratic paper of the state, pronounced the new constitution "the very best Constitution ever framed by a free people"; and predicted its adoption "by

a large majority on the first Monday in August," 1851. The editor of the Indianapolis *Indiana State Journal,* premier Whig organ
of Indiana, said the constitution "contained much that is objectionable," but had "so many redeeming features" that he would
vote for it, trusting that its errors would be corrected by "its future amendment." This Whig editor emphasized that he would
vote against the exclusion of blacks "as contrary to the spirit
which should characterize the Christian age in which we live."
The *Indiana State Sentinel,* however, vigorously supported exclusion of blacks and their colonization elsewhere. The Indianapolis
Indiana Statesman, a Democratic organ with free soil sympathies,
concluded that the constitution's "redeeming qualities" overbal-
anced its "defects," and forecast its adoption "by at least a two
thirds vote."[125]

The referendum on August 4, 1851, gave an overwhelming
verdict for the new constitution. Official returns from all ninety-
one counties yielded 113,230 ballots for and 27,638 against adoption, thus 80.38 percent of the voters supported the new document. The electorate gave an even larger percentage of its vote
for black exclusion and colonization. Official returns from the
ninety-one counties provided 113,828 ballots for these items and
only 21,873 against them. Statewide, 83.88 percent of the vote approved the article containing these efforts to prevent further immigration of blacks to the state and to persuade those already resident in the state to emigrate elsewhere.[126]

Many changes were imbedded in the Constitution of 1851.
Among the principal changes were: (1) biennial sessions of the
General Assembly, limited to sixty-one consecutive days, with
special sessions limited to forty such days; (2) local and special
legislation was forbidden for a number of subjects, plus the requirement that whenever possible all laws must be general and
uniform throughout the state; (3) no further state debt allowed,
save for a few specified and restricted situations; (4) the state prohibited from becoming a stockholder in any bank or corporation,
or loaning its credit to any individual or corporation; (5) popular
election required for additional state and local officials, with an
increase in shorter terms and limited tenure for them; (6) a man-

date that the General Assembly must establish a general and uniform system of common schools, equally open to all and free of
tuition; and (7) further immigration of blacks and mulattoes was
forbidden, plus an effort to persuade such persons already resident of the state to emigrate elsewhere. There are also important
differences between the Constitution of 1816 and that of 1851.
The former was shorter and more precise, reflecting liberal Jeffersonian Republicanism of the early nineteenth century, with the
General Assembly as the dominant branch of state government.
The latter, much longer and far more detailed, blended concepts
of Jacksonian Democracy with a vigorous emphasis on economic
laissez faire reflecting Indiana's burdensome and lingering financial experience arising from the breakdown of the System of 1836
during the late thirties and early forties.

CHAPTER 9

JEFFERSONIAN DEMOCRACY REINTERPRETED, 1816–1829

FROM STATEHOOD through the presidency of James Monroe, ending March 3, 1825, Indiana was under the sway of the Jeffersonian Republicans. There was no rival party, nor were the Jeffersonian Republicans an organized party.[1] If any candidate for office ever avowed himself a Federalist, evidence of it has not been found. Candidates were at times denounced as Federalists, but the political rhetoric arising from such denunciation illustrates the unpopularity of the Federalists rather than their existence. The Jeffersonian Republicans, however, were a modified version of the mother lode that had developed in the 1790s. Indiana's Constitution of 1816, with its rigid mandate against slavery, universal suffrage for white males, and ballot or secret voting, added democratic aspects to traditional Jeffersonian Republicanism. Moreover, Indiana voters quickly developed a strong attachment to both western sectionalism and the union of the states. The voters increasingly looked to the federal government for a rapid rolling back of Indian titles, a liberal policy concerning disposition and sale of land from the public domain, tariff protection, and federal aid for internal improvements.

Indiana had a modest role as a member of the United States during the teens and twenties. She had the two senators allotted each state, plus one congressman to March 3, 1823, then three congressmen to the early thirties. Federal policies generally served western interests in a suitable manner, hence there was strong support for and attachment to the federal government. Especially during the last half of the twenties, in federal politics citizens disagreed more about personalities than issues. Despite the political rhetoric, there was much in common concerning the issues sustained by both the Jacksonians (Democratic Republicans) and anti-Jacksonians (National Republicans). While mainly preoccupied with domestic politics, there was sympathy expressed for independence and liberal movements in other countries, particularly Greece and the revolting Spanish colonies of Central and South America. Distrust of England, combined with a nascent expansionism, at times stirred thought of American expansion westward to the Pacific Ocean. Indiana citizens to a substantial degree turned their backs on Europe and optimistically anticipated the spread of liberty and independence, American style, over a New World that would be a citadel of republicanism in contrast to the dominance of monarchy and corruption in the Old World.

Soon after Indiana completed her transition to statehood Monroe became president. Shortly after the General Assembly convened at Corydon in November, 1816, it had named Jesse L. Holman of Dearborn County, Joseph Bartholomew of Clark County, and Thomas H. Blake of Knox County presidential electors. It was probably not accidental that they respectively represented eastern, middle, and western sections of the state. In choosing electors the assembly observed that there was not time to elect them "in their respective districts," and noted its desire to embrace the earliest opportunity to support "genuine republican men and measures" as evidence of the "political character" of the infant commonwealth. Despite the protest of Congressman John W. Taylor of New York that Indiana had entered the Union too late to participate in the presidential election, her three electoral votes were cast for and counted for Monroe.[2]

Presidential politics created almost no ripples in Indiana during the teens and early twenties. In the summer of 1819 the state was honored with the first visit of an incumbent president. Monroe, accompanied by General Andrew Jackson, visited Corydon; and the next day Governor Jennings presided over a dinner in their honor at Jeffersonville. A toast which declared Monroe "First in office—First in the affections of his country," reportedly drew nine cheers.[3] Next year the governor called the legislature into session in November to enable Indiana to take part in the presidential election. Again naming electors from eastern, central, and western portions of the state, the General Assembly chose Daniel J. Caswell of Franklin County, John H. Thompson of Clark County, and Nathaniel Ewing of Knox County respectively.

A Corydon paper stated that it was "understood that they will vote for James Monroe for President," which they did.[4]

Meantime, at the August election in 1816, five weeks after the adjournment of the Corydon convention, Indiana elected her first congressman. At stake was the selection of an individual to serve until March 3, 1817, when Madison's administration terminated. Allan D. Thom of Clark County, William Hendricks of Jefferson County, and George R. C. Sullivan of Knox County became candidates. Thom and Sullivan professed that they entered the race at the behest of others, while Thom and Hendricks were branded "caucus" nominees.[5] On the eve of the voting Sullivan withdrew in favor of Thom, but Hendricks won by a lopsided majority.[6] Thom was apparently a supporter of Thomas Posey over Jennings in the gubernatorial contest, and it seems certain that Hendricks and Jennings cooperated in favor of each other.[7] When Congress convened on December 2, 1816, Hendricks was seated that day.[8]

Before completing his initial week in the House, Hendricks sought confidential information from a constituent about "party and policy" and possible strong opposition if he sought reelection the ensuing August. In the spring of 1817 a Corydon paper announced Hendricks as a candidate for reelection, and Reuben W. Nelson, editor of the Corydon *Indiana Herald*, offered himself as a rival.[9] The Vincennes *Western Sun* opened its columns to vigorous attacks on the incumbent congressman. "Justice & Truth" charged Hendricks and Senator James Noble with playing petty politics concerning payments to militiamen who had served in the War of 1812 in order to discredit Senator Waller Taylor. They and Governor Jonathan Jennings were said to be "without either public or individual merit," hence should be "discarded as unworthy servants" in contrast to Taylor, the one good man representing Indiana in Washington.[10] But Nelson's campaign fizzled about a month before the election when Thomas Posey, former territorial governor, entered the fray. Nelson endorsed Posey and withdrew from the campaign. The *Western Sun* praised Posey's military service, and "A Voter" claimed that the health of the old soldier and venerable patriot had been restored.[11] Nonetheless, Hendricks trounced Posey by an even larger margin than that by which Jennings had defeated Posey for governor the preceding year.[12]

Congressman Hendricks easily won additional terms in 1818 and 1820. In both instances he piled up overwhelming majorities against Nelson, carrying the western as well as the middle and eastern sections of the state. In 1818 Hendricks won nearly all counties, in 1820 only Knox went for Nelson. At the latter election several counties, including Wayne with its 1,785 votes, gave unanimous support for Hendricks.[13] Thus, during the early years of statehood Congressman Hendricks established himself as the most popular politician in the state so far as the voters were concerned.

While Hendricks established a strong political base as Indiana's congressman, Waller Taylor and James Noble served in the United States Senate. Because the federal constitution required that they be named by the General Assembly, their election was delayed until after this body convened in November, 1816. Prior to its convening a Vincennes paper listed Taylor, Noble, Jesse L. Holman, James Scott, and Elias McNamee as candidates. Soon after the legislature met it assembled in joint session and, voting concurrently for two senators, chose Taylor and Noble on the first ballot. Both men were natives of Virginia and lawyers, but Noble resided at Brookville while Taylor had close association with residents from the western counties. Had the voting been strictly along east-west sectional lines, Taylor could not have won election. He probably received most of the votes of western legislators, plus several from eastern members to gain election by the barest possible majority. Noble, who showed more strength than Taylor, perhaps gained his majority mainly from eastern legislators who easily controlled the assembly. Although the new senators were in Washington when Congress convened on December 2, the Senate denied them their seats until December 12, the day after Indiana's formal admission to the Union.[14]

Because senatorial rotation limited Taylor's initial term to less than three years, it lapsed March 3, 1819. Taylor seldom visited Indiana after his elevation to the Senate, but in the summer of 1818 he returned, presumably seeking support for another term.[15] The *Western Sun* staunchly endorsed his reelection, scoffing at the suggestion that Judge Isaac Blackford of the Supreme Court had an equal hold with Taylor on popular affection. While commending Blackford, its editor lavished praise on Taylor, asserted that no sincere friend of the judge would bring him forward in opposition to Taylor, and published anonymous items having similar views. In December, 1818, the General Assembly chose Taylor for a new six-year term. James Scott, another judge on the Supreme Court, was his leading rival in the balloting.[16] As in 1816 Taylor probably received the preponderance of the votes from legislators in the western counties, but he could not have won except for at least several votes from the eastern counties.

With Senator Noble's term ending on March 3, 1821, the question of his reelection came before the General Assembly the preceding December. In September, 1820, Boon wrote John Tipton from Evansville that he was on an electioneering tour with General Noble. After returning to his home at Brookville, Noble thanked Tipton for his "friendly letters" to certain individuals, adding that he had "met with much friendship from the members of the Legislature in the Western part of the State." When the assembly balloted in December, Noble won a second term by the slenderest possible majority, with Jesse L. Holman, a member of the Supreme Court who also lived in the eastern section, his nearest rival.[17]

The congressional election of 1822 aroused considerable interest among Indiana voters. Hendricks resigned his congressional seat, held from statehood, to run for governor, making necessary a special election to replace him for the remainder of his term which expired March 3, 1823. Because of the increase in population arising from the federal census of 1820, Indiana was entitled to three congressmen for the 1823–1825 term. Anticipating this increase, the General Assembly divided the state into First (western), Second (central), and Third (eastern) districts. They all bordered on the Ohio River and extended northward, making it possible to add new counties to them prior to the next general apportionment. No county was divided in forming these districts.[18] Both the special and regular congressional elections were held concurrently on August 5, 1822.

The competition to replace Congressman Hendricks was principally between Governor Jennings and Davis Floyd, a president judge of one of the circuit courts. Some weeks after the judge became a candidate, Jennings, already seeking election in the Second District, reported that from different parts of the state he had been solicited to indicate his willingness to complete Hendricks' term. The governor expressed this willingness.[19] Floyd responded that he had not anticipated such formidable opposition, and countered that he had entered the race because of his own reflection rather than at the behest of numerous friends. The judge noted his twenty-two years of residence in Indiana and stood on his record of public service. Jennings defeated Floyd by a little more than a two to one margin.[20]

For the regular election in the First District the contest was largely between William Prince of Gibson County and Charles Dewey of Orange County. A third aspirant, John Ewing of Knox County, withdrew early in favor of Dewey, stressing the importance of improving the navigation of such rivers as the White and Wabash.[21] "An Elector" asked candidates to state their views concerning improvement of the Wabash River, predicting that none could obtain the vote of the people without pledging this support. Dewey, a former resident of New England, was termed a Federalist who had opposed and obstructed the War of 1812. He was accused of having advanced Federalist principles since coming to Indiana, but Dewey affirmed his commitment to republicanism. Prince, who arrived in Indiana before 1800, had held a variety of territorial and state offices. He had fought with General William Henry Harrison at the Battle of Tippecanoe in 1811, and he was credited with having won cessions of land from the Indians while serving as a federal agent to them.[22] The venerable Prince defeated Dewey by a comfortable margin.[23]

For awhile it appeared that Jennings would be the only durable candidate in the Second District. Then several weeks before the election James Scott, a member of the Supreme Court who had been the runnerup against Senator Taylor at his reelection in 1818, entered the fray.[24] As the campaign neared its close "An Old Resident" leveled various charges at Jennings, including those that he had tried to defeat the Tippecanoe Campaign of 1811 and had sought to monopolize certain offices. In a slashing attack on the governor's character, "An Old Resident" asserted that after having proclaimed a day of fasting and prayer the chief executive had spent the night preceding this observance "at a public house in Charlestown, in the fashionable vice of drinking, card playing, &c. &c." Then next day, while the people of the area engaged in private acts of devotion, Jennings slumbered at a private house. To this salvo Jennings vowed: "I gambled not, nor was I intoxicated." The governor offered certificates affirming that he had inquired about a church service on the day of prayer and fasting, but on learning that service had commenced much earlier he declined to enter because of his policy not to enter such services late or leave them early. "Tom Blunt" proclaimed that Jennings had served the people well in various posts, had championed their rights, had more talents than Scott, and asserted that even his most violent enemies had never questioned his integrity.[25] Jennings won over Scott by a substantial majority, but the architect of statehood was unable to match Hendricks' popularity as a congressional vote-getter.[26]

In the more densely populated Third District, mainly within the Whitewater Valley, John Test of Franklin County was opposed by Ezra Ferris and Samuel C. Vance of Dearborn County.[27] "Moral Duty" supported Test over Ferris and denounced as false reports that Test wanted all public officials appointed without a popular vote. "A Free Man" acknowledged Test's ability, but doubted his integrity and labeled him a "law candidate" sustained by lawyers. Ferris was pictured as a public servant of unblemished integrity, while Vance was touted for his military career including service in Arthur St. Clair's campaign against the Indians in 1791.[28] Test was a strong plurality winner who ran best in counties in the upper portion of the district.[29] In this, as in the other congressional contests of 1822, personalities and local considerations, rather than important issues, prevailed. Moreover, it may be safely presumed that winners and losers alike were Jeffersonian Republicans.

Meantime, statehood had not ended Indiana's heavy dependence upon the federal government. Because Indian relations and disposition of the public domain were controlled by the United States, the progress of settlement and economic development was much influenced by federal policy regarding these key items.

Since roughly only one third of the state had been cleared of Indian titles, and that principally in southern Indiana, locating the permanent state capital and opening a network of roads connecting them to it had to be delayed. The three leading tribes were the Miami, found mainly in the upper Wabash and Maumee valleys; the Potawatomi, spread thinly over most of the remaining area north of the Wabash and some of the area south of the river; and the Delaware, situated chiefly along the upper portion of the West Fork of White River from near where Indianapolis was later established to above the subsequent site of Muncie. The defeat of the Indians during the War of 1812 and the substantial decline of British influence among them as a consequence of this conflict greatly weakened their ability to hold back the advancing tide of American settlers. As historian John B. Dillon, himself a pioneer, described the situation: "A sense of security pervaded the minds of the people. The hostile Indian tribes, having been overpowered, humbled, and impoverished, no longer excited the fears of the pioneer settlers, who dwelt in safety in their plain log cabin homes, and cultivated their small fields without the protection of armed sentinels. The numerous temporary forts and blockhouses . . . were either converted into dwelling houses, or suffered to fall into ruins."[30]

Both presidential and congressional policy strongly favored the settlers over the Indians. In addressing Congress in 1817, President James Monroe observed the progress of settlement in the Old Northwest, "which the rights of nature demand and nothing can prevent," but he insisted on the "duty to make new efforts for the preservation, improvement, and civilization of the native inhabitants." Increasingly the president emphasized that the Indians must be civilized and incorporated into white society or be removed. From 1809, when Governor William Henry Harrison completed a series of cessions, through the War of 1812, the Indians of the Indiana area had surrendered no further titles. With the ending of this conflict a series of "peace and friendship" treaties were negotiated with the Indians, which confirmed prewar boundaries but obtained no new cessions.[31] Early in 1818 the Indiana legislature urged the federal government to obtain further cessions from the Indians. In support of this request Congressman Hendricks said this was necessary to make it possible to locate the site for the permanent state capital, open Three Per Cent roads connecting with it, and foster relations between the residents of northern Indiana with citizens in other parts of the state.[32] In treaties negotiated between 1817 and 1821 —and principally by the New Purchase treaties of 1818—except for numerous reserves to individual Indians, the Indian title was largely liquidated for all but most of the northern third of Indiana. To obtain the title to millions of acres of land, the United States paid large sums for tribal annuities. The federal government also assumed various debts of the Indians, paid costs concerning their removal, and made appropriations to educate and "civilize" them.[33] As a consequence of these treaties, the Delaware left Indiana for the West in 1820;[34] and the Kickapoo and Wea[35] did likewise about this time. The cessions secured from 1817 to 1821, and the payments resulting from them and the surveying of the land for sale, made possible a rapid advance of settlement into central Indiana, and to a modest extent into northern Indiana during the 1820s.

While Indian titles were being rolled back, Isaac McCoy and his wife began their missionary labors among the Indians. After McCoy had served as minister of the Maria Creek Baptist Church near Vincennes, in 1818 the McCoys established a log cabin mission among the Wea and Kickapoo on Raccoon Creek in present Parke County. For two years their efforts to educate and Christianize the Indians were largely fruitless. A small number of white and Indian children and at least one black attended their mission school. In 1820 the mission was moved to Fort Wayne, attracting about forty Miami, Potawatomi, and mixed blood children by the end of its initial year. Once more success was meager. Both missions received modest financial aid from the Baptists, while that at Fort Wayne was sustained in part from federal appropriations for civilizing the Indians. In 1822 the McCoys transferred to Niles, Michigan, and continued their missionary efforts mainly among the Potawatomi. The problems encountered at Raccoon Creek and Fort Wayne helped persuade McCoy that removal of the Indians and their separation from the whites was essential for their conversion to Christianity and civilization.[36]

In contrast to the sacrificial efforts of the McCoys was the ruthless murder of nine Indians, principally women and children, in the spring of 1824 near Pendleton. Five settlers were indicted for these killings, but one man escaped and was not found. The remaining four were convicted in the Madison County Circuit Court and sentenced to be hung. Concerned about the reaction of the Indians to the brutal murders, the federal government assisted in the prosecution of the offenders and arranged for Indians to witness some of the hangings. An Indianapolis editor termed the murders outrageous, while a Lawrenceburg editor contended that justice demanded executions to assure the Indians that their grievances would not be ignored by their white brethren. Three of the convicted men were hung, but Governor Ray spared the life of a youthful offender by a last minute pardon.[37] Oliver H. Smith, who helped prosecute the whites, later termed their trials the only ones "where convictions of murder were ever had, followed by the execution of white men, for killing Indians, in the United States."[38]

As land was ceded by the natives, it was surveyed and placed on sale through federal land offices.[39] When new areas were available for purchase they were advertised and tracts were sold to the highest bidders. Thereafter, unsold tracts could be bought for minimum terms in accordance with existing legislation. But even at initial sales competition was at times avoided or at least reduced. In describing beginning sales at Crawfordsville in the twenties, Sandford Cox explained: "There is but little bidding against each other. The settlers, or 'squatters,' as they are called by speculators, have arranged matters among themselves to their general satisfaction." Moreover, "If a speculator makes a bid, or shows a disposition to take a settler's claim from him, he soon sees the white of a score of eyes snapping at him, and at the first opportunity he crawfishes out of the crowd."[40]

When Indiana became a state, federal land was sold according to the Harrison Land Law of 1800 as amended in 1804. The act of 1800 provided that tracts first be offered for sale at public auction to the highest bidders, in units of not less than 320 acres for not less than $2 per acre. The remaining acreage in a land district could be bought, without bidding, at the minimum price in units of 320 acres or above. If purchased on credit, one twentieth the cost was due as a down payment, the remainder payable in four equal annual installments, the initial one within forty days after the down payment. Fees required, interest owed, and discounts allowed could make the actual cost either more or less than $2 per acre. But if a tract was not fully paid for within five years of paying the first installment, all of it reverted to the federal government for resale. If the resale yielded a return above the costs involved, the surplus was to be paid the original purchaser. The act of 1804 made it possible to buy land in tracts as low as 160 acres. From this time a quarter section could be obtained for roughly $320, if payment was completed within five years.[41]

Sales from the federal domain within Indiana began in southeastern Indiana during the early 1800s from the Cincinnati Land Office. They began at land offices in Vincennes and Jeffersonville in 1804 and 1807 respectively, these being the only such offices in the state under the credit system. Indiana land, however, was sold from offices in Ohio until well beyond 1820, while Illinois land was purchased from the office at Vincennes until after this time.[42] Prior to the War of 1812 combined sales at Vincennes and Jeffersonville averaged less than 50,000 acres annually, then soared to an average of more than 500,000 acres annually during the boom years 1816 to 1818 inclusive. Gross sales from these offices to the end of the credit system on June 30, 1820, aggregated 2,490,736.17 acres for a total of $5,137,350.20 at an average price of $2.06 per acre.[43] Meantime, starting in 1806 relief laws had allowed an extension of time to make payments and other concessions to reduce forfeiture and resale of tracts because of delinquency. Even so, at the end of 1820, six months after termination of credit sales, a balance of $2,214,168.63 remained outstanding at the Indiana offices.[44] A series of additional relief laws, continuing until at least the early 1830s, afforded debtors a mix of options such as surrendering part of the acreage contracted for, using prior payments to complete purchase of acres retained; completing payment, with the price reduced to $1.25 per acre; or obtaining further time to pay the sum owed.[45] By the 1840s the federal government had obtained $3,524,161.18 for 1,678,639.82 acres sold on credit at the Vincennes and Jeffersonville offices for an average of $2.09 per acre. If sales of land within Indiana from Ohio offices were added to the above, and that of Illinois land sold from Vincennes subtracted, the aggregate for both *gross* and *net* sales would probably be significantly increased.[46]

From the beginning of the credit system it became apparent that an increasing debt was creating problems for both purchasers and the federal government. Would-be buyers in large numbers found it impossible to make payments on schedule, and members of Congress found it expedient to deal gently with defaulters. Settlers were generally reluctant to bid against land forfeited by neighbors, and the system spawned the keeping and updating of detailed records about original and installment payments. Moreover, from the start there had been those who contended that tracts should be sold to settlers at reduced prices for cash in smaller units than available in the laws of 1800 and 1804. But not until the deflation and economic distress, accompanying the Panic of 1819, did Congress end credit sales, and provide that starting July 1, 1820, tracts as low as eighty acres could be bought for $100 in cash. Senator James Noble and Congressman William Hendricks voted against this law, but Senator Waller Taylor voted for it. An editor at Corydon branded Taylor's support not "representative of the interest and feelings of the State of Indiana." An editor at Vincennes, however, approved the cash system as being of equal benefit to the nation and individuals.[47] During the twenties the acreage sold for cash averaged much less annually than that sold for credit in the boom years of the teens. Nevertheless, the law of 1820 became a boon to western settlement and to the federal treasury.[48]

As land passed from the Indians to settlers and speculators, farms and villages grew in number and size, increasing the need for transportation facilities connecting Indiana with other parts of the country. So great was this need and so meager were state resources that Hoosiers looked to the federal government for their financing. Since the United States retained title to the domain of Indiana, Hoosiers frequently argued that this sapped their ability to finance transportation projects. Congressman

Hendricks asserted in 1820 that because of this situation states created from the public domain had lost "resources and wealth, almost inexhaustible," depriving them of equality in the Union with the original states. Indiana probably gained more than it lost by federal control of the domain, but claiming otherwise was fostered by a desire for liberal federal grants of land and money on behalf of internal improvements.[49] Presidents Madison and Monroe and many other Republicans for a time tempered their advocacy of federal aid to internal improvements by making it subject to a constitutional amendment, but leading Indiana politicians presumed that Congress already had this power.[50]

In the teens and first half of the twenties Indiana increasingly sought federal largesse for key transportation projects. Congress was urged to hasten extension of the National Road through Indiana, then on to the Mississippi; buy stock to help an Indiana company open a canal on the Indiana side of the Ohio River Falls at Louisville; and make a liberal grant of land to enable Indiana to build a canal connecting the navigable points on the Wabash and Maumee rivers.[51] As the latter item suggests, Hoosiers were eager to obtain improved transportation facilities with the middle states of the Atlantic Seaboard. Indiana members of Congress also supported various transportation projects desired by other states and parts of the country.[52] During the presidential campaign of 1824 supporters of Adams, Clay, and Jackson alike presented their candidates as favorable to federal aid for internal improvements. Early in 1825 Congressman Jacob Call, an avowed Jacksonian from the lower Wabash Valley, protested that residents of western states paid millions for federal land, while Congress gave only modest aid for extension of the National Road to them in contrast to immense sums spent in eastern states for defense and internal improvements.[53]

Sentiment for increased tariff protection also grew, especially after the Panic of 1819. In messages to the legislature Governors Jennings and Hendricks stressed the need to curtail imports, particularly of fine fabrics. The appetite for such items during the boom of the teens was viewed as an important factor in draining specie from the West, with baneful effects on banks and persons in debt for land under the credit system.[54] Both individuals and the General Assembly urged protection for agriculture as well as manufacturing.[55] Following the Panic of 1819 some legislators sought to have members agree to wear only items of domestic manufacture. One who called himself "The Censor," exhorted the casting aside of all foreign fashions and splendor to wear "only the products of American manufactures." Such wear should be considered patriotic and honorable, he asserted, with the suggestion that "let the female that appears clothed in the works of her own hands receive all the respect and attention that is sought by a splendid display of foreign finery."[56] The tariff of 1824, a triumph for augmented protection, was supported by Senators Noble and Taylor and Congressmen John Test and William Prince.[57] In the 1824 presidential campaign proponents of Adams, Clay, and Jackson presented their favorite as for tariff protection.[58]

While the desire for federal aid to internal improvements and additional tariff protection increased, strong hostility existed toward the Second United States Bank. Owned in part by the United States, this institution commenced in January, 1817, and served as fiscal agent for the federal treasury. Indiana's state constitution, drafted in June, 1816, two months after the national bank had been chartered, implicitly prohibited the opening of its branches within the commonwealth. This prohibition might not have withstood review by the federal Supreme Court, but no branch was established and this question remained moot. Branches, however, which served Indiana, were founded at the border cities of Cincinnati and Louisville. Owners of the First State Bank of Indiana, which was established in 1817, and the owners of an earlier chartered bank at Madison, immediately discovered that the ability to have their paper accepted at land offices or to obtain federal money on deposit was much influenced by policies and practices of the Second United States Bank. During the teens and early twenties Secretary of the Treasury William H. Crawford at times restrained the national bank in its restrictions on western banks.[59]

As a debtor and undeveloped area, eager for loans but with scant security for them, Hoosiers frequently ignored the abuses of local banks and magnified those of the national bank. In the spring of 1818 fourteen western members of Congress, including all three Indiana members, protested the "monopolizing and depressing policy of the United States Bank" and its western branches which they asserted threatened the general prosperity of the country. Asking that "western paper" in good standing and paying specie be accepted at land offices, the protesters claimed that the "par value of the paper currency of Indiana is not doubted by any." The credit of Indiana's two banks was considered "equal to any in the western country."[60] In addressing the General Assembly at the end of 1818, Governor Jennings charged that the national bank was trying to destroy local banks and obtain a monopoly for its paper in payment of debts to the United States. Debtors, especially those owing for land, were said to be suffering heavy losses on account of this situation. Early the next year, but in advance of the Panic of 1819, Congressman Hendricks termed the report of a House committee which had investigated that bank "an *expose* of a series of improprieties on the part of the directors, not perhaps equalled in the history of any other moneyed institution." Rather than amending the bank's charter, the congressman preferred it be forfeited so "that a few moneyed capitalists at Philadelphia should no longer govern the circulating medium of our country, and lay their heavy hand on any district of the community they might think proper to press."[61] Newspaper editors also castigated the national bank. The Corydon *Indiana Gazette* urged repeal of its charter and regretted that only a small minority, including Indiana's lone congressman, William Hendricks, seemed "to support the cause of a suffering people, against the voracious host of *Bankers, stock jobbers, shavers* and *Swindlers.*"[62]

Amid the flood of criticism John Ewing of Vincennes raised his voice in defense of the Second United States Bank. In a Fourth of July address in 1818, he declared that freedom and prosperity were not endangered "by any internal or external cause, so much as by *a system of banking*, now become general in almost every village in the western country." Observing that a number of banks had failed, and predicting that many more would, Ewing described the federal bank as "a solid national institution, that is now decried by all tottering establishments." Congress, Ewing asserted, had wisely provided it as a safeguard for the people. If Indiana could obtain a branch, her citizens would be materially benefited; and a safe national currency would replace the unsafe local paper. At the next legislative session the House passed a bill to prohibit a branch within the state, but the Senate did not approve this measure.[63] Nonetheless, with the demise of the discredited First State Bank and nearly all other western banks during the early twenties, accompanied by gradual economic recovery, criticism of the national bank waned.[64]

Hostility to slavery also characterized the teens and early twenties. Although slavery and involuntary servitude existed on a meager scale in the territorial period, the antislavery element scored a triumph in 1810 when the assembly repealed legislation sustaining involuntary servitude. This victory was reaffirmed in the Constitution of 1816 which mandated that there "shall be neither slavery nor involuntary servitude" in Indiana. Moreover, declaring that slavery and such servitude "can only originate in usurpation and tyranny," the framers asserted that the constitution could never be altered to permit the existence of either. During 1820 the state Supreme Court interpreted this mandate to be retroactive, thus officially ending slavery. The next year it made the same decision regarding involuntary servitude.[65]

Slavery brought troublesome questions regarding the return of fugitive slaves. Masters at times offered monetary awards for help toward recovery of escaped slaves.[66] According to federal law, a claimant or his agent could, without a warrant, arrest his alleged fugitive in another state and take such person before a federal judge or state magistrate. If the evidence of ownership offered by the claimant was convincing, a certificate was issued authorizing return of the person seized to the presumed owner. Persons aiding a fugitive or interfering with his capture were subject to stiff penalties.[67] Nevertheless, in addressing the first state legislature in November, 1816, Governor Jennings urged legislators to consider a law more effectually to prevent "unlawful attempts to seize and carry into bondage persons of colour legally entitled to their freedom," while keeping individuals owing service to citizens of other states from finding "a refuge from the possession of their lawful owners." The assembly responded with an act imposing heavy fines on persons knowingly aiding escaped slaves, and it afforded personal liberty safeguards not in the federal law. In seeking a fugitive a claimant had to obtain an arrest warrant from a judge or justice of the peace; await the outcome of a jury trial, in which testimony was heard by both fugitive and claimant; and pay the costs of the trial. If the outcome favored the claimant, the person sought could be taken from the state. Individuals seizing and taking persons contrary to these safeguards were branded "guilty of man stealing."[68]

Writing in 1817 at the behest of the Kentucky legislature, Governor Gabriel Slaughter protested to Jennings that difficulties were being experienced in reclaiming slaves from Indiana. Without specifying details, Slaughter added: "our citizens complain of serious obstructions to the recovery of their property." Governor Jennings recommended that the General Assembly make further provision to restrain slaves from fleeing to Indiana to escape their owners, and to enable either circuit or Supreme Court judges to decide such cases, with the aid of a jury, without delay.[69] A House committee, chaired by Samuel Milroy of Washington County, charged that unprincipled individuals had tried "to seize and carry away people of color, as slaves, who were free, and as much entitled to the protection of the laws, as any citizen of Indiana." Hoosiers, the committee asserted, were of "one sentiment" against "people of color migrating, in any circumstance, to this state." If not restricted such migration "would in time, become an evil, of not much less magnitude, than slavery itself." Nevertheless, it was a solemn duty to protect these "degraded and much injured people" from "miscreants" who had repeatedly attempted to carry them "into perpetual slavery." The assembly adjourned without modifying its personal liberty legislation, but the ensuing session provided for the expedition of jury trials concerning persons claimed as fugitive slaves.[70]

This confrontation over fugitive slaves led to an appeal by a resident of Kentucky from an Indiana circuit court to the federal district court for Indiana. In 1818 Judge Benjamin Parke of the federal court ruled that congressional enactments superseded state legislation regarding fugitive slaves. But by granting that a state might exercise concurrent power "for different purposes, but not for the attainment of the same end," Parke left uncertain what state laws might cover.[71] In any event, Indiana's continued support of personal liberty legislation was spurred by the fact that during 1818 Robert Stephens, a Kentucky legislator, and accomplices forcibly seized a black woman called Susan from a residence at Corydon and returned her to the Bluegrass State. Although Susan was an escaped slave, her status was under review in the Harrison County Circuit Court, resulting in an indictment against Stephens and two accomplices for manstealing. Governor Jennings made efforts to obtain extradition of the trio for trial in the circuit court, but Governor Slaughter steadfastly refused extradition insisting that federal law was above state law regarding fugitive slaves.[72] Perhaps with the Stephens case in view, the Indiana legislature added the requirement that persons convicted of manstealing be given from ten to one hundred stripes on their bare backs. The assembly also enacted a resolution urging Indiana members of Congress to attempt to prevent legislation that would deprive any Indiana resident "claimed as a fugitive from service of a legal constitutional trial, according to the laws of" Indiana.[73]

The spirited controversy between Indiana and Kentucky persisted while Jennings was governor. Indiana declined to repeal its personal liberty safeguards; Kentucky refused to extradite Stephens and his associates; and Congress failed to add personal liberty protection to its fugitive slave legislation. In March, 1821, Governor Jennings sought aid from President Monroe regarding the dispute with Kentucky, but it is uncertain whether Monroe responded to this request. In his message to the General Assembly late in 1822, Governor Boon, who completed Jennings' second term, stressed the need for conciliation with Kentucky, and the obligation to return fugitive slaves; but he made no mention of personal liberty items. A few weeks after his term began in December, Governor Hendricks indicated that he had not renewed an application for the extradition of Stephens. During 1823 the indictment against Stephens and his accomplices was dropped.[74]

In the mid-twenties the General Assembly softened its personal liberty legislation. The revised code of 1824 included a penalty for aiding a fugitive owing service in another state, while it provided a much stiffer penalty and imprisonment at hard labor for removing persons from Indiana without a proper claim. But the act regarding fugitives avoided the word mansteal ing, and it allowed for a trial by jury *only* on appeal from the decision of a justice of the peace or a judge. If an appeal were made, security for the costs which would ensue must be paid in advance. In these and other ways the law favored the claimant over the black whose status was in question. At the legislative session early in 1825, when personal liberty legislation was proposed but rejected, Senator John H. Thompson protested that the code of the previous year had destroyed jury trials so far as persons of color were concerned. By the mid-twenties Indiana's personal liberty legislation, at best only partially effective, had principally been abandoned.[75]

While Indiana and Kentucky disputed about fugitive slaves, the controversy regarding the admission of Missouri stirred sectional animosities between free and slave states. The Ordinance of 1787 had made the Ohio River the boundary between freedom and slavery, but the latitude of Missouri, immediately across the Mississippi from the mouth of the Ohio, made it an uncertain borderland. When Congress gave serious consideration to statehood for Missouri at its session in 1818–1819, Indiana, though heavily populated by southerners, had considerable antislavery sentiment. Thus, when the Tallmadge amendment proposed to exclude the *further* introduction of slavery following admission and give freedom at age twenty-five to children of slaves born thereafter, Congressman William Hendricks supported both items when the amendment passed the House. Although the amendment failed in the Senate, Senators James Noble and Waller Taylor, natives of Virginia, likewise voted for the further exclusion of slavery; and Noble also voted to free children of slaves, but Taylor opposed this provision.[76] The session ended without an enabling act for Missouri, but Congress approved one for her southern neighbor, Arkansas, with Hendricks and Noble recorded for and Taylor against the further exclusion of slavery.[77]

When the admission of Missouri was considered at the 1819–1820 session, the House initially had a majority for exclusion of the further introduction of slavery but the Senate staunchly favored leaving this decision to its people. Maine's request for statehood, however, caused southerners in particular to link its admission with that of Missouri, making possible a free state to match an expected slave state. Both houses of Congress approved linkage, with Hendricks and Noble against and Taylor for it. Only two other northern senators voted as Taylor did. When the Thomas amendment was offered to admit slavery in Missouri but exclude it north of 36° 30′ Hendricks, Noble, and Taylor voted nay. In evaluating opponents and proponents of the Missouri Compromise of 1820—allowing Maine and Missouri to decide slavery for themselves, but with exclusion of slavery north of 36° 30′—an historian of the Missouri controversy considers Hendricks, Noble, and Taylor its opponents.[78]

While the controversy continued both Hendricks and Noble voiced their opposition to slavery. Hendricks condemned slavery as a moral as well as a national evil. He contended that "the great work of emancipation and colonization, which has to commence some day, will be easier to commence now than half a century to come." Taylor, who apparently owned slaves in Virginia, privately doubted the wisdom of excluding slavery and some of his votes, especially that for linking Maine and Missouri, contributed to the Compromise of 1820.[79] Indiana editorial reaction was mixed, but some editors who had asked for exclusion of slavery expressed support for compromise or at least recognized its need to strengthen the bonds of union.[80] When Missouri's new constitution prohibited free blacks and mulattoes from becoming residents, Hendricks and Noble continued to vote for exclusion of slavery and for removal of this prohibition as the price of admission. Taylor, however, joined the majority in both houses in adopting the second or Missouri Compromise of 1821 which permitted further introduction of slavery and for practical purposes left the status of free blacks and mulattoes to be determined by Missourians.[81] The persistent opposition of Hendricks and Noble to further slavery in Missouri more closely represented Indiana sentiment than did the voting of Taylor. On the other hand, in this national crisis Taylor, rather than his colleagues, contributed toward compromise, conciliation, and national harmony.

Though mainly occupied with domestic politics, Hoosiers also gave consideration to relations with other countries. As for Americans generally, for the most part they focused their attention mainly upon developments in the New World. The defeat suffered by the Indians in the War of 1812 and the waning of British influence among them ended the serious conflict which had intermittently perturbed the Ohio Valley and Old Northwest since the middle of the previous century. The purchase of Louisiana and the decline of Spanish power in the New World had made secure the hold of the United States on the Mississippi trade artery, the route over which the preponderance of Indiana's imports and exports were conveyed. Distrust of England remained, but peace prevailed to the end of the pioneer era, except for the Mexican War in 1846–1848. The small federal garrison at Fort Wayne was terminated in 1819, and three years later Fort Harrison, the state's only remaining military post, was evacuated.[82] Concern about the Indians, however, had not yet disappeared. A Vincennes newspaper carried the comment that "abandonment of Fort Wayne" had been impolitic because that area was "infested with Indians" throughout a vast region.[83]

Venerating liberty and freedom as fruits of the American Revolution, Hoosiers cherished their republican government and contrasted it with monarchical rule in Europe where kings rather than people were sovereign. The efforts of leading European powers to suppress movements and revolts toward republics or liberal monarchies were frequently abhorred and denounced as oppressive and tyrannical. European life and institutions were viewed as corrupt and inferior to American life and institutions. Fourth of July observances, with their extremely patriotic overtones, pictured Americans as free and virtuous, owing their independence, liberties, and republican government to the guidance of Providence. Thus, it seemed, America's destiny could best be served by isolation from European affairs as much as possible. On the other hand, America's interests and destiny required a favored position, above European countries, concerning affairs of the New World. In a superficial and romantic manner, the growth of independent and republican governments, with the blessings of liberty and freedom largely American style, was anticipated for the New World. But mixed with this optimistic idealism was a practical concern about trade, military security, and national power which begat a strong tendency toward expansionism.

The revolt of the Spanish colonies of Latin America, commencing in the first decade of the 1800s and cresting in the late teens and early twenties, afforded an outlet for mixing idealism about republican government with dreams of expansion. At a Fourth of July observance "to celebrate the grand national festival" at Fort Harrison in 1816, one of the toasts was to "The patriot champions of liberty in South America—engaged in the cause of the rights of man, may they triumph over their oppressors, and may we shortly hail them as brethren and founders of another republic."[84] Two years later Congressman Hendricks hailed "the Patriots of South-America" for their "firm and steady pace, to liberty and independence." Suggesting that the patriots needed no alliance with any country to achieve success, and apparently thinking of American experience, Hendricks added: "They will remember the origin of their liberties, and prize them in proportion to what they cost."[85] The desire of the Monroe administration to secure Florida by negotiation encouraged the president to emphasize neutrality regarding the revolting Spanish colonies and delay recognizing them as independent republics. Senators Taylor and Noble voted for the Florida purchase treaty of 1819 which gave the United States clear title to all of Florida, while surrendering its claim to Texas and strengthening that to the Oregon country. With Spanish ratification of this treaty late in 1820, recognition of some of the revolting colonies soon followed. Hendricks welcomed news that Spain had ceded Florida and advised constituents that this enabled the United States to check piracy in the Gulf of Mexico. The congressman added that the friends of liberty and philanthropy would be gratified "to see the mild and salutary influence of the Republic extended beyond the summit of the Rocky Mountains, to the Columbia, on the shores of the Pacific ocean." Glossing over American surrender of claim to Texas, Hendricks predicted "from her position and population" Texas "will incline and attach herself to the United States." Mexico was expected to break away from Spain and become a republic.[86]

Visions of expansion, however, were not limited to reaching the distant Pacific. An Indianapolis editor in 1823, after stating that Cuba must soon change masters or become independent, termed this island "the key of the gulf of Mexico." Noting Cuba's importance for American trade and expressing concern about its falling into British hands, the editor suggested that its possession by the United States would have advantages "almost incalculable, in a commercial point of view." Thus, "it is almost impossible to suppress a wish that it may soon be attached to our territories." A few years earlier Editor Stout of Vincennes quoted a paper which asserted that ere long Canada and other British territory "on this continent, will belong to us, if not by conquest, by the own free will of the colonists themselves." Later Stout quoted a Louisville paper which observed that the question of the free navigation of the St. Lawrence and transfer of Canada to the United States had been agitated in papers of the Atlantic area. The Kentucky editor suggested that negotiations for American navigation of the St. Lawrence should end favorably if based on the British precedent "that a nation inhabiting the bank or banks of a river, above, has the right to ascend or descend it, from and to the ocean—even through the territory of other powers." Moreover, the United States "should at least own the country on the south side of the St. Lawrence, from the out-let of Lake Ontario to the ocean." The Kentucky editor viewed conjectures that the United States would probably become too vast and unwieldy as "without foundation" because the American "government is not . . . like any that has preceded it. It is one of *opinion*—not of *force*; and as long as the people are intelligent and virtuous, we need not fear the effects of new acquisition, either of territory or of numbers." Presuming the answer self-evident, the editor asked if the acquisition of Louisiana had, as had been predicted, weakened "the bond of union between the states?"[87]

With these unduly optimistic sentiments and aspirations it is not surprising that the Indiana General Assembly enthusiastically supported the Monroe Doctrine, which the president proclaimed to Congress late in 1823. Monroe's emphasis on isolation from European affairs and the special interest and role which the United States should have in the affairs of the New World were closely akin to these sentiments and aspirations. Early in 1824 the assembly affirmed that the "sentiment expressed" by the chief executive, "both as it respects our foreign relations and domestic policy, meet our decided approbation." In his message legislators recognized "the immortal principles of '76." Aware that what Monroe said was especially linked to developments in South America, Hoosier lawmakers explained that their "sympathetic feelings" and "best wishes" had been excited as they had "witnessed the resistance of our brethren of South America, to the merciless tyranny of Spain, and seen with joy, the Eagle of Liberty expand his wings over a sister Continent."[88]

But members of the assembly had not completely turned their backs against Europe. They also expressed sympathy and admiration for the Greeks engaged in "bursting the chains of Turkish despotism, and struggling for the rights and glory of their ancestors." The Greeks should be given as much countenance and encouragement as consistent with the duties of neutrality. Meantime, "the resurrection of that freedom in her sons, which raised their forefathers to the pinnacle of glory," was eagerly anticipated. Thus, despite preoccupation with developments in the New World, sympathy and verbal encouragement were at times extended to European movements toward liberty and representative government. Congressman Hendricks, in commenting upon revolutionary movements in Europe, discerningly viewed the French Revolution as the beginning of a new era in government. Its principles and advocates were slumbering for a time, but "the former superstitious veneration for legitimacy and the rights of kings, will probably never be restored, and the idea of representative government which it brought into view . . . may yet change entirely the complexion of Europe."[89] The expansionist mood voiced by Hoosiers did not reach its fruition until the 1840s, while meantime the liberty and freedom associated with representative government and republics showed more promise in

Europe than in Latin America. The Indiana pioneers owed more to their European, and especially their English heritage, than they at times realized.

In contrast to the presidential election of 1820, which created only ripples among Indiana voters, that of 1824 made big waves. With President Monroe not a candidate, several individuals, all Jeffersonian Republicans who blended personal and sectional rivalries in varying degrees, were given major consideration. During 1822 and 1823 three members of Monroe's cabinet received much attention, including Secretary of State John Quincy Adams of Massachusetts; Secretary of the Treasury William H. Crawford of Georgia; and Secretary of War John C. Calhoun of South Carolina. The growing political role and sectionalism of the West was manifested in the consideration extended Speaker of the House Henry Clay of Kentucky, and General Andrew Jackson of Tennessee. Lesser attention was bestowed on De Witt Clinton of New York, hailed for his support of the nearly completed Erie Canal. Late in 1823, after observing that his Indianapolis debating club had weighed the qualifications of Clay, Jackson, Crawford, Calhoun, Adams, and Clinton, Calvin Fletcher commented that the presidential election had become the topic of legislative bodies in each state; the hobby of every newspaper; and the chitchat of the counting rooms of merchants, the barrooms of inns, and the firesides of farmers.[90]

Popular interest in the presidential campaign of 1824 was stimulated because for the first time the state's electors were chosen by the voters rather than the General Assembly. There was much diversity of opinion whether Indiana's five electors should be selected from separate districts or on a general ticket. "Unus," who supported Jackson, urged election by districts, charging that advocates of the general ticket plan sought to increase the state's bargaining power to enable dealers in office to barter with "the wholesale hucksters of the Metropolis." Governor Hendricks advised Clay that his friends at the 1822–1823 legislative session had preferred the district method for fear he could not carry a general ticket. Early in 1824, however, the assembly provided for popular election on a general ticket.[91]

During the first half of the twenties there was an upsurge of popular sentiment against presidential nominations by congressional caucus. In December, 1823, state Senator John H. Thompson presented resolutions denouncing such nominations as "opposed to the genius and purest principles of our republican institutions" as well as contrary to the spirit and meaning of the federal constitution. Declaring it the "legitimate and exclusive right of the people of the United States to elect a President and Vice-President without the aid or influence of caucus nominations," the resolutions termed the "exercise [of] this invaluable privilege, either by Congress or State Legislatures" beyond legislative authority. The senators split eight for and eight against these resolutions, but Lieutenant Governor Ratliff Boon broke the tie in favor of passage. The House, however, neither approved these nor other resolutions critical of congressional caucus nominations.[92] Governor William Hendricks, responding to Clay's solicitation of an endorsement from the Indiana legislature, advised the Kentuckian that, despite the fact that his friends were a majority in both houses, even his "warmest friends would not venture on the proposition of a [legislative] caucus nomination in your favor." The danger was too great that the result would be unfavorable, the governor explained.[93]

At a poorly attended congressional caucus in February, 1824, Crawford won its endorsement for president. Senator James Noble attended and presumably voted for the Georgian. Noble vigorously defended his participation, viewing the caucus as an effort to produce union, as an expression of sentiment not binding on any voter, and as consistent with the manner in which federal and state officials had traditionally been put forward. By use of the caucus the Federalists had been dislodged and Thomas Jefferson made president, Noble stated, for which "from his youthful days, he said amen!"[94] But the unpopularity of the congressional caucus, combined with Crawford's serious and continued poor health, weakened support for him in Indiana.[95] By the early months of 1824 the contest within the state had largely narrowed to Adams, Clay, and Jackson.

Since the legislature made no provision concerning how presidential electors should be nominated, proponents of candidates had some difficulty determining which five individuals would form their respective tickets. During April an Adams ticket was announced in the press, at times with the comment that it had been named by his friends. Jesse L. Holman, a member of the ticket, wrote Clay that it had been formed "by the friends of Mr. Adams, in the Indiana Legislature," his name having been added without his knowledge or consent.[96] In May editors announced a ticket on behalf of Clay, and the next month the staunchly pro-Clay Indianapolis *Gazette* confirmed the slate, proclaiming that it had been "Adopted by the people of Indiana . . . ." In a subsequent issue the Clay spokesman asked editors to print the Clay ticket as agreed upon, omitting the names of two additional persons who had earlier announced and then had withdrawn. With perhaps a jab at advocates of Adams, the spokesman explained that two extra candidates had been brought out because "the people had to bring about a selection unaided by a Legislative or Congressional caucus—and were of course liable to some misunderstandings previous to its adoption."[97] Although various local meetings had been held, and some of them formed correspondence committees as they expressed ideas about electors and issues, the Clay ticket probably was formed by a limited number of his legislative and other friends.[98]

Forming an electoral ticket for Jackson proved difficult. Near the end of June, Elihu Stout of the Vincennes *Western Sun* announced five men as the Jackson or People's Ticket, adding, without explanation, that he had been authorized to release it. Asserting that Jackson's friends were numerous and increasing, Stout warned that "want of concert would insure defeat—but in UNION, there is STRENGTH." Meantime, more than five persons had been announced as Jackson electors, and want of concert continued as still others were added to the list. At least twice during July Stout revised the Jackson slate, but the surplus of aspirants continued. Unless the Jacksonian vote could be restricted to five individuals, it might be so diffused that part or all of a rival slate would be successful.[99] To avert such a calamity, Stout proposed a "certain shield" to make victory possible. "A general convention, county committees of correspondence, and township committees of vigilance," the veteran editor asserted, "will secure to us such a ticket as will produce unanimity among ourselves, and afford general satisfaction—will secure the certain and speedy diffusion of information, and will secure such diligence, activity and attention throughout the state, on the day of election, as will render success certain[.]" Stout called upon Jacksonians to hold county meetings during August and name delegates to a state convention at Salem on Monday, September 9, "to nominate an electoral ticket" for Jackson and make such other arrangements as the good of the cause required. Each county meeting was asked to name a county correspondence committee of five members and township vigilance committees of three persons. Various counties held such meetings, named delegates to the state convention, and some of them formed county and township committees.[100]

The resulting state convention held its one-day session at Salem on September 16. According to its proceedings, eighteen delegates from thirteen of the fifty-one counties which participated in the presidential balloting were in attendance. An electoral ticket of five members was agreed upon, and a general correspondence or state central committee of three persons was formed and empowered "to fill up any vacancies which may occur in the electoral ticket and take such measures as may be necessary to insure its success[.]" Counties lacking correspondence committees were urged to establish them. Three thousand copies of the electoral slate and five hundred copies of an approved address to the people of the state were ordered printed for general distribution.[101] Although the Salem convention included delegates from a minority of the counties, and they were probably selected by a small number of citizens, it achieved the basic objective Stout had proposed for it. Moreover, it established key practices and features upon which subsequent conventions and party organization were developed.

As the presidential campaign advanced, Adams gained the endorsement of most Indiana newspapers.[102] Proponents extolled him for his integrity, unquestioned personal character, staunch commitment to republicanism, and outstanding qualifications to serve as president. They presented the secretary of state as one who would serve the interests of the country, an advocate of internal improvements and tariff protection, and an opponent of slavery. Doubtless with jabs at Clay and Jackson, the comment of an eastern paper that Adams "fights no duels, tells no lies, and drinks very little, if any whiskey," was quoted.[103] Opponents played on western bias against Yankees and Federalists. Adams was portrayed as a diplomat who had been willing to sacrifice American interest concerning navigation of the Mississippi. He was pictured as having so long hobnobbed abroad with kings, princes, and noblemen that he had acquired more knack for political intrigue and become more versed in court etiquette than Talleyrand. Branded an aristocrat, his conversion to republicanism was doubted, and critics sought to convince voters that he was still a Federalist. Critics also questioned whether Adams would promote western interests by supporting federal aid for internal improvements and increased tariff protection.[104]

For a time it seemed as if the competition would be largely between Adams and Clay. The speaker's friends presented him as a westerner and plain old-fashioned republican untainted by corruption. If elected he would reduce the federal bureaucracy, make appointments on the basis of merit, and give jobs to sons of the poor as well as of the rich. Experienced in both domestic politics and foreign affairs, he had proven his strong commitment to internal improvements and tariff protection, while in diplomacy he had steadfastly held out for American navigation of the Mississippi to its mouth. Though admittedly a slaveholder, as most presidents had been, it was claimed that he had done more to ameliorate the lot of oppressed Africans from bondage than had Adams. A pro-Adams editor suggested that to prefer Clay over Adams voters "must first learn to disregard all distinction between right and wrong—between freedom and *slavery*—between a man polluted with the crimes of gaming and duelling, and one whose moral character is 'without spot and blemish.'"[105] Clay was described as a part of the eastern political establishment, which engaged in political intrigue, and used patronage and secret caucuses to gain office. His support for the Second United States Bank and his legal services on its behalf were viewed as a desire for personal gain and an effort to use this monied institution in reaching the presidency.[106]

As the November balloting neared Jackson's strength alarmed friends of Adams and Clay. Old Hickory's emotionally charged disciples offered him as the hero of warfare against the British and Indians, picturing him as one of the few politicians who was a veteran of the great American Revolution for freedom and independence. Described as a westerner, committed to both internal improvements and tariff protection, Jackson, his advocates insisted, had not tainted himself by engaging in intrigue and corruption with eastern politicians. Thoroughly dedicated to republican principles, and especially government by the people, the general was in the race, his friends emphasized, not by personal choice but by a draft from the people. "Unus" contended that the contest was "between political honesty and integrity on the one side—and intrigue, and corruption and infamy on the other." Only if Jackson won would victory accrue to the people. Boldly presenting Jackson as one of the great men of all times, "Unus" averred that Providence had given him for the hour when "the liberty and independence of the world" were at stake and "the dreadful contest between the despots of the earth, & freeborn man, must be decided." With dripping sarcasm "Unus" appealed to western prejudice by asking: "Has he been to Europe? Has he ever bowed in the halls of royalty? Has he ever kissed a king's hand or a pope's toe? Has he ever played cards with royal dukes, dined with nobility, or intrigued with queens or princesses? Has he ever figured in a caucus, or rioted on the spoils of the public treasury?"[107]

Opponents sharpened their attack on General Jackson as the election neared. They often admitted his achievements as a military man, but claimed that he lacked acquaintance with both domestic and foreign affairs. "Backwoodsman" affirmed that it was "absolutely necessary" that a "chief magistrate should be something more than a victorious general." An Adams editor quoted an item which stated that as president Jackson would so elevate the military over civil authority that only "Turkey, abject and degraded by despotism, could tolerate" his rule. "Omega" tersely stated that "Rome had her Caesar, England her Cromwell, and

France her Bonaparte, and these United States should profit by their example." Spraying grapeshot at random, "Omega" reported that Jackson had killed a fellow citizen in a duel; imprisoned a federal judge, following the Battle of New Orleans, for having issued a civil process against him; altered the sentence of a military court, then hanged a man; tried to restrict suffrage to freeholders while a member of the Tennessee constitutional convention; and threatened to cut off the ears of a member of Congress because of comments about his role in the Seminole War. Moreover, Jackson reportedly had so little regard for religion, morality, and the good order of society that he had taken "*another man's wife*, and it is said still lives with her." Mingled with assaults on Jackson's personal character and qualifications were doubts whether he could be trusted to sustain federal aid and tariff protection.[108]

Local polls, often taken at militia gatherings, frequently favored Jackson with Clay ahead of Adams. After the Salem convention Stout optimistically observed: "But little, if any doubt now remains, of the vote of Indiana going for the HERO OF [NEW] ORLEANS—and an opinion seems to be gaining ground that he will be elected without troubling congress upon the matter."[109] Though only a plurality winner, Jackson garnered a considerable margin over Clay with Adams a weak third. Clay, however, carried more counties than Jackson, running well in those on and near the Wabash and West Fork of White River, perhaps because voters there thought him more trustworthy than Jackson concerning federal aid to internal improvements. Jackson ran best in counties of south-central and southeastern Indiana, thence up the Whitewater Valley to Wayne County. Wayne and neighboring Randolph were the only counties which favored Adams. The returns suggest a strong preference for western candidates, but Jackson's triumph cannot safely be viewed as a democratic upheaval. Indiana had had universal suffrage for white males and secret voting from statehood; various older and more developed counties went for Jackson, while Clay won several of the newer and less developed counties in central Indiana; and the aggregate vote for the three presidential tickets was far below that for the congressional races of 1824, even less than the vote for governor in 1822 when Hendricks ran without opposition. Jackson's *plurality* victory probably resulted largely from his personal popularity as a military hero, the view that he was in a special way the candidate of the people, and the feeling that he was a westerner not identified with the eastern political establishment.[110]

Jackson also won a plurality in the electoral college, but Adams was second with Crawford a distant third and Clay in fourth place. The House of Representatives had to choose from among the three frontrunners, but many believed that Clay would be the kingmaker.[111] After the House had elected Adams on February 9, but before the result was known, a Hoosier editor at Richmond, Indiana, who had spoken harshly of Clay during the campaign, responded to the allegation that a corrupt bargain was being negotiated whereby Clay would support Adams in return for being named secretary of state. "I would as soon believe that any one of the other candidates is politically corrupt," the editor stated, "as I would that Mr. Clay is. His whole public life forbids such a belief." Another pro-Adams editor at Indianapolis, presumably unaware that Adams had been chosen, insisted that Clay's "freedom from intrigue is proverbial," and warned that such allegations would unite all elements against Jackson and assure success for Adams. In the same issue, under date of February 22, this editor inserted a brief postscript on an inside page, saying: "We stop the press to announce the highly interesting and important intelligence of the result of the Presidential election. JOHN QUINCY ADAMS is elected President of the United States, for four years from and after the 4th of March next. The information was communicated by the Post Master at Vernon, who received it from the Post Master at Madison. The news come [*sic*] to Madison in 2½ days from Wheeling by steam boat. ADAMS had 13 states—JACKSON 7—and CRAWFORD 4."[112] Although Congressmen Jonathan Jennings and John Test almost certainly preferred Adams, they joined Congressman Jacob Call, a Jacksonian, in casting Indiana's vote for Old Hickory. Editor Stout, expressing surprise that the popular will had been disregarded, added that Jackson's friends could console themselves "under the firm conviction, that the voice of the American people was in his favor." Stout made no reference to a possible corrupt bargain between Adams and Clay, but it soon became evident that schism had replaced consensus regarding presidential politics in Indiana.[113]

In the midst of the presidential campaign, Hoosiers elected three congressmen on August 2, 1824. All candidates were presumably Jeffersonian Republicans who sought office mainly on the basis of issues and personal considerations rather than presidential preferences. In the First or western district, incumbent William Prince did not seek reelection. By May Ratliff Boon of Warrick County, Jacob Call of Knox County, and Thomas H. Blake of Vigo County were the leading candidates.[114] "Hickory," who noted that Call and Blake were both lawyers, judges, and bachelors with military experience, described Blake as having been born under the "genial smoke" of the national capital. Thus he had become an intriguing courtier, acquainted with the levee, drawing room, and etiquette of fashion. Call was presented as having been born and educated in the West, where he had acquired its habits and become completely identified with its interests. "Hickory" ignored the homespun Boon who had resigned as lieutenant governor to make the race. Shortly before the voting Robert M. Evans staunchly denied that he had circulated the story, branded as false, that Boon had told him of having joined a Baptist church for the sole purpose of seducing a young woman who belonged to it. Despite this seduction story, Boon was an easy plurality winner over runnerup Call and third place Blake.[115]

In the Second or middle district, Congressman Jonathan Jennings faced tough opposition from Jeremiah Sullivan of Madison. The incumbent declared his support for tariff protection and internal improvements. If the presidential election devolved upon the House of Representatives, Jennings promised to vote for the candidate preferred by the people.[116] "Plato" argued for rotation in office, said to have been favored by the immortal Washington, and he emphasized Sullivan's republican principles, talents, and acquirements as well as his "prudence, modesty, temperance, morality and urbanity." Apparently responding to this thinly veiled attack on Jennings, "A Farmer" countered that "we find men *loud* in the censure of *slave-holding* and *dram drinking* pushing Jerry and his *slave votes*" against Jennings who opposed both the "*principle* and *practice*" of slavery. "A Farmer" lashed out at the hypocrisy of those who term every gentleman who drinks "spirits on any *occasion* a *Sot*," while some of them drink in the back room of a store or at a candidate's house on election day. "Q" denied that Washington had advocated rotation in office, saying had he been forced from office at Jennings' age he would have gone to his grave with a small margin of fame. Though Sullivan gave the former governor the strongest competition of his congressional career prior to his defeat in 1831, Jennings eked out a narrow margin to win a new term.[117]

In the Third or eastern district, Congressman John Test won reelection by a plurality. His closest rival was youthful James Brown Ray, like Test, also from Franklin County. Daniel J. Caswell, of Dearborn County, was third.[118]

If any of the congressional candidates who completed the campaign publicly avowed their presidential preferences before the August voting, the author has not found convincing evidence regarding their preferences. Of the three winners, it is almost certain that Jennings and Test favored Clay over either Jackson or Adams. Though various writers have termed Boon a Jacksonian, adequate evidence to support this is needed. Among the losers, most likely Call preferred Jackson, and Blake and Ray favored Clay. What preferences, if any, Sullivan and Caswell had are uncertain.

The death of Congressman Prince in early September resulted in a special election to choose his successor on November 8, the day of the presidential balloting. The competition narrowed mainly to Boon, Call, and Blake, and then to Call and Blake,[119] both of whom promised to vote according to popular preference if the House of Representatives were called upon to name the president. Call, however, proclaimed his personal support of Jackson; and Blake stated his intent to vote for Clay. The two candidates endorsed federal aid to improve navigation of rivers, especially the Wabash. Call suggested that a canal connecting the Wabash with the lakes would reduce dependence on the New Orleans market, facilitate transportation of troops and supplies in time of war, and "amply compensate the national government in cutting the proposed canal, and removing the obstructions in our rivers."[120] Call won a thin edge over Blake, even though the electoral balloting had favored Clay. Blake contended that votes received after the governor certified Call the victor turned the outcome in his favor, but the House of Representatives seated Call, making him the first avowed Jacksonian congressman from Indiana.[121]

Soon after the voters named Call to replace Prince, the General Assembly elected a successor to Senator Waller Taylor whose term expired March 4, 1825. The latter had served since statehood, but following his reelection in 1818 he seldom visited Indiana. A native of Virginia, he generally spent time between congressional sessions there, doubtless explaining why as early as 1822 he was termed the *"Virginia Indiana Senator"* by an anonymous writer. In November, 1824, an Indianapolis editor announced Governor William Hendricks, Congressman Jonathan Jennings, and Judge Isaac Blackford of the Supreme Court as candidates to succeed Taylor. The editor presumed one of these men would be elected "as it is *very probable* that Waller Taylor Esq. who resides in Virginia . . . *will not again* trouble the Legislature of Indiana for their suffrages."[122] This trio of incumbents belonged to the officeholding elite, having held important offices from statehood. Moreover, they sought election to the Senate without resigning their high offices. Blackford had been on the Adams electoral ticket, while Hendricks and Jennings had apparently preferred Clay for president.

As Hendricks, Jennings, and Blackford sought support from legislators, criticism of an officeholding elite became an issue. "Alpha" disliked what he termed an electioneering tour by "our *smiling* governor," charging that his frequent resignations indicated a "restlessness" that reflected "most unfavourably, of the purity of his republicanism." The political careers of the governor and congressman, "Alpha" acidly observed, "remind us of what we have heard of skilful gamblers, who, colluding, by dexterously packing and shuffling cards, are enabled to divide the profits which inexperience and credulity had brought to their unhallowed board." Several weeks later "Beta" intensified the attack on Hendricks and Jennings, saying: "Without talents of a very high order they have succeeded, by dint of electioneering and management, in keeping the honors and emoluments of high responsible offices divided between themselves. Alternately resigning and making room for each other, they have played a game which has made the people of this state the derision of their neighbors." The political rhetoric from "Alpha" and "Beta" was perhaps intended to aid Judge Blackford.[123] Meanwhile, enroute to the national capital for a congressional session starting in December, Jennings wrote his brother-in-law that his election would be almost certain if Hendricks were out of the way.[124]

In January, the two houses met in joint session to elect a successor to Taylor. On the two initial ballots Blackford led Hendricks by one vote, with Jennings a poor third. Thereafter, with most of those who had voted for Jennings most likely switching to Hendricks, the governor led and gained a bare majority on the fourth ballot. The final ballot was not strictly along east-west sectional lines, otherwise Hendricks would have had a larger margin. Blackford must have secured some votes from eastern counties, especially as Senator John Ewing of Knox County insisted that he was not the only western legislator who voted for Hendricks.[125] Despite the closeness of the outcome, Hendricks won a significant triumph, while the poor showing of Jennings, coming on the heels of his stiff competition from Sullivan in winning reelection as a congressman, was a setback. A surprising result was the heavy support for Judge Blackford, and the prominence he gained by nearly winning the prize.

The congressional elections of 1826, like those of 1824, largely emphasized local and personal considerations rather than presidential politics. In March a pro-Adams editor commented that he had "heard of no opposition to the present worthy incumbent, Jonathan Jennings." By securing an almost unanimous vote in the Second District without an opponent in the field, Jennings vindicated himself from his near defeat by Jeremiah Sullivan two years before.[126] In the Third District, Oliver H. Smith, a youthful lawyer from Connersville in Fayette County, challenged incumbent John Test.[127] Smith charged Test with duplicity in supporting Noah Noble over Enoch McCarty to succeed Lazarus Noble as receiver of the Indianapolis Land Office. An anonymous writer, perhaps a proponent of Smith, pictured Test as lacking in candor and as a wheeler and dealer concerning patronage.[128] Smith later wrote that stump speaking was then coming into fashion, and his "strong voice, reaching to the very extremes of the largest crowds," was an asset. The two rivals made a joint appearance in Switzerland County. From his residence at Connersville, Smith rode horseback on roughly a 225 mile round trip through largely unsettled wilderness to campaign in the Fort Wayne area.[129] In the August balloting Smith defeated the incumbent by more than a thousand votes, however, he secured only ten votes in Allen County, of which Fort Wayne is the county seat, against 101 for Test.[130]

In the First District Thomas H. Blake and Dr. Lawrence Shuler, both residents of Terre Haute in Vigo County, opposed Ratliff Boon of Warrick County who sought reelection.[131] Since the Wabash River flowed through a number of counties in this district, it is not surprising that the contemplated Wabash and Erie Canal was an important issue. Shuler, defending himself from the accusation that he opposed the canal and improvement of navigation on the Wabash, insisted that no "person of good sense" in the area opposed either of these items. Seven citizens of the Vincennes area termed it "idle, preposterous, and certainly inconsistent with candour and generosity, to accuse any of the present candidates" of unfriendly views toward internal improvements.[132] Editor Stout of the Vincennes *Western Sun*, a staunch Jacksonian, supported Boon whom he called a zealous friend of internal improvements. "Vigo," presumably from the Terre Haute area, pleaded with voters of Knox County to help elect Blake over Boon. Blake was said to have been the earliest legislator to introduce a resolution concerning improvement of navigation on the Wabash, while Boon was claimed to be unfriendly to its improvement and to the Wabash and Erie Canal. Blake, not Shuler, "Vigo" insisted, was the candidate of the northern counties. Blake's defeat by Boon two years earlier was attributed to Jacob Call having divided the vote of the north with Blake. Weeks passed after the August voting with the outcome in doubt between Blake and Boon. Blake ran best in the northern counties,

Boon in those of the south as did Shuler. The latter's inroads against Boon tipped the scales in favor of Blake by a razor thin margin.[133]

None of the leading congressional candidates in 1826 seems to have run as an avowed Jacksonian, though Shuler and possibly Boon may have privately preferred Jackson to Adams. Although apparently none of the winners publicly sought support on the basis of his presidential preference, it is reasonable to conclude that all three preferred Adams as against Old Hickory. The election, however, of Blake, who had openly preferred Clay over Boon in 1824 was a plus for the Adams administration.

Several months after the congressional elections, the legislature convened in December to elect a senator for the term starting March 4, 1827. James Noble, who had held the position from statehood, was a candidate along with Congressman Jennings and Judge Blackford, both of whom had lost to Hendricks nearly two years earlier.[134] Personal and sectional considerations loomed large in the competition. In June, 1826, "Legion" asserted that "The western half of Indiana is now without any representation in the Senate of the United States. Attention to the advancement of the Canal project is necessary to ensure the assistance of Congress." Perhaps with John Ewing's previous desertion of Blackford in view, "Legion" asked local candidates to the legislature for "plain, direct, and unequivocal answers" to whether they would vote for a resident of the Wabash country for the Senate whether he be Blackford or another of "equal or superior character and standing?" Moreover, if elected, pledged "to certain men or measures," would a representative of the people have "a right to change his mind, adopt new opinions, and act contrary to his pledge?" In a private letter to John Tipton, Ewing vowed his preference for "either Jennings or Noble to Blackford," but explained that his vote would be "subservient to the grand object of the canal and improvement bills"; then bluntly added that Blackford should "resign his Judgeship if tired of it; he has been a *Candidate* and *Judge* long and often, enough."[135]

Despite western support for Blackford, the odds favored Noble. The Indianapolis *Gazette*, published in Jennings' congressional

district, described the former governor and incumbent congressman as having "acquired a popularity perhaps superior to any man
in the state," but thought he should be satisfied with the high office already held to which he had only recently been reelected.
The editor believed it was not "the wish of the people, that Gen.
Noble, whose public services are so well appreciated, should be
sent into private life in this manner." Similar views were expressed
by an editor in Brookville, Noble's hometown. After stressing Noble's beneficial service, the fact that Jennings already had been
elected for three additional years of congressional service was
noted. Considering Jennings' influence in the House, there
seemed no need to change his status at the expense of the people
of the state. The editor argued that Blackford would be more useful to the state as a Supreme judge, a position which "ought to sa-
tiate his ambition, and satisfy any man." "Q" disliked the three
frontrunners, and considered "republican institutions" endangered if the "plebian ranks" were ignored. Noble, "Q" stated, had
already held his position too long.[136]

When the legislators voted in December Noble led on every
ballot, and won on the fourth. Blackford gave Noble less competition than he had Hendricks, while Jennings, though he trailed
throughout, ran stronger than he had against Hendricks. Blackford almost certainly got most of the votes from legislators in the
western counties, while Noble probably gained the preponderance of those from the eastern ones. Jennings' strength most
likely came largely from the middle counties, with its decline after the initial ballot aiding Noble more than Blackford.[137] Noble's
third successive election to the Senate established him as a "pa-
trician" among the officeholding elite. Jennings and Blackford,
having sustained two senatorial defeats within two years, suffered
loss of political stature. Thereafter, Jennings completed his career
as a congressman; and Blackford, who had also lost the governorship to James Brown Ray in 1825, continued on the state
Supreme Court until 1853. Inasmuch as Noble, Jennings, and
Blackford all apparently preferred Adams over Jackson, the reelection of Noble apparently had no unusual significance as regards presidential politics.

Although congressional and senatorial elections of the mid-twenties revolved mainly around local and personal considerations, thereafter presidential politics played a more significant role in them. During the previous decade candidates had principally sought office on their own with informal assistance from friends and followers. But the schism in Jeffersonian Republican ranks, arising from the presidential election of 1824–1825, soon caused congressional and senatorial candidates, in varying degrees, to run as supporters of a particular presidential faction. After having served both in the federal House and Senate Oliver H. Smith looked back to his congressional campaign of 1826 and described this transition from personal to party campaigning. "There was fun [in campaigning] in those days," Smith observed in a nostalgic vein. "We had no parties then, and there was some life in a contest —very different from after times, when the candidates had to be engrafted into the party stock, and drew all their life and strength from the party to which they belonged."[138]

Meantime, numerous Jacksonians, many of whom contended that Old Hickory had been unjustly denied the presidency, were eager to vindicate the general by electing him over Adams in 1828. Clay's support of Adams for president in the House election early in 1825, followed by his becoming secretary of state in the new administration, had made him and Adams leading targets of the Jacksonian faction. Consequently a coalition of friends of the secretary and president developed as an Adams-Clay or administration faction. Within Indiana the Adams-Clay element had significant advantages as they met the challenge from the Jacksonians. The aggregate vote for the electoral tickets on behalf of Adams and Clay had exceeded that for Jackson. In addition, friends of Adams and Clay had a decisive majority in the state legislature. On the other hand, Adams had received less than one fourth of Indiana's popular vote for electors, reflecting in significant part western bias against him as a New Englander and concern about his Federalist background.[139] Though allied with Adams, Clay could not take all of his followers with him.

Among Hoosiers, the coalition of friends of Adams and Clay was hastened and strengthened by the naming of Clay as secretary of state. Most advocates of Clay were doubtless aware that this office had frequently been a steppingstone to the presidency. Senator William Hendricks voted to confirm Clay as secretary, while Senator James Noble, though absent when the voting occurred, praised Clay's distinguished talents for the post and tried in vain to have his vote recorded for the Kentuckian.[140] Thomas H. Blake, an unsuccessful congressional candidate the previous November who had publicly expressed his preference for Clay as president, assured the secretary that his "conduct" in the presidential election had been "warmly approved" by his friends. Blake asserted that the friends of Adams and Clay were "harmonizing in the most perfect accord," but he noted that there was occasional "muttering" from some Jacksonians. In an optimistic vein Blake commented that "the cause of the General is certainly down, such a turbulent spirit can not be revived among us." Judge Jesse L. Holman, an Adams elector in 1824, likewise wrote Clay about the close affinity between his friends and those of Adams. Also viewing Jackson's popularity as a temporary aberration, the judge explained that the clamor "a few noisy politicians have raised against the course you have pursued . . . reaches us only as the distant thunder, & dies away among us without an echo."[141] Unfortunately for the Adams-Clay faction, the Jacksonian movement was not a temporary aberration but a swelling tide which mounted extremely partisan criticism against the administration, and then won a sweeping victory for Jackson in 1828. This despite the fact that the policies of the administration were widely popular within Indiana, especially regarding internal improvements and the tariff.

The political status of the Adams administration probably would have increased had the president made judicious use of his appointive power. This the president declined to do and persons holding offices generally received reappointment, if their duties appeared to be properly performed, even if they were of or at least sympathetic to the Jacksonians. Continuity of federal appointees especially applied to Indiana. For instance, John Badollet, register of the Vincennes Land Office from 1804, and Samuel Gwathmey, register at the Jeffersonville Land Office from 1807, were given new four-year appointments near the end of the Adams presidency.[142] John Tipton, Indian agent in northern Indiana since 1823, continued to hold this political plum which itself controlled considerable patronage, despite his vote for Jackson in 1828.[143] Samuel Milroy, a Jackson elector in 1824, was named to inspect land offices in Illinois.[144] But when Lazarus Noble, receiver of the land office at Brookville, died in 1825 while moving the office to Indianapolis, in the scramble to become his successor support of the administration was apparently an important consideration. At least the appointment went to Noah Noble, brother of Senator James Noble as well as of the deceased. A Brookville correspondent, Amos Lane, advised Clay that Noah was "well qualified," and as popular as any man in the state. Moreover, he had voted for Clay in 1824, and on various occasions had expressed approval of the outcome of the presidential contest.[145] But the net effect of Adams' practices regarding appointments, especially for Indiana, was to perpetuate an officeholding elite which was overwhelmingly of the Adams-Clay faction.[146]

As discussed in a previous chapter, by the mid-twenties Hoosiers had caught the internal improvements fever. They especially desired federal aid for projects which directly or indirectly offered connections with the eastern seaboard. President Adams' early and repeated endorsement of congressional power to appropriate land or money for transportation projects, particularly because it was not qualified by constitutional scruples such as had been expressed by Monroe and Madison, struck a responsive chord among Indiana residents.[147] Near the close of the initial congressional session under Adams, Senator Hendricks told his constituents that the administration had "taken a stand more favourable to the new states" concerning congressional power "to construct roads and canals, than any former one."[148]

Perhaps no four years in the pioneer era brought Indiana as much significant federal aid for internal improvements as occurred while Adams was president. During 1826 and 1827 United States engineers made canal surveys in Indiana, financed by congressional appropriations. The most substantial aid received was the grant in March, 1827, of five sections of land for each mile of the prospective Wabash and Erie Canal. Terming this donation "liberal," Senator Hendricks added that it would, "if judiciously managed, make the canal." This same year Congress provided a section of land for each mile of what became the Michigan Road, extending from Michigan City to Madison via Indianapolis. On learning of these grants and related items Hugh B. McKeen exulted to John Tipton: "Huza for Indiana her fortune is made[.]"[149] During 1828 Congress earmarked $500 for a federal survey of obstructions to navigation of the Wabash River from its mouth to its reception of the Eel River, then anticipated as the probable western terminal for the Wabash canal. As the Adams administration ended, Congress made an appropriation of $50,000 to begin construction of the National Road across the state.[150] Hoosiers failed to secure aid for other projects, notably a canal on the Indiana side of the Ohio River Falls. But in 1826 when Congress purchased $100,000 of stock to aid a Kentucky company dig a canal on the southern side of the Falls, Senators Noble and Hendricks voted for the purchase.[151]

For the appropriations received, however, Indiana was much indebted to both the Jacksonians and the Adams-Clay faction. Because the administration never controlled both houses of Congress and each faction included opponents as well as proponents of federal aid, votes from both factions were essential to its approval. This support was generally greatest among members of Congress who came from the Middle Atlantic and western states. Within Indiana the internal improvements issue transcended factional lines. Adams-Clay men correctly pointed out that many Jacksonians, especially those from the South, were not sympathetic to such aid, while Jacksonians correctly noted that their support had been essential in obtaining appropriations for Indiana. Hence, during the congressional and presidential campaigns of 1828 leaders of the Jacksonian and Adams-Clay factions alike used political rhetoric to persuade voters that they rather than their opponents were more to be trusted as regards internal improvements.[152]

Vigorous support for tariff protection was closely linked with the desire for federal aid to internal improvements. Protection was expected to stimulate local manufacturing, decrease dependence on foreign imports, reduce the unfavorable balance of trade with its drain of specie from Indiana, and make the country stronger economically and more self-sufficient in case of another war with England.[153] Since agriculture was the dominant occupation, it is not surprising that there was a demand to protect manufacturing based on agricultural products. Early in 1829 a House committee, chaired by John Dumont of Switzerland County, after viewing agriculture and manufacturing as "the only causes of wealth," expressed optimism that flax, hemp, and wool, perhaps also cotton and silk, could become important in augmenting agricultural and manufacturing output. If leading individuals would wear only "domestic clothing" and "ladies would clothe themselves with fabrics of their own construction," such a change could be advanced. The committee recommended that county agricultural societies be established to award prizes for the best specimens of clothing from "cotton, silk, hemp, flax, or wool," with awards "exclusively to females, for the best specimens of hats or bonnets, make [sic] of either grass or straw, the growth of Indiana." The committee also urged that legislators "be requested to clothe themselves in domestic" prior to the next legislative session. A similar proposal about legislative garb had failed at the preceding session, along with a suggested amendment pledging members not to "use any spiritous or strong liquors but Indiana whiskey" for a year.[154] Meantime, the General Assembly had adopted a resolution calling upon Indiana members of Congress to use reasonable efforts to "restrain" the importation of hemp, raw wool, and woolens and afford full protection to all items of American growth and manufacture. Some members of the assembly, at least most of whom were Jacksonians, wanted western interests given additional consideration by explicit request for protection on behalf of iron, lead, and whiskey as well as hemp, wool, and woolens.[155]

Hoosier protectionists could not always agree concerning which items to protect. After Senators Hendricks and Noble had voted against lowering the duty on salt in 1827, a committee of the Indiana House, which noted the shortage of salt for curing and packing pork and complained that its price was high because of monopolistic control, advocated repeal of the duty on salt.[156] That same year Congressmen Jennings and Boon voted against a bill which favored protection to woolens, apparently because western agricultural interests were not adequately covered.[157] Nonetheless, all five members of Congress from Indiana voted for the tariff of 1828 which raised protection to a new high and included increases on such items as woolens, wool, hemp, flax, and iron. This measure was a hodgepodge compromise with heavy political overtones that passed because of substantial support from both Jacksonians and Adams-Clay men. Its support came principally from the Middle Atlantic and western states, while Jacksonians from southern states were largely in opposition to its passage.[158] Nevertheless, in the congressional and presidential elections of 1828, within Indiana, both Jacksonians and administration supporters frequently presented themselves and their presidential candidate as advocates of protection. Even so, by the late twenties there was a waning of protectionist sentiment and a trend in favor of eliminating or at least reducing duties on articles of common consumption, including salt, sugar, tea, and coffee, while leaving duties on costly fabrics, hard liquors, and other items purchased mainly by persons of more than modest wealth. The favorable federal fiscal situation, with the rapid decline of the federal debt, encouraged this trend.[159]

Hoosiers also were much concerned about Indian relations and public land policy. When Adams became president in 1825, Indian titles, except for tracts of varying size in central Indiana, had been cleared from the region south of the Wabash and Maumee rivers. Above these rivers, except for an irregular strip north of the Wabash from the Illinois border eastward more than halfway across the state and a narrow slice along the eastern portion of the boundary with Michigan, almost all the land was yet held by the Indians. For practical purposes, only the Miami and Potawatomi remained in Indiana. The Miami retained land on or near much of the route through which the contemplated Wabash and Erie Canal would pass.[160] This consideration, coupled with the influx of settlers into central Indiana, caused legislators and others to urge further extinguishment of Indian titles, accompanied in some instances with comments about the need for early removal of the Miami and Potawatomi from the state.[161] Treaties with these tribes in 1826 and 1828 reduced Indian holdings along the route of the anticipated canal, in northeastern Indiana, and adjoining the western part of the Michigan border. They also ended Indian title to various tracts in central Indiana, cleared the title along the Indiana shore of Lake Michigan, and resulted in the Michigan Road which north of the Wabash River bisected Potawatomi territory, weakening tribal control over the area.[162] These cessions prepared the way for commencement of the Wabash and Erie Canal and a system of internal improvements, fostered the flow of settlers across central Indiana, and to a lesser extent into northern Indiana. But the increased annuities provided by these treaties encouraged the Indians, supported by some traders, to resist removal from the state. In reporting about the negotiation of the 1826 treaties the commissioners emphasized that it was "impossible" to persuade the Miami and Potawatomi to emigrate. "Time, the destruction of the game, and the approximation of our settlements," the commissioners explained, "are necessary before this measure can be successfully proposed to them."[163]

The decrease of Indian holdings in northern Indiana, and especially around Fort Wayne, set the stage for removal to Logansport of the state's only federal Indian agency. John Tipton, Indian agent at the Summit City from 1823, persistently contended that the agency could better serve the interest of the Indians if moved westward to a region occupied more by Indians and less so by whites. Since regulation of trade with the tribesmen and distribution of presents and annuities among them were leading functions of the agency, there was considerable to be said in favor of this contention but Tipton was doubtless influenced by his significant speculation in land in the Logansport area. For the most part citizens of Fort Wayne and traders of eastern Indiana and western Ohio had a vested interest in preventing removal. Senator James Noble and Congressman Oliver H. Smith joined with such citizens and traders in opposing the transfer, while Senator William Hendricks, Congressman Thomas H. Blake, and apparently Congressman Jonathan Jennings, plus a number of citizens and traders west of Fort Wayne, supported it.[164] President Adams finally approved the removal, effected in 1828.

Federal policy regarding disposition of the public domain remained basically unchanged. The 1820 law, making eighty-acre tracts available for a minimum of $100 in cash, persisted. Sales from Indiana land offices ranged from a low of 154,558.51 acres in 1824 to a high of 346,527.51 acres in 1829 during the twenties. According to the *Indiana Journal*, for the decade as a whole they sold more acreage than those of any state.[165] Meantime, relief legislation to debtors for credit purchases to 1820 was extended and at times modified. President Adams, Hoosier legislators, and members of Congress from both rival parties gave support to the relief acts which continued into the early thirties.[166]

While there was no major change in land policy under Adams, support grew, especially from western states, for graduation and cession. Modest interest in these proposals had been manifest during the first half of the twenties. Advocates of graduation asked for step by step reduction of the price of public lands, mainly according to the time they had been on the market, with unsold lands being donated to the states when the price became nominal. Proponents of cession requested that the federal government cede the public domain to the state in which it was located. As the twenties advanced Senator Thomas Hart Benton, of Missouri, became known for his persistent and vigorous support of graduation. Despite considerable support, including endorsement by a resolution of the legislature of Indiana, graduation failed to win the approval of Congress.[167]

Indiana's Senator William Hendricks became one of the staunchest proponents of cession. He insisted that the landed domain rightfully belonged to the states in which it was located, else they would not have the same rights and sovereignty and be on an equal status with the original states.[168] His senatorial colleague, James Noble, called cession a "dangerous" proposition that "would injure the new States" but he termed Benton's plan for graduation worthy of consideration. Samuel Milroy, an early Jacksonian, approved cession as a means whereby "the national domain, or national purse" could be used to help the states build internal improvements. If the "unsold lands" could be obtained for this purpose, Milroy asserted, he "would be willing to receive the favour, at the hand of *Either* of the *Grate Political* parties—or both . . . ."[169] Early in 1829 the Indiana legislature declared its "exclusive right, to the soil and eminent domain, of all the unappropriated lands within" its borders. The debate on this item in the Indiana House indicates much interest in obtaining land from the public domain for support of internal improvements. David Wallace, later governor of Indiana, opposed the measure as one "fraught with much confusion and great mischief." He commented that a majority of the House believed that it "would be extremely unpopular, and calculated to injure the member" voting against the memorial. Nonetheless, Wallace said he could not "for the sake of floating with the popular current, consent to make a compromise with conscience" and vote for its adoption.[170] With much of the federal debt yet to be liquidated, the federal government bearing heavy costs regarding acquisition and disposition of the public domain, and most states having little or none of the public domain, neither graduation nor cession stood any chance of congressional approval during the twenties.

Although the main focus of the Adams administration was on domestic politics, significant attention was given to relations with other countries. Despite the fact that the president had had much success as a diplomat, efforts to resolve Anglo-American differences about trade on the oceans, to open trade with the British West Indies, and to obtain compensation from France for damage to American shipping during the Napoleonic era were unsuccessful. The extremely partisan sniping of the Jacksonians concerning these items and the Panama Congress of 1826 added to the difficulties and frustrations which President Adams and Secretary Clay faced in negotiating with representatives of other nations.[171] Indiana members of Congress, however, gave these officials substantial support. When the administration recommended that representatives be sent to the Panama Congress, called by Latin American countries to discuss matters of common concern, both Hoosier senators voted to confirm their appointment; and they, plus all three Indiana congressmen, sustained an appropriation to finance the mission.[172]

Distrust of European powers, notably England and France, stimulated interest in the Panama Congress. Congressman John Test insisted that the security of the United States and advancement of trade made American representation essential. President Washington's warning about political connections with foreign nations, Test contended, was meant for European powers. Political connections with republican governments such as those of our Latin American neighbors, the congressman explained, "are not liable to the same objections with those of regal or monarchical character. It is never the interests of Republics to acquire Territory beyond what is necessary to their physical strength, or to secure them against the encroachments of an enemy." Nevertheless, Test concluded that Spain, by not preventing pirates and marauders from using Cuba as a base against the United States, had "long since" given Americans "good cause to seize the Island of Cuba" from her. Suppose, Test suggested, that England purchase Cuba, thus threaten the security of the United States and control of the Mississippi trade artery; that France regain part of Louisiana from Spain; and that Spain reassert her claim to territory east of the Sabine River (the western boundary of the state of Louisiana). There would then be the very real possibility of England's "goring" the United States "on the North, the East, and the South," while France on the western border disputes "the very soil upon which you tread, and which was paid for by the sweat of your brows." The Monroe Doctrine of 1823, which Test interpreted as telling European governments that interference with the government of the Spanish republics by any power other than Spain would be viewed as an attack upon the principles of free governments, was described "like a voice from Heaven" and desirable American policy "toward our sister Republics in the South."[173] Before the Panama Congress met, a Richmond editor endorsed the principle that "the United States CANNOT CONSENT to the occupation of the islands of Cuba and Porto Rico, by any European power, other than Spain," under any contingency. Near the end of 1826 the Indiana Senate overwhelmingly declared that it was wise to "abstain from every species of involvement in the concerns of foreign nations," but warmly approved the course pursued by Adams concerning the Panama Congress as favorable to South American independence.[174]

Although late in 1826 Governor James Brown Ray suggested that the proposed Michigan Road would have great military importance if Americans had to meet the "old enemy" in the North, Indiana residents showed no eagerness for another conflict with England. The editor of the Richmond paper that had been adamant against any power other than Spain controlling Cuba or Puerto Rico, after commenting about the long dispute regarding the northeastern border with Canada, added: "Enough blood has already been shed in disputes for American territory—and we hope that an amicable disposition may settle this question to mutual satisfaction." Two years later Senator Hendricks noted the continuation of disputes regarding portions of the continental border with Canada. He explained that the Convention of 1818, providing joint occupation between the United States and England for a vast area west to the Rocky Mountains, had been renewed for an indefinite period. Hendricks observed that the proposed occupation of the mouth of the Columbia River by Americans was a "measure not likely to be adopted until all questions of boundary in that quarter be settled."[175]

Though eager to maintain isolation from European affairs, Hoosiers continued to express sympathy and admiration for the persistent but unsuccessful attempt of the Greeks to gain independence from Turkey. In the summer of 1825 a Lawrenceburg paper rejoiced in what it considered to be the rapid progress of the Greeks toward liberty and freedom. Senator Hendricks and Congressman Oliver H. Smith viewed with concern the terrible plight of the Greeks and looked to aid from European powers as a possible means of tipping the scales in their favor. Early in 1827 the Lawrenceburg paper observed that citizens of New York and Philadelphia had contributed $800 for relief of the beleaguered Greeks, then commented that local citizens had but little hard cash to spare, but would doubtless "throw in a few barrels of *pork* to help the good cause, if called upon."[176] As such utterances suggest, Hoosiers were more aware of their European heritage than much of their rhetoric suggests.

Meantime, scarcely had Adams been inaugurated when the fes-tering political sores arising from the election of 1824–1825 caused the Jacksonians to become intent on elevating Old Hickory to the presidency in the next election. Soon after the inauguration a pro-Adams editor in eastern Indiana observed that a Tennessee paper had already announced Jackson for president commencing March 4, 1829, then sarcastically commented that the announce-ment was "*In time.*" Some months later another pro-Adams editor, first noting that Jackson had resigned from the federal Senate and again been nominated for president, tersely commented: "But 'tis all in vain,—he has run his best race." In October, 1826, Elihu Stout, the veteran editor who had staunchly supported Jackson in 1824, informed his readers that the mails had been "barren of news," while "The presidential question, and the local affairs of the states, occupy the columns of almost every paper."[177]

During 1827 the campaign to elect the general gained momen-tum. Citizens of Switzerland County met at Vevay and com-menced the year by adopting resolutions in his favor. They rec-ommended him because he was one of the few surviving soldiers of the American Revolution; for his conduct during the War of 1812; on account of his popularity with the great body of citizens throughout the Union, while "unpledged to any particular course of measures"; and in the belief that he would "collect around him and call to his aid the talents and integrity of the land." A county correspondence committee of five was chosen and authorized to name ten persons as a vigilance committee for each township. Friends of General Jackson were asked "to call meetings, in their several counties, and adopt similar resolutions."[178] In reporting the Switzerland County gathering, Stout proclaimed that "notwithstanding the apparent strength of the Administration among the officeholders and office seekers in this state, the cause of the people, and of the people's man, is gaining ground contin-ually among those most deeply interested—the people." As evi-dence that the "people's man" was "gaining ground," Stout de-clared that within a few months the Lawrenceburgh *Indiana Palladium*, the Vevay *Switzerland Guest*, and Salem *Annotator* had come "out decidedly" for Jackson.[179] Whereas the Jacksonians emphasized Jackson the man as the candidate of the people against the political establishment, friends of Adams and Clay stressed the attachment of the administration to federal aid for internal improvements and tariff protection, the importance of these issues to Indiana, and the threat to them should Jackson become chief executive. Pro-Adams editors expressed concern that Jackson had declined to make clear his views on these issues and was supported by southerners from slave states who were opposed to them.[180]

In January, 1828, both the Jacksonians and Adams-Clay men held state conventions which chose electoral tickets. During the preceding November "Citizen" had called upon friends of Jackson to meet at their respective county seats on Saturday, December 15, to name committees of correspondence and delegates to a state convention at Indianapolis on January 8. This date, the anniversary of Jackson's triumph over the British at New Orleans during the War of 1812, indicates a desire to capitalize on national pride and the general's military fame. A number of counties held meetings which named delegates to the state convention, appointed or made provision for the appointment of county and township committees, and expressed enthusiastic support of Old Hickory. These gatherings frequently hailed Jackson for his firm commitment to republicanism, as one unsullied by political intrigue and corruption, and as a man pure and unpledged coming from the very bosom of the people. Adams was castigated as a "decided" aristocrat and Federalist, for his corrupt bargain with Clay, as hostile to western interests, and an opponent of universal suffrage.[181] About forty-seven persons from approximately twenty-five of the fifty-eight counties that took part in the ensuing election attended the state convention, according to its proceedings. Dr. Israel T. Canby, a delegate from Jefferson County, chaired the convention which met January 9 and 10. An electoral ticket of five members was adopted "by unanimous consent" by the convention; fifteen persons were named a "general superintendence" or state central committee; local Jacksonians were urged to establish county correspondence and township vigilance committees; and an address on "behalf of the Democratic Republicans" of the state was adopted.[182]

This address, which served as a party platform, used inflated rhetoric in viewing "with serious alarm" the "extraordinary political crisis" facing the nation. It claimed that Jackson had won a plurality of both the popular and electoral vote in 1824, only to have the "rights of the people trampled upon" by the House election of Adams, apparently achieved through corruption, bargain, and intrigue. With seemingly a grudging admission of the popularity of key measures of the Adams administration, the address insisted that until elected president he had "ever opposed the best interests of the Western country." Jackson's ability and integrity were exalted; his great military achievements pointed to with pride; and his voting record proclaimed as having established him as "the honest but prudent, the sincere and zealous but consistent friend of Internal Improvements and Domestic Manufactures." Chairman Canby enjoined the delegates to refute the calumny that the Democratic Republicans were engaged in a mere personal contest. "The cause of Jackson is the cause of our country, its liberties and constitution," he exhorted.[183]

Hardly had the Jackson convention adjourned when the Adams-Clay men or National Republicans convened for a similar meeting at the capital. In early December "A Citizen" had called upon friends of internal improvements and domestic manufactures to hold county meetings and send delegates "to take into consideration the next Presidential election" at a convention in Indianapolis January 12.[184] Various counties elected delegates to this convention, made provision for county and township organization, and adopted resolutions staunchly supporting internal improvements and the tariff. Jackson's commitment to these issues was much questioned, often with the suggestion that his friends came mainly from states which had raised objection to them. Jackson was pictured as a military chieftain, at times as a very successful one, but frequently as an individual too rash and arbitrary to be entrusted with the supreme civil power of the country. The "hackneyed charge of a corrupt bargain" between Adams and Clay was viewed as abusive political rhetoric.[185] According to its proceedings, the pro-Adams state convention held formal sessions on January 12, 14, and 16, with about twenty-seven "delegated" and approximately forty-nine "friendly citizen" members, making a total of seventy-six persons in attendance from forty-four counties. John Watts, a veteran of the American Revolution and a "delegated member" from Dearborn County, served as chairman. The convention "unanimously adopted" an electoral slate of five individuals; named a state or "Central Committee" of fifteen persons; asked friends of internal improvements and domestic manufactures, favorable to the reelection of Adams, to meet at county seats on February 22 (Washington's birthday) or soon thereafter to establish county correspondence and township vigilance committees; and approved a platform expressing "entire confidence" in the Adams administration.[186]

The platform emphasized issues rather than personalities. The policy of the administration "in fostering Internal Improvements and Domestic Manufactures" was vigorously commended, and the aid of Indiana's five members of Congress in support of these policies was gratefully acknowledged. Contending that "Gen. Jackson stands *virtually committed* and *pledged* to Southern policy and Southern measures," the platform insisted that no Indiana voter friendly to the American System could consistently support his election "without an *explicit* and public declaration on his part, that he will recommend and foster Internal Improvements and Domestic Manufactures." The platform declared that Clay's role in the election of Adams had been prompted by "pure and patriotic motives" by "one who is still the ornament of the *West* and the benefactor of his country." An address to citizens of the state reinforced and elaborated these items. It asserted that the Adams administration had given Indiana "all the Internal Improvements that have ever been made or projected by the General Government"; afforded generous relief to debtors for land purchases; provided protection to agriculture as well as to manufacturing; and achieved all this while reducing the national debt. Adams was pictured as an able, experienced, and tested statesman having superb moral character and capacity. Jackson, however, was termed "*untried* as a Statesman"; described as "either unwilling to *avow*, or desirous to *conceal* his opinions" about internal improvements and tariff protection; and presented as a candidate whose principal support came from seven slave states staunchly opposed to these two measures.[187]

Almost immediately members of the Indiana Senate poured oil on the political fires as they maneuvered for partisan advantage. Senator John Milroy, a delegate from Lawrence County to the Jackson convention, who had been named to its state central committee, offered to present resolutions asking the governor to correspond with General Jackson to solicit his views about internal improvements and a protective tariff. His proposed resolutions also called upon the governor to solicit from Adams what his views had been against the organization of Louisiana and the coalition formed between him and Clay. Milroy refused to submit his resolutions unless members agreed to approve them unchanged. Whereupon William Graham of Jackson County, a delegate at the recent Adams convention, introduced resolutions asking the governor to solicit from Jackson an explicit statement of his views about the tariff and internal improvements. Their preamble described the confusion which existed because the general's friends in western states urged his election on the ground that he favored these measures while his supporters in Virginia, the Carolinas, Georgia, Tennessee, Alabama, and Mississippi advocated his election because of his opposition to them. Graham's resolutions were quickly read three times and passed by a vote of fourteen to five, the voting presumably at least largely along partisan lines.[188]

Governor James Brown Ray, resorting to his oft-used effervescent and pompous style, wrote Jackson as required by the Senate. Ray assured Jackson that Hoosiers had "not ceased to venerate the victorious General, who, aided by the brave sons of freedom, preserved New Orleans," but he explained that in selecting "public servants" that "*principles* and *measures*" had to have priority over attachment to fallible men. After emphasizing that the western and northern states could "never support any administration or party . . . composed of anti-tariff and anti-internal improvement men," Ray asked Jackson for an explicit statement of his current views concerning these issues.[189] In a cagey response, subject to varying interpretations, the presidential aspirant replied that his "opinions, *at present*, are precisely what they were in 1823 and 4," when communicated by letter to Dr. L. E. Coleman of

Warrenton, North Carolina, "and when I voted for the present tariff [1824] and appropriations for internal improvement."[190] A pro-Adams editor warned that it amounted to "abandoning a certainty for an uncertainty to prefer Gen. Jackson [over Adams] on account of his devotion to the American system."[191] Nonetheless, in view of the election returns, Jackson's reply to Ray apparently reassured his followers and gained him votes in Indiana.

Although issues were discussed, the presidential contest between adjournment of the state conventions in January and the voting in November gave much consideration to hashing and rehashing personal charges and countercharges. The National Republicans stressed their commitment and that of Adams to the tariff and internal improvements, while questioning Jackson's attachment to these issues. They maintained that regardless of his views his administration would be captive to southerners who held contrary opinions. Friends of the president continued to stress his character, unusual ability, and distinguished and statesmanlike service to the nation. In contrast, proponents of Adams often described Jackson as a distinguished military chieftain who had tarnished his achievements by acts of oppression, tyranny, and insubordination. His mediocre civilian career had included opposition to universal suffrage for whites, early and current ties with Federalism, and association with the treasonable activities of Aaron Burr. His personal character had been marred by dueling, gambling, trading of black slaves, and tavern brawls. In a slashing attack on both the public and private life of Jackson, an address from the Adams State Central Committee admonished Hoosiers to show by their "votes that ours is a government of Laws, of Religion, of Morals, and of Peace, and that to obtain the highest office in the gift of enlightened freemen a man must exhibit other qualifications than those of a MILITARY CHIEFTAIN."[192]

The Democratic Republicans stoutly defended their candidate and vigorously assailed Adams. Though their statements were at times subject to varying interpretations, the Jacksonians affirmed and reaffirmed their and their candidate's attachment to the tariff and internal improvements. Portraying Jackson as one of the great men of the age, well qualified for civilian as well as military service, his supporters presented him as an honest and incorruptible man who would serve the interests of the people. Adams was described as an aristocrat who had retained strong Federalist leanings, opposed universal suffrage for whites, and had a long record of hostility to western interests. Repeatedly Jacksonians embellished the accusation that Adams had become president as a result of political intrigue which included a corrupt bargain that made Clay secretary of state, thus thwarting the will of the sovereign people and tainting republican virtue. Both Senators Noble and Hendricks were explicit that they had no knowledge of a corrupt bargain or even of either a direct or indirect understanding between Adams and Clay, but their statements probably had meager impact on popular opinion. The mood of most Hoosiers seems to have been expressed by "A Mechanic" who declared that the people had "taken a fancy to one Andrew Jackson, a hero who has often shown how much he loved his country, by exposing his life in her service; and who, moreover, has always had a mortal hatred to bargain and sale in political matters."[193]

In the voting on November 3 electors pledged to Jackson won Indiana by a landslide, receiving about 22,100 votes to 16,950 for those pledged to Adams. Popular interest in the election is indicated from the fact that the aggregate of votes cast was about two and one-half times that four years earlier, and slightly above that for the gubernatorial election a few months previous. Jackson won a majority in three fourths of the counties, winning all but two that had gone for him in 1824. He was victorious in nearly all counties of the Whitewater Valley south of Wayne; likewise in the interior or middle counties stretching from the Ohio River northward; and he ran better in counties on or near the Wabash and West Fork of White River than he had four year earlier, carrying most of them. Adams won several counties on or near the National Road, including Wayne and Marion, and scattered others. Jackson's improved showing in the Wabash and White River counties affords evidence that voters in this area, strongly attached to internal improvements, had confidence that he would support federal aid for such improvements. Since as in 1824 many older and more developed counties went for Jackson, while various new and less developed ones sustained Adams, the general's triumph cannot properly be viewed as a victory for frontier democracy over aristocratic elements.[194]

Jackson's wide margin over Adams, fueled by western bias and personal preference, elated his followers. After observing that the "long and bitter contest is over," Editor Stout advised the "*hot tongued . . .* of both parties, to 'keep cool,' and 'judge the tree by its fruits[.]'" The Vincennes editor urged that none condemn Jackson "in anticipation of imaginary evil" and asserted that "too much of the vilest abuse" had been showered on both candidates. A pro-Adams editor, noting that Jackson had been fairly elected by a large majority, termed it the duty of every republican to submit to the popular will and look upon every act of Jackson in the most charitable light. If the new administration became as good as that of Adams' had been, the friends of Adams had a duty to support it.[195] But the joy of success and vindication was especially sweet to the ardent Jacksonians. When the Jackson electors met at Indianapolis in December their five votes for Old Hickory were "announced by a discharge of FIVE ROUNDS from a six pounder." Stout approvingly quoted an unnamed editor who gloried in the role that people of the West had played in electing "'a man who is virtually a BACKWOODS-MAN. A man who has grown grey in the wilderness of America, one who has seen a small community of civilization, hemmed in by savages and wild beasts, spreading its social & harmonizing influence, until it became a great nation[.]'"[196] The *spirited* elation of some Jacksonians is indicated by the manner in which Thomas J. Evans and Congressman Ratliff Boon observed Jackson's inauguration on March 4, 1829. In a jovial vein, Evans wrote John Tipton: "On the morning of the 4th I was with Col Boon & was by him Jacksonised with a glass of gin[.] Whisky you know has been said to be a Jackson liquid but that was when the presidency was in expectancy, now when hope has ended in fruition gin must be the substitute[.]"[197]

Despite Jackson's decisive triumph over Adams in the November voting, in the congressional races which terminated in August only one avowed Jacksonian was successful. Of the incumbents, all seeking reelection, Congressmen Thomas H. Blake and Oliver

H. Smith were openly for Adams while Jonathan Jennings, not publicly committed to either presidential candidate, had generally sustained the measures of the Adams administration. The Adams-Clay men, who controlled state politics, were less inclined than the Jacksonians to urge voters to let their preference for Jackson or Adams determine for whom they would vote to represent them in Congress. The Jacksonians, however, hungry for office and eager to ride on Jackson's coattails in winning other offices, asked voters to elect congressmen committed to Jackson. Thus the "presidential question" became involved in the congressional elections in varying degrees. Candidates from both presidential factions entered the competition in all three districts, but informally on their own since the use of conventions to nominate congressmen had not yet developed.

In the large First District, drawn mainly from counties of the Wabash Valley, the "presidential question" had a dominant role. For a time it seemed that Samuel Judah, one of the founders of the Jackson party in Indiana and a Vincennes lawyer, would challenge Blake. But Ratliff Boon, a Jackson elector in 1828 who had served in Congress from 1825 to 1827, and been narrowly defeated for reelection by Blake in 1826, became a candidate. Judah graciously withdrew and urged the party faithful to unite in support of Boon. [198] Hoisting high the Jacksonian flag, Editor Elihu Stout exhorted: "The race will be between Mr. Boon, and col. Blake. It is hoped the friends of Jackson, the republicans, and friends of liberty, will do their duty." Stout proclaimed that Blake had reported that "'he has nailed his flag to the mast, and will *sink* or *swim* with the present administration[.]'" In a letter to John Tipton, Boon stressed that "The Administration men *will* act in *Concert*" with his success depending largely upon the "unanimity" of Jacksonians. Suggesting that the congressional elections would "give tone to the November election for president," Boon emphasized, "Let the *line be drawn*, and we are safe."[199]

When Blake returned home from the annual congressional session in early June, the incumbent insisted that his remarks had been misquoted. He said he had merely promised to "'sink or swim *with the cause* of the present administration'" meaning the cause of internal improvements, tariff protection, and extensive relief to purchasers of public lands. "I am for measures in preference to men," Blake explained, and however "devoted to Henry Clay" or any other member of the Adams administration, should Jackson be elected he would cheerfully and zealously support his administration in the same cause. Following his explanation, "Many Friends of Jackson" put forth a seven-page circular contending that Blake had pledged his support to the Adams administration, not just some of its measures. The circular argued that election of a Jacksonian Congress was essential to the success of a Jacksonian presidency. The experience of the recent congressional session was referred to as proving that it would be "infinitely better" for the country and Andrew Jackson that he "remain a private citizen, than succeed to the Presidency with a majority of Congress opposed to his administration."[200] Friends of Blake contended that Boon's commitment to internal improvements and the tariff was less reliable than that of Blake. A Terre Haute editor charged that in northern counties of the district Boon sought election on the popularity of Jackson, as a man of the people, and not on a sectional basis, but inferred that south of White River Boon had appealed to voters on the ground that the interests of the north were different from those of the southern area.[201] Boon's modest margin over Blake renewed his interrupted tenure in Congress, and it afforded a favorable omen for Jacksonian victory in November. Boon thus became the second avowed Jacksonian congressman from Indiana.[202]

In the Second District, mainly comprising counties in the middle of the state between the Ohio and Wabash rivers, Jonathan Jennings, the independent incumbent, was challenged by candidates from the rival presidential factions. By mid-June, Lieutenant Governor John H. Thompson, an Adams man, and Henry S. Handy, Jacksonian editor of the Salem *Annotator*, were in the race.[203] In a circular to voters, Thompson proclaimed his support for tariff protection for every article of American growth and manufacture; claimed that he had been the first Indiana legislator to seek relief legislation for overburdened purchasers of public land under the credit system; and ignored the internal improvements issue. Congressman Jennings affirmed his commitment to tariff protection, federal aid for internal improvements, relief legislation for purchasers of land, and more liberal terms for selling public land. After stating that he approved "The general measures of the present administration," the incumbent promised that if reelected and a new administration came into office he would "support the measures proposed" whenever he could do so consistent with the trust imposed on him. Handy probably held views on the issues similar to those espoused by Jennings, however, on the eve of the election he withdrew his candidacy.[204] Jennings buried Thompson in a landslide, affording substantial evidence of his personal popularity with the electorate regardless of their presidential preferences.[205]

In the Third District, located principally in the Whitewater Valley, the congressional campaign became a contest within a contest. Congressman Oliver H. Smith faced opposition from John Test, a former congressman and supporter of Adams and his administration, whom Smith had unseated two years earlier, as well as from Jonathan McCarty, a member of the 1824 Jackson electoral ticket.[206] Smith affirmed his commitment to federal aid for internal improvements and tariff protection—measures doubtless also endorsed by Test and McCarty. The incumbent declared that he would vote for Adams, but if Jackson were elected he would sustain the measures of his administration that were consistent with the interests of his constituents and the country. After returning to Indiana from the congressional session, Smith withdrew from the canvass. He explained that otherwise the majority would be defeated by a minority—meaning, though Test's name was not mentioned, that he and Test would so divide the pro-Adams vote that McCarty would be the victor by being the sole candidate of the Jacksonian minority.[207] The Indianapolis *Gazette*, an administrative organ, attributed Smith's withdrawal to there being "two administration candidates and one Jacksonian" in the field. Commending Smith and hoping that his action would "not hereafter be forgotten," the *Gazette* observed that "The Jacksonians will now be suffered to draw the line, and will be met on equal grounds."[208] Test's sizable victory over McCarty doubtless resulted mainly from his support from the more numerous Adams-Clay element.[209]

The "presidential question" was much involved in the congressional elections of 1828, but the voting was not rigidly along lines of preference for Jackson or Adams. Jackson electors carried the First District by a much larger margin than did Boon, making it almost certain that Boon rode to victory on Jackson's coattails. In the Third District Jackson electors ran considerably ahead of McCarty, but they failed to win a majority from its counties. Jackson electors ran extremely well in the Second District, but the outcome affords substantial evidence that the independent Jennings was strongly supported by proponents of Adams and Jackson alike. Compared to the 1826 congressional elections, however, the exchange of Test for Smith and the reelection of Jennings represented no change of importance but the triumph of Boon was a decided plus for the Jacksonians.[210] Thus, with the congressional and presidential campaigns of 1828, *organized and rival political parties* had their beginning in Indiana.

CHAPTER 10

JACKSONIAN DEMOCRACY REINTERPRETED, 1829–1841

THE PREFERENCE OF HOOSIERS for Jackson over Adams in the presidential election of 1828 was not the harbinger of a democratic revolution. From statehood there had been universal suffrage for white males, ballot or secret voting, and popular election of the governor and some local officials. Moreover, the General Assembly met annually, with the electorate choosing all the representatives and one third of the senators each August. Both in 1824 and 1828 the voters had named the presidential electors. This considerable degree of political democracy for its time was deeply rooted in Jeffersonian Republicanism and strongly reinforced by an egalitarian economic base. Slavery, only meagerly established in the territorial era, was prohibited by the Constitution of 1816.[1] The rural and largely undeveloped economy principally rested upon farmers of modest means, plus trades, merchants, and household manufacturing. During the thirties Hoosiers were more eager to advance their economy than to reform their political system.

When Old Hickory became president, among Hoosiers Jacksonians or Democratic Republicans and anti-Jacksonians or National Republicans generally held similar views on the leading political questions. Both parties vigorously supported federal aid for internal improvements, substantial tariff protection, early removal of the Indians, and a liberal policy for disposition of the public domain. On the other hand, both parties had largely ignored the bank issue during the last half of the twenties. Whether for or against Old Hickory, party leaders were staunchly for western interests but also strongly devoted to the Union. The overwhelming majority of Indiana citizens, despite their hostility to slavery, were not inclined to interfere with slavery in the states where it already existed.

Party cleavage increased during the thirties, but at times loyalty to individuals prevailed over party preference. Under Adams the

Jacksonians had pressed their attack against the administration, but under Jackson the National Republicans became the attackers. After Old Hickory's triumph in 1828, Editor Elihu Stout of the *Western Sun*, the general's early and devoted advocate, commented that the "long and bitter contest" was over and he hoped for the "return of peace and harmony among all classes, and parties." But when Jackson delivered his inaugural the pro-Adams Indianapolis *Gazette* considered it more like "Speeches usually delivered by the British Kings at the opening of Parliament" than previous inaugurals. The inaugural was correctly described as only "a faint and imperfect outline" of the new president's intended course as well as subject to conflicting interpretations. The *Gazette* contended that the new cabinet represented views that jeopardized both tariff protection and federal aid to internal improvements. Concern was also expressed about the chief executive's remarks that he had a mandate from the people to reform abuses in the federal patronage.[2]

Immediately upon becoming president, Jackson set about ousting National Republicans from federal offices in Indiana. Dr. Israel T. Canby, defeated Jacksonian candidate for governor in 1828, and other party leaders urged removals as a means of rewarding party faithful and strengthening the Democratic Republicans. He especially supported the removal of Noah Noble, receiver of the Indianapolis Land Office and a prominent National Republican, but John Tipton and others unsuccessfully opposed his dismissal.[3] The Indianapolis *Gazette*, which had preferred Adams over Jackson, observed that those who had "supported Mr. Adams, have reason to 'tremble in their pumps.'" Another pro-Adams editor commented that "the whole Yanke[e] nation has felt the force of the Hickory broom."[4] Before the end of 1830 all registers and receivers at the five Indiana land offices, except John Badollet who had served as register at Vincennes since 1804, had been replaced.[5] John Tipton, Indian agent at Logansport, who like Badollet was a Jacksonian, also escaped removal.[6] Charles Dewey, attorney for the federal district court for Indiana, and John Vawter, its marshal, were succeeded by Samuel Judah and William Marshall respectively.[7] Many Indiana postmasters were removed.[8]

These partisan removals aroused the indignation of the National Republicans who had enjoyed a near monopoly of state as well as federal offices during the Adams administration. The Indianapolis *Indiana Journal*, a leading National Republican organ, commented that the proscriptive system fostered the inclination "to live by public employment and be exempted from ordinary labour," with a resultant lower standard of performance. If a man could not retain office during good behavior, then "the security of his fidelity to the public" would be eliminated. Moreover, if rotation was a Jacksonian principle, why had the veteran officeholder, John Badollet, been retained? The *Indiana Journal* expressed concern about converting "the Post Office into a political machine" for party advantage. A Centerville editor deplored the ousting of gray haired veterans of the American Revolution to make room for unprincipled office seekers. Should offices become the spoils of victory, "Virtue, morality, wisdom, modesty, patriotism, experience and qualifications will then be banished from all our public stations, and the grave of these must be the grave of our Liberty."[9] Badollet confided his "disappointment & allarm" to Albert Gallatin, adding: "The havoc has begun in this state, the best & most tried officers are unmercifully removed, & their stations filled by partisans, not even the post master of the most obscure country village can escape[.]"[10] Both before and after his elevation to the Senate in 1832, John Tipton expressed disapproval of removals on partisan grounds. The politically independent Senator William Hendricks, writing in the summer of 1830, stated that he had "always disapproved" removals and believed them "the chief cause of all the murmurings against" the Jackson administration.[11]

Apologists for Old Hickory defended removals as necessary to preserve republican government. Editor Elihu Stout considered them "essential to the prosperity and duration of our free institutions," hence the president had "been compelled to make" dismissals. The Indianapolis *Gazette*, which became a supporter of Jackson during 1829 despite its advocacy of Adams in 1828, emphasized that the general owed his election to "the bone and sinew of the country," who were "men of small capital" and on that account had greater interest in republican institutions. A Lawrenceburg editor declared that if people knew that the loudest bawlers about removals were "disappointed office seekers, hirelings, and disbanded officers," little concern would exist regarding them.[12] The Indianapolis *Indiana Democrat*, a staunch proadministration journal, vigorously sustained the removal policy in a series which continued through several issues. Prior to Jackson's election, it emphasized, "an almost perfect system of official nobility" had been established so that a "common man, or plebian" had about the same prospect of obtaining an office as a plebian would have had of claiming "privileges of the patricians of Rome" before the Gracchi. "The principle of rotation in office," the capital city editor proclaimed, "corrects many evils." Hence, the time had come to end the patronage monopoly of the "purse proud" Adams-Clay men and give Jacksonians their share of state and federal offices.[13]

Old Hickory's widespread use of removals to reward partisans quickly resulted in domination of federal offices in Indiana passing to the Jacksonians. Thereafter, Jackson and Van Buren generally filled vacancies from the party faithful. Early in 1838 the Whig editor of the Indianapolis *Indiana Journal* viewed Van Buren's use of the "*spoils principle*" as an important reason why he should be overthrown. As Van Buren's term neared its end, this editor accused the lame duck incumbent of making wholesale nominations of friends to office, charging him with "impudence" for allegedly filling some offices which would not become vacant until after Harrison became president. The Whig spokesman, however, exhibited a hankering for Whig appointees when he asked why did Van Buren "not wait but two short months and let the offices be filled by the 'People's President?'"[14] The integrity and efficiency of the federal civil service in Indiana apparently suffered during the thirties. Calvin Fletcher, who had preferred Jackson for president in 1824, commented in his diary that during the general's four initial years as executive "the weak & corrupt . . . filled all the federal offices" in the state. The very men who had controlled the patronage, Fletcher added, had themselves been turned out for corruption in office.[15]

Meantime, a future governor and an Indiana land speculator gained important federal positions at the national capital. In 1836

Henry L. Ellsworth, a large-scale owner of land in Tippecanoe and other counties, became commissioner of the Patent Office. In this position, which he held until 1845, Ellsworth encouraged agricultural progress. Late in 1836 James Whitcomb was named commissioner of the General Land Office, at the time when land sales were at their peak in both the state and nation, and held this position until 1841. The initial Hoosier to hold this significant post, Whitcomb learned French and Spanish to enable him to read records in these languages.[16]

While the Jackson administration came under attack for introducing *partisan* removals to Indiana politics, its policy about federal aid for internal improvements was unclear. A bipartisan consensus therefor had developed in the state during the Adams administration. Democratic Republicans had maintained that such aid would not be jeopardized if the general were elected president. Under Adams, Congress, with bipartisan support, had approved significant grants of land to help Indiana finance the Wabash and Erie Canal and the opening of the Michigan Road. As the presidency of Adams ended Congress made an initial appropriation of $50,000 toward extending the National Road across the state. As yet, however, construction had not commenced on any of these important projects.[17] It would seem that an undeveloped frontier state with meager fiscal resources and limited population (343,031 in 1830) would have been satisfied with this largesse. Congressman Jonathan Jennings advised his constituents that Indiana had "obtained, a much greater proportion of the public resources, in comparison to her population" than a large majority of the states. Though expressing decided approval for internal improvements, he warned that conflicts and jealousies would ensue among the states unless "equal justice" were extended them.[18] Nevertheless, at its session in 1829–1830 the General Assembly asked Congress for federal engineering surveys concerning a canal through central Indiana, connecting the proposed Wabash and Erie Canal with the Ohio River, and regarding removal of obstructions from the White River and its east and west forks. It also sought a donation of land to help pay for a good "clay turnpike" with "suitable" bridges on the approximately 120 miles of the Great Western Mail Stage Route between New Albany and Vincennes. All three projects were presented as having national importance. The pro-Jackson *Western Sun* claimed that everyone in its part of the state approved the request concerning the postal route.[19]

Before the General Assembly had another opportunity to solicit further aid, in May, 1830, Jackson explained his views about internal improvements in the Maysville Road Veto. Branding this road a local route within Kentucky, the president contended that both fiscal and constitutional considerations mandated that federal aid be limited to items of truly national importance. The president reaffirmed his friendship for internal improvements, and he urged an amendment to the constitution spelling out the proper role of the federal government regarding transportation projects.[20] National Republicans charged that the veto showed Jackson's lack of commitment to western interests, indicated the importance of attachment to measures over men, illustrated his dominance by southerners, and vindicated their warnings that his election would set back internal improvements. Something had to be done to appease the "passions of the south," a Terre Haute editor mused, "and western interests were the most convenient sacrifice." Ezra Rodgers of Fayette County, who said he had proudly supported Jackson in 1828, termed him "no longer worthy the support of the West." Henry Clay, "the great Western Champion of the American System," would have his support in 1832 as he had had in 1824. The Indianapolis *Indiana Journal* predicted "a powerful defection from the administration" in consequence of the Maysville and similar vetoes.[21] Democratic Republicans responded that Old Hickory only opposed local improvements. They praised him for his efforts to end the national debt, reduce taxes, and prevent the squandering of federal money on numerous local improvements. A Lawrenceburg editor pointed to the president's approval of a new appropriation for the National Road as evidence that he "rejects *sectional* improvements," but not "those that are *national* in character." An editor at the capital estimated that it would require $100,000,000 to complete the public works for which surveys had been made or ordered. Thus, save for the

Maysville veto millions would have been squandered on innumerable local works, with an everlasting debt saddled upon the nation, leaving important works like the National Road unfinished. Jackson was right, the *Western Sun* asserted, in lessening the debt and reducing taxes. After this was accomplished the people could decide whether it would be expedient to have money from an overflowing treasury applied to a well digested system of internal improvements.[22]

Despite the Maysville veto Hoosier legislators augmented their requests for federal aid to transportation projects. They solicited help for roads, railroads, canals, harbors, and removal of obstructions from the Wabash and other rivers.[23] A legislator from Dearborn County, in urging Senator Tipton to sustain federal aid for a canal or railroad in the Whitewater Valley, remarked that if Congress did not react favorably it "surely will not charge us for asking—in as much as all states are in the habbit of begging[.]"[24] Congress turned a deaf ear to nearly all such appeals, but before Jackson left office it appropriated an aggregate of $58,000 toward a lighthouse and harbor at Michigan City[25] and "loaned" Indiana $286,751.48 of the federal surplus revenue pursuant to the distribution and deposit act of 1836.[26]

Lack of federal aid for removal of obstructions to navigation of the Wabash River caused much disappointment among supporters as well as opponents of the administration. In 1832 the president pocket vetoed a bill which included $20,000 for its improvement, then in 1834 he killed a bill whose only appropriation provided a like sum for this purpose. A leading opposition organ declared that Jackson had been inconsistent in approving aid for harbors and "small creeks" on the eastern seaboard, and for the Cumberland which ran near his estate in Tennessee, while refusing deserved aid to the Wabash on constitutional grounds. The pro-Jackson *Indiana Democrat*, however, argued that the executive had been guided by constitutional principles. His second veto was explained on the ground that the Wabash and Erie Canal had not been completed and ports of entry had not been established on the Wabash as for the Cumberland and other rivers.[27] In 1834 Senator Tipton protested that millions were appropriated to improve "rivers and small streams east of the mountains." If only ten, twenty, or fifty miles long, Tipton told his colleagues, "you call them rivers, and we improve them." Before electing a successor to Jackson, Tipton admonished, the "voters should ascertain whether candidates are for or against improving our rivers; and no one holding the opposite doctrine need expect one-fourth of the votes in the valley of the Mississippi."[28] Bills appropriating $50,000 for improving the Wabash passed the Senate in 1835 and 1836, but failed in the House.[29] Thus the Wabash, whose improvement, Senator Hendricks said, plus completion of the Wabash and Erie Canal, would "form a perfect inland navigation between New York and New Orleans, on the shortest and most eligible route" was denied federal aid.[30]

While Van Buren was president both the economic and political context were unfavorable to federal aid for transportation projects. The Panic of 1837 quickly changed the federal surplus into a treasury deficit, and the disastrous consequences of state internal improvement systems fostered a return to laissez faire. Nevertheless, stimulated in part by the catastrophic fiscal situation arising from the System of 1836, Hoosiers continued to ask Congress for land and money on behalf of roads, railroads, canals, the System of 1836, harbors, and rivers.[31] Before the Van Buren administration ended, March, 1841, two further installments of surplus revenue totaling $573,502.96 were gained from the distribution act of 1836. In 1838 Congress provided $150,000 for the Cumberland Road within Indiana, and $60,733.59 for the harbor at Michigan City, ending such grants under Van Buren.[32] Democrats and Whigs alike were unhappy with the diminution of federal aid for internal improvements. Early in 1840 Congressman Tilghman A. Howard described the terrible condition of the National Road and pleaded for an appropriation toward its completion within the state. Howard, the Democratic nominee for governor that year, called this road the greatest of all national works. He predicted that it would be extended to the Rocky Mountains "and *through them*, if it cannot be constructed over them" to some great trading center on the Pacific. Asserting that millions had been spent on roads, lighthouses, harbors, and rivers in the East, Howard asked how congressmen could support these appropriations and "for constitutional reasons, not a dollar to the Cumberland road?" Was it "the *salt water* that makes it constitutional to make harbors," the Indiana spokesman sarcastically inquired.[33] During the depression of the late thirties and early forties, federal revenue from the sale of land in Indiana plummeted, with the same effect on the Three Per Cent Fund. But in 1841 Congress approved extension of the land grant for the Wabash and Erie Canal to help finance its continuation from the mouth of the Tippecanoe River to Terre Haute.[34]

While many Hoosiers became disappointed with the lack of federal aid for transportation projects, others became disappointed because of reduced tariff duties. The bipartisan protectionist movement of the last half of the twenties peaked in the early thirties. All Indiana members of Congress had voted for the augmented tariff of 1828, and in the presidential election of that year within Indiana Jacksonians and anti-Jacksonians vied in affirming their support for protection. The National Republicans, however, predicted that a Jackson administration could no more be trusted on this issue than it could for internal improvements.[35] Despite the bipartisan consensus for protection, some Hoosiers indicated a willingness to have duties lowered. In announcing for reelection in 1831, Congressman Ratliff Boon, vigorously pro-Jackson, advocated reduced duties on necessities such as coffee, tea, salt, and sugar. The politically independent congressman, Jonathan Jennings, also seeking reelection, urged that the duty on sugar be lowered. There was nothing in the world, Jennings said, comparable to the "*protection* extended to the sugar planters of the United States." While the tariff of 1832 was being debated, Senator William Hendricks, also politically independent, proclaimed that he held "the protective principle sacred" but he "would cheerfully vote to take the duties off teas, coffee, dye stuffs, and such like articles."[36] At the legislative session of 1831–1832 the Indiana Senate adopted a resolution endorsing "a protecting tariff to encourage home industry, and render us independent of foreign nations," by a three to one margin. Seven Jacksonians, though professing support for protection, condemned the resolution for its "blind and unqualified adherence" to the tariff of 1828, which they said even its friends admitted needed modification. The protesters stressed protection for agriculture and commerce as well as manufacturing, and they suggested that ending some duties and lowering rates on items of "prime necessity" would "lighten the burdens of the poor" and "tend to repress sectional complaints" and thus "destroy the already germinating seeds of disunion . . . ."[37] To National Republicans, however, the Jacksonians were endangering tariff protection by abandoning or at least weakening this key principle of the American System.[38]

Amid southern threats to resort to nullification against the tariff, in July, 1832, Congress reduced duties to roughly the level of 1824. Bipartisan support resulted in about a two to one margin for the new tariff in both houses of Congress. All five Indiana members of Congress, four of whom were Jacksonians, voted for passage.[39] While the legislation was under consideration, Senator John Tipton advised a constituent that "a modification of the Tariff is loudly called [for] in the south and stoutly opposed in the north but the west I hope will be able to bring the extremes nearer each other and save the Country." Nevertheless, in spite of tariff reduction and Jackson's stern and vigorous proclamation against nullification, as the year ended a delegate convention in South Carolina declared the tariff null and void within that state from and after March 4, 1833.[40] Indiana's firm commitment to the Union of the states, by Hoosiers regardless of party, was persuasively demonstrated before and during the nullification crisis. When talk of nullification surfaced in 1828, Governor James Brown Ray admonished legislators that "The union of these states is the people's only sure charter for their liberties and independence." The states, he said, "must be kept together *peacibly* (*sic*) if we can, *forcibly* if we must." In his inaugural three years later, Governor Noah Noble asserted that "in the integrity of the Union consists our glory and strength, and upon its continuance depend our peace, prosperity and happiness as a nation."[41] Even before they learned of Jackson's proclamation against nullification, Elisha M. Huntington and Calvin Fletcher, both anti-Jacksonians, insisted in letters to Senator Tipton that the Union must be preserved. "*Resist nullification unto blood, if necessary to save the Union,"* Huntington pleaded. Fletcher urged that partisan politics be forgotten and the rebellion in South Carolina be crushed. "Dont wait till it gethers like the snow ball that is rolld—," Fletcher exhorted.[42] The Indianapolis *Indiana Journal*, though staunchly antiadministration, declared the president's proclamation "a production of great force and power, and well calculated to meet the present crisis." Early in 1833 the General Assembly, overwhelmingly anti-Jacksonian in the Senate and strongly Jacksonian in the House, denounced nullification and asked South Carolinians "to pause ere it be too late to save themselves from ruin." The assembly emphasized that "devotion to party should be lost in devotion to country" as Americans sought the "means best calculated to prevent the temple of our union from crumbling into ruins."[43]

In efforts to resolve the nullification crisis Hoosier members of Congress were more inclined to hold a sword over South Carolina than to extend an olive branch. All five members voted for the revenue collection or Force Bill. But Senators Tipton and Hendricks disliked lowering the tariff under duress of threatened nullification; and they, plus Congressman Jonathan McCarty, opposed passage of the Compromise Tariff of 1833. This measure, which provided a gradual lowering of duties over the ensuing decade, had the support of Congressmen Ratliff Boon and John Carr.[44] In informing constituents about the compromise tariff, Tipton said that the North and West had "yielded much" for a measure "supported by men of all parties with the hope of quieting the southern nullifyers." Tipton and Hendricks concurred in the view that the crisis would pass without the shedding of blood. Hendricks was adamant that South Carolina "must abandon her position, or there must be consequences the most unpleasant."[45] Jacksonians tended to praise the chief executive for the peaceful termination of the crisis, while National Republicans hailed Henry Clay as the able compromiser who once more had shown his statesmanship.[46]

Pursuant to the Compromise of 1833 tariff duties were gradually reduced until 1842 when they approximated the 20 percent level. During this period anti-Jacksonians were generally more

supportive of protection than Jacksonians, this cleavage being evident in congressional and presidential elections.[47] The extreme
spread between these positions is illustrated by remarks of Congressmen Henry S. Lane and Ratliff Boon. Lane, a Whig, recommended that the tariff laws be extensively modified by laying "a
sufficient tax on foreign luxuries" to enable Congress to distribute
the proceeds from land sales among the states. Had Clay's land bill
for distribution been adopted, Lane suggested in 1841, already Indiana would have received over $4,000,000 therefrom. Lane com-
mented that this sum was adequate to pay half of the state's internal improvement debt. If funded, the interest from the principal
would pay the interest on the state debt "without a resort to taxation" or educate "every child within her borders for all time to
come." Boon, rabidly pro-Jackson, in 1836 urged that federal revenue from tariff duties and land sales be trimmed to cover only the
truly essential costs of government. "Above this," Boon exhorted,
"the pockets of the people are the safest repositories for their own
money." He "opposed *in toto*" the raising "of surplus revenue for
distribution among the several States of this Union."[48]

Meantime, Jacksonian policy regarding banking received much
attention among Hoosiers. The Constitution of 1816 had implicitly prohibited the establishment of a branch of the Second Bank
of the United States, which commenced in 1817, within Indiana,
but the constitutionality of this denial had not been tested. Moreover, from the demise of the First State Bank in 1822 until the
start of the Second State Bank in 1834, Indiana had no chartered
bank except for the intermittent existence of the Farmers and Mechanics Bank of Indiana at Madison. During the teens branches of
the Second Bank of the United States were established near the
state border at Cincinnati and Louisville. Because a large proportion of Indiana's population lived in an area tributary to these two
trading centers, these branches had much influence over the circulation of currency within the commonwealth. During the period 1824–1831 the bank was largely ignored in the presidential
campaign of 1828 and likewise in the congressional elections under Adams. As yet, the Second Bank of the United States had not
become a basic issue dividing Jacksonians and anti-Jacksonians.[49]

In 1831 and early 1832 efforts were made toward the establishment of branches within Indiana. In February, 1832, the General Assembly requested the president and directors of the bank "to locate and establish one or more branches in this state." Representative Marinus Willett, a Jacksonian from Rush County, protested this action. He condemned the bank as a "*monied institution*" beyond the control of the state which threatened the freedom of elections and was contrary to both "the very letter and spirit" of the state constitution.[50] In March, 1832, three individuals solicited the support of Senator John Tipton for a branch at Lafayette.[51]

At the 1831–1832 session of Congress an unsuccessful effort was made to recharter the bank. The Indiana Senate, overwhelmingly anti-Jacksonian, urged Hoosier members to sanction a recharter "with or without amendments, but guard the institution against any disproportionate increase of government control." In protesting this action seven Jacksonian senators recognized that the bank had "been of great public advantage in affording commercial facilities and in aiding the fiscal operations of the national government," yet they insisted on amendments which would regulate it more closely and reduce the power of its board.[52] Senator William Hendricks, an independent, voted for recharter, but Indiana's four Jacksonians in Congress were divided on this question. Senator Tipton and Congressman Ratliff Boon voted for recharter, but Congressmen John Carr and Jonathan McCarty voted contrary thereto. Jackson's lengthy veto of the recharter bill, which argued that the measure was unconstitutional and harmful to the best interests of the country, could not be overridden, but Hendricks and Tipton joined in the effort to muster a two-thirds vote to do so.[53] Editor Elihu Stout, a devoted Jacksonian, called the veto "an able document" that "proves conclusively the unconstitutionality of the Bank." In printing the message Stout termed it "gratifying to those who love constitutional law."[54] A meeting at Indianapolis supported the veto, but the *Indiana Journal*, a National Republican organ, was probably correct in asserting that the gathering had been gotten up by Jacksonian officeholders and office hunters. In private correspondence two

Jacksonians offered criticism of the veto. Edward A. Hannegan advised Senator Tipton that the veto had injured his chance of being elected to the legislature; and Isaac C. Elston called it "a hard pill," but he thought he had successfully "explained its effect away" in his area.[55] The triumph of Jackson over Clay in the presidential election of 1832, in which the bank was a major issue, indicated widespread approval for the veto among partisans of the president.[56] Upon learning of the veto the *Indiana Journal* declared that the fond hopes of the people had been blighted by the arbitrary decision of the executive. Because of facilities afforded by the bank, the editor stated, the "country was prosperous, improvements were progressing rapidly, and an extraordinary degree of confidence existed among the various members of the community." To help avert terrible consequences, he urged voters to unite and support their own interests at the forthcoming presidential election.[57] In August roughly three hundred persons called for a meeting of Marion County citizens opposed to the veto. Asserting that the veto "will have a tendency to drain our country of money, stop the improvement, and blight the prospects of the west, creating great sacrifices and embarrassments," the conveners announced the protest meeting for the courthouse at noon on September 8. The resulting gathering, represented by the *Indiana Journal* as the largest political meeting ever held in the county, resolved to use all just means to obtain a recharter of the bank, insisted that the time had come to support measures over men, and endorsed the election of Clay over Jackson for president.[58]

Since the bank charter remained in effect until January 1, 1837, under normal circumstances the institution would have had several years remaining whether rechartered or not. But the vehemence of Jackson's attack on the bank and the emphasis on the bank question in the presidential campaign of 1832 made recharter a political as well as an economic issue. The president decided to cripple and weaken the "monster" by transferring the federal deposits from its coffers to local banks. Despite some embarrassment, Jackson obtained a secretary of the treasury willing to do his bidding and the order to transfer deposits to local banks became effective October 1, 1833.[59] Next March the Senate adopted a resolution which called the reasons for the removal policy unsatisfactory and insufficient, then the Senate censured Jackson on the basis that he had assumed power and authority contrary to the laws and constitution. William Hendricks voted that the reasons given for removal had been insufficient, but against censure. John Tipton voted against declaring the reasons inadequate and against censure.[60] In April, 1834, the six Democratic congressmen from Indiana voted against restoring the federal deposits to the bank, but the one Whig congressman voted for their restoration. At this time five of the Democrats voted for a resolution stating that the bank should not be rechartered, one Democrat voted against this resolution, and the Whig representative missed the vote on this item.[61] In destroying the "monster," Old Hickory made banking a leading issue in separating Democrats from National Republicans within Indiana. And in contrast to the situation regarding internal improvements, Indiana Democrats in Congress, with Tipton a notable exception, usually sustained the president.

When Van Buren became president the federal deposits were in local banks around the country, and prosperity was at a peak. Hardly had Van Buren been inaugurated, however, when the Panic of 1837 led to a general suspension of specie payments by banks and fiscal stringency for the federal treasury. Whigs argued that the panic and distressed fiscal and economic circumstances were caused mainly by Jacksonian policies, particularly by the destruction of the Second Bank of the United States and the transfer of treasury deposits to less secure and less well-managed local banks.[62] Many Whigs advocated another United States Bank. Van Buren and Democratic members of Congress, however, generally wished control of banking left with the states and the separation of the federal government from banking. Though the concept of an Independent or Subtreasury system was discussed under Jackson, the movement therefor gained strength at the special session of Congress in the fall of 1837. Its establishment, however, was delayed until 1840, with the voting by Hoosier members of Congress almost entirely along party lines.[63]

Discussion of internal improvements, the tariff, banking, and other issues stimulated party controversy concerning senatorial and congressional elections. Though Jackson easily had carried Indiana against Adams in 1828, Congressman Ratliff Boon was the only avowed Jacksonian among Indiana's five members of Congress as the general began his administration. When Old Hickory became president, Senators William Hendricks and James Noble, whose terms expired in 1831 and 1833 respectively, represented Indiana. But if either of them openly became a member of either of the emerging political parties, this writer has not found convincing evidence of same.[64] Hence, it is not surprising that when Hendricks came up for reelection in December, 1830, he did not seek reelection as a member of either party. In May, 1829, Philip Sweetser, an anti-Jacksonian, offered to support Indian Agent John Tipton as the only person he believed could defeat Hendricks. Sweetser asked Tipton if he would permit his friends to make preparations for his election in lieu of Hendricks. Several weeks later Tipton made a cagey reply asking for time to review the matter confidentially with "some 6, 8 or 10 friends," while responding that the "incumbant is my friend and without some strong reason we should not desert friends nor then unless the public good require it[.]"[65] Congressman Jennings, while seeking reelection in 1829, wrote Tipton that he would not be a candidate for the Senate. He stated that Sweetser "wanted to put Hendricks down," and that Isaac Howk had "long disliked Hendricks." Their strategy, Jennings said, was to support "a Jackson man" who could defeat Hendricks with "some votes" from National Republicans.[66] During 1830 the competition seems to have been mainly between Hendricks and Boon, with Tipton wavering on the sidelines.[67] As the legislative session neared, Noah Noble, an anti-Jacksonian, wrote Tipton: "Each side [party] seems to wait for the other to make a move on the political checker-board. The Clay men think if they bring out another you [the Jacksonians] will unite on Hendricks and your side think if they formally *announce* a candidate, the Clay boys will stick to Hendricks."[68] Despite continued bipartisan support on the eve of the election Tipton advised Calvin Fletcher "that it is not best to use my name for the Senate."[69]

When the General Assembly met in joint session on December 18, Hendricks won reelection on the fourth ballot. He led on every ballot, with Boon always second, gaining his election with 44 votes to 26 for Boon, 9 for John Law, and 3 for Charles Dewey.[70] Since Boon possibly got all of the Jacksonian vote, it appears that National Republicans, many of whom probably preferred Law or Dewey, gave Hendricks sufficient votes to make him the victor. After the election the Madison *Indiana Republican*, a National Republican paper, termed Hendricks a friend of "Domestic Manufacturers, Internal Improvements, and Henry Clay." But the *Indiana Democrat*, a Jacksonian organ which had opposed his reelection, observed that despite Hendricks' friendship for Clay the incumbent's recent actions in Congress and his pledges made his election favorable to the administration. A more accurate assertion seems to have been made by the *Indiana Democrat*, after Hendricks completed his initial term, when it said: "he is guided in his official acts by principles instead of a blind devotion to parties and to men."[71]

Not long after Hendricks gained reelection, Senator James Noble, who had represented Indiana since statehood, died in Washington during February, 1831, while Congress was in session. In August Governor James Brown Ray named Robert Hanna to replace Noble "*until superseded by a successor.*"[72] Meantime, in April Tipton wrote Calvin Fletcher that the time had "come when correct men no *matter whethe[r] Jackson* or *Clay* men should be" elected for both state and general government. Though Tipton claimed that he had "no desire for a seate in the Senate," his comment that he would "never seek it nor decline it" seems to suggest otherwise. This same month Jesse L. Holman, a National Republican who had served on the Supreme Court from statehood until 1830, announced that he was a candidate.[73] In September Samuel Judah, one of the founders of the Jackson party in Indiana, became a candidate. In an address to the public Judah committed himself to "support a tariff for *revenue* so adjusted as will *best protect* our own industry and manufactures" and provide items of general use, not grown or manufactured in the United States, "at the cheapest rate." Judah affirmed his support of congressional appropriations for internal improvements "so general in . . . nature, and important to the interests of the union, or of several states, as to be national." As soon as the federal debt was paid, he favored reduction of the federal revenue; and the president's plan for distribution of any surplus revenue. He also favored graduation as the best land policy for the West, condemned both *nullification* and *consolidation* as extreme doctrines, and ignored the question of banking.[74] Support was also manifested for Thomas H. Blake and James Rariden, both National Republicans.[75] Interim appointee Robert Hanna informed legislators that he would like to be continued in office.[76] The Indianapolis *Indiana Journal* urged that a National Republican be chosen. It asserted that Hendricks had won reelection by the friends of Clay over the opposition of Jacksonians, but had since "shown as great a degree of subserviency to the powers that be as could be expected of any of the avowed supporters of General Jackson." Because neither party acted in concert, Tipton was afforded considerable bipartisan support. He was doubtless pleased with the assurance from Senator Hendricks: "You have nothing to fear from me."[77] But with the National Republicans a majority on joint ballot, the outcome was uncertain.[78]

When the legislature met in joint session on December 8, 1831, six ballots were taken without an election. Apparently most Jacksonians voted for Judah, while most National Republicans voted for either Holman or Blake, until the sixth ballot when it seems that Tipton drew significant bipartisan support. Next day a seventh ballot elected Tipton with 55 votes to 36 for runnerup Holman, 5 for Blake, 3 for Judah, and 6 ballots blank or for unnamed persons. Editor Elihu Stout of the *Western Sun* termed Tipton "a sincere friend of the present administration and of Gen. Jackson" who had received from "many of his political opponents . . . a cordial and efficient support."[79] Like Hendricks the previous year, Tipton was indebted to the National Republicans for his election. National Republicans admonished Tipton to act independently of partisan politics and support measures beneficial to Indiana, doubtless meaning such items as tariff protection, the Second Bank of the United States, and federal aid for internal improvements. The significant bipartisan support for Tipton's elevation to the Senate is convincing evidence that party discipline and cleavage had not become rigid.[80]

Several months preceding Tipton's election to the United States Senate, Indiana voters elected their first solid bloc of Jacksonian congressmen. From statehood most congressional elections had been held in even years, however, the 1828–1829 legislative session moved them to odd years. This change was possibly made to prevent these elections in the same year as presidential elections in view of Jackson's demonstrated popularity with the voters. Whatever the motivation, in 1831 incumbents Ratliff Boon, a Jacksonian; Jonathan Jennings, an independent; and John Test, a National Republican sought reelection.[81]

In the First District, carved largely from the Wabash Valley, John Law, a National Republican, challenged Boon. The incumbent announced that he had twice voted for Jackson, and would vote for him in 1832 if he became a candidate. Boon asserted that the greater proportion of taxes should come from duties on articles used mainly by the rich. He proclaimed that he had always been and remained a "decided friend" of internal improvements, but aid therefor should be distributed fairly among the states, with increased benefit to western states, as proposed by the president.[82] Law sustained the National Republican cause concerning these issues, but Boon won by a slender margin.[83] In the Second District, extending northward through the middle of the state, several candidates entered against Jennings who had represented it since 1822. In May, 1830, John Carr wrote Tipton: "If our old Friend Jonathan Jennings does not reform his habbits he will be dessuaded from becoming a Candidate for Congress at the Election in 1831[.]" After Carr, a Jackson elector in 1824, became a candidate, "A Voter" eulogized him as the son of a Revolutionary veteran, a volunteer who had "done his duty" at Tippecanoe and in the War of 1812, and as one of the earliest friends of Jackson in Indiana.[84] Although Carr obtained not much more than one third of the vote, he won over William W. Wick, his nearest rival, with Jennings a weak third. Jennings' defeat, and the tragedy of his last years amid intemperance and poverty, should not obscure his significant contributions as territorial delegate to Congress, president of the Corydon Constitutional Convention, first state governor, and congressman.[85] The contest in the Third District, mainly located in the Whitewater Valley, had an ironic twist. In 1826, in a duel between National Republicans, Oliver H. Smith had defeated John Test, then seeking his third term. Two years later Test, plus Jonathan McCarty, a Jacksonian, vied against Smith, causing the latter to withdraw saying that otherwise the Jacksonian minority would elect McCarty. Test then regained his congressional seat by a considerable majority over his Jacksonian rival. In 1831, however, Smith, Test, and McCarty entered the fray, and McCarty won a plurality victory over his National Republican rivals.[86] Thus, Boon, Carr, and McCarty, "all Jacksonians," as Editor Stout happily noted, were elected as Indiana's representatives in the House. But, as the *Indiana Journal* observed, at least one, and perhaps two, seats had been won because the National Republican vote had not been concentrated on a single candidate. The National Republican organ boasted that in the voting for governor and members of the General Assembly, the Jacksonians had "sustained a Waterloo defeat."[87] Moreover, as the preceding pages have indicated, the reelection of Senator Hendricks in 1830 and the initial election of Tipton to the United States Senate in 1831 had been achieved with significant National Republican support over the opposition of avowed Jacksonians. Hence, if the Democratic Republicans were to make Indiana a Jacksonian state, it was important for them to gain control of the General Assembly on joint ballot as well as to carry the state for Old Hickory in the 1832 presidential election.

Although some had presumed that perhaps Jackson would serve only one term, soon after his inauguration in 1829 an Indianapolis editor reported that he was more and more constrained to believe that the president would seek reelection. But, the editor explained, this would not be from his eagerness to continue, rather from the impossibility of his friends uniting on anyone else. During 1830 John Carr, a Jacksonian, told John Tipton that he hoped the general's health would permit him to run again. Otherwise, Carr explained, he feared that the competition between Van Buren and Calhoun would split the party and lead to

Clay's election as president.[88] Early in 1831 the *Indiana Democrat* gleefully proclaimed "'THE LONG AGONY IS OVER,'" explaining that it was "distinctly understood" that the president would serve "the people of the Union . . . for a second term, should they again honor him with their confidence."[89]

In the fall of 1831 the pro-Clay editor of the *Indiana Journal* proposed that every county name one or more delegates to a state convention at Indianapolis on the first Monday in November to select delegates to the party's national convention. In succeeding issues the editor encouraged county conventions, at times giving favorable reports about them.[90] After the Clay editor reported that the Knox County Convention had been large and enthusiastic, the *Western Sun* scoffed that not more than *"fifteen* persons," and probably fewer, had attended.[91] The National Republican State Convention convened on November 7, and completed its session the next day.[92] According to the proceedings only thirty-three delegates were seated from twenty counties, however, twelve persons from nine other counties also were given seats. The convention named three delegates to the party's national convention at Baltimore in December.[93] A correspondence committee, consisting of one person from each county, was named and asked to promote the great interests and cause of the party. The platform adopted by the convention branded Jackson unworthy of reelection, and emphasized the party's devotion to the American System. It declared that internal improvements and tariff protection had been brought into jeopardy under Jackson, who had vetoed the former and treated the latter with contempt. And the president's repeated attacks on the circulating currency of the country, which had been brought to "perfection unequalled" by the federal bank, had produced a "general alarm in the community." Jackson was charged with: failing to protect the treaty rights of the Cherokee Indians against the harsh laws of Georgia; injuring the civil service by removing nearly a thousand friends of the Adams administration, often replacing them with inexperienced and incompetent men; naming more members of Congress to office than all previous presidents combined; and with having broken his solemn assurance that he would not seek a second term.

For these and other reasons, the times demanded the splendid talents, illustrious services, and tried patriotism of Henry Clay to save and sustain the American System.

About a month after the National Republican Convention adjourned, the Jackson State Convention met at Indianapolis on December 12, and completed its work on that day.[94] The editor of the *Indiana Democrat* had apparently suggested this date to enable Jacksonians to name delegates to their national convention at Baltimore in May.[95] About 121 delegates were seated from approximately forty counties, and twenty-one additional persons were given seats and voting privileges. Five delegates were named for the Baltimore convention,[96] an electoral ticket was chosen, and twenty-four individuals were appointed to a state central committee. This committee was authorized to plan the presidential campaign, and the delegates were urged to help establish county correspondence and local vigilance committees. The Jacksonian platform lavishly praised and vigorously defended "the venerable patriot" and his administration. Jackson's "'*Judicious*'" tariff was affirmed as what the people had desired, but it needed modifications to remove its sectional and oppressive features. The true American system would protect "infant manufactures without granting them monopolies"; and provide sufficient revenue without unnecessary tax burdens. Speedy payment of the national debt would enable Congress to fulfill all the regular and incidental engagements of the government. Other than these oblique comments, the internal improvement issue was ignored; and no mention was made of banking. Treaties of commerce and friendship, which had been negotiated with various countries, were touted as evidence of the president's diplomatic and executive skill. His Indian removal policy, described as humanely pursued, was termed consistent with that of Monroe, Calhoun, and Adams. In short, so varied were the achievements of the administration that none should "be preferred before the venerable and hoary headed patriot of the Revolution, who for the last time will call upon his country to sustain him."

Delegates from Indiana participated in the national conventions of the two major parties, the first they had held. At Baltimore in December, 1831, the National Republicans unanimously and enthusiastically nominated Henry Clay for president. John Sergeant of Pennsylvania was nominated for vice president.[97] Then in May, 1832, the Democratic convention at Baltimore formally ratified the choice of Jackson as its candidate for president. While the Indiana delegates staunchly supported Old Hickory's renomination, they reluctantly pledged their support for Martin Van Buren, Jackson's choice for running mate, after voting for Senator Richard M. Johnson of Kentucky.[98]

During the presidential campaign of 1832 the differences between the Jacksonians and their opponents were greater than they had been in the presidential campaign of 1828. Indiana Jacksonians had become less supportive of the Second United States Bank, a protective tariff, and federal aid for internal improvements than four years earlier. Though staunchly devoted to the Union of the states, they emphasized states' rights and strict construction more than they had in the twenties. And they continued to try to convince voters that theirs was the party of the common people in contrast to the National Republicans sustained by aristocrats.[99] The Whigs, led by Henry Clay, father of the American System, supported the bank, tariff, and internal improvements much as they had in 1828. But admiration for and loyalty to Old Hickory, more than differences between the parties, seems to have swayed Hoosiers. "No state," the *Indiana Journal* declared, "has a greater interest in the measures . . . vetoed by the present administration. No state will suffer more by the destruction of the U. S. Bank, or the withholding of appropriations for the improvement of the country." As the election neared, this paper exhorted that "No part of the United States is under greater obligations to Mr. Clay than Indiana." Clay, it said, had taken the lead on behalf of the National Road through Indiana, and had championed tariff protection and internal improvements, both of vital interest to Indiana. This editor called the impending election the most vital ever in Indiana. He asserted that the election of Jackson and Van Buren would "prostrate the hopes of the west, and endanger the liberties of the country."[100]

As the campaign progressed the popularity of the old soldier and folk hero of many westerners augured well for his triumph over Clay. In February, a correspondent from Greencastle sent Senator Tipton the names of fifteen men "who go the hole hog" for Old Hickory. The next month a voter from Crawfordsville asked the senator to say "to ourr venerabel Chieaff . . . that his Strenth is daly increesing in this parte of th state . . . ." Tipton was informed "that th prarys of the people are evry where offerd up for his helth and prosperity for it seams thrugh him and by his pattrotism th constution is to be perservd." As April ended Edward A. Hannegan advised Tipton, from Covington, that despite rumors to the contrary "that so far from loosing we are gaining upon the Wabash." Then in June, a citizen from Washington, Indiana, aptly wrote the senator: "I believe the state is Jackonizing very fast, you know that the state is republican therefore will fall in with the Old General measures."[101] The August elections, in which the Democratic Republicans gained legislative seats, adding to the gains they had made the previous year, was a favorable omen for the Jacksonians. In the November voting for electors, Jackson won about 31,400 votes to approximately 25,250 for Clay, defeating him by a larger margin than he had Adams in 1828. In the electoral college the incumbent defeated Clay much more decisively than he had Adams four years earlier. Old Hickory's reelection triumph, making three times in succession that he had won Indiana, appears to have been more a personal than a party victory. Clay won only sixteen of the sixty-six counties, running best in the Whitewater Valley and carrying scattered counties elsewhere mainly near and around the boundary of the state. Jackson won more votes and more counties than Clay on or close to the Wabash River where internal improvement sentiment was strong. He made almost a grand sweep of the interior counties of central and southern Indiana.[102] Editor Elihu Stout declared that the president had placed his veto on the bank bill and the people in turn had placed "their *veto* upon both Mr. Clay, and the Bank." The *Indiana Journal*, which had devotedly supported Clay, asked that so far as possible partisan strife be laid aside for the good of the country. Judicious measures, not the election of a particular man, it said, caused prosperity and made liberties permanent. An editor at Madison satirically commented: "Old Hickory can do no wrong. His popularity can stand any thing! Huzza for Old Hickory!!! Down with Henry Clay. Down with the American System. Down with the Bank. Huzza for British Manufactories! Huzza for local banks *without capital*! Good times are coming—spurious paper money is coming—Van Buren is coming."[103]

Several weeks after Jackson's reelection, the General Assembly met in joint session to elect a successor to Senator Tipton. Although the incumbent considered himself a Jacksonian, he at times voted more with the National Republicans than with staunch followers of Old Hickory. For much of 1832, Congressman Ratliff Boon and federal district attorney Samuel Judah, both stalwart Jacksonians, appeared to be the incumbent's most determined opponents. The National Republicans apparently wanted to ensure Tipton's reelection, unless convinced that they could elect one of their leaders. In May Isaac Howk, a prominent National Republican, advised the senator that if he wished reelection that he knew of no man in the state who "could defeat your wishes." Howk suggested that some "clamorous friends of Gen. Jackson" were trying to "elect a more *thorough going*" Jacksonian in preference to Tipton.[104] During May Judah wrote Tipton that he had himself "given way often enough," and owed something to his friends and "to the sacrifices I have made for the party."[105] Late in July Boon asked Tipton for permission to indicate to his friends, and to Judah if necessary, that Judah had "expressed his determination to *ruin*" him if he (Boon) persisted as a candidate for the Senate. Soon after the state election in August, Tipton granted this request. Tipton told Boon: "I do not feel anxious to run. one of us with the aid of the other can be elected over any man in the state[.] if we divide we are both left out, *down forever*." Boon probably, and understandably, considered this response devious and less than honest. In November Boon bluntly wrote Tipton that he had "stronger Claims upon the support of the Jackson party in Indiana" than any of the candidates for the Senate. His letter concluded: "I cannot consent to withdraw my name under existing circumstances, be the result what it may."[106] A gain in the number of Jacksonian legislators at the August election, plus Jackson's sizeable triumph over Clay in winning Indiana's presidential electors in November, perhaps increased support for Boon. But on the eve of the senatorial election Judah's prospects were blasted by allegations that he had acted improperly as federal district attorney regarding charges against the receiver of the Vincennes Land Office. This situation removed Judah as a candidate, but it aided Jonathan McCarty, one of the fathers of the Jacksonian party in Indiana, who had some months earlier become a candidate.[107] When the legislature met in joint session on December 8, twelve ballots were taken, with Tipton leading on every tally. Two days later, Tipton mustered fifty-four of the 103 votes cast, winning election to the United States Senate on the nineteenth ballot. Sorting out what happened amid intrigue and manipulation is tricky, however, it appears that Tipton won more votes from National Republicans than from Jacksonians. Clearly the out and out Jacksonians could not elect a senator from their ranks. Aaron Finch, a Jacksonian, told Tipton that William Marshall had been "compelled for th purpose of enshureing your Election to buy up a Jackson and a Clay man or two." Marshall cautiously reported to Tipton that his friends "had to do many things that I assure [you] was disagreeable."[108] Tipton, who for practical purposes was a member of both major parties, wrote his friend Calvin Fletcher: "to *party* I owe nothing and will go for my whole country."[109]

Not long after Tipton's return to the Senate the congressional campaigns of 1833 began to stir. Since Indiana's population had considerably more than doubled during the twenties, in 1832 Congress gave the state seven in lieu of its three previous congressmen. No county was split in establishing the new districts, but their number per district was reduced. Four districts were carved from counties on or entirely south of the National Road, and two of the three remaining districts included counties south of this thoroughfare.[110] Jacksonians tended to draw the party line to increase the vote for their candidates. The *Indiana Democrat* urged the election of men who would uphold the president's veto against rechartering the United States Bank and sustain other measures of his administration.[111] Not surprisingly, however, the National Republicans—who had three times lost the state to

Jackson in presidential elections—opposed drawing the party line in choosing congressmen. The *Indiana Journal* insisted that such elections should be based on talent, integrity, and commitment to measures beneficial to constituents. The country, this paper asserted, needed a respite from the excitement of the late presidential campaign, and it was "high time that every species of man-worship were entirely discountenanced . . . ."[112] The candidates divided somewhat along party lines regarding federal policy about the bank, tariff, public lands, and internal improvements. District conventions were considered to nominate candidates, but most candidates probably were self-announced. In at least one district there was a joint discussion of the issues by rival candidates, and several candidates issued campaign circulars considering the issues at stake.[113] The voting in August resulted in a sweeping victory for the Jacksonians. Incumbents Ratliff Boon, John Carr, and Jonathan McCarty were reelected in the first, third, and fifth districts respectively. Amos Lane, George L. Kinnard, Edward A. Hannegan, and John Ewing were elected to initial terms in the fourth, sixth, seventh, and second districts, "all thorough going, dyed in the wool dervises [*sic*], except our own member," the pro-Clay Vincennes *Gazette* declared.[114]

Jacksonian victories in the congressional elections of 1831 and 1833, combined with Old Hickory's decisive victory over Clay in 1832, however, failed to give the Democrats firm control over federal politics concerning Indiana. In the Senate, William Hendricks, an independent, and John Tipton, who considered himself a Jacksonian, both at times voted with the opposition on important issues. Moreover, Democratic congressional victories had been much influenced by Jackson's personal popularity, with less than desirable consensus about issues. The unpopularity of Vice President Martin Van Buren, widely presumed to be the heir apparent, was a drag on party unity. While Jackson trounced Clay in 1832, the National Republicans continued to have the upper hand in state politics; and Clay had many followers staunchly devoted to him and his policies. In this general context the Whig party of Indiana was born. In May the *Indiana Journal*, the leading National Republican organ of the state, explained that several citizens from

Marion County had requested a meeting at Indianapolis on May 17 to consider "the late measures of the general government." All who opposed "the usurpations of the Executive," favored "a sound currency," opposed "measures calculated to destroy public confidence and produce distress and bankruptcy," and desired "to preserve in their full vigor the constitution and the laws" were "invited to attend and participate." The heading for these remarks referred to the May 17 meeting as a "WHIG MEETING." This meeting "unanimously" resolved that "the question which is now convulsing the nation is not '*Bank or no Bank*,' but Constitution or no Constitution, liberty or despotism." A second resolution, so adopted, resolved that "the friends of true liberty in this state should unite as the whigs of Indiana in sustaining the Constitution." President Jackson was condemned for removing federal deposits from the bank contrary to the wishes and action of Congress, and for his disposition to take power given to Congress by the constitution and concentrating it in his hands. According to the *Indiana Journal*, despite the short notice, farmers attended the meeting from every corner of the county; the attendance was large, but the number present was not exactly known; and never had there been "a more determined spirit" than was shown at this one. The *Indiana Democrat* referred to the meeting as one by "the enemies of the Republican administration . . . that the *military parade* had brought together from different quarters." After the "military were dismissed," this Jacksonian paper noted, those present assembled at the courthouse "where the orators were ready *cut and dry* to appear before them." Following this meeting the former National Republicans became known as Whigs without any basic modification of their policies.[115]

The congressional elections of 1835, the last under General Jackson, gave Whigs their initial test of strength against the Democrats. All incumbent congressmen, six Democrats and one Whig, sought reelection. As the campaign ended, in five districts the rivalry was between one Whig versus one Democrat, but it is uncertain whether either party used a district convention to nominate its candidate. The six incumbent Democrats had attested to their staunch support of Old Hickory the previous year by voting against taking federal deposits from local banks and returning them to the United States Bank.[116] The liquidation of the national debt amid the prosperity of the mid-thirties augured well for the Democrats. The six Democrats—Ratliff Boon, John Carr, Amos Lane, Jonathan McCarty, George L. Kinnard, and Edward A. Hannegan—were all reelected, though McCarty, with two rivals, was only a plurality winner. John W. Davis, a Democrat whom John Ewing, a Whig, had defeated by two votes in 1833, was an easy victor over Ewing. Boon, a Jacksonian loyalist, won his fourth consecutive term, his fifth in all. Although the Democrats clobbered their Whig rivals in the congressional elections, the latter retained their dominant voice in the General Assembly.[117]

Meantime, the presidential campaign of 1836 was well advanced. In the fall of 1833 a Tammany Hall celebration at New York City credited Colonel Richard M. Johnson and his brave Kentucky volunteers for the glorious victory at the Battle of the Thames, October 5, 1813, in which the colonel was presumed to have killed Tecumseh.[118] In November, 1833, Senator John Tipton, a close political friend of Johnson, began a series of three articles boosting the colonel over Van Buren as successor to Jackson. Using the pseudonym "A Voter," Tipton credited Jackson with good intentions but harshly condemned his removal of tried and capable officeholders for partisans, some of whom had abused his trust in them. The senator opposed having the party's state convention dictate Indiana's preference for president, but he insisted that "a large majority of the people" were for Johnson. Next month the Democratic State Convention selected delegates to the party's forthcoming national convention at Baltimore in May, 1835, but adjourned without instructing them for either the colonel or vice president. Later "A Voter" asked: "Can it be possible that the friends of Johnson, who are a majority in Indiana, will barter their rights and those of one of their bravest warriors and purest patriots, and allow him made Vice President to the man he can distance?"[119] On January 8, 1834, Johnson visited Indianapolis and delivered an oration in commemoration of Old Hickory's illustrious victory over the British at New Orleans on that date in 1815. During the gubernatorial canvass of 1834, Governor Noble as Whig candidate for reelection had made statements which some construed to be an endorsement of Johnson for the presidency.[120]

The Indiana movement for Johnson, however, helped serve as midwife to an Indiana movement to elect William Henry Harrison to replace Andrew Jackson. During the fall citizens of Indianapolis, apparently mainly Jacksonians, invited Colonel Johnson and General Harrison to speak there in October to help celebrate the victory won over the British and Indians "by the American forces under Gen. Harrison and Col. Johnson" on October 5, 1813. Johnson sent his regrets but agitated the political waters by comments about "the gallant regiment" he had commanded on that occasion. Harrison also sent his regrets, but added oil to the fire by briskly asking who ever heard of Jackson's victory at New Orleans over the British in 1815 being attributed to one of his colonels. The glory belonged to the army he had commanded. If he had had any associate, the general acidly commented, it had been Governor Isaac Shelby of Kentucky, not Colonel Johnson.[121] Among Indiana Jacksonians there was also consideration of Lewis Cass, of Michigan; John McLean, of Ohio; and Hugh L. White, of Tennessee.[122] By the early months of 1835, however, Van Buren's nomination seemed assured with Colonel Johnson as his probable running mate. State Treasurer Nathan B. Palmer, a Democrat, counseled Tipton that a national convention was "the best mode of consentrating [*sic*] the strength and operations of the friends of the administration that can be devised." In January the Vincennes *Western Sun* concurred with Senator Thomas Hart Benton, of Missouri, that Van Buren was the most acceptable and electable Democratic candidate.[123] On the eve of the party's national convention at Baltimore in May, 1835, the *Indiana Democrat* predicted the vice president's nomination since most of the states had pledged their delegates to him. This paper strongly recommended Johnson for vice president, calling him the particular favorite of farmers, mechanics, and workingmen who were the "bone and sinew of our country." At the Baltimore convention Indiana's nine votes were cast for Van Buren, whose nomination was declared unanimous on the initial ballot. The state's nine

votes were cast for Colonel Johnson as the nominee for vice president, and he was chosen on the initial ballot by more than the
two-thirds majority required by the convention. The *Indiana
Democrat* averred that as Van Buren became better known he was
"becoming more and more the favorite of the people of Indiana,"
and would defeat any candidate of the opposition "by a large majority . . . ."[124]

While Johnson failed to become the presidential nominee of
the Democrats, friends of Harrison sought to make him the nominee of the Whigs. As early as June, 1834, the *Indiana Journal* said
it was premature to view Clay or any man as the only candidate
upon whom the Whigs could unite. This Whig paper emphasized
that "parties should be formed with reference to *principles* and not
men"; however, Hoosier Whigs gave much consideration to men,
and especially to William Henry Harrison, their former territorial governor and hero of the War of 1812. During 1834 and 1835
they also gave consideration to Henry Clay, of Kentucky; Daniel
Webster, of Massachusetts; Hugh L. White, of Tennessee; and
John McLean, of Ohio.[125] While on an electioneering tour to Indiana in May and June of 1835, which included visits to Indianapolis and the site of the Battle of Tippecanoe, Harrison was
enthusiastically received with Democrats participating in cere-
monies and dinners along the way. The *Indiana Journal* commented about Harrison's visit to the Tippecanoe Battle Ground
"where, nearly 24 years ago, he perilled his life in defence of his
country." The *Indiana Democrat* noted that Edward A. Hannegan
had paid eloquent tribute to the hero of Tippecanoe during the
visit to the site of the battle.[126] Soon after this tour the *Indiana
Journal* called Harrison a gallant gentleman and an enlightened
statesman who had been brought forth "by the people—*the real
democracy of the country*, not your *office-holding democrats*." Thousands who had supported Jackson, it said, would support Harrison
over Van Buren. Amid such puffing of Harrison the *Indiana Democrat* wryly observed that some opposition papers "are getting
over their dread of *Military Chieftains*" since hoisting the Harrison banner.[127] When the Whig or Harrison State Convention
met at Indianapolis, December 14–15, about two hundred dele-

gates from approximately forty-five counties were seated.[128] President Marston G. Clark, veteran Indian fighter who had been with Harrison at Tippecanoe, told delegates that on the "bloody field of Tippecanoe" he more than once heard Harrison's "voice cheering us to the charge against the savage foe." The convention unanimously nominated Harrison for president, named a committee to select an electoral ticket on his behalf, and stressed the need for party organization at state, county, and township levels. The address of the convention to the people stated that the presidential contest was not "for *party* ascendancy," but to return power to the people, defend the constitution, and protect the interests of Indiana and the West. It lauded Harrison for his commitment to republicanism, and his mild use of the powers vested in him while governor of Indiana Territory. The platform credited Harrison with having cleared Indian titles from vast areas of the West; voted for graduation, preemption, and other liberal land policies; and supported federal appropriations for the National Road and the Wabash and Erie Canal.

A few weeks after the Harrison State Convention the Jacksonians, calling themselves "Democratic Republicans," held their state convention at Indianapolis, January 8–9.[129] Approximately 281 delegates from about sixty-three counties attended. A large number of other persons in attendance were accepted as members, perhaps making it the largest such convention at the capital to that time. Because Van Buren and Johnson had been nominated at the party's national convention at Baltimore nine months earlier, the convention's main purposes were to form an electoral ticket on their behalf, develop party organization, and persuade voters to sustain Old Hickory by supporting Van Buren and Johnson. Party organization was much emphasized, beginning with the state committee and continuing through congressional district, county, and township committees. The address of the convention portrayed the Democrats as the party of the people, states' rights, and strict construction in contrast to the Whigs as the party of aristocrats, consolidationists, and liberal constructionists in the Federalist tradition. Jackson, it proclaimed, had defeated the "consolidationists, or federalists" in 1828 and 1832 as

Jefferson had in 1800. And his administration had maintained the military in strict subordination to civilian authority; liquidated the national debt, creating a surplus of millions in the treasury; defeated recharter of the United States Bank; and changed the tariff to protect agriculture as well as eastern manufactures. Van Buren and Johnson were credited with having uniformly supported Jackson, and as always having been firmly attached to democracy.

Discussion of men not measures dominated the presidential campaign in Indiana. According to the Whig address to the people, Van Buren had opposed the War of 1812, was the candidate of the party of "*office-holders* and *office-expectants*," and "the *enemy*" of the dearest interests of Hoosiers. As the campaign continued these criticisms were repeated; and Van Buren was said to have had early ties with the Federalists, opposed universal suffrage as a member of a New York constitutional convention, voted against aid for the National Road, voted to curb petitions regarding slavery, and had long practiced intrigue. One editor reported that the vice president rode "in a *three thousand* dollar coach, imported from England, American manufacture not being quite the thing for the New York nabob." One editor quipped: "Take Martin Van Buren from Jackson, and Jackson remains—take Jackson from Martin Van Buren and O [zero] remains."[130] According to the address of the Democrats to the people, Harrison had been named secretary of the Northwest Territory and then governor of the Indiana Territory by that early Federalist, John Adams. Moreover, as territorial governor he had helped establish "the foul blot of slavery" in Indiana, and thereby desecrated her "soil with a degraded population" in spite of the efforts of the fathers of the republic to have it "remain forever the exclusive and hallowed abode of freemen." As the campaign continued such criticisms were repeated; and Harrison was said to have helped establish slavery, even for white men, when territorial governor; and with having favored and fostered the Roman Catholic Church while serving in this capacity. One editor described Harrison as a mediocre military leader who had suffered many defeats; and had caused needless loss of life at the Battle of Tippecanoe by "encamping upon a creek pointed out by his savage foes, without a breast work or other protection . . . ." This editor declared that Harrison had had a political career with "no official act . . . which evinces any superior intellect or patriotism"; and viewed him as the dupe of designing politicians.[131]

Issues were discussed, but not in a consistent and systematic manner. Generally speaking most Democrats opposed, while many Whigs favored recharter of the United States Bank; and Whigs were more favorable to distributing surplus federal revenue to the states than were the Democrats. Partisans in both parties indicated continued support for internal improvements, and especially for the National Road. Neither party gave much attention to the tariff question. Van Buren was presented as one who would faithfully follow Jacksonian policies. Harrison advised a correspondent that he opposed federal aid for internal improvements, save for projects of real national importance. But he straddled the bank question, though he asserted that the government should experiment with handling its fiscal affairs without a national bank. Harrison criticized Jackson by saying that the veto power and party control over Congress should be used sparingly.[132]

As might be expected, Democrats and Whigs alike predicted that their party would carry Indiana.[133] About two months before the voting, the *Indiana Journal* suggested that by a remarkable coincidence every president had taken office in his sixty-second year, the age Harrison would be if elected. This Whig organ further noted that most states were expected to elect their presidential electors on November 7, the anniversary of the Battle of Tippecanoe. Its editor declared: "There is no doubt that Gen. Harrison is destined for the Presidency."[134] The voting in Indiana on November 7 resulted in a landslide victory for the Hero of Tippecanoe. The vote for Van Buren exceeded that for Jackson over Clay in 1832, but Harrison's margin of about 8,300 over his rival was larger than Old Hickory's had been over Clay. Harrison ran well in southern, central, and northern Indiana. He won the eighteen counties which had supported Clay, plus many others, giving him fifty-six of the seventy-six counties. The former territorial governor ran especially well in counties in or near the Whitewater Valley, in those through which the National Road passed, and he gained most of those bordering the Ohio, Wabash, and Maumee rivers.[135] Harrison's overwhelming triumph over Van Buren in Indiana was more a personal than a party victory. Van Buren, an easterner and a nonmilitary man, was no match against Harrison, a westerner and a hero of warfare against the British and Indians. Moreover, Harrison was viewed by many as the candidate of the people, as Jackson had been in his successful campaigns. Not to be overlooked is the fact that the election came amid the peak prosperity of the thirties when the Whig dominated General Assembly had recently adopted the widely approved Internal Improvements System of 1836. Thousands of Hoosiers deserted Old Hickory for another western military hero. In no other way could Jackson's margin of 6,150 votes over Clay have been supplanted by a margin of 8,300 votes for Harrison over Van Buren. Nonetheless, Van Buren won more electoral votes than the Whig candidates combined to replace his mentor. Johnson, however, got only a plurality of the electoral vote, but was chosen vice president over Francis Granger on the initial vote therefor by the Senate. Senators John Tipton and William Hendricks voted for Johnson, and they supported Van Buren's elevation to the presidency, at least to a limited extent.[136]

About a month after the landslide vote for Harrison, the General Assembly declined to reelect Senator William Hendricks whose term expired March 3, 1837. As Frederick D. Hill has noted, by the end of 1835 there had been speculation about Governor Noah Noble and former Congressman Oliver H. Smith, both Whigs, as probable candidates against Hendricks.[137] Noble was midstream in his second term, and ineligible for reelection. The *Indiana Democrat* had published an article by "Corn Planter" urging the election of only "*'original* and *thoroughgoing* Jackson men'" to office. In June, 1836, this Jacksonian organ called for the election of a "genuine republican" and "true republican" who would "carry into full operation the measures of the administration." With opposition to Hendricks emerging from partisans in both parties, the prospects for the independent Hendricks were unfavorable; and especially so after the Whigs won majority control of both legislative houses at the election in August.[138] During

November the *Indiana Democrat*, perhaps to sow division between Noble and Smith, published an item by "Indianian" favoring Smith over Noble, claiming that Smith would be less objectionable to the Van Buren men. The paper then followed with an item by "Hoosier" who contended that Noble, the bosom friend of Clay who had done more than anyone else to carry Indiana for Harrison, should be elected senator.[139] Immediately preceding the election the *Indiana Journal*, which favored Noble over Smith, explained that his promise not to use the office of governor as a steppingstone to another office, made in 1831, applied only to that election. It noted that he had twice been elected governor by a large majority, and asserted that a very large portion of the people desired his election to the Senate.[140] Meantime, there were reports as the presidential campaign ended that Hendricks had endorsed Van Buren.[141] When the legislature voted in joint session on December 8, 1836, Smith won election on the ninth ballot, obtaining seventy-nine votes against sixty-three for Noble, one for Hendricks, and three scattering. Both the voting and contemporary comments afford convincing evidence that the basic competition was between Noble and Smith, with Noble preferred by most Whigs but Smith winning because he got more Democratic votes than the governor.[142]

Smith's triumph as the first Indiana Whig in the federal Senate was followed by a near Whig sweep in the congressional elections of 1837. On January 2, a special election was held in the Sixth District to choose a successor to Congressman George L. Kinnard, a Democrat, who had suffered a miserable death from burns caused by the explosion of a steamboat boiler while he was enroute to Washington for a new session of Congress.[143] William Herod, a Whig, and William W. Wick, who had deserted the National Republicans to support Van Buren in 1836, vied to complete Kinnard's term which ended March 3, 1837. Both advocated distribution of surplus federal revenue to the states, and federal aid for completion of the National Road across Indiana. Herod stressed that he favored Harrison over Van Buren, while Wick promised liberal support for the Van Buren administration but claimed that he was not a strict party man.[144] Herod defeated

Wick by 210 votes in a district which had gone Democratic in the two preceding congressional elections.[145] This omen, coming on the heels of Harrison's landslide victory over Van Buren among Hoosier voters and Smith's election to the United States Senate, suggested that perhaps the Whigs were about to grasp control of federal as well as state politics within Indiana. With a number of men being mentioned as congressional aspirants, an editor mused that most of them were doomed to defeat, reminding him of the poet who said:

> "Ah who can tell how hard it is to climb
> The steep where fame's proud temple shines afar,
> Who can tell how many a soul sublime
> Hath felt the influence of mailgnant [sic] star."[146]

With the onset of the Panic of 1837 in May, "'fame's proud temple'" became less promising to Democrats than it had been when the year commenced. While all seven congressional districts had elected Democrats in 1835, Ratliff Boon in the First District was the only Democrat to win reelection.[147] Amos Lane, in the Fourth District, lost to George H. Dunn, a Whig, who won his first and only term. Herod, the Whig who had replaced the deceased Kinnard, trounced ex-Governor James Brown Ray by a huge margin.[148] In the Fifth District, Jonathan McCarty, elected as a Democrat in 1835, ran as a Whig but was defeated by James Rariden, a Whig he had defeated in 1835. McCarty lost in spite of Henry Clay's appeal via Noah Noble urging Whigs to support him because of his recent unflinching opposition to Jackson's administration and to help make room for needed converts.[149] Ewing, a Whig, regained the seat in the Second District that he had lost two years earlier. William Graham and Albert S. White, both Whigs, easily won initial terms in the Third and Seventh districts respectively. After the voting in August, the Vincennes *Western Sun* declared: "The delegation from Indiana will now consist of six Federalists [Whigs] and one Republican [Democrat]." The *Indiana Democrat* agreed with the *Western Sun* about the outcome, and it contended that merchants and national bank men associated with Nicholas Biddle had alarmed voters by attributing all the difficulties from the panic on the Democrats. Such criticism, and the Harrison sweep of the previous November, it said, had been too much for Democrats to overcome, however, the Whig triumph would not be a lasting one. The *Indiana Journal* viewed the election of six Whig congressmen "as the most complete, signal, and brilliant [victory] ever achieved by one political party over another." This Whig editor asserted that "Van Burenism is swept from Indiana," and he predicted that if Harrison should obtain the next Whig nomination for president that the "Vanites" would not even nominate electors. Indiana was proclaimed as "'THE WHIG STATE.'"[150]

The senatorial election in December, 1838, afforded Whigs a possibility of increasing their control over federal politics within Indiana. Despite bipartisan encouragement to Senator Tipton that he seek another reelection, in May, 1838, he announced his "settled purpose" to retire at the end of his term on March 3, 1839.[151] This announcement increased speculation about his possible successor. Among Whigs, ex-Governor Noah Noble, former Congressman Thomas H. Blake, and Supreme Court Judge Charles Dewey were prominently considered. On the Democratic side, Congressman Ratliff Boon and Tilghman A. Howard, federal district attorney for Indiana since 1833, were mentioned. The Vincennes *Western Sun* staunchly supported Boon as the candidate of the people who would sustain Jacksonian policies.[152] The *Indiana Democrat* blasted Noble as the proscriptive head of an Indianapolis Junto, and the one most responsible for the state's excessive and costly internal improvement system.[153] The bank question, policy regarding internal improvements, and the financial straits of the country were discussed largely along party lines.[154] The annual election in August had increased the already sizeable Whig majority in the General Assembly making it almost certain that a Whig would be elected. Before the voting, Noble, after stating that two years previous a distinguished citizen had defeated him "without a general concurrence of the Whigs," asked that his name be withdrawn from consideration "either finally, or for a time sufficient to allow an opportunity for the choice of another . . . ."[155] Thirty-six ballots were required when the voting occurred on December 7, 8, and 11. On ballots one through seven, Whigs Blake, Dewey, and Milton Stapp all gained significant support, while Noble got from one to four votes. On most of the remaining ballots Blake and Noble got more votes than Dewey and Stapp, then on the last several votes Albert S. White, who had received no votes until the thirty-second ballot quickly gained election with seventy-five votes on the thirty-sixth ballot. Boon and Howard were the Democrats who fared best, but neither was any threat to the Whig contenders. White, however, owed his victory to about forty-eight Whigs and twenty-seven Democrats.[156] The *Indiana Journal* called White "a firm and talented Whig" who would give "entire satisfaction" to his party and the people of the state. Its editor, however, explained that he had preferred Noble, whom it commended for his role regarding the election. The *Indiana Democrat* viewed White as a Federalist, but a gentleman whom it respected.[157] With White's elevation to the Senate, both senators and six of the state's seven congressmen were Whigs.

The near monopoly of Indiana senators and congressmen, gained by the Whigs during 1836–1838, was shattered in the congressional elections of 1839. Five Whig incumbent congressmen—John Ewing, William Graham, George H. Dunn, James Rariden, and William Herod sought new terms. Albert S. White, the remaining Whig incumbent, had been elevated to the Senate; and the lone Democrat, Ratliff Boon, who had won six terms, was not a candidate for the first time since 1824. Most of the Democratic candidates, and some who were Whigs, were nominated by congressional district conventions. Except in the Fifth District where Jonathan McCarty, a Whig, and William Thompson, a Democrat, opposed Rariden, by election day in August the rivalry was on a one-to-one basis. The Democrats made more use of district conventions to foster consensus and unity; they also announced publication of a campaign organ, the *Expunger*, to inspire the party faithful to action.[158] With the country in the midst of a severe depression, the Democrats advocated the separation of the government from banking, favored an independent treasury, and opposed recharter of the United States Bank.[159] The *Indiana*

Democrat contended that the election of Democratic congress-men would help elevate Harrison to the presidency by showing that Indiana had generously supported him but would not go for Clay.[160] In the First District views about religion muddied the political waters. George H. Proffit, the Whig candidate, was charged with having kicked a Bible out of his house and having "'administered the Sacrement with corn bread and butter milk.'"[161] Robert Dale Owen, his Democratic opponent, was accused of having denied the existence of a Supreme Being and abolition of the ordinance of marriage. "Mr. Owens entertains notions pernicious to the good order of society," the *Indiana Journal* declared, "and the people should know it."[162] Two weeks later this premier Whig organ of Indiana said: "we condemn the practice, as unchristian and unbecoming, of a candidate who is urging his claims upon the people to a political office, to publicly address his fellow-citizens on the subject of religion." The editor suggested that when a candidate makes "long and public professions of Christianity, we set him down as a hypocrite," and "a drawback to the progress of true religion."[163] When the votes were counted in August, Rariden in the Fifth District was the only Whig incumbent reelected. But George H. Proffit, a Whig, defeated Robert Dale Owen in the First District which the veteran Boon had vacated. Democrats John W. Davis, John Carr, Thomas Smith, William W. Wick, and Tilghman A. Howard won the Second, Third, Fourth, Sixth, and Seventh districts respectively. The *Indiana Journal* acknowledged that the Whigs had been *"Defeated and Routed—Rowed up Salt River, to the very head waters ! ! ! !"* The *Western Sun* gleefully asserted: "the state of Indiana has been redeemed, regenerated, and disinthralled." The *Indiana Democrat* viewed the outcome as indicating that the Democrats were the stronger of the two parties because of its congressional victories, and because the large majority of Whigs in the previous legislative session had been converted to a "decided majority" of Democrats.[164]

Meantime, while Hoosiers divided into rival political parties, they maintained an overwhelming consensus for early removal of the Indians. According to Indian Agent John Tipton, as of 1831 there were between five and six thousand tribesmen in the state, including about twelve hundred Miami with the remainder Potawatomi. The latter held title to about three million acres, mainly located in the central and western parts of northern Indiana. The Miami retained the Big Miami Reserve, of thirty-four miles square, and numerous small tracts along or near the upper Wabash River totaling over nine thousand acres.[165] But because of the lucrative trade with the Indians some Hoosiers were not eager to hasten their exit. Towns such as Fort Wayne, Huntington, Peru, Logansport, and South Bend, and their tributary areas, were very dependent upon the trade, especially since payments for annuities and otherwise to the tribesmen swelled in the thirties. Among the prominent traders were William G. and George W. Ewing, Allen Hamilton, Samuel Hanna, Alexis Coquillard, Francis Comparet, Lathrop M. Taylor, Cyrus Taber, and Miami chiefs Jean B. Richardville and Francis Godfroy. The Indian trade, often combined with speculation in land, provided a considerable economic base for various pioneer families. Hugh McCulloch, who was personally acquainted with a number of traders, later observed that men who dealt "fairly with white men did not hesitate to practise the most shameful impositions in their dealing with Indians." He could not remember "more than two or three" traders who had treated the Indians "with perfect fairness."[166] The Ewings, perhaps the largest but not the most scrupulous of traders, sought to delay removal. In 1837, when the major Potawatomi removal was preparing, George W. Ewing told the secretary of war: "Nor shall those Indians ever go out of Indiana until we are paid [our claims against them] if it is in my power to prevent them."[167] Nevertheless, the demand for removal of the Potawatomi and Miami increased during the thirties. The location of the Michigan Road through the Indian area in 1830, construction of the Wabash and Erie Canal beginning in 1832, and launching of the System of 1836 augmented this demand. The spread of settlements into northern Indiana and the hostility toward Indians generated by the Black Hawk War of 1832 increased eagerness for their removal. Tipton and others argued that because the Indians had rejected efforts to educate, civilize, and

Christianize them, their relocation west of the Mississippi, away from vices acquired from the whites, would afford them another opportunity to progress toward a civilized society. And the vigor with which the Jackson administration sustained removal made the political context favorable.[168]

In treaties concluded between 1832 and 1840 the Potawatomi and Miami surrendered their tribal holdings within Indiana. The initial cessions under President Jackson were negotiated in 1832 by Jonathan Jennings, John W. Davis, and Marks Crume. In three treaties portions of the Potawatomi ceded land in Indiana, Illinois, and part of Michigan, except for numerous small reservations to "bands" and individual Potawatomi. According to these treaties the United States agreed to pay the Potawatomi annuities totaling $880,000, provide them goods worth $247,000, and assume their debts totaling $111,879. An aggregate of $1,238,879 was pledged for these items.[169] During 1834, 1836, and 1837 fourteen supplemental treaties were concluded with various bands or groups of Potawatomi, resulting in the cession of scattered tracts, and the promise to make additional payments, largely in goods or money, totaling $105,440.[170] Liquidating claims of the Miami to land in Indiana proved more difficult than it was for the Potawatomi. The Miami not only possessed very fertile soil near the route of the Wabash and Erie Canal, but they were more united than the Potawatomi and led by the very capable Chief Jean B. Richardville. Moreover, some of the traders wished to delay their removal. Nevertheless, in treaties negotiated in 1834, 1838, and 1840 the Miami surrendered their tribal holdings in the state, and in the last treaty agreed to move beyond the Mississippi by 1845. These treaties included numerous grants of land to individual Miami, especially to Chiefs Richardville and Francis Godfroy. As the table which follows indicates, considerable payments were made to hasten removal.[171]

Treaty	Annuities	Cash	Debts
1834	$100,000	$58,000	$ 50,000
1838	12,568	60,000	150,000
1840	250,000	0	300,000

The removal of the Potawatomi and Miami was both gradual and incomplete. The largest single removal of the Potawatomi, appropriately called the Trail of Death, occurred in 1838. Some tribesmen had agreed to leave the land they had ceded by early August of that year, but Indians planted crops for summer and fall harvest; and white squatters moved onto Indian tracts to establish preemption claims in anticipation of their departure. Skirmishes which followed between whites and Indians resulted in loss of property and threatened loss of life. Indian Agent Abel C. Pepper, superintendent for the removal, and citizens of the area appealed to Governor David Wallace for a military force to preserve the peace. The governor called upon Senator John Tipton to recruit one hundred volunteers and report to Pepper "for service" with the men in his command "armed and equipped."[172] In letters prior to his appointment Tipton had said the Indians "*must go*" and he had commenced gathering volunteers preparatory to their removal. Tipton quickly forcibly rounded up many tribesmen, including Menominee who insisted that he had not consented to either cession or removal; and he and other Indians were compelled to emigrate.[173] The removal force left Twin Lakes, near Plymouth, on September 4; and it arrived in what became the state of Kansas on November 4. Tipton escorted the removal party to near Danville, Illinois, from where William Polke completed the removal. The Indians were ill prepared for the long and difficult journey, made largely by foot but partially by horseback and wagon. They suffered from severe thirst, intense heat, clouds of dust, rain, snow, mud, and bitter cold. Inadequate food added to sickness along the way, and about forty-three of the Potawatomi died before or soon after their arrival in the West. About 750 Indians reached Kansas.[174] Polke reported that the Indians preferred complaints against the government because houses had not been prepared for them nor had the land been cultivated as promised in treaties. He urged that such promises be fulfilled. One Indian complained that "They had been taken from their homes affording them plenty, and brought to a desert—a wilderness—and were now to be scattered as the husbandman scattered his seed."[175] Some Potawatomi had gone west earlier, and removals of lesser numbers followed until by the early fifties perhaps not more than several hundred of them remained in Indiana, while part of the Potawatomi who had emigrated soon returned after their removal.[176] Although the Miami had promised to emigrate by 1845, their partial removal largely took place in 1846. Their leaving was delayed because many tribesmen had been exempted from emigration. These exemptions hastened cessions of land, but they encouraged Indians not exempted to try to avoid emigration. In 1846, with a military force available to compel removal, if force was required, the major Miami exodus occurred. On October 6 three canal boats, loaded with Indians, removal personnel, and baggage, left Peru for Fort Wayne via the Wabash and Erie Canal. At Fort Wayne, a mecca for the Miami, additional Miami and baggage were added, plus additional boats; and the expedition proceeded by canal into Ohio and thence via canal to Cincinnati. From this city the party continued by steamboat to Kansas City, then to their reservation in Kansas, arriving on November 9. They were spared much of the hardship and suffering endured by the Potawatomi, but there were six deaths enroute and only 323 Miami were delivered to their new location.[177] John W. Dawson, who witnessed their departure from Fort Wayne, described their mournful goodby to their beloved area: "Well I remember the sober, saddened faces, the profusion of tears, as I saw them hug to their bosoms a little handful of earth which they had gathered from the graves of their dead kindred" as they left Fort Wayne. Dawson observed: "many a bystander was moved to tears at the evidences of grief he saw before him."[178] A smaller removal followed in 1847, but less than half of the Miami became permanent residents of the West since those who never emigrated plus those who returned constituted a majority of the tribe.[179]

By the 1830s the process by which land was *supposed* to pass from the Indians to the settlers was well established. According to this process only the federal government could acquire land from the Indians; only the federal government could have it surveyed; and land could be sold only through federal land offices. Surveying often began before ceded tracts were vacated, with the initial public sale of land usually soon after its survey. Following public sale the remaining acreage could be purchased at the minimum price. Settling on land before its survey, though common, was illegal. In 1838 Senator John Tipton stated, with exaggeration, that "the people of four entire counties"—Lake, Newton, Porter, and Pulaski—had been squatters as had some residents of Miami and other counties.[180] In 1836 squatters in Lake County organized a Squatters' Union and drafted a constitution which established a system of registering and defending their claims. Solon Robinson, of Crown Point, was named register of claims, and 476 persons signed the constitution. At the initial public auction in 1839, squatters who desired to buy their tracts secured them at the minimum price of $1.25 per acre. For aiding them Robinson became known as the "King of the Squatters."[181] While many easterners and some westerners viewed squatters as a lawless and unruly lot, Hoosier politicians generously defended them. In 1835, after a colleague from Rhode Island condemned squatting as "something very like stealing," Congressman Edward A. Hannegan bristled. Squatters, he said, were better off than the workingmen of the large factories of Rhode Island; and, he stressed, making land available to the "industrious poor" in small parcels would increase the wealth of the nation. Three years later, Congressman Ratliff Boon asserted that a majority of the white population of the new states and territories had been squatters, and the government was more indebted to them for the value of the public domain than to any other element. Boon recounted how he had left Kentucky twenty-seven years earlier, with a wife and four small children, to become a squatter in Indiana. In Boon's words: "my nearest neighbor was a hostile Indian, and my only shelter from the storm, and my protection from danger, was an open *camp*; and the bark of the elm tree when spread upon the cold earth served both as my floor and my carpet. And, for more than five long years, the meal of which my daily bread was made I had to grind on a hand mill." Land policy, Boon added, should be changed to favor those who had borne such hardships, rather than the speculator who fared best under existing law. Early in 1841 Senator Albert S. White urged that preemption be granted squatters, to hasten the extension of Anglo-Saxon civilization "to the shores of the Pacific

ocean . . . ." Northwestern Indiana, he suggested, had been settled by squatters, and "A more orderly, industrious, or better regulated community, is not to be found."[182]

Some modification of federal land policy was effected under
Presidents Jackson and Van Buren. The law of 1820, which ended
the credit system and made possible the purchase of tracts as small
as eighty acres for $100 in cash, was amended in 1832 to permit
sales as small as forty acres for $50. Early in the thirties relief leg-
islation on behalf of buyers under the credit system apparently
terminated.[183] Land offices continued in operation at Vincennes,
Jeffersonville, Indianapolis, Fort Wayne, and Crawfordsville; and
another, opened at La Porte in 1833, was moved to Winamac in
1839. In both the state and nation land sales peaked amid the
prosperity of the mid-thirties. During the thirties more than one
third of the federal domain of Indiana passed to private ownership. In the years 1835, 1836, and 1837 more than one million
acres were sold annually, with over three million sold in the peak
year of 1836. Indiana land offices, especially those in the northern
half of the state, truly did a "land office business" in the thirties.[184]

Discussion persisted concerning four major proposals for disposition of the federal domain. Advocates of cession asked that
Congress donate, or at least sell the domain at a nominal price, to
the states in which it was located. Proponents of preemption
wanted squatters to have priority in buying their tracts at minimum price. Champions of graduation sought a step by step lowering of the price until a low minimum was achieved, with land
unsold donated to the states in which it was situated. Those who
favored distribution generally wanted the price unchanged, or
only slightly lowered, with surplus federal revenue distributed
among all states per some formula. All four proposals had variations regarding details, and at times two or more of them were
supported concurrently. Cession had considerable support among
Indiana politicians, but it had no realistic chance of adoption
while the states, having none of the federal domain, controlled
Congress. Senator William Hendricks continued to support cession in the thirties, as he had under President Adams; and cession
gained increased consideration in the late thirties when John C.

Calhoun championed its cause.[185] Temporary and special pre-emption laws continued to be passed, and were much supported by Indiana politicians, but not until 1841 was a general and con-tinuing preemption law achieved. By this time westerners had an increased voice in Congress and many Whigs as well as numerous Democrats had become its supporters.[186] Westerners in particular, Hoosiers included, gave much support for graduation as they did for cession and preemption.[187]

With the swelling of revenue from sales of the public domain and the approaching liquidation of the national debt in the early thirties, support for distribution grew. The need of various states for money to finance internal improvements fostered a desire for federal aid via distribution. Henry Clay, its best known sponsor, obtained passage of a distribution bill in 1833, only to have it ve-toed by President Jackson. Senator William Hendricks, an inde-pendent in politics, voted for the bill's passage, as did Congress-man Jonathan McCarty, a Jacksonian. But three Jacksonians, Senator John Tipton, Congressman Ratliff Boon, and Congress-man John Carr opposed passage.[188] Hendricks explained that by "contending for that which we prefer, but have no prospect of getting," an estimated $1,000,000 would be lost to Indiana (1833–1837) that would be gained from distribution. The pro-National Republican *Indiana Journal* expressed similar views, and it praised Hendricks and McCarty for their course. The *Western Sun*, faith-ful to Old Hickory, was delighted with the veto.[189] Nonetheless, with the national debt paid and the surplus revenue mounting amid the prosperity of the middle thirties, another distribution bill passed in 1836, which President Jackson signed. Senators Hendricks and John Tipton voted for passage, as did six of Indi-ana's seven Democratic congressmen.[190] With evident delight Tipton estimated that Hoosiers would receive about $1,000,000 during the initial year of the surplus distribution, thus enabling "Indiana to push forward her great schemes of internal improve-ment with spirit and economy."[191] Congressman Ratliff Boon, who had vigorously opposed distribution and strongly recom-mended decreasing federal revenue, said he had voted for the bill with great reluctance. He stated that the surplus resulted from a revenue system which taxed "the many for the benefit of the few." Such a system, Boon asserted, "humbugged" the people; and the revenue should be reduced to meet the legitimate needs of government, "and leave the surplus where it should be—in the pockets of its rightful owners."[192]

Early in 1837 it appeared that Indiana would receive $1,147,005.92 in federal surplus revenue during this year. Half of this sum was received before the Panic of 1837 began in May, and a third installment was obtained in June.[193] Then, with federal land sales and revenue plummeting, President Van Buren, who had succeeded Jackson in March, called Congress into a special session starting September 1. Van Buren advised Congress that at least most of the fourth installment money would be needed to meet existing appropriations, hence it "should be withheld."[194] At first a bill for indefinite postponement of distribution passed the Senate 28 to 17, and the House 119–117. Senator Oliver H. Smith voted against such postponement, which Senator Tipton also opposed but he was not among the voters. In the House Congressman Ratliff Boon supported indefinite postponement, but his Whig colleagues—George H. Dunn, John Ewing, William Graham, William Herod, James Rariden, and Albert S. White—opposed this action. After the House voted to reconsider the bill's passage, a modified bill, calling for suspension until January 1, 1839, passed the House 118 to 106 and was concurred with by the Senate by a count of 30 to 2.[195] Though the distribution bill had been explicit that deposits were subject to recall, Tipton asserted that Indiana had a right to expect the fourth installment. He argued that its faithful payment would transfer money from the banks to the states and then into circulation as "a permanent relief measure." The *Indiana Journal*, staunchly pro-Whig, asserted: "This was the only measure by which the west ever received back any of the vast amount drawn from her by the general government, and just at the moment when the country is most in need of it it is withdrawn." Any member of Congress from the West who had voted for the postponement was branded "a traitor to the interests of his constituents . . . ." Congressman James Rariden blamed the Democrats for the economic and fiscal distress, and he insisted that the fourth installment be paid. Tipton advised a correspondent that he had opposed postponement of the fourth installment "under the belief that the faith of this govrt was pledged to the states, that witholding it might retard the resumption of specie payment by our banks and compell them to press thier [sic] debtors and distress the people." In any event, distribution ceased for the Jackson-Van Buren era.[196]

Questions relating to the public domain, internal improvements, the tariff, and banking—all much interrelated—were not the only domestic concerns of Hoosiers. Considerable attention was given to the status of blacks in the state, and national policy concerning slavery gained consideration during the Jackson-Van Buren era, 1829–1841. Although blacks approximated only about 1 percent of the population from statehood to mid-century, there was much discrimination against them based, in varying degrees, upon custom, legislation, and the state constitution. The constitution vigorously prohibited slavery, but it denied suffrage to blacks and excluded them from the militia.[197] At a meeting of a colonization society at Indianapolis in 1834, Daniel D. Pratt observed that blacks could not vote, hold office, or testify in courts except against other blacks. Though nominally free, he explained, yet there was "not a feature in our institutions but reminds them that they are objects of contempt and ridicule—that they are *not* our equals. While they live and move among us they are not *of* us. There exists antipathies which can never be eradicated." Foreseeing no hope for improvement of their condition, Pratt endorsed the colonization of free blacks in Africa. Three years later Samuel Merrill, also supporting colonization, commented that in the United States "the black man is considered an inferior being," and in portions thereof denied freedom. Merrill added: "Law in general, refuses his testimony; and prejudice, still stronger than law, degrades him among the lowest of his species."[198] An important legal right, however, the ownership of property, was allowed blacks. A number of blacks, often as members of rural settlements, acquired land and other property. Blacks also became barbers, carpenters, brickmasons, coopers, shoemakers, blacksmiths, teamsters, cooks, waiters, and stewards.[199]

During the twenties and thirties Hoosiers gave support to the movement for colonizing free blacks in Africa or elsewhere. Early in 1820, while the legislature was in session at Corydon, the Indiana Colonization Society was organized as an auxiliary of the American Colonization Society, founded three years earlier. The meeting that organized the state society strongly condemned slavery, urged Indiana citizens to check its extension, and adopted a constitution advocating the colonization of blacks in Africa. Governor Jonathan Jennings was elected president of the Indiana Colonization Society, which apparently died not long after its meeting at Corydon in December, 1820. In announcing this meeting, an editor at Corydon said that citizens generally wished to "be freed, as much as possible, from a mixt population," and wished that "the Africans should have a home of their own."[200] At the first session of the legislature at Indianapolis in 1825, the General Assembly approved a resolution of the Ohio legislature which urged that colonization be linked with a plan for gradual emancipation of all slaves in the United States. Four years later the legislature urged federal aid for the American Colonization Society to "more speedily" remove "the colored population" from the country.[201]

The Indiana Colonization Society was revived at Indianapolis in 1829. Its statement of purpose noted laws in slaves states requiring freed slaves to leave their borders, and declared: "The existence of these laws, and in the increasing desire to be rid of the evil of slavery, is continually pouring in upon the free states a flood of suspected and unwelcome population." Judge Jesse L. Holman was named president of the society.[202] Collections to help finance colonization were taken, often in churches on or near the Fourth of July, but blacks resisted colonization and very few of them responded to it.[203] At the annual meeting of the Indiana Colonization Society in 1830, slavery was termed incompatible with republican institutions, and the managers of the society exalted Liberia as a place for colonization. The society apparently soon languished, but was revived in 1845.[204] While the colonization movement sought to encourage blacks to leave Indiana, the General Assembly attempted to decrease the number of them coming to the state. An act of 1831 mandated that blacks entering the state give bond, with good and sufficient security, that they would not become a public charge and also as incentive for their good behavior. This legislation did not apply to blacks already in the state, and it placed no restrictions on ownership of property. Whether it checked black immigration is uncertain, but, if so, it appears to have been only modest since the number of blacks almost doubled during the thirties.[205]

During the thirties Indiana citizens showed growing concern about issues regarding slavery. A state senator who protested against the law of 1831 to restrict the immigration of blacks, declared that Indiana was not "entirely clear of the sin of slavery" since she had participated with other states "in legislating for the District [of Columbia] and maintaining the existence of slavery there for the last fourteen years, and has not as yet uttered a word of complaint." As the decade advanced, Congress received memorials from Hoosiers for the abolition of slavery in the District.[206] Members of Congress from Indiana, especially its Whig members, usually voted against the tabling of such memorials which prevented their consideration by relevant committees.[207] In 1837 Congressman Amos Lane contended that Congress had power to regulate slavery in the District, but he viewed its exercise "fearfully dangerous to the tranquillity of the Union." Senator John Tipton, however, said Congress had no such authority. Attempts by free state citizens to disturb property rights regarding slaves, Tipton warned, "distracts the peace of the country and endangers the existence of the Union."[208] Hoosier politicians were largely agreed that Congress had no authority over slavery in the slave states. In 1836 six of the state's seven Democratic congressmen supported this view, as did four of its Whig congressmen two years later.[209] The *Indiana Journal*, the state's premier Whig organ, hoped that the day was not distant when the nation would be free of slavery, but it was emphatic that the slave states, and they alone, could end such bondage. Congressman Ratliff Boon and Senator John Tipton argued that the federal constitution recognized slavery. Congressman Amos Lane asserted that even the "wildest fanatic" did not claim that Congress had power over slavery in the states.[210] At its session of 1838–1839, the General Assembly, dominated by Whigs, declared that interference with slavery, without the consent of the slaveholding states, "either by Congress or the state legislatures, is contrary to the compact by which those states became members of the Union."[211]

By the late thirties, however, there was increasing concern about the prospective addition of new states by territorial expansion. Even before Texas gained independence from Mexico in 1836, Senator Tipton advised his constituents of his opposition to its annexation. "Her climate may incline her people to use slave labor," he suggested. Tipton added: "While we should scrupulously refrain from interfering with this institution in the States of our Union where it now exists, we should also be careful to do nothing that will tend to its farther propagation among us."[212] Hoosiers, especially Quakers, sent resolutions to Congress opposing the extension of slavery through territorial expansion, at times making explicit their opposition to the addition of Texas as a slave state.[213]

Meanwhile, the efforts of masters to recover escaped slaves gave Hoosiers vivid reminders of the harsher aspects of slavery. The federal Fugitive Slave Law of 1793 enabled a claimant or his representative to seize an alleged fugitive and take such person before a federal judge or state magistrate. If an official viewed the escapee as belonging to the claimant, he gave the latter a certificate for the return of such person to slavery. This law included penalties for harboring a fugitive or obstructing his or her recovery.[214] Opposition to fugitive slave legislation had existed from territorial days. By the thirties a modest number of Hoosiers, particularly Quakers and members of some other Protestant groups, supported the Underground Railroad in its efforts on behalf of escaped slaves and free blacks. After their emigration from North Carolina to Newport (Fountain City) in 1826, the Levi Coffin home became a station on the Underground Railroad. Coffin later estimated that by 1847 more than two thousand fugitives had stayed with the family, at times for weeks or months. Coffin asserted that "It was never too cold or stormy, or the hour of night too late, for my wife to rise from sleep, and provide food and comfortable lodging for the fugitives" who "generally came to us destitute of clothing, and were often barefooted." Many of

Coffin's fellow Quakers disapproved of such aid, some refused to do business with him, however, other Quakers made clothes and helped fugitives in various ways.[215] But many Hoosiers, especially public officials, supported the fugitive slave law and declined to aid the Underground Railroad. In some instances free blacks were forcibly removed from the state, at times without a hearing before an appropriate official. At other times, claimants falsely persuaded judges that free blacks were their slaves.[216] In 1837 the legislature of Kentucky asked the legislature of Indiana for protection against the seduction and concealment of slaves. Governor Noah Noble responded that Indiana had "religiously abstained" from interfering with the "domestic institutions of her sister States." The Senate Judiciary Committee concurred, averring that Indiana had "carefully avoided any interference with the delicate and exciting question of slavery."[217]

Starting about 1836 local antislavery societies were formed. In this year the Decatur County Anti-Slavery Society was organized by persons who had belonged to the Decatur County Colonization Society. During this year some young men at Hanover College formed an antislavery society whose constitution declared that slaves had a right to be free in the United States. By the early forties perhaps a dozen or so local antislavery societies had been founded, but most of them were apparently short lived. These societies were often associated with local churches, but their membership at times crossed denominational lines. Societies formed by Quakers were more numerous than for any other religious body, and they were especially found in east-central Indiana.[218] In September, 1838, five years after the formation of the American Anti-Slavery Society, about forty-four delegates representing local antislavery societies in approximately a dozen counties organized a State Anti-Slavery Society at Milton, in Wayne County. According to the preamble of the new society, its purposes were to awaken public opinion against slavery by appealing to the hearts and consciences of men; disseminate knowledge about the evils of slavery, including the duty and safety of immediate emancipation; and elevate the character of the black population by promoting its moral and intellectual improvement. The founding convention deprecated the formation of separate political parties devoted to abolition, but it approved the questioning of candidates about issues regarding slavery. The convention endorsed the free labor movement which sought to end slavery by boycotting the buying and selling of goods whose production involved slave labor. The new society urged Hoosiers to petition Congress for the end of slavery in the District of Columbia. The State Anti-Slavery Society seems not to have held an annual meeting until 1841 when nearly two thousand people reportedly attended. Daniel Worth, a Methodist preacher, was its president, but most of the other officers were Quakers. Quakers also dominated the State Female Anti-Slavery Society, organized about this time; and in 1841 the Indiana State Wesleyan Anti-Slavery Society was established.[219] Although church members largely nourished these societies, they immediately became divisive forces within denominations. Both ministers and laymen often opposed membership in antislavery societies and the holding of their meetings in church buildings.[220]

By the early forties antislavery sentiment spilled over into party formation, though on a negligible scale. As early as 1824 James Duncan, a Presbyterian minister at Vevay, had condemned slavery as a sin contrary to moral law, natural rights, republican principles, and the teachings of both the Old and New Testaments. Duncan urged voters to support men who favored freedom.[221] With the formation of antislavery societies candidates were "questioned" about their views regarding slavery. In the presidential election of 1840, a tiny step was taken with the organization of the Liberty party. In Indiana this new party, dedicated to the abolition of slavery, polled only thirty votes scattered over four counties. Nonetheless, slavery had become directly involved in the political arena.[222] As the forties began many Hoosier politicians considered slavery an evil, but most of them viewed slavery within the states as beyond the control of the federal government. At the same time, however, there was an increasing desire to prevent the addition of new slave states into the Union.

While domestic politics received the major attention during the Jackson–Van Buren era, relations with other countries had considerable importance. The absence of major wars in Europe, combined with the Atlantic Ocean as a defense shield, gave the United States an opportunity to grow in population and strength, while expanding into the Mississippi Valley free of conflict with other countries. When Jackson became president Senator William Hendricks advised his constituents that the "foreign relations of the country" were "gratifying to the friends of peace." Hendricks observed that questions were pending with Great Britain concerning commerce and the boundary between Maine and Canada. He noted that claims against France for damages to American shipping arising from the Napoleonic wars remained unsettled. But these items, the senator observed, threatened "no inquietude to the country"; and the warfare between Russia and Turkey, and Turkey and Greece, "have little or no effect on our commerce, remote as those theatres of war are from the Atlantic ports of Europe." Hendricks also noted that for years a "strong squadron" had been maintained in the Atlantic to protect American "commerce against the pirates which continually infest those seas."[223] In 1833 Senator John Tipton told Hoosiers: "Our commerce covers every sea, protected from piracy by our tars, and we have peace with all the world."[224]

Though the United States remained aloof from participation in European affairs, Indiana citizens often expressed interest in efforts toward liberty and freedom in the Old World. When revolutions swept over much of Europe in 1830, Indiana's youthful Governor James Brown Ray effervescently told legislators: "The genius of liberty, from soaring triumphant with the Eagle and star-spangled banner of America, has taken her flight across the Atlantic, to career for a while, with the lilies and tri-colours of France." After describing France as having become a *Republican Monarchy*," Ray expressed the hope that liberty and freedom would take root in Europe and "visit the republicks of South America, bleeding under their misrule and factions," and make them independent of Spain. Early in 1831 the anti-Jacksonian editor of the *Indiana Journal* predicted that "The progress of free principles is onward; and the time appears to be rapidly approaching, when no king will run the hazard of opposing popular sentiment." But as the liberal and national uprisings subsided Editor Elihu Stout commented that "the brave but unfortunate Poles have bled in vain."[225] A decade later Major Gaspard Tochman, who had participated in the Polish uprising of the early thirties, lectured in Indianapolis about Polish history and the struggle of the Poles for independence. A meeting, chaired by former Governor David Wallace, expressed deep sympathy concerning "the calamities which have befallen the Poles in the destruction and dismemberment of their country" at the hand of tyrannical power. The meeting expressed the hope that "Poland will again be free, will again become a refuge and a home for the oppressed and persecuted, and a beacon light, in the midst of the dark and besotted nations of the old world, to the friends of Liberty and Free Government."[226]

The reopening of trade with the British West Indies had been an object of American diplomacy since independence. In negotiations regarding this trade, Secretary of State Martin Van Buren tried to conciliate the British by criticism of the manner in which the Adams administration had conducted negotiations about this issue. But the stalemate continued and the impatient Jackson threatened to cut off trade with Canada if the West Indian trade was not opened. Congress, however, authorized concessions to the British if concessions were made to the United States. The British removed certain restrictions, and in the fall of 1830 President Jackson proclaimed the opening of the West Indian trade. Indiana Jacksonians touted this development as evidence of Old Hickory's skill as a diplomat, but an opposition organ suggested that perhaps changed circumstances rather than "superior skill" had been responsible for the outcome.[227]

Although by a treaty ratified in 1832 the French government agreed to pay about $5,000,000 as compensation for damages to American shipping during the Napoleonic era, in 1833 payment was not begun as had been promised. Late the next year, with no payment yet received, Jackson recommended that Congress authorize reprisals against French property if payment was not soon commenced. Congress, however, did not authorize reprisals; but amid talk of possible war between France and the United States, in 1835 France made an appropriation, payable after Jackson made satisfactory explanation for the language he had used when he had recommended reprisals.[228] Before knowing this response from France, Senator Tipton urged forbearance. National honor, he said, might make war unavoidable, but he cherished the expectation that "our first friend and most ancient ally" would "ultimately do us entire justice." Senator Hendricks feared war, unless the promised payments were made, but he noted that both countries strongly desired peace about a matter in which the money involved was "as dust" when "compared with the expenses of a war to either nation." Congressman John Ewing, Indiana's sole Whig member of Congress, considered the United States unprepared for war. He thought the people were for the utmost forbearance with France to keep the peace.[229] Jackson made no formal apology, but in addressing Congress late in 1835 he mitigated his remarks and expressed regret that his previous remarks had irritated the French. In the summer of 1836 Senator Tipton informed the citizens of Indiana that the French had commenced payment of compensation for the longstanding damages. He credited the outcome to the "friendly mediation" of Great Britain and the "firmness" of President Jackson.[230]

As the controversy with France eased, American interest in and concern about Texas increased. About the time Mexico secured independence from Spain in the early twenties, the United States had surrendered its claim to the area which became Texas. But during the twenties and thirties Texas was mainly settled by Americans from the lower Mississippi Valley, making it an American enclave detached from the principal areas of Mexican settlements. Meantime, there were continued and unsuccessful efforts to settle claims of Americans for damages sustained during revolutions in Mexico. Mexico understandably did not wish to lose her Texan outpost or weaken her feeble control over the vast region between Texas and the Pacific.[231] But the Texas War for Independence, 1835–1836, aroused much sympathy for the Texans among Hoosiers as with Americans generally. Early in 1836 Editor Elihu Stout, a veteran Jacksonian, observed that thus far success had attended the Texans, then added: "may it continue with them to the end." The Whig editor of the *Indiana Journal* asserted that the Mexicans by their cruel conduct of the war had "thrown themselves without the pale of civilization, and should be placed in the same scale with the Cannibals of New Zealand and the wild savages of North America." After General Sam Houston defeated Santa Anna at the Battle of San Jacinto in April, 1836, and took the Mexican leader prisoner, the *Indiana Democrat* predicted that this "glorious victory" would terminate the conflict and compel Santa Anna to recognize the independence of Texas. Despite Jackson's official stance of neutrality, both Jackson and numerous Americans throughout the country favored the Texans in their aspirations for independence.[232]

Most Americans, especially Democrats, quickly favored the recognition of Texas as an independent state. Not long after Santa Anna promised independence under duress of circumstances Senator William Hendricks voted for resolutions calling for recognition of Texas as soon as it had established a successful government performing the usual functions of an independent state. Senator John Tipton, who did not participate in the voting, viewed recognition as premature. Tipton was emphatic that he preferred Texas as a sister republic rather than as a slave state within the United States.[233] At this same session, that of 1835–1836, when the House voted 135 to 56 for an appropriation for a minister to Texas, to be named by the president at as early a date as he thought proper, three of Indiana's seven Democratic congressmen voted for passage, two against, and two were nonvoters. Then the House approved 128 to 20 for recognition whenever satisfactory information was available that Texas had established a government capable of performing the duties and obligations of an independent power. Four Hoosier congressmen voted therefor, while the remaining three were nonvoters.[234] In December, 1836, President Jackson, in two messages to Congress, urged caution concerning recognition of Texas as an independent country. But shortly before Jackson's presidency ended both the House and Senate authorized him to recognize Texas at his discretion, which he did on March 3, 1837, his last day as president, thus sparing Van Buren this troublesome decision.[235] Concern about possible war with Mexico, widespread opposition to annexation of a slave state, and uncertainty about what the British and French might do caused the question of the possible annexation of Texas to remain largely in limbo until near the end of Van Buren's administration. In addition, uncertainty about the outcome of boundary disputes with Britain, concerning both the northeastern and northwestern borders, also fostered caution about actions that might engender conflict with Mexico on the southwestern border.[236]

CHAPTER 11

WESTERN EXPANSION AMID SECTIONAL STRIFE, 1841–1850

Important changes occurred concerning Indiana's role in national politics as the forties advanced. Party organization increased and became more emphasized than previously. Personal preferences remained important in winning elections, but after Harrison's death in 1841 loyalty to party grew and issues between the major parties were much emphasized. Questions regarding money and banking, the tariff, and internal improvements persisted, but waned in importance as items about territorial expansion and slavery gained prominence. The Democrats remained more attached to states' rights than the Whigs, and they suffered less from sectional cleavage than their opponents. Both parties were staunchly western in their outlook, yet vigorous in their devotion to the Union of the states. The Liberty-Free Soil party, though modest in strength, stirred the political waters, especially as the slavery issue intensified. Relations with other countries, particularly with Britain and Mexico, were threatening during much of the decade. Indiana's augmenting population gave Hoosiers a significantly larger voice than previously in national politics, its congressmen increasing from seven in 1841 to ten through the election of 1851. Having ranked eighteenth among the states in population in 1820, Indiana rose to tenth in 1840, and seventh in 1850.[1]

Within Indiana the presidential election of 1840 was more a culmination of the politics of the thirties than a transition to that of the forties. In both 1828 and 1832 Hoosier voters had generously sustained General Andrew Jackson, but in 1836 and 1840 they generously supported General William Henry Harrison. In the last two contests numerous Hoosiers switched from one military hero and westerner to another; a switch much encouraged because Martin Van Buren, Harrison's opponent, was an easterner and nonmilitary man against whom many voters were prejudiced.[2] Even before Van Buren's inauguration on March 4, 1837, the movement began among Hoosiers to make Harrison his successor. In December, 1836, the *Indiana Journal*, the premier Whig organ of the state, proclaimed the "People's Nomination For President, WILLIAM HENRY HARRISON" to replace Van Buren in 1841. After asserting that Van Buren could easily have been defeated in 1836, had the Whigs voted in strength in Pennsylvania, Virginia, and North Carolina, its editor declared: "'Sink or swim, survive or perish,' we therefore go for HARRISON, the Constitution, and the supremacy of the laws." During July, 1837, the *Indiana Journal* indicated that Hugh L. White, Daniel Webster, Henry Clay, and Harrison were all qualified to be president; and it agreed that a national convention should make a party nomination. In October it pledged support to the nominee of a national convention, but warned that Webster "cannot receive the support of the West in preference to either Harrison or Clay." A short time later this paper called a convention unnecessary because: "The people have already made their choice, and it has fallen upon Gen. William Henry Harrison, of Ohio."[3] Nevertheless, late in 1837 the *Indiana Journal* and other Whig papers urged a state convention to name delegates to a national convention to select the party's nominee for president. Perhaps mindful of the lack of Whig consensus in 1836, the Rushville *Herald* admonished: "'*The spirit of compromise, of concession, as to men, must predominate to insure success.*'" Although the *Indiana Journal* affirmed principles in preference to men as the motto of the Whigs, Hoosier Whigs were trimming their sails to the political winds to elect a western military hero. As county conventions elected delegates to a state convention, January 22, 1838, was set for its meeting at Indianapolis.[4] The resulting Whig State Convention expressed the opinion that Harrison was the choice of Indiana voters to succeed Van Buren, but it pledged support to Henry Clay should he be the nominee. The address of the convention to the people of Indiana referred to Harrison and Clay as "the common property of the whole Union," and proclaimed that with either as the nominee "victory will be complete" if there be concert and union among Whigs of the United States.[5] Soon after the convention adjourned, the Richmond *Palladium* commenced publication of "FOR PRESIDENT WILLIAM HENRY HAR-RISON" at the head of its editorial comments.⁶

Nearly three years elapsed from the Whig State Convention until November 2, 1840, when Indiana voters would choose their presidential electors. The *Indiana Journal* continued the listing of Harrison as the people's choice for president, while promising to support Clay should he become the nominee. When Webster withdrew from the contest in the summer of 1839, its editors praised him warmly and viewed his action a boon for Harrison.⁷ The heavy losses suffered by Whigs in the congressional elections of 1839 apparently fostered support among Indiana voters for Harrison over Clay. Nonetheless, the *Indiana Journal* reaffirmed its support for Clay, if nominated.⁸ Several weeks later Henry Clay sought information from Senator Oliver H. Smith about his prospects in Indiana, only to be told that they were unfavorable.⁹

The nomination of General Harrison by the Whig National Convention at Harrisburg, Pennsylvania, in December, 1839, delighted Hoosier Whigs. Several weeks earlier county conventions had begun electing delegates to a Whig State Convention for the purpose of nominating presidential electors and preparing for the presidential and gubernatorial campaigns of 1840.¹⁰ According to the *Tri-Weekly Journal* this convention, which met at the capital January 16, 1840, "was the *largest* political assemblage ever convened" in the state. This Whig press emphasized that in spite of the coldest and most inclement weather of the winter that delegates "poured into town from every quarter. They came in companies of from one to one hundred, to a late hour at night, and hundreds arrived on the morning of the 16th."¹¹ Mingling pageantry, music, and political rhetoric, the delegates endorsed the nomination of Harrison and Tyler as "the best selection that could be made." Harrison was commended as a soldier-statesman-patriot, a friend of Indiana and of the West, a tried and unerring democrat, and an honest man of practical good sense. Tyler was described as "a man of spotless integrity and unimpeached honor" and *"'one of the straightest disciples of Jeffersonian Democracy, that Virginia ever knew.'"* According to the address and resolutions approved by the convention, Jacksonian policies had replaced the sound circulation of the Second United States Bank with numerous weak state banks having an overexpanded and depressed circulation; by refusing needed federal aid had forced states to become heavily indebted for systems of internal improvement; had caused a decline in exports versus imports to other countries; and had turned the country from prosperity to depression. Moreover, the extravagance of the Van Buren administration was shamefully indicated by the spending of $25,000 to refurnish the "President's house" to make it fit for "the courtly *Martin the First.*" This even though shortly before it had been furnished at great expense for General Jackson, but what was good "enough for the 'Old Hero' would not suit his princely successor." To emphasize the Whigs as the party of the people, the delegates resolved that all of its existing party organization in the state be dissolved, with power returned to the people for rebuilding the organization from state to local levels. Doubtless to make it easier for Democrats to vote for Harrison and Tyler, Samuel Judah, one of the founders of the Jacksonian party in Indiana, was elected president of the convention; and Jonathan McCarty, an early Jacksonian and an elector for Jackson in 1824, was named an elector for Harrison and Tyler.[12]

Meanwhile, Hoosier Democrats for the most part supported the renomination and reelection of Van Buren and Johnson. The *Indiana Democrat* called the *Indiana Journal* announcement of Harrison as the nominee of the people, made before Van Buren's inauguration, premature and unprecedented. The Democratic paper said the people were fair, and wanted the new administration to be judged by its acts. The *Western Sun*, staunchly Democratic, termed Van Buren's inaugural one of the ablest documents ever presented to an American public. If its principles were implemented, the Van Buren administration would be "triumphantly sustained by the Democracy of the Union."[13] Late in 1837 a meeting of Democratic citizens and legislators at the capital "unanimously" resolved that the principles of the Van Buren administration "are but carrying out the doctrines of Thomas Jefferson, as urged at that day in opposition to the policy of John Adams and Alexander Hamilton," supported by the United States

Bank "to sustain Federal principles." Early in 1838 an address of Democratic politicians asserted that "the question of a National bank or no National Bank" was the "great question" dividing the rival parties. Moreover, Henry Clay, who earlier denounced the bank, had become its firm advocate. The address commended Van Buren "for a noble effort to prevent the unholy alliance of Bank and State," and Vice President Johnson for his effort "to prevent the yet more dangerous union of Church and State."[14] At the Democratic State Convention at the capital on January 8, 1840, the delegates "unanimously" called President Van Buren "an upright statesman, and a chief magistrate of high talents, sound judgment, and firm purpose," and pledged its support to his reelection as well as that of Vice President Johnson. In listing the names of the electoral ticket on their behalf the *Western Sun* added the motto: "'Union, Concession, Harmony.—Every thing for the Cause—Nothing for Men.'"[15] When the Democratic National Convention met at Baltimore in May it gave a "unanimous" vote for the nomination of Van Buren on the initial ballot. Unable, however, to achieve consensus about the nominee for vice president, it left each state free to vote for whomever it preferred. The Indiana delegates supported Johnson's nomination.[16]

Within Indiana, the presidential campaign of 1840 stirred more excitement, included more hoopla, and engendered more emotion than any other political contest of the pioneer era. Characterized by marches, processions, bands, doggerel, banners, slogans, barbecues, and the like, the political orations were long on sound and short on substance. Newspapers, mainly weeklies and extremely partisan, were replete with political announcements, charges and counter-charges, public documents, anonymous communications of an abusive nature, and glowing accounts of meetings which favored their partisan slant. Editorial views were not confined to editorial columns, and they pervaded and colored the news generally. The Whigs, even more than the Jacksonians had earlier, emphasized such campaigning; and in doing so they beat the Democrats at their own game.[17]

A mammoth gathering at the Tippecanoe Battleground starting on May 29 was the principal event which illustrates how Hoosier Whigs used excitement, hoopla, and emotion in support of Harrison's election for president. Calvin Fletcher's diary for May 25 notes that "companys" arriving from Cambridge City, Connersville, Columbus, Madison, and elsewhere had filled the streets of the capital with persons headed for the battleground. He suggested that fifty thousand people were expected to attend, including those who would travel by steamboats from Cincinnati and Louisville. As Professor R. C. Buley has stated: "For days in advance the delegations converged on selected rendezvous and then advanced to the battleground. Weeks had been spent preparing banners, floats, food, and speeches. Delegations from Illinois, Michigan, Kentucky, Tennessee, and Indiana vied with each other for noise, music, outfits, and enthusiasm. It had rained for days and the roads were deplorable, but it made no difference. By boat and by stage, ox team, horseback, and on foot through the mud over corduroy roads they came." Decades later, David Turpie noted that the thousands who attended the battleground meeting had come "by land and water in every kind of conveyance: in wagons, in huge log cabins mounted on wheels, in long canoes painted and decorated with party emblems." He observed that the "tents, wagons, flags, banners and streamers" gave the assemblage the appearance of a military encampment but lacking an orderly arrangement. Speakers from various stands proclaimed the achievements and qualifications of General Harrison, and warmly praised the men who had fought with him at Tippecanoe. As a youngster Turpie and other schoolboys listened as the veterans of this battle told and relived details of the fighting which had commenced near daybreak.[18] The *Indiana Journal* reported that estimates of the attendance ran from thirty to fifty thousand, but it estimated there had been about thirty thousand including at least five thousand ladies. At the battleground one delegation had a banner reading: "*'Old Tip did the fighting and we'll do the voting'*"; and another said: "*'A vote from a cabin goes as far as a vote from a palace.'*" The *Indiana Democrat* suggested that the attendance had been "estimated from 5,000 to 60,000." This Democratic organ presumed an attendance of "about eight thousand men, women and children; whigs, loafers and democrats; decent, indecent and rowdies, together with a great collection of gamblers, horse jockeys, negroes and hucksters." "The pilgrimage to Tippecanoe" had been "a ridiculous *farce*," but "Folly has often enlisted great armies." Reason alone, the Democratic editor declared, should prompt political opinions, but the Whigs had tried to excite feelings by crying hero, and displaying blue and orange flags, and appealing to feelings and prejudice.[19]

Nevertheless, issues as well as charges and countercharges were discussed during the presidential canvass. Generally speaking Hoosier Whigs contended that Jackson's transfer of the federal deposits from the United States Bank to local banks, which Democrats had supported, had crippled an institution with a sound circulation of bank notes. As a result, they said, local banks had greatly overissued a depreciated currency which had in turn been a major cause of the depression of the late thirties. Many Democrats staunchly defended Jackson's transfer of the deposits, and supported Van Buren's proposal that federal money be deposited in an Independent Treasury divorced from banking. Each party blamed the other for the halt in appropriations for continuing the National Road through Indiana, and both wanted additional federal aid for internal improvements. Whigs asserted that Indiana would have received a much larger sum from distribution, save for inadequate Democratic support for it. Whether so or not, the federal deficit, which accompanied the depression and downward tumbling of sales from the public domain, largely ended distribution. The tariff was not a major issue, in part because the reductions agreed upon in 1833 had not been completed. Whigs vied with Democrats in insisting that they were the party of the people versus the officeholders, aristocrats, and persons tainted with Federalism. Harrison's military ability and achievements were touted by the Whigs, but considered mediocre by some Democrats. Whigs charged that Van Buren had: been a Federalist; opposed the War of 1812; proposed a property qualification for voting; advocated suffrage for free blacks; tried to create a standing army; as president lived extravagantly at cost to taxpayers—living more like a king than the president of a republic; and that he was an eastern politician opposed to the interests of the West. Democrats charged that Harrison had: been a Federalist; supported the odious Alien and Sedition Laws; been responsible for slavery and a property qualification for voting while governor of Indiana Territory; for years lived at public expense because of salary and payments received from state and federal offices and positions; and that he was the abolition candidate for president.[20] Harrison never made clear and consistent statements about what his basic policies would be if he became president. In a letter to Harmar Denny and in a speech at Dayton, Harrison pledged that he would serve but one term, would use the veto power very sparingly, and regard Congress as the proper source for legislation. He expressed concern that the federal government might unduly overshadow the states, in large part because of the influence of federal officeholders. He talked out of both sides of his mouth regarding banking, and loosely declared that: "*'This* [federal] *Government is now a practical monarchy!'*" "If the Augean stable is to be cleansed," Harrison asserted, "it will be necessary to go back to the principles of Jefferson."[21]

In mid-October Hoosier Democrats sought to rally Jacksonians to their support by staging a huge celebration at the capital in honor of Van Buren's running mate, Vice President Johnson. The *Indiana Democrat* referred to Johnson as the hero of the Battle of the Thames in which Tecumseh had been killed. "One of the wounds" he had sustained there, the avid editor asserted, "has never yet healed, but still occasionally bleeds." The equally avid editor of the rival *Indiana Journal*, after commenting that the Democrats had engaged a brass band and were preparing flags, banners, and so forth for the occasion, observed: "not long since [they] affected holy horror at the Whig exhibitions of music, banners, flags, log cabins, &c. insisting that such things had a demoralizing tendency." The *Indiana Democrat* claimed that about thirty thousand people conducted Johnson into the city, making it the largest meeting ever convened by the Democracy of Indiana. William W. Wick presented Vice President Johnson as "the real Hero" of the Battle of the Thames, then Johnson spoke and held "the audience in almost breathless attention" for "more than three hours and a half . . . ." The *Indiana Journal*, however, estimated attendance at only four to six thousand, of whom perhaps one fourth to one third were Whigs, present in honor of the colonel. Moreover, his speech had not been up to the caliber expected, and Johnson had talked more than an hour about the "whole minutia" of the Battle of the Thames.[22] Several months earlier Tilghman A. Howard, the Democratic nominee for governor in 1840, had declined an invitation to a public dinner, saying: "It is not Democratic, and would be to a certain extent, imitating the folly of our antagonists. Freemen ought to meet together to reason on public interests . . . and my wish is to have no demonstration, no procession, no flags, no drums, nor any other exhibition unworthy of a free, thinking, orderly community."[23] Howard's worthy ideal, however, was largely ignored by Democrats and Whigs alike amid the ballyhoo of the presidential campaign of 1840.

As November 2 neared, it seemed almost certain that Harrison would triumphantly carry Indiana. On the eve of the state election in August, Democratic Congressman William W. Wick had agreed with Calvin Fletcher that Van Buren would be defeated. The victory of the Whig candidate for governor by the decisive margin of about 8,700 votes augured well for Harrison in November.[24] George W. Ewing's belated resignation as a proposed elector for Van Buren, plus his explanation that he would not attend the celebration for Johnson at the capital because he could not "*SUPPORT THE SUB-TREASURY SYSTEM,*" embarrassed the Democrats.[25] Indiana's nine electors were won for General Harrison by approximately 11,700 votes, and in the electoral college he obtained 234 votes against 60 for Van Buren.[26] Democratic papers blamed their stunning loss on votes Whigs received from such groups as abolitionists, nullifiers, tariff men, and ministers. They also claimed that roughly 20,000 illegal votes had been cast by Whigs, but this accusation seems dubious.[27] The comment of the *Indiana Democrat* that "thousands who supported General Jackson . . . have voted for Harrison" indicates a major reason for the defeat of Old Hickory's successor.[28] Perhaps equally important is the explanation by Godlove S. Orth, a Whig, that the Whigs had avoided "highstrung Whig doctrine" during the campaign.[29] Four factors largely explain the stunning defeat of

Jackson's protege in Indiana in 1840: the enormous personal popularity of Harrison; the substantial unpopularity of Van Buren, both as a man and as a politician; the impact of hard times under Van Buren as president; and Whig avoidance of "high-strung Whig doctrine" for emphasis on excitement, hoopla, and emotion.

Harrison's sweeping victory in Indiana, plus Whig majorities in both houses of Congress, gave the Whigs their first chance to control federal policies.[30] But having nominated Harrison without adopting a national platform, and leaving issues to be variously interpreted from state to state, it remained to be seen whether consensus could be obtained for key policies. Even before Harrison's inauguration, the pro-Whig *Indiana Journal* approvingly quoted an editorial in the *National Intelligencer* urging a special session of Congress at the earliest practical time to change the measures of the federal government.[31] As Van Buren's administration ended, this paper commented: "Yesterday, the most corrupt, blighting and paralyzing administration that ever cursed a free Republic, went out of power; and, we trust, and sincerely believe that one which will prove itself of the best and most wholesome, made its advent."[32] Harrison's inaugural, however, was silent about distribution and the tariff; and he neither approved nor disapproved a national bank. The new president stressed that legislative power was vested in Congress, and he explained that the veto should never be used against ordinary legislation. Harrison pledged that under no circumstances would he serve a second term. The *Western Sun* published the inaugural, and appropriately observed that it was "not more conspicuous for what it does say, than for what it does not."[33] Although the inaugural left unclear the extent of Harrison's agreement with policies urged by Clay, his cabinet was composed largely of men favorable to the Kentuckian. Under date of March 17 the president called for a special session of Congress to begin May 31, but one month after assuming the presidency Harrison became the first president to die in office. In announcing the melancholy news, the *Indiana Journal* said: "Our town, the *Union*, is in mourning. A great man has fallen in Israel." Amid the outpouring of tributes and memorializing, the *Western Sun*, at Vincennes where Harrison had lived as territorial governor, tersely commented: "One short month witnessed his ascent to the summit of human greatness, and his passage to the tomb."[34]

Indiana Whigs soon had concern about John Tyler's accession to the presidency. But at first the *Indiana Journal* declared: "There will be no change in the general policy of the Administration. The same policy and measures will characterize it that would have characterized it had Gen. Harrison lived." The Richmond *Palladium* called Tyler's inaugural "replete with the true spirit" and "Whig all over." Calvin Fletcher, however, observed: "It is feard [*sic*] that Tyler will recommend a Southern policy—no national bank or rather no national currency—no protecting duties or taxes upon luxuries &c but we trust otherwise." The *Indiana Democrat* reported that an eastern paper had indicated that the new president was opposed to a national bank, a protective tariff, and distribution of federal land proceeds. If so, the measures of his administration might approximate those advocated by Democrats.[35] In publishing Tyler's inaugural and two related documents, the *Indiana Journal* asserted: "They are correct and satisfactory exponents of his political creed, and will place him high in the confidence and esteem of the Whigs and all other true patriots." This Whig organ affirmed that Tyler was "decidedly" opposed to the Independent Treasury, and he would sanction any constitutional measure from Congress for restoration of a sound currency. Also that he favored a protective tariff to avoid direct taxation, and distribution of the proceeds from the public lands. But Tyler's inaugural on April 9 did not mention the bank, tariff, or distribution. His comment that he would sanction "any constitutional measure" from Congress for restoring "a sound circulating medium" left uncertain whether he would approve a national bank.[36]

Harrison's call for a special session of Congress starting May 31 caused the election of Indiana's seven congressmen to be advanced from the first Monday in August, 1841, to Monday, May 3.[37] Apparently party nominees were principally selected by congressional district conventions. Of the four Democratic incumbents—John Carr, John W. Davis, Thomas Smith, and William W. Wick—all but Wick were down to the wire candidates for reelection. Of the three Whig incumbents—Henry S. Lane, George H. Proffit, and James Rariden—only the first two were candidates when the voting occurred.[38] In urging the election of former Governor David Wallace in the Sixth District, the *Indiana Journal* suggested that a tariff to raise revenue and avoid direct taxes, repeal of the Independent Treasury, distribution of proceeds from the public domain, and an appropriation for the Cumberland Road were "measures loudly called for by the people." This Whig organ emphasized that it was important for Whigs to gain a "decisive majority" in Congress; otherwise, Democrats, aided by a few southern Whigs with "peculiar notions," could prevent adoption of reform measures. Within Indiana, the Whigs gained a decisive victory, reelecting Lane and Proffit plus election of James H. Cravens, Richard W. Thompson, David Wallace, and Joseph L. White. Andrew Kennedy, the sole Democratic winner, seemingly won because he had two rivals whose total vote far exceeded his.[39] The *Indiana Journal* called the six Whigs "able and faithful men" who would do their duty in adopting measures of the new administration necessary for the prosperity and welfare of the country. The *Indiana Democrat* called the Whig victors Federalists, and it attributed their election to an inadequate understanding by the people of what would be the impact of Whig policies concerning a national bank, the tariff, and distribution.[40]

When the special session met on May 31, the clash between Tyler and Henry Clay regarding a national bank soon became apparent. In his message to Congress the next day Tyler expressed: strong opposition to modifying the Compromise Tariff of 1833, which called for reduction of duties for one more year; opposition to assumption of state debts; vigorous support for distribution of proceeds from land sales to the states; an emphasis on the need for a national currency of uniform value; a desire for a fiscal agency in lieu of a national bank; and he urged repeal of the Independent Treasury. Several days later Senator Clay introduced a resolution emphasizing the need for: repeal of the Independent Treasury; the incorporation of "a bank adapted to the wants of the people and of the Government"; the raising of adequate revenue from tariff duties, combined with a temporary loan; and distribution of the proceeds from public land sales to the states. The *Indiana*

Journal indicated concern that Tyler had not recommended more decidedly a national bank, a high tariff, and distribution. These measures, it said, had been "most unequivocally" sustained by the people in electing Harrison and their congressmen. Hence, "Short of nothing else will they be satisfied."[41] Clay introduced a bill to repeal the Independent Treasury; and another to establish a national bank. Since the president and senator both favored repeal of the Independent Treasury, the Whigs easily overwhelmed the Democrats to repeal it by a vote of 29 to 18 in the Senate and 134 to 87 in the House. All Indiana members of Congress but Kennedy, the lone Democrat, supported repeal.[42] The Senate then adopted the bank bill 26 to 23, and the House passed it 128 to 98. All Indiana members of Congress but Kennedy supported passage. Tyler, however, vetoed the bank bill, contending it was unconstitutional and contrary to views he had long held. The Senate voted 25 to 24 to override the veto, with Smith and White for the override; and the House voted to nullify the veto by a count of 103 to 80, with four Indiana Whigs against the veto, one Whig not voting, and Kennedy and Proffit supporting it.[43] Since both houses fell short of a two-thirds majority, the veto killed Clay's bank bill.

Among Hoosier editors, as for members of Congress, for the most part those who were Whigs approved and Democrats opposed a national bank. While the bank bill was pending the Fort Wayne *Sentinel* asserted that the proposed bank was unconstitutional, and neither necessary nor useful "in the legitimate business transactions of the country." This Democratic paper commended Tyler for his veto, thereby saving the finances of the government from "foreign stock-jobbers, American brokers and bank shavers." Moreover, it asked, if the Whigs expected Harrison and Tyler to approve a bank bill against their principles, why had they not said so before their election? The *Indiana State Sentinel*, Indiana's leading Democratic press, called Clay's bank bill a measure to swindle laborers and farmers. It said that every Whig paper in the state, except one, had committed itself to such a bank, yet not one of them had dared make it an issue in the presidential election. On the Whig side the *Indiana Journal* hailed passage of

Clay's bank bill with the declaration: "We shall have a National Bank, and that is glory enough for one Administration." Its editor branded the veto power "a prerogative of despots that should not be permitted to grow in our democratic soil." Nonetheless, its Whig editor viewed Tyler an honorable man who might yet approve a compromise bank bill. Whigs were urged to support the administration, but this recommendation was coupled with a prediction that Tyler would not seek election to a term on his own. The South Bend *Free Press*, vigorously Whig, attacked the "*acting president*" for his veto, and branded his treachery "not surpassed by that of a Benedict Arnold . . . ."[44] Congressman Proffit, the only Whig who opposed the bank bill and voted to sustain the veto, defended the president. Whig victory, he said, had been achieved with the help of Jacksonians who wanted abuses reformed. Proffit associated the bank bill with the Kentuckian's presidential ambitions, and he declared that "he never could have Mr. Clay for his President."[45]

While the stalemate regarding banking continued, Congress considered land policy. As states carved from the federal domain grew in number, sentiment for distribution to the states of proceeds from land sales and the granting of preemption to settlers increased. By the forties, however, proceeds from land sales were far below what they had been in the thirties. The demand for distribution was further increased as states with heavy internal improvement debts looked to possible federal aid through distribution.[46] In December, 1840, Indiana's new Whig governor, Samuel Bigger, ecstatically endorsed distribution, estimating that thereby the Hoosier State could "safely" expect to receive "30,000,000 of dollars." With such a sum, Indiana could pay its existing debts, finance additional internal improvements, reduce taxes, and provide "the most liberal provision for the benefit of common schools, and the general promotion of education." At the legislative session of 1840–1841, the state Senate, voting along party lines, concurred with a committee report advocating distribution. The General Assembly adopted a resolution in its support, and another asking that preemption be combined with distribution.[47] During the special session in the summer of 1841, Congress approved an act providing for both distribution and preemption. This measure passed the House 116 to 108, and the Senate 28 to 23, with Whigs largely for and Democrats largely against passage. But a proviso was added that if tariff duties were raised above the level permitted by the Compromise Tariff of 1833, distribution would be suspended. The six Hoosier Whig congressmen voted for this legislation, while Andrew Kennedy, the lone Democrat, voted against it. Senators Oliver H. Smith and Albert S. White, both Whigs, voted for passage, but Smith supported and White opposed the proviso.[48] Before passage Kennedy condemned the measure as an attempt to create a national debt, establish a national bank, and increase the tariff. But he "would most cheerfully" have supported preemption "if it were not found in such bad company!" Senator Smith, speaking as chairman of the Committee on Public Lands, asserted that preemption had so few opponents that argument for it was unnecessary. He defended distribution, contending that the Compromise Tariff of 1833 presumed that revenue from land would not be needed to finance the federal treasury, and distribution would return much needed revenue to the West. The *Indiana Journal* hailed the distribution and preemption act, and declared that it was worth five times the cost of the special session of Congress. But in contrast to the rosy forecast of Governor Bigger, this Whig editor quoted Senator White as asserting that it would provide Indiana more than $130,000 annually, "thus diminishing the taxes of the people by that amount." The editor of the *Western Sun* hoped in vain that Tyler would veto the measure. Early in 1842, after stating that Indiana's share from distribution for 1841 would be $34,836, or about 5 cents per Hoosier, the *Indiana State Sentinel* sarcastically commented that Hoosiers would soon get rich under the new act. This Democratic editor jabbed that the amount so received would be collected from the people in some other form, plus enough more to pay the Whigs for collecting it.[49]

As the special session neared adjournment on September 13, Congress adopted a second bank bill. It called for a *fiscal corporation*, but it proposed a modified version of a national bank. The House passed this bill 125 to 94, with Kennedy against approval,

Proffit not voting, and the five other Whigs from Indiana for passage. In the Senate the bill was advanced to third reading by a count of 27 to 22, Smith and White sustaining this action. It then passed the Senate without amendment and without a roll call. Tyler quickly vetoed the bill, insisting that it would establish a bank not warranted by the constitution. By a tally of 103 to 80 the House tried in vain to override the veto.[50] Congressman Richard W. Thompson declared that "the president has disappointed and deceived me" by his bank vetoes. He said he had believed that Tyler would support a bank, and had so stated in his congressional campaign. Congressman Henry S. Lane, claiming that nine tenths of the Whigs wanted a national bank, asked: "What right had John Tyler to allow his name . . . on the Whig ticket, if he was not a Bank man?" The president, Lane said, had "trampled" Whig principles "under foot, and acted basely and treacherously to the Whig party." But Congressman George H. Proffit suggested that several prominent Whigs had voted against the initial bank bill, which he had "reluctantly" voted for. Proffit explained that he thought Tyler favored a fiscal institution, free of constitutional objections. Nor had he abandoned Whig principles since he had sanctioned repeal of the Independent Treasury, distribution, a naval appropriation, and "every other measure" the majority had passed "except the Bank bill." The *Indiana Journal*, however, greeted news of the second veto with the comment that "it is regarded here as sealing the fate of President Tyler with the Whigs." After the Whigs had suffered defeats in elections around the country during the summer and fall, its editor asserted that most Whigs had lost confidence in Tyler; and in many states Whigs must suffer defeat until dissensions were healed and they could act in concert. The editor appealed to Tyler to unite in support of Whig principles and unity, and he insisted that Whigs could not change their basic course. The *Western Sun* rejoiced in the moral courage and adherence to principle manifested by Tyler in the second bank bill veto, and its Democratic editor admonished: "no party ever can remain stable and firm, without some *fixed principles* to operate upon, *even before an election*."[51]

As the special session ended, a large majority of Whigs in Congress parted company with Tyler. His two vetoes had prevented recharter of a national bank, a basic item in the Whig program. Whether the vetoes resulted more from constitutional scruples or personal and political considerations have been variously interpreted, as have the impact of the presidential aspirations of rivals Tyler and Clay. A caucus of Whig members of Congress, after accusing Tyler of treachery to Whig principles and being motivated by personal ambition in vetoing the bank bills, in effect read him out of the party so far as they were concerned. Following this action all cabinet members but Webster resigned, and Tyler obtained a cabinet dominated by his friends rather than those of Clay. Proffit was the only Indiana Whig in Congress who supported Tyler.[52] In 1843 the president named Proffit minister to Brazil, but his service ended in 1844 when the Senate declined to confirm a regular appointment for him.[53]

At the regular session from early December, 1841, through the end of August, 1842, the split between Tyler and the Whigs widened. In his message to Congress as the session began, the president stressed the need for a sound currency of uniform value, warned against an overexpansion of state banks, and expressed ideas about an acceptable fiscal corporation. An administration bill for a fiscal agency was quickly set aside by Congress with only modest consideration. Many Whigs opposed it because it did not provide for a national bank, while most Democrats wanted the Independent Treasury restored.[54] The session, however, gave major attention to tariff legislation. In his message Tyler suggested that tariff duties could include protection for manufacturing as well as provide increased revenue, but he noted that the land act of the previous session required the end of distribution if tariff duties rose above the general level of 20 percent. With borrowing already necessary to finance the federal treasury, higher duties were favored by most Whigs but opposed by the preponderance of southern Whigs. During the summer of 1842 Congress passed two tariff bills, both raising duties above the 20 percent level *while distribution continued*, and Tyler vetoed them. He indicated, however, his willingness to have duties rise above 20 percent, if distribution ceased. Unable to override the vetoes, Congress passed and the president approved the Tariff of 1842 which increased duties considerably above the 20 percent level, *minus the continuation of distribution*. Hence, land proceeds and tariff duties would both accrue to the federal treasury. The vote on the Tariff of 1842 reflected considerable party and sectional cleavage. Most Whigs, save a minority mainly from the South, sustained passage; most Democrats, except for a minority largely from the Middle Atlantic states, opposed passage; and in the Old Northwest Whigs and Democrats divided both for and against its passage.[55] Though principally a Whig measure, it passed the House by the razor thin margin of 104 to 103; and the Senate by the equally close margin of 24 to 23.[56]

At the congressional session of 1841–1842, unsuccessful efforts were made to curb the veto power of the president. Senator Henry Clay proposed amending the constitution to permit a majority in both houses to nullify a presidential veto, but his resolution seems not to have come to a vote.[57] After Tyler's veto of the second bank bill, in the summer of 1842 a House committee, chaired by former President John Quincy Adams, recommended such an amendment. The majority of this committee asserted that Tyler had assumed powers not vested in him by the constitution, and declared that his four vetoes within fifteen months had "struck with apoplexy" the power of Congress to enact laws essential for the welfare of the people. The House voted 99 to 90 for the amendment. Congressman John M. Botts, of Virginia, promised to introduce impeachment charges against the president at the ensuing session; and Congressman Kenneth Rayner, of North Carolina, said that he "among others, was in favor of an impeachment of the President," but he explained that Adams thought "the time for that had not yet come."[58] At the next congressional session Botts accused Tyler of corruption, malconduct, and high crimes and misdemeanors; and he asked that a committee investigate impeachment charges, "which he stood prepared to prove, by testimony the most conclusive" but the request was defeated 127 to 84. Four congressmen from Indiana, all Whigs, voted for the proposed committee.[59] In both houses of Congress prominent Whigs advocated curbing the veto power, while prominent Democrats defended it and the manner in which it had been exercised.[60] Whigs in Gibson County called Tyler's vetoes "subversive of the great principles of a Republican Government," and declared that this power should be "'plucked from the Constitution.'" Whigs in St. Joseph County explained that as true Whigs they had lost confidence in Tyler, and they termed his use of the veto power more daring, impudent, and unreasonable than that of any president. But the pro-Democratic *Western Sun* noted that Democrats in Sullivan County viewed Tyler entitled to the "everlasting gratitude" of his countrymen for his patriotic use of the veto power. A township meeting of Democrats in Marion County resolved that "John Tyler has nobly sustained, by his vetoes and protest, the Constitution of the U.S., the sovereignty of the States, and the dignity of his office." The considerable use of the veto by Presidents Jackson, Van Buren, and Tyler, versus its limited and cautious use by former presidents, made the pros and cons of such a veto a political question. Various Whig politicians supported changing the constitution so that a mere majority of Congress could nullify a veto, but most Democratic politicians staunchly upheld this constitutional provision.[61]

While the Whigs in Congress were being weakened by intra-party division and conflict with President Tyler, within Indiana Whig power was declining. The large majorities in both houses which the Whigs had won in 1840, by the 1842–1843 session had been replaced by a legislature of seventy-seven Whigs and seventy-three Democrats, with the former a majority in the Senate and the latter a majority in the House, *when the session opened in December, 1842.*[62] At this time the competition for election of a successor to Senator Oliver H. Smith, whose term would expire March 3, 1843, focused on this Whig incumbent versus Tilghman A. Howard, who had been the Democratic nominee for governor in 1840.[63] With party cleavage intensifying, the prospects for Smith's reelection seemed very favorable. The House, however, refused to meet with the Senate in joint session to elect a senator until January 24. Meanwhile, as a result of a vacancy in each house special elections had replaced Whigs with Democrats; and the House, dominated by Democrats, had resolved a contested election regarding

DeKalb and Steuben counties by unseating Enos Beall, a Whig, in favor of Madison Marsh, a Democrat. Hence, when the voting for senator began the legislative membership had changed to seventy-five Whigs and seventy-five Democrats, with seventy-six votes required for an election.[64] The outcome was made even more uncertain because Senator David Hoover, a Democrat from Wayne County where Whigs were usually dominant, had apparently promised to vote for Smith; and Senator Daniel Kelso, a Whig from Switzerland County where Democrats were usually dominant, had apparently promised to vote for a Democrat. In the first five tries, Smith won from seventy to seventy-five votes, Howard from seventy-three to seventy-four votes. Hoover voted for Smith on the first and second ballots. Thereafter, Hoover never voted for Smith, but he did not join Kelso, who supported Edward A. Hannegan on all ballots, until the final one when he also supported Hannegan. Marsh sustained Howard until the sixth ballot when he voted for Hannegan, who won election by obtaining seventy-six votes to sixty-nine for Smith, four for Joseph G. Marshall, and one for Howard. Separating the wheat from the chaff to decide who was most responsible for the outcome appears impossible.[65] The *Indiana Journal* blamed Hoover and Kelso for Smith's defeat but it called Hannegan's election "infinitely better . . . than would have been the choice of Tilghman A. Howard." The *Indiana State Sentinel* termed the election "the best we could have hoped for under the circumstances." Its Democratic editor referred to Howard as "the favorite of the Democracy of Indiana," adding that "Our Howard will yet rise; his name and fortunes are identified with Hoosier Democracy, and will yet soar above the ruins of federal whiggery." But though Howard had fallen, Hannegan was described as "of the pure Democratic Stamp," opposed to a national bank, against distribution, and for a revenue tariff. The Fort Wayne *Sentinel*, after saying that it, in common with the entire Democratic party, had preferred Howard, termed Hannegan a fine Democrat of splendid talents.[66]

While the Democrats elected Hannegan to the Senate by the narrowest possible margin, seven months later they triumphed over the Whigs in the congressional elections of 1843. The con-

gressional apportionment of the previous year had increased Indiana's membership in the House of Representatives from seven
to ten. Only five states gained a larger representation than that
given the Hoosier State. For the first time Congress mandated
that congressmen be elected by single districts; however, such districts had prevailed in Indiana from statehood.[67] Both Whigs and
Democrats, with perhaps a few exceptions, nominated their candidates in district conventions.[68] With Democratic strength rising
and six of the seven incumbent congressmen Whigs, the Democrats sharply attacked their rivals. They emphasized their support
of the Independent Treasury and a revenue tariff, and their opposition to distribution, often claiming that the Whigs favored distribution, a protective tariff, and a national bank. Generally
speaking the reverse of these issues was sustained by the Whigs,
though with less ardor than during the thirties.[69] The *Indiana
State Sentinel* exclaimed that notwithstanding that the Whigs
"have already created a National Debt of some Thirty Millions,
they are determined to increase it." And the federal treasury had
invited proposals "for a NEW LOAN of SEVEN MILLIONS
OF DOLLARS . . . ." Moreover, they had: "KILLED one President," tried to make another politically infamous, made their
party the laughingstock of the country by quarrelling among
themselves, and had not redeemed a single promise they had
made at the last presidential election. The *Indiana State Journal*,
after stating that stable and prosperous conditions had prevailed
under John Quincy Adams, asserted that the twelve years of the
Jackson-Van Buren administrations had: destroyed the national
bank, exploded a system of state banks, trebled national costs,
grossly corrupted the civil service, and caused a national debt
which made the treasury hopelessly bankrupt. In addition, the
Democrats, by promising to support Tyler for reelection, had induced him to become a traitor to Whig policies promised by Harrison.[70] After the Evansville *Journal* had reportedly objected that
Robert Dale Owen, candidate in the First Congressional District,
was "*an Englishman*" because he had been born in Scotland, the
Indiana State Sentinel asserted that Owen was an American citizen
who "supports American interests and principles; and we should

rather support an Englishman, Irishman, Scotchman, German, or anything else, *who supports American principles*, than a man born in America, who is an advocate of *British Whiggery*, like the Editor of the Evansville Journal."[71] In the race between William J. Brown, a Democrat, and David Wallace, his Whig opponent, the *Indiana State Sentinel* denied that Brown had been making speeches against the Washingtonians. "Besides," its editor jabbed, "Gov. Wallace is not a temperance man, by a *jug full*, and Brown could not profit much by making war on the Washingtonian cause. Who drinks the most *liquor*, Brown or Wallace? Let Wallace's Washingtonian friends answer this question."[72]

At the voting on August 7, 1843, the Democrats won a sweeping victory. For the first time since parties had developed they won majorities in both houses of the General Assembly; and they elected James Whitcomb as their initial governor. In the congressional elections they won eight of the ten seats. Andrew Kennedy, a Democrat, was the only incumbent reelected; however, Democrats John W. Davis and Thomas Smith, who had served previously, were returned to Congress. Democrats William J. Brown, Thomas J. Henley, Robert Dale Owen, John Pettit, and Joseph A. Wright, plus Whigs Samuel C. Sample and Caleb B. Smith, won initial terms. The dominance which Hoosier Democrats gained over the congressional delegation in this election was retained throughout the forties.[73] Moreover, the sweeping victories they won in 1843 hastened the transition to a new generation of Democrats as issues regarding expansion and slavery came to the fore.

When Congress convened on December 4, 1843, the Whigs retained a modest majority in the Senate, but the huge majority they had had in the House for two years became an even larger majority for the Democrats.[74] Meantime, the Whigs had parted company with President Tyler. This situation made it impossible for the Whigs to reestablish a national bank, and impossible for the Democrats to reestablish the Independent Treasury. Nor could any significant change be made in the Tariff of 1842; and the heavy reduction of proceeds of land sales, combined with substantial Democratic opposition, made it impossible for the Whigs to restore distribution.[75] Nevertheless within Congress—and within Indiana—considerable bipartisan support existed for federal aid, in land or money, on behalf of internal improvements.[76] A bill for the improvement of western rivers and harbors, approved by President Tyler in June, 1844, which made some appropriations of money for items affecting Indiana, was supported by the three Indiana Whig members of Congress, and by six of the nine Democratic members.[77] A related bill, however, which made appropriations for eastern rivers and harbors, was supported by the three Whig members, with Senator Hannegan as the only Democrat who voted for its passage.[78] In the spring of 1845 another western rivers and harbors bill passed Congress with the approval of every Indiana member of Congress but Thomas J. Henley who was a nonvoter. A proposed amendment which was defeated, that would have given $300,000 each to Ohio, Indiana, and Illinois for prosecution of the National Road, received the support of all ten Hoosier congressmen.[79] These votes suggest that Indiana Whigs in Congress were for internal improvements on a national basis, while most of their Democratic colleagues were mainly supportive of such improvements only for their state or section.

While domestic politics were largely stalemated during the second half of Tyler's administration, important developments occurred regarding relations with other countries. Of major concern when Tyler became president was the longstanding dispute with Great Britain about the boundary between Maine and Canada; irritation from border incidents growing out of an 1837 uprising against the Canadian government, resulting in the sinking of an American ship known as the *Caroline*; and continued British searching of American ships on the high seas as well as impressment of Americans into British service.[80] Soon after the Harrison-Tyler administration began the *Indiana Journal*, the state's leading Whig paper, asserted that "our rights and territory have been encroached upon from Maine to Oregon," because the British, unchecked by the previous administration, had "grown bold and insolent." Nevertheless, the new administration was expected to maintain an honorable peace. The staunchly Democratic *Western Sun* approvingly quoted a New York paper which said: "'The man who would unnecessarily embroil the United States in a war with England, is a murderer and a wretch—hanging is too good for him. Peace between these countries, is the peace of the world.'" But the *Indiana Democrat* vigorously claimed that the United States owned all the territory in dispute with Great Britain, concerning both the boundary of Maine and the "northwest *territories*." It said that British claims to these areas seemed to make war or disgrace inevitable, with war preferred if "*necessary* to prevent dishonor." This Democratic paper declared: "We hope and tr[u]st there is that spirit in the American people, which will cause them gladly to court the sword, flame, blood and devastation before they yield to British tyranny."[81] During 1842 Lord Ashburton of Great Britain and Secretary of State Daniel Webster, both of whom sought compromise, negotiated a treaty that gave most of the disputed area in the northeast to Maine, provided for the mutual extradition of criminals, and called for joint patrols to suppress the African slave trade. In notes, not a part of the treaty, the British representative made soothing comments about impressments and searching of American ships, and expressed regret concerning the sinking of the *Caroline*.[82] The American Senate ratified the treaty by the decisive vote of 39 to 9, with Indiana's two senators, Whigs Oliver H. Smith and Albert S. White, sustaining ratification. The bill passed by the House for implementation of the treaty, approved 137 to 40, was supported by three Indiana congressmen, opposed by two of them, and the remaining two were nonvoters. In addressing the next legislative session, Governor Samuel Bigger, a Whig, observed: "The recent treaty with Great Britain has banished all apprehension of war from our borders, and has secured to us a bloodless and satisfactory adjustment of an unpleasant controversy with a great and powerful nation."[83] Mutual compromise and a peaceful settlement was a major contribution of the Webster-Ashburton Treaty of 1842.

The new treaty, however, left unresolved the boundary concerning the Oregon country in the Northwest. Since 1818 the United States and Britain had considered Oregon under their joint control. The principal interest of the British had been the fur trade, mainly that of the powerful Hudson's Bay Company. By the early 1840s American interest in Oregon was building. During the last half of the thirties American missionaries, especially Methodists and Presbyterians, commenced efforts among the Indians of the fertile Willamette Valley. The missionaries advertised the climate and fertile soil of Oregon in inflated terms. As early as 1839 some emigrants arrived, and by 1845 there were several thousand American settlers in Oregon.[84] In 1841 the *Indiana Journal* warned of the "nameless difficulties and privations to be encountered" in emigrating to a place where war might ensue with the British, including bloody deeds of savage [Indian] warfare. Surprise was expressed at the "disposition to venture so far west! —so far from government security—so far from the comforts of life —so far from friends—so far from civilization . . . ." Early in 1842 Tilghman A. Howard, the unsuccessful Democratic nominee for governor in 1840, advocated the immediate organization of a territorial government for Oregon. He spoke of the mild and healthful climate of the area whose "occupation would ultimately . . . open up to us the commerce of the Indies on the West." The settlement of the vast region from California to the Russian territory on the north by Americans, Howard asserted, would result in its occupation "by a civilized people speaking our language, and ultimately yielding to the influence of free institutions in the American sense of the term." If an appropriate government were organized in Oregon, Howard predicted that within five years "10,000 families" would be there.[85]

The interest of Hoosiers regarding Oregon rose rapidly in the mid-forties. Early in 1843 the legislature urged Congress to organize a territorial government for the area, and establish fortifications and posts "sufficiently strong" to protect its settlers. The memorial declared that "the settlement of no other Territory ever promised to afford such increasing sources of trade, revenue, or power to the country, east of the Mississippi, or to be more essential to the future peace and prosperity of the Union . . . ." A year later the legislature asserted that the territory of Oregon "rightfully belongs" to the United States. This memorial complained of "the insatiate avarice, and grasping spirit of the British government . . . directed to its subjugation and conversion"; and asked for "the immediate occupation, organization, and adequate defence of the Oregon Territory, peacably [*sic*] if we can, forcibly if we must."[86] In September, 1843, the *Western Sun* said possession of the Oregon Territory was essential to American security, with every day "adding to the necessity of having the matter settled." Early in 1844 Congressman Robert Dale Owen proposed that the president be required to serve notice for ending joint occupation of Oregon with Great Britain. He described Oregon as a vast area, extending from 42° to 54° 40', and more than one-fourth larger than the original thirteen states. "This negotiating about what does not belong to us," the British-born Owen declared, "is not only an unprofitable but [is] a dangerous affair." Exhibiting the spirit of Manifest Destiny, Owen proclaimed: "Oregon is our land of promise. Oregon is our land of destination . . . . Two thousand American citizens are already indwellers in her valleys. Five thousand more—ay, it may be twice that number—will have crossed the mountain passes before another year rolls round. While you are legislating, they are emigrating; and whether you legislate for them or not, they will emigrate still." Shortly after Owen spoke, Senator Edward A. Hannegan made a bellicose speech, urging the end of joint occupation, and the extension of American laws over Oregon. Every inch of the area from 42° to 54° 40' belonged to the United States, Hannegan claimed, hence there was nothing to negotiate, nor would he yield "one inch" of it to avoid war. "Let England dare to stoop on the Oregon, and, my head for it, she will never, never again resume her lofty poise," Hannegan asserted, and "When she attempts to rise, she will find her wings clipped and her talons harmless."[87]

Meantime, there was developing concern about the extension of slavery as a result of westward expansion. The possible annexation of Texas worried many Whigs who feared that its addition as a slave state would add strength to their Democratic rivals. Opinions about Texas were also influenced by the schism between Tyler and the Whigs; raids and counterraids by the Texans and the Mexicans; uncertainty about British and French designs regarding Texas; the fiscal weakness of Texas, plus its political divisions; and the possibility that annexation would lead to war with Mexico.[88] In October,1841, the staunchly Democratic *Indiana State Sentinel* noted that annexation was strongly opposed in northern and eastern parts of the United States, but predicted that with the rapid increase of population in the Southwest, and admission of two states therefrom, this might in a year or two "perhaps reconcile the free States to its acquisition." Two years later a Whig paper at South Bend asserted: "The Northern Whigs, as a body, are openly . . . against the annexation of Texas to the Union, which would form 10 more Slave states, and thus give that interest a preponderance in both branches of Congress." About this time a Democratic organ at Fort Wayne stated: "The citizens of the free States are we believe generally opposed to the annexation of Texas, on the ground that it would be increasing the power of the slave-holders." After reading Tyler's message to Congress in December, 1843, Calvin Fletcher observed in his diary: "His heart is bent on receiving Texas into the Union but there is no party able to do that. As the present Congress is organized the Slave states have a decided advantage—A Southern Speaker."[89]

During 1844 it became evident, as Fletcher had surmised, that President Tyler's heart was bent on the annexation of Texas. At the congressional session of 1843–1844 memorials were received for and against annexation. Those for it came overwhelmingly from states of the lower South, those against overwhelmingly from New England and the Old Northwest.[90] In June, 1844, Indiana Senator Albert S. White told his colleagues that he held in his hand a memorial in opposition to annexation from the Society of Friends, which stated that it represented not less than twenty-five thousand members in Illinois, Indiana, and western Ohio. He said the memorial opposed annexation because it would uphold, continue, and extend slavery and lead to "an unjust war with a friendly nation now at peace with us." The views of the memorialists, White said, also represented the sentiments of a large majority of the intelligent and respectable westerners. Such sentiments, he forecast, would within eighteen months be "the universal sentiments" of a very large majority of the citizens of the United States. Hence, annexation "will be a dead question within that period." Several months earlier, however, the Indiana House of Representatives rejected a resolution against annexation by a vote of

51 to 45, with Whigs preponderantly voting against and Democrats preponderantly and successfully voting for its rejection.[91]

In April, 1844, however, President Tyler had submitted to the Senate a treaty for the annexation of Texas. Soon after its submission Henry Clay and Martin Van Buren, widely expected to be their party's presidential nominees, released letters in opposition to annexation. Ex-Congressman Tilghman A. Howard, a Democrat, viewed "the acquisition of Texas of great moment to the United States." "I think Democrats should not be too prompt in taking ground against Texas," Howard said, "as it will react, and the country will go for it, or I am mistaken." Another Democrat, Congressman Robert Dale Owen serving his initial term, made a major speech in which he insisted that the United States had both a right and duty to annex Texas. The right existed because the Lone Star State had successfully maintained its independence for eight years. If war with Mexico should result therefrom, he said there was no "real danger . . . of any war that a couple of regiments of good Kentucky riflemen could not terminate in a fortnight." Owen indicated his dislike of slavery, but charged that "modern abolitionism" had slowed rather than hastened its decline. Contending that adding Texas to the Union would serve the national interest, the Hoosier congressman said he agreed with Andrew Jackson that "the golden moment" for its "reannexation" had arrived.[92] On June 8, however, the Senate, by a vote of 35 to 16, refused to ratify the treaty for annexation of Texas. Only one Whig supported ratification as senators from northern states voted overwhelmingly against and those from southern states mainly for ratification. Indiana Senator Albert S. White voted with Whigs against ratification, while his Democratic colleague, Edward A. Hannegan, was a nonvoter.[93] Tyler failed to obtain annexation of Texas at this time, but contrary to White's prediction the question of annexation, rather than becoming a dead issue, gained augmented importance. Moreover, issues regarding slavery and western expansion had become intermingled and divisive within parties as well as between the North and South.

Although the annexation of Texas became a major issue in the presidential canvass of 1844, it had not been a major issue during the three preceding years. Various men had been mentioned as possible party nominees for president, but before the end of 1841 former President Van Buren was viewed as the frontrunner for his party, and Henry Clay emerged as such for the Whigs. During 1843 and 1844 President Tyler, having been repudiated by the Whigs, emerged as a wild card in presidential politics.[94] Within Indiana, Clay early became the favorite of Hoosier Whigs. Less than six months after Tyler succeeded Harrison, the Knightstown *Courier* disavowed him and endorsed Clay as the Whig candidate for 1844. It suggested that a national nominating convention was unnecessary because by "unanimous impulse all eyes" were turned upon Clay as the choice of the Whigs. In quoting this endorsement the *Indiana Journal*, premier Whig press of the state, affirmed that "the Whig party of Indiana are unanimous in the desire" to have Clay its candidate. During 1842 some Clay clubs were organized in Indiana.[95] By October of that year the Rushville *Whig* and *Indiana Journal* had named Clay their choice for president. In September, 1843, the *Indiana State Sentinel* stated that "all, or nearly all" of the Whig papers were "attached to the car of Henry Clay."[96] Meantime, as 1842 and 1843 advanced, among Hoosiers Lewis Cass, of Michigan, seems to have afforded more competition for Van Buren than former Vice President Richard M. Johnson of Kentucky. While commenting on Whig papers for Clay, this leading Democratic organ of the state declared its preference for Van Buren. It, however, called Cass and Johnson "two highly deserving men"; said that Johnson was very strong in southern Indiana near the Ohio River, with many friends elsewhere; and that Cass was equally strong in the Wabash country, with many friends in central Indiana. The *Sentinel* reported the preferences of various Democratic papers, nine of which preferred Van Buren, four Cass, and one Johnson.[97] At a state convention at the capital in January, 1843, the Whigs instructed their delegates to the party's national convention to support Henry Clay for "President as the first choice of the Whig party of the State." At their next such convention a year later they tagged the Kentuckian as their "first" and "decided choice for President of the United States." A state convention of "Young

Whigs," meeting on the same day, enthusiastically endorsed Clay, not as a "'northern man with southern principles,'" but as a "'Western man with American principles'" who "under Providence [is] destined to restore prosperity to our nation."[98] Meanwhile, at their state convention at Indianapolis in January, 1843, the Democrats expressed no preference for president. They, however, named a committee to correspond with "the distinguished individuals," considered Democratic candidates for president and vice president, to obtain their views about stated issues and whether they would abide by and support the nominees of the party's national convention. The Democratic State Convention which met at the capital a year later, apparently was comprised largely of members preferring either Van Buren or Cass. The convention made no endorsement, but instructed its presidential electors "to support the nominee of the National convention for President and Vice President." The address of this convention concerning national policy, without naming "the five distinguished individuals" spoken of as Democratic candidates, declared that there "is not one but whose irreproachable character, commanding abilities, and eminent public services, would deserve and adorn any official station in the gift of the people."[99]

The major party state conventions in January of 1843 and 1844 expressed views which indicate that cleavage between Whigs and Democrats had increased versus what they had been in the late twenties and early thirties. Generally speaking—and as preceding pages of this chapter illustrate—Democrats opposed and Whigs favored a national bank, considerable tariff protection, and significant distribution of the proceeds of federal land sales to the states. Each blamed the other for failure to obtain desired federal appropriations for prosecution of the National Road, removal of obstructions to the Ohio and Wabash rivers, and improvement of the harbor at Michigan City. At times Whigs advocated, while Democrats resisted, efforts to curb the veto power of the president, and to limit his tenure to a single term. Party cleavage had become greater than it had been since party formation in the mid-twenties. The resolutions of their conventions early in 1843 and 1844 confirm Whig support for a national bank, considerable tariff protection, and distribution; and Democratic opposition to these measures. But their resolutions and addresses were silent about Oregon, Texas, and slavery.[100] Despite their division about key issues, each party contended that it was the true heir of the Revolutionary Fathers, while linking the opposition with Federalism and aristocracy; blamed their rivals for the hard times of the late thirties and early forties; and considered their policies essential for a return to better times. Both Whigs and Democrats painted their opponents as dominated by officeholders and office seekers, who served their selfish interests and often fleeced the public. In 1843 the Whig State Convention explained that the party had been unable to implement its policies because of "the Executive veto!" A year later the next such convention stated that with the death of "the Patriarch of the West" the Whig administration had been "buried in the grave of General Harrison" by Tyler's betrayal of the party which had elected him. The Democratic State Convention of 1843 pointed out that it had been the Whigs, not they, who had extolled and elected Tyler. Their convention the next year charged that in 1840 the Whigs had misled and deceived the voters about their policies; "set afloat falsehoods and slanders of every description" against the Van Buren administration; and then when Tyler vetoed the bank bill, consistent with his long and well known views, they had cried "from Maine to Georgia, that they had been cheated and betrayed . . . ."[101]

In May, 1844, both major parties held their national nominating conventions at Baltimore. In a one day session on May 1, the Whigs enthusiastically nominated Clay by acclamation, then chose Theodore Frelinghuysen of New Jersey for vice president. Their brief platform called for "a well-regulated currency," and a "tariff for revenue to defray the necessary expenses of the government" combined with "discriminating" protection to domestic labor. Whether this presumed the need for a national bank and increased protection was not explained, but these remarks suggest a reduced commitment to these key items of Clay's American System. Distribution was advocated, as was "a single" term for the executive. The *Indiana State Journal* approved the nominations of Clay and Frelinghuysen as an opportunity "to perfect the objects of 1840, and to secure the fruits of a revolution stolen and turned to ashes by Treachery."[102]

Although early in 1844 Van Buren still appeared to be his party's presidential choice, at the Democratic National Convention in Baltimore, May 28–30, another won the prize. Soon after Van Buren and Clay affirmed their opposition to the annexation of Texas ex-Congressman Tilghman A. Howard, in warning Democrats not to be hasty in "taking ground against Texas," observed that Van Buren's letter had "given great dissatisfaction to the Southern members," and "Cass [is] often mentioned concerning the nomination." Early in May seven Indiana Democratic members of Congress reportedly signed a card expressing doubts whether Van Buren could be elected. One of them, Congressman Thomas J. Henley, wrote William H. English that "We *must* have a new candidate or be defeated," commenting "I think with [Lewis] Cass or Dick [Richard M. Johnson] we could go it with a *rush* . . . ."[103] Even so, except for the adoption of the rule requiring a two-thirds majority for nomination, Van Buren would probably have become the nominee since he won a majority of the votes on the initial ballot at the party's national convention. Van Buren and Cass were the principal rivals on the first seven ballots, but Van Buren never attained a majority after the first count. On the eighth ballot James K. Polk of Tennessee, who had previously not received even one vote, forged ahead of Van Buren; and on the ninth he won much more than the required two-thirds majority. Indiana gave nine votes for Cass and three for Van Buren on the four initial ballots, Cass eleven and Van Buren one on the next three tries, and its twelve votes for Polk on the final count. George M. Dallas of Pennsylvania was nominated for vice president. The Democratic platform stressed that the federal government had "limited powers" which should be "strictly" constructed; and considered a national bank, distribution, and a general system of internal improvements measures denied the general government. It branded a national bank "dangerous to our republican institutions and the liberties of the people"; and declared the separation of federal money "from banking institutions . . . indispensable" for the safety of federal funds. Modification of the veto power was opposed, accompanied by the assertion that this power had "thrice saved the American people from the corrupt and tyrannical domination of the Bank of the United States." The Democrats said the government should not "foster one branch of industry to the detriment of another," or "cherish the interests" of one part of the country to the injury of another without explaining what this meant about tariff rates. One plank insisted that the rights of immigrants to become citizens and own land must not be abridged; and another emphasized that slavery was exclusively a matter for the states to decide, with abolitionists viewed as endangering "the stability and permanency of the Union" of the states. Perhaps the most important plank was the one that affirmed America's "clear and unquestionable" title to all of Oregon, and asked for "the reoccupation of Oregon and the re-annexation of Texas, at the earliest practicable period."[104]

Polk and Clay were the principal rivals for the presidency in 1844, but two other nominees had a role in the campaign which mixed emerging with waning issues. The Liberty party, opposing any extension of slavery and asking for its gradual abolition, nominated James G. Birney who had been its candidate four years before. A motley group of Whigs and Democrats nominated President Tyler, who vigorously sought the early annexation of Texas.[105] With Polk and the Democrats jumping on the expansionist bandwagon Clay tried to explain and soften his opposition to annexation of Texas, however in August Tyler withdrew in favor of Polk. Birney remained in the race in spite of the argument of some Whigs that his persistence might help make Polk the victor. Both Whigs and Democrats had members who wished to curb political and other privileges of immigrants, but each party sought to convince the foreign born that it was their best friend. Polk wooed friends of tariff protection in Pennsylvania and other manufacturing states by explaining that he had sanctioned "moderate discriminating duties" to obtain needed revenue and "afford reasonable incidental protection to our home industry." During a southern tour Clay assured voters that the advance of industry beyond the infant stage made tariff protection less necessary. Since the Whigs had softened their support for a national bank and a protective tariff, and the Democrats were evasive on the tariff, the gap between them narrowed concerning these issues. Party views about distribution remained clashing, but with land proceeds much reduced this item had diminished importance. Whigs called Polk a man of mediocre ability, claimed that he came from a family that had supported Tories during the American Revolution, asserted that he had opposed pensions for Revolutionary soldiers and their widows, and considered him a free trader serving British interests. Some predicted that his election would lead to disunion, others that it would result in war with Mexico. Democrats portrayed Clay as a gambler, frequent duelist, addicted to profanity, and a man motivated by arrogance and selfish ambition. They described Polk as the candidate of the people, versus Clay as the candidate of the aristocrats. Democrats said they promoted the interest and welfare of the people, whereas the Whigs advanced the wealth and power of the few at the expense of the many.[106] The popular vote in November was extremely close, both nationally and in various states, but Polk gained 170 electoral votes against 105 for Clay and none for Birney.[107]

Indiana's twelve electoral votes for Polk, following the Democratic sweep in the state election of the previous year, gave Hoosier Democrats the dominant voice as spokesmen for Hoosiers in both federal and state politics for the first time since parties had commenced in the twenties. Polk beat Clay in Indiana by about 2,350 votes; however, he got approximately 18,500 more votes than Van Buren had in 1840 while Clay received only about 4,600 more than Harrison had.[108] Why so large an increase for Polk, so modest a one for Clay? Among the factors which seem to have produced this result are: the extraordinary popularity of Harrison and the substantial unpopularity of Van Buren in 1840; the considerable popularity of Polk in 1844 versus strong and long standing bias against Clay; Polk's vigorous support of western expansion, offering the prospect for early acquisition of both Oregon and Texas; the fiscal insolvency arising from the System of 1836, for which the Whigs were considered largely responsible; the increase in German and Irish voters, most of whom probably voted for Polk; the gain in support for the Liberty party, largely at the expense of the Whigs; the increased emphasis of the Whigs on issues in contrast to their stress on hoopla and emotion in 1840; and the trend toward economic laissez faire which the Democrats supported more than did the Whigs. Whatever the influences, from the mid-forties until the Civil War, the Democrats, not the Whigs or Republicans who succeeded them in the fifties, for the most part spoke for Hoosiers in both state and federal politics.

The congressional and state elections in August, 1845, strengthened Democratic dominance over Hoosier politics. Soon after the voting in August, Godlove S. Orth, a Whig, advised Schuyler Colfax: "we are beaten, both branches of the Legislature are against us—and the congressional representation stands as in the last congress . . . ." Nevertheless, Orth declared, with undue optimism: "Indiana is a Whig State," and he explained how they could elect their candidate for governor in 1846. "Instead of drawing an elevated line, unbending and unchangeable, and battling to raise public opinion to its level," Orth counseled, "we must come down a little, slacken the stern rule when necessary, meet public opinion, even if only midway at the desired goal—in a word, we must 'stoop to conquer.'"[109] The congressional election gave the Democrats eight versus two congressmen for the Whigs, repeating their overwhelming triumph achieved in 1843. Six of the eight incumbent Democrats—John W. Davis, Thomas J. Henley, Andrew Kennedy, Robert Dale Owen, John Pettit, and Thomas Smith—were reelected. Incumbent Democrat William J. Brown did not seek reelection, but was replaced by William W. Wick of the same party. Incumbent Democrat Joseph A. Wright lost to Edward W. McGaughey, a Whig, but Democrat Charles W. Cathcart defeated Whig incumbent Samuel C. Sample. Caleb B. Smith, a Whig, won reelection. By this time Owen and Davis had achieved national stature. Owen was suggested to Andrew Jackson for consideration as a member of Polk's cabinet, but he was not so named. When Congress convened in December, 1845, Davis became the first Hoosier to be elected speaker of the House of Representatives.[110]

Meantime, at the legislative session of 1844–1845, a successor to Albert S. White, Indiana's second and last Whig senator, would normally have been chosen by the General Assembly. Although the Whigs and Democrats each had twenty-five senators, the Whigs had a majority of nine members in the House. The *Indiana State Journal* understandably asserted that the election of a Whig had been "rendered certain." The *Western Sun*, though strongly Democratic, presumed that "the Federalists," as it called the Whigs, would be able "to elect their Senator."[111] According to a law of 1831 the election of a new senator was required since White's term would expire March 3, 1845.[112] But the Senate, presided over by Lieutenant Governor Jesse D. Bright, a Democrat, repeatedly refused to meet in joint session for an election, with Bright frequently casting the deciding vote. Whig editors contended that Senate Democrats had failed to uphold the laws and constitution of the state, while Democratic editors vigorously defended their refusal on the claim that the Whigs had inflated their strength in the legislature for this session by gerrymandering the districts from which members were elected. Moreover, some Democrats argued, theirs was the majority party, hence they should elect the senator for the majority was entitled to prevail over the minority.[113] As many Democrats had doubtless hoped, at the election in August, 1845, they gained a twelve vote margin over the Whigs in the House with each party having twenty-five senators. Before the new legislature met in December, Governor James Whitcomb, Lieutenant Governor Bright, Congressman Robert Dale Owen, and Joseph A. Wright were among the Democrats considered as a successor to White.[114] Apparently a Democratic legislative caucus opted for Bright, who gained election on the initial ballot by winning eighty votes to sixty-six for Joseph G. Marshall, the Whig candidate, with two votes blank. Bright's election occurred December 6, five days after the congressional session of 1845–1846 had commenced, and nine months after his term should have begun on March 4, 1845.[115] The *Indiana State Sentinel* asserted that Bright's election exhibited the "entire harmony and concert of the Democratic Party in Indiana," but this appears to have been more rhetoric than fact. The *Indiana State Journal* suggested that the rank and file of the Democracy would doubtless be astounded at the outcome "as three fourths of them, no doubt, preferred the election of Governor Whitcomb." The "political tricksters," it said, had defeated the will of the Democratic majority. This Whig editor called Bright's election "A Triumph of matter over mind." Calvin Fletcher termed Bright "a 4th rate lawyer," and he stated that with Senators Hannegan and Bright representing Indiana: "We have now 2 very ordinary men to fill that important place."[116] However Bright's elevation to the United States Senate may be viewed, his election thereto, after his role in preventing an election at the previous session, if not dishonorable, at least was not entirely honorable for him or his party.

Meantime, in his inaugural on March 4, 1845, and his message to Congress in December following, President Polk had indicated his basic policies and priorities regarding domestic politics. He emphasized that the federal government had limited powers which should be strictly construed, but he was emphatic that the Union of the states must be preserved. The new president advocated: a revenue tariff, with limited incidental protection; reestablishment of the Independent Treasury, but no national bank; strict frugality in federal expenditures, and speedy extinguishment of the national debt; increased preemption rights and graduation concerning public lands; continuation of the executive veto by the executive; and insisted that slavery in the states had been both recognized and protected by the federal constitution. The staunchly Democratic Vincennes *Western Sun* called the inaugural "an able, and patriotic state paper," but the Richmond *Palladium*, staunchly Whig, considered it "very common place . . . and a mishmash of occasional sensible sentiment with much that is silly." The *Indiana State Journal* wryly described Polk's inaugural as coming from "an accidental nominee" rather than from "an accidental President" as chief executive. This paper expressed concern that Polk's administration would destroy the Tariff of 1842, extend and reestablish the "odious Sub-Treasury," and fail to make appropriations for western harbors and the Cumberland Road.[117] At a meeting in Indianapolis early in 1845 Democratic editors had unanimously adopted a "creed of principles and measures" which had much in common with Polk's utterances in his inaugural and first annual message.[118]

At the congressional session which began December 1, 1845, and ended August 10, 1846, the Democrats had majorities in both houses. Indiana contributed to this dominance for both of her senators and eight of her congressmen were of this party.[119] After Congressman John W. Davis won reelection in August, 1845, the *Western Sun* expressed its pleasure that Indiana's "able and distinguished Representative" was likely to be elected to the third ranking position in the government. Because Indiana was "the sixth State in the Union" in population and "conservative and Democratic in her character," this paper thought the Hoosier State was entitled to have Davis as speaker of the House. When Congress convened Davis was so elected by a decisive majority, becoming the first Hoosier to win this position.[120] At this session Congress approved several key items of Polk's domestic program, including the reestablishment of the Independent Treasury. In discussing the House bill therefor, Congressman Caleb B. Smith asserted that its reestablishment had not been called for by the presidential campaign; contended that Jacksonian measures and tinkering had destroyed a sound currency, convertible in gold or silver, resulting in financial revulsions and disasters. He labeled the Independent Treasury such "a miserable humbug" and "so impracticable" that it had never been implemented. Moreover, Smith said, it could be justified only for "a hard-money currency exclusively." Congressman William W. Wick, a Democrat, declared that at least in his district the Independent Treasury had been openly avowed, both in the presidential election of 1844 and the congressional election of 1845. Wick expressed the view that "the Democracy of Indiana is prepared to defy the world, the flesh, the devil, and the banks"; and would "sponge out their banks" except that then the "rotten circulation of shinplasters" from nearby Whig states "would be flooded in upon us in the absence of a paper circulation of our own . . . ." The House, reflecting the hard money sentiment of many Democrats, amended the bill to require that all payments to the government be in gold or silver. This amendment was adopted 108 to 73, and the bill passed the House by the lopsided margin of 123 to 67. The Senate amended the measure to permit payments to the federal treasury in treasury notes as well as in gold and silver, and then approved the Independent Treasury by a tally of 28 to 25. In both houses the voting was mainly along party lines, making the reestablishment of the Independent Treasury a Democratic triumph.[121] The act eliminated all connection with banks concerning the receiving, holding, and disbursing of federal money. The subtreasuries would receive, safeguard, and make payments in silver, gold, or treasury notes. Though much opposed by Whigs and elements in the business community, the Independent Treasury continued as the basic mode of handling federal finances until the early twentieth century.[122]

While the Democratic controlled Congress easily reestablished the Independent Treasury, it obtained tariff reduction with great difficulty. Revision downward, with emphasis on revenue and incidental protection, was a key object of Polk's administration.[123] Especially by the midforties, at the national level sentiment pro and con the tariff reflected a considerable degree of party cleavage as well as a considerable degree of sectional division. Within Indiana, party cleavage had become pronounced, in contrast to the last half of the twenties and early thirties when there had been significant bipartisan consensus for tariff protection. After adoption of the Whig Tariff of 1842, which significantly augmented protection, James Whitcomb, while candidate for governor in 1843, authored a pamphlet vigorously contending that protective duties were both inexpedient and unconstitutional. Such duties, he argued, encouraged smuggling and monopoly, and aided manufacturers at the expense of farmers and laborers. Whitcomb supported such protection if incidental to revenue considerations, with imports and exports regulated by competition. Senator Oliver H. Smith, Indiana's first Whig in the United States Senate, responded to Whitcomb in a pamphlet which vigorously defended protection as both expedient and constitutional. Protection, he argued, did not increase prices, encourage smuggling and monopoly, or aid manufacturers at the expense of farmers and laborers. Smith offered quotations from Washington, Jefferson, Madison, Monroe, Calhoun, and Jackson to support the point that the "old Republicans," in contrast to contemporary Democrats, had endorsed protection as desirable and constitutional.[124]

Shortly before Polk became president, the state's leading Democratic organ insisted that talk of protecting American labor by tariffs, "when more than nine-tenths of the labor of the country is engaged in raising productions, of which we now have a large surplus, and always must have, so long as we have so much unoccupied soil, and which cannot for ages to come, be consumed by any amount of population that can here be profitably engaged in manufactures is an absurdity." Soon after Polk's inauguration, Indiana's leading Whig press, after asserting that "locofoco demagogues" had repeatedly denounced the Tariff of 1842 as "a tax upon the poor for the benefit of the rich," challenged the Democrats—having "a locofoco President, Senate, and H. of Representatives"—to remedy "the evils of which they had complained."[125]

The Polk administration pressed hard for substantial tariff reduction. As the congressional session of 1845–1846 got under way the *Indiana State Journal* considered the tariff views of Secretary of the Treasury Robert J. Walker more alarming and demagogic than those of Polk. The secretary's "whole effort," it said, "seems to be to create the impression that the effect of the Tariff is to benefit one class and to oppress all others." When the administration's tariff bill was under discussion in June, 1846, Congressman Robert Dale Owen described tariff protection as part of an antiquated system of "legal intermeddling with commerce" having precedents in the Middle Ages. The Hoosier Democrat contended that protective legislation lessened competition, raised prices, and legislated "money from the pockets of one class into the pockets of another, without any value received to justify the transfer." Owen agreed that "a temporary tariff for protection . . . to defend the young plants of enterprise until they shoot up to an independent growth" might have "benefits to overbalance its injustice." The congressman said the pending measure provided rates above that anticipated by the Compromise Tariff of 1833, but its friends in the West and South were willing to concede much to "brethren from the manufacturing States" who were urged to meet them in the same spirit of concession and conciliation.[126] The Walker-administration tariff bill, as amended, passed the House 114 to 95, with a number of Democrats joining

Whigs in opposition to passage. Modestly further amended in the Senate, it required the deciding vote of Vice President George M. Dallas, from protectionist Pennsylvania, to advance the measure to its third reading and then passage by the close margin of 28 to 27.[127] In contrast to the Whig Tariff of 1842, the Walker Tariff of 1846 was a Democratic measure. A rapidly expanding economic base and returning prosperity augmented the revenue from the moderate rates of the new tariff. This situation also afforded a favorable context for continuing the Independent Treasury and the growth of banking under state regulation. In short, early in Polk's administration, two key items of Clay's American System were buried.

Although Indiana Democrats gave overwhelming support to Polk's policies concerning the Independent Treasury and tariff, they often parted company with the president regarding internal improvements for western roads, rivers, and harbors. During the last half of the forties the General Assembly sought appropriations of land or money for constructing or completing such items as making the Wabash and St. Joseph rivers navigable; building a harbor at Michigan City; completing the National Road within Indiana; building a canal around the Falls of the Ohio, on the Indiana shore; constructing a railroad from Indianapolis to Peru; and building a clay or macadamized road from Bloomington to Columbus via Nashville.[128] Despite Polk's caution about approving internal improvement bills, the congressional session of 1845–1846 adopted a Western Rivers and Harbors bill which, according to Polk, appropriated $1,378,450 "to be applied to more than forty distinct and separate objects of improvement." The only item within Indiana designated $40,000 for improvement of the harbor at Michigan City. This measure passed the House by a margin of 109 to 92, and the Senate advanced it to third reading by a vote of 34 to 16, then passed it without a roll call. Indiana's two Whig congressmen and four of their Democratic colleagues voted for passage, however, three of the Democrats were nonvoters and Robert Dale Owen voted against passage.[129] President Polk vetoed this legislation, contending that many of its items were "of a local character," thus unconstitutional inasmuch as the federal constitution had not "conferred upon the Federal Government the power to construct works of internal improvement within the States, or to appropriate money from the Treasury for that purpose." He termed the measure inexpedient, largely appropriating money "for objects which are of no pressing necessity" at a time when means should be husbanded to meet the cost of the Mexican War. The House voted 97 to 91 to override the veto, but this was far short of the two-thirds majority needed to nullify the veto.[130]

Polk's vehement opposition to federal appropriations for internal improvements slowed such aid during his presidency. While the Western Rivers and Harbors bill of 1846 was under discussion, John Pettit vowed that he was "a strict constructionist" but he contended that such appropriations as it contained were authorized by the constitution. This Democratic congressman warned that the House would never approve a "reduction of the tariff" until the rivers and harbors bill "in its substantial provisions, was passed." A short time later Senator Edward A. Hannegan, in discussing another internal improvement bill, declared that he could not support an appropriation for improving the navigation of part of the Tennessee River "without at the same time insisting upon a similar measure in behalf of the Illinois, Wabash, and other rivers . . . upon which so great a loss of life and property annually occurred for want of a paltry sum to remove the obstructions to their navigation."[131] During Polk's administration Indiana Whigs generally supported federal aid for western rivers, harbors, and roads. Hoosier Democrats, however, were much divided concerning these appropriations. Polk's vigorous and persistent opposition to such aid, the increasing interest on states' rights, and the renewal of emphasis on economic laissez faire all tended to make internal improvements, except for those truly national, the responsibility of states and especially private enterprise.[132]

Before Polk reached midpoint in his administration he had obtained the reestablishment of the Independent Treasury, a tariff mainly for revenue, and had put a brake on the expansion of federal appropriations for internal improvements. Meantime, items about expansion and slavery were increasingly overshadowing other issues as they became intertwined with relations concerning other countries. Polk was an ardent expansionist, however, he considered slavery an issue to be settled by territorial or state legislatures without the intervention of Congress. His election on a platform calling for the reannexation of Texas and the reoccupation of Oregon intensified the movement for the immediate annexation of Texas to the Union.[133] But before Polk's inauguration as president, Tyler recommended and Congress adopted a joint resolution for its immediate annexation. This resolution passed the House by a tally of 120 to 98, and the Senate without a roll call vote. Tyler approved the resolution on March 1, three days before his term ended.[134] In debating this resolution sharp cleavage developed along partisan lines. Congressman Caleb B. Smith, a Hoosier Whig, insisted that the constitution made no provision for the annexation of Texas or any foreign country. He said a state of war existed between Texas and Mexico, and he viewed robbing Mexico of Texas by force like a "war of conquest" in imitation of the ancient Roman republic. Annexation, Smith argued, might bring commercial and other obligations because of Texan treaties with other countries; would make the United States responsible for the large debt of Texas; and extend slavery and increase the number and power of the slave states. "Our territory," Smith suggested, "is already sufficiently extensive to promote the welfare of all." Samuel C. Sample, also from Indiana, generally concurred with the views of his Whig colleague. From both a military and commercial point of view he thought the United States safer without Texas. If the country had "caught the spirit of conquest . . . it had reached its meridian." Sample and Smith both insisted that the compromises of the constitution concerning slavery must be respected.[135] Congressman Robert Dale Owen, an Indiana Democrat, contended that Texas had won her independence and become a sovereign state, hence annexation was for Texas and the United States to decide. Owen suggested that annexation would diminish slavery by drawing off slaves from the northern states, inducing gradual emancipation among them; and likewise in other slave states because "Slavery, like monarchy, is a temporary evil." Owen emphasized that the Union of sovereign states, provided the emphasis was on less rather than more central government, could extend "its blessings" over all of North America. Another Indiana Democrat, Congressman Thomas J. Henley, asserted that Texas could not be kept out of the Union, and he predicted that opposition to its annexation would become as odious as had that of those who had sought to create a separate confederacy for New England.[136]

In his inaugural on March 4, 1845, Polk announced his intention to consummate "the reannexation of Texas . . . at the earliest practicable period." The president noted the vast fertile soil and "genial climate" of Texas. Its annexation, he said, would help protect New Orleans and the southwestern frontier from hostile aggression. To those who believed that "our system of confederated States could not operate successfully over an extended territory," the president responded that experience had shown that it "may be safely extended to the utmost bounds of our territorial limits" while becoming stronger as it expanded. When Congress met in December the executive reported that Texas had agreed to the terms of annexation; and he stated that strong reasons existed for quickly admitting "Texas into the Union upon an equal footing with the original States."[137] Two weeks later the House adopted a resolution for admission of the Lone Star State by the overwhelming margin of 141 to 58; and the Senate advanced the resolution therefor to third reading by the large margin of 31 to 13, then passed it without a roll call vote.[138] Polk signed the resolution of admission on December 29; and the two senators from Texas were seated in March, 1846, followed by that of its two representatives during June.[139]

Meanwhile, augmenting emigration to Oregon increased the need to resolve rival British and American claims concerning this large area. Polk's election on a platform calling for the "reannexation" of Texas and the "reoccupation" of Oregon caused some to view these items as twin measures to be achieved together. Although Tyler sought to hasten the annexation of Texas after Polk's triumph in the presidential election, he exhibited no such haste regarding Oregon. He repeated, however, his previous recommendations that American laws be extended over Oregon, and that military posts be established along the route to make it safer to emigrate there. Early in 1845 the Indiana legislature, dominated by Whigs, affirmed American title to all of Oregon, and urged that joint occupation with Britain be terminated.[140] Robert Dale Owen, as he had at the previous session, opposed granting land rights to American settlers in Oregon, in part for lack of "exclusive sovereignty" over its area. But he strongly advocated the end of joint occupancy. The latter, he argued, would be more likely to encourage negotiation, and less likely to cause war than the former. Congressman Andrew Kennedy, another Indiana Democrat, spoke in hostile and uncompromising terms. Viewing all of Oregon as "indisputably" American, Kennedy urged that Congress extend laws over it, "let the consequences be what they may." And if England resorted to war: "Let us begin the melee by whipping the *bully* first." Gentlemen had no fear of doing their duty when Mexico threatened war over Texas, Kennedy jabbed, but with some gentlemen Oregon is "a horse of another color." He charged the British with having paid money to Indians for American scalps whether "torn from the head of the warrior, the lovely female, or the helpless infant." The congressman predicted that after expanding to the Pacific Ocean the "resistless wave" of Americans would occupy "the shores of the Pacific until it includes the entire American continent, from Behring's Straits to Cape Horn." This "great and glorious destiny," Kennedy proclaimed, "is written on the map of the world, by the finger of God." Senator Albert S. White, Hoosier Whig, called himself a friend of Oregon, but he supported a compromise settlement with Great Britain and asked for the maintenance of good faith in treaty stipulations.[141]

Polk's zigzag course concerning Oregon was in contrast to his unwavering support for the prompt admission of Texas. But "reoccupation" of all of Oregon made war with Britain a possible result. In his inaugural, March 4, 1845, Polk proclaimed American title to Oregon "'clear and unquestionable,'" but he did not expressly claim all of it to 54° 40', nor did he ask for termination of joint occupation. Nine months later in his first annual message to Congress Polk explained that since former administrations had sought compromise at the forty-ninth degree, and negotiations on this basis were pending when he became president, he deemed it his "duty not abruptly to break it off." Since then, however, "wholly inadmissable" British demands showed that an acceptable compromise could not be effected. Hence, the negotiation had been ended and American "title to the whole Oregon Territory" had been asserted. The president urged Congress to extend American laws over settlers in Oregon, have military forts erected and mounted riflemen recruited to protect emigrants enroute there, and serve notice for termination of joint occupation. With termination achieved, Polk emphasized, "national honor and interest" would require that "the national rights in Oregon" be "firmly maintained."[142] This bellicose language was responded to in kind in England, but a majority in both houses of Congress, including Whigs generally and a number of Democrats, preferred compromise to risking war with Great Britain.[143]

Hoosier Whigs were more inclined to delay a showdown with Britain than were Hoosier Democrats. A Whig paper at South Bend, after reporting that emigrants from the Mississippi Valley were pouring into Oregon, commented: "The country is becoming daily more and more Americanized; and thus a few short years will give us *peaceably*, what at all hazards the Union *must* have, the whole of Oregon." The *Indiana State Journal*, the state's leading Whig organ, published a series of articles by "L. B." who reviewed the historical background regarding claims to Oregon and efforts to resolve them. This anonymous writer emphasized that it was unrealistic to expect the British to surrender claim to all of Oregon after having refused earlier to compromise at the forty-ninth parallel. "L. B." strongly recommended compromise at this parallel, saying that such a division had been supported by Presidents Madison, Monroe, and John Quincy Adams. "That the Oregon question will lead to hostilities," "L. B." said, "no man in his senses can, for a moment, seriously believe. For such a controversy to create serious difficulty between two kindred nations, closely united by mutual commercial relations, is ridiculous."[144] The *Indiana State Journal* insisted that there was no danger that the Polk administration would have war with England regarding

Oregon or any question. "A Southern administration will never go to war with that power," it said, because in such a "war the British Possessions in North America would be annexed to the Union, making five more free States!" About this time, at least three Indiana Democratic papers respectively proclaimed: "54° 40′ 'is ours, and we must have it'"; "if war was avoidable only at the expense of republican institutions on the Pacific Coast, 'then LET IT COME'"; and "'Peace, if practicable—war, if necessary.'"[145]

During the early months of 1846 Congress debated at length whether to mandate abrogation of joint occupation. Finally, in April it adopted a resolution urging "a speedy and amicable" adjustment of differences, while giving the president the authority to give notice of abrogation at his discretion. This resolution passed the House by a count of 141 to 47, and the Senate by the even stronger margin of 42 to 10. Among Hoosier congressmen only its two Whigs, Caleb B. Smith and Edward W. McGaughey, and one Democrat, Robert Dale Owen, voted for its adoption. In the Senate Jesse D. Bright voted against the resolution, while his Democratic colleague, Edward A. Hannegan, was a nonvoter. Owen's support for the resolution made him the only Hoosier Democrat who supported negotiation and compromise rather than serving notice of abrogation.[146] Senator Hannegan vowed that he would never consent to surrender, by treaty or otherwise, "one foot" of Oregon south of 54° 40′. Rather than peace on "degrading and dishonorable terms," he said, a "war, even of extermination, would be far preferable." He asserted that "Texas and Oregon were born in the same instant, nursed and cradled in the same cradle," then charged that with Texas admitted its "peculiar friends turned and were doing all they could to strangle Oregon!" Fear of Punic faith, the senator explained, had caused him to vote against the admission of Texas because the Oregon question remained unresolved.[147] Congressmen Andrew Kennedy, Charles W. Cathcart, and William W. Wick also spoke in bellicose tones for all of Oregon north to 54° 40′. Kennedy noted that the South had been supported in gaining Texas, hence it should reciprocate in kind in acquiring Oregon. He described Oregon as "the inch of ground" upon which a "fulcrum" could be planted providing a lever that would make it possible to stretch "one hand to the Eastern world through the Pacific chain, and the other to Europe through the Atlantic chain, grasping the trade of the world . . . ." From the impact of the steam locomotive and magnetic telegraph, Cathcart suggested, "all the people of this continent may be moulded to one mind." Oregon's acquisition, he predicted, would make possible "the vision of State after State coming into this great temple of freedom, and burning their incense upon an altar consecrated to the enjoyment of civil and religious liberty." Wick declared himself "for Oregon and against a war; but for Oregon, war or no war." He claimed all of Oregon and was "ready to claim all the continent, upon the principle of manifest destiny," however, he wanted no "mixed races in our Union, nor men of any color except white, unless they be slaves." Cathcart stressed the manufacturing and commercial potential of Oregon, and observed that the "harbors of Oregon, fronting a barbarous world, afford admirable facilities for carrying on trade; and barbarous nations are always the best customers of civilized people."[148]

Other Hoosiers spoke in more moderate terms, including some Democrats. Congressman Caleb B. Smith, a Whig, opposed mandating abrogation of joint occupation. It would lead to war within a year, he said, because England "cannot recede without being disgraced in the eyes of the universal world." Moreover, with emigration to Oregon rapidly increasing, in "a few years . . . we shall be strong enough in Oregon to maintain our claims to the whole territory." Smith expressed his concern that Americans "were imbued with too strong a belief that it was their destiny . . . to conquer or overrun the whole continent, at least of North America." "Such expansion," he said, "would soon excite . . . the hostility of the whole world, and bring upon us their united forces in arms."[149] Robert Dale Owen strongly defended Polk's policy concerning Oregon, and he supported moderation and compromise. He emphasized that the area most in dispute was the limited area north and west of the Columbia River, south of the forty-ninth parallel. The Indiana Democrat anticipated the development of "a great line of communication with China and the East Indies . . . through Oregon," the acquisition of which he considered "almost worthless" unless it embraced the excellent harbors at Puget Sound. He called war a terrible alternative, but said that if "in spite of our averting efforts, the blow must be given, let it be in the spirit of the old adage, 'he gives twice, who gives quickly.'" Giving notice that joint occupation would be ended would facilitate negotiations, whereas granting land titles while occupation continued would be contrary to its terms and perhaps more likely to cause war.[150] As the discussion neared its conclusion, Wick modified his position and supported Polk's policy concerning Oregon. He argued that the Whigs and a Whig president had so "slandered" and encumbered the American title to Oregon that Polk had to offer a compromise similar to previous offers. He asserted that public opinion "would not justify a war for that portion of Oregon between the parallels of 49° and 54° 40′." "A large majority of either branch of Congress," Wick declared, "would yield up that part of Oregon north of latitude 49°, in extinguishment of the encumberance and claim held and made by Great Britain, and to secure the blessings of peace."[151]

As the debate about Oregon dragged on, it became apparent that both the British and American governments preferred compromise to conflict. Despite Polk's blistering reassertion of American claim to all of Oregon after the British rejected his initial proposal, through diplomatic finesse he made it known that if the Senate so advised he would accept the forty-ninth parallel as the northern boundary of Oregon, provided the right of navigating the Columbia River was not granted the British. On June 6 the president received a proposal from the British for acceptance of the forty-ninth parallel, with navigation of the Columbia limited to persons associated with the Hudson's Bay Company. Polk disliked this concession to the fur trading company, but its acceptance may have been influenced from a desire not to risk war with Britain in addition to the war with Mexico which had begun several weeks earlier.[152] In sending the British proposal to the Senate, he promised to follow its advice whether it should be accepted or rejected. Nevertheless, the president stated that his opinions about Oregon remained as given to Congress when the session began—when he had reasserted American claim to it north to 54°

40'. The Senate quickly approved the British proposal, without change, by the overwhelming bipartisan majority of 38 to 12, thus advising Polk to accept the compromise offer. Senator Edward A. Hannegan voted against approval, and his Democratic colleague, Jesse A. Bright, was a nonvoter. Polk then submitted a treaty, embracing the compromise terms, which the Senate ratified on June 18 by a decisive and bipartisan majority of 41 to 14. Indiana's two senators, Hannegan and Bright, voted against ratification.[153]

The annexation of Texas in 1845 and partition of Oregon in 1846 only partly satisfied the desire of Polk and many other Americans for territory, particularly in the Southwest at the expense of Mexico. This desire made slavery and expansion dominate issues for the rest of Polk's presidency. Previously these questions had been subordinated largely to considerations of party and national unity. By the mid-forties, however, as antislavery became mainly a northern and free state movement, northerners grew increasingly concerned that southwestern expansion would not only extend slavery but also bring political dominance to southern slave states. This concern affected many northerners who were modestly antislavery. The rapid admission of Texas as a slave state, in contrast to the delay in organizing a territorial government for Oregon, free of slavery, augmented this concern.[154] As Congress was about to adjourn in August, 1846, the House, by the very large margin of 108 to 44, added an amendment prohibiting slavery to a bill to establish a territorial government for Oregon, then passed it without a roll call vote. With few exceptions, the votes against slavery came from free states of the North, including many Democrats and Whigs generally. Seven Indiana congressmen, two Whigs and five Democrats, voted for the prohibition. The Senate, in which slave states had much more voting power than they had in the House, gave the bill only negligible consideration, then tabled it, thus postponing the organization of a civil government for Oregon.[155]

Meantime, the outbreak of war with Mexico in May, 1846, further stirred party and sectional division about slavery and expansion. Before the war began Polk had been eager to acquire at least Upper California and New Mexico from Mexico. Some expansionists wanted to obtain much of Mexico. During the summer of 1845 Polk had sent a naval squadron to the coast of Mexico and troops to the Rio Grande River, which he viewed as the western boundary of Texas but in an area that Mexico claimed as rightfully hers. These military forces were to fight only to defend themselves. Early in May, 1846, however, Polk decided to ask Congress for war against Mexico on the basis of its unwillingness to pay claims owed Americans for damage to persons and property of Americans, and its unwillingness to negotiate a peaceful settlement of issues between the two countries. But prior to the completion of his proposed call for war with Mexico, the president learned that Mexican troops had crossed the Rio Grande, attacked American soldiers, taken prisoners, and killed or wounded about fifteen Americans. In asking Congress for a declaration of war against Mexico on May 11, Polk reported that "Mexico has passed the boundary of the United States, has invaded our territory and shed American blood upon the American soil." The president asserted that Americans had long suffered from injuries to persons and property at the hands of Mexicans, and he said the Mexican government had refused to negotiate with a minister he had sent concerning a peaceful solution of items in dispute. The war message presumed that American title to Texas ran west to the Rio Grande River.[156] The House approved a declaration of war against Mexico by the large margin of 174 to 14. No Hoosier congressmen voted against the declaration, but two of them were nonvoters. The Senate adopted the declaration by the near unanimous vote of 40 to 2. Senator Jesse D. Bright voted for the declaration, however, his Democratic colleague, Edward A. Hannegan, was a nonvoter. The president signed the declaration on May 13. It stated that the war existed "by the act of the Republic of Mexico"; and authorized the president to raise up to fifty thousand volunteers, to serve twelve months or until the end of the war, to bring the conflict to "a speedy and successful" conclusion. The sum of $10,000,000 was appropriated to finance the war.[157]

Hoosiers strongly supported the men who were fighting against Mexico, but they differed much about the causes of the war and terms for its conclusion. Whigs were much more critical of the war than were Democrats, but diversity of views existed within both parties. As the conflict commenced, a bipartisan meeting at Indianapolis, with citizens from other parts of the state present, endorsed energetic measures for a speedy and successful termination of the fighting. But the adoption of a resolution declaring that Mexico had started the war by invading American territory and had caused "the shedding of American blood upon American soil"; and another resolution calling for repelling "the enemy from our soil," carrying "the War into the enemy's country" and planting "the Star Spangled Banner in the city of Mexico, upon the Halls of the Montazumas, as the best mode to secure an honorable peace," drew a strong disclaimer from Editor John D. Defrees of the *Indiana State Journal*. This Whig editor, who had been secretary of the meeting, emphasized that there had been no diversity of views about "willingness to repel an invading foe from our borders," but many thought that carrying the war to Mexico City would make "a War of aggression and Conquest, rather than one of defence." The Richmond *Palladium*, another leading Whig paper, commented: "Mr. Polk and his cabinet succumbs to England; but is determined to whip the poor, puny and half-starved Mexicans. They declare our title to 'all of Oregon' to be 'clear and unquestionable'; and do not pretend to have any claim to California, yet intend to have it. Who can be enthusiastic in such a war, 'conceived in sin, and brought forth in iniquity?'" A Whig editor at Fort Wayne, stirring the prejudice of Americans toward Mexicans, commented: "The Mexicans are said to be the filthiest race of modern times. The country literally swarms with fleas, ticks, bugs, and vermin of all kinds." The Mexicans were said to have "diseases wholly unknown in the United States," and their women were reported to "pass most of their time in drinking gin and picking the lice from each other's persons." The editor ended his comments by saying: "This intelligence will be interesting to those who are volunteering 'to revel in the halls of Montezuma.'"[158] Congressman Caleb B. Smith castigated the Democratic majority in the lower house of Congress for causing an "unjustifiable war," preventing proper discussion of its causes, and denouncing criticism as treason. This Hoosier Whig claimed that

Polk had started the war by invading the territory of a sister republic "without the consent or sanction of Congress, and without the knowledge of the people." Its purpose, Smith charged, was to acquire "California, and perhaps other provinces of Mexico," for the object "of extending and perpetuating the power and influence of the South." He called for an end to "these odious hostilities with a neighboring Republic" and the restoration of peace. Congressman Thomas Smith, a Democrat who voted for the war, stated that the war "was to make Mexico respect our rights, to come to a fair settlement with us, and give us the boundary we are entitled to; and not an inch" more. Smith thought the United States was entitled to the Rio Grande boundary, but it would be "rather too much" to ask for California; and he opposed annexing Mexico at the point of a bayonet. He declared that he "was as much opposed to carrying our institutions at the point of the bayonet, as our religion by the stiletto, the bowie-knife, and the mouth of the cannon." The *Indiana State Journal* probably spoke for most Whigs when it said of them: "They believe that it [the war] was unnecessarily provoked and made by the President; but, being made, and the public resources embarked in its prosecution, it becomes an affair of the country, and not of the administration. In this view they will vote every dollar required for its vigorous prosecution and to secure a speedy and honorable peace. Notwithstanding this, they intend holding those in power, who brought this calamity upon the country, responsible for their acts, and it is a fear of this responsibility that prompts them to misrepresent the positions occupied by the Whig party."[159]

The Mexican War quickly augmented party and sectional strife about territorial expansion and slavery. Many northerners, especially Whigs, felt betrayed that Polk had at once pressed for and obtained Texas as a slave state, but partitioned Oregon with Britain and left it without an organized territorial government. These Whigs, and some northern Democrats, were also displeased with Polk's opposition to internal improvements and his emphasis on tariff reduction. As the congressional session of 1845–1846 ended in August, as yet no territorial government had been organized for Oregon. At the same time Polk's desire for additional territory in the Southwest intensified the concern that slavery might be significantly extended and tip political dominance in Congress in favor of the slave states.[160] On Saturday, August 8, with adjournment set for noon, August 10, Polk tossed Congress a bombshell by requesting $2,000,000 for use in obtaining the cession of territory from Mexico. A House bill to appropriate the requested sum, after the Wilmot Proviso excluding slavery from any territory so acquired was added as an amendment by the decisive margin of 83 to 64, was then passed by a count of 87 to 64. This item was considered under pressure of time, with members of Congress strongly divided along both party and sectional lines.[161] Congressman Robert Dale Owen, who apparently voted for the proviso, argued that if the appropriation were refused, then both at home and abroad the inference would be that peace was not desired with Mexico. The Hoosier Democrat stressed that achieving peace was the main goal, and with a weak opponent like Mexico he was "willing to purchase a boundary, instead of fighting for it." William W. Wick, Owen's Democratic colleague, asserted that he was "decidedly friendly" to the appropriation. He hoped territory would be acquired from Mexico, but to say in advance "what laws may not exist" in territory to be acquired would be "not merely counting our chickens before they are hatched, but even before the eggs are laid."[162] The Senate received the bill, with the Wilmot Proviso attached, on Monday about an hour before the session ended, but a filibuster prevented any Senate action on it.[163] Northern Whigs, plus various northern Democrats, had made Polk's requested appropriation hostage to the Wilmot Proviso. Meantime, Senator John C. Calhoun, of South Carolina, had added fuel to the sectional and party cleavage by his insistence that slavery could not be excluded from any state or territory without violating the federal constitution.[164]

When Congress reconvened in December, 1846, Polk repeated his request for an appropriation to secure territory from Mexico, and discussion of the Wilmot Proviso principle was reignited. The president told Congress that the war had not been "waged with a view to conquest," explained that temporary governments had been established for some "conquered provinces," and he sought an appropriation for the cost of maintaining "possession and authority" over conquered areas. But he made no comment about the status of slavery in such areas, nor in his repeated recommendation that a territorial government be established for Oregon.[165] In January bills proposing $3,000,000 to the president for use in negotiating an end to the Mexican War were introduced in both houses. The House, by a vote of 115 to 106, added the Wilmot Proviso principle to the bill, after which it passed by the same vote. Indiana's two Whig congressmen and five of their Democratic colleagues voted for exclusion of slavery in any territory so obtained. One Whig and seven Democrats from Indiana then voted for its passage. Meantime, the Senate, by the large margin of 32 to 21, rejected the exclusion against slavery, then passed the bill without a roll call vote. Hoosier Democratic Senators Edward A. Hannegan and Jesse D. Bright voted against the exclusion of slavery, but presumably favored the bill's passage.[166] The stalemate was broken when the House, by the narrow margin of 102 to 97, agreed to omit the exclusion of slavery; and approved the appropriation of the $3,000,000 by the considerable majority of 115 to 82. The two Whig congressmen from Indiana and three of their Democratic colleagues voted for the exclusion of slavery, then five Hoosier Democrats helped pass the appropriation measure. As of early 1847 the two Indiana Whigs in Congress were strongly for the exclusion of slavery from any territory acquired from Mexico, while its ten Democrats were divided on this item. Its two Democratic senators and most of its Democratic congressmen seemed to prefer to delay resolution of the slavery issue until the war was over and additional territory was secured. As one historian has observed: "Polk had his money, but he had further solidified Northern opposition to the war and to slavery."[167]

The $3,000,000 appropriation granted Polk for use in acquiring new territory increased division among Hoosiers about the causes, conduct, and aims of the war. Democrats Andrew Kennedy, Robert Dale Owen, and Edward A. Hannegan generally defended the Polk administration regarding these items.

Kennedy termed critics who called the war unjust to be unpatriotic. "They knew the war had been forced upon us," he said.
Owen reminded colleagues that when the war was called "unholy,
unrighteous, damnable; the President's war," that these words
were heard in Mexico. He asked: "what chance [have we] of terminating the war, while the enemy is daily fed with hopes, that,
divided in feeling and distracted in counsel, we cannot, for any
length of time, conduct military operations with vigor, or prosecute them with success?" Owen suggested that roughly the areas
of California and New Mexico should be obtained as indemnity
for the "war thrust upon us without provocation." The Indiana
Democrat vigorously opposed adding territory from the more
settled portions of Mexico, where the language, customs, and religion were "all differing from ours"; and their prejudices were
"against us." But if "wild territory" mainly inhabited by Indians
were obtained, it, like Oregon, would be settled by Americans
taking "with them our language, our laws, and our republican institutions." Senator Hannegan urged energetic prosecution of the
war to a successful conclusion. "The road to the city of Mexico is
the road to peace," he stated. Like Owen, however, Hannegan
wanted only "vacant and unoccupied territory" from Mexico. The
Mexicans, he declared, were "a mongrel race" unsuited for representative government. No "sane and intelligent man in the
United States," Hannegan said, would favor annexing all of Mexico even if she offered herself for annexation. He considered agitation of the slavery question concerning additional territory both
premature and detrimental to the war effort. Why, he asked, "kin-
dle a flame on either side about this matter now," as there will be
time to make laws once new areas are obtained.[168]

Meanwhile, some Democrats joined with Whigs in criticism of
the Mexican War. Congressman Caleb B. Smith continued his
sharp criticism by castigating Polk for having caused an unnecessary war that might have been avoided had the president, after
annexing Texas, not sent the "army to advance and invade a Mexican province, to which we had no manner of claim whatsoever."
To critics who termed it unpatriotic to inquire about the war's
causes while the fighting continued, Smith responded: "Yes, wait

till Mexico was first conquered—then annexed—till thousands and thousands of our brave citizen soldiers had perished in battle, or by the diseases of a sickly climate; wait till millions on millions of the public treasure should have been expended, and a national debt created that must press like an incubus upon us and our children; wait till we had made our name a reprobation to mankind; . . . [and] then sit down and coolly inquire what we have been fighting for." The Whig congressman opposed acquiring any territory from Mexico or any extension of slavery. "Where," Smith challenged, "was the northern man who dared . . . express the opinion that we were ever to admit more slave territory into this Union?" Congressman John Pettit, a Democrat, declared that he would "not support any proposition that will tolerate, even for a moment, a further extension of slavery, believing, as I do, it is a curse—a curse to mankind—a curse to the world." Pettit preferred that no territory be obtained from Mexico rather than have "slave territory" acquired. In August, 1847, John Law, a Democrat and friend of Van Buren, advised the former president: "The Truth is the Mexican War is not popular in the thinking and reflecting majority of our party . . . ." Law added: "We want no addition of slave states."[169] When Congressmen Edward W. McGaughey and Caleb B. Smith voted against an army appropriation bill, the *Indiana State Sentinel* pounced on them, saying: "Indiana has but two federalists in Congress, and they both vote for the Mexicans." After Governor James Whitcomb called for more volunteers to fight the war in the spring of 1847, a staunchly Whig paper at Richmond commented: "Volunteers *may* be found; but we had hoped the people of Indiana being convinced that the war with Mexico is designed alone to secure the annexation of territory upon which to establish the institution of slavery, would refuse to aid the President in his unholy scheme." Several weeks later this paper observed: "Our Recruiting officer left this place, as he came, 'solitary and alone'; not one convert to follow in his train. If Polk wants men to fight his wars he must look for them elsewhere—they are not to be found in old Wayne." But a few months earlier a Whig organ at Muncie had suggested: "We are one of those who think it wrong at *this time* to argue the justice or injustice of the war: it is enough that it is now on our hands, and it is the duty of every American . . . to contribute his mite towards bringing it to a speedy and triumphant termination. When it is ended, we can enquire into the causes, and fix the responsibility on those public officers whose duty it was to conduct the affairs of the government."[170]

Issues concerning the Mexican War increased party and sectional divisions, and opposition to the spread of slavery helped produce a Whig majority in the House for the congressional session of 1847–1848. The Democrats, however, retained their majority in the Senate.[171] At Indiana's congressional elections in August, 1847, the Whigs gained two seats, electing four congressmen against six for the Democrats. Indiana's two Democratic senators, Edward A. Hannegan and Jesse D. Bright, continued in office through Polk's term as president.[172] Early in 1848 the House defeated a resolution, by the large margin of 135 to 41, which suggested peace with Mexico on the basis of no indemnity from Mexico for the cost of the war, a modest compromise regarding the boundary between the United States and Mexico, but with Mexico to pay all just claims due Americans when the war began. Two Hoosier Whigs voted for this resolution, the other two Whigs and five Democrats opposed it, with one Democrat a nonvoter.[173] Immediately thereafter, by the razor thin margin of 82 to 81, the House declared that the war had been *"unnecessarily and unconstitutionally begun by the President of the United States."* Three Indiana Whigs voted for this declaration, five Democrats opposed it, and one from each party was a nonvoter.[174] In March, 1848, the Senate ratified the peace treaty with Mexico, submitted by President Polk, by a tally of 38 to 14. Senators Hannegan and Bright voted for approval. By this treaty the United States obtained roughly 525,000 square miles from which were carved the states of California, Nevada, and Utah, most of New Mexico and Arizona, and parts of Colorado and Wyoming. In securing this vast and largely unsettled area, except for a considerable number of Indians, the United States agreed to pay Mexico $15,000,000; and to assume the claims of Americans against Mexicans to an aggregate of about $3,500,000. Thereby several hundred miles of

California's balmy coastal area were added to the United States, providing excellent harbors for trade, and establishing a southwestern border easier to maintain and defend than it had been before the war.[175]

The acquisition of this extensive region intensified the urgency to determine federal policy about slavery in the territories. In December, 1847, Polk had recommended territorial governments for areas of New Mexico and California, which he said "should never be surrendered to Mexico"; and he once more urged such a government for Oregon. Though silent about slavery in these areas, he apparently preferred that this question be determined by their residents.[176] Later, during consideration of the peace treaty, Hannegan and Bright voted against a proposal to prohibit slavery in the area acquired from Mexico. Four months later when the Senate approved a bill for territorial governments in Oregon, California, and New Mexico the Hoosier senators voted against such a prohibition. On August 2, 1848, as adjournment neared, by the overwhelming count of 128 to 71 the House passed a bill, applying only to Oregon, which prohibited slavery. All ten Indiana congressmen, except John Pettit, voted for its adoption. Pettit, who opposed slavery in the territories, argued that slavery could not exist in a federal territory unless it was authorized by Congress. The bill regarding Oregon was amended in the Senate, by a margin of 33 to 21, so that the Missouri Compromise or 36° 30' line was extended to the Pacific for all federal territories. Hannegan and Bright voted for this compromise, which Polk supported, but all ten Hoosier congressmen refused to concur; and the House likewise refused by the decisive margin of 121 to 82. As the session ended the Senate agreed with the House amendment excluding slavery in Oregon by a vote of 29 to 25, with Hannegan and Bright for its passage.[177] Polk disliked the prohibition of slavery in Oregon, however, he approved the act with the explanation that "Oregon lies far north of 36° 30', the Missouri and Texas compromise line."[178]

Throughout the Mexican War Democrats often contended that it was premature to establish policy about slavery in territory yet to be obtained from Mexico. As indicated above, although

Senators Hannegan and Bright had voted in favor of extending the Missouri Compromise line to the Pacific, none of the Hoosier congressmen, Democrat or Whig, concurred with this proposal which had Polk's support. As Polk's administration approached its end on March 4, 1849, opposition to slavery in federal territories increased among Hoosier politicians. In December, 1848, when the General Assembly was about to elect a senator to succeed Hannegan, several Democratic possibilities for his seat were asked if they believed Congress had the right to exclude slavery in federal territories; and, if so, would they vote for its prohibition. Hannegan, the incumbent, said Congress had such power; and he pledged himself to obey any instructions given him by a majority of the legislature. Governor James Whitcomb stressed his long opposition to slavery, and he promised to vote against it in the territories. John Law and Ebenezer M. Chamberlain said they would vote to exclude slavery. Robert Dale Owen reaffirmed his opposition to the Wilmot Proviso, but he also agreed to vote to exclude slavery.[179] The legislature, heavily dominated by Democrats, elected Governor Whitcomb to succeed Hannegan, giving Whitcomb 75 votes to only 15 for Hannegan on the initial ballot.[180] Several weeks later both the Democratic and Whig state conventions, in nominating candidates for governor for the state election in 1849, called for the exclusion of slavery from the area acquired as a result of the Mexican War. On this item they concurred with the platform of Indiana's newly established Free Soil party. In short, so far as their state platforms were concerned, all three parties had adopted the Wilmot Proviso principle of 1846. But since this principle had been affirmed amid threats of disunion from southern states, it remained to be seen whether Hoosiers would or would not make concessions regarding slavery if such seemed necessary to preserve the Union.[181]

NOTES

CHAPTER 1

1 An especially valuable sketch of Jennings is that by Dorothy Riker, "Jonathan Jennings," *Indiana Magazine of History*, XXVIII (1932), 223–239. Also see Logan Esarey (ed.), *Messages and Papers of Jonathan Jennings, Ratliff Boon, William Hendricks, 1816–1825* (Indianapolis, 1924), 27–28; William Wesley Woollen, *Biographical and Historical Sketches of Early Indiana* (Indianapolis, 1883), 29–41. According to Riker, pp. 223–228, 238, Jennings was born in 1784, "probably in Hunterdon County, New Jersey." While a boy his family moved to Fayette County, western Pennsylvania, where Jennings had some instruction in Latin, Greek, and mathematics at the Cannonsburg grammar school. William Hendricks and William [W.] Wick were among his classmates at this school. In April, 1807, Jennings was admitted to the practice of law at Vincennes. Here he performed some clerical duties at the federal land office, for the territorial legislature, and for the Vincennes University Board of Trustees. By late 1808 Jennings had located in Clark County, where he resided until his death July 26, 1834.

2 Unless otherwise indicated, the discussion and quotations concerning the Constitution of 1816 which follow are based on this document as found in Charles Kettleborough, *Constitution Making in Indiana* (3 vols., Indianapolis, 1916, 1930), I, 83–125. For other concise reviews of the Constitution of 1816, see John D. Barnhart, *Valley of Democracy: The Frontier Versus the Plantation in the Ohio Valley, 1775–1818* (Bloomington, Ind., 1953), 188–196; John D. Barnhart and Dorothy L. Riker, *Indiana to 1816: The Colonial Period* (Indianapolis, 1971), 448–463; R. Carlyle Buley, *The Old Northwest: Pioneer Period, 1815–1840* (2 vols., Indianapolis, 1950), I, 70–78.

3 Kettleborough, *Constitution Making in Indiana*, I, 83–88, 107–108, 112–115, 117.

4 The powers exercised by the General Assembly were not all spelled out in the constitution. For the most part this body exercised any power not contrary to the state or federal constitution.

5 *Ibid.*, 89–96, 101–102, 106. Pursuant to the federal constitution the General Assembly also elected two members of the United States Senate.

6 *Ibid.*, 96–103, 106.

7 *Ibid.*, 103–107.

8 *Ibid.*, 102, 105–107, 118, 119. The office of recorder was omitted in Jennings' official election notice of June 29, 1816. *Ibid.*, 128–129. Dorothy Riker

(ed.), *Executive Proceedings of the State of Indiana, 1816–1836* (Indianapolis, 1947), 8, points out that the first election for this office was held in February, 1817.

9 *Ibid.*, 120–124, 116.

10 *Ibid.*, 121–122. See *ibid.*, 128–129, for Jennings' writ of election to the sheriff of Knox County, and the sheriff's call for the election on August 5, 1816.

11 Thomas Posey to Alexander Devin, Frederick Rapp, David Robb, and James Smith, in Karl J. R. Arndt (ed.), *A Documentary History of the Indiana Decade of the Harmony Society, 1814–1824* (2 vols., Indianapolis, 1975, 1978), I, 232; Vincennes *Western Sun*, July 6, 13, 1816; Vevay *Indiana Register*, July 8, 1816.

12 Vincennes *Western Sun*, July 20, 27, 1816. In the July 27 issue Editor Elihu Stout states: "I am at times almost tempted to fear that I am too partial to those who are not Mr. Jennings's blind admirers—for with me his fortress has never beeh [*sic*] inaccessible."

13 Jonathan Jennings to Josiah Meigs, July 13, 1816, in Clarence Edwin Carter (ed.), *The Territorial Papers of the United States* (vols. 1–28, Washington, D.C., 1934–1975), VIII, 436; Indiana *House Journal*, 1816–17, p. 3. According to Dorothy Riker and Gayle Thornbrough (comps.), *Indiana Election Returns, 1816–1851* (Indianapolis, 1960), 137, the official returns for this election had not been found. They cite the Vincennes *Western Sun*, August 17, 24, 1816, giving the vote from four counties, showing 621 votes for Jennings and 1,399 for Posey. These returns, however, were incomplete.

14 Indiana *House Journal*, 1816–17, p. 3; Riker and Thornbrough (comps.), *Indiana Election Returns, 1816–1851*, p. 159. The four counties whose votes had been received for lieutenant governor gave 1,786 for Harrison, 147 for Vawter. The speaker of the House announced that Abel Findley had received 18 votes for lieutenant governor; John Johnson, 14; Davis Floyd, 13; Amos Lane, 12. These returns were also incomplete.

15 See Kettleborough, *Constitution Making in Indiana*, I, 124–125, for convention delegates; *A Biographical Directory of the Indiana General Assembly* (2 vols., Indianapolis, 1980, 1984), Volume 1, *1816–1899*, Volume 2, *1901–1984*, I, 437, for members of the first legislature; and Gayle Thornbrough and Dorothy Riker (eds.), *Journals of the General Assembly of Indiana Territory, 1805–1815* (Indianapolis, 1950), 953–957, for members of the territorial legislature. The delegates who sat in the first legislative session were: Patrick Beard (Baird), John Boone, James Brownlee, Thomas Carr, Sr., John DePauw, Ezra Ferris, Davis Floyd, John K. Graham, William Graham, Joseph Holman, John Johnson, Dann (Dan) Lynn, Samuel Milroy, James Noble, Dennis Pennington, and William Polke.

16 Indiana *House Journal*, 1816–17, p. 4; Indiana *Senate Journal*, 1816–17, p. 3.

17 Indiana *House Journal*, 1816–17, pp. 10–12.

18 *Ibid.*, 9, 28. On the only ballot New defeated Alexander Holton 23 to 11; there is no tally for the election of Lane; and Lilly received 18 votes to 17 for Milo Davis.

19 *Ibid.*, 85–86. All three judges were elected on initial ballots. Parke got 20 votes to 13 for General Washington Johnston and 1 for Jesse Olds; Raymond obtained 30 votes to 6 for Alexander Dunn and 1 for Jesse Olds; and Test won 21 votes to 16 for John Watts. Parke, soon appointed federal district judge for Indiana, declined appointment; Jennings gave William Prince a recess appointment, and the next legislative session elected him for continuation as associate judge. Riker (ed.), *Executive Proceedings of the State of Indiana, 1816–1836*, pp. 22n, 23, 25, 62.

20 Indiana *Senate Journal*, 1816–17, pp. 58–59, 61–62. Johnson served less than a year before his death in 1817, and Jennings gave Isaac Blackford a recess appointment as his successor. Late in 1817 the Senate, without a dissenting vote, confirmed Blackford for the remainder of Johnson's term. Blackford served on the state Supreme Court from 1817 to 1853. *Ibid.*, 1817–18, pp. 13, 25; Riker (ed.), *Executive Proceedings of the State of Indiana, 1816–1836*, pp. 42, 43, 60, 303, 306; *A Biographical Directory of the Indiana General Assembly*, I, 27.

21 See below, Chapter 9, pp. 453, 455, concerning these elections.

22 According to Riker (ed.), *Executive Proceedings of the State of Indiana, 1816–1836*, pp. 21–23, Jennings commissioned New as secretary of state November 7; Lane and Lilly as treasurer and auditor November 16; Test as circuit judge December 18, Raymond and Parke as circuit judges December 21; and Holman, Johnson, and Scott December 28. Secretary New, elected November 6, began the executive journal on November 7.

23 For the act of admission, see *Annals of Congress*, 14 Congress, 2 session, 1348. See below, Chapter 9, p. 455, regarding the seating of Indiana members of Congress.

24 For the law extending federal legislation over Indiana, see *ibid.*, 1337–1338; for appointment of Parke, Blake, and Vawter, see *Journal of the Executive Proceedings of the Senate of the United States . . .* (3 vols., Washington, D.C., 1828), III, 73. The Indiana House of Representatives "unanimously" urged Parke's appointment, and the Indiana Senate supported it, perhaps likewise, but its vote is not recorded. Indiana *House Journal*, 1816–17, p. 59; Indiana *Senate Journal*, 1816–17, p. 41.

25 For items in the constitution about counties, see Kettleborough, *Constitution Making in Indiana*, I, 102, 104–107, 117–122.

26 *Ibid.*, 121–122; *Laws of Indiana*, 1816–17, pp. 109–117, 154.

27 *Laws of Indiana*, 1816–17, pp. 119–125; Riker (ed.), *Executive Proceedings of the State of Indiana, 1816–1836*, p. 12. Riker's introduction, pages 1–12, offers considerable information about the transition from territorial to state government.

28 *Laws of Indiana*, 1816–17, pp. 125–130. As indicated in the citations given in the index to Louis B. Ewbank and Dorothy L. Riker (eds.), *The Laws of Indiana Territory, 1809–1816* (Indianapolis, 1934), separate charters had been given to at least these ten towns during the territorial era: Brookville, Centerville (Centreville), Charlestown, Jeffersonville, Lawrenceburg, Lexington, Salem,

Salisbury, Vevay, and Vincennes. The law for the incorporation of towns limited voting to qualified voters who had been local residents for six months and had either pursued a trade or occupation, or had become a freehold owner of property in the town. The act for the regulation of Salem is in *ibid.*, 724–727, since Salem does not appear in the index.

[29] Unless otherwise indicated, in the ensuing discussion items about *ordinary state expenditures* and *ordinary state revenue* are based on the annual reports of the state treasurer as found in: *Acts* (special), 1817–18, p. 123 (fiscal 1816–17); Indiana *House Journal*, 1818–19, pp. 71–72 (fiscal 1817–18); *ibid.*, 1819–20, pp. 42–43 (fiscal 1818–19); Indiana *Senate Journal*, 1820–21, pp. 22–24 (fiscal 1819–20); Indiana *House Journal*, 1821–22, pp. 26–27 (fiscal 1820–21); Indiana *Senate Journal*, 1822–23, pp. 32–34 (fiscal 1821–22). Donald F. Carmony, "Historical Background of the Restrictions Against State Debt in the Indiana Constitution of 1851," *Indiana Magazine of History*, XLVII (1951), 130, estimates that territorial government costs averaged about $10,000 from 1800 to 1816, with approximately two thirds of the cost provided by the federal treasury. Usual and ongoing costs of state government, paid for from taxes and borrowing, are considered ordinary expenditures. Special funds created for designated purposes are not so considered. At times reports of the state treasurer do not make it clear whether particular items are or are not ordinary expenditures, however, the items in question are negligible from 1816 to 1822. Legislative costs also included items which were listed as incidental, specific, or miscellaneous costs during the rest of the pioneer era. Judicial costs were presumably almost entirely for compensation to the three supreme judges and their assistants. During fiscal 1820–21 the sum of $100 first appeared as pay to an attorney general. House rent, when listed by the treasurer as a separate item, has been counted as an executive cost. When not so listed this item was probably buried among legislative expenses. Miscellaneous items spent by authority of the governor were termed contingent costs. Items listed as miscellaneous in the tables regarding expenditures and revenues, consist of items which fit no other category in these tables. Two special funds, the Saline and the Indianapolis funds, had their beginnings in these years. There is room for some honest differences in interpreting and segregating ordinary expenditures and ordinary revenue from other items in the annual reports of the treasurer, but it is believed that the data offered regarding same is a *close approximation of such expenditures and revenues*. The Saline Fund included money from the sale or rental of salt springs; the Indianapolis Fund included money from the sale of lots from the site of the state capital.

[30] *Laws of Indiana*, 1816–17, p. 171; *Acts* (special), 1817–18, pp. 67–68. As indicated in Kettleborough, *Constitution Making in Indiana*, I, 119, the Constitution of 1816 restricted pay to legislators to a maximum of $2 per day of service, and $2 for every twenty-five miles of "travel on the most usual route" to and from sessions prior to 1819. Moreover, an increase in pay could not be effective at the session approving it. For beginning and closing dates of sessions from

1818 to 1822, see John G. Rauch and Nellie C. Armstrong, *A Bibliography of the Laws of Indiana, 1788–1927* (Indianapolis, 1928), 68.

31 *Laws of Indiana*, 1816–17, pp. 148, 161, 171; *Acts* (special), 1817–18, pp. 67, 81, 83. According to the constitution the salaries given these judicial and executive officials was the maximum allowed prior to 1819. The constitution prohibited either an increase or decrease in salary of the governor during his elected term, while that for judges could not be decreased during their terms. Kettleborough, *Constitution Making in Indiana*, I, 119, 97, 105.

32 Sheriffs as collectors were allowed 9 percent of the state *tax revenue* collected for obtaining it, plus some fees and commissions and minus some penalties. Whether their percentage averaged more or less than 9 percent is uncertain, but this percentage is presumed to be roughly the sum received by sheriffs. *Laws of Indiana*, 1816–17, pp. 138–139; *ibid*, 1817–18, pp. 266–268. No other percentage for collectors has been found in legislation about assessing and collecting taxes for 1816–22. As indicated below, Chapter 3, note 44, during 1822–31 collectors were allowed 9 percent of the tax revenue collected, subject to modification by fees, commissions, and penalties.

33 Concerning the items included in this $30,800 owed the bank, and when they were borrowed, see Donald F. Carmony, Indiana Public Finance, 1816–1826 (Ph.D. dissertation, Indiana University, 1940), 167–168. The suit against unnamed citizens of Harrison County resulted from a bond that Dennis Pennington, John Tipton, Davis Floyd, and others had executed to the state to obtain the mandate in the Constitution of 1816 that Corydon "shall be the seat of Government of the state of Indiana, until the year eighteen hundred and twenty-five and until removed by law." Kettleborough, *Constitution Making in Indiana*, I, 118, 138–139, 146; Justin E. Walsh, *The Centennial History of the Indiana General Assembly, 1816–1978* (Indianapolis, 1987), 4–5.

34 Indiana *House Journal*, 1816–17, p. 11; *Laws of Indiana*, 1816–17, pp. 132–133; *ibid.*, 1817–18, p. 259. During 1816–1822, the state tax levy was only on land, not on either improvements thereon or on personal property.

35 Indiana *House Journal*, 1820–21, pp. 11–12, 186.

36 *Laws of Indiana*, 1820–21, pp. 8–9, 40–44, 90–91.

37 See letters from "C" in Corydon *Indiana Gazette*, October 25, November 1, 8, 1821; Indiana *House Journal*, 1821–22, pp. 18–19.

38 *Laws of Indiana*, 1821–22, pp. 105–110; Corydon *Indiana Gazette*, January 21, 1822. Representative General Washington Johnston, of Knox County, commented: "*The Poll tax.*—It has always been considered in an odious light in the United States, and should be resorted to only in cases of emergency. The principal reason of its continuance at the last session, was two-fold—1st. to include those persons in the new purchase whose lands could not be taxed by the articles of compact with the United States, by which we became an independent state, and—2dly. to reduce the tax on lands properly taxable, and augment the revenue." Johnston explained that "those above 50 . . . contend, that being then in the decline of life, they should be viewed with a favorable eye, and receive some

little exemption—The young dislike it (and in fact they dislike all direct taxation) because wealth, and not age, should support our government in its fiscal concerns." Vincennes *Western Sun*, October 5, 1822.

39 Vincennes *Indiana Centinel & Public Advertiser*, November 11, 1820; Corydon *Indiana Gazette*, February 1, 1821; Indiana *House Journal*, 1821–22, pp. 348–349. For the act establishing the office of attorney general, see *Laws of Indiana*, 1821–22, pp. 72–74.

40 Vincennes *Western Sun*, April 6, 1822, quoting Lawrenceburgh *Oracle*; Richmond *Weekly Intelligencer*, September 4, 1822.

41 As indicated in Kettleborough, *Constitution Making in Indiana*, I, 81–83, as part of the quid pro quo for federal grants of land and money, the Constitutional Convention of 1816 agreed that starting December 1, 1816, federal lands sold in Indiana would be free of both state and local taxation for five years after its purchase. Hence, such land was tax exempt until 1822. The highest levy on first rate land, in effect less than half of the Jennings-Boon period, levied only $1.20 on eighty acres of such land. Moreover, males who owned no land were not taxed for state revenue until the poll tax of 50 cents became effective for 1822.

42 For the principal legislation regarding the assessing and collecting of state revenue, 1816–22, see *Laws of Indiana*, 1816–17, pp. 131–140; *ibid.*, 1817–18, pp. 256–273; *ibid.*, 1818–19, pp. 66–67; *ibid.*, 1819–20, pp. 150–153; *ibid.*, 1820–21, pp. 8–9; *ibid.*, 1821–22, pp. 105–108.

43 For instance, see report of House Ways and Means Committee, Indiana *House Journal*, 1820–21, pp. 184–186; comments of Auditor Lilly, *ibid.*, 79; comments of Governor Boon, *ibid.*, 1822–23, p. 11.

44 The unfavorable context for banking is emphasized in Logan Esarey, *State Banking in Indiana, 1814–1873* (Bloomington, Ind., 1912), 219–223, 227–229, 241–242.

45 Kettleborough, *Constitution Making in Indiana*, I, 115. For examples of unchartered banks in territorial Indiana, see Carmony, Indiana Public Finance, 1800–1826, pp. 556–559; Esarey, *State Banking in Indiana, 1814–1873*, p. 226.

46 The charters are in Ewbank and Riker (eds.), *Laws of Indiana Territory, 1809–1816*, pp. 747–763. For the beginning of the Vincennes bank, see Vincennes *Western Sun*, December 3, 24, 1814; Arndt (ed.), *Indiana Decade of the Harmony Society*, I, 82, 195. Regarding the Madison bank, see Vincennes *Western Sun*, April 13, 1816; Vevay *Indiana Register*, July 8, 1816.

47 *Laws of Indiana*, 1816–17, pp. 185–191; Vincennes *Western Sun*, March 22, 1817.

48 For examples of this error, see Esarey, *State Banking in Indiana, 1814–1873*, pp. 227–229; Logan Esarey, *A History of Indiana: From Its Exploration to 1850* (2 vols., Fort Wayne, Ind., 1924), I, 266–267; Buley, *The Old Northwest*, I, 572; John D. Barnhart and Donald F. Carmony, *Indiana: From Frontier to Industrial Commonwealth* (4 vols., New York, 1954), I, 305–306. Although Carmony made this error years ago, he finds solace in the fact that his mentors for Indiana history, Logan Esarey and R. Carlyle Buley, had made the same error. The arrangement

calling for taking stock subscriptions at fourteen different places seemed to suggest the organization of fourteen branches. Realization of this error was prompted by the observation that both the adoption law and Constitution of 1816 prohibited more than one branch for any three counties.

⁴⁹ For the association of these and other leaders, see Esarey (ed.), *Messages and Papers of Jennings, Boon, Hendricks*, 124–132, 140–150, 172–215, 226–232 *passim*; *Laws of Indiana*, 1816–17, pp. 185–186, naming persons to help obtain subscriptions for additional stock. For Jennings' resignation, see Corydon *Indiana Gazette*, November 27, 1819.

⁵⁰ *American State Papers, Finance*, IV, 713–714. For related items concerning inclusion of the First State Bank for receipt of federal deposits, see *ibid.*, 521–522, 524–525, 783, 796, and *passim*.

⁵¹ *Ibid.*, 262–263, 362–364, 718–719, 796, 819–820, and *passim*.

⁵² *Ibid.*, III, 734–739; IV, 688, and *passim*.

⁵³ Vincennes *Western Sun*, March 8, 1817; Arndt, *Indiana Decade of the Harmony Society*, I, 440–442. Arndt indicates that the petition to the legislature including this request was apparently drafted about January, 1818.

⁵⁴ Vincennes *Western Sun*, May 1, 1819; Indiana *House Journal*, 1819–20, pp. 13, 14, 64–66, 112–113, 156, 329–331, 334 and *passim*.

⁵⁵ Vincennes *Western Sun*, June 10, July 22, 1820.

⁵⁶ *Biographical Directory of the Indiana General Assembly*, I, 440–442, for members of the 1820–21 versus the 1819–20 session; Corydon *Indiana Gazette*, December 7, 1820, for Jennings' letter requesting information and the item about the Vevay officer who used this branch for benefit of himself and friends; Indiana *House Journal*, 1820–21, pp. 8–11, for the governor's remarks; Brookville *Enquirer*, December 19, 1820, for comment of the Brookville editor. Because the data about credits and debits for the parent bank and branches, as in the Corydon *Indiana Democrat*, December 7, 1820, are apparently both incomplete and inaccurate, these data are taken from the parent bank and branch bank statements as found in Vincennes *Indiana Centinel-Extra*, December 23, 1820. Esarey (ed.), *Messages and Papers of Jennings, Boon, Hendricks*, 124–133, uses the *Indiana Gazette* as the source about credits and debits and related items, but his data have various errors.

⁵⁷ Indiana *House Journal*, 1820–21, pp. 14, 16, 26, 35–36, 97–99, 100–101, 113, 248–249, 290–292 and *passim*; Corydon *Indiana Gazette*, December 14, 1820; *Laws of Indiana*, 1820–21, pp. 11–13, 34–36, the former applying to unchartered banks, the latter to those chartered. Since the Constitution of 1816 prohibited unchartered banks, part of this legislation seems to have been de facto recognition of banking contrary to the constitution.

⁵⁸ Vincennes *Western Sun*, February 3, 1821; Vincennes *Indiana Centinel*, February 17, 1821. As noted in note 60 below, the Steam Mill Company apparently owed the bank about $91,000.

⁵⁹ Vincennes *Indiana Centinel*, March 10, 1821; Vincennes *Western Sun*, March 17, 1821, quoting Vincennes *Indiana Centinel*; *American State Papers, Finance*, III, 738–739.

60 Vincennes *Western Sun*, June 16, 1821; Corydon *Indiana Gazette*, June 28, 1821; Vincennes *Western Sun*, July 28, 1821, quoting Louisville *Public Advertiser*. The last citation includes an item about "'$91,000, or thereabouts'" which the company had obtained from the bank.

61 Vincennes *Indiana Centinel*, June 16, 1821; Corydon *Indiana Gazette*, August 30, 1821; Vincennes *Western Sun*, June 23, 1821. According to *Biographical Directory of the Indiana General Assembly*, I, 91, Daniel was a Gibson County lawyer who had served in the House of Representatives at two previous sessions. Hence, he was probably well acquainted with the management of the First State Bank.

62 Indiana *House Journal*, 1821–22, pp. 15–17; Corydon *Indiana Gazette*, October 25, 1821. Both the Charlestown *Indiana Intelligencer and Farmer's Friend*, October 31, 1821, and the Madison *Indiana Republican*, November 8, 1821, quoted the *Indiana Gazette* concerning this item. Regarding return of bonds from the federal government and payment of the state debt to the bank, see Carmony, Indiana Public Finance, 1800–1826, pp. 168–169, 583–584.

63 *Laws of Indiana*, 1821–22, pp. 61, 48–52.

64 Vincennes *Western Sun*, March 9, 23, May 4, 1822. This paper carried announcements of bank dividends, declared by its officials, often at from 8 to 10 percent, in its issues for May 31, November 29, 1817, June 6, December 12, 1818, June 5, 1819, June 16, 1821. The payment in May, 1817, came the same month that the first federal deposits were received. The announcements for 1817 were by Isaac Blackford as cashier, later a member of the state Supreme Court, who declined to vote when the status of the bank came before the court in 1823. See note 66 below. It is an understatement to suggest that the payment of these, and perhaps additional dividends, reflects unfavorably on the fairness, honesty, and integrity of the directors of the First State Bank. Since payments on stock subscribed were made from time to time, perhaps frequent stock dividends were a means of helping stockholders increase the amount of *paid for* stock which they held.

65 Vincennes *Western Sun*, July 6, 13, 1822; Corydon *Indiana Gazette*, July 18, 1822; Esarey, *State Banking in Indiana, 1814–1873*, pp. 240–241.

66 Vincennes *Western Sun*, November 22, December 6, 13, 1823; Indianapolis *Gazette*, November 25, 1823, quoting Corydon *Indiana Gazette*; Indianapolis *Western Censor, & Emigrants Guide*, December 1, 1823. According to the Indianapolis *Gazette*, previous to the decision Judge Isaac Blackford left the bench because of having real estate transactions with the bank that might be affected by the Supreme Court decision. As mentioned in note 64 above, Blackford had been cashier of the bank in 1817. See also *The President, Directors, and Company of the Bank of Vincennes, the State Bank of Indiana v. the State of Indiana* in *Indiana Reports*, I, 267–285.

67 *Indiana Gazetteer* (1849), 120. The Indianapolis *Indiana State Sentinel* (semi-weekly), May 16, 1849, in noting forthcoming publication of this *Indiana Gazetteer*, states: "Mr. SAMUEL MERRILL has been for some time engaged in compiling it . . . ." Pages 125 and 298 of the *Gazetteer* have comments which

seem to connect with Merrill's removal of the capital to Indianapolis in 1824 and a visit to Madison in 1816.

68 Madison *Indiana Republican*, March 6, 1817; Vincennes *Western Sun*, July 5, 1817. In 1821 the Lawrenceburg branch reportedly declined to respond to a request from the governor concerning its situation on the ground that such an investigation was contrary to its charter. Evansville *Gazette*, May 15, 1821; Esarey (ed.), *Messages and Papers of Jennings, Boon, Hendricks*, 184–185.

69 For instance, see Vincennes *Western Sun*, February 28, 1818, September 20, 1820, January 6, 1821, January 5, 1822; Corydon *Indiana Gazette*, September 17, 1820, February 1, 1821, March 28, 1822; Indianapolis *Gazette*, July 13, 1822, January 11, 1825, November 30, 1826.

70 For correspondence about the Madison bank for federal deposits and early deposits in the bank, see *American State Papers, Finance*, III, 739–741; *ibid.*, IV, 692, 701 (for draft of $140,000 pending against the bank according to letter of September 18, 1821), 725, 739–740, 744 (May 11, 1820, letter of Hendricks and Noble), 746–747, 752, 757, 759, 956–957.

71 Esarey, *State Banking in Indiana, 1814–1873*, pp. 225–226; *U.S. Statutes at Large*, 22 Congress, 1 session, IV, 569; Indianapolis *Indiana Democrat*, October 13, 1832; Vincennes *Western Sun*, October 13, 1832, quoting [Lawrenceburgh] *Indiana Palladium*.

72 *Laws of Indiana*, 1834–35, p. 165; *Indiana Gazetteer* (1849), 120.

73 Concerning Jennings' appointment and the resulting treaty, see below, pp. 27, 29.

74 Vincennes *Western Sun*, February 22, 1817, October 3, 1818 (quotation). For other attacks on Jennings, see February 15, March 1, 15, 29, April 12, 1817, August 22, September 5, 26, 1818.

75 Jennings to Harrison, October 3, 1818, Indiana *House Journal*, 1818–19, pp. 47–48.

76 Christopher Harrison, "Lieutenant and acting Governor of the State of Indiana," to editor of Jeffersonville *Indianian*, Corydon, November 2, 1818, in Vincennes *Western Sun*, November 14, 1818. Harrison says he received Jennings' letter October 13, got the seal on the 17th, and returned to Corydon on the 30th to learn that Jennings had obtained it.

77 Vincennes *Western Sun*, November 14, 28, 1818.

78 Kettleborough, *Constitution Making in Indiana*, I, 97, 118–119, 99. In the letter cited in note 76 above, Harrison refers to constitutional provisions against a governor holding another federal or state office, or more than one lucrative office, as the basis for his view that Jennings "had virtually and constitutionally abdicated his office of Governor of this state."

79 Indiana *House Journal*, 1818–19, pp. 5–6, 6–7; Indiana *Senate Journal*, 1818–19, pp. 7–8.

80 Indiana *House Journal*, 1818–19, pp. 12–14, 18. In his address Jennings made no comment about his service as Indian commissioner or his dispute with Harrison.

81 *Ibid.*, 14–15, 25–26, 28–29; Indiana *Senate Journal*, 1818–19, pp. 19–20. Harrison mentioned the "statement of facts" he had given the public in the Jeffersonville *Indianian* (see note 76 above), which he said had appeared in nearly every newspaper in the state. He also offered additional comment in support of his claim that Jennings had held a federal commission.

82 Indiana *House Journal*, 1818–19, pp. 42–50. The three witnesses seem to have suffered poor eyesight, hearing, or memory on Jennings' behalf! As indicated in Dorothy Riker, *Unedited Letters of Jonathan Jennings* (Indianapolis, 1932), 240, quoting the Madison *Western Clarion*, July 24, 1822, several years after the dispute with Harrison, Jennings explained why he had become a commissioner, and said of his commission: "I destroyed it in disgust." He also asserted that the auditor of state had given a certificate indicating that he had neither asked for nor received any pay from the state while negotiating with the Indians.

83 Indiana *House Journal*, 1818–19, pp. 41–42, 55–56. Opponents of Jennings were probably more concerned about making political capital from the dispute between Jennings and Harrison than in the constitutionality of Jennings having served as a commissioner to treat with the Indians.

84 *Ibid.*, 12–13, 55–56, for key House votes about joining with the Senate in hearing communications from Jennings, and then for ending its investigation. In considering the revision between eastern and western counties, Harrison, Washington, and Jackson are counted with the eastern counties, all other counties as western.

85 Vincennes *Western Sun*, January 2, 1819; Corydon *Indiana Gazette*, February 13, 1819. The editor of the latter paper said that the [Lawrenceburgh] *Dearborn Gazette* was misinformed on the subject of claiming that Jennings had received pay as governor while serving as commissioner.

86 Madison *Indiana Republican*, April 3, 1819; Corydon *Indiana Gazette*, April 3, May 8, 1819; Brookville *Enquirer and Indiana Telegraph*, April 9, 23, 1819; Vincennes *Western Sun*, April 10, 17, 1819.

87 Jonathan Woodbury to Tipton, April 11, 1819, in Nellie A. Robertson and Dorothy Riker (eds.), *The John Tipton Papers* (3 vols., Indianapolis, 1942), I, 155–156; Brookville *Enquirer and Indiana Telegraph*, April 23, 1819; Corydon *Indiana Gazette*, May 8, 1819, for Jennings' announcement of his candidacy. Woodbury indicated that some in southeastern Indiana had brought Judge "Holdman" forward as a candidate for governor, but he thought he would "Stand but a poor poll" for this office.

88 Vincennes *Western Sun*, May 29, June 5, 19, July 17, 24, 31, 1819. For quoted items see issues for June 19 and July 24.

89 *Ibid.*, July 3, 1819. In its issue for June 26, 1819, the *Western Sun* quoted the Charlestown *Indiana Intelligencer* saying that it had received a letter from Holman in the last mail stating that he was not a candidate for governor.

90 Vincennes *Western Sun*, July 17, 24, 31, 1819. See issue of July 31 for quoted comments.

91 Riker and Thornbrough (comps.), *Indiana Election Returns, 1816–1851*, pp. 137–138. In announcing the vote to the General Assembly on December 7, 1819, the speaker of the House reported the vote for governor as: Jennings, 9,168; Harrison, 2,007; Samuel Carr, 80; Peter Allen, 1. Evidently the speaker had not received the vote of various counties. Indiana *House Journal*, 1819–20, p. 26. These six western counties voted for Jennings: Orange, Pike, Posey, Spencer, Vigo, Warrick; whereas Knox, where Stout's paper was published, and adjoining Gibson gave majorities to Harrison. Posey County, where the Harmonists lived, gave Jennings 410 votes to 93 for Harrison suggesting that the governor probably obtained the preponderance of the Harmonist vote.

92 Corydon *Indiana Gazette*, January 9, 30, February 13, May 22, 1819; Madison *Indiana Republican*, February 27, May 15, 22, 1819. Sketches of Boon, Clark, DePauw, and Pennington are in *Biographical Directory of the Indiana General Assembly*, I, 31, 64–65, 99, 311.

93 Corydon *Indiana Gazette*, June 5, 12, 1819; Riker and Thornbrough (comps.), *Indiana Election Returns, 1816–1851*, p. 186n.

94 Corydon *Indiana Gazette*, July 10, 31, 1819; Vincennes *Western Sun*, July 17, 24, 1819.

95 Unofficial returns for twenty counties show 7,397 votes for Boon and 3,882 for DePauw. Riker and Thornbrough (comps.), *Indiana Election Returns, 1816–1851*, pp. 159–160. The vote, as announced by the speaker to the General Assembly, gives Boon 7,150 and DePauw 3,422, plus meager votes for four other individuals. Indiana *House Journal*, 1819–20, p. 26.

96 Indiana *House Journal*, 1819–20, pp. 105–114; Indiana *Senate Journal*, 1819–20, p. 62. Lane got 27 votes to 10 for James B. Slaughter; Lilly received 36 votes, with none against him.

97 Indiana *Senate Journal*, 1820–21, pp. 15, 32–33, 48–49, 54; Indiana *House Journal*, 1820–21, pp. 40–41, 69–70, 77. On the initial ballot New received 21 votes; Armstrong Brandon, 13; Harbin H. Moore, 3. Perhaps reflecting the committee's criticism, before adjournment the legislature enacted a law, which the governor signed, making it the duty of the secretary or his deputy to be at his office every day in the year, except Sundays, from the hours of ten to twelve. *Laws of Indiana*, 1820–21, pp. 101–102.

98 Kettleborough, *Constitution Making in Indiana*, I, 89, 91. The constitution authorized the General Assembly to require an enumeration of voters within two years after its first session as a basis for a legislative apportionment, but this option was not used. After the aggregate of voters reached 22,000, the number of representatives could not exceed one hundred and that of senators was limited to a maximum of fifty.

99 For the enumeration of 1815 and the apportionment of 1816, see *ibid.*, 68–69, 122–123. Much information about the 1816 apportionment is in Leon H. Wallace, "Legislative Apportionment in Indiana: A Case History," *Indiana Law Journal*, XLII (1966), 10–15 and Appendix B–1 and B–2. This scholarly study, with its massive data and summary tables, is an indispensable source about leg-

islative apportionments in Indiana from territorial days to the middle 1960s. As Wallace notes, a supplemental report about the 1815 enumeration added an estimated 223 additional voters for Harrison County. This item as well as the addition of two new counties and the growing and shifting nature of the population were probably considered by the convention delegates in making the legislative apportionment for the new state. For maps showing the apportionment by counties for both representatives and senators, see Walsh, *Centennial History of the Indiana General Assembly*, 730–732.

[100] The precedent that districts having plural representation elect them on an at large basis further suggests the attachment to county lines by the framers of the constitution.

[101] Principally from state enumerations of voters preceding apportionments and from the apportionments, the author has assembled considerable data which indicate that throughout the pioneer era newer and less settled sections of the state were usually given somewhat more representation in the House of Representatives than they were entitled to in proportion to their number of voters. For the apportionment of 1816 the author considers the following as counties of the eastern part of Southern Indiana: Clark, Dearborn, Franklin, Jefferson, Harrison, Jackson, Switzerland, and Washington; its western counties as: Gibson, Knox, Orange, Perry, Posey, and Warrick. Wayne County, in the eastern part of Central Indiana, was the only other organized county at this time. Since county lines frequently changed in the pioneer era, at times it is uncertain whether some counties were mainly in Southern, Central, or Northern Indiana.

[102] For counties added from 1816 to 1821, see George Pence and Nellie C. Armstrong, *Indiana Boundaries: Territory, State, and County* (Indianapolis, 1933), 30–37, 146–157. This source indicates numerous changes in boundaries and size of counties in these years. Pence and Armstrong name thirty-eight counties in the apportionment of 1821, however, as indicated *ibid.*, 228–229, 406–407, 614–615, 650–651, at least the four counties of Bartholomew, Greene, Morgan, and Parke did not become *organized* counties until after the passage of the apportionment act which, as cited in note 106 below, was approved on January 2, 1821. The four counties named were presumably included in anticipation of their early organization.

[103] *Laws of Indiana*, 1816–17, pp. 194, 199, 207, 210; *ibid.*, 1817–18, p. 176. For the one exception, see note 98, above. As noted in the Indianapolis *Indiana Journal*, January 2, 1841, Senator Charles H. Test, a Whig senator from Wayne County, suggested that "attaching counties to districts of Senators already elected" would not be without precedent since for years the legislature had attached new counties to districts of incumbent senators.

[104] *Laws of Indiana*, 1819–20, pp. 141–143, 95–96. Pages 95–96 give a law requiring John Vawter to count voters in the New Purchase, "lately acquired from the Indians," which area had not yet been organized into counties.

[105] Brookville *Enquirer*, May 16, 1820; Indiana *Senate Journal*, 1820–21, pp. 94–95, for the secretary's comment. See Indiana *House Journal*, 1820–21, pp. 74–

75, reporting the enumeration of voters for about two thirds of the counties. With 63,897 residents and 12,112 voters according to the territorial count of 1815, this suggests approximately one voter for every 5.28 residents. Since the federal census of 1820 reported a population of 147,178 inhabitants, on this same ratio of voters to population there would have been 27,875 voters in 1820.

106 *Laws of Indiana*, 1820–21, pp. 87–90. Both the *Western Sun* and Governor James B. Ray asserted that the 1821 apportionment was based on one senator for 1,800 voters and one representative for every 700 voters. These items suggest roughly 28,800 and 30,100 voters respectively. Vincennes *Western Sun*, February 3, 1821; Indiana *House Journal*, 1825–26, p. 44. Ray's comment was made to the legislature that made the next general legislative apportionment. According to *Biographical Directory of the Indiana General Assembly*, 575, the legislative apportionment of 1821 included thirty-eight counties in representative districts, but only thirty-seven counties for senatorial districts since Morgan County was included for a representative district but was not included for a senatorial district. As indicated in *Laws of Indiana*, 1821–22, pp. 35–38, Morgan County was created by an act approved December 31, 1821, effective February 15, 1822. As noted below, Chapter 3, note 105, Morgan and other counties were given representation in the General Assembly by an interim or special appropriation act of 1823. The inclusion of Morgan in a representative district may have been an error. But as may be seen *ibid*., 1820–21, pp. 63–66, an act, approved soon after the general apportionment act created Parke County, attached it to Vigo County for a representative district, and to Greene, Owen, Sullivan, and Vigo counties for a senatorial district. Hence Parke County is considered as part of the apportionment of 1821. The apportionment maps in Walsh, *Centennial History of the Indiana General Assembly*, 733–734, and the apportionment data in *Biographical Directory of the Indiana General Assembly*, I, 575–589, illustrate the confusing nature of the legislative apportionment of 1821.

107 The data about distribution of representatives among Southern, Central, and Northern Indiana is merely a close approximation of the actual distribution. Changing county lines make for some inconsistency in areas designated as Southern, Central, and Northern Indiana, and some representative districts were partially in two of these three areas. Of the thirty-eight counties named in the 1821 apportionment of representative districts the author considers the following as eastern counties of Southern Indiana counties: Bartholomew, Clark, Dearborn, Floyd, Franklin, Harrison, Jackson, Jefferson, Jennings, Ripley, Scott, Switzerland, and Washington; its western counties as: Crawford, Daviess, Dubois, Gibson, Greene, Knox, Lawrence, Martin, Monroe, Orange, Perry, Pike, Posey, Spencer, Sullivan, Vanderburgh, and Warrick. The eastern counties of Central Indiana: Fayette, Randolph, Union, and Wayne; its western counties as: Morgan, Parke, Owen, and Vigo. As yet there was no county in Northern Indiana, but as noted in Pence and Armstrong, *Indiana Boundaries*, 704–709, a strip along the eastern border of Indiana, north to the Michigan line, was included as part of Randolph County.

[108] Kettleborough, *Constitution Making in Indiana*, I, 107–108. The property qualification for voting had been eliminated in 1811, but payment of a county or territorial tax remained a requirement until statehood. *Ibid.*, 58–59.

[109] Francis S. Philbrick (ed.), *The Laws of Indiana Territory, 1801–1809* (Springfield, Ill., 1930, reprinted Indianapolis, 1931), 393 (law of 1807); Ewbank and Riker (eds.), *Laws of Indiana Territory, 1809–1816*, pp. 37–38, 67, 230–231 (law of 1811), 490 (law of 1814).

[110] *Journal of the Convention of the Indiana Territory* . . . (Louisville, Ky., 1816), reprinted in *Indiana Magazine of History*, LXI (1965), 15, 22–23; Kettleborough, *Constitution Making in Indiana*, I, xxvii–xxix.

[111] *Laws of Indiana*, 1820–21, pp. 136–137; Vincennes *Western Sun*, May 12, 1821; Vincennes *Indiana Centinel*, June 30, 1821; Kettleborough, *Constitution Making in Indiana*, I, xxviii–xxix.

[112] Indiana *Senate Journal*, 1821–22, pp. 92, 101; Vincennes *Western Sun*, August 11, 1821; Vincennes *Indiana Centinel*, August 11, 1821. The *Centinel*, after saying Knox County had favored "*balloting*" nearly two to one added, probably much too optimistically, "and there is little doubt that nine tenths of the votes in the state will support the correctness of our choice."

[113] Indiana *House Journal*, 1821–22, pp. 222–226, 325–326; Indiana *Senate Journal*, 1821–22, pp. 107, 222–223.

[114] Indiana *House Journal*, 1821–22, pp. 326–327; Indiana *Senate Journal*, 1821–22, pp. 222–223. For a very comprehensive discussion of oral versus ballot voting from the constitutional convention through the legislative session of 1821–22, plus some of the key documents resulting in a reaffirmation of ballot voting, see Kettleborough, *Constitution Making in Indiana*, I, xxvii–xxxiii, 140–144.

[115] *Laws of Indiana*, 1816–17, pp. 85–92. When two or more counties were joined for a representative or senatorial district, the county returns were given the sheriffs of the counties who met and jointly issued certificates of election to the persons having the most votes. If a tie resulted, the sheriffs chose the winner by lot. Perhaps because this legislation was not entirely clear concerning the settlement of contested local elections by the commissioners, an act of the ensuing session made this authority explicit. *Ibid.*, 1817–18, p. 175.

[116] Kettleborough, *Constitution Making in Indiana*, I, 92, 96–97.

[117] *Laws of Indiana*, 1816–17, pp. 87, 90; Kettleborough, *Constitution Making in Indiana*, I, 116.

[118] Madison *Indiana Republican*, July 24, 1819. For examples of these and related criticisms, see *ibid.*, July 27, August 31, 1820; Corydon *Indiana Gazette*, August 10, 1820. Also see Walsh, *Centennial History of the Indiana General Assembly*, 78–81.

[119] Corydon *Indiana Gazette*, August 8, 1822. The 1816 Constitution provided that voters were entitled to vote in the county of their residence; the law of 1817, cited in note 115 above, provided for voting places in all townships but it did not restrict voters to those places. Not until 1845 was a law passed that required voters to cast their ballots in their townships of residence.

120 The federal census of 1810 reported 24,520 inhabitants; the territorial census of 1815, 63,897; the federal census of 1820, 147,178. The author *estimates* that the number was roughly 80,000 in December, 1816, when Congress admitted Indiana.

121 Buley, *The Old Northwest*, I, 432–436, 459–465. For vivid descriptions concerning the hardships and hazards of pioneer travel and transportation, see *passim* comments in Harlow Lindley (ed.), *Indiana as Seen by Early Travelers . . .* (Indianapolis, 1916); Shirley S. McCord (comp.), *Travel Accounts of Indiana, 1679–1961 . . .* (Indianapolis, 1970), 79–195; Oliver H. Smith, *Early Indiana Trials and Sketches* (Cincinnati, 1858). As such sources suggest very similar hardships and hazards existed throughout the pioneer era.

122 John Candee Dean (ed.), *Journal of Thomas Dean* (Indianapolis, 1918), 294, 298; McCord (comp.), *Travel Accounts of Indiana, 1679–1961*, p. 117; Smith, *Early Indiana Trials and Sketches*, 118–119.

123 George R. Wilson, *Early Indiana Trails and Surveys* (Indianapolis, 1919), 349–401. The Buffalo Trace, connecting Louisville and Vincennes, was an especially important trail. *Ibid.*, 349–350, 364–367. For the predominance of forested land, see R. O. Petty and M. T. Jackson concerning "Plant Communities," 264–294, in Alton A. Lindsey (ed.), *Natural Features of Indiana* (Indianapolis, 1966). See pp. 284–285 for map suggesting the approximate distribution of forests, wetlands, and prairies as of 1816. *Ibid.*, 288, states that "approximately 13% of the Indiana landscape" was prairie in 1816.

124 George R. Wilson and Gayle Thornbrough, *The Buffalo Trace* (Indianapolis, 1946), 245; *Laws of Indiana*, 1821–22, p. 167, providing that the Three Per Cent Fund roads should be "opened forty-eight feet wide, and take off all timber even with the ground; except such as are eighteen inches and upwards, which shall be cut at the usual height of twelve inches."

125 *Laws of Indiana*, 1816–17, pp. 72–84, quotations, 78, 81.

126 *Ibid.*, 1818–19, pp. 69–74; *ibid.*, 1821–22, pp. 38–42. As stated in the Northwest Ordinance of 1787, as part of an "unalterable" compact, except by the common consent of the original states and the people and states of the territory, the land and property of nonresidents could not be taxed higher than for residents. Kettleborough, *Constitution Making in Indiana*, I, 31–32.

127 Madison *Indiana Republican*, August 3, 1820; Vincennes *Western Sun*, October 5, 1822.

128 *Laws of Indiana*, 1819–20, pp. 97–112. As indicated *ibid.*, 1820–21, pp. 21–23, *ibid.*, 1821–22, pp. 45–46, 124–127, various changes were made regarding the location of these roads.

129 Indiana *House Journal*, 1818–19, pp. 21–23. See above, note 41, regarding this fund and the quid pro quo.

130 *Laws of Indiana*, 1821–22, pp. 152–169.

131 Corydon *Indiana Gazette*, July 18, 1822 (money received); Vincennes *Western Sun*, May 11, 1822 (road labor); Indianapolis *Gazette*, September 21, 1822 (road labor).

132 Indiana *House Journal*, 1821–22, pp. 287–288. The protesters were: General Washington Johnston, Knox County; James Brown Ray, Franklin County; John Tipton and David G. Mitchell, Harrison County; William B. Chamberlain, Switzerland County. Ray was the only representative of a non-river county.

133 Richmond *Weekly Intelligencer*, March 27, 1822, quoting [Corydon?] *Indiana Gazette*; Vincennes *Western Sun*, April 13, May 11, 1822.

134 Charles Henry Ambler, *A History of Transportation in the Ohio Valley . . .* (Glendale, Calif., 1932), 31, 38–42, 73–74; Leland D. Baldwin, *The Keelboat Age on Western Waters* (Pittsburgh, 1941), 47–49, 52, 67–68, 85–86, 124–125, 181–182; Buley, *The Old Northwest*, I, 413–415, 520–521, 530–531; Louis C. Hunter, *Steamboats on the Western Rivers: An Economic and Technological History* (Cambridge, Mass., 1949), 35, 54–60; Albert L. Kohlmeier, *The Old Northwest as the Keystone of the Arch of American Federal Union: A Study in Commerce and Politics* (Bloomington, Ind., 1938), 2–3.

135 Vincennes *Western Sun*, February 8, April 19, July 5, 1817, May 15, 1819; Indianapolis *Gazette*, June 1, 1822; Ambler, *A History of Transportation in the Ohio Valley*, 42–43, 48–49, 162; Baldwin, *Keelboat Age on Western Waters*, 42–45, 61–67, 87, 139, 180–181, 191–195; Buley, *The Old Northwest*, I, 412–413, 427–428; Hunter, *Steamboats on the Western Rivers*, 22, 25–26, 35, 52–60.

136 Vincennes *Western Sun*, July 1, 1815, May 9, 1818; Madison *Indiana Republican*, February 6, March 8 ("Harriet"), 1817, March 13, 1819; Ambler, *History of Transportation in the Ohio Valley*, 48, 61, 107–131; Baldwin, *Keelboat Age on Western Waters*, 190–195; Buley, *The Old Northwest*, I, 416–444; Hunter, *Steamboats on the Western Rivers*, 3–43.

137 Kettleborough, *Constitution Making in Indiana*, I, 32. According to the ordinance this item was part of the articles of compact that would "forever remain unalterable," except by common consent of the original states and the people and states of the territory.

138 *Laws of Indiana*, 1819–20, pp. 58–61. This enactment is discussed in Ewbank and Riker (eds.), *Laws of Indiana Territory, 1809–1816*, pp. 43–52, plus comment about a territorial precedent for it, and evidence that the decade of the twenties was the peak time for such legislation about rivers as public highways.

139 Logan Esarey, *Internal Improvements in Early Indiana* (Indianapolis, 1912), 61.

140 Buley, *The Old Northwest*, I, 427, 429, 432–435; Smith, *Early Indiana Trials and Sketches*, 116, 118–119, 168–169, 285; Robertson and Riker (eds.), *John Tipton Papers*, I, 180–184, 258, 261–262.

141 *Laws of Indiana*, 1818–19, pp. 74–76, giving such authority to county commissioners. For examples of laws authorizing toll bridges, see *Acts* (special), 1817–18, pp. 43–53; *Laws of Indiana*, 1818–19, pp. 111–114, 132–133, 135–138.

142 *Laws of Indiana*, 1817–18, pp. 292–296.

CHAPTER 2

1 Alton A. Lindsey (ed.), *Natural Features of Indiana, 1816–1966* (Indianapolis, 1966), x. As explained in note 3 below, the white population was considerably more at statehood than the 63,900 number given by Lindsey.

2 *Ibid.*, 279–281, 288–292, 547 (quotations). The two scholars are W. C. Bramble and F. T. Miller of Purdue University.

3 U. S. Bureau of the Census, *Seventh Census of the United States, 1850*, I, lxxxii. According to this source, in 1850 there were 5,046,543 acres of improved farmland and 7,746,879 acres of unimproved farmland from a total of about 23,000,000 acres within the state. The estimate of 80,000 settlers, excluding Indians, is only a rough estimate. There was no census taken at the time of statehood. The territorial census of 1815 as reported by Charles Kettleborough, *Constitution Making in Indiana* (3 vols., Indianapolis, 1916, 1930), I, 68–69, reported 63,897 settlers. As given in Donald F. Carmony, *A Brief History of Indiana* (Indianapolis, 1966), 61, the federal census of 1810 reported 24,520 residents; that of 1820, 147,178. Since the territorial census of 1815 was completed during the first half of that year, by which time the War of 1812 had ended with increased migration following, the 80,000 total seems a reasonable estimate.

4 Lindsey (ed.), *Natural Features of Indiana*, 57–90 *passim*, especially pp. 57–61, and map, p. 69, showing general soil regions and leading types of soil. R. Carlyle Buley, *The Old Northwest: Pioneer Period, 1815–1840* (2 vols., Indianapolis, 1950), I, 159, states: "For thousands of years generations of trees had seeded, grown, fallen, and rotted to add a layer of humus to the subsoil."

5 Lindsey (ed.), *Natural Features of Indiana*, 156–180 *passim*. See p. 172 for map about frost free periods and map, p. 94, regarding annual rainfall.

6 Agriculture as the economic base and principal foundation for trade and manufacturing is indicated by succeeding pages this chapter, especially pp. 46, 51–61, 67–73.

7 Buley, *The Old Northwest*, I, 235–236; John D. Barnhart and Donald F. Carmony, *Indiana: From Frontier to Industrial Commonwealth* (4 vols., New York, 1954), I, 418–419. Not until 1840 did the federal census indicate that Indiana had an urban area of 2,500 or more, this number being the minimum to be called an urban area. As noted *ibid.*, II, 14–16, in 1850 Indiana's population was 95.5 percent rural and 91.4 percent rural in 1860.

8 Albert Ludwig Kohlmeier, *The Old Northwest as the Keystone of the Arch of American Federal Union: A Study in Commerce and Politics* (Bloomington, Ind., 1938), 1–4; John H. Garland (ed.), *The North American Midwest: A Regional Geography* (Urbana, Ill., 1955), 5–6, 9–10.

9 Buley, *The Old Northwest*, I, 138–239, Chapter IV, "Pioneer Life—The Material Side," gives an impressive and detailed account of the pioneers as *generalists*, especially regarding how they fed, clothed, housed, and otherwise provided for themselves. Note his comment, p. 140, about the idea that pioneer life was simple.

[10] Logan Esarey, *The Indiana Home* (Bloomington, Ind., 1953), 73.

[11] *Congressional Globe*, 25 Cong., 2 session, VI, 436; *A Biographical Directory of the Indiana General Assembly* (2 vols., Indianapolis, 1980, 1984), Volume 1, *1816–1899*, Volume 2, *1901–1984*, I, 31.

[12] Esarey, *The Indiana Home*, 24–25. See *ibid.*, i–iv, x, for a picture of Esarey's boyhood home and Buley's tribute to Esarey. Buley states that Esarey "grew up in the hills of southern Indiana in a period in which many of the pioneers were still alive. He worked on the farm, swam in the Ohio River, played baseball, attended village school, listened to tall tales and reminiscences at the general store and blacksmith shop, and read books."

[13] Buley, *The Old Northwest*, I, 142.

[14] *Ibid.*, 142–145. For other and somewhat different comments about selecting a home site and building log cabins, see Esarey, *The Indiana Home*, 24–28, with illustrations of some tools; Barnhart and Carmony, *Indiana*, I, 241–245.

[15] Buley, *The Old Northwest*, I, 159–164 (quotes 159, 162–164). For other accounts of clearing forest land for cultivation, see Esarey, *The Indiana Home*, 73–79, with illustrations of tools used; Barnhart and Carmony, *Indiana*, I, 345–350.

[16] See citation to federal census of 1850 in note 3 above.

[17] Buley, *The Old Northwest*, I, 170–174 (quote 171); Esarey, *The Indiana Home*, 78–79; Barnhart and Carmony, *Indiana*, I, 348–349; William C. Latta, *Outline History of Indiana Agriculture* (Lafayette, Ind., 1938), 30–31; Robert Leslie Jones, *History of Agriculture in Ohio to 1880* (Kent, Ohio, 1983), 261–262, 264–266. As the comments of Esarey versus those of Buley concerning the jumping shovel suggest, Esarey was personally much more familiar with farming practices. Jones also was well informed about farming practices.

[18] Barnhart and Carmony, *Indiana*, I, 350–351, based on data from the federal census returns of 1840 and 1850.

[19] *Ibid.*, I, 351–353; Buley, *The Old Northwest*, I, 169–170, 174–176; Esarey, *The Indiana Home*, 86–88, 95, 96–97; Latta, *Outline History of Indiana Agriculture*, 44–48, 70–71, 81–82, 137–139; Jones, *History of Agriculture in Ohio to 1880*, pp. 50–55, 272–274. See Percy Wells Bidwell and John I. Falconer, *History of Agriculture in the Northern United States, 1620–1860* (New York, 1925; reprint, 1941), 341, for a useful summary of corn production in the United States for 1840, 1850, and 1860 by states and by regions, plus the per capita produced by each state and its percent of the national total. According to this table Indiana produced 7.5 percent of the corn in 1840, 8.9 percent in 1850, and 8.5 percent in 1860.

[20] Buley, *The Old Northwest*, I, 169–170 (quote), 174–182 *passim*; Barnhart and Carmony, *Indiana*, I, 350–351, 353; Esarey, *The Indiana Home*, 88–90, 93–94; Latta, *Outline History of Indiana Agriculture*, 48–50, 70–71, 79–80, 137, 139–140; Jones, *History of Agriculture in Ohio to 1880*, pp. 58–70, 262–272; Bidwell and Falconer, *History of Agriculture in the Northern United States, 1620–1860*, p. 323, for a useful summary of wheat production in the United States for 1840, 1850, and 1860 by states and by regions, plus the per capita production per state and its percentage of the national total. According to this table Indiana produced 4.8

percent of the wheat in 1840, 6.3 percent in 1850, and 9.7 percent in 1860. Here and elsewhere it should be noted that census data are generally neither complete nor fully accurate. Also that crop output varies from year to year.

21 Barnhart and Carmony, *Indiana*, I, 350–351, 353; Latta, *Outline History of Indiana Agriculture*, 49–50, 70–71; Buley, *The Old Northwest*, I, 176, 177–178; Jones, *History of Agriculture in Ohio to 1880*, pp. 49, 55–58; Bidwell and Falconer, *History of Agriculture in the Northern United States, 1620–1860*, pp. 351, 355, and 358 respectively give the same data for oats, rye, and barley production in the United States as for corn and wheat in preceding citations. According to these pages, for oats Indiana produced 4.9 percent of the national total in 1840, 3.9 percent in 1850, and 3.1 percent in 1860. For rye, .7 percent in 1840, .6 percent in 1850, and 2.2 percent in 1860. For barley, .7 percent in 1840, .9 percent in 1850, and 2.4 percent in 1860.

22 Barnhart and Carmony, *Indiana*, I, 354; Buley, *The Old Northwest*, I, 182–183, 222, 366; Latta, *Outline History of Indiana Agriculture*, 53–54, 70–71; Jones, *History of Agriculture in Ohio to 1880*, pp. 239–242, 249, 250–258; Bidwell and Falconer, *History of Agriculture in the Northern United States, 1620–1860*, pp. 243–246, 359–365, 384–386. According to *ibid.*, 383, Indiana produced .8 percent of the tobacco of the country in 1840, .5 percent in 1850, 1.9 percent in 1860; pp. 361–362, 6.6 percent of the flaxseed and 7.6 percent of the flax fiber in 1850, 21.1 percent and 2 percent respectively in 1860; p. 386, 3.1 percent of the hops in 1840, 2.6 percent in 1850, and .3 percent in 1860. This source has no such data for hemp.

23 Barnhart and Carmony, *Indiana*, I, 354; Buley, *The Old Northwest*, I, 186–187; Latta, *Outline History of Indiana Agriculture*, 71; Jones, *History of Agriculture in Ohio to 1880*, pp. 244–245.

24 Barnhart and Carmony, *Indiana*, I, 354–355; Buley, *The Old Northwest*, I, 182; Esarey, *The Indiana Home*, 92–93; Latta, *Outline History of Indiana Agriculture*, 50–51, 70–71, 137, 140–143; Jones, *History of Agriculture in Ohio to 1880*, pp. 65, 124–125, 245–246; Bidwell and Falconer, *History of Agriculture in the Northern United States, 1620–1860*, pp. 159–161, 366–372, 367 (census data). Indiana produced 1.7 percent of the total United States hay production in 1840, 2.9 percent in 1850, and 3.3 percent in 1860.

25 Barnhart and Carmony, *Indiana*, I, 245–246, 353–354; Buley, *The Old Northwest*, I, 182, 185–186, 217–219; Latta, *Outline History of Indiana Agriculture*, 51, 71–72; Esarey, *The Indiana Home*, 86, 95–96; Jones, *History of Agriculture in Ohio to 1880*, pp. 230–234; Bidwell and Falconer, *History of Agriculture in the Northern United States, 1620–1860*, pp. 373–379, 375 (census data). According to Bidwell and Falconer Hoosiers produced 1.4 percent of the potatoes of the country in 1840, 3.2 percent in 1850, and 3.5 percent in 1860.

26 Barnhart and Carmony, *Indiana*, I, 245–246, 353–354; Buley, *The Old Northwest*, I, 83–86, 155, 183–184 (quote, 184), 217–222, 339–340; Esarey, *The Indiana Home*, 42–43, 44, 49–55, 96; Latta, *Outline History of Indiana Agriculture*, 52–53, 72, 248–253; Jones, *History of Agriculture in Ohio to 1880*, pp. 213–230;

Bidwell and Falconer, *History of Agriculture in the Northern United States, 1620–1860*, pp. 243, 380–382.

[27] Barnhart and Carmony, *Indiana*, I, 245–246; Buley, *The Old Northwest*, I, 155–157 (quote, 155), 215–216, 224–225, 543–546; *ibid.*, II, 324–325; Esarey, *The Indiana Home*, 46–49; Latta, *Outline History of Indiana Agriculture*, 54–55, 71.

[28] Buley, *The Old Northwest*, I, 148–154, 158–159, 213–217; Esarey, *The Indiana Home*, 97–98; Barnhart and Carmony, *Indiana*, I, 245–246, 358, 359; Latta, *Outline History of Indiana Agriculture*, 57, 226, 234. For items about Mr. Hog, Madame Cow, and Miss Hen, see this chapter, pp. 57–59, 61.

[29] Barnhart and Carmony, *Indiana*, I, 355–356; Latta, *Outline History of Indiana Agriculture*, 45–46 (quotes); Buley, *The Old Northwest*, I, 177.

[30] Barnhart and Carmony, *Indiana*, I, 356; Latta, *Outline History of Indiana Agriculture*, 55, 72.

[31] Barnhart and Carmony, *Indiana*, I, 356–357; Buley, *The Old Northwest*, I, 158–159 (quote), 187–189, 478–481; Esarey, *The Indiana Home*, 97–98; Latta, *Outline History of Indiana Agriculture*, 55 (quote), 72–74, 168; Jones, *History of Agriculture in Ohio to 1880*, pp. 120–124; Bidwell and Falconer, *History of Agriculture in the Northern United States, 1620–1860*, pp. 435–441, 436 (data on hogs). According to the latter source Indiana had 6.2 percent of the hogs of the country in 1840, 7.4 percent in 1850, and 9.2 percent in 1860. Per thousand of population Indiana had 2,367 hogs in 1840, 2,290 in 1850, and 2,295 in 1860. Concerning Mr. Hog's "unmerited humiliation," as the text states, this refers to the time when "he was ordered to be destroyed by the government"—enclosed in parentheses—a jab at the killing of pigs under the Roosevelt New Deal in the 1930s. Buley once emphasized to the author that this comment was in the text from Esarey, not his addition; however, both Buley and Esarey had very similar views about Roosevelt and his New Deal.

[32] Barnhart and Carmony, *Indiana*, I, 356–358; Latta, *Outline History of Indiana Agriculture*, 56–57, 72, 75, 168–170, 234 (quote); Buley, *The Old Northwest*, I, 158, 187, 189–190, 216–217, 478–481; Jones, *History of Agriculture in Ohio to 1880*, pp. 77–82, 88, 99–103, 181–192; Bidwell and Falconer, *History of Agriculture in the Northern United States, 1620–1860*, pp. 166–167, 223–224, 227–229, 264–265, 388–390 (number of neat cattle), 392–393, 403–404, 424–427 (cheese and butter output), 434 (number of dairy cattle). According to *ibid.*, 389, Indiana had 4.2 percent of the neat cattle in 1840, 4 percent in 1850, and 4.2 percent in 1860. Indiana also had 904 neat cattle per thousand of population in 1840, 723 in 1850, and 792 in 1860. In 1850 Indiana had 288 dairy cattle per thousand of population, 269 in 1860. The state had 4.5 percent of the country's total of dairy cows in 1850, 4.2 percent in 1860.

[33] Barnhart and Carmony, *Indiana*, I, 356, 358; Buley, *The Old Northwest*, I, 187, 190–191; Esarey, *The Indiana Home*, 29, 79–84; Latta, *Outline History of Indiana Agriculture*, 56 (quote), 72, 75, 181–183; Jones, *History of Agriculture in Ohio to 1880*, pp. 139–154; Bidwell and Falconer, *History of Agriculture in the Northern United States, 1620–1860*, pp. 166–167, 183, 217–223, 406–420, 409

(number of sheep), 411 (wool production). According to the federal censuses Indiana had 3.5 percent of the sheep of the United States in 1840, 5.1 percent in 1850, and 4.4 percent in 1860. In 1840 there were 986 sheep per thousand Hoosiers, 1,136 in 1850, and 734 in 1860. Concerning wool Hoosiers produced 3.5 percent of the national total in 1840, 5 percent in 1850, and 4.2 percent in 1860.

34 Barnhart and Carmony, *Indiana*, I, 356, 358–359; Buley, *The Old Northwest*, I, 187, 191–192 (quotes), 317, 478–481; Latta, *Outline History of Indiana Agriculture*, 31 (quote), 57, 72, 75–76 (quote), 168; Esarey, *The Indiana Home*, 78–79, 85–86; Jones, *History of Agriculture in Ohio to 1880*, pp. 158–178; Bidwell and Falconer, *History of Agriculture in the Northern United States, 1620–1860*, pp. 443–447, 445 (data regarding number), 447 (quote). According to the latter source Indiana had 5.6 percent of the horses and mules of the country in 1840, 6.6 percent in 1850, and 7.4 percent in 1860. In 1840 there were 351 horses and mules per thousand population in Indiana, 325 in 1850, and 407 in 1860.

35 Latta, *Outline History of Indiana Agriculture*, 57 (quote), 76, 226 (quotes); Barnhart and Carmony, *Indiana*, I, 359; Buley, *The Old Northwest*, I, 234; Bidwell and Falconer, *History of Agriculture in the Northern United States, 1620–1860*, p. 442; Esarey, *The Indiana Home*, 83–85.

36 Barnhart and Carmony, *Indiana*, I, 345–359 *passim*; Buley, *The Old Northwest*, I, 138–239 *passim*; Latta, *Outline History of Indiana Agriculture*, 35–83 *passim*. The views expressed are generalizations based on these and various other sources the author has read from time to time.

37 Barnhart and Carmony, *Indiana*, I, 357–358; Buley, *The Old Northwest*, I, 171, 175–176, 177–178, 180–181, 187–193; Latta, *Outline History of Indiana Agriculture*, 73–109, 168–280 *passim*, 307–316, 353–370. Although Latta's account of Indiana agriculture is a pioneering study, its information, comments, and illustrations make it an extremely valuable study of Hoosier agriculture during the period from statehood through the early decades of the 1900s.

38 *Laws of Indiana*, 1828–29, pp. 9–11; *ibid.* (general), 1834–35, pp. 87–91, 90–91 (quotes). Both laws are discussed briefly in Latta, *Outline History of Indiana Agriculture*, 269–270. For a concise statement regarding early periodicals about agriculture in Indiana, see Barnhart and Carmony, *Indiana*, II, 65.

39 For a copy of this report, see Indiana *Documentary Journal*, 1835–36, Doc. No. 23, pp. 1–4. According to Dorothy Riker (ed.), *Executive Proceedings of the State of Indiana, 1816–1836* (Indianapolis, 1947), 277, on April 10, 1835, the governor named Samuel Moor, John Owen, Moses Henkle, Larkin Syms, and James Blake to the State Board of Agriculture for terms of five years. As indicated in Barnhart and Carmony, *Indiana*, II, 62, a Knox County Agricultural Society was in existence in 1810 with Governor William Henry Harrison as its president.

40 Indiana *Documentary Journal*, 1835–36, Doc. No. 23, pp. 14–15.

41 *Ibid.*, 16–21 (quotes 17, 18, 19, 20, 21). See Latta, *Outline History of Indiana Agriculture*, 278–279, 314, 316–318 for efforts during the fifties and sixties which led to the opening of Purdue University for students in March, 1874. On p. 318

Latta states that Purdue's School of Agriculture was not established until the fall of 1879.

⁴² Latta, *Outline History of Indiana Agriculture*, 271–274. In 1851 the State Board of Agriculture was revived, and increased emphasis and success followed regarding both the efforts of the state board and county agricultural societies as indicated *ibid.*, 273–280; Barnhart and Carmony, *Indiana*, II, 60–65. For the law reestablishing the State Board of Agriculture, see *Laws of Indiana* (revised), 1851–52, pp. 98–100. The first state fair was held in 1851. The annual reports of the State Board of Agriculture, especially for the years 1851–59, are an extremely valuable source for miscellaneous items about pioneer farming, often with regard to farming in particular counties. As indicated in Logan Esarey, *A History of Indiana: From Its Exploration to 1850* (2 vols., Fort Wayne, Ind., 1924), II, 1004–1006, a law of 1852 required the trustees of Indiana University to establish an "agricultural department," and a university catalog in 1853 announced such a department; however, it apparently died a stillbirth or in very early infancy.

⁴³ Kohlmeier, *The Old Northwest as the Keystone of the Arch of American Federal Union*, 1–3; Garland (ed.), *The North American Midwest*, 5–6.

⁴⁴ Kohlmeier, *The Old Northwest as the Keystone of the Arch of American Federal Union*, 4, 7–9, 20, 31–35, 51–56, 82–92, 115–123; Buley, *The Old Northwest*, I, 410, 530–531, 536–539; *ibid.*, II, 319–324. These sources list various other exports.

⁴⁵ Kohlmeier, *The Old Northwest as the Keystone of the Arch of American Federal Union*, 7, 21, 35–37, 56–57, 92–93, 123–127; Buley, *The Old Northwest*, I, 234–235, 543–544, 554–555, 558–560. The sources cited list additional miscellaneous imports.

⁴⁶ Kohlmeier, *The Old Northwest as the Keystone of the Arch of American Federal Union*, 6–9, 16–20, 92–95, 120–128; Buley, *The Old Northwest*, I, 530, states: "Until 1840 and after, the flatboat on the Ohio and Mississippi was the means by which the great bulk of the produce of the Northwest was conveyed to market."

⁴⁷ Kohlmeier, *The Old Northwest as the Keystone of the Arch of American Federal Union*, 21, 36, 56, 92–93; Buley, *The Old Northwest*, I, 215, 543–544 (quote); *ibid.*, II, 324.

⁴⁸ Barnhart and Carmony, *Indiana*, I, 360–361, citing Rolla M. Tryon, *Household Manufactures in the United States, 1640–1860* (Chicago, 1917), 308, 344–347, 188–241 (comprehensive discussion of household processes); Buley, *The Old Northwest*, I, 202–225, for concise discussion of various household processes.

⁴⁹ Barnhart and Carmony, *Indiana*, I, 362–363, based on *Seventh Census of the United States, 1850*, I, 789–790. The exact meaning of some of the names used for what tradesmen did is not clear, and the difference between particular trades is at times uncertain. Perhaps both the census takers and the tradesmen themselves had trouble deciding what classification best fitted numerous tradesmen. The 4,679 blacksmiths and whitesmiths were apparently what Indiana residents have usually called blacksmiths. H. G. Emery and K. G. Brewster (eds.), *The*

New Century Dictionary of the English Language . . . (3 vols., New York, 1927), III, 2205, offers this explanation about a whitesmith: "A tinsmith; also, a worker in iron who finishes or polishes, in distinction to one who forges." *Ibid.*, I, 603, in explaining the process of forging, adds strong support to the conclusion that the 4,679 tradesmen were what have usually been called blacksmiths. This dictionary has very helpful explanations about what is embraced in various of the other trades listed in the 1850 federal census. The three *Indiana Gazetteers* of 1826, 1833, and 1849 have numerous *passim* items about pioneer trades or crafts.

50 Buley, *The Old Northwest*, I, 227; Baynard Rush Hall, *The New Purchase, or Seven and A Half Years in the Far West*, edited by James Albert Woodburn (Princeton, N. J., 1916), 278. Hall's reference to "the Purchase" refers to the cessions of the Indians in 1818 which freed Indian claims to much of Indiana.

51 Barnhart and Carmony, *Indiana*, I, 364–365, with sources indicated.

52 *Seventh Census of the United States, 1850*, II, 789–790. Male workers numbered 13,748; 692 were females.

53 *Eighth Census of the United States, 1860*, II, 142–145, 659. Male workers numbered 20,023; females 732. These data show that as of 1860 manufacturing was based overwhelmingly upon products from agriculture and timber. It was doubtless equally if not even more so in 1850. For the twenty leading industries of 1860 according to the federal census returns, see Barnhart and Carmony, *Indiana*, I, 238–239.

54 Barnhart and Carmony, *Indiana*, I, 365–366, quoting *Indiana Gazetteer* (1849), 39. Concerning persistence of the agrarian base, along with much rural population and urban decentralization, see Barnhart and Carmony, *Indiana*, II, 427, which states: "Undoubtedly the most significant economic development among the Hoosiers in the half-century after 1900 was the triumph of manufacturing over agriculture, through which Indiana had become more industrial than agricultural by 1920." Also for *passim* items about industrialization, rural population, and urban decentralization, see *ibid.*, II, chapters 23 and 28, pp. 426–453, 531–550. It should be noted that the agricultural and rural elements were slow to yield political power to the industrial and urban elements for some decades after 1920.

55 Dorothy Riker and Gayle Thornbrough (eds.), *Messages and Papers Relating to the Administration of Noah Noble, Governor of Indiana, 1831–1837* (Indianapolis, 1958), 409; Indiana *House Journal*, 1835–36, pp. 267–269.

56 Riker and Thornbrough (eds.), *Messages and Papers of Noah Noble*, 488–489; *Laws of Indiana* (general), 1836–37, pp. 108–109; Walter Brookfield Hendrickson, *David Dale Owen: Pioneer Geologist of the Middle West* (Indianapolis, 1943), 28–29. Owen's letter about specimens is in the Indianapolis *Indiana Democrat*, April 12, 1837, and in the Indianapolis *Indiana Journal*, April 15, 1837. In its issue for April 8, 1837, the *Indiana Journal* made favorable comment regarding Owen's appointment and predicted that the state would benefit from his efforts. Also see Barnhart and Carmony, *Indiana*, II, 268–276, for additional items about the establishment of geological surveys for Indiana.

⁵⁷ David Dale Owen, *Report of a Geological Reconnoisance [sic] of the State of Indiana; Made in the Year 1837* (Indianapolis, 1838), 21; Hendrickson, *David Dale Owen*, 28–40 (quotes 28, 30).

⁵⁸ Dorothy Riker (ed.), *Messages and Papers Relating to the Administration of David Wallace, Governor of Indiana, 1837–1840* (Indianapolis, 1963), 181; *Laws of Indiana* (general), 1838–39, p. 54; Hendrickson, *David Dale Owen*, 38–41.

⁵⁹ For general accounts, see Barnhart and Carmony, *Indiana*, I, 362–363, 365; *ibid.*, II, 268–289; Buley, *The Old Northwest*, I, 546–549; Lindsey (ed.), *Natural Features of Indiana*, 131–155. For comments of Governor Wallace, see Indiana *House Journal*, 1838–39, p. 33; *ibid.*, 1839–40, p. 27. Concerning soil, climate, and trees as leading resources for agriculture, see this chapter, pp. 45–46.

⁶⁰ This paragraph, and the concluding paragraph of this chapter, are an interpretative essay. They are intended to raise key questions and provoke research and thought. The interpretations given by the author have been influenced by items in the previous pages of this chapter and by the comments found in a number of pioneer newspapers as well as in his general reading about the pioneer era. Regarding the division of labor between women and girls versus men and boys, in addition to the preceding pages of this chapter, see Buley, *The Old Northwest*, I, 138–394 *passim*; Esarey, *The Indiana Home*, 3–99 *passim*. The basic division of labor between women and girls versus men and boys seems pretty well established, but items about morality and abuses between men and women have not been so established.

⁶¹ Buley, *The Old Northwest*, I, 239, 309 (quote).

CHAPTER 3

¹ Madison *Western Clarion*, March 27, 1822; Indianapolis *Gazette*, April 3, 1822, indicating Madison *Indiana Republican* as its source.

² Indianapolis *Gazette*, April 3, 1822. As this issue notes, Governor Hendricks and Congressman Jennings were seeking an exchange of positions.

³ For examples, see Corydon *Indiana Gazette*, April 18, May 9, June 27, July 25, 1822; Vincennes *Western Sun*, April 20, May 11, June 15, July 27, 1822; Richmond *Weekly Intelligencer*, April 24, May 8, June 19, July 31, 1822; Indianapolis *Gazette*, May 11, 25, June 8, July 13, 1822.

⁴ Frederick Dinsmore Hill, William Hendricks: Indiana Politician and Western Advocate, 1812–1850 (Ph.D. dissertation, Indiana University, 1972), 72–73. This dissertation is a comprehensive and significant study of William Hendricks.

⁵ Vincennes *Western Sun*, August 10, 1822; Indiana *House Journal*, 1822–23, p. 23. The Indianapolis *Gazette*, August 24, 1822, and the Richmond *Weekly Intelligencer*, September 18, 1822, state that Hendricks won without opposition. The *Gazette*, August 10, 1822, reports 315 votes for Hendricks in Marion County with 2 votes "Scattering."

⁶ Indianapolis *Gazette*, February 11, May 25, 1822; Vincennes *Western Sun*, May 4, 1822; Corydon *Indiana Gazette*, May 9, 1822. The three rivals were

David H. Maxwell, Monroe County; William Polke, Knox County; Erasmus Powell, Dearborn County. Concerning their legislative and other service, see *A Biographical Directory of the Indiana General Assembly* (2 vols., Indianapolis, 1980, 1984), Volume 1, *1816–1899*, Volume 2, *1901–1984*, I, 266, 316, 317.

⁷ Dorothy Riker and Gayle Thornbrough (comps.), *Indiana Election Returns, 1816–1851* (Indianapolis, 1960), pp. 160–161, giving unofficial returns, with about a dozen and a half counties missing, indicate 6,614 votes for Boon; 3,469 for Polke; 3,168 for Powell; 2,309 for Maxwell. Somewhat higher totals, showing Boon a strong plurality winner, with returns incomplete, were reported by the speaker of the House. Indiana *House Journal*, 1822–23, pp. 16–17, 23.

⁸ Indiana *House Journal*, 1822–23, pp. 39–40, 81, 92–93. Merrill received 32 votes against 25 for Lane, Lilly 55 votes against 3 for Reuben Kidder. For Merrill's legislative service, see *Biographical Directory of the Indiana General Assembly*, I, 270.

⁹ For elections of Congressman Boon and Senator Hendricks, see Chapter 9, pp. 484, 487.

¹⁰ At the session of 1823–24, the last at Corydon, Ray was elected president pro tem of the Senate on the first ballot; at the session early in 1825, the first at Indianapolis, he was reelected on the initial ballot. He had been elected to the Senate on August 5, 1822, hence his term expired with the election on August 1, 1825. Indiana *Senate Journal*, 1823–24, pp. 237–238; *ibid.*, 1825, pp. 5, 18–19. For his term as senator and earlier year as a representative, see *Biographical Directory of the Indiana General Assembly*, I, 322–323, 442–446.

¹¹ Dorothy Riker (ed.), *Executive Proceedings of the State of Indiana, 1816–1836* (Indianapolis, 1947), 275; John G. Rauch and Nellie C. Armstrong, *A Bibliography of the Laws of Indiana, 1788–1927* (Indianapolis, 1928), 68.

¹² Indiana *Senate Journal*, 1825, pp. 4, 5, 18–19, 122, 195–197; Vincennes *Western Sun*, February 26, 1825. Ewing contended that it would be contrary to the constitution for Ray to serve as governor subsequent to the ensuing August election at which time his senatorial term would expire.

¹³ Riker (ed.), *Executive Proceedings of the State of Indiana, 1816–1836*, pp. 275–276. Ray filed a certificate with the secretary of state explaining that he had become "acting governor," and would "during the term he administered the government" do so to the best of his ability. Thus, Ray left open when his tenure as governor would end. The Constitution of 1816, by providing that lacking a governor or lieutenant governor that the president pro tem shall "administer the Government, until he shall be superseded by a Governor or Lieutenant Governor," perhaps gave Ray constitutional authority to serve until the person elected in August became governor in December. Charles Kettleborough, *Constitution Making in Indiana* (3 vols., Indianapolis, 1916, 1930), I, 100. For another discussion of Ray's succession to the office of governor, see Dorothy Riker and Gayle Thornbrough (eds.), *Messages and Papers Relating to the Administration of James Brown Ray, Governor of Indiana, 1825–1831* (Indianapolis, 1954), 23–26.

14 Indianapolis *Gazette*, January 25, March 1, 8, 22, April 5, 1825; Richmond *Public Leger*, February 12, 1825; Lawrenceburgh *Indiana Palladium*, February 25, 1825; Vincennes *Western Sun*, March 5, 26, April 2, 1825. As March ended, Reuben W. Nelson announced himself for governor, but withdrew as a candidate late in May. Indianapolis *Gazette*, April 19, June 7, 1825.

15 Ray to Clay, October 5, 1825, in James F. Hopkins (ed.), *The Papers of Henry Clay* (7 vols., Lexington, Ky., 1959–1982), IV, 721–722; Riker and Thornbrough (comps.), *Indiana Election Returns, 1816–1851*, pp. 8–9.

16 Riker and Thornbrough (eds.), *Messages and Papers of James Brown Ray*, 35–36, quoting Indianapolis *Gazette*, June 7, 1825.

17 Indianapolis *Gazette*, March 15, 22, 1825.

18 *Ibid.*, April 12, May 31, June 7, 14, July 12, 1825.

19 *Ibid.*, March 15, June 21, 1825.

20 *Ibid.*, July 19, 1825, quoting Brookville *Enquirer*. For similar criticism by "Marion," see *ibid.*, July 12, 1825.

21 Indianapolis *Indiana Journal*, June 14, July 5, 1825.

22 Indianapolis *Gazette*, July 5, 1825; Indianapolis *Indiana Journal*, July 12, 19, 1825.

23 Vincennes *Western Sun*, March 26, 1825, quoting Madison *Indiana Republican*; Indianapolis *Indiana Journal*, July 19, 1825, for item by "A friend to the Constitution."

24 Richmond *Public Leger*, July 23, 1825.

25 *Ibid.*, July 9, 30, 1825. For items concerning certificates, at times quoted from other papers, see *ibid.*, July 30, 1825, Vincennes *Western Sun*, July 30, 1825, and Indianapolis *Indiana Journal*, July 26, 1825.

26 The election returns, missing for six counties and for those counties listed are official for only Dearborn County, as found in Riker and Thornbrough (comps.), *Indiana Election Returns, 1816–1851*, pp. 138–139, show 13,852 votes for Ray against 12,165 for Blackford. The speaker of the House reported 13,040 for Ray, 10,418 for Blackford. The totals given for Ray and Blackford omit the votes for two counties which are reported as having given Ray a majority of 482 votes. Indiana *House Journal*, 1825–26, p. 23.

27 Indianapolis *Indiana Journal*, August 16, 1825; Vincennes *Western Sun*, August 27, 1825.

28 Indianapolis *Indiana Journal*, August 9, 1825; Lawrenceburgh *Indiana Palladium*, September 9, 1825.

29 Indiana *Senate Journal*, 1825–26, pp. 4, 8; Indiana *House Journal*, 1825–26, pp. 8, 14–15. After the House voted one member changed his vote, making the count 29 to 16 for inviting Ray.

30 Indiana *Senate Journal*, 1825–26, pp. 12–13; Indiana *House Journal*, 1825–26, pp. 23–26. Both sources have related items concerning Ray's inauguration as governor, especially during the first three days of the session. After Ray's inauguration the legislature appropriated $352.80 "for his services" from the first

Monday in August, 1825, to the third day of the session when his elected term as governor began. *Laws of Indiana*, 1825–26, p. 9.

31 Lawrenceburgh *Indiana Palladium*, May 13, 1825, quoting Evansville *Gazette*. For persons considered candidates, see Indianapolis *Gazette*, January 18, February 15, March 1, April 12, 19, May 31, 1825; Indianapolis *Indiana Journal*, February 15, May 10, July 5, 1825; Richmond *Public Leger*, May 28, 1825. Among the persons considered were Elisha Harrison, General Washington Johnston, William Cotton, Joseph Warner, Dennis Pennington, Samuel Milroy, and John H. Thompson.

32 Concerning the legislative experience of these three candidates and two of them as members of the Corydon Constitutional Convention, see *Biographical Directory of the Indiana General Assembly*, I, 275–276, 311, 389–390; Kettleborough, *Constitution Making in Indiana*, I, 124–125.

33 Indianapolis *Indiana Journal*, May 31, 1825.

34 Indianapolis *Gazette*, July 12, 1825; Vincennes *Western Sun*, March 26, 1825.

35 Indianapolis *Gazette*, May 10, 1825; Lawrenceburgh *Indiana Palladium*, June 24, 1825. According to Riker (ed.), *Executive Proceedings of the State of Indiana, 1816–1836*, p. 352, Milroy and Thompson resigned their seats June 7 and May 6 respectively.

36 Riker and Thornbrough (comps.), *Indiana Elections Returns, 1816–1851*, pp. 161–162, reporting returns, missing for most counties, and for those counties listed are official only for Dearborn County indicate: Thompson, 6,416; Milroy, 4,470; Pennington, 931; Johnston, 609; Harrison, 429; Warner, 31. To compare the vote for lieutenant governor with that for presidential electors, see *ibid.*, 4–9. The speaker of the House reported returns, also incomplete, showing: Thompson, 10,781; Milroy, 7,496; Pennington, 1,496; Harrison, 1,434; Johnston, 851; scattering, 84. Indiana *House Journal*, 1825–26, p. 23.

37 Indiana *House Journal*, 1825, p. 34. On the final ballot Wick got 33 votes; Enoch D. John, 27; James B. Slaughter, 2.

38 *Ibid.*, 1825–26, pp. 123–124. Merrill received 61 votes with none against him. Lilly gained 34 votes to 27 against him and one scattering, on the fourth ballot.

39 Late in 1829 Treasurer Merrill reported 28,500 taxable polls and 1,874,710 taxable acres for 1822; 48,500 taxable polls and 3,595,177 taxable acres for 1829. Indiana *House Journal*, 1829–30, p. 73.

40 *Ibid.*, 1822–23, pp. 36–37.

41 Except when otherwise *explicitly indicated*, items regarding ordinary expenditures and ordinary revenues from 1822 to 1831 are from or based on data in the annual reports of the state treasurer as found in the Indiana *Senate Journal*, 1823–24, pp. 23–26 (fiscal 1822–23); Indiana *House Journal*, 1825, pp. 43–46 (fiscal 1823–24); *ibid.*, 1825–26, pp. 59–61 (fiscal 1825); *ibid.*, 1826–27, pp. 66–68 (fiscal 1825–26); *ibid.*, 1827–28, pp. 47–50 (fiscal 1826–27); *ibid.*, 1828–29, pp. 42–45

(fiscal 1827–28); *ibid*, 1829–30, pp. 71–73 (fiscal 1828–29); *ibid*., 1830–31, Appendix A, 1–3 (fiscal 1829–30); *ibid*., 1831–32, Appendix A, 5–8 (fiscal 1830–31). See above, Ch. 1, note 29, for explanation of the difference between ordinary expenditures and ordinary revenues versus other expenditures and revenues. With the increase of special funds (1822–31), it is more difficult to separate ordinary expenditures and ordinary revenues from expenditures and revenues for special funds than for the period 1816–22. But the sums that are doubtful are believed to be modest. See Ch. 1, and accompanying table p. 11 for ordinary state expenditures, 1816–22. Special funds observed in the annual report of the treasurer, 1822–31, include these funds: Indianapolis, Saline, State Seminary, County Seminary, Michigan Road, Wabash and Miami Canal (Wabash and Erie Canal).

[42] The Constitution of 1816 provided for thirty-nine members of the General Assembly; the legislative apportionments of 1821 and 1826 raised the total to fifty-nine and seventy-nine respectively. Late in 1829 Treasurer Merrill reported that legislative and printing costs had increased about $5,000 during the seven preceding years. For increase in number of legislators in 1821 and 1826 respectively, see Ch. 1, pp. 31–34; this chapter, 102–103.

[43] Judicial circuits numbered three in 1816; four in 1818; five in 1821; seven in 1830. *Laws of Indiana*, 1816–17, p. 15; *ibid*., 1817–18, p. 358; *ibid*., 1821–22, pp. 74–79; *ibid*., 1829–30, p. 42. Judicial payments were mainly for compensation to judges of the Supreme Court, president judges of the circuit courts; and, starting in fiscal 1825, for payments for circuit prosecutors for the circuit courts. During 1822–25 modest payments were made for an attorney general; and during 1828–31 payments were added for probate judges.

[44] As for the years 1816–22, during 1822–31 collectors of tax revenue were allowed 9 percent of the total collected as their compensation for obtaining it. Since collectors were at times allowed some fees and commissions, the amount retained by collectors cannot be determined with complete accuracy but 9 percent seems to be a rough approximation. *Laws of Indiana* (revised), 1823–24, pp. 351–352; *Laws of Indiana*, 1828–29, p. 88; *ibid*. (revised), 1830–31, p. 441.

[45] For miscellaneous costs, 1816–22, see Chapter 1, tables of ordinary expenditures, for payments to tax collectors. The large percentage gain in miscellaneous expenditures apparently resulted in significant part because items which had been "buried" among other costs, particularly legislative costs, began to be segregated as "incidental allowances," "special allowances," or "special appropriations" in the annual reports of the treasurer for 1825–28, with the term "special appropriations" becoming generally used thereafter. Miscellaneous costs include: $1,444.00 for "tract books and copies," $633.51 for presidential elections, $248.59 for impeachments, and $70.00 for the Committee on Education, plus items listed as Specific Appropriations, Incidental Allowances, and Special Allowances. For 1825–26 the treasurer listed $20 for the "librarian's salary," among legislative costs. Such an item may have been included previously, without saying so in the treasurer's annual report. The context indicates that the State Library was mainly to serve state officials.

46 Corydon *Indiana Gazette*, September 24, 1823; Indiana *House Journal*, 1827–28, p. 32. Concerning the treasury notes, $19,872 was spent for their redemption, $1,395.28 for interest; $5,000 was required to pay principal owed the Harmonists, and $734 for interest; $2,673.12 was paid on account of loans from the First State Bank, apparently a mix of interest and principal; $1,160.81 in interest was paid the Indiana State Seminary Fund; and $55.41 was expended for territorial warrants.

47 See note 41 above for citations and explanation regarding ordinary revenues. Concerning ordinary state revenues, 1816–22, see Chapter 1.

48 *Laws of Indiana* (revised), 1823–24, pp. 338–339, reaffirmed the levies on land as inherited from the Jennings-Boon period. For tax levies, 1816–22, see Chapter 1.

49 Indiana *House Journal*, 1825, p. 18; *Laws of Indiana*, 1825, pp. 67–68.

50 Indiana *House Journal*, 1825–26, pp. 45–46; *ibid.*, 1826–27, pp. 63–64; *Laws of Indiana*, 1826–27, p. 68. The *Laws of Indiana* (revised), 1830–31, pp. 426–427 have the same levy on land as for the 1827 law. The revised codes of 1823–24 and 1830–31 both include a levy of 25 cents per $100 of stock in a bank, but this levy seems to have yielded meager revenue at most.

51 *Laws of Indiana* (revised), 1823–24, pp. 338–339, 353; *ibid.*, 1830–31, pp. 426–428. Examples of miscellaneous exemptions include an act of 1822 which exempted persons over fifty, not freeholders, those unable to follow a useful occupation, and "idiots and paupers" from the poll tax. An act of 1826 exempted veterans from payment of the poll tax. *Ibid.*, 1821–22, p. 107; *ibid.*, 1825–26, p. 68.

52 Indianapolis *Gazette*, June 29, 1824; Thomas H. Blake to Henry Clay, July 30, 1825, in Hopkins (ed.), *Papers of Henry Clay*, IV, 560–561; Lawrenceburgh *Indiana Palladium*, October 7, 1826.

53 Indiana *House Journal*, 1826–27, pp. 56, 160–161; *ibid.*, 1828–29, p. 269. Richardson Terrill was the Indiana artist. What Terrill asked for the portrait is unknown, but it was probably a nominal sum.

54 *Ibid.*, 1821–22, pp. 347–348; *ibid.*, 1825–26, p. 46. Ray made much the same recommendations at the ensuing session. *Ibid.*, 1826–27, p. 64.

55 For instance, see *ibid.*, 1821–22, p. 349; *ibid.*, 1827–28, pp. 234–235; Indianapolis *Gazette*, June 29, 1824, July 4, 18, August 1, 1826.

56 Indianapolis *Indiana Journal*, January 2, 1830.

57 *American State Papers, Public Lands*, III, 498–499, 492–493. The memorial has not been found among laws and resolutions for the session of 1820–21, but its content is indicated in these citations to *American State Papers*. For a more extended discussion of Indiana's effort to have the five-year exemption clause abrogated during the twenties, see Donald F. Carmony, Indiana Public Finance, 1800–1826 (Ph.D. dissertation, Indiana University, 1940), 240–250.

58 *Indiana Acts* (special), 1823–24, pp. 111–112; *ibid.*, 1830–31, pp. 193–194.

59 Indianapolis *Gazette*, March 28, June 6, July 4, 18, August 1, 1826; *Biographical Directory of the Indiana General Assembly*, I, 128–129, 240, 449; Indiana *House Journal*, 1826–27, p. 62.

60 Indiana *House Journal*, 1827–28, pp. 279–282.

61 Vincennes *Western Sun*, February 2, 1828; Indianapolis *Indiana Journal*, January 2, 1830. The Indianapolis *Gazette*, January 8, 1828, after noting the closely divided sentiment in the House regarding a bill to value property in anticipation of the ad valorem plan, said most members favored the plan but for some future time.

62 Among the principal laws concerning the assessing and collecting of taxes from 1822–31 are the following: *Laws of Indiana* (revised), 1823–24, pp. 338–355; 1825, pp. 13–14, 63–72; 1825–26, pp. 68–69; 1826–27, pp. 66–68; 1827–28, pp. 80–82; 1828–29, p. 88; (revised), 1830–31, pp. 426–445.

63 For examples of concern about inadequate collection of state taxes, see Governor Hendricks to the General Assembly in Indiana *House Journal*, 1822–23, pp. 35–36, and 1823–24, pp. 16–18; Governor Ray to the General Assembly, *ibid.*, 1825–26, p. 46; Auditor Lilly regarding delinquency of collectors, *ibid.*, 1823–24, pp. 276–278, Treasurer Merrill about delinquency, 1820–24, *ibid.*, 1825–26, p. 61; suggestions of Noah Noble, former collector for Franklin County, *ibid.*, 1825, pp. 73–74; Vincennes *Western Sun*, February 7, 1824; Corydon *Indiana Gazette*, June 9, 1824.

64 *Laws of Indiana* (revised), 1823–24, p. 127; *ibid.*, 1825, pp. 70–71.

65 Indiana *House Journal*, 1831–32, Appendix A, 7–8.

66 Kettleborough, *Constitution Making in Indiana*, I, 121; Indiana *House Journal*, 1816–17, p. 11; *ibid.*, 1817–18, p. 7.

67 Jennings told the General Assembly, at the beginning of its third session, that "Nearly all" the territorial laws had been repealed. Indiana *House Journal*, 1818–19, p. 20. Even a casual examination of the laws of the first two sessions shows that much legislation had been passed adapting the laws to statehood. General Washington Johnston's *A Compend of the Acts of Indiana From the Year Eighteen Hundred and Seven Until That of Eighteen Hundred and Fourteen, Both Inclusive*, was published at the press of Elihu Stout, Vincennes, 1817. Rauch and Armstrong, *Bibliography of the Laws of Indiana, 1788–1927*, p. 13.

68 Corydon *Indiana Gazette*, December 18, 1819; Indiana *House Journal*, 1821–22, p. 19.

69 *Laws of Indiana*, 1821–22, pp. 16–19; Indiana *House Journal*, 1821–22, p. 232; Indiana *Senate Journal*, 1822–23, pp. 54–55. Parke explained that information about his appointment had not reached him until after the previous session had adjourned. Although the *House Journal* did not record any vote about Parke's appointment, the Vincennes *Western Sun*, January 5, 1822, indicating General Washington Johnston as its source, reported that Parke had been elected "'by a majority of three votes over Judge [James] Scott, on the 6th ballot.'"

70 Vincennes *Western Sun*, December 21, 1822. The diversity of views and maneuvering is indicated in Indiana *House Journal*, 1822–23, pp. 78–81, 84–86, 89–91, 95–99, 108–109, 127, 169–170, 187, 242, 248–249, 253–254.

71 *Laws of Indiana*, 1822–23, pp. 25–26; Indiana *House Journal*, 1822–23, pp. 253–254; Indiana *Senate Journal*, 1822–23, p. 211. Neither the House nor Sen-

ate journal names any rival against Hendricks, and the latter states that he gained 31 votes to win election on the seventh ballot. Since there were nearly twice this number of legislators, perhaps most of those who did not support Hendricks preferred that the General Assembly make the revision.

72 Indiana *House Journal*, 1823–24, pp. 27–31. Hendricks expressed generous acknowledgment for aid regarding the revision received from Judge Parke of the federal district court, Judges Jesse L. Holman and James Scott of the Supreme Court, and Treasurer Samuel Merrill. Conspicuous for its absence was any acknowledgment to Judge Isaac Blackford of the Supreme Court. Possibly Blackford had been a rival of Hendricks concerning the revision of the laws, or perhaps they were already rivals for election to the United States Senate in 1825.

73 For this decision and the lists of bills or laws to begin in each house, see Indiana *Senate Journal*, 1823–24, pp. 15, 22, 26, 34–36. *Ibid.*, pp. 36–38, offer examples of the procedure and scrutiny which followed. As indicated in Rauch and Armstrong, *Bibliography of the Laws of Indiana, 1788–1927*, p. 68, the session of 1823–24 was longer than any since statehood.

74 *Laws of Indiana* (revised), 1823–24, aggregating 438 pages, were printed as a separate volume. *Ibid.*, 256–257, for reaffirmation of the status of the common law and a declaration of the laws in force. A separate volume of *Indiana Acts* (special), 1823–24, including laws enacted at the session, also resulted from this session.

75 Indiana *House Journal*, 1823–24, pp. 288–289, 323–324. The Richmond *Public Leger*, October 15, 1825, commenting on a report attributed to Nathan B. Palmer, that to obtain selection as reviser Hendricks had promised to make the revision without compensation, then accepted compensation for the revision. Palmer, the *Leger* added, had since acknowledged the last charge to be false.

76 For examples, see Indiana *House Journal*, 1825–26, pp. 196–197; *ibid.*, 1826–27, pp. 167–168, 201; *ibid.*, 1827–28, pp. 288–289, 414–417; Indiana *Senate Journal*, 1827–28, pp. 43–44; *ibid.*, 1830–31, pp. 49–50.

77 Richmond *Public Leger*, February 3, 1827; Vincennes *Western Sun*, October 20, 1827.

78 Indiana *House Journal*, 1827–28, pp. 30–32, 414–417. Riker and Thornbrough (eds.), *Messages and Papers of James Brown Ray*, 296n–297n, indicate that Edward Livingston revised a civil code for Louisiana, adopted in 1825, but the criminal code he prepared was not adopted. Particularly in view of the ensuing comment from Stevens, the item quoted from him may have been written with tongue-in-cheek.

79 Indiana *House Journal*, 1829–30, p. 42; Indiana *Senate Journal*, 1829–30, pp. 130–132, 141–142. Four members of this committee expressed disapproval of the report.

80 Indiana *Senate Journal*, 1830–31, pp. 87–88; Indiana *House Journal*, 1830–31, p. 103. Senate members appointed were William Graham, William C. Linton, John T. McKinney, Stephen C. Stevens, and James Whitcomb. House members appointed were Ezra Ferris, William Herod, David Hillis, Amory

Kinney, and David Wallace. These men were a distinguished group for a pioneer legislature. Ferris and Graham had been members of the 1816 Constitutional Convention; Wallace served in that of 1850–51; Stevens and McKinney became members of the Supreme Court; Wallace and Hillis became lieutenant governor; Wallace and Whitcomb became governor; Herod, Graham, and Wallace became congressmen; Whitcomb became commissioner of the General Land Office for the United States and a member of the federal Senate. Brief sketches of these men are included, in alphabetical order, in *Biographical Directory of the Indiana General Assembly*, Volume I.

81 For a sample of the discussion pro and con concerning the revision by a joint committee of the legislature versus by a reviser or revisers, see Indianapolis *Indiana Journal*, December 18, 1830. As indicated in Rauch and Armstrong, *Bibliography of the Laws of Indiana, 1788–1927*, p. 68, the session of 1830–31, which began December 6 and ended February 10, was the longest since statehood, but only several days longer than that of 1823–24 which reviewed and approved the revision submitted by William Hendricks with some modifications.

82 *Laws of Indiana* (revised), 1830–31, pp. 334, 335–359, and 330 respectively for these items.

83 *Ibid.*, 539–540; *Acts* (special), 1830–31, p. 171, for the act mandating the secretary of state to append "explanations of the technical phrases and terms used in said laws."

84 For an indication of legislation regarding these subjects from 1822–31, see *Laws of Indiana* (revised), 1823–24, pp. 166–179; (revised), 1830–31, pp. 215–222.

85 Indiana *House Journal*, 1822–23, p. 12; *Laws of Indiana*, 1822–23, pp. 18–20. Boon stated that thus far no penalty had been affixed for failure of clerks to forward returns, but as note 86 indicates this seems to have been incorrect.

86 Indiana *House Journal*, 1825–26, p. 46; *Laws of Indiana*, 1825–26, p. 20. This law made clerks liable for the penalties imposed for neglect of duties according to the act of January 7, 1818. *Ibid.*, 1817–18, pp. 168–169. This act made clerks liable for a fine not to exceed $500 for failing to forward returns regarding the vote for governor and lieutenant governor.

87 For examples of editors' complaints about delay in election results, see Lawrenceburgh *Indiana Palladium*, August 30, September 13, December 13, 1828; Centreville *Western Times*, September 5, 1828; Indianapolis *Gazette*, September 11, 1828; Indianapolis *Indiana Journal*, September 25, 1828. *Laws of Indiana*, 1829–30, pp. 49–50. The reduced delinquency after 1830 versus that for the period 1816–28 may be noted in reviewing election results for governor from 1816 to 1849 in Riker and Thornbrough (comps.), *Indiana Election Returns, 1816–1851*, pp. 137–158.

88 Kettleborough, *Constitution Making in Indiana*, I, 96–97; Indiana *House Journal*, 1823–24, p. 18.

89 *Laws of Indiana*, 1825–26, pp. 18–20. Concerning the vigorous hassle between the House and Senate, see Indianapolis *Indiana Journal*, December 20,

1825, and these selected citations: Indiana *House Journal*, 1825–26, pp. 9, 19, 70, 73, 95, 102, 111, 137–138; Indiana *Senate Journal*, 1825–26, pp. 44–45, 83.

[90] For examples of items about confining voters to their township of residence, see Indiana *House Journal*, 1825–26, p. 22; *ibid.*, 1828–29, pp. 63–64; *ibid.*, 1829–30, p. 95; Indiana *Senate Journal*, 1827–28, pp. 31, 58.

[91] Vincennes *Western Sun*, January 10, 1829. One legislator contended that the Constitution of 1816 extended the right to vote to any place in the county.

[92] For examples of opposition to treating, see *ibid.*, April 10, 1824; Indianapolis *Gazette*, March 14, 1826; Indianapolis *Indiana Journal*, May 7, 1829. For legislation against treating, see *Laws of Indiana* (revised), 1823–24, p. 170; *ibid.*, 1830–31, p. 219.

[93] According to the federal census returns, Indiana's population jumped from 147,178 in 1820 to 343,031 in 1830. John D. Barnhart and Donald F. Carmony, *Indiana: From Frontier to Industrial Commonwealth* (4 vols., New York, 1954), I, 408.

[94] Indiana *House Journal*, 1825, pp. 18–19; *ibid.*, 1825–26, pp. 11–14. The returns for fifty-one of the fifty-two counties, by the secretary of state, indicate 36,977 voters according to the enumeration of 1825. The author has estimated that Clay, the missing county, had about 400 voters, making an aggregate of approximately 37,377 voters.

[95] So stated in the Indianapolis *Indiana Journal*, January 17, 1826. Governor Ray had advised legislators that this was the ratio used for the 1821 apportionment. Ray commented: "To continue this ratio, would make a considerable addition to your present number, and to increase it so as to avoid an addition of your number, would necessarily lessen the number of Senators and Representatives from particular districts." The governor waffled by recommending "consideration of . . . a proper regard to the rights of representation, at the same time keeping in view such economy of expenditure as the situation of our finances require." Indiana *House Journal*, 1825–26, p. 44.

[96] For the act of 1826, apportioning representation among fifty-three counties, see *Laws of Indiana*, 1825–26, pp. 5–6. Fountain County, not embraced in the enumeration of 1825, made the fifty-third county. As noted in George Pence and Nellie C. Armstrong, *Indiana Boundaries: Territory, State, and County* (Indianapolis, 1933), 44–45, 352–353, Fountain County was established after the enumeration of 1825 had been made. If an ideal apportionment of legislators was possible, each representative (or each senatorial) district would be based upon the same number of voters. The respect for county lines made considerable inequality in the number of voters from district to district inevitable. The innovation whereby Fayette and Union counties, in addition to obtaining a separate representative for the ensuing five year apportionment period, secured one who *floated* back and forth between them, afforded the possibility of reducing the inequality in the number of voters represented from district to district. The system of *floats*, which really floated in the apportionment of 1846, is discussed in Leon H. Wallace, "Legislative Apportionment in Indiana: A Case History," *Indiana Law Journal*, 42 (1966), 15–21.

[97] According to the Indianapolis *Indiana Journal*, January 3, 10, 17, 1826, the Senate passed an apportionment bill based on one representative per 700 voters and one senator per 1,800 voters. The House rejected this bill and passed one calling for one representative per 1,000 voters and one senator per 2,500 voters, but the ratio desired by the Senate was adopted.

[98] For the apportionment of 1826 Southern Indiana includes these 14 eastern counties: Bartholomew, Clark, Dearborn, *Decatur*, Floyd, Franklin, Harrison, Jackson, Jefferson, Jennings, Ripley, Scott, Switzerland, and Washington; and these 17 western counties: Crawford, Daviess, Dubois, Gibson, Greene, Knox, Lawrence, Martin, Monroe, Orange, Perry, Pike, Posey, Spencer, Sullivan, Vanderburgh, and Warrick. Central Indiana counties include these 11 eastern counties: Fayette, *Hamilton, Henry, Johnson, Madison, Marion*, Randolph, *Rush, Shelby*, Union, and Wayne; and these 10 western counties: *Clay, Fountain, Hendricks, Montgomery, Morgan*, Owen, Parke, *Putnam, Vermillion*, and Vigo. *Allen*, the only Northern Indiana county, is an eastern county. The apportionment of 1826 attached large unorganized portions of the northern half of the state to organized counties for both House and Senate districts. The 16 counties in *italics* had not been *organized* in time to be embraced in the apportionment of 1821.

[99] See Indianapolis *Indiana Journal*, December 25, 1830, for the enumeration by counties; Indiana *House Journal*, 1830–31, pp. 26–27 (Ray's comments). The enumeration was reported to both houses December 13, 1830, but the journals for that day do not have a copy of the report. *Ibid.*, 95; Indiana *Senate Journal*, 1830–31, pp. 89–90.

[100] Indianapolis *Indiana Journal*, December 25, 29, 1830, January 1, 5, 22, 29, 1831.

[101] *Laws of Indiana* (revised), 1830–31, pp. 503–504. Counties considered Southern Indiana embraced these 14 eastern counties: Bartholomew, Clark, Dearborn, Decatur, Floyd, Franklin, Harrison, Jackson, Jefferson, Jennings, Ripley, Scott, Switzerland, and Washington; and these 17 western counties: Crawford, Daviess, Dubois, Gibson, Greene, Knox, Lawrence, Martin, Monroe, Orange, Perry, Pike, Posey, Spencer, Sullivan, Vanderburgh, and Warrick. Central Indiana counties included these 13 eastern counties: *Delaware*, Fayette, Hamilton, *Hancock*, Henry, Johnson, Madison, Marion, Randolph, Rush, Shelby, Union, and Wayne; and these 14 western counties: *Boone*, Clay, *Clinton*, Fountain, Hendricks, Montgomery, Morgan, Owen, Parke, Putnam, *Tippecanoe, Warren*, Vermillion, and Vigo. Northern Indiana had these 2 eastern counties: Allen, *Elkhart*; and these 3 western counties: *Carroll, Cass*, and *St. Joseph*. A few legislative districts included territory for which counties had not yet been organized. The ten counties in *italics* had not been organized in time to be included in the apportionment of 1826.

[102] Indiana *House Journal*, 1830–31, pp. 223–224, 237–240. Of the 11 representatives who protested the legislative apportionment, and the 30 who defended it, according to *Biographical Directory of the Indiana General Assembly*, I, 455–456, the protesters included 6 Jacksonians, 4 Adams men, and 1 represen-

tative whose politics was unknown; and the defenders included 9 Jacksonians, 12 Adams men, 4 probable Adams men, and 5 whose politics were unknown. This illustrates rather convincingly that local and personal considerations, not party cleavage, had determined the apportionment. All of the protesters, according to Walsh, represented Southern Indiana counties, but about the same number of the defenders also represented Southern Indiana counties. The reapportionment of 1831, because of the large increase in population of Central Indiana counties, left fewer representatives for distribution to Southern counties, hence some of them had reduced representation; and this was probably the principal basis for their protest, especially as most of the protesters were from the counties of Dearborn, Floyd, Harrison, and Washington which suffered reductions.

103 Riker and Thornbrough (eds.), *Messages and Papers of James Brown Ray*, 572n (Zenor); Indianapolis *Indiana Journal*, January 22, 1831. For related information about the apportionment of 1831, see Wallace, "Legislative Apportionment in Indiana," *Indiana Law Journal*, XLII, 16–17; Walsh, *Centennial History of the Indiana General Assembly*, 64–65, 730, 741–742.

104 For an explanation of voters remaining in counties of residence until new apportionment districts were formed, see Chapter 1, pp. 30–31.

105 Pence and Armstrong, *Indiana Boundaries*, 158–159, 320–321, 434–435, 580–581, 614–615, 694–695, 716–717, 740–741. The seven counties were Decatur, Henry, Marion, Morgan, Putnam, Rush, and Shelby. According to *ibid.*, 37, these "seven counties were created, all in, or extending into, the New Purchase." The maps cited indicate that they were overwhelmingly within the New Purchase, obtained from the Indians in 1818.

106 Indianapolis *Gazette*, February 25, August 10, September 28, 1822.

107 Indiana *House Journal*, 1822–23, pp. 13–14; *Laws of Indiana*, 1822–23, pp. 110–111. Regarding passage, see Indiana *House Journal*, 1822–23, pp. 81, 222, 273–274; Indiana *Senate Journal*, 1822–23, pp. 134, 145, 170, 253–254, 269. For maps illustrating the counties composing these new districts, see Walsh, *Centennial History of the Indiana General Assembly*, 730, 735–736. The interim apportionment of 1823 established a representative district for the counties of Hamilton, Johnson, Madison, and Marion; a second district for the counties of Decatur, Henry, Rush, and Shelby; and a third district for the counties of Montgomery, Putnam, and Wabash. The eight counties that composed the first two of these representative districts were also created into an additional senatorial district, while the counties of the third representative district were "attached" to the existing senatorial district composed of the counties of Greene, Morgan, Owen, Parke, Sullivan, and Vigo. Hence this act added three representative districts and one new senatorial district.

108 Indiana *House Journal*, 1827–28, pp. 152–154; *Laws of Indiana*, 1828–29, p. 12. The committee contended that an item in the articles of compact of the Ordinance of 1787, asserting that residents should always be entitled to "a proportionate representation of the people in the legislature," applied and was obligatory. For maps illustrating the counties composing these new districts, see

Walsh, *Centennial History of the Indiana General Assembly*, 730, 739–740. The interim apportionment of 1829 gave one representative to a district consisting of the counties of Allen and Cass, and all the country north thereof to the state line; two representatives to the district for Carroll, Fountain, Montgomery, Tippecanoe, and Warren; and two representatives for the counties of Hamilton, Hancock, Henry, and Madison, and all country north thereof to the state line, not attached to another county. The counties of Allen, Cass, Delaware, and Randolph, and all the country north thereof to the state line were formed in a new senatorial district, with one senator. An additional senator was given the senatorial district created for the counties of Carroll, Montgomery, Putnam, and Tippecanoe, plus counties attached to certain territory per an act of January 24, 1828.

[109] Indiana *Senate Journal*, 1828–29, p. 248. As noted in Oliver H. Smith, *Early Indiana Trials and Sketches* (Cincinnati, 1858), 76–77, Smith said, perhaps with exaggeration, that the apportionment of 1823 hastened removal of the seat of government to Indianapolis "years sooner than it would otherwise have been." And as indicated in Nellie A. Robertson and Dorothy Riker (eds.), *The John Tipton Papers* (3 vols., Indianapolis, 1942), II, 132–133, Representative Thomas J. Matlock advised Tipton that the reapportionment of 1829 would no doubt "be of infinite importance in all our efforts to promote the wabash canal." He explained that a bill "on this subject" had been lost by a vote of 29 to 29, and efforts to reconsider the bill had proved abortive. The laws for the interim apportionments of 1823 and 1829, as cited in this and the preceding note, indicate that part of the additional representation was given counties which had been included in the five year reapportionments.

[110] Kettleborough, *Constitution Making in Indiana*, I, 71–76. This was one of the donations given as a quid pro quo for exemption of federal land from taxation for five years subsequent to its sale.

[111] *Ibid.*, xxv–xxvii, 118, 127, 138–139, 146. Also see Ethel Cleland, "New Facts About the Corydon State House," *Indiana Magazine of History*, IX (1913), 14–19; Walsh, *Centennial History of the Indiana General Assembly*, 4–5 , 131. Despite the considerable information contained in these sources, questions remain concerning what understandings, perhaps as much informal as formal, existed about the bond and the use by the state of buildings while the capital remained at Corydon. Also see Walsh, *Centennial History of the Indiana General Assembly*, 4, 4n.

[112] Indiana *House Journal*, 1818–19, p. 22; *ibid.*, 1819–20, p. 20.

[113] *Laws of Indiana*, 1819–20, pp. 18–20; Corydon *Indiana Gazette*, March 23, 1820; Vincennes *Western Sun*, May 13, 1820. The commissioners and the counties indicated for them were: Joseph Bartholomew, Clark; John Conner, Fayette; Jesse B. Durham, Jackson; Thomas Emmerson (Emison), Knox; John Gilliland, Switzerland; George Hunt, Wayne; Stephen Ludlow, Dearborn; William Prince, Gibson; Frederick Rapp, Posey; John Tipton, Harrison. As indicated in *Biographical Directory of the Indiana General Assembly*, I, 440, this commission was composed entirely of individuals who were not members of the legislative session which named it.

114 The official journal (or report) regarding location of the capital is in Indiana *House Journal*, 1820–21, pp. 24–26. The commissioners elected Hunt chairman. Tipton's account, more complete and detailed than the official journal, is in Robertson and Riker (eds.), *John Tipton Papers*, I, 195–210. Tipton makes various references to the presence of Governor Jennings with the commissioners. He begins his account by saying that he and the governor left Corydon May 17, adding: "(we took with us Bill a Black Buoy)[.]" On December 28, 1818, in a letter to Josiah Meigs about land surveys across the "West Branch of White river," Jennings stated that "it is not unlikely that our permanent seat of Government will be situated ere long on this stream." Dorothy Riker, *Unedited Letters of Jonathan Jennings* (Indianapolis, 1932), 224. This letter, and the convening of the commission at Conner's residence, suggest that apparently the principal duty of the commission was to determine *which site* along White River should be selected for the permanent capital. Both the official journal and Tipton's account indicate the participation of all the commissioners except William Prince, who is not mentioned in either record.

115 Madison *Indiana Republican*, June 22, 1820, quoting [Charlestown] *Indiana Intelligencer*; Salem *Tocsin*, June 10, 1820, quoting [Vincennes] *Indiana Centinel*. As noted in Gayle Thornbrough, Dorothy Riker, and Paula Corpuz (eds.), *The Diary of Calvin Fletcher* (9 vols., Indianapolis, 1972–1983), II, 4, 4n, poor drainage and flooding were problems for the capital site in spite of statements about its dryness.

116 Indiana *House Journal*, 1820–21, p. 7; *Laws of Indiana*, 1820–21, pp. 44–53, quotations on 45, 47, 53.

117 *Laws of Indiana*, 1820–21, p. 53; Vincennes *Indiana Centinel & Public Advertiser*, January 13, 20, 1821. For an account, anything but conclusive, about the naming of Indianapolis, see Jacob Piatt Dunn, *Indiana and Indianans* (5 vols., Chicago, 1919), I, 363–365. The Vincennes *Indiana Centinel & Public Advertiser*, December 2, 1820, has a lengthy article by "An Indianian" urging that the permanent capital be named Tecumseh, explaining that the name was musical and that Tecumseh had been a great leader of his people.

118 For the election of James W. Jones, Christopher Harrison, and Samuel P. Booker as commissioners, see Indiana *House Journal*, 1820–21, pp. 282–283; for the act legalizing Harrison's acts "as if the same had been done by a majority" of the commissioners, see *Laws of Indiana*, 1821–22, pp. 18–19.

119 Carmony, Indiana Public Finance, 1800–1826, pp. 336–337. On December 4, 1822, Ralston presented the Senate with "a map of the donation, for the use of the General Assembly," and the Senate thanked him "for the elegant plat of Indianapolis" received from him. Indiana *Senate Journal*, 1822–23, p. 20. This source says the map was deposited in the office of the secretary of state.

120 Dunn, *Indiana and Indianans*, I, 362–363, has a copy of the Ralston plat, with comments about it and the quote attributed to Ralston.

121 Corydon *Indiana Gazette*, September 13, 1821. This notice, dated June 10, 1821, also appeared in the Vincennes *Indiana Centinel & Public Advertiser*,

June 23, 1821. Early in 1821 the General Assembly had memorialized Congress praying that the National Road pass through Indianapolis. *Laws of Indiana,* 1820–21, pp. 142–144.

[122] Indiana *House Journal,* 1825–26, pp. 95–96; Thornbrough, Riker, and Corpuz (eds.), *Diary of Calvin Fletcher,* I, 41, 41n–42n. According to the *Indiana Gazetteer* (Indianapolis, 1849), 254–255, one lot sold for $560, another for $500, apparently the highest prices paid.

[123] Indiana *House Journal,* 1834–35, pp. 73–74, for report of Treasurer Samuel Merrill concerning revenue, by years, to November 30, 1834.

[124] Riker and Thornbrough (eds.), *Messages and Papers of James Brown Ray,* 154–155, 185 (remarks of Ray), 269–270, 408–410. For what seems to have been the initial relief legislation to purchasers of lots from the capital donation, see Indianapolis *Indiana Journal,* December 15 [13], 1825; *Laws of Indiana,* 1825–26, pp. 61–62.

[125] *Laws of Indiana,* 1821–22, pp. 135–139; Pence and Armstrong, *Indiana Boundaries,* 28–29, 34–35, 37–38, 580–581; Jacob Piatt Dunn, *Greater Indianapolis* (2 vols., Chicago, 1910), I, 47–53, 112–113.

[126] *Laws of Indiana,* 1821–22, pp. 136–137, appropriating $8,000; *Acts* (special), 1823–24, pp. 10–11, appropriating "the further sum" of $5,996 for furniture and other items; *Laws of Indiana,* 1825–26, pp. 60–61, appropriating $915.97 for "payment of the balance due" contractors for building the courthouse; Charles H. Test to his wife, December 12, 1826, Charles H. Test Collection, Lilly Library, Indiana University, Bloomington.

[127] Thornbrough, Riker, and Corpuz (eds.), *Diary of Calvin Fletcher,* I, 102.

[128] *Laws of Indiana* (revised), 1823–24, pp. 370–372; *Acts* (special), 1823–24, pp. 113–114; Indiana *House Journal,* 1823–24, pp. 188, 298–301 (protest by Pennington and Zenor); Indiana *Senate Journal,* 1823–24, pp. 123, 133–134. The House vote is given as 25 to 17, but only 16 noes are listed.

[129] Indianapolis *Gazette,* August 24, 1824; Indiana *Senate Journal,* 1825, pp. 7–8, for Merrill's report about the sale of property and removal to Indianapolis. Merrill received $52.52 for property sold at Corydon, and he reported the removal cost as $118.07, or $65.55 more than gained at the sale. For some unknown reason Merrill was allowed to keep the $65.55 plus only $60.50; he was also given a bonus of $100 for his personal expense and trouble in making the removal. *Laws of Indiana,* 1825, pp. 10–12. For an oft quoted account of the removal, probably by Merrill, see *Indiana Gazetteer* (1849), 125.

[130] Indiana *House Journal,* 1825, pp. 19–20; *Laws of Indiana,* 1825, p. 11, the house to be located along Washington Street, opposite the state house square. Early in 1827 Merrill was allowed *up to $30* for painting "the house and offices built for the auditor and treasurer." *Laws of Indiana,* 1826–27, p. 11.

[131] *Laws of Indiana,* 1826–27, pp. 4–5, for the appropriation of $4,000; *ibid.,* 1827–28, pp. 3–4, $2,040 additional for house for governor; *ibid.,* 1828–29, p. 85, $653.15 additional for house for governor. The last of these acts authorized the agent for the Indianapolis Fund to deduct from the sum appropriated any

amount considered proper if on completion the house was found defective or improperly finished.

132 *Ibid.*, 1827–28, p. 136. See Dunn, *Greater Indianapolis*, I, 102–103, for a picture and description of the residence for the governor.

133 For examples of discussion about possible use of the Governor's House as a capitol—or by the Marion County Seminary, or its sale to the highest bidder —see Indiana *House Journal*, 1828–29, pp. 243–248; *ibid.*, 1829–30, pp. 157–159, 324–328; *ibid.*, 1830–31, pp. 258–259. As indicated in *Acts* (special), 1830–31, p. 171, the Indianapolis agent was to fix up rooms in the Governor's House for offices for the secretary of state and auditor of public accounts. He was also to have the building repaired "by cleaning out the cellar, having shutters hung to the cellar windows, and the leaks in the roof stopped."

134 See *Laws of Indiana*, 1825, p. 11, allowing "the Governor for the time being . . . two hundred dollars annually for house rent." At the session of 1828–29 a House committee proposed to add wings to the Governor's House and convert it into a capitol; and build a house for the chief executive on the square reserved for a state house, so that $200 yearly in house rent for the executive could be saved. Indiana *House Journal*, 1828–29, pp. 245, 247.

135 Riker and Thornbrough (eds.), *Messages and Papers of James Brown Ray*, 57–58, 116–117, 123–124. In February, 1826, Ray wrote Secretary of State Henry Clay seeking his aid for appointment as a commissioner to treat with the Indians for land which, he said, the General Assembly desired for construction of a Wabash and Erie Canal. Hopkins (ed.), *Papers of Henry Clay*, V, 82.

136 Vincennes *Western Sun*, July 15, 1826; Kettleborough, *Constitution Making in Indiana*, I, 97. Not noted by the *Sun* was a related section of the constitution which stated that "No persons shall hold more than one lucrative office at the same time, except as in this constitution is expressly permitted." *Ibid.*, I, 118–119. This item was used later against Ray in the discussion by legislators concerning whether his service as commissioner had been in violation of the constitution.

137 According to treaty proceedings in Robertson and Riker (eds.), *John Tipton Papers*, I, 576–592, negotiations began September 20 and ended October 23, 1826. Ray arrived September 23 and seemingly remained until October 23. For outcome of the negotiations, see pp. 116–118 and Chapter 9, pp. 496–497.

138 Indiana *Senate Journal*, 1826–27, p. 6; Indiana *House Journal*, 1826–27, pp. 9–10.

139 Indiana *House Journal*, 1826–27, pp. 16–17, 28.

140 The Indianapolis *Gazette*, December 7, 14, 22, 1826, offers proceedings and speeches about Craig's resolution for the second, third, and fourth days of the session. The Indiana *House Journal*, 1826–27, pp. 9–10, 13, 14, 15, 16–17, 28–31, indicates such consideration during these three days.

141 Indianapolis *Gazette*, December 7, 14, 22, 1826. Quotes from Hurst and Hays are in the December 14 issue. The Indianapolis *Indiana Journal*, December 12, 1826, gives close to half of its four-page issue to speeches pro and con

Craig's resolution. Despite differences, its account and that of the *Gazette* cover much the same ground.

[142] Indiana *House Journal*, 1826–27, pp. 29, 30–31; Indiana *Senate Journal*, 1826–27, pp. 16–17.

[143] Indiana *House Journal*, 1826–27, pp. 49–52. Ray, like Jennings, rather than arguing the constitutionality of his service, emphasized the benefits resulting from his service to negotiate with the Indians. Representative General Washington Johnston, who staunchly defended and supported Ray, explained that he had opposed Jennings when he had acted in a similar capacity but had since changed his view. Indianapolis *Gazette*, December 7, 1826. That Ray apparently applied for and perhaps received compensation of $440 for his service as Indian commissioner, plus travel allowance, is indicated in Riker and Thornbrough (eds.), *Messages and Papers of James Brown Ray*, 225, 247–248, 257–258; Robertson and Riker (eds.), *John Tipton Papers*, I, 688–689, 699–700.

[144] Indiana *House Journal*, 1826–27, pp. 300–304, 307–310. The speaker named John T. McKinney, Stephen C. Stevens, and Morris Morris members of the committee.

[145] *Ibid.*, 479; Indianapolis *Gazette*, May 16, 1826. As indicated in Kettleborough, *Constitution Making in Indiana*, I, 102, the constitution made no residence requirement for the auditor and treasurer; however, Indiana residence was doubtless presumed.

[146] Indiana *House Journal*, 1826–27, p. 484.

[147] *Ibid.*, 491.

[148] *Ibid.*, 479–480.

[149] *Ibid.*, 484–485. Merrill also stated that at times [Henry P.] Coburn, Judge [Bethuel F.] Morris, [Benjamin I.] Blythe, and James M. Ray had done work for him during his absences.

[150] *Ibid.*, 489–491. Wick said that at different times Andrew Ingraham [Ingram], Samuel Merrill, Austin W. Morris, James M. Ray, and "probably others" had been "employed" in his office. Whether Wick meant employed for pay is uncertain.

[151] For salaries and per diem, see Chapter 1, p. 12.

[152] Indiana *House Journal*, 1826–27, pp. 316–319, 324–329. After the session ended Ray explained to a correspondent that he had overdrawn $50 on his house rent account while "nearly at all times large sums" were underdrawn on his salary account, and that the whole affair had been basely colored and perverted. Riker and Thornbrough (eds.), *Messages and Papers of James Brown Ray*, 211–212.

[153] Indiana *House Journal*, 1826–27, pp. 475–477.

[154] *Ibid.*, 329–336, 512–514. On page 329 Merrill stated "That no money has ever been advanced or loaned by him as Treasurer, out of the Treasury of state, either to officers of state, or members of the present House of Representatives, in anticipation of their services." Nevertheless, how advances were made and items about them cleared seems unclear.

155 *Ibid.*, 489, 491–492. For a misunderstanding and controversy regarding Merrill's role in issuing military commissions in 1825, see *ibid.*, 477–479 (comment of investigating committee), 485–488 (comment of Merrill), 492–494 (comment of Wick), 514 (comment of Merrill).

156 *Ibid.*, 479–483. Lilly stated that suits had been instituted against all but two delinquent county collectors to whom the legislature had given additional time to make settlement.

157 *Ibid.*, 470, 479. The ensuing discussion perhaps explains the omission of the auditor from this evaluation.

158 *Ibid.*, 470 471. If the committee submitted a bill indicating the proper respective duties of the auditor and treasurer, it has not been found.

159 *Ibid.*, 474.

160 *Ibid.*, 477–479. The pages cited in note 157 cover criticism of Merrill's role concerning issuance of military commissions.

161 *Ibid.*, 471–472, 479.

162 *Ibid.*, 470–495. As indicated, *ibid.*, 522–524, the manner in which the select committee investigated the state offices appears to have been even more casual and informal than the manner in which the state offices had been conducted. See also remarks of Merrill, *ibid.*, 512–514.

163 *Ibid.*, 485; Lawrenceburgh *Indiana Palladium*, January 27, 1827; Indianapolis *Gazette*, February 2, 1827.

164 Merrill's denunciation of Ray appeared in the Indianapolis *Gazette*, June 19, 1827, and is reprinted in Riker and Thornbrough (eds.), *Messages and Papers of James Brown Ray*, 218–226, quotations, 221–224, as a response to criticisms against Merrill which had appeared in "the three last numbers" of this pro-Ray paper—the issues of May 22, June 15, 12, 1827.

165 Indianapolis *Gazette*, July 3, 1827. From late June through December, 1827, at least a dozen items appeared in the *Gazette* in support of Ray.

166 Riker and Thornbrough (eds.), *Messages and Papers of James Brown Ray*, 239–248, quoting excerpts from this pamphlet, plus notes commenting pro and con about the evidence.

167 Thornbrough, Riker, and Corpuz (eds.), *Diary of Calvin Fletcher*, I, 147; Robertson and Riker (eds.), *John Tipton Papers*, I, 784–785.

168 Indianapolis *Gazette*, July 10, September 4, December 11, 1827, January 8, 1828; Indianapolis *Indiana Journal*, October 9, 1827; Vincennes *Western Sun*, February 2, 1828.

169 Robertson and Riker (eds.), *John Tipton Papers*, II, 11–12; Vincennes *Western Sun*, September 25, 1824, January 19, 26, February 16, 1828. The proceedings of the Jackson convention, perhaps incomplete as found in the *Western Sun*, January 19, 26, 1828, do not indicate a nomination of Canby. The Indianapolis *Gazette*, February 19, 1828, notes an item from the [Lawrenceburgh] *Palladium*, stating that a Madison paper was publishing a letter, written by Canby, in which he says he declines "being considered a candidate for Governor, in consequence of urgent private business requiring his absence from the state some length of time."

170 The issues of the Lawrenceburgh *Indiana Palladium* for March, 1, 8, 15, 22, 29, April 5, 1828, list only Ray and Thompson as candidates for governor but starting April 12 Thompson's name no longer appears. The Vincennes *Western Sun*, April 12, 1828, quotes the Charlestown *Advocate* that it was "'authorized again to state, that Mr. Thompson will not be a candidate.'" The Indianapolis *Indiana Journal*, January 31, 1828, indicates Thompson as a nondelegate member of the Adams State Convention, 1828.

171 Indianapolis *Indiana Journal*, January 31, May 15, 29, 1828; Vincennes *Western Sun*, May 24, 1828; *Biographical Directory of the Indiana General Assembly*, I, 280.

172 For a copy of the proposal to Ray, as adopted by the Jackson State Committee, May 7, 1828, and Ray's response dated May 15, see Riker and Thornbrough (eds.), *Messages and Papers of James Brown Ray*, 343–346.

173 *Ibid.*, 348–350. As the ensuing discussion makes clear, Ray insisted that the remarks attributed to him were a gross misrepresentation of what he had said. Presumably Jocelyn was trying to turn Jacksonians against Ray.

174 *Ibid.*, 350–353.

175 Indianapolis *Indiana Journal*, July 24, 1828, for Canby's July 5 announcement, saying he had yielded to numerous communications asking him to become a candidate; Lawrenceburgh *Indiana Palladium*, July 5, 1828, quoting Salem *Annotator*, June 21, 1828. Canby's comments seem to say that he had at least been the informal candidate of the Jackson State Convention in January.

176 Riker and Thornbrough (eds.), *Messages and Papers of James Brown Ray*, 357–366, quoting Indianapolis *Gazette*, July 17, 1828, quotes on 359, 364, 365. As reported on pp. 354–355, in a public meeting at Indianapolis on July 12, Noah Noble and others charged that during the last legislative session Ray had told the Adams men that he was one of them; and since his correspondence with the Jacksonians in May Ray had made remarks critical of Jackson, and had contributed five dollars toward costs of the Adams party. *Ibid.*, 354–355, according to the Indianapolis *Gazette*, July 31, 1828, Ray admitted having made such a contribution.

177 The official returns for all fifty-eight counties are in Riker and Thornbrough (comps.), *Indiana Election Returns, 1816–1851*, pp. 140–141. Ray and Canby got an equal number of votes in Greene County. See *ibid.*, 10–13, showing that Jackson received about 22,100 votes in November versus about 17,000 for Adams.

178 Riker and Thornbrough (eds.), *Messages and Papers of James Brown Ray*, 369–370, quoting Lawrenceburgh *Indiana Palladium*, October 18, 1828, quoting the Indianapolis *Gazette*. As sources cited in note 177 indicate, Jackson received about 9,850 more votes than Canby, while the count for Adams exceeded that for Moore about 6,100. The combined vote for Jackson and Adams was approximately 15,950 more votes than the combined vote for Canby and Moore, whereas Ray received 15,131 votes. Thus, Ray drew much support from partisans of both Jackson and Adams; and the aggregate of votes cast for governor roughly approached that for president.

179 Indianapolis *Indiana Journal*, June 5, 1828; *Biographical Directory of the Indiana General Assembly*, I, 311, 369. The *Indiana Journal*, January 31, 1828, lists Stapp as a delegate to the Adams State Convention, January, 1828; the Indianapolis *Gazette*, June 5, 1828, called Pepper a "decided Jacksonian" who would presumably draw the (party) line in politics.

180 Riker and Thornbrough (comps.), *Indiana Election Returns, 1816–1851*, pp. 162–163, official for all counties, shows 17,895 votes for Stapp, and 17,262 for Pepper. Concerning the Michigan Road as an issue, see Lawrenceburgh *Indiana Palladium*, August 2, 30, October 4, 11, 1828; Indianapolis *Indiana Journal*, August 21, 1828.

181 Lawrenceburgh *Indiana Palladium*, September 13, 1828, mentioning John Scott, Benjamin I. Blythe, Morris Morris, Harvey Gregg, and B. F. Wallace for auditor; William Wick and Henry P. Thornton for secretary of state; and commenting that it had not heard of any person announced against Merrill. These names had been mentioned in the Indianapolis *Gazette*, August 28, 1828.

182 Indiana *House Journal*, 1828–29, p. 41. The four votes against Merrill are listed as "scattering," with no names given.

183 *Ibid.*, 41–42; Indianapolis *Gazette*, February 19, 1828, announcing Lilly's death. Blythe resigned as Indianapolis agent April 5, 1828, and was commissioned auditor to succeed Lilly the same day. Riker (ed.), *Executive Proceedings of the State of Indiana, 1816–1836*, pp. 278, 288.

184 Indiana *House Journal*, 1828–29, pp. 40–41.

185 For previous members of the Supreme Court, 1816–30, see Chapter 1, pp. 8–9, and note 20.

186 For items before, during, and after the legislative session, charging that Ray was trying to use appointments to the Supreme Court to enhance his prospect for election to the United States Senate, see I. George Blake, *The Holmans of Veraestau* (Oxford, Ohio, 1943), 21–23; Riker and Thornbrough (eds.), *Messages and Papers of James Brown Ray*, 624–625; Robertson and Riker (eds.), *John Tipton Papers*, II, 324–325, 348–349; Smith, *Early Indiana Trials and Sketches*, 144–145; William Wesley Woollen, *Biographical and Historical Sketches of Early Indiana* (Indianapolis, 1883), 57.

187 Indiana *Senate Journal*, 1830–31, pp. 159, 230–231.

188 *Ibid.*, 255–257. There was some confusion about when the terms of the previous judges expired. Ray stated that their terms began December 28, 1823, and ended December 28, 1830. According to Riker (ed.), *Executive Proceedings of the State of Indiana, 1816–1836*, pp. 303, 306, Blackford, Holman, and Scott had been commissioned December 29, 1823; their terms ended December 27, 1830; and Blackford, McKinney, and Stevens were commissioned January 28, 1831.

189 Indiana *Senate Journal*, 1830–31, pp. 259–261, 277–278, 347–355. The Senate report says the terms of Blackford, Holman, and Scott had ended December 27, not December 28 as indicated by Ray. Since the 1816 Constitution

explicitly limited terms of Supreme Court justices to seven years, presumably Indiana was without an official Supreme Court for about one month. Kettleborough, *Constitution Making in Indiana*, I, 105–106, Sections 4, 10.

190 Indiana *Senate Journal*, 1830–31, pp. 388, 394–396. Some senators who voted for McKinney voted against Stevens, and some who voted for Stevens voted against McKinney. Perhaps the vote had been arranged to make approval as narrow as possible.

191 *Ibid.*, 408, 543–545. For a different version of Watts' remarks, see Indianapolis *Indiana Democrat*, February 12, 1831. As indicated in Kettleborough, *Constitution Making in Indiana*, I, 94, no legislator during his elected term was eligible to any office "the appointment of which" was vested in the General Assembly. Watts' comment that the elevation of McKinney and Stevens to the court at least violated the spirit of the constitution was justified. As indicated in Indiana *Senate Journal*, 1830–31, pp. 87–88, Stevens and McKinney had been named to the Senate committee to act with the House in revising the laws. Since Stevens was named first, presumably he was its chair.

192 Riker and Thornbrough (comps.), *Indiana Election Returns, 1816–1851*, pp. 128–131. It is possible, however, that some of the small number of votes listed as "scattering" were for Ray. Soon after the legislature adjourned Ray commented in a letter to the editor of the Indianapolis *Indiana Democrat*, February 26, 1831: "from the time I became a candidate, this winter, for the Senate of the U. States, in Congress, to fill a place to become vacant two years hence" that Aristocrats, friends of opposing candidates, "certain disappointed Senators, who could not lash me into their selection of Judges"; etc. formed "one general *conspiracy*" to ruin his prospects "at the *outset*."

193 Riker and Thornbrough (comps.), *Indiana Election Returns, 1816–1851*, pp. 8–9, 76–77, 127, 138–139.

194 See pp. 98–99, this chapter, for Ray's promise to prepare such a code without cost to the state. Ray's explanation of the status of his effort re the code is in Indiana *Senate Journal*, 1830–31, pp. 59, 63–64.

195 *Ibid.*, 230, 246, 503.

196 *Ibid.*, 503, 249–250 (Ray's response), 504–505, 546–552 (related items from Ray), 169, 500–511, Appendix D, 1–4, for quibbling before and after Ray's response.

197 Travel conditions, 1816–22 are described in Chapter 1, pp. 38–39.

198 *Indiana Gazetteer* (1849), 126; Shirley S. McCord (comp.) *Travel Accounts of Indiana, 1679–1961* (Indianapolis, 1970), 117; Madison *Indiana Republican*, October 7, 1829; Smith, *Early Indiana Trials and Sketches*, 583–584. Smith states that Hager had been on the road fifteen days, and would require three more to reach Indianapolis.

199 Indianapolis *Indiana Journal*, February 2, 1831; Thornbrough, Riker, and Corpuz (eds.), *Diary of Calvin Fletcher*, I, 163–164.

200 Thornbrough, Riker, and Corpuz (eds.), *Diary of Calvin Fletcher*, I, 104–129, 131, 172–173.

201 Indianapolis *Indiana Journal*, February 19, 1829, June 5, 1828; Smith, *Early Indiana Trials and Sketches*, 88. Smith adds: "There were no railroads across the mountains then, stages were 'all the go,' and traveling on horseback [for such trips?] fast going out of fashion. But the General [Senator Noble] stuck to the old mode all his life."

202 George Bush to Absalom Peters, February 18, 1828, and Isaac Coe to Peters, November 4, 1828, in American Home Missionary Society Papers, Lilly Library, Indiana University, Bloomington, and Indiana Division, Indiana State Library, Indianapolis; Lawrenceburgh *Indiana Palladium*, August 30, 1828.

203 *Laws of Indiana* (revised), 1823–24, pp. 360–362; *ibid.* (revised), 1830–31, pp. 450–451, 133 (election of supervisors). The road labor and tax levied by the code of 1831 were the same as that established in 1825. *Laws of Indiana*, 1825, pp. 74–76.

204 *Laws of Indiana* (revised), 1823–24, pp. 355–367 *passim*; *ibid.* (revised), 1830–31, pp. 445–455 *passim*. These codes suggest the general content and trends regarding legislation for opening and maintaining roads.

205 Regarding legislation for improvement of roads, 1816–22, see Chapter 1, pp. 39–40.

206 *Laws of Indiana*, 1821–22, pp. 152–169, listing and naming the twenty-two roads included in the initial appropriation from the Three Per Cent Fund; Indiana *House Journal*, 1831–32, Appendix B, 1–4, indicating that fifty-five appropriations had been made concerning roads and ten for rivers, but not giving the names of the roads and rivers. In each category there were two items for which no expenditures had been made. This report, by Benjamin I. Blythe, shows only $1,725 spent on rivers. But $147.34 listed as spent on the Wabash Fund presumably should be counted as spent for river improvement.

207 Indianapolis *Gazette*, July 8, 1823, June 1, 1824.

208 Riker and Thornbrough (eds.), *Messages and Papers of James Brown Ray*, 85–86. For examples of similar criticism, see Vincennes *Western Sun*, April 13, May 11, 1822; Indianapolis *Gazette*, September 21, 1822; Indiana *Senate Journal*, 1825, pp. 65, 103–104; Indiana *House Journal*, 1827–28, p. 54.

209 *Laws of Indiana*, 1828–29, pp. 98–101; *Acts* (special), 1830–31, pp. 154–166.

210 For examples of bridges authorized under supervision of county commissioners, see *Laws of Indiana* (revised), 1823–24, pp. 366–367; *ibid.* (revised), 1830–31, pp. 453–454. For examples of acts authorizing toll bridges by individuals, see *Laws of Indiana*, 1822–23, pp. 97–100; *ibid.*, 1825, pp. 40–43; *ibid.*, 1828–29, pp. 142–143; *Acts* (special), 1830–31, pp. 9–11, 25–28. See Chapter 1, pp. 43–44 concerning bridges, 1816–22.

211 Smith, *Early Indiana Trials and Sketches*, 176; *Laws of Indiana*, 1825, pp. 81–82, 58–59. The original act appropriating $100,000 for roads, and that of 1831 appropriating $400 to each county, illustrate *passim* use of the Three Per Cent Fund for building bridges. *Laws of Indiana*, 1821–22, pp. 152–169; *Acts* (special), 1830–31, pp. 154–166.

212 Lawrenceburgh *Indiana Palladium*, June 26, July 3, 31, September 25, 1830. As indicated in *Acts* (special), 1830–31, pp. 25–28, at the ensuing legislative session the Lawrenceburgh Bridge Company was incorporated to build a toll bridge over Tanner's Creek. As may be noted in Louis B. Ewbank and Dorothy L. Riker (eds.), *The Laws of Indiana Territory, 1809–1816* (Indianapolis, 1934), 737–747, seventeen years earlier a Lawrenceburgh Bridge Company had been incorporated to build a bridge over Tanner's Creek, also as a toll bridge.

213 Lawrenceburgh *Indiana Palladium*, February 3, 1827.

214 *Laws of Indiana* (revised), 1823–24, pp. 208–211; *ibid.* (revised), 1830–31, pp. 259–264.

215 Indianapolis *Gazette*, May 11, 1822; Lawrenceburgh *Indiana Palladium*, March 29, 1828.

216 Indianapolis *Gazette*, September 12, 1826; Vincennes *Western Sun*, September 30, 1826.

217 Lawrenceburgh *Indiana Palladium*, September 16, 1826. The ensuing discussion about the Ohio River point for the Michigan Road strongly illustrates this rivalry.

218 *Laws of Indiana*, 1827–28, pp. 47–55. Noah Noble was one of the commissioners to establish the proposed corporation. Upon completion of contracts for their portion of the turnpike, the "undertakers" or contractors received certificates which could be transferred to others. When the turnpike was completed, holders of certificates were to become stockholders of the corporation. The Indianapolis *Gazette*, May 22, 1828, and the Indianapolis *Indiana Journal*, May 29, 1828, announced meetings to let contracts for building this turnpike, but no further information has been found regarding it.

219 Indiana *House Journal*, 1829–30, p. 18. Ray also envisioned a railroad from some point on the Ohio River to the Wabash and Erie Canal, via Indianapolis; and a railroad from Fort Wayne through the Whitewater Valley to Lawrenceburg, suggesting that perhaps a canal had been reported impractical for this route.

220 *Laws of Indiana*, 1828–29, pp. 92–97 (Levenworth Turnpike Company, to build a road twenty or more miles toward Indianapolis); *ibid.*, 1829–30, pp. 60–69 (New Albany and Vincennes Turnpike Company); *ibid.*, 70–81 (Hamilton, Rossville, and Richmond Turnpike Company); *ibid.*, 82–84 (White Water and Miami Turnpike Company). The Levenworth Turnpike Company was to be organized in a manner similar to that for the Indianapolis and White Water Turnpike Company. The three corporations, authorized in 1829–30, were to be organized by individuals who had purchased stock in them.

221 *Laws of Indiana*, 1827–28, p. 47. Acts about turnpikes had varying specifications about how they should be sloped from their center; the use of sand, gravel, stones, and lumber for the roadbed; and bridges.

222 *Annals of Congress*, 15 Cong., 1 session, I, 1113–1114; U. S. *Statutes at Large*, 19 Cong., 2 session, IV, 234–235.

223 *Laws of Indiana*, 1827–28, pp. 87–88; Riker and Thornbrough (eds.), *Messages and Papers of James Brown Ray*, 402–408 (report of commissioners); Robert-

son and Riker (eds.), *John Tipton Papers*, II, 72–73 (also 48–50, 58). The commissioners were John I. Neely, Gibson County; John McDonald, Daviess County, Chester Elliott, Warrick County. All were from southwestern counties where the road was not likely to pass. Perhaps legislators expected them to give more consideration to the general interest than if they had come from areas more likely to have a stronger chance to have it pass through their area. As indicated in Robertson and Riker (eds.), *John Tipton Papers*, II, 141–142, 168n–169n, South Bend had its beginnings at the southern bend of the St. Joseph in the late twenties and early thirties.

[224] Indianapolis *Gazette*, December 25, 1827; Indianapolis *Indiana Journal*, January 3, 1828.

[225] Indiana *House Journal*, 1828–29, pp. 223–229, 302–303, 318–323, 334–338, 344–345 (various House votes); *Laws of Indiana*, 1829–30, pp. 111–114; Indianapolis *Gazette*, January 7, 1830.

[226] For items suggesting this possibility, see Lawrenceburgh *Indiana Palladium*, January 9, 16, 30, June 5, 1830; Indianapolis *Indiana Democrat and State Gazette*, June 10, 1830. The Indianapolis *Indiana Journal*, July 14, 1830, stated that the Michigan Road, from Indianapolis to Napoleon, had been located on the state road from the capital to Lawrenceburg. Thus, there was an overlap of the two roads for about sixty-five miles to Napoleon, *less distant from Lawrenceburg than from Madison.* This item stated that contracts for opening the Michigan Road were lower between Indianapolis and Napoleon than near Madison and immediately north of Indianapolis.

[227] *Laws of Indiana*, 1829–30, pp. 114–116 (Noble's appointment, letting of contracts, how road to be built); Riker and Thornbrough (eds.), *Messages and Papers of James Brown Ray*, 522–523, 563–564 (Ray's opposition and subsequent criticism); Indiana *House Journal*, 1830–31, pp. 92–95 (contracts let). The Indianapolis *Indiana Journal*, July 14, 1830, giving Noble and "others" as its sources, stated that at Madison contracts were let on 15 miles at an average of $498.25 per mile; 15 miles at Shelbyville, $96 per mile; 11 miles at Means's (between Shelbyville and Indianapolis), $149 per mile; 7 miles south of Indianapolis, $105 per mile; 17 miles north of Indianapolis, $444 per mile. See p. 139, this chapter, concerning how the Cumberland Road was to be opened and graded.

[228] Riker and Thornbrough (eds.), *Messages and Papers Relating to the Administration of Noah Noble, Governor of Indiana, 1831–1837* (Indianapolis, 1958), 72–74 (Noble's report, 1830–31); Indianapolis *Indiana Journal*, November 5, 1831 (land sales); Riker and Thornbrough (eds.), *Messages and Papers of James Brown Ray*, 688 (land sales).

[229] R. Carlyle Buley, *The Old Northwest: Pioneer Period, 1815–1840* (2 vols., Indianapolis, 1950), I, 446–447; Indiana *House Journal*, 1825, pp. 16–17 (comments of Governor Hendricks); *ibid.*, 1830–31, pp. 19–20 (comments of Governor Ray).

[230] *Laws of Indiana*, 1820–21, pp. 142–144; *ibid.*, 1822–23, p. 152; *Acts* (special), 1823–24, pp. 110–111; *Laws of Indiana*, 1827–28, pp. 144–145; *ibid.*, 1828–29, pp. 151–152, 154–155; *Acts* (special), 1830–31, pp. 186–188.

231 Indianapolis *Indiana Journal*, June 12, July 10, October 30, 1827.

232 U.S. *Statutes at Large*, 20 Cong., 2 session, IV, 351–352; Indiana *House Journal*, 1829–30, pp. 109–114, for report by Johnson and Milroy. The aggregate of contracts for cutting, removing, and grubbing was $33,889 for the 143 miles let for an average of only $236.98 per mile.

233 U.S. *Statutes at Large*, 21 Cong., 1 session, IV, 427–428; *ibid.*, 21 Cong., 2 session, IV, 469–470.

234 The Indianapolis *Gazette*, August 14, 1827, announced that several towns had been laid off and lots advertised for sale on the National Road, including Georgetown, Knightstown, and Raysville. In October, 1830, Governor Ray wrote the federal secretary of war that the National Road "passes through the following towns, viz. Richmond, Centreville, Louisville, Raysville, Knightstown, Greenfield, Indianapolis, Terre Haute." Riker and Thornbrough (eds.), *Messages and Papers of James Brown Ray*, 549. A law authorized contractors to exclude persons "with horses, wagons, or carriages" from use of the road while construction was in progress. *Laws of Indiana*, 1831–32, pp. 86–87.

235 Indiana *House Journal*, 1826–27, pp. 41–42. Ray said that Indiana was "washed by the great and useful Ohio river" for at least 300 miles; that the "beautiful Wabash . . . meanders along and through another portion of her boundary, upwards of five hundred miles"; and the "White rivers run through her centre upwards of three hundred miles." He mentioned the "Whitewater and Blue rivers" as the smaller streams within the "inhabited" part of Indiana.

236 Albert L. Kohlmeier, *The Old Northwest as the Keystone of the Arch of American Federal Union: A Study in Commerce and Politics* (Bloomington, Ind., 1938), 1–21; John Garretson Clark, *The Grain Trade in the Old Northwest* (Urbana, Ill., 1966), 1–51.

237 Buley, *The Old Northwest*, I, 4, 520–521, 530–532. During the 1850–51 Constitutional Convention, Robert Dale Owen and two other delegates commented about their experiences as flatboatmen down the Mississippi. Owen asserted that one of these colleagues had made "fifteen or twenty" such trips. *Report of the Debates and Proceedings of the Convention for the Revision of the Constitution of the State of Indiana, 1850* (2 vols., Indianapolis, 1850, reprinted 1935), I, 527–528.

238 Vincennes *Western Sun*, June 17, 1826; Indianapolis *Gazette*, June 19, 1828, quoting Bloomington *Gazette*; Lawrenceburgh *Indiana Palladium*, October 16, 1830. Also see *Indiana Gazetteer* (1826), 50–51, 79–80, 83–84, 122, and perhaps other *passim* comments.

239 Leland D. Baldwin, *The Keelboat Age on Western Waters* (Pittsburgh, 1941), 49, 67–68, 89, 124–126.

240 *Ibid.*, 61–65, 86–87, 191–195; Buley, *The Old Northwest*, I, 412–413, 427–428.

241 Buley, *The Old Northwest*, I, 419, 428–429; George Rogers Taylor, *The Transportation Revolution, 1815–1860* (New York, 1951), 136–137.

242 Vincennes *Farmers and Mechanics Journal*, May 15, 1823. The Vincennes *Western Sun*, May 10, 1823, also called the "Florence" the "first Steam boat that

has ever ascended the Wabash" River. Two years earlier the Vincennes *Indiana Centinel*, March 17, 1821, announced: "We hear that a *Steam Boat* will shortly pay her respects to Vincennes. She is expected hourly[.]" Apparently this boat never arrived. It is quite possible, however, that steamers had at least entered the Wabash before 1823.

243 Vincennes *Western Sun*, March 13, April 3, May 22, 1824; *Western Register & Terre-Haute Advertiser*, May 19, 1824. The latter source states that it took the steamer "only" four days and three hours to make the trip from Louisville, despite being detained twenty-one hours and fifteen minutes enroute. It also states that this was the third steamboat arrival at Terre Haute.

244 Vincennes *Western Sun*, March 25, April 15, 22, 1826. The issue of April 15 notes arrival of the "American" "destined for Lafayette"; that of April 22 notes its return from there.

245 *Ibid.*, February 13, 1830.

246 Indianapolis *Indiana Journal*, April 14, 1830 ("Paragon"). As this discussion suggests, there was no one *head* for steamboat navigation on the Wabash River. How far boats could ascend depended on such factors as: the level and nature of the water flow, the size and construction of boats, and the economic base to be served. When the Wabash and Erie Canal, to connect navigable points on the Maumee and Wabash rivers, was begun, the mouth of the Tippecanoe River was to be its western terminal. But soon the terminal was moved to Lafayette, later to Terre Haute, and then even to Evansville on the Ohio River. Regarding western terminals for the canal, see pp. 185–188, 194–197, 241, 346–348.

247 George L. Murdock to Tipton, Cincinnati, February 11, 1831, in Robertson and Riker (eds.), *John Tipton Papers*, II, 394.

248 Indianapolis *Gazette*, May 1, 1828, quoting *Western Register [&] Terre-Haute [Advertiser]*, April 19. The "Cincinnati" was not called the first steamer to proceed up the Vermillion, but it may have been the first.

249 The Indianapolis *Indiana Journal*, March 26, 1831, states that for three or four years past Noble had made efforts to induce boats to ascend the river and thereby induce legislative appropriations for its improvement. This issue also has a letter of Noble, January 15, 1830, offering to contract to pay a reward of $200 for ascent of a steamboat to Indianapolis, plus $100 additional if Noblesville and "Andersontown" were reached. Noble notes that he had made a similar proposition the previous year.

250 *Ibid.*, May 15, 1828, December 11, 30, 1829, March 31, April 14, May 12, 1830. According to these sources the "Victory" and "Traveller" delivered freight for merchants at Spencer and other places in the area.

251 *Ibid.*, April 16, 1831. The *Indiana Journal* said it was sorry to learn that the stone was not of proper construction for its intended purpose. Logan Esarey, *A History of Indiana: From Its Exploration to 1850* (2 vols., Fort Wayne, Ind., 1924), I, 303, states that on the return the boat "ran on a bar at Hog Island, a few miles down, and lay there till winter." No citation is offered for this item, however.

[252] For example, see *Laws of Indiana*, 1822–23, pp. 15–18, 133–134, 142; *ibid.*, 1825–26, pp. 43–49; *ibid.*, 1829–30, pp. 93–94, 97. See Chapter 1, pp. 43–44, regarding such legislation, 1818–22, and the context and background for it.

[253] Barnhart and Carmony, *Indiana*, I, 277–278, 280–281; Logan Esarey, *Internal Improvements in Early Indiana* (Indianapolis, 1912), 51, 60–63.

[254] Indiana *House Journal*, 1831–32, Appendix B, 1–4, giving status of the Three Per Cent Fund as of December 1, 1831. In detailing the expenditures from the fund, the Three Per Cent agent lists items regarding ten rivers, which indicate $2,050 appropriated for them, with $1,725 spent on them. The report also indicates that $4,675.86 had been appropriated to the "Wabash Fund," with only $147.34 thereof spent. These two items indicate $6,725.86 appropriated with $1,872.34 spent, leaving unspent a balance of $4,853.52. As indicated in the Indiana *House Journal*, 1832–33, pp. 320–321, a select committee explained that the Wabash Fund had had its beginning in 1824 with $2,902.97 of Three Per Cent money earmarked for it. Then $2,000 additional had been appropriated from the fund in 1828, leaving a balance of $4,646.64 in the Wabash Fund.

[255] Francis S. Philbrick (ed.), *The Laws of Indiana Territory, 1801–1809* (Springfield, Ill., 1930, reprinted Indianapolis, 1931), 154–163; Buley, *The Old Northwest*, I, 433–435.

[256] *Laws of Indiana*, 1816–17, pp. 219–228; *ibid.* (special), 1817–18, pp. 57–67.

[257] Vincennes *Western Sun*, May 22, 1819, quoting Jeffersonville *Indianian* (May 8); J. Bigelow to John Francis Dufour, April 20 (1819), Dufour Collection, Indiana Division, Indiana State Library; Indiana *House Journal*, 1820–21, p. 135. The committee report indicated that individuals had subscribed $108,650 in stock, the state $10,000. In the pioneer era stock was frequently obtained with a modest down payment, as this report illustrates.

[258] *Acts* (special), 1823–24, pp. 78–81; Indiana *Senate Journal*, 1825, pp. 46–48; Louis C. Hunter, *Steamboats on the Western Rivers: An Economic and Technological History* (Cambridge, Mass., 1949), 181–184, 233–234. Hunter offers useful information about the hazard to commerce arising from the Falls, and about the circumstances which resulted in a canal constructed by the Louisville and Portland Canal Company.

[259] Concerning the System of 1836 and fiscal insolvency, see Ch. 5, pp. 232–233; Ch. 6, pp. 287–288, 293–294, 309–312.

CHAPTER 4

[1] Although party lines were not tightly drawn in the General Assembly from 1828–31, party listings offered in *A Biographical Directory of the Indiana General Assembly* (2 vols., Indianapolis, 1980, 1984), Volume 1, *1816–1899*, Volume 2, *1901–1984*, I, 452–456, indicate the greater strength of the anti-Jacksonians over the Jacksonians in these years. The political ties of some members, however, are uncertain.

2 Israel T. Canby to John Tipton, January 25, 1830, in Nellie A. Robertson and Dorothy Riker (eds.), *The John Tipton Papers* (3 vols., Indianapolis, 1942), II, 242–243; Indianapolis *Indiana Journal*, November 10, 1830, February 26, March 5, 1831.

3 *Biographical Directory of the Indiana General Assembly*, I, 294, 369, states that Noble and Stapp were National Republicans or anti-Jacksonians. The comment, quoted from Canby, indicates the same. As noted in Dorothy Riker and Gayle Thornbrough (comps.), *Indiana Election Returns, 1816–1851* (Indianapolis, 1960), 8–9, Scott had been an elector for Adams in 1824. In its July 23, 1831, issue the Indianapolis *Indiana Journal* reported that papers at Charlestown and New Albany had been instructed to withdraw Scott's name as a candidate, apparently leaving, it said, only Noble, Stapp, and Read as candidates.

4 Joseph Holman to John Tipton, December 18, 1830, in Robertson and Riker (eds.), *John Tipton Papers*, II, 379. The proceedings of the Jackson meeting, perhaps incomplete, as found in the Vincennes *Western Sun*, January 22, 1831, and Indianapolis *Indiana Democrat*, January 1, 1831, make no mention of Tipton's nomination for governor. Possibly Tipton was mainly concerned in winning election to the United States Senate at the legislative session of 1831–32, hence attempting to obtain and retain support therefor from legislators in both parties.

5 Indianapolis *Indiana Democrat*, May 7, 1831; Indianapolis *Indiana Journal*, May 7, 14, 1831.

6 *Biographical Directory of the Indiana General Assembly*, I, 294, 323. For Noble's service for the Michigan Road, see Chapter 3, p. 139 and note 227. According to William Forest Shonkwiler, The Land Office Business in Indiana (Master's thesis, Indiana University, 1950), 47–48, Read served as receiver from April 1, 1831 to 1839.

7 Both circulars, dated May 10, 1831, are in the Madison *Indiana Republican*, June 16, 1831.

8 Indianapolis *Indiana Democrat*, May 14, 1831. The address, dated May 2, 1831, was signed by James Blake, chairman, and A. F. Morrison, secretary (and editor of the *Indiana Democrat*).

9 Dorothy Riker and Gayle Thornbrough (eds.), *Messages and Papers Relating to the Administration of Noah Noble, Governor of Indiana, 1831–1837* (Indianapolis, 1958), 17–18; Indianapolis *Indiana Journal*, May 7, 14, June 11, July 2, 23, 1831; Indianapolis *Indiana Democrat*, May 7, June 25, 1831; Madison *Indiana Republican*, May 19, 26, June 23, 1831. In its issue of April 9, 1831, before Read was announced as a candidate for governor, the *Indiana Democrat* reported that Read had become receiver of the land office at Jeffersonville. It intimated that he probably would serve in the land office for only a limited period until another was appointed as such. This issue expressed the view that Read had not yet decided to be a candidate for governor, but might conclude to stand a poll.

10 Riker and Thornbrough (comps.), *Indiana Election Returns, 1816–1851*, pp. 141–143. Complete county returns, official for all but three counties, indicate

that Noble received 23,518 votes; Read, 21,002; Stapp, 6,984; Scott, 61; Robert Hanna, Jr., 1. Of the 64 counties, Noble won 34 by at least a plurality vote, gaining a majority vote in most of them. In like manner Read won 27 counties, and Stapp won 3.

[11] Lawrenceburgh *Indiana Palladium*, November 13, 1830; Indianapolis *Indiana Journal*, February 19, 26, 1831; Vincennes *Western Sun*, February 19, 1831. Among those mentioned as candidates: Dennis Pennington, James G. Read, James Gregory, Ross Smiley, William C. Linton, David Wallace, Alexander S. Burnett.

[12] The Indianapolis *Indiana Journal*, May 7, 14, 1831, contended that the "caucus" that picked Read for governor chose Amos Lane, of Dearborn County, for lieutenant governor. Lane's withdrawal letter in the Indianapolis *Indiana Democrat*, July 2, 1831, offers strong evidence that he had been the choice of Jacksonian leaders for lieutenant governor. Also see Vincennes *Western Sun*, May 14, June 4, July 16, 1831.

[13] Riker and Thornbrough (comps.), *Indiana Election Returns, 1816–1851*, pp. 164–165. Complete county returns, official for all but three counties, show that Wallace received 22,801 votes; Smiley, 17,502; Gregory, 7,163; Lane, 157; with lesser totals to a few others.

[14] According to the *Biographical Directory of the Indiana General Assembly*, I, 457–458, the two parties were about evenly divided in the House, but the anti-Jacksonians had a two to one margin in the Senate, thus an overall majority in the 1831–32 session. For Jacksonian triumph in all three elections, see Chapter 10, pp. 532–533.

[15] Indianapolis *Indiana Journal*, August 13, 1831; Vincennes *Western Sun*, August 20, 27, 1831.

[16] Indianapolis *Indiana Journal*, December 3, 1831; *Indiana House Journal*, 1831–32, pp. 45–46; *ibid.*, 1832–33, p. 33. Merrill received 100 votes to 4 for unnamed persons; Morris 61 votes to 39 for Abraham W. Harrison, plus 4 for unnamed persons; Sheets 71 votes to 29 for Morrison, with 5 votes for unnamed persons.

[17] Indianapolis *Indiana Democrat*, August 31, September 28, 1833.

[18] Indianapolis *Indiana Journal*, November 9, 1833.

[19] Based on proceedings in Indianapolis *Indiana Democrat*, December 11, 1833. After listing the delegates from counties, on motion, additional Jacksonians present from about a dozen counties were seated as members. Since Read had become receiver of the Jeffersonville Land Office in 1831, he had left Daviess County and become a resident of Clark County. From early October, 1833, until the convention met the *Indiana Democrat* published many items about county meetings to elect delegates, and items from other papers supporting the convention.

[20] *Ibid.*, December 11, 1833; Indianapolis *Indiana Journal*, January 4, 1834, quoting [Terre Haute] *Wabash Courier*; Paris C. Dunning to Noah Noble, February 21, 1834, in Riker and Thornbrough (eds.), *Messages and Papers of Noah*

Noble, 236–237. As indicated *ibid.*, 253–254, in April Dunning promised Noble any assistance in his power concerning an anticipated visit to Monroe County. Dunning was elected lieutenant governor as a Democrat in 1846, and became governor in 1848 after Governor James Whitcomb was elected to the United States Senate.

21 The Indianapolis *Indiana Journal*, March 1, 1834, listed Noble and Read for governor and Wallace and Culley for lieutenant governor as the only presumed candidates for these offices. On April 5, it asked opposition papers to list Noble as a candidate for reelection, otherwise the public might think there was no candidate except "him who was brought out by the *Caucus.*"

22 For the agreement and its modification, see Riker and Thornbrough (eds.), *Messages and Papers of Noah Noble*, 225–226, 240–241, 242–243, 244–245, 250–251, 261–262, 291, 293–296.

23 Read's circular, dated June, 1834, is in Vincennes *Western Sun*, July 26, 1834; that by Noble in Riker and Thornbrough (eds.), *Messages and Papers of Noah Noble*, 272–292, quoted from Indianapolis *Indiana Journal*, July 19, 1834. Noble's circular is a vigorous attack on Read, from whose circular he quotes at length.

24 Indianapolis *Indiana Democrat*, March 1, June 7, 13, 20, July 4, 11, 1834; Indianapolis *Indiana Journal*, April 19, June 7, 14, July 19, 26, August 1, 1834; Riker and Thornbrough (eds.), *Messages and Papers of Noah Noble*, 251–252, 263–264, 296–297, 299–300. Relevant items are also included in the circulars cited in the preceding note.

25 Riker and Thornbrough (comps.), *Indiana Election Returns, 1816–1851*, pp. 143–145, 166–167; Indianapolis *Indiana Democrat*, August 8, 1834. According to official returns from all counties Noble obtained 36,773 votes against 27,257 for Read; and Wallace polled 38,108 votes to 20,364 for Culley.

26 Indianapolis *Indiana Journal*, August 16, 23, 1834; Vincennes *Western Sun*, December 20, 1834. Only two governors had sought reelection: Jennings in 1819, Ray in 1828.

27 *A Biographical Directory of the Indiana General Assembly*, I, 463–464, offers evidence that the Whigs apparently outnumbered Democrats at the 1834–35 session. The Indianapolis *Indiana Journal*, September 26, October 10, 1834, claimed that a majority of members in both houses were opposed to the Jacksonians. Years later the Indianapolis *Indiana State Sentinel*, April 18, 25, 1843, a Democratic organ, said the 1834–35 session had 17 Whigs and 13 Democrats in the Senate, and 46 Whigs to 30 Democrats in the House.

28 Dorothy Riker (ed.), *Executive Proceedings of the State of Indiana, 1816–1836* (Indianapolis, 1947), 289, 291n; Riker and Thornbrough (eds.), *Messages and Papers of Noah Noble*, 229; Indianapolis *Indiana Journal*, February 22, 1834; Vincennes *Western Sun*, February 22, 1834.

29 Indiana *House Journal*, 1834–35, p. 50. Palmer secured 97 votes to 6 for unnamed persons; Morris 101 votes to 2 for unnamed persons.

30 Unless otherwise indicated, items about ordinary state expenditures and ordinary state revenues are from or based on annual reports of the state treasurer

in Indiana *House Journal*, 1832–33, pp. 51–53; *ibid.*, 1833–34, pp. 59–61; *ibid.*, 1834–35, pp. 70–71; Indiana *Documentary Journal*, 1835–36, Doc. 1, pp. 1–3; *ibid.*, 1836–37, Doc. 2, pp. 1–3; *ibid.*, 1837–38, Doc. 11, pp. 1–3. The separation between items which are ordinary expenditures and revenues versus those from special funds is somewhat more difficult to make for the thirties than it was for the teens and twenties. Among the special funds noted in these annual reports of the treasurer are: Indianapolis, Michigan Road, Saline, Indiana College, Congressional Township, and County Seminary.

[31] For the number of counties and legislators in the apportionments of 1826, 1831, and 1836, respectively, see Chapter 3, pp. 102–105, and pp. 161–163, this chapter. The increased length of session laws and journals is evident compared with those for the teens and twenties. Moreover, with the 1835–36 legislative session, publication of the Indiana *Documentary Journal* began adding many pages not printed in the House and Senate journals. As noted in Riker (ed.), *Executive Proceedings of the State of Indiana, 1816–1836*, pp. 717–720, the number of circuit courts was established at three in 1816; five in 1821; seven in 1830; and nine in 1836.

[32] It is possible that some of the prison costs were paid from the Indianapolis Fund, but, if so, this is thought to have been a modest sum. In his report for 1831–32 the treasurer lists prison costs among the "Ordinary expenditures [.]" In that for 1834–35 the treasurer notes that the Indianapolis Fund is "set apart, especially to the erection of that edifice [the first state capitol.]" The reports of the treasurer for 1834–35, 1835–36, and 1836–37 seem to indicate that roughly $20,000 to $25,000 of tax revenue was spent on completing the state capitol. It also seems that about $1,451.78 of tax revenue for 1837 was collected toward payment of interest on internal improvement loans during 1837. As noted in note 147, Chapter 5, $40,000 of the tax revenue levied in 1837, the final year under Governor Noble, was used to pay interest on the bonded debt for internal improvements during the ensuing period 1837–43. Costs for state prison and capitol, not taken from tax revenue, were apparently paid from the Indianapolis Fund—derived from the sale of lots on the federal donation of four sections of land for a state capitol. Payments of interest on the state bonded debt, not taken from tax revenue, were overwhelmingly paid from loans from bondholders.

[33] See *Laws of Indiana* (revised), 1830–31, p. 441, reaffirming the allowance to collectors of 9 percent of the state tax collected. No change in this rate was found in checking laws regarding the assessing and collecting of taxes from 1831–37, nor is any indicated by Riker and Thornbrough (eds.), *Messages and Papers of Noah Noble*, 38–40, in their discussion of such legislation. Miscellaneous expenditures were overwhelmingly for "special appropriations," but included $1,232.86 for cost of presidential elections; $666.78 for geological surveying; and $306.32 for refunding revenue received from estates without heirs.

[34] Unless otherwise indicated, items about ordinary state revenues are from or based on annual reports of the treasurer as cited in note 30 above.

35 *Laws of Indiana* (revised), 1830–31, pp. 426–427; Riker and Thornbrough (eds.), *Messages and Papers of Noah Noble*, 38–39. Treasurer Merrill said in December, 1832, that the "rates of taxation" had "continued the same since the year 1826 . . . ." Indiana *House Journal*, 1832–33, p. 53. No evidence has been found to indicate any change in state tax levies between 1831 to 1836.

36 *Laws of Indiana* (general), 1834–35, pp. 12–22; *ibid.* (general), 1835–36, pp. 25–39; *ibid.* (general), 1836–37, pp. 110–113. The levy for 1836 authorized county boards to deduct 5 percent of state revenue for their county in support of common schools, but this item was repealed in the levy for 1837. The levy of 1836 set aside 12 1/2 cents of the poll tax for support of common schools, but the levy of 1837 ended this and left the poll tax at 50 cents.

37 For discussion of the ad valorem system during the twenties, see Donald F. Carmony, Indiana Public Finance, 1800–1826 (Ph.D. dissertation, Indiana University, 1940), 302–305. A bill to value property preparatory for the ad valorem plan was indefinitely postponed in the House by a vote of 39 to 35 at the 1831–32 session; at the 1833–34 session a similar bill passed the House but failed in the Senate. Indiana *House Journal*, 1831–32, p. 220; *ibid.*, 1833–34, p. 479; Indiana *Senate Journal*, 1833–34, p. 351.

38 Indiana *House Journal*, 1832–33, pp. 222–224; Richard W. Thompson to Noah Noble, June 9, 1835, in Riker and Thornbrough (eds.), *Messages and Papers of Noah Noble*, 372. The Ways and Means Committee was chaired by Nathan B. Palmer of Jefferson County, which borders the Ohio River.

39 Indiana *House Journal*, 1834–35, p. 39; *Laws of Indiana* (general), 1834–35, pp. 12–22; Indianapolis *Indiana Democrat*, February 27, 1835.

40 Indiana *House Journal*, 1835–36, p. 24; *Laws of Indiana* (general), 1835–36, pp. 29, 34.

41 *Laws of Indiana* (general), 1835–36, pp. 25–26, 82; *ibid.* (general), 1833–34, p. 343.

42 See remarks of Noble in Indiana *House Journal*, 1834–35, pp. 39–40; *ibid.*, 1836–37, pp. 28–29. Also see Indianapolis *Indiana Democrat*, August 31, 1836; "E" in Indianapolis *Indiana Journal*, July 16, 1836.

43 For examples, see *Laws of Indiana*, 1832–33, p. 41; *ibid.* (local), 1834–35, p. 6.

44 Indiana *House Journal*, 1834–35, p. 40; Charles H. Test, Jr., to Noah Noble, January 20, 1836, in Riker and Thornbrough (eds.), *Messages and Papers of Noah Noble*, 438–439; Indiana *House Journal*, 1836–37, p. 29.

45 Indianapolis *Indiana Democrat*, June 8, 1836; Indianapolis *Indiana Journal*, April 23, 1836, quoting Richmond *Palladium*; *Laws of Indiana* (general), 1836–37, p. 75. The Constitution of 1816 prohibited any increase or decrease in the salary of a governor during a term for which he had been elected, and it prohibited an increase in the compensation of legislators until after the close of the session which provided the increase. Charles Kettleborough, *Constitution Making in Indiana* (3 vols., Indianapolis, 1916, 1930), I, 97, 119.

46 Enoch D. John to Noah Noble, March 21, 1837, in Riker and Thornbrough (eds.), *Messages and Papers of Noah Noble*, 542–543; Indianapolis *Indiana*

Democrat, April 19, 1837; Indianapolis *Indiana Journal*, April 15, May 13 (quoting [Salem] *Indiana Monitor*), 1837.

⁴⁷ Riker and Thornbrough (eds.), *Messages and Papers of Noah Noble*, 201–202.

⁴⁸ Indianapolis *Indiana Journal*, January 4, 18, 1834. Also *ibid.*, January 4, 8, 11, 18, 1834, for related items.

⁴⁹ *Laws of Indiana*, 1833–34, pp. 3–4. See Justin E. Walsh, *The Centennial History of the Indiana General Assembly, 1816–1978* (Indianapolis, 1987), 744–745, for maps showing changes resulting from this special apportionment. This interim apportionment gave representation to some new counties, but it also changed the representation for some other counties.

⁵⁰ Riker and Thornbrough (eds.), *Messages and Papers of Noah Noble*, 411; *Laws of Indiana* (general), 1835–36, pp. 3–5, for the apportionment act. The constitution established fifty and one hundred as the maximum for senators and representatives respectively.

⁵¹ As noted in George Pence and Nellie C. Armstrong, *Indiana Boundaries: Territory, State, and County* (Indianapolis, 1933), 64–66, in 1835 the legislature created 15 *paper* counties from parts of Central and especially Northern Indiana. They were: Adams, DeKalb, Fulton, Jasper, Jay, Kosciusko, Marshall, Newton, Noble, Porter, Pulaski, Starke, Steuben, Wells, and Whitley. As for earlier paper counties, until *organized*, these counties were attached to organized counties for legislative districts. When these counties became organized is at times uncertain because of inadequate or even conflicting data. From legislation regarding apportionments, both general and special, plus data about when the votes of these counties were counted separate from other counties in state elections, I tried to discover when they in fact became organized counties. Of the 15 counties, I concluded that only Adams, Fulton, Kosciusko, Marshall, Noble, and Porter warrant inclusion in the apportionment of 1836. But this and later apportionments as in *Biographical Directory of the Indiana General Assembly*, I, 575–581; Walsh, *Centennial History of the Indiana General Assembly*, 745–752; and Riker and Thornbrough (comps.), *Indiana Election Returns, 1816–1851*, pp. 402–408, mingle *paper* and *organized* counties together in listing apportionments. Neither this method, nor mine, seems as relevant and appropriate as desirable. As indicated in Pence and Armstrong (eds.), *Indiana Boundaries*, 34–36, 154, Delaware and Wabash counties had been created as paper counties, however, none of the three sources, cited above, mentions them in the apportionment of 1821.

⁵² See Riker and Thornbrough (comps.), *Indiana Election Returns, 1816–1851*, pp. 402–403, for their listing of the votes for each county; Walsh, *Centennial History of the Indiana General Assembly*, 745–746, for maps showing counties involved in this apportionment.

⁵³ There were 76 organized counties in the apportionment of 1836. Per this apportionment, roughly 42 percent of the representatives were elected by the voters in Indiana's 31 southern counties, 46 percent by the voters in its 28 central counties, and 12 percent by the voters in its 17 northern counties. The 14 eastern counties of Southern Indiana were: Bartholomew, Clark, Dearborn, De-

catur, Floyd, Franklin, Harrison, Jackson, Jefferson, Jennings, Ripley, Scott, Switzerland, and Washington; its 17 western counties: Crawford, Daviess, Dubois, Gibson, Greene, Knox, Lawrence, Martin, Monroe, Orange, Perry, Pike, Posey, Spencer, Sullivan, Vanderburgh, and Warrick. The 14 eastern counties of Central Indiana were: Delaware, Fayette, Grant, Hamilton, Hancock, Henry, Johnson, Madison, Marion, Randolph, Rush, Shelby, Union, and Wayne; its 14 western counties: Boone, Clay, Clinton, Fountain, Hendricks, Montgomery, Morgan, Owen, Parke, Putnam, Tippecanoe, Vermillion, Vigo, and Warren. The 9 eastern counties of Northern Indiana were: Adams, Allen, Elkhart, Huntington, Kosciusko, LaGrange, Miami, Noble, and Wabash. Its 8 western counties were: Carroll, Cass, Fulton, La Porte, Marshall, Porter, St. Joseph, and White. The following 13 counties were not included in the apportionment of 1831: Adams, Fulton, Grant, Huntington, Kosciusko, LaGrange, La Porte, Miami, Marshall, Noble, Porter, Wabash, and White.

54 *Laws of Indiana*, 1831–32, pp. 262–263; *ibid*. (general), 1834–35, p. 32.

55 For examples see Indiana *House Journal*, 1831–32, pp. 142–143; *ibid*., 1832–33, p. 70; *ibid*., 1833–34, p. 77; *ibid*., 1835–36, pp. 296–297; *ibid*., 1836–37, p. 135. Some of these references support legislation "to confine" voters to their townships of residence.

56 *Laws of Indiana*, 1833–34, p. 78; Indiana *Senate Journal*, 1834–35, pp. 128–129, 179; *Laws of Indiana* (general), 1836–37, p. 82.

57 Riker (ed.), *Executive Proceedings of the State of Indiana, 1816–1836*, p. 311. According to Riker, Stevens submitted his resignation, effective March 1, in a letter dated February 15, 1836. The Indianapolis *Indiana Journal*, April 23, 1836, has an advertisement dated February 20, 1836, indicating that Stevens had resigned his seat on the Supreme Court, had located at Madison, and resumed his practice of law.

58 Riker and Thornbrough (eds.), *Messages and Papers of Noah Noble*, 456–457, 493; Riker (ed.), *Executive Proceedings of the State of Indiana, 1816–1836*, p. 311; Indiana *Senate Journal*, 1836–37, pp. 351–352.

59 Indianapolis *Indiana Democrat*, June 1, 1836; Indianapolis *Indiana Journal*, June 4, 1836.

60 Riker and Thornbrough (eds.), *Messages and Papers of Noah Noble*, 540, 541–542, 544–545, 547, 594; Vincennes *Western Sun*, April 1, May 13, 1837; Indianapolis *Indiana Journal*, May 13, 1837.

61 Stephen C. Stevens to Noah Noble, April 29, 1837, in Riker and Thornbrough (eds.), *Messages and Papers of Noah Noble*, 547, 594; Indianapolis *Indiana Journal*, June 3, 1837; Vincennes *Western Sun*, June 17, 1837; Gayle Thornbrough, Dorothy Riker, and Paula Corpuz (eds.), *The Diary of Calvin Fletcher* (9 vols., Indianapolis, 1972–1983), I, 434.

62 Indiana *Senate Journal*, 1833–34, p. 44. For the intermittent existence of the Madison bank, see Chapter 1, pp. 17–18, 24–25. Banking services rendered by merchants, unincorporated private "bankers," and corporations such as insurance companies appear to be a virgin field in need of careful study, but this

volume does not cover this aspect of banking in the pioneer era. An early study, which includes much useful comment regarding the Second State Bank of Indiana, is *State Banking in Indiana, 1814–1873* (Bloomington, Ind., 1912), by Logan Esarey.

63 *Laws of Indiana*, 1827–28, pp. 127–130. This law directed the state treasurer, as superintendent of the loan office, to loan only the money received from the seminary townships in Monroe and Gibson counties, plus other revenue on behalf of Indiana College (formerly Indiana State Seminary). The session which established the Second State Bank provided that revenue from saline lands be loaned in like manner. *Ibid.*, 1833–34, pp. 326–327.

64 Indiana *House Journal*, 1829–30, p. 290; Indiana *Senate Journal*, 1829–30, pp. 170–171, 203–205; Indianapolis *Indiana State Gazette*, February 11, 1830; Indiana *Senate Journal*, 1830–31, pp. 114–115, 169, 174, 358–359.

65 *Laws of Indiana*, 1831–32, p. 288; Indiana *Senate Journal*, 1831–32, pp. 115–116; Indiana *House Journal*, 1831–32, pp. 432–434.

66 Nicholas Biddle to Noah Noble, February 25, 1832, in Riker and Thornbrough (eds.), *Messages and Papers of Noah Noble*, 100–101; J. B. Semans, Jacob Walker, and Samuel Hoover to John Tipton, March 7, 1832, in Robertson and Riker (eds.), *John Tipton Papers*, II, 542.

67 See *Laws of Indiana* (local), 1834–35, p. 165, for legislation allowing the Madison bank three additional years to collect debts due it. A bill in the House to revive and continue this bank for twenty years was indefinitely postponed by a vote of 42 to 33. Indiana *House Journal*, 1834–35, pp. 426, 452–453.

68 Indiana *House Journal*, 1832–33, pp. 22–23. Noble did not recommend a state bank, but he apparently favored one.

69 Vincennes *Western Sun*, December 22, 1832, quoting Indianapolis *Indiana Democrat*; Indianapolis *Indiana Journal*, January 2, February 23, 1833.

70 For reports by legislators of constituent support, see Indiana *House Journal*, 1832–33, pp. 267, 322; Indiana *Senate Journal*, 1832–33, pp. 99, 195, 231, 270, 305. According to the Indianapolis *Indiana Journal*, January 19, 23, 1833, the bank bill passed the House 41 to 28; according to the Indianapolis *Indiana Democrat*, January 30, February 9, 1833, it lost in the Senate by two votes. Both papers suggested that a majority of the senators favored a state bank, but had differences about details.

71 Indiana *Senate Journal*, 1832–33, p. 354; Thornbrough, Riker, and Corpuz (eds.), *Diary of Calvin Fletcher*, I, 186–187, 188, 190n, 194–197; John Tipton to Calvin Fletcher, February 7, 1833, in Robertson and Riker (eds.), *John Tipton Papers*, II, 800–801. The Indianapolis *Indiana Democrat*, January 26, February 9, 1833, viewed Fletcher's resignation as proper and consistent with the right of constituents to instruct their representatives. Considering a legislator as an agent of the people, it regarded resignation as an obligation if a legislator could not vote consistent with the known desire of his constituents.

72 Indianapolis *Indiana Democrat*, March 2, 16, 23, June 15, 1833; Indianapolis *Indiana Journal*, May 4, 1833.

73 Indianapolis *Indiana Democrat*, September 28, October 26 (quote), December 7, 1833; Indianapolis *Indiana Journal*, November 16, 1833; Indiana *House Journal*, 1833–34, pp. 23–24.

74 Indiana *Senate Journal*, 1833–34, pp. 41–47. Merrill was responding to a resolution, which he quotes, adopted by the Senate at the previous session.

75 *Ibid.*, 43–44, including quotes.

76 *Ibid.*, 42, 45 (quotes).

77 Indiana *House Journal*, 1833–34, p. 352; Indiana *Senate Journal*, 1833–34, p. 268. Some amendments were made after these votes were taken. According to the political ties of legislators as given in *Biographical Directory of the Indiana General Assembly*, I, 461–462, in the House 27 Jacksonians voted for and 10 Jacksonians voted against passage, while in the Senate the Jacksonian vote for and against was 5 and 6 respectively. In the House 19 anti-Jacksonians voted for and 14 anti-Jacksonians voted against passage, while in the Senate the anti-Jacksonian vote for and against was 10 and 5 respectively. The vote of 3 representatives and 2 senators, whose political ties are not listed, were all for passage. The Jacksonians were responsible for passage of the bank bill in the House, but Senate approval required the support of senators whose politics are listed as unknown. Although a bipartisan measure, passage seems more indebted to Democratic than anti-Jackson support.

78 For instance, see Indianapolis *Indiana Democrat*, January 8, 11, 15, 1834; Indianapolis *Indiana Journal*, January 8, 15, 1834. Both papers, especially for the period from December, 1833, through early February, 1834, have much material about questions concerning establishment of the Second State Bank.

79 John Tipton to Calvin Fletcher, January 6, 1834, in Robertson and Riker (eds.), *John Tipton Papers*, III, 9. Also see Congressman John Ewing to Noah Noble, January 18, 1834, in Riker and Thornbrough (eds.), *Messages and Papers of Noah Noble*, 219–220, reluctantly recommending approval for a state bank. Ewing explained that he had concluded that a national bank could not be rechartered, however, he considered state banks a poor substitute for it as well as of doubtful validity under the federal constitution.

80 Indiana *House Journal*, 1837–38, p. 18. The remarks of such political leaders as Noble, Ewing, and Tipton suggest that probably many anti-Jacksonians reluctantly supported the Second State Bank largely because they had concluded that a national bank could not be continued. Perhaps this reluctance explains why a lesser proportion of anti-Jacksonians than Jacksonians voted for the charter of the Second State Bank.

81 For the charter, see *Laws of Indiana*, 1833–34, pp. 12–38.

82 *Ibid.*, 12–13, 18–19, 28–30, 33–35. If a branch could not profitably use the full $80,000 of state stock, the unused part could be transferred to another branch.

83 *Ibid.*, 13, 16, 18–30, 36–38.

84 *Ibid.*, 17–19, 24–25, 34, 37–38.

85 *Ibid.*, 14–17, 19, 32–33.

[86] *Ibid.*, 15–16, 35–36.

[87] Indiana *House Journal*, 1833–34, pp. 463–466, 469–472. The chief competitors of Merrill were John Sering and Gamaliel Taylor. For related information and comments that Isaac Blackford and Tilghman A. Howard were also talked of for president, see Thornbrough, Riker, and Corpuz (eds.), *Diary of Calvin Fletcher*, I, 214–215, 220, 221n.

[88] See report of President Merrill in Indiana *House Journal*, 1834–35, pp. 66–67. Even in 1840, New Albany, the largest town in the state, had only 4,226 residents according to the federal census. John D. Barnhart and Donald F. Carmony, *Indiana: From Frontier to Industrial Commonwealth* (4 vols., New York, 1954), I, 418–419.

[89] Indiana *House Journal*, 1834–35, pp. 22–24 (loan), 66–69 (Merrill's report). According to the charter, before a branch could open individual subscribers must pay $30,000 *in specie* as their initial payment on $80,000 of stock, with the remainder due *in specie* in two equal annual installments; and the state must pay $50,000 *in specie* as its initial payment on $80,000 of stock, with the remainder due paid *in specie* in two annual installments. Thus each branch would have $80,000 *in specie* at its start, with an additional $80,000 *in specie* due within two years. *Laws of Indiana*, 1833–34, pp. 29–30.

[90] Riker and Thornbrough (eds.), *Messages and Papers of Noah Noble*, 312–313 (proclamation); Indiana *House Journal*, 1834–35, pp. 19–20.

[91] Indiana *Senate Journal*, 1835–36, p. 70; Indiana *House Journal*, 1835–36, pp. 152–160 (quote, 153).

[92] Indiana *House Journal*, 1837–38, p. 192.

[93] *Ibid.*, 415.

[94] Indiana *Senate Journal*, 1836–37, p. 101. According to Merrill the new branch had paid a dividend of 5 percent for the last half of its initial year.

[95] For examples of interest in additional branches, see Indiana *House Journal*, 1835–36, pp. 50–51, 56, 60, 138, 143, 177, 270; Indiana *Senate Journal*, 1835–36, pp. 103, 399; Indiana *House Journal*, 1836–37, pp. 157, 187, 197; Indiana *Senate Journal*, 1836–37, p. 276. Among the places where individuals sought branches for their town or area were: Michigan City, La Porte, Kosciusko County, La Porte County, Elkhart County, Jeffersonville, Laurel, and Mount Vernon.

[96] Indiana *Senate Journal*, 1837–38, p. 59.

[97] *Laws of Indiana* (general), 1835–36, pp. 21–23 (approval by General Assembly); Indiana *Senate Journal*, 1836–37, pp. 101–105 (approval by branch banks and state bank board). Such approvals for amendments were required by the charter. *Laws of Indiana*, 1833–34, pp. 34–35.

[98] Hugh McCulloch, *Men and Measures of Half a Century* (New York, 1889), 71–72, 85. For other contemporary accounts about travel conditions, see Shirley S. McCord (comp.), *Travel Accounts of Indiana, 1679–1961* (Indianapolis, 1970), 139–176, *passim*. As a recently arrived immigrant from New England, McCulloch was doubtless amazed at the contrast between roads and streets in Indiana versus those in New England.

[99] Thornbrough, Riker, and Corpuz (eds.), *Diary of Calvin Fletcher*, I, 178, 259, 387; Logansport *Herald*, November 23, December 28, 1837. See Fletcher's diary, pp. 204, 246, 247, 259, 299, 310–313, 363, 384–387, for additional comments about travel conditions.

[100] *Laws of Indiana* (revised), 1830–31, pp. 450–453, 133–134; *ibid.* (general), 1835–36, p. 32. An act approved in 1837 allowed persons owing a road tax to discharge his tax in labor at the rate of 75 cents per day. *Ibid.* (general), 1836–37, pp. 104–105. As indicated in the Indianapolis *Indiana Journal*, January 21, 1832, Senator John Dumont gave strong support for placing the responsibility for road labor more on the owners of land. For labor and taxes regarding local roads, 1816–31, see Chapter 1, pp. 39–40, Chapter 3, pp. 133–134.

[101] Indiana *House Journal*, 1835–36, p. 132. At the previous session another House committee noted the swelling of legislation about roads, the increased cost resulting from the legislation, and suggested a desire for Three Per Cent revenue as a basic cause for all the legislation. *Ibid.*, 1834–35, pp. 298–299.

[102] In December, 1831, the Three Per Cent agent reported commissioners and appropriations for over fifty Three Per Cent roads. According to this report $119,294.32 had been received for this fund and largely spent on roads. *Ibid.*, 1831–32, Appendix B, p. 3.

[103] *Indiana Gazetteer* (2nd edition, Indianapolis, 1833), 16; preceding note, and Indiana *Senate Journal*, 1837–38, pp. 159–163. See table concerning ordinary state revenue 1831–37, this chapter, p. 156.

[104] *Acts* (special), 1830–31, pp. 154–166; *Laws of Indiana*, 1832–33, pp. 51–64; *ibid.* (general), 1835–36, pp. 72–74; *ibid.* (general), 1836–37, p. 86.

[105] *Ibid.*, 1831–32, p. 83. Such an act had been recommended by a Senate committee on roads. *Ibid.*, p. 318.

[106] Indiana *House Journal*, 1834–35, pp. 15–16. For examples of similar comments by Noble and legislative committees, see *ibid.*, 1833–34, p. 21; *ibid.*, 1834–35, pp. 298–299; *ibid.*, 1835–36, pp. 132–134.

[107] *Ibid.*, 1835–36, pp. 132–134. Noble agreed that the people had benefitted from the widespread dispersal of the fund. *Ibid.*, 1834–35, p. 15.

[108] According to a Senate committee, annual pay to the agent, who received 2 percent of the fund's revenue as his compensation from 1825 through 1828, and 3 percent thereafter, grew from $120.70 in 1825 to a peak of $623.74 for 1831. The committee estimated that the agent's duties declined one half during these years. An act of 1833 reduced the compensation to $150 per annum; an act in 1835 ended the agency, transferred his duties to the state treasurer, and added $100 yearly to his regular salary. Indiana *Senate Journal*, 1832–33, pp. 369–371; *Laws of Indiana*, 1832–33, p. 45; *ibid.* (general), 1834–35, pp. 75–76.

[109] U.S. *Statutes at Large*, IV, 351–352, 427, 469–470, 557, 649, 680, 772; *ibid.*, V, 71, 195, 228. Some of these appropriations state that they were an obligation against the Two Per Cent Fund agreed to with statehood, whereby Congress promised to use 2 percent of the net sales from public land in Indiana for building a road or roads leading to the new state.

110 R. Carlyle Buley, *The Old Northwest: Pioneer Period, 1815–1840* (2 vols., Indianapolis, 1950), I, 463; *Laws of Indiana* (local), 1837–38, pp. 449–450. The appropriation acts, cited in the preceding note, have various items about the objects for which the money should be used. The assembly asserted that a large appropriation was owed because of the Two Per Cent Fund and large volume of sales from the public domain within the state.

111 Philip D. Jordan, *The National Road* (Indianapolis, 1948), 169–173; Lee Burns, *The National Road in Indiana* (Indianapolis, 1919), 222–228; Indianapolis *Indiana Democrat*, September 28, 1833. Speaking in the Senate in 1836, Senator William Hendricks said the National Road was "the principal thoroughfare of emigration" from the eastern states to the central portions of Ohio, Indiana, and Illinois. *Congressional Debates*, 24 Cong., 1 session, XII, Pt. 1, pp. 631–632.

112 Geneal Prather, The Building of the National Road (Master's thesis, Indiana University, 1941), 74, 86–87, 103–104, 107–108, 111–118, and *passim*.

113 Prather, Building of the National Road, 56, 68–69, 72–73, 82–93, 96–97, 98. Proceeds from sale of the federal land grant for the Michigan Road aggregated $241,173.65 for 1831–36, and totaled $252,136.87 as of 1840. *Ibid.*, 106, 120.

114 Indiana *House Journal*, 1836–37, p. 21; *ibid.*, 1837–38, pp. 15–16; Indiana *Senate Journal*, 1836–37, pp. 239–241; Indianapolis *Indiana Democrat*, January 17, 1837. No evidence has been found to show that any money to improve the Michigan Road was spent from the state treasury during the pioneer era.

115 Prather, Building of the National Road, 128, 131, 132–134, and *passim*. Also see items cited in preceding note.

116 *Laws of Indiana*, 1833–34, p. 200; *ibid.* (general), 1836–37, pp. 95–96.

117 Comments about turnpike construction by contemporary engineers are in Indiana *Senate Journal*, 1836–37, pp. 295–296, 393–394. The initial citation indicates the cost of a turnpike from Mount Vernon to Princeton, via New Harmony, at $3,655.72 per mile.

118 Examples of incorporation acts concerning turnpikes are in *Laws of Indiana*, 1832–33, pp. 147–161; *ibid.* (local), 1834–35, pp. 8–16, 24–31, 35–42, 66–73; *ibid.* (local), 1836–37, pp. 113–119, 133–139, 153–154, 157–158, 225–228, 254–260, 299–305. For two turnpikes included in the Internal Improvements System of 1836 and their projected cost, see p. 196, this chapter. According to the *Indiana Gazetteer* (1833), 16, several turnpike charters had been granted but "none of them have yet been carried into operation."

119 *Laws of Indiana* (revised), 1830–31, pp. 259–264 (quotation, 262). Ferry keepers were required to pay from $2 to $10 yearly to the county treasury, but the county board could exempt ferry keepers on streams that were often impassable from payment of any fee.

120 Vincennes *Western Sun*, April 12, 1834, quoting (Paoli) *Indiana Patriot*; *Laws of Indiana* (revised), 1830–31, p. 262.

121 *Laws of Indiana* (revised), 1830–31, pp. 453–454.

122 For examples of charters to private companies to build bridges, see *Laws of Indiana*, 1831–32, pp. 150–160; *ibid.* (local), 1834–35, pp. 87–90, 98, 99–104, 174–176. For examples of Three Per Cent money for bridges, see *ibid.* (local), 1834–35, pp. 154–157, 159–163; *ibid.* (local), 1836–37, pp. 31–32, 294–296, 367–368. For bridges supported from the Michigan Road Fund, see *ibid.* (general), 1836–37, pp. 64–66.

123 The appropriation acts of 1830, 1831, 1832, and 1836 made explicit authorization for bridges. That for 1831 for a bridge over White River "near" Indianapolis; that for 1832 for bridges over the East and West forks of Whitewater River; that for 1836 for materials for a bridge over the Wabash River near Terre Haute. U.S. *Statutes at Large*, IV, 427, 469, 557; *ibid.*, V, 71, 228.

124 *Laws of Indiana*, 1831–32, pp. 166–173, 276; Riker and Thornbrough (eds.), *Messages and Papers of Noah Noble*, 113–114, 161.

125 Thornbrough, Riker, and Corpuz (eds.), *Diary of Calvin Fletcher*, I, 291, 396, 424, 426; *ibid.*, II, 131, 139, 263; *ibid.*, III, 117, 140, 250. As noted *ibid.*, II, 139, in 1840 Fletcher said he had about $4,000 in this bridge for which he had "never realized one cent" in dividends, but hoped to later. Also see Jehu Z. Powell, *History of Cass County, Indiana* (2 vols., Chicago, 1913), I, 207.

126 See Barnhart and Carmony, *Indiana*, I, 293–294, concerning this line and another opened between Vincennes and Terre Haute later the same year.

127 Vincennes *Western Sun*, May 6, 1826, January 5, 1828.

128 Indianapolis *Gazette*, June 5, 1828, quoting Madison *Indiana Republican*, reporting that John Wilson had a contract for a weekly stage between Madison and Indianapolis. In its issue of August 21 and several subsequent issues, the *Gazette* carried an advertisement that a stage left Madison at 8 a.m. and Indianapolis at 7 a.m. on Thursdays, arriving at Indianapolis and Madison respectively at 5 p.m. on Sunday. Vernon, Columbus, and Franklin were principal points on the route of about ninety miles. It is worth noting that Madison was the nearest Ohio River town to Indianapolis.

129 For examples of items regarding these and other lines, see Indianapolis *Indiana Journal*, July 14, 1830, May 12, 26, July 7, 14, 1832, May 15, 1835; Indianapolis *Indiana Democrat*, May 15, 1835, June 1, 15, 1836, May 3, June 7, July 5, 1837; Vincennes *Western Sun*, May 26, 1832, January 26, 1833; Logansport *Herald*, October 19, 1837.

130 Indianapolis *Indiana Democrat*, June 15, 1836.

131 Barnhart and Carmony, *Indiana*, I, 294; Buley, *The Old Northwest*, I, 465–466; Indianapolis *Indiana Journal*, May 12, 1832; Indianapolis *Indiana Democrat*, June 1, 1836. Apparently the shortening of time between departures and arrivals arose mainly from longer hours of travel and increased travel at night.

132 Concerning these items, including fares, see references cited in notes 128, 129, and 131 above.

133 Lawrenceburgh *Indiana Palladium*, November 27, 1830; Vincennes *Western Sun*, September 12, 1835.

134 *Laws of Indiana* (revised), 1837–38, pp. 569–571. This was probably the first such law in Indiana since the Vincennes *Western Sun*, October 21, 1837, commented about such a law in Ohio and urged that it be imitated in Indiana.

135 Samuel Milroy to John Tipton, December 16, 1831, in Robertson and Riker (eds.), *John Tipton Papers*, II, 469. Also see Israel T. Canby to Tipton, December 22, 1831, *ibid.*, 473, writing from Crawfordsville, in which Canby stated that "We are full of rail roads here," but had wisely decided it was premature to do anything about them.

136 For the eight initial charters, see *Laws of Indiana*, 1831–32, pp. 173–236. For examples of further charters and amendments to charters, see *ibid.*, 1832–33, p. 146; *ibid.* (local), 1834–35, pp. 16–24, 47–61, 63, 66–73, 105–106; *ibid.* (local), 1836–37, pp. 20, 27–28, 106–113, 119–124, 154, 228–242, 246–254.

137 Vincennes *Western Sun*, March 24, April 14, 1827 (Baltimore and Ohio); Indianapolis *Indiana Journal*, July 31, 1827 (Baltimore and Ohio); Albert L. Kohlmeier, *The Old Northwest as the Keystone of the Arch of American Federal Union: A Study in Commerce and Politics* (Bloomington, Ind., 1938), 22–29, *passim* (Charleston to Lake Michigan); Indiana *House Journal*, 1835–36, pp. 23–24 (Governor Noble regarding Lawrenceburg and Indianapolis).

138 Indianapolis *Indiana Journal*, July 19, 1834 (quoting Shelbyville *Transcript*), July 31, 1835; Edward H. Chadwick, *Chadwick's History of Shelby County, Indiana* (Indianapolis, 1909), 260. Chadwick states that the road at Shelbyville was made entirely of wood.

139 As stated p. 196, the railroad was to commence at Madison, on the Ohio River, and terminate at Lafayette, on the Wabash River.

140 Indiana *Senate Journal*, 1837–38, p. 240.

141 *Laws of Indiana* (general), 1835–36, p. 90; *ibid.* (local), 1836–37, pp. 357, 361.

142 *Laws of Indiana*, 1831–32, p. 94; *ibid.*, 1833–34, pp. 167–168; *ibid.* (local), 1836–37, pp. 365, 374, 380, 396–398.

143 Vincennes *Western Sun*, June 25, 1836; Harold Lee O'Donnell, *Newport and Vermillion Township: The First 100 Years, 1824–1924, Vermillion County, Indiana* (Danville, Ill., 1969), 37; *The Pioneers of Morgan County: The Memoirs of Noah J. Major*, edited by Logan Esarey (Indianapolis, 1915), 402. At a meeting at Evansville regarding railroads in 1832, a speaker asserted that for the five or six previous years an average of three to five thousand boatmen had ascended the Ohio to that point, nearly all of whom were destined for Wabash and White River counties "on their return from the southern market." Vincennes *Western Sun*, September 29, 1832.

144 Leland D. Baldwin, *The Keelboat Age on Western Waters* (Pittsburgh, 1941), 191–195; Buley, *The Old Northwest*, I, 427–428.

145 For example, the Indianapolis *Indiana Journal*, January 14, 1837, has an advertisement by forwarding and commission merchants at Madison increasing charges for receiving and forwarding goods to other merchants.

146 Vincennes *Western Sun*, September 1, 1832. The editor said that the "Vincennes" was owned by Samuel and Thomas Emison and others. He termed the

Emisons "enterprising citizens" who had built and launched the first flatboat on the Wabash above Vincennes in 1807 or 1808. It was also noted that the Emisons had been part owners of the "General Hanna," said to have been the first steamboat owned by citizens upon the Wabash.

147 *Ibid.*, April 30, 1836.

148 According to the Indianapolis *Indiana Democrat*, January 10, 1837, the "Phenomenon" arrived at Fort Wayne in 1836, and was hailed as the first steamer there. The South Bend *Free Press*, March 28, October 28, 1837, reported two arrivals of the "Matilda Barny" there during 1837.

149 Ronald R. Boyce (ed.), *Regional Development and the Wabash Basin* (Urbana, Ill., 1964), v, 9–11. See map, p. 10, showing the Wabash River's drainage area.

150 Indiana *House Journal*, 1833–34, pp. 218–219, 223. At the previous session a Senate committee expressed the "absolute necessity" for improving navigation of the Wabash if the "anticipated usefulness of the Wabash and Erie canal" was to be realized. Indiana *Senate Journal*, 1832–33, p. 287.

151 *Laws of Indiana*, 1833–34, pp. 346–350. For the state appropriation of $50,000 for the improvement of navigation on the Wabash River, see p. 196, this chapter and Chapter 10, p. 520 for Jackson's veto of a bill for this purpose.

152 *Laws of Indiana*, 1833–34, pp. 372–373; *ibid.* (local), 1835–36, pp. 397–398; *ibid.* (local), 1836–37, pp. 433–434 (quotes), 442–444.

153 U.S. *Statutes at Large*, V, 130, 187, 268. In 1834 Congress appropriated $5,000 for a lighthouse at or near Michigan City, and three years later added $3,000 to complete it *at Michigan City. Ibid.*, IV, 721; *ibid.*, V, 184.

154 Barnhart and Carmony, *Indiana*, I, 279–280, 294–298; Buley, *The Old Northwest*, I, 500–503, 613–614; Logan Esarey, *Internal Improvements in Early Indiana* (Indianapolis, 1912), 74–76, 78–101; Charles R. Poinsatte, *Fort Wayne During the Canal Era, 1828–1855* (Indianapolis, 1969), 23–37.

155 Indiana *House Journal*, 1831–32, Appendix F, 1–8. The commissioners contended that a canal would cost less than a railroad, and also be more desirable.

156 *Ibid.*, 1831–32, pp. 194–195; Indiana *Senate Journal*, 1831–32, pp. 167–168; *Laws of Indiana*, 1831–32, pp. 3–8 (quotations, 4–5). According to political preferences of legislators as in *Biographical Directory of the Indiana General Assembly*, I, 457–458, in the House 22 Jacksonians, 19 anti-Jacksonians, and 1 whose politics is uncertain voted for passage; 13 Jacksonians and 18 anti-Jacksonians against passage. In the Senate 4 Jacksonians and 14 anti-Jacksonians voted for passage; 5 Jacksonians and 7 anti-Jacksonians against passage. Thus, passage was by bipartisan support. This source also indicates that the vote against passage came entirely from counties south of the National Road, plus some votes from Wayne and Marion astride the road. The opposition vote was especially strong from counties in the lower third of the state. Hence, the opposition vote was strongly sectional; it was also strongly bipartisan.

157 Austin W. Morris to John Tipton, January 12, 1832, in Robertson and Riker (eds.), *John Tipton Papers*, II, 497; Paul Fatout, *Indiana Canals* (Lafayette, Ind., 1972), 51.

158 Logansport *Cass County Times*, March 2, 1832; Indiana *House Journal*, 1832–33, pp. 99–105 (annual report of canal commissioners). The commissioners also noted the "commencement" of the canal on February 22 (p. 99).

159 Indiana *House Journal*, 1833–34, pp. 163–164 (annual report of canal commissioners). Concerning the Irish as canal workers and their fighting among themselves, see Poinsatte, *Fort Wayne During the Canal Era, 1828–1855*, pp. 59–64.

160 *Laws of Indiana*, 1833–34, pp. 49–50; Indianapolis *Indiana Journal*, July 31, 1835, quoting Fort Wayne *Sentinel*; Indiana *House Journal*, 1835–36, p. 13. In authorizing an additional loan of $400,000, the guarantee that the state would repay the loan with interest should the proceeds of the canal and the canal itself be inadequate therefor was "irrevocably" guaranteed.

161 Indiana *House Journal*, 1834–35, pp. 237, 242–245, 246–251 (quotes, 243). The commissioners reported that engineering surveys suggested it would cost more to continue the canal on the south side of the Wabash than to keep it on the north side.

162 Indiana *Senate Journal*, 1836–37, pp. 146–147. The location and method of crossing were determined by the Wabash and Erie Canal Commissioners pursuant to legislative direction. *Laws of Indiana* (general), 1834–35, pp. 27–28.

163 For the canal's ultimate extension to Evansville, see pp. 185–188, 194–197, this chapter; Chapter 5, p. 241, and note 20; Chapter 6, pp. 346–348.

164 For the 1829 compact, see Dorothy Riker and Gayle Thornbrough (eds.), *Messages and Papers Relating to the Administration of James Brown Ray, Governor of Indiana, 1825–1831* (Indianapolis, 1954), 492–499. For the compact of 1834, see *Laws of Indiana*, 1833–34, pp. 359–361. For acceptance of the 1834 compact, see Riker and Thornbrough (eds.), *Messages and Papers of Noah Noble*, 237–238, 318.

165 Indianapolis *Indiana Journal*, June 17, 1837, quoting Fort Wayne *Sentinel*; Indiana *Senate Journal*, 1837–38, p. 182.

166 Indiana *Senate Journal*, 1837–38, p. 644. Because canal tracts were sold on credit, proceeds were received over a period of years.

167 John Tipton to Howard Stansbury, November 8, 1835, in Robertson and Riker (eds.), *John Tipton Papers*, III, 179–180; Indiana *Senate Journal*, 1836–37, p. 229.

168 Indiana *House Journal*, 1837–38, p. 13.

169 Calvin Fletcher to Elijah Fletcher (his brother), February 6, 1833, in Thornbrough, Riker, and Corpuz (eds.), *Diary of Calvin Fletcher*, I, 195–196.

170 Indiana *House Journal*, 1834–35, p. 14.

171 These and related items concerning ideas about a system, with the Wabash and Erie Canal as the trunk line to the Atlantic Seaboard, are discussed in the references cited in note 154 above.

172 Indianapolis *Indiana Democrat*, January 20, 1835; Indianapolis *Indiana Journal*, February 3, 1835; Nathan B. Palmer to John Tipton, February 18, 1835, in Robertson and Riker (eds.), *John Tipton Papers*, III, 127; Noah Noble to

Howard Stansbury, April 24, 1835, in Riker and Thornbrough (eds.), *Messages and Papers of Noah Noble*, 367.

173 Thornbrough, Riker, and Corpuz (eds.), *Diary of Calvin Fletcher*, I, 266, 271–272; Indianapolis *Indiana Democrat*, August 5, 1835; Indianapolis *Indiana Journal*, August 28, 1835. Fletcher mentions that he and Williams included an eastern, middle, and western canal in their calculations—items basic in the System of 1836 as adopted.

174 Three installments of this series appear in the Indianapolis *Indiana Democrat*, October 14 (quote by "H"), 21, 1835, and in the Indianapolis *Indiana Journal*, October 16, 23, 1835. In commenting on the two initial installments in the *Indiana Democrat*, Fletcher states that they were "written by Jesse Williams Engineer in order to prepare [the] public mind. The Editer says we *can go* $10 million." Thornbrough, Riker, and Corpuz (eds.), *Diary of Calvin Fletcher*, I, 279.

175 Indiana *Senate Journal*, 1835–36, pp. 107–220, for report of Engineer Howard Stansbury concerning railroads and turnpikes; *ibid.*, 239–317, for report of Engineer Jesse L. Williams regarding canals (quotes, 255, 256–257).

176 Indiana *House Journal*, 1835–36, pp. 19–23; Indianapolis *Indiana Democrat*, December 11, 1835.

177 Indiana *Senate Journal*, 1835–36, pp. 226–239 (quotes, 234, 135 [235]).

178 Indiana *House Journal*, 1835–36, p. 232; Indiana *Senate Journal*, 1835–36, p. 446; *Biographical Directory of the Indiana General Assembly*, I, 465–466. According to the last citation in the House 4 Whigs, 13 Democrats, and 1 probable Democrat voted against passage; in the Senate 4 Whigs and 8 Democrats so voted. In the House 35 Whigs and 21 Democrats voted for passage; in the Senate 12 Whigs, 6 Democrats and 1 whose politics is uncertain so voted. The opposition vote by Whigs and Democrats alike was mainly from the same areas. In addressing the legislature in December, 1836, Noble reported that the items in the system "do not accommodate the interests, nor enlist the feelings of our citizens of Jackson, Scott, and Clark counties, nor of those south of the New Albany and Vincennes Road, and therefore they complain of its injustice." He added that counties from south of this road had named delegates to a convention at Jasper to consider measures to present their claims to the legislature, while the three counties named sought credit from the state on behalf of the proposed Columbus and Jeffersonville Railroad. Indiana *House Journal*, 1836–37, p. 28. For one legislator's comment about the maneuvering and compromising concerning items in the System of 1836 and their routes, see Senator Othniel L. Clark to John Tipton, January 25, 1836, in Robertson and Riker (eds.), *John Tipton Papers*, III, 213–214.

179 John B. Dillon, *A History of Indiana* . . . (Indianapolis, 1859), 569. Barnhart and Carmony, *Indiana*, I, 276–277, 294–298, emphasize that a system of internal improvements had been discussed and anticipated from the early years of statehood.

180 Indianapolis *Indiana Journal*, January 19, 1836; Indianapolis *Indiana Democrat*, January 19, 1836. Calvin Fletcher's enthusiasm for the system is at-

tested by his comment "that as a state Indiana by liberal & wise legislation is to be under the smiles of a kind Providence to be exalted among the nations of the earth." Noting that Samuel Merrill did not share his optimism, Fletcher observed: "He fears that this bill will ruin our state financially & morally. I do not believe it." Thornbrough, Riker, and Corpuz (eds.), *Diary of Calvin Fletcher*, I, 301–303.

[181] Vincennes *Western Sun*, January 30, 1836; Indianapolis *Indiana Journal*, February 13, 1836, quoting an anonymous communication from Peru dated January 20, 1836. Concerning a big celebration at Evansville, see Indianapolis *Indiana Journal*, May 21, 1836, quoting at length from the Evansville *Journal*, and the Indianapolis *Indiana Democrat*, May 25, 1836, quoting at length from the Evansville *Republican*. For a large celebration at Brookville, see Indianapolis *Indiana Democrat*, August 24, 1836, and Indianapolis *Indiana Journal*, September 24, 1836. Probably no event since statehood had been as widely and favorably celebrated as that regarding adoption of the Internal Improvements System of 1836. If the Central Canal was not extended through Muncie, a feeder canal was to be constructed to connect Muncie with the main line.

[182] *Laws of Indiana* (general), 1835–36, pp. 6–21. If Ohio would not approve having a short portion of the Whitewater Canal within its borders, a railroad from near Harrison, Ohio, was to be substituted from there to Lawrenceburg and be located entirely within Indiana.

[183] *Ibid.*, 1836–37, p. 67.

[184] *Ibid.*, 1835–36, pp. 10–11, 20. As here made explicit, borrowing was *authorized*, up to $10,000,000, at interest not over 5 percent, for not to exceed twenty-five years. The Canal Fund Commissioners were "authorized and required" to secure "a loan or loans, from time to time," as "directed by the Board of Internal Improvement," per these limitations. The state irrevocably pledged to complete the works in the system "so soon as the interest of the State will justify . . . ." An act of 1832 had established what became known as the Canal Fund Commissioners, consisting of three individuals, to secure loans for construction of the Wabash and Erie Canal. An act of 1837 specified that the Canal Fund Commissioners should be known as the Fund Commissioners. *Laws of Indiana*, 1831–32, pp. 3–8; *ibid.* (general), 1836–37, pp. 66–68.

[185] *Ibid.* (general), 1835–36, pp. 6, 9–12. The three existing Wabash and Erie Canal Commissioners were named members of the Board of Internal Improvement, and the board was made responsible for the canal as well as the system. Members served three year terms, staggered so that three were appointed annually. No member of the General Assembly, and no state official, could serve as a member of the board during the term for which they had been appointed or elected. The next legislative session required that members of the board be elected by a separate majority vote of each house, with the vote recorded in the legislative journals. *Ibid.*, 1836–37, p. 92.

[186] Indiana *Senate Journal*, 1836–37, pp. 131, 143; *ibid.*, 1837–38, pp. 181, 192. The data given are taken from the first and second annual reports of the

Board of Internal Improvement. According to these reports contracts totaling $402,162 were let for the Wabash and Erie Canal during 1836, with $10,018 paid for construction; during 1837 an additional $340,135.17 was paid for construction on the canal.

187 Indiana *House Journal*, 1836–37, pp. 19, 28.

188 *Ibid.*, 127–128, 145, 265, 356–357; Indianapolis *Indiana Democrat*, December 27, 1836. The *Indiana Democrat* refers to the bill as the Calf Bill. During the previous summer, under the pseudonym of "Tullius," Owen had advocated additions to the system and some modifications of the works it embraced. The three installments in this series are in the *Indiana Democrat*, June 8, 29, July 20, 1836, and the Vincennes *Western Sun*, June 4, 25, July 23, 1836. For identification of Owen as "Tullius," and considerable discussion about the series and the failure of his bill, see Richard William Leopold, *Robert Dale Owen: A Biography* (Cambridge, Mass., 1940), 143, 146–150.

189 Indiana *House Journal*, 1836–37, pp. 268–270.

190 Indiana *Senate Journal*, 1836–37, pp. 202, 238–239. Dumont suggested that all except priority works be delayed until they would not be burdensome regarding taxes or oppressive to agricultural interests by increasing the price of labor to an "immoderate degree."

191 Indianapolis *Indiana Journal*, January 28, 1837.

192 Indianapolis *Indiana Democrat*, January 27, 1837.

193 Indiana *Senate Journal*, 1836–37, pp. 22–23 (Noble's comments), 82 (committee referral), 329–337 (quotes from report, 331, 332, 337). The committee incorrectly reported the aggregate cost of the works south of the National Road as $9,304,691, but the items embraced therein aggregate $9,364,694. The report estimated that it would cost $1,800,000 to construct the Erie and Michigan Canal, whereas no appropriation therefor had been made in 1836. (But the General Assembly had "irrevocably pledged" the faith of the state to start within a decade and ultimately complete a canal or a railroad from Fort Wayne via Goshen and South Bend to Lake Michigan at or near Michigan City.) The magnitude of the fiscal situation facing the state in 1837 is better understood when it is realized that the state's tax collections for the ordinary costs of state government averaged only $50,946.94 per year during 1831 to 1837; and $258,005.25 during 1837 to 1843. Sixteen senators were named to the Senate Committee on Canals and Internal Improvements when the session began, twelve of whom were Whigs and four were Democrats. Eight Whigs and two Democrats voted for the system, and one Democrat had voted against it. Although no names were added to this report, it seems reasonable to presume that it represents the basic views of a substantial majority of the committee. *Ibid.*, pp. 25, 43; *Biographical Directory of the Indiana General Assembly*, I, 465, 467. See Indiana *Senate Journal*, 1835–36, pp. 444–446 [445], for the vote of senators for and against adoption of the system.

194 Indianapolis *Indiana Journal*, February 11, 1837.

CHAPTER 5

[1] The political balance in the General Assembly, 1837–43, is based on compilation of party ties in *A Biographical Directory of the Indiana General Assembly* (2 vols., Indianapolis, 1980, 1984), Volume 1, *1816–1899*, Volume 2, *1901–1984*, I, 469–485.

[2] Gayle Thornbrough, Dorothy Riker, and Paula Corpuz (eds.), *The Diary of Calvin Fletcher* (9 vols., Indianapolis, 1972–1983), I, 265; Dorothy Riker (ed.), *Messages and Papers Relating to the Administration of David Wallace, Governor of Indiana, 1837–1840* (Indianapolis, 1963), 3–9.

[3] Indianapolis *Indiana Democrat*, November 9, 30, 1836. The state central committee explained that it had issued the call for a state convention in compliance with duties given it at the party's state convention in January, 1835.

[4] Indianapolis *Indiana Journal*, January 28, 1837; Indianapolis *Indiana Democrat*, February 8, 15, 1837.

[5] Indianapolis *Indiana Democrat*, January 10, 27, 1837.

[6] *Ibid.*, March 16, 1837. In its issue of April 22, 1837, the Indianapolis *Indiana Journal* contended that the *Indiana Democrat*, after learning that it was inexpedient to draw party lines, had encouraged Thomas H. Blake, Morgan, and David Hillis to run for governor. The *Indiana Journal* announced Morgan as a candidate in its issue of February 25, 1837, but on April 1, 1837, it reported that he no longer considered himself a candidate, leaving that field entirely to Wallace.

[7] For Taylor's candidacy and withdrawal, see Indianapolis *Indiana Democrat*, May 3, July 5, 1837; for Dumont's candidacy, see Indianapolis *Indiana Journal*, May 6, 1837.

[8] Indianapolis *Indiana Journal*, June 3, July 22, 29, August 5, 1837. In his inaugural in December, 1837, Wallace said he had staunchly opposed classification, and still believed that it would result in prostration of the system, but he proposed a modified form of concurrent construction. Indiana *House Journal*, 1837–38, pp. 34–35.

[9] Indianapolis *Indiana Journal*, July 8, August 5, 1837 (quote).

[10] See especially Dumont's address in Indianapolis *Indiana Democrat*, April 26, June 27, July 19, 1837.

[11] *Ibid.*, July 5, 1837.

[12] *Ibid.*, April 19, May 17, July 5, 1837, including quotations from other papers regarding these and others charges.

[13] *Ibid.*, July 19 (quotes), August 2, 1837. See Indianapolis *Indiana Journal*, July 22, 1837, for a defense of Wallace's private character.

[14] Indianapolis *Indiana Democrat*, June 27, 1837, quoting New Albany *Gazette*.

[15] Indianapolis *Indiana Democrat*, July 26, 1837.

[16] Edward A. Hannegan to John Tipton, July 18, 1837, in Nellie A. Robertson and Dorothy Riker (eds.), *The John Tipton Papers* (3 vols., Indianapolis, 1942), III, 415–416; Dorothy Riker and Gayle Thornbrough (comps.), *Indiana Election Returns, 1816–1851* (Indianapolis, 1960), 145–148, giving election re-

turns, official for all but four counties, showing 46,067 for Wallace and 36,915 for Dumont; Oliver H. Smith, *Early Indiana Trials and Sketches* (Cincinnati, 1858), 131–132.

17 See *passim* issues of the Indianapolis *Indiana Journal* and Indianapolis *Indiana Democrat* from late April through mid-June, 1837. In its issue of January 27, 1837, the *Indiana Democrat* stated that friends of Pepper had asked that his name be announced as a candidate for lieutenant governor; in its issue of March 4, 1837, the *Indiana Journal* said it had been authorized to announce Hillis as a candidate. For brief sketches of Hillis and Pepper, see *Biographical Directory of the Indiana General Assembly*, I, 184–185, 311.

18 Indianapolis *Indiana Journal*, June 17, 1837 (Pepper's withdrawal); Indianapolis *Indiana Democrat*, July 12, 1837 (Burnett's entry); Riker and Thornbrough (comps.), *Indiana Election Returns, 1816–1851*, pp. 168–170, complete for all counties but unofficial for four of them, gives Hillis 49,535 votes to 22,829 for Burnett. See *Biographical Directory of the Indiana General Assembly*, I, 47, for a sketch of Burnett.

19 Indiana *House Journal*, 1837–38, pp. 66–67; *Biographical Directory of the Indiana General Assembly*, I, 469–471, giving political ties of members of the legislature. For examples of this lambasting and responses to it, see Indianapolis *Indiana Democrat*, November 2, 9, 1836, February 15, March 1, 8, 1837; Indianapolis *Indiana Journal*, November 5, 19, 1836, March 4, 11, August 26, 1837.

20 Indiana *House Journal*, 1836–37, p. 41; *Biographical Directory of the Indiana General Assembly*, I, 467–469, regarding political ties of legislators. The Indianapolis *Indiana Democrat*, December 13, 1836, boasted that Brown had won because of superior merit and Sheets' unpopularity. The rival Indianapolis *Indiana Journal*, December 14, 1836, described Sheets as energetic and faithful but its admission that it might take exception to some of his acts as secretary perhaps indicates dissatisfaction with his conduct of the office.

21 Indiana *House Journal*, 1837–38, pp. 31–36 (quotes, pp. 31, 35–36).

22 *Ibid.*, 14–15.

23 Indiana *Senate Journal*, 1837–38, pp. 181–182, 184. See pp. 180–192, for an overview of board efforts during 1836–37, its initial year.

24 *Ibid.*, Table A, following p. 460. According to this report $1,241,767.66 had been spent on the system, $360,983.06 on the Wabash and Erie Canal, and $15,221.22 on general contingencies.

25 *Ibid.*, 122–125. The related report is in Indiana *Documentary Journal*, 1837–38, Doc. 13. The General Assembly gave the fund commissioners authority to make a compromise settlement with the Cohens of Baltimore and the Josephs of New York from debts due for Indiana bonds previously sold them. *Laws of Indiana* (revised), 1837–38, p. 356. This act, however, did not prohibit the further sale of bonds on credit, which practice had made possible these defaults.

26 Indiana *House Journal*, 1837–38, p. 13; Indiana *Senate Journal*, 1837–38, pp. 182–183. The General Assembly earnestly requested Ohio to make its portion

of the canal the same depth and width as that from Fort Wayne to the Ohio border so that the canal would be the same size from Fort Wayne to Lake Erie. *Laws of Indiana* (local), 1837–38, pp. 443–444.

[27] Indiana *Senate Journal*, 1837–38, pp. 183–184; *Laws of Indiana* (local), 1837–38, p. 451. For examples of earlier interest in extending the canal to Terre Haute, perhaps even to the Ohio River, see Indiana *House Journal*, 1834–35, p. 167; *ibid.*, 1835–36, pp. 54, 124; Indiana *Senate Journal*, 1834–35, p. 127; Indianapolis *Indiana Journal*, January 8, 1836; Vincennes *Western Sun*, January 24, 1835. Also see Governor Noah Noble to James Whitcomb, Commissioner of the General Land Office, November 12, 1837, in Dorothy Riker and Gayle Thornbrough (eds.), *Messages and Papers Relating to the Administration of Noah Noble, Governor of Indiana, 1831–1837* (Indianapolis, 1958), 568–570.

[28] Indiana *Senate Journal*, 1838–39, pp. 308–310. The commissioners reported that had they borrowed an additional $1,000,000, as authorized, in bonds, the interest due in 1839 would have been $341,769.25.

[29] *Ibid.*, 9.

[30] *Ibid.*, 9–12. Also see pp. 13–17.

[31] *Ibid.*, 14–15. If such measures were adopted, Wallace said, the state would be able to finish its "present undertakings" and do something for the Michigan Road, rapidly going to decay.

[32] *Ibid.*, 17–20.

[33] *Ibid.*, 161–164 (commissioners), 68–69 (treasurer).

[34] *Laws of Indiana* (general), 1838–39, pp. 3–8, 29–30.

[35] *Ibid.*, 27–28, 15–17.

[36] *Ibid.*, 77; Indianapolis *Indiana Journal*, November 17, 1838, says cars had been placed on the road November 10 and immediately commenced regular trips; Riker (ed.), *Messages and Papers of David Wallace*, 152–153; Thornbrough, Riker, and Corpuz (eds.), *Diary of Calvin Fletcher*, II, 31. At the previous session the Madison to Lafayette Railroad via Indianapolis had been changed to a turnpike between Indianapolis and Lafayette; and the railroad between Indianapolis and Madison had been restricted to a single track line. *Laws of Indiana* (revised), 1837–38, pp. 354–355. According to the Indianapolis *Indiana Journal*, November 12, 1841, railroad cars, propelled by locomotives, had commenced ascending the steep incline hill at Madison earlier that month, by which time twenty-nine miles of the line were in operation north to within six miles of Vernon.

[37] See annual report of the board for 1838–39, in Riker (ed.), *Messages and Papers of David Wallace*, 355–375, especially pp. 355–361 (quote, 358). The board gives the total of such contracts as $3,414,121, however, the data given add up to $3,410,111.

[38] Thornbrough, Riker, and Corpuz (eds.), *Diary of Calvin Fletcher*, II, 116, 119; Indianapolis *Indiana Journal*, August 24, 1839 (Noble to contractors).

[39] Riker (ed.), *Messages and Papers of David Wallace*, 365–366, has a copy of the order as in the board's annual report for 1838–39.

⁴⁰ *Ibid.*, 288–301 (quote, 295), for annual report of Commissioners Milton Stapp and L. H. Scott. They principally concern themselves with items pertaining to the system and the trunk line canal, but offer information about related items.

⁴¹ *Ibid.*, 410–420, especially p. 412. See below, note 45, regarding the political composition of this committee.

⁴² Different individuals gave different estimates regarding the suspended debt which varied somewhat from time to time. In October, 1840, Treasurer Nathan B. Palmer itemized it as totaling $3,559,791.34; in December, 1842, Agent Michael G. Bright, after examining the debts arising from internal improvements, estimated this debt as "about $4,000,000," but listed items totaling $4,210,456.72. Gayle Thornbrough (ed.), *Messages and Papers Relating to the Administration of Samuel Bigger, Governor of Indiana, 1840–1843* (Indianapolis, 1964), 74–75, 579–580.

⁴³ See Chapter 4, p. 156, for table concerning ordinary state revenue 1831–37.

⁴⁴ Riker (ed.), *Messages and Papers of David Wallace*, 372–374. As indicated in *Biographical Directory of the Indiana General Assembly*, I, 235, 294, Samuel Lewis and Noah Noble were Whigs. The politics of the third member, John A. Graham, is unknown, but it seems likely that he was also a Whig.

⁴⁵ Riker (ed.), *Messages and Papers of David Wallace*, 411–412, 420. The names attached to this report are Thomas J. Henley, chairman, of Clark County; Elwood Fisher, Switzerland County; John I. Morrison, Washington County; and John L. Spann, Jennings County. Fisher, Morrison, and Spann represented counties not directly provided for by the System of 1836. Their comments may have been influenced more by this fact than by their politics. *Biographical Directory of the Indiana General Assembly*, I, 474–476, for political ties and counties represented. According to the last source cited, all four representatives were Democrats. Henley and Fisher respectively represented Clark and Switzerland counties, both bordering on the Ohio River; Morrison and Spann respectively represented Washington and Jennings counties, both adjoining counties bordering on the Ohio. No project in the System of 1836 extended into Switzerland; a short section of the New Albany and Lafayette Turnpike, via Crawfordsville, was projected through the western edge of Clark; part of this turnpike was to cross Washington via Salem; and the contemplated Madison to Lafayette Railroad, via Indianapolis, was to extend across the middle of Jennings. Hence, the four Democrats represented counties which were very closely dependent on the all important Ohio-Mississippi trade artery.

⁴⁶ Riker (ed.), *Messages and Papers of David Wallace*, 361–362 (board), 336 (Wallace); *Laws of Indiana* (local), 1839–40, p. 243.

⁴⁷ Riker (ed.), *Messages and Papers of David Wallace*, 326–333, especially pp. 328, 330, 332. Wallace explains that it would probably take $212,620 to meet the interest on improvement bonds due January 1, 1840, thus the author has presumed that approximately this amount would be required for payment on July 1, 1840. Wallace estimated that the levy of 30 cents per $100 of taxable property

for 1839 would yield $294,000 for this purpose. As may be seen *ibid.*, 367–369, the improvement board, using different data, reached somewhat different views about the debt and interest thereon. Any attempt to bring consistency out of these data would be an exercise in confusion!

48 *Ibid.*, 370–371. This comment favorable to turning works over to private enterprise, coming from a committee chaired by Noah Noble, helps illustrate that the return to economic laissez faire in the 1840s was a bipartisan movement born in significant part from dire economic necessity. The board suggested that such associations proposed to take over the state bonds for the works.

49 According to *Biographical Directory of the Indiana General Assembly*, I, 474–476, the 1839–40 session had 25 Whigs and 22 Democrats in the Senate; 61 Democrats and 39 Whigs in the House.

50 *Laws of Indiana* (general), 1839–40, pp. 17–21. For an indication of divergent views about this bill, which the governor allowed to become law without his signature, see Riker (ed.), *Messages and Papers of David Wallace*, 331n–332n.

51 Indiana *Documentary Journal*, 1839–40, pp. 192–195. The committee estimated that it would require $444,390 to pay interest on the improvement debt during fiscal 1840–41 (January 1 and July 1, 1840). Only the name of Chairman Elisha Long is attached to the report which submitted a bill calling for the proposed increase in tax levies. Division within the committee is suggested by the explanation that a majority of it believed that "although the taxes appear oppressive, the people will sustain the credit of the State," therefore the majority recommended its passage.

52 *Laws of Indiana* (general), 1839–40, pp. 6–10, reproducing the tax law of 1836, plus a joint resolution declaring it in effect for the ensuing year.

53 *Ibid.*, 51–52; Indianapolis *Indiana Journal*, March 7, 1840. Also see Riker (ed.), *Messages and Papers of David Wallace*, 328n–329n, for additional information about the wrangling between the House and Senate concerning the tax bill, the board, and related items. Riker concluded: "The crux of the matter seemed to be the effort of the Democratic House to get rid of Milton Stapp as fund commissioner and the Senate [Whig controlled] determination to keep him."

54 The Indianapolis *Indiana Journal*, October 5, 1839, named William Hendricks, Amos Lane, Nathan B. Palmer, William J. Brown, Gamaliel Taylor, Samuel Milroy, and Robert Dale Owen as persons being considered. As indicated in Robertson and Riker (eds.), *John Tipton Papers*, III, 820–821, and Vincennes *Western Sun*, March 9, 1839, quoting other papers, there were strong expressions of support for John Tipton prior to his death in early April, 1839.

55 Indianapolis *Indiana Democrat*, September 25, October 9, 1839; Indianapolis *Indiana Journal*, October 12, 1839.

56 Indianapolis *Indiana Journal*, September 28, November 2, 16, 1839; David Wallace to Samuel Judah, September 23, 1839, in Riker (ed.), *Messages and Papers of David Wallace*, 269.

57 Based on the proceedings in the Indianapolis *Indiana Democrat*, January 14, 1840. The resolution establishing the committee provided that delegates from

each county name a member of it, such member to have voting power equal to the number of senators and representatives his county had in the legislature. The Vincennes *Western Sun*, January 25, 1840, quoting the Indianapolis *Indiana Democrat*, says the committee consisted of seventy-two members who, after an hour's deliberation, "unanimously" endorsed Howard and Tuley.

58 Based on the proceedings in the Indianapolis *Tri-Weekly Journal*, January 22, 1840. The resolution establishing the committee provided that it consist of one person from each congressional district, named by the county delegation of the district, with districts having the same voting power as they have senators and representatives in the legislature.

59 *Ibid.*, January 20, 1840. As shown in Riker (ed.), *Messages and Papers of David Wallace*, 270n, the Terre Haute *Enquirer*, February 15, 1840, reported that it believed the initial ballot for governor had been: Wallace 38, McCarty 47, Bigger 33, John W. Payne 32; second ballot: McCarty 61, Bigger 56, Wallace 23, Payne 17; on the third ballot Wallace's friends largely supported Bigger and he received 84 votes, McCarty 72, and Wallace 4. The editor attributed McCarty's defeat to a grudge Caleb B. Smith had against him.

60 Concerning Bigger, see Thornbrough (ed.), *Messages and Papers of Samuel Bigger*, 4–5; *Biographical Directory of the Indiana General Assembly*, I, 25. Regarding Howard, see *Biographical Directory of the American Congress, 1774–1927*; William Wesley Woollen, *Biographical and Historical Sketches of Early Indiana* (Indianapolis, 1883), 262–272.

61 Indianapolis *Tri-Weekly Journal*, January 20, 1840; Vincennes *Western Sun*, January 25, 1840.

62 Indianapolis *Tri-Weekly Journal*, January 20, 1840.

63 *Biographical Directory of the Indiana General Assembly*, I, 160 (sketch of Hall); Indianapolis *Indiana Journal*, March 7, 1840, for a favorable sketch of Hall and an unfavorable one of Tuley. This paper claimed that Hall had been elected to the board without his knowledge or consent, and had attended but one meeting of it.

64 From the address in the Indianapolis *Indiana Democrat*, January 14, 1840. The address deprecated the heavy use which had been made of both public and private credit, and recommended "a constitutional curb to a system of Public Debt" and a gradual return from the unbounded use of private credit. This illustrates how the debacle resulting from the System of 1836 fostered an abandonment of state efforts to develop the economy in favor of a return to economic laissez faire.

65 From the address in the Indianapolis *Tri-Weekly Journal*, January 22, 1840.

66 Indianapolis *Indiana Democrat*, March 11, 1840; Riker (ed.), *Messages and Papers of David Wallace*, 422–423 (Bigger's resignation); Vincennes *Western Sun*, May 2, 1840.

67 Tilghman A. Howard to N(athaniel) West, Washington, D.C., February 24, 1840, in Vincennes *Western Sun*, March 21, 1840, indicating that his acceptance letter had been forwarded under date of January 18, which suggests an

unusually quick response for that time; Howard to Citizens of the Seventh Congressional District, Washington, D.C., March 27, 1840, in Indianapolis *Indiana Democrat*, April 15, 1840, stating that "positive injunctions" of duty required his remaining at his post until adjournment—adding that the use of his name regarding the gubernatorial election had been "without my consent, and against my often-expressed wishes."

[68] See Howard to unnamed correspondent, Washington, D.C., May 30, 1840, in Woollen, *Biographical and Historical Sketches of Early Indiana*, 265–266, stating that he will leave Washington "at the very earliest day, and hurry home" and "be at several points yet in Indiana before the election." According to the *Congressional Globe*, 26 Cong., 1 session, VIII, 458, 510, on June 11 Congressman William W. Wick obtained a two weeks leave of absence for Howard; on July 6 the speaker laid before the House a letter from Indiana's governor enclosing Howard's resignation.

[69] Thornbrough, Riker, and Corpuz (eds.), *Diary of Calvin Fletcher*, II, 196 (Indianapolis speech). For evidence that he probably started campaigning in southeast Indiana, see Indianapolis *Indiana Democrat*, March 18, June 20, 1840; Indianapolis *Indiana Journal*, August 22, 1840.

[70] Indianapolis *Indiana Journal*, June 6, 1840, quoting Madison *Banner*, April 15. According to the South Bend *Free Press*, July 24, 1840, Bigger expressed similar views to citizens of St. Joseph County as the campaign neared its end.

[71] Tilghman A. Howard to George Burton Thompson, Washington, D.C., February 14, 1840, in Indianapolis *Indiana Democrat*, June 27, 1840; Howard to Citizens of the Seventh Congressional District, *ibid.*, April 15, 1840. In the Vincennes *Western Sun*, July 25, 1840, Howard reaffirmed views very similar to those of Thompson.

[72] Indianapolis *Indiana Democrat*, August 1, 1840.

[73] *Ibid.*, May 30, July 25 ("Backwoodsman"), 1840.

[74] Indianapolis *Indiana Journal*, August 1, 22, 1840; Indianapolis *Indiana Democrat*, July 18, 1840.

[75] For the outcome of the largely official vote for governor and lieutenant governor respectively, see Riker and Thornbrough (comps.), *Indiana Election Returns, 1816–1851*, pp. 148–150, 170–172. Hall got 62,874 votes against 53,687 for Tuley. According to *Biographical Directory of the Indiana General Assembly*, I, 477–479, the new House had 78 Whigs and 22 Democrats; the new Senate, 33 Whigs and 14 Democrats.

[76] See p. 206, this chapter, for previous elections of these three officials.

[77] For the outcome of ballots cast and persons involved, see Indiana *House Journal*, 1840–41, pp. 57–58. On the presumption that the thirty-six Democrats cast at least nearly all their votes against Dunn, Sheets, and Morris, and the fact that the opposition votes were significantly more than thirty-six votes in each instance against the winners, it is reasonable to presume that a Whig minority was part of the opposition in each election. *Biographical Directory of the Indiana General Assembly*, I, 109, 294, identifies Dunn and Noel as Whigs.

78 Thornbrough, Riker, and Corpuz (eds.), *Diary of Calvin Fletcher*, II, 253–254; Indianapolis *Indiana Democrat and Spirit of the Constitution*, December 12, 1840.

79 See report of the board to the General Assembly, dated November 30, 1840, in Thornbrough (ed.), *Messages and Papers of Samuel Bigger*, 101–102.

80 From the annual report of Treasurer Palmer, dated October 31, 1840, *ibid.*, 71–77. Palmer explained that his listing of items constituting the public debt was nearly but not precisely correct. He noted that his fellow fund commissioner Milton Stapp did not consider items 3, 4, and 5 of his listing part of the state debt. The act establishing the System of 1836 authorized the issuance of bonds on behalf of the Lawrenceburgh and Indianapolis Railroad up to $500,000, however, this item is often not viewed as part of the System of 1836.

81 Indiana *House Journal*, 1840–41, pp. 35–37. During the session Noah Noble, president of the Board of Internal Improvement, submitted a report to the Senate in which he reported that $5,316,335 had been spent on the system to November 1, 1840; and that its completion would increase the aggregate cost to $18,469,573. Regarding the Wabash and Erie Canal, an estimated $1,843,114 had been spent or obligated for it to November 1, 1840; and its final cost was anticipated to be $2,056,634. Indiana *Documentary Journal*, 1840–41, Sen. Doc. 8, pp. 146–149.

82 Indiana *House Journal*, 1840–41, pp. 37–38.

83 *Ibid.*, 38–40.

84 *Ibid.*, 40–44.

85 Thornbrough, Riker, and Corpuz (eds.), *Diary of Calvin Fletcher*, II, 278, 284–285. About a month earlier Fletcher had confided to his diary that Indiana had been "guilty of much folly," been "branded extravegant profligate," been "guided by wicked counsellers . . . in the weak & selfish plans of demagogues. She is now bankrupt—degraded." *Ibid.*, 255. Fletcher's early and strong support of the System of 1836 is indicated in Chapter 4, pp. 191–192, 195.

86 According to *Biographical Directory of the Indiana General Assembly*, I, 477–479, 33 Whigs and 14 Democrats were members of the Senate; and 78 Whigs and 22 Democrats of the House. Two changes in the House added one Democrat at the expense of the Whigs during the session.

87 See Indiana *Documentary Journal*, 1840–41, Sen. Doc. 6, pp. 117–121 (committee report); Indianapolis *Indiana Journal*, January 9, 1841 (content of bill). The Indiana *Documentary Journal* by its comments *suggests* the content of the bill offered. According to the Indiana *Senate Journal*, 1840–41, pp. 57, 58, nine senators, all from counties having no system works passing through them, were named to the select committee; and as noted in *Biographical Directory of the Indiana General Assembly*, I, 477, five members were Whigs, four were Democrats.

88 Indiana *Documentary Journal*, 1840–41, House Doc. 26, pp. 345–352 (quotes, 346, 348). Committee members signing the report were: Caleb B. Smith, Fayette County; Samuel Howe Smydth, Daviess County; Thomas

Dowling, Vigo County; Daniel Stratton, Wayne County; Williamson Terrell, Bartholomew County and part of Brown County; John D. Defrees, St. Joseph County. William Jones, Spencer County, dissented from the report. Party membership and counties represented are as indicated in *Biographical Directory of the Indiana General Assembly*, I, 478–479.

[89] Indiana *Documentary Journal*, 1840–41, House Doc. 27, pp. 353–355. This report was signed by Jesse Morgan, Rush County, and Aaron Rawlings, Scott County. Both were Whigs.

[90] *Laws of Indiana* (general), 1840–41, pp. 207–208. The bill passed the Senate 27 to 17, the House 52 to 44. Indiana *Senate Journal*, 1840–41, p. 463; Indiana *House Journal*, 1840–41, pp. 638–639. In the Senate 17 Whigs and 10 Democrats voted for passage, 15 Whigs and 2 Democrats against passage; in the House 50 Whigs and 2 Democrats were for passage, 24 Whigs and 20 Democrats against passage. Thus Democratic support was essential for passage in the Senate, but not the House. Party ties and counties represented are given in *Biographical Directory of the Indiana General Assembly*, I, 477–479.

[91] *Laws of Indiana* (general), 1840–41, p. 209.

[92] *Ibid.*, 214–218, 200.

[93] Indiana *House Journal*, 1840–41, pp. 814–815; Indianapolis *Indiana Journal*, February 20, 1841. The *Indiana Journal*, friendly to Noble, declared that Noble's friends had elected him even though he had "preemptorily refused" to be a candidate.

[94] *Laws of Indiana* (general), 1840–41, pp. 47–48.

[95] *Ibid.*, 202–204, 192–196. As indicated *ibid.* (general), 1841–42, pp. 85–86, the provision for investment of such funds in bank stock was largely repealed at the ensuing session, and entirely so for practical purposes as concerned state stock.

[96] See pp. 251–252, this chapter, for savings anticipated from these changes.

[97] *Laws of Indiana* (general), 1840–41, pp. 218, 210–213, 219.

[98] See Noble's report as fund commissioner, dated November 22, 1841, in Indiana *Documentary Journal*, 1841–42, Sen. Doc. 1, pp. 2–3; N. M. Rothschild & Sons to William Henry Harrison, London, April 2, 1841, in Thornbrough (ed.), *Messages and Papers of Samuel Bigger*, 236–238; Samuel Bigger to Noah Noble, May 17, 1841, *ibid.*, 238–240.

[99] Thornbrough (ed.), *Messages and Papers of Samuel Bigger*, 245–247 (Noble's circular statement); Philip Mason to Noble, June 29, 1841, *ibid.*, 243–244. For other items indicating that the default was at least not entirely unexpected, see *ibid.*, 211 (Samuel Judah), 248 (George H. Dunn); Thornbrough, Riker, and Corpuz (eds.), *Diary of Calvin Fletcher*, II, 278, 284–285, 319–320.

[100] Indiana *House Journal*, 1841–42, pp. 13–18 (quotes, 13, 15, 18). All items listed, as constituting the state debt, pp. 15–16, except the $1,727,000 for the Wabash and Erie Canal, appear to have been items in either the bonded or unfunded debt for internal improvements.

[101] *Ibid.*, 19–20.

102 Ebenezer M. Chamberlain to Editor, Goshen *Democrat*, December 11, 1841, in Thornbrough (ed.), *Messages and Papers of Samuel Bigger*, 349–350. See Indiana *House Journal*, 1835–36, p. 232, for Chamberlain's vote for the system; and *Biographical Directory of the Indiana General Assembly*, I, 465, for his being a member of the House as a Democrat.

103 According to *Biographical Directory of the Indiana General Assembly*, I, 480–482, at the legislative session of 1841–42, there were 28 Whigs and 22 Democrats in the Senate, 53 Democrats and 47 Whigs in the House.

104 For the Senate resolution creating the committee and its members, see Indiana *Senate Journal*, 1841–42, pp. 28–29, 50–51. Its members, their politics, and counties represented as indicated in *Biographical Directory of the Indiana General Assembly*, I, 480, were: Joseph C. Eggleston, Whig, Switzerland; Ebenezer M. Chamberlain, Democrat, Elkhart, Kosciusko, and Whitley; Samuel W. Parker, Whig, Fayette and Union; Thomas D. Baird, Whig, Fulton, Marshall, and St. Joseph; Nathaniel West, Democrat, Marion.

105 For the House resolution creating the committee and its members, see Indiana *House Journal*, 1841–42, pp. 32–35, 270. Its members, their politics, and counties represented as indicated in *Biographical Directory of the Indiana General Assembly*, I, pp. 480–482, were: Edward A. Hannegan, Democrat, Fountain; John D. Defrees, Whig, St. Joseph; John S. Simonson, Democrat, Clark; Joseph G. Marshall, Whig, Jefferson; William J. Brown, Democrat, Marion; John S. Davis, Whig, Floyd; Ethan A. Brown, Democrat, Dearborn; James Ritchey, Democrat, Johnson; Robert M. Cooper, Whig, Henry. During the investigation William B. Mitchell, Democrat, Elkhart, replaced Simonson.

106 For report of the Senate committee, see Indiana *Documentary Journal*, 1841–42, Sen. Doc. 2, pp. 141–629 (quotes, 144, 180). As indicated *ibid.*, 181, the three Whig members signed the report without reservation. Chamberlain and West, the two Democrats, objected that the report tended to exonerate Noah Noble concerning his knowledge about fictitious payments for the Madison and Indianapolis Railroad; and Chamberlain contended that it had inappropriately exonerated Jesse L. Williams from blame. For House committee report, see *ibid.*, House Doc. 12, pp. 215–468. No signatures are attached to this report. For much additional comment about items criticized, persons blamed, and some charges that were tried in court, see Thornbrough (ed.), *Messages and Papers of Samuel Bigger*, 344n–347n.

107 Ebenezer M. Chamberlain to Editor, Goshen *Democrat*, January 29, 1842, in Thornbrough (ed.), *Messages and Papers of Samuel Bigger*, 428–431.

108 The annual report of Treasurer George H. Dunn for 1841–42, in Indiana *Documentary Journal*, 1842–43, House Doc. 2, Statement B, following p. 16, covering revenue from and costs of works in the system for the period March 1 to October 31, 1842, shows $15,007.62 in revenue from the Whitewater Canal, Northern Division Central Canal, Madison and Indianapolis Railroad, and the New Albany and Vincennes Road; and shows expenditures aggregating $37,570.28 for modest construction, maintenance, and related items for the Erie

and Michigan Canal, Southern Division Central Canal, Northern Division Central Canal, Whitewater Canal, New Albany and Vincennes Road, Jeffersonville and Crawfordsville Road, Madison and Indianapolis Railroad, and the Cross Cut Canal—not counting $6,752.51 for contingencies for the fund commissioners and Board of Internal Improvement.

109 For examples of discussion about payment or nonpayment of interest and principal on the bonded debt, 1841–47, see pp. 228–234, this chapter; and Ch. 6, pp. 293–295, 310–312.

110 Indiana *Documentary Journal*, 1841–42, House Doc. 14, pp. 479–485 (quotes, 481). According to the Indiana *House Journal*, 1841–42, p. 29, the House Ways and Means Committee embraced: Thomas J. Henley, Chairman, Democrat, Clark; William Wines, Democrat, Vigo; Wilson Thompson, Democrat, Fayette; John Hendricks, Democrat, Shelby; John H. Bradley, Whig, La Porte; John Steele Davis, Whig, Floyd; and Samuel Goodnow, Whig, Jefferson. The report was signed only by Henley, however, the three Whigs expressed their concurrence with its recommendations and conclusions, but dissented from its premises and assertions that former executives and legislatures intentionally deceived the people concerning the system. All Democrats probably concurred with the report. The politics of members and counties represented are in *Biographical Directory of the Indiana General Assembly*, I, 481–482.

111 *Laws of Indiana* (general), 1841–42, p. 73. See p. 246, this chapter, for the 1841 tax levy. The act establishing the system stated: "For the punctual payment of the interest and final redemption of the principal of all sums of money which may be borrowed" the state "irrevocably pledged and appropriated" the canals, railroads, and turnpikes, and the income from them, "the sufficiency of which . . . the State of Indiana doth hereby irrevocably guarantee." *Ibid*. (general), 1835–36, pp. 10–11.

112 *Ibid*. (general), 1841–42, p. 120. For the appropriation of $1,500,000 in state scrip to pay contractors, see pp. 214–215. An act of 1842 authorized the issue of such notes to pay principal and interest due branches of the Second State Bank (for money advanced the state for internal improvements in 1839). *Ibid*., 82–83. According to the report of the state auditor in 1844, the $1,500,000 of notes had been issued during 1840, 1841, and 1842, but largely in 1840; $722,640 in treasury notes had been issued in 1842 to pay the debt owed the branches of the state bank. Indiana *Documentary Journal*, 1844–45, Pt. I, Doc. 1, pp. 44–46.

113 *Laws of Indiana* (general), 1841–42, pp. 3–21 (quotes, 18, 19). Agents or commissioners to supervise and protect respectively the interests of the Wabash and Erie Canal, Erie and Michigan Canal, Madison and Indianapolis Railroad, Whitewater Canal, and the New Albany and Vincennes Road were to be elected for a term of two years by joint ballot of the General Assembly. If agents were needed for other works, the state treasurer was to appoint them. *Ibid*., 18–20. No additional company could be organized for completion of the Whitewater Canal, since another act of the session had approved such a company. *Ibid*., 21. As may be noted, *ibid*. (general), 1840–41, p. 208, the act of the previous session

classifying the works had authorized the creation of private companies to complete unfinished parts of any work under the direction of the Board of Internal Improvement, but it seems that no companies were formed pursuant to this legislation.

114 *Laws of Indiana* (general), 1841–42, pp. 22–23; Indiana *House Journal*, 1841–42, p. 643. Bright won 81 votes to 60 for John Law of Vincennes, also a Democrat; 4 votes were reported blank. See *Biographical Directory of the Indiana General Assembly*, I, 38, 230–231, for sketches of Bright and Law.

115 Indiana *House Journal*, 1841–42, p. 436; Indiana *Senate Journal*, 1841–42, pp. 500–501. In the House 33 Whigs and 21 Democrats voted for passage, 10 Whigs and 23 Democrats opposed approval; in the Senate 17 Whigs and 12 Democrats voted for passage, 9 Whigs and 10 Democrats opposed approval. Party politics determined according to party ties in *Biographical Directory of the Indiana General Assembly*, I, 480–482.

116 Indiana *House Journal*, 1841–42, pp. 487–489. Party ties of protesters and counties they represented are in *Biographical Directory of the Indiana General Assembly*, I, 481–482.

117 Marshall S. Wines to Citizens of Allen County, February 22, 1842, in Thornbrough (ed.), *Messages and Papers of Samuel Bigger*, 436–439; William B. Mitchell to Editor, Goshen *Democrat*, January 26, 1842, *ibid.*, 424–426. Wines and Mitchell were among the Democrats who had signed the protest of the twenty-two House members.

118 Indiana *House Journal*, 1843–44, p. 634. In his annual message to the General Assembly on December 5, 1843, Governor Bigger reported that no such bonds had been bought by companies, and he added that "we cannot reasonably expect any relief" from this source. *Ibid.*, 18. The author has found no evidence of bonds surrendered for this purpose.

119 Thornbrough (ed.), *Messages and Papers of Samuel Bigger*, 446–448, 391n, 627–629, respectively for these organizations. Thornbrough, *ibid.*, 11–12, incorrectly states that all three companies were organized pursuant to the general law of 1842 for transfer of works to private companies. The White Water Valley Canal Company, however, was organized under a special incorporation act, approved January 20, 1842, as evidenced in *Laws of Indiana* (local), 1841–42, pp. 37–45. Moreover, the general law of 1842, approved eight days later, explicitly exempted the White Water Valley Canal Company from its application, as stated in *ibid.* (general), 1841–42, p. 21.

120 Indiana *House Journal*, 1842–43, p. 21; *ibid.*, 1843–44, p. 15.

121 The Madison and Indianapolis Railroad was apparently the only state sponsored internal improvement taken over and successfuly completed under private auspices.

122 *Laws of Indiana* (general), 1841–42, pp. 28–29; *ibid.* (general), 1842–43, pp. 63–64.

123 According to the *Biographical Directory of the Indiana General Assembly*, I, 482–485, when the session began the Senate had 31 Whigs and 19 Democrats;

the House 46 Whigs and 54 Democrats. During the session changes in members favored the Whigs, but the majorities remained unchanged.

124 Indiana *Documentary Journal*, 1842–43, House Doc. 4, p. 86. How much the "average taxpayer" made annually is unknown, but the Goshen *Democrat*, September 14, 1843, in contrasting the early economy of the West versus the East, commented: "Many and many is the man who does not handle five dollars of money in a year."

125 Indiana *House Journal*, 1842–43, p. 20; *Laws of Indiana* (general), 1842–43, pp. 74–75.

126 Indiana *House Journal*, 1843–44, pp. 15, 20.

127 When commenced the western terminal was located at the mouth of the Tippecanoe River. For a contrary view about the relationship between the canal and system, see Thornbrough (ed.), *Messages and Papers of Samuel Bigger*, 12–13, which asserts that the canal was "a kind of collateral project to" the system.

128 See report of fund commissioners in Thornbrough (ed.), *Messages and Papers of Samuel Bigger*, 135–137. Expenditures consisted of two items: $1,738,780.83½ for construction costs, and $339,801.38 to pay interest on the bonded debt for the canal. The principal sources of revenue had been: $1,687,000 as net proceeds from the bonded debt of $1,727,000; and $288,415.01 as net proceeds from the sale of canal lands. Only $8,612.77 had been obtained from tolls on the canal. The fund commissioners are not explicit that these data apply to the Wabash and Erie Canal above the Tippecanoe River, but both the content of the data and other data which follow confirms this conclusion.

129 *Ibid.*, 100. As indicated in Indiana *House Journal*, 1840–41, p. 220, the House Committee on Canals and Internal Improvements objected to the issuance of treasury notes, "both on grounds of expediency and constitutional right . . . ." The action of the preceding legislature regarding treasury notes to pay sums due contractors for works on the system was viewed as contrary to the federal constitution which prohibited states from issuing bills of credit.

130 *Laws of Indiana* (general), 1840–41, pp. 199–200. The certificates given by the board to contractors could be exchanged for any number of smaller certificates, not exceeding the total exchanged for them; and they were to bear interest from the date of issue. The title of this law authorized payments to contractors on the canal *east* of the Tippecanoe River.

131 Indiana *Documentary Journal*, 1840–41, Sen. Doc. 8, pp. 148–149.

132 As noted on page 215, this chapter, in 1839 the Wabash and Erie Canal had been restricted to its own funds for its further construction.

133 Thornbrough (ed.), *Messages and Papers of Samuel Bigger*, 96–98. Noah Noble and Jesse L. Williams were the only members of the board at this time. Indiana *Documentary Journal*, 1840–41, Sen. Doc. 8, pp. 148–149.

134 *Laws of Indiana* (local), 1840–41, pp. 215–216; Thornbrough (ed.), *Messages and Papers of Samuel Bigger*, 230–233, has a copy of Bigger's letter dated March 7, 1841.

135 Thornbrough (ed.), *Messages and Papers of Samuel Bigger*, 308–309; Vincennes *Western Sun*, August 13, 1842, quoting the Toledo *Blade*.

136 Fort Wayne *Sentinel*, July 15, 1843. Also see Charles R. Poinsatte, *Fort Wayne During the Canal Era, 1828–1855* (Indianapolis, 1969), 75–76.

137 Vincennes *Western Sun*, August 5, 1843, quoting the Lafayette *Journal*.

138 Indiana *Documentary Journal*, 1843–44, House Doc. 4, pp. 115–118.

139 See *ibid.*, 47–48, 78–79, for report of the state auditor that receipts for the canal east of the Tippecanoe River to November 1, 1842, included $140,194.79 in treasury notes; and $133,538.04 in Wabash and Erie Canal scrip; and *ibid.*, 1843 44, House Doc. 4, p. 109, in which the auditor indicates the issue of $58,223.24 in scrip for the canal east of Tippecanoe. From these data, however, it is not clear precisely how much of such paper money was issued for the canal east of Tippecanoe to November 1, 1843. These two reports of the auditor have *passim* items about repair and maintenance costs, but also see the report of Commissioner S. Fisher, *ibid.*, 1842–43, House Doc. 6, pp. 155–162; *ibid.*, 1843–44, Sen. Doc. 3, pp. 19–24. In the latter report Fisher states: "Many of the wooden structures [of the canal] first erected are now much decayed." He suggested that $40,000 to $50,000 should be expended for repairs during 1843–44.

140 See *ibid.*, 1843–44, Doc. No. 4, Statement No. 13, following p. 132, for the auditor's explanation that $1,727,000 in bonds had been issued for the canal between 1832 and 1839. The initial $100,000 carried 6 percent interest; the remaining $1,627,000 5 percent; making $87,350 of interest due annually. Thus, presumably, unpaid interest, aggregating $393,075, had accumulated from the suspension of interest payments from July 1, 1841 to December, 1843.

141 For completion of the Wabash and Erie Canal to Evansville via Terre Haute, see Chapter 6, pp. 345–347.

142 Except as otherwise indicated, items concerning state expenditures and state revenue are based on annual reports of the treasurer in Indiana *Documentary Journal*, 1838–39, House Doc. 5, pp. 36–37; *ibid.*, 1839–40, House Doc. 3, pp. 46–47; *ibid.*, 1840–41, House Doc. 4, pp. 70–71; *ibid.*, 1841–42, House Doc. 5, pp. 54–55; *ibid.*, 1842–43, House Doc. 2, pp. 14–15; *ibid.*, 1843–44, House Doc. 3, pp. 22–23. Concerning ordinary state expenditures for 1831–37, see table in Chapter 4, p. 154. *Fiscal years usually covered the period from November 1 through October 31 of the ensuing year.* In the annual reports of the treasurer, on which the table of expenditures is based, printing and stationery are usually listed as separate items. Though listed separately from legislative costs, presumably they were principally spent for the printing and publishing of the legislative journals and session laws. Although specific costs are miscellaneous expenditures, their growing volume warrants listing them separately. The column regarding miscellaneous costs includes: $27.77 for incidental costs, $200 for the deaf and dumb (1842–43), $674.40 for presidential elections, $1,182.07 as refunds of money collected from estates without heirs, $2,833.22 for geological surveys (1837–39), and $4,575.53 spent as refunds from taxes collected. Among the special funds indicated, but not always by their usual names, are: Common

School, County Seminary, Indianapolis, Internal Improvement, Michigan Road, Saline, and State College or University Fund.

[143] See Chapter 4, pp. 161–163, indicating 105 legislators for the apportionment of 1831, and 147 legislators for that of 1836; and pp. 267–268, this chapter indicating 150 legislators for that of 1841. The judicial circuits increased from seven in 1831, to nine in 1838, and twelve in 1843. *Laws of Indiana* (revised), 1830–31, pp. 142–146; *ibid.*, 1837–38, pp. 164–171; *ibid.*, 1842–43, pp. 646–664. Each judicial circuit had a president judge whose salary was paid by the state.

[144] See pp. 245–249, this chapter, for the increased payments. For lengthening of legislative sessions, see John G. Rauch and Nellie C. Armstrong, *A Bibliography of the Laws of Indiana, 1788–1927* (Indianapolis, 1928), 68; for the increased size of journals and volumes of laws, see library shelves regarding them.

[145] See comment of the auditor in Indiana *Documentary Journal*, 1843–44, House Doc. 4, p. 74, stating that formerly collectors had been allowed 9 percent of the tax collected. He estimated that it had cost "nearly" 5 percent of the tax revenue to collect the tax for 1842 under the new law of 1841. The new legislation allowed collectors 8 percent on the first $1,000 collected; 7 percent on the portion between $1,000 and $2,000; 6 percent on the portion between $2,000 and $3,000; 5 percent on the portion between $3,000 and $4,000; 4 percent on the portion between $4,000 and $5,000; and 3 percent on any amount over $5,000. The collector was allowed eight cents per mile of travel to and from the capital to pay the revenue collected. *Laws of Indiana* (general), 1840–41, pp. 31, 34. These provisions are also in *ibid.* (revised), 1842–43, pp. 220–221. It is presumed that collectors retained 9 percent of the revenue collected from 1837–41, and 5 percent for 1841–43. This presumption is thought to be a close *approximation* of the sums collectors actually obtained.

[146] For taxes levied from 1837–43, see *Laws of Indiana* (general), 1836–37, p. 112; *ibid.*, 1838–39, pp. 27–28; *ibid.*, 1839–40, pp. 8–10; *ibid.*, 1840–41, pp. 47–48; *ibid.*, 1841–42, p. 73; *ibid.*, 1842–43, pp. 74–76. The levy for 1837 provided that it continue until changed, and it apparently did so without confirming legislation at the 1837–38 session. The levy of 1841 provided that if necessary revenue earmarked for internal improvements could be used for ordinary costs. Taxes levied for a particular year were largely collected during the ensuing year.

[147] As observed in the tables about ordinary expenditures and ordinary revenues for state government, 1837–43, costs aggregated $681,547.66 versus $1,568,851.38 for revenues, thus leaving a surplus of $887,303.72 not needed to cover ordinary costs; and presumably was *very largely* used to pay debts concerning the Internal Improvements System of 1836 and the Wabash and Erie Canal. But tax money was also used to pay some costs of the building of the First State Capitol, completed in the mid-thirties; and tax revenue was not the only source used to pay system and canal debts. These considerations, plus the fact that revenue levied in one year was in part collected and largely spent in a succeeding year or years; that fiscal reports frequently mingled items regarding costs with those concerning special funds; and the fact that items were not always reported in the

same manner from year to year makes it extremely difficult, and perhaps impossible, to determine in an accurate and precise manner how much tax revenue was spent from year to year for interest and principal on internal improvements. According to the state auditor during the fiscal years 1837–38, 1838–39, 1839–40, and 1840–41 at least about $377,838 was spent to pay interest on the bonded debt for internal improvements. And according to the state auditor at least $546,265 was expended during fiscal years 1841–42 and 1842–43 to redeem treasury notes issued pursuant to the law of 1842 which had resulted in the issue of $1,500,000 in treasury notes for payment of sums owed contracts on internal improvement projects. Indiana *Documentary Journal*, 1840–41, House Doc. 3, pp. 32, 46 (for interest on bonded debt); *ibid.*, 1850–51, Pt. 1, Doc. 17, p. 313 (for redemption of treasury notes). The auditor indicates that $40,000 of the money paid for interest on the bonded debt came from revenue arising from the tax levy of 1837. This tax levy had been the first to include a levy for payment of either the principal or interest of the internal improvement debt. Hence, at least $924,103 of tax money was apparently spent for payment of interest on the bonded debt and to pay interest and principal for redemption of treasury notes, regarding the unfunded or domestic debt, during 1837–43. Since this exceeds the amount of surplus revenue for this period, presumably part of the payments for internal improvements was covered by other revenues such as borrowing for internal improvements and revenue received from the sale of Wabash and Erie Canal land sales.

148 Indiana *Documentary Journal*, 1840–41, House Doc. 3, pp. 32–46. Morris gave 481/4 cents as the average for 1837; 421/2 cents for 1838; $2.76 for 1839; and about 363/5 cents for 1840.

149 See pp. 245–249, this chapter, for discussion pro and con on the increases.

150 Indianapolis *Indiana Democrat*, August 15, 1838, September 4, 1839; Indianapolis *Indiana Journal*, January 9, 1841.

151 Indiana *House Journal*, 1840–41, p. 14; Indianapolis *Democrat and Spirit of the Constitution*, January 13, 1841.

152 Indiana *Senate Journal*, 1841–42, p. 78; Indiana *House Journal*, 1841–42, pp. 170–171; *Biographical Directory of the Indiana General Assembly*, I, 480–481, for politics of Gregory and Millikan.

153 Indiana *House Journal*, 1842–43, pp. 771–772; Indiana *Senate Journal*, 1842–43, p. 649. Nine Democrats and five Whigs protested passage, arguing that the bill had not been given adequate consideration, nor allowed consideration of reduced per diem, fees, and salaries during the session. They said they could not vote for reduction of per diem to $2 for the next session, while allowing members to pocket $3 for the existing session! Politics of the protesters is in *Biographical Directory of the Indiana General Assembly*, I, 483–485. The Vincennes *Western Sun*, a prominent Democratic organ, in its February 25, 1843 issue, admonished the people to remember that the Democrats had a majority in the House whereas the Federalists [Whigs] had a majority in the Senate.

154 For reports of the three officials about their salaries and other payments to them, see Indiana *Documentary Journal*, 1840–41, House Docs. 36–38, pp.

469–474; for the report of the House select committee, see Indiana *House Journal*, 1840–41, pp. 231–235.

155 *Laws of Indiana* (general), 1840–41, pp. 132–133. As previously, considerable of the new salaries was to be paid from other than tax revenue. Both the treasurer and auditor were to have $400 of their salary paid from the "college or loan office fund"; $200 for both the auditor and secretary was to be paid from proceeds of the Wabash and Erie Canal lands. The residue of their salaries was to be paid from the state treasury. All fees received by the secretary of state for copying records, making deeds, and the like were to be paid to the state treasurer, and so reported by the secretary annually.

156 Indianapolis *Indiana State Sentinel*, September 13, 1842. The editor estimated that compensation paid local and state officials, residing in Marion County, was more than double the value of wheat raised in the county; and that of the 974,966 bushels of corn annually produced within the county only 119,766 bushels were left to feed hogs after paying officeholders!

157 *Ibid.*, December 27, 1842. According to West's bill the president of the Senate and speaker of the House would receive per diem of $3; and the secretary of state was to act as state librarian, the treasurer as "keeper" of the capitol, both without pay for such duties.

158 Indiana *Documentary Journal*, 1842–43, Sen. Doc. 7, pp. 443–450 (quotes, 448, 449–450, 445). Regarding committee members and their politics, see Indiana *Senate Journal*, 1842–43, p. 25; *Biographical Directory of the Indiana General Assembly*, I, 482–483.

159 Indiana *House Journal*, 1842–43, pp. 501–502, 617. Concerning committee members and their politics, see *Biographical Directory of the Indiana General Assembly*, I, 483–485.

160 Regarding the tax base, assessing and collecting, see Chap. 1, pp. 13, 15–16; Chap. 3, pp. 88–93; Chap. 4, pp. 155, 158–159, and this chapter, p. 246.

161 Indiana *House Journal*, 1837–38, pp. 33–34; *ibid.*, 1838–39, pp. 20–21; *ibid.*, 1839–40, pp. 15–16; *ibid.*, 1840–41, pp. 15–16.

162 *Ibid.*, 1840–41, p. 40.

163 Indiana *Documentary Journal*, 1838–39, House Doc. 5, p. 39 (treasurer), and House Doc. 12, pp. 173–174, 177–184 (auditor, quote, 173).

164 Indiana *House Journal*, 1838–39, pp. 268–270 (House committee), 470, 525 (bill submitted).

165 Indiana *Documentary Journal*, 1840–41, House Doc. 15, pp. 233–236 (Morris regarding his proposals), 237–274 (the seven bills).

166 *Laws of Indiana* (general), 1840–41, pp. 3–48. The assessor was elected every other year, the treasurer every third year, and the auditor every fifth year.

167 *Ibid.*, 34–36, 39. Land sold from school sections, except that sold before 1834 on which "the credit of ten years" had not expired, was also taxable. *Ibid.*, 35.

168 Vincennes *Western Sun*, September 11, 1841; Indianapolis *Indiana State Sentinel*, October 11 [12], 1841.

169 Indiana *Documentary Journal*, 1841–42, House Doc. 4, pp. 22–27. As noted on p. 24, the sum reported as saved included savings concerning both county and state revenue.

170 Indiana *House Journal*, 1841–42, pp. 35, 51–52; Indiana *Senate Journal*, 1841–42, pp. 209, 258. The bill passed the House 74 to 21, but was laid on the table in the Senate 23 to 22.

171 Indiana *Senate Journal*, 1841–42, pp. 209–213, 212, 272–273; Indiana *House Journal*, 1841–42, pp. 291–292. According to these journals, the reorganization bill passed the Senate 23 to 22, then lost in the House 48 to 45. The *House Journal*, however, names only 47 members voting for rejection. As indicated in *Biographical Directory of the Indiana General Assembly*, I, 480–482, in the Senate 22 Whigs and 1 Democrat voted for passage; 3 Whigs and 19 Democrats against passage. In the House 6 Whigs and 41 Democrats sustained rejection; 38 Whigs and 7 Democrats opposed rejection.

172 Indiana *Senate Journal*, 1841–42, pp. 294–296; Indiana *House Journal*, 1841–42, pp. 332–333. According to these journals, repeal passed the Senate 24 to 21; the House 60 to 33. But the *House Journal* names 59 for and 34 against repeal. According to the politics of members in *Biographical Directory of the Indiana General Assembly*, I, 480–482, in the Senate 6 Whigs and 18 Democrats voted for repeal; 19 Whigs and 2 Democrats against repeal. In the House 18 Whigs and 41 Democrats voted for repeal; 28 Whigs and 6 Democrats against this action. For the law repealing the board, see *Laws of Indiana* (general), 1841–42, p. 126. Additional items about repeal of the state equalization board are in Thornbrough (ed.), *Messages and Papers of Samuel Bigger*, 264n–266n.

173 The Second State Bank was not just one bank, or a parent bank with branches, *but a banking system having separate units or "branches" operating as banks in towns of the state. The unit or "branch" at Indianapolis had the same authority, limitations, and responsibilities as the other units.*

174 Indiana *House Journal*, 1836–37, p. 24; Thornbrough, Riker, and Corpuz (eds.), *Diary of Calvin Fletcher*, I, 296–297, 333, 398–399, 413, 414, 419, 420, 422–423.

175 Thornbrough, Riker, and Corpuz (eds.), *Diary of Calvin Fletcher*, I, 426–427, 427–428.

176 *Ibid.*, 428–429. Fletcher noted that the board had received a complaint from part of the branch board at Lawrenceburg alleging corruption by its cashier, and that a company owing the "Tarre Haute branch" $140,000 had failed. Logan Esarey, *State Banking in Indiana, 1814–1873* (Bloomington, Ind., 1912), 258–259, indicates that the federal deposits remained with the bank "till drawn in the regular course of business."

177 Thornbrough, Riker, and Corpuz (eds.), *Diary of Calvin Fletcher*, I, 429. President Merrill wrote Secretary of the Treasury Levi Woodbury, May 20, 1837, that the board had been in session when news arrived of the suspension by banks at Cincinnati and eastern cities, and that it immediately recommended "'a

similar course to the branches for the present.'" He told Woodbury that the bank's "'intire solvency is unquestionable.'" *Ibid.*, 429n–430n.

178 Indianapolis *Indiana Journal*, May 20, 1837. The charter of the bank explicitly prohibited a suspension of specie payments. It also asserted that no amendment could ever be added authorizing suspension of specie payments; and the General Assembly had pledged "the faith of the state" to the creditors of the bank that no such amendment would ever be made. *Laws of Indiana*, 1833–34, pp. 14, 34–35.

179 Indianapolis *Indiana Journal*, May 20, 1837. Based on minutes of the meeting for which A. F. Morrison and Douglass Maguire were secretaries. Since Morrison was a well-known Democrat and Maguire likewise as a Whig, their roles as well as the content of the minutes suggest that this was a bipartisan meeting. Austin W. Morris, a Whig, and son of Auditor Morris Morris, proposed the resolution for an early convening of the legislature.

180 *Ibid.* McCarty, a Whig, chaired the meeting.

181 Indianapolis *Indiana Democrat*, May 31, 1837.

182 Indianapolis *Indiana Journal*, May 20, 1837; Indianapolis *Indiana Democrat*, May 31, 1837.

183 Indianapolis *Indiana Democrat*, June 7, September 27, 1837.

184 *Ibid.*, October 4, 1837, quoting *Indianian*.

185 Indiana *House Journal*, 1837–38, pp. 17–19 (Noble); Indiana *Senate Journal*, 1837–38, pp. 59–61 (Merrill); Indiana *House Journal*, 1837–38, pp. 30–37 (Wallace).

186 Indiana *House Journal*, 1837–38, pp. 173–177. The report has Judah's name attached as chairman, but omits the names of members. According to *ibid.*, 43, nineteen representatives had been appointed to the committee. *Biographical Directory of the Indiana General Assembly*, I, 470–471, indicates that fourteen were Whigs, five Democrats.

187 Indiana *Senate Journal*, 1837–38, pp. 529–535, 535–549, for majority and minority reports respectively. The majority report was signed by Paris C. Dunning, Aaron Finch, Henry W. Hackett, Andrew Kennedy, all Democrats; and George B. Thompson, Whig. The minority report by William Elliott, Democrat; and Thomas D. Baird, David H. Colerick, Richard W. Thompson, all Whigs. Political ties are in *Biographical Directory of the Indiana General Assembly*, I, 469–470.

188 *Laws of Indiana* (local), 1837–38, pp. 442–443. According to the Indianapolis *Indiana Journal*, February 10, 1838, the joint resolution approving the suspension as justified passed the House 63 to 35, with an "immaterial amendment" after having "formerly passed the Senate by a large majority."

189 See Indiana *House Journal*, 1837–38, pp. 822–826, for Coe's account of the initial bank convention in New York; and *ibid.*, 815–822, for his three letters to James M. Ray, cashier of the bank, offering further information about it. See Indianapolis *Indiana Journal*, April 21, 28, May 19, 1838, regarding the adjourned convention in New York, including a letter from Law and Lanier about how they voted.

190 The Indianapolis *Indiana Journal*, May 19, 1838, reported that the state bank board had authorized Merrill to correspond with other banks about an

early resumption. Also see Indiana *Senate Journal*, 1838–39, p. 105, for Merrill's comment about resumption.

191 Thornbrough, Riker, and Corpuz (eds.), *Diary of Calvin Fletcher*, II, 24, 25.

192 Indianapolis *Indiana Journal*, October 19, 1839; Indianapolis *Indiana Democrat*, October 23, 1839.

193 Thornbrough, Riker, and Corpuz (eds.), *Diary of Calvin Fletcher*, II, 124, 126. Such references to "foreigners," apparently meaning strangers or persons from other areas, are common in this period.

194 As indicated in Riker (ed.), *Messages and Papers of David Wallace*, 342–343, in December, 1839, Wallace commented to legislators: "The measure of total suspension, recently adopted by the banks of Pennsylvania, Maryland and other states, I am happy to say, has not been followed by the State bank of Indiana. The board . . . refused to authorize it; but, very properly, left the question open" for determination "by the people themselves in the several bank districts." As noted in Thornbrough (ed.), *Messages and Papers of Samuel Bigger*, 302, late in 1841 Bigger told legislators: "During the past year, most of the Banks in the Western, Middle and Southern States, have suspended specie payments. Ten of the branches of the State Bank also, it is understood, have not uniformly paid specie on their notes when demanded, and probably the three others would have refused if their notes had been presented in large amounts from abroad." For related items, see *ibid.*, 375–376, 540; Thornbrough, Riker, and Corpuz (eds.), *Diary of Calvin Fletcher*, II, 124; Indianapolis *Indiana Journal*, May 19, 1838, November 2, 1839; Indiana *Senate Journal*, 1841–42, pp. 95–96.

195 Thornbrough (ed.), *Messages and Papers of Samuel Bigger*, 106–107.

196 Thornbrough, Riker, and Corpuz (eds.), *Diary of Calvin Fletcher*, II, 273–274, 275; Indianapolis *Indiana Journal*, February 13, 1841, for convention proceedings. James F. D. Lanier and Mason C. Fitch also represented the Second State Bank at this meeting. The proceedings include letters from banks in Illinois, Tennessee, and Louisiana declining to send representatives.

197 Indianapolis *Indiana State Sentinel*, September 7, October 11 [12], 1841.

198 Indianapolis *Indiana Journal*, November 12, 1841; Indianapolis *Indiana State Sentinel*, November 2, 1841, quoting Goshen *Democrat*.

199 Thornbrough (ed.), *Messages and Papers of Samuel Bigger*, 304–305.

200 Indiana *House Journal*, 1841–42, pp. 223–224 (committee report), 491–492; Indiana *Senate Journal*, 1841–42, p. 132; *Laws of Indiana* (general), 1841–42, pp. 82–84.

201 Indianapolis *Indiana Journal*, May 18, 1842; Thornbrough (ed.), *Messages and Papers of Samuel Bigger*, 509–510.

202 Thornbrough (ed.), *Messages and Papers of Samuel Bigger*, 540, 540n–541n; Fort Wayne *Sentinel*, July 9, 1842, quoting Louisville *Journal*.

203 William Gerald Shade, *Banks or No Banks: The Money Issue in Western Politics, 1832–1865* (Detroit, 1972), 61; R. Carlyle Buley, *The Old Northwest: Pioneer Period, 1815–1840* (2 vols., Indianapolis, 1950), II, 287.

204 Indiana *Senate Journal*, 1838–39, p. 108. Loans to directors totaled $493,549; to other stockholders, $914,530; to nonstockholders, $2,156,361, for an aggregate of $3,564,440.

205 Riker (ed.), *Messages and Papers of David Wallace*, 312–315.

206 Thornbrough (ed.), *Messages and Papers of Samuel Bigger*, 104, 511–512; Indiana *Documentary Journal*, 1843–44, House Doc. 5, pp. 277–278.

207 Indiana *House Journal*, 1837–38, pp. 389–510. See pp. 389–402, for main body of the report signed by Samuel Judah, George H. Proffit, Marks Crume, and Ebenezer M. Chamberlain. As indicated in *Biographical Directory of the Indiana General Assembly*, I, 470–471, Judah and Proffit were Whigs, Crume and Chamberlain were Democrats. The remarks of the committee about the responsibility of the state to establish a sound circulating medium, maintain a proper proportion of specie, control "expansions and contractions," and increase the number of branches and aggregate of banking capital suggest that members of the committee were novices about the possibilities and limitations of banks.

208 Indiana *House Journal*, 1837–38, p. 391. For further comments regarding domination of the branches by private interests, also see pp. 391–397.

209 *Ibid.*, 394–395, 398, and *passim*.

210 *Ibid.*, 396–397, 400, and *passim*. As the committee notes, the Constitution of 1816 had given the General Assembly authority to establish branches, not exceeding one for every three counties. Charles Kettleborough, *Constitution Making in Indiana* (3 vols., Indianapolis, 1916, 1930), I, 115.

211 Indiana *House Journal*, 1837–38, pp. 395, 401. The committee, chaired by Judah, had asked the branches to respond to thirty-eight questions. The branches at Lafayette, Vincennes, Lawrenceburg, Bedford, Indianapolis, and Evansville, the committee observed, had failed either to respond to one or more questions or had made evasive responses.

212 Indiana *Senate Journal*, 1841–42, pp. 343–344, 362–364, 381–382, 388, 428–429; Indiana *House Journal*, 1841–42, pp. 368–370, 386–387, 403. Palmer's vote to charter the Second State Bank is recorded *ibid.*, 1833–34, p. 352. His tenure as state treasurer and role as speaker of the House when the bank was chartered is indicated in *Biographical Directory of the Indiana General Assembly*, I, 304. See note 103 for the political makeup of the two houses.

213 *Laws of Indiana* (general), 1841–42, p. 174.

214 Indiana *Documentary Journal*, 1842–43, Sen. Doc. 6, pp. 83–441. Pages 85–110 are the main body of the report; 112–152, afford much detail about assets and liabilities of the branches; 153–156, list directors and branch officials; 157–163 has copy of the sixty-seven questions Palmer asked of each branch; 166–441, contain responses from branches to these questions. This report is an extremely important document concerning the Second State Bank.

215 *Ibid.*, 86, 88–89.

216 *Ibid.*, 86–87.

217 *Ibid.*, 90–93.

218 *Ibid.*, 106–107, 96–98, 96. For instance, at Indianapolis former branch directors Samuel Henderson, James Blake, and Daniel Yandes were delinquent on sums of $10,000, $13,400, and $7,236 respectively; and early in 1841 Nicholas McCarty had been given an extension of time for payment of $35,000 which he owed. *Ibid.*, 165–166. Alexis Coquillard, a former director at South Bend, was delinquent for $34,116.18, plus interest. *Ibid.*, 271. At the Evansville branch Director John Shanklin, including Shanklin and Johnston, was overdue $10,193; and President John Mitchell was delinquent $2,751. *Ibid.*, 213, 217. The cashier of the much criticized Lawrenceburg branch, perhaps in an effort to embarrass Merrill and members of the state bank board, reported that no debts were then owed by officers of the state bank or any branch but that Merrill, Mason C. Fitch, John Sering, and James F. D. Lanier had respectively repaid loans of $1,220.33, $3,800, $2,000, and $5,000. *Ibid.*, 179.

219 Thornbrough, Riker, and Corpuz (eds.), *Diary of Calvin Fletcher*, II, 140–141, 216–217, 256.

220 *Ibid.*, 437–438, 461–462.

221 *Ibid.*, 470–471.

222 Indiana *Senate Journal*, 1842–43, pp. 156, 158.

223 Indiana *Documentary Journal*, 1843–44, House Doc. 5, pp. 279–280. See table regarding ordinary expenditures, 1837–43, this chapter, p. 243. Ordinary state expenditures averaged $113,591.27 annually for 1837–43.

224 *Ibid.*, 1842–43, Sen. Doc. 8, pp. 451–463 (quotations, 455–456). Merrill attributed much of the criticism of the bank to partisanship.

225 For charter provisions about branches, see *Laws of Indiana*, 1833–34, pp. 12–13.

226 Indianapolis *Indiana Democrat*, May 22, July 17, 1835; Poinsatte, *Fort Wayne During the Canal Era, 1828–1855*, pp. 86–90; Riker and Thornbrough (eds.), *Messages and Papers of Noah Noble*, 385, for governor's proclamation, dated November 17, 1835, declaring the bank organized and ready for business. In organizing new branches private stock subscriptions were subscribed before state stock was subscribed.

227 Indianapolis *Indiana Journal*, January 8, 1836; Riker (ed.), *Messages and Papers of David Wallace*, 113–115, 195, 310; South Bend *Free Press*, May 19, 26, 1838.

228 Thornbrough, Riker, and Corpuz (eds.), *Diary of Calvin Fletcher*, I, 280, regarding early interest of Elston; Riker (ed.), *Messages and Papers of David Wallace*, 113–115, 310; Gladys Bull Nicewarner, *Michigan City, Indiana: The Life of a Town* (Michigan City, 1980), 94–96; Indianapolis *Indiana Democrat*, February 28, 1839, saying operations will commence March 12, 1839.

229 See Riker (ed.), *Messages and Papers of David Wallace*, 195, 310–311, for items by President Merrill about branches approved for Logansport and Rushville, 1838, for which private stock subscriptions were opened in June, 1839, with the appropriate amount of stock subscribed for them. But the state, having no money to pay for its initial installment, had made no call on subscribers for their payments. The Indianapolis *Indiana Journal*, May 18, 1839,

noted the state's inability to pay installments for Rushville and Logansport. It announced that the sixteenth branch had been "located at Crawfordsville, a flourishing town of 2000 inhabitants, and the county seat of Montgomery county." The legislative journals, especially for the sessions of 1836–37, 1837–38, have *passim* items about possible branches at scattered places in southern as well as in central and northern Indiana.

230 *Laws of Indiana*, 1833–34, pp. 34–35.

231 Indiana *House Journal*, 1835–36, pp. 18, 158, 154.

232 *Laws of Indiana* (general), 1835–36, pp. 21–23; Indiana *Senate Journal*, 1836–37, pp. 104–105, for statement of Merrill concerning approval of amendments.

233 Jesse L. Williams to James B. Johnson, July 5, 1838, in Riker (ed.), *Messages and Papers of David Wallace*, 141–142. Williams, Indiana's principal engineer for internal improvements, indicated *concentration of operations* as the other possible alternative.

234 *Ibid.*, 154–168 (quote, 159). Among other items, Wallace did not explain how proceeds from land sales could be diverted to buy bank stock rather than be used for construction of the canal; or, if so used, how construction costs would be paid. For Merrill's remarks, see *ibid.*, 196–197.

235 *Laws of Indiana* (general), 1838–39, pp. 15–17. As the ensuing paragraphs indicate, this legislation was never carried into effect as no such additional branches were established and the capital of the Second State Bank was soon reduced rather than enlarged. Also see Thornbrough (ed.), *Messages and Papers of Samuel Bigger*, 22–23.

236 See annual report of President Merrill in Indiana *Documentary Journal*, 1839–40, House Doc. 6, pp. 79–80, explaining his inability to obtain loans for increase of capital and branches of the Second State Bank pursuant to the legislation of 1839.

237 Riker (ed.), *Messages and Papers of David Wallace*, 386–391 (quote, 387), has Merrill's account about this negotiation. As indicated in Thornbrough, Riker, and Corpuz (eds.), *Diary of Calvin Fletcher*, II, 142, 143–144, several days before Merrill submitted his account the House committees regarding the bank had called for his removal as president of the bank, plus removal of state bank directors Calvin Fletcher and Robert Morrisson. Merrill's role concerning the negotiation with the Morris Canal and Banking Company had been strongly criticized by the committee. Shortly after Merrill's account was received the House voted 51 to 47 to remove him and the two directors, but the Senate indefinitely postponed the resolution for removal, 27 to 20. Late in 1842, Michael G. Bright, in his detailed report on how the state bank had been conducted, reported that only a few thousand dollars had been received from the collateral given by the Morris Canal and Banking Company, and no more was anticipated. Thornbrough (ed.), *Messages and Papers of Samuel Bigger*, 23, 346n, 347n.

238 Thornbrough (ed.), *Messages and Papers of Samuel Bigger*, 533–539 (quote, 537). As may be observed *ibid.*, 72, 105, 319, 321, 452, 480, near the end of 1842

the state owed various branches $294,000 for having advanced this sum *in antic-*
ipation of the fourth surplus of federal revenue; and $722,640 for advances made
by various branches in 1839 for internal improvement works.

239 *Ibid.*, 610–612; *Laws of Indiana* (general), 1842–43, pp. 53–56.

240 Indiana *Documentary Journal*, 1843–44, House Doc. 5, pp. 276–277. Concerning approval of the bank and branches for this reduction, see Thornbrough,
Riker, and Corpuz (eds.), *Diary of Calvin Fletcher*, II, 477–478, 479, 483.

241 Indiana *Senate Journal*, 1842–43, p. 156; Indiana *Documentary Journal*,
1843–44, House Doc. 5, pp. 276–277, 284.

242 *Laws of Indiana* (general), 1839–40, pp. 33–34; Indiana *Documentary Journal*, 1840–41, House Doc. 39, pp. 475–477. The secretary of state reported an
aggregate of 119,974 polls, but the county totals add up to 121,169. The returns
for some counties seem to be estimates.

243 Indiana *House Journal*, 1840–41, p. 14; Indianapolis *Indiana Journal*, December 26, 1840. As reported in *Report of the Debates and Proceedings of the Convention for the Revision of the Constitution of the State of Indiana, 1850* (2 vols., Indianapolis, 1850, reprinted 1935), I, 999, as a delegate to the Indiana
Constitutional Convention of 1850–51, Wallace commented that despite "overwhelming pecuniary embarrassments" his proposed reduction in the total of legislators had been "entirely disregarded." The editor's remark about "full representation in the House" apparently meant that many counties would lose their
separate representative if significant reduction occurred.

244 Indianapolis *Indiana Journal*, January 2, 1841; William Berry to Editors,
Bloomington *Post*, December 29, 1840, in Thornbrough (ed.), *Messages and Papers of Samuel Bigger*, 156–157. For political ties of Test and Berry, see *Biographical Directory of the Indiana General Assembly*, I, 24, 386, 477.

245 According to *Biographical Directory of the Indiana General Assembly*, I, 477–
479, the Whigs had more than a two to one margin in the Senate, and more than
a three to one edge in the House. For the apportionment committees, see Indiana *Senate Journal*, 1840–41, pp. 56–58 (committee members), 83 (instruction
regarding apportionment); Indiana *House Journal*, 1840–41, pp. 73–74, 170
(committee members). The politics of committee members as listed in *Biographical Directory of the Indiana General Assembly*, indicate that the Senate apportionment committee had nine Whigs and two Democrats; the initial House
committee thirteen Whigs and one Democrat; the second House committee
twenty-two Whigs and no Democrats.

246 Indiana *Senate Journal*, 1840–41, pp. 165–167; Indiana *House Journal*,
1840–41, pp. 267–272. The Senate vote is recorded as 33 to 10 for passage, but
the *Journal* shows thirty-four votes for and nine against. According to political
ties in *Biographical Directory of the Indiana General Assembly*, I, 477–479, in the
Senate five Whigs and four Democrats voted against passage; in the House eighteen Whigs and ten Democrats voted against passage.

247 Senator Johnson Watts, a Whig from Dearborn County and a member
of the Senate Committee on Reapportionment, introduced a bill to lower the

number of senators to thirty-six and representatives to seventy-five; Senator Copeland P. J. Arion, a Whig from Jefferson County, proposed that there be forty-two senators and eighty-four representatives. Indiana *Senate Journal*, 1840–41, pp. 141–142, 165–166; Indianapolis *Indiana Journal*, January 2, 9, 1841. Watts and Arion are identified as Whigs in *Biographical Directory of the Indiana General Assembly*, I, 8, 410, 477.

[248] *Laws of Indiana* (general), 1840–41, pp. 48–50. The number of voters for particular counties is found in Indiana *Documentary Journal* cited in note 242 above. Since there were reported to be 121,169 voters in the state, ideally each of the 100 representatives would have represented 1,212 voters. Leon H. Wallace, "Legislative Apportionment in Indiana: A Case History," *Indiana Law Journal*, XLII (1966), 18–19 and Appendix D, offers much detail about disparity in representation among counties. Justin E. Walsh, *The Centennial History of the Indiana General Assembly, 1816–1978* (Indianapolis, 1987), has maps showing both representative and senatorial districts for this reapportionment. *Ibid.*, pp. 66–67, asserts that the Whig dominated legislature used floats in such a way as to give Whigs extra votes when United States senators were to be elected at the 1842–43 and 1844–45 sessions. The evidence offered, however, seems inadequate to sustain this conclusion. For objections of Shelby County legislators, see Indiana *Senate Journal*, 1840–41, pp. 293–294; Indiana *House Journal*, 1840–41, pp. 682–684.

[249] *Laws of Indiana* (general), 1840–41, p. 50.

[250] *Ibid.* (general), 1842–43, p. 86. Concerning the confusion in Posey and Vanderburgh counties, see Thornbrough (ed.), *Messages and Papers of Samuel Bigger*, 507.

[251] Thirty-two of the 87 organized counties in the apportionment of 1841 were in Southern Indiana. Its 15 eastern counties were: Bartholomew, *Brown*, Clark, Dearborn, Decatur, Floyd, Franklin, Harrison, Jackson, Jefferson, Jennings, Ripley, Scott, Switzerland, and Washington; its 17 western counties were: Crawford, Daviess, Dubois, Gibson, Greene, Knox, Lawrence, Martin, Monroe, Orange, Perry, Pike, Posey, Spencer, Sullivan, Vanderburgh, and Warrick. The 30 counties of Central Indiana included these 16 eastern counties: *Blackford*, Delaware, Fayette, Grant, Hamilton, Hancock, Henry, *Jay*, Johnson, Madison, Marion, Randolph, Rush, Shelby, Union, and Wayne; its 14 western counties were: Boone, Clay, Clinton, Fountain, Hendricks, Montgomery, Morgan, Owen, Parke, Putnam, Tippecanoe, Vermillion, Vigo, and Warren. The 25 counties of Northern Indiana embraced these 13 eastern counties: Adams, Allen, *DeKalb*, Elkhart, Huntington, Kosciusko, LaGrange, Miami, Noble, *Steuben*, Wabash, *Wells*, and *Whitley*; its 12 western counties were: *Benton*, Carroll, Cass, Fulton, *Jasper*, *Lake*, La Porte, Marshall, Porter, *Pulaski*, St. Joseph, and White. The 11 counties in *italics* had not been organized in time for inclusion in the apportionment of 1836.

[252] See Chapter 3, pp. 99–102.

[253] Indiana *Senate Journal*, 1834–35, p. 212; Indianapolis *Indiana Democrat*, January 2, 1835.

254 Indianapolis *Indiana Democrat*, December 13, 1836; *Laws of Indiana* (local), 1836–37, p. 431. Recent "immigrants" as used here presumably referred to those from other states as well as from other countries.

255 Indiana *House Journal*, 1837–38, p. 21. The governor explained that the work of the judges had been slowed by the death of one judge and the delay in getting his successor on the bench. As indicated in Rauch and Armstrong, *Bibliography of the Laws of Indiana, 1788–1927*, p. 68, the session of 1837–38 was the longest of any subsequent to statehood. But in the late thirties augmented consideration of questions about banking and internal improvements resulted in longer sessions than previously.

256 Indianapolis *Indiana Journal*, February 17, 24, 1838; *Laws of Indiana* (local), 1837–38, pp. 440–441; Indianapolis *Indiana Journal*, January 2, 1841 (Test's comment). At the next legislative session both House and Senate committees observed that some acts approved for the revision had not been printed in the new code. Indiana *House Journal*, 1838–39, p. 175; Indiana *Senate Journal*, 1838–39, pp. 6, 311–312.

257 *Laws of Indiana* (revised), 1837–38, p. 398.

258 *Ibid.* (local), 1837–38, p. 441; *ibid.* (local), 1838–39, p. 344.

259 Indiana *Senate Journal*, 1840–41, p. 91; *Laws of Indiana* (general), 1840–41, p. 150. Isaac Blackford, Charles Dewey, and Jeremiah Sullivan were the judges who so responded.

260 Indiana *Senate Journal*, 1841–42, pp. 115–116; *Laws of Indiana* (general), 1841–42, p. 148.

261 Indiana *Senate Journal*, 1842–43, pp. 64–66. For comment regarding how review of the revision was commenced by the assembly, see Representative John Jackson to Editor, Goshen *Democrat*, December 23, 1842, in Thornbrough (ed.), *Messages and Papers of Samuel Bigger*, 560.

262 *Laws of Indiana* (revised), 1842–43, p. 1030.

263 *Ibid.* (revised), 1837–38, pp. 154, 244–259; *ibid.* (revised), 1842–43, pp. 100, 121–154. Concerning the election code for 1831–37, see Chapter 3, pp. 99–102.

264 Vincennes *Western Sun*, November 28, 1840.

265 *Laws of Indiana* (revised), 1837–38, pp. 245–246; *ibid.* (revised), 1842–43, pp. 127, 129.

266 Discussion of this item, except as otherwise indicated, is based on Indiana *Documentary Journal*, 1842–43, House Doc. 11, pp. 211–239, which offers sealed testimony regarding the voting by commissioners of DeKalb and Steuben counties, statements by Marsh and Beall, and related items arising from the review of this election by the House of Representatives. As noted *ibid.*, 219, Shoemaker testified that the word "Representative" and Madison Marsh's name were on the same "piece of paper."

267 *Ibid.*, 213–234. See p. 212 for members of the elections committee, embracing four Democrats and three Whigs as indicated in *Biographical Directory of the Indiana General Assembly*, I, 483–485. As noted in Kettleborough, *Constitution Making in Indiana*, I, 92, the House of Representatives was the final judge regarding contested elections of its members.

268 Indiana *Documentary Journal*, 1842–43, House Doc. 11, pp. 235–238. According to *Biographical Directory of the Indiana General Assembly*, I, 483–485, all votes for ejection of Beall and for seating of Marsh came from Democrats; all votes against rejection of Beall and against seating of Marsh from Whigs. Beall did not participate in the voting, nor did two Democrats. Marsh, not having been seated, could not participate.

269 Indianapolis *Indiana Journal*, December 14, 1842. As early as its issue of August 23, 1842, the Indianapolis *Indiana State Sentinel* quoted the vigorously Democratic Goshen *Democrat* explaining that Marsh had discovered a vote for him in DeKalb County which the Whigs had rejected, adding: "We therefore set down Madison Marsh, Democrat, as elected." Both the *Indiana Journal* and the *Indiana State Sentinel* have *passim* items about this contested election, at times quoted from other papers.

270 If Beall had not replaced Marsh, the author believes that Senator Smith, a Whig, would probably have been reelected.

271 Indiana *House Journal*, 1840–41, pp. 227–228, 280–281; Indiana *Senate Journal*, 1840–41, pp. 213–214. The House, after rejecting the bill 43 to 45, reconsidered its vote and passed the bill 55 to 39. At the next session a bill to restrict voting to townships of residence was indefinitely postponed in the House by a tally of 47 to 45. Indiana *House Journal*, 1841–42, p. 347.

272 Indianapolis *Indiana Journal*, January 16, 1841. As used here the term "foreigners" probably mainly referred to strangers or persons from other counties, rather than those from other countries.

273 For instance, see *Laws of Indiana* (general), 1841–42, p. 157; *ibid.* (general), 1842–43, pp. 97, 104, 109, for legislation applying to the counties of Cass, DeKalb, Franklin, Hamilton, Lake, La Porte, Porter, St. Joseph, Shelby, Steuben, Tippecanoe, and Union.

274 Indianapolis *Indiana State Sentinel*, October 17 and November 7, 1843. The earlier issue has a brief notice from the Corydon [*Harrison*] *Gazette* that Owen and a friend voted in Harrison County contrary to law, and the latter issue quotes a letter Owen wrote to the New Harmony *Statesman* explaining his voting in Harrison County. Owen's letter explains that he cut off the names of county candidates from a ticket, and voted for governor, lieutenant governor, and congressman—striking out his own name for the latter office and voting for John W. Payne, his Whig rival from Harrison County, who in turn voted for Owen. The *Indiana State Sentinel* regarded Owen's explanation as satisfactory and charged that three or four Whigs had illegally voted outside their congressional districts. In its issue of September 26, 1843, the *Sentinel* reported that the grand jury of Adams County had indicted Robert Hanna, federal marshal for Indiana, and Moody Parke, Whig mayor of Madison, for illegally voting in Adams County at the late state election.

275 Thornbrough, Riker, and Corpuz (eds.), *Diary of Calvin Fletcher*, I, 386. It seems probable that Fletcher would not have tried to vote for Harrison unless he knew that voting was at times permitted in such circumstances.

[276] See Walsh, *Centennial History of the Indiana General Assembly*, 80–81, 83, 223.

[277] Riker (ed.), *Messages and Papers of David Wallace*, 253; *Biographical Directory of the Indiana General Assembly*, I, 82, 213.

[278] For previous members of the Supreme Court, see Chapter 1, pp. 8–9; Chapter 4, pp. 159–160, 163–164.

[279] Dorothy Riker (ed.), *Executive Proceedings of the State of Indiana, 1816–1836* (Indianapolis, 1947), 311; Indiana *House Journal*, 1836–37, pp. 28–29. The quotation about salary is from Noble, not Stevens.

[280] Indiana *House Journal*, 1836–37, p. 29; Stephen C. Stevens, et al., to Charles Dewey, May 30, 1836, in Riker and Thornbrough (eds.), *Messages and Papers of Noah Noble*, 456; Indianapolis *Indiana Democrat*, June 1, 1836.

[281] Riker and Thornbrough (eds.), *Messages and Papers of Noah Noble*, 540 (McKinney's death), 547 (Stevens to Noble), 540n, 594n (Sullivan appointment).

[282] Riker (ed.), *Messages and Papers of David Wallace*, 84 (nomination of judges); Indiana *Senate Journal*, 1837–38, pp. 106, 117–118 (approval of nominations). At the previous session Dewey's recess appointment had been extended for completion of Stevens' term, the Senate approving Noble's nomination of him 43 to 0. *Ibid.*, 1836–37, pp. 351–352.

[283] Leander J. Monks *et al.* (eds.), *Courts and Lawyers of Indiana* (3 vols., Indianapolis, 1916), I, 204–205. See *ibid.*, 208–244 for roster of court docket from 1816–46. Charles W. Taylor (comp.), *Biographical Sketches and Review of the Bench and Bar of Indiana* (Indianapolis, 1895), 32–41 *passim*, offers very favorable views about Blackford, Dewey, and Sullivan by John Coburn.

CHAPTER 6

[1] For National Republican-Whig domination of state politics from the midtwenties to the election of 1843, see political division of the General Assembly for each session from 1843–44 through 1849–50 as follows based on *A Biographical Directory of the Indiana General Assembly* (2 vols., Indianapolis, 1980, 1984), Volume 1, *1816–1899*, Volume 2, *1901–1984*, I, 485–502.

1843–44	Senate—26 D, 24 W;	House—55 D, 45 W
1844–45	Senate—25 D, 25 W;	House—45 D, 54 W (Only 99 representatives. Jefferson Co. had only two representatives although it was entitled to three.)
1845–46	Senate—25 D, 25 W;	House—56 D, 44 W
1846–47	Senate—26 D, 24 W;	House—46 D, 54 W
1847–48	Senate—25 D, 25 W;	House—49 D, 51 W
1848–49	Senate—27 D, 23 W;	House—60 D, 40 W
1849–50	Senate—29 D, 21 W;	House—59 D, 41 W

2 Indiana *Documentary Journal*, 1842–43, House Doc. 4, pp. 83–86. These items from Morris' report have been considered part of the bonded debt for the System of 1836 and Wabash and Erie Canal: $7,306,028 for "Internal Improvements," presumably the System of 1836; $1,727,000 for the Wabash and Erie Canal; $980,000 for increase of state stock in the Second State Bank (to earn dividends to help pay interest on the bonded debt); and $294,000 for advances to the state from branches of the Second State Bank in anticipation of such amount from federal surplus revenue in 1837. In noting annual interest due, Morris does not include interest concerning the last of these items. As noted in note 54 below, the auditor's report for the ensuing year shows a larger total due for the bonded debt for internal improvements; including $456,000 of bonds for the Madison and Indianapolis Railroad, apparently not included in the previous report and apparently having been issued before 1842. *Ibid.*, 1843–44, House Doc. 4, pp. 129–132, and statements 12 and 13. The item of $980,000 regarding bank stock, though intended to obtain dividends to help pay interest on the bonded debt, was a part of the bonded debt for the bank. As noted in the table of ordinary state expenditures, in Chapter 5, p. 243, such expenditures average $113,591.27.

3 Indianapolis *Indiana Journal*, November 9, 1842. In its issue for December 14, 1842, the *Indiana Journal* observed that the Brookville *American* had endorsed John H. Bradley, La Porte County, for lieutenant governor if Hall declined renomination. The *Indiana Journal* commented that James H. Collins, Jr., Floyd County, had also been mentioned for this office; and it called Bradley and Collins Whigs of "handsome abilities" for nomination if Hall declined. Concerning Bradley and Collins as Whig senators, see *Biographical Directory of the Indiana General Assembly*, I, 482–483.

4 Indianapolis *Indiana Journal*, December 30, 1842. See *ibid.*, January 11, 1843, explaining that Gibson County Whigs had expressed their entire confidence in the honor, integrity, and ability of Governor Bigger; and had approved a resolution promising support of the state convention's nominee for lieutenant governor since Samuel Hall, their fellow townsman, declined being a candidate.

5 Indianapolis *Indiana State Sentinel*, September 6, 1842. For political background of Milroy and Kennedy, see *Biographical Directory of the Indiana General Assembly*, I, 275–276, 217.

6 Indianapolis *Indiana State Sentinel*, September 20, 1842, quoting Goshen *Democrat*, September 8, 1842. The Indianapolis *Indiana State Sentinel*, October 11, 1842, noting items from Lawrenceburg *Gazette*, November 4 and 8, 1842, noting items from Wilmington *Register*, indicating Amos Lane and Abel C. Pepper as possible gubernatorial candidates, plus Pepper's declining to be one. Presumably Tilghman A. Howard, the popular Democratic nominee for governor in 1840, was not prominently considered for renomination because he had become the party favorite for election to the United States Senate at the legislative session of 1842–43.

7 Indianapolis *Extra State Sentinel*, January 31, 1842; Indianapolis *Indiana State Sentinel*, September 6, 1842. Both issues name Nathaniel West, Nathan B.

Palmer, Nathaniel Bolton, James P. Drake, John Cain, Alexander F. Morrison, and William J. Brown as members of the Democratic State Central Committee. In its issue for September 20, 1842, the *Sentinel* quotes the Goshen *Democrat*, September 8, 1842, suggesting that "if any such body be in existence, that the Central Committee at the Capital . . . call for a State Convention on the glorious 8th of January, ensuing." In the pioneer era the Democrats frequently held state conventions on January 8, the anniversary of Jackson's celebrated victory over the English at New Orleans in 1815.

[8] Indianapolis *Indiana Journal*, November 2, 30, 1842. For concurrence by Whig papers, see *ibid.*, November 2, 9, 16, December 7, 1842. From November, 1842, into January, 1843, the *Indiana Journal* and the *Indiana State Sentinel* have various *passim* items about delegates elected and other actions of county conventions.

[9] Indianapolis *Indiana State Sentinel*, November 1, 1842.

[10] Indiana *House Journal*, 1842–43, pp. 310, 371; Indiana *Senate Journal*, 1842–43, pp. 235, 296. Both journals indicate no legislative session on January 9 or 17. Representative John H. Bradley and Senator James H. Collins, Jr., Whigs, made the motions favorable to the Democrats for January 9; Representative Amzi Lewis Wheeler and Senator James Ritchey, Democrats, reciprocated for the Whigs for January 17. Various legislators in both parties were members of their party convention. For politics of Bradley, Collins, Wheeler, and Ritchey, see *Biographical Directory of the Indiana General Assembly*, I, 482–485.

[11] Unless otherwise indicated, items about the convention are based on the proceedings in Vincennes *Western Sun*, January 28, 1843. Its proceedings, however, do not name the delegates seated or the counties represented. Concerning Brown and Bayless respectively, see *Biographical Directory of the Indiana General Assembly*, I, 40, and Gayle Thornbrough, Dorothy Riker, and Paula Corpuz (eds.), *The Diary of Calvin Fletcher* (9 vols., Indianapolis, 1972–1983), II, 448n. Those named to the State Central Committee were: Nathan B. Palmer, Nathaniel West, John Lister, Demas McFarland, Powell Howland, George A. Chapman, Julius Nicolai (Nicholi), James P. Drake, and James Blake. The inclusion of Nicolai, a German grocer at Indianapolis, who Calvin Fletcher said had arrived poor and became "worth 12 or 13 thousand dollars," was perhaps a bid for the votes of Germans who were increasing in number. Fletcher admired Nicolai who soon became a member of the board of the Indianapolis branch of the state bank. *Ibid.*, II, 512–513, 530, 546, 548, 568. Since Palmer was named first, presumably he was chairman of the committee.

[12] Items regarding the content of the address, unless otherwise indicated, are from the Vincennes *Western Sun*, February 18, 1843. According to the proceedings Alexander F. Morrison proposed a committee to prepare an address, and since he is listed first among its five members it is presumed that he was its chairman and possibly its principal author.

[13] This statement about Whig domination of state offices and the state bank and internal improvement boards and the fund commissioners seems to be at

least a close approximation of what their role had been. The comment that before 1840 "occasionally a scattering crumb fell to a Democrat," but thereafter Democrats had been "ostracised" from office, seems to reflect a hardening of party lines as the forties began.

14 Except as otherwise indicated, items about the Whig convention are based on its proceedings in the Indianapolis *Indiana Journal*, January 21, 1843. Regarding Pennington and Gurley respectively, see *Biographical Directory of the Indiana General Assembly*, I, 311, and Thornbrough, Riker, and Corpuz (eds.), *Diary of Calvin Fletcher*, II, 309, 495. The proceedings as cited do not name the delegates or the counties represented in the convention. The following were named to the Whig State Central Committee: Noah Noble, Theodore J. Barnett, George W. Stipp, John S. Bobbs, Austin W. Morris, all of Marion County; John S. Davis, Floyd County; Henry Cooper, Allen County; Caleb B. Smith, Fayette County; Jesse Conrad, Vigo County; William Brown Butler, Vanderburgh County. Since Noble was named first, presumably he was chairman.

15 Indianapolis *Indiana Journal*, January 25, 1843. In publishing this address the editor called it "admirable," noting that it came from the pen of John D. Defrees, St. Joseph County. As indicated *ibid.*, January 21, 1843, Defrees was chairman of the committee which presented the address to the convention which "unanimously adopted" it.

16 Indianapolis *Indiana State Sentinel*, January 17, 1843. As noted in John W. Miller, *Indiana Newspaper Bibliography* (Indianapolis, 1982), 275–276, the *Indiana State Sentinel* had been founded at the capital in 1841 by George A. and Jacob Page Chapman. The quoted items suggest the biting nature of their attack on the Whigs.

17 Fort Wayne *Sentinel*, January 21, February 4, 1843 (quoting Goshen *Democrat*); Indianapolis *Indiana State Sentinel*, January 31, 1843, quoting Madison *Courier*, January 21. According to the Wilmington *Register*, as quoted in the *Indiana State Sentinel*, January 24, 1843, an individual just returned from the capital reported that about 1,500 had attended the Democrat State Convention, whose proceedings had been "conducted in perfect harmony and unison of feeling." For examples of other Democratic papers endorsing Whitcomb and Bright, see Indianapolis *Indiana State Sentinel*, January 31, February 21, 1843; Vincennes *Western Sun*, January 14, 28, 1843.

18 Indianapolis *Indiana Journal*, January 16, 1843.

19 Indianapolis *Indiana State Sentinel*, January 17, 1843. No evidence of any formal caucus nominations has been observed. *Ibid.*, January 31, 1843, quotes the Franklin *Democrat*, January 13, saying that in his initial canvass for governor Bigger had said he would not consent to serve more than one term. In its issue for July 4, 1843, the *Sentinel* made this same claim. No trustworthy evidence has been found in support of this claim.

20 Indianapolis *Indiana Journal*, January 21, 1843; Indianapolis *Indiana State Sentinel*, January 24, 1843. The *Journal* asserted that at least a thousand delegates

had attended the Whig State Convention, while the *Sentinel* claimed that there were never more than 450 individuals present, including legislators and local residents. Attendance at political meetings was often inflated or deflated according to party bias.

21 *Biographical Directory of the Indiana General Assembly*, I, 413; William Wesley Woollen, *Biographical and Historical Sketches of Early Indiana* (Indianapolis, 1883), 81–93. For Whitcomb's vote against the bank and for the system, see Indiana *Senate Journal*, 1833–34, p. 268; *ibid.*, 1835–36, p. 446. As Whitcomb passed through Lafayette enroute to Terre Haute in 1841, he declared his "abiding confidence in the virtue and intelligence of the people" as the "cardinal principle" of his political creed. If Democrats avoided petty dissensions, mere personal ambition, and moved in "one unbroken phalanx, animated alone by correct principle and love of liberty," Whitcomb observed, political success would be theirs. Indianapolis *Indiana State Sentinel*, December 7, 1841, quoting Lafayette *Advertiser*, November 25, 1841.

22 Indianapolis *Indiana Journal*, January 16, 1843; Indianapolis *Indiana State Sentinel*, January 17, 1843. Governor Whitcomb's marriage to Mrs. Martha Ann Renick Hurst in March, 1846, and her death in July, 1847, after giving birth to a daughter who became the wife of Claude Matthews, a Democrat who served as governor of Indiana, 1893–97, is noted in Woollen, *Biographical and Historical Sketches of Early Indiana*, 92. The Whitcomb-Hurst marriage is noted in Indianapolis *Indiana Democrat*, April 3, 1846; her death is noted in Indianapolis *Indiana State Sentinel*, July 21, 24, 1847, including a lengthy obituary.

23 Indianapolis *Indiana State Sentinel*, January 24, 1843; Indianapolis *Indiana State Journal*, May 24, June 28, July 26, 1843.

24 Indianapolis *Indiana State Journal*, March 22, 29, April 5, 12, 19, 1843; Indianapolis *Indiana State Sentinel*, April 4 (quotes), 11, 18, 25, May 2, 9, 16, 23, June 6, 13, 20, July 4, 18, 1843. In its initial article the *Journal* sets forth the principal claims and charges elaborated in the series, and its last article summarizes them. In the series by the *Sentinel*, consisting of at least thirteen installments, the basis and continuing emphasis is on Whig responsibility for the fiscal debacle resulting from the System of 1836.

25 Indianapolis *Indiana State Sentinel*, April 11, 1843, quoting Terre Haute *Wabash Express*, April 5, 1843. The *Sentinel* said it liked the spirit of this comment, but protested that it had never charged the Whigs with exclusive responsibility and had always admitted the partial responsibility of the Democrats. As noted above, note 21, Whitcomb had voted for the system. Bigger had not been a legislator when it had been adopted.

26 Goshen *Democrat*, February 23, 1843. Also quoted in the Vincennes *Western Sun*, April 1, 1843. For similar castigation of the Whigs by the Fort Wayne *Sentinel*, see issue of March 25, 1843; by the Indianapolis *Indiana State Sentinel*, February 21, March 28, May 16, 1843, plus the series cited in note 24 above. Dr. E. W. H. Ellis was editor of the Goshen *Democrat*. Ellis said execution of the system had been entrusted to Noah Noble, Caleb B. Smith, Dr. Isaac Coe, Milton

Stapp, Jesse Williams, and other prominent Whigs who had "squandered" the state's money.

27 As the ensuing pages of this chapter indicate, such data were calculated variously in the 1840s. A somewhat different calculation had been given by Governor Bigger in his message to the General Assembly in December, 1841, following the initial default on interest due on the bonded debt due July 1, 1841, preceding. Gayle Thornbrough (ed.), *Messages and Papers Relating to the Administration of Samuel Bigger, Governor of Indiana, 1840–1843* (Indianapolis, 1964), 319–322.

28 Indianapolis *Indiana State Journal*, May 31, June 7, 1843.

29 *Ibid.*, April 12, 26, May 31, 1843.

30 *Ibid.*, June 28, July 26 (quote), 1843.

31 Indianapolis *Indiana State Sentinel*, June 13, 20, 1843.

32 As noted p. 295, this chapter, the possibility of a compromise with creditors (bondholders) had been suggested as early as 1842.

33 Indiana *House Journal*, 1833–34, p. 352; Indiana *Senate Journal*, 1833–34, p. 268. The *Indiana State Sentinel*, May 23, 1843, however, said it was not impossible and not improbable that the bank would again suspend if Whigs won the legislature in the August voting, but it would be obliged to continue if the Democrats won.

34 In his inaugural Whitcomb commented about the distress and embarrassments suffered from overbanking; in his annual address to the legislature in December, 1844, he reported about the funded debt of the Second State Bank and loans to the state from certain branches; and his annual address, December, 1845, makes no mention of banking. Indiana *House Journal*, 1843–44, pp. 33–38; *ibid.*, 1844–45, pp. 18–28; *ibid.*, 1845–46, pp. 14–23. In none of these addresses did he speak in support of or in opposition to the bank.

35 Indianapolis *Indiana State Journal*, April 12, 1843; Indianapolis *Indiana State Sentinel*, May 2, 16, 1843. In its issue for May 2 the *Sentinel* stated that Bright had resigned as senator. According to *Biographical Directory of the Indiana General Assembly*, I, 37, Bright resigned April 22, 1843.

36 Indianapolis *Indiana State Sentinel*, April 25, July 4, May 23 (quote), 1843.

37 Indianapolis *Indiana State Journal*, July 26, 1843.

38 *Ibid.*, May 10, 24, July 12, 26, 1843. The wording of the charge varies, the wording quoted is from the issue of July 12. The Whigs offered certificates in support of this accusation and the claim that Whitcomb had been a Clay man before he became a Jacksonian. For denials of these charges, see Vincennes *Western Sun*, May 20, 1843; Indianapolis *Indiana State Sentinel*, May 30, July 11, August 1, 1843.

39 Indianapolis *Indiana State Sentinel*, September 6, 20, 1842. For biographical sketches of Deming and Harding, see *Biographical Directory of the Indiana General Assembly*, I, 98, and Etta Reeves French, "Stephen S. Harding: A Hoosier Abolitionist," *Indiana Magazine of History*, XXVII (1931), 207–229.

40 Indianapolis *Indiana State Sentinel*, May 9, 30, 1843; Indianapolis *Indiana State Journal*, May 31, June 7, 1843. In its issue for May 31 the *Journal* empha-

sized Whig support for tariff protection, distribution, and a sound national currency. It also contended that the Democrats were playing both sides of the abolition question, and warned that the election of either John C. Calhoun or Lewis Cass would lead to the annexation of Texas and the expansion of slavery in the United States.

41 Indianapolis *Indiana State Sentinel*, June 13, July 4, 18, 1843; Indianapolis *Indiana State Journal*, June 21, 28 (quotation), August 2, 1843; Vincennes *Western Sun*, July 29, August 5, 1843. This controversy is discussed at length in Jane Shaffer Elsmere, *Henry Ward Beecher: The Indiana Years, 1837–1847* (Indianapolis, 1973), 181–187; Robert D. Clark, "Matthew Simpson, the Methodists, and the Defeat of Samuel Bigger, 1843," *Indiana Magazine of History*, L (1954), 23–33. The author has frequently heard this explanation for Bigger's defeat during the last half century, but it seems less and less convincing as one digs into the newspapers and legislative records of the early 1840s! According to Woollen, *Biographical and Historical Sketches of Early Indiana*, 80, in 1846 he heard Bishop Edward R. Ames of the Methodist church say: "It was the amen corner of the Methodist church that defeated Governor Bigger, and I had a hand in the work."

42 Indianapolis *Indiana State Journal*, July 26, 1843. The *Journal* reminded Whigs that one vote had caused them to lose the election of a United States senator earlier in 1843. For this election, see Chapter 11, pp. 591–592, and note 65.

43 For instance, see *ibid.*, May 24, July 5, 26, 1843; Indianapolis *Indiana State Sentinel*, April 25, July 18, 25, 1843.

44 Fort Wayne *Sentinel*, August 12, 1843; Indianapolis *Indiana State Sentinel*, August 15, 1843.

45 According to Dorothy Riker and Gayle Thornbrough (comps.), *Indiana Election Returns, 1816–1851* (Indianapolis, 1960), 150–153, 173–175, election returns—complete for all counties and official for all but one county—show that Whitcomb received 60,784 votes; Bigger, 58,721 votes; and Deming, 1,683 votes. For lieutenant governor Bright obtained 60,982; Bradley, 56,963 votes; and Harding, 1,677 votes. As may be seen in Indiana *House Journal*, 1843–44, pp. 29–30, in announcing these returns to members of the legislature the speaker of the House gave somewhat different totals for most of them. See note 1, this chapter, for the political makeup of the General Assembly.

46 For instance, see Indianapolis *Indiana State Sentinel*, August 22, 29, 1843; Indianapolis *Indiana State Journal*, August 23, 30, 1843; Vincennes *Western Sun*, September 23, 1843, quoting Madison *Courier.*

47 Indianapolis *Indiana State Sentinel*, September 12, 1843, quoting Greensburg *Repository*, September 2, 1843, and then responding thereto.

48 The Indianapolis *Indiana State Journal*, July 5, 1843, stated that there had been an increase of about two thousand naturalized voters, "a large proportion of which our opponents very graciously place down to themselves." In *ibid.*, August 23, 1843, this Whig paper quoted the Evansville *Journal* which considered the German and English vote for Robert Dale Owen, a Democrat, a significant

factor in his recent congressional victory. In the midforties a recent German immigrant to Marshall County wrote: "Since you all know what democracy means, you may know that the greater number of immigrants here are democrats, because they have never been aristocrats anyway." Donald F. Carmony (ed.), "Letter Written by Mr. Johann Wolfgang Schreyer," *Indiana Magazine of History*, XL (1944), 289.

[49] The Liberty party got 1,269 of its votes, or about three fourths of its total of 1,683, in the forty counties which favored Bigger; and only 414 votes in the forty-seven counties favoring Whitcomb.

[50] Indianapolis *Indiana State Sentinel*, August 22, 1843; Goshen *Democrat*, August 31, 1843. In its issue of October 17, 1843, the *Sentinel* renewed and strongly emphasized its support of Palmer. Then in its issue of November 16, 1843, the *Democrat* reported that Palmer would probably be elected treasurer, and renewed its emphasis that the auditor should be selected from northern Indiana. It named L. S. Chittenden, Allen County; Amzi L. Wheeler, Marshall County; and Horatio J. Harris, of Carroll County, as northern Indiana Democrats, any one of whom it would be glad to see elected auditor.

[51] Indianapolis *Indiana State Sentinel*, September 19, 1843, quoting Goshen *Democrat*, September 7, 1843, quoting Fort Wayne *Sentinel*, September 2, 1843 (barb in Fort Wayne *Sentinel* and response of *Indiana State Sentinel*); Indianapolis *Indiana State Journal*, November 8, 1843. The Fort Wayne *Sentinel*, September 23, 1843, in commenting about its appeal for election of persons outside of Indianapolis stated: "Rotation in office we consider the true democratic doctrine." But Palmer had been a faithful public servant and it would "cheerfully" acquiesce in his election as treasurer if its friends generally favored him.

[52] For election of Mayhew, see Indiana *House Journal*, 1843–44, pp. 120–121, 123–124, 128–129, 130–132, 145; for that of Harris, *ibid.*, 145–146, 157–158. For comments of Fletcher about Mayhew and Harris respectively, see Thornbrough, Riker, and Corpuz (eds.), *Diary of Calvin Fletcher*, II, 560, 561.

[53] For the status of the System of 1836 and the Wabash and Erie Canal when Whitcomb became governor, see pp. 298–300, this chapter.

[54] Indiana *Documentary Journal*, 1843–44, House Doc. 4, pp. 129–132. In computing the debt from data given by Morris, these items, totaling $11,901,000 have been counted as part of the bonded debt for internal improvements: (1) $8,451,000 for "internal improvement bonds," presumably for the system; (2) $980,000 for bonds to increase state stock in the Second State Bank (*intended* to earn dividends to help pay interest on the bonded debt); (3) $456,000 for Madison and Indianapolis Railroad bonds (part of the system); (4) $294,000 for bonds as reimbursement for advances made to the state in anticipation of this sum from federal surplus revenue of 1837; and (5) $1,720,000 for bonds for the Wabash and Erie Canal.

[55] As noted in Thornbrough (ed.), *Messages and Papers of Samuel Bigger*, 74, 320, and 579–580 respectively, in 1840 Treasurer Nathan B. Palmer estimated the suspended debt at $3,559,791.34; in 1841 Governor Bigger estimated it at

$3,381,000; and in 1842 State Agent Michael G. Bright gave items totaling $4,210,456.72 as the aggregate of the suspended debt. The amounts given varied from time to time according to the items included, and then as items were collected therefrom. Sums thereof were collected from time to time, both before and after surrender of the Wabash and Erie Canal to the trustees according to the Butler Bill of 1847, but this author found no reliable data to indicate what the actual loss was from the suspended debt.

56 Federal census data as cited in John D. Barnhart and Donald F. Carmony, *Indiana: From Frontier to Industrial Commonwealth* (4 vols., New York, 1954), I, 408, show a population of 685,866 for Indiana in 1840; 988,416 in 1850. Three quarters of a million is a rough estimate for December, 1843. A correspondent in the Vincennes *Western Sun*, March 25, 1843, commented: "We are a very poor people, although our gross annual products somewhat exceed thirty millions of dollars. We probably have 120,000 families—their average gross product is about $250, each annually, and their average surplus product is about sixteen dollars each annually." Presuming the debt to be about $12,000,000 and the interest on the debt to be $720,000 yearly, this would be "six dollars each family" or more "than a third of our surplus product in the best of times, and probably half of it now." To pay this amount in additional taxes, the correspondent said, "we will not, we cannot." What the actual family income was is uncertain, but this comment suggests the limited and undeveloped nature of the pioneer economy.

57 Thornbrough (ed.), *Messages and Papers of Samuel Bigger*, 116–118, 324–326, 493–496.

58 Indianapolis *Indiana State Sentinel*, July 21, 1841; Indianapolis *Indiana State Journal*, December 15, 1841.

59 Indianapolis *Daily State Sentinel*, January 22, 1842.

60 For table of tax levies 1837–43, see Chapter 5, p. 246. For appropriation of $1,500,000.00 in scrip in payment of contractors for works on internal improvements, giving priority to payment of this debt, see *ibid.*, 214–215.

61 For persistent efforts by Chamberlain for repudiation of the suspended debt, see Thornbrough (ed.), *Messages and Papers of Samuel Bigger*, 352, 391, 423. Comments of Chamberlain support the view that Democrats were more favorable to such repudiation than were Whigs.

62 Indiana *Documentary Journal*, 1841–42, House Doc. 14, p. 482. The four Democratic members were Chairman Thomas J. Henley, William Wines, Wilson Thompson, John Hendricks; the three Whigs were John H. Bradley, John S. Davis, Samuel Goodnow. The Whigs concurred with the recommendation of the majority, but dissented from its premises. They said the people of Indiana "will eventually pay every dollar of the public debt, which they honestly owe." For committee members, see Indiana *House Journal*, 1841–42, p. 29; for their politics, *Biographical Directory of the Indiana General Assembly*, I, 481–482. As indicated in Thornbrough (ed.), *Messages and Papers of Samuel Bigger*, 353–354, 421–423, Senator Chamberlain was also an avid proponent of buying bonds at low prices to redeem them.

63 See this chapter, pp. 288, 294, 354; Ch. 11, pp. 584–585, 586–587, 589–590, 593, 594, for strong Whig support for distribution, but modest revenue therefrom during the forties.

64 Indianapolis *Indiana State Sentinel*, July 5, 1842; Indianapolis *Indiana State Journal*, December 30, 1842. The *Sentinel* said: "We'll set a ball in motion on this subject one of these days. We know a good deal about this matter—more than nine-tenths of the politicians in the State. Look out for developments." As noted on p. 295, this chapter, early in 1843 the Democratic State Convention mentioned negotiation with bondholders as one way to reduce the debt for internal improvements.

65 Indiana *House Journal*, 1843–44, pp. 15 (Bigger), 35 (Whitcomb). A year later Whitcomb reaffirmed this view and cleverly added that the opinion advanced by his predecessor in his last message "'that we cannot now pay the interest on the public debt,' is universally entertained among the people of the State." *Ibid.*, 1844–45, p. 23.

66 See letters from N. M. Rothschild and Sons in Thornbrough (ed.), *Messages and Papers of Samuel Bigger*, 250–251, 236–238.

67 Indianapolis *Indiana Journal*, June 22, 1842. The "English" bondholders included at least two Americans, resident in London, George Peabody and Benjamin Wiggin. A few signers explained that they were signing for others; and the transmittal letter noted that many bondholders, living at a distance from London, had been unable to sign but had sent letters expressing perfect accord with the statement. N. M. Rothschild and Baring Brothers were among the signers. Nearly fifty names were attached to the memorial. The transmittal letter, memorial, and names of its signers are also in the Indianapolis *Indiana State Sentinel*, June 14, 1842. The transmittal letter and memorial, minus the names of signers, is in Thornbrough (ed.), *Messages and Papers of Samuel Bigger*, 439–444.

68 Indiana *Documentary Journal*, 1843–44, House Doc. 18, pp. 394–396. This memorial is also in Thornbrough (ed.), *Messages and Papers of Samuel Bigger*, 614–617.

69 Logansport *Telegraph*, April 16, 1842, quoting New York *Express*; Indiana *House Journal*, 1842–43, p. 19.

70 Goshen *Democrat*, September 14, 1843. The *Democrat* stated that Bigger had sought federal aid via distribution "which would have sunk us deeper in the mire," while Whitcomb's policy "was to husband the resources of the State, gather up the fragments of public property, pay off our domestic debt, and be active in preparation for the time when the liquidation of the whole debt shall become practicable."

71 Indianapolis *Indiana State Sentinel*, March 29, 1842.

72 Indiana *House Journal*, 1843–44, pp. 33, 36; *ibid.*, 1844–45, pp. 19–21, 23. Whitcomb emphasized that it was far more burdensome to pay a debt to another country than to fellow citizens because the former drained specie from the debtor country.

73 *Ibid.*, 1844–45, p. 23.

74 *Ibid.*, 344, 480–481, 542, 593, for House action; Indiana *Senate Journal*, 1844–45, pp. 353–354, 661–662, for passage by Senate in amended form. Since the bill did not pass both houses with the same content, it failed. The Indianapolis *Indiana State Sentinel*, January 23, 1845, asserted, probably correctly, that the Whigs had inserted Whitcomb's name in place of Bright to embarrass him in his future recommendations with the legislature, impose duties on him that would require him to leave the state, and make him a target for moneyed men to shoot at.

75 Indiana *Senate Journal*, 1844–45, pp. 11–12, 156, 242–243. For members of the select committee and the accompanying bill, see Indiana *Documentary Journal*, 1844–45, Pt. II, Doc. 5, pp. 27–34. The bill closely followed the terms of the resolution submitted by Defrees, the interest remaining at 3 percent per annum, but the new bonds would be redeemable after thirty rather than twenty-five years. See pp. 30–31, for quoted items. Three members of the select committee, Defrees, David P. Holloway, and Robert G. Cotton were Whigs; the two other members, Ransom W. Akin and Albert G. Hutton, were Democrats. See *Biographical Directory of the Indiana General Assembly*, I, 488. The Indianapolis *Indiana State Journal*, December 7, 1844, has an item, unsigned, concerning the Defrees proposal, which suggests the belief that it "will be satisfactory to our bond-holders, and within the ability of our people to accomplish."

76 Indiana *House Journal*, 1844–45, pp. 389–390; Indianapolis *Indiana State Journal*, January 29, 1845, quotes Leslie as saying, "That this liberal proposition will be accepted, we have not only the assurance of an agent of the bond-holders, now here at the capital in person, but also the published proposals of an authorized number of the bond-holders themselves, as submitted to this House in the special message of the Executive."

77 Indiana *House Journal*, 1844–45, pp. 515–519. For members of the committee and their politics, see above, note 75.

78 *Ibid.*, 521–527 (quotation, 523). Vandeveer calculated the bonded debt for internal improvements at $10,828,000, presumed accumulated interest totaling $4,888,080, for the nine years January 1, 1841, to January 1, 1850, making an aggregate of $15,716,080.

79 For tax levies, 1837–1850, see Chap. 5, p. 246; Chap. 6, p. 319.

80 According to John Denis Haeger, *The Investment Frontier: New York Businessmen and the Economic Development of the Old Northwest* (Albany, N. Y., 1981), 202, 204, 209–217, and Chapter 11, *passim*, debt settlements had been made in Michigan and Illinois, with Butler having effected the one in Michigan.

81 *Proceedings of the Canal Convention, Assembled at Terre-Haute, May 22, 1845, For the Purpose of Considering the Best Mode of Applying the Proceeds of the Liberal Grant of Land by the General Government, Towards Extending the Wabash and Erie Canal to the Ohio River, at Evansville* (Terre Haute, Ind., 1845). Butler's address is on pp. 8–14, of this sixteen page publication. The quoted items are on pp. 9, 10, 13. Senator Edward A. Hannegan, Democrat, was president of the convention; Charles I. Battell and Richard A. Clements, vice-presidents, were both Whigs. *Biographical Directory of the Indiana General Assembly*, I, 17, 68, 165.

[82] *Proceedings of the Canal Convention,* 6–7. Richard W. Thompson, a Whig, and a former representative in Congress, submitted the report and resolutions for the committee concerning them. Senator Hannegan and Congressman Joseph A. Wright, a Democrat, both strongly urged extension of the canal to Evansville as a measure linked with liquidation of the internal improvement debt owed bondholders. As the proceedings indicate, Congress had recently granted Indiana an additional grant of land to help finance such an extension. As indicated on p. 15, at its final session the convention resolved "without a dissenting voice: That we, as citizens of Indiana, scoff at the idea of repudiation; we know we are in debt, *we acknowledge the corn,* and we earnestly request those who are to represent us in the coming legislature, to make some arrangement for the gradual liquidation of our state debt."

[83] Indiana *House Journal,* 1845–46, pp. 15–20. Quoted items are on pp. 15, 18, 19.

[84] Francis Hovey Stoddard, *The Life and Letters of Charles Butler* (New York, 1903), 227–229. Several days prior to the governor's message Butler wrote his wife: "The prospects are altogether discouraging, and almost everybody says that *nothing* can be done. Politicians, on both sides, are afraid to move. It is really amazing to see what a paralysis hangs upon this people." Butler added: "It is certain that if the question is not now settled it never will be; the people will go into repudiation." *Ibid.,* 226–227.

[85] Indiana *Documentary Journal,* 1845–46, Pt. II, Doc. 8, pp. 55–66. Quoted items are on pp. 55, 56, 59. In his letter of December 10, 1845, addressed to the governor for his presentation of it to the General Assembly, Butler offered much detail about terms for a compromise settlement. As noted in Stoddard, *Life and Letters of Charles Butler,* 229–231, Whitcomb and other persons had read Butler's letter in advance of its presentation to the members of the legislature. Butler wrote his wife that "The letter is very much complimented by the few to whom I have submitted it, among whom are the best men I can find here; they think it will save the debt and the people."

[86] Indiana *House Journal,* 1845–46, pp. 114, 129; Indiana *Senate Journal,* 1845–46, pp. 93–94, 96–97, 98. Both houses named one member from each of the state's twelve judicial circuits, providing geographical representation to all parts of the state. Despite a considerable Democratic majority in the House, Speaker John S. Simonson, a Democrat, named six Democrats and six Whigs. In the Senate, evenly divided between the parties, Lieutenant Governor Jesse D. Bright, Democrat, named seven Democrats and five Whigs, giving the Democrats a majority of the committee's total membership. For the politics of members and the counties they represented, see *Biographical Directory of the Indiana General Assembly,* I, 490–492. The Indianapolis *Indiana State Sentinel,* December 25, 1845, states that Joseph Lane became chairman of the committee.

[87] Indiana *Documentary Journal,* 1845–46, Pt. II, Doc. 21, pp. 238–240. See *ibid.,* Doc. 8, pp. 55–76, for Butler's presuming that the bonded debt for internal improvements had been $11,090,000 on July 1, 1841. These pages have

much elaboration and data relevant to the content of his first proposition. In submitting his first proposition Butler included a proviso that the canal would be completed to the Ohio River "by the year 1853 . . . ."

88 Stoddard, *Life and Letters of Charles Butler*, 237–245. Quotes are on pp. 237, 238, 241, 242, 244. The item about repudiation of three to four million dollars doubtless concerned the suspended debt for which the principal had never been received.

89 Indiana *Documentary Journal*, 1845–46, Pt. II, Doc. 21, p. 240; Stoddard, *Life and Letters of Charles Butler*, 245–246.

90 Indiana *Documentary Journal*, 1845–46, Pt. II, Doc. 21, pp. 241–242, 243–248, for relevant data; Stoddard, *Life and Letters of Charles Butler*, 245–246.

91 Stoddard, *Life and Letters of Charles Butler*, 246–249.

92 For a copy of the bill, see Indiana *Documentary Journal*, 1845–46, Pt. II, Doc. 22, pp. 249–260. For its introduction, see Indiana *House Journal*, 1845–46, p. 371; Indiana *Senate Journal*, 1845–46, pp. 380–381.

93 See pp. 300–305, this chapter, for Butler's first proposed compromise toward a debt settlement. He regarded the Whigs as more favorable therefor than the Democrats, but he concluded: "Both parties are pledged to the proposition, and my hope is that now the Legislature will act." Stoddard, *Life and Letters of Charles Butler*, 253–254.

94 *Ibid.*, 252–259. Quotes are on pp. 253, 259. According to 259–260, the item about a popular referendum was defeated 49 to 41.

95 Indiana *House Journal*, 1845–46, pp. 506–507. According to the Indianapolis *Indiana State Sentinel*, January 22, 1846, in presenting this amendment Charles Secrest reported that at first Butler had refused to accept it, but "He would now do so."

96 Indiana *House Journal*, 1845–46, pp. 537–539; Stoddard, *Life and Letters of Charles Butler*, 261–262.

97 Stoddard, *Life and Letters of Charles Butler*, 266–269; Haeger, *The Investment Frontier*, 221.

98 Indiana *Senate Journal*, 1845–46, p. 618; Indiana *House Journal*, 1845–46, pp. 594, 622, for House acceptance of Senate amendments. Butler, in commenting about Governor Whitcomb's signing of the bill, though ill, states: "He signed it in bed in my presence, saying that it was one of the most gratifying acts of his life." Stoddard, *Life and Letters of Charles Butler,* 269. Although Butler at first viewed Whitcomb as timid and cautious, as consideration of the bill continued he indicated appreciation for strong support for the compromise settlement from both Whitcomb and Lieutenant Governor Jesse D. Bright. *Ibid.*, 226–228, 242, 250, 255–258, 262–263, 269, and *passim.*

99 A check regarding the politics of legislators as listed in *Biographical Directory of the Indiana General Assembly*, I, 490–492, shows that in the House 33 Whigs and 28 Democrats voted for passage of the Butler Bill of 1846; while 9 Whigs and 24 Democrats opposed passage. In the Senate 15 Whigs and 16 Democrats voted for passage, 6 Democrats and 9 Whigs in opposition to

passage. Of the 24 members of the joint committee which submitted the bill, 9 Whigs and 5 Democrats voted for passage, 1 Whig and 6 Democrats against passage, and 1 Whig and 2 Democrats did not vote. Note 86, above, indicates sources for members of the joint committee.

[100] *Laws of Indiana* (general), 1845–46, pp. 3–18. Thomas H. Dowling, a Whig representative from Vigo County who had voted for passage of the Butler Bill of 1846, gave an excellent summary of its content in the Indianapolis *Indiana State Sentinel*, February 5, 1846, quoting the Terre Haute *Wabash Express*. Dowling indicated that this measure transferred the responsibility for $6,500,000 of the principal from the state to the revenue from the Wabash and Erie Canal.

[101] Indianapolis *Indiana State Journal*, December 3, 1845, January 7, 21, 1846.

[102] Indianapolis *Indiana State Sentinel*, January 29, February 19, 1846.

[103] *Ibid.*, February 19, 1846. Butler made this comment in a friendly exchange between himself and about three dozen legislators.

[104] Haeger, *The Investment Frontier*, 221–222. Haeger's account is based on Butler's report to the legislature and also that to the bondholders. The source cited in the preceding note also includes important information concerning why Butler agreed to the amendment making the Wabash and Erie Canal responsible for half of the principal as well as half of the interest.

[105] During debate over the Butler Bill of 1846 various legislators indicated that the importance of and the revenue anticipated from the canal were being overvalued. For instance, see Indianapolis *Indiana State Journal*, January 28, 1846; Indianapolis *Indiana State Sentinel*, January 22, 1846.

[106] Indiana *Documentary Journal*, 1846–47, Pt. I, Doc. 5, p. 112.

[107] Haeger, *The Investment Frontier*, 222; Indiana *House Journal*, 1846–47, pp. 15–17, 32–33 (quotations, 16, 33).

[108] Indiana *Documentary Journal*, 1846–47, Pt. II, Doc. 6, pp. 71–74. For related information, see *ibid.*, 72, 75–76, for statement by J. Horsley Palmer, who Butler refers to as chairman of the "London committee of bondholders."

[109] Indiana *House Journal*, 1846–47, pp. 511–512; Indiana *Senate Journal*, 1846–47, p. 604. The *Senate Journal* gives the vote as 24 to 19 for passage, but only 18 senators are listed as having so voted. According to politics of legislators in *Biographical Directory of the Indiana General Assembly*, I, 493–495, in the House 39 Whigs and 31 Democrats voted for passage; 15 Whigs and 15 Democrats against passage. In the Senate 13 Whigs and 11 Democrats supported passage, and 8 Whigs and 10 Democrats opposed passage. This source lists Representative John Deam, who opposed passage, as probably a Democrat. The Indiana *House Journal*, 1846–47, p. 656, lists Deam as a Democrat.

[110] Indiana *House Journal*, 1846–47, pp. 651–657. Page 656 lists the 30 representatives, their politics, and the counties represented by them. Senator Joseph Robinson, a Whig, charged that the revised Butler Bill had been "concocted in England, drafted by a learned barrister in the inner temple of her Majesty, Queen Victoria . . . ." He said it would particularly benefit speculators who had

made modest payments for bonds, persons who became trustees for completion of the canal, and owners of large tracts of land whose value would be enhanced by completion of the canal. Robinson further claimed that Butler, as an agent of the American Land Company, held in his name "large tracts of lands lying in the region of country, through which" the canal would pass. Indianapolis *Indiana State Journal*, February 16, 1847, quoting Greensburg *Repository*. As indicated in Haeger, *The Investment Frontier*, 71–73, 105–107, 110, 126–127, 230–232, and *passim*, Butler was much involved in large scale land speculation and economic development in the Old Northwest, especially in Michigan, Ohio, and Illinois, but the extent to which he was so involved in the Wabash Valley, if at all, is uncertain.

111 *Laws of Indiana* (general), 1846–47, pp. 3–38. The quoted item is on p. 8.

112 Indianapolis *Indiana State Journal*, February 9, 1847. Thompson was an experienced legislator as indicated in *Biographical Directory of the Indiana General Assembly*, I, 388–389. Perry County, bordering the Ohio River upstream from Evansville, which Thompson represented, had been among the counties for which immediate benefit of importance had not been anticipated from the System of 1836.

113 Jacob Piatt Dunn, *Indiana and Indianans* (5 vols., Chicago, 1919), I, 403–405; Logan Esarey, *A History of Indiana: From Its Exploration to 1850* (2 vols., Fort Wayne, Ind., 1924), I, 432–434, 435–436.

114 *Laws of Indiana*, 1831–32, pp. 4–5; *ibid*. (general), 1835–36, pp. 10–11.

115 For tax levies 1837–1850, see Chapter 5, p. 246; Chapter 6, p. 319.

116 Indiana *House Journal*, 1844–45, pp. 34–37.

117 Thornbrough, Riker, and Corpuz (eds.), *Diary of Calvin Fletcher*, II, 533–534. See *ibid*., 550–551, for Whitcomb's response, November 9, 1843, to Fletcher's letter to him, dated September 25, 1843, in which Whitcomb concurs with much that Fletcher had written to him. Also see *ibid*., 562, for Fletcher's comment: "I have a high regard for W.'s talants & his good intentions to administer the government of the state correctly but I have no regard for the leaders of both political parties."

118 See pp. 296–297, this chapter, for comments of Editor Ellis and Governor Whitcomb professing the inability of citizens to pay taxes required to meet claims of bondholders concerning internal improvement debts.

119 As indicated in *Laws of Indiana* (general), 1843–44, pp. 13–14, about one week after becoming governor Whitcomb signed a law reducing the annual salary of the governor and Supreme judges from $1,500 to $1,300; presidents of circuit courts from $1,000 to $800; salary of treasurer and auditor remained at $1,000, but with loss of $400 for clerk hire; and that of the secretary of state remained at $800, with loss of $300 for clerk hire. Legislators continued to receive $3 per diem for the first six weeks of a session, but only $1.50 per diem thereafter, plus $3 for every twenty-five miles of travel to and from a session. As president of the Senate, the lieutenant governor received the same compensation as legislators received. The per diem for doorkeepers, secretaries of the Senate, and

clerks of the House could not exceed that paid legislators. This law stipulated that hereafter no compensation could be given a private secretary to the governor from the state treasury. Since the Constitution of 1816 prohibited decreasing the salary of the governor and judges during the terms for which they had been elected or appointed, their reductions were not immediately effective. Charles Kettleborough, *Constitution Making in Indiana* (3 vols., Indianapolis, 1916, 1930), I, 97, 105, 119. Regarding the decreased length of sessions, see John G. Rauch and Nellie C. Armstrong, *A Bibliography of the Laws of Indiana, 1788–1927* (Indianapolis, 1928), 68–69.

[120] In the ensuing discussion about ordinary expenditures and ordinary revenue, unless otherwise indicated, items are based on annual reports of the state treasurer as found in Indiana *Documentary Journal*, 1844–45, Pt. I, Doc. 2, pp. 60–63; *ibid.*, 1845–46, Pt. I, Doc. 2, pp. 67–70; *ibid.*, 1846–47, Pt. I, Doc. 2, pp. 59–63; *ibid.*, 1847–48, Pt. I, Doc. 1, pp. 7–11; *ibid.*, 1848–49, Pt. I, Doc. 2, pp. 99–103; *ibid.*, 1849–50, Pt. I, Doc. 1, pp. 7–11; *ibid.*, 1850–51, Pt. I, Doc. 3, pp. 137–145. According to a law of 1841 the county treasurer was allowed a percentage of the state tax revenue collected as his compensation for collecting it. He was allowed 8 percent of the first $1,000 collected, with reduced percentages as additional thousands were collected, and finally only 3 percent of the revenue collected in excess of $5,000. He was also allowed 8 cents per mile of travel to and from the capital for making payment of the state tax from his county. *Laws of Indiana* (general), 1840–41, pp. 31, 34. These provisions are also in *ibid.* (revised), 1842–43, pp. 220–221; and *ibid.* (revised), 1851–52, I, 286–287. Late in 1843 the state auditor reported that it cost nearly 5 percent to collect the revenue of 1842, and this official reported that it cost a fraction more than 4 percent to collect the revenue of 1845. Indiana *Documentary Journal*, 1843–44, House Doc. 4, p. 74; *ibid.*, 1845–46, Pt. I, Doc. 1, pp. 43–44. The author has estimated that it probably cost roughly 5 percent of the revenue to collect it during the years 1843–50, but this estimate could perhaps be as much as 1 percent too high.

[121] Legislative, judiciary, and other expense cannot be calculated with complete accuracy. Legislative costs presumably embraced at least nearly all expenditures listed as legislative expenses, public printing and binding of laws, and distribution of laws and journals. Moreover, some legislative costs are doubtless included under expenditures for stationery and fuel and specific appropriations. Judicial costs were for the Supreme Court, president judges of the circuit courts, probate judges, and prosecuting attorneys—largely for salaries. Miscellaneous costs totaled $15,445.53, and included these items: $7,129.81 for tax revenue refunded; $5,610.58 in lost revenue for 1845–46; $1,194.45 cost of presidential elections; $1,014.48 in 1849–50 for some costs of the Constitutional Convention 1850–51; refund of $461.21 from money from estates having no heirs; and $35.00 refunded from sale of copies of revised statutes. Among the special funds included in annual reports of the treasurer, at time by differing names, are: Bank Tax, College or University, Common School, Congressional Township, Indi-

anapolis, Michigan Road, Saline, Surplus Revenue, Three Per Cent, and Wabash and Erie Canal fund.

122 During the period 1816–50, in listing expenditures the state treasurers have *no category indicating expenditures for education paid for from tax revenue.* Some such costs, probably meager in amount, are buried within other categories of expense. For instance, as early as fiscal 1821–22, $140 was paid the Committee on Education. Indiana *Senate Journal*, 1822–23, p. 33.

123 Esarey, *History of Indiana*, I, 492–494; *Laws of Indiana*, 1817–18, pp. 331–332; *ibid.* (revised), 1837–38, pp. 333–334; *ibid.* (general), 1839–40, pp. 71–72. Especially during the thirties and early forties unsuccessful efforts were made to obtain federal grants of land and state appropriations on behalf of the blind, deaf and dumb, and insane. For examples, see *Acts* (special), 1830–31, pp. 188–189; Indiana *House Journal*, 1836–37, p. 186; *ibid.*, 1837–38, p. 83; *Congressional Globe*, 25 Cong., 3 session, VII, 166; *ibid.*, 26 Cong., 1 session, VIII, 212; Indiana *Senate Journal*, 1841–42, p. 83; *ibid.*, 1842–43, p. 144. Benevolent costs for 1843–50 include: $43,809.79 for the education of the blind; $87,849.58 for the Deaf and Dumb Asylum; and $103,370.66 for the Indiana Hospital for the Insane, called the Lunatic Asylum in some of the reports of the treasurer.

124 Thornbrough, Riker, and Corpuz (eds.), *Diary of Calvin Fletcher*, I, 239. The Vincennes *Western Sun*, February 21, 1835, quoting the Indianapolis *Indiana Democrat*, which stated that Hays was totally consumed by a fire which he had set; and that an attempted rescue failed because the key to his door broke in the lock and the door had to be forced open.

125 Indiana *House Journal*, 1841–42, pp. 594–599. Quotes on pp. 595, 597, 598. According to the committee, Ohio's lunatic asylum had achieved cures for slightly more than 86 percent of those whose insanity had been of recent origin, and one third of those who had long been insane had been cured.

126 Dunn, *Indiana and Indianans*, II, 980–983, 987–1004; *Indiana Gazetteer* (1849), 136–149. Early in 1843 the General Assembly appropriated $200 for James McLean, a deaf and dumb person of Parke County, said to have taught "deaf and dumb orphans and indigent children of Indiana for fifteen months past" without adequate compensation. *Laws of Indiana* (local), 1842–43, p. 189. A comprehensive, factual, and scholarly study of the beginnings and early development of Indiana's benevolent and correctional institutions is much needed.

127 Indiana *House Journal*, 1850–51, p. 28.

128 *Ibid.*, 1839–40, pp. 833–834. At the ensuing session, 1840–41, both Rufus Haymond, prison visitor, and Governor David Wallace recommended that the state take over management of the prison. Indiana *Documentary Journal*, 1840–41, Pt. I, House Doc. 10, pp. 135–141; Indiana *House Journal*, 1840–41, pp. 14–15.

129 Indiana *House Journal*, 1840–41, pp. 276–280; *Laws of Indiana* (general), 1840–41, pp. 136–140.

130 Indiana *House Journal*, 1841–42, pp. 44–46. After this Wort suggested locating the prison on a fifteen to twenty acre site, affording space for suitable facilities, outside Jeffersonville.

131 *Ibid.*, 46–50. All quotes on p. 50.

132 *Ibid.*, 25–27; *Laws of Indiana* (general), 1841–42, p. 98.

133 Indiana *House Journal*, 1842–43, pp. 657–658, 761.

134 Concerning construction of the new prison, see annual report of Warden William Lee, 1846–47, in Indiana *Documentary Journal*, 1846–47, Pt. II, Doc. 4, p. 119. See *ibid.*, 119–138, for his complete report. Lee considered the new prison better than the old one, but he indicated that conditions were deplorable in the new prison. For comments by Dix, see Indianapolis *Indiana State Sentinel*, February 12, 1846, quoting Cincinnati *Gazette*.

135 Data concerning ordinary state revenue, 1843–50, are from annual reports of the state treasurer as cited in note 120 above. As the ensuing discussion explains, the major portion of the tax revenue was used for costs arising from the System of 1836 and the Wabash and Erie Canal rather than for ordinary state expenditures.

136 For the tax levies, see *Laws of Indiana* (general), 1842–43, pp. 74–76; *ibid.*, 1843–44, pp. 50, 120; *ibid.*, 1844–45, pp. 50–51; *ibid.*, 1845–46, p. 65; *ibid.*, 1846–47, pp. 47–48; *ibid.*, 1847–48, pp. 71–72; *ibid.*, 1848–49, p. 99; *ibid.*, 1849–50, pp. 153–154. For the most part taxes levied at the session of 1842–43 for collection during 1843 were received at the treasury during the fiscal year of 1843–44, and likewise for succeeding levies. Fiscal years normally ran from November 1 through October 31 of the ensuing year.

137 Concerning tax levies and their context, 1816–43, see Ch. 5, pp. 249–250.

138 For the reappraisements of real estate in 1845 and 1851, see *Laws of Indiana* (general), 1845–46, pp. 108–109; *ibid.*, 1850–51, pp. 11–19.

139 Indiana *Documentary Journal*, 1847–48, Pt. I, Doc. 2, pp. 89–91.

140 For Whitcomb's remarks, see Indiana *House Journal*, 1847–48, pp. 125–126; *ibid.*, 1848–49, pp. 19–20; and *ibid.*, 1849–50, pp. 18–19, for remarks by Governor Paris C. Dunning. For such comments by auditors, see Indiana *Documentary Journal*, 1844–45, Pt. I, Doc. 1, pp. 29–31; *ibid.*, 1845–46, Pt. I, Doc. 1, pp. 20–21, 42–47; *ibid.*, 1848–49, Pt. I, Doc. 4, pp. 188–195.

141 Indiana *Documentary Journal*, 1850–51, Pt. I, Doc. 1, pp. 57–58.

142 *Laws of Indiana* (general), 1850–51, pp. 11–19, 27–38; *ibid.* (revised), 1851–52, I, 273–276. As may be observed in Indiana *Documentary Journal*, 1850–51, Pt. I, Doc. 17, p. 296, the House Ways and Means Committee said assessors "scarcely ever executed" their duties with proper diligence, care, and impartiality. It declared that "A large amount of the invisible wealth of the State has for years entirely escaped taxation, thereby making the burdens of taxation rest the heavier upon the farming interest."

143 The state, having become bankrupt, began to pay part of the interest and principal of its debt for the Wabash and Erie Canal and System of 1836 from state tax revenue.

144 Indiana *Documentary Journal*, 1850–51, Pt. I, Doc. 17, p. 313. This source shows the sums paid on a yearly basis for these two items. Pages 306–323 afford much summary data about what the total bonded debt for the System of 1836

and the Wabash and Erie Canal had been; concerning such bonds as had been surrendered for new state stocks, per the Butler Bill of 1847; items about expenditures made on various debts, 1843–50; and related items.

145 See details regarding surrender of bonds, 1847–50, offered by the House Ways and Means Committee, *ibid.*, 306–309.

146 Indiana *House Journal*, 1842–43, pp. 443–447. Abel C. Pepper replaced George P. Buell, also a Democrat; William Daily and James P. Drake respectively replaced Robert Morrisson and William T. T. Jones, both Whigs. Thornbrough, Riker, and Corpuz (eds.), *Diary of Calvin Fletcher*, II, 470, 470n; Thornbrough (ed.), *Messages and Papers of Samuel Bigger*, 526, 526n.

147 Goshen *Democrat*, August 31, 1843; Vincennes *Western Sun*, October 7, 1843.

148 Indianapolis *Indiana State Sentinel*, October 17, 1843, quoting both the Greencastle *Patriot* and the Madison *Courier*.

149 Indianapolis *Indiana State Sentinel*, August 22, October 3, 1843.

150 *Ibid.*, October 17, 1843, quoting New Albany *Democrat*; *ibid.*, October 24, 1843, quoting *Grant County Herald* [Marion *Democratic Herald*]; *ibid.*, November 14, 1843, quoting Goshen *Democrat*. Issues of the *Sentinel* from August through November, 1843, have *passim* additional items about whether a Whig or Democrat should succeed Merrill.

151 For instance, see Indianapolis *Indiana State Sentinel*, September 19, 26, November 14, 28, 1843; Vincennes *Western Sun*, September 16, 1843. Former Governor James Brown Ray ruefully observed that he had held "no office" since his tenure as governor, and he asked the people to suggest to their legislators "the expediency" of his election "in the place of Samuel Merrill." Indianapolis *Indiana State Sentinel*, September 26, 1843; Vincennes *Western Sun*, October 7, 1843.

152 Thornbrough, Riker, and Corpuz (eds.), *Diary of Calvin Fletcher*, II, 523. Fletcher indicates that Merrill was then at odds with him and some other members of the branch bank board at Indianapolis.

153 Indiana *House Journal*, 1843–44, pp. 345–349; Indiana *Senate Journal*, 1843–44, pp. 246–252. No vote is recorded for Ray, but some of the scattered vote may have been for him. As may be noted in Thornbrough, Riker, and Corpuz (eds.), *Diary of Calvin Fletcher*, III, 5n, Merrill wrote his brother that he had received about ten Democratic votes, but had lost that of five or six Whigs. He said twice as many Democrats "had promised" to support him, but he had never been "sanguine" of the outcome.

154 Indiana *House Journal*, 1848–49, pp. 46–47; Indiana *Senate Journal*, 1848–49, pp. 43–44; Indianapolis *Indiana State Journal*, December 18, 1848. As shown in Riker and Thornbrough (eds.), *Indiana Election Returns, 1816–1851*, p. 53, Mace was a Democratic presidential elector in 1848. According to *Biographical Directory of the Indiana General Assembly*, I, 257, Mace was successively Whig, Democrat, Fusion, and Republican. The legislative journals show that Morrison received 53 votes to 47 for Mace in the House; and 34 votes to 14 for Mace, with one ballot blank, in the Senate.

155 Dumont was elected on the first ballot, obtaining 94 votes to 3 for Morrison, with 2 blank votes and 1 for Henry Swyhart in the House; and 35 to 12 for Morrison in the Senate. Indiana *House Journal*, 1853, pp. 106–107; Indiana *Senate Journal*, 1853, pp. 90–92. For the earlier and later comments about Morrison by Fletcher, see Thornbrough, Riker, and Corpuz (eds.), *Diary of Calvin Fletcher*, III, 5–6; *ibid.*, V, 179–180. Fletcher, commenting about Morrison, wrote: "An old professional rival in the law who was a violent opponent one sided & bitter[.] But as a president of the Bank has been extraordinary in fair decision."

156 Convincing information about political ties of members of the branch and state bank boards of the Second State Bank has not been found. But it seems certain that especially prior to 1843, they were overwhelmingly Whigs. Thereafter, even though Democrats gained additional representation, most likely board members remained principally Whigs. The author's *impression* is that the bank was mainly operated by merchants and other businessmen who acted more as businessmen than as politicians.

157 Indiana *Documentary Journal*, 1843–44, House Doc. 5, pp. 277–279, 280.

158 *Ibid.*, 283–285. These data are from part of the annual report prepared by Cashier James M. Ray about the status of the bank as of November 18, 1843. The demise of the Second Bank of the United States in the late thirties had left a void which perhaps enhanced the status of the Second State Bank.

159 The annual reports of the president, 1843–50, include a section about the bank's resources and liabilities prepared by Cashier Ray. The data about capital, suspended debt, and specie are taken from these sections as found in Indiana *Documentary Journal*, 1844–45, Pt. I, Doc. 7, pp. 116–117; *ibid.*, 1845–46, Pt. I, Doc. 6, pp. 114–115; *ibid.*, 1846–47, Pt. I, Doc. 7, pp. 130–131; *ibid.*, 1847–48, Pt. I, Doc. 5, pp. 165–166; *ibid.*, 1848–49, Pt. I, Doc. 7, pp. 268–269; *ibid.*, 1849–50, Pt. I, Doc. 5, pp. 121–122; *ibid.*, 1850–51, Pt. I, Doc. 15, pp. 277–278. These sources indicate the capital, suspended debt, and specie as of November each year. See Chapter 5, p. 265, for an amendment to the charter in 1837 allowing note circulation to be an average of two and one half times its paid in capital but never more than three times same.

160 For sections of the bank reports giving annual profits as of November, see *ibid.*, 1844–45, Pt. I, Doc. 7, p. 115; *ibid.*, 1845–46, Pt. I, Doc. 6, p. 112; *ibid.*, 1846–47, Pt. I, Doc. 7, p. 128; *ibid.*, 1847–48, Pt. I, Doc. 5, p. 162; *ibid.*, 1848–49, Pt. I, Doc. 7, pp. 266–267; *ibid.*, 1849–50, Pt. I, Doc. 5, p. 119; *ibid.*, 1850–51, Pt. I, Doc. 15, p. 275. Since some revenue was used to build up a surplus fund, the actual profits were somewhat larger than stated in these reports. Concerning reinstatement of the Lawrenceburg branch on February 26, 1844, see *ibid.*, 1844–45, Pt. I, Doc. 7, p. 111. This source also reports the South Bend branch as "gradually emerging from its late crippled condition," and "now only subject" to restrictions common to all branches. Creation of three new branches is discussed in Chapter 5, pp. 264–265.

161 Thornbrough, Riker, and Corpuz (eds.), *Diary of Calvin Fletcher*, III, 142, 205; *ibid.*, IV, 147; Indianapolis *Indiana State Journal*, January 7, 21, 1846. Ac-

cording to the *Journal* on November 15, 1845, the specie reserve in gold and silver totaled $1,079,368.26.

162 *Journal of the Convention of the People of the State of Indiana to Amend the Constitution* (Indianapolis, 1851, reprinted 1936), 99–101. Ray estimated that for the six remaining years of the charter an additional $390,000 would be earned for the Common School Fund, bringing its aggregate to $1,390,000—the sum the state had borrowed in bonds to help establish the Second State Bank.

163 Indiana *Senate Journal*, 1847–48, pp. 320, 639 (veto); Indiana *House Journal*, 1847–48, pp. 406–407, 469.

164 Indiana *Senate Journal*, 1848–49, pp. 45–46, 52, 57–58; Indiana *House Journal*, 1848–49, pp. 83–84, 104, 312–314, 326–328, 367. The House amended the bill to require that new branches would have to be established before the end of 1851, then approved the bill with 38 Whigs and 20 Democrats for passage; 1 Whig and 38 Democrats opposed. The Senate concurred with this amendment.

165 Indiana *Documentary Journal*, 1849–50, Pt. I, Doc. 5, p. 120. In his annual report about the bank, dated December 8, 1849, President Morrison said the state bank board had assented to four new branches, and had "urged the assent of the Branches" but some of them had not yet assented.

166 *Laws of Indiana*, 1833–34, p. 17. Moreover, an act of 1832 had prohibited the use of bank notes from any territory or other state in units of less than $5 in payment of debts due. What impact this enactment had is uncertain. *Ibid.*, 1831–32, pp. 269–270.

167 Indianapolis *Indiana Journal*, December 21, 1839; Indianapolis *Indiana Democrat*, December 13, 1839.

168 Indiana *House Journal*, 1840–41, p. 24. At this session the Whigs had their peak membership in the legislature, having 33 senators to 14 for the Democrats; and 77 representatives versus 23 for the Democrats, with one seat changing from Whig to Democrat during the session.

169 *Laws of Indiana* (general), 1840–41, pp. 202–204 (issue of small notes by state bank), 120–121 (other issue of small notes prohibited). This legislation was closely associated with an effort to gain revenue for payment of interest on the bonded debt for internal improvements by increasing state stock in the Second State Bank. In short, the Sinking Fund for liquidation of the bonded debt for the bank—apart from miscellaneous costs and payment of interest on the bonded debt for the bank—would be used for this purpose. And the money so diverted, plus interest at 6 percent, would be a debt to the Sinking Fund for ultimate liquidation of the bonded debt for the bank, with any surplus earmarked for the support of common schools. Related items sought to gain additional revenue from levies on both state and private bank capital. A careful reading of sections 113 and 114 of the bank charter seems to indicate that this proposed diversion of revenue from the Sinking Fund was contrary to the charter. *Ibid.*, 1833–34, pp. 35–36.

170 The bill authorizing small notes passed the House 64 to 26; the Senate 27 to 16. The item about issuance of small notes, and their taxation at 1 percent of

their amount, however, was expressly subject to its approval by the state and branch bank boards as an amendment to the charter. Indiana *House Journal*, 1840–41, pp. 190, 448–451; Indiana *Senate Journal*, 1840–41, pp. 426, 430–431. For passage of the bill prohibiting small notes, except by the state bank, see Indiana *House Journal*, 1840–41, pp. 215–216; Indiana *Senate Journal*, 1840–41, pp. 304–305.

171 Thornbrough, Riker, and Corpuz (eds.), *Diary of Calvin Fletcher*, II, 281. Fletcher explains that members of the state bank board "seem to complain of want of firmness on [the part of] the President [Merrill] & will refuse to accept the small bill law. That is the privilege to issue 1 million in 3 years at 1 per cent bonus & at the same time with a privilege to tax (additionally) the old bank stock & state stock. This the board seem to think has been countenanced by the President too much."

172 *Laws of Indiana* (general), 1840–41, pp. 192–196. This law, however, provided that in addition to revenue from the Sinking Fund for liquidation of the bonded debt for establishing the bank, that the Surplus Revenue, (Indiana) College, Saline, and State Bank School funds also be converted into money for state stock in the bank, with cooperation of the bank in their management. The Indianapolis *Indiana Journal*, January 17, 1842, explains that concessions had been made by the legislature after the bank refused to issue notes according to the previous law.

173 Indiana *Documentary Journal*, 1841–42, House Doc. 9, pp. 112–113; Indianapolis *Indiana Journal*, April 24, 1841. According to the Indianapolis *Indiana Journal*, January 17, 1842, the state and branch bank boards had quickly accepted the new legislation about small notes as an amendment to the bank's charter. For comments for and against the issuing of small notes, see Thornbrough (ed.), *Messages and Papers of Samuel Bigger*, 158, 193–195, 198, 209–210, 224. As indicated *ibid.*, 198, 209–210, Representative Samuel Judah estimated that the state treasury would have obtained at least $80,000 in revenue had the 1 percent tax on their issue prevailed, but this item was among those not adopted "in consequence of the opposition of the Bank men."

174 *Laws of Indiana* (general), 1841–42, pp. 85–86. This law, however, allowed counties which had decided to convert part of their portion of the federal surplus revenue into bank stock to do so. The bill prohibiting conversion of the special funds into bank stock passed the House with 48 Democrats and 2 Whigs for and 2 Democrats and 42 Whigs against passage. The Senate passed the bill without a roll call vote, but 21 Democrats and 12 Whigs voted for its engrossment to third reading, with 1 Democrat and 14 Whigs against engrossment. Indiana *House Journal*, 1841–42, pp. 362, 366; Indiana *Senate Journal*, 1841–42, pp. 456–458, 471–472, 484. Concerning the bitter fights between Democrats and Whigs over this legislation, see Thornbrough (ed.), *Messages and Papers of Samuel Bigger*, 396–398n, for comments of Senator Ebenezer M. Chamberlain; and Indianapolis *Indiana State Sentinel*, January 17, 1842; Indianapolis *Indiana Journal*, January 17, 1842.

[175] Indiana *Documentary Journal*, 1844–45, Pt. I, Doc. 7, p. 112. The Senate approved extension of the privilege of issuing small notes by the narrow margin of 25 to 23, with 18 Whigs and 7 Democrats for, and 7 Whigs and 16 Democrats against passage. In amended form it passed the House 44 to 24, with 44 Whigs and no Democrats for, and 2 Whigs and 22 Democrats against passage. Indiana *Senate Journal*, 1844–45, pp. 224–225, 317–318, 649–651; Indiana *House Journal*, 1844–45, pp. 571–572, 577–578, 593–594. Each party had 25 senators, and the House had 54 Whigs and 45 Democrats.

[176] Indiana *Documentary Journal*, 1845–46, Pt. I, Doc. 6, p. 110. Morrison's interpretation may have been influenced by the shift in control of the General Assembly which gave the Democrats 56 representatives to 44 for the Whigs, with each party having 25 senators.

[177] Indianapolis *Indiana State Sentinel*, December 18, 1845, January 8, 1846 (quoting Goshen *Democrat*). The Delphi *Oracle*, as quoted *ibid.*, January 1, 1846, warned that "the more favors banks receive at the hands of the people the more they swindle them in return."

[178] Indianapolis *Indiana State Sentinel*, January 8, 1846; Indianapolis *Indiana State Journal*, January 21, 1846, quoting New Albany *Democrat*. See *Indiana State Sentinel*, January 1, 8, 15, 1846, for further criticism of Democratic papers against the continuing issue of small notes.

[179] In the House a bill authorizing continued issue of small notes was defeated 57 to 29; 14 Whigs and 15 Democrats voting for, and 26 Whigs and 31 Democrats opposing passage. Indiana *House Journal*, 1845–46, pp. 484–485. Political ties given are as indicated in *Biographical Directory of the Indiana General Assembly*, I, 491–492. Perhaps a number of legislators, particularly Whigs, opposed passage on the ground that such power already existed. As of November 16, 1850, the Second State Bank had an aggregate of $3,548,267.50 of notes in circulation, including $643,535.50 in units of less than $5 but not less than $1. Indiana *Documentary Journal*, 1850–51, Pt. I, Doc. 15, pp. 277–278.

[180] Vincennes *Western Sun*, June 5, 1819; Indiana *House Journal*, 1821–22, p. 238.

[181] Vincennes *Western Sun*, June 24, July 1, 8, 18, 22 (Fourth of July toast), 29, November 4 (quote from "Corn Planter"), 1820.

[182] Indianapolis *Indiana State Sentinel*, April 5, 1842, February 26, 1846.

[183] Fort Wayne *Sentinel*, May 10, 1845. Late in 1843 Calvin Fletcher commented that the election of a president of the Second State Bank to succeed Merrill may have been delayed in part "by Democrats who want no bank at all . . . ." Thornbrough, Riker, and Corpuz (eds.), *Diary of Calvin Fletcher*, II, 563–564.

[184] Indianapolis *Indiana Democrat*, November 21, 1838. This paper, edited by John Livingston, suggested that free banking could be regulated by legislation like that which had been adopted in New York State, or otherwise as the legislature decided. While insisting that the General Assembly had such power, Livingston explicitly declined to say whether he favored or opposed such legislation.

185 Indiana *House Journal*, 1838–39, p. 67. The resolution also appears in the Indianapolis *Indiana Democrat*, December 15, 1838.

186 Indiana *House Journal*, 1838–39, pp. 55 (committee members), 181–185 (committee report). The committee included 16 Whigs and 5 Democrats according to *Biographical Directory of the Indiana General Assembly*, I, 472–474. Although Judah says the committee had directed him to report what followed, the report was probably at least largely his views, and almost certainly not those of most of the committee. Under date of December 14, 1836, Judah had advised Governor Noah Noble that "the present [banking] system is not sufficient for the wants of the State" and "the Scotch System with Insurance powers—must take, and I do most sincerely hope it may." Dorothy Riker and Gayle Thornbrough (eds.), *Messages and Papers Relating to the Administration of Noah Noble, Governor of Indiana, 1831–1837* (Indianapolis, 1958), 502. Earlier that year the Vincennes *Western Sun*, March 19, 1836, published in Knox County which Judah represented in the House, had an item giving information about the Safety Fund Banks of New York State. For Noble, Hanna, and Parke as members of the Corydon Constitutional Convention of 1816, see Kettleborough, *Constitution Making in Indiana*, I, 124–125; and *Biographical Directory of the Indiana General Assembly*, I, 472–473, for Hanna as a member of the House for the session of 1838–39.

187 Indianapolis *Indiana Democrat*, February 20, 1839. As shown in Indiana *House Journal*, 1838–39, pp. 501–502, the House postponed the free banking bill by a count of 58 to 34. Voting for postponement were 40 Whigs and 18 Democrats, while 12 Whigs and 22 Democrats opposed. Of the 16 Whigs on the judiciary committee, 11 voted for and 4 voted against postponement, with 1 not voting. Of the 5 Democrats, 3 voted for postponement, 1 opposed postponement, and 1 did not vote. Judah voted against postponement, as did Owen though the latter was not on the committee. Owen, the judiciary committee, and the *Indiana Democrat* all make note of the New York Safety Fund Banks and the earlier "Scotch" system as part of the background and context for the development of free banking. The seeming cooperation between Owen and Judah is interesting and worthy of note. Fritz Redlich, *The Molding of American Banking: Men and Ideas* (New York, 1951), 5, 65–66, 187, 188, 197, 198, and *passim*, suggests that the concept of free banking was imbedded in the Scotch banking system.

188 Indianapolis *Indiana Democrat*, September 18, 1839; Indiana *House Journal*, 1840–41, p. 24; Thornbrough, Riker, and Corpuz (eds.), *Diary of Calvin Fletcher*, II, 444.

189 For this mandate, see Kettleborough, *Constitution Making in Indiana*, I, 355–358, and 411–412, for explanation of it by a committee chaired by Robert Dale Owen.

190 See note 1 for political division of both parties for the sessions of 1843–44 through 1845–46.

191 Richmond *Palladium*, September 24, 1845, quoting Lafayette *Tippecanoe Journal*; Indianapolis *Indiana State Journal*, October 29, 1845. All of these men

had had legislative experience, considerable in most instances. See sketches of them in *Biographical Directory of the Indiana General Assembly*, Volume 1.

192 Smith's statement, October 29, 1845, is in Indianapolis *Indiana State Journal*, November 5, 1845. Smith said: "in no event can I consent to the use of my name in connection with" the office of governor.

193 J. Herman Schauinger (ed.), "The Letters of Godlove S. Orth, Hoosier Whig," *Indiana Magazine of History*, XXXIX (1943), 368, 370, 371, 374, 376.

194 Indianapolis *Indiana State Journal*, January 7, 14, 1846. Thompson apparently anticipated the nomination of Marshall. Shortly before the convention met, Orth wrote Schuyler Colfax: "if Marshall refuses to lend his name to the Convention . . . I will undoubtedly be nominated." Orth had written Colfax that if nominated for governor his running mate "must reside on, or near the Ohio river, in the vicinity of the Pocket—." Schauinger (ed.), "Letters of Godlove S. Orth," *Indiana Magazine of History*, XXXIX, 376, 373. G. Burton Thompson, of Perry County, may have been the person Orth had in mind as his proposed running mate if he became the nominee for governor.

195 Indianapolis *Indiana State Journal*, August 20, 1845, quoting Lawrenceburg *Beacon*. The Whig editor asserted that Major J. P. Dunn, of the Lawrenceburg *Beacon*, was one of the most active and talented leaders of the "Young Democracy" of the state. See *ibid.*, November 12, October 1, 1845, concerning the charge about an understanding that Bright would become the nominee for governor.

196 For examples of views of county conventions regarding the Democratic nominee for governor, see Indianapolis *Indiana State Sentinel*, November 27, December 4, 18, 25, 1845. Regarding Bright's election to the United States Senate, see Chapter 11, pp. 608–609. Shortly before the Democratic convention met, Orth—at Indianapolis on behalf of his nomination for governor by the Whigs—wrote Colfax that despite intrigues against Whitcomb he would become his party's nominee for governor unless he withdrew his name. Schauinger (ed.), "Letters of Godlove S. Orth," *Indiana Magazine of History*, XXXIX, 377.

197 Unless otherwise indicated, items about the Democratic State Convention are based on its proceedings as in Indianapolis *Indiana State Sentinel*, January 15, 1846. In listing delegates by counties, there is no listing for Marion County. The call and date for the convention, made by the party's central committee, is *ibid.*, October 2, 23, 1845. The convention named a new state committee.

198 Unless otherwise indicated, items about the Whig State Convention are based on its proceedings as in Indianapolis *Indiana State Journal*, January 14, 1846. After indicating uncertainty whether the Whig State Central Committee, which had acted for the presidential campaign of 1844, considered itself empowered to call a state convention to nominate candidates for governor and lieutenant governor, the *Indiana State Journal* proposed January 9, 1846, at the capital as the time and place for the convention, subject to the concurrence of Whig editors. After considering their response favorable, the suggested date and place were confirmed. See *ibid.*, October 8, 15, 22, 1845. The editor asserted that a

state central committee had been named by Whig legislators at the session of 1844–45, but explained that their names had not been published. The party's state convention named a new Whig State Central Committee.

[199] Indianapolis *Indiana State Sentinel*, January 15, 1846; Indianapolis *Indiana State Journal*, January 21, 1846; Esarey, *History of Indiana*, I, 539. The *Journal*, January 28, 1846, quotes various Whig papers endorsing the Whig ticket, usually with enthusiasm.

[200] Schauinger (ed.), "Letters of Godlove S. Orth," *Indiana Magazine of History*, XXXIX, 379. As indicated on p. 306 and note 99, this chapter, the Butler Bill of 1846 received strong bipartisan approval, but a higher proportion of Whigs than Democrats voted for its approval. To Colfax, Orth suggested: "Whig papers had better not laud the measure too highly." But, Orth added, as "the law of the land" with "a majority of the votes" in its favor from Whigs, Whigs dare not oppose the bill. In a wistful vein Orth commented: "If nothing had been done this winter [by the legislature about a debt settlement], what an awful reckoning had there been against Whitcomb." Such views perhaps explain why Orth withdrew as a candidate for governor.

[201] Indianapolis *Indiana State Journal*, January 21, 1846. As indicated in *Biographical Directory of the Indiana General Assembly*, I, 262, Marshall had not been in the legislature when the system was adopted, nor when the Butler Bill had been adopted.

[202] Indianapolis *Indiana State Journal*, January 14, April 8, 29, July 1, 1846. The *Journal* granted that Whitcomb had favored passage of the Butler Bill in the caucus of the Democrats, and in the lobby of the House, but stated that "*evidence of such favor cannot be found on paper.*" *Ibid.*, April 8, 1846.

[203] *Ibid.*, May 20, 1846. When various salaries were reduced at the initial legislative session under Whitcomb, the salary of the governor was reduced from $1,500 to $1,300, effective for the ensuing term because the Constitution of 1816 prohibited any change in such salary during the term for which a governor had been elected. The *Journal* claimed that Whitcomb had pledged to waive his constitutional right and take only the reduced salary, but had taken the $1,500 salary for his initial year.

[204] *Ibid.*, February 18, 1846, quoting Bloomington *Herald*.

[205] Indianapolis *Indiana State Sentinel*, January 29, 1846; Indianapolis *Indiana State Journal*, April 8, 1846, quoting Greencastle *Patriot*.

[206] Indianapolis *Indiana State Journal*, May 13, 1846, quoting Indianapolis *Indiana State Sentinel*, quoting LaGrange *Democrat*, April 29, 1846. The latter paper also charged that Marshall had inappropriately suddenly gained property worth $12,500 while serving as an attorney for Edward Beckwith, said to have defrauded the state concerning construction of the Madison and Indianapolis Railroad. See *Indiana State Journal*, June 17, 1846, for Marshall's vigorous and lengthy refutation of the charges against him.

[207] For instance, see Indianapolis *Indiana State Journal*, February 11, April 29, July 1, 1846.

208 *Ibid.*, June 10, 1846. Also see issues for June 3 and 17, 1846.

209 *Ibid.*, February 11, July 1, 1846. Concerning appointments to the Supreme Court, see pp. 342–345, this chapter.

210 For instance, see *ibid.*, January 21, March 25, July 1, 1846.

211 *Ibid.*, July 1, 22, 1846. According to Calvin Fletcher, State Agent Michael G. Bright paid himself, James Morrison, and Governor Whitcomb $500 each regarding the state suit against Dr. Isaac Coe, accused of malversations as a fund commissioner to borrow money for internal improvements. Thornbrough, Riker, and Corpuz (eds.), *Diary of Calvin Fletcher*, III, 365–366. Marshall and Fletcher served as attorneys for Coe in this case. *Ibid.*, 87–88, 228, 319.

212 Indianapolis *Indiana State Sentinel*, January 29, 1846.

213 *Ibid.*, July 3, 1845, quoting Brookville *Franklin Democrat*. For biographical data about Stevens and his devotion to the abolition of slavery, see Woollen, *Biographical and Historical Sketches of Early Indiana*, 353–359; *Biographical Directory of the Indiana General Assembly*, I, 371–372. For data about Harding, see French, "Stephen S. Harding: A Hoosier Abolitionist," *Indiana Magazine of History*, XXVII, 207–229. When, where, and by whom Stevens and Harding were nominated is not apparent.

214 Schauinger (ed.), "Letters of Godlove S. Orth," *Indiana Magazine of History*, XXXIX, 379; Indianapolis *Indiana State Journal*, February 11, July 15, 1846.

215 Indianapolis *Indiana State Journal*, March 18, April 22, 1846.

216 *Ibid.*, April 15, 1846. In its issue of April 29, the editor reported his understanding that Whitcomb and Marshall had spent several days preparing for an early commencement of their campaigns.

217 *Ibid.*, May 13, 1846. The Indianapolis *Indiana State Sentinel*, February 26, 1846, asserted some "whig papers, the Evansville Courier, for example, speak of Mr. Orth as a *repudiator*." It is possible that Orth anticipated probable defeat for election as lieutenant governor, hence chose to seek reelection to his seat in the Senate, which he won. *Biographical Directory of the Indiana General Assembly*, I, 300.

218 Indianapolis *Indiana State Journal*, June 3, 1846; *Biographical Directory of the Indiana General Assembly*, I, 372. Stevenson, a prominent farmer, had served in both houses of the legislature, and he had been speaker of the House. Like Marshall he had not been in the General Assembly when the System of 1836 had been adopted, nor when the Butler Bill of 1846 was approved.

219 Indianapolis *Indiana State Journal*, June 10, 17, July 1, 8, 1846. If Marshall made all the speeches scheduled for him, from July 8 through August 3, he made twenty-four speeches in twenty-one counties, usually at county seats, normally riding horseback roughly fifteen to twenty miles per day. His speeches were scheduled mainly for central and east-central Indiana, and on the lower line of the Wabash and Erie Canal to Evansville. No speeches, however, were scheduled on Sundays. *Ibid.*, July 8, 15, 22, 1846; Woollen, *Biographical and Historical Sketches of Early Indiana*, 443.

220 Thornbrough, Riker, and Corpuz (eds.), *Diary of Calvin Fletcher*, III, 283, 245.

221 Indianapolis *Indiana State Journal*, September 16, 1846.

222 Riker and Thornbrough (comps.), *Indiana Election Returns, 1816–1851*, pp. 150–155. This source gives complete and official returns for 1846; the same for 1843, except that returns for Daviess County are unofficial. In 1846 Grant, Hamilton, Henry, Randolph, and Wayne counties gave 1,059 votes for Stevens. In these counties Marshall perhaps attracted some votes which would otherwise have gone for Stevens. For the total vote, Whitcomb won 50.65 percent of the vote; Marshall, 47.52 percent; and Stevens, 1.82 percent.

223 As noted in Indianapolis *Indiana State Sentinel*, September 3, 1846, quoting the Goshen *Democrat*, about a dozen counties which favored Whitcomb over Marshall elected Whigs over Democrats to the legislature.

224 Indiana *House Journal*, 1846–47, pp. 86–87. Hanna won on the third ballot, obtaining 76 votes to 72 for Mayhew; Maguire won on the second ballot, securing 75 votes to 71 for Harris, 1 for G. P. R. Wilson, and 1 blank vote. For a sketch of Hanna, see *Biographical Directory of the Indiana General Assembly*, I, 164–165. Concerning Maguire, see John H. B. Nowland, *Sketches of Prominent Citizens of 1876* (Indianapolis, 1877), 100, 103; Miller, *Indiana Newspaper Bibliography*, 273–274, 289.

225 Indianapolis *Indiana State Journal*, December 22, 29, 1846; Schauinger (ed.), "Letters of Godlove S. Orth," *Indiana Magazine of History*, XXXIX, 382–383. Orth had unsuccessfully supported Schuyler Colfax for auditor. *Ibid.*, 380–383.

226 Indiana *House Journal*, 1844–45, pp. 317–319, 325–326; Indianapolis *Indiana State Journal*, January 8, 1845; Indianapolis *Indiana State Sentinel*, January 9, 1845.

227 The legislative session of 1844–45 required each county assessor to "make a complete list of the resident white male inhabitants above the age of twenty one years" within his county as of March 1, 1845, then forward a certificate reporting the number of voters in each township and the total for the county to the state auditor by June 1. *Laws of Indiana* (general), 1844–45, pp. 25–26. See Indiana *Documentary Journal*, 1845–46, Pt. II, Doc. 1, pp. 5–7, for voters per county as reported by the assessor. For the enumeration of 1840 and the legislative reapportionment of 1841, see Chapter 5, pp. 267–270.

228 Indianapolis *Indiana State Sentinel*, January 23, 1845; Indiana *House Journal*, 1845–46, pp. 22–23.

229 Indianapolis *Indiana State Journal*, December 3, 1845. A Whig editor at Rushville said a reduction in number would cause business to be done "more expeditiously," less expensively, and help secure the election of better men. *Ibid.* Representative Joel Vandeveer, a Democrat from Orange County, sought a reduction to a maximum of 30 senators and 60 representatives; Senator Hugh Hamer, a Whig from Lawrence County, sought a reduction of the number of senators to not less than 30 or more than 40; that of representatives to not less than 60 or more than 80. Indiana *House Journal*, 1845–46, p. 31; Indiana *Senate Journal*, 1845–46, p. 215.

230 Indiana *House Journal*, 1845–46, pp. 31, 41 (committee members), 422 (House passage); Indiana *Senate Journal*, 1845–46, p. 362.

231 Unless otherwise indicated items about the reapportionment of 1846 are based on the law in *Laws of Indiana* (general), 1845–46, pp. 25–27; Leon H. Wallace, "Legislative Apportionment in Indiana: A Case History," *Indiana Law Journal*, XLII (1966), 19. Thirty-three of the 90 organized counties in the apportionment of 1846 were in Southern Indiana. The 16 eastern counties of Southern Indiana were: Bartholomew, Brown, Clark, Dearborn, Decatur, Floyd, Franklin, Harrison, Jackson, Jefferson, Jennings, Ohio, Ripley, Scott, Switzerland, and Washington; its 17 western counties were: Crawford, Daviess, Dubois, Gibson, Greene, Knox, Lawrence, Martin, Monroe, Orange, Perry, Pike, Posey, Spencer, Sullivan, Vanderburgh, and Warrick. The 18 eastern counties of Central Indiana were: Blackford, Delaware, Fayette, Grant, Hamilton, Hancock, Henry, Jay, Johnson, Madison, Marion, Randolph, Richardville (Howard), Rush, Shelby, Tipton, Union, and Wayne; its 14 western counties were: Boone, Clay, Clinton, Fountain, Hendricks, Montgomery, Morgan, Owen, Parke, Putnam, Tippecanoe, Vermillion, Vigo, and Warren. The 13 eastern counties of Northern Indiana were: Adams, Allen, DeKalb, Elkhart, Huntington, Kosciusko, LaGrange, Miami, Noble, Steuben, Wabash, Wells, and Whitley; its 12 western counties were: Benton, Carroll, Cass, Fulton, Jasper, Lake, La Porte, Marshall, Porter, Pulaski, St. Joseph, and White. Howard, Ohio, and Tipton counties had not been in the apportionment of 1836. As the ensuing note explains, Starke and Newton had not yet become organized counties.

232 Although there are 91 counties listed in the legislative apportionment of 1846, Starke was then a *paper* or unorganized county. As noted in George Pence and Nellie C. Armstrong, *Indiana Boundaries: Territory, State, and County* (Indianapolis, 1933), 64–66, 746–749, Starke remained a paper county until 1850 when it became an organized county. As indicated *ibid.*, 620–625, Newton, organized in 1860, became the last of the ninety-two organized counties.

233 Wallace, "Legislative Apportionment in Indiana," *Indiana Law Journal*, XLII, 15–16, 19. See *ibid.*, Appendix E–1, E–2, E–3, for many examples of inequalities in both senatorial and representative districts. For maps showing districts, see Justin E. Walsh, *The Centennial History of the Indiana General Assembly, 1816–1978* (Indianapolis, 1987), 730, 749–750. Neither Wallace nor Walsh explain that Starke was a *paper* rather than an *unorganized* county. This distinction also is not made in Riker and Thornbrough (comps.), *Indiana Election Returns, 1816–1851*, pp. 406–407.

234 As indicated in *Laws of Indiana* (general), 1845–46, pp. 25–26, the apportionment of senatorial districts includes much the same counties as for that of 1841. *Ibid.*, 1840–41, pp. 48–50. Moreover, the 1846 apportionment provides that the counties of Miami and Wabash, combined for a senatorial district, shall not elect a senator until 1847. In like manner LaGrange and Elkhart counties comprised a senatorial district, but could not elect a senator until 1847. Meanwhile, these four counties were attached to other senatorial districts until then.

Wallace, "Legislative Apportionment in Indiana," *Indiana Law Journal*, XLII, 18–20, 25–31, indicates that the complications arising from floats and the formation of senatorial districts had much influence on the provisions of the Constitution of 1851 concerning how legislative districts should be established.

235 Concerning the revision of 1852, see Kettleborough, *Constitution Making in Indiana*, I, 344–345; *Laws of Indiana* (revised), 1851–52, Volumes I and II.

236 As may be observed in *Laws of Indiana* (revised), 1851–52, I, 260–273, the election code of 1852 is much like that of 1843.

237 *Ibid.* (general), 1842–43, pp. 82–83; *ibid.*, 1843–44, pp. 51, 46, 52–53; *ibid.*, 1849–50, pp. 71–72, 74–76; *ibid.*, 1850–51, pp. 85–86, 90–91.

238 Kettleborough, *Constitution Making in Indiana*, I, 107; *Laws of Indiana* (general), 1841–42, p. 157; *ibid.*, 1842–43, pp. 97, 104, 109; *ibid.*, 1843–44, pp. 71, 72. These laws applied to the counties of Adams, Cass, DeKalb, Franklin, Hamilton, Jay, Lake, La Porte, Porter, St. Joseph, Shelby, Steuben, Tippecanoe, and Union. As noted *ibid.*, 1843–44, p. 71, such legislation for Lake was soon repealed.

239 *Laws of Indiana* (general), 1844–45, pp. 7–8; Indianapolis *Indiana State Sentinel*, February 6, 1845; Thornbrough, Riker, and Corpuz (eds.), *Diary of Calvin Fletcher*, III, 171.

240 Indiana *House Journal*, 1845–46, p. 160; *Laws of Indiana* (general), 1849–50, pp. 72–73, 75; *ibid.*, 1850–51, p. 87; Kettleborough, *Constitution Making in Indiana*, I, 304.

241 *Laws of Indiana* (local), 1836–37, p. 434; *ibid.*, 1840–41, p. 218; *ibid.*, 1841–42, p. 186. As indicated in Riker and Thornbrough (comps.), *Indiana Election Returns, 1816–1851*, pp. 4, 10, 14, 21, 29, 38, 53, from 1824 through 1848 Indiana voters elected their presidential electors within the period November 2–8; and always on an at large basis. But as noted *ibid.*, 3, the General Assembly named Indiana's presidential electors in 1816 and 1820.

242 U.S. *Statutes at Large*, 28 Cong., 2 session, V, 721; *Laws of Indiana* (general), 1847–48, pp. 29–30.

243 Governor Ray had made the first major shakeup in 1831.

244 Thornbrough, Riker, and Corpuz (eds.), *Diary of Calvin Fletcher*, III, 105, 105n. As indicated in *Biographical Directory of the Indiana General Assembly*, I, 27, 100, 378–379, Blackford was a Democrat, while Dewey and Sullivan were Whigs. Blackford, however, had been a Whig.

245 Indiana *Senate Journal*, 1844–45, pp. 544–546. According to party ties given in *Biographical Directory of the Indiana General Assembly*, I, 44, 62, 336–337, 488, three experienced Democratic senators—George P. Buell, Sr., Joseph W. Chapman, and William Rockhill—joined with 25 Whigs against confirmation of Wick and Morrison.

246 Indiana *Senate Journal*, 1844–45, pp. 582–583, 633–635. In these votes no Whig voted for confirmation, joined by a varying number of Democrats. According to *Biographical Directory of the Indiana General Assembly*, I, 60, 386, Chamberlain was a Democrat, while Test was a Whig in 1840 and a Democrat in 1848.

247 Indiana *Senate Journal*, 1844–45, pp. 700–703. On the final voting 19 Democrats voted for confirmation of Wick and Chamberlain.

248 Indianapolis *Indiana State Journal*, January 15, 1845; Indianapolis *Indiana State Sentinel*, January 23, 1845. In its issue for February 6, 1845, the *Sentinel* stated that Blackford was the only Democrat who had ever been named to the Supreme Court, and that Governor Wallace had reappointed him because he did not dare to incur "the certain odium" had Blackford not been reappointed. On January 13 Calvin Fletcher called on Whitcomb and "told him that much mischief would ensue if he did not appoint Judges Dewey & Sullivan to Sup. bench that his party had postponed the Senatorial election which would be thrown into the next years canvass [for governor?] & to carry the question of the non appointment of the Judges also would break him & his party down." Fletcher added: "He informed me he should do *about* right or *about* as would please me." Thornbrough, Riker, and Corpuz (eds.), *Diary of Calvin Fletcher*, III, 108.

249 Indianapolis *Indiana State Journal*, January 22, 1845 (interim terms for Dewey and Sullivan); Indianapolis *Indiana State Sentinel*, December 25, 1845, January 1, 1846 (quoting Vincennes *Western Sun*).

250 Indiana *Senate Journal*, 1845–46, pp. 487–488, 533–534; Indianapolis *Indiana State Sentinel*, January 15, 1846. The *Sentinel* said both men "are *firm* in politics, [but] there is no *bitterness* about them." The inference apparently is that both were Democrats.

251 Indianapolis *Indiana State Journal*, January 28 (interim terms for Dewey and Perkins), February 4, 1846 (comment regarding Sullivan and Perkins). *Ibid.*, March 18, 1846, the *Journal* charged Whitcomb with having used the judicial nominations, first in an effort to gain election to the United States Senate, then to win reelection as governor.

252 Indiana *Senate Journal*, 1846–47, pp. 219–220, 545–547, 620–621. As indicated in *Biographical Directory of the Indiana General Assembly*, I, 493, seven of the votes for Perkins were from Whigs, possibly cast with the hope that sustaining him might gain Democratic votes to elect Dewey over Smith.

253 Indianapolis *Indiana State Journal*, February 2, 9, 1847.

254 Indiana *Senate Journal*, 1847–48, pp. 70–72, 215–216. As indicated in *Biographical Directory of the Indiana General Assembly*, I, 495–496, Senators Elias Murray and Lovell Harrison Rousseau were the two Whigs who supported Smith's elevation to the Supreme Court.

255 There is much need for a comprehensive and scholarly history of the Indiana Supreme Court, but Charles W. Taylor (comp.), *Biographical Sketches and Review of the Bench and Bar of Indiana* (Indianapolis, 1895), 36–41, 43, and Leander J. Monks *et al.* (eds.), *Courts and Lawyers of Indiana* (3 vols., Indianapolis, 1916), I, 198–207, are considerably more generous to Dewey and Sullivan than to Perkins and Smith.

256 U.S. *Statutes at Large*, 28 Cong., 2 session, V, 731–732; Indiana *House Journal*, 1845–46, pp. 16–17; *Laws of Indiana* (general), 1845–46, pp. 58–61.

257 See initial report of the trustees to the General Assembly in Indiana *Documentary Journal*, 1847–48, Pt. II, Doc. 6, pp. 191–277, especially 195–196, 203–204, 209–210. *Ibid.*, 201, 266, explains that the canal was "nearly" finished to Coal Creek; and that $4,154.50 had been spent on construction between Coal Creek and Covington.

258 *Ibid.*, 201–205, 247–250. The cost of completing the canal from Coal Creek to Terre Haute was estimated at $350,000; with $1,560,371 as the probable cost from Terre Haute to Evansville.

259 *Ibid.*, 202; *ibid.*, 1849–50, Pt. II, Doc. 11, pp. 253–256; *ibid.*, 1850–51, Pt. II, Doc. 3, pp. 145–147, 149–150; *ibid.*, 1853, Pt. II, Doc. 7, pp. 327, 330–332, 336–337, 345–346; *ibid.*, 1853, pp. 6, 16–17, 22 (paging irregular, documents not numbered, near end of volume).

260 The revenue from tolls and water rents, July 1, 1847 to December 1, 1859:

Year	Revenue	Source
1847	$ 77,742.05	Indiana *Documentary Journal*, 1847–48, Pt. II, Doc. 6, p. 266
1847–48	145,414.82	*Ibid.*, 1848–49, Pt. II, Doc. 5, p. 157
1848–49	139,665.28	*Ibid.*, 1849–50, Pt. II, Doc. 11, p. 293
1849–50	160,632.82	*Ibid.*, 1850–51, Pt. II, Doc. 3, p. 184
1850–51	187,074.20	*Ibid.*, 1851–52, Pt. I, Doc. 7, p. 249
1851–52	187,392.15	*Ibid.*, 1853, Pt. II, Doc. 7, p. 349
1852–53	181,204.28	*Ibid.*, 1853, p. 47 [in next to last item]
1853–54	180,535.65	*Ibid.*, 1855, p. 824 [paging irregular]
1854–55	140,399.53	*Ibid.*, 1855, Pt. II, Doc. 3, p. 139
1855–56	113,423.47	*Ibid.*, 1857, Pt. II, Doc. 6, p. 299 [Pt. II is a separate volume]
1856–57	60,165.08	*Ibid.*, 1857, Pt. II, Doc, 4, p. 191
1857–58	63,996.44	*Ibid.*, 1859, Pt. I, Doc. 3, p. 322
1858–59	48,278.10	*Ibid.*, 1859, Pt. I, Doc. 3, p. 319

The revenue was very largely from tolls.

At times finding items in the Indiana *Documentary Journals*, especially for those of the 1850s and later, is somewhat like looking for a needle in a haystack. Generally items reported to or during a particular legislative session are published as a volume or volumes for that session. For instance, such items for the legislative session of 1847–48 become a volume or volumes for the 1848–49 session. But many annual reports are made early in sessions, hence such for 1846–47 are normally found in the volume or volumes for 1847–48. But with the end of annual sessions in 1851–52, many annual reports—for 1851–52 and 1852–53 become mingled with items arising from the session of 1853, and are at times scattered through three volumes. Moreover, there is no consistent practice followed regarding how documents are numbered (some are not numbered), paged, or arranged. Moreover, there are times when items, not found on the page or pages cited, are found as cited elsewhere in the item concerning it. In

December, 1845, when entering negotiation with Indiana about a compromise debt settlement, Charles Butler enclosed data supplied by engineers which estimated that the Wabash and Erie Canal would yield revenue of $96,400 for 1847; climb to $232,200 in 1850; and rise to $368,600 for 1855. Indiana *Documentary Journal*, 1845–46, Pt. II, Doc. 8, p. 76.

261 Indiana *House Journal*, 1857, pp. 1095–1114 (quotes, 1108, 1096). As early as 1851 the trustees expressed concern about the impact of railroad competition on the canal. Indiana *Documentary Journal*, 1851–52, Pt. I, Doc. 7, p. 242. In 1857 the trustees emphasized that the "continued diminution of the tolls of the Canal," resulting from "the competition of the railways," had been fully explained in previous reports. *Ibid.*, 1857, Pt. II, Doc. 4, p. 173.

262 Indiana *Documentary Journal*, 1859, Pt. I, Doc. 3, pp. 293–295. James F. D. Lanier, formerly of Madison, was chairman of this committee.

263 *Ibid.*, Pt. I, Doc. 3, pp. 293–295, 305–318; *ibid.*, 1875, Pt. II, Doc. 10, pp. 3–5. According to the latter source, the Wabash and Erie Canal Company had contracted for the canal above Terre Haute in 1866, had spent $436,345.52 on its operation and maintenance to the spring of 1874, while obtaining only $274,019.41 in tolls and water rents. Paul Fatout, *Indiana Canals* (Lafayette, Ind., 1972), especially pp. 147–148, 157–181, offers considerable information about the demise of the Wabash and Erie Canal, first below and then above Terre Haute. This account, however, is less scholarly than desirable.

264 Kettleborough, *Constitution Making in Indiana*, I, cxxvii–cxxx; *ibid.*, II, 18–19, 34–35, 40–41, 79–80, 81–84, 86–88.

265 *Memorial of the Holders of Certificates of Stock of the Wabash and Erie Canal, Issued by the State of Indiana, to the People of the State of Indiana* (not paged, December, 1870). This seven-page item was found in the Indiana University Library, Bloomington.

266 Kettleborough, *Constitution Making in Indiana*, I, cxxx–cxxxii; *ibid.*, II, 88–92, 95–112.

267 According to Fatout, *Indiana Canals*, 176–177, the Wabash and Erie Canal "died in debt for more than $18 million" and its sale yielded "total receipts" of only $160,096. Elbert Jay Benton, *The Wabash Trade Route in the Development of the Old Northwest* (Baltimore, 1903), 86–87, says receipts from the sale were but $96,260; and "The bondholders received from the sale about 9$^1/_2$ per cent. of their investment." Benton states that the receivership, arising from the sale, was not discharged until October 2, 1897. In 1869 Governor Conrad Baker asserted that if the state assumed the debt thrown upon the canal the total would be about $15,000,000. Early in 1875 Governor Thomas A. Hendricks reported that Jonathan K. Gapin, in his suit late in 1874 to have the canal put in receivership, had indicated that the debt dependent on the canal, including principal and interest, was "over" $16,000,000. Indiana *House Journal*, 1869, p. 36; *ibid.*, 1875, p. 640.

268 *Laws of Indiana*, 1872, pp. 11–12; Indiana *Documentary Journal*, 1875, Pt. I, 87 (paging irregular). According to the state auditor, 161 bonds had been

redeemed in 1873, 1874, and 1875, for which $553,942.23 had been paid in principal and interest, leaving 30 bonds outstanding.

269 Thornbrough, Riker, and Corpuz (eds.), *Diary of Calvin Fletcher*, II, 394; Indianapolis *Indiana Journal*, November 16, 1842; Vincennes *Western Sun*, January 6, 1844.

270 Thornbrough, Riker, and Corpuz (eds.), *Diary of Calvin Fletcher*, III, 124–125, 255, 361; Fort Wayne *Sentinel*, March 4, 1848, quoting Goshen *Democrat*.

271 Indianapolis *Indiana Democrat*, September 12, 1838; Indianapolis *Indiana Journal*, November 10, 1838.

272 Indianapolis *Indiana Statesman*, December 31, 1851; Plymouth *Marshall County Republican*, February 17, 1859.

273 Indianapolis *Indiana Journal*, July 13, 1839; Indianapolis *Indiana State Sentinel*, August 1, 1843; Indianapolis *Indiana State Journal*, January 5, 1847.

274 *Laws of Indiana* (revised), 1837–38, pp. 493–504 (quote, 493). Legislation regarding road labor and taxes was frequently not general and consistently uniform throughout the state. Thus, as noted in this code, pp. 495, 504, exceptions were made concerning road legislation as it applied to the counties of Lawrence, Daviess, Washington, Monroe, Brown, Greene, and Owen.

275 *Ibid.*, 495–498.

276 *Ibid.*, 498–500.

277 *Ibid.* (revised), 1842–43, pp. 339–341. As observed *ibid.*, 339, for Dearborn County the road tax could be up to 15 cents per $100 of taxable real estate. The items about furnishing a substitute or working out taxes at 75 cents per day for required labor, and about credit for three days of labor for every day worked with a plow or wagon and team of horses or oxen, were the same as in the 1838 code. For the remainder of this code, see *ibid.*, 100, 119, 120, 134, 135, 325–343. This code mandated the county boards of counties through which either the National or Michigan road passed to have road supervisors keep them in repair "in the same manner" as provided for the act of February 17, 1838, regarding roads and highways. *Ibid.*, 1041.

278 *Ibid.* (revised), 1851–52, I, 307–316, 462–468; *ibid.*, II, 436, 444. For items about road labor and road tax, see I, 463–466. A separate item, p. 468, permitted the township trustees to "levy an additional tax for road purposes," on all land within their township at not to exceed one and three fourths cents per acre if such increase was supported by a majority of its voters. General legislation regarding roads often allowed numerous variations and exceptions in its application from county to county. For instance, see the indices to the laws for the period 1837–50.

279 Indiana *House Journal*, 1843–44, pp. 169–170; *ibid.*, 1841–42, pp. 517–518.

280 Unless otherwise indicated, items regarding these codes are based on them as found in *Laws of Indiana* (revised), 1837–38, p. 500; *ibid.*, 1842–43, pp. 333–334. Except as otherwise noted, the ensuing discussion about bridges is also based on these codes.

281 See the indices to local laws, enacted at annual sessions, 1837–50, under bridges and incorporations, for frequent examples of toll bridges authorized by special acts of the General Assembly.

282 *Laws of Indiana* (revised), 1851–52, I, 201–203. In accordance with the Constitution of 1851, which mandated a general law whenever "applicable," this code has a general act for the incorporation of bridge companies which allowed existing bridge companies to receive its benefits by complying with it. *Ibid.*, 197–200; Kettleborough, *Constitution Making in Indiana*, I, 319.

283 Indiana *Senate Journal*, 1842–43, pp. 563–564.

284 *Laws of Indiana* (revised), 1837–38, pp. 302–306; *ibid.*, 1842–43, pp. 343–348, 235. Unless otherwise indicated, the ensuing discussion is based on these codes.

285 *Ibid.*, 1851–52, I, 295–297, 356.

286 *Ibid.*, 1842–43, p. 977. But the law concerning ferries declared that a licensed ferrykeeper who failed to "set over" any person or property "without unnecessary delay" during daylight was subject to a fine not exceeding $100 and liability to the injured party in a civil action. *Ibid.*, 347.

287 *Ibid.*, 343–348, *passim*, for the law regarding ferries.

288 *Ibid.*, 334.

289 *Ibid.*, 1837–38, pp. 124, 215, 218, 302–306, 500; *ibid.*, 1851–52, I, 197–203, 295–297, 356.

290 Indiana *Senate Journal*, 1837–38, pp. 159–163; Indiana *Documentary Journal*, 1843–44, House Doc. 1, pp. 1–5. Both sources indicate $574,148.58 as the aggregate of legislative appropriations from the fund since statehood. According to the latter source a balance of $8,819.09 was due the fund from the state treasury which had used this sum to meet expenses of state government.

291 Late in 1854 the state auditor reported a balance of $32.13 in the Three Per Cent Fund, explaining that no additional money had been received since February, 1844. Indiana *Documentary Journal*, 1855, Pt. I, Doc. 5, p. 287.

292 Concerning land sales and revenue from the Three Per Cent Fund, see p. 354, this chapter.

293 Indiana *Documentary Journal*, 1874–75, pp. 32–34 (third document, documents paged separately); *ibid.*, 52–53 (second document, paged separately).

294 For examples of consideration of this item, see Indiana *Senate Journal*, 1840–41, pp. 48–49; Indiana *Documentary Journal*, 1848–49, Pt. I, Doc. 2, pp. 110–111; *ibid.*, 1853, pp. 27–30 (first document, paged separately).

295 Indianapolis *Indiana Journal*, January 13, 1835; Indianapolis *Indiana Democrat*, October 12, 1836; Indiana *House Journal*, 1836–37, pp. 112, 414, 422–423; *Laws of Indiana* (local), 1836–37, pp. 157–158. On the vote regarding engrossment, Owen's bill was lost 46 to 35. The author's *hunch* is that "Tullius" was Robert Dale Owen! Resolutions about use of "wooden blocks" and cost of a "wood paved road" were introduced at the two ensuing sessions of the General Assembly. Indiana *House Journal*, 1837–38, p. 282; *ibid.*, 1838–39, p. 157.

296 Indiana *Senate Journal*, 1837–38, pp. 328–342, especially 332–333, 337, 339. Adams' estimate regarding cost for the Michigan Road was based on the use of wooden blocks 9″ by 6″, and a road consisting of a 16′ width of such blocks plus 2′ of curbing. He suggested that "no better timber" could be desired for these blocks than "the oak found in abundance in the vicinity of the road." *Ibid.*, 333, 342.

297 Indianapolis *Indiana State Journal*, May 14, 1845, quoting Richmond *Palladium*; Charles R. Poinsatte, *Fort Wayne During the Canal Era, 1828–1855* (Indianapolis, 1969), 240–242, quoting Fort Wayne *Sentinel*, February 15, May 24, November 15, 22, 29, 1845. For a summary review of the plank road era in the Middle West, see Carl Abbott, "The Plank Road Enthusiasm in the Antebellum Middle West," *Indiana Magazine of History*, LXVII (1971), 95–116.

298 For instance, see Abbott, "Plank Road Enthusiasm in the Antebellum Middle West," *Indiana Magazine of History*, LXVII, 98–99, 102, 104, 108–112; Indianapolis *Indiana State Journal*, September 30, 1846, February 16, 1847, January 1, 1849; Indiana *House Journal*, 1849–50, p. 25; *ibid.*, 1850–51, pp. 25–26. The advantages of plank roads were proclaimed by Robert Dale Owen in his *A Brief Practical Treatise on the Construction and Management of Plank Roads . . .* (New Albany, Ind., 1850), Chapter 1.

299 Indianapolis *Indiana State Journal*, January 1, 1849, quoting a letter from William M. Gillespie, author of a manual regarding the making of roads; Indianapolis *Indiana State Sentinel*, December 4, 1847, quoting Logansport *Telegraph*, November 13, 1847.

300 Special legislation regarding charters for plank road companies apparently commenced at the legislative session of 1848–49. For such legislation at this and the ensuing session, see *Laws of Indiana* (local), 1848–49, pp. 78–83, 110–115, 126, 195–201, 245–250, 317–322, 330–337, 422–428, 459–464; *ibid.*, 1849–50, pp. 92–98, 110–115, 119–127, 168–173, 190–191, 216–222, 225–230, 316–318, 321–326, 357–362, 365–371, 447–448, 488–524, 535–537, 540–542. Much additional legislation concerning special charters was approved at the session of 1850–51. From at least the session of 1847–48 charters regarding plank road companies were also authorized according to general laws. *Ibid.* (general), 1847–48, pp. 24–25; *ibid.*, 1848–49, pp. 88–93; *ibid.*, 1849–50, pp. 145–149; *ibid.*, 1850–51, p. 138.

301 Indianapolis *Indiana State Journal*, May 14, 1845, quoting Richmond *Palladium*; *ibid.*, September 30, 1846; *First Annual Report of the Indiana State Board of Agriculture* (1852), 274–281, *passim*; Abbott, "Plank Road Enthusiasm in the Antebellum Middle West," *Indiana Magazine of History*, LXVII, 97 (diagram), 99–100. For a comprehensive and detailed account about construction of plank roads, see Owen, *A Brief Practical Treatise on the Construction and Management of Plank Roads*, Chapters 4–7.

302 Indiana *House Journal*, 1850–51, p. 25; *ibid.*, 1853, p. 71. Since, as already noted, parts of routes for plank roads did not have to be made of planks, it is possible that such sections were also counted in reporting plank road mileage.

Moreover, it is possible that roads approaching completion were reported as already completed.

303 *First Annual Report of the Indiana State Board of Agriculture*, 274–281, *passim*; Abbott, "Plank Road Enthusiasm in the Antebellum Middle West," *Indiana Magazine of History*, LXVII, 113–116.

304 Dorothy Riker and Gayle Thornbrough (Eds.), *Messages and Papers Relating to the Administration of James Brown Ray, Governor of Indiana, 1825–1831* (Indianapolis, 1954), 273–285. Ray's remarks about railroads illustrate the ornate, pompous, verbose, and meandering style Ray frequently used.

305 These eight charters are in *Laws of Indiana*, 1831–32, pp. 173–236. Five of the eight lines had a terminal on the Ohio River.

306 For the "railroad" at Shelbyville, 1834, see Chapter 4, pp. 182–183. Considerable information regarding railroads and the charters for them to 1850 is in Victor M. Bogle, "Railroad Building in Indiana, 1850–1855," *Indiana Magazine of History*, LVIII (1962), 211–232.

307 Before the Constitution of 1851 became effective, railroad charters were at least usually authorized by special acts of the General Assembly. With a modest number of exceptions, charters and amended charters are found in the annual volumes regarding local laws. They may be located by reference to entries in the indices in these volumes regarding railroads and incorporations.

308 Indiana *Senate Journal*, 1837–38, p. 240.

309 These charters may be located as suggested in note 307 above. Also see Bogle, "Railroad Building in Indiana, 1850–1855," *Indiana Magazine of History*, LVIII, 213–217. On the basis of his detailed study of charters, Bogle estimated that a hundred or more separate charters were issued from 1832–50, aggregating more than four thousand miles of railways, with twenty-five lines having terminals on the Ohio River.

310 Riker and Thornbrough (eds.), *Messages and Papers of James Brown Ray*, 234–237; Indianapolis *Indiana State Journal*, December 3, 1849.

311 Some charters authorized other states and the United States to buy stock in railroad companies, but the author has no evidence that such subscriptions were made. Various charters reserved the right of Indiana to subscribe stock, but it seems that none was subscribed except for the Madison and Indianapolis Road as stated below in note 313. At times local units of government were empowered to buy stock in lines passing through their part of the state. Late in 1850 Governor Wright vigorously objected to what he viewed as excessive purchase of railroad stock by counties and towns. Indiana *House Journal*, 1850–51, pp. 25–26.

312 Barnhart and Carmony, *Indiana*, II, 24, 27–28.

313 *Laws of Indiana* (local), 1842–43, pp. 132–133; Thornbrough (ed.), *Messages and Papers of Samuel Bigger*, 446–448, 563–564n, 633. Though the law of 1843 gave operation of the railroad to the Madison and Indianapolis Railroad Company, the net earnings on the portion which the state had completed were to be paid the state and then be invested in stock of the company. Calvin

Fletcher indicates that the road was nearly completed to Columbus by the fall of 1843. Thornbrough, Riker, and Corpuz (eds.), *Diary of Calvin Fletcher*, II, 542–543, 553.

314 Thornbrough, Riker, and Corpuz (eds.), *Diary of Calvin Fletcher*, III, 408–409; Elsmere, *Henry Ward Beecher*, 80, 300–301; Thornbrough, Riker, and Corpuz (eds.), *Diary of Calvin Fletcher*, II, 105–106.

315 Barnhart and Carmony, *Indiana*, II, 29, for table regarding railroad mileage in Indiana, 1845–60, pursuant to Henry V. Poor (comp.), *Manual of the Railroads of the United States, 1868–1869* (vols. 1–57, New York, 1868–1924), I, 20–21; Indiana *House Journal*, 1850–51, p. 25. Contemporary accounts about railroads as "completed" or in "operation" at times infer more than is normally presumed by these words. For instance, in reporting the beginning of traffic on the Indianapolis and Bellefontaine Railroad in October, 1850, Calvin Fletcher commented that "the track half way was only a temporary arrangement." Thornbrough, Riker, and Corpuz (eds.), *Diary of Calvin Fletcher*, IV, 232.

316 *Indiana Gazetteer* (1849), 28–29, 214, 278, 378; Thornbrough, Riker, and Corpuz (eds.), *Diary of Calvin Fletcher*, IV, 221–223, 241.

317 *Indiana Gazetteer* (1849), 33, 333, 380; Frank F. Hargrave, *A Pioneer Indiana Railroad: The Origin and Development of the Monon* (Indianapolis, 1932), 49, 52–55. Hargrave says "the first train passed over the entire distance of thirty-five miles" on January 14, 1851.

318 Thornbrough, Riker, and Corpuz (eds.), *Diary of Calvin Fletcher*, IV, 64–65, 231–232; Indianapolis *Indiana State Journal* (daily), December 31, 1850; Bogle, "Railroad Building in Indiana, 1850–1855," *Indiana Magazine of History*, LVIII, 217.

319 Hargrave, *A Pioneer Indiana Railroad*, 54, has a table, "published in November, 1850," which he considers "a fairly accurate summary" of Indiana's railroad mileage; and George S. Cottman, "Internal Improvements in Indiana," *Indiana Magazine of History*, III (1907), 158, has data showing such mileage completed by "the latter part" of 1850 "according to the U. S. census." Neither Hargrave nor Cottman, however, cite the exact source for their information. Their data regarding Indiana railroads are as follows:

Railroad	Construction Mileage per Cottman	Hargrave	Construction Mileage Progress per Hargrave
Madison and Indianapolis	86	88	0
Shelbyville and Edinburgh	16	16	0
Shelbyville and Knightstown	27	26	0
Shelbyville and Rushville	20	19	0
Indianapolis and Bellefontaine	28	28	55
New Albany and Salem	35	27	73
Jeffersonville	16	8	58
	228	212	186

Hargrave lists 12 other roads under construction, for mileage totaling 993, but it seems unlikely that construction was actually in progress on the scale this suggests. Cottman states: "There are more than 1000 miles of railroad surveyed and in a state of progress." Poor, *Manual of the Railroads of the United States, 1868-1869,* I, 20–21, gives these items regarding railroad mileage in Indiana to 1850: 1845, 30; 1846, 30; 1847, 42; 1848, 86; 1849, 86; 1850, 228.

[320] Indiana *House Journal,* 1853, p. 71; Barnhart and Carmony, *Indiana,* II, 28–29, 33; Bogle, "Railroad Building in Indiana, 1850–1855," *Indiana Magazine of History,* LVIII, 220–221. Bogle estimates aggregate mileage as 1,407 in 1855, and he gives apparent mileage for each of twenty lines.

[321] Indiana *Documentary Journal,* 1857, Pt. II, Doc. 6, pp. 285–287. In 1874 the trustees of the Wabash and Erie Canal estimated that total revenue (receipts) from the canal, July 1 to December 1, 1874, had been $4,891,485.73; aggregate expense had been $4,850,377.74; leaving a balance of $41,107.99. The costs given, however, add up to $4,861,376.81. Indiana *Documentary Journal,* 1875, Pt. II, pp. 12–13, near the end of the volume (this volume has irregular paging, no numbering of documents).

CHAPTER 7

[1] Much useful information about education in pioneer Indiana is available in Richard G. Boone, *A History of Education in Indiana* (New York, 1892; reprint, Indianapolis, 1941), and William A. Rawles, *Centralizing Tendencies in the Administration of Indiana* (New York, 1903). For useful shorter accounts, see John D. Barnhart and Donald F. Carmony, *Indiana: From Frontier to Industrial Commonwealth* (4 vols., New York, 1954), I, 255–275, II, 105–128; R. Carlyle Buley, *The Old Northwest: Pioneer Period, 1815–1840* (2 vols., Bloomington, Ind., 1950), II, 326–416, *passim*; Logan Esarey, *A History of Indiana: From Its Exploration to 1850* (2 vols., Fort Wayne, Ind., 1924), I, 328–335, II, 679–713, 988–1020; James H. Madison, *The Indiana Way: A State History* (Indianapolis, 1986), 53, 108–115. For a review of scholarly publications about education in Indiana and suggestions for further research, see William J. Reese, "Indiana's Best Public School Traditions: Dominant Themes and Research Opportunities," *Indiana Magazine of History,* LXXXIX (1993), 289–334. For a general background, see Carl K. Kaestle, *Pillars of the Republic: Common Schools and American Society, 1780–1860* (New York, 1983); and Carl K. Kaestle, "Public Education in the Old Northwest: 'Necessary to Good Government and the Happiness of Mankind,'" *Indiana Magazine of History,* LXXXIV (1988), 60–74.

[2] Charles Kettleborough, *Constitution Making in Indiana* (3 vols., Indianapolis, 1916, 1930), I, 112–114. Italics added for emphasis. See 76, 81–82, for congressional grant of an additional congressional township for the support of higher education.

[3] *Laws of Indiana,* 1816–17, pp. 104–109. If a "fit person" was not available within a township, such a person from another township could be named super-

intendent. Upon election of the three township trustees, the superintendent lost his office, and his duties were then performed by the trustees.

4 *Ibid.*, 1818–19, pp. 57–59. According to this law, money was to be appropriated to each school "agreeable to the number of its scholars." This law was supplementary to that cited in the preceding note. Neither law made any provision for district officials; hence, the three township trustees were responsible for any school or schools within their respective townships.

5 *Ibid.*, 1820–21, pp. 139–140. The committee members, in order named, were John Badollet and David Hart, Knox County; William W. Martin, Washington County; James Welsh, Switzerland County; Daniel I. Caswell, Franklin County; Thomas C. Searle, Jefferson County; John Todd, Clark County. Possibly Badollet was chairman of the committee. According to *A Biographical Directory of the Indiana General Assembly* (2 vols., Indianapolis, 1980, 1984), Volume 1, *1816–1899*, Volume 2, *1901–1984*, I, 441, no member of the committee was in the legislature when appointed.

6 See Indiana *House Journal*, 1821–22, pp. 128–149, for the report by Caswell, chairman, and Todd and Welsh. On pages 128–130 the report explains that because of sickness and death of some members and nonattendance of others, the committee had not been able to draft a bill as had been requested.

7 *Ibid.*, 131–132, 136.

8 *Ibid.*, 135. See pages 133–134, 139–142 regarding the preference for credit over cash sales.

9 *Ibid.*, 138.

10 *Ibid.*, 135–142.

11 *Ibid.*, 143. The committee stated further that to require "the people of a district, to support a school against their will, might be considered an infringment [*sic*] of their natural rights . . . ."

12 *Ibid.*, 141–143. The extremely optimistic calculations of the committee seem to have been based upon the anticipation that all proceeds from sections 16 would be consolidated into a State Congressional Township Fund, whereas, proceeds from sections 16 were distributed to the residents of the respective townships. Perhaps the committee hoped Congress would permit the state to have a single centralized fund rather than 950 decentralized ones. For an introductory overview concerning the management and mismanagement of the township funds, and the immense variation in their yield from township to township, see Boone, *History of Education in Indiana*, 168–180. Congressional townships were bounded by artificial survey lines, but schools were located with consideration to such items as roads, swamps, lakes, clearings, villages, hills, and rivers. Hence, there was much variety in the distances children had to walk to get to school and the nature of the routes they used.

13 Indiana *House Journal*, 1821–22, pp. 142–143.

14 *Laws of Indiana* (revised), 1823–24, pp. 379–385. This act was entitled "An Act incorporating Congressional Townships, and providing for Public Schools therein."

15 *Ibid.*, 379–381. The township trustees were elected concurrently for terms of three years. They elected one of their number as clerk, and another as treasurer.

16 *Ibid.*, 381–382.

17 *Ibid.*, 384.

18 *Laws of Indiana*, 1825, pp. 93–94.

19 *Laws of Indiana* (revised), 1830–31, pp. 463–480.

20 *Ibid.*, 463–464, 473–474.

21 *Ibid.*, 475–477.

22 Boone, *History of Education in Indiana*, 30–42, 87–128, *passim.* As indicated on p. 120, increased tax support for schools and consolidation of the numerous Congressional Township Funds into a single fund, were later changes.

23 Indiana had a population of 147,178 in 1820; 343,031 in 1830; 685,866 in 1840; and 988,416 in 1850 according to federal census returns. Barnhart and Carmony, *Indiana*, I, 408.

24 For an overview of laws and developments about public common schools, 1830–1850, see Boone, *History of Education in Indiana*, 30–42, 87–128. For a concise overview, see Barnhart and Carmony, *Indiana*, I, 255–268, 275.

25 See sources cited in preceding note.

26 Although it leaves many questions about these funds unanswered, Boone's *History of Education in Indiana*, 164–217, is a useful source of general information about them. For the quotation from Superintendent Larrabee, see p. 174.

27 Dorothy Riker and Gayle Thornbrough (eds.), *Messages and Papers Relating to the Administration of Noah Noble, Governor of Indiana, 1831–1837* (Indianapolis, 1958), 61, 143–144.

28 Indianapolis *Indiana Journal*, November 9, 1833. The Association thanked "the proprietors of the Protestant Methodist Church, for the privilege of using their house." The Indianapolis *Indiana Democrat*, November 16, 1833, has an account of the meeting at Madison. Both papers give names of those in attendance.

29 Indianapolis *Indiana Journal*, November 9, 1833.

30 Riker and Thornbrough (eds.), *Messages and Papers of Noah Noble*, 207–208.

31 *Laws of Indiana*, 1833–34, pp. 57–59, 334–335. Also see Boone, *History of Education in Indiana*, 78–80, for their chartering. Boone concluded that the seminary at Madison never opened; however, see Indiana *Senate Journal*, 1834–35, pp. 382–388, and the Vincennes *Western Sun & General Advertiser,* February 8, 1834, for accounts of its opening. According to Boone, 181–182, no money from the Saline Fund went to support common schools until the 1840s.

32 Riker and Thornbrough (eds.), *Messages and Papers of Noah Noble*, 329–330.

33 *Ibid.*, 514–516, quoting Indianapolis *Indiana Journal,* January 21, 1837.

34 *Ibid.*, 521–523, quoting Madison *Common School Advocate*, May, 1837. As noted, the age regarding school attendance is indicated as "between 5 and 21," then as "between 5 and 20" years of age.

35 *Ibid.*, 523–524.

36 *Ibid.*, 518–521.

37 Charles W. Moores, *Caleb Mills and the Indiana School System* (Indianapolis, 1905), 363–638, for the six messages and information about Mills and his messages. Mills had a very important role in improving and extending public common schools; however, his basic ideas and emphases have much in common with the basic ideas and emphases of the State Education Convention of January 3–4, 1833.

38 Riker and Thornbrough (eds.), *Messages and Papers of Noah Noble*, 517–18.

39 Indianapolis *Indiana Journal*, January 13, 1838.

40 *Ibid.*, January 12, 1839. See Dorothy Riker (ed.), *Messages and Papers Relating to the Administration of David Wallace, Governor of Indiana, 1837–1840* (Indianapolis, 1963), 474–475; Gayle Thornbrough (ed.), *Messages and Papers Relating to the Administration of Samuel Bigger, Governor of Indiana, 1840–1843* (Indianapolis, 1964), 212–218, for 1840 and 1841 recommendations that a state superintendent of common schools be established as a separate office. *Ibid.*, 218n, indicates that in 1843 the state treasurer was made ex-officio state superintendent of common schools.

41 Concerning provisions in the Constitution of 1851 about common schools, see Kettleborough, *Constitution Making in Indiana*, I, 346–349.

42 Indiana *Documentary Journal*, 1846–47, Pt. I, Doc. No. 4, pp. 91–92. In his short inaugural address, as his term began, Whitcomb said nothing about education. *Ibid.*, Pt. I, Doc. No. 9, pp. 241–242.

43 *Ibid.*, Pt. II, Doc. No. 10, pp. 127–130.

44 Moores, *Caleb Mills and the Indiana School System*, 398–404.

45 *Ibid.*, 409–411, 414.

46 *Ibid.*, 410–411, 417–418.

47 *Ibid.*, 411.

48 Indiana *House Journal*, 1846–47, p. 387; Indiana *Senate Journal*, 1846–47, p. 360. Henry Secrest, who introduced the House resolution, was a Democrat, born in Kentucky, and a lawyer. James H. Henry, who introduced the resolution in the Senate, was a Democrat, and a lawyer, birthplace unknown. *Biographical Directory of the Indiana General Assembly*, I, 348, 180, 493–494.

49 Indianapolis *Indiana State Journal*, February 9, 1847. The committee to make plans for the convention in May comprised: Rev. Henry Ward Beecher, James M. Ray, Rev. Edward R. Ames, Rev. John S. Bayless, and Ovid Butler. Beecher was a Presbyterian minister, Ames and Bayless were Methodist ministers. See Gayle Thornbrough, Dorothy Riker, and Paula Corpuz (eds.), *The Diary of Calvin Fletcher* (9 vols., Indianapolis, 1972–1983), III, 341–343, for comments about the Indianapolis meeting held at "Mr. Gurlys church." (Rev. Phineas Gurley was a Presbyterian minister.) As this source indicates, at that time Fletcher was involved with William Slade, former governor of Vermont, in efforts to secure better qualified teachers, including women.

50 Indianapolis *Indiana State Journal*, May 25, 1847.

51 Thornbrough, Riker, and Corpuz (eds.), *Diary of Calvin Fletcher*, III, 380–383. Judge Amory Kinney, Richard W. Thompson, Rev. Edward R. Ames, and

Sylvester Scovel were members of the committee chaired by Butler. Kinney was a lawyer; Thompson a Whig politician; Ames a Methodist minister; Scovel president of Hanover College. Ovid Butler, a lawyer, later was much involved in founding what became Butler University, established by the Disciples of Christ.

52 *Ibid.*, 380–383. The proceedings are in Indianapolis *Indiana State Journal*, June 1, 15, 1847; Indianapolis *Indiana State Sentinel* (semi-weekly), June 5, 9, 1847.

53 Indiana *Documentary Journal*, 1847–48, Pt. II, Doc. No. 5, pp. 163–165. Pages 161–175 include the entire address. Names attached are: E[dward] R. Ames, J[eremiah] Sullivan, T[imothy] R. Cressey, R[ichard] W. Thompson, J[ames] H. Henry, S[olomon] Meredith, and James Blake. As indicated in note 48, Henry had presented the Senate resolution recommending the May, 1847, State Education Convention. *Biographical Directory of the Indiana General Assembly*, I, 180, 485–498, shows that Henry, a Democrat, served in the Senate at the 1847–48 and 1848–49 sessions when the General Assembly considered legislation desired by advocates of better schools.

54 Indiana *Documentary Journal*, 1847–48, Pt. II, Doc. No. 5, pp. 163–165. The committee did not claim that half of the existing teachers were females but that "the proportion of females should be much greater . . . ."

55 *Ibid.*, 165–167.

56 *Ibid.* Note 40 indicates that the treasurer of state had been made ex-officio state superintendent of common schools in 1843.

57 *Ibid.*, 167–168.

58 *Ibid.*, 168–174 (quotes 170, 173).

59 Indianapolis *Indiana State Journal*, November 30, 1847. In contrasting conditions in Indiana with those in older states, the address commented: "We have but few men of wealth. The great mass . . . are really poor compared with older States. But few of our children have ever seen their grandsires or the brothers or sisters of their parents—and in truth, no reliable provisions are made for their education. Now what must be the feelings of the dying emigrant father? He is leaving no property for his children beyond his funeral day. None of his relatives are near to throw around those orphans their guardian care, and at the same time, no system of education is in existence to furnish them with that intellectual furniture which constitutes the greatest temporal wealth. He leaves them in poverty, in ignorance, to the cold charities of a land of strangers and exposed to every temptation." Indiana *Documentary Journal*, 1847–48, Pt. II, Doc. No. 5, p. 174.

60 Unless otherwise indicated, items about the bill are as explained by the committee in Indiana *Documentary Journal*, 1847–48, Pt. II, Doc. No. 5, pp. 141–160 (quotations, 147–149). As p. 160 indicates, the bill is signed by A[mory] Kinney, O[liver] H. Smith, and Calvin Fletcher. For significant information about this bill, its drafting and content, see Thornbrough, Riker, and Corpuz (eds.), *Diary of Calvin Fletcher*, III, 382n, 424–429. The committee explained that with a tax of one tenth of a mill, a man owning no taxable property would pay

only a 25 cent poll tax; one owning $500 of taxable property would pay 85 cents: a 25 cent poll tax, 30 cents for state tax, and 30 cents for township tax. When the tax became one cent, the owner of $500 of taxable property would pay $1.25 per year: 25 cents for poll tax, 50 cents for state tax, and 50 cents for township tax.

61 Indiana *Documentary Journal*, 1847–48, Pt. II, Doc. No. 5, pp. 152–159. The committee estimated that Indiana had 18,999 district trustees and 2,430 township trustees.

62 *Ibid.*, 159.

63 *Ibid.*, 159–160. For a synopsis of the bill, see Indianapolis *Indiana State Journal*, December 21, 1847. See *ibid.*, January 4, 1848, for "an outline of . . . principal arguments by which the provisions of the bill are enforced." The committee of three did not ask that the law about schools be submitted to the voters for approval on a county option basis. It is evident that the committee thought that on this basis various counties might reject such legislation but believed that the statewide vote would result in its approval for all counties.

64 Moores, *Caleb Mills and the Indiana School System*, 430. For the entire message, see 429–500.

65 *Ibid.*, 433–437 (quotation, 437). According to the federal census of 1840 persons over twenty, who could neither read nor write, were illiterate. Mills tends to equate illiteracy with lack of intelligence.

66 *Ibid.*, 444–445.

67 *Ibid.*, 438–448 (quotations, 443, 446).

68 *Ibid.*, 449–455 (quotations, 449, 450, 455).

69 *Ibid.*, 456–467 (quotations, 465, 458). As noted on pages 417–418, in his previous address Mills had urged the appointment of county superintendents.

70 *Ibid.*, 458–460.

71 For Whitcomb's comment, see Indiana *Documentary Journal*, 1847–48, Pt. I, Doc. No. 7, pp. 196–197. For law authorizing the referendum for or against free schools, see *Laws of Indiana* (general), 1847–48, pp. 48–49. For Calvin Fletcher's caustic comments concerning legislative defeat of the school bill, see Thornbrough, Riker, and Corpuz (eds.), *Diary of Calvin Fletcher*, III, 431–432, 434; *ibid.*, IV, 5, 8, 12–15. In IV, 8, 13, Fletcher states: "The old unfortunate system of internal improvements have excluded all the old settlers or men of early standing from the Legislature. Set of strangers & young men knowing very little if anything about the state or its wants are the governors." He regretted the defeat of the common school bill by the Senate but thought "it will work together for good. It was a matter of interest to me rather I felt a desire to live to see a general system of free schools in which any child the poorest could be taught free of charges."

72 Thornbrough, Riker, and Corpuz (eds.), *Diary of Calvin Fletcher*, IV, 42–44, used as the source for the convention and copy of the appeal for support from the press. Henry F. West, editor of the *Common School Advocate*, and Rev. Timothy R. Cressey, a Baptist minister, were the other members of the committee chaired by Fletcher. The proceedings of the convention are in the Indianapolis

Indiana State Journal (tri-weekly), May 10, 1848. The appeal to the press is in Indianapolis *Indiana State Journal*, June 12, 1848. Thornbrough, Riker, and Corpuz (eds.), *Diary of Calvin Fletcher*, IV, 43n, state that the address appeared "in many other papers throughout the state during June."

73 Moores, *Caleb Mills and the Indiana School System*, 501–502; Boone, *History of Education in Indiana*, 105–108.

74 For a sampling of views pro and con free public common schools on a statewide basis, see Boone, *History of Education in Indiana*, 87–112 *passim;* Barnhart and Carmony, *Indiana*, I, 255–262; Madison, *The Indiana Way*, 108–115. For much relevant comment about elements pro and con free public common schools, see Moores, *Caleb Mills and the Indiana School System*, 397–638.

75 For the governor's silence, see Indiana *House Journal*, 1848–49, pp. 17–27. For the school law of 1849, see *Laws of Indiana* (general), 1848–49, pp. 123–131.

76 Moores, *Caleb Mills and the Indiana School System*, 538–543, 548–549 (quotes, 543–545). Mills explains the returns of votes cast were not available for eight counties, of which six had favored and two opposed the law. The author presumes that for the most part the elements for and against the law of 1849 are similar to the same concerning the vote for and against free schools in 1848.

77 Kettleborough, *Constitution Making in Indiana*, I, 346–349 (quote, 346).

78 Boone, *History of Education in Indiana*, 143–164 (quote, 145).

79 *Ibid.*, 114. Also see pages 42–58 for an overall view of county seminaries.

80 *Laws of Indiana*, 1817–18, pp. 355–357; *ibid.*, 1823–24 (revised), 116–120; *ibid.*, 1830–31 (revised), 489–495. According to *Laws of Indiana*, 1816–17, p. 155, the state treasurer was to retain county seminary money until authorized to transfer it to others; *ibid.*, 1818–19, pp. 67–68, required county seminary trustees, "if an opportunity can be had," to loan seminary money at 6 percent annually.

81 Boone, *History of Education in Indiana*, 42–58; Barnhart and Carmony, *Indiana*, I, 267–271; Walter J. Wakefield, "County Seminaries in Indiana," *Indiana Magazine of History*, XI (1915), 148–161.

82 Indiana *House Journal*, 1834–35, p. 19 (quote from Noble); Boone, *History of Education in Indiana*, 47 (report of state treasurer), 44 (county seminary buildings).

83 Boone, *History of Education in Indiana*, 42–58 (quote, 49); Barnhart and Carmony, *Indiana*, I, 267–271; Kettleborough, *Constitution Making in Indiana*, I, 347. In the pioneer era secondary education, like primary and college education, was mainly under private and denominational auspices as indicated in Boone, *History of Education in Indiana*, 59–86; John Hardin Thomas, "The Academies of Indiana," *Indiana Magazine of History*, X (1914), 331–358 and XI (1915), 8–39.

84 Barnhart and Carmony, *Indiana*, I, 271 (quotation); Buley, *The Old Northwest*, II, 387–388. For the minutes of the trustees of Vincennes University from 1806 to 1849, see J. Robert Constantine (ed.), "Minutes of the Board of Trustees for Vincennes University," *Indiana Magazine of History*, LIV (1958), 313–364; LV (1959), 247–293; LVII (1961), 311–367; LIX (1963), 323–387; LX (1964),

159–198. The introductory comments and notes included by Constantine are useful as a guide to the contents of the minutes. No minutes of the trustees were found for the period April 24, 1824, to October 3, 1828.

   85 Barnhart and Carmony, *Indiana*, I, 271–272; Buley, *The Old Northwest*, II, 372, 387–389; Boone, *History of Education in Indiana*, 353–355; James Albert Woodburn, *History of Indiana University, 1820–1902* (2 vols., Bloomington, Ind., 1940).

   86 These sources give 1824 as the opening date for the Indiana State Seminary: Boone, *History of Education in Indiana*, 19, 31; Buley, *The Old Northwest*, I, 122; and Woodburn, *History of Indiana University*, I, 16. These sources give 1825 as the date: Barnhart and Carmony, *Indiana*, I, 271; Buley, *The Old Northwest*, II, 388; Thomas D. Clark, *Indiana University: Midwestern Pioneer* (4 vols., Bloomington, Ind., 1970–1977), I, 30–31. In 1987 the Indiana University Board of Trustees decided the Indiana State Seminary opened in 1824. The evidence pro and con is subject to differing interpretations. Although Buley gives 1824 as the date in Volume I, in Volume II he gives the date as "probably May 1, 1825."

   87 Barnhart and Carmony, *Indiana*, I, 271–273; Buley, *The Old Northwest*, II, 388–393.

   88 Indiana *Documentary Journal*, 1848–49, Pt. II, Doc. No. 6, pp. 277–278, 284–286.

   89 *Ibid.*, 286–288.

   90 Frank S. Baker, *Glimpses of Hanover's Past, 1827–1977* (Seymour, Ind., 1978), 15, 28–34, 43–49; Boone, *History of Education in Indiana*, 410–412; Barnhart and Carmony, *Indiana*, I, 273.

   91 James Insley Osborne and Theodore Gregory Gronert, *Wabash College: The First Hundred Years, 1832–1932* (Crawfordsville, Ind., 1932); Boone, *History of Education in Indiana*, 412–414; Barnhart and Carmony, *Indiana*, I, 273; Buley, *The Old Northwest*, II, 402–403, 406.

   92 William Warren Sweet, *Indiana Asbury-DePauw University, 1837–1937* (New York, 1937), 27–41, 42–43, 65–66, 58; Boone, *History of Education in Indiana*, 414–417; Barnhart and Carmony, *Indiana*, I, 273.

   93 John F. Cady, *The Centennial History of Franklin College* (Franklin, Ind., 1934), 9–44, 47; Boone, *History of Education in Indiana*, 417–418; Buley, *The Old Northwest*, II, 407–408; Barnhart and Carmony, *Indiana*, I, 273.

   94 Thomas J. Schlereth, *The University of Notre Dame: A Portrait of Its History and Campus* (Notre Dame, Ind., 1977), 3–10, 26; Boone, *History of Education in Indiana*, 424–426; Barnhart and Carmony, *Indiana*, I, 273–274, 275.

   95 Opal Thornburg, *Earlham: The Story of the College, 1847–1962* (Richmond, Ind., 1963), 28–43, 78–79; Boone, *History of Education in Indiana*, 419–421.

   96 Indiana *House Journal*, 1849–50, p. 27.

   97 Moores, *Caleb Mills and the Indiana School System*, 473–478. As indicated *ibid.*, 423–428, in his initial address to the legislature Mills had expressed similar ideas about dissolving Indiana University and dividing its proceeds among selected colleges.

[98] *Ibid.*, 559–561, 571–577 (quotations 572, 560). For Mills' comments about dissolving Indiana University and diverting proceeds from it to selected colleges and universities in his third and fourth addresses to the legislature, see *ibid.*, 522–527, 537–538. In his sixth address submitted to the legislature, *ibid.*, 578–638, Mills elaborates what needs to be done for common schools and omits his proposal about dissolving Indiana University. It is interesting to note that he begins this address with a comment about "that distinguished educator, the late Dr. Wylie, so long the able and efficient head of the State University . . . " (p. 578), and expresses the hope "that the day is not far distant, when the funds of the State University will be taxed to establish a [normal school] department at the seat of government . . . ." (p. 613).

[99] Thornbrough, Riker, and Corpuz (eds.), *Diary of Calvin Fletcher*, II, 257–258. According to *Biographical Directory of the Indiana General Assembly*, I, 282, Austin W. Morris was state auditor, 1828–44, a Whig, a lawyer, a Methodist, and a member of the Asbury Board of Trustees. See Chapter 8, pp. 440–442, for both the defense of and criticism of Indiana University by delegates to the Constitutional Convention of 1850–51.

CHAPTER 8

[1] Charles Kettleborough, *Constitution Making in Indiana* (3 vols., Indianapolis, 1916, 1930), I, 84, 111–112 (quoted items). For a copy of the Constitution of 1816, see *ibid.*, 83–125.

[2] Dorothy Riker and Gayle Thornbrough (comps.), *Indiana Election Returns, 1816–1851* (Indianapolis, 1960), 367–373; Kettleborough, *Constitution Making in Indiana*, II, 607–612. According to Riker and Thornbrough, largely official returns from 37 of the 47 counties for the referendum of 1823 provided 15,113 votes against and only 3,804 for a convention; that of 1828, with largely official returns from 46 of the 58 counties, 19,671 votes against and 10,607 votes for a convention; and that of 1840, official returns from 71 of the 87 counties, 63,820 votes against and only 12,798 for a convention. Somewhat different returns, but with useful additional comments, are in Kettleborough as cited.

[3] For comments of "Junius," see Vincennes *Western Sun*, March 8, 1823, quoting Corydon *Indiana Gazette*. Kettleborough, *Constitution Making in Indiana*, I, xli–lxi, 138–163, offers much relevant information about these three and other changes considered during the teens, twenties, and thirties.

[4] Corydon *Indiana Gazette*, April 9, 1823; Vincennes *Farmers & Mechanics Journal*, June 26, 1823. Kettleborough, *Constitution Making in Indiana*, I, xlvii–l (quote, p. xlvii), states: "But there is tolerably conclusive evidence that the real reason for calling a constitutional convention was to eliminate from the Constitution the provision excluding slavery and involuntary servitude from the State."

[5] Indianapolis *Gazette*, April 26, 1823, quoting Corydon *Indiana Gazette*. See Kettleborough, *Constitution Making in Indiana*, I, 124–125, for delegates to the Constitutional Convention of 1816, and *A Biographical Directory of the Indiana*

General Assembly (2 vols., Indianapolis, 1980, 1984), Volume 1, *1816–1899*, Volume 2, *1901–1984*, I, 443–444, for members of the legislative session of 1822–23 that called the referendum. Patrick Beard, William Graham, Nathaniel Hunt, Dennis Pennington, and David Robb were members of both bodies.

⁶ Indiana *House Journal*, 1848–49, p. 25. For much information regarding interpretation of the twelve year clause, see Kettleborough, *Constitution Making in Indiana*, I, xxxiii–xl, 153–154, 164, 171–179.

⁷ See Kettleborough, *Constitution Making in Indiana*, I, 404–413, for an explanation of these changes by a special committee of ten delegates.

⁸ Indiana *Senate Journal*, 1845–46, pp. 45, 48, 76, 103, 267–268, 511–512, 536 (Senate bill), and 163, 183, 610–611 (Senate passage of House bill); Indiana *House Journal*, 1845–46, pp. 100, 148, 176, 192, 611–612, 637–638. According to *Biographical Directory of the Indiana General Assembly*, I, 490–492, the House had 56 Democrats, 44 Whigs; each party had 25 senators.

⁹ Riker and Thornbrough (comps.), *Indiana Election Returns, 1816–1851*, pp. 373–375; Indiana *House Journal*, 1846–47, p. 22; Kettleborough, *Constitution Making in Indiana*, II, 612–614. Riker and Thornbrough give official figures; Kettleborough gives returns according to the report of the secretary of state which show 32,468 votes for and 27,123 against a convention. According to *Biographical Directory of the Indiana General Assembly*, I, 493–495, the Senate had 26 Democrats, 24 Whigs; the House 45 Democrats, 1 probable Democrat, and 54 Whigs.

¹⁰ Indiana *Senate Journal*, 1846–47, pp. 36, 45, 94–95, 220–221, 224–225, 294–295, 388–391, 448 (Senate bill); Indiana *House Journal*, 1846–47, pp. 561, 620–621. According to the politics of legislators as in *Biographical Directory of the Indiana General Assembly*, I, 493–495, in the Senate 22 Democrats and 2 Whigs voted for passage; 21 Whigs and 1 Democrat against passage; in the House 9 Democrats, 1 probable Democrat, and 48 Whigs supported indefinite postponement; 35 Democrats and 2 Whigs opposed indefinite postponement. For much additional information about the referendum of 1846, its outcome, and the legislative response thereto, see Kettleborough, *Constitution Making in Indiana*, I, lxi–lxxii, 165–183.

¹¹ Indiana *House Journal*, 1846–47, pp. 278–283 (quotations, 280, 283); Indiana *Senate Journal*, 1846–47, 220–221. The Whig protesters were John Dowling, Francis H. Fry, Jonathan S. Harvey, Samuel Stewart, John Yaryan. As indicated in Kettleborough, *Constitution Making in Indiana*, I, 111–112, the constitution stated that a convention "should be" called if "a majority of all the votes given at such election" favored a convention; and the call was "agreed to by a majority of all the members elected to both branches of the General assembly . . . ." While the majority required by the popular vote is less explicit than desirable, Orth was correct that the approval by the Senate had been less than that explicitly required by the constitution. But opponents could argue that the bill of rights gave the legislature power to call a convention at any time.

[12] Indiana *Senate Journal*, 1848–49, pp. 95, 118, 124, 244–245, 269–270, 531, 572; Indiana *House Journal*, 1848–49, pp. 421, 532–533. According to *Biographical Directory of the Indiana General Assembly*, I, 498–500, the Senate had 27 Democrats, 23 Whigs; the House, 60 Democrats, 40 Whigs. In the Senate the bill passed with 25 Democrats and 9 Whigs for passage; 1 Democrat and 11 Whigs against passage. In the House 47 Democrats and 33 Whigs voted for approval; no Democrat and 2 Whigs against approval.

[13] For the vote on the referendum and for governor, see Riker and Thornbrough (comps.), *Indiana Election Returns, 1816–1851*, pp. 375–377, 155–158, respectively. Kettleborough, *Constitution Making in Indiana*, II, 615–616, gives the same returns as Riker and Thornbrough. For much additional information regarding the referendum of 1849, see *ibid.*, I, lxxii–lxxvi, 183–189.

[14] Indianapolis *Indiana State Sentinel* (semi-weekly), May 16, 1849; Indiana *House Journal*, 1849–50, pp. 21–22. Editor Schuyler Colfax of the South Bend *St. Joseph Valley Register*, in the issue of January 25, 1849, said he was "decidedly in favor of" a constitutional convention as he had already stated. He explained that in 1846, when the county had voted the other way, he had voted for that referendum.

[15] Indiana *Senate Journal*, 1849–50, pp. 11–12, 125–126, 190, 233, 268–273, 289–295, 308–311, 321–324, 377–378, 586–587, 595–596, 630, 637–638, 659–660, 673–674, 691, 749, 810; Indiana *House Journal*, 1849–50, pp. 499, 508, 517, 524–534, 649–650, 691, 708–709, 736, 767. In the House 34 Democrats and 20 Whigs voted for passage; 21 Democrats and 17 Whigs opposed passage. For the election of delegates, see *Laws of Indiana* (general), 1849–50, pp. 29–34. The legislature authorized the governor, auditor, and treasurer to provide "suitable accommodations" for the convention "either in the Representative's Hall or in the Masonic Hall, or in other suitable building" at their option provided the "entire rent" did not exceed $100 per month. *Ibid.*, 250–251.

[16] Fort Wayne *Times*, February 21, 1850; Fort Wayne *Sentinel*, February 23, 1850; Kettleborough, *Constitution Making in Indiana*, I, 212–213, quoting *Daily Lafayette Courier*, March 1, 1850.

[17] Unless otherwise indicated, here and elsewhere in this chapter, these data are based on a broadside by "Baker & McFarland," entitled "Members of the Convention to Amend the Constitution of the State of Indiana, Assembled at Indianapolis, October, 1850, Giving Name, Age, Post Office, County Represented, Nativity, Years in State, Boarding House, Occupation, Politics, Married or Single, and Remarks." This item is listed in Cecil K. Byrd and Howard H. Peckham, *A Bibliography of Indiana Imprints, 1804–1853* (Indianapolis, 1955), 370. The broadside may be found in the Indiana Division, Indiana State Library, Indianapolis. The author has a photocopy of it. Baker and McFarland indicate that 94 delegates were Democrats, with one of them listed as Locofoco; 53 Whigs, including one listed as Independent Whig; and one each as Free Soil, Conservative, and Independent. The Indianapolis *Indiana State Sentinel*, August 29, 1850, and the Indianapolis *Indiana State Journal*, August 31, 1850, both state

there were 96 Democrats and 54 Whigs. For much more about the election of delegates, see Kettleborough, *Constitution Making in Indiana*, I, lxxvi–lxxxiii, 194–217; *ibid.*, II, 639–642.

¹⁸ *Journal of the Convention of the People of the State of Indiana to Amend the Constitution* (Indianapolis, 1851, reprinted 1935), 3–12; *Report of the Debates and Proceedings of the Convention for the Revision of the Constitution of the State of Indiana, 1850* (2 vols., Indianapolis, 1850, reprinted 1935), I, 3–9. According to the *Convention Journal*, 8, 12, 48, 118, of the remaining original delegates, four arrived the afternoon of the first day; one each arrived on October 8, 12, 23. For sketches of Carr and English, see *Biographical Directory of the Indiana General Assembly*, I, 55, 119, respectively.

¹⁹ *Convention Journal*, 12–17, 22–23, 55–56; *Convention Debates*, I, 9–13, 25–32, 59. For clues regarding possible informal agreements among Democrats, see *ibid.*, I, 6, 11, 29–30.

²⁰ *Convention Debates*, I, 25–30. See pp. 31–32, for a vigorous defense of having a stenographer by Robert Dale Owen. For further items about employment of a stenographer, both pro and con, see 30–32, 59; *ibid.*, II, 1262–1266. William C. Foster, a Democrat, argued that two assistant secretaries would be enough. He urged his Democratic friends to practice the economy pledges they had made in seeking election. *Ibid.*, I, 11.

²¹ *Convention Journal*, 17, 27–28. As noted on p. 33, this practice began October 10, after which it persisted, with delegates and visiting clergy at times also offering prayer. The resolution concerning opening each day with prayer, offered by James G. Read, a Democrat from Clark County, was apparently accepted without discussion, as indicated in *Convention Debates*, I, 13, 41.

²² *Convention Journal*, 8, 21, 34–39, 57–58; *Convention Debates*, I, 5–7, 22, 45–46. Also see Kettleborough, *Constitution Making in Indiana*, I, 223–231, for the rules initially adopted, pp. 231–232, for rules later adopted, and pp. 232–234, for rules proposed and rejected.

²³ *Convention Journal*, 17–18 (quote, p. 18), 24–25, 30–31, 40–42, 52–54 (committee members); *Convention Debates*, I, 13–21, 34–39, 41, 42–43, 47–48, 53–58. See *Convention Journal*, 52–54, for the twenty-two standing committees and their members. Two additional committees, one concerning elections and another accounts, were named.

²⁴ *Convention Journal*, 25–26, 158, 174–175; *Convention Debates*, I, 39–40, 255–258. The *Debates* offer no discussion regarding either of Kilgore's proposals. Six Whigs, one "conservative," and four Democrats voted against tabling the first proposal: Henry J. Bowers, Samuel Frisbie, David Kilgore, Hiram Prather, Henry G. Todd, and Johnson Watts were the Whigs; William Steele, the Conservative; and James W. Borden, Thomas Chenowith, Daniel Kelso, and Zachariah Tannehill were the Democrats. Kettleborough, *Constitution Making in Indiana*, II, 640, lists Daniel Kelso as a Whig; Baker and McFarland list him as a Democrat, as does *Biographical Directory of the Indiana General Assembly*, I, 216–217, 499, the latter page reference being to the legislative session of 1848–49. In

the 1850–51 Constitutional Convention material in the William H. English Collection held by the Indiana Historical Society Library, Indianapolis, Kelso's son, James P. Kelso, wrote to English in an undated letter from Newport, Kentucky, that his father "Was a Democrat after 1844."

25 *Convention Debates*, I, 537, 548. Rariden mentioned apprehension about "the great expenditure" for a convention and the "great diversity of opinions" anticipated in explaining his vote against calling a convention.

26 *Convention Journal*, 166, 354, 360; *Convention Debates*, II, 1068–1069. Chapman's role regarding the Indianapolis *Indiana State Sentinel* and other papers is indicated in John W. Miller, *Indiana Newspaper Bibliography* (Indianapolis, 1982), 265, 275, 454.

27 *Convention Journal*, 53. The committee chaired by Bright included seven Democrats: Bright, Walter E. Beach, Mark A. Duzan, Benjamin R. Edmonston, Smith Miller, Rudolphus Schoonover, Ross Smiley; and two Whigs, Othniel L. Clark, Thomas D. Walpole. The committee chaired by Newman had four Whigs: Newman, Hiram Allen, Melchert Helmer, Samuel Pepper; and three Democrats: Daniel Crumbacker, Smith Miller, Henry T. Snook.

28 *Ibid.*, 60, 87–89.

29 *Convention Debates*, I, 94–95 (Read), 96–97 (Allen), 97 (Murray), 94 (Clark), 95–96 (Biddle).

30 *Ibid.*, II, 1061 (Niles), 1062 (Edmund D. Taylor, Democrat), 1064–1065 (Daniel Read, Democrat), 1066–1067 (Daniel Kelso, Democrat).

31 *Ibid.*, II, 1063–1064 (Pettit), 1064 (Clark), 1065 (Newman).

32 *Convention Journal*, 166–170 (quote, p. 169), 470–471; *Convention Debates*, II, 1223–1225 (quotes, p. 1224). As indicated p. 1225, Read's proposed amendment was amended, by acclamation, to add the word "'BUNCOMBE'" to the end of it. The word "buncombe," now and then found among legislative records and newspaper comments of the pioneer era, by its usage seems roughly the equivalent of humbug. The words in brackets are as in the *Debates*.

33 *Convention Journal*, 492–494; *Convention Debates*, II, 1249–1250 (Read), 1252 (Smith), 1248–1253 (related remarks). According to the *Convention Journal*, James B. Foley, a Democrat, proposed to amend Read's amendment by making the compensation sought by Read that for the delegates. Foley's amendment was tabled without a roll call vote. As may be observed in the *Convention Debates*, II, 1224, 1250, two delegates indicate that in 1842 the legislature had adopted a law limiting sessions to six weeks. The author has not found such legislation for either the 1841–42 or 1842–43 sessions, but the session of 1843–44 limited compensation to $3 per day for the first six weeks of a session, and $1.50 thereafter, plus allowance for travel to and from the session. *Laws of Indiana* (general), 1843–44, p. 13. As may be observed in John G. Rauch and Nellie E. Armstrong, *A Bibliography of the Laws of Indiana, 1788–1927* (Indianapolis, 1928), 68–69, the sessions, starting with that of 1843–44, were shorter than they had generally been during the thirties.

34 *Convention Journal*, 512–514, 619–620, 926–927, 930–931; *Convention Debates*, I, 1276–1279 (Robinson quotations, pp. 1277–1278), 1473–1474.

35 *Convention Journal*, 63, 95, 168 (committee report), 416–417 (Holman amendment), 431–433, 912, 915; *Convention Debates*, I, 102 (Stevenson), 109 (Wolfe), 107 (Chapman), 102 (Kelso), 103 (Clark); *ibid.*, II, 1093 (Hovey). For additional remarks pro and con, see *ibid.*, I, 102–113; *ibid.*, II, 1089–1098, 1124–1125. As indicated in *Convention Journal*, 415–418, 431, Kelso made unsuccessful efforts to have the Holman amendment defeated. On what appears to have been his final effort, Kelso lost 91 to 39.

36 *Convention Journal*, 413–414 (vote for), 428–429, 430, 915, 936, 942; *Convention Debates*, II, 1086 (Read), 1119 (Pettit), 1085–1086 (Bright). For further remarks by those quoted, and by other delegates, see 1084–1088, 1113–1121, 2008–2011, 2014.

37 *Convention Journal*, 428, 433–438 (proposal, vote on, vote on proviso), 455–456 (referral vote), 926, 931; *Convention Debates*, II, 1117–1118, 1128–1141, 1196–1197, 1383–1385, 1431–1434, 1128 (Morrison), 1128–1129 (Niles), 1132–1133 (McClelland), 1134–1135 (Read), 1130 (Bascom). As indicated in the *Convention Journal*, 926, 930–932, although this item was referred to the revision committee with the proviso attached, it seems that this committee did not include the proviso as part of the new constitution. Nor is the provision found in the copy of the constitution as in *Convention Debates*, II, 2066–2077, or in Kettleborough, *Constitution Making in Indiana*, I, 295–375.

38 Indiana *House Journal*, 1848–49, pp. 23–24.

39 *Convention Journal*, 216–217. See note 27, this chapter, for the members on and political ties of this committee.

40 See *ibid.*, 744–746, 766–767, indicating that this article passed second reading without a roll call vote, then was adopted by the overwhelming vote of 116 to 13. For the items included as this article was referred to the revision committee, see p. 927, section 1, and pp. 931–932, sections 22 and 23, as same were revised by the revision committee. Kettleborough, *Constitution Making in Indiana*, I, 318–319, sections 22 and 23, also has these items as in the Constitution of 1851. For a discussion of same, see *Convention Debates*, II, 1765–1772, 1813–1816.

41 *Convention Journal*, 438, 596–597, 743–744, 746–748, 762–763, 796–797, 938, 943.

42 *Convention Debates*, II, 1420–1422 (Stevenson, Newman, Borden, Chapman), 1766 (Dobson), 1421 and 1801 (Pettit), 1803 (Wallace). For further discussion about which laws should be general and whether county boards should be given power to pass local laws, by these and other delegates, see 1420–1422, 1763–1773, 1801–1805, 1813–1816.

43 Kettleborough, *Constitution Making in Indiana*, I, 89, 91, 122–123.

44 *Convention Journal*, 166–167 (section 2). In submitting his report Bright explained that the committee was reporting concerning items which had been referred to it, "without coming to a conclusion upon all of them," for the consideration of the convention.

45 For further items regarding the number of senators and representatives, see *ibid.*, 188, 354–358, 361–366, 372–376, 385–387, 910, 914. For the Prather

amendment establishing the maximum number of senators at 50 and representatives at 100, and its approval, see 358, 374–376, 385–387.

46 *Ibid.*, 407, 801, 815, 928, 932. As indicated in *Convention Debates*, II, 1407,
1585, and 1880, these items were apparently adopted without any debate. As proposed and passed part of the second section provided that the first election of
members of the General Assembly should be according to the apportionment
made by the legislature at its session of 1850–51. The Committee on Revision,
Arrangement, and Phraseology, chaired by Robert Dale Owen, modified this item
to require that the second as well as the first election of members of the General
Assembly should be according to the legislative apportionment of 1850 51.

47 *Convention Journal*, 166–172 (section 3), 376–379, 387–388, 475–477, 487–
491, 541–542, 984. See 487, 542, for approval and passage of this amendment
without a roll call vote.

48 *Convention Debates*, I, 269 (Shoup), 264–265 (Nave), 274–275 (Stevenson),
270–274 (Chapman, quotation 270), 267–268 (Pepper), 264 (Bascom). See 262–
276, for further discussion about the basis for representation by these and other
delegates.

49 *Ibid.*, I, 980–989, 990–1008; *ibid.*, II, 1009–1016, 1022–1036, 1037–1048,
for the December 5, 6, 7, 9 discussions. As noted in Ch. 4, p. 162, the number
of representatives first reached 100 in 1836; that of senators reached 50 in 1841.
Ch. 5, pp. 267–270. Thereafter, these maximums remained unchanged.

50 *Ibid.*, II, 1049 (Pettit), 1034–1035 (Morrison); *ibid.*, I, 997–998 (Stevenson).
Pettit meant that if the representative ratio called for 3,000 voters to make a representative district, then counties having only 2,000 voters would have an equal
voice with those having 3,000. In this manner two counties with 6,000 voters
would have two representatives, while three counties with 2,000 voters would
have three representatives.

51 *Ibid.*, I, 983–984 (Kelso), 986 (Ritchey); *ibid.*, II, 1009–1016, especially pp.
1009–1013 (Borden). Borden strongly objected to the use of floats in apportioning representatives. Concerning floats, see Leon H. Wallace, "Legislative
Apportionment in Indiana: A Case History," *Indiana Law Journal*, 42 (1966), 15–
21, 27. Kelso stated: "Now there are two legitimate modes on which to base a
representation—either on population or on territory—the one or the other.
Now, of the two, in the State of Indiana, I maintain that that of territory is the
most proper."

52 Kettleborough, *Constitution Making in Indiana*, I, 89, 312.

53 *Convention Debates*, II, 1029 (Stevenson), 1030 (Borden and Nave), 1049–
1050 (Colfax), 1049 (Pettit). For additional discussion about single districts, see
ibid., I, 100–101, 992–993; *ibid.*, II, 1009–1016, 1028–1031, 1048–1050, 1231,
1241–1248, 1320. The important role which Stevenson and Colfax had concerning this item is indicated in *Convention Journal*, 78, 167, 188, 356–357, 377,
387–388, 475–477, 487, 541–542, 984.

54 *Convention Debates*, I, 269–270 (Smith), 980–981 (Nave). Nave suggested
that abolition of the Senate would save money; that if senators were elected for

four years they would "remain so long in office that they forget the objects for which they were elected." Moreover, rather than having acted as a check against "improvident and hasty legislation" they had aided such legislation. The *Convention Journal*, 160, has nothing regarding Smith's comments which appear in the *Debates*, but p. 354 of the *Journal* notes that Nave's proposal was immediately tabled.

55 *Convention Debates*, I, 998–1000. See Chapter 5, pp. 267–270, regarding Wallace's disregarded recommendation about reducing the number of senators and representatives.

56 Kettleborough, *Constitution Making in Indiana*, I, 96, 97, 99; *Convention Journal*, 177–180. As shown *ibid.*, p. 53, the members of this committee as originally appointed were: Alexander F. Morrison, Cromwell W. Barbour, Erastus K. Bascom, John Beard, George A. Gordon, Jesse Morgan, William F. Sherrod, Alexander C. Stevenson, Benjamin Wolfe. According to Baker and McFarland's listing Beard was a Free Soiler; Barbour, Morgan, and Stevenson, Whigs; the others were Democrats, giving them a majority of the committee.

57 For the votes, see *Convention Journal*, 534–536, 545–546. For the comments of delegates, see *Convention Debates*, II, 1315 (Morrison and Smith), 1321–1322 (Borden and Cookerly). The *Convention Journal* shows that the effort to limit governors to terms of two years, with eligibility for a maximum of four years in any period of six, was defeated 55 to 53 although the tally is given as 52. *Convention Debates* gives the correct vote.

58 *Convention Journal*, 264 (Mowrer's proposal), 405–406 (Mowrer's proposal rejected), 534–536 (Edmonston amendment rejected); *Convention Debates*, II, 1073 (comments of Edmonston, Mowrer, Read, Smith). Two lieutenant governors—Ratliff Boon for Jonathan Jennings, and Paris C. Dunning for James Whitcomb—had succeeded to the governorship, 1816–50. The fact of these two successions probably was an important consideration in the decision to retain the office of lieutenant governor *to be filled by the voters of the state*. According to the Constitution of 1851 as well as that of 1816 the lieutenant governor had to meet the same qualifications as were required of the governor; he presided over the Senate, and gave the casting vote to break tie votes; and he received the same compensation as the speaker of the House while presiding over the Senate, then the salary allowed the governor if he became the executive. Kettleborough, *Constitution Making in Indiana*, I, 99–100, 323–326. Under the new constitution the lieutenant governor, like the governor, was elected for terms of four years, however, the lieutenant governor, unlike the governor, was eligible for immediate re-election. Moreover, the controversy and constitutional questions about President Pro Tem of the Senate James Brown Ray succeeding Hendricks, at a time when the office of lieutenant governor was vacant, may also have been an important factor in the decision to retain an elective lieutenant governor.

59 *Convention Journal*, 177–179, for the section as reported to the convention; Kettleborough, *Constitution Making in Indiana*, I, 98, 330–331, for such sections in the constitutions of 1816 and 1851.

60 *Convention Debates*, I, 225–226 (Gibson, Read, Wallace); *ibid.*, II, 1317–1318, 1641 (sharing power); *Convention Journal*, 68, 538, 693–694, 701.

61 *Convention Debates*, II, 1317–1318. For an overview of how this section developed, see *ibid.*, I, 225–226; *ibid.*, II, 1317–1318, 1641, 1649; *Convention Journal*, 67, 68, 120, 133, 136, 178–179, 538, 693–694, 701, 935, 941.

62 Kettleborough, *Constitution Making in Indiana*, I, 101–102; *Convention Journal*, 166, 168–169, 170–171 (majority and minority reports), 177–180 (Committee on the Executive).

63 *Convention Journal*, 432–433, 541, 547–551, 556–562, 610–612, 750–751, 935–936, 941–942; *Convention Debates*, II, 1320, 1322–1332, 1345–1352, 1447–1449, 1787. As indicated in the *Convention Journal*, 556–559, on motion of John B. Howe, a Whig, the delegates by a vote of 68 to 44 voted to strike out the section received from the Committee on the Executive and report the relevant section from the Constitution of 1816 for consideration regarding the veto power. See *Convention Debates*, II, 1345–1352, 1447–1449, for significant explanatory comment about modifications made to the section.

64 *Convention Debates*, II, 1323 (Rariden), 1323–1327 (Biddle), 1327–1328 (Pettit), 1328–1329 (Owen), 1346–1347 (Read), 1349 (Kelso). In the address to voters, summarizing changes made in drafting the new constitution, submitted by a select committee chaired by Robert Dale Owen, is this comment: "If a bill is presented to the Governor within three days of the close of the session and he fail to return it, it shall be a law, unless he file the bill, together with his objections, in the office of the Secretary of State, within five days after the adjournment. By the old Constitution, he might hold it over until the next session, and then return it, with his objections." *Ibid.*, 2043–2044.

65 Kettleborough, *Constitution Making in Indiana*, I, 328.

66 *Convention Journal*, 129. As indicated on p. 53, the members of this committee were James G. Read, Thompson P. Bicknell, William Bracken, Alexander S. Farrow, Samuel Frisbie, George W. Moore, and Daniel Mowrer. Bicknell, Farrow, and Frisbie were Whigs, the other members were Democrats. Under the Constitution of 1816 the secretary of state served four year terms, the treasurer and auditor three year terms, all with no restriction on indefinite reelection. Kettleborough, *Constitution Making in Indiana*, I, 101, 102. As indicated in *Convention Debates*, I, 218–219, the report concerning the secretary, treasurer, and auditor was the first one submitted to the convention by any of its standing committees.

67 *Convention Journal*, 175–176. For the further development of this report and the resulting provisions concerning these officials in the new constitution, see *ibid.*, 183–186, 188–190, 192–193, 198–199, 247–248, 935–936, 942–943; *Convention Debates*, I, 277–278 (Foster), 277 (Hall and Read), 281–282 (Dobson), 280–281 (Pettit), 287–288 (Watts). For additional discussion by these and other delegates, see 276–285, 300–315, 329–339. Presumably Dobson either spoke inaccurately or else was inaccurately reported by the stenographer for four times some eight hundred thousand dollars would be far in excess of two millions.

⁶⁸ *Convention Journal,* 247–248. In this and various other votes it seems that once a consensus was achieved, concerning an item about which there was much disagreement, that some delegates voted for sections that did not represent their first preferences. A reading of the discussion, especially in this instance, makes it impossible to believe that only seven delegates had first preferences which conflicted with this decision.

⁶⁹ *Ibid.,* 207–209. As noted *ibid.,* pp. 53, 75, the original members of the Committee on the Organization of the Courts of Justice were John Pettit, chairman, Samuel (I. or J.) Anthony, Oliver P. Davis, James Lockhart, Beattie Mc-Clelland, Christian C. Nave, and Thomas Smith, all Democrats; and Horace P. Biddle, William McKee Dunn, John B. Howe, James Rariden, Elias S. Terry, and Henry P. Thornton, all Whigs. One day later Cromwell W. Barbour, John S. Newman, and John B. Niles, all Whigs, were added to the committee. The political ties indicated are as in the table of delegates by Baker and McFarland as explained above, note 17. According to this table the members were all lawyers, except Davis and Smith. But at that time many men had more than one profession or occupation. Such is indicated for most of the members of this committee whose sketches are in *Biographical Directory of the Indiana General Assembly,* Volume 1. The *Convention Journal,* 4, 381, in listing Anthony as a delegate, then as among delegates whose credentials had been approved, has the initial as J; however, p. 988, listing money allowed delegates for mileage traveled, the initial is P. The *Convention Debates,* I, 3, in listing Anthony as a delegate, has the initial as I. The broadside by Baker and McFarland and the *Biographical Directory of the Indiana General Assembly,* I, 7, 488, 508, 511, use I rather than J. Probably the initial was I.

⁷⁰ See Kettleborough, *Constitution Making in Indiana,* I, 103–107, concerning the judiciary as provided in the Constitution of 1816. Concerning Nave's proposal and its adoption, see *Convention Journal,* 705–706; *Convention Debates,* II, 1652–1659.

⁷¹ Concerning Pettit's persistent efforts, see *Convention Journal,* 208–209 (minority report favored by Pettit), 704–705 (tabled), 713–714 (recommitted), 727–729 (passed). For discussion of this item, see *Convention Debates,* II, 1652–1659, 1679–1683 (Pettit quote, p. 1680), 1718–1724.

⁷² See Kettleborough, *Constitution Making in Indiana,* I, 339–345, for this and *other sections* regarding the judiciary as in the new constitution.

⁷³ *Convention Journal,* 207–209, 706–707, 715, 938, 944; *Convention Debates,* II, 1659–1660, for comments by Pettit, Dunn, and other delegates. Before its passage the term of the clerk was reduced from six to four years, with no limitation on reelection.

⁷⁴ *Convention Journal,* 208, 707–708; *Convention Debates,* II, 1663.

⁷⁵ *Convention Journal,* 207, 707, 708–709, 715, 938, 944; *Convention Debates,* II, 1660–1663, 1671, 1684.

⁷⁶ *Convention Journal,* 120, 209, 719, 748–749, 900; *Convention Debates,* II, 1660–1662, 1698.

[77] *Convention Debates*, II, 1660–1663. As noted in the *Convention Journal*, 717, 734, Auditor Erastus W. H. Ellis reported that during the preceding five years the state had paid fees, for attorneys attending suits brought by or against the state, for a total of $1,960.

[78] Kettleborough, *Constitution Making in Indiana*, I, 104–106; *Convention Journal*, 207–209.

[79] *Convention Journal*, 708, 709, 715–716, 719–722, 723–726, 737–739, 939, 944; *Convention Debates*, I, 362–363; *ibid.*, II, 1663–1671, 1675–1679, 1684–1694, 1698–1708, 1710–1712, 1724–1728, 1735–1737. For examples of unsuccessful efforts to have circuit judges serve four rather than six years as well as efforts to restrict eligibility for reelection, see *Convention Journal*, 719–722, 737–739. The discussion about circuit courts ranged far and wide, at times with emphasis on efforts to make the circuit court judge also serve as judge of the probate court.

[80] *Convention Debates*, II, 1663–1665 (Holman), 1668 (Hovey), 1669 (Kilgore). For further discussion about the probate system by these and other delegates, see 1663–1672, 1675–1679, 1684–1694, 1698–1708, 1710–1712, 1724–1728. As indicated in the preceding note, this discussion was closely associated with that regarding circuit courts. As shown in the *Convention Journal*, 708, 724, Holman's amendment to have the circuit judge hold at least two terms of circuit court and three terms of probate, in each county of his district annually, was rejected 78–48.

[81] *Convention Journal*, 120, 209, 723, 739–740, 939, 944, 968; *Convention Debates*, II, 1676, 1709, 1737.

[82] *Convention Journal*, 149–150 (committee report), 312 (amendment), 338–339 (passage), 940, 945; *Convention Debates*, I, 256–257, 843–844, 929. Leander J. Monks *et al.* (eds.), *Courts and Lawyers of Indiana* (3 vols., Indianapolis, 1916), I, 131–132, states: "The Justices' court was one of considerable importance in our early history." The *substance* of the section regarding justices is the same in the 1816 and 1851 constitutions, except that justices served terms of five years under the old constitution. As indicated in the *Convention Journal*, 53–54, the Committee on County and Township Organization consisted of five Democrats and five Whigs. The Democrats were: Thomas Smith, chair, and Charles Alexander, Othniel Beeson, Thomas Gootee, Thomas A. Hendricks; the Whigs were: Cromwell W. Barbour, Othniel L. Clark, Benoni C. Hogin, Robert C. Kendall, Hiram Prather.

[83] *Convention Journal*, 710–711 (Frisbie), 789–790 (Foster), 796 (section reported). As indicated in note 17 this chapter and the text it supports, unless otherwise suggested, occupations of delegates are based on the Baker and McFarland broadside about the delegates.

[84] *Convention Debates*, II, 1717 (Kelso), 1847 (Foster and Kelso); *Convention Journal*, 796, 860–861, 878–879 (passed), 940, 945. It was while the author studied Indiana history under Logan Esarey in the 1930s that he developed his abiding interest in its further research and study.

85 *Convention Debates*, I, 645–647 (Read), 658 (Owen), 661–662 (Niles), 689–691 (Dunn), 698–699 (Rariden).

86 *Convention Journal*, 138–139. The Committee on State Debt and Public Works originally included four Democrats and three Whigs. The Whigs were Chairman Samuel Hall, Douglass Maguire, John Zenor; the Democrats were Thomas Chenowith, Robert H. Milroy, James Ritchey, Daniel Trembly. Later Smith Miller, Democrat, and John B. Howe, Whig, were added. *Ibid.*, pp. 54, 422.

87 *Ibid.*, 274–275 (amendment), 277–278 (passed), 954, 957. For the discussion regarding this section, see *Convention Debates*, I, 652–655, 664–665.

88 *Convention Journal*, 138–139 (section 3), 275, 278–281 (Allen amendment), 281–284, 287–291 (passed). *Ibid.*, pp. 954, 957, indicates that the two sections were merged to form section 5 of Article 10 of the new constitution. For the discussion of this section, see *Convention Debates*, I, 652–664, 664–692, 693–715, 725–741. The discussion of these sections considered whether the delegates did or did not have a right to prohibit the sovereign people from borrowing. But it also included much about the pros and cons of banking and whether the state should or should not be allowed to hold stock in banks after the expiration of the charter of the Second State Bank; and regarding who was responsible for the fiscal debacle arising from the System of 1836.

89 For differing views about banking, see Chapter 6, pp. 321–332.

90 *Convention Journal*, 193–197, for the various reports; *Convention Debates*, I, 329, for comments of Hamilton. Johnson Watts, a Whig and member of the committee, remarked: "I wish to disclaim all connection with the report made by the minority of this committee, and also with the majority report. I could endorse neither." Schuyler Colfax observed: "For some time it was extremely doubtful whether any proposition at all could be agreed upon by a majority of this committee, and whether all the reports would not be minority reports." *Ibid.*, I, 329. As indicated in the *Convention Journal*, 54, 75–76, as originally appointed the Committee on Currency and Banking consisted of six Democrats and five Whigs. The Whigs were Allen Hamilton, chairman, Schuyler Colfax, Melchert Helmer, Henry G. Todd, Johnson Watts; the Democrats were James Dick, John Piatt Dunn, Franklin Hardin, Samuel P. Mooney, George G. Shoup, Edmund D. Taylor. The next day three Democrats were added: George W. Carr (president of the convention), Abel C. Pepper, and Joseph Ristine; and one Whig, Horace P. Biddle.

91 As noted in *Convention Debates*, I, 647–664, 664–692, 693–715, 725–741, a significant discussion of banking took place during November 21, 22, 23, in connection with the discussion of state debt, which included *passim* comments about banking and internal improvements. A further and prolonged discussion about banking occurred during January 1–16. *Ibid.*, II, 1399, 1414–1420, 1424–1425, 1426–1430, 1436–1447, 1449–1457, 1458–1473, 1474–1534, 1535–1561, 1564–1640, 1641–1645. The voting and related items regarding the discussion of banking are in the *Convention Journal*, 193–197, 273–275, 277–281, 281–284, 287–291, 584–588, 595, 601, 606–610, 612–613, 620–630, 632–641, 644–651, 653–664, 665–692, 695–700, 955–956, 958–959.

92 Such views are frequently found in *Convention Debates*, as cited in the preceding note.

93 Moreover, as indicated in the *Convention Journal*, 280–281, in the discussion about state debt during November, a proviso leaving the state the option of buying stock in "a State bank" was tabled 65 to 55.

94 *Convention Debates*, II, 1426–1429 (Hamilton quotation, p. 1429), 1524–1525 (Colfax). For the Colfax proposal and its rejection, see *Convention Journal*, 628–630.

95 *Convention Debates*, II, 1621–1624 (quotations, pp. 1621–1622, 1623); *Convention Journal*, 672–676. See *ibid.*, 955–956, 958–959, for the sections regarding banking as adopted for the new constitution.

96 *Convention Journal*, 407–409. As indicated in Kettleborough, *Constitution Making in Indiana*, I, 114, the Constitution of 1816 mandated that money paid for exemption from militia duty in times of war, and fines assessed for breach of the penal laws, be applied to support county seminaries. As noted in the *Convention Journal*, 54, nine delegates were named to the Committee on Education. The Democrats were: Chairman John I. Morrison, William C. Foster, Edward R. May, Dixon Milligan, William R. Nofsinger; the four Whigs were: James E. Blythe, James R. M. Bryant, Willis W. Hitt, Alexander C. Stevenson.

97 *Convention Journal*, 408, 801, 815; *Convention Debates*, II, 1858, 1880.

98 *Convention Journal*, 408, 807–808, 815–817 (passage); *Convention Debates*, II, 1867–1869, 1880–1883. Although the *Convention Journal* shows eight votes against passage, it lists only seven delegates who so voted. The *Convention Debates* indicates seven negative votes, but lists only six voters!

99 *Convention Journal*, 408, 801–803, 808–809, 817–818; *Convention Debates*, II, 1858–1861 (Read and Morrison), 1883–1884. See 1888–1891, for speech of James R. M. Bryant, which includes data about school attendance, illiteracy, and population per county.

100 *Convention Journal*, 408, 803–804; *Convention Debates*, II, 1862. *Ibid.*, 1880, states that section 2 was taken up and passed, but this seems to be an error.

101 *Convention Journal*, 408, 804.

102 *Ibid.*, 68; *Convention Debates*, II, 1885 (Bascom), 1864 (Shoup), 1885 (McClelland). In the pioneer era, as in this instance, "foreign students" often meant students from other *states!*

103 *Convention Debates*, II, 1886–1888 (Read), 1888–1892 (Bryant quotations, pp. 1888, 1891).

104 *Convention Journal*, 818–820. See pp. 940–941, 953–954, for sections regarding education as referred to the revision committee; and 945–946, 956–957, for same as referred back by the revision committee for concurrence of the convention. The sections as they appear in the Constitution of 1851 are also in Kettleborough, *Constitution Making in Indiana*, I, 346–349.

105 *Convention Journal*, 32, 68, 137–138 (report). As seen *ibid.*, 52–53, the Committee on the Rights and Privileges of the Inhabitants of the State, as originally appointed, included six Democrats: Robert Dale Owen, chairman, George

Berry, Jacob Page Chapman, Joseph Coats, John A. Graham, William R. Haddon; and three Whigs: Elias Murray, John B. Niles, Hiram Prather.

106 For the November phase of this discussion, see *Convention Debates*, I, 438–459, 460–462, 561–592, 592–600, 600–634, 635–644, 664. See John D. Barnhart and Donald F. Carmony, *Indiana: From Frontier to Industrial Commonwealth* (4 vols., New York, 1954), I, 414–415: Indiana had 7,165 Negroes in 1840 and 11,262 in 1850.

107 *Convention Debates*, I, 438–441 (Howe), 441, 592–600 (Gregg quotations, pp. 592, 593, 597), 455–459 (Colfax quotations, pp. 456, 457, 458). Gregg stated: "Let no one infer from my remarks that I desire to place the white and the colored emigrant upon the same degree of social and political equality—that I would exclude the one as well as the other, or admit them both upon the same footing." *Ibid.*, I, 597.

108 *Ibid.*, I, 449–453 (Foster quotations, pp. 449, 450, 451), 572–576 (Rariden quotations, pp. 573, 575), 461–462 (Pettit), 566–568 (Robinson).

109 For examples of these memorials, see *Convention Journal*, 81, 94, 101, 164, 207, 243, 264, 273, 303, 308, 359, 664.

110 *Ibid.*, 267–273, for the proposals, items approved, committee members, and adoption of Owen's resolution. For the discussion, from Kent's proposal to adoption of Owen's resolution, see *Convention Debates*, I, 561–592, 600–634, 635–644. See 561–562, and 644, for Kent's explanation why he thought such a committee was needed, and Alexander F. Morrison's appeal that delegates trust the committee to reflect their opinions as reflected in the votes they had given. The five Democrats on the select committee were Kent, David M. Dobson, William Steele Holman, Joel B. McFarland, Robert Dale Owen; the five Whigs were John B. Howe, Douglass Maguire, John B. Niles, James Rariden, Alexander C. Stevenson.

111 *Convention Journal*, 652; *Convention Debates*, II, 1586, 1787–1801, 1816–1820, 1931–1934.

112 *Convention Journal*, 652, 751–753, 767–768. On second reading William McKee Dunn, a Whig from Jefferson County, moved to add: "'And that the members of this Convention be required, whenever they see a Negro in the State, to catch him and take him out.'" The amendment was defeated 114 to 15. See *ibid.*, p. 752, indicating that "come into and settle" was changed to "come into or settle . . . ."

113 *Ibid.*, 652, 753–756, 768–770. See pp. 754, 960, indicating that "less than ten, or more," was changed to "not less than ten, nor more . . . ."

114 *Ibid.*, 652, 756–758, 770–773. Page 772 indicates that 33 delegates opposed passage of this section, but only 32 delegates were named; also that 106 delegates voted for passage, but only 100 are named.

115 *Ibid.*, 652, 758–759. Page 758 refers to this item as section 3, but the context indicates that it is section 4.

116 *Ibid.*, 652, 759–760, 776. As noted on pp. 759–760, the item about "if adopted by the people" was deleted.

117 *Ibid.*, 652, 760–762, 776–777. An amendment to table this section was rejected 73 to 58. An amendment that this section would not become a part of the constitution, unless approved by a majority of all the votes given at the election when this item was submitted at a referendum, was defeated 87 to 44.

118 For the section as proposed by the committee, adopted by the convention, and as revised by the committee that prepared the final draft of the constitution, see *ibid.*, 652 (as reported by the select committee), 960–962 (as sections 1, 2, 3, 5 referred to the revision committee and reported back by it), 977–981 (as section 6 referred to and reported back from the revision committee). Section 6, after passage, *ibid.*, pp. 776–777, by a course not entirely clear, emerged as found on p. 981. These sections are also in Kettleborough, *Constitution Making in Indiana*, I, 360–363, 373.

119 *Convention Journal*, 692–693. As noted *ibid.*, p. 54, James Ritchey, a Democrat, was chair of this committee that included two other Democrats, Benjamin R. Edmonston and Amzi L. Wheeler, plus two Whigs, James Crawford and Elias Murray. Regarding section 2, if two or more amendments were submitted concurrently they must be voted on separately; and no additional amendments could be submitted while other amendments were pending. And at least three months prior to the election of legislators, whose concurrence was necessary for submission of amendments to the voters, the proposed amendments were to be published.

120 *Ibid.*, 444–445, 497. Read's proposal was a close approximation of section 2, except it specified that amendments could not be proposed by the legislature "oftener than once in ten years." For comments by the delegates named and others, see *Convention Debates*, II, 1258–1260.

121 See *Convention Journal*, 830–831, and 831–833, 837–839, respectively, for the tabling of section 1, then amendment of section 2. See *Convention Debates*, II, 1913, indicating no discussion about section 1; and pp. 1913–1919, 1938–1940, for the discussion about section 2.

122 *Convention Journal*, 840–842, 856–857; *Convention Debates*, II, 1941, 1952–1954, concerning the section restoring the two omitted items. For the sections regarding amendments, as referred to the revision committee and reported back from it, see *Convention Journal*, 975–977. Also see Kettleborough, *Constitution Making in Indiana*, I, 367–369.

123 *Convention Debates*, II, 1938 (Pettit). For the discussion regarding preference for use of conventions, see 1258–1260, 1913–1919, 1938–1940, 1941, 1952–1954, *passim*.

124 Kettleborough, *Constitution Making in Indiana*, I, 370–374, giving the schedule for the transition to the new constitution, and the item mandating the separate vote on black exclusion and colonization.

125 Indianapolis *Indiana State Sentinel*, February 20, 27, 1851; Indianapolis *Indiana State Journal* (tri-weekly), February 19, 1851; Indianapolis *Indiana Statesman*, February 19, 1851. But in the *Indiana State Journal* (daily), May 6, 1850, the editor endorsed colonization of blacks "as the right move for them"; and on May 10, 1851, declared that he would not vote for the new constitution.

126 Riker and Thornbrough (comps.), *Indiana Election Returns, 1816–1851*, pp. 388–390. Support for adoption of the constitution increased across the state from south to north, with Southern Indiana averaging 74.84 percent for approval; Central Indiana, 81.16 percent; and Northern Indiana, 89.91 percent. The reverse was true for black exclusion and colonization, with Southern Indiana 91.60 percent for the same; Central Indiana, 81.66 percent; and Northern Indiana, 73.43 percent. Only Ohio County opposed adoption of the constitution, but two other Ohio River counties, Switzerland and Vanderburgh, approved by modest margins. Starke County gave a unanimous vote for approval, and several other northern counties had ten or less votes in opposition. Only four counties voted against exclusion and colonization. They were Elkhart, LaGrange, and Steuben, bordering on Lake Michigan with a significant portion of settlers from New England stock, and Randolph County in east central Indiana, with considerable Quakers as settlers.

CHAPTER 9

1 The terms Jeffersonian Democracy and Jeffersonian Republicanism are considered synonymous, but the latter wording is more common and relevant to the Indiana sources used than the former. The practical monopoly which the Jeffersonian Republicans held over Indiana from 1816 to 1825 is also indicated in the preceding chapters about state politics.

2 Indiana *House Journal*, 1816–17, p. 23; *Laws of Indiana*, 1816–17, p. 251; *Annals of Congress*, 14 Cong., 2 session, 947–949; Dorothy Riker and Gayle Thornbrough (comps.), *Indiana Election Returns, 1816–1851* (Indianapolis, 1960), 3.

3 Corydon *Indiana Gazette*, June 26, 1819; *ibid.*, July 10, 1819, quoting Jeffersonville *Indianian*, July 3, 1819. Also see Nellie A. Robertson and Dorothy Riker (eds.), *The John Tipton Papers* (3 vols., Indianapolis, 1942), I, 159.

4 Indiana *House Journal*, 1820–21, pp. 7, 38–39; Corydon *Indiana Gazette*, November 30, 1820; Riker and Thornbrough (comps.), *Indiana Election Returns, 1816–1851*, p. 3.

5 Vincennes *Western Sun*, July 6, 13, 20, 27, 1816.

6 *Ibid.*, August 3, 17, 1816; Riker and Thornbrough (comps.), *Indiana Election Returns, 1816–1851*, p. 71, giving unofficial returns for four counties. In December, 1816, Hendricks indicated that he thought his majority had been between 3,500 and 4,000. Karl J. R. Arndt (comp. and ed.), *A Documentary History of the Indiana Decade of the Harmony Society, 1814–1824* (2 vols., Indianapolis, 1975, 1978), I, 274. Hendricks was elected to complete the unexpired term that Territorial Delegate Jonathan Jennings had commenced in 1815.

7 Arndt (comp. and ed.), *Indiana Decade of the Harmony Society*, I, 232, 241, 373, 518, has items suggesting a close political association between Posey and Thom.

8 *Annals of Congress*, 14 Cong., 2 session, 230.

9 Hendricks to Samuel Milroy, December 6, 1816, in Frederick Dinsmore Hill, William Hendricks: Indiana Politician and Western Advocate, 1812–1850

(Ph.D. dissertation, Indiana University, 1972), 63; Vincennes *Western Sun*, May 10, 1817 (quoting Corydon *Indiana Gazette* concerning Hendricks), June 7, 1817 (Nelson's announcement). Hill's comprehensive and thoughtful study of Hendricks, 15–20, 62–71, offers additional information about Hendricks' elections to Congress in 1816, 1817, 1818, and 1820.

10 For series by "Justice & Truth," see Vincennes *Western Sun*, February 15 (quotations), March 1, 15, 29, April 12, 1817. For other anonymous criticism, see *ibid.*, March 29, July 12, 26, 1817. Critics described Hendricks as the caucus nominee, put forth by politicians.

11 *Ibid.*, July 12, 26, 1817.

12 Riker and Thornbrough (comps.), *Indiana Election Returns, 1816–1851*, pp. 71–72, giving returns for all counties, with unofficial returns for four of them. On this basis the total for Hendricks was 5,693, that for Posey 3,778.

13 *Ibid.*, 72–74; Hill, William Hendricks, 68–70. According to Riker and Thornbrough (comps.), *Indiana Election Returns, 1816–1851*, pp. 72–74, official returns, with the vote lacking from Daviess and Sullivan counties, show 9,955 votes for Hendricks to 1,118 for Nelson; returns for 1820, official for all but four counties, give 16,331 votes for Hendricks and 1,623 for Nelson.

14 Vincennes *Western Sun*, September 21, 28, October 5, 12, 26, 1816; Indiana *House Journal*, 1816–17, pp. 16, 17–18; Riker and Thornbrough (comps.), *Indiana Election Returns, 1816–1851*, p. 127. With thirty-nine members of the General Assembly, twenty votes were required for election. On the initial vote Noble received 26 votes; Taylor, 20; Scott, 16; Holman, 3; Ezra Ferris, 2; Davis Floyd, 2; Walter Wilson, 2; Elias McNamee, 1. For biographical sketches of Noble and Taylor respectively, see Gayle Thornbrough and Dorothy Riker (eds.), *Journals of the General Assembly of Indiana Territory, 1805–1815* (Indianapolis, 1950), 998, and Robertson and Riker (eds.), *John Tipton Papers*, I, 113n. For seating of the senators, see *Annals of Congress*, 14 Cong., 2 session, 9–10, 31.

15 Vincennes *Western Sun*, July 18, 1818, states that Taylor had participated in a Fourth of July observance at nearby Bruceville. Donald E. Baker, Waller Taylor: The Virginia Indiana Senator (paper delivered at the Indiana History Conference, Indianapolis, November 8, 1969; copy of paper in possession of Donald F. Carmony), gives significant information about Taylor's senatorial career and his persistent residence in Virginia.

16 Vincennes *Western Sun*, October 10, 24, November 14, 1818; Riker and Thornbrough (comps.), *Indiana Election Returns, 1816–1851*, p. 127. Taylor got 21 votes; Scott, 15; Blackford, 2. Riker and Thornbrough make no mention of a second ballot, but the Indiana *Senate Journal*, 1818–19, pp. 32–33, states there were two ballots.

17 Ratliff Boon to Tipton, September 13, 1820, in Robertson and Riker (eds.), *John Tipton Papers*, I, 227–228; James Noble to Tipton, October 14, 1820, *ibid.*, 228–229; Riker and Thornbrough (comps.), *Indiana Election Returns, 1816–1851*, p. 127. Noble received 20 votes; Holman, 13; Davis Floyd, 4. With thirty-nine members of the legislature, twenty votes were required for an election.

18 For the congressional districts, *Laws of Indiana*, 1821–22, pp. 43–45. For a map of the three districts and the counties in each, see Justin E. Walsh, *The Centennial History of the Indiana General Assembly, 1816–1978* (Indianapolis, 1987), 783.

19 Corydon *Indiana Gazette*, April 18, May 9, 30, June 27, July 18, 25, 1822; Indianapolis *Gazette*, June 15, 1822 (Jennings' willingness to complete Hendricks' term, dated June 8, 1822). When Hendricks resigned is uncertain, but Jennings as governor issued a proclamation for the election of a successor to Hendricks on June 7, 1822. Dorothy Riker (ed.), *Executive Proceedings of the State of Indiana, 1816–1836* (Indianapolis, 1947), 221. At this election Congressman Hendricks was seeking election as governor, and Governor Jennings was seeking election as a congressman.

20 Corydon *Indiana Gazette*, July 18, 1822 (Floyd's statement); Riker and Thornbrough (comps.), *Indiana Election Returns, 1816–1851*, pp. 74–75, for nearly complete returns, mainly official, showing 13,211 votes for Jennings and 5,926 for Floyd. According to the Corydon *Indiana Gazette*, July 18, 1822, Reuben W. Nelson and Henry P. Thornton had withdrawn from the race.

21 Vincennes *Western Sun*, April 13, 20, 27, May 4, 11, June 8, 29, July 6, 27, 1822. The May 11 issue has Ewing's withdrawal.

22 Examples of charges and countercharges, *ibid.*, May 11 ("An Elector"), May 18 (John Ewing), 1822; Evansville *Gazette*, June 15 (attack on Dewey), 1822; Vincennes *Western Sun*, July 6 (Dewey's response), 20, 27, 1822. For an excellent and comprehensive sketch of Prince, see Thornbrough and Riker (eds.), *Journals of the General Assembly of Indiana Territory, 1805–1815*, pp. 1005–1009.

23 Complete and largely official returns in Riker and Thornbrough (comps.), *Indiana Election Returns, 1816–1851*, p. 76, show 4,137 votes for Prince and 3,067 for Dewey.

24 Corydon *Indiana Gazette*, April 18, May 9, 30, June 27, July 4, 18, 25, 1822. The *Indiana Gazette* included Scott in its list of candidates on June 27. Scott's letter announcing his candidacy, dated July 5, 1822, is in Indianapolis *Gazette*, July 20, 1822.

25 Madison *Western Clarion*, July 24, 1822, quoting [Salem] *Indiana Farmer* ("An Old Resident" and Jennings' response), July 31, 1822 ("Tom Blunt"). For further attacks on Jennings, see Vincennes *Western Sun*, May 18 (editorial comment), July 20, 1822 ("Farmer Reuben"); Corydon *Indiana Gazette*, July 18, 1822 ("Sidney"). Jennings' denial, however, did not embrace card playing or drinking!

26 Riker and Thornbrough (comps.), *Indiana Election Returns, 1816–1851*, pp. 76–77. Official returns for all counties, except two for which returns are missing, give 3,971 votes for Jennings and 2,598 for Scott.

27 Richmond *Weekly Intelligencer*, April 24 and *passim* through July 31, 1822.

28 *Ibid.*, June 12 ("Moral Duty"), 26 ("A Free Man"), 1822. Also *ibid.*, June 12, 19, 26, July 31, 1822, for related items.

29 Riker and Thornbrough (comps.), *Indiana Elections Returns, 1816–1851*, p. 77, with returns missing from one county and official for all but one county for

which returns are given, list 3,178 votes for Test, 2,238 for Vance, and 1,425 for Ferris.

30 R. Carlyle Buley, *The Old Northwest: Pioneer Period, 1815–1840* (2 vols., Indianapolis, 1950), I, 104–105, 109–110; John D. Barnhart and Dorothy L. Riker, *Indiana to 1816: The Colonial Period* (Indianapolis, 1971), 402–411; John D. Barnhart and Donald F. Carmony, *Indiana: From Frontier to Industrial Commonwealth* (4 vols., New York, 1954), I, 200–202; John B. Dillon, *A History of Indiana . . .* (Indianapolis, 1859), 563. Although the Indians had been overpowered by the end of 1813, loss of life and property by the settlers and Indians on a modest scale continued into at least 1814 and 1815. For example, see Vincennes *Western Sun*, March 19, April 23, 30, August 13, September 3, 10, December 3, 10, 24, 1814, March 4, 11, 18, 25, April 8, May 13, 1815, September 6, 1817.

31 James D. Richardson, *Compilations of the Messages and Papers of the Presidents, 1789–1917* (20 vols., Washington, D.C., 1897–1917), II, 9, 16 (quotation), 45–46, 79–80, 92, 189, 261; George Dewey Harmon, *Sixty Years of Indian Affairs: Political, Economic, and Diplomatic, 1789–1850* (Chapel Hill, N.C., 1941), 88–89, 137; Buley, *The Old Northwest*, I, 104–105, 109–110.

32 Hill, William Hendricks, 23. Hill states that Hendricks sent Monroe a copy of the legislature's request, although a copy of the request has not been found among the laws for the session of 1817–18.

33 Harmon, *Sixty Years of Indian Affairs*, 137–142; Buley, *The Old Northwest*, I, 110–113. Charles C. Royce (comp.), *Indian Land Cessions in the United States* (U.S. Bureau of American Ethnology, *Eighteenth Annual Report, 1896–1897*, Washington, D.C., 1899), 684–689, 692–693, 699–705, indicates when and where these cessions were made, plus comments about them. His maps, numbers 19 and 20, suggest areas covered by the cessions. Royce also cites where the treaties may be found in Charles J. Kappler (ed.), *Indian Affairs: Laws and Treaties* (2 vols., Washington, D.C., 1904). Maps regarding Indian cessions are not always accurate, cessions at times duplicated or overlapped other cessions, tribal claims were often in dispute, and the terms of cessions frequently included imprecise language. In addition, their interpretation was often complicated because the Indians did not understand their terms and implications.

34 Royce (comp.), *Indian Land Cessions in the United States*, 692–693, map 19, concerning the treaty completed at St. Mary's, Ohio, October 3, 1818; Harmon, *Sixty Years of Indian Affairs*, 139; Buley, *The Old Northwest*, I, 112; C. A. Weslager, *The Delaware Indians: A History* (New Brunswick, N. J., 1972), 350–355, 359–363, 380–381. Weslager states that 1,346 Delaware were removed from Indiana in 1820.

35 Royce (comp.), *Indian Land Cessions in the United States*, 692–693, 700–701, maps 19–20 (Wea), 696–699, maps 19, 20 (Kickapoo); Harmon, *Sixty Years of Indian Affairs*, 138–140; Buley, *The Old Northwest*, I, 112.

36 George A. Schultz, *An Indian Canaan: Isaac McCoy and the Vision of an Indian State* (Norman, Okla., 1972), 7–9, 11–15, 24–56, 67–69, and *passim*. At Fort Wayne McCoy helped organize a Baptist church whose "membership included

one full Indian, one half-blood Indian, and one Negro." *Ibid.*, 58. *Mrs. McCoy made very important contributions to these missions.*

37 Accounts of these ruthless atrocities against the Indians at times differ about the number of men involved as well as the number executed. The author's account is mainly indebted to George Chalou, "Massacre on Fall Creek," *Prologue*, IV (1972), 109–114; Oliver H. Smith, *Early Indiana Trials and Sketches* (Cincinnati, 1858), 51–53, 55–57, 177–179. Also see Sandford C. Cox, *Recollections of the Early Settlement of the Wabash Valley* (Lafayette, Ind., 1860), 9–11. Every existing newspaper in Indiana may have carried items about these murders and trials. See *passim* issues of papers such as the Indianapolis *Gazette*, Indianapolis *Indiana Journal*, Corydon *Indiana Gazette*, Lawrenceburgh *Indiana Palladium*, Vincennes *Western Sun*, and Richmond *Public Leger* from about March, 1824 through June, 1825. The pardoning of youthful John Bridge is confirmed in Riker (ed.), *Executive Proceedings of the State of Indiana, 1816–1836*, p. 321.

38 Smith, *Early Indiana Trials and Sketches*, 179. This item is stated in different words on page 57. Smith wrote in the 1850s, but his recollections suggest that the principal facts about this episode had remained in his memory.

39 For a discussion of surveying and how it was done, see Buley, *The Old Northwest*, I, 95, 115–123; Barnhart and Carmony, *Indiana*, I, 220–223.

40 Cox, *Recollections of the Early Settlement of the Wabash Valley*, 17–18. As shown in Buley, *The Old Northwest*, I, 94–99, 106, 115, from colonial days squatters had been a perplexing problem concerning land sales.

41 U. S. *Statutes at Large*, II, 73–78; Buley, *The Old Northwest*, I, 103–104; Benjamin Hibbard, *A History of the Public Land Policies* (Madison, Wis., 1965), 68–72.

42 William Forest Shonkwiler, The Land Office Business in Indiana (Master's thesis, Indiana University, 1950), ii–iv, 19–33. Each land office had a receiver to whom payments were made, and a register who kept the official record of tracts sold. Malcolm J. Rohrbaugh, *The Land Office Business: The Settlement and Administration of American Public Lands, 1789–1837* (New York, 1968), 23–25, 31–32, 75–78, offers a comprehensive account of the duties of these officials.

43 Shonkwiler, The Land Office Business in Indiana, 19–23, 144 (summary table).

44 Buley, *The Old Northwest*, I, 106–108, 133; Hibbard, *History of Public Land Policies*, 92–95; *American State Papers, Public Lands*, III, 645.

45 Buley, *The Old Northwest*, I, 134–136; Hibbard, *History of Public Land Policies*, 94–97.

46 Shonkwiler, The Land Office Business in Indiana, 144, citing *Senate Documents*, 27 Cong., 3 session, 5. See Shonkwiler, ii–iii, concerning sale of Indiana land from Ohio offices, and Illinois land from Vincennes.

47 Buley, *The Old Northwest*, I, 105–109; Hibbard, *History of Public Land Policies*, 87–92; *Annals of Congress*, 16 Cong., 1 session, I, 489 (Senate vote), II, 1901 (House vote); Corydon *Indiana Gazette*, March 30, 1820; Vincennes *Indiana Centinel & Public Advertiser*, May 20, 1820. The transition to cash sales was approved

in the Senate, 31 to 7; in the House, 133 to 23. The opposition votes came principally from members from western states.

48 Shonkwiler, The Land Office Business in Indiana, 145. Since more Indiana land was sold from Ohio offices than Illinois land sold from Indiana offices, actual sales of Indiana land were larger than the aggregate of sales from Indiana land offices.

49 Annals of Congress, 16 Cong., 1 session, II, 1353–1354. Thomas Donaldson, The Public Domain: Its History, with Statistics (Washington, D.C., 1884), 523–524, estimates that the cost of acquiring, surveying, and selling the public domain, plus costs of Indian cessions and removals to 1883, exceeded the net revenue from sales of land by $126,428,484.89. Whatever this balance was, it seems reasonable to conclude that federal ownership and control of the public domain brought significant political and economic benefits to Indiana.

50 Richardson, Messages and Papers of the Presidents, I, 567–568, 584–585 (Madison); ibid., II, 17–18, 142–143, 190–191, 216–217, 255–256 (Monroe). Passim items in this chapter illustrate strong support for federal grants of land and money for internal improvements. Also see ibid., II, 144–183, for a very detailed and comprehensive statement by Monroe concerning his views regarding internal improvements.

51 Concerning federal aid, see Ch. 1, pp. 41–42; Ch. 3, pp. 134–135, 139–140, 144–145; Ch. 4, pp. 176–180. Also see Hill, William Hendricks, 44–48.

52 For example, see Annals of Congress, 18 Cong., 1 session, I, 136, 294; Congressional Debates, 18 Cong., 2 session, I, 333, 361.

53 Congressional Debates, 18 Cong., 2 session, I, 242–243. See pp. 476–484, this chapter, for internal improvements as an issue in the presidential campaign of 1824. The Indianapolis Gazette, December 16, 1823, strongly sustained congressional support for internal improvements to strengthen the ties that bind the country together.

54 Indiana House Journal, 1818–19, p. 21; ibid., 1819–20, p. 17; ibid., 1820–21, pp. 10–11; ibid., 1821–22, pp. 17–18; ibid., 1822–23, p. 37; ibid., 1825, pp. 12–13. The governors indicated the need to develop domestic manufacturing as a means of reducing the dependence on European imports. These messages presumably gave implicit support for tariff protection to curb exports, but they did not explicitly call for such protection.

55 Vincennes Indiana Centinel & Public Advertiser, June 10, November 4, 1820; Indianapolis Gazette, March 29, September 2, December 16, 1823; Vincennes Western Sun, July 24, 1824; Richmond Public Leger, March 27, December 18, 1824. See Acts (special), 1823–24, p. 116, for memorial supporting a tariff to encourage the manufacture of domestic fabrics.

56 Indiana House Journal, 1819–20, pp. 131, 259–260; Brookville Enquirer and Indiana Telegraph, January 28, 1820. It appears that no law was passed about wearing only items of domestic manufacture.

57 Annals of Congress, 18 Cong., 1 session, I, 738–744, 751, 754–757, 759, 765–766; II, 1419–1430, 1607, 2620–2629, 2631–2635, 2669, 2671–2675. Congress-

man Jennings did not vote for passage, but his other votes suggest that he probably favored passage. *Ibid.*, II, 2621, 2627–2629, 2633–2634, 2673–2674.

[58] For the tariff as an issue in the presidential election of 1824, see pp. 479–480.

[59] For banking in early Indiana, see Chapter 1, pp. 17–25.

[60] *American State Papers, Finance*, V, 66. Six of the protesters were from Ohio (including William Henry Harrison, Indiana's territorial governor), three from Kentucky, two from western Pennsylvania, and three from Indiana—Senators Noble and Taylor and Congressman Hendricks, comprising all of Indiana's members of Congress. The two Indiana banks referred to were presumably the recently organized First State Bank of Indiana and the Farmers and Mechanics Bank of Madison.

[61] Indiana *House Journal*, 1818–19, pp. 23–24; Noble E. Cunningham, Jr., *Circular Letters of Congressmen to their Constituents, 1789–1829* (3 vols., Chapel Hill, N.C., 1978), III, 1046.

[62] Corydon *Indiana Gazette*, February 27 (repeal charter), March 20 (concerning Hendricks), 1819. For other adverse criticisms, see *ibid.*, October 26, 1820; Brookville *Enquirer and Indiana Telegraph*, February 5, 1819; Madison *Indiana Republican*, May 8, 15, 1819; Vincennes *Western Sun*, May 6, 1820.

[63] Vincennes *Western Sun* (extra), July 11, 1818; Indiana *House Journal*, 1818–19, pp. 17, 78–79, 90, 132, 149; Indiana *Senate Journal*, 1818–19, pp. 85, 87.

[64] In doing substantial research in newspapers and legislative documents for the middle and late twenties, the author generally has found meager references to banking, while often finding many items about tariff protection and especially internal improvements.

[65] Barnhart and Riker, *Indiana to 1816*, p. 360; Charles Kettleborough, *Constitution Making in Indiana* (3 vols., Indianapolis, 1916, 1930), I, 112, 117; Emma Lou Thornbrough, *The Negro in Indiana Before 1900: A Study of a Minority* (Indianapolis, 1958), 24–29. The Vincennes *Western Sun*, June 27, 1818, has an ad offering to sell a black woman and two children for cash.

[66] For examples, see Madison *Indiana Republican*, June 8, 15, August 24, 1820; Vincennes *Western Sun*, January 29, April 16, 1825.

[67] Emma Lou Thornbrough, "Indiana and Fugitive Slave Legislation," *Indiana Magazine of History*, L (1954), 201–202.

[68] Indiana *House Journal*, 1816–17, p. 11; *Laws of Indiana*, 1816–17, pp. 150–152. See Louis B. Ewbank and Dorothy L. Riker (eds.), *The Laws of Indiana Territory, 1809–1816* (Indianapolis, 1934), 138–139, for a law approved in 1810 providing penalties for illegal removal of blacks from Indiana.

[69] Indiana *House Journal*, 1817–18, pp. 9–10 (Jennings' remarks), 47–50 (Slaughter's protest and Jennings' response).

[70] *Ibid.*, 1817–18, pp. 47, 50–52; *Laws of Indiana*, 1818–19, pp. 64–65.

[71] Vincennes *Western Sun*, November 21, 1818 (Parke's decision). The case is discussed in Thornbrough, "Indiana and Fugitive Slave Legislation," *Indiana Magazine of History*, L, 204–205.

72 Some items regarding Susan and her capture are uncertain and not always described in the same manner, but apparently she was kidnapped more than once. For a summary view, see Thornbrough, "Indiana and Fugitive Slave Legislation," *Indiana Magazine of History*, L, 207–214. For relevant correspondence and documents, see Logan Esarey (ed.), *Messages and Papers of Jonathan Jennings, Ratliff Boon, William Hendricks, 1816–1825* (Indianapolis, 1924), 47–52, 98–109, 134–137, 223, 277, 455–456; Robertson and Riker (eds.), *John Tipton Papers*, I, 146–147, 171, 173–174, 221–222. The latter source seems to indicate that Tipton, as sheriff of Harrison County, was more sympathetic to Kentucky slaveholders than to Jennings in this controversy.

73 *Laws of Indiana*, 1818–19, pp. 64–65, 141–142.

74 Indiana *House Journal*, 1822–23, p. 14 (Boon); Indiana *Senate Journal*, 1822–23, p. 146 (Hendricks); Thornbrough, "Indiana and Fugitive Slave Legislation," *Indiana Magazine of History*, L, 213–214. Boon explained that the governor of Kentucky had solicited the naming of commissioners by Ohio, Kentucky, Indiana, and Illinois to try to resolve differences about fugitive slaves. The Indiana Senate and House voted for the naming of commissioners to meet with those of Kentucky but, unable to concur about the conditions involved, commissioners were not authorized. Indiana *Senate Journal*, 1822–23, pp. 240, 254–255, 257, 273, 277; Indiana *House Journal*, 1822–23, pp. 303, 311–312, 319.

75 *Laws of Indiana* (revised), 1823–24, pp. 142, 143, 221–222; Indiana *Senate Journal*, 1825, pp. 92, 98, 117–119, 132–134. So far as the author has learned, neither Governors Boon nor Hendricks sought the extradition of Robert Stephens as Governor Jennings had; and the efforts of the latter to give a degree of protection to fugitive slaves, and blacks claimed as such, apparently were largely abandoned after he resigned as chief executive. Jennings' efforts against "manstealing," although unsuccessful, seem to have been a further effort for the elimination of slavery in Indiana, begun in the territorial period and proclaimed in the Constitution of 1816. During the late teens and early twenties the Corydon *Indiana Gazette* and Vincennes *Western Sun* have numerous items concerning policy about fugitive slaves and related items.

76 The Tallmadge amendment passed the House, but was in part rejected in the Senate and the two houses failed to agree hence it did not pass. Donald E. Baker, The Fearful Contest: Indiana Views the Missouri Controversy, 1819–1821 (unpublished paper, 1971, in possession of author), 9–10; Glover Moore, *The Missouri Controversy, 1819–1821* (Lexington, Ky., 1953), 52–55. Baker's manuscript is a comprehensive study of Indiana views toward and reaction to the Missouri Compromise.

77 Baker, The Fearful Contest: Indiana Views the Missouri Controversy, 10–11; Moore, *The Missouri Controversy*, 59–62.

78 Baker, The Fearful Contest: Indiana Views the Missouri Controversy, 26–27, 32–36, 41–42; Moore, *The Missouri Controversy*, 100, 107–111. As Baker notes, after repeated votes against the 36° 30′ line, Hendricks voted for it,

apparently expecting slavery to develop south of the line and with it prohibited north of the line.

[79] *Annals of Congress*, 16 Cong., 1 session, II, 1344–1355 (Hendricks' quote, p. 1355); Corydon *Indiana Gazette*, March 23, 1820 (Noble); Baker, The Fearful Contest: Indiana Views the Missouri Controversy, 6, 33 (Taylor).

[80] For examples of editorial comment for and against, and otherwise related to the Missouri question, see Corydon *Indiana Gazette*, March 2, August 10, December 28, 1820; Brookville *Enquirer*, March 2, 16, 23, November 21, December 5, 1820; Vincennes *Indiana Centinel*, April 1, 1820; Vincennes *Western Sun*, March 18, 25, April 1, 15, 1820; Madison *Indiana Republican*, March 9, 31, May 25, 1820. For many additional editorial comments, plus comments of Fourth of July speakers and anonymous contributors, see Baker, The Fearful Contest: Indiana Views the Missouri Controversy, 8–78 *passim*, including quoted items.

[81] Baker, The Fearful Contest: Indiana Views the Missouri Controversy, 69–83; Moore, *The Missouri Controversy*, 155–159.

[82] Both the Vincennes *Western Sun*, June 5, 1819, and Vincennes *Indiana Centinel*, June 19, 1819, quoting Dayton (Ohio) *Watchman*, say the post at Fort Wayne had been evacuated. Blackford Condit, *The History of Early Terre Haute from 1816 to 1840* (New York, 1900), 39–40, states that Fort Harrison, the post at Terre Haute, ceased to be a military post in 1822. Francis Paul Prucha, *A Guide to the Military Posts of the United States, 1789–1895* (Madison, Wis., 1964), 5–8, includes both Fort Wayne and Fort Harrison as military posts for 1817, but neither for 1822.

[83] Brookville *Enquirer and Indiana Telegraph*, September 24, 1819, quoting Vincennes *Indiana Centinel*.

[84] Vincennes *Western Sun*, August 3, 1816. Other toasts hailed George Washington and those who won freedom by the American Revolution; voiced strong attachment to the American union of states; and, referring to the War of 1812, expressed pride in its military achievements.

[85] Cunningham, *Circular Letters of Congressmen*, III, 1016–1017.

[86] *Journal of the Executive Proceedings of the Senate of the United States . . .* (3 vols., Washington, D.C., 1828), III, 177–178, 242–244; Cunningham, *Circular Letters of Congressmen*, III, 1138–1139. The Florida treaty was ratified February 24, 1819, without a dissenting vote; but since more than the allowed time of six months passed before the Spanish Cortes approved it, it was ratified again on February 19, 1821. Taylor and Noble voted yea on both occasions. The vote in 1819 was 34–0; that in 1821 was 40–4. The opposition votes were cast by senators from Kentucky and Tennessee.

[87] Indianapolis *Gazette*, May 10, 1823; Vincennes *Western Sun*, November 4, 1820, quoting the *Metropolitan*; *ibid.*, October 25, 1823, quoting Louisville *Public Advertiser*. The *Western Sun* carried items about the wealth of Texas, the development of trade between the Pacific coast and the East Indies, and related items. For instance, see issues for August 12, November 25, 1820, February 17, 1821, March 23, June 15, 1822.

88 *Acts* (special), 1823–24, pp. 109–110.

89 *Ibid.*; Cunningham, *Circular Letters of Congressmen*, III, 1158–1159. For additional examples of friendly sentiments for liberal and independence movements in Europe, see Indianapolis *Gazette*, April 3, 1822, April 12, May 3, September 16, 23, 1823, June 22, 1824.

90 Gayle Thornbrough, Dorothy Riker, and Paula Corpuz (eds.), *The Diary of Calvin Fletcher* (9 vols., Indianapolis, 1972–1983), I, 96, 99; Vincennes *Western Sun*, January 26, March 9, November 23, 30, December 7, 1822, July 12, 26, September 6, 1823; Indianapolis *Gazette*, March 6, 18, June 8, 1822, March 22, September 9, 1823; Richmond *Weekly Intelligencer*, March 20, June 19, 1822.

91 Vincennes *Western Sun*, November 1, 1823; James F. Hopkins (ed.), *The Papers of Henry Clay* (11 vols., Lexington, Ky., 1959–1992), III, 552; *Laws of Indiana* (revised), 1823–24, pp. 174–179. For further comments about election of delegates by districts versus general ticket, see Vincennes *Western Sun*, December 23, 1820, July 28, 1821, June 14, July 12, 26, December 20, 1823; Indianapolis *Gazette*, June 7, December 16, 1823; Thornbrough, Riker, and Corpuz (eds.), *Diary of Calvin Fletcher*, I, 100.

92 Indiana *Senate Journal*, 1823–24, pp. 38, 58–59; Indiana *House Journal*, 1823–24, pp. 80, 90, 182–183, 186–187. Indiana *Senate Journal*, 1823–24, pp. 59, 65–66, has protests from four senators against passage of Thompson's resolution. A protest which included the name of James Brown Ray, soon to become governor, deprecated caucusing but stated: "if there should be a caucus, which may result to the injury of the west, let Indiana have her weight there."

93 William Hendricks to Henry Clay, December 22, 1823, in Hopkins (ed.), *Papers of Henry Clay*, III, 551–552. In its issue of September 9, 1823, the Indianapolis *Gazette*, a pro-Clay organ, had condemned nomination by congressional caucus, contending that since Monroe's reelection the people had resolved to choose the president without interference from any delegated or self-constituted body.

94 Edward Stanwood, *A History of the Presidency, 1788–1897* (2 vols., Boston, 1928), I, 130–131. For Noble's defense of his participation, see *Annals of Congress*, 18 Cong., 1 session, I, 374–375; Indianapolis *Gazette*, May 18, 1824, quoting Centreville *Western Emporium*, March 31, 1824. Noble's comments and his friendship for Crawford strengthen the presumption that he voted for Crawford.

95 Chase C. Mooney, *William H. Crawford, 1772–1834* (Lexington, Ky.), 249, 259–260, 263.

96 Indianapolis *Gazette*, April 6, 1824; Corydon *Indiana Gazette*, April 14, 1824, quoting [Salem] *Indiana Farmer*; Jesse L. Holman to Henry Clay, October 24, 1825, in Hopkins (ed.), *Papers of Henry Clay*, IV, 756–758. The Adams electors, from the political elite of the state, were Isaac Blackford, Knox County; Jesse L. Holman, Dearborn County; James Scott, Clark County; Christopher Harrison, Washington County; and David H. Maxwell, Monroe County. The first three were members of the state Supreme Court, Harrison had been lieutenant governor, and Maxwell had served as speaker of the House of Representatives.

97 Corydon *Indiana Gazette*, May 12, 1824; Vincennes *Western Sun*, May 22, 1824; Indianapolis *Gazette*, June 8, 29, 1824. The Clay electors were Marston G. Clark, Washington County; James Rariden, Wayne County; Moses Tabbs, Knox County; William W. Wick, Marion County; and Walter Wilson, Gibson County.

98 Indianapolis *Gazette*, February 17, March 23, April 13, May 11, 18, July 20, October 5, 1824. If friends of Adams used such meetings and committees, the author has found no evidence of them.

99 Vincennes *Western Sun*, June 26, July 10, 31, 1824. For additional examples of surplus aspirants as electors, see Corydon *Indiana Gazette*, May 5, June 2, 9, July 7, 21, 1824; Richmond *Public Leger*, June 12, 19, 26, July 31, October 2, 1824.

100 Vincennes *Western Sun*, July 31, 1824. Editor Stout suggested that each county name a delegate or delegates proportionate to its "representation in the legislature," for the convention at Salem. For examples of county meetings, naming delegates and at times committees, see *ibid.*, August 21, 29, September 4, 11, 1824; Evansville *Gazette*, August 26, September 2, 1824.

101 Vincennes *Western Sun*, September 25, 1824. The Jackson electors chosen by the convention were John Carr, Clark County; Jonathan McCarty, Fayette County; Elias McNamee, Knox County; Samuel Milroy, Washington County; and David Robb, Gibson County. Dr. Israel T. Canby, Jefferson County, Samuel Beach, Clark County, and Jesse B. Durham, Jackson County, were named the general correspondence committee, which Canby apparently chaired. Samuel Milroy was elected convention chairman, and Jacob Call, Knox County, was chosen convention secretary.

102 The Corydon *Indiana Gazette*, May 19, 1824, quoted the Centreville *Western Emporium* that so far as could be learned the fourteen [weekly] newspapers of the state had presidential preferences as follows: for Adams, Richmond *Public Leger*, Centreville *Western Emporium*, Lawrenceburgh *Oracle*, Salem [*Indiana*] *Farmer*, Charlestown *Indiana Intelligencer* [*and Farmers' Friend*], Corydon [*Indiana*] *Gazette*, Evansville *Gazette*; for Clay, Indianapolis *Gazette*, Indianapolis *Censor*, Madison [*Indiana*] *Republican*, Vevay [*Indiana*] *Register*; as "Half Adams and half Clay," Brookville *Enquirer*; as doubtful, Vincennes *Western Sun* and Connersville [*Indiana*] *Statesman*. Thomas W. Howard, "Indiana Newspapers and the Presidential Election of 1824," *Indiana Magazine of History*, LXIII (1967), 204–206, concurs with this listing, except that he counts the Brookville *Enquirer* for Clay and the Vincennes *Western Sun* for Jackson. Howard has a variety of useful comments about the issues as well as the personal charges and countercharges concerning this election.

103 Howard, "Indiana Newspapers and the Presidential Election of 1824," *Indiana Magazine of History*, LXIII, 193, quoting Charlestown *Indiana Intelligencer and Farmers' Friend*, May 29, 1824, quoting Hartford (Connecticut) *Mirror*.

104 For a sampling of items pro and con Adams, see Indianapolis *Gazette*, May 17, 24, June 21, November 25, 1823, March 2, May 18, July 20, August 24, 1824; Vincennes *Western Sun*, January 17, May 29, June 26, July 3, 17, 24, 1824; Rich-

mond *Public Leger*, May 22, 29, July 24, August 21, 28, October 9, 1824. These citations about Adams, and those for notes 106 and 108 below, often include items about rival candidates.

105 Richmond *Public Leger*, May 15, 1824.

106 For a sampling of items pro and con Clay, see Indianapolis *Gazette*, September 2, 9, November 25, 1823, January 20, March 2, 16, June 15, July 20, September 21, November 2, 1824; Vincennes *Western Sun*, December 20, 1823, January 10, 17, 24, April 17, May 29, June 5, 12, 19, 26, July 3, 17, October 23, 1824; Richmond *Public Leger*, May 22, June 5, October 9, 1824.

107 Vincennes *Western Sun*, December 13, 1823, January 3, February 7, 1824.

108 The quotations are respectively from *ibid.*, January 10, 1824; Richmond *Public Leger*, August 7, 1824, quoting *National Crisis*; Indianapolis *Gazette*, October 26, 1824. For a sampling of items pro and con Jackson, see Vincennes *Western Sun*, August 23, November 1, December 13, 1823, January 3, 10, 17, February 7, April 24, May 29, August 7, 1824; Indianapolis *Gazette*, September 9, 1823, March 2, July 20, October 26, 1824; Richmond *Public Leger*, May 22, 1824. The address of the Jackson State Convention in the Indianapolis *Gazette*, October 12, 1824, exalts Jackson's personal qualities as the candidate of the people, but is silent regarding the key issues of tariff protection and federal aid to internal improvements.

109 Vincennes *Western Sun*, September 25, 1824. For examples of polls and victory forecasts, see *ibid.*, August 7, 21, October 9, 23, 30, 1824; Indianapolis *Gazette*, October 26, 1824.

110 Riker and Thornbrough (comps.), *Indiana Election Returns, 1816–1851*, pp. 4–9, give official returns for all counties. The vote for Jackson electors varied from a low of 7,418 to a high of 7,444; Clay electors, 5,311 to 5,321; Adams electors, 3,071 to 3,093. For the vote for congressmen and governor, see *ibid.*, 77–79, 138.

111 Concerning the electoral vote and Adams' election by the House, see Stanwood, *History of the Presidency*, I, 134–141. A table on page 141 indicates that Indiana's three congressmen voted for Jackson.

112 Richmond *Public Leger*, February 19, 1825; Indianapolis *Indiana Journal*, February 22, 1825.

113 Vincennes *Western Sun*, February 26, 1825. The Richmond *Public Leger*, March 5, 1825, has a letter from Congressman John Test, dated February 9, 1825, in which Test states: "'The presidential question is decided by a single ballot . . . . Indiana voted unanimously for Andrew Jackson.'"

114 Vincennes *Western Sun*, February 21, March 13, April 3, 10, 17, 1824; Indianapolis *Gazette*, February 24, March 9, June 8, 1824; Corydon *Indiana Gazette*, April 14, May 5, 1824. According to Riker (ed.), *Executive Proceedings of the State of Indiana, 1816–1836*, p. 284, Boon resigned as lieutenant governor January 30, 1824.

115 *Western Register & Terre-Haute Advertiser*, June 9, 1824; Evansville *Gazette*, July 8, 1824; Riker and Thornbrough (comps.), *Indiana Election Returns*,

1816–1851, pp. 77–78, official and complete, give Boon 4,281 votes, Call 3,222, Blake 2,661.

[116] Indianapolis *Gazette*, February 24, April 13, 1824; Corydon *Indiana Gazette*, July 21, 1824 (Jennings' declaration).

[117] Corydon *Indiana Gazette*, July 21, 28, 1824. "A Farmer" said it was a notorious fact that Sullivan had voted against a resolution to censure Waller Taylor for voting to admit slaves into Arkansas Territory. Complete returns, official for all counties but Madison, show Jennings 4,680 votes and Sullivan 4,119. Riker and Thornbrough (comps.), *Indiana Election Returns, 1816–1851*, pp. 78–79.

[118] Indianapolis *Gazette*, February 24, June 8, 1824; Richmond *Public Leger*, March 27, May 29, June 5, 1824; Riker and Thornbrough (comps.), *Indiana Election Returns, 1816–1851*, p. 79, indicating official returns for all counties but Randolph and Ripley, show Test 3,434 votes, Ray 2,471, Caswell 1,388.

[119] Vincennes *Western Sun*, September 11, 25, October 2, 9, 23, November 6, 1824; Evansville *Gazette*, September 16, 23, October 7, 1824.

[120] Vincennes *Western Sun*, October 2, 9, 1824, respectively for statements by Blake and Call. As indicated in the Evansville *Gazette*, October 7, 1824, Robert M. Evans, in withdrawing from the contest, stated that he, like Blake, favored Clay for president; and that although Boon's sentiments were not precisely known he was "supposed" to be for Crawford.

[121] According to Riker and Thornbrough (comps.), *Indiana Election Returns, 1816–1851*, pp. 79–80, giving official returns for all counties but Hendricks, show Call received 2,155 votes, Blake 2,087, and Boon 36. The following have items pro and con whether Call or Blake had obtained the most votes at this election: Vincennes *Western Sun*, January 22, February 5, March 19, 26, 1825, April 1, 1826; Indianapolis *Indiana Journal*, January 18, 1825. According to the *Biographical Directory of the American Congress, 1774–1927*, p. 778, Call served in Congress "from December 23, 1824, to March 3, 1825; [and] died by suicide April 20, 1826."

[122] Indianapolis *Gazette*, October 19, 1822, November 30, 1824.

[123] *Ibid.*, October 12, November 30, 1824. For this and similar comments, see Hill, *William Hendricks*, 112–117.

[124] Jennings to David G. Mitchell, November 18 and December 1, 1824, in Dorothy Riker, *Unedited Letters of Jonathan Jennings* (Indianapolis, 1932), 252–254.

[125] Riker and Thornbrough (comps.), *Indiana Election Returns, 1816–1851*, p. 127. The election occurred January 12, 1825, with the voting as follows:

	1st ballot	2nd ballot	3rd ballot	4th ballot
William Hendricks	25	29	31	32
Isaac Blackford	26	30	30	30
Jonathan Jennings	10	2	0	0
Scattering	1	1	1	0

Ewing said he voted once for Blackford, but claimed that neither his vote for Blackford, nor his absence from voting, would have elected him. Ewing scoffed at the idea of Blackford being considered a "western candidate" because of his "occasional residence" at Vincennes. Ewing asserted that Hendricks had more merit, and that he objected to Blackford having traversed the state in search of votes. Vincennes *Western Sun*, February 26, 1825.

126 Indianapolis *Indiana Journal*, March 14, 1826; Riker and Thornbrough (comps.), *Indiana Election Returns, 1816–1851*, pp. 81–82, giving official returns for all counties except Crawford and Scott for which returns are lacking, show 7,913 votes for Jennings, with 43 scattered votes.

127 Indianapolis *Gazette*, November 22, 1825, February 28, March 7, April 18, August 1, 1826; Lawrenceburgh *Indiana Palladium*, January 13, May 6, August 5, 1826. For a time Noah Noble, Amos Lane, and Samuel Vance were also mentioned as candidates.

128 Smith's statement and that of the anonymous writer are in Lawrence-burgh *Indiana Palladium*, July 15, 1826. For Test's response and related items, see *ibid.*, July 22, 29, September 23, 1826.

129 Smith, *Early Indiana Trials and Sketches*, 80–82. Smith says people turned out "by thousands" to hear the candidates; and for their joint appearance at Allenville in Switzerland County, "The whole country was there." Smith's details, however, are not always accurate. Most likely the crowds were much smaller than Smith indicates. According to Smith, "Stump speaking was just coming in fashion."

130 Riker and Thornbrough (comps.), *Indiana Election Returns, 1816–1851*, p. 82. Official returns for all counties indicate 6,015 votes for Smith, and 4,946 for Test.

131 Vincennes *Western Sun*, February 25, March 25, May 20, August 5, 1826. According to Condit, *The History of Early Terre Haute from 1816 to 1840*, pp. 124–125, and an obituary notice in the *Western Sun*, August 11, 1827, Shuler resided in Vincennes before moving to Vigo County in 1825.

132 Vincennes *Western Sun*, July 11, 29, 1826. As indicated *ibid.*, July 29 (extra), 1826, Shuler stressed his support of federal aid to improve navigable streams, the Wabash and Erie Canal, and tariff protection to aid domestic manufacturing.

133 *Ibid.*, July 6, 1826; "Vigo" "To the Citizens of Knox County," broadside in Indiana Division, Indiana State Library; Riker and Thornbrough (comps.), *Indiana Election Returns, 1816–1851*, pp. 80–81, has complete returns, official for all counties but Putnam, showing 5,223 votes for Blake, 5,202 for Boon, and 1,723 for Shuler. The delay and uncertainty about the outcome are indicated in Vincennes *Western Sun*, September 16, 23, October 14, 1826.

134 Indianapolis *Gazette*, November 7, 1826; Lawrenceburgh *Indiana Palladium*, November 18, 1826. The *Gazette* said Jennings and Noble had announced themselves; the *Indiana Palladium* stated that Jennings, Noble, and Blackford, all men of standing and well-known throughout the state, were understood to be candidates.

135 Vincennes *Western Sun*, June 3, 1826; Ewing to Tipton, June 5, 1826, in Robertson and Riker (eds.), *John Tipton Papers*, I, 537–539.

136 Indianapolis *Gazette*, November 7, December 7, 1826, quoting Brookville *Franklin Repository*; Lawrenceburgh *Indiana Palladium*, December 2, 1826 ("Q"). The Brookville editor stressed Noble's contributions regarding early Indian treaties; numerous relief acts to purchasers of public land; recent exertions in obtaining federal engineers, at the cost of the federal government, to make surveys for contemplated Indiana canals. Suggesting that Jennings had influence as a congressman, Noble as a federal senator, and Blackford as a Supreme judge, the editor viewed their continued service in these positions as in the public interest.

137 Riker and Thornbrough (comps.), *Indiana Election Returns, 1816–1851*, p. 127. The election was on December 12, with the voting as follows:

	1st ballot	2nd ballot	3rd ballot	4th ballot
James Noble	32	35	38	40
Isaac Blackford	24	24	26	28
Jonathan Jennings	22	20	15	10

After a visit to Indiana by William Henry Harrison in the fall of 1826, during which time he met Jennings and Blackford at Vincennes and Princeton, Harrison wrote Henry Clay, November 12, 1826, that Blackford "will get the members from the West end of the State with the exception of one or two & those will be in favor of Noble. The center Districts are generally for Jennings But there also Noble will break in upon him. I think upon the whole that Nobles prospects are best[.]" Hopkins (ed.), *Papers of Henry Clay*, V, 918.

138 Smith, *Early Indiana Trials and Sketches*, 80.

139 The party ties as indicated in *A Biographical Directory of the Indiana General Assembly* (2 vols., Indianapolis, 1980, 1984), Volume 1, *1816–1899*, Volume 2, *1901–1984*, I, 447–453, show that supporters of Adams significantly outnumbered those of Jackson at each annual legislative session from 1825 to 1829.

140 *Senate Executive Journal*, III, 436, 441; Lawrenceburgh *Indiana Palladium*, March 25, 1825, quoting Noble's statement from the *National Intelligencer*.

141 Blake to Henry Clay, July 30, 1825, in Hopkins (ed.), *Papers of Henry Clay*, IV, 561; Holman to Clay, October 24, 1825, *ibid.*, 757.

142 *Senate Executive Journal*, III, 627, 634. The continued tenure of these two officials is noted in Rohrbaugh, *The Land Office Business*, 182, 273–274, 293.

143 The author is unaware how Tipton voted in 1824, but in 1835 he asserted that he had "never been a partisan but . . . voted for Genl Jackson in 1828 & 1832 . . . ." Tipton to Alexander F. Morrison, January (?), 1835, in Robertson and Riker (eds.), *John Tipton Papers*, III, 118. For letters to Tipton during 1827 and 1828, which seem to indicate his being considered a Jacksonian by correspondents, see *ibid.*, I, 769–770, 784–785, 817–821; *ibid.*, II, 39–40, 61–62, 73–74.

144 Samuel Milroy to Tipton, May 2, 1827, *ibid.*, I, 706–707. Before learning of his appointment Milroy commented: "If the patronage of the Government

. . . is to be dispensed as rewards, for services heretofore rendered, or anticipated; I have nothing to expect from Washington City—." As stated in note 101 above, Milroy had been chairman of the Jackson State Convention in 1824, which named him one of its five electors.

145 *Senate Executive Journal*, III, 460–461, 471. Noah Noble was given a recess appointment, then confirmed for a regular appointment on January 4, 1826. Amos Lane, later a Jacksonian congressman, recommended Noah over two "violent Jackson men." Senator James Noble, writing Clay on behalf of his brother, asserted that within "four hours" after the death of Lazarus while "relatives was preparing the corpse for the *grave*," that "Abner McCarty, and others mounted horses in every direction" seeking recommendations on their behalf as successor to the deceased. Hopkins (ed.), *Papers of Henry Clay*, IV, 708, 710–711. The Richmond *Public Leger*, December 3, 1825, after saying it understood there had been nearly fifty applicants for this vacancy, mused: "Ah, these 'loaves and fishes' of Uncle Sam's, they're enticing!" *This early reference to Uncle Sam is worthy of note!*

146 Leonard Dupee White, *The Jeffersonians: A Study in Administrative History, 1801–1829* (New York, 1951), 355–357, 380–381, 414–415; David Walter Krueger, Party Development in Indiana, 1800–1832 (Ph.D. dissertation, University of Kentucky, 1974), 157–158, 166.

147 For Adams' support of internal improvements, see Richardson, *Messages and Papers of the Presidents*, II, 298–299, 306–308, 316, 360–361, 388–389, 416–417.

148 Cunningham, *Circular Letters of Congressmen*, III, 1324.

149 *Ibid.*, III, 1379 (Hendricks); Robertson and Riker (eds.), *John Tipton Papers*, I, 677 (McKeen). For comments by Governor Ray about canal surveys in 1826 and 1827, and grants for the Wabash and Erie Canal and Michigan Road, see Dorothy Riker and Gayle Thornbrough (eds.), *Messages and Papers Relating to the Administration of James Brown Ray, Governor of Indiana, 1825–1831* (Indianapolis, 1954), 133–136, 171–172, 274–275.

150 U. S. *Statutes at Large*, IV, 289, 352.

151 *Congressional Debates*, 19 Cong., 1 session, II, Pt. 1, pp. 619–620. According to *House Journal*, 19 Cong., 1 session, 506, 510, this item passed the House without a roll call vote.

152 According to George Dangerfield, *The Awakening of American Nationalism, 1815–1828* (New York, 1965), 242–243, 273–274, from the beginning the Adams administration had no real control over the Senate and only a shaky control over the House, while the congressional elections of 1826 left the opposition in control of both houses.

153 In addition to items concerning tariff protection in the ensuing pages, see *Acts* (special), 1823–24, p. 116 (domestic manufacturing); *Laws of Indiana*, 1827–28, pp. 143–144 (hemp, cotton, raw wool, and woolens); series by "Fenelon" in Indianapolis *Indiana Journal*, June 26, July 3, 10, 24, August 7, 21, 28, September 4, 1827, quoting Lawrenceburgh *Indiana Palladium*; Cunningham, *Circular*

Letters of Congressmen, III, 1378, 1422, 1431, 1527; Riker and Thornbrough (eds.), *Messages and Papers of James Brown Ray*, 75–77, 283, 389.

¹⁵⁴ Indiana *House Journal*, 1828–29, pp. 498–500; *ibid.*, 1827–28, p. 450.

¹⁵⁵ *Laws of Indiana*, 1827–28, pp. 143–144; Indiana *House Journal*, 1827–28, pp. 412–413; Indiana *Senate Journal*, 1827–28, pp. 63–64. "Unus," a staunch Jacksonian, said: "it was the farmer, and not the manufacturer, who required additional protection." He stressed the need for increased protection for producers of whiskey, hemp, and wool. Vincennes *Western Sun*, February 23, 1828.

¹⁵⁶ *Congressional Debates*, 19 Cong., 2 session, 254, 267; Indiana *House Journal*, 1827–28, pp. 118–119. Buley, *The Old Northwest*, I, 543–546, discusses the harsh criticism among westerners about price fixing and other unsavory practices that characterized salt production during the twenties and thirties.

¹⁵⁷ Indianapolis *Gazette*, April 3, 1827. This pro-Adams editor said Jennings and Boon had voted with the friends of Jackson. He explained that because Boon was "an open Jacksonian" his vote was not much of a surprise, but since Jennings had "pursued a '*neutral*' course" his vote had been a surprise.

¹⁵⁸ *Congressional Debates*, 20 Cong., 1 session, IV, Pt. 2, pp. 2470–2471; *ibid.*, IV, Pt. 1, p. 786; Edward Stanwood, *American Tariff Controversies in the Nineteenth Century* (2 vols., Boston, 1903), I, 243–290; F. W. Taussig, *The Tariff History of the United States* (New York, 1889), 86–103.

¹⁵⁹ In 1829 Congressman Oliver H. Smith, a protectionist, noted the favorable fiscal situation and predicted that with the liquidation of the national debt about 1835 duties could be removed from articles of common production, not produced in the United States, such as tea, coffee, and spices. At this time Senator William Hendricks expressed similar views. Cunningham, *Circular Letters of Congressmen*, III, 1527, 1543.

¹⁶⁰ For earlier cessions and related items, see pp. 458–460. When Adams became president, no cession had been made since 1821.

¹⁶¹ For examples of comments about the canal, settlements, and shrinking of Indian claims, see *Acts* (special), 1823–24, p. 112; *Laws of Indiana*, 1825–26, pp. 90–91; *ibid.*, 1828–29, pp. 155–156; Riker and Thornbrough (eds.), *Messages and Papers of James Brown Ray*, 57–58, 79–80; Charles R. Poinsatte, *Fort Wayne During the Canal Era, 1828–1855* (Indianapolis, 1969), 11–12; Vincennes *Western Sun*, March 18, April 1, 1826.

¹⁶² Royce (comp.), *Indian Land Cessions in the United States*, 716–717, 722–723, maps 19 and 20 (Potawatomi), 716–717, 720, maps 19 and 20 (Miami); Harmon, *Sixty Years of Indian Affairs*, 272–276.

¹⁶³ See Harmon, *Sixty Years of Indian Affairs*, 273–274, for a letter of Commissioner Lewis Cass concerning the Miami treaty of 1826, saying: "'its acquisition was highly important to the State of Indiana, as it [area ceded] interrupts the continuity of her settlements, and prevents her from entering upon that system of internal improvements to which she is invited by nature, policy and interest.'" Concerning reluctance of the Indians to make cessions and their opposition to removal, see Robertson and Riker (eds.), *John Tipton Papers*, I, 598–606

(quotation, 601), 576–592, respectively for the report of the commissioners and treaty proceedings.

164 Poinsatte, *Fort Wayne During the Canal Era*, 15–19; Bert Anson, *The Miami Indians* (Norman, Okla., 1970), 185–186; Robertson and Riker (eds.), *John Tipton Papers*, I, 11, 19–22, 26. For a selection of documents for and against removal, see *ibid.*, I, 622–623, 651–653, 658, 681–683, 701; *ibid.*, II, 5–7, 13–15, 17–18, 20–21, 31–36, 38–39, 43, 52–53, 81–84, 107–108, 118, 179.

165 Shonkwiler, The Land Office Business in Indiana, 145; Indianapolis *Indiana Journal*, January 22, 1831. According to the *Indiana Journal*, 2,169,149 acres had been sold at Indiana land offices from July 1, 1820, through December 31, 1829, exceeding that of any other state with Alabama ranked next followed by Ohio. Shonkwiler's yearly totals indicate that 2,170,140.90 acres of Indiana land were sold in this period. Presumably Indiana cash sales would have been larger than this in the twenties, except for the fact that during this decade money was also being spent for payment of land bought under the credit system, from 1800 to 1820. Concerning credit sales and their later liquidation, see pp. 461–464. It should be noted that some Indiana land, not counted in the preceding, was being sold in Ohio; and that some land in Illinois, sold from the Vincennes office, is included.

166 For instance, see Richardson, *Messages and Papers of the Presidents*, II, 305, 390–391; *Laws of Indiana*, 1825–26, pp. 87–88; *ibid.*, 1826–27, p. 104; *ibid.*, 1827–28, pp. 140–142; *ibid.*, 1828–29, pp. 150–151; Cunningham, *Circular Letters of Congressmen*, III, 1327–1328, 1340–1341, 1379–1380, 1419, 1431–1432. Some of the resolutions cited also sought certain preemption rights.

167 Hibbard, *A History of the Public Land Policies*, 289–296; *Laws of Indiana*, 1825–26, pp. 87–88. The resolution, endorsed by the legislature, approved graduation by a memorial adopted by the General Assembly in 1824; however, such a memorial has not been found. When seeking reelection as governor in 1834, Noah Noble said that in 1828 he had been one of the few "Land Officers" who had supported Benton's views for graduation. Dorothy Riker and Gayle Thornbrough (eds.), *Messages and Papers Relating to the Administration of Noah Noble, Governor of Indiana, 1831–1837* (Indianapolis, 1958), 281.

168 For examples of Hendricks' persistent and vigorous support of cession from 1826 to 1829, see *Congressional Debates*, 19 Cong., 1 session, II, 591–597; *ibid.*, 19 Cong., 2 session, 48–50; *ibid.*, 20 Cong., 1 session, 15–18, 151–166; *ibid.*, 20 Cong., 2 session, 58–59. As early as 1820, while a congressman, Hendricks had supported the principle of cession. *Annals of Congress*, 16 Cong., 1 session, 1353–1354.

169 *Congressional Debates*, 20 Cong., 1 session, 577–582; Samuel Milroy to John Tipton, December 10, 1827, in Robertson and Riker (eds.), *John Tipton Papers*, I, 817–821.

170 *Laws of Indiana*, 1828–29, pp. 152–153; Hill, William Hendricks, 187–191; Indianapolis *Indiana Journal*, January 31, February 5, 12, 19, 26 (Wallace quotation), 1829.

171 Dangerfield, *The Awakening of American Nationalism, 1815–1828*, pp. 243–267 *passim*.

172 *Congressional Debates*, 19 Cong., 1 session, II, Pt. 1, 151, 671; *ibid.*, II, Pt. 2, p. 2514. Hendricks advised his constituents that he had "voted for this mission in every shape and form" that it had been presented to the Senate. Cunningham, *Circular Letters of Congressmen*, III, 1328.

173 *Congressional Debates*, 19 Cong., 1 session, II, Pt. 2, pp. 2458–2471. Quoted items respectively, pages 2463, 2469, 2470, 2461.

174 Richmond *Public Leger*, April 15, 1826; Indiana *Senate Journal*, 1826–27, pp. 115–116. The resolution was adopted 18 to 2.

175 Indiana *House Journal*, 1826–27, p. 51; Richmond *Public Leger*, December 8, 1827; Cunningham, *Circular Letters of Congressmen*, III, 1435.

176 Lawrenceburgh *Indiana Palladium*, August 26, 1825; Cunningham, *Circular Letters of Congressmen*, III, 1382, 1421–1422, 1435, 1544; Lawrenceburgh *Indiana Palladium*, February 17, 1827.

177 Centreville *Western Emporium*, March 26, 1825; Richmond *Public Leger*, November 5, 1825; Vincennes *Western Sun*, October 21, 1826. In its issue of March 24, 1827, the Lawrenceburgh *Indiana Palladium* denied having come out for either Adams or Jackson.

178 Vincennes *Western Sun*, February 17, 1827, quoting *National Republican*.

179 *Ibid.*; Indianapolis *Gazette*, April 17, November 6, 13, 27, 1827.

180 Lawrenceburgh *Indiana Palladium*, November 17, 1827. This call also appears in the Indianapolis *Indiana Journal*, November 20, 1827, asking citizens of "Indianapolis" to hold meetings at their respective county seats, presumably meaning Indiana rather than Indianapolis. The substance of the calls is the same in both papers.

181 For examples of county meetings, not all held on December 15, see Indianapolis *Gazette*, December 18, 1827, January 1, 1828; Vincennes *Western Sun*, December 8, 1827, January 12, 1828; Lawrenceburgh *Indiana Palladium*, December 8, 22, 1827; Indianapolis *Indiana Journal*, January 3, 1828. The Lawrenceburgh *Indiana Palladium*, December 15, 1827, has a lengthy address by Arthur St. Clair hailing Jackson and castigating Adams in an extremely partisan manner.

182 From proceedings of the convention as in Lawrenceburgh *Indiana Palladium*, January 19, 26, 1828. The electors were Benjamin V. Beckes, Knox County; Ratliff Boon, Warrick County; Jesse B. Durham, Jackson County; William Lowe, Monroe County; and Ross Smiley, Union County.

183 *Ibid.*, January 19, 1828, has both the address and remarks by Canby. *Ibid.*, January 26, 1828, names the following as the committee to prepare the address: Samuel Judah, Arthur St. Clair, Paris C. Dunning, Marenus Willitt (Marinus Willett), Thomas Fitzgerald, Alexander F. Morrison, and Henry S. Handy. Since Judah is named first and reported the address, presumably he was chairman.

184 Indianapolis *Indiana Journal*, December 4, 1827.

185 For examples of county meetings, see Vincennes *Western Sun*, January 5, 1828; Lawrenceburgh *Indiana Palladium*, January 5 (quote), 12, 1828; Indi-

anapolis *Indiana Journal*, January 10, 1828; Indianapolis *Gazette*, January 15, 1828.

186 Indianapolis *Indiana Journal*, January 31, 1828. The electors were James Armstrong, Monroe County; Joseph Bartholomew, Clark County; Isaac Montgomery, Gibson County; Joseph Orr, Putnam County; and John Watts, Dearborn County.

187 Indianapolis *Indiana Journal*, January 31, 1828. The committee to prepare the address consisted of John Law, J. C. S. Harrison, John H. Farnham, B. F. Morris, Ebenezer Sharpe, James Rariden, David H. Maxwell, Horace Bassett, Isaac Howk, William Graham, Harbin H. Moore, Philip Sweetser, and Merrit (Merit) S. Craig. Since Law is named first and reported the address, presumably he was chairman.

188 Indiana *Senate Journal*, 1827–28, pp. 225–227. Milroy protested Graham's resolutions as an attack on Jackson's integrity and consistency, insisting that his senatorial record showed him "the firm and decided friend of internal improvements" and tariff protection. If Jackson's friends wrote him "he would give his views in full, which would shut the mouths of his enemies on such subjects," Milroy asserted. Thirteen senators, most of whom had voted for Graham's resolution, said they had had no intention of seeking Jackson's opinions until Milroy presented his resolutions. *Ibid.*, 255–256, 260.

189 Riker and Thornbrough (eds.), *Messages and Papers of James Brown Ray*, 319–328, for Ray's letter to Jackson, January 30, 1828. Quotations are on pages 321, 322, 324. Ray's letter included a copy of Graham's resolutions, noted Indiana's vigorous attachment to federal aid for internal improvements and tariff protection, and said the state had voted for Jackson in 1824 in the belief that his administration would liberally encourage internal improvements and domestic manufactures.

190 *Ibid.*, 338–341, giving Jackson's response, dated February 28, 1828. The Coleman letter is in the Indianapolis *Gazette*, April 8, 1828, although it had appeared earlier in the Vincennes *Western Sun*, June 26, 1824, quoting the Raleigh (North Carolina) *Star*. Like Jackson's response to Ray, it is fuzzy enough to be subject to differing interpretations.

191 Indianapolis *Indiana Journal*, May 8, 1828. The Richmond *Public Leger*, April 16, 1828, another pro-Adams paper, commented: "But, anxious as the General is to be thought above all concealment, he avoids the points, and makes a few vague and general remarks."

192 For examples of items friendly to Adams and critical of Jackson, see Indianapolis *Gazette*, February 26, March 18, June 26, September 25, 1828; Indianapolis *Indiana Journal*, March 6, May 8, 15, June 5, October 2, 30, 1828; Lawrenceburgh *Indiana Palladium*, September 27, October 11, 1828; *Address of the Administration Standing Committee to Their Fellow-Citizens of Indiana* [1828], 1–22, in Indiana Historical Society Library, Indianapolis. Quotation is on page 17.

193 For items friendly to Jackson and critical of Adams, see Vincennes *Western Sun*, April 26 (undated address of Jackson Central Committee), May 24, 31,

October 4, 11, 18, 25, 1828; Lawrenceburgh *Indiana Palladium*, September 6 (quotation), 27, November 1 (Jackson Central Committee address dated October 18), 1828. The Indianapolis *Indiana Journal*, October 16, 1828, has letters from Noble and Hendricks in which both make explicit statements of their lack of evidence against a corrupt bargain involving Clay and Adams.

[194] Official returns for all counties but Harrison which are unofficial and Carroll which are missing have about 22,100 votes for Jackson electors and 16,950 voters for Adams electors. Riker and Thornbrough (comps.), *Indiana Election Returns, 1816–1851*, pp. 10–13. *Ibid.*, pp. 140–141 and 4–9, have the vote for governor in 1828 and for president in 1824.

[195] Vincennes *Western Sun*, November 15, 29, 1828; Centreville *Western Times*, December 6, 1828.

[196] Indianapolis *Gazette*, December 4, 1828; Vincennes *Western Sun*, December 13, 1828.

[197] Thomas J. Evans to John Tipton, March 13, 1829, in Robertson and Riker (eds.), *John Tipton Papers*, II, 152–153.

[198] According to the Vincennes *Western Sun*, January 26, 1828, friends of Jackson in Knox and other counties of the First District had repeatedly expressed a desire that Judah become a candidate. The editor added that he had been informed that all delegates from counties of the district at the recent (Jackson State) Convention at Indianapolis had expressed a similar desire. Though disclaiming knowledge of Judah's intent, Editor Stout presumed that Judah would "hold himself at the disposition of his political friends." Under date of July 31, 1827, which appeared in the *Sun* August 11, 1827, Boon had advised voters of the district that he had determined not to be a congressional candidate for the 1828 election. See *ibid.*, March 29, 1828, for Judah's withdrawal, and Stout's announcement of Boon's candidacy.

[199] Vincennes *Western Sun*, March 29, 1828; Ratliff Boon to John Tipton, April 29, 1828, in Robertson and Riker (eds.), *John Tipton Papers*, II, 39–40. The *Sun* stated that it had been authorized to announce Boon as a candidate. In the issue of April 5, 1828, Stout admitted that he had given only the substance of what Blake had said; and that Blake's actual statement had been that he was "'willing to sink or swim with the cause of the present administration[.]'" In a speech defending the Adams administration, Blake is reported as having used the words as quoted by Stout. *Congressional Debates*, 20 Cong., 1 session, IV, Pt. 1, pp. 1152–1154.

[200] Vincennes *Western Sun*, June 28, 1828, for Blake's communication to voters; *An Address to the Friends of Andrew Jackson, in the First Congressional District of Indiana* [Salem, July 1, 1828], pamphlet in Indiana Division, Indiana State Library, 1.

[201] *Western Register & Terre-Haute Advertiser*, June 7, 14, 28, July 19, 1828.

[202] Complete returns, official for all counties but Knox and Morgan, indicate 7,272 votes for Boon, 6,671 for Blake. Riker and Thornbrough (comps.), *Indiana Election Returns, 1816–1851*, pp. 82–83. See note 121 above concerning Call as a previous Jacksonian congressman.

203 The Indianapolis *Indiana Journal*, June 19, 1828, states that these three men had been announced in the papers as candidates. According to *ibid.*, January 31, 1828, Thompson, from Clark County, had been a member of the Adams State Convention. As indicated in the Lawrenceburgh *Indiana Palladium*, January 19, 1828, Handy had been a delegate to the Jackson State Convention which named him to the party's State Central Committee.

204 Indianapolis *Indiana Journal*, July 24, 1828, has both circulars. No withdrawal statement by Handy has been found, but the *Indiana Journal*, July 31, 1828, omits his name from the roster of candidates. The fact that almost no votes were cast for him seems conclusive evidence of Handy's withdrawal.

205 Riker and Thornbrough (comps.), *Indiana Election Returns, 1816–1851*, pp. 83–84. Official returns, complete for all counties but Jackson and Scott, show 7,659 votes for Jennings, 2,785 for Thompson, and 3 for Handy.

206 The Lawrenceburgh *Indiana Palladium*, May 3, 1828, listed Smith as a candidate; by May 24, 1828, it added Test and McCarty. The Indianapolis *Indiana Journal*, May 29, 1828, referred to Test of Dearborn County and McCarty of Fayette County (as was Smith) commenting: "Test and Smith, decided friends of the Administration and its measures—M'Carty of Gen. Jackson."

207 Indianapolis *Gazette*, June 5, July 3, 1828.

208 *Ibid.*, June 19, 1828.

209 Riker and Thornbrough (comps.), *Indiana Election Returns, 1816–1851*, p. 84. Official returns for all counties report 6,867 votes for Test, 5,433 for McCarty.

210 These conclusions are based upon the author's summary tabulation of how counties voted in the three congressional districts in the presidential versus the congressional elections. There are minor differences in the two sets of data, but they are not sufficient to make the conclusions expressed questionable.

CHAPTER 10

1 Regarding the somewhat democratic nature of state government, see Chapter 1, pp. 1–10.

2 Vincennes *Western Sun*, November 15, 1828; Indianapolis *Gazette*, March 26, 1829.

3 David Walter Krueger, Party Development in Indiana, 1800–1832 (Ph.D. dissertation, University of Kentucky, 1974), 214–216, 218–223. Krueger states that Canby, Tipton, William Marshall, Henry S. Handy, Jonathan McCarty, and William H. Hurst conferred with the president-elect in Washington during January, 1829.

4 Indianapolis *Gazette*, March 26, 1829; Centerville *Western Times*, April 11, 1829.

5 Indianapolis *Indiana Democrat and State Gazette*, April 15, 1830; Vincennes *Western Sun*, April 24, 1830. Both papers list persons who had been confirmed at the Indiana land offices. At Vincennes John D. Woolverton became receiver

vice John C. S. Harrison, resigned. At Jeffersonville William H. Hurst became receiver vice Andrew P. Hay, removed; and William Lewis became register vice Samuel Gwathmey, removed. At Indianapolis James P. Drake became receiver vice Noah Noble, removed; and Arthur St. Clair became register vice Robert Hanna, removed. At Fort Wayne Jonathan McCarty became receiver vice Joseph Holman, removed; and Robert Brackenridge became register vice Samuel C. Vance, removed. At Crawfordsville Israel T. Canby became receiver vice Ambrose Whitlock, removed; and Samuel Milroy became register vice Williamson Dunn, removed. All incumbents, except Harrison, are reported as having been removed. Had he not resigned presumably he would have been removed.

    6 In 1835 Tipton wrote that he had "never been a partisan but have voted for Genl Jackson in 1828 & 1832," was a supporter of the Jackson administration, but had often voted with the opposition on important measures. Nellie A. Robertson and Dorothy Riker (eds.), *The John Tipton Papers* (3 vols., Indianapolis, 1942), III, 118, and *passim*; items in this chapter sustain these comments. Although in 1829 Badollet indicated that he had preferred Jackson in 1828, he was an unusually honest and highly regarded civil servant who was register of the Vincennes Land Office, 1804–36. Gayle Thornbrough (ed.), *The Correspondence of John Badollet and Albert Gallatin, 1804–1836* (Indianapolis, 1963), 21, 25–26, 290; Malcolm J. Rohrbaugh, *The Land Office Business: The Settlement and Administration of American Public Lands, 1789–1837* (New York, 1968), 182, 293.

    7 *Journal of the Executive Proceedings of the Senate of the United States* (Washington, D.C., 1887), IV, 9, 41–42, 72. According to this source, Dewey had been removed and Vawter's term had expired.

    8 For examples of postal changes, see Vincennes *Western Sun*, June 20, 27, July 11, August 22, September 26, 1829. According to the Indianapolis *Indiana Journal*, April 14, 1830, all but two or three of the post offices worth keeping had "undergone the *reforming* operation of the present Administration."

    9 Indianapolis *Indiana Journal*, May 28, September 10, 1829, March 31, 1830; Centerville *Western Times*, July 11, 1829. For examples of similar criticisms, see Indianapolis *Indiana Journal*, July 2, August 13, 27, October 8, 1829; Centerville *Western Times*, May 23, August 22, 1829.

    10 John Badollet to Albert Gallatin, August 14, 1829, in Thornbrough (ed.), *Correspondence of John Badollet and Albert Gallatin*, 289–290, 296.

    11 Robertson and Riker (eds.), *John Tipton Papers*, II, 176, 181, 508, 519, 585; Indianapolis *Indiana Journal*, June 23, 1830, for letter by Hendricks.

    12 Vincennes *Western Sun*, June 20, 1829; Indianapolis *Gazette*, August 27, September 10, October 15, 1829; Lawrenceburgh *Indiana Palladium*, May 15, 1830. As early as February 8, 1817, Stout supported limited tenure for officeholders.

    13 Installments II through V of this series are in Lawrenceburgh *Indiana Palladium*, October 2, 9, 16, 23, 1830. Quoted items are from issues of October 2 and 9. For additional examples of support for removals, see Vincennes *Western Sun*, October 10, 1829; Indianapolis *Gazette*, November 5, 1829.

14 Indianapolis *Indiana Journal*, February 3, 1838, January 16, 1841.

15 Gayle Thornbrough, Dorothy Riker, and Paula Corpuz (eds.), *The Diary of Calvin Fletcher* (9 vols., Indianapolis, 1972–1983), I, 415–416. Fletcher named Israel T. Canby, William Hurst, Samuel Judah, and William Marshall as the officeholders who had been turned out. For information about charges against Jacksonian appointees, see Robertson and Riker (eds.), *John Tipton Papers*, II, 661, 683, 686, 762–763, 765–766, 851, regarding the defalcation and removal of Canby as receiver of the Crawfordsville Land Office; *ibid.*, 715, 724, 725, 728, 737–738, regarding the situation which led to the removal of Judah as attorney for the federal district court for Indiana; *ibid.*, 492, 763, regarding anticipated suit against Marshall on his bond as marshal for the Indiana district court; *ibid.*, 840, 843–845, 851, 861, regarding removal of Samuel Milroy as register of the Crawfordsville Land Office. According to the *Senate Executive Journal*, IV, 135, 200, Hurst had been removed and Marshall had resigned. Judah's removal as district attorney was announced in Vincennes *Western Sun*, May 4, 1833. Rohrbaugh, *Land Office Business*, 286–287, 291, offers detail about Canby, stating that he owed the government $39,013.31 at the time of his removal in 1832. Rohrbaugh views John Badollet as a noteworthy example "of character and integrity" among land office officials. *Ibid.*, 182, 293.

16 Concerning Ellsworth, see Paul W. Gates, *The Farmer's Age: Agriculture, 1815–1860* (New York, 1960), 190–192, 299–300, 330–331, 366–367. Concerning Whitcomb, see Thomas Donaldson, *The Public Domain: Its History, with Statistics* (Washington, D. C., 1884), 166; William Wesley Woollen, *Biographical and Historical Sketches of Early Indiana* (Indianapolis, 1883), 82–83. According to Gates, Ellsworth, from Connecticut, took up residence at Lafayette after retiring from the Patent Office.

17 Regarding bipartisan support for federal aid for internal improvements, see Chapter 9, pp. 493–494.

18 Jennings' circular to his constituents is in Indianapolis *Indiana Journal*, April 16, 1829.

19 *Laws of Indiana*, 1829–30, pp. 174–175, 177–178; Vincennes *Western Sun*, January 2, 1830.

20 The Maysville Road Veto, May 27, 1830, is in James D. Richardson, *Compilations of the Messages and Papers of the Presidents, 1789–1917* (20 vols., Washington, D. C., 1897–1917), II, 483–493; *Senate Journal*, 21 Cong., 1 session, 306–307, 340–341, 381–382; *House Journal*, 21 Cong., 1 session, 586–587, 763–764; Indianapolis *Indiana Journal*, July 28, 1830. As the citations to the journals indicate, Hendricks and Noble voted to advance the Maysville Road bill to its third reading, but it passed without a roll call vote. Boon and Test voted for passage, but Jennings did not participate in this vote. Of Indiana's five members of Congress, Senators William Hendricks and James Noble, and Congressmen John Test and Ratliff Boon (an avid Jacksonian) voted to override the veto; while Congressman Jonathan Jennings sustained the veto.

21 Terre Haute *Western Register*, June 19, 1830; Indianapolis *Indiana Journal*, July 7, 1830 (regarding Rodgers), June 23, July 14, September 15, December 1, 1830. For further and similar comment, see *ibid.*, June 9, 16, July 28, August 4, 18, 1830.

22 Lawrenceburgh *Indiana Palladium*, June 19, 1830; Indianapolis *Indiana State Gazette*, July 22, 1830; Vincennes *Western Sun*, July 24, August 14, 1830. For further and similar comment, see Lawrenceburgh *Indiana Palladium*, June 12, July 10, 1830; Vincennes *Western Sun*, June 12, 19, 26, July 3, 1830; Indianapolis *Indiana State Gazette*, July 29, 1830.

23 For examples of these requests, see *Special Acts of Indiana*, 1830–31, pp. 178, 180, 181–182, 183–185, 186–188, 192–193; *Laws of Indiana*, 1832–33, pp. 232, 236–237, 238, 244–245; *ibid.* (local), 1834–35, pp. 269–271, 274–275, 276, 278–280; *ibid.* (local), 1836–37, pp. 429, 433–434, 436–437, 442–444.

24 David Guard to John Tipton, Indianapolis, January 13, 1834, in Robertson and Riker (eds.), *John Tipton Papers*, III, 12.

25 U. S. *Statutes at Large*, IV, 721; V, 130, 184, 187. The sum of $5,000 was appropriated for the lighthouse in 1834, plus an additional $3,000 in 1837 to complete it; $20,000 was appropriated for the harbor in 1836, then an additional $30,000 in 1837. In 1837 $5,000 was also appropriated for a lighthouse at City West.

26 See report of state treasurer in Indiana *Senate Journal*, 1837–38, pp. 281–282. As noted in *Laws of Indiana* (general), 1836–37, p. 97, the General Assembly pledged it would repay all such loans when requested by the treasurer of the United States.

27 Indianapolis *Indiana Journal*, September 8, 1832, July 19, 26, 1834; Indianapolis *Indiana Democrat*, July 25, August 22, 1834.

28 *Congressional Debates*, 23 Cong., 2 session, XI, Pt. 1, pp. 9–14. The quoted items are on p. 13.

29 Robertson and Riker (eds.), *John Tipton Papers*, III, 93, 132–133, 296.

30 *Congressional Debates*, 23 Cong., 2 session, XI, Pt. 1, pp. 85–86.

31 For examples of these requests, see *Laws of Indiana* (local), 1837–38, pp. 439, 441, 445, 446–447, 449–450, 451, 452–453; *ibid.* (local), 1838–39, pp. 341–342, 343, 345, 349, 354, 356, 358; *ibid.* (local), 1839–40, pp. 244, 250–251, 253, 255–256. From statehood there has been much discussion, often superficial and highly partisan, whether residents of Indiana contribute more for the support of the federal government than it reciprocates to them. In December, 1839, during the Depression of 1837 and after the blowup of the Internal Improvements System of 1836 a few months earlier, Governor David Wallace, a Whig, offered members of the General Assembly data which he said showed that for the four previous years Indiana had contributed to the support of the federal government "at the ruinous rate of two millions of dollars a year . . . ." A bipartisan committee responded with data suggesting that from various earlier and recent federal grants of land and money, plus revenue available from taxes on land within Indiana which had been purchased from the federal government, made "a grand

aggregate of 42,883,150 dollars." However these data are interpreted, they illustrate that federal aid to Indiana and its residents *played a role of enormous importance while Indiana was in the pioneer era.* Concerning views of the governor and committee, see Dorothy Riker (ed.), *Messages and Papers Relating to the Administration of David Wallace, Governor of Indiana, 1837–1840* (Indianapolis, 1963), 338–339, views of the governor (also 323–343, for context); 393–399, views of the committee; and 376–381, views of a Senate Democrat.

32 Indiana *Senate Journal,* 1837–38, pp. 281–282 (surplus revenue); U.S. *Statutes at Large,* V, 228 (Cumberland Road), 268 (harbor at Michigan City).

33 *Congressional Globe,* 26 Cong., 1 session, VIII, Appendix, 189–193. The quoted items are on p. 192.

34 For the plummeting of land sales, see pp. 557–562, this chapter. For extension of the land grant for the Wabash and Erie Canal to Terre Haute, see Chapter 5, p. 241.

35 For party views regarding the tariff, see Ch. 9, pp. 494–496.

36 For the respective statements by Boon and Jennings, see Vincennes *Western Sun,* March 19, July 2, 1831. For remarks of Hendricks, see *Congressional Debates,* 22 Cong., 1 session, VIII, Pt. 1, p. 615.

37 Indiana *Senate Journal,* 1831–32, pp. 96, 111–113, 122, 321–323, 340–342, 399–401. The quoted items are on 341, 321–322. According to *ibid.,* 122, 323, the seven who voted against and then protested the resolution were: John De-Pauw, Thomas Givens, Joseph M. Hayes, John M. Lemon, James T. Pollock, David Robb, James Whitcomb. As indicated in *A Biographical Directory of the Indiana General Assembly* (2 vols., Indianapolis, 1980, 1984), Volume 1, *1816–1899,* Volume 2, *1901–1984,* I, 457, the protesters were all Jacksonians, while nearly all of those who supported the resolution were anti-Jacksonians.

38 For examples of this view, see Indianapolis *Indiana Journal,* April 7, December 1, 1830, October 29, 1831. Late in 1831 Governor Noah Noble wrote Tipton, commending him as almost "the only efficient friend" of Jackson who had not "surrendered in part or entire, his opinions" concerning the tariff and internal improvements. Dorothy Riker and Gayle Thornbrough (eds.), *Messages and Papers Relating to the Administration of Noah Noble, Governor of Indiana, 1831–1837* (Indianapolis, 1958), 79.

39 *Congressional Debates,* 22 Cong., 1 session, VIII, Pt. 1, p. 1219; *ibid.,* VIII, Pt. 3, pp. 3830–3831. The four Jacksonians were Senator Tipton, Congressmen Boon, Carr, McCarty. The fifth member, Senator Hendricks, is considered an independent, not openly a member of either party.

40 John Tipton to James B. Slaughter, March 27, 1832, in Robertson and Riker (eds.), *John Tipton Papers,* II, 563; Richardson, *Messages and Papers of the Presidents,* II, 640–656, for Jackson's proclamation.

41 Indiana *House Journal,* 1828–29, pp. 15–16; *ibid.,* 1831–32, p. 35.

42 Robertson and Riker (eds.), *John Tipton Papers,* II, 742, 747–748. Their letters are dated December 11 and 14, while Jackson's proclamation is dated December 10.

43 Indianapolis *Indiana Journal,* December 26, 1832; *Laws of Indiana,* 1832–33, pp. 238–240. For the political makeup of the General Assembly, see *Biographical Directory of the Indiana General Assembly,* I, 459–460.

44 For passage of the Force Bill, see *Congressional Debates,* 22 Cong., 2 session, IX, Pt. 1, p. 688; *ibid.,* IX, Pt. 2, p. 1903. For passage of the tariff, see *ibid.,* IX, Pt. 1, pp. 808–809; *ibid.,* IX, Pt. 2, pp. 1810–1811. For opposition voiced by Tipton and Hendricks, see John Tipton to Calvin Fletcher, January 11, February 7, 1833, in Robertson and Riker (eds.), *John Tipton Papers,* II, 771–772, 801; Frederick Dinsmore Hill, William Hendricks: Indiana Politician and Western Advocate, 1812–1850 (Ph.D. dissertation, Indiana University, 1972), 277.

45 Robertson and Riker (eds.), *John Tipton Papers,* II, 805–806; Vincennes *Western Sun,* March 30, 1833.

46 Indianapolis *Indiana Democrat,* March 2, 9, 1833; Indianapolis *Indiana Journal,* March 2, May 4, 1833.

47 See pp. 524–525 and note 46, this chapter.

48 *Congressional Globe,* 26 Cong., 2 session, IX, Appendix, 262–266 (quotations, 264–265); *Congressional Debates,* 24 Cong., 1 session, XII, Pt. 4, pp. 4318–4320.

49 For the role of banking in the presidential election of 1828, see pp. 502–509.

50 *Laws of Indiana,* 1831–32, p. 288; Indiana *House Journal,* 1831–32, pp. 432–434; *Biographical Directory of the Indiana General Assembly,* I, 417, 458, listing Willett as a Jacksonian. See Riker and Thornbrough (eds.), *Messages and Papers of Noah Noble,* 100–101, for acknowledgment of the legislative request concerning branches by bank president Nicholas Biddle, also of a memorial from "many" legislators for a branch at Indianapolis, with a statement that these items will be submitted to the bank board for its consideration.

51 Robertson and Riker (eds.), *John Tipton Papers,* II, 542. See Vincennes *Western Sun,* July 2, 1831, for a letter of Congressman Boon to Samuel Judah, June 17, 1831, with a comment about a possible branch at Vincennes.

52 Indiana *Senate Journal,* 1831–32, pp. 96, 111–113, 122, 321–323, 340–342. The quotes are on pp. 341, 322 respectively. According to *Biographical Directory of the Indiana General Assembly,* I, 457–458, the Senate was more than two to one anti-Jacksonian. One of the protesters was James Whitcomb, elected governor in 1843 as the first Democrat to gain this office.

53 For votes of Hendricks and Tipton for passage and then to override, see *Congressional Debates,* 22 Cong., 1 session, VIII, Pt. 1, pp. 1073, 1296. As indicated *ibid.,* VIII, Pt. 3, pp. 3838–3839, 3852, Boon voted against postponing the recharter bill, Carr and McCarty voted for postponement; Carr and McCarty voted against ordering the bill to third reading, Boon did not vote on this item; and the bill passed the House without a roll call vote. The Indianapolis *Indiana Journal,* July 14, 1832, stated: *"Mr. Boon voted for the bill, and Messrs. Carr and McCarty voted against it!!"* The veto message is in Richardson, *Messages and Papers of the Presidents,* II, 576–591.

54 Vincennes *Western Sun*, July 21, 28, 1832. In its issue of October 13, 1832, the *Western Sun* published President Madison's veto of an 1815 bill for a federal bank.

55 Indianapolis *Indiana Journal*, September 1, 1832; Robertson and Riker (eds.), *John Tipton Papers*, II, 665, 687.

56 For Jackson's overwhelming reelection in 1832, despite his opposition to the federal bank, see pp. 533–538.

57 Indianapolis *Indiana Journal*, July 21, 1832.

58 *Ibid.*, August 25, September 1, 15, 1832. This paper comments that most of those who initiated the meeting were farmers, but well-known anti-Jacksonians had a very large role in the deliberations. See *ibid.*, September 15, 1832, and *passim* to the presidential election in November for items about other meetings protesting the veto. The call for the September 8 meeting indicated that the failure of the president to approve the congressional appropriation of $20,000 for the improvement of the Wabash River would be considered. This veto was strongly condemned at the county meeting on September 8.

59 Robert V. Remini, *Andrew Jackson and the Course of American Democracy, 1833–1845* (New York, 1984), 166–168; Glyndon G. Van Deusen, *The Jacksonian Era, 1828–1848* (New York, 1959), 80–84.

60 *Congressional Debates*, 23 Cong., 1 session, X, Pt. 1, p. 1187. For comments of Tipton critical of removal and favorable to recharter, see Robertson and Riker (eds.), *John Tipton Papers*, III, 32, 34, 283, 330–331, 441. For views of Hendricks, see Hill, *William Hendricks*, 262–265; *Congressional Debates*, 23 Cong., 1 session, X, Pt. 2, pp. 1805–1811.

61 *Congressional Debates*, 23 Cong., 1 session, X, Pt. 3, pp. 3474–3476. Democrats Boon, Carr, Hannegan, Kinnard, Lane, and McCarty voted against restoration of the federal bank and for keeping deposits in state banks. Ewing, the National Republican, voted opposite the Democrats for both items. Boon, Carr, Hannegan, Kinnard, and Lane voted for a resolution that the United States Bank should not be rechartered, McCarty voted against the same, with Ewing not voting. Soon after this vote McCarty said he had always opposed the bank as chartered, but favored a national bank with proper modifications. *Ibid.*, X, Pt. 4, pp. 4499–4501.

62 For examples of Whig comments about causes of the panic and resulting economic distress, see Indianapolis *Indiana Journal*, May 27, October 7, 14, 1837, June 2, 1838, September 14, October 19, 1839, August 20, 1841. Also see speech of Senator Oliver H. Smith in *Congressional Debates*, 25 Cong., 1 session, XIV, Pt. 1, pp. 123–133, in which he attributes the crisis and embarrassments to "the destruction of the national bank, and the removal of the deposites, in the first instance, as the great moving cause" (p. 127). For Democratic comments and counterattack, see Indianapolis *Indiana Democrat*, June 7, September 13, 27, October 25, 1837, April 20, July 11, 1838, June 26, 1839.

63 At the special session in the fall of 1837 Senators Oliver H. Smith, Whig, and John Tipton, Democrat, voted against passage of the Independent Treasury

bill; Congressmen George H. Dunn, John Ewing, William Graham, William Herod, James Rariden, and Albert S. White, Whigs, voted to lay the bill on the table, but Ratliff Boon, Democrat, voted against the same. When the Independent Treasury bill passed Congress in 1840 Senators Smith and Albert S. White, Whigs, voted against passage. In the House Congressmen John Carr, John W. Davis, and Thomas Smith, Democrats, voted for passage; George H. Proffit and James Rariden, Whigs, and William W. Wick, Democrat, voted against passage; Tilghman A. Howard, Democrat, did not vote. *Congressional Debates*, 25 Cong., 1 session, XIV, Pt. 1, p. 511; *ibid.*, XIV, Pt. 2, pp. 1685–1686; *Senate Journal*, 26 Cong., 1 session, 131; *House Journal*, 26 Cong., 1 session, 1175–1177.

64 For examples of varying views about the political status of Hendricks, see Hill, *William Hendricks*, 136–153 *passim*; Krueger, *Party Development in Indiana, 1800–1832*, pp. 228–234 *passim*.

65 Philip Sweetser to John Tipton, May 13, 1829, in Robertson and Riker (eds.), *John Tipton Papers*, II, 166–167; Tipton to Sweetser, June 20, 1829, p. 176. Sweetser claimed that Hendricks had won election to the Senate "by a deception of one vote practised upon myself . . . ."

66 Jonathan Jennings to John Tipton, July 25, 1829, *ibid.*, 181–182. Jennings emphasized that he would not be a candidate for the federal Senate.

67 See Hill, *William Hendricks*, 137–144, for a comprehensive and very useful account about the maneuvering concerning politicians regarding Hendricks, Boon, Tipton, and others from 1829 until the election in December, 1830.

68 Noah Noble to John Tipton, October 15, 1830, in Robertson and Riker (eds.), *John Tipton Papers*, II, 355–356.

69 John Tipton to Calvin Fletcher, December 2, 1830, *ibid.*, 377. In this letter Tipton said that even if he were "sure of an election it would be a loss. I have got my Indians right again and can do the *State*, the *canal* and my *friends* more good as Indian Agent than as a Senator for two years." For examples of bipartisan support for Tipton, see *ibid.*, 271, 280–281, 293, 318, 348–349, 361. According to *Biographical Directory of the Indiana General Assembly*, I, 455–456, of the 84 members of the 1830–31 legislative session, 42 were anti-Jacksonians, 5 were probably likewise; 27 were Jacksonians, 1 was probably likewise; and the political connection of 9 is unknown.

70 Indiana *House Journal*, 1830–31, pp. 137–138. The vote for Boon was 26, 28, 24, and 26 respectively.

71 Madison *Indiana Republican*, December 23, 1830, quoted in Hill, *William Hendricks*, 148; Indianapolis *Indiana Democrat*, December 25, 1830; *ibid.*, March 26, 1831, quoted in Hill, *William Hendricks*, 148, 149.

72 Dorothy Riker (ed.), *Executive Proceedings of the State of Indiana, 1816–1836* (Indianapolis, 1947), 286; Dorothy Riker and Gayle Thornbrough (eds.), *Messages and Papers Relating to the Administration of James Brown Ray, Governor of Indiana, 1825–1831* (Indianapolis, 1954), 676.

73 John Tipton to Calvin Fletcher, April 28, 1831, in Robertson and Riker (eds.), *John Tipton Papers*, II, 406; Vincennes *Western Sun*, April 30, 1831, quoting Centerville *Western Times*, April 16, 1831.

[74] Vincennes *Western Sun*, September 17, 1831. Judah's address is dated September 10. Judah offered the Wabash and Erie Canal, the Wabash River, the Cumberland Road, and the mail route between Louisville and St. Louis, via Vincennes, as examples of internal improvements worthy of congressional aid.

[75] Robertson and Riker (eds.), *John Tipton Papers*, II, 446, 460; Krueger, Party Development in Indiana, 1800–1832, pp. 265–266.

[76] Indianapolis *Indiana Journal*, December 17, 1831, for statement to legislators, dated November 23. Hanna stated that he had lived above the influence of party, but he was vague about his views on issues. He had served as a member of the Corydon Constitutional Convention in 1816, and as register of the land office at Brookville and then Indianapolis, 1820–29. He later served in both houses of the General Assembly. *Biographical Directory of the Indiana General Assembly*, I, 164.

[77] Indianapolis *Indiana Journal*, December 3, 1831; Logan Esarey (ed.), *Messages and Papers of Jonathan Jennings, Ratliff Boon, William Hendricks, 1816–1825* (Indianapolis, 1924), 286–287. Concerning bipartisan support for Tipton, see Robertson and Riker (eds.), *John Tipton Papers*, II, 445–446, 447–448, 455, 457–458, 460, 461.

[78] According to *Biographical Directory of the Indiana General Assembly*, I, 457–458, the 1831–32 legislative session included 57 anti-Jacksonians, 46 Jacksonians, and 1 member of unknown political tie. In addition, one seat was occupied for a time by a member of unknown tie, then by an anti-Jacksonian. With an aggregate of 105 members, the anti-Jacksonians had a modest majority.

[79] Indiana *House Journal*, 1831–32, pp. 41–42, 44; Vincennes *Western Sun*, December 17, 1831.

[80] For examples, see Robertson and Riker (eds.), *John Tipton Papers*, II, 463, 464, 465. See I. George Blake, *The Holmans of Veraestau* (Oxford, Ohio, 1943), 23–26, for information about Holman's role and status concerning this election.

[81] *Laws of Indiana*, 1828–29, pp. 28–29. For years and dates of congressional elections, 1816–28, see Dorothy Riker and Gayle Thornbrough (comps.), *Indiana Election Returns, 1816–1851* (Indianapolis, 1960), 71–84.

[82] Vincennes *Western Sun*, March 19, 1831. Boon, however, wanted a reduction of duties on such articles of common use as salt, sugar, coffee, and tea.

[83] *Western Register & Terre-Haute Advertiser*, March 26, 1831. As reported in Riker and Thornbrough (comps.), *Indiana Election Returns, 1816–1851*, pp. 84–85, official returns for all counties but one show 11,280 votes for Boon and 10,849 for Law. On the basis of Law's statement in the *Western Register* and the comment of David Burr in a letter to John Tipton, May 23, 1832, in Robertson and Riker (eds.), *John Tipton Papers*, II, 607, Law is presumed to have been a National Republican devoted to Clay.

[84] John Carr to John Tipton, May 29, 1830, in Robertson and Riker (eds.), *John Tipton Papers*, II, 279. In its issue of April 16, 1831, the Indianapolis *Indiana Democrat* announced Carr as a candidate, praised his record, and noted that he had cast an electoral vote for Jackson in 1824. The statement by "A Voter" is in *ibid.*, May 28, 1831, quoting the Logansport *Potawattimie & Miami Times*,

May 8, 1831. The language used and information offered by "A Voter" suggest that John Tipton, a resident of Logansport, probably wrote this statement.

85 Riker and Thornbrough (comps.), *Indiana Election Returns, 1816–1851*, pp. 85–86. Returns, official for all counties but one, recorded 4,854 votes for Carr; 4,605 for Wick; 1,680 for Jennings; 1,486 for John H. Thompson; 732 for James Brown Ray; and 453 for Isaac Howk. For evidence about Jennings' tragic bout with poverty and intemperance, see Robertson and Riker (eds.), *John Tipton Papers*, II, 181, 279, 629–630, 630n, 666–667, 863; *ibid.*, III, 48, 57, 64–65, 72, 74, 79. In lamenting Jennings' death in 1834 Senator John Tipton stated: "he has been usefull to me and to my Country, a man of more untarnished Honour never lived—and but for his inordinate thirst for liquor he might have lived and been a most usefull Citizen many years." *Ibid.*, III, 72. Also see sketch of Jennings in Woollen, *Biographical and Historical Sketches of Early Indiana*, 39–41.

86 Riker and Thornbrough (comps.), *Indiana Election Returns, 1816–1851*, p. 86. Official returns for all counties resulted in 6,238 votes for McCarty, 5,297 for Smith, and 3,107 for Test.

87 Vincennes *Western Sun*, August 27, 1831; Indianapolis *Indiana Journal*, August 27, 1831. In comparing votes the *Indiana Journal* counted the three winners as Jacksonians; Law, Test, and Smith as Clay men or National Republicans. In the Second District it counted Wick, Thompson, and Howk as Clay men, and listed "Governors Jennings and Ray, on the fence."

88 Indianapolis *Gazette*, June 11, 1829; John Carr to John Tipton, Charlestown, May 29, 1830, in Robertson and Riker (eds.), *John Tipton Papers*, II, 280. The editor of the *Gazette* considered it highly probable that the presidential contest would be between Clay and Jackson.

89 Indianapolis *Indiana Democrat*, February 12, 1831. The Indianapolis *Indiana Journal*, January 15, 1831, had reported the rumor that Jackson had declined being a candidate.

90 Indianapolis *Indiana Journal*, September 10, 17, 24, October 1, 15, November 5, 1831.

91 *Ibid.*, October 15, 1831; Vincennes *Western Sun*, October 29, 1831.

92 Unless indicated otherwise, items regarding the National Republican State Convention are from its proceedings in Indianapolis *Indiana Journal*, November 12, 1831. Resolutions, preambles, and addresses adopted by state conventions, which indicate party issues and views, are considered as the state party platform. The attendance was probably reduced because the convention met before the legislative session began and Clay was the presumed favorite.

93 The delegates were: John I. Neely, Gibson County, First Congressional District; Isaac Howk, Clark County, Second Congressional District; George H. Dunn, Dearborn County, Third Congressional District. All three were convention delegates from their respective counties.

94 Unless otherwise indicated, items regarding the Jackson State Convention are from its proceedings in Vincennes *Western Sun*, January 7, 1832. The proceedings indicate that the convention completed its work on December 12.

95 Indianapolis *Indiana Democrat*, September 3, 17, 1831, calling for a Democratic Republican State Convention at Indianapolis on the second Monday in December, 1831, with delegates elected by county conventions of the party.

96 The delegates were: Congressmen Ratliff Boon, John Carr, Jonathan McCarty; John Tipton, recently elected senator; and Samuel Milroy, of Carroll County. The delegates were to help select "a suitable person to be run for Vice President . . . on the Ticket with Andrew Jackson."

97 Edward Stanwood, *A History of the Presidency, 1788–1897* (2 vols., Boston, 1928), I, 157; Indianapolis *Indiana Journal*, December 27, 1831. In its abstract of the proceedings the *Indiana Journal* indicates that at least two delegates attended from Indiana, but does not name them. Since Isaac Howk was named to the committee to prepare an address to the people of the United States, his attendance may be presumed. This address is in the *Indiana Journal*, January 4, 1832.

98 Stanwood, *History of the Presidency, 1788–1897*, I, 159–162; John Tipton to Calvin Fletcher, May 25, 1832, in Robertson and Riker (eds.), *John Tipton Papers*, II, 614. This convention adopted the rule and established the precedent that its party's nominations for president and vice president must be approved by not less than two thirds of the delegates. For examples of Indiana's preference for Johnson over Van Buren, see *ibid.*, 525, 526, 533, 538–539, 541–542, 544, 552, 562–563, 571, 588.

99 For a sample of Jacksonian views, from county conventions late in 1831 through the election of presidential electors in November, 1832, see Vincennes *Western Sun*, December 3, 1831, January 14, October 20, 27, November 3, 1832. For a discussion that considers differences between views expressed by Indiana Jacksonians in the 1820s versus those in the early thirties, see Krueger, Party Development in Indiana, 1800–1832, pp. 248–254, and 254–303 *passim*.

100 Indianapolis *Indiana Journal*, August 18, October 6, November 3, 1832. For a further sampling of views espoused by National Republicans, see other items in the issues of the *Indiana Journal* as cited, plus the issues of September 15, 29, 1832.

101 Robertson and Riker (eds.), *John Tipton Papers*, II, 526, 554, 592, 625.

102 Riker and Thornbrough (comps.), *Indiana Election Returns, 1816–1851*, pp. 10–20. *Ibid.*, 20, shows 27 votes for the Anti-Masonic electoral ticket. Fayette County has been counted for Clay, but his vote over Jackson was negligible. For the electoral vote in 1832 versus 1828, see Stanwood, *History of the Presidency, 1788–1897*, I, 149, 164. Oliver H. Smith, who knew and admired Clay, said that no man in America had been better qualified to be president than Clay, but he failed to achieve the presidency "because Mr. Clay voted for John Quincy Adams against Gen. Jackson, in the House of Representatives, and then accepted from Mr. Adams the office of Secretary of State." Oliver H. Smith, *Early Indiana Trials and Sketches* (Cincinnati, 1858), 134.

103 Vincennes *Western Sun*, December 8, 1832; Indianapolis *Indiana Journal*, December 5, 1832; Madison *Indiana Republican*, November 22, 1832.

[104] Isaac Howk to John Tipton, May 10, 1832, in Robertson and Riker (eds.), *John Tipton Papers*, II, 600. For examples of early and bipartisan efforts on behalf of Tipton, see *ibid.*, 470, 496–497, 499, 506–507, 510–511, 544–545. For examples of comments about National Republicans as possible candidates, see *ibid.*, 607, 658–659, 705–706, 708, 712, 718–719.

[105] Samuel Judah to John Tipton, May 30, 1832, *ibid.*, 618. Tipton's response, if any, has not been found.

[106] *Ibid.*, 667–668, 683–684, 714. Boon interpreted Tipton as having said that if they both ran, "'a *Clay* man, will be the senator.'" Boon added: "Now Sir, if you are disposed to produce these results which you have predicted, by your runing for the senate, you can do so." In November Boon said Tipton had told him that he "did not *wish* to be reelected to the senate."

[107] For comments regarding allegations against John D. Woolverton, receiver at the Vincennes Land Office, and the impact of this situation on Judah, see *ibid.*, 124n, 715, 724, 725, 728, 729, 737–738. Concerning McCarty as a candidate for the Senate, see 701–702, 711–712, 718–719, 724, 735, 749–750, 773.

[108] Indiana *House Journal*, 1832–33, pp. 48–50, 62–63, 65–67. For a summary of the voting ballot by ballot, see Riker and Thornbrough (comps.), *Indiana Election Returns, 1816–1851*, pp. 129–130. For comments by Finch and Marshall, see Robertson and Riker (eds.), *John Tipton Papers*, II, 737–738, 742–743. For other comments about the voting and its outcome, see 727–728, 731–733, 735, 737–751, 773. As noted, p. 773, Jordan Vigus reported to Tipton that twenty-four Clay men stood by him during the voting on the first day, and he presumed their number increased by the end of the election; and that only sixteen Jacksonians could be found for him when the voting began.

[109] John Tipton to Calvin Fletcher, January 11, 1833, in Robertson and Riker (eds.), *John Tipton Papers*, II, 771–772. In this letter the wily Tipton vented his ire at Boon and McCarty, incumbent Jacksonian congressmen, saying of them: "I would indeed be relieved could the Reps. in the next Cong. be men of *common sense* and *good feelings*. McCty and Boon are worse than no men here[.] we could do better without them.—" As this comment suggests, intrigue and manipulation within party ranks were at times more bitter than that between rivals from opposing parties.

[110] U.S. *Statutes at Large*, IV, 516; *Laws of Indiana*, 1832–33, pp. 3–4. For a map showing the congressional districts and their counties, see Justin E. Walsh, *The Centennial History of the Indiana General Assembly, 1816–1978* (Indianapolis, 1987), 785.

[111] Indianapolis *Indiana Democrat*, April 6, June 8, 1833. An anonymous writer, but clearly a staunch Jacksonian, warned against candidates who had favored recharter of the United States Bank and high tariff protection, then later showed fondness for Jacksonian measures they had violently opposed. Vincennes *Western Sun*, June 8, 1833.

[112] Indianapolis *Indiana Journal*, July 6, 1833. "One of the People," apparently a National Republican, urged candidates to state their opinions on paper,

and leave no room for dodging or sliding around. Since there was no debate about economy, rights of the people, and the right of instruction not much need be said about them. However, emphasis should be given to their views about such items as rechartering the federal bank and disposal of proceeds from public lands. *Ibid.*, June 15, 1833.

113 For examples of issues discussed in campaign circulars, see Vincennes *Western Sun*, April 13, 1833 (circular by John W. Davis), May 11, 1833 (circular by Robert M. Evans); Indianapolis *Indiana Democrat*, January 5, 1833 (circular of Alexander F. Morrison), June 22, 1833 (circular of George Craig). Also see Vincennes *Western Sun*, May 25, 1833, quoting (Terre Haute) *Wabash Courier*, for lengthy report of a joint discussion of issues by several candidates. Steps were taken toward some district conventions, but whether any meeting worthy of being called a district convention occurred is uncertain. See Indianapolis *Indiana Democrat*, March 9, 16, 23, April 6, June 29, 1833. *Ibid.*, June 1, 1833, states that James Rariden declined being a candidate in the Fifth District because friends of Clay had nominated Oliver H. Smith in preference to him.

114 Vincennes *Gazette*, September 7, 1833. The official returns for all counties are in Riker and Thornbrough (comps.), *Indiana Election Returns, 1816–1851*, pp. 87–90. Ewing beat his Jacksonian opponent, John W. Davis, his closest rival, by two votes. The Jacksonians won their districts by a majority count in every instance. Boon won over five rivals; Hannegan over three; Lane and Kinnard over two; and Carr and McCarty over one opponent. James Brown Ray, who had been governor, 1825–31, got only sixteen votes as one of the rivals of Kinnard.

115 Indianapolis *Indiana Journal*, May 10, 24, 1834; Indianapolis *Indiana Democrat*, May 24, 1834. The *Indiana Journal*, May 31, 1834, states that the "Salem Annotator" (Salem *Western Annotator*) had objected to the use of the word Whig because it infers the opposite term (Tory) for the opposition party. The *Indiana Democrat*, May 31, 1834, comments about an item in the Terre Haute *Wabash Courier* suggesting an individual who would be a valuable addition to the "WHIG" cause in Indiana.

116 For the six congressmen who voted against requiring local banks to take their deposits to the U.S. Bank, see pp. 526–527.

117 Complete returns for all districts, by counties and official for all counties but one, are in Riker and Thornbrough (comps.), *Indiana Election Returns, 1816–1851*, pp. 90–93, with political ties listed for all but John Finley and Jacob B. Lowe. The Indianapolis *Indiana Democrat*, September 2, 1835, states that Kinnard and Lowe had declared for Van Buren for president and Johnson for vice president in 1836. As noted in Chapter 4, p. 151, in 1834 Lowe ran second to James G. Read for nomination as governor by the Jacksonians. Hence, Lowe is presumed to be a Democrat, who lost to Kinnard, also a Democrat. In the other six districts, apart from the 2,353 votes for Finley, Democrats garnered 31,078 votes versus 23,095 for the Whigs. As indicated in *Biographical Directory of the Indiana General Assembly*, I, 465–466, 56 Whigs, 50 Democrats, 1 probable

Democrat, and 1 whose political connection is unknown were elected to the legislative session of 1835–36.

[118] Indianapolis *Indiana Democrat*, November 2, 1833, quoting New York *Working Man's Advocate*. The Indianapolis *Indiana Journal*, August 3, 1833, had published an item, reportedly at the request of local friends of Johnson, recommending him as a candidate for president. This Whig organ seems to have cooperated with Tipton concerning items about Johnson, presumably to stir division among Indiana Jacksonians. As shown in Robertson and Riker (eds.), *John Tipton Papers*, II, 525, 533, 544, 562–563, 571, 588, 611n, 614, Tipton had strongly supported Johnson for vice president in 1832. *Ibid.*, 838–839, 840, 857–858, 860; and III, 5, 10, 11, 65, 77, 108, 119, show that Tipton was strongly for Johnson for president in 1836.

[119] Robertson and Riker (eds.), *John Tipton Papers*, II, 841–843, 849–850; *ibid.*, III, 6–9. The proceedings of the Democratic State Convention in Indianapolis *Indiana Democrat*, December 11, 1833, indicate that the convention did not endorse either Johnson or Van Buren. An attempt to have Johnson endorsed "as well qualified" failed.

[120] Indianapolis *Indiana Democrat*, January 11, 15, 1834. This paper states that the celebration at which Johnson spoke was participated in "by the citizens of Indianapolis and vicinity, and many members of the legislature, without distinction of party." Concerning Noble's role regarding Johnson for president, see Riker and Thornbrough (eds.), *Messages and Papers of Noah Noble*, 35, 36n, 262n.

[121] Indianapolis *Indiana Democrat*, September 19, 26, 1834. For responses by Johnson and Harrison, see Vincennes *Western Sun*, November 8, 1834. *Ibid.*, October 11, 1834, states that celebrations commemorating the Battle of the Thames had been held in several states.

[122] For instance, see Robertson and Riker (eds.), *John Tipton Papers*, III, 10–11, 65, 108, 119, 124, 125–126, 128, 145; Riker and Thornbrough (eds.), *Messages and Papers of Noah Noble*, 35, 224–225, 245–246, 355–356.

[123] Nathan B. Palmer to John Tipton, February 18, 1835, in Robertson and Riker (eds.), *John Tipton Papers*, III, 127–128; Vincennes *Western Sun*, January 24, 1835.

[124] Indianapolis *Indiana Democrat*, May 2, June 5 (convention proceedings), July 3 (Indiana favorite and victor), 1835. According to *ibid.*, June 5, 1835, the following were seated as delegates from Indiana: Thomas B. Brown, John Cain, John DuBois, Livingston Dunlap, Jesse Jackson, N. Jackson, Samuel Milroy, Alexander F. Morrison, Daniel Reid, John Spencer, and Marinus Willett.

[125] Indianapolis *Indiana Journal*, June 7, 1834. For examples of consideration of candidates among citizens of Indiana, see Riker and Thornbrough (eds.), *Messages and Papers of Noah Noble*, 36–37, 224–225, 246, 355–356, 380–381, 384. Also see Indianapolis *Indiana Journal*, December 26, 1834, January 6, July 31, August 21, September 18, 1835, January 1, 1836.

[126] Indianapolis *Indiana Journal*, June 19, 1835; Indianapolis *Indiana Democrat*, June 19, 1835. Calvin Fletcher called the tour "an electioneering campaign

for [the] Presidency or trying to ascertain the public pulse" regarding the presidency. In mid-December Fletcher confided to his diary: "I shall not support Genl. Harrison for reasons hereafter expressed." Thornbrough, Riker, and Corpuz (eds.), *Diary of Calvin Fletcher*, I, 256, 290. Nothing has been found regarding Fletcher's reasons for this statement; however, as indicated *ibid.*, p. 386, while at Madison on election day, he offered to vote the Harrison ticket but was refused a ticket.

127 Indianapolis *Indiana Journal*, July 31, August 14, 1835; Indianapolis *Indiana Democrat*, August 19, 1835.

128 Items about the Harrison State Convention and its address, unless indicated otherwise, are from its proceedings in the Indianapolis *Indiana Journal*, December 18, 1835. Although in fact a Whig convention, the word Whig is not found in the proceedings cited, and the proceedings state that delegates were chosen by the friends of Harrison. The convention named a State Central Committee of sixteen persons, and urged the establishment of county and township committees to cooperate with the state committee for success of the party nominees.

129 Items concerning the Democratic Republican State Convention, unless otherwise indicated, are based on proceedings in the Indianapolis *Indiana Democrat*, January 12, 1836, and its resolutions and address to the people as in its issue of February 2, 1836. The convention placed much emphasis on party organization. It named a State Central Committee of sixteen persons, established a committee for each of the seven congressional districts, created correspondence committees for nearly all counties, and asked the latter to create township committees. The state, congressional, and county committees were empowered with authority to fill their own vacancies—an important step toward continuing party organization. See *ibid.*, September 30, October 7, 1835, regarding the calling of the convention; and *ibid.*, September 30, 1835, January 8, 1836, *passim*, for county meetings and selection of delegates to the convention.

130 Indianapolis *Indiana Journal*, December 18, 1835 (Whig address), June 18, 1836 (Van Buren's coach), July 2, 1836, quoting Lawrenceburgh *Indiana Palladium* (Jackson minus Van Buren). For a sampling of items against Van Buren, see Indianapolis *Indiana Journal*, June 18, 25, July 16, 23, August 27, September 17, October 22, 1836. For a sampling of responses to such criticism, see Indianapolis *Indiana Democrat*, April 13, May 25, June 29, July 6, 13, 20, September 14, 21, 28, November 2, 1836; Vincennes *Western Sun*, August 20, 1836.

131 Indianapolis *Indiana Democrat*, February 2, 1836 (quotations from Democratic Republican address); February 17, 1836 (quotations concerning role of Harrison at Tippecanoe, and criticism of his political career). For a sampling of these and other items against Harrison, see *ibid.*, February 17, May 4, July 13, 20, September 7, 14, 21, October 12, 19, November 2, 1836; Vincennes *Western Sun*, November 5, 1836. For a sampling of responses to such criticism, see Indianapolis *Indiana Journal*, June 18, 25, September 3, 17, October 8, 15, November 5, 1836.

132 This summary view is based on items cited in the two preceding notes, plus items cited in proceedings of the party state conventions as found in notes 128 and 129 above. See William Henry Harrison to Sherrod Williams, May 1, 1836, in Indianapolis *Indiana Journal,* June 18, 1836, in which Harrison at length indicated his support for distribution of surplus revenue from sales of public lands to the states, as proposed by Henry Clay; stressed that no money should be taken from the federal treasury for internal improvements, except for items of strictly national importance; explained that distribution of surplus revenue from land sales among the states would provide means to make needed internal improvements, and help preserve harmony among the states; denied that he had ever been identified with the Federalist party; emphasized that he was not the candidate of the bank party, and gave examples of his earlier opposition to the United States Bank, but agreed that a bank might be chartered with terms that would meet his approval; and criticized Jackson's use of the veto power.

133 For instance, see Vincennes *Western Sun,* February 6, 1836; Indianapolis *Indiana Democrat,* July 27, August 24, 1836; Indianapolis *Indiana Journal,* May 14, July 30, September 10, 1836.

134 Indianapolis *Indiana Journal,* September 10, 1836. In its issue of November 2, 1836, the Indianapolis *Indiana Democrat* lists states with 170 votes that beyond all doubt would go for Van Buren and Johnson, with 148 electoral votes needed to elect. This paper calls their election "certain, beyond all doubt." Indiana was not listed among states certain for Van Buren and Johnson. The *Indiana Journal* was only partially correct about the ages at presidential inaugurations.

135 Riker and Thornbrough (comps.), *Indiana Election Returns, 1816–1851,* pp. 14–28. In 1836 Harrison got about 41,300 votes against 33,000 for Van Buren; in 1832 Jackson gained 31,400 votes against 25,250 for Clay.

136 As shown in Stanwood, *History of the Presidency, 1788–1897,* I, 184–188, Van Buren won 170 votes (total the *Indiana Democrat* predicted according to note 134 above); Harrison, 73; White, 26; and Webster, 14. As seen in *Congressional Debates,* 24 Cong., 2 session, XIII, Pt. 1, pp. 738–739, although Indiana's electors had voted for Francis Granger of New York, Harrison's running mate, for vice president, Tipton and Hendricks voted for Johnson over Granger. Despite the fact that Tipton had fought with Harrison at the Battle of Tippecanoe in 1811, his support for Van Buren and Johnson is affirmed in Robertson and Riker (eds.), *John Tipton Papers,* III, 202, 207, 314–315; and Hendricks' support of Van Buren and Johnson is indicated in Hill, *William Hendricks,* 292–298.

137 Hill, *William Hendricks,* 247–250.

138 *Ibid.,* 250, quoting Indianapolis *Indiana Democrat,* November 25, 1835; Indianapolis *Indiana Democrat,* June 15, 1836. The *Biographical Directory of the Indiana General Assembly,* I, 467–469, indicates that for the session of 1836–37, 27 Whigs and 20 Democrats were elected to the Senate, 54 Whigs and 46 Democrats to the House, giving the Whigs 81 versus 66 members on joint ballot, with 74 votes required to elect a senator.

[139] Indianapolis *Indiana Democrat*, November 16, 30, 1836.

[140] Indianapolis *Indiana Journal*, December 7, 1836. See Indianapolis *Indiana Democrat*, November 30, 1836, for "Many Citizens" to Noble, arguing that Noble had made such a pledge in 1831 as a binding and continuing obligation.

[141] See Indianapolis *Indiana Democrat*, November 30, 1836, for the claim of "A Wabash Citizen" that Hendricks had reportedly avowed himself a Van Buren man; William Henry Harrison to Noah Noble, December 3, 1836, in Riker and Thornbrough (eds.), *Messages and Papers of Noah Noble*, 466–467, in which Harrison insists that Hendricks had exerted himself against his election; and Hill, *William Hendricks*, 292–298.

[142] Riker and Thornbrough (comps.), *Indiana Election Returns, 1816–1851*, p. 131. For contemporary comments, see Indianapolis *Indiana Democrat*, December 13, 1836; Indianapolis *Indiana Journal*, December 10, 20, 1836; Thornbrough, Riker, and Corpuz (eds.), *Diary of Calvin Fletcher*, I, 389–390; Robertson and Riker (eds.), *John Tipton Papers*, III, 319–320, 330, 334; Smith, *Early Indiana Trials and Sketches*, 68–69, 86, 141–143. In its issue of December 20, 1836, the *Indiana Journal* strongly defended Noble and emphasized its regret that he had not been elected senator.

[143] Concerning the accident and resulting death of Kinnard, see Indianapolis *Indiana Democrat*, November 23, 30, December 13, 1836; Robertson and Riker (eds.), *John Tipton Papers*, III, 317, 318.

[144] For announcements of candidacy by Wick and Herod respectively, see Indianapolis *Indiana Journal*, December 10, 23, 1836. For additional items about their views and campaigns, see *ibid.*, December 20, 23, 27, 1836; Indianapolis *Indiana Democrat*, December 13, 1836. As indicated in Thornbrough, Riker, and Corpuz (eds.), *Diary of Calvin Fletcher*, I, 389, and Robertson and Riker (eds.), *John Tipton Papers*, III, 329, Fletcher announced himself as a candidate then withdrew after discussion with Herod, in which both agreed that if they competed Wick would win.

[145] Riker and Thornbrough (comps.), *Indiana Election Returns, 1816–1851*, pp. 93, 92, 89. As noted *ibid.*, 6, Wick had been a Clay elector in 1824.

[146] Vincennes *Western Sun*, January 7, 1837, quoting Terre Haute *Wabash Courier*.

[147] For the result of the congressional elections of 1835 versus those of 1837, see Riker and Thornbrough (comps.), *Indiana Election Returns, 1816–1851*, pp. 90–97.

[148] Herod received 9,635 votes to 5,888 for Ray. Although Ray thanked the voters for their generous support, and made note of the fact that he had won Marion County, where he had lived for twelve years, he plaintively commented: "Whilst my political sun has set forever in a cheerless sky, deep is my regret, that it did not go down under circumstances, that would have justified me in saying that my country had been grateful." See Ray's statement to voters of the district in Indianapolis *Indiana Democrat*, August 30, 1837.

[149] Henry Clay to Noah Noble, June 20, 1837, in Riker and Thornbrough (eds.), *Messages and Papers of Noah Noble*, 551–553. The Indianapolis *Indiana*

Journal, August 26, 1837, emphasized that both Rariden and McCarty were Whigs, with the result decided between them on local and personal grounds. It is probable, however, that Democratic votes for Rariden gave him the victory over McCarty. Worth noting is the comment of the Indianapolis *Indiana Democrat*, August 9, 1837, that Rariden had been elected over McCarty, "the political turncoat and bosom friend of N Noble."

150 Vincennes *Western Sun*, August 26, 1837; Indianapolis *Indiana Democrat*, August 23, 1837; Indianapolis *Indiana Journal*, August 26, 1837.

151 John Tipton to John Livingston (editor, Indianapolis *Indiana Democrat*), May 7, 1838, in Robertson and Riker (eds.), *John Tipton Papers*, III, 623–625. Tipton said many reasons had caused his decision; and he emphasized the need to provide for the care and education of his young children, also that he "must be very soon on the decline of life." See pp. 582–589, for an earlier and lengthy letter to Livingston in which Tipton indicated his intention to retire, and stated that such had been announced to several gentlemen as early as 1833. But, as noted pp. 756–757, 763–764, 767–768, 770–771, 776–777, 778–779, efforts on behalf of his reelection continued into the election. Moreover, as may be seen pp. 767–768, less than a month before the voting Tipton sent Nathaniel West the names of members of the legislature "that I think are not unfriendly to me." He added: "I wish all to understand that I do not ask a re election & that I have told my friends to unite on Boone, Carr, Howard, Pepper, Milroy or west, or on the most prominant man . . . but do not use my name unless you have good reason to believe you can suceede nor unless you are confident that no other Democrat can be electd[.]" Perhaps the wily Tipton believed that there was no reasonable chance that any Democrat could be elected, hence he was not a candidate unless his election seemed assured! As indicated in Indianapolis *Indiana Democrat*, May 16, 1838, Indianapolis *Indiana Journal*, May 19, 1838, Vincennes *Western Sun*, May 26, 1838, these papers all spoke quite favorably of the public service which Tipton had rendered Indiana.

152 In its issue of October 6, 1838, the Indianapolis *Indiana Journal* stated that the election of Noah Noble, Charles Dewey, Milton Stapp, John Dumont, Thomas H. Blake, Thomas J. Evans or any other honest and capable Whig would give satisfaction to the Whigs. However, it stated the conviction that two thirds of the people were anxious for Noble's election, and added that his claims for the office were superior to those of anyone else. In its issue of May 23, 1838, the Indianapolis *Indiana Democrat* published an item by "AN OLD DEMOCRAT" naming the following Democrats as possible successors to Tipton: General Tilghman A. Howard, James Whitcomb, Samuel Milroy, John Carr, Abel C. Pepper, and Nathaniel West. The Vincennes *Western Sun*, June 30, July 14, September 29, October 20, November 3, 1838, plugged hard for the election of Ratliff Boon as a true Jacksonian. Much related comment is found *passim* in issues of these papers, especially during the fall of 1838.

153 Indianapolis *Indiana Democrat*, March 9, July 11, 18, September 5, 1838.

154 For examples of comments about issues, see *ibid.*, May 23, June 27, October 10, 17, 1838; Indianapolis *Indiana Journal*, June 30, July 14, August 4, October 6, 1838.

155 See Indianapolis *Indiana Journal*, December 22, 1838, for Noble's statement dated December 6. Noble said he was "assured that a majority of the Whigs" preferred him, but their number was not sufficient to secure his election because they could not act in concert. The comment of the editor seems to indicate that Noble issued his statement after the Whigs had been unable to agree on their preferred candidate. The context and comments suggest that Noble perhaps anticipated that after other Whigs had battled for the nomination that the party then would turn to him. The state election in August had resulted in 27 Whigs and 20 Democrats being elected to the Senate, 57 Whigs and 43 Democrats to the House, giving the Whigs 84 members to 63 for the Democrats when voting in joint session. *Biographical Directory of the Indiana General Assembly*, I, 472–474.

156 Indiana *Senate Journal*, 1838–39, pp. 45–53, 55–64, 80–88, 91–99, showing how members voted on each ballot. According to the politics of legislators in *Biographical Directory of the Indiana General Assembly*, I, 472–474, on the final ballot 48 Whigs and 27 Democrats voted for White. See Riker and Thornbrough (comps.), *Indiana Election Returns, 1816–1851*, pp. 132–133, for a tabulation of the voting for all thirty-six ballots.

157 Indianapolis *Indiana Journal*, December 15, 22, 1838; Indianapolis *Indiana Democrat*, December 15, 1838.

158 For nominations by congressional district conventions, see Indianapolis *Indiana Journal*, May 4 (Proffit, First), May 11 (Ewing, Second), April 6 (Thomas J. Evans, Seventh), January 19 (Howard, Seventh), 1839; Vincennes *Western Sun*, March 30 (Davis, Second), 1839; Indianapolis *Indiana Democrat*, May 1 (Smith, Fourth, and William Thompson, Fifth), 1839. According to *ibid.*, February 20, 1839, the *Expunger* would be published for four months prior to the August election by J. Livingston, editor of the *Indiana Democrat*. See Riker and Thornbrough (comps.), *Indiana Election Returns, 1816–1851*, pp. 93–97, for those elected and those defeated in 1837.

159 For examples of such discussion, see Vincennes *Western Sun*, March 2, 16, 30, 1839; Indianapolis *Indiana Democrat*, April 17, 24, May 1, 1839; Indianapolis *Indiana Journal*, April 13, June 23, July 27, 1839. As indicated in *Indiana Democrat*, June 26, July 10, 1839, and *Indiana Journal*, April 27, 1839, Whig responsibility for the fiscal crisis arising from the System of 1836 was emphasized by some Democrats.

160 Indianapolis *Indiana Democrat*, July 3, 17, 1839.

161 Indianapolis *Indiana Journal*, July 13, 1839. This charge also was made, same substance, in its issue of July 6, 1839. The *Indiana Journal* attributed this charge to Van Buren advocates and pronounced it groundless, which seems likely.

162 *Ibid.*, July 13, 1839. In its issue of July 10, 1839, the Indianapolis *Indiana Democrat* comments on attacks against Owen as an infidel and because of his

little book on moral physiology, notes his political stature and contribution to education, and indicates that Owen earlier held views which he since thinks were a little extravagant; and others which, had prudence been consulted, would not have been published. Also see Richard William Leopold, *Robert Dale Owen: A Biography* (Cambridge, Mass., 1940), 165–167.

163 Indianapolis *Indiana Journal*, July 27, 1839.

164 Riker and Thornbrough (comps.), *Indiana Election Returns, 1816–1851*, pp. 97–100; Indianapolis *Indiana Journal*, August 10, 1839; Vincennes *Western Sun*, August 17, 1839; Indianapolis *Indiana Democrat*, September 4, 1839. In its issue for August 17, 1839, the *Indiana Journal* stated: "Their [the Whig] defeat did not result from a lack of numbers, but from a want of union and action." In this same issue the Richmond *Palladium* is quoted which emphasized that the Whigs had not adequately presented the national issues at stake to the people; and in the *Journal* issue of August 31 the Greencastle *Visitor* is quoted which declared: "We have only to attribute our defeat to carelessness on our part, in suffering our opponents to make the issue upon the popularity of Mr. Clay. Indiana ever will stand by her old governor, but for Henry Clay, she never will cast her vote." As noted in *Biographical Directory of the Indiana General Assembly*, I, 474–476, the legislative elections in August gave the Democrats 22 senators and 61 representatives, against 25 senators and 39 representatives for the Whigs, giving the Democrats an aggregate of 83 to 64 for the Whigs on joint ballot.

165 John Tipton to John H. Eaton, April 5, 1831, in Robertson and Riker (eds.), *John Tipton Papers*, II, 399–400. Estimates about the number of Indians vary considerably. The Lawrenceburgh *Indiana Palladium*, May 9, 1829, stated that Indiana had 4,050 Indians according to a report from the secretary of war.

166 Hugh McCulloch, *Men and Measures of Half a Century* (New York, 1889), 102.

167 George W. Ewing to Benjamin F. Butler, February 12, 1837, in Robertson and Riker (eds.), *John Tipton Papers*, I, 42n. See William G. Ewing to Tipton, February 3, 1830, *ibid.*, II, 245, stating that it would be desirable to permit the Indians "to occupy back & unimportent situations for a while, as their increased annuity will be of material benefit in the first settleing of our country . . . ."

168 For arguments for Indian removal, see John Tipton to Thomas L. McKinney, January 31, 1830, *ibid.*, II, 243–244; and speeches of Tipton and John W. Davis respectively in *Congressional Debates*, 22 Cong., 1 session, VIII, Pt. 1, pp. 1075, 1076, 1083; *ibid.*, 24 Cong., 2 session, XIII, Pt. 1, pp. 1149–1150. Also see *Laws of Indiana*, 1828–29, pp. 155–156; *ibid.*, 1829–30, pp. 176–177; *Special Acts*, 1830–31, pp. 180–181; *Laws of Indiana*, 1832–33, pp. 241–242, 243–244; *ibid.* (local), 1834–35, pp. 277–278. For commentary about the possibility that removal would result in the "civilization" of the Indians, see Bernard W. Sheehan, *Seeds of Extinction: Jeffersonian Philanthropy and the American Indian* (Chapel Hill, N. C., 1973), 3–12, 243–245, 274–275, and *passim*. In 1830 Congress approved a law providing for tribal lands west of the Mississippi to tribes east of this river who would exchange their existing lands for same and remove thereto. U. S. *Statutes at Large*, IV, 411–412.

169 *Senate Documents*, 58 Cong., 2 session, No. 319 (2nd ed., 2 vols.), II, 256–258, 268–270, 272–274. The treaties also promised additional miscellaneous payments. The second of them promised to supply goods, farming utensils, and other needed articles required if the Potawatomi decided to emigrate from Indiana.

170 *Ibid.*, II, 318–320, 333, 339–341, 343–344, 349–351, 362–363. These treaties also promised additional miscellaneous payments, including items associated with removals. Some treaties called for payment of debts owed by Indians, but such payments were to be deducted from promised payments. Various of these treaties provided for emigration from Indiana by 1838, one said by 1839.

171 *Ibid.*, II, 315–318, 384–388, 393–394. The annuity payments were to be $10,000 yearly for ten years, then $12,568 yearly for ten years, and then $12,250 yearly for twenty years. If debts assumed exceeded the sums indicated, the shortage would be taken from annuity payments, if less than the debts, the surplus would be added to annuity payments. The table does not include various miscellaneous payments promised by these treaties, such as costs of removals. According to Paul Wallace Gates in Robertson and Riker (eds.), *John Tipton Papers*, I, 49, from 1818 to 1840 the United States ceded Richardville 44 1/4 sections of land and paid him $31,800; and in the same period gave Godfroy 17 sections of land and $17,612. For evaluations of Richardville, see *ibid.*, 15, 547; Bert Anson, *The Miami Indians* (Norman, Okla., 1970), 188–190, 208–209.

172 Abel C. Pepper to David Wallace, August 26, 1838, in Riker (ed.), *Messages and Papers of David Wallace*, 147; David Wallace to John Tipton, August 27, 1838, and Tipton to Wallace, August 27, 1838, in Robertson and Riker (eds.), *John Tipton Papers*, III, 675–676. For related items, see Riker (ed.), *Messages and Papers of David Wallace*, 148–150, 150, 180; Robertson and Riker (eds.), *John Tipton Papers*, III, 660–663, 682–685, 715–716, 719–720; Irving McKee, *The Trail of Death: Letters of Benjamin Marie Petit* (Indianapolis, 1941), 81–84, 87.

173 Robertson and Riker (eds.), *John Tipton Papers*, III, 672, 673, 676–682, 687–688; "Journal of an Emigrating Party of Pottawattomie Indians, 1838," *Indiana Magazine of History*, XXI (1925), 316–317. Tipton or his aide probably wrote the portion of the journal here cited. Although Menominee refused to cede land or agree to removal, he was nonetheless forced to emigrate. Robertson and Riker (eds.), *John Tipton Papers*, III, 246–247, 259–260, 301–302, 304–305, 312–313, 325–326, 391–392, 686–687, 713–715, 720.

174 "Journal of an Emigrating Party of Pottawattomie Indians, 1838," *Indiana Magazine of History*, XXI, 317–336 *passim*. Also see McKee, *The Trail of Death*, 90–92, 95, 98–101, 128–131; R. David Edmunds, *The Potawatomis: Keepers of the Fire* (Norman, Okla., 1978), 267–268.

175 William Polke to Carey A. Harris, November 10, 1838, in Dwight L. Smith (ed.), "A Continuation of the Journal of an Emigrating Party of Potawatomi Indians, 1838, and Ten William Polke Manuscripts," *Indiana Magazine of History*, XLIV (1948), 408; "Journal of an Emigrating Party of Pottawattomie Indians, 1838," *ibid.*, XXI, 334.

[176] Edmunds, *The Potawatomis*, 246–247, 251, 254–256, 261–264, 266–268, 270–271, 273–274; John D. Barnhart and Donald F. Carmony, *Indiana: From Frontier to Industrial Commonwealth* (4 vols., New York, 1954), I, 213, 216.

[177] Anson, *The Miami Indians*, 217–226; Charles R. Poinsatte, *Fort Wayne During the Canal Era, 1828–1855* (Indianapolis, 1969), 99–103.

[178] Bert J. Griswold, *The Pictorial History of Fort Wayne, Indiana* (2 vols., Chicago, 1917), I, 379.

[179] Anson, *The Miami Indians*, 228–229, 266.

[180] *Congressional Globe*, 23 Cong., 2 session, VI, Appendix, 133–135. Tipton explained that as Indian agent he had warned settlers against trespassing on public lands, but that legislation against it had not "in a single instance" been enforced for many years. For an 1831 warning of Tipton to trespassers, while he was Indian agent, see Robertson and Riker (eds.), *John Tipton Papers*, II, 453.

[181] Herbert Anthony Kellar (ed.), *Solon Robinson: Pioneer and Agriculturist* (2 Vols., Indianapolis, 1936), I, 10–12, 66–76.

[182] *Congressional Debates*, 23 Cong., 2 session, XI, Pt. 2, pp. 1353–1358; *Congressional Globe*, 25 Cong., 2 session, VI, 436; *ibid.*, 26 Cong., 2 session, IX, Appendix, 74–78.

[183] U. S. *Statutes at Large*, IV, 503 (1832 law).

[184] Finding accurate and consistent data about land office sales in Indiana during the pioneer period seems impossible. According to a report of Commissioner Richard M. Young in 1849, during 1829–36, 7,624,029.07 acres were sold; for the years 1837–40, 2,303,881.26 acres. According to Young Indiana land sales totaled 1,547,500.21 acres in 1835; 3,016,960.77 acres in 1836; and 1,131,327.84 acres in 1837—the only years before 1848 when Indiana sales aggregated more than a million acres.

[185] Hill, *William Hendricks*, 186–194, 233–241, offers much information about support for cession, at times linked with graduation, by Hendricks and other Hoosiers. For a more general view, see Benjamin Hibbard, *A History of the Public Land Policies* (Madison, Wis., 1965), 190–194. At its session in 1828–29 the General Assembly asked Congress to cede the public domain within the state to Indiana; at the session of 1833–34, it asked for graduation to a minimum price then sale of the residue to Indiana at this minimum. *Laws of Indiana*, 1828–29, pp. 152–153; *ibid.*, 1833–34, p. 364.

[186] Concerning preemption legislation, 1829–41, see Hibbard, *History of the Public Land Policies*, 144–170; Roy M. Robbins, *Our Landed Heritage: The Public Domain, 1776–1936* (Princeton, N. J., 1942), 48–50, 64–65, 74–85. The General Assembly adopted various resolutions regarding preemption. For instance, see *Laws of Indiana*, 1832–33, pp. 233–234 (continue preemption act of 1832 for two years); *ibid.* (local), 1835–36, p. 390 (continue certain preemptions); *ibid.* (local), 1836–37, pp. 444–446 (remedy evils in preemption laws); *ibid.* (local), 1840–41, p. 217 (supporting Benton's "log cabin" bill for distribution, plus continuing preemption). For examples of speeches vigorously approving the principle of preemption, see *Congressional Debates*, 23 Cong., 1 session, X, Pt. 4, pp. 4471–

4472 (Jonathan McCarty, Jacksonian); *Congressional Globe*, 25 Cong., 2 session, VI, 436 (Ratliff Boon, Jacksonian); *ibid.*, 26 Cong., 2 session, IX, Appendix, 67–74 (Oliver H. Smith, Whig), 74–78 (Albert S. White, Whig).

187 Hibbard, *History of the Public Land Policies*, 295–301. As explained in note 185, graduation was often linked with cession.

188 *Congressional Debates*, 22 Cong., 2 session, IX, Pt. 1, p. 235; *ibid.*, Pt. 2, pp. 1920–1921; Richardson, *Messages and Papers of the Presidents*, III, 56–69 (veto message). For general background and context, see Hibbard, *History of the Public Land Policies*, 174–184; Robbins, *Our Landed Heritage*, 55–58.

189 Hill, William Hendricks, 237, quoting Madison *Indiana Republican*, March 21, 1833; Indianapolis *Indiana Journal*, May 18, 1833; Vincennes *Western Sun*, December 21, 1833.

190 U. S. *Statutes at Large*, V, 52–56; *Congressional Debates*, 24 Cong., 1 session, XII, Pt. 2, pp. 1845–1846; *ibid.*, Pt. 4, pp. 4379–4380. Democratic congressmen who voted for passage were: Ratliff Boon, John Carr, Edward A. Hannegan, George L. Kinnard, Amos Lane, and Jonathan McCarty. Their fellow Democrat, John W. Davis, did not participate in the voting. For the general background regarding the distribution act of 1836, see Hibbard, *History of the Public Land Policies*, 183–184; Robbins, *Our Landed Heritage*, 69–70. The distribution act of 1836 called for depositing surplus revenue above $5,000,000 with the states in four quarterly payments during 1837, interest free, but subject to recall. Its recall, however, was not anticipated and was never required.

191 Robertson and Riker (eds.), *John Tipton Papers*, III, 294–295. Tipton said that money spent by state legislatures would be spent with "a more rigid accountability . . . than is generally observed when disbursed by the United States." Indiana's expenditures for the System of 1836 *were decidedly not characterized by rigid accountability.*

192 *Congressional Debates*, 24 Cong., 2 session, XIII, Pt. 2, pp. 1967–1969. For similar comments earlier made by Boon, see *ibid.*, 24 Cong., 1 session, XII, Pt. 4, pp. 4318–4320.

193 Indiana *Senate Journal*, 1837–38, pp. 281–282, for report by Treasurer Nathan B. Palmer that $286,751.48 had been received January 25, 1837, same sum on March 22, 1837, and also June 9, 1837. (The fourth installment was never received.)

194 Richardson, *Messages and Papers of the Presidents*, III, 321–322 (special session call), 343 (advice of Van Buren).

195 For the voting in the Senate, see *Congressional Debates*, 25 Cong., 1 session, XIV, Pt. 1, pp. 45, 422; the House vote, *ibid.*, 1104, 1135–1136, 1148, 1149, 1151. Concerning the modified bill only Herod, Rariden, and White voted for the amendment postponing payment to January 1, 1839. For Tipton's opposition to indefinite postponement, see *ibid.*, 421–422. In short, Boon sustained indefinite postponement, which all other Indiana members opposed; and presumably Herod, Rariden, and White merely preferred limited to indefinite postponement. For the resulting legislation, see U. S. *Statutes at Large*, V, 201.

[196] *Congressional Debates,* 25 Cong., 1 session, XIV, Pt. 1, pp. 421–422 (Tipton), 858–861 (Rariden); John Tipton to Henry B. Milroy, October 1, 1837, in Robertson and Riker (eds.), *John Tipton Papers,* III, 446–447; Indianapolis *Indiana Journal,* October 7, 1837.

[197] According to U. S. Bureau of the Census, *Negro Population in the United States, 1790–1915,* pp. 44–45, 51, in 1800 there were 298 blacks in Indiana or 5.3 percent of the total; 630 and 2.6 percent, 1810; 1,420 and 1 percent, 1820; 3,632 and 1.1 percent, 1830; 7,168 and 1 percent, 1840; 11,262 and 1.1 percent, 1850; 11,428 and .9 percent, 1860. For constitutional restrictions, see Charles Kettleborough, *Constitution Making in Indiana* (3 vols., Indianapolis, 1916, 1930), I, 107, 109.

[198] Indianapolis *Indiana Journal,* August 1, 1834, February 11, 1837. For an overview of discriminations against blacks, see Emma Lou Thornbrough, *The Negro in Indiana Before 1900: A Study of a Minority* (Indianapolis, 1958), 119–127, 142–143, 151–153, 159–163, 171–172, and *passim.*

[199] Thornbrough, *The Negro in Indiana,* 133–142.

[200] Corydon *Indiana Gazette,* January 20, February 3, October 12 (quote), November 23, December 14, 28, 1820.

[201] *Laws of Indiana,* 1825, pp. 105–106; *ibid.,* 1828–29, pp. 153–154.

[202] Indianapolis *Indiana State Gazette,* November 5, 12, 1829. Thornbrough, *The Negro in Indiana,* 75, notes formation of the Indiana Colonization Society in 1829, but makes no mention of the earlier formation at Corydon.

[203] For examples of such financing, see Vincennes *Western Sun,* July 3, 1830, June 13, 1840; Indianapolis *Indiana Journal,* June 23, 1832, July 6, 1833, June 25, 1836, June 23, 1838. For resistance to colonization among blacks, see Thornbrough, *The Negro in Indiana,* 78–80.

[204] Indianapolis *Indiana Journal,* January 26, 1831; Thornbrough, *The Negro in Indiana,* 80. The annual meeting urged that blacks "be removed and their places supplied with intelligent freemen . . . ."

[205] *Laws of Indiana* (revised), 1830–31, pp. 375–376; Thornbrough, *The Negro in Indiana,* 55–63. The 1831 law is repeated in *Revised Statutes,* 1837–38, pp. 418–419. This restrictive legislation was strongly condemned by seven senators who interpreted the statement in the Indiana constitution that "all men are born equally free, independent and have certain natural, inherent and unalienable rights" as embracing blacks. The protesters were James Blair, Calvin Fletcher, Samuel Frisbie, Amaziah Morgan, Abel Lomax, John Sering, and Daniel Worth —all anti-Jacksonians or Adams men according to *Biographical Directory of the Indiana General Assembly,* I, 455. At the ensuing legislative session, a report from the judiciary committee, submitted by Senator James Whitcomb, vigorously defended the restrictive law of 1831. With various states, both slave and free, trying to prohibit or at least restrict the presence of blacks, the report said that before its passage the "influx" of blacks "was daily and rapidly augmenting," often with "aged and infirm slaves" who had been freed among those coming to the state. Such a population, the report predicted, would threaten "the peace of

society, the contamination of public morals, an increased number of paupers with a corresponding increase of taxation," and bring "the danger of that gradual amalgamation of the species . . . which the canons of nature seem to forbid." Indiana *Senate Journal*, 1831–32, p. 394. See note 197 above regarding the increase of blacks in the 1830s.

206 Indiana *Senate Journal*, 1830–31, p. 533. For examples of such memorials, see *Congressional Debates*, 24 Cong., 2 session, XIII, Pt. 1, p. 706; *Congressional Globe*, 25 Cong., 2 session, VI, 101, 291; *ibid.*, 25 Cong., 3 session, VII, 104, 203; *ibid.*, 26 Cong., 1 session, VIII, 158. Women were among the signers of some of these petitions.

207 For instance, see *Congressional Debates*, 24 Cong., 1 session, XII, Pt. 4, pp. 4052–4054, May 26, 1836. Indiana's seven Democratic congressmen divided as follows concerning such memorials: Ratliff Boon and George L. Kinnard for tabling, John Carr, Amos Lane, and Jonathan McCarty against tabling; with John W. Davis and Edward A. Hannegan not voting. *Congressional Globe*, 25 Cong., 2 session, VI, 45, December 21, 1837, in which Boon voted for tabling; and Whigs George H. Dunn, John Ewing, William Graham, William Herod, James Rariden, and Albert S. White voted against tabling. *Ibid.*, 25 Cong., 3 session, VII, 28, December 12, 1838, in which Whigs Dunn, Ewing, Graham, Herod, Rariden, and White voted against tabling, with Boon not voting.

208 *Congressional Debates*, 24 Cong., 2 session, XIII, Pt. 2, p. 1720 (Lane); *ibid.*, Pt. 1, pp. 706–708 (Tipton). As indicated in Hill, *William Hendricks*, 279–280, Senator Hendricks voted to receive memorials regarding the abolition of slavery in the District of Columbia.

209 *Congressional Debates*, 24 Cong., 1 session, XII, Pt. 4, pp. 4031–4032; *Congressional Globe*, 25 Cong., 3 session, VII, 23, 25. In 1836 Democrats Ratliff Boon, John Carr, Edward A. Hannegan, George L. Kinnard, Amos Lane, and Jonathan McCarty voted that the states had no such authority; in 1838 Whigs George H. Dunn, William Graham, William Herod, and Albert S. White voted that the states had no such authority, with Whigs John Ewing, James Rariden, and Democrat Ratliff Boon not voting.

210 Indianapolis *Indiana Journal*, July 30, 1836; *Congressional Debates*, 23 Cong., 2 session, XI, Pt. 2, pp. 1394–1395 (Boon); *ibid.*, 24 Cong., 2 session, XIII, Pt. 1, p. 706 (Tipton); *ibid.*, Pt. 2, p. 1720 (Lane).

211 *Laws of Indiana* (local), 1838–39, p. 353.

212 Robertson and Riker (eds.), *John Tipton Papers*, III, 299–300. Tipton also declared: "We have already a territory sufficiently extensive to support a powerful nation, are at this time, if united, able to maintain our Independence against the world in arms." Tipton hoped Texas would become a sister republic.

213 For examples of these memorials, presented from 1837–39, see *Congressional Globe*, 25 Cong., 2 session, VI, 27, 101, 181, 291; *ibid.*, 3 session, VII, 170. According to the Indianapolis *Indiana Journal*, December 14, 1836, a joint resolution of the legislature opposing the annexation of Texas had passed to second reading.

214 U. S. *Statutes at Large*, I, 302–305. This law did not require that the claimant obtain a warrant before seizing an alleged fugitive, it did not require hearing of testimony from the fugitive, and it had no provision for a jury trial.

215 Levi Coffin, *Reminiscences of Levi Coffin* . . . (Cincinnati, 1876), 106–107, 113 (quotation).

216 Thornbrough, *The Negro in Indiana*, 39–44, 99–118 *passim*; William M. Cockrum, *History of the Underground Railroad as It was Conducted by the Anti-Slavery League* (Oakland City, Ind., 1915), *passim*. Cockrum's account has errors and embellishments, but used with care it is useful regarding the suffering and sacrifices endured by fugitive slaves, and the liability of free blacks to enslavement. Calvin Fletcher at various times aided blacks, both free and slaves. For examples, see Thornbrough, Riker, and Corpuz (eds.), *Diary of Calvin Fletcher*, I, 166–168, 322–324, 455–456; II, 18, 120.

217 Riker and Thornbrough (eds.), *Messages and Papers of Noah Noble*, 599–600; Indiana *Senate Journal*, 1837–38, p. 297.

218 Marion Clinton Miller, The Antislavery Movement in Indiana (Ph.D. dissertation, University of Michigan, 1938), 34–35, 64–75, 258–259.

219 *Ibid.*, 66–70, 73–75; Coffin, *Reminiscences of Levi Coffin*, 224–225. .

220 Miller, The Antislavery Movement in Indiana, 58–64, 74–76, 94–95, 258; L. C. Rudolph, *Hoosier Zion: The Presbyterians in Early Indiana* (New Haven, Conn., 1963), 119–120, 152–153.

221 James Duncan, *A Treatise on Slavery: In Which is Shewn Forth the Evil of Slave Holding, both from the Light of Nature and Divine Revelation* (Vevay, Ind., 1824).

222 Miller, The Antislavery Movement in Indiana, 78–79, 84.

223 Vincennes *Western Sun*, April 4, 1829. For an extremely useful and comprehensive discussion of relations between the United States and other countries during the Jackson-Van Buren era, see David M. Pletcher, *The Diplomacy of Annexation: Texas, Oregon, and the Mexican War* (Columbia, Mo., 1973), 1–110 *passim*.

224 Robertson and Riker (eds.), *John Tipton Papers*, II, 807. For examples of similar comments, see *ibid.*, III, 293–294 (Tipton); Indianapolis *Indiana Democrat*, April 6, 1833 (Jonathan McCarty); Vincennes *Western Sun*, April 11, 1835 (John Ewing). Early in 1841 Senator Oliver H. Smith presented a memorial to the Senate from citizens of Indiana praying that Congress recognize the independence of Haiti and establish commercial relations with it.

225 Riker and Thornbrough (eds.), *Messages and Papers of James Brown Ray*, 551–553; Indianapolis *Indiana Journal*, January 12, 1831; Vincennes *Western Sun*, November 19, 1831.

226 Indianapolis *Indiana Journal*, February 13, 1841. See *ibid.*, February 6, 1841, for comments about Tochman and his lectures in Indianapolis and elsewhere.

227 Van Deusen, *The Jacksonian Era*, 100–101; Vincennes *Western Sun*, May 21, 1831 (comment of Jackson State Central Committee); Indianapolis *Indiana Journal*, November 3, 1830.

228 For an overview of this controversy, see Van Deusen, *The Jacksonian Era*, 101–103; Richardson, *Messages and Papers of the Presidents*, III, 100–107 (Jackson's remarks, 1834), 152–160 (Jackson's remarks, 1835).

229 Robertson and Riker (eds.), *John Tipton Papers*, III, 134–136; Vincennes *Western Sun*, April 18, 11, 1835 (Hendricks and Ewing respectively). In this paper for April 4, 1835, Congressman Ratliff Boon vigorously supported Jackson's policy concerning the claims against France.

230 Indianapolis *Indiana Democrat*, February 2, 1836; Robertson and Riker (eds.), *John Tipton Papers*, III, 293.

231 For a scholarly overview of American relations with Texas and Mexico from the early twenties through the presidency of Van Buren, see Pletcher, *The Diplomacy of Annexation*, 31–86.

232 Vincennes *Western Sun*, January 2, 1836; Indianapolis *Indiana Journal*, June 11, 1836; Indianapolis *Indiana Democrat*, May 25, 1836. For examples of other comments about sympathy, financial aid, or volunteers for Texas, see Vincennes *Western Sun*, November 14, 28, December 12, 1835, April 23, May 21, 1836; Indianapolis *Indiana Democrat*, December 18, 1835, January 22, April 27, 1836. For Jacksonian policy regarding Texas, see Pletcher, *The Diplomacy of Annexation*, 68–72.

233 *Senate Journal*, 24 Cong., 1 session, 516–517; circular of Tipton to the people of Indiana, ca. July 4, 1836, in Robertson and Riker (eds.), *John Tipton Papers*, III, 299–300.

234 *House Journal*, 24 Cong., 1 session, 1100–1101, 1218–1221. On the initial vote Ratliff Boon, John Carr, and John W. Davis supported passage; George L. Kinnard and Amos Lane opposed passage; and Edward A. Hannegan and Jonathan McCarty were nonvoters. On the second vote Carr, Kinnard, Lane, and McCarty sustained passage; Boon, Davis, and Hannegan were nonvoters.

235 Richardson, *Messages and Papers of the Presidents*, III, 237–238, 265–269, 281–282; *House Journal*, 24 Cong., 2 session, 546–548; *Senate Journal*, 24 Cong., 2 session, 310, 317–318. Hannegan, Lane, and McCarty voted for passage; Boon, Carr, Davis, and Kinnard were nonvoters. Hendricks voted for passage, Tipton against. All Indiana members of Congress, except Tipton, apparently supported recognition of Texas as the Jackson administration ended.

236 The Vincennes *Western Sun*, July 29, 1837, approved Jackson's action in recognizing the independence of Texas, and commented: "Never again can she be brought under the control of the Mexicans." Also see Pletcher, *The Diplomacy of Annexation*, 73–88.

CHAPTER 11

1 For congressional districts as established in 1833 and 1843, see Justin E. Walsh, *The Centennial History of the Indiana General Assembly, 1816–1978* (Indianapolis, 1987), 785–786. Indiana's ranking in population is noted in John D.

Barnhart and Donald F. Carmony, *Indiana: From Frontier to Industrial Commonwealth* (4 vols., New York, 1954), I, 408.

2 As indicated in Dorothy Riker and Gayle Thornbrough (comps.), *Indiana Election Returns, 1816–1851* (Indianapolis, 1960), 10–20, Jackson was elected by very significant majorities in 1828 and 1832; and Harrison likewise in 1836 and 1840. *Ibid.*, 21–37.

3 Indianapolis *Indiana Journal*, December 7, 1836, July 22, October 28, November 18, 1837. In its issue for December 7, the *Indiana Journal* vowed to list Harrison as the people's choice "until his election and the certain triumph of correct principles in 1840."

4 Concerning Whig consensus for a state convention January 22, 1838, see Indianapolis *Indiana Journal*, December 2, 16, 30, 1837, January 6, 1838; Richmond *Palladium*, December 9, 1837, quoting Rushville *Herald*. Regarding county conventions to select delegates to the state convention, see Indianapolis *Indiana Journal*, December 2, 1837, January 6, 13, 20, 1838; Richmond *Palladium*, December 9, 23, 1837.

5 Richmond *Palladium*, February 3, 1838 (convention proceedings); Indianapolis *Indiana Journal*, March 24, 1838 (convention address).

6 Richmond *Palladium*, February 3, 1838.

7 For examples, see Indianapolis *Indiana Journal*, March 3, 1838, July 13, 27, 1839.

8 *Ibid.*, August 17, September 21, 1839.

9 For Henry Clay to Oliver H. Smith, Ashland, September 14, October 5, 1839, and Smith to Clay, Indianapolis, September 28, 1839, see Oliver H. Smith, *Early Indiana Trials and Sketches* (Cincinnati, 1858), 251–254. Clay asked Smith: "Was the result of your late [congressional] elections owing to the use of my name in connexion with the Presidential office?" Smith responded: "on that class who joined us under the Harrison flag we can not rely, should you be the candidate." Smith considered the outcome doubtful in Indiana if the contest was between Clay and Van Buren, but he believed "General Harrison could get a majority of this State against Mr. Van Buren." Smith explained that Clay had many devoted friends in Indiana, but those who had "joined us under the Harrison flag" have not forgotten the contest between you and their idol General Jackson; and they "retain a deep-rooted prejudice against you, repeating the oft-refuted charge of bargain, intrigue and management, between you and Mr. Adams, and they are beyond the reach of reason or arguments."

10 For calling and fixing the date of the Whig State Convention, see Indianapolis *Indiana Journal*, August 31, September 7, 26, November 9, 16, 23, 30, December 7, 1839. Concerning county conventions electing delegates to the convention, see *ibid.*, October 26, 1839, and succeeding issues *passim* through January 18, 1840. The nomination of Harrison over Clay at Harrisburg, and that of John Tyler as his running mate is explained in Edward Stanwood, *A History of the Presidency, 1788–1897* (2 vols., Boston, 1928), I, 193–196.

11 Indianapolis *Tri-Weekly Journal*, January 20, 1840.

12 Unless otherwise indicated items about the Whig State Convention are based on its proceedings in *ibid.*, January 22, 1840. Whigs throughout the state were urged to hold county meetings on February 22, Washington's birthdate, to "effect a complete whig organization in every county and township in Indiana." Whigs were also asked to organize Tippecanoe clubs in every township, with each club to select its own speakers.

13 Indianapolis *Indiana Democrat*, January 17, 1837; Vincennes *Western Sun*, March 25, 1837. In its issue for January 6, 1838, the *Western Sun* quoted a letter from Andrew Jackson, dated December 21, 1837, denying that he had "for a moment harbored the thought that the administration of Mr. Van Buren would not be successful." The former president said all of Van Buren's official acts "manifested his determination to conform his administration to that construction of the constitution, which has been claimed and sustained by the republican party."

14 Vincennes *Western Sun*, January 13, February 24, 1838, both issues quoting Indianapolis *Indiana Democrat*.

15 From proceedings of the convention as in Vincennes *Western Sun*, January 25, 1840. For examples of county conventions preparatory to the state convention, see *ibid.*, October 5, 26, November 9, 16, 23, 1839; Indianapolis *Indiana Democrat*, September 25, October 2, November 21, 1839.

16 See proceedings of the convention in Arthur M. Schlesinger, Jr. and Fred L. Israel (eds.), *History of American Presidential Elections, 1789–1968* (4 vols., New York, 1971), I, 714–732. The proceedings are in part found in Vincennes *Western Sun*, May 30, June 6, 1840, especially items about the nomination for vice president.

17 Much detail regarding the presidential campaign of 1840 is found *passim* issues of the Indianapolis *Indiana Journal*, Indianapolis *Indiana Democrat* (becomes *Indiana Democrat and Spirit of the Constitution* in August), and Vincennes *Western Sun*, especially from January through October, 1840. For a comprehensive account of the hoopla nationally, which includes items about Indiana, see Robert Gray Gunderson, *The Log-Cabin Campaign* (Lexington, Ky., 1957). For examples of concise accounts, see R. Carlyle Buley, *The Old Northwest: Pioneer Period, 1815–1840* (2 vols., Indianapolis, 1950), II, 223–259; Freeman Cleaves, *Old Tippecanoe: William Henry Harrison and His Time* (New York, 1939), 314–328.

18 Gayle Thornbrough, Dorothy Riker, and Paula Corpuz (eds.), *The Diary of Calvin Fletcher* (9 vols., Indianapolis, 1972–1983), II, 184; Buley, *The Old Northwest*, II, 249–251; David Turpie, *Sketches of My Own Times* (Indianapolis, 1903), 64–67. Fletcher noted "that 7 or 8 Small boys have run away to attend the battle ground celebration." He also expressed "fears & apprehensions as to their welfare" concerning two of his sons who joined the advancing groups, but observed that he "must leave them in the hands of our Heavenly Father." Gunderson, *The Log-Cabin Campaign*, 117–118, indicates that the Tippecanoe Battleground celebration was one of the most important observances of this kind regarding the presidential campaign of 1840.

¹⁹ Indianapolis *Indiana Journal,* June 6, 13, 1840; Indianapolis *Indiana Democrat,* June 6, 1840. The *Indiana Journal,* May 30, 1840, is a two rather than the usual four page issue. This, the issue says, was because all the workmen in the establishment but one had gone to the battleground.

²⁰ For a potpourri of discussions about these items, see Indianapolis *Indiana Journal,* February 29, March 7, 14, April 11, May 23, June 20, 27, July 18 (extra), 25, August 8, 15, 22, September 12, 26, October 3, 31, 1840; Indianapolis *Indiana Democrat,* February 4, 7, March 18, April 8, May 6, 13, August 14, 23, September 4, 11, October 2, 23, 1840; Vincennes *Western Sun,* March 14, 21, June 20, 27, July 4, 11, 18, 25, August 1, 8, 15, 22, September 26, October 10, 1840. *Passim* issues of these papers for March through October have additional items about these and related items. Also see Richmond *Palladium,* September 5, October 10, 1840, and *passim.*

²¹ William Henry Harrison to Harmar Denny, n.p., n.d., in Indianapolis *Indiana Journal,* September 19, 1840; and *ibid.,* September 26, 1840, for Harrison's speech at Dayton about two weeks earlier. In addition, on September 12, 1840, this paper republished Harrison's letter to Sherrod Williams, May 1, 1836, which it had published during the presidential campaign of 1836.

²² Indianapolis *Indiana Democrat,* September 11, 18, October 16, 1840; Indianapolis *Indiana Journal,* September 26, October 17, 1840. The editor of the *Indiana Journal,* after noting in its issue of September 26 that Johnson was to be conveyed through the streets by "four *gray* horses," asked "Would not *black* be a more pleasing color to the distinguished guest for the horses?" Apparently the editor was aware of the supposition of many that Johnson lived with a black woman. Calvin Fletcher recorded that Johnson was escorted down Washington Street "by a band of music & 2500 or 3000 horsemen," and that "12000 or 15000" were at the grove where the vice president spoke. Thornbrough, Riker, and Corpuz (eds.), *Diary of Calvin Fletcher,* II, 242–243. As indicated in *Indiana Democrat,* September 11, October 16, 1840, and Vincennes *Western Sun,* September 26, October 31, 1840, Johnson spoke in a number of Indiana towns in the weeks before the election in November.

²³ Tilghman A. Howard to Dear Sir, Washington City, May 30, 1840, in William Wesley Woollen, *Biographical and Historical Sketches of Early Indiana* (Indianapolis, 1883), 265–266.

²⁴ Thornbrough, Riker, and Corpuz (eds.), *Diary of Calvin Fletcher,* II, 209; Riker and Thornbrough (comps.), *Indiana Election Returns, 1816–1851,* 148–150.

²⁵ Indianapolis *Indiana Democrat,* October 9, 23, 1840; Richmond *Palladium,* October 10, 1840; Vincennes *Western Sun,* October 17, 1840, quoting Logansport *Herald* referring to Ewing as another traitor; Indianapolis *Indiana Journal,* October 31, 1840, quoting Logansport *Telegraph* for letter of George W. Ewing, Peru, October 6, 1840. As these sources indicate Tilghman A. Howard replaced Ewing on the electoral ticket for Van Buren.

²⁶ Riker and Thornbrough (comps.), *Indiana Election Returns, 1816–1851,* pp. 29–37; Stanwood, *History of the Presidency, 1788–1897,* I, 202–204. Riker and

Thornbrough give official returns for all counties. Harrison won majorities for his electors in 61 counties, Van Buren electors won in 24 counties, and in 2 counties the votes were not entirely for either set of electors. Harrison won majorities in Southern, Central, and Northern counties, however, Van Buren carried some counties in all three areas.

27 Indianapolis *Indiana Democrat*, November 7, 14, December 12, 1840, January 29, 1841; Vincennes *Western Sun*, January 9, 23, 1841.

28 Indianapolis *Indiana Democrat*, November 14, 1840.

29 J. Herman Schauinger (ed.), "The Letters of Godlove S. Orth, Hoosier Whig," *Indiana Magazine of History*, XXXIX (1943), 366–368, for letter of Orth to Schuyler Colfax, August 16, 1845. Orth wrote: "Look at the campaign of '40, straight-laced Whiggery could not have excited a single throb of noble enthusiasm in the breasts of the people, but old things & old politicians were either laid aside, or compelled to follow in the wake of a new sect or species of tacticians." Orth explained: "Instead of drawing an elevated line, unbending and unchangeable, and battling to raise public opinion to its level, . . . we must 'stoop to conquer.'"

30 Both Joel H. Silbey, *The Shrine of Party: Congressional Voting Behavior, 1841–1852* (Pittsburgh, 1967), 22, 49; and Oscar Doane Lambert, *Presidential Politics in the United States, 1841–1844* (Durham, N. C., 1936), 18, agree that the Whigs had substantial majorities in both houses when Congress met in special session May 31, 1841.

31 Indianapolis *Indiana Journal*, February 27, 1841, quoting *National Intelligencer* (n.p., n.d.). In its issue for March 6, 1841, the *Indiana Journal* indicated the necessity for a special session, saying it seemed certain Harrison would call one.

32 *Ibid.*, March 6, 1841. For Calvin Fletcher's caustic indictment of the Jackson-Van Buren administrations, see Thornbrough, Riker, and Corpuz (eds.), *Diary of Calvin Fletcher*, II, 293.

33 James D. Richardson, *Compilations of the Messages and Papers of the Presidents, 1789–1917* (20 vols., Washington, D. C., 1897–1917), IV, 5–21; Vincennes *Western Sun*, March 20, 1841.

34 Richardson, *Messages and Papers of the Presidents*, IV, 21–23; Indianapolis *Indiana Journal*, April 17, 1841; Vincennes *Western Sun*, April 17, 1841. For examples of tributes and memorials, see *passim* issues of both papers during April and May, 1841. Also see Richmond *Palladium*, April 10, 17, 1841; Thornbrough, Riker, and Corpuz (eds.), *Diary of Calvin Fletcher*, II, 305, 309, 321.

35 Indianapolis *Indiana Journal*, April 17, 1841; Thornbrough, Riker, and Corpuz (eds.), *Diary of Calvin Fletcher*, II, 305; Richmond *Palladium*, April 17, 1841; Indianapolis *Indiana Democrat*, April 23, 1841, quoting Philadelphia *Spirit of the Times* (n.d.).

36 Indianapolis *Indiana Journal*, April 24, 1841; Richardson, *Messages and Papers of the Presidents*, IV, 36–39. There was no formal inauguration of Tyler, but his address of April 9 is considered his inaugural.

37 Richardson, *Messages and Papers of the Presidents*, IV, 21; *Laws of Indiana* (general), 1840–41, p. 144. This advance in the time for the congressional election

had been authorized before the call was issued for the special session. As noted in Riker and Thornbrough (comps.), *Indiana Election Returns, 1816–1851*, pp. 84–122, congressional elections were usually held on the first Monday in August during odd years in the thirties and forties, about four months before the convening of the new Congress. Since the old Congress had ended March 3, 1841, the advance was necessary for Hoosier congressmen to sit in the special session. For the governor's proclamation setting the date for the special election, see Gayle Thornbrough (ed.), *Messages and Papers Relating to the Administration of Samuel Bigger, Governor of Indiana, 1840–1843* (Indianapolis, 1964), 235–236.

³⁸ See Indianapolis *Indiana Journal, passim*, January through April, regarding congressional district conventions. Concerning incumbent congressmen, see Riker and Thornbrough (comps.), *Indiana Election Returns, 1816–1851*, pp. 97–101.

³⁹ Indianapolis *Indiana Journal*, April 17, 24, 1841. A national bank, however, was not mentioned as a measure called for by the people. Riker and Thornbrough (comps.), *Indiana Election Returns, 1816–1851*, pp. 101–105.

⁴⁰ Indianapolis *Indiana Journal*, May 15, 1841; Indianapolis *Indiana Democrat*, May 7, 1841.

⁴¹ Richardson, *Messages and Papers of the Presidents*, IV, 40–51 (especially pp. 43–48); *Senate Journal*, 27 Cong., 1 session, 24; Indianapolis *Indiana Journal*, June 12, 1841.

⁴² *Senate Journal*, 27 Cong., 1 session, 22–23, 35–37, 163–164; *House Journal*, 27 Cong., 1 session, 344–345. Indiana's two Whig senators were Oliver H. Smith and Albert S. White; its six Whig congressmen were James H. Cravens, Henry S. Lane, George H. Proffit, Richard W. Thompson, Joseph L. White, and David Wallace.

⁴³ *Senate Journal*, 27 Cong., 1 session, 51, 125, 193–194; *House Journal*, 27 Cong., 1 session, 288, 324–326, 511–513; Richardson, *Messages and Papers of the Presidents*, IV, 63–68 (veto message).

⁴⁴ Fort Wayne *Sentinel*, June 26, August 28, 1841; Indianapolis *Indiana State Sentinel*, August 17, 24, 1841; Indianapolis *Indiana Journal*, August 20, 27, 1841; South Bend *Free Press*, August 27, 1841.

⁴⁵ *Congressional Globe*, 27 Cong., 1 session, 371. In its issue for September 10, 1841, the Indianapolis *Indiana Journal* expressed regret in announcing to Whigs that George H. Proffit "has withdrawn from among them." He had, the editor added, connected himself with the "'Other wise party.'" The editor predicted that after reflection Proffit would return to the Whig party.

⁴⁶ Frederick Jackson Turner, *The United States, 1830–1850: The Nation and Its Sections* (New York, 1935), 494–496; Benjamin Hibbard, *A History of Public Land Policies* (Madison, Wis., 1965), 184–188. See *ibid.*, pp. 103, 106, for federal land sales in the forties versus the thirties.

⁴⁷ Thornbrough (ed.), *Messages and Papers of Samuel Bigger*, 121–126; Indiana *Documentary Journal*, 1840–41, Sen. Doc. 9, pp. 161–165; *Laws of Indiana* (local), 1840–41, pp. 217, 223–224. Bigger never mentioned preemption, but de-

clared that neither graduation nor cession had "even a probability" of adoption. In the state Senate 32 Whigs voted for and 11 Democrats voted against distribution. Party ties presumed as in *A Biographical Directory of the Indiana General Assembly* (2 vols., Indianapolis, 1980, 1984), Volume I, *1816–1899*, Volume 2, *1901–1984*, I, 477.

48 *House Journal*, 27 Cong., 1 session, 175, 188, 221–223, 433–439; *Senate Journal*, 27 Cong., 1 session, 76, 78, 86, 207, 216, 221–222, 227. The six Whig congressmen are named in note 42.

49 *Congressional Globe*, 27 Cong., 1 session, Appendix, 103–105, 456–459; Indianapolis *Indiana Journal*, July 23, September 17, 1841; Vincennes *Western Sun*, September 4, 1841; Indianapolis *Indiana State Sentinel*, February 22, 1842.

50 *House Journal*, 27 Cong., 1 session, 267, 409–410, 459, 511–513; *Senate Journal*, 27 Cong., 1 session, 212–213, 220, 228–230, 232–233, 234–235, 255; Richardson, *Messages and Papers of the Presidents*, IV, 68–72.

51 *Congressional Globe*, 27 Cong., 1 session, Appendix, 471–476, 393–394, 389–390 (remarks of Thompson, Lane, and Proffit, respectively); Indianapolis *Indiana Journal*, September 24, October 29, 1841; Vincennes *Western Sun*, September 18, 25, 1841. The South Bend *Free Press*, September 24, 1841, opposed the second bank veto, and stressed that Whigs must remain true to their principles, even when their president opposed them. In its issue for November 5, 1841, this Whig press quoted the New Orleans *Picayune* as saying: "We yesterday saw a likeness of Gen. Jackson on the vignette of a bank note. It would be just as appropriate to have a figure-head of Father Matthew over a distillery door." Appropriately stated, and worth noting is that during the early 1990s Jackson's picture appears on federal reserve bank notes valued at $20, while Alexander Hamilton, who helped father the First United States Bank, has his face relegated to notes in units of $10!

52 Maurice G. Baxter, *One and Inseparable: Daniel Webster and the Union* (Cambridge, Mass., 1984), 308–312; Turner, *The United States, 1830–1850*, pp. 497–500; Glyndon G. Van Deusen, *The Jacksonian Era, 1828–1848* (New York, 1959), 158–161.

53 Smith, *Early Indiana Trials and Sketches*, 359–360; *Senate Journal*, 28 Cong., 1 session, 413. The Senate rejected Proffit 33 to 8; Hannegan voted for rejection, Albert S. White was a nonvoter.

54 Richardson, *Messages and Papers of the Presidents*, IV, 82–87; Baxter, *Daniel Webster and the Union*, 313–314. Baxter offers a concise account of the administration bill for a fiscal corporation, and its lack of serious congressional consideration.

55 Baxter, *Daniel Webster and the Union*, 314–316; Turner, *The United States, 1830–1850*, pp. 503–508; Van Deusen, *The Jacksonian Era, 1828–1848*, pp. 164–166; Richardson, *Messages and Papers of the Presidents*, IV, 81–82, 180–189.

56 *House Journal*, 27 Cong., 2 session, 1151, 1385–1387; *Senate Journal*, 27 Cong., 2 session, 629. The Tariff of 1842 was voted for by three Whig congressmen from Indiana: George H. Proffit, Richard W. Thompson, and David Wallace; opposed by Whigs James Cravens and Henry S. Lane as well as Democrat

Andrew Kennedy; and Whig Joseph L. White was a nonvoter. Senators Oliver H. Smith and Albert S. White voted for its engrossment. It is possible that Cravens and Lane voted against the Tariff of 1842 in the hope of obtaining higher duties in another bill, or perhaps to avoid the end of distribution.

[57] *Senate Journal*, 27 Cong., 2 session, 58, 119, 136, 153, 166, 187, 191, 203; *Congressional Globe*, 27 Cong., 2 session, 69, 164–167, 200, 221, 259–260, 266. Clay also unsuccessfully proposed that naming the secretary of the treasury and the treasurer be given to Congress; and that members of Congress be made ineligible to appointment to any civil office during the term for which they were elected.

[58] *House Journal*, 27 Cong., 2 session, 1254–1257, 1295–1297, 1346–1353 (quotation, 1351); *Congressional Globe*, 27 Cong., 2 session, 909–910.

[59] *House Journal*, 27 Cong., 3 session, 157–160, 163–164; *Congressional Globe*, 27 Cong., 3 session, 144–146. Four Indiana congressmen—James H. Cravens, Henry S. Lane, Richard W. Thompson, and Joseph L. White—voted for the committee; two Whigs—George H. Proffit and David Wallace—voted against it, as did Andrew Kennedy, Democrat.

[60] *Congressional Globe*, 27 Cong., 2 session, 69, 164–167, 200, 221, 259–260, 266, 871–875, 878–883, 894–901, 905–911.

[61] Indianapolis *Indiana Journal*, October 29, 1841, June 15, 1842; Vincennes *Western Sun*, October 22, 1842; Indianapolis *Indiana State Sentinel*, November 8, 1842. For additional examples of Whig concern and criticism about the veto power and its use by presidents, see Indianapolis *Indiana Journal*, December 5, 1840, June 12, July 16, November 12, 26, December 3, 1841, October 11, 1843. Also see speech of Congressman Caleb B. Smith in Richmond *Palladium*, August 16, 1848.

[62] According to the *Biographical Directory of the Indiana General Assembly*, I, 482–485, there were 31 Whigs and 19 Democrats in the Senate, 46 Whigs and 54 Democrats in the House when the session began.

[63] As indicated in Smith, *Early Indiana Trials and Sketches*, 353–355, and Woollen, *Biographical and Historical Sketches of Early Indiana*, 266–267, Smith and Howard viewed each other as their principal rival. For evidence of widespread support for Howard by Democrats, see Indianapolis *Indiana State Sentinel*, June 7, August 16, 23, 30, September 6, 20, 27, October 11, 18, 25, November 1, 8, 15, 22, 1842.

[64] The refusal of the House to convene in joint session until January 24, 1843, is indicated in Indiana *Senate Journal*, 1842–43, pp. 34–35, 86–87, 88–91, 296–297, 338–340, 344–346. Concerning the two special elections and the replacement of Beall by Marsh, see *Biographical Directory of the Indiana General Assembly*, I, 482–485. The replacement of Representative Beall, a Whig, by Marsh, a Democrat, and that of Senator Samuel Howe Smydth, a Whig, by Abner M. Davis, a Democrat, gained two votes for the Democrats. In another election Representative Ezekiel L. Dunbar, a Democrat, was succeeded by Samuel P. Mooney, also a Democrat.

65 Amid claims and counterclaims, and apparently promises and counter-promises, what was actually promised is uncertain. As noted in Smith, *Early Indiana Trials and Sketches*, 353–354, Smith insists that Hoover had given "unequivocal" assurance that he would vote for him all the time; and that Kelso had given "positive assurances" on his behalf. As may be noted in Thornbrough (ed.), *Messages and Papers of Samuel Bigger*, 619–620, soon after the election Hoover declared that "both parties" would say they had not been deceived because he had said that he "did not expect to vote for Smith more than twice." Hoover asserted that it had been "at all times admitted and by both parties" that if Smith or Howard could be elected it would be on the first or second ballot.

66 Indianapolis *Indiana Journal*, January 25, 1843; Indianapolis *Indiana State Sentinel*, January 31, 1843; Fort Wayne *Sentinel*, February 4, 1843.

67 For use of single districts for Indiana congressional elections, 1816–51, see Riker and Thornbrough (comps.), *Indiana Election Returns, 1816–1851*, pp. 71–126; for the congressional distribution of 1842, see U. S. *Statutes at Large*, V, 491. New York, Pennsylvania, Ohio, Virginia, and Tennessee, in this order, obtained more representatives than Indiana. Kentucky and Massachusetts got ten representatives.

68 For items regarding district conventions, see Indianapolis *Indiana State Sentinel*, March 7, April 25, May 2, 9, 30, 1843, and *passim*; Indianapolis *Indiana State Journal*, April 12, 26, May 3, 10, 24, 1843, and *passim*; Vincennes *Western Sun*, March 25, April 29, May 13, 1843, and *passim*.

69 For examples of comments regarding these and related issues, see Indianapolis *Indiana State Sentinel*, January 24, April 25, May 30, June 13, July 4, 11, 1843; Indianapolis *Indiana State Journal*, May 10, 24, August 2, 1843; Vincennes *Western Sun*, May 27, June 24, July 1, 1843.

70 Indianapolis *Indiana State Sentinel*, June 27, July 4, 1843; Indianapolis *Indiana State Journal*, August 2, 1843.

71 Indianapolis *Indiana State Sentinel*, July 25, 1843. For criticism of Owen's earlier views about religion and economic issues, see Indianapolis *Indiana State Journal*, June 28, July 12, 1843.

72 Indianapolis *Indiana State Sentinel*, August 8, 1843, commenting about earlier reports that the state librarian was said to have been circulating.

73 Riker and Thornbrough (comps.), *Indiana Election Returns, 1816–1851*, pp. 105–109. The index and previous pages indicate which men had prior congressional service. Whig incumbents David Wallace and Joseph L. White sought reelection but were defeated. Incumbents George H. Proffit, Richard W. Thompson, James H. Cravens, and Henry S. Lane were not standing for reelection. According to *ibid.*, 110–122, Democrats won eight of the ten congressional seats against two for the Whigs in the election of 1845; six against four for the Whigs in 1847; and eight against one for the Whigs and one for the Free Soilers in 1849. For a map of the congressional districts pursuant to the apportionment of 1843, see Walsh, *Centennial History of the Indiana General Assembly*, 786. For Democratic victories in gubernatorial and legislative elections of 1843, see Ch. 6, pp. 290–291.

[74] Lambert, *Presidential Politics in the United States, 1841–1844*, p. 67. Speaking of the Twenty-eighth Congress which convened December 4, 1843, Lambert states: "The House was Democratic, the Senate Whig, and the President stood separate and apart from either of them. If there were three parties, each held a position by which it could negative the power of the other." According to *Congress A to Z* (Washington, D.C., 1988), 497, this Congress began with 28 Whigs and 25 Democrats in the Senate, 79 Whigs and 142 Democrats in the House; two years earlier there had been 28 Whigs and 22 Democrats in the Senate, 133 Whigs and 102 Democrats in the House.

[75] Lambert, *Presidential Politics in the United States, 1841–1844*, p. 67. Lambert comments: "If the House should re-enact a Sub-Treasury system it would be defeated in the Senate. If the Senate should bring up another bank bill it would be opposed by both the House and the President, whose vetoes would ever stand in its way. Both the House and the Senate would turn deaf ears to the President's recommendations. Three parties were in office, but none in power. All legislation that existed must remain for the time in status quo." Despite Lambert's overstatement of the situation, there is substantial truth in his observations. For the huge drop in proceeds from land sales during the forties versus the thirties, see Hibbard, *History of the Public Land Policies*, 103, 106, 184–190.

[76] It is a myth to conclude that the Hoosier pioneers were generally opposed to federal aid, and especially so as regards internal improvements. During 1841–45, while Tyler was president, the Indiana General Assembly asked for federal aid, in money or land, on behalf of a variety of internal improvements. As indicated in *Laws of Indiana* (local), 1841–42, pp. 178, 183–185, aid was sought on behalf of a harbor at the mouth of the St. Joseph River on Lake Michigan; a harbor at Michigan City on Lake Michigan; extension of the Wabash and Erie Canal to Terre Haute; and on behalf of the National Road. And *ibid.* (local), 1842–43, pp. 184, 189–190, 193–196, 199, on behalf of making the Grand Rapids of the Wabash River navigable; improving navigation on the Mississippi, Ohio, Wabash, and "other important" rivers; extension of the Wabash and Erie Canal to Terre Haute; a harbor at Michigan City; and improving navigation of the Wabash River from its mouth to Lafayette. And *ibid.* (local), 1843–44, pp. 173–179, on behalf of completing the Wabash and Erie Canal from Terre Haute to Evansville; on behalf of the National Road; removing obstacles to navigation of the Mississippi, Ohio, and Wabash rivers; repairing bridges on the National Road; building the Central Canal from Indianapolis north to the Wabash and Erie Canal; constructing a canal on the Indiana side of the Ohio River Falls; completing a harbor at Michigan City; erecting a lighthouse at the harbor at City West on Lake Michigan. And *ibid.* (local), 1844–45, pp. 293–298, 300–301, for improving navigation of the Wabash River; completing the Wabash and Erie Canal from Terre Haute to Evansville; for construction of the Northern Cross Railroad in Illinois and Indiana; making a clay or macadamized road from Bloomington to Columbus via Nashville; on behalf of the National Road; on behalf of the harbor at Michigan

City; and constructing the Central Canal from Indianapolis north to the Wabash and Erie Canal.

77 *House Journal*, 28 Cong., 1 session, 837–838; *Senate Journal*, 28 Cong., 1 session, 317; U. S. *Statutes at Large*, V, 661–662. This bill passed the House 108 to 72, the Senate 32 to 6. Among its appropriations were $100,000 to improve the Ohio River from Pittsburgh to the Ohio River Falls; $180,000 to improve the Ohio River below the Ohio River Falls, and the Mississippi, Arkansas, and Missouri rivers; $20,000 for improvement of the harbor at the mouth of the St. Joseph River on Lake Michigan; and $25,000 for improvement of the harbor on Lake Michigan at Michigan City. The last item was the only exclusively Indiana appropriation. The three Whig members from Indiana, Congressmen Samuel C. Sample and Caleb B. Smith and Senator Albert S. White, voted for passage. Among Democrats, Congressmen William J. Brown, Thomas J. Henley, Andrew Kennedy, Thomas Smith, and John Pettit voted for passage, as did Senator Edward A. Hannegan; and Congressmen John W. Davis, Robert Dale Owen, and Joseph A. Wright voted against passage.

78 *House Journal*, 28 Cong., 1 session, 938–939, 1085–1086; *Senate Journal*, 28 Cong., 1 session, 317–318. This bill passed the House 96 to 79, the Senate 32 to 8. Senators White and Hannegan, plus Congressmen Sample and Caleb B. Smith voted for passage; Congressmen Davis, Owen, Thomas Smith, Wright, and Kennedy voted against passage; Congressmen Brown, Henley, and Pettit were nonvoters. As noted in Richardson, *Messages and Papers of the Presidents*, IV, 330–333, Tyler vetoed this bill. The House vote to override failed 104 to 84. Congressmen Brown, Sample, and Smith voted to override; Davis, Henley, Owen, Thomas Smith, and Wright voted against an override; and Congressmen Kennedy and Pettit were nonvoters.

79 *House Journal*, 28 Cong., 2 session, 513–515, 483–484, 493–494; *Senate Journal*, 28 Cong., 2 session, 257–258. Both senators and all congressmen but Henley, a nonvoter, voted for passage. According to the Richmond *Palladium*, March 15, 1845, and the Vincennes *Western Sun*, March 22, 1845, Tyler gave this bill a pocket veto. The bill passed the House 105 to 97, the Senate 27 to 11.

80 Baxter, *Daniel Webster and the Union*, 318–337 *passim*; David M. Pletcher, *The Diplomacy of Annexation: Texas, Oregon, and the Mexican War* (Columbia, Mo., 1973), 9–25 *passim*; Van Deusen, *The Jacksonian Era, 1828–1848*, pp. 170–176. Baxter has a very helpful map regarding the disputed boundary between Maine and Canada.

81 Indianapolis *Indiana Journal*, March 13, 1841; Vincennes *Western Sun*, April 16, 30, 1842; Indianapolis *Indiana Democrat*, March 5, 1841. For other comments about war or peace between the United States and Great Britain, see Indianapolis *Indiana Journal*, March 6, 13, October 15, 22, 1841, March 23, April 20, June 15, 1842; Indianapolis *Indiana Democrat*, March 12, 26, April 2, 30, May 26, 1841; Indianapolis *Indiana State Sentinel*, July 21, August 4, September 7, October 5, 11, 19, 26, November 2, 21, 1841, March 15, 22, May 10, 17, 31, 1842; Vincennes *Western Sun*, March 13, 1841; Fort Wayne *Sentinel*,

March 27, 1841, May 14, 1842. The latter two papers, both Democratic, were more conciliatory toward Britain than the *Indiana Democrat.*

[82] Baxter, *Daniel Webster and the Union,* 338–352, especially pp. 350–352; Pletcher, *The Diplomacy of Annexation,* 24–26.

[83] *Senate Journal,* 27 Cong., 2 session, Appendix, 699; *House Journal,* 27 Cong., 2 session, 222, 491, 495–496; Thornbrough (ed.), *Messages and Papers of Samuel Bigger,* 490. George H. Proffit, Richard W. Thompson, and Joseph L. White, all Whigs, voted for implementation of the treaty; James H. Cravens, Whig, and Andrew Kennedy, Democrat, voted against implementation; and Henry S. Lane and David Wallace, both Whigs, were nonvoters. While the Indianapolis *Indiana Journal,* November 16, 1842, commended the Webster-Ashburton Treaty, the Indianapolis *Indiana State Sentinel,* June 13, 1843, asserted that "Jackson or Van Buren might have been quite as successful in arranging the affair, if like Mr. Webster, they had shown a willingness to permit Great Britain to dictate the terms of settlement, and finally to give the British Government all it asked."

[84] Pletcher, *The Diplomacy of Annexation,* 101–110, 214–217; Ray Allen Billington, *The Far Western Frontier, 1830–1860* (New York, 1956), 41–115 *passim.* See Pletcher, p. 91, for a map of the Oregon country between the Rocky Mountains and the Pacific Ocean, between 42° to 54° 40'.

[85] Indianapolis *Indiana Journal,* April 10, 1841; Indianapolis *Indiana State Sentinel,* March 8, 1842. Howard explained that in a speech at Bloomington the previous year, he had set forth many reasons for the "immediate occupation" of Oregon, since which numerous inquiries had been received from persons who seemed to think he had been authorized to organize an emigrating company to it.

[86] *Laws of Indiana* (local), 1842–43, pp. 194–195; *ibid.* (local), 1843–44, p. 176. Neither memorial made *explicit claim to all of Oregon north to 54°40'.* The first recognized the existence of conflicting claims, and stressed the validity of United States title from the forty-second to the forty-ninth parallel.

[87] Vincennes *Western Sun,* September 9, 1843; *Congressional Globe,* 28 Cong., 1 session, 178–179, 185–186 (Owen), 312–314 (Hannegan), Appendix, 243–246 (Hannegan). Another Democrat, Congressman Andrew Kennedy, as shown *ibid.,* Appendix, 264–265, declared: "But, sir, if you suppose that the West will yield one acre—ay, one inch—of our northwestern territory, as long as there is a man left to defend it, then, sir, you or I have mistaken the character of that western people, who have driven the red man before them like the morning mist before the rays of a clear, cloudless sun."

[88] For an overview of the situation regarding Texas and Mexico during the Tyler administration, see Pletcher, *The Diplomacy of Annexation,* 64–88, 113–182; Van Deusen, *The Jacksonian Era, 1828–1848,* pp. 109–110, 176–191.

[89] Indianapolis *Indiana State Sentinel,* October 26, 1841; Norman E. Tutorow, "Whigs of the Old Northwest and Texas Annexation, 1836–April, 1844," *Indi-*

ana Magazine of History, LXVI (1970), 66, quoting Richmond *Palladium*, October 21, 1843, quoting South Bend *Free Press*; Fort Wayne *Sentinel*, December 9, 1843; Thornbrough, Riker, and Corpuz (eds.), *Diary of Calvin Fletcher*, II, 559.

90 *House Journal*, 28 Cong., 1 session, 424, 612–613, 822; *Senate Journal*, 28 Cong., 1 session, 216, 237, 238; *Congressional Globe*, 28 Cong., 1 session, 175, 346, 365, 408–409, 410, 428, 492, 542, 600, 607, 609, 615, 617–618, 619, 658. If the General Assembly enacted resolutions for or against the annexation of Texas, 1841–45, the author failed to find them in the laws of the annual legislative sessions.

91 *Congressional Globe*, 28 Cong., 1 session, 647; Indiana *House Journal*, 1843–44, p. 100. According to Tutorow, "Whigs of the Old Northwest and Texas Annexation, 1836–April, 1844," *Indiana Magazine of History*, LXVI, 67, in voting on the House resolution Whigs voted 87 percent against rejection and the Democrats sustained rejection with 85.5 percent of their vote. Tutorow, p. 68, states: "In conclusion, objection to the acquisition of Texas in the Old Northwest prior to 1842 was largely bipartisan and was based primarily upon antislavery principles, though the argument that the United States should not become too large was gaining currency." As noted in Ch. 10, p. 565, and note 212, in 1836 Senator John Tipton, a Democrat, had opposed annexation of Texas in part because the United States already had a "sufficiently extensive" territory. In discussing the memorial from the Society of Friends, White explained that it came from Quakers not "united with abolitionists."

92 Charles Sellers, "Election of 1844," in Schlesinger and Israel (eds.), *History of American Presidential Elections, 1789–1968*, I, 814–817, 822–828; Woollen, *Biographical and Historical Sketches of Early Indiana*, 268–269 (giving letter of Howard, dated Washington, April 29, 1844, to an unnamed person); *Congressional Globe*, 28 Cong., 1 session, Appendix, 696–701 (Owen's speech), May 21, 1844. The letters released by Clay and Van Buren were dated May 27, 1844.

93 *Senate Journal*, 28 Cong., 1 session, Appendix, 421–438 (vote, 438); Pletcher, *The Diplomacy of Annexation*, 149.

94 Sellers, "Election of 1844," in Schlesinger and Israel (eds.), *History of American Presidential Elections, 1789–1968*, I, 747–759; Stanwood, *History of the Presidency, 1788–1897*, I, 206–211; Van Deusen, *The Jacksonian Era, 1828–1848*, pp. 180–182. James Buchanan, Lewis Cass, John C. Calhoun, and Richard M. Johnson were also considered as possible nominees by the Democrats; Winfield Scott and Daniel Webster were among those considered by the Whigs.

95 Indianapolis *Indiana Journal*, September 17, 1841 (quoting the *Courier* and affirming Clay as the choice of Indiana Whigs). Regarding early formation of Clay clubs, see *ibid.*, June 8, July 20, 1842. For the minutes of a Clay club, see Donald F. Carmony (ed.), "Minutes of a Clay Club, Shelby County, Indiana, 1843–1844," *Indiana Magazine of History*, LVI (1960), 153–171.

96 Indianapolis *Indiana Journal*, August 10, 1842, quoting Rushville *Whig*; *ibid.*, October 26, 1842; Indianapolis *Indiana State Sentinel*, September 19, 1843.

97 Indianapolis *Indiana State Sentinel*, September 12, 1843. According to *ibid.*, September 19, 1843, the Goshen *Democrat*, Indianapolis *Indiana State Sentinel*, Richmond *Jeffersonian*, Lafayette *Eagle*, Bloomington *Democrat*, Noblesville *Little Western*, Brookville *Democrat*, Marion *Herald*, and Covington *People's Friend* were listed for Van Buren; the Greencastle *Patriot*, Mishawaka *Tocsin*, Delphi *Oracle*, and Lawrenceburgh *Beacon* were listed for Cass; and the New Albany *Democrat* for Johnson. The preferences of the following papers, presumably all Democratic, were indicated as unknown: Fort Wayne *Sentinel*, Lafayette *Standard*, Crawfordsville *Review*, Paoli *American*, Vincennes *Sun*, New Harmony *Statesman*, Frankfort *Observer*, Salem *Republican*, Vevay *Palladium*, Madison *Courier*, Charlestown *Southern Indianian*, and Valparaiso *Republican*. In its issue of September 16, 1843, the *Sentinel* reported the Fort Wayne *Sentinel* for Van Buren; in that of October 17, 1843, the *Sentinel* quoted: the Frankfort *Observer* for Cass; the Mishawaka *Tocsin* for Cass; the Franklin *Democrat* for Johnson; and the Vincennes *Sun* for Johnson.

98 Indianapolis *Indiana Journal*, January 21, 1843; Indianapolis *Indiana State Journal*, January 24, 1844. All quoted items are from proceedings of these conventions.

99 Vincennes *Western Sun*, January 28, 1843, January 27, February 3, 1844. All quoted items are from convention proceedings or the address.

100 For views expressed by the Whig conventions, see Indianapolis *Indiana Journal*, January 21, 25, 1843; Indianapolis *Indiana State Journal*, January 31, 1844. For the same by the Democratic conventions, see Vincennes *Western Sun*, January 28, February 18, 1843, January 27, February 3, March 30, 1844.

101 Indianapolis *Indiana Journal*, January 25, 1843; Indianapolis *Indiana State Journal*, January 31, 1844; Vincennes *Western Sun*, February 18, 1843, February 3, 1844.

102 Sellers, "Election of 1844," in Schlesinger and Israel (eds.), *History of American Presidential Elections, 1789–1968*, I, 761, 807; Stanwood, *History of the Presidency, 1788–1897*, I, 220–221 (quotes from platform); Indianapolis *Indiana State Journal*, May 11, 1844.

103 Woollen, *Biographical and Historical Sketches of Early Indiana*, 268–269 (letter dated April 29, 1844); Oscar S. Dooley, Presidential Campaign and Election of 1844 (Ph.D. dissertation, Indiana University, 1942), 279–280 (for comment about card from seven Indiana Democrats); Thomas J. Henley to William H. English, Washington City, May 11, 1844, William H. English Collection, Indiana Historical Society Library, Indianapolis. According to Dooley the Indiana members who signed were Senator Edward A. Hannegan and Congressmen William J. Brown, John W. Davis, John Pettit, Thomas Smith, Joseph A. Wright, and Thomas J. Henley. Vincennes *Western Sun* and Fort Wayne *Sentinel*, both in their issue of June 1, 1844, have a copy of a letter from Lewis Cass to Edward A. Hannegan, Detroit, May 10, 1844, in which Cass affirms his support for the immediate annexation of Texas.

[104] Based on convention proceedings in Sellers, "Election of 1844," in Schlesinger and Israel (eds.), *History of American Presidential Elections, 1789–1968*, I, 829–852 (quotations from platform, 850–851).

[105] Stanwood, *History of the Presidency, 1788–1897*, I, 216–221.

[106] Sellers, "Election of 1844," in Schlesinger and Israel (eds.), *History of American Presidential Elections, 1789–1968*, I, 773–796 *passim*; Lambert, *Presidential Politics in the United States, 1841–1844*, pp. 163–193 *passim*; Eugene Holloway Roseboom, *A History of Presidential Elections* (New York, 1957), 130–134; Van Deusen, *The Jacksonian Era, 1828–1848*, pp. 186–190. Concerning Polk and Clay regarding the tariff, see Sellers, "Election of 1844," in Schlesinger and Israel (eds.), *History of American Presidential Elections, 1789–1968*, I, 775–778, 853; Arthur C. Cole, *The Whig Party in the South* (Washington, D. C., 1913), 100–101.

[107] Stanwood, *History of the Presidency, 1788–1897*, I, 222–224; Lambert, *Presidential Politics in the United States, 1841–1844*, pp. 194–196. Both Stanwood and Lambert give data concerning the popular vote showing 1,337,243 for Polk, 1,299,062 for Clay, and 62,300 for Birney. These totals, however, exclude South Carolina, the only state where the voters did not choose their electors.

[108] Riker and Thornbrough (comps.), *Indiana Election Returns, 1816–1851*, pp. 29–52. Polk received about 70,200 votes, Clay 67,850, and Birney 2,100. In 1840 Harrison gained 63,250 votes, Van Buren 51,700, and Birney 30 votes.

[109] Godlove S. Orth to Schuyler Colfax, August 16, 1846, in Schauinger (ed.), "The Letters of Godlove S. Orth, Hoosier Whig," *Indiana Magazine of History*, XXXIX, 366–368. Orth stated that the Whigs were beaten in both houses of the legislature, but as noted in the ensuing paragraph the Senate had an equal number of Whigs and Democrats.

[110] Riker and Thornbrough (comps.), *Indiana Election Returns, 1816–1851*, pp. 105–113; Richard William Leopold, *Robert Dale Owen: A Biography* (Cambridge, Mass., 1940), 188; *Biographical Directory of the American Congress, 1774–1927*, pp. 205, 886.

[111] According to the *Biographical Directory of the Indiana General Assembly*, I, 488–490, each party had 25 senators, and the Whigs had 54 representatives to 45 for the Democrats (there were only 99 representatives because Jefferson County, which was entitled to three representatives, had only two at the session); Vincennes *Western Sun*, August 24, 1844; Indianapolis *Indiana State Journal*, August 10, 1844. In its issue for December 11 the *Indiana State Journal*, after advising Democrats that they could not count on support from any Whig concerning the election of a secretary of state or United States senator, commented: "There is not one man among them who is willing to be placed on the same roll of infamy with *Dan Kelso*." See pp. 607–609, and notes 112–116, when the Whigs thought, with considerable basis, that they, not the Democrats, should have elected a federal senator.

112 *Laws of Indiana* (revised), 1831–32, pp. 101–102; *ibid.* (general), 1844–45, p. 92, reaffirming the law of 1831. Walsh, *Centennial History of the Indiana General Assembly*, 52, states that "no law appointed a time or required the attendance of either house" regarding election of United States senators.

113 For examples of such comments by Democrats, see Indianapolis *Indiana State Sentinel*, January 2, 9, 16, 23, 30, February 6, 1845, including quotations from and comments about views of other Democratic papers; for Whig comments, see Indianapolis *Indiana State Journal*, January 1, 15, March 19, 1845. Concerning the refusal of the Senate to a meeting with the House, and Bright at various times casting the decisive vote for refusal, see Indiana *Senate Journal*, 1844–45, pp. 31–32, 52–58, 90–91, 92–94, 174–176, 229–230, 278, 295–296, 443–446, 498–502.

114 *Biographical Directory of the Indiana General Assembly*, I, 490–492. Each party had 25 senators, but the House had 56 Democrats against 44 Whigs, giving the Democrats a majority of 81 to 69 on joint ballot. For Democrats considered as successor to incumbent Senator White, see Indianapolis *Indiana State Sentinel*, September 25, 30, December 11, 1845; Vincennes *Western Sun*, October 4, 1845; Indianapolis *Indiana State Journal*, October 1, 22, November 12, December 3, 1845. This Whig paper predicted that as the result of a "bargain" Governor Whitcomb would be elected to the United States Senate, with Lieutenant Governor Bright becoming the Democratic candidate for governor in 1846. It also urged that Whigs stick to their principles, and not support any Democrat.

115 Indiana *Senate Journal*, 1845–46, p. 50; *Senate Journal*, 29 Cong., 1 session, 69. Presumably since Bright was a candidate Senator James G. Read, a Democrat, presided over the election and announced Bright's success over Marshall. The Indianapolis *Indiana State Journal*, December 10, 1845, reported that two Whigs, representing Democratic counties, voted for Bright, and contrasted this commendable conduct with the course pursued in 1842–43 when two Democrats, pledged to support a Whig senator, "violated that pledge!" Had the two Democrats honored their pledge, the *Journal* said, Marshall "would this day be occupying a seat in the U. S. Senate . . . ." An item in the Indianapolis *Indiana State Sentinel*, December 11, 1845, including a comment by Senator James G. Read, infers that Bright had been the caucus choice of the Democrats. As indicated in Charles Kettleborough, *Constitution Making in Indiana* (3 vols., Indianapolis, 1916, 1930), I, 98, since Senator White's term had expired on March 3, 1845, Governor Whitcomb could have named an interim successor to White. Moreover, in its issue of January 18, 1845, the Vincennes *Western Sun* had stated that if the session of 1844–45 adjourned without electing a senator "it will become the duty of the Governor to fill that vacancy by special appointment."

116 Indianapolis *Indiana State Sentinel*, December 11, 1845; Indianapolis *Indiana State Journal*, December 10, 24, 1845; Thornbrough, Riker, and Corpuz (eds.), *Diary of Calvin Fletcher*, III, 209–210.

117 Richardson, *Messages and Papers of the Presidents*, IV, 373–379, 402–410, 414; Vincennes *Western Sun*, March 15, 1845; Richmond *Palladium*, March 12, 1845; Indianapolis *Indiana State Journal*, March 5, 19, 26, October 1, 1845.

118 Indianapolis *Indiana State Sentinel*, January 15, 1846.

119 Silbey, *The Shrine of Party*, 67, 245n (note 1); *Congress A to Z*, 497; Charles Sellers, *James K. Polk, Continentalist, 1843–1846* (Princeton, N. J., 1966), 310–313. Silbey and *Congress A to Z* concur that there were 143 Democrats and 77 Whigs in the House, 31 Democrats and 25 Whigs in the Senate.

120 Vincennes *Western Sun*, March 29, October 4, 1845; *Biographical Directory of the American Congress, 1774–1927*, pp. 205, 886. The Indianapolis *Indiana State Sentinel*, January 9, 1845, commenting on a quote from another paper supporting Governor Whitcomb as postmaster general in Polk's cabinet, said Whitcomb was "fully competent" for any position in Polk's cabinet. The *Congressional Directory*, 11–18, cited above, listing all cabinet members to 1861, names Caleb B. Smith, Lincoln's secretary of the interior, as the initial Hoosier to serve in a president's cabinet. As indicated in Barnhart and Carmony, *Indiana*, I, 408, Indiana ranked eighteenth among the states in population in 1820, tenth in 1840, and seventh in 1850.

121 *Congressional Globe*, 29 Cong., 1 session, 574, 575; *House Journal*, 29 Cong., 1 session, 619–622; *Senate Journal*, 29 Cong., 1 session, 467. Concerning the bill's content and party line voting, see Sellers, *James K. Polk, Continentalist, 1843–1846*, pp. 468–470; Van Deusen, *The Jacksonian Era, 1828–1848*, pp. 205–206. For reestablishment of the Independent Treasury, Democratic Congressmen Charles W. Cathcart, Thomas J. Henley, Robert Dale Owen, John Pettit, Thomas Smith, and William W. Wick voted for passage; two Democrats, Congressmen Andrew Kennedy and Speaker John W. Davis, were nonvoters; and Congressmen Edward W. McGaughey and Caleb B. Smith, Whigs, voted nay. Democratic Senators Edward A. Hannegan and Jesse D. Bright voted for passage. The vote in the House regarding payment only in gold and silver, among Hoosiers, was the same as for passage, except that Thomas Smith joined the Whigs in opposition.

122 U. S. *Statutes at Large*, IX, 59–66; Van Deusen, *The Jacksonian Era, 1828–1848*, pp. 205–206.

123 For Polk's views about the tariff, see pp. 605–606, 609, 612–613.

124 [James Whitcomb], *Facts for the People in Relation to a Protective Tariff; Embracing a Brief Review of the Operation of Our Tariff Laws Since the Organization of the Government, Including That of 1842* (1843); Oliver H. Smith, *The Other Side of "Facts for the People," in Relation to a "Protective Tariff,"* "by an Indianian" (1843). According to the Fort Wayne *Sentinel*, June 3, 1843, the pamphlet by Whitcomb had its beginning as an address before the Democratic State Convention in January, 1843. The copy in the Indiana Historical Society Library, Indianapolis, indicates that it was initially published as having been written "By an Indianian." The author, however, has based his remarks on the

copy found in the Vincennes *Western Sun*, May 13, 20, 27, 1843, and on Smith's copy in his *Early Indiana Trials and Sketches*, 298–332. For examples of contrasting views of Democrats versus Whigs regarding the tariff during 1843, see Indianapolis *Indiana State Sentinel*, January 24, March 28, April 18, 25, May 2, June 20, August 1, November 7, 1843; Indianapolis *Indiana State Journal*, April 12, May 10, 17, 31, August 2, October 11, November 1, December 6, 1843; Fort Wayne *Sentinel*, February 11, October 7, December 9, 1843.

125 Indianapolis *Indiana State Sentinel*, February 6, 1845; Indianapolis *Indiana State Journal*, August 20, 1845.

126 Indianapolis *Indiana State Journal*, December 24, 1845; *Congressional Globe*, 29 Cong., 1 session, 1002–1006. Concerning the tariff reduction sought by Walker, see Sellers, *James K. Polk, Continentalist, 1843–1846*, pp. 451–452, and 453–470 *passim*.

127 *House Journal*, 29 Cong., 1 session, 1029–1030; *Senate Journal*, 29 Cong., 1 session, 451–454. For party split and sectional aspects of the voting, see Sellers, *James K. Polk, Continentalist, 1843–1846*, pp. 457, 467; Edward Stanwood, *American Tariff Controversies in the Nineteenth Century* (2 vols., Boston, 1903), II, 75–76, 79–80; Turner, *The United States, 1830–1850*, pp. 554–559. Of Indiana's ten congressmen, five Democrats, Charles W. Cathcart, Thomas J. Henley, Andrew Kennedy, Thomas Smith, and William W. Wick voted for passage; Democrats John W. Davis, speaker, Robert Dale Owen, and John Pettit were nonvoters. Senators Hannegan and Bright voted for passage. Davis and Owen presumably also favored passage.

128 In this period as during the early forties, the General Assembly sought federal grants of land or money for a variety of internal improvements. As indicated in *Laws of Indiana* (local), 1844–45, pp. 293–294, 294–295, 296–297, 298, 300–301, aid was sought on behalf of improving the Wabash River; completing the Wabash and Erie Canal from Terre Haute to Evansville; constructing the Northern Cross Railroad in Indiana and Illinois; making a clay or macadamized road connecting Bloomington and Columbus via Nashville; construction of the National Road; constructing the harbor at Michigan City; constructing the Central Canal from Indianapolis north to the Wabash and Erie Canal. And *ibid.* (general), 1845–46, pp. 121, 123–124, 127–128, 129, 130–131, 134, on behalf of improving navigation of the St. Joseph River; construction of the Buffalo and Mississippi Railroad from Toledo to Chicago; improving navigation of the Wabash River; continuing building the National Road; completing the harbor at Michigan City; constructing a canal around the Falls of the Ohio on the Indiana side. And *ibid.* (general), 1846–47, pp. 147–148, 150–151, 157, 161, 162–163, on behalf of extending the Wabash and Erie Canal from the mouth of the Tippecanoe River to Terre Haute; for draining lands and building roads in Gibson County; "Mr. Whitney" for constructing a railroad from Lake Michigan to the Pacific Ocean; constructing the Buffalo and Mississippi Railroad; building a clay

or macadamized road within Brown County. And *ibid.* (general), 1847–48, pp. 106–107, on behalf of completing the National Road. And *ibid.* (general), 1848–49, pp. 152–153, 158, 162–163, on behalf of completing a harbor at Michigan City; construction of railroads within Indiana; construction of the Indianapolis and Peru Railroad.

129 *House Journal,* 29 Cong., 1 session, 546–547, 563–564; *Senate Journal,* 29 Cong., 1 session, 443. Four Democratic congressmen—Charles W. Cathcart, Thomas J. Henley, Thomas Smith, and William W. Wick—voted for passage, as did the two Whigs, Congressmen Edward G. McGaughey and Caleb B. Smith. Three Democrats—John W. Davis, Andrew Kennedy, and John Pettit—were nonvoters; and the remaining Democrat, Robert Dale Owen, voted against the bill. The item appropriating $40,000 for the harbor at Michigan City passed 99 to 81. On this vote, Owen and the six colleagues who voted for passage of the bill, voted for this item; and the three nonvoters remained the same as for the bill. Senator Edward A. Hannegan voted to advance the bill to third reading, while Senator Jesse D. Bright was a nonvoter. See the following note for source of item quoting Polk.

130 Richardson, *Messages and Papers of the Presidents,* IV, 460–466 (quotations, 460, 461, 465); *House Journal,* 29 Cong., 1 session, 1218–1219. Six congressmen voted to override the veto: Democrats Charles W. Cathcart, Thomas J. Henley, Thomas Smith, and John Pettit, and Whigs Edward G. McGaughey and Caleb B. Smith. Of the four remaining Democrats, Robert Dale Owen and William W. Wick voted not to override, and Speaker John W. Davis and Andrew Kennedy were nonvoters.

131 *Congressional Globe,* 29 Cong., 1 session, 462–463 (Pettit), 1084 (Hannegan).

132 Although the National Road was perhaps the best constructed road in Indiana, it was difficult and hazardous to travel well beyond 1850. See Ch. 6, pp. 345-347 for extension of the Wabash and Erie Canal to Evansville via Terre Haute.

133 For Polk's views regarding slavery, see David M. Potter, *The Impending Crisis, 1848–1861* (New York, 1976), 67–73; Richardson, *Messages and Papers of the Presidents,* IV, 376–377, 640–642. Also see pp. 604–605, regarding annexation as an issue in the presidential campaign of 1844.

134 Richardson, *Messages and Papers of the Presidents,* IV, 343–345 (Tyler's recommendation); *House Journal,* 28 Cong., 2 session, 259–265, 527–529; *Senate Journal,* 28 Cong., 2 session, 113, 215–221. Indiana's eight Democratic congressmen—William J. Brown, John W. Davis, Thomas J. Henley, Andrew Kennedy, Robert Dale Owen, John Pettit, Thomas Smith, Joseph A. Wright—all voted for annexation; the two Whig congressmen, Samuel C. Sample and Caleb B. Smith, voted against annexation. Senator Edward A. Hannegan, Democrat, voted to advance the annexation resolution to third reading; Senator Albert S. White, Whig, voted against the same. The resolution was advanced to third reading by a vote of 27 to 25. As indicated in Pletcher, *The Diplomacy of*

Annexation, 180–182, a larger proportion of southerners than of northerners, and of Democrats than Whigs, voted for annexation.

135 *Congressional Globe,* 28 Cong., 2 session, Appendix, 78–81 (Smith), 71–73 (Sample). Both Smith and Sample said they would respect the compromises of the constitution regarding slavery.

136 *Ibid.,* 109–113 (Owen), 74–78 (Henley).

137 Richardson, *Messages and Papers of the Presidents,* IV, 379–381, 386–388.

138 *House Journal,* 29 Cong., 1 session, 71–72, 108–114, 157, 172; *Senate Journal,* 29 Cong., 1 session, 50, 64, 68, 75. Both Whig congressmen from Indiana, Edward W. McGaughey and Caleb B. Smith, voted against admission; Democratic Congressmen Charles W. Cathcart, Thomas J. Henley, Robert Dale Owen, John Pettit, Thomas Smith, William W. Wick voted for admission; and Speaker John W. Davis and Congressman Andrew Kennedy, Democrats, were nonvoters. Senator Edward A. Hannegan voted to advance the admission bill to third reading, but his Democratic colleague, Jesse D. Bright, as the *Senate Journal* shows, did not take his seat until after the measure had passed.

139 U. S. *Statutes at Large,* IX, 108 (admitting resolution); *Biographical Directory of the American Congress, 1774–1927,* p. 211, for seating of Texan senators and representatives.

140 Richardson, *Messages and Papers of the Presidents,* IV, 257–258, 337–338; *Laws of Indiana* (local), 1844–45, p. 300. This resolution claims all of Oregon south of 52°, but as presented to the House by Congressman Samuel C. Sample claim is made to all of Oregon, from 54° 40' south. *House Journal,* 28 Cong., 2 session, 310. As indicated in *Biographical Directory of the Indiana General Assembly,* I, 488–490, the General Assembly which passed this resolution had 45 Democrats and 54 Whigs in the House, with each party having 25 senators.

141 *Congressional Globe,* 28 Cong., 2 session, 222 (Owen), Appendix, 137–138 (Kennedy), 47–48 (White).

142 Richardson, *Messages and Papers of the Presidents,* IV, 381, 392–397. For a comprehensive view of Polk's course regarding Oregon, see Pletcher, *The Diplomacy of Annexation,* 229–253, 261, 270–272, 296–351, 377–382, 402–417.

143 Pletcher, *The Diplomacy of Annexation,* 240–241, 296–305, 381–383, 402–415; Frederick Merk, *The Oregon Question: Essays in Anglo-American Diplomacy and Politics* (Cambridge, Mass., 1967), 229–230, 346–347, 380–381, 386–388.

144 South Bend *St. Joseph Valley Register,* September 19, 1845; Indianapolis *Indiana State Journal,* August 20, September 3, 17, 24, October 1, 1845. The identity of "L. B." has not been found.

145 Indianapolis *Indiana State Journal,* November 26, 1845; Leopold, *Robert Dale Owen,* 194, quoting [New Harmony] *Indiana Statesman,* November 29, 1845, [Indianapolis] *Indiana State Sentinel,* November 15, 1845, and Indianapolis *Indiana Democrat,* November 28, 1845.

146 *House Journal,* 29 Cong., 1 session, 700–709; *Senate Journal,* 29 Cong., 1 session, 260–261. The Democratic congressmen from Indiana who voted

against the resolution were Charles W. Cathcart, Thomas J. Henley, Andrew Kennedy, John Pettit, Thomas Smith, and William W. Wick. Owen's role for moderation, as a member of the conference committee which submitted the resolution adopted, is noted in Leopold, *Robert Dale Owen*, 200–202. Leopold states that Owen was the only Democrat in the Old Northwest, from either house, who supported passage.

147 *Congressional Globe*, 29 Cong., 1 session, 109–110, 379, 388 (quotations, 110, 388). As indicated *ibid.*, 110, Hannegan made his comments about not surrendering "one foot" of Oregon on December 30, 1845. In mid-February, as the Oregon debate persisted, the Hoosier Democrat explained why he had voted against the annexation of Texas even though he had favored its immediate annexation, saying: my "course had been induced by an apprehension in my mind that, if the Texas question were settled before final action on Oregon, I apprehended Punic faith—Punic faith."

148 *Ibid.*, 179–181 (Kennedy), 322–324 (Cathcart), Appendix, 199–201 (Wick).

149 *Ibid.*, 158–160.

150 *Ibid.*, 135–136, Appendix, 146–151.

151 *Ibid.*, Appendix, 695–697.

152 Pletcher, *The Diplomacy of Annexation*, 404–407, 410–414. See note 143 for citations regarding the tendency toward compromise in both Britain and the United States.

153 Richardson, *Messages and Papers of the Presidents*, IV, 449–450; *Senate Journal*, 29 Cong., 1 session, Appendix, 547–555.

154 Pletcher, *The Diplomacy of Annexation*, 172–207, 352–376 *passim*; Sellers, *James K. Polk, Continentalist, 1843–1846*, pp. 213–266 *passim*; Potter, *The Impending Crisis*, 1–89 *passim*.

155 *House Journal*, 29 Cong., 1 session, 1240, 1244–1247; *Senate Journal*, 29 Cong., 1 session, 492, 506; Sellers, *James K. Polk, Continentalist, 1843–1846*, p. 479. The two Whig congressmen from Indiana, Caleb B. Smith and Edward W. McGaughey, and Democrats Charles W. Cathcart, Thomas J. Henley, Robert Dale Owen, John Pettit, and William W. Wick voted for prohibition of slavery. Democrats John W. Davis, Andrew Kennedy, and Thomas Smith were nonvoters.

156 Pletcher, *The Diplomacy of Annexation*, 352–392; Sellers, *James K. Polk, Continentalist, 1843–1846*, pp. 398–409; Richardson, *Messages and Papers of the Presidents*, IV, 437–443 (quote, 442).

157 *House Journal*, 29 Cong., 1 session, 792–793, 796–797, 804–806, 809; *Senate Journal*, 29 Cong., 1 session, 287–289, 292–293; U. S. *Statutes at Large*, IX, 9–10. Democratic Congressmen Charles W. Cathcart, Thomas J. Henley, Andrew Kennedy, Robert Dale Owen, John Pettit, Thomas Smith, and William W. Wick voted for passage, as did Whig Congressman Edward W. McGaughey. Congressman John W. Davis, the Democratic speaker, was a nonvoter. Whig Congressman Caleb B. Smith was also a nonvoter, but some weeks later he

explained that had illness not prevented his attendance he would have voted for passage to support the troops fighting the war. *Congressional Globe*, 29 Cong., 1 session, Appendix, 1118. The act declaring war also authorized the president to call militiamen into service.

158 Indianapolis *Indiana State Journal*, May 20, 1846; Richmond *Palladium*, June 23, 1846; Fort Wayne *Times & People's Press*, June 6, 1846.

159 *Congressional Globe*, 29 Cong., 1 session, Appendix, 1115–1118 (Caleb B. Smith), 910–911 (Thomas Smith); Indianapolis *Indiana State Journal*, January 5, 1847.

160 Pletcher, *The Diplomacy of Annexation*, 458–461; Potter, *The Impending Crisis*, 18–21; Sellers, *James K. Polk, Continentalist, 1843–1846*, pp. 468–481.

161 According to the *Congressional Globe*, 29 Cong., 1 session, 1211–1218 (votes, 1217–1218), the vote on the Wilmot Proviso and then passage were as indicated, however, there is no recording of this vote. The account of the deliberation of the House on this bill as found in the *House Journal*, 29 Cong., 1 session, 1272–1278, 1283–1287, differs from that in the *Congressional Globe*. Robert Dale Owen's opposition to the Wilmot Proviso is emphasized in Leopold, *Robert Dale Owen*, 207–210. The ensuing discussion gives significant clues regarding how Indiana congressmen voted on both the Wilmot Proviso and passage of the appropriation with the proviso attached.

162 *Congressional Globe*, 29 Cong., 1 session, 1216 (Owen), 1217–1218 (Wick).

163 *Senate Journal*, 29 Cong., 1 session, 524, 527, 530. *Ibid.*, Appendix, 558–563, has related items which *seem to suggest* that Senators Jesse Bright and Edward A. Hannegan opposed the proviso; and that Bright favored the appropriation and Hannegan opposed it. The ensuing pages give important clues about their views on these matters.

164 *Congressional Globe*, 29 Cong., 2 session, 453–455; Potter, *The Impending Crisis*, 59–62.

165 Richardson, *Messages and Papers of the Presidents*, IV, 494–495, 504.

166 *House Journal*, 29 Cong., 2 session, 194, 343–350. Hoosier Democrats Robert Dale Owen and William W. Wick voted against the proviso, but for passage with the proviso attached; Democrats Charles W. Cathcart, Thomas J. Henley, Andrew Kennedy, John Pettit, and Thomas Smith voted for both the proviso and passage; Democrat John W. Davis, speaker of the House, was a nonvoter. Edward W. McGaughey and Caleb B. Smith, the two Whigs, voted for the proviso; McGaughey voted against and Smith for passage. When the Senate bill was advanced to third reading, 29 to 24, Democrats Bright and Hannegan voted for advancement. *Senate Journal*, 29 Cong., 2 session, 112, 252–253.

167 *House Journal*, 29 Cong., 2 session, 470, 474–476, 500–504; Pletcher, *The Diplomacy of Annexation*, 475. During House consideration of concurrence with the Senate bill, Democrats Henley, Owen, and Wick voted against adding the proviso to the Senate bill, then for concurrence with the bill; Democrats Cathcart and Kennedy voted to add the proviso, and also supported concurrence;

Democrat Pettit voted for the proviso, but was a nonvoter on concurrence; Democrats Thomas Smith and Speaker Davis were nonvoters on both items. The two Whigs, McGaughey and Caleb B. Smith, voted to add the proviso, and against concurrence.

168 *Congressional Globe*, 29 Cong., 2 session, 47–48 (Kennedy), 106–110 (Owen), 515–517 (Hannegan).

169 *Ibid.*, 180–182 (Pettit), 122–124 (Smith); John Law to Martin Van Buren, August 2, 1847, quoted in Roger H. Van Bolt, "Hoosiers and the Western Program, 1844–1848," *Indiana Magazine of History*, XLVIII (1952), 275.

170 Indianapolis *Indiana State Sentinel*, March 11, 1847 (McGaughey and Smith called Federalists); Richmond *Palladium*, April 27, June 1, 1847; Muncie *Journal*, January 16, 1847.

171 Pletcher, *The Diplomacy of Annexation*, 552–557; Van Deusen, *The Jacksonian Era, 1828–1848*, pp. 241–244; *Congress A to Z*, 497.

172 Riker and Thornbrough (comps.), *Indiana Election Returns, 1816–1851*, pp. 110–118, 134. One Whig, Caleb B. Smith, was reelected, and three other Whigs—George G. Dunn, Elisha Embree, and Richard W. Thompson—were elected. Four Democrats—Charles W. Cathcart, Thomas J. Henley, John Pettit, and William W. Wick—were reelected, and two other Democrats, John L. Robinson and William Rockhill, were elected. Robert Dale Owen, the only incumbent Democrat seeking reelection, was defeated by Embree.

173 *House Journal*, 30 Cong., 1 session, 175–180. Two Whigs, Smith and Thompson, voted for this resolution; the other two Whigs, Dunn and Embree, joined with Democrats Cathcart, Henley, Robinson, Rockhill, and Wick in opposition to passage. Pettit, a Democrat, was a nonvoter. The resolution proposed that the boundary between the United States and Mexico be established at or near the desert between the Nueces and Rio Grande rivers—the area which both countries had claimed prior to the war.

174 *Ibid.*, 183–185. Three Whigs—Dunn, Smith, and Thompson—voted for this resolution; five Democrats—Cathcart, Henley, Robinson, Rockhill, and Wick—voted against it; Embree, Whig, and Pettit, Democrat, were non-voters. Abraham Lincoln, Whig congressman from Illinois, voted for this resolution.

175 *Senate Journal*, 30 Cong., 1 session, 644–645. See *ibid.*, 609–646, for Senate proceedings resulting in ratification. For discussions of the treaty and its ratification, see Pletcher, *The Diplomacy of Annexation*, 549–550, 557–563, 569–570; Van Deusen, *The Jacksonian Era, 1828–1848*, pp. 235–240, 244–245.

176 Richardson, *Messages and Papers of the Presidents*, IV, 542, 558–559. Polk's views about slavery, culminating in June, 1848, when he committed his support for extension of the Missouri Compromise or 36°30′ line to the Pacific, are indicated in Potter, *The Impending Crisis*, 67–73.

177 *Senate Journal*, 30 Cong., 1 session, 633, 562–564, 589–590; *House Journal*, 30 Cong., 1 session, 1154–1156, 1244–1246. See *Congressional Globe*, 30 Cong., 1 session, Appendix, 716–719, for Pettit's contention that slavery could

not exist in a territory, unless authorized by Congress. He viewed the Northwest Ordinance of 1787 as binding for Oregon.

178 Richardson, *Messages and Papers of the Presidents*, IV, 606–610 (quotation, 608).

179 See statements of Hannegan, Whitcomb, Law, Chamberlain, and Owen in Indianapolis *Indiana State Sentinel*, December 14, 1848. Much the same information is also in Indianapolis *Indiana State Journal*, December 18, 1848. The latter explained that three weeks previous it had predicted that any of the aspirants, if necessary to ensure success, would come out in favor of preventing the introduction of slavery in the new territories.

180 Riker and Thornbrough (comps.), *Indiana Election Returns, 1816–1851*, p. 134. Caleb B. Smith, the strongest Whig rival, received 53 votes. According to "Justice" in the Indianapolis *Indiana State Journal*, December 25, 1848, Whitcomb had been the choice of a Democratic caucus, and the Democratic aspirants had all agreed to abide by its decision.

181 Barnhart and Carmony, *Indiana*, I, 405–407.

BIBLIOGRAPHY

This bibliography is *preponderantly based on sources used in the research for and the writing of this book*. With meager exceptions, the items listed are quoted, cited, or referred to in its pages. The author's primary purpose has been to write *a history of the state of Indiana for the period 1816 to 1850*. Major emphasis has been given to Indiana's political and constitutional history, however, much attention has been given to its population, economy, internal improvements, banking, state finances, fiscal insolvency, education, and miscellaneous items. Considerable emphasis also has been given to Indiana's role within and attitude toward the Union of the States.

Since most sources used are relevant to various subjects, the bibliography has been organized under these general categories:

    I. State Documents.
    II. Federal Documents.
    III. Newspapers.
    IV. Secondary Books.
    V. Diaries, Letters, and Reminiscences.
    VI. Articles.
    VII. Dissertations, Theses, and Unpublished Papers.

The research and writing for this volume has been based mainly on primary sources. Comments by and discussions with mentors, colleagues, and students through the years have given the author an increased understanding of and appreciation for what Indiana was like in the pioneer era. Moreover, since the author gained his elementary education in one-room, red-brick country schools; lived for a short time in a log cabin; and did farm labor before mechanization made horses and mules unnecessary, he has an affinity with pioneer life. And, having served on various state committees and commissions, an augmented understanding has been gained about how the political process and government function.

I. STATE DOCUMENTS

The most important state documents are the laws of Indiana and the Constitutions of 1816 and 1851, plus the publications which led to their adoption. As will be apparent from the listing and comments, particularly significant are the books compiled or edited by Dorothy Riker and Gayle Thornbrough.

Their meticulously edited documents are extremely relevant and valuable for the study of Indiana in its pioneer era. Since Indiana was the second state carved from the Old Northwest Territory, the background and precedents for some its laws are in Theodore Calvin Pease (ed.), *The Laws of the Northwest Territory, 1788–1800* (Springfield, Ill., 1925). Concerning the Indiana territorial period, 1800–1816, these volumes are very useful: Francis S. Philbrick (ed.), *The Laws of Indiana Territory, 1801–1809* (Springfield, Ill., 1930; reprinted Indianapolis, 1931); Louis B. Ewbank and Dorothy L. Riker (eds.), *The Laws of Indiana Territory, 1809–1816* (Indianapolis, 1934); William Wesley Woollen, Daniel Wait Howe, and Jacob Piatt Dunn (eds.), *Executive Journal of Indiana Territory, 1800–1816* (Indianapolis, 1900); Gayle Thornbrough and Dorothy Riker (eds.), *Journals of the General Assembly of Indiana Territory, 1805–1815* (Indianapolis, 1950); and Clarence E. Carter (ed.), *The Territory of Indiana, 1800–1816* (vols. 7 and 8, Washington, D. C., 1939).

From statehood in 1816 to 1850 the laws, arising from annual sessions of the legislature, were printed in one or two volumes for each session. Whether called general, local, special, revised, or merely laws or acts of Indiana, they were usually a mix of local and general laws. Beginning in the 1830s—with the chartering of the Second State Bank in 1834 and the Internal Improvements System of 1836—the annual volumes of the laws are generally larger than previously. The revised codes of 1824, 1831, 1843, and 1852 are quite useful in reviewing change versus continuity regarding particular items or subjects.

Throughout the period 1816–1850 the proceedings of the Senate and House of Representatives were published in separate volumes for each legislative session. Generally speaking these journals offer modest information about the pro and con deliberations concerning the introduction, consideration, and passage or defeat of proposed laws and resolutions. But they include messages of the governors, reports from committees and state officials, roll call votes, and miscellaneous items which afford much information about issues and concerns of the day and the circumstances of pioneer life. The legislative journals increased in size during the thirties and forties after Indiana abandoned economic laissez-faire with the chartering of the Second State Bank in 1834 and the adoption of the Internal Improvements System of 1836. Hence, as Senate and House proceedings increased in length, starting with the session of 1834–1835, various Senate and House documents were published in a *Documentary Journal*. At times two such volumes were published, one for Senate and another for House documents. Often some of the same documents appeared in the *Documentary Journal* as in the Senate and/or House journals.

Several sources offer information about pioneer legislators, and the laws and journals resulting from their sessions. John G. Rauch and Nellie C. Armstrong, *A Bibliography of the Laws of Indiana, 1788–1927* (Indianapolis, 1928), gives the dates for legislative sessions, indicates by whom the laws were published, and notes whether the laws were adopted at regular or special sessions.

Cecil K. Byrd and Howard H. Peckham, *A Bibliography of Indiana Imprints, 1804–1853* (Indianapolis, 1955), indicates who published the laws for legislative sessions, and lists libraries where the laws for various sessions were available. Byrd and Peckham also note who published the Senate, House, and Documentary journals, and where they were available. Dorothy Riker and Gayle Thornbrough (comps.), *Indiana Election Returns, 1816–1851* (Indianapolis, 1960), offers data about votes for and against legislative candidates, notes party ties when known, and provides detailed information about legislative apportionments. Justin E. Walsh, *The Centennial History of the Indiana General Assembly, 1816–1878* (Indianapolis, 1987), notes key legislative officers by sessions, offers very useful information about the background and experience of legislators, and has maps illustrating legislative apportionments by counties. *A Biographical Directory of the Indiana General Assembly*, Vol. I, *1816–1899* (Indianapolis, 1980), offers concise sketches of legislators, lists members by legislative sessions, indicates their politics when known, and details legislative apportionments by counties.

There are more primary sources regarding the Constitution of 1851 than for the Constitution of 1816. The *Journal of the Convention of the Indiana Territory*, for the drafting of the Constitution of 1816, was printed by Butler and Wood (Louisville, 1816). A copy of the journal is in the *Indiana Magazine of History*, LXI (1965), 77–156, edited by Donald F. Carmony. The debates of this convention were not published. For the Indianapolis Constitutional Convention, 1850–1851, which drafted the Constitution of 1851, a lengthy journal and two fat volumes of debates were published. They are known as the *Journal of the Convention of the People of the State of Indiana to Amend the Constitution* (Indianapolis, 1851; reprint, 1935), and *Report of the Debates and Proceedings of the Convention for the Revision of the Constitution of the State of Indiana, 1850* (2 vols., Indianapolis, 1850 [1851]; reprint, 1935). Hubert H. Hawkins (comp.), *Indiana's Road to Statehood* (Indianapolis, 1961), has a copy of the Constitution of 1816 and key documents leading to its adoption.

An extremely helpful source concerning the drafting of sections of the Constitutions of 1816 and 1851 is Charles Kettleborough, *Constitution Making in Indiana* (vol. I, Indianapolis, 1916; reprint, 1971), pp. 83–125 and 295–375. Kettleborough also offers much information and relevant documents contributing to the revision of both constitutions. An invaluable guide to the journal and debates of the Constitutional Convention of 1850–1851 is that by Jessie P. Boswell (comp.), *Index to the Journal and Debates of the Indiana Constitutional Convention, 1850–1851* (Indianapolis, 1938). Pages 79–125 give citations to both the journal and debates leading to the sections drafted in the Constitution of 1851. Pages 129–136 give what seems to be the most accurate listing of the officers and delegates of the convention. A broadside, printed by the Indianapolis *Indiana State Sentinel*, obviously in 1850, entitled *Members of the Convention to Amend the Constitution of the State of Indiana, Assembled at Indianapolis, October,*

1850, contains much information regarding the age, postal address, county or counties represented, years in Indiana, boardinghouse, occupation, politics, whether married or single, and miscellaneous comments of the delegates except for those elected to fill vacancies.

Among primary sources of indispensable value are several volumes about the administration of Indiana's governors, 1800–1843. They are: Logan Esarey (ed.), *Messages and Letters of William Henry Harrison* (2 vols., Indianapolis, 1922); Logan Esarey (ed.), *Messages and Papers of Jonathan Jennings, Ratliff Boon, William Hendricks, 1816–1825* (Indianapolis, 1914); Dorothy Riker and Gayle Thornbrough (eds.), *Messages and Papers Relating to the Administration of James Brown Ray, Governor of Indiana, 1825–1831* (Indianapolis, 1954); Dorothy Riker and Gayle Thornbrough (eds.), *Messages and Papers Relating to the Administration of Noah Noble, Governor of Indiana, 1831–1837* (Indianapolis, 1958); Dorothy Riker (ed.), *Messages and Papers Relating to the Administration of David Wallace, Governor of Indiana, 1837–1840* (Indianapolis, 1963); and Gayle Thornbrough (ed.), *Messages and Papers Relating to the Administration of Samuel Bigger, Governor of Indiana, 1840–1843* (Indianapolis, 1964). Unfortunately there are no such volumes for Governors James Whitcomb, 1843–1848, Paris C. Dunning, 1848–1849, and Joseph A. Wright, 1849–1857. My research was hampered and made less complete because these papers have not been published. I hope that this extremely valuable series will soon be continued so that selections of similar papers will before long be published for the administrations of all Indiana governors.

A variety of books afford important primary sources regarding Indiana in the pioneer period. Of particular value are: Dorothy Riker and Gayle Thornbrough (comps.), *Indiana Election Returns, 1816–1851* (Indianapolis, 1960); George Pence and Nellie C. Armstrong, *Indiana Boundaries: Territorial, State, and County* (Indianapolis, 1933); Dorothy Riker (ed.), *Executive Proceedings of the State of Indiana, 1816–1836* (Indianapolis, 1947); Charles W. Moores, *Caleb Mills and the Indiana School System* (Indianapolis, 1905); and Karl J. R. Arndt (comp. and ed.), *A Documentary History of the Indiana Decade of the Harmony Society, 1814–1824* (2 vols., Indianapolis, 1975, 1978). For primary sources about agriculture, see Herbert Anthony Kellar (ed.), *Solon Robinson: Pioneer and Agriculturist* (2 vols., Indianapolis, 1936); *First Annual Report of the Indiana State Board of Agriculture* (1852), and *Second Annual Report of the Indiana State Board of Agriculture: For the Year 1852* (Indianapolis, 1853), plus succeeding volumes in this series. A variety of documents regarding pioneer Indiana are in Gayle Thornbrough and Dorothy Riker (comps.), *Readings in Indiana History* (Indianapolis, 1956); and in Ralph D. Gray (ed.), *The Hoosier State: Readings in Indiana History* (2 vols., Grand Rapids, Mich., 1980). For samples of relevant travel accounts, see Harlow Lindley (ed.), *Indiana As Seen by Early Travelers* (Indianapolis, 1916); Shirley S. McCord (comp.), *Travel Accounts of Indiana, 1679–1961* (Indianapolis, 1970); and *passim* items in Reuben G. Thwaites (ed.), *Early Western Travels, 1748–1846* (32 vols., Cleveland, 1904–1907).

II. FEDERAL DOCUMENTS

In the preparation of this book considerable research was done in federal documents. Documents regarding Indiana's status as a federal territory are found in Clarence Edwin Carter (comp. and ed.), *The Territory Northwest of the River Ohio, 1787–1803* (vols. 2, 3, Washington, D. C., 1934); Clarence E. Carter (ed.), *The Territory of Indiana, 1800–1816* (vols. 7, 8, Washington, D. C., 1939); Theodore C. Pease (ed.), *The Laws of the Northwest Territory, 1788–1800* (Springfield, Ill., 1925); Francis S. Philbrick (ed.), *The Laws of Indiana Territory, 1801–1809* (Springfield, Ill., 1930); Louis B. Ewbank and Dorothy L. Riker (eds.), *The Laws of Indiana Territory, 1809–1816* (Indianapolis, 1934); Gayle Thornbrough and Dorothy Riker (eds.), *Journals of the General Assembly of Indiana Territory, 1805–1815* (Indianapolis, 1950); and William Wesley Woollen, Daniel Wait Howe, and Jacob Piatt Dunn (eds.), *Executive Journal of Indiana Territory, 1800–1816* (Indianapolis, 1900). Useful documents concerning Indiana's territorial status are also in Charles Kettleborough, *Constitution Making in Indiana* (vol. 1, Indianapolis, 1916; reprint, 1971), and Hubert H. Hawkins (comp.), *Indiana's Road to Statehood* (Indianapolis, 1961).

Items about federal legislation concerning Indiana are found in *Statutes at Large of the United States of America, 1789–1873* (17 vols., Boston, 1850–1873). Discussion pro and con legislation is in the *Debates and Proceedings in the Congress of the United States, 1789–1824* (42 vols., Washington, D. C., 1834–1856), known as the *Annals of Congress*; the *Register of Debates in Congress, 1825–1837* (29 vols., Washington, D. C., 1825–1837), known as *Congressional Debates*; and *Congressional Globe, Containing the Debates and Proceedings, 1833–1873* (109 vols., Washington, D. C., 1834–1873). The *Journal of the House of Representatives of the United States*, and the *Journal of the Senate of the United States*, both published annually 1789–1850, are excellent sources for information about bills introduced, changes made concerning them, and whether they passed.

A variety of other books were useful regarding federal documents. Among those of particular value are: James D. Richardson, *Compilations of the Messages and Papers of the Presidents* (20 vols., Washington, D. C., 1897–1917); *Biographical Directory of the American Congress, 1774–1927* (Washington, D. C., 1928); *American State Papers: Documents, Legislative and Executive of the Congress of the United States* (38 vols., Washington, D. C., 1832–1861), covering sessions of Congress, 1789–1838. Its volumes regarding public lands, Indian affairs, and finance have significant documents relevant to pioneer Indiana. Noble E. Cunningham, Jr., *Circular Letters of Congressmen to Their Constituents, 1789–1829* (3 vols., Chapel Hill, N. C., 1978), includes some informative letters of Indiana congressmen to their constituents.

Of much value regarding Indian affairs and public lands are Charles J. Kappler (ed.), *Indian Affairs: Laws and Treaties* (2 vols., Washington, D. C., 1904); Charles C. Royce (comp.), *Indian Land Cessions in the United States* (U. S. Bureau of American Ethnology, *Eighteenth Annual Report, 1896–1897*, Washington, D. C., 1899); and Thomas Donaldson, *The Public Domain: Its History, with*

Statistics (Washington, D. C., 1884). Miscellaneous books used include: *Journal of the Executive Proceedings of the Senate of the United States.* . . . (3 vols., Washington, D. C., 1828); Robert Brent Mosher (comp.), *Executive Register of the United States, 1789–1902* (Washington, D. C., 1905); and U. S. Bureau of the Census, *Negro Population in the United States, 1790–1915* (Washington, D. C., 1915). Other census returns of the U. S. Bureau of the Census for 1800, 1810, 1820, 1830, 1840, 1850, and 1860 offer much information about population, crafts and trades, manufacturing, and agriculture. Considerable summary census information is in U. S. Bureau of the Census, *Historical Statistics of the United States, 1789–1945* (Washington, D. C., 1949).

III. NEWSPAPERS

Indiana newspapers are an invaluable source of information concerning Indiana in the pioneer era. The first newspaper was the *Indiana Gazette*, which Elihu Stout commenced at Vincennes in 1804. A fire destroyed his press in 1806, but the next year Stout began the Vincennes *Western Sun*. By December, 1816, when Indiana became a state, more than a half dozen papers had been established. By 1850 perhaps several thousand papers had been commenced, the preponderance of which were weeklies. The mortality rate among them was high, many dying in their infancy. Frequently newspapers missed publication of weekly issues, at times lapsing for weeks or even months. By the forties some papers, especially those located in the larger towns, appeared biweekly, triweekly, or even daily, particularly in connection with annual sessions of the General Assembly. Apparently none was published on Sundays. Pioneer papers seldom had more than a few hundred subscribers who were usually charged no more than $2.50 annually, at times payable in rags, firewood, potatoes, whiskey, or miscellaneous goods or services.

Most pioneer papers give much attention to politics. During the initial decade of statehood, possibly without exception, they sustained some brand of Jeffersonian Republicanism. As loosely organized political parties developed, starting in the midtwenties, most papers soon became ardently devoted to one party and a vigorous critic of the rival party. For the most part their columns were colored with partisan bias, with facts often distorted, and generally minus any separation of editorial views and news. The pioneer press usually gave limited consideration to local news, nevertheless now and then significant items about the context and nature of pioneer life were included. Considerable attention was given to national politics and relations with other countries, but such information was often weeks or even months old. Generally speaking pioneer newspapers consisted of only four pages, varied much in size, and were printed in small and often old type. Pages one and four were usually printed first, hence the most recent news normally appeared on pages two and three, the inside pages. Fortunately for historians the pioneer press was almost always printed on rag paper, and the pages are generally much better preserved than those printed during World War II.

Newspapers published at the capital are especially important sources of information about Indiana in its pioneer era. From late 1816 through most of 1824 the Corydon *Indiana Gazette*, largely friendly to Jonathan Jennings, was the leading paper at the state's first capital. The first paper at Indianapolis, which succeeded Corydon as the capital in 1825, also called the *Indiana Gazette*, was established early in 1822. It lacked any consistent political coloration, but after changes of name and ownership in 1829 it became the Indianapolis *Indiana Democrat and State Gazette*, staunchly committed to the Jacksonians. In 1841 the paper passed to the Chapman brothers as the *Indiana State Sentinel*, vigorously supportive of the Democrats. Meantime, in 1823 the *Western Censor, & Emigrants Guide*, much opposed to the Jacksonians, became the second paper at Indianapolis. Early in 1825 it became the *Indiana Journal*, and in the early forties the *Indiana State Journal*, a staunch supporter of the Whigs. The Indianapolis *Indiana Statesman*, 1850–1852, reflected the free soil tendencies emerging in the Democracy. It also has items of significance about the drafting of the Constitution of 1851, as do both the *Indiana State Sentinel* and the *Indiana State Journal*. A sampling of newspapers in the numerous towns and villages of the state is also helpful in understanding Indiana in its early decades as a state. Of very great value to historians are the files of the Vincennes *Western Sun*, which Elihu Stout controlled until 1845. This veteran editor, one of the founders of the Jacksonian party in Indiana, later a supporter of the Democrats against the Whigs, enhanced the historical value of his paper by generous copying of items, about politics and otherwise, from various newspapers around the state. This copying from other papers was fairly common among the pioneer press.

The papers listed below, alphabetically by towns and villages, are quoted, cited, or referred to in this book. Their names are often abbreviated, with the actual names at times unknown or at least uncertain. The research done in them is significantly greater than the quotations, citations, and references to them perhaps indicate.

Bloomington *Gazette, Herald, Democrat.*
Brookville *Franklin Democrat, Democrat.*
Brookville *Enquirer, Enquirer and Indiana Telegraph.*
Brookville *Franklin Repository.*
Centerville *Western Emporium.*
Centerville *Western Times.*
Charlestown *Indiana Intelligencer, Indiana Intelligencer and Farmer's Friend.*
Charlestown *Southern Indianian.*
Connersville *Indiana Statesman.*
Corydon *Indiana Gazette.*
Covington *People's Friend, Friend.*
Crawfordsville *Review.*
Delphi *Oracle.*
Evansville *Gazette.*
Evansville *Journal.*

Evansville *Republican*.
Evansville *South-Western Sentinel*.
Fort Wayne *Sentinel*.
Fort Wayne *Times, Times and People's Press*.
Frankfort *Observer*.
Greencastle *Indiana Patriot, Patriot*.
Greencastle *Visiter*.
Greensburg *Repository*.
Indianapolis *Indiana Democrat, Democrat*.
Indianapolis *Indiana Democrat and State Gazette*.
Indianapolis *Indiana Democrat and Spirit of the Constitution*.
Indianapolis *Indiana Journal, Indiana State Journal*.
Indianapolis *Indiana State Sentinel, Indiana Sentinel*.
Indianapolis *Indiana Statesman*.
Indianapolis *Western Censor, & Emigrants Guide, Western Censor*.
Jeffersonville *Indianian*.
Lafayette *Advertiser*.
Lafayette *Courier*.
Lafayette *Indiana Eagle*.
Lafayette *Standard*.
Lafayette *Tippecanoe Journal, Journal*.
Lawrenceburg *Political Beacon*.
Lawrenceburg *Dearborn Gazette*.
Lawrenceburg *Indiana Palladium*.
Lawrenceburg *Indiana Oracle*.
Logansport *Cass County Times*.
Logansport *Herald*.
Logansport *Telegraph, Canal Telegraph*.
Logansport *Potawattimie and Miami Times*.
Madison *Courier*.
Madison *Indiana Republican*.
Madison *Western Clarion*.
Mishawaka *Tocsin*.
Muncie *Journal*.
New Albany *Democrat*.
New Albany *Gazette*.
New Harmony *Indiana Statesman*.
Noblesville *Little Western*.
Paoli *True American*.
Paoli *Indiana Patriot*.
Plymouth *Marshall County Republican*.
Richmond *Jeffersonian*.
Richmond *Palladium*.
Richmond *Public Leger*.

Richmond *Weekly Intelligencer.*
Rushville *Indiana Herald and Indiana Gazette.*
Salem *Indiana Farmer.*
Salem *Indiana Monitor.*
Salem *Washington Republican.*
Salem *Tocsin.*
Salem *Western Annotator, Annotator.*
Shelbyville *Transcript.*
South Bend *Free Press.*
South Bend *St. Joseph Valley Register.*
Terre Haute *Wabash Enquirer.*
Terre Haute *Wabash Courier.*
Terre Haute *Wabash Express.*
Terre Haute *Western Register, Western Register and Terre Haute Advertiser.*
Valparaiso *Republican.*
Vevay *Indiana Palladium.*
Vevay *Indiana Register.*
Vincennes *Western Sun, Western Sun and General Advertiser.*
Vincennes *Indiana Centinel, Indiana Centinel and Public Advertiser.*
Vincennes *Farmers & Mechanics Journal.*
Wilmington *Indiana Register, Dearborn County Register.*

The best source regarding when and where newspapers were published, and where files of them may be found, is John W. Miller, *Indiana Newspaper Bibliography* (Indianapolis, 1982). Miller's bibliography, pages 519–520, gives a number of references to other sources concerning particular periods or various kinds of Indiana newspapers. Miller covers newspapers to 1980. Not included in Miller's bibliography is Donald F. Carmony, *The Pioneer Press in Indiana* (Indianapolis, 1954).

IV. SECONDARY BOOKS

Several general histories of Indiana have been published. The earliest of them was that by John B. Dillon, *A History of Indiana . . .*(Indianapolis, 1843). Revised in 1859, it added perceptive comments about Indiana's development to the 1850s. Dillon merits being known as the "Father of Indiana History." The initial two-volume history of Indiana was that by William Henry Smith, *The History of the State of Indiana From the Earliest Explorations by the French to the Present Time* (2 vols., Indianapolis, 1897). In the two decades after Indiana's centennial of statehood in 1916, three general histories appeared. The first was by Jacob Piatt Dunn, *Indiana and Indianans* (2 vols., Chicago, 1919). The second was by Logan Esarey, *A History of Indiana: From Its Exploration to 1850* (2 vols., Fort Wayne, 1924). Then came Charles Roll, *Indiana: One Hundred and Fifty Years of American Development* (2 vols., Chicago, 1931). The last of these general histories was authored by John D. Barnhart and Donald F. Carmony, *Indi-*

ana: From Frontier to Industrial Commonwealth (4 vols., New York, 1954). The publication by Barnhart and Carmony, and that by Roll, were accompanied by two volumes of biographical sketches, while that by Dunn included three such volumes. James H. Madison, *The Indiana Way: A State History* (Indianapolis, 1986), is a recent one volume history of Indiana. All these histories have their strengths and weaknesses.

Several historical accounts are mainly interpretive essays. In order of publication they are: John Bartlow Martin, *Indiana: An Interpretation* (New York, 1947); Irving Leibowitz, *My Indiana* (Englewood Cliffs, N. J., 1964); William E. Wilson, *Indiana: A History* (Bloomington, Ind., 1966); Howard H. Peckham, *Indiana: A Bicentennial History* (New York, 1978); Dwight W. Hoover, *A Pictorial History of Indiana* (Bloomington, Ind., 1980); and Patrick J. Furlong, *Indiana: An Illustrated History* (Northridge, Calif., 1985). Some of the essays in Donald F. Carmony (ed.), *Indiana: A Self-Appraisal* (Bloomington, Ind., 1966), are relevant to Indiana in the pioneer era.

The author is indebted to numerous secondary books in addition to those indicated in the two preceding paragraphs. With few exceptions, those listed below have been quoted, cited, or referred to in this volume. These books are not grouped by subjects because generally they are relevant to several subjects. Such books are listed in alphabetical order by author:

Charles Henry Ambler, *A History of Transportation in the Ohio Valley* . . . (Glendale, Calif., 1932).

Bert Anson, *The Miami Indians* (Norman, Okla., 1970).

Leland D. Baldwin, *The Keelboat Age on Western Waters* (Pittsburgh, 1941).

John D. Barnhart, *Valley of Democracy: The Frontier Versus the Plantation in the Ohio Valley, 1775–1818* (Bloomington, Ind., 1953). No study of the pioneer era in Indiana is complete without reference to Barnhart's intensive research and writings concerning migration patterns, southern influence on Indiana, and constitutional, governmental, and political developments.

John D. Barnhart and Dorothy L. Riker, *Indiana to 1816: The Colonial Period* (Indianapolis, 1971).

Charles Henry Bartlett, *Tales of Kankakee Land* (New York, 1904).

Maurice D. Baxter, *One and Inseparable: Daniel Webster and the Union* (Cambridge, Mass., 1984). In addition to providing an excellent biography of Webster, Baxter offers much valuable information about American politics and foreign relations from the 1820s to midcentury.

Elbert Jay Benton, *The Wabash Trade Route in the Development of the Old Northwest* (Baltimore, 1903).

Percy Wells Bidwell and John I. Falconer, *History of Agriculture in the Northern United States, 1620–1860* (1925; reprint, New York, 1941).

Ray Allen Billington, *The Far Western Frontier, 1830–1860* (New York, 1956).

I. George Blake, *The Holmans of Veraestau* (Oxford, Ohio, 1943).

Richard D. Boone, *A History of Education in Indiana* (New York, 1892; reprinted, Indianapolis, 1941). Old, but has very useful information.

Edward Gaylord Bourne, *The History of the Surplus Revenue of 1837 . . .* (New York, 1885).

Ronald R. Boyce (ed.), *Regional Development and the Wabash Basin* (Urbana, Ill., 1964).

R. Carlyle Buley, *The Old Northwest: Pioneer Period, 1815–1840* (2 vols., Indianapolis, 1950). Buley provides a variety of indispensable items about pioneer life, including quotations from newspapers no longer available.

Lee Burns, *The National Road in Indiana* (Indianapolis, 1919).

Alfred L. Burt, *The United States, Great Britain and British North America From the Revolution to the Establishment of Peace After the War of 1812* (New Haven, 1940).

Amos W. Butler, *Indiana: A Century of Changes in the Aspects of Nature* (Indianapolis, 1895).

John F. Cady, *The Centennial History of Franklin College* (Franklin, Ind., 1934).

Donald F. Carmony, *A Brief History of Indiana* (Indianapolis, 1966).

Edward H. Chadwick, *Chadwick's History of Shelby County, Indiana* (Indianapolis, 1909).

Victor C. Clark, *History of Manufacturing in the United States* (3 vols., New York, 1949). Has extremely useful information.

Grace Julian Clarke, *George W. Julian* (Indianapolis, 1923).

Freeman Cleaves, *Old Tippecanoe: William Henry Harrison and His Time* (New York, 1939).

William M. Cockrum, *History of the Underground Railroad as It Was Conducted by the Anti-Slavery League* (Oakland City, Ind., 1915).

Arthur Charles Cole, *The Whig Party in the South* (Washington, D. C., 1913).

Blackford Condit, *The History of Early Terre Haute from 1816 to 1840* (New York, 1900).

Fassett A. Cotton, *Education in Indiana, 1793–1934* (Bluffton, Ind., 1934).

George Dangerfield, *The Awakening of American Nationalism, 1815–1828* (New York, 1965).

John B. Dillon, *The National Decline of the Miami Indians* (Indianapolis, 1897).

Seymour Dunbar, *A History of Travel in America* (Indianapolis, 1915).

James Duncan, *A Treatise on Slavery: In which is Shewn Forth the Evil of Slave Holding, both from the Light of Nature and Divine Revelation* (Vevay, Ind., 1824). An early treatise against slavery.

Jacob Piatt Dunn, *Greater Indianapolis* (2 vols., Chicago, 1910).

Jacob Piatt Dunn, *Indiana and Indianans* (5 vols., Chicago, 1919).

R. David Edmunds, *The Potawatomis: Keepers of the Fire* (Norman, Okla., 1978).

Jane Shaffer Elsmere, *Henry Ward Beecher: The Indiana Years, 1837–1847* (Indianapolis, 1973).

Logan Esarey, *The Indiana Home* (Crawfordsville, Ind., 1943). Esarey's recollections and comments about pioneer life are classic and sprinkled with wit, wisdom, and some exaggeration.

John Mack Faragher, *Sugar Creek: Life on the Illinois Prairie* (New Haven, Conn., 1986). Although Faragher's Sugar Creek concerns life on the primitive Illinois prairie, it is equally applicable to similar areas of Indiana.

Paul Fatout, *Indiana Canals* (West Lafayette, Ind., 1972).

John H. Garland (ed.), *The North American Midwest: A Regional Geography* (Urbana, Ill., 1955).

Paul W. Gates, *The Farmer's Age: Agriculture, 1825–1860* (New York, 1960).

Dorothy Burne Goebel, *William Henry Harrison: A Political Biography* (Indianapolis, 1926).

Bert J. Griswold, *The Pictorial History of Fort Wayne, Indiana* (2 vols., Chicago, 1917).

Robert Gray Gunderson, *The Log-Cabin Campaign* (Lexington, Ky., 1957).

John Denis Haeger, *The Investment Frontier: New York Businessmen and the Economic Development of the Old Northwest* (Albany, N. Y., 1981). Haeger notes that eastern investors had an important role in making possible the Internal Improvements System of 1836, and in the negotiations resulting in Indiana's repudiation of millions of the debt owed therefor.

Holman Hamilton, *Zachary Taylor: Soldier in the White House* (Indianapolis, 1951).

Samuel B. Harding, *Indiana University, 1820–1904* (Bloomington, Ind., 1904).

Frank F. Hargrave, *A Pioneer Railroad: The Origin and Development of the Monon* (Indianapolis, 1932).

George Dewey Harmon, *Sixty Years of Indian Affairs: Political, Economic, and Diplomatic, 1789–1850* (Chapel Hill, N. C., 1941).

Walter Brookfield Hendrickson, *David Dale Owen: Pioneer Geologist of the Middle West* (Indianapolis, 1943).

Benjamin Hibbard, *A History of the Public Land Policies* (Madison, Wis., 1965).

Arthur J. Hope, *Notre Dame: One Hundred Years* (Notre Dame, Ind., 1943).

Louis C. Hunter, *Steamboats on the Western Rivers: An Economic and Technological History* (Cambridge, Mass., 1949).

Robert Leslie Jones, *History of Agriculture in Ohio to 1880* (Kent, Ohio, 1983). Jones' history of agriculture in Ohio is also very revealing about agriculture in pioneer Indiana.

Philip Dillon Jordan, *The National Road* (Indianapolis, 1948).

Albert Ludwig Kohlmeier, *The Old Northwest as the Keystone of the Arch of American Federal Union: A Study in Commerce and Politics* (Bloomington, Ind., 1938). Historians are much indebted to Kohlmeier for convincing evidence that geographical location and trade routes strengthened Indiana's devotion to the Union of the States, with a willingness to make reasonable compromise for its preservation.

Oscar Doane Lambert, *Presidential Politics in the United States, 1841–1844* (Durham, N. C., 1936).

William C. Latta, *Outline History of Indiana Agriculture* (Lafayette, Ind., 1938). Although old, Latta's work is an essential source concerning agriculture in its pioneer stage.

Chelsea L. Lawlis, *Vincennes University in Transition: The Making of a Comprehensive Community College* (Vincennes, Ind., 1982).

Richard William Leopold, *Robert Dale Owen: A Biography* (Cambridge, Mass. and London, 1940).

Alton A. Lindsey (ed.), *Natural Features of Indiana, 1816–1866* (Indianapolis, 1966). This book, edited by Lindsey, is a significant and needed volume concerning Indiana's natural features as they were in the pioneer era.

Daniel McDonald, *Removal of the Pottawattomie Indians from Northern Indiana . . .* (Plymouth, Ind., 1899).

George B. Manhart, *DePauw Through the Years* (Greencastle, Ind., 1962).

Frederick Merk, *The Oregon Question: Essays in Anglo-American Diplomacy and Politics* (Cambridge, Mass., 1967).

William Alfred Millis, *The History of Hanover College from 1827 to 1927* (Hanover, Ind., 1927).

Leander J. Monks, *et al.* (eds.), *Courts and Lawyers of Indiana* (3 vols., Indianapolis, 1916).

Chase C. Mooney, *William H. Crawford, 1772–1834* (Lexington, Ky., 1974).

Glover Moore, *The Missouri Controversy, 1819–1821* (Lexington, Ky., 1953).

Powell A. Moore, *The Calumet Region: Indiana's Last Frontier* (Indianapolis, 1959). Has significant items regarding counties south of Lake Michigan.

Gladys Bull Nicewarner, *Michigan City, Indiana: The Life of a Town* (Michigan City, Ind., 1980).

Harold Lee O'Donnell, *Newport and Vermillion Township: The First 100 Years, 1824–1924, Vermillion County, Indiana* (Danville, Ill., 1969).

James Insley Osborne and Theodore Gregory Gronert, *Wabash College: The First Hundred Years, 1832–1932* (Crawfordsville, Ind., 1932).

Robert Dale Owen, *A Brief Practical Treatise on the Construction and Management of Plank Roads . . .* (New Albany, Ind., 1850).

Madge E. Pickard and R. Carlyle Buley, *The Midwest Pioneer: His Ills, Cures, & Doctors* (Crawfordsville, Ind., 1945).

David M. Pletcher, *The Diplomacy of Annexation: Texas, Oregon, and the Mexican War* (Columbia, Mo., 1973). Pletcher offers a detailed and scholarly study concerning Texas and Oregon during the 1830s and 1840s, and the ensuing Mexican War, 1846–1848.

Charles R. Poinsatte, *Fort Wayne During the Canal Era: 1828–1855* (Indianapolis, 1969).

David M. Potter, *The Impending Crisis, 1848–1861* (New York, 1976).

Jehu Z. Powell, *History of Cass County, Indiana* (2 vols., Chicago, 1913).

William A. Rawles, *Centralizing Tendencies in the Administration of Indiana* (New York, 1903). Although old, Rawles' study of centralization in Indiana state government is useful regarding the tendency therefor in the pioneer era.

Fritz Redlich, *The Molding of American Banking: Men and Ideas* (2 vols., New York, 1951).

Robert V. Remini, *Andrew Jackson and the Course of American Democracy, 1833–1845* (New York, 1984).

Roy M. Robbins, *Our Landed Heritage: The Public Domain, 1776-1936* (Princeton, N. J., 1942).

Malcolm J. Rohrbaugh, *The Land Office Business: The Settlement and Administration of American Public Lands, 1789-1837* (New York, 1968). Rohrbaugh's volume is especially informative regarding how land sales and land office business were conducted amid evasions and abuses.

Charles Roll, *Colonel Dick Thompson: The Persistent Whig* (Indianapolis, 1948).

L. C. Rudolph, *Hoosier Zion: The Presbyterians in Early Indiana* (New Haven, Conn., 1963).

Thomas J. Schlereth, *The University of Notre Dame: A Portrait of Its History and Campus* (Notre Dame, Ind., 1977).

Arthur M. Schlesinger, Jr., and Fred L. Israel (eds.), *History of American Presidential Elections, 1789-1968* (4 vols., New York, 1971).

George A. Schultz, *An Indian Canaan: Isaac McCoy and the Vision of an Indian State* (Norman, Okla., 1972).

William Gerald Shade, *Banks or No Banks: The Money Issue in Western Politics, 1832-1865* (Detroit, 1972).

Bernard W. Sheehan, *Seeds of Extinction: Jeffersonian Philanthropy and the American Indian* (Chapel Hill, N. C., 1973).

Joel H. Silbey, *The Shrine of Party: Congressional Voting Behavior, 1841-1852* (Pittsburgh, 1967).

James H. Smart (ed.), *The Indiana Schools and the Men Who Have Worked in Them* (Cincinnati, 1876).

Willard H. Smith, *Schuyler Colfax: The Changing Fortunes of a Political Idol* (Indianapolis, 1952).

Edward Stanwood, *American Tariff Controversies in the Nineteenth Century* (2 vols., Boston, 1903).

George W. Starr, *Industrial Development of Indiana* (Bloomington, Ind., 1937).

B. R. Sulgrove, *History of Indianapolis and Marion County, Indiana* (Philadelphia, 1884).

William Warren Sweet, *Indiana Asbury-DePauw University, 1837-1937* (New York, 1937).

F. W. Taussig, *The Tariff History of the United States* (New York, 1889).

Charles W. Taylor (comp.), *Biographical Sketches and Review of the Bench and Bar of Indiana* (Indianapolis, 1895).

George Rogers Taylor, *The Transportation Revolution, 1815-1860* (New York, 1951). Taylor affords a very readable and informative overview of transportation in the pioneer era in a scholarly manner.

Emma Lou Thornbrough, *The Negro in Indiana Before 1900: A Study of a Minority* (Indianapolis, 1958). Although not as comprehensive as desirable regarding the pioneer era, Thornbrough has written the most useful account available concerning the role and status of Negroes in Indiana during the nineteenth century.

Opal Thornburg, *Earlham: The Story of a College, 1847–1962* (Richmond, Ind., 1963).

Payson Jackson Treat, *The National Land System, 1785–1820* (New York, 1910).

Rolla M. Tryon, *Household Manufactures in the United States, 1640–1860* (Chicago, 1917). Has extremely useful information.

Frederick Jackson Turner, *The United States, 1830–1850: The Nation and Its Sections* (New York, 1935).

Glyndon G. Van Deusen, *The Jacksonian Era, 1828–1848* (New York, 1959).

Justin E. Walsh, *The Centennial History of the Indiana General Assembly, 1816–1978* (Indianapolis, 1987). Walsh has given a significant and scholarly account of Indiana politics and government for the pioneer era. He has very useful tables about various aspects of politics and government.

C. A. Weslager, *The Delaware Indians: A History* (New Brunswick, N. J., 1972).

Leonard Dupee White, *The Jeffersonians: A Study in Administrative History, 1801–1829* (New York, 1951).

George R. Wilson, *Early Indiana Trails and Surveys* (Indianapolis, 1919).

George R. Wilson and Gayle Thornbrough, *The Buffalo Trace* (Indianapolis, 1946).

James Albert Woodburn, *History of Indiana University, 1820–1902* (2 vols., Bloomington, Ind., 1940).

Theophilus A. Wylie, *Indiana University: Its History from 1820, When Founded, to 1890* (Indianapolis, 1890).

V. DIARIES, LETTERS, AND REMINISCENCES

Donald F. Carmony (ed.), "Letter Written by Mr. Johann Wolfgang Schreyer," *Indiana Magazine of History*, XL (1944), 283–306.

Levi Coffin, *Reminiscences of Levi Coffin . . .* (Cincinnati, 1876).

Sandford C. Cox, *Recollections of the Early Settlement of the Wabash Valley* (Lafayette, Ind., 1860).

John Candee Dean (ed.), *Journal of Thomas Dean* (Indianapolis, 1918).

Logan Esarey (ed.), *The Pioneers of Morgan County: The Memoirs of Noah J. Major* (Indianapolis, 1915).

Baynard Rush Hall, *The New Purchase, or Seven and a Half Years in the Far West* (Princeton, N. J., 1916), ed. by James Albert Woodburn.

John F. Hopkins (ed.), *The Papers of Henry Clay* (11 vols., Lexington, Ky., 1959–1992).

Oliver Johnson, *A Home in the Woods: Oliver Johnson's Reminiscences of Early Marion County* (Indianapolis, 1951).

"Journal of An Emigrating Party of Pottawattomie Indians, 1838," *Indiana Magazine of History*, XXI (1925), 316–336.

George W. Julian, *Political Recollections, 1840 to 1872* (Chicago, 1884).

James F. D. Lanier, *Sketch of the Life of J. F. D. Lanier* (New York, 1870).

Hugh McCulloch, *Men and Measures of Half a Century* (New York, 1889).

Irving McKee, *The Trail of Death: Letters of Benjamin Marie Petit* (Indianapolis, 1941).

John H. B. Nowland, *Sketches of Prominent Citizens of 1876* (Indianapolis, 1877).

Dorothy Riker (ed.), *Unedited Letters of Jonathan Jennings* (Indianapolis, 1932).

Nellie A. Robertson and Dorothy Riker (eds.), *The John Tipton Papers* (3 vols., Indianapolis, 1942).

J. Herman Schauinger (ed.), "The Letters of Godlove S. Orth, Hoosier Whig," *Indiana Magazine of History,* XXXIX (1943), 365–400.

Dwight L. Smith (ed.), "A Continuation of the Journal of An Emigrating Party of Potawatomi Indians, 1838, and Ten William Polke Manuscripts," *ibid.,* XLIV (1948), 393–408.

John C. Smith, *Reminiscences of Early Methodism in Indiana* (Indianapolis, 1879).

Oliver H. Smith, *Early Indiana Trials and Sketches* (Cincinnati, 1858).

Francis Hovey Stoddard, *The Life and Letters of Charles Butler* (New York, 1903).

W. P. Strickland (ed.), *An Autobiography of Peter Cartwright: The Backwoods Preacher* (New York, 1857).

Gayle Thornbrough (ed.), *The Correspondence of John Badollet and Albert Gallatin, 1804–1836* (Indianapolis, 1963).

Gayle Thornbrough, Dorothy Riker, and Paula Corpuz (eds.), *The Diary of Calvin Fletcher* (9 vols., Indianapolis, 1972–1983).

David Turpie, *Sketches of My Own Times* (Indianapolis, 1903).

William Wesley Woollen, *Biographical and Historical Sketches of Early Indiana* (Indianapolis, 1883).

VI. ARTICLES

Carl Abbott, "The Plank Road Enthusiasm in the Antebellum Middle West," *Indiana Magazine of History,* LXVII (1971), 95–116.

Louis J. Bailey, "Caleb Blood Smith," *ibid.,* XXIX (1933), 213–239.

John D. Barnhart, "Sources of Indiana's First Constitution," *ibid.,* XXXIX (1943), 55–94.

John D. Barnhart, "The Southern Influence in the Formation of Indiana," *ibid.,* XXXIII (1937), 261–276.

Victor M. Bogle, "Railroad Building in Indiana, 1850–1855," *ibid.,* LVIII (1962), 211–232.

R. Carlyle Buley, "The Political Balance in the Old Northwest, 1820–1860," *Studies in American History Inscribed to James Albert Woodburn* (Bloomington, Ind., 1926), 405–455.

Charles E. Canup, "Temperance Movements and Legislation in Indiana," *Indiana Magazine of History*, XVI (1920), 1–37, 112–151.

Donald F. Carmony, "Fiscal Objection to Statehood in Indiana," *ibid.*, XLII (1946), 311–321.

Donald F. Carmony, "Historical Background of the Restrictions Against State Debt in the Constitution of 1851," *ibid.*, XLVII (1951), 129–142.

George Chalou, "Massacre on Fall Creek," *Prologue*, IV (1972), 109–114.

Robert D. Clark, "Matthew Simpson, The Methodists, and the Defeat of Samuel Bigger, 1843," *Indiana Magazine of History*, L (1954), 23–33.

Ethel Cleland, "New Facts about the Corydon State House," *ibid.*, IX (1913), 14–19.

Etta Reeves French, "Stephen S. Harding: A Hoosier Abolitionist," *ibid.*, XXVII (1931), 207–229.

Paul Wallace Gates, "Land Policy and Tenancy in the Prairie Counties of Indiana," *ibid.*, XXXV (1939), 1–26.

Thomas H. Greer, "Economic and Social Effects of the Depression of 1819 in the Old Northwest," *ibid.*, XLIV (1948), 227–243.

Elfrieda Lang, "An Analysis of Northern Indiana's Population in 1850," *ibid.*, XLIX (1953), 17–60.

Val Nolan, Jr., "Caleb Mills and the Indiana Free School Law," *ibid.*, XLIX (1953), 81–90.

Frederick L. Paxson, "The Railroads of the 'Old Northwest' Before the Civil War," *Transactions* of the Wisconsin Academy of Sciences, Arts, and Letters, XVII (1911), 243–274.

Dorothy Riker, "Jonathan Jennings," *Indiana Magazine of History*, XXVIII (1932), 223–239.

Ernest V. Shockley, "County Seats and County Seat Wars in Indiana," *ibid.*, X (1914), 1–46.

John Hardin Thomas, "The Academies of Indiana," *ibid.*, X (1914), 331–358; XI (1915), 8–39.

Emma Lou Thornbrough, "Indiana and Fugitive Slave Legislation," *ibid.*, L (1954), 201–228.

Norman E. Tutorow, "Whigs of the Old Northwest and Texas Annexation, 1836-April, 1844," *ibid.*, LXVI (1970), 56–69.

Roger H. Van Bolt, "The Hoosiers and the 'Eternal Agitation,' 1848–1850," *ibid.*, XLVIII (1952), 331–368.

Roger H. Van Bolt, "Hoosiers and the Western Program, 1844–1848," *ibid.*, 255–276.

Leon H. Wallace, "Legislative Apportionment in Indiana: A Case History," *Indiana Law Journal*, XLII (1966), 1–76, plus Appendices A–Y.

Walter Jackson Wakefield, "County Seminaries in Indiana," *Indiana Magazine of History*, XI (1915), 148–161.

George R. Wilson, "The First Public Land Surveys in Indiana; Freeman's Lines," *ibid.*, XII (1916), 1–33.

VII. DISSERTATIONS, THESES, AND UNPUBLISHED PAPERS

Donald E. Baker, The Fearful Contest: Indiana Views the Missouri Controversy, 1819–1821 (Unpublished paper, 1971, in possession of Donald F. Carmony).

Donald E. Baker, Waller Taylor: The Virginia-Indiana Senator (Unpublished paper, ca. 1969, in possession of Donald F. Carmony).

Vonneda Dunn Bailey, The Germans in Indiana (M. A. thesis, Indiana University, 1946).

Donald F. Carmony, Indiana Public Finance, 1800–1826 (Ph.D. dissertation, Indiana University, 1940).

James Victor Chittick, The Greater Indiana: A Study of the Movement of Hoosiers to Other States (M. A. thesis, Indiana University, 1940).

H. Brooklyn Cull, James F. D. Lanier: Banker, Patriot (M. A. thesis, Indiana University, 1952).

Oscar S. Dooley, Presidential Campaign and Election of 1844 (Ph.D. dissertation, Indiana University, 1942).

Richard Alan Gantz, Henry Clay and the Harvest of Bitter Fruit: The Struggle with John Tyler, 1841–1842 (Ph.D. dissertation, Indiana University, 1986).

Frederick Dinsmore Hill, William Hendricks: Indiana Politician and Western Advocate, 1812–1850 (Ph.D. dissertation, Indiana University, 1972).

David Walter Krueger, Party Development in Indiana, 1800–1832 (Ph.D. dissertation, University of Kentucky, 1974).

Elfrieda Lang, Immigration to Northern Indiana, 1800–1850 (Ph.D. dissertation, Indiana University, 1950).

Lois McDougald, Negro Migration into Indiana, 1800–1860 (M. A. thesis, Indiana University, 1945).

Marion Clinton Miller, The Antislavery Movement in Indiana (Ph.D. dissertation, University of Michigan, 1938).

Geneal Prather, The Building of the Michigan Road (M. A. thesis, Indiana University, 1941).

William Forest Shonkwiler, The Land Office Business in Indiana (M. A. thesis, Indiana University, 1950). A very useful summary regarding federal land sales in Indiana.

William W. Wimberly II, Missionary Reforms in Indiana, 1826–1860: Education, Temperance, Antislavery (Ph.D. dissertation, Indiana University, 1977).

INDEX

Ad valorem taxes, 94, 155; adoption of, 155, 157, 158; education, 380; firm establishment of, 249; General Assembly and, 94; increases in, 242; non-adoption of, 95; Thompson on, 157.

Adams, John Quincy, 674n, 764n, 800n, 801n, 804n, 806n, 809n, 810n; charges and countercharges, 507; competition with Clay, 480–481; elected president, 483; foreign relations difficulties, 499; impeachment of Tyler, 590; Indiana newspaper endorsements, 479–480; internal improvements, 464, 493; Jackson favored over, 482; nomination for president, 478; presidential candidacy, 476; removal of Indiana Indian agency, 498; tariff protection, 465; use of appointive power, 492–493.

Adams, Julius W., timber to improve roads, 355–356.

Adams-Clay coalition, 491–492; internal improvements aid, 494, 503; state conventions, 503–506; tariff protection, 503.

Agricultural school, 65–66.

Agricultural societies, 63–64; depression and collapse of, 66; Indiana product usage, 495; short life of, 66.

Agriculture, 62, 63; basis of manufacturing, 68–69; clearing areas for, 63; crop rotation, 63; diversification of, 62; economy and, 46, 63; exports, 67; extensiveness, 62; importance of, 73; improvements, 62; labor and, 207; manure, fertilizer, and straw, 63; seed improvements, 63; soci-eties, 63–64; subsistence farming, 62–63; tariff protection for products made from, 495; textbook on, 64; tools, 62, 63; traditional practices, 62.

Akin, Ransom W., 739n.

Alexander, Charles, 785n.

Allen, Hiram, 779n; biennial legislative sessions, 411; University Fund for common schools, 442.

Allen, Peter, 643n.

Allheart, Vulcanus, 71.

Ambler, Charles Henry, 648n.

American Anti-Slavery Society, 566.

American style independence, Indiana's support of, 453.

Ames, Bishop Edward R., 735n, 770n, 771n.

Annotator (Salem), on Canby's withdrawal, 126–127; pro-Jackson, 502.

Anthony, Samuel, 784n.

Antislavery, 622; element, 467–468, 470; societies, 566–567.

Appalachian Mountains barrier, 46, 67.

Apples, 55.

Appleseed, Johnny, 55, 56.

Arion, Copeland P. J., 726n.

Armstrong, James, 809n.

Asbury College, 399–400; Indiana Central Medical College and, 400.

Ashburton, Lord (Alexander Baring), 596.

Association for the Improvement of Common Schools in Indiana, 371; teachers' college, 372.

Attorney general, delinquent collectors and, 17; election as state official, 430.

Auditor, constitutional convention changes, 428–429; county collectors, 118, 121–122; salaries, 12, 120, 247; session pay reduction, 247; taxes, 123; term of, 4; tract books, 119, 121–122.

Badollet, John, 492, 768n, 812n, 813n; National Republicans, 516; register at Vincennes, 515.
Baird, Thomas D., 711n, 720n.
Baker, Conrad, 761n; Wabash and Erie Canal debt, 347–348.
Baldwin, Elihu, 376.
Baltimore and Ohio railroad, 182.
Bank of Vincennes, 18; Brown president of, 22; depository for federal money, 19; insolvency of, 22–23; state bank, 18; statement by cashier of, 21.
Bankers' Weekly Circular (New York), on Second State Bank, 325.
Banking, 436–439; abolition of, 329–330; Democrats and National Republicans, 528; development of, 17; free, 437; Jacksonians, 525–528; private enterprises taking over, 321; privileged or monopolistic, 17; proposals for consideration 436–438; state participation in, 164; state sponsored systems, 146; unfavorable context for, 17; Van Buren, 528.
Banks, capital invested in, 437; encouragement for, 330–332; failures, 168–169, 258–259; free banking, 330–332; gap in chartered, 525; House of Representatives, 20; modest legislation for, 22; notes from other states, 164; private, 330; restrictions on, 437; Second State Bank, 253–254; state not stockholder in, 437; territorial charters, 18.
Baring Brothers, 738n.
Barley, 51, 53.
Barnett, Theodore J., 732n.

Barnhart, John D., 57; on factory system, 72.
Barshare plows, 50.
Bartholomew, Joseph, 668n, 809n; presidential elector, 453; site selection for state capital, 108.
Bascom, Erastus K., 780n, 781n, 782n; number of legislators, 421; simple wording of bills, 416; University Fund, 440.
Bassett, Horace, 809n.
Battell, Charles I., 739n.
Bayless, Rev. John S., 280, 731n, 770n.
Beach, Samuel, 800n.
Beach, Walter E., 779n.
Beall, Enos, 273, 727n, 728n, 844n; unseated by House, 592.
Beard, John, 782n.
Beard, Patrick, 634n, 776n.
Beckes, Benjamin V., 808n.
Beckwith, Edward, 754n.
Beecher, Rev. Henry Ward, 360, 770n; State Common School Convention, 381.
Beeson, Othniel, 785n.
Benton, Thomas Hart, 807n, 832n; public domain lands, 498.
Berries, 55.
Berry, George, 787n, 788n.
Berry, William, 725n; size of legislature, 268.
Bicknell, Thompson P., 783n.
Biddle, Horace P., 784n, 786n; annual legislative sessions, 411; bills and governor's veto, 427.
Biddle, Nicholas, 166, 690n, 783n, 816n.
Bidwell, Percy Wells, 61, 650n, 651n, 652n, 653n.
Bigelow, J., 682n.
Bigger, Samuel, 705n, 707n, 708n, 710n, 711n, 713n, 714n, 715n, 721n, 722n, 724n, 730n, 732n, 733n, 734n, 735n, 736n, 738n, 765n, 842n; candidate for second term, 279; distribution, 586; governor, 202, 221; gubernatorial candidacy, 219, 282, 332; internal im-

provement debt, 229, 288, 294; internal improvements, 219, 224–225, 236, 238; Internal Improvements System of 1836, pp. 218–219, 222; judge of circuit court, 219; life of, 217; Madison and Indianapolis Railroad Company, 236; nomination for governor, 217; obligations to creditors, 237; public debt, 237–238; renomination of, 279; revision of law code, 272; road taxes, 351; state debt, 225–226, 229–230; state prison, 316; treaty with England, 596; Wabash and Eel River Canal Company, 236; Wabash and Erie Canal, 239; White Water Valley Canal Company, 236.

Birney, James G., 851n; presidential candidacy, 605.

Black Hawk War of 1832, p. 554.

Blackford, Isaac, 635n, 640n, 658n, 663n, 675n, 692n, 727n, 729n, 758n, 759n, 791n, 803n, 804n; constitutional convention, 408; Friends of Common Education, 373; gubernatorial candidacy, 82, 125; loss of political stature, 490; on Ray, 84; other offices run for, 130; reappointment as judge, 128, 342; senatorial candidacy, 486–487, 489–490; speaker of the House of Representatives, 8; State Common School Convention, 382; unanimous reelection of, 276.

Blacks, colonization linked to emancipation of slaves, 562; colonizing Africa by, 447, 562–564; denying suffrage to, 562; excluded from militia, 562; free blacks as slaves, 468; intense prejudice against, 442–445; leaving Indiana, 442; mindset against, 442–444; opposition to immigration of, 442; personal liberty legislation, 470; property ownership, 562; referendum on rights of, 449–450; restrictions on, 446, 447; rights and privileges, 442, 443–444, 445–446; status of, 562; voting, 34.

Blacksmiths, 70–71; plows, 51.

Blair, James, 834n.

Blake, I. George, 675n.

Blake, James, 635n, 653n, 683n, 723n, 731n, 771n.

Blake, Thomas C., 9.

Blake, Thomas H., 216, 335, 661n, 702n, 828n; congressional candidacy, 484, 488–489, 510–511; election as congressman, 489; Indian agency transfer, 497; Jackson's downslide, 492; praising Clay, 492; presidential elector, 453; senatorial candidacy, 531, 551–552; successor to Prince, 485–486; support for Adams, 509–510; tax on land, 92.

Blind citizens, 314.

Blythe, Benjamin I., 86, 128, 262, 672n, 673n, 675n.

Blythe, James E., 399, 787n.

Board of Internal Improvement, 197, 210–211; Burr and unaccounted for funds, 189; future of, 222; internal improvements, 212–213; Noble and, 210; reducing size of, 209, 210, 215; sale of canal lands, 238–239; state debt report, 211–212; terminating, 234; Wabash and Erie Canal, 210–211.

Board of Public Instruction, 373.

Bobbs, John S., 732n.

Bolton, Nathaniel, 731n.

Booker, Samuel P., 669n.

Boon, Ratliff, 19, 643n, 657n, 664n, 782n, 791n, 797n, 801n, 802n, 803n, 806n, 808n, 810n, 813n, 815n, 817n, 818n, 819n, 821n, 822n, 823n, 828n, 833n, 835n, 837n; candidate for successor to Prince, 485–486; congressional candidacy, 484, 488–489, 510–511, 532; congressional nominations, 477; constitution recognizes slavery, 564; county interim appointments, 106; distribution bill, 560; distribution money, 561; election as congressman, 82, 484, 511; elections, 100; Hendricks and, 530; internal im-

Boon, Ratliff, (cont.)
provements, 532; Jackson, 509;
Jacksonians, 529; Judah, 538; Kentucky, 469; lieutenant governor, 29–
30; new settler, 48; protective tariffs, 522, 532; reelection as
congressman, 532, 540; reelection
as lieutenant governor, 81; reelection of, 542, 550; retirement of,
552; Second United States Bank,
526; senatorial candidacy, 529, 538–
539, 551–552; squatters, 558; tariff
laws, 525; tariff on woolens, 496;
taxes, 560–561.
Boone, Richard G., 394; free common
schools, 391; seminaries, 395;
Wabash College, 399.
Borden, James W., 778n, 780n, 781n;
apportioning legislators, 422; constitutional amendments, 448; four-
year executive term, 424; justice of
the peace limit, 433; legislative districts, 422; voters practicing law in
courts, 433–434.
Borden, John W., county board, 418.
Botts, John M., impeachment charges
against Tyler, 590.
Bower, Henry J., 778n.
Boyce, Ronald R., 697n.
Bracken, William, 783n.
Bradley, John H., 712n, 730n, 731n,
735n, 737n; gubernatorial candidacy, 332; nomination for lieutenant governor, 282.
Bramble, W. C., 649n.
Brandon, Armstrong, 19, 643n.
Brewster, K. G., 654n.
Bridge, John, 794n.
Bridges, 135–136, 180; as public utilities, 353–354; Congressional appropriations for, 180; conveying
stone for building, 143; financing,
180, 351–352; floating, 136; National and Michigan roads, 180; necessity for, 351; Ohio River at
Louisville, 180; reliance on local
government, 352; road taxes, 351;
toll, 135, 180, 351, 352.

Bright, Jesse D., 735, 739, 740n, 741n,
779n, 780n, 852n, 853n, 855n,
856n, 858n; candidacy for lieutenant governor, 280; election to
Senate, 608–609; joint occupation
of Oregon, 619; Mexican War, 623;
presiding over Senate, 608; slavery,
627; winning U.S. Senate race, 332.
Bright, Michael G., 705n, 713n, 724n,
734n, 737n, 753, 755n; Committee
on the Legislative Department,
410; debt bondholders, 299; number of legislators, 419; Second State
Bank stock, 266; state agent for internal improvements, 235; title of
bill, 415.
British law, references to, 97.
Brown, David, 22.
Brown, Ethan Allen, 240, 711n; Democratic state convention, 280.
Brown, Thomas B., 824n.
Brown, William J., 703n, 711n, 850n,
855n; congressional candidacy, 594;
election as congressman, 594; reelection of, 221; secretary of state,
206.
Brownlee, James, 634n.
Bryant, James R. M., 787n; Common
School Fund, 439; secondary education, 441–442.
Buchanan, James, 849n.
Buckwheat, 51.
Buell, George P., 747n, 758n.
Buley, Dr. R. Carlyle, blacksmiths, 70–
71; concentration of settlements,
49; denuding forests, 50; furnishings in log cabins, 49; girls, 78;
grafting fruit trees, 56; hard life of
women, 78; hogs, 58; honey, 56;
horses, 60–61; life in villages and
country towns, 46; long rifle and
woodsman's ax, 49–50; mulberries,
55; salt, 68; Second State Bank surviving bank failures, 259; selection
of home site, 48–49; Tippecanoe
Battleground campaign, 578; typical
plow, 50.
Bull plows, 50.

Burnett, Alexander J., 323.
Burnett, Alexander S., 206, 684n, 703n.
Burr, David, 189, 819n.
Bush, George, 677n.
Business, government staying out of, 435; self-regulation of, 435.
Butler Bill of 1846, p. 306; support of first draft of, 307–308; Whitcomb administration, 336.
Butler Bill of 1847, bonded debt surrendered for certificates, 310; bondholders declining to surrender bonds, 320–321; changes from Butler Bill of 1846, p. 310; opposition to, 309–310; passage of, 309; proponents' views, 310–311; settlement contrary to guarantees, 312; state obligations to bondholders, 311–312; Wabash and Erie Canal, 310, 321.
Butler, Benjamin F., 830n.
Butler, Brown, 732n, 739n.
Butler, Charles, 740n, 741n, 742n, 743n, 761n; compromise settlement, 302–305; English stockholders' wishes for canal, 309; Indiana's arrangement for bondholders, 308–309; internal improvement debt, 301–302; Wabash and Erie Canal, 308–309; Whitcomb and Bright, 304.
Butler, Ovid, 382, 770n, 771n.

Cain, John, 731n, 824n.
Calhoun, John C., 735n, 849n; excluding slavery, 626; presidential candidacy, 476; support for cessation, 560.
Call, Jacob, 800n, 802n; candidate as successor to Prince, 485–486; congressional candidacy, 484; National Road, 464; seated by House of Representatives, 486.
Canada, adding to United States, 474; disputes over border with, 501.
Canals, 144–145; aid for, 41; commission to build, 145; federal aid for, 115; network of, 174–175; suitability of Indiana for, 192; survey from Fort Wayne to Michigan City, 196; unsuccessful attempt at building, 144; Wabash and Erie Canal, 185–189; Whitewater Valley, 191.
Canby, Dr. Israel T., 673n, 674n, 683n, 696n, 800n, 811n, 812n, 813n; election as governor, 146; gubernatorial candidacy, 125, 126; Jackson, 504; Jacksonian state convention, 503; National Republicans, 514; on Noble and Stapp, 146; withdrawal of candidacy, 126.
Carmony, Donald F., 57; factory system, 72.
Carr, George W., 786n, 820n; president, 1850–51 Constitutional Convention, 408; constitutional convention committee, 409.
Carr, John, 800n, 815n, 816n, 817n, 818n, 819n, 820n, 821n, 823n, 833n, 835n, 837n; congressional candidacy, 532, 583; distribution bill, 560; election as congressman, 532, 553; on Jackson, 533; on Jennings, 532; reelection of, 540, 542; Second United States Bank, 526.
Carr, Thomas, Sr., 634n, 643n.
Carter, Clarence Edwin, 634n.
Cass, Lewis, 240, 735n, 806n, 849n, 850n; competition for Van Buren, 601; Democratic support, 602; Indian commissioner, 116; presidential candidacy, 543, 604; treaty with Potawatomi, 137.
Caswell, Daniel I., 768n.
Caswell, Daniel J., congressional candidate, 485; presidential elector, 453.
Cathcart, Charles W., 853n, 854n, 855n, 856n, 857n, 858n, 859n; congressional election, 607; Oregon, 619, 620.
Cattle, 59.
Centinel (Vincennes), on voting by ballot, 34–35.

Central Canal, 195–196, 236.
Cereal crops, 52.
Chadwick, Edward H., 696n.
Chamberlain, Ebenezer M., 711n, 722n, 737n, 750n, 758n, 759n, 860n; internal improvement debt, 294; on Coe and Stapp, 232; on Noble and Williams, 231; opposition to slavery, 632; Second State Bank, 322; Supreme Court judge, 343.
Chamberlain, William B., 648n.
Chapman, George A., 731n, 732n.
Chapman, Jacob Page, 732n, 788n; county board municipal status, 418; hasty legislation, 414; limitations for General Assembly, 410; number of legislators, 421.
Chapman, Joseph W., 758n, 780n, 781n.
Chenowith, Thomas, 778n, 786n.
Chickens, 61.
Child labor and agriculture, 62.
Chittenden, L. S., 736n.
Churchman, William H., 314.
Circuit court, 5; associate judges, 5, 403; clerk, 5, 10; clerk, associate justices, recorder, and commissioners, 9; commissioners, 10; Constitution of 1816, p. 432; constitutional provisions, 432–433; held three times a year, 432; judge acting as probate judge, 432; judges, 5; number of, 432; president judges election, 8; prosecuting attorney, 433; sheriff, 10; term of office, 432.
Civil commissions, 121, 122.
Clark, Marston G., 29, 800n; on Harrison, 545.
Clark, Othniel L., 699n, 779n, 785n; legislative sessions, 411, 412; minority passing laws, 414.
Clay, 75, 77.
Clay, Henry, 92, 658n, 661n, 671n, 799n, 800n, 801n, 804n, 805n, 810n, 820n, 821n, 826n, 827n, 830n, 838n, 844n, 849n, 851n; advocates of, 492; annexation of Texas, 600; competition with Adams, 480–

481; counties carried by, 482; distribution bill, 560; followers of, 540; Hoosier Whigs and, 601; internal improvements aid, 464; Jackson favored over, 482; national bank, 577, 584–585; nomination for president, 478, 536, 603–604; political corruption, 483; presidential candidacy, 476, 601, 602; presidential veto power, 590; prospects in Indiana, 575; slavery, 480; state convention support, 574; state nomination of, 535; tariff protection, 465; Wabash and Erie Canal, 240; Whig support, 601.
Cleland, Ethel, 668n.
Clements, Richard A., 739n.
Clerk, terms of, 5–6.
Climate, 45.
Clinton, De Witt, presidential candidate, 476.
Clover, 54.
Coal, 75, 76.
Coats, Joseph, 788n.
Coburn, Henry P., 672n.
Coe, Dr. Isaac, 232, 677n, 720n, 733n, 755n; specie payments, 256.
Coffee, importing, 56.
Coffin, Levi, 565, 836n.
Cohens of Baltimore, 207–208, 209, 703n.
Colerick, David H., 720n.
Colfax, Schuyler, 335, 753n, 754n, 777n, 781n, 786n; blacks, 443–444, 444; legislative districts, 422–423; state bank and free banking, 438.
Collectors, state revenue collectors fees, 88.
Colleges and universities, 396; advocates, 441–442; Asbury College, 399–400; detractors, 440–441; Earlham College, 400; Franklin College, 400; Hanover Academy, 398–399; Hanover College, 399; Indiana Baptists Manual Labor Institute, 400; Indiana Central Medical College, 400; Indiana University, 397–398; Notre Dame, 400; religious

denominations, 396; trust funds, 440; Vincennes University, 396; Wabash College, 399.

Collins, James H., Jr., 730n, 731n.

Commerce, growth of, 67; relationship with politics, 66.

Commissioners, roads, 41, 42.

Committee on Canals and Internal Improvements, classifying improvements, 226; prioritizing projects, 198; reports on additional works, 199.

Common Law, 95–99, 130–131, 270–272.

Common School Advocate, on State Common School Convention, 382.

Common School Fund, 383, 439.

Common schools, 365–366; administrative supervision of, 387; apathy toward education, 375; bill for improving and extending, 385–387; Board of Public Instruction, 373; building of, 366–367; caliber of, 384; changes in legislation for, 373–374; competent teachers, 366, 372; comprehensive legislation for, 366–368; Congressional Township Fund, 370; Constitution of 1851, p. 394; county superintendents, 386, 388; dismal picture of, 379; district libraries, 386–387; equal distribution of funds to, 392; essential elements, 383–385; family or religious auspices, 368; free to all students, 383; funds, 370, 377; hindrances to establishing, 375; inadequacy of, 393–394; increased centralization of, 386; increasing taxes for, 389; indictment of, 382–383; interest waning in, 372–373; legislation of 1824, pp. 366–367; legislation of 1831, pp. 367–368; modest progress toward, 393–394; moral education, 376; morality and religion, 389; neglect of, 379–380; obstacles to, 385; organized movements for, 378; public, 369–370; qualified teachers, 375, 384; reasons for low esteem of, 380;

religion and, 389; response by governor and legislature to, 390; school law of 1849, pp. 392–393; selecting textbooks, 386; State Board of Education, 386–387; state superintendent, 377, 384, 386; strengthening, 378; support from legislature, 380–381; taxes, 370–371, 383, 385, 387, 388; teachers, 367–368, 384; townships, 370; uniform system of, 439; University Fund, 442; *versus* cost of private schools, 385; *versus* elementary education, 439–440.

Comparet, Francis, 554.

Compromise Tariff of 1833, p. 524; duties raised above limit of, 587; Tyler's opposition to, 584.

Congress, bridge appropriations, 180; presidential electors, 342; presidential veto power, 590–591; Whig majorities, 582.

Congressional elections of 1843, pp. 592–594.

Congressional Township Fund, 370, 388.

Congressmen, campaigns of 1833, p. 539; Democratic landslide, 553; election of 1824, pp. 484–486; election of 1826, pp. 487–489; election of first Indiana, 6; election party controversies, 529; Jacksonian, 532; presidential elections influence on, 491; Whig strengths, 541–542.

Conner, John, 27, 668n.

Conner, William, 107.

Conrad, Jesse, 732n.

Conference committee reports (Constitution of 1851), banking, 436–439; free banking, 437; justice of the peace courts, 433; prosecuting attorney, 433; public education, 439–442; state bank, 437; white male voters practicing law in courts, 433–434.

Constitution of 1816, pp. 1–2; antislavery element, 467; banking article, 330; biennial election of legislators, 403; chances to amend, 403; circuit court associate judges, 403; circuit

Constitution of 1816, (cont.)
courts, 432; conciseness of, 403; Constitution of 1851 differences, 451; constitutional convention, 403; education, 363–364; impeachment trials, 403; interim apportionment, 106; Jeffersonian Republicanism, 452; never amended, 403; privileged or monopolistic banking, 17; proposed amendments to, 403–404; reapportionment mandates, 341; referendums, 403–404, 404; revision and referendum of 1846, pp. 405–406; Second United States Bank, 525–526; seminaries, 394–395; state officials, 26; state university, 396–397; support for, 403; territorial laws, 96; transition to statehood, 6–9.

Constitution of 1851, amending, 447–448; amendments, 448–449; blacks, 447, 449–450; common schools, 394; Constitution of 1816 differences, 451; date of effect of, 449–450; features, 450–451; free banking, 332; General Assembly, 410; lawyers' requirements, 433–434; public support for, 450; reapportionment mandates, 341; referendums, 449–450; voting, 342; Wabash and Erie Canal, 348.

Constitutional convention, attorney general, 430; bills, 415–416; calling, 448; choosing delegates, 407–408; county board powers, 417–419; courts, 430; drafting constitution, 408–409; executive department, 423–426; General Assembly, 405, 410–412; governor, 425–429; governor and lieutenant governor terms of office, 424; Internal Improvement System of 1836, p. 405; Jacksonian Democracy and, 405; judicial changes, 429–433; laws, 415; laws enactment, 414–415; legislative apportionment, 419–422; legislative approval, 406–407; legislative districts, 420, 422–423; legislative sessions, 412–414; lieutenant governor, 424–425; momentum for, 405; number of legislators, 419–422; officers and rules for, 408; referendums for, 403–407, 448, 449; revisions to constitution, 409–410; Second State Bank, 405; Senate, 406; single legislative branch, 423; state debt, 434–435; state law, 417; state law *versus* local law, 416–417; Supreme Court, 430–431, 431–432; suspensive veto, 426–428; treasurer, auditor, and secretary of state, 428–429; voting, 449; what government should and should not do, 434–436.

Constitutional government and laissez faire economics, 434–435.

Constitutional provisions for circuit court, 432–433.

Cookerly, Grafton F., 424.

Cooper, Henry, 732n.

Cooper, Robert M., 711n.

Coquillard, Alexis, 723n; trading with Indians, 554.

Corn, 51–52; uses for, 52; yields, 52.

Coroner, election of first, 6–7.

Corydon, 107.

Corydon Constitutional Convention, costs, 12; Jennings, 1; private banking bill, 331.

Cotton, Robert G., 739n.

Cotton, William, 659n.

Counties, clerk, 5–6; free common schools, 391; General Assembly, 32; governing board, 9; legislative districts, 422–423; legislative seats, 31–32; manufacturing, 72; new, 9; northern, 161; office vacancies, 100; organized, 162; plural representation, 33; prosecutors, 10; reapportionment, 105; recorder, 5–6; sheriff, 5; sheriff and coroner, 6, 10; state roads, 177; surveyors, 10; taxation without representation, 106; Three Per Cent Fund, 177; treasurer, 10; voters, 32–33.

County auditor and yearly tax duplicates, 250.

County boards, ferries, 179; powers, 417–419.

County clerks, election returns, 100–101.

County collectors, 121–122.

County commissioners, responsibilities for roads, 39; road districts, 350; road taxes, 40; supplies from, 35, 36.

County government, clerk, associate justices, recorder, and commissioners, 9–10; transition to, 9.

County taxes, 16–17.

County treasurer, 250.

Courier (Knightstown), on Clay, 601.

Courier (Madison), on Bright, 285; on Second State Bank, 322.

Courthouse, 110; government use of, 112.

Courts, vesting judicial power in, 430; voters practicing law in, 433–434.

Cox, Jonathan P., 275.

Cox, Sandford, 461.

Craftsmen, 69–70.

Craig, Merit S., 116, 671n, 809n.

Cravens, James H., 842n, 843n, 845n, 848n; classification of internal improvements, 226; election as congressman, 584.

Crawford, James, 789n, 802n.

Crawford, William H., congressional endorsement for president, 477; federal depositories, 19; presidential candidacy, 476; Second United States Bank, 465.

Crawfordsville Road, 197.

Cressey, Timothy R., 771n, 772n.

Crops, 51–55; farm animal destruction of, 57; pests and diseases, 57.

Crosscut Canal, contracts, 197; finishing, 236.

Crowe, John Finley, 38.

Crumbacker, Daniel, 779n.

Crume, Marks, 722n; Indian cessions, 555.

Cuba, 474.

Culley, David V., 151, 685n.

Cumberland Road, 143, 521.

Cunningham, Noble E., Jr., 796n.

Daily, William, 747n.

Dairy cattle, 59.

Dairy products, 56.

Dallas, George M., 604.

Dams for mills, 183.

Dangerfield, Wallace, 807n, 808n.

Daniel, Richard, 23, 640n.

Davidson, Andrew, 342–343.

Davis, Abner M., 844n.

Davis, John Steele, 711n, 712n, 732n, 737n.

Davis, John W., 818n, 823n, 830n, 833n, 835n, 837n, 847n, 850n, 853n, 854n, 855n, 856n, 857n, 859n; congressional candidacy, 583–584; election as congressman, 542, 553; Indian cessions, 555; re-election of, 594, 607, 610; speaker of House of Representatives, 607, 610.

Davis, Milo, 634n.

Davis, Oliver P., 784n.

Dawson, John W., 557.

Deaf and dumb citizens, 314.

Dean, John Candee, 647n.

Dean, Thomas, 38.

Debt, American bondholders, 296–297; Bigger on, 225–226; compromise settlement on, 301–302; debt on bonded, 295–296; English creditors, 296; Hoosiers sacrificing to pay, 293; Indiana unable to pay, 295; liquidation of, 321; national, 560; Noble on, 228–229; not meeting obligations of, 297–298; obtaining money to pay, 228; reasons for contracting, 435; state limit, 435; strict limitations on, 434–435; taxes and, 435; unpaid interest, 293; Wabash and Erie Canal, 306–307.

Decatur County Anti-Slavery Society, 566.

Deere, John, 51.

Defrees, John D., 624, 710n, 711n, 732n, 739n; exchanging bonds, 299; Whigs and Democrats, 337–338.

Delaware Indians, 459, 460.

Deming, Dr. Elizur, 289, 734n, 735n.

Democrat (Goshen), on extending small notes, 329; on Merrill, Palmer, and Dunn, 292; on Milroy and Kennedy, 279; on resumption of specie payment, 258; on Second State Bank, 322, 323, 328–329; on Whigs, 323, 336; on Whitcomb and Bright, 285.

Democratic Republicans, 115; campaign for governor, 150–151; congressional elections, 149; Jackson, tariffs, and internal improvements, 507–508; on Jackson, 504; similarities with National Republicans, 452, 513; state convention, 151, 545–546; voting party lines, 147.

Democrats, banking, 333; candidate against Wallace, 203; candidates for governor, 333; Clay, 606; congressional delegation, 594; congressional elections, 553; congressional elections of 1843, pp. 592–594; differences from Whigs, 602–603; federal politics, 540; Johnson, 577, 580–581; key legislative committees (1840–41), 268; National Bank, 577; national convention, 536, 604–605; political dominance, 607; promises to voters, 281–282; Second State Bank, 541–542; Second United States Bank, 547; Senate majority, 594; slavery and Mexican War, 631–632; State Central Committee, 280, 281; state convention, 203, 216–218, 279–280, 280–282, 333–334, 602; state policy, 281; states' rights, 573; Van Buren, 543–544, 577; Van Buren and Johnson, 575; victory in legislature, 291; Whig opponents, 542; Whigs, 282, 334.

DePauw, John, 29–30, 634n, 643n, 815n.

Depression, collapse of agricultural societies and, 66.

Depression of 1819, economic recovery from, 87.

Depression of 1839, p. 257.

Devin, Alexander, 634n.

Dewey, Charles, 216, 727n, 729n, 758n, 759n, 828n; interim appointments as judge, 343–344; qualifications of, 345; republicanism, 457; senatorial candidacy, 457, 551–552; Supreme Court, 164, 276, 343.

Dick, James, 786n.

Dill, James, 27.

Dillon, John B., 699n; Indians, 459; Internal Improvements System of 1836, p. 194.

Dix, Dorothea L., 746n; Indiana state prisons, 316.

Dobson, David M., 780n, 783n, 788n; courts deciding cases, 426; executive and pardoning power, 426; regional problems and county boards, 418; treasurer, 429.

Dowling, John, 776n.

Dowling, Thomas H., 709n, 710n, 742n.

Drake, James P., 731n, 747n, 812n.

Drinking water, 38.

DuBois, John, 824n.

Ducks, 61.

Dufour, John Francis, 19, 144, 682n.

Dumont, Ebenezer, 324.

Dumont, John, 693n, 702n, 703n, 748n, 828n; ad valorem tax system, 94–95; agriculture and manufacturing, 495; gubernatorial candidacy, 204; internal improvement classification, 204–205; poll taxes, 93.

Dunbar, Ezekiel L., 844n.

Duncan, James, 836n; abolition of slavery, 567.

Dunlap, Livingston, 824n.

Dunn, Alexander, 635n.

Dunn, George G., 859n.

Dunn, George H., 710n, 711n, 818n, 820n, 835n; congressional candidacy, 552; distribution money, 561; election as congressman, 550; treasurer, 221, 292.

Dunn, Gregory H., 272.

Dunn, Jacob Piatt, 669n, 670n, 671n, 743n, 753n, 786n; state obligations to bondholders, 311.

Dunn, John P., 437.
Dunn, William McKee, 784n, 788n; clerk of Supreme Court, 431; state debt, 435.
Dunn, Williamson, 812n.
Dunning, Paris C., 151, 684n, 685n, 720n, 746n, 782n, 808n; colleges and universities, 400; constitutional convention, 407; nomination for lieutenant governor, 333; railroads, 359.
Durham, Jesse B., 668n, 800n, 808n.
Duzan, Mark A., 779n.

Eads, William, 19.
Earlham College, 400.
East-west railroads, 46.
Eaton, John H., 830n.
Economy, agriculture, 46, 63; corn, 51–52; Depression of 1819, p. 87; expansion and development of, 37–38; exports, 67; geographical context, 46; growth of, 67–68; imports, 67–68; imports over exports, 37; individual enterprise, 345; laissez-faire, 164, 345, 434–435; lumber, 46; Ohio-Mississippi River waterway, 47; rapidly advancing, 321; rivers, 37; roads, 37; rural and agrarian, 293–294; trade routes, 47; trade with Atlantic Seaboard, 37–38.
Edmonston, Benjamin R., 779n, 782n, 789n; lieutenant governor, 425.
Education, ad valorem taxes, 380; annual conventions for, 377; apathy toward, 375; common school versus elementary education, 439–440; competent teachers, 366; county superintendents, 386; federal revenue, 374; high ideals for, 363–364; higher, 440–441; important and desirable, 375; no tax support for, 363; parents and religious denominations, 363; primary, 371; private schools, 375–376; proceeds from section 16 supporting, 363; public,

439–442; school law of 1849, pp. 392–393; school year length, 374; secondary, 394–395; secondary and higher, 387; slow development of, 363; State Board of Education, 386–387; state superintendent, 384, 386, 439; taxes, 375; township superintendents of schools, 364.
Educational legislation, Board of Public Instruction, 373; county board examiners' statistics, 373–374; federal revenue for education, 374; Friends of Common Education and, 373–374; licensed teachers, 374; money apportioned to districts, 374; school year length, 374; state Common School Convention, 382.
Eggleston, Joseph C., 711n.
Eggleston, Miles C., 203; Supreme Court, 164.
Eggs, dependency on, 56, 57; types, 56.
Elected officials, absences from office, 119–120, 122; aid given to, 123; duties fulfilled by others, 120; impeachment trials of, 403; monies advanced to, 121; salaries, 120–121.
Election elite, 486–487; perpetuating, 493.
Election law of 1817, p. 37.
Elections, additional places for holding, 163; attorney general, 430; changes in code, 163; clerks, 35; conduct of, 35; congressional, 552–553; constitutional convention, 448; counting votes, 36; county clerk, 100, 162; election elite, 486–487; first congressman, 8; first governor, 7; free common schools, 390–392; General Assembly, 163; governor and lieutenant governor, 100, 101; gubernatorial campaign of 1822, p. 81; gubernatorial campaign of 1825, p. 82; gubernatorial campaign of 1840, pp. 215–221; improper voting, 36–37; inspector, 35; items concerning, 99–100; judges, 35, 36; legislative session of 1820–21, p. 34;

Elections, (cont.)
lieutenant governor of 1825, pp. 85–86; local, state, and presidential laws, 272–273; moved to odd years, 532; opening polls, 35; political dominance and reapportionment, 103; presidential electors, 115; presidential of 1824, pp. 476–484; presidential preferences and party ties influencing, 115; reliable data, 100–101; religion and slavery issues, 289–290; reporter, 431; returns lacking, 100; Sabbath of Liberty, 37; secret ballots, 99; senatorial and congressional, 529; sheriff, 431; state bank issue, 167–168; Supreme Court clerk, 431; township and county vacancies, 100; valid ballots, 273–274; voter or candidate contesting, 101; voters, 37, 275; voting, 35–36, 37, 101–102, 274–275; Whig strength, 541–542; Whigs, 332.

Elementary education, family or religious auspices, 368; *versus* common schools, 439–440.

Elliott, Chester, 679n.

Elliott, William, 720n.

Ellis, Dr. E. W. H., 292, 297, 733n, 785n; delinquency of taxpayers, 320.

Ellsworth, Henry L., commissioner of Patent Office, 518, 813n.

Ellsworth, Henry W., 240.

Elston, Isaac C., 264; Jackson's veto, 527.

Embree, Elisha, 859n; bill codifying laws, 270.

Emery, H. G., 654n.

Emison, Thomas, 43, 668n, 696n, 697n.

England, avoidance of war with, 501; boundary between Maine and Canada, 595; controversy over Oregon, 596–597, 618–619.

English, William H., 850n; secretary of constitutional convention, 408.

Enquirer (Brookville), criticism of Blackford, 83.

Esarey, Logan, 633n, 638n, 639n, 641n, 648n, 649n, 650n, 651n, 652n, 653n, 654n, 681n, 682n, 696n, 697n, 719n, 743n, 745n, 819n; farm families, 47, 48; Farmers and Mechanics Bank, 24, 44; hogs, 59; lawyers and saloon keepers, 434; mulberries, 55; pioneer life, 48; pioneer schools, 394; pork, 57; state obligations to bondholders, 311; Whitcomb and Marshall, 335.

Europe, corruptness of life in, 474; distrust of powerful nations, 500–501; French Revolution, 475; Greece, 475; isolation from, 472–473, 475; liberty and freedom in, 568–569; Polish struggle for independence, 569; republics or liberal monarchies, 472; revolutions, 568; Test's suggestions to, 500.

Evans, Robert M., 802n; Boon, 484.

Evans, Thomas J., 509, 810n, 828n.

Ewbank, Louis B., 635n, 638n, 644n, 648n, 678n.

Ewing, Charles, 457.

Ewing, George W., 830n, 840n; trading with Indians, 554; Van Buren elector, 581.

Ewing, John, 82, 657n, 691n, 803n, 804n, 818n, 823n, 835n, 837n; congressional candidacy, 552; distribution money, 561; election as congressman, 540; Jennings or Noble over Blackford, 489; reelection as congressman, 550; Second United States Bank, 466–467; U.S. unprepared for war, 570; voting for Hendricks, 487.

Ewing, Nathaniel, 19, 23; presidential elector, 453.

Ewing, William G., 554.

Exclusion article, 447, 450.

Expansionism and war with Mexico, 622–626.

Expenditures, critics of, 16.

Exports, agricultural, 67; dependence on Mississippi River, 67, 131; flatboats, 183; Noble on, 147; rivers, 140–141, 183; value of, 68; wheat, 52.
Express (New York), on Hoosiers not meeting obligations of debt, 297.
Expunger, Democratic campaign paper, 552.

Factory system, 71–72.
Falconer, John I., 61, 650n, 651n, 653n.
Farm animals, cattle, 59; chickens, 61; ducks, 61; geese, 61; hogs, 58–59; horses, 60–61; mules, 60–61; oxen, 61; sheep, 60.
Farm families, labor performed by, 47, 48.
Farmers and Mechanics Bank of Madison, 18, 525; expiration of charter, 24; federal deposits, 24; intermittent existence of, 164; specie payment, 24.
Farnham, John H., 809n.
Farrow, Alexander S., 783n.
Fatout, Paul, 697n.
Federal district court, 9.
Federal government, cessions from Indians, 460; control over domain of Indiana, 463–464; dependence on, 458–459; Indian relations, 458; Indiana's dominance in, 610; Indians, 460; public domain, 458; roads and canals, 41; tariff protection, 464–465; transportation projects and aid, 464; transportation systems, 463–464.
Federal land, credit system, 463; debtor options on, 462–463; Land Law of 1820, p. 463; payments on, 462; purchasing on credit, 462; sales of, 462–463; selling, 461–462; small tracts of, 463.
Federal land offices, former Indian land, 461.
Federalists, 452.

Feeder Dam, local control of, 236–237.
Ferguson, Benjamin, classifying internal improvements projects, 198–199.
Ferries, 44, 135–136; county boards and, 179; establishment of, 352–353; importance of, 179; necessity for, 351; private ownership of, 136, 353; public utility nature of, 179–180, 353–354; regulation of, 352–353; toll rates, 179.
Ferris, Ezra, 634n, 663n, 664n, 791n, 793n; senatorial candidacy, 458.
Finances, benevolent purposes, 242; solvency and stability of, 321; statewide problems, 293–294; Wallace on crisis of, 214.
Finch, Aaron, 539, 720n.
Findley, Able, 634n.
Finley, John, 823n.
First State Bank, 525; branches of, 18–19; charter forfeited, 23; collapse of, 20; depository for federal money, 19–20; epitaph for, 24; insolvency of, 14; noninterest-bearing treasury notes, 15; opposition to, 21; political and economic leaders, 19; precarious status, 21; quo warranto suit against, 23; Second United States Bank and, 465; state government borrowing money from, 14.
Fiscal affairs, 87.
Fiscal corporation, 587–589.
Fisher, Elwood, 705n.
Fisher S., 715n.
Fitch, Mason C., 721n, 723n.
Fitzgerald, Thomas, 808n.
Flatboats, 43, 140–141; exports, 183; increase of, 183.
Flax, 53–54.
Fletcher, Calvin, 94, 673n, 676n, 690n, 691n, 693n, 695n, 698n, 699n, 700n, 704n, 708n, 709n, 710n, 719n, 721n, 723n, 724n, 725n, 728n, 731n, 743n, 748n, 750n, 751n, 759n, 762n, 765n, 766n, 771n,

Fletcher, Calvin, (cont.)
772n, 773n, 813n, 816n, 818n, 822n, 824n, 825n, 827n, 834n, 836n, 839n, 840n, 841n; annexation of Texas, 599; bad condition of roads, 348; bank failures, 253; Blythe, 262; bridge over Wabash at Logansport, 180; common school education committee, 381; controversy between Ray and Merrill, 12; Dunn, 222; elections, 338; federal offices, 517; free schools, 390; frozen roads, 132; Hays' death, 314; Indiana University, 401–402; internal improvements, 191–192, 192, 195; internal improvements fund commissioners, 190; John N. Wick, 120; Madison and Indianapolis Railroad, 210; McCarty, 262; moving capital to Indianapolis, 112; preservation of Union, 523; presidential candidates of 1824, p. 476; private banking, 332; railroad line between Indianapolis and Madison, 360; resigning from Senate, 167; roads, 175; Second State Bank, 172, 254, 262, 323, 324, 325; slow and hazardous roads, 133; specie payment, 256–257; Stapp paying interest on debt, 226; State Common School Convention, 382; Tippecanoe Battleground crowds, 578; unsettled markets, 253; Van Buren defeat, 581; voting, 275, 341–342; Wallace, 202; Whitcomb, 312.

Fletcher, Elijah, 698n.

Floating bridges, 136.

Florida purchase treaty of 1819, p. 473.

Floyd, Davis, 456–457, 634n, 637n, 791n, 792n.

Foley, James B., 779n.

Force Bill, 524.

Fordham, Elias P., 109–110.

Foreign relations, 472; Adams, 499–500; boundary of Maine and Canada, 595; disputes with Canada over border, 501; European powers, 500–501; French compensation for shipping damages, 569–570; Greece, 501; importance of, 568–572; isolation from, 472–473, 501; Latin American neighbors, 500; Mexico, 570–571; no involvement with, 500; Oregon, 596–597; Panama Congress, 499–500; Polish uprisings, 569; Spain, 500; threatening, 573; Tyler, 595–598; war with England, 501; West Indies, 569.

Forests, 45; denuding, 50; farming cleared lands, 63; preparing land for cultivation, 49; trails and, 39; virgin hardwood trees, 45.

Foster, William C., 778n, 783n, 785n, 787n; blacks, 444; reapportionment of legislators, 419; treasurer, auditor, and secretary of state, 428; voters practicing law in courts, 433, 434.

Fowler, Harvey, 408.

France, compensation for shipping damages, 569–570; damage to American shipping, 499; possible war with, 569–570.

Franklin College, 400.

Franklin Democrat (Brookville), on Stevens and Harding, 337.

Free and slave states, 470.

Free banking, 330–332, 437; bipartisan support for, 331–332; compromise on, 438.

Free common schools, referendum of 1848, pp. 390–392; taxes, 391–392.

Free Press (South Bend), on Tyler, 586.

Frelingheysen, Theodore, 603–604.

French Revolution, 475.

Friends of Common Education, 373–374; advantages of education, 375; Board of Public Instruction, 373; county board examiners, 373–374; federal revenue for education, 374; laws about schools, 374–375; legislation for common schools, 373–374; licensed teachers, 374; money apportioned to districts, 374; school year length, 374.

Frisbie, Samuel, 778n, 783n, 834n; voters practicing law in courts, 433.
Fry, Francis H., 776n.
Fugitive Slave Law of 1793, pp. 565–566.

Gallatin, Albert, 812n.
Gapin, Jonathan K., 761n.
Gazette (Indianapolis), on Adams' supporters, 515; on Jackson, 514, 515; on Jacksonians, 540; on new courthouse, 113; on Noble, 489–490; on Ray, 83, 124; on Smith's withdrawal, 512.
Geese, 61.
General Assembly, ad valorem tax system, 94; banking legislation, 22; biennial sessions, 410–412; blacks entering state, 563–564; Butler Bill of 1846, p. 306; charters for railroads, 358–359; colonization linked to emancipation of slaves, 562; common schools, 390; compromise settlement, 303–305; Constitution of 1851, p. 410; constitutional amendments, 448–449; county representation, 32; debt settlement bill, 306; debt, invasions, insurrection, and public defense, 435; Democratic majority, 278; Democrats, 292; distribution, 586; electing successor to Tipton, 538; election of officials by, 8–9; election of successor to Taylor, 486–487; elections of 1840, pp. 221–222; enacting laws, 2; importance of knowledge, 365; imported goods, 495; internal improvement contractors, 214–215; internal improvement debt, 233–234, 300; internal improvements, 518–519; Jennings and Harrison, 26; judicial power, 2; land owner road obligations, 39–40; Lane and Lilly, 30; laws about schools, 374–375; legislative power, 2; local agencies power to make laws, 417; Marion County government, 111; Monroe Doctrine, 475; oral voting, 35; per diem, 160; personal liberty legislation, 470; presidential electors, 453; property taxes, 294; public buildings in Indianapolis, 113–114; public officials, 2; qualifications and elections of members, 36; review by electorate, 2–3; revision of laws, 99; river transportation, 42–44; Second State Bank, 256, 260, 264–265, 265, 327–328; Second United States Bank, 165–166; sessions, 2; single legislative branch, 423; size and apportionment, 3; specie payment, 258; state bank, 17–18, 170–171; Supreme Court, 6; tariffs, 465; voters, 30; Wabash and Erie Canal, 347–348; Whig majority, 221, 226, 339.
General property taxes, 155; adoption of, 158; advocates, 157; all-inclusiveness of, 250–251; exemptions from, 158–159.
Generalists, 47, 62.
Geographical context, 46; Appalachian Mountains barrier, 46; Ohio-Mississippi River waterway, 47; rivers, 46.
Geographical location, 67.
Gibson, Thomas W., 783n; governor's abuse of pardons, 425.
Gillespie, William M., 764n.
Gilliland, John, 668n.
Givens, Thomas, 815n.
Godfroy, Francis, land grants to, 555; trading with Indians, 554.
Goodnow, Samuel, 712n, 737n.
Gootee, Thomas, 785n.
Gordon, George A., 782n.
Government, business, 435; ordinary costs, 241–242.
Governor, candidates for 1828, pp. 125–128; changes to office of, 423–426; contest for first, 7; election of 1819, p. 28; election of 1840, pp. 215–221; election of first, 6; increases in pay, 242; Liberty party candidate, 289; pardons, 425–426; power of, 3–4; residence on Gover-

Governor, (cont.)
nor's Circle, 114; salary, 12; Second State Bank, 288–289; state bank, 170–171; term of, 3, 424; veto power, 425–428.
Governor's Circle, 114.
Governor's contingency fund and ordinary expenditures, 88.
Graham, Christopher C., 448.
Graham, John A., 705n, 788n.
Graham, John K., 634n.
Graham, William, 634n, 663n, 664n, 776n, 809n, 818n, 835n; congressional candidacy, 552; distribution money, 561; election as congressman, 550; gubernatorial candidacy (1828), 125; Jackson, 506.
Grand Rapids of Wabash River, 227.
Granger, Francis, 826n.
Grant County Herald (Marion), on Second State Bank, 323.
Grasses, 54.
Greece, sympathy for, 475, 501.
Gregg, Harvey, 675n.
Gregg, Milton, 408; blacks and mulattoes, 443.
Gregory, James, 149, 684n, 717n.
Gregory, Robert C., legislator's per diem, 246.
Grist mills, 43.
Guard, David, 814n.
Gurley, Rev. Phineas D., 282, 732n, 770n.
Gwathmey, Samuel, 492, 812n.

Hackett, Henry W., 720n.
Haddon, William R., 788n.
Half-faced camp, 48.
Hall, Baynard Rush, 396, 655n, 707n, 708n; on blacksmiths, 71.
Hall, Samuel, 217, 730n, 783n, 786n; candidate for second term, 279; election as lieutenant governor, 221; legislature, 435; political background of, 218; state debt, 435; treasurer, auditor, and secretary of state, 428–429; Whig nomination for lieutenant governor, 217.

Hamer, Hugh, 756n.
Hamilton, Alexander, 843n.
Hamilton, Allen, 786n; banking proposals, 436–438; state bank and free banking, 438; trading with Indians, 554.
Handy, Henry S., 808n, 811n; congressional candidacy, 511–512; withdrawal of candidacy, 512.
Hanna, Robert, 331.
Hanna, Robert, Jr., 335, 684n, 728n, 752n, 756n, 812n, 819n; captains steamboat to Indianapolis, 143; private banking, 331; replacing Noble as senator, 530; senatorial candidacy, 531.
Hanna, Samuel, elected treasurer, 339; trading with Indians, 554.
Hannegan, Edward A., 240, 702n, 711n, 739n, 740n, 823n, 833n, 835n, 837n, 843n, 847n, 850n, 853n, 855n, 856n, 857n, 858n, 860n; election as congressman, 540; election as senator, 592; excluding slavery, 627; internal improvement loans, 294; internal improvements, 614; Jackson, 527, 537; joint ownership of Oregon, 598; Mexican War, 623; Polk administration, 627, 628; reelection of, 542; senatorial candidacy, 592; squatters, 558; Wallace, 2–5.
Hanover Academy, 398–399.
Hanover College, 399.
Harbors, 184–185, 421, 613.
Hardin, Franklin, 786n; general banking law, 437.
Harding, Stephen S., 289, 734n, 735n, 755n; Abolition candidate, 337.
Hardwood forests, 45.
Harmonie, 55.
Harmonists, 60.
Harney, John H., 397.
Harris, Carey A., 831n.
Harris, Horatio J., 736n, 756n; election as auditor, 292–293.
Harrison, Abraham W., 684n.
Harrison, Christopher, 641n, 642n, 643n, 669n, 799n; agent for Three

Per Cent Fund, 42; canal commissioner, 145; candidacy against Jennings, 29; commissioner to plat Indianapolis, 109; first lieutenant governor, 8; governor, 8; resignation as lieutenant governor, 27–28; right and authority to administer government, 25; state seal, 25.

Harrison, Elisha, 659n.

Harrison, John C. S., 809n, 812n.

Harrison, William Henry, 653n, 710n, 796n, 804n, 824n, 825n, 826n, 827n, 838n, 840n, 841n, 851n; basic policies, 580; cessions from Indians, 459; death of, 582; Indiana, 543, 547–548, 573–576, 581; internal improvements, 547; Jackson, 547; Johnson, 543; legislative power in Congress, 582; negatives against, 546–547; nomination of, 544–545, 575; personal popularity, 582; state convention choice, 574; veto power, 582; vilification of, 25.

Harrison Land Law of 1800, pp. 461–462.

Harrison State Convention, 544–545.

Hart, David, 768n.

Harvey, Jonathan S., 776n.

Hay, Andrew P., 812n.

Hay, John D., 19.

Hay production, 54.

Hayes, Joseph M., 815n.

Haymond, Rufus, 745n.

Hays, John, 314.

Hays, Joseph H., 117.

Helmer, Melchert, 779n, 786n.

Hemp, 53–54.

Henderson, Samuel, 723n.

Hendricks, John, 252, 712n, 737n.

Hendricks, Thomas A., 761n, 785n.

Hendricks, William, 130, 633n, 656n, 657n, 662n, 663n, 664n, 694n, 706n, 790n, 791n, 792n, 793n, 796n, 797n, 803n, 806n, 807n, 808n, 810n, 812n, 813n, 815n, 817n, 818n, 827n, 835n, 837n; Adams, 493; Canadian border, 501; canal commissioner, 145; canal on Ohio River Falls, 494; candidate for reelection, 454–455; cessation of public domain to states, 498; Clay, 477, 492; congressional candidacy, 454; debt liquidation and reduced tax rates, 87; declined for renomination, 548; distribution bill, 560; election as senator, 486; election of, 80, 454; exemption for government land, 93; Farmers and Mechanics Bank, 24; favorable state finances, 87; first congressman, 8; foreign relations, 568; French Revolution, 475; governor and lieutenant governor elections, 101; gubernatorial candidacy, 456; import tariff protection, 464; Indian agency transfer, 497; Indiana presidential electors, 476; Indians and locating state capital, 460; Jackson, 528; joint English-American occupation, 501; levy on land, 91; lowering tariff, 524; north-south military road, 137; original law code, 270; political parties, 529; public buildings in Indianapolis, 113; public domain, 464; reelection as congressman, 455; reelection to Senate, 530; references to British law, 97; removal from office, 516; republican government, 473–474; resigning congressional seat, 456; reviser of territorial law, 97; Second United States Bank, 466, 526; senatorial candidacy, 486–487; slavery, 470, 471; small tracts of federal land, 463; South American republican governments, 473; strong political base, 455; support for candidacy of, 80; support for cessation, 559; sympathy for Greece, 501; tariff on salt, 495; tariffs on common consumables, 522; Texas, 571; voting, 540; Wabash and Erie Canal, 494; Wabash River, 521.

Hendrickson, Walter Brookfield, 655n, 656n; Owen's survey of Indiana, 75.

Henkle, Moses, 653n.

Henley, Thomas J., 705n, 712n, 737n, 847n, 850n, 853n, 854n, 855n,

Henley, Thomas J., (cont.)
856n, 857n, 858n, 859n; annexation of Texas, 616; Cass and Johnson, 604; election as congressman, 594; reelection of, 607.
Henry, James H., 770n, 771n.
Herald (Rushville), on compromise, 574.
Herod, William, 663n, 664n, 818n, 827n, 833n, 835n; congressional candidacy, 549, 552; distribution money, 561; election as congressman, 549–550; tax burdens, 300.
Hill, Frederick Dinsmore, 548, 656n, 793n.
Hillis, David, 663n, 664n, 702n, 703n; candidate for lieutenant governor, 206.
Hitt, Willis W., 787n.
Hogin, Benoni C., 785n.
Hogs, 58–59.
Holloway, David P., 739n.
Holman, Jesse L., 663n, 675n, 791n, 799n, 819n; Adams, 478; candidacy for governor, 28, 82; Clay and Adams, 492; Indiana Baptists Manual Labor Institute, 400; Indiana Colonization Society, 563; presidential elector, 453; Ray, 276; reappointment as judge, 128; senatorial candidacy, 455, 456, 530; Supreme Court, 9.
Holman, Joseph, 634n, 635n, 642n, 683n, 812n.
Holman, William Steele, 788n; circuit judges, 432; legislature voting, 414–415.
Holton, Alexander, 634n.
Homes, best site for, 48; half-faced camp, 48; lean-to, 49; open-faced camp, 49; primitive types of log cabins, 49; providing shelter with, 48; selecting site for, 48; tradesmen associated with, 70.
Honey, importing, 56.
Hoover, David, 592.
Hoover, Samuel, 690n, 845n.
Hopkins, James E., 658n.

Hops, 53–54.
Horses, 60–61.
Hoshour, Samuel K., 395.
House Committee on Public Expenditures, 248–249.
House Committee on Public Lands, 93.
House Committee on State Debt, 213.
House of Representatives, banking suggestions, 20; Committee on Education, 73; criticism of Second State Bank operations, 259–261; Democratic majority, 237; dominance by southern Indiana counties, 32; governor and lieutenant governor, 36; impeachment, 2; improvement bond financing, 230–231; Jennings and Harrison, 26–27; Lunatic Asylum, 314; membership, 3; oral voting, 35; Ray, 118; State Common School Convention recommendation, 381; Ways and Means Committee, 91.
House Ways and Means Committee, Bright, 299; improvement debt, 300; interest payments, 233; reduced legislative compensation, 248; state finances, 320; tax levies, 215.
Hovey, Alvin P., probate judges, 432–433; Senate, 414.
Howard, Thomas W., 800n.
Howard, Tilghman A., 216, 692n, 707n, 708n, 730n, 818n, 828n, 840n, 844n; election as congressman, 553; Internal Improvements System of 1836, pp. 218–219, 219–220; life of, 217; National Road, 521–522; Oregon, 597; public dinner, 581; Second State Bank, 260; senatorial candidacy, 551–552, 591–592; Van Buren, 221; Van Buren and Cass, 604.
Howe, John B., 783n, 786n, 788n; blacks and mulattoes, 443.
Howk, Isaac, 809n, 820n, 821n, 822n; Hendricks, 529; Tipton, 538.

Howland, Powell, 731n.
Hudson's Bay Company, 596.
Hunt, George, 668n, 669n.
Hunt, Nathaniel, 776n.
Hunter, Louis C., 648n, 682n.
Huntington, Elisha M., 523.
Hurst, Benjamin, 671n; presidential appointments of governor, 117.
Hurst, William H., 811n, 812n, 813n.
Hutton, Albert G., 739n.

Imports, 67–68; coffee, 56; curtailing, 464–465; federal tariff protection, 464–465; honey, 56; keelboats, 183–184; Mississippi River, 67, 131; rivers, 141, 183; salt, 56; steamboats, 183–184; sugar, 56; tea, 56; value of, 68.
Incorporation of towns, 10.
Independent Treasury, 610, 611, 613.
Indian removal, 553–557.
Indiana, American style independence, 453; antislavery sentiment, 470; congressional districts, 456; federal government, 452; federal legislation over, 9; federal senators and representatives, 52; first congressman, 454; foreign relations, 452–453, 472; geographical context, 46; geological and topographical survey of, 73, 74; hardwood forests, 45; Indian titles, 459; member of United States, 452–453; presidential electors, 476; republican government, 472–473; stage lines, 181; transition to statehood, 1, 9; Wilmot Proviso, 632.
Indiana Central Medical College, 400.
Indiana College, 396, 397. See also Indiana State Seminary and Indiana University.
Indiana Colonization Society, 563–564.
Indiana Constitutional Convention of 1850–1851, p. 278.
Indiana Democrat (Indianapolis), on *Indiana Journal* and Harrison, 576;

on Bigger, 219, 220; on British tyranny, 595; on circuit court judges, 245; on Democratic congressmen, 553; on Democrats, 580; on Dewey, 164, 276; on Dumont, 205; on federal aid, 520; on Federalist victory, 584; on free banking and state land lottery, 331; on governor and lieutenant governor, 152; on Harrison, 581; on Hendricks, 530; on internal improvements, 191, 204–205, 220; on Jackson, 534, 539; on Jacksonian state convention, 535; on Jacksonians, 548; on Johnson, 580; on judges salaries, 160; on legislators' per diem, 245–246; on military presidents, 544; on Morgan, 204; on Morris family, 206; on Morris, Brown, and Palmer, 222; on Noble, 193; on Noble and Williams, 220; on private banks, 330; on Read, 147; on removal from office, 516; on revision of laws, 270, 271; on Second State Bank, 255, 264; on small notes from banks, 326; on Smith, 549; on specie payments, 255, 257, 257–258; on state bank, 167, 168; on state convention, 150–151, 203; on Taylor, 204; on Texas, 571; on Tippecanoe Battleground crowds, 578–579; on U.S. Senate, 160–161; on Van Buren, 543, 544; on Wallace, 203, 205, 216; on Whigs, 541, 550–551, 553; on White, 552.
Indiana Gazette (Indianapolis), on referendum of 1823, p. 404; on Second United States Bank, 466; on slavery, 404; on state finances, 15–16.
Indiana Journal (Indianapolis), on bank failures, 257; on Beall, 274; on Bigger and Bradley, 285–286; on Bigger and Hall, 279; on Blackford, 84; on British, 595; on First Butler Bill of 1846, p. 307; on Clay, 536, 601; on congressional elections, 540; on Democrats, 215, 580–581; on Dewey, 164; on distribution and

Indiana Journal (Indianapolis), (cont.)
  preemption act, 587; on distribution
  bill, 560; on elections, 149; on European liberty, 568–569; on federal
  government policies, 582; on Harrison, 544, 547, 574, 575, 582; on
  Hoover and Kelso, 592; on internal
  improvement debt, 307; on internal
  improvements, 192, 200, 204, 220–
  221; on Jackson, 524, 526, 536; on
  Jacksonians, 152, 532; on keeping
  office, 516; on law code, 271; on
  legislature, 267–268; on Maysville
  Road Veto, 519; on Merrill and
  Morris, 149; on Mexican War, 571;
  on national bank, 585–586; on National Republicans, 531; on Noble,
  153, 549; on Noble and Stapp, 146;
  on Oregon, 597; on Owen, 553,
  593; on partisan strife, 537; on post
  office, 516; on postponing distribution, 560; on property taxes, 160–
  161; on Ray, 83, 84–85; on Ray and
  Blackford, 83; on Read, 147; on
  roads, 348; on Scott, 146; on Second United States Bank, 527; on
  slavery, 564; on small notes from
  banks, 326; on special apportionment, 161; on specie payments,
  254–255, 258; on Stapp and Pepper,
  127; on state bank, 167, 168; on
  state convention, 150, 534; on state
  officials' pay, 245; on steamboat in
  Indianapolis, 142, 143; on tariff,
  584; on Tippecanoe Battleground
  campaign, 578; on Tyler, 583, 585,
  588; on Van Buren, 517; on Wabash
  and Erie Canal, 240; on Wallace,
  216; on Whigs, 280, 541, 551, 553,
  574, 584; on Whitcomb and Bright,
  285; on White, 552; on White,
  Webster and Clay, 574.
Indiana Palladium (Lawrenceburg), on
  Jackson, 502.
Indiana Republican (Madison), on Hendricks and Clay, 530.
Indiana State Journal (Indianapolis), on
  Bigger, 290; on Bigger and Whit-

comb, 289; on Bright, 289, 333,
  608–609; on Butler Bill approval,
  336; on candidates for governor,
  332; on Clay and Frelinghuysen,
  603–604; on common schools, 385;
  on Constitution of 1851, p. 450; on
  creditors of state debt, 295; on Democrats, 333; on Democrats and
  Deming, 290; on elections, 337; on
  First Butler Bill of 1846, p. 307; on
  internal improvement debt, 294,
  307; on internal improvements,
  287; on Jackson.-Van Buren administrations, 593; on legislators, 339–
  340; on Marshall, 336; on Mexican
  War, 624, 625; on new blood in office, 292; on Oregon, 618; on Orth
  and Marshall, 337; on Polk, 609; on
  roads, 356; on Second State Bank,
  325; on State Common School
  Convention, 381–382; on state conventions, 335; on Sullivan and
  Dewey, 344; on voting, 290; on
  Walker, 612; on war with England,
  619; on Whig state convention,
  334; on Whigs, 608; on Whigs and
  Democrats, 337–338; on Whitcomb, 286, 287, 288, 336, 343, 344.
Indiana State Seminary, 396–397.
Indiana State Sentinel (Indianapolis),
  on annexation of Texas, 598–599;
  on banks, 330; on Bigger, 289; on
  Bigger and Bradley, 285, 286; on
  black governor, 289–290; on blacks,
  450; on Bright, 608; on Brown and
  Wallace, 594; on Clay, 601; on Constitution of 1851, pp. 449–450; on
  constitutional convention, 407; on
  Democratic state convention, 280;
  on distribution and preemption act,
  587; on First Butler Bill of 1846, pp.
  307–308; on governor, 279; on
  Hannegan, 592; on internal improvement debt, 288, 294, 295,
  297–298, 307–308; on internal improvement problems, 287; on legislators, 339–340; on legislators'
  salaries, 247; on Marshall, 336; on

Mexican sentiments, 629; on Morrison, 328, 329; on national bank, 585; on new blood in office, 292; on Owen, 593–594; on Palmer, 292; on politics and judicial appointments, 343; on Second State Bank, 322; on Smith and Perkins, 344; on state conventions, 335; on voting, 291, 341; on Whigs, 289, 593; on Whitcomb, 286–287, 291, 343; on Whitcomb and Bright, 285.

Indiana State Wesleyan Anti-Slavery Society, 567.

Indiana Statesman (Indianapolis), on Constitution of 1851, p. 450.

Indiana Teachers' Seminary (Madison), 372.

Indiana University, 397–398; advocates, 441–442; detractors, 440–441; importance to state, 398; normal school, 440; regents, 401; status of, 397–398; trust funds, 442; University Boarding House, 397.

Indianapolis, beauty and fertility of site, 111; civil townships, 111; courthouse, 110, 112; crossroads for transportation, 181; donation lots, 110–111; Governor's Circle, 110; grid pattern, 110; housing county and state officials, 112; market site, 110; Market Street, 110; Meridian Street, 110; Michigan Road, 349; naming streets, 110; National Turnpike, 111; permanent capital, 41, 107–108, 112; plan of town, 111; platting, 108, 109–110; plots sold in, 111; Pogue's Run, 110; protests over move to, 112–113; public buildings, 108–109; removal of state capital to, 112–113; roads, 114; slow growth of, 114; state house, 110; town government, 111–112; Washington Street, 110, 348–349, 349.

Indianapolis and White Water Turnpike Company, 137.

Indianapolis Fund, 636n; courthouse appropriations, 112; public buildings in Indianapolis, 113–114.

Indians, Black Hawk War of 1832, p. 554; clearing Indiana of titles by, 459; clearing remaining titles of, 497; compelling immigration of, 556; concern about, 472, 496–497; Delaware, 459, 460; Kickapoo, 460; land passing to settlers, 557–558; lucrative trade with, 554; Miami, 459, 554; missionaries to, 460–461; moving agency to Logansport, 497; murders of, 461; negotiating treaties with, 555; New Purchase treaties of 1818, p. 460; pioneers preferred over, 459; Potawatomi, 459, 496, 554; presidential and congressional policy on, 459–460; relations, 458; removal of, 553–557; surveying land of, 557–558; Wea, 460.

Ingraham, Andrew, 672n.

Institutions for blind and deaf, 314.

Interim apportionment of 1823, p. 106.

Internal Improvement Board, financial crisis, 207–208.

Internal improvements, 336; Adams, 493–494; Adams-Clay coalition aid, 494; aid to, 614; American bondholders complaints, 296–297; Bigger, 224–225; bond financing, 231; bond rate of interest, 212–213; bonded debt, 295–296; bondholders, 310; bonds, 294–295; bonds on credit, 213; canal opponents and proponents, 186–187; canal surveys, 493; classifying, 226–227; cost of labor, 207; debt, 211–212, 297–298, 301–302; debt interest accumulating, 293; downfall of, 212–213; engineering surveys for, 192–193; English bondholders complaints, 294–295; federal aid, 595; federal aid and tariff protection, 494–495; federal aid for, 115, 464, 518–519, 536; federal surveys, 518–519; fraud and corruption, 213; fraud and mismanagement, 230–231; generated revenues, 190; growth of population

Internal improvements, (cont.)
and wealth, 190; interest and principle on bonds, 348; interest on, 207, 209–210; interest payments, 213, 229; Jackson, 518–519, 519–520; Jacksonians, 494; labor and provisions cost, 212; liquidating bonds and interest, 294; liquidating debt, 288; local control, 236–237; long-term borrowing, 190; loose practices and wasteful expenditures, 232; Maysville Road Veto, 519–520; momentum for, 191–192; Morris Canal and Banking Company, 211; necessary decisions for, 191; Noble, 190–191; not completing, 234; optimism over, 189–190; paying contractors, 214–215; paying debt, 312; paying interest on, 233–234, 299–300; paying principle and interest in toto, 232; Polk, 613–614; private associations, 214; private companies, 226; problems, 287–288; projects, 213; Read, 147; redeeming bonds, 232; repudiation of debt, 300, 312; state financial condition, 213; state financing, 560; state participation in, 164; state sponsored systems, 146; support for, 152; surplus distribution money, 560–561; suspended debt, 227; suspension of, 211; taxes, 193, 200, 233, 249; transportation network, 190; unfunded or domestic debt, 294; Wabash and Erie Canal, 185–189, 306–307, 493–494; Wallace, 209; Whig and Democratic support for, 547.
Internal Improvements Fund Commissioners, fiscal disaster, 207–208.
Internal Improvements System of 1836, pp. 175, 185, 190; abandonment of, 378; additions to, 197–198; appropriations, 196–197; approval of, 158; Bigger and Howard, 218–219; bonds, 208; canals, 358; classification of projects, 197–198; costs and legislators, 199–200; cutting expenditures, 210; debt, 210; downfall of, 213; financial crisis from, 405; fiscal insolvency, 222; foundation of, 201; interest owed on, 237; legislative approval of, 194; no projects completed in, 278; paying interest on, 233–234; payment for, 232–233; policy to follow on, 204; private companies, 234, 235, 236; problems with, 232; projects, 195–196, 197; removal of Indians, 554; state agent for, 234–235; state sponsored turnpikes, 179; suspension in 1839, p. 293; ultimate cost, 202; unfinished projects, 222; Wabash River, 184; Wallace, 206–207; Whigs, 252.
Internal Revenue System of 1836, taxes, 320.
Irish potatoes, 54.
Iron, 75.

Jackson, Andrew, 674n, 801n, 804n, 809n, 810n, 815n, 817n, 821n, 838n, 841n, 843n, 848n; Adams and Clay, 482; campaign, 481, 502–503; censured by Senate, 528; charges and countercharges, 507; counties carried by, 482; election as president, 492, 509; filling vacancies, 517; Indiana voting for, 508–509; internal improvements, 464, 518–519, 519–520; internal improvements and tariffs, 506–507; Maysville Road Veto, 519–520; National Republicans, 514–516; nomination for president, 478; opponents, 481–482; plurality in electoral college, 483; popular vote for, 483–484; popularity of, 536–538; presidential candidacy, 476, 491–492; recognition of Texas, 571; reelection as president, 537; renomination for president, 502, 536; reprisals toward France, 569–570; Second State Bank, 526; second term, 533–534; Second United States Bank, 527–528; tariff protec-

tion, 465; victory in Indiana, 482–483; visit to Indiana, 453; Wabash River, 520; West Indies, 569.
Jackson, Jesse, 824n.
Jackson, John, 727n.
Jackson, N., 824n.
Jackson State Committee, on Ray as Jacksonian gubernatorial candidate, 125–126.
Jacksonian Democracy, 405.
Jacksonians, banking, 525–528; Clay and Adams, 491; congressional races, 509–510; congressional victory for, 540; congressmen, 532; federal offices in Indiana, 517; federal policies concerning Indiana, 540–541; gubernatorial candidacy, 146–147; internal improvements aid, 494; Jackson, 504; Noble, 148; opponents, 536; party unity and Van Buren, 540; problems created by, 576; Read, 147; state conventions, 503–506, 535, 545–546; Tipton, 147.
Jeffersonian Republicans, 452; Constitution of 1816, p. 452; schism, 491.
Jeffersonville and Crawfordsville Road, 237.
Jeffersonville Ohio Canal Company, 144.
Jennings, Jonathan, 130, 633n, 634n, 635n, 639n, 641n, 642n, 643n, 656n, 662n, 669n, 790n, 792n, 797n, 802n, 803n, 804n, 806n, 811n, 813n, 815n, 818n, 820n; accomplishments, 532–533; Adams, 510; adapting laws to statehood, 96; attacks on character of, 457–458; congressional candidacy, 456–457, 484–485, 511–512, 532; Corydon Constitutional Convention, 1; current revenue made equal to current costs, 14–15; education, 8; election as governor, 6; election to Congress, 1; Enabling Act, 1; federal commission, 27; First State Bank, 19, 20, 21; first state constitution, 1; fiscal prospects (1816–1817), 14;

governor, 1, 8, 27; gubernatorial candidacy (1828), 125; House of Representatives, 1; immigrants and law, 96; import tariff protection, 464; Indian agency, 497; Indian cessions, 555; Indian commissioner, 25; Indiana Colonization Society, 563; ineligibility for reelection, 80; internal improvements, 518; loss of political stature, 490; Monroe and Jackson, 453; negotiations with Indians, 27; New Purchase, 27, 29; not running for Senate, 529; permanent state capital, 107, 108; popularity of, 29; presidential electors, 453–454; reducing tariffs on sugar, 522; reelection as governor, 29; reelection to Congress, 485, 487, 512; replacement as governor, 25; resignation of, 26; right to retain office, 25; roads and canals, 41; second term candidacy for governor, 28; Second United States Bank, 466; senatorial candidacy, 455–456, 486–487, 489–490; slaves, 467–468, 468; specie payment, 21; statute law, 96; Supreme Court, 9; tariffs, 496; tax revenue, 14–15; transition to statehood, 1.
Jocelyn, Augustus, 126, 674n.
John, Enoch D., 86, 160, 659n, 687n.
Johnson, James B., 724n.
Johnson, John, 634n, 635n, 680n; nomination to Supreme Court, 9.
Johnson, Richard M., 152, 849n, 850n; competition for Van Buren, 601; election as vice president, 548; Indiana support for, 543–544, 545–546; Jackson's victory at New Orleans, 542; nomination for president, 543–544; vice presidential candidate, 544; Wabash and Erie Canal, 240.
Johnston, General Washington, 96, 635n, 637n, 638n, 648n, 659n, 662n, 672n; landowners and roads, 40; on revising territorial laws, 96.
Jones, James W., 669n.

Jones, Robert Leslie, 650n, 651n, 652n, 653n.
Jones, William T. T., 710n, 747n.
Jordan, Philip D., 694n.
Josephs of New York, 703n.
Judah, Samuel, 706n, 710n, 720n, 722n, 750n, 752n, 808n, 810n, 813n, 816n, 819n, 822n; ad valorem taxes, 94; common law and English statutes, 98; federal district court attorney, 515; improper actions, 539; internal improvements, 530–531; nullification and consolidation, 531; private banking bill, 331; protective tariffs, 530; Second State Bank, 255–256; senatorial candidacy, 530, 538–539; treating voters, 275; Whig convention, 575.
Judges, constitutional convention, 429–433; costs, 12; elections, 35; growth in number of, 242; salaries, 12, 159–160, 164, 242.
Judicial branch, 4; circuit courts, 5; costs 1822–1831, p. 153; justices of the peace, 5; Supreme Court, 5.
Jump plows, 50.
Jumping shovel plows, 50–51.
Justice of the peace courts, 433.
Justices of the peace, 5; term, 433.

Keelboats, 43, 141; imports, 183–184.
Kelso, Daniel, 778n, 783n, 785n, 845n, 851n; apportioning legislators, 422; legislation by majority, 414; per diem compensation, 412; Smith, 592; suspensive veto, 427–428; voters as lawyers, 434.
Kelso, James P., 779n.
Kendal, Robert C., 785n.
Kennedy, Andrew, 279, 720n, 730n, 844n, 847n, 848n, 853n, 854n, 855n, 856n, 857n, 858n; distribution, 587; election as congressman, 584; Oregon, 617, 619–620; Polk administration, 627, 628; reelection of, 594, 607.
Kent, Phineas M., 788n; separation of whites and blacks, 446.

Kentucky, reclaiming slaves from Indiana, 468–469.
Kickapoo Indians, 460.
Kidder, Reuben, 657n.
Kilgore, David, 778n; Constitution of 1816, p. 409; probate system, 432; reporter elections, 431; special apportionments, 161–162.
Kinnard, George L., 817n, 823n, 827n, 833n, 835n, 837n; death of, 549; election as congressman, 540; reelection of, 542.
Kinney, Amory, 390, 663n, 664n, 770n, 771n.
Knight, Jonathan, National Road, 140.
Kohlmeier, Albert L., 648n, 649n, 654n, 680n; Appalachian Mountain barrier, 67; commerce and trade and politics, 66; importance of salt, 68; leaving stumps standing, 50; Northern and Southern politicians, 47.

Labor, agricultural, 62, 207; child, 62; cooperation of genders, 77–78; gender divisions of, 77; internal improvements, 207; Wabash and Erie Canal, 187.
Land, agriculture, 62; bought from federal government, 93; changing policy on, 558; distribution to states, 586–587; exemptions, 91; federal government, 91; federal land, 461–462; federal policy on, 559, 586–587; federal revenue from sale of, 522; former Indian, 461; Harrison Land Law of 1800, pp. 461–462; inequality of assessment of, 17, 94; initial plowing, 50–51; law of 1820, p. 559; Ohio, 462; passing from Indians to settlers, 557–558; preemption, 586–587; purchasing on credit, 462; revised tax code of 1824, p. 91; revised tax code of 1831, p. 91; road tax on, 39; sales, 559; squatters, 558; successive clearing of, 50; surveying Indian, 557–558; taxes, 87, 91.

Land Law of 1804, pp. 461–462.
Land Law of 1820, pp. 461–462.
Land offices, 462–463, 492, 493, 515.
Landowner road taxes, 39–40.
Lane, Amos, 149, 634n, 635n, 643n, 657n, 684n, 706n, 730n, 803n, 833n, 835n, 837n; Adams, 493; election as congressman, 540; reelection of, 542; slavery, 564.
Lane, Daniel C., 19; election as treasurer, 8; examination of conduct of, 81; reelection as treasurer, 30.
Lane, Henry S., 335, 842n, 843n, 844n, 845n, 848n; congressional candidacy, 583–584; gubernatorial candidacy, 332; modification of tariff laws, 525; national bank, 588; reelection of, 584.
Lanier, James F. D., 720n, 721n, 723n, 761n; bank failures, 253; specie payment, 256.
Larrabee, William C., 370.
Latta, William C., 650n, 651n, 652n, 653n, 654n; beef and chicken, 57; cattle, 59; chickens, 61; county agricultural societies, 66; crop pests and diseases, 57; hogs, 58; horses, 60; livestock, 57–58; poultry, 61; sheep, 60.
Law, bill titles, 415; civil and criminal, 98–99; civil code of Louisiana, 130–131; codification and revision of, 95–99, 270–272; elections, 272–273; enacting, 414–415; English statutes, 97, 98; General Assembly revision of, 99; immigrants and, 96; local agencies power to make, 417; local law, 416–417, 417; logrolling, 415; Ray, 130–131; revised code of 1831, p. 99; rivers as public highways, 143–144; territorial laws, 96; too few legislators passing, 414; uniform state law, 417; valid ballots, 273–274; wording of bills, 415–416.
Law, John, 713n, 720n, 809n, 819n, 820n, 859n; congressional candidacy, 532; Mexican War, 629; slavery, 632; specie payment, 256.

Lawrenceburg and Indianapolis Railroad, construction of, 182; purchase of stock in, 196.
Lawrenceburg and Indianapolis Railroad Company, 182.
Lawyers, requirements to practice, 433–434.
Lean-to, 49.
Lee, William, 746n.
Legislators, apportionment, 31, 419–423; biennial elections, 403; compensation, 12, 242, 247–249; expanded number of, 242; Internal Improvements System of 1836, pp. 199–200; number of, 419–422; Ray, 116, 130–131; reapportionment of 1821, p. 33; reducing number of, 339–340; representation, 33–34.
Legislature, biennial sessions of, 405; Butler Bill of 1847, pp. 309–310; common schools, 380–381, 385–387; compensation fixed by law, 412–414; costs 1822–1831, pp. 153, 155; county, township, and town government, 5; Democrats, 291; distribution of seats, 31; educational system bills, 365; First State Bank, 15; ineligibility for, 3; internal improvements, 210, 234; land tax, 14; legislative district definition, 420; lengthening sessions, 242, 412; local law, 417; payment of unfunded or domestic debt, 234; per diem costs, 245–247; public domain lands, 499; reapportionment of, 102–103, 155; reapportionment of 1826, pp. 102–103; reapportionment of 1831, pp. 103–104; reapportionment of 1841, pp. 269–270; reduction in, 267–268; regular and special sessions, 413; stagecoach penalties, 181–182; Three Per Cent Fund, 177; veto, 426–427.
Lemon, John M., 815n.
Leopold, Richard William, 701n.
Leslie, Frederick, 739n; on converting existing improvement bonds, 299.
Lewis, Samuel, 705n.
Lewis, William, 812n.

Liberty party, abolition of slavery, 567; Birney as presidential candidate, 605; first candidate for governor, 289; slavery, 337; Whigs, 291, 337.

Liberty-Free Soil party, 573.

Licensing teachers, 374.

Lieutenant governor, changes to office of, 423–426; during governor's absence, 26; duties of, 4; election of first, 6, 8; eliminating office of, 424–425; salary, 12; term of office, 424.

Life in agricultural society, 78–79.

Lilly, William H., 634n, 635n, 643n, 657n, 659n, 662n, 673n, 675n; absences from capital, 119; conduct of, 81; death, 128; election as auditor, 8; fourth term as auditor, 86; Jennings, 27; reelection as auditor, 30.

Limestone, 75; oolitic, 77.

Lindley, Harlow, 647n.

Lindsey, Alton A., 45, 649n, 656n.

Linton, William C., 663n, 684n.

Lister, John, 731n.

Livestock. See Farm animals.

Livingstone, John, 751n, 828n.

Lockhart, James, 784n.

Log cabins, 49.

Logrolling, 415.

Lomax, Abel, 834n.

Long, Elisha, 94, 706n.

Long rifle, 49–50.

Lowe, Jacob B., 151, 823n.

Lowe, William, 808n.

Lowry, William G., 133.

Ludlow, Stephen, 668n.

Lumber, 46.

Lunatic Asylum, 314.

Lynn, Dann, 634n.

Macadamized roads. See Turnpikes.

Mace, James, 323, 747n.

Maclure, William, 74.

Madison, James, 676n, 817n; internal improvements, 464.

Madison and Indianapolis Railroad, classifying, 226, 227; completion of, 210, 235, 236; contracts on projects, 197; tax levies on, 227; stock in, 317, 319.

Madison and Indianapolis Railroad Company, 236; no taxes paid on stock of, 317, 319; unfinished line, 360.

Madison and Napoleon Turnpike Company, 355.

Maguire, Douglass, 720n, 756n, 786n, 788n; elected auditor, 339; Madison and Indianapolis Railroad, 317, 319; property tax assessments, 317, 319.

Mail, stagecoach network and, 180–181.

Major, Noah F., 696n.

Manual Labor Seminary, 372. See also Wabash Manual Labor College and Teachers' Seminary.

Manufacturing, agricultural produce, 68–69; average yearly wage, 72; categories of, 68–69; centers, 73; counties noted for, 72; craftsmen, 69–70; factory system, 71–72; growth of, 67; industries by dollar amount, 72; tradesmen, 69–70; value of products, 72.

Maple sugar, 56.

Marion County, beginning government, 111; courthouse, 112.

Marsh, Madison, 273, 727n, 728n, 844n; seated by House, 592.

Marshall, Joseph G., 216, 711n, 753n, 754n, 755n, 756n; gubernatorial candidacy, 332, 335; strong qualifications of, 335; taking campaign to voters, 337–338.

Marshall, William, 813n; marshal for federal district court, 515; Tipton, 539.

Martin, William W., 768n, 811n.

Mason, Philip, 710n; internal improvements interest payments, 229.

Matlock, Thomas J., 668n.

Matthews, Claude, 733n.

Maxwell, David H., 657n, 799n, 809n; Board of Internal Improvement, 197; gubernatorial candidacy, 82.

May, Edward R., 787n.

Mayhew, Royal, 736n, 756n; common schools, 379; election as state treasurer, 292, 293.

Maysville Road Veto, 519–520.

McCarty, Abner, 805n.

McCarty, Jonathan, 216, 800n, 811n, 812n, 815n, 816n, 817n, 821n, 822n, 823n, 828n, 833n, 835n, 836n, 837n; congressional candidacy, 512–513, 532, 552; distribution bill, 560; Harrison and Tyler, 575; reelection of, 540, 542; Second United States Bank, 526; senatorial candidacy, 539; tariffs, 524.

McCarty, Nicholas, 262, 707n, 723n; branch suspension, 254.

McClelland, Beattie, 780n, 784n; election of sheriff, 431; Indiana University and foreign students, 441; Latin terms in bills, 415–416; reporter elections, 431.

McCord, Shirley S., 647n, 676n, 692n.

McCoy, Isaac, 793n; missionary to Indians, 460–461.

McCulloch, Hugh, 175, 692n; bank failures, 253; traders cheating Indians, 554.

McDonald, David, 398.

McDonald, John, 679n.

McFarland, Demas, 731n.

McFarland, Joel B., 788n.

McGaughey, Edward W., 853n, 855n, 856n, 857n, 858n, 859n; army appropriations, 629; congressional election, 607; Oregon, 619.

McKeen, Hugh B., and Michigan Road, 494.

McKinney, John T., 663n, 664n, 672n, 675n, 676n; approval by Senate, 276; death, 164, 276; state Supreme Court, 128.

McKinney, Thomas L., 830n.

McLean, James, 314, 745n.

McLean, John, 543.

McNamee, Elias, 791n, 800n; senatorial candidacy, 455.

Meat, dependency on, 56; types, 56; wild animal, 56–57.

Meigs, Josiah, 634n, 669n.

Men, as providers, 78; labor on roads, 133–134; tasks done by, 77; taxable property and roads, 350, 351; working on roads, 349–350.

Menominee, 831n; compelling immigration of, 556.

Meredith, Solomon, 771n.

Merrill, Samuel, 640n, 641n, 657n, 659n, 660n, 662n, 663n, 670n, 672n, 673n, 675n, 684n, 687n, 691n, 692n, 700n, 719n, 720n, 721n, 723n, 724n, 747n, 750n; absences from capital, 119; aid given elected officials, 123; assessed and collected taxes, 95; bank failures, 168–169, 254; black colonization of Africa, 562; county collectors and tract books, 121–122; election as treasurer, 81; finding successor to, 321–324; fulfilling duties while absent, 120; Morris Canal and Banking Company loan, 266; move to Indianapolis, 112; plots sold in Indianapolis, 111; Ray, 123–124; reelection of, 149; removal of state items to Indianapolis, 113; resignation as treasurer, 153; sale of state items at Corydon, 113; Second State Bank, 153, 172, 254, 256, 259, 263, 265, 327; Second United States Bank, 164–165; specie payment, 258; specie payments, 257; state bank, 173; tax delinquencies, 95; third term as treasurer, 86, 128.

Metal craftsmen, 70.

Mexican War, 622–626; criticism of, 628–630; party and sectional divisions, 630–631; peace treaty with Mexico, 630–631; Polk, 630; volunteers for, 629–630; Whigs, 623–624.

Miami Indians, 459, 496, 554; Big Miami Reserve, 554; missionaries to, 460; payments to, 555; removal of, 497, 557; surrender tribal holdings, 555.

Michigan City, as commerce center, 184–185.

Michigan Road, 137–138; bad condition of, 175; bridges, 180; construction through Indian territory, 554; donations of land for, 494; federal aid, 178; federally donated sections, 178–179; financing, 139, 178; importance of, 178; military importance of, 500; Noble, 139, 147; rivalry over, 138–139; turnpikes intersecting, 137.

Militia, issuance of commissions, 121; ordinary expenditures, 88.

Milk, 57.

Miller, F. T., 649n.

Miller, Smith, 779n, 786n.

Milligan, Dixon, 787n.

Millikan, James P., 717n; comments on legislators' per diem, 246.

Mills, Caleb, 376, 770n, 773n, 775n; common schools, 379–380, 380, 388–389, 389, 391, 393; denominational and private schools, 389; Indiana University, 401; paying for good schools, 388; proper education of youth, 388–389; religion, 380; state supported colleges and universities, 400–401; statewide common schools, 387–388; superintendents, 380; Wabash College, 399.

Milroy, John, Jackson and Adams, 506.

Milroy, Samuel, 27, 634n, 659n, 680n, 696n, 706n, 730n, 786n, 790n, 800n, 804n, 805n, 809n, 812n, 813n, 821n, 824n, 828n, 834n; approves cession of public domain to states, 498–499; classifying internal improvements projects, 198; free blacks treated as slaves, 468; gubernatorial candidacy, 125, 279; inspecting land offices, 493; qualifications for governor, 203–204; railroads, 182; Ray and Merrill, 124.

Milroy, Thomas, candidate for lieutenant governor, 85; Corydon Constitutional Convention, 86; Jackson, 86; resignation of Senate seat, 86.

Minerals, 73–77.

Mississippi River, exports and imports, 67, 131.

Missouri, admission of to United States, 470; blacks and mulattoes, 471.

Missouri Compromises of 1820 and 1821 p. 471.

Mitchell, David G., 648n, 802n.

Mitchell, John, 723n.

Mitchell, William B., 711n, 713n; internal improvement debt, 235–236.

Monks, Leander J., Sullivan, Dewey, and Blackford, 277.

Monopolistic banking, 17.

Monroe Doctrine, 500; General Assembly support of, 475.

Monroe, James, federal aid for internal improvements, 464; Florida purchase, 473; Indiana presidential electoral votes, 453; Indians, 459; South America, 474; visit to Indiana, 453.

Montgomery, Isaac, 809n.

Mooney, Samuel P., 786n, 844n.

Moor, Samuel, 653n.

Moore, George W., 783n.

Moore, Harbin H., 643n, 674n, 809n; gubernatorial candidacy, 125.

Morality and common schools, 389.

Morgan, Amaziah, 834n.

Morgan, Jesse, 702n, 710n, 782n.

Morris, Austin W., 672n, 697n, 720n, 732n, 775n; Wabash and Erie Canal, 186–187.

Morris, Bethuel F., 112, 672n, 809n.

Morris, Morris, 672n, 675n, 684n, 708n, 717n, 720n, 730n; elected auditor, 128; fifth term as auditor, 221–222; internal improvements, 237, 278; loss of election as auditor, 292; loss of election as treasurer, 292; reelection of, 149, 206; reelection to third term, 153; taxes, 242, 245, 249–250, 251–252.

Morris Canal and Banking Company, canal fund, 212, 238; suspends bond payments, 211; Second State Bank, 266.

Morrison, Alexander F., 683n, 684n, 720n, 731n, 782n, 788n, 804n, 808n, 824n; apportioning legislators, 422; executive department, 423–424; governor's term, 424; simple wording of bills, 415; state political convention, 150.

Morrison, James, 323, 755n; Second State Bank, 323–324, 324, 328; secretary of state, 128, 149–150; Supreme Court judge, 342, 343.

Morrison, John I., 395, 705n, 787n; common schools, 439; constitutional convention, 406; education in Indiana, 440; state superintendent, 439, 440.

Morrison, Robert, 724n, 747n.

Mowrer, Daniel, 424–425, 782n, 783n.

Mulattoes, leaving Indiana, 442; opposition to immigration of, 442; prejudice against, 442–445; rights and privileges, 442, 443–444, 445–446.

Mules, 60–61.

Murdock, George L., 681n.

Murray, Elias, 759n, 788n, 789n; annual legislative sessions, 411.

National bank, 577; Clay and Tyler, 584–585; fiscal corporation, 587–588; Hoosier opposition to, 585–586; modified version, 587–588.

National Republicans, 115; Adams, 507; congressmen, 540; internal improvements and tariff protections, 504, 505; Jackson, 516; merit, 151; national convention, 535–536; prominence of, 150. See also Whigs.

National Road, 137–138; bridges, 180; congressional appropriations for, 140; construction of, 178; financing of, 139; imperfect results of, 177; Indiana segment, 140, 178; terrible condition of, 521–522; Two Per Cent Fund, 139; western U. S., 464.

Natural resources, 45, 77.

Nave, Christian C., 781n, 784n; counties, 422; number of legislators, 423; single legislative branch, 423; Supreme Court members, 430–431.

Neely, John I., 679n, 820n.

Nelson, Reuben W., 658n, 792n; congressional candidacy, 454; withdrawal from race, 454.

New, Robert A., 634n; election as secretary of state, 8; Jennings, 27; not seeking third term, 86; reelection as secretary of state, 30; state seal and, 25.

New Albany and Vincennes Road, 197.

New Purchase treaties, 27, 106, 460.

Newman, John S., 779n, 780n, 784n; legislative sessions starting on Monday, 412; powers of county board, 418; uniform state laws, 417.

Nicholi, Julius, 731n.

Niles, John B., 780n, 784n, 786n, 788n; internal improvement projects and private enterprise, 435; legislative sessions starting on Monday, 411–412; simple wording of bills, 415.

No Bank element, 329–330.

Noble, James, 19, 130, 634n, 791n, 796n, 798n, 813n; canal on Ohio River Falls, 494; cessation of public domain, 498; Clay, 492; Crawford, 477; death, 530; election as senator, 9, 455–456, 490; Farmers and Mechanics Bank, 24; Florida purchase, 473; Indian agency transfer, 497; new states excluding slavery, 470; political parties, 529; private banking bill, 331; road travel, 133; slavery, 471; small tracts of federal land, 463; tariff on salt, 495.

Noble, Lazarus, 493.

Noble, Noah, 19, 662n, 674n, 677n, 678n, 679n, 681n, 683n, 684n, 685n, 686n, 687n, 688n, 689n, 690n, 691n, 698n, 699n, 701n, 704n, 705n, 706n, 709n, 710n, 711n, 714n, 720n, 723n, 732n, 733n, 752n, 792n, 803n, 804n,

Noble, Noah, (cont.)
805n, 807n, 810n, 812n, 815n, 818n, 824n, 827n, 828n, 829n; ad valorem plan, 157–158; anti-Jacksonians, 147; Board of Internal Improvement, 210, 215; canals, 192; candidacy for governor, 146; candidate for reelection, 151–152; classification of internal improvements, 207; Clay supporters versus Jacksonians, 529; competent teachers, 372; eastern county support, 148; election as governor, 148–149; exports and transportation, 147; fair apportionments, 162; Friends of Common Education, 373; ineligibility for Senate nomination, 548; ineligibility for third term, 202; internal improvements, 190–191, 192–193, 227; Jacksonians, 148; Johnson, 542–543; Johnson Democrats, 152; judges revising law code, 271; judges' wages, 159–160; Michigan Road, 139, 147, 178; party support, 148; population and special apportionments, 161; public common schools, 371; receiver of land office, 493; school system, 372–373; Second State Bank, 264; semiannual interest on debt, 228–229; seminary funds, 395; senatorial candidacy, 551–552; slavery, 148; specie payment, 255; state bank, 166, 168, 169, 174; steamboats on White River, 142; Supreme Court appointments, 163–164; proposes agricultural and geological surveys of state, 64, 73, 74; tariff legislation, 147; tariff of 1824, p. 465; tax system, 157; tenure, 150; Three Per Cent Fund, 177; Union of states, 523; Wabash and Erie Canal, 239.
Noel, William T., 221, 708n.
Nofsinger, William R., 787n.
Northwest Ordinance of 1787, pp. 43, 470; increase in legislative representation, 106.
Notre Dame, 400.

Nuts, 55.
Nutt, Cyrus, 399.

O'Donnell, Harold Lee, 696n.
Oats, 51, 53.
Ohio, Wabash and Erie Canal extension in, 188–189, 214, 239, 240.
Ohio-Mississippi River waterway, 47; imports and, 183–184.
Ohio River bridge at Louisville, 180.
Old Northwest, 66.
Olds, Jesse, 635n.
Oolitic limestone, 77.
Open-faced camp, 49.
Oracle (Delphi), on Milroy and Kennedy, 279.
Oral voting, 34.
Ordinary expenditures, state government, 12; 1822–1831, pp. 87–88, 89, 153, 155; 1837–1843, pp. 241–242, 243; 1843–1850, pp. 312, 313, 314; benevolent expenses, 314; contingent items, 12; executive department, 88; financing, 312; governor and lieutenant governor, 12; governor's contingency fund, 88; insane, 314; judges' salaries, 12; legislative and judicial costs, 87–88; legislative salaries, 12; militia, 88; prison costs, 315–316; state government, 38; state library, 88; state prison, 88; state revenue collectors, 12, 88; territorial debt, 12; treasurer, auditor, and secretary of state salaries, 12; wolf scalps, 88.
Ordinary revenues, 1822–1831, pp. 88, 90, 91, 156; 1837–1843, p. 244; 1843–1850, pp. 316–317, 318; exceeding expenditures, 320.
Oregon, abrogation of joint occupation, 619–620; American claim to, 617–618; boundary and England, 596–597; compromise on, 621–622; Hoosier interest in, 597; Hudson's Bay Company, 596; reoccupation of, 616–618; territorial government, 597–598.

Orr, Joseph, 809n.

Orth, Godlove S., 753n, 754n, 755n, 756n, 841n, 851n; candidate for lieutenant governor, 335; constitutional convention, 406; gubernatorial candidacy, 332, 335; Liberty party, 337; replaced as candidate for lieutenant governor, 337; Whigs, 336, 607.

Otto, William T., 398.

Owen, David Dale, 656n; coal deposits, 76; exploring mineral lands for government, 76; geological survey of state by, 74–75; iron deposit, 75; renewal of appointment, 75; Richard Owen, 76.

Owen, John, 653n, 655n.

Owen, Richard, 76.

Owen, Robert Dale, 198, 279, 680, 701n, 706n, 728n, 735n, 752n, 763n, 764n, 778n, 781n, 783n, 786n, 787n, 788n, 829n, 830n, 847n, 853n, 854n, 855n, 856n, 857n, 858n, 859n, 860n; annexation of Texas, 600, 615; blacks, 442; blacks and mulattoes, 446–447; congressional candidacy, 553; election as congressman, 594; General Assembly, 448; general banking law, or bank restraining law, 330, 331; internal improvement disaster, 218; joint occupancy of Oregon, 598, 617, 619; national stature of, 607; Polk, 620–621, 627, 628; protective tariffs, 612; reelection of, 607; regular and special legislative sessions, 413; remodeling constitution, 448; slavery, 615–616, 632; state debt, 435; state equalization of taxes, 251; veto power of governor, 427; voting, 275; Wilmot Proviso, 626; wooden turnpike, 355.

Oxen, 61.

Palladium (Richmond), on Harrison, 574–575; on Mexican War, 624; on Polk, 609; on roads, 356; on Tyler, 583; on Whig state convention, 280.

Palmer, J. Horsley, 742n.

Palmer, Nathan B., 279, 663n, 685n, 687n, 698n, 705n, 706n, 709n, 722n, 730n, 731n, 736n, 833n; Board of Internal Improvement, 215; fiscal situation of state, 223–224; internal improvements, 191, 209–210; nominating presidential candidate, 543; Second State Bank, 260–262, 322; taxes, 249–250; Three Per Cent Funds, 354; treasurer of state, 153, 206; defeated for reelection, 221.

Panama Congress, 499–500.

Panic of 1819, p. 465.

Panic of 1837, pp. 202, 550; specie payments, 528.

Parke, Benjamin, 8; federal district judge, 9; fugitive slaves, 469; private banking, 331; statute laws, 96.

Parke, Moody, 635n, 662n, 663n, 728n, 752n.

Parker, Samuel W., 711n; voting at county seat, 275.

Patriot (Greencastle), on Second State Bank, 322.

Paul, John, 8.

Payne, John W., 707n, 728n.

Peabody, George, 738n.

Pence, George, 644n, 665n, 670n, 688n.

Pennington, Dennis, 29, 335, 634n, 637n, 643n, 659n, 684n, 732n, 776n; candidate for lieutenant governor, 85; Corydon Constitutional Convention, 86; incumbent judges, 128; protests move to Indianapolis, 112–113; Ray, 85; Whig state convention, 282.

Pepper, Abel C., 206, 675n, 703n, 730n, 747n, 786n, 828n, 831n; candidate for lieutenant governor, 127–128; military force to keep peace between whites and Indians, 556.

Pepper, Samuel, 779n, 781n; number of legislators, 421.

Perkins, Charles H., Supreme Court judge, 343, 344.
Perkins, Samuel E., 343–344.
Personal liberty legislation, 470.
Pests and diseases in crops, 57.
Peters, Absalom, 677n.
Pettit, John, 417, 780n, 781n, 783n, 784n, 788n, 847n, 850n, 853n, 854n, 855n, 856n, 857n, 858n, 859n; apportioning legislators, 421–422; college and university trust funds, 440; constitutional amendments, 449; counties, 423; election as congressman, 594; executive branch, 429; judicial department, 429; legislative sessions starting on Monday, 412; reelection of, 607; slavery, 629; Supreme Court clerk, 431; Supreme Court members, 430–431; title of bill, 415; trust funds and Indiana University, 442; uniform state law and county board, 418–419; veto power of governor, 427; whites and blacks, 445.
Philbrick, Francis S., 646n, 682n.
Pioneers, agricultural society, 78–79; agriculture of, 62; clearing of land, 50; concentration of settlements, 49; Esarey on, 48; food dependencies, 56–57; generalists, 47, 62; home site, 48; labor, 62; land for cultivation, 49; land passing from Indians, 557–558; log cabins, 49; shelter, 48.
Plowing, 49–51.
Poinsatte, Charles R., 697n.
Political parties, beginnings of, 513; Democratic Republicans, 115; emergence of, 115; gubernatorial election of 1831, p. 146; loyalty to, 513–514; National Bank, 577; National Republicans, 115; Ray, 115; state politics, 146.
Politics, changes in, 278; commerce or trade, 66; Indiana voice in, 573; reapportionment and dominance in, 103; southern slave states, 47;

Supreme Court involvement with, 130; transitions, 114–115.
Polk, James K., 854n, 856n, 857n, 858n, 859n; annexation of Texas, 616; cessation of Mexican territory, 626–628; domestic politics, 609–611; election as president, 606; expansionism, 615–618; Independent Treasury, 610–611; Indiana election of, 606–607; internal improvements, 613–614; preservation of Union, 609; presidential candidacy, 604; reoccupation of Oregon, 616–618; slavery issue, 622.
Polke, William, 81, 634n, 657n, 831n, 851n, 853n; Michigan Road, 178; removal of Indians, 556.
Poll taxes, 787; common schools, 392; end to, 157; exemptions, 91, 159; increases in, 215, 317; lowering, 91; objections to, 92–93; Veterans of American Revolution and, 159.
Pollock, James T., 815n.
Pork, 57.
Posey, Thomas, 7, 19, 634n, 790n; congressional candidacy, 454–455.
Potatoes, 57.
Potawatomi Indians, 459, 496; land held title to, 554; missionaries to, 460; payments to, 555; removal from state, 497, 556–557; surrender tribal holdings, 555; Trail of Death, 556–557.
Poultry, 61.
Powell, Erasmus, 657n.
Powell, Jehu Z., 695n.
Prather, Hiram, 694n, 778n, 785n, 788n.
Pratt, Daniel D., 562.
Precipitation, 45–46.
President, curbing veto power of, 590–591.
Presidential campaign of 1840, excitement caused by, 577–581; issues, 579–580.
Presidential election of 1824, pp. 476–484; congressional nominations,

477; Indiana electors, 476; popular interest in, 476.
Presidential election of 1840, Harrison, 573.
Presidential election of 1844, Birney, 605; Polk and Clay, 605.
Presidential electors, 453–454; candidate tickets, 478–479; method of selection of, 477–478; state convention, 479.
Prince, William, 27, 635n, 668n; death, 485; election to Senate, 457; not seeking reelection, 484; successor to, 485; tariff of 1824, p. 465.
Prison, building new, 315–316, 316; expenditures, 155; increase in costs of, 242; leasing to highest bidder, 315; ordinary expenditures, 88; poor condition of, 315–316; taxes, 153.
Probate judges, circuit court judges, 432.
Proffit, George H., 198, 722n, 818n, 842n, 843n, 844n, 845n, 848n; congressional candidacy, 553, 583–584; election as congressman, 553; minister to Brazil, 588; national bank, 586; reelection of, 584.
Property taxes, common schools, 392; criticisms of assessment, 317, 319–320; extending levy, 214; firm establishment of, 249; increases in, 242, 317; redeeming treasury notes, 233; reduction of, 215, 294; state debt, 228.
Prosecutors, 242.
Protective tariffs, 612; Democrats less supportive of, 536; reductions in, 522–524, 611–613; Senate, 522–523; southern threats of nullification against, 523.
Public domain, cession advocates, 559; cession to states, 498–499; disposition of, 458, 498–499, 559–560; distribution advocates, 559, 560; graduation advocates, 498, 559; preemption advocates, 559.

Public land policy, Hoosiers and, 496–497, 498–499, 558–561.

Quakers, antislavery societies, 566; State Anti-Slavery Society, 567; State Female Anti-Slavery Society, 567.

Railroads, anticipation of, 182; Baltimore and Ohio, 182; charters, 182, 358–359; completed in Indiana, 360–361; connecting Indianapolis with Madison, 359–360; construction of, 182–183, 360–361; developing network of, 174–175; east-west, 46; first successful, 182; importance of, 357–358; Lawrenceburg and Indianapolis Railroad, 182, 196; Madison to Lafayette, 196; paper network of lines, 182, 358–359; proposed lines, 182, 613; rapid advance of, 361; Wabash and Erie Canal, 347, 361.
Ralston, Alexander, 669n; design of capital, 110; platting state capital, 109–110.
Rapp, Frederick, 634n, 668n.
Rariden, James, 779n, 783n, 784n, 788n, 800n, 809n, 818n, 823n, 828n, 833n, 835n; bills and governor's veto, 427; congressional candidacy, 552; distribution money, 561–562; election as congressman, 550; gubernatorial candidacy (1828), 125; advocates keeping most of old constitution, 409–410; senatorial candidacy, 531; state debt, 435–436; whites elevated over blacks, 444–445.
Rauch, John G., 637n, 657n, 662n, 663n, 664n, 716n.
Rawlings, Aaron, 710n.
Ray, James Brown, 130, 645n, 648n, 657n, 658n, 661n, 662n, 665n, 666n, 667n, 670n, 671n, 672n,

Ray, James Brown, (cont.)
673n, 674n, 675n, 676n, 677n, 678n, 679n, 680n, 720n, 747n, 758n, 765n, 782n, 799n, 805n, 806n, 809n, 818n, 820n, 823n, 827n; absences from capital, 119–120; acting governor, 82; ad valorem tax system, 94; Adams, 126; Adams and Jackson, 126–127; needs assistant for revising laws, 98–99; attacks on age eligibility of, 85; civil and criminal law, 98–99; concurrently holding offices, 117–119; congressional candidacy, 485; controversies about, 116–119; county election returns lacking, 100; Dewey, 276; drawing money from treasury, 122; editorials in support of, 124; election as governor, 82–83, 84; English statutes and common law, 98; European liberty, 568; expenditures to, 120–121; financing roads, 135; Holman and Scott, 276; House investigation of payments to, 118; Indian commissioner, 116; Indiana Supreme Court, 129; interim governor, 84; Jackson, 506–507; Jacksonian gubernatorial candidate, 125–126; laws for state, 130–131; liquidation of public debt, 88; low esteem of, 99; McKinney and Stevens, 129, 276; membership in Senate, 130; Merrill, 123–124; Michigan Road, 500; Noble, 530; objections to poll tax, 92–93; pardoning Indian murderer, 461; plots sold in Indianapolis, 111; political has-been, 115; political neutrality of, 125–126; political parties, 115; population growth and reapportionment, 103–104; Potawatomi, 137; railroad extensions, 359; railroads, 357–358; reelection of, 127; rivers, 140; succession as governor, 82; turnpikes, 137; Union of states, 523; Watts, 129–130.
Ray, James M., 672n, 673n, 748n, 749n, 770n; Second State Bank, 325.
Raymond, David, 8, 635n.

Rayner, Kenneth, 590.
Read, Daniel, 398, 824n; business, 435; foreign words in bills, 416; advocates state superintendent of public instruction, 439–440; University Fund, 441; veto power of governor, 427.
Read, James G., 147, 151, 683n, 684n, 778n, 780n, 782n, 783n, 786n, 787n, 789n, 823n, 852n; amendments to constitution, 448; caucus or convention candidate, 152; constitutional convention, 409; eliminating office of lieutenant governor, 424–425; holding federal appointment while campaigning, 148; internal improvements, 147; Jacksonians, 147, 152; party support, 148; per diem compensation of legislators, 412–413; receiver of Jeffersonville Land Office, 147; tariff support, 148; title of bill, 415; treasurer, auditor, and secretary of state, 429; triennial legislative sessions, 410–411; Wabash and Erie Canal, 152.
Real estate, taxes, 250.
Reapportionment, 3, 32, 102–103, 161–163, 339–341; codification and revision of, 96–99; compromises, 104; Constitution of 1816, p. 341; Constitution of 1851, p. 341; constitutional convention, 419–422; county lines, 103; floats, 340–341; House protests against, 105; increase in population, 341; inequality of, 105, 341; interim apportionment of 1823, p. 106; intervals, 102; legislators (1821), 33; new counties, 105; New Purchase, 106; number of legislators, 242; of 1826, pp. 102–103; of 1831, pp. 103–104; of 1841, pp. 269–270; organized counties, 162; paper districts, 162; political dominance and, 103; population growth and, 103–104; senatorial districts, 104; Whigs, 267.
Recorder, 6; terms of, 5–6.
Referendum of 1823, p. 404.
Referendum of 1846, p. 405–406.

Referendum of 1849, p. 404.
Religion, common schools and, 389; issues in campaign of 1843, pp. 289–298.
Reporter, 431.
Representative government, 475–476.
Republican government, 472–473; mixing with expansion, 473–474.
Revised law code of 1831, p. 99.
Richardville, Jean B., 554–555.
Ristine, Joseph, 786n; county seminary system and state university, 440.
Ritchey, James W., 711n, 731n, 786n, 789n; Constitution of 1816, p. 409; apportioning legislators, 422.
Rivers, 140–141; bank maintenance, 179; bridges, 180; crossings of, 179; dams for mills, 183; destroying or injuring navigation, 43–44; difficulties in navigating, 38; economy and, 37; exports, 140–141, 183; federal aid for improving, 520–521; ferries, 44; flatboats, 43, 140–141, 141, 183; geographical context, 46; grist mills, 43; hazards to transportation, 38, 44; importance of travel on, 43–44; imports, 141, 183; keelboats, 43, 141; man-made obstructions, 174; Northwest Ordinance of 1787, pp. 43–44; public highway, 143–144, 183; sawmills, 43; steamboats, 141; Three Per Cent Fund, 144; transportation on, 42–44.
Road taxes, 176, 350, 351; bridges, 351; nonresidents, 351.
Roads, 132–136; bad condition of, 38, 132, 175, 348–349; commissioners, 39, 41, 42, 135; connecting settlements and towns, 40–41; county districts of, 350; cutting and opening, 132; economy, 37; federal aid, 41, 115; financing of, 134–135; frozen, 133; Indianapolis, 114; labor, 39, 176, 133–134, 349–350; land owner obligations for, 39–40; linking settlements, 37; little improvement to, 132; local government, 352; location and relocation of, 176; Michigan

Road, 137–138; north-south military, 137–138; obstacles, 39; opening, 131; opening and repairing, 174; plank roads, 355–357; public, 39–42; responsibility for, 133, 175–176, 349–350; surveyors, 41; taxable property and, 350, 351; taxes, 39, 134; Three Per Cent Fund, 134–135, 176–177; travel slow and hazardous, 133; unnecessarily obstructing, 350; wooden, 356–357.
Robb, David, 634n, 776n, 800n, 815n.
Robinson, John L., 859n.
Robinson, Joseph, 742n, 743n, 788n; blacks as good as whites, 445; legislative sessions, 413.
Robinson, Solon, 558.
Rockhill, William, 758n, 859n.
Rodgers, Ezra, 519.
Rodman, William, 135–136.
Root crops, 55.
Rope-making, 54.
Rothschild and Sons of London, 710n, 738n; default of improvement debt, 295–296; Harrison, 229.
Rothschilds & Baring, 301.
Rousseau, Lovell Harrison, 759n.
Rye, 51, 53.
Ryors, Alfred, 398.

Sabbath of Liberty, 37.
Salaries of elected officials, 120–121.
Saline Fund, 636n.
Salt, 75; importance of, 68; importing, 56; tariffs, 495–496.
Sample, Samuel C., 847n, 855n, 856n; annexation of Texas, 615; election as congressman, 594; gubernatorial candidacy, 332.
Sandstone, 76.
Sawmills, 43.
School law of 1849, pp. 392–393.
Schools, common, 365–366; district or neighborhood, 371–372; English language only, 364–365; income for, 364. See also Common schools; Taxes.

Schooner, Rudolphus, 779n.
Schreyer, Johann Wolfgang, 736n.
Scott, James, 635n, 663n, 791n, 792n, 799n; gubernatorial candidacy, 82, 146; nomination to Supreme Court, 9; other offices run for, 130; Ray, 276; reappointment as judge, 128; senatorial candidacy, 455, 456–457.
Scott, John, 675n, 683n, 684n.
Scott, L. H., 705n.
Scott, Rev. Samuel, 396.
Scott, Winfield, 849n.
Scovel, Sylvester, 771n.
Searle, Thomas C., 768n.
Second State Bank, 525; amendments to charter, 174, 264–265; authorized banking, 329–330; banking monopoly of, 405; branch suspension, 254–256; branches, 171, 174, 256, 264, 325–326; charter, 171–172, 200; criticisms of, 253, 255, 259–261; Democrats, 322; establishment of, 152; expiration of charter, 437; financial upheavals, 258–259; foundation of, 200; gubernatorial election of 1843, pp. 288–289; increased capital, 174, 210, 265; increased dividends, 325; Merrill, 153, 172; opposition to, 321–323; other bank failures and, 253–254; panic and depression, 252; partial suspensions, 257; performance of, 260–262; replacement for Merrill, 321–324; revenue from state stock, 265–266; small notes, 326–330; specie payment, 252–253, 256, 257, 324; state and private stock, 266; state and private stockholders, 171, 172; state borrowing from, 253; strength and prosperity of, 173, 202, 267, 321, 324–325; suspended debt of borrowers, 324; suspension of bonds for, 211; weakened status in 1843, p. 324; weakening of, 278–279; Whigs, 252.
Second United States Bank, 18, 164–165; branches, 165–166, 465, 525, 526; defense of, 466–467; First

State Bank as federal depository, 19; First State Bank policies affected by, 465; hostility toward, 465, 536; improprieties of, 466; Jackson, 527–528; loss of charter, 166; magnifying abuses of, 465–466; national government finances, 526; policies of, 466; prohibited in Indiana, 465, 525–526; public advantage of, 526; unsuccessful at rechartering, 526–527; Whigs, 283–284.
Secondary education, 394–395; colleges and universities, 396; Hanover Academy, 398–399; Hanover College, 399; Indiana College, 396; Indiana State Seminary, 396–397; Indiana University, 397–398; lack of support for, 440–441; seminaries, 394–395; state university, 396–397; Wabash College, 399.
Secondary schools, Asbury College, 399–400; Earlham College, 400; Franklin College, 400; Indiana Baptists Manual Labor Institute, 400; Notre Dame, 400.
Secrest, Charles, 741n.
Secrest, Henry, 770n.
Secretary of state, constitutional convention, 428–429; salaries, 12, 120, 247; session pay reduction, 247; term of, 4.
Semans, J. B., 690n.
Seminaries, 394–395.
Senate, ballot voting, 35; Committee on Agriculture, 66; improvements fraud and mismanagement, 230–231; Jackson, 528; membership, 3; protective tariffs, 522–523; public officials, 2; refusing to elect senator, 608; Second State Bank, 256; Whigs, 237.
Senate Finance Committee, 247–248.
Sentinel (Indianapolis), on banks, 330; on Bigger, 290; on constitutional conventions, 407; on First Butler Bill of 1846, p. 308; on Hannegan, 592; on internal improvement debt, 308; on new blood in office, 292; on

payment to bondholders, 308; on Van Buren, 601; on voting, 290, 291; on Whigs and Whitcomb, 290; on Whitcomb and Bright, 285.

Sergeant, John, nomination for vice president, 536.

Sering, John, 692n, 723n, 834n; on Second United States Bank opening branches in Indiana, 165–166; proposal for state bank, 165.

Settlements, roads connecting, 40–41.

Shade, William Gerald, 259.

Shakers, 60.

Shanklin, John, 723n.

Sharpe, Ebenezer, 809n.

Sheep, 60.

Sheets, William, 206, 684n, 703n, 708n; secretary of state, 150, 221.

Shelby, Isaac, 543.

Sheriff, collecting taxes due state, 17; election of, 431; election of first, 6–7; terms of, 5.

Sherrod, William F., 782n.

Shoemaker, Henry, 273, 727n.

Shonkwiler, William Forest, 683n.

Shoup, George G., 786n; number of legislators, 420; state university, 440–441.

Shovel plows, 50–51.

Shuler, Dr. Lawrence, 803n; congressional candidacy, 488–489.

Silk, 54; mulberry trees and, 65.

Simonson, John S., 711n, 740n.

Simpson, Rev. Matthew, 399.

Slaughter, Gabriel, 468.

Slaughter, James B., 643n, 659n, 815n.

Slavery, 622; annexation of Texas, 599; antislavery societies, 566–567; Clay, 480; compromise on, 471; condemning, 563; constitution recognition of, 564; James Dunkin and abolition of slavery, 567; extension of, 598–599; federal policy on, 631–632; free and slave states, 470, 471; free slaves leaving state, 563; Fugitive Slave Law of 1793, pp. 565–566; further introduction of, 471; growing concern about, 337, 564–

565; hostility toward, 467; interference with, 565, 566; issues in campaign of 1843, pp. 289–290; Mexican War, 622–626; Missouri Compromise of 1820, p. 471; national policy on, 562; personal liberty legislation, 470; politics and, 567; recovering escaped slaves, 467–469, 565–566; restoration of, 404; territorial expansion and, 565; Texas, 625; Underground Railroad, 565–566; Wilmot Proviso, 626–628.

Smiley, Ross, 149, 151, 684n, 779n, 808n.

Smith, Caleb B., 216, 707n, 709n, 732n, 733n, 844n, 847n, 853n, 855n, 856n, 857n, 858n, 859n, 860n; annexation of Texas, 615; army appropriations, 629; classifying improvements, 226; election as congressman, 594; Independent Treasury, 610; Oregon, 619, 620; Mexican War, 624–625, 628–629; reelection of, 607.

Smith, Hezekiah S., eliminating office of lieutenant governor, 425.

Smith, James, 634n.

Smith, Oliver H., 39, 647n, 648n, 668n, 677n, 703n, 771n, 806n, 817n, 821n, 836n, 838n, 842n, 844n; Adams, 509–510; bridges, 135; Compromise Tariff of 1833, p. 587; condition of roads, 132, 133; congressional candidacy, 487–488, 512, 532; distribution, 587; distribution money, 561; election as senator, 549; Greece, 501; gubernatorial candidacy, 332; Indian agency transfer, 497; party campaigning, 491; preemption opponents, 587; prosecuting whites who murdered Indians, 461; protective tariffs, 611; senatorial candidacy, 591–592; treaty with England, 596; Wallace and Dumont, 206.

Smith, Thomas, 784n, 785n, 818n, 847n, 850n, 854n, 855n, 856n,

Smith, Thomas, (cont.)
857n, 858n, 859n; congressional candidacy, 583–584; election as congressman, 553; governor's term, 424; justices of the peace, 433; reelection of, 594, 607; single legislative branch, 423; time requirements for legislature, 413; war with Mexico, 625.
Smith, Thomas L., Supreme Court judge, 343, 344, 345.
Smydth, Samuel Howe, 709n, 844n.
Snook, Henry T., 779n.
Soil, 45.
Sorin, Rev. Edward, 400.
South Carolina nullification crisis, 523–524.
Southern slave states, 47.
Spann, John L., 705n.
Spencer, John, 824n.
Squatters, 558.
St. Clair, Arthur, 808n, 812n.
St. Lawrence River, American navigation of, 474.
Stagecoach network, 180–181.
Stansbury, Howard, 698n, 699n.
Stapp, Milton, 232, 335, 683n, 684n, 705n, 706n, 709n, 733n, 734n, 828n; Board of Internal Improvement, 215; candidate for lieutenant governor, 127–128; gubernatorial candidacy, 146; president pro tem of Senate, 85; semiannual interest on debt, 226; senatorial candidacy, 552.
State Anti-Slavery Society, 566–567.
State bank, 437; authorized capital, 169; Bank of Vincennes, 18; branch boards, 170; branches, 172; charter, 169–170, 171–172; compromise on, 438; directors, 18, 170; election issue, 167–168; establishment of, 17–18, 437; General Assembly and governor's control of, 170–171; increasing capital of, 213; investing funds, 228; loans to state, 18; management and control of, 170; movement for another, 165; Noble, 166; organization of, 172; political sup-

port for, 167; president, 170; proponents, 168–169; restrictions and safeguards, 171. See also First State Bank; Second State Bank.
State Board of Agriculture, 63, 64; agricultural school, 65–66; annual report, 64; culture of silk, 65.
State Board of Education, 386–387; district libraries, 386–387; selecting textbooks, 386.
State capital, donation lots, 110–111; Governor's Circle, 110; Indians and location of, 460; naming, 109; permanent, 107–108; platting, 108, 109–110; public buildings, 108–109; removal to Indianapolis, 112–113; site selection of, 107–108; time restrictions of Corydon, 107.
State Common School Convention, 381; Blackford, 382; committee of seven, 382–385; common schools, 382–383; educational legislation, 382; importance of, 381–382; May, 1848, p. 390; Whitcomb, 382.
State conventions, 203; Adams-Clay coalition, 503–506; Democratic gubernatorial candidates, 216–217; Jacksonians, 535; National Republicans, 534–535; need for, 150–151; nominating candidates at, 151; pro-Clay, 534–535; public schools, 373; rhetoric and, 335–336; Whigs, 217.
State debt, 211–212; Bigger, 229–230; bonds on credit, 230; embarrassing fiscal situation of, 223–224; interest from borrowed money, 230; obtaining money to pay, 228; property taxes, 228.
State Education Convention of 1837, pp. 373–375; common schools, 376; friends of education convention, 376; public common schools, 375–376.
State Education Convention of 1839, pp. 377–378.
State Female Anti-Slavery Society, 567.

State house, 110.

State library, money spent on, 242; ordinary expenditures, 88; peak expenditures, 314.

State loan office, 165.

State officials, holding other offices, 26; increased salaries, 245; low salaries of, 248; supplemental payments to, 159.

State roads, 41, 42; county control over relocation, 176, 177.

State university, 396–397; maintenance of, 439; no necessity for, 440–441.

Statehood, transition to, 6–9; campaigning by office seekers, 6; contracts, actions, rights, suits, claims and prosecutions, 6; Corydon Constitutional Convention costs, 12; county elections, 6–7; fines, penalties and forfeitures, 6; fiscal burdens for citizens, 10–11; governor, lieutenant governor, and congressman, 6; oaths by appointees, 6; territorial courts, 6; territorial legislation, 6.

States, free and slave states, 471; slavery, 471; territorial expansion, 565.

Steamboats, 141; Big Vermillion River, 184; imports, 141, 183–184; limitations of, 143; Maumee and St. Joseph rivers, 184; Ohio and Wabash rivers, 184–185; Wabash River, 141–142, 184; White River, 141, 142–143.

Steele, William, 778n.

Stephens, Robert, 797n; takes slave from Indiana, 469.

Stephenson, Alexander C., apportioning legislators, 422.

Stevens, Stephen C., 663n, 664n, 672n, 673n, 675n, 676n, 689n, 729n, 755n, 756n; Abolition gubernatorial candidacy, 337; body of laws, 98; Ray, 99; reluctant approval by Senate, 276; resigns judgeship, 276; Supreme Court, 129, 160, 163.

Stevenson, Alexander C., 755n, 780n, 781n, 782n, 787n, 788n; candidate for lieutenant governor; counties, 422; county board powers, 417; few legislators passing laws, 414; number of legislators, 420–421; General Assembly, 448.

Stewart, Samuel, 776n.

Stipp, George W., 732n.

Stout, Elihu, 634n, 662n, 810n, 812n; First State Bank, 20; Hendricks, 80–81; incumbent governor, 26; Internal Improvements System of 1836, p. 195; Jackson, 478–479, 502, 509; Jacksonians, 153; Jennings, 25; legislators and banks, 20; Polish uprisings, 569; political parties, 514; removal from office, 516; Second State Bank, 525; Second United States Bank, 537; Texas War for Independence, 570–571.

Stratton, Daniel, 710n.

Streams, crossing flooded, 133; dams for mills, 143; impediments, 143–144; public highways, 183; unbridged, 38.

Suffrage, blacks and women, 34; denying to blacks, 562; universal white male, 513.

Sugar, 56.

Sullivan, George R. C., 454.

Sullivan, Jeremiah, 727n, 729n, 758n, 759n, 771n; completing McKinney's term, 164; congressional candidacy, 484–485; qualifications of, 345; reappointment as judge, 343; Supreme Court judge, 276.

Supreme Court, changes in membership (1837–1843), 275–277; clerk, 431; clerk, sheriff, and reporter, 431–432; Democratic judges, 342; Jennings, 9; members and election of, 430–431; politics, 130; second major shakeup, 342–343; territorial courts to, 6.

Surveyors, 41.

Suspensive veto, 426–428.

Sweetser, Philip, 809n, 818n; Tipton, 529.

Swinney, Thomas, 240.

Switzerland Guest (Vevay), on Jackson, 502.

Swyhart, Henry, 748n.

Syms, Larkin, 653n.

Tabbs, Moses, 800n.

Taber, Cyrus, 554.

Tannehill, Zachariah, 778n.

Tariff of 1824, p. 465.

Tariff of 1842, p. 590.

Tariff protection, articles of common consumption, 496; Compromise Tariff of 1833, p. 524; Force Bill, 524; gradual reduction of, 524–525; increased, 464–465; internal improvements and, 494–495; items protected by, 495–496; reduced duties, 522–524; Tariff of 1842, p. 590; Tyler, 589–590.

Taxes, ad valorem, 94, 155; assessed and collected, 95, 250; balances due state, 123; broadening of base, 249; collection by sheriff, 17; common schools, 370–371, 383, 385, 387, 388, 389, 391–392; county, 16–17; debt and, 435; denominational and private schools, 389; equalization of, 250, 251–252; exemption on land, 93; expansion of base, 153; general property, 155; increase in revenues (1821–1822), 16; increases in, 242–245; internal improvements, 193, 200, 210, 237, 249, 320; land, 91, 251; land assessment, 17; land bought from federal government, 91; levies 1837–1843, p. 246; levies 1844–1850, p. 319; levies on land, 87; levies on Madison and Indianapolis Railroad, 227; lowering rates, 87; poll tax, 87, 157; public debt with, 15; rating land for, 16–17; real estate, 250; reduction of rate, 88, 91; revenue 1843–1850, p.

317; revenue from, 251; revenue meeting costs, 153; revenue retained at treasury, 88; revenues, 155; revised legislation, 251; road taxes, 39; roads, 134; schools, 365–366; state bank shares, 171–172; state equalization board, 251–252; state prison and state capital costs, 153; too high, 92; Whigs, 228.

Taylor, Edmund D., 786n.

Taylor, Gamaliel, 203, 692n, 702n, 706n.

Taylor, John W., 453.

Taylor, Lathrop M., 554.

Taylor, Waller, 130, 802n; compromise and national harmony, 472; discrediting, 454; elected senator, 9; election of successor to, 486–487; Florida purchase, 473; Missouri Compromise of 1821, p. 471; second term in Senate, 455–456; slavery, 470, 471; small tracts of federal land, 463; tariff of 1824, p. 465.

Tea, 56.

Teachers, common schools, 367–368; competent, 366, 372; licensed, 374; qualified, 375, 384; salaries, 384.

Terrell, Williamson, 710n.

Terrill, Richardson, 661n.

Territorial debt, 12.

Terry, Elias S., 784n; attorney general and prosecuting attorney, 431–432; prosecuting attorney in circuit courts, 433.

Test, Charles H., 160, 644n, 670n, 687n, 725n, 727n, 758n, 793n; law code of 1838, p. 271; reduction in legislature, 268; Supreme Court judge, 342–343; voting at county seat, 275.

Test, John, 8, 181, 203, 801n, 803n, 813n; congressional candidacy, 487–488, 512–513, 532; election to Congress, 485, 512–513; European nations, 500; Monroe Doctrine of 1823, p. 500; Panama Congress, 500; Spain, 500; tariff of 1824, p. 465.

Texas, American recognition of, 571; annexation, 565, 572, 598–600, 615–616; annexation by Mexico, 570–571; Mexican War, 622–626; slavery, 625; Texas War for Independence, 570–571.

Thom, Allan D., 454.

Thompson, George Burton, 332, 708n, 720n, 753n; Butler Bill of 1847, pp. 310–311.

Thompson, John H., 659n, 674n, 820n; Adams and Clay, 86; blacks and jury trials, 470; candidate for lieutenant governor, 85; congressional candidacy, 511–512; gubernatorial candidacy (1828), 125; nominations for president and vice president, 477; presidential elector, 453; relief for debtors, 86; resignation of state Senate seat, 86; secretary of state, 339; special apportionments, 161.

Thompson, Richard W., 687n, 720n, 740n, 743n, 770n, 771n, 842n, 843n, 844n, 845n, 848n, 859n; ad valorem tax, 157; election as congressman, 584; gubernatorial candidacy, 332; internal improvements, 218–219; Second State Bank, 173; Tyler, 588.

Thompson, William, congressional candidacy, 552.

Thompson, Wilson, 712n, 737n.

Thornton, Henry P., 675n, 784n, 792n; attorney general, 432.

Three Per Cent Fund, 41–42; bridge over Muscatatuck River, 136; county boards, 177; diminishing proceeds, 355; Harrison, 42; internal improvement debt interest, 354; Michigan Road, 180; National and Michigan roads, 178; Noble, 177; permanent state capital, 107; rivers, 144; roads, 41, 134–135, 176–177; sale of public land, 354.

Times (Fort Wayne), on constitutional convention delegates, 407.

Timothy, 54.

Tipton, John, 124, 125, 142, 637n, 648n, 668n, 669n, 671n, 673n, 675n, 679n, 681n, 683n, 690n, 691n, 696n, 697n, 698n, 699n, 702n, 791n, 804n, 807n, 810n, 811n, 812n, 814n, 815n, 816n, 817n, 818n, 819n, 820n, 821n, 822n, 828n, 830n, 831n, 832n, 833n, 834n, 836n, 837n; annexation of Texas, 565; bipartisan support of, 531–532; bridge over Wabash, 180; distribution bill, 560; distribution money, 561, 562; election as senator, 531; foreign relations, 568; illegal squatters, 58; Indian agency, 497; Indian agent, 493, 515; Indian commissioner, 116; Indian peace, 556; Indians left in Indiana, 554–555; Jackson, 528, 537; Jacksonians, 147; Johnson, 543–544; protective tariffs, 523; reelection to Senate, 539; opinions on removal from office, 516; retirement, 551; rivers, 520–521; Second United States Bank, 526; senatorial candidacy, 529, 530, 538–539; slavery, 564; state bank, 167, 169; state capital, 108; supporting country not party, 539; tariffs, 524; Texas as separate republic, 571; treaty with Potawatomi, 137; voting, 540; Wabash and Erie Canal, 189.

Tobacco, 53–54.

Tochman, Gaspard, 569.

Todd, Henry G., 778n, 786n.

Todd, John, 768n.

Toll bridges, 135, 180, 351, 352.

Towns, incorporation of, 10; life in, 46; roads connecting, 40–41.

Townships, assessors, 16–17; common schools, 370; election inspectors, 35; office vacancies, 100; school districts, 365; seminaries, 363–364; superintendents of schools, 364; township trustees and schools, 364.

Tract books, 121–122.

Trade, Ohio-Mississippi River waterway, 47; relationship with politics, 66; routes, 47.

Tradesmen, 69–70; blacksmiths, 70–71; building homes, 70.

Trail of Death, 556–557.

Trails, 39, 132–136; forests and, 39; obstacles, 39; opening, 131.

Transportation, bridges, 135–136; canal connecting Wabash and Maumee rivers, 132; canals, 144–145; efforts to improve, 185; federal aid for projects, 463–464, 520, 521–522; ferries, 135–136; financing network, 190; flooded streams, 133; generated revenues, 190; growth of population and wealth, 190; improving facilities, 131–132, 174–175, 464; Indianapolis as important crossroads for, 181; key projects and federal aid, 464; Mississippi River, 131; Noble, 147; political parties on, 345; private enterprises taking over, 321; public roads, 39–42; rivers, 42–44, 44, 140–141; roads, 132–136; role of federal government, 519–520; Three Per Cent Fund, 41–42; trade routes, 131–132; trails, 132–136; trails and roads, 131; turnpikes, 136–137.

Travel, bad conditions of, 38–39; Dean and party, 38; drinking water, 38; land and rivers, 44; public roads, 39–42; slow and hazardous, 133; trails, 39.

Treasurer, advanced payments to state officials, 118; constitutional convention changes, 428–429; salaries, 12, 120, 247; session pay reduction, 247; state loan office establishment, 165; term of, 4.

Treasury notes, 14.

Treating voters, 275.

Trembly, Daniel, 786n.

Tri-Weekly Journal (Indianapolis), on Bigger, 217; on Whig state convention, 575.

Tuley, Benjamin S., 216, 217, 707n, 708n; political background of, 218.

Turnpikes, 136–137; charters to private companies for, 179; developing network of, 174–175; Indianapolis and White Water Turnpike Company, 137; interest in, 179; Michigan Road, 137; New Albany to Vincennes, 196; rivalries among river towns and, 137; state sponsored, 179; survey from Jeffersonville to Crawfordsville, 196.

Turpie, David, Tippecanoe Battleground campaign, 578.

Two Per Cent Fund, and National Road, 139.

Tyler, John, 838n, 846n; annexation of Texas, 599–600; becomes president, 583; Clay, 584–585; Compromise Tariff of 1833, p. 584; domestic policies, 594–595; fiscal corporation, 589; foreign relations, 595–598; new cabinet members, 589; nomination of, 575, 576–577; presidential candidacy, 605; sound currency, 589; state banks, 589; tariff bills, 589–590; tariff protection, 589–590; vetoes by, 590–591; Whigs, 589–590, 594–595.

Unbridged streams, 38.

Underground Railroad, 565–566.

United States, admission of Missouri as state, 470; Canada and, 474; Cuba and, 474; expansion of, 473–474; free and slave states, 470; growth of, 568; isolation from Europe, 472–473; life in, 474; New World developments, 472; republican government with expansion, 473–474.

University Fund, 440; common schools, 442; generating income from, 441.

Van Buren, Martin, 825n, 829n, 837n, 839n, 840n, 841n, 848n, 850n, 859n; annexation of Texas, 600; defeat of, 580–581; Democratic support, 602; distribution money, 561; election as president, 548; extravagance of, 576; federal deposits, 528; filling vacancies, 517; hard times under, 582; Howard, 221; Indiana support for, 545–546; Jackson, 547; nomination for president, 543–544; nomination for vice president, 536; presidential candidacy, 601, 604; renomination of, 576–577; transportation projects, 521–522; unpopularity of, 540, 546, 573, 582; Wabash and Erie Canal, 240.

Vance Arthur, 136.

Vance, Samuel C., 793n, 803n, 812n; senatorial candidacy, 458.

Vandeveer, Joel, 300, 739n, 756n.

Vawter, John, 8, 635n, 644n, 812n; federal district court marshal, 9.

Vegetables, 54–55.

Vevay, 55.

Vigus, Jordan, 19, 187, 822n; Canby, 125.

Villages, life in, 46.

Vincennes Steam Mill Company, 22.

Vincennes University, 396.

Voters, apportionments and, 30; county enumeration of, 32–33; federal government role, 452; influencing, 37; No Bank element, 329–330; practicing law in courts, 433–434; Union of states, 452; western sectionalism, 452.

Voting, 35–36, 101–102; ballot, 35; blacks and women, 34; county seat, 37, 102, 274–275; Democratic Republicans, 147; improper, 36–37; National Republicans, 147; oral, 34, 35; secret ballots, 99; in township of residence, 341–342; universal white male suffrage, 513; valid ballots, 273–274.

Wabash and Erie Canal, 175, 185–189; bonds sold for, 208; borrowing for, 187; commissioners and loans for, 190; compact with Ohio on, 188–189; continuing construction of, 238; continuous navigation, 187; Cross Cut Canal, 236; data on proceeds of, 209; distances navigable, 213–214; donations of land for, 493–494; estimating costs from, 239; extending contracts for, 215; extending western terminal, 187; extension of land grant on, 522; extension to, 196–197, 241, 346; failure to finish feeders for, 293; favored status of, 238; favoritism and corruption of officials, 189; federal government financing route to Vincennes, 345–346; federal land grant, 208; financial disaster for bondholders, 346–347; financing, 238–239; fragile financial basis, 240–241; General Assembly, 347–348; greater time and costs of, 189; Indians, 554; interest owed on, 237; internal improvement debt, 301–302, 306–307, 345; labor, 187; managed by trustees, 346; middle section open for navigation, 187; necessary decisions for, 191; Ohio portion, 208, 214, 239, 240; open for navigation, 240, 345; opponents, 186; outstanding contracts on, 210–211; plans to complete, 301; plummeting revenues, 347; portage between Fort Wayne and Huntington, 186; predictions on, 208; proponents, 186–187; railroads, 347; repair and maintenance costs, 241; revenue, 194, 212; rising expenditures of, 207; sale to pay debt, 348; stimulating wheat growing, 51; taxes, 320; trustees for, 307; Wallace, 206–207.

Wabash and Erie Canal Commissioners, 186; canals, 193–194.

Wabash College, 399; beginnings, 372.

Wabash Courier (Terre Haute), on state conventions, 151.

Wabash Manual Labor College and Teachers' Seminary, 372, 399.

Wabash River, bridge at Logansport, 180; federal aid denied for, 521; improving navigation on, 184; remov-

Wabash River, (cont.)
ing obstructions, 196, 520; steam-boats, 141–142, 184; survey for obstructions, 494.
Walker, Jacob, 690n.
Walker, Robert J., 612.
Walker Tariff of 1846, pp. 612–613.
Wallace, David, 334, 643n, 644n, 656n, 664n, 684n, 685n, 702n, 703n, 704n, 705n, 706n, 707n, 720n, 721n, 722n, 723n, 724n, 725n, 729n, 745n, 759n, 780n, 782n, 783n, 814n, 831n, 842n, 843n, 844n, 845n, 848n; banks issuing small notes, 327; Board of Internal Improvement, 209; candidate for reelection, 151–152; classifying internal improvements, 206–207; congressional candidacy, 584, 594; decrease in legislators, 267–268; Dunning, 334; election as congressman, 584; election as governor, 205–206; election as lieutenant governor, 149; free banking, 331; governor, 202; governor's pardoning power, 425; gubernatorial candidacy, 202, 203; internal improvements, 204, 209; Internal Improvements System of 1836, pp. 206–207; iron industry in Indiana, 77; life of, 202–203; limiting House and Senate, 423; Noble, 202; Owen, 75–76; Polish uprisings, 569; public domain lands, 499; reduction of per diem costs, 245–247; reelection of, 152; Second State Bank, 255, 265; state financial crisis, 214; Supreme Court judges, 276; taxes, 249; Wabash and Erie Canal, 206–207, 209, 214; Whigs, 216; Whitcomb, 334.
Wallace, Leon H., 665n, 667n, 726n; reapportionment, 340.
Walpole, Thomas D., 779n.
Walsh, Justin E., 637n, 644n, 667n, 668n, 688n.
Warner, Joseph, 659n.

Washington, George, 798n.
Watts, John, 635n, 676n, 809n; Adams-Clay state convention, 505; McKinney and Stevens, 130; Ray, 129–130.
Watts, Johnson, 725n, 726n, 778n, 783n, 786n; banks, 437; gubernatorial candidacy, 332; treasurer, auditor, and secretary of state, 429.
Wea Indians, 460.
Webster, Daniel, 826n, 849n; treaty with England, 596; Wabash and Erie Canal, 240.
Webster-Ashburton Treaty of 1842, p. 596.
Welsh, James, 768n.
West, Henry F., 772n.
West, Nathaniel, 279, 707n, 711n, 718n, 730n, 731n, 828n; state officials' salaries, 247.
West Indies, opening trade with, 499; trading with, 569.
Western Sun (Vincennes), on Blackford, 85, 455–456; on Canby, 125; on Democrats, 577; on distribution bill, 560; on elections, 149; on Great Western Mail Stage route, 519; on Harrison, 28–29, 582–583; on Hendricks and Noble, 454; on Howard, 217; on internal improvements, 488; on Jackson, 478, 520; on Jennings, 7, 28; on Jennings and Posey, 7; on legislature's revision of law, 96–97; on Noble, 152–153; on Oregon territory, 598; on Polk, 609; on Posey, 454; on Ray, 85; on Second State Bank, 322; on Taylor, 455–456; on Tipton, 531; on Tyler, 587, 588, 591; on Van Buren, 576; on voting, 34; on war with England, 596; on Whigs, 550, 553, 608; Stout as editor of, 125.
Wheat, 51, 52–53.
Wheeler, Amzi Lewis, 731n, 736n, 789n.
Whig (Rushville), on Clay, 601.
Whig State Central Committee, replaces Orth with Stevenson, 338.

Whigs, bank support, 536; birth of, 540–541; Clay, 601, 602; congressional victory, 584; declining power of, 591–592; Democrats, 542, 602–603; domination of state politics, 202; federal and state politics, 550–552; federal revenue to states, 547; fiscal and economic woes, 284; General Assembly, 221; gubernatorial candidates, 332; Harrison, 544, 577–579; initial test of strength, 541–542; Internal Improvements System of 1836, p. 252; internal improvements, 283, 536, 595; Jackson, 541; Jacksonian policies, 283; Liberty party, 337; lieutenant governor victory, 206; majorities in Congress, 582; majority in General Assembly, 153, 226, 339; Marshall, 336–337; Mexican War, 623–624; motto, 574; national conventions, 575, 603–604; peak strength, 278; political campaigns, 283; Polk, 606; public domain, 295; reapportionment of 1841, p. 267; Second State Bank, 252, 267; Second United States Bank, 283–284, 547. See also National Republicans.

Whitcomb, James, 279, 663n, 664n, 685n, 704n, 733n, 734n, 735n, 736n, 738n, 739n, 740n, 741n, 743n, 746n, 754n, 755n, 756n, 759n, 770n, 772n, 815n, 816n, 828n, 834n, 852n, 853n, 860n; commissioner of General Land Office, 518; common schools, 378–379, 392; constitutional convention, 405–406; consumption exceeding income, 312; Democratic judges, 342; Dewey and Sullivan, 343–344; English bondholders, 309; first Democratic governor, 278; fiscal and economic conditions, 309; governor, 291, 594; gubernatorial candidacy, 280; improvement for bondholders, 302; internal improvement debt, 288; internal improvements, 298–299; life of, 286; local laws, 416–417,

417; Mexican War, 629–630; protective tariffs, 611; reducing number of legislators, 340; reelection as governor, 333, 338–339; referendum of 1849, p. 404; Second State Bank, 324, 325, 326; slavery, 632; State Common School Convention, 382; state financial problems, 293–294; strong qualifications of, 335; Supreme Court, 344, 345; uniform state laws, 417; voters, 337–338.

White, Albert S., 240, 818n, 826n, 833n, 835n, 842n, 843n, 844n, 847n, 852n, 855n; annexation of Texas, 599, 600; distribution, 587; distribution money, 561; election as congressman, 550; election as senator, 552; Oregon, 617; squatters' rights, 558–559; treaty with England, 596.

White, Hugh L., consideration as presidential candidate, 543.

White, James, 323.

White, Joseph L., 842n, 844n, 845n, 848n; election as congressman, 584.

White River, 141.

White Water Valley Canal Company, 236.

Whitewater Canal, 195; classifying, 226, 227; contracts on projects, 197; finishing, 236.

Whitlock, Ambrose, 812n.

Whitney, Asa, 359.

Wick, John N., 120.

Wick, William W., 84, 633n, 672n, 673n, 675n, 708n, 758n, 800n, 818n, 820n, 827n, 853n, 854n, 855n, 856n, 857n, 858n, 859n; absences from capital, 120; congressional candidacy, 532, 549, 583–584; congressional election, 607; defeat as secretary of state, 128; election as congressman, 553; election as secretary of state, 86; Independent Treasury, 610; issuance of commissions, 121; Johnson, 580; Mexican War, 626; Oregon, 619, 620, 621; Supreme Court judge, 342, 343; Van Buren, 581.

Wiggin, Benjamin, 738n.
Willett, Marinus, 808n, 816n, 824n; protests federal banking in Indiana, 166, 526.
Williams, Jesse L., 699n, 711n, 714n, 724n, 734n; Board of Internal Improvement, 215; canals, 192; internal improvement projects, 191–192; railroads, 182–183, 358; Second State Bank, 265; superiority of railroad to Wabash and Erie Canal, 361–362; Wabash and Erie Canal, 187, 192, 336, 346.
Williams, Sherrod, 826n, 840n.
Willard, William, 314.
Wilmot Proviso, 626–628; Indiana, 632.
Wilson, George R., 647n, 756n.
Wilson, John, 695n.
Wilson, Walter, 800n.
Winemaking, 55.
Wines, Marshall S., 713n; internal improvement debt, 235–236; private companies and internal improvements, 235.
Wines, William, 712n, 737n.
Wolf scalps, costs, 155; ordinary expenditures, 88.
Wolfe, Benjamin, 414, 782n.
Women, as keepers of household, 78; hard life of, 78; tasks done by, 77; unable to vote, 34.

Woodburn, James Albert, 655n.
Woodbury, Jonathan, 642n.
Woodbury, Levi, 719n.
Woodsman's ax, 49–50.
Woodworking craftsmen, 70.
Woollen, William Wesley, 633n, 675n.
Woolverton, John D., 811n, 822n.
Wort, Samuel, 745n; prisons, 315–316.
Worth, Daniel, 834n.
Wright, Joseph A., 278, 740n, 765n, 847n, 850n, 855n; on deaf, insane, and blind, 315; election as congressman, 594; Indiana State Seminary, 397; railroads, 360, 361; wooden roads, 357.
Wylie, Andrew, 376; Friends of Common Education, 373; Indiana College, 397.
Wylie, Theophilus A., 397.

Yandes, Daniel, 723n.
Yaryan, John, 776n.
Young, Richard M., 832n.

Zenor, John, 786n; fair reapportionment, 105; protesting move to Indianapolis, 112–113.